RECEIVED

JAN 1 1 2013

COURT OF APPEAL
SIXTH APPELLATE DISTRICT

SEARCH AND SEIZURE

A Treatise

on the

Fourth Amendment

FIFTH EDITION

West's Criminal Practice Series

By

Wayne R. LaFave

David C. Baum Professor of Law Emeritus
and Professor Emeritus in the Center for Advanced Study
The University of Illinois

Volume 1
Sections 1.1 to 2.7

WEST®

A Thomson Reuters business

For Customer Assistance Call 1-800-328-4880

Mat #41352950

ISBN 978-0-314-61387-5

To Loretta ~

"It is as absurd to pretend that one cannot love the same woman always, as to pretend that a good artist needs several violins to execute a piece of music."

(Honore de Balzac)

PREFACE TO FIFTH EDITION

In the Preface to the 1978 first edition of this Treatise, I observed that "the flow of appellate decisions dealing with arrest, search and seizure continues unabated." This flow has in no sense diminished over the past thirty-four years, and thus—just as it became necessary to publish a second edition in 1986, a third edition in 1996, and then a fourth edition in 2004—it is now time for a fifth edition, likewise substantially revised and expanded from the preceding one.

During the last thirty-four Terms of the Supreme Court, the Court decided 205 cases involving issues within the compass of this Treatise. Many of those decisions have brought about very significant developments. Illustrative of those decided since publication of the fourth edition are:

- *Arizona v. Gant*, concerning search of vehicles incident to arrest (included within entirely new § 7.1, especially in subsections (c) and (d))
- *Arizona v. Johnson*, concerning frisk of traffic stop passengers (§ 9.6(a))
- *Brendlin v. California*, concerning the standing of vehicle passengers to question the lawfulness of the stopping of the vehicle (§ 11.3(e))
- *Brigham City v. Stuart*, concerning warrantless entry of premises to give emergency aid (§ 11.3(e))
- *Davis v. United States*, concerning application of the exclusionary rule in the event of overruled precedent (§ 1.3(h))
- *Florence v. Board of Freeholders*, concerning strip search of arrestees upon their entry into a pretrial detention facility (§ 5.3(c))
- *Georgia v. Randolph*, concerning the effect of refusal to consent by one co-occupant upon the consent of another (§ 8.3(d))
- *Herring v. United States*, concerning the inapplicability of the exclusionary rule to "isolated negligence attenuated from the arrest" (§ 1.6(i))
- *Hudson v. Michigan*, concerning the inapplicability of the exclusionary rule in "knock-and-announce" violations (§§ 1.2(b), 1.6(h), 11.4(a))
- *Illinois v. Caballes*, concerning the *Terry* scope limitation on temporary detentions, as applied to traffic stops (§ 9.3(b), (f))

- *Kentucky v. King*, concerning police-created exigent circumstances (§ 6.5(b))
- *Safford Unified School District # 1 v. Redding*, concerning strip search of students (§ 10.11(b))
- *Samson v. California*, concerning suspicionless searches of parolees (§ 10.10(c), (d), (e))
- *United States v. Grubbs*, concerning anticipatory search warrants (§ 3.7(c))
- *United States v. Jones*, concerning the trespass theory and GPS tracking (§§ 2.1(e), 2.7(f))

Where recent cases decided by the Supreme Court or lower appellate courts have suggested a need for attention to issues not considered or only considered in passing in the prior edition, I have again (as in the second, third and fourth editions) added new subsections. Thus, the reader will find herein new discussion of several Fourth Amendment problems which have taken on added importance in the last few years:

- whether the exclusionary rule is sometimes inapplicable at a criminal trial because the social costs outweigh the deterrence benefits ((§ 1.6(h), (i))
- whether the pre-*Katz* trespass theory remains as an alternative basis for finding that a Fourth Amendment search has occurred (§ 2.1(e))
- whether the aggregation of a large volume of personal data on private citizens and the sophisticated "mining" of this data to discover suspicious patterns of activity and persons involved therein constitutes a search (§ 2.7(e))
- whether special rules apply to execution of a search warrant at a congressional office (§ 4.1(i))
- whether a search of third parties is required in response to a request for discovery by the defense (§ 5.4(d))
- whether search of a vehicle incident to arrest is limited by the arrestee's "possibility of access" (§ 7.1(c))
- whether search of a vehicle incident to arrest is lawful when undertaken for "offense-related evidence" (§ 7.1(d))
- whether a protective sweep of a vehicle is sometimes permissible to ensure the safety of police investigating nearby (§ 7.4(i))
- whether the *Terry* reasonable suspicion standard requires suspicion of a particular crime or only of criminality generally (§ 9.5(c))

Some of these new subsections have required renumbering of subsequent subsections. Otherwise, the old section and subsection designations have been retained, which means that usually (but not inevitably) references to the fourth edition in earlier cases and commentary will be valid for this edition as well.

Because of the Supreme Court cases and developments mentioned earlier, to say nothing of an untold number of other court decisions and developments in analysis worthy of note, this fifth edition (as with the second, third and fourth) is substantially larger than its predecessor—a circumstance which seems to attend all works of this nature.[1] Here, as with the prior editions, my intention has been to "report in a systematic and orderly fashion the current state of Fourth Amendment law" and also "to present a critical assessment of how the Supreme Court and the lower courts have fared in their ongoing and challenging enterprise of giving content and meaning to the Fourth Amendment."[2] Though the documentation in this fifth edition is heavier than in the fourth, reflecting especially the intervening

---

[1] Professor Anthony Amsterdam has recounted "the progress of the apocryphal author of the celebrated treatise called Jones on Easements. The first sentence of the first edition began: 'There are fourteen kinds of easements recognized by the law of England.' But the work was well received, and the author labored to produce a second edition, in two volumes, which necessarily began: 'There are thirty-nine kinds of easements.' After the author's death, the treatise was scrupulously updated by his literary scions and now appears in a solid 12-volume sixth edition beginning with the sentence; 'It is impossible to say how many kinds of easements are recognized by the law of England.'" Amsterdam, Perspectives on the Fourth Amendment, 58 Minn.L.Rev. 349, 374–75 (1974).

I leave it to the reader to determine how many different kinds of searches and seizures are discussed in this fifth edition.

[2] Especially as to the latter, I have drawn upon my post-first edition work elsewhere on Fourth Amendment issues: LaFave, The Smell of Herring: A Critique of the Supreme Court's Latest Assault on the Exclusionary Rule, 99 J.Crim.L. & Criminology 757 (2009); LaFave, The Routine Traffic Stop from Start to Finish: Too Much "Routine," Not Enough Fourth Amendment, 102 Mich.L.Rev. 1843 (2004); LaFave, The Fourth Amendment as a "Big Time" TV Fad, 53 Hastings L.J. 265 (2001); LaFave, Computers, Urinals and the Fourth Amendment: Confessions of a Patron Saint, 94 Mich.L.Rev. 2553 (1996); LaFave, The Present and Future Fourth Amendment, 1995 U.Ill.L.Rev. 111; LaFave, Mapp Revisited: Shakespeare, J., and Other Fourth Amendment Poets, 47 Stan.L.Rev. 261 (1995); Commentaries on search and seizure issues in O.J. Simpson case, in 1994 WESTLAW 530213, 530235, 530236, 541760, 559215, 562135; LaFave, Police Rulemaking and the Fourth Amendment: The Role of the Courts, in "Discretion and Criminal Justice: The Tension Between Individualization and Uniformity" at 211 (L. Ohlin & F. Remington, eds. 1993); LaFave, Pinguitudinous Police, Pachydermatous Prey: Whence Fourth Amendment "Seizures"?, 1991 U.Ill.L.Rev. 729 (1991); LaFave, The Fourth Amendment: A Bicentennial Checkup, 26 Valp.U.L.Rev. 223 (1991); LaFave, Controlling Discretion by Administrative Regulations: The Use, Misuse, and Nonuse of Police Rules and Policies in Fourth Amendment Adjudication, 89 Mich.L.Rev. 442 (1990); LaFave, Constitutional Rules for Police: A Matter of Style, 41 Syrac.L.Rev. 849 (1990); Entries on Reasonable Expectation of Privacy and Plain View Doctrine for "Encyclopedia of the American Constitution Supplement" (1990); Entries on Katz v. United States, Chimel v. California, Payton v. New York, and Marshall v. Barlows, Inc. for "Oxford Companion to the Supreme Court of the United States" (1990); LaFave, The Fourth Amendment Today: A Bicentennial Appraisal, 32 Vill.L.Rev. 1061 (1987); LaFave, The Fourth Amendment: "Second to None in the Bill of Rights," 75 Ill.B.J. 424 (1987); Entry on Searches and Seizures in "Encyclopedia of the American Constitution" (1987); LaFave, Being Frank About the Fourth: On Allen's "Process of 'Factualization' in the Search and Seizure Cases," 85 Mich.L.Rev. 427 (1986); LaFave, The Forgotten Motto of Obsta Principiis in Fourth Amendment Jurisprudence, 28 Ariz.L.Rev. 291 (1986); LaFave, A Fourth Amendment Fantasy: The Last (Heretofore Unpublished) Search and Seizure Decision of the Burger Court, 1986 U.Ill.L.Rev. 669 (1986); LaFave, "The Seductive Call of Expediency": United States v. Leon, Its Rationale and Ramifications, 1984 U.Ill.L.Rev. 895; LaFave,

eight years of case law and commentary,[3] I must again caution that it is not my intention to provide a jurisdiction-by-jurisdiction laundry list of citations on every conceivable point. Much of the Fourth Amendment jurisprudence is highly fact-oriented, and in the main I have utilized case citations with brief parenthetical descriptions or quotations so that the reader may readily ascertain how subtle factual differences can affect the application of doctrine in the infinite variety of circumstances which arise.

Most of the work on this fifth edition was completed during the 2011-12 academic year and the summer following. I much appreciate the continued support I have received from Dean Bruce Smith and the College of Law.

WAYNE R. LAFAVE

November, 2012

"Seizures" Typology: Classifying Detentions of the Person to Resolve Warrant, Grounds and Search Issues, 17 U.Mich.J.L.Ref. 417 (1984); LaFave, Fourth Amendment Vagaries (Of Improbable Cause, Imperceptible Plain View, Notorious Privacy, and Balancing Askew), 74 J.Crim.L. & Crim. 1171 (1983); LaFave, Supreme Court Report: Nine Key Decisions Expand Authority to Search and Seize, 69 A.B.A.J. 1740 (1983); LaFave, The Fourth Amendment in an Imperfect World: On Drawing "Bright Lines" and "Good Faith," 43 U.Pitt.L.Rev. 307 (1982).

[3] I have included in this edition Supreme Court cases through the Term ending in June 2012, plus lower court cases and commentary up to June 2012.

PREFACE TO FIRST EDITION

At least in the years following the Supreme Court's landmark decision of *Mapp v. Ohio*[1] in 1961, it is beyond question that the Fourth Amendment has been the subject of more litigation than any other provision in the Bill of Rights. Indeed, I would be willing to wager (at least a modest amount) that during this period lawyers and judges have spilled more words over the Fourth Amendment than all of the rest of the Bill of Rights taken together. As perusal of any recent volume of law reports will attest, the flow of appellate decisions dealing with arrest, search and seizure continues unabated.

The fifty-four words which make up the Fourth Amendment are not particularly illuminating. The Amendment first declares that it is a "right of the people" to be secure "against unreasonable searches and seizures," but there is no hint as to precisely what activities "unreasonable." The second or warrant clause Amendment sets out certain requirements for warrants, but they are of the stated in general terms which are not self-defining, such as that warrants must issue upon "probable cause." It has been necessary for the Supreme Court and the lower federal and state courts to give "concrete and contemporary meaning to that brief, vague, general, unilluminating test."[2]

This is no mean task. It "is inescapably judgmental," and in "the pans of judgment sit imponderable weights,"[3] to say, therefore, as Justice Frankfurter put it some years ago, that "[t]he course of true law pertaining to searches and seizures *** has not *** run smooth,"[4] is not to suggest that the courts have performed ineptly in this undertaking. Rather, this observation (which is still apt today) merely reflects the inherent difficulties in developing a sound body of Fourth Amendment jurisprudence.

Certainly much progress has been made. In pre-*Mapp* days, the contours of the Fourth Amendment were largely undefined. This is no longer true; since *Mapp* many thousand appellate deci-

---

[1] 367 U.S. 643, 81 S.Ct. 1684, 6 L.Ed.2d 1081 (1961).

[2] Amsterdam, Perspectives on the Fourth Amendment, 58 Minn.L.Rev. 349, 353-54 (1974).

[3] Id. at 354.

[4] Chapman v. United States, 365 U.S. 610, 81 S.Ct. 776, 5 L.Ed.2d 828 (1961) (concurring op'n).

sions addressing a wide variety of Fourth Amendment issues have been published, and thus we know much more now than we did just a few decades ago. This is not to suggest, however, that the task has been completed. As some issues are finally put to rest, still others surface and cry out for resolution. Pieces are continuously being added to the Fourth Amendment mosaic, but as this occurs others fall away and somehow its borders still seem indeterminate. And the addition of more and more pieces does not necessarily reveal more clearly the overall design. As the Supreme Court recently observed, it has not yet been possible to reduce "Fourth Amendment law to complete order and harmony."[5]

For a confirmed Fourth Amendment buff such as myself, this state of affairs has been the source of continued excitement and opportunity. During my time in academe, which approximates the post-*Mapp* years, I have devoted much of my research and writing efforts to one subject: the Fourth Amendment.[6] I have never been in want of grist for my mill. Because the Amendment, which occupies "a place second to none in the Bill of Rights,"[7] has spawned a seemingly endless stream of litigation, there has always been a ready supply of Fourth Amendment issues deserving critical commentary. In these endeavors, I have never found myself in jeopardy of exhausting the subject (although, at times, I have felt somewhat exhausted by the subject).

After mining this particular lode of constitutional law for several years, I felt that I had achieved a fair degree of expertise in the subject. But it proved to be a humbling experience as well. Somehow, the more I learned about the Fourth Amendment, the more there seemed to be which remained to be mastered, and

---

[5] Coolidge v. New Hampshire, 403 U.S. 443, 91 S.Ct. 2022, 29 L.Ed.2d 564 (1971).

[6] See W. LaFave, Arrest: The Decision to Take a Suspect Into Custody (1965); LaFave, Probable Cause from Informants: The Effects of Murphy's Law on Fourth Amendment Adjudication, 1977 U.Ill.L.F. 1; LaFave, "Case by Case Adjudication" Versus "Standardized Procedures": The *Robinson* Dilemma, 1974 Supreme Court Rev. 127; LaFave, Warrantless Searches and the Supreme Court: Further Ventures Into the "Quagmire," 8 Crim.L.Bull. 9 (1972); LaFave, "Street Encounters and the Constitution: *Terry, Sibron, Peters* and Beyond," 67 Mich.L.Rev. 39 (1968); LaFave, Administrative Searches and the Fourth Amendment: The *Camara* and *See* Cases, 1967 Supreme Court Rev. 1 (1968); LaFave, Search and Seizure: "The Course of True Law. . . Has Not. . . Run Smooth," 1966 U.Ill.L.F. 255 (1966); LaFave, Improving Police Performance Through the Exclusionary Rule-Part II: Defining the Norms and Training the Police, 30 Mo.L.Rev. 566 (1965); LaFave, Improving Police Performance Through the Exclusionary Rule-Part I: Current Police and Local Court Practices, 30 Mo.L.Rev. 391 (1965); LaFave & Remington, Controlling the Police: The Judge's Role in Making and Reviewing Law Enforcement Decisions, 63 Mich.L.Rev. 987 (1963); LaFave, Detention for Investigation by the Police: An Analysis of Current Practices, 1962 Wash.U.L.Q. 331 (1962).

[7] Harris v. United States, 331 U.S. 145, 67 S.Ct. 1098, 91 L.Ed. 1399 (1947) (Frankfurter, J., dissenting).

this is what prompted me to commence the present, more ambitious undertaking some four years ago. For one thing, for my own satisfaction I wanted to produce a more systematic and comprehensive analysis of the entire range of contemporary Fourth Amendment issues. Secondly, and perhaps more importantly, it was my hope that I could produce a treatise on this subject which would be of aid to lawyers, judges, law teachers and students, and others who have occasion to confront in their professional or scholarly pursuits the many challenging problems posed by the Amendment and the great mass of reported decisions interpreting it. It will remain for others to judge how well I have succeeded in this latter objective.

As will be apparent from examination of the Table of Contents for this treatise, I have attempted to encompass within these volumes virtually all aspects of Fourth Amendment law. There is one notable exception, however, which merits a few words of explanation here. Though I have discussed at various points certain fundamental Fourth Amendment issues which exist with respect to the practices of eavesdropping and wiretapping, I have not attempted to cover in detail the limits upon that particular kind of activity, especially the unique restrictions which are applicable to the issuance and execution of eavesdropping-wiretapping warrants. These restrictions, although often grounded in the Fourth Amendment, are elaborated and particularized in Title III of the Crime Control Act of 1968,[8] and litigation concerning them has for the most part focused upon this legislation. Because a complete analysis of Title III and the cases decided thereunder would be a book in and of itself,[9] I have not attempted to bring that subject within the present undertaking.

I have tried to report in a systematic and orderly fashion the current state of Fourth Amendment law. In particular, it has been my purpose to record accurately and completely what issues have been decided by the Supreme Court and how they have been resolved, what issues not decided by the Court have been confronted with some degree of regularity by lower courts and how these issues have generally been decided, and what issues have by and large not been treated by the appellate courts. I have, of course, given the closest attention to the United States Supreme Court's Fourth Amendment decisions, for those opinions are the primary source to which lawyers and lower courts look when seeking guidance on the Amendment's content and meaning. However, I have examined hundreds upon hundreds of lower court opinions as well, for it is these cases which provide a

[8] 18 U.S.C.A. §§ 2510-2520.

[9] See J. Carr, The Law of Electronic Surveillance (1977); National Lawyers Guild, Raising and Litigating Electronic Surveillance Claims in Criminal Cases (1977); M. Paulsen, The Problems of Electronic Surveillance (1977).

real sense of the range of situations in which Fourth Amendment issues arise in practice and which reveal how formidable is the task of articulating principles to govern those situations which are intellectually sound but yet practical and readily understandable. Only by looking at such a great number of decisions is it possible "to see in the round rather than the flat, and to gain some understanding of the whole in action."[10] But while several thousand cases are cited in this work, I have not attempted to present a jurisdiction-by-jurisdiction laundry list of citations relating to every conceivable Fourth Amendment issue. To do so would require a substantially longer treatise or one of lesser depth and, in my judgment, would not materially advance what I perceive as the unique merits of this study.

Although I do not deprecate the value of an accurate account of the current state of the law, especially concerning a subject matter as vast and diverse as the Fourth Amendment, it has been my intention from the outset to produce something more than this. I have, at many points throughout this treatise, attempted to present a *critical* assessment of how the Supreme Court and the lower courts have fared in their ongoing and challenging enterprise of giving content and meaning to the Fourth Amendment. I have not been reluctant to express my own opinions on these matters, and I have tried to develop in an understandable and lucid way the reasoning underlying my views. Likewise, I have from time to time indicated my own judgments as to how various unresolved questions ought to be decided. Many of the issues in this field, as previously noted, are exceedingly difficult and complex, and thus I would not be so bold as to suggest that the positions I have taken are invariably beyond dispute or criticism. I do think, however, that the viewpoints expressed herein are worthy of consideration by those who by design or necessity have occasion to wrestle with Fourth Amendment questions. Whether my own perspective is in a particular instance accepted or rejected, I would hope that an appraisal of my views by lawyers and judges would aid in some small way in the development of a more sound and cohesive Fourth Amendment jurisprudence.

The research and writing of this treatise was greatly facilitated by the fact that on two occasions I was able to take a leave of absence from my regular duties at the University of Illinois College of Law. During the 1974-75 academic year, by virtue of the generous support of Dean John E. Cribbet, I was able to take an extended sabbatical leave. During the 1977-78 academic year, as a result of a Fellowship from the John Simon Guggenheim Foundation and an appointment as an Associate at the University of Illinois Center for Advanced Study, I was again able to be on leave. To Dean Cribbet, the Guggenheim Foundation, and the

---

[10] K. Llewellyn, The Common Law Tradition—Deciding Appeals 263 (1960).

Center, I express my heartfelt appreciation for their vital support.

During the gestation period of this treatise, I was fortunate to be aided by a series of able student assistants who helped me in a variety of ways—from the preparation of memoranda on selected topics to the tedious but essential task of checking footnote citations. These assistants were: James Conley; Robert Graham; Dale Gronemeier; Charles Knight; Robert Maganuco; and James Tueth. Over the entire four-year period, Carol Haley has aided me immensely by typing drafts, proofreading and cheerfully performing endless other necessary chores. Brenda Masters typed the final manuscript, and James LaFave and Theresa LaFave assisted with the processing of the research notes and the final manuscript. To all of them, I express my sincere thanks for their valuable contributions. In addition, I am grateful for the helpful insights and reactions provided by a number of my colleagues at the College of Law who cheerfully (or, at least resignedly) endured hearing more about the Fourth Amendment than they may have wanted to know.

I must also mention here what I hope is apparent in the treatise itself, namely, that I have been aided considerably in forming my own judgments about various Fourth Amendment issues by the thoughtful analysis others have given to many of those questions. I have profited from lead articles and student pieces appearing in the law reviews; they are too numerous to be listed here, but are cited at appropriate points throughout the treatise. In addition, I have benefited from the careful attention which many federal and state appellate judges have given to extremely difficult Fourth Amendment questions. Confronted with the responsibility of decision and the necessity of resolving the particular issue presented by the facts of the case (burdens which do not befall the law review commentator or text writer), they have had to develop Fourth Amendment theory under the most trying of circumstances.

Finally, I must acknowledge my indebtedness to my good friend and former mentor, Professor Frank J. Remington of the University of Wisconsin Law School. He taught me how to think clearly about the complexities of constitutional criminal procedure and how to write about the law. To the extent that this treatise manifests some facility in either respect, he is responsible. To the extent that it falls short, it is because I failed to learn better from Frank's instruction and example.

WAYNE R. LAFAVE

November, 1978

THE AUTHOR

Wayne R. LaFave received his Bachelor of Science, Bachelor of Laws and Doctor of Juridical Science degrees from the University of Wisconsin, where he was named to Phi Beta Kappa and the Order of the Coif. Since 1961 he has been on the faculty of the College of Law at the University of Illinois. At that institution, he is now Professor Emeritus in the College of Law and the Center for Advanced Study, and continues to conduct research at the College. He has also taught at the law schools of the University of Michigan and Villanova University.

Over the years, Professor LaFave has been active in several endeavors seeking improvements in criminal justice administration. He was a member of the Committee on Rules of Practice and Procedure of the Judicial Conference of the United States, the ABA Task Force on Technology and Law Enforcement, and the ABA Committee on Criminal Justice in a Free Society, and was Chairman of the Illinois Supreme Court Committee on Criminal Justice Programs. He has also served as Reporter/Draftsman for the Advisory Committee on the Federal Rules of Criminal Procedure of the Judicial Conference of the United States, the Uniform Rules of Criminal Procedure project of the National Conference of Commissioners on Uniform State Laws, and the Standards for Criminal Justice project of the American Bar Association.

Professor LaFave has also been involved in many research and educational efforts of national scope regarding the administration of criminal justice. For example, he participated for many years in the American Bar Foundation's empirical Survey of the Administration of Criminal Justice in the United States. He was a member of the Editorial Board for four-volume Encyclopedia of Crime and Justice, and served as consultant and contributing writer for the Public Broadcasting System's "Search and Seizure: The Supreme Court and the Police," shown nationally in 1992 and 1993.

LaFave has written extensively for the law reviews in the areas of criminal law and criminal procedure, especially on the subject of arrest, search and seizure, and he has also written several books on criminal law and procedure. For West, in addition to the present work, he has authored or co-authored two other multi-volume practitioners' treatises, six casebooks, five hornbooks, and one shorter student text. Many of these works have been quoted or cited by the U.S. Supreme Court in over a hundred and forty cases, and in well over ten thousand reported opinions in all. Of the later total, nearly seven thousand of those cases referred to a prior edition of this Search and Seizure treatise. LaFave's work has also been cited in over seven thousand law review articles.

As one legal periodical put it, "Professor LaFave undoubtedly is the reigning expert on the law of search and seizure." Or, in the words of one appellate court, LaFave has become the Fourth Amendment's "patron saint."

WestlawNext™

THE NEXT GENERATION OF ONLINE RESEARCH

WestlawNext is the world's most advanced legal research system. By leveraging more than a century of information and legal analysis from Westlaw, this easy-to-use system not only helps you find the information you need quickly, but offers time-saving tools to organize and annotate your research online. As with Westlaw.com, WestlawNext includes the editorial enhancements (e.g., case headnotes, topics, key numbers) that make it a perfect complement to West print resources.

- FIND ANYTHING by entering citations, descriptive terms, or Boolean terms and connectors into the WestSearch™ box at the top of every page.

- USE KEYCITE® to determine whether a case, statute, regulation, or administrative decision is good law.

- BROWSE DATABASES right from the home page.

- SAVE DOCUMENTS to folders and add notes and highlighting online.

SIGN ON: next.westlaw.com
LEARN MORE: store.westlaw.com/westlawnext
FOR HELP: 1–800–WESTLAW (1–800–937–8529)

Summary of Contents

Volume 1

Volume 2

Volume 3

Volume 4

Summary of Contents by Section

Volume 1

Volume 2

Volume 3

CHAPTER 5 SEIZURE AND SEARCH OF PERSONS AND PERSONAL EFFECTS

CHAPTER 6 ENTRY AND SEARCH OF PREMISES

CHAPTER 7 SEARCH AND SEIZURE OF VEHICLES

Volume 4

CHAPTER 8 CONSENT SEARCHES

CHAPTER 9 STOP AND FRISK AND SIMILAR LESSER INTRUSIONS

Volume 5

CHAPTER 10 INSPECTIONS AND REGULATORY SEARCHES

Volume 6

CHAPTER 11 ADMINISTRATION OF THE EXCLUSIONARY RULE

Table of Contents

Volume 1

CHAPTER 2 PROTECTED AREAS AND INTERESTS

Volume 2

CHAPTER 3 PROBABLE CAUSE

CHAPTER 4 SEARCH WARRANTS

Volume 3

CHAPTER 5 SEIZURE AND SEARCH OF PERSONS AND PERSONAL EFFECTS

CHAPTER 6 ENTRY AND SEARCH OF PREMISES

CHAPTER 7 SEARCH AND SEIZURE OF VEHICLES

Volume 4

CHAPTER 8 CONSENT SEARCHES

CHAPTER 9 STOP AND FRISK AND SIMILAR LESSER INTRUSIONS

Volume 5

CHAPTER 10 INSPECTIONS AND REGULATORY SEARCHES

Volume 6

CHAPTER 11 ADMINISTRATION OF THE EXCLUSIONARY RULE

CHAPTER 1

THE EXCLUSIONARY RULE AND OTHER REMEDIES

§ 1.1 Origins and purposes of the exclusionary rule

Research References

West's Key Number Digest
Criminal Law ∞394.1(3), 394.4; Searches and Seizures ∞12, 23

Legal Encyclopedias
C.J.S., Criminal Law §§ 770 to 773, 778 to 792; Searches and Seizures §§ 2 to 6, 9 to 12, 14 to 15, 24, 29 to 30, 32 to 34, 47 to 48, 99 to 102

Introduction

In this Chapter, attention is given to various actual or potential remedies for violation of the Fourth Amendment. Without passing judgment at this point upon the relative efficacy of these various remedies, it may nonetheless be said with confidence that the practicing lawyer most frequently encounters the Fourth Amendment in the context of proceedings to determine whether the fruits of a search or seizure are to be admitted into evidence in a criminal case. It is primarily because of the exclusionary rule that courts are called upon to meet the seemingly unceasing challenge of marking the dimensions of the protections flowing from the Fourth Amendment. Thus, it is appropriate to begin this Treatise with a brief historical survey of the origins and purposes of the exclusionary rule.[1]

§ 1.1(a) Origins of the Fourth Amendment[2]

A leading Fourth Amendment scholar has noted: "Alone among those constitutional provisions which set standards of fair conduct

---

[Section 1.1]

[1]That is, the Fourth Amendment exclusionary rule, which is one of several constitutional exclusionary rules, quite different from one another. See J. Tomkovicz, Constitutional Exclusion: The Rules, Rights, and Remedies That Strike the Balance Between Freedom and Order (2011).

[Section 1.1(a)]

[2]For a more thorough account, see W. Cuddihy, The Fourth Amend-ment: Origins and Original Meaning, 602-1791 (2009); J. Landynski, Search and Seizure and the Supreme Court ch. 1 (1966); N. Lasson, The History and Development of the Fourth Amendment to the United States Constitution (1937); L. Levy, Original Intent and the Framers' Constitution 221-46 (1988); T. Taylor, Two Studies in Constitutional Interpretation (1969); A. Taslitz, Reconstructing the Fourth Amendment: A History of Search and Seizure, 1789–1868 (2006); Clancy,

for the apprehension and trial of accused persons, the Fourth
Amendment provides us with a rich historical background rooted
in American, as well as English, experience; it is the one
procedural safeguard in the Constitution that grew directly out of
the events which immediately preceded the revolutionary
struggle with England."[3]

In England, the power to search was long used as a means of
restricting freedom of the press.[4] A licensing system was
introduced by Henry VIII in 1538,[5] and vast powers of search
were conferred on those who enforced the system. The Star
Chamber,[6] and later the Parliament,[7] authorized virtually
unlimited search powers to seek out books and other publications.
It was not until the impeachment of a justice for his issuance of
general warrants that the Parliament recognized, in 1685, "the
idea that general warrants were an arbitrary exercise of

The Framers' Intent: John Adams, His
Era, and the Fourth Amendment, 86
Ind.L.J. 979 (2011); Clancy, The Rule
of History, 70 Ohio St.J.Crim.L. 811
(2010) (review of Cuddihy book); Cloud,
A Conclusion in Search of a History to
Support It, 43 Tex. Tech L.Rev. 29
(2010); Cloud, The Fourth Amendment
During the Lochner Era: Privacy,
Property, and Liberty in Constitutional
Theory, 48 Stan.L.Rev. 555 (1996);
Davies, Can You Handle The Truth?
The Framers Preserved Common-Law
Criminal Arrest and Search Rules in
"Due Process of Law"—"Fourth Amend-
ment Reasonableness" is Only a
Modern, Destructive, Judicial Myth,
43 Tex. Tech L.Rev. 51 (2010); Davies,
How the Post-Framing Adoption of the
Bare-Probable-Cause Standard Drasti-
cally Expanded Government Arrest
and Search Power, 73 Law & Contemp.
Probs. 1 (Summer 2010); Davies,
Correcting Search-and-Seizure
History: Now-Forgotten Common-Law
Warrantless Arrest Standards and the
Original Understanding of "Due
Process of Law," 77 Miss.L.J. 1 (2007);
Davies, Recovering the Original Fourth
Amendment, 98 Mich.L.Rev. 547
(1999); Maclin & Mirabella, Framing
the Fourth, 109 Mich.L.Rev. 1049
(2011) (reviewing Cuddihy book);
Michael, Reading the Fourth Amend-
ment: Guidance From the Mischief
That Gave It Birth, 85 N.Y.U.L.Rev.
905 (2010); Oliver, The Modern History
of Probable Cause, 78 Tenn.L.Rev. 377
(2011); Smith, The Fourth Amendment, 1789–1868: A Strange History,
5 Ohio St.J.Crim.L. 663 (2008); Steinberg, The Uses and Misuses of Fourth
Amendment History, 10 U.Pa.J.
Const.L. 581 (2008); Stewart, The
Road to Mapp v. Ohio and Beyond:
The Origins, Development and Future
of the Exclusionary Rule in Search and
Seizure Cases, 83 Colum.L.Rev. 1365,
1372–80 (1983); Thomas, Stumbling
Toward History: The Framers' Search
and Seizure World, 43 Tex. Tech L.Rev.
199 (2010).

For more recent history, describing "the trajectory of search and seizure doctrine" as developed by the
Supreme Court from the 1914 *Weeks*
decision forward, see the thoughtful
discussion in Davies, The Supreme
Court Giveth and the Supreme Court
Taketh Away; The Century of Fourth
Amendment 'Search and Seizure'
Doctrine, 100 J.Crim.L. & Criminology 933 (2010).

[3] J. Landynski, Search and
Seizure and the Supreme Court 19
(1966).

[4] See F. Siebert, Freedom of the
Press in England: 1476-1776 (1952).

[5] F. Siebert, Freedom of the Press
in England: 1476-1776 at 48 (1952).

[6] F. Siebert, Freedom of the Press
in England: 1476–1776 at 84–85
(1952).

[7] F. Siebert, Freedom of the Press
in England: 1476-1776 at 173–76
(1952).

governmental authority against which the public had a right to be safeguarded."[8] But it was many years later before judicial rulings against such warrants were forthcoming, first in *Wilkes v. Wood*[9] and later in the most famous case of *Entick v. Carrington*,[10] where Lord Camden sustained a trespass verdict in favor of the victim of a general warrant. He declared, "if this point should be determined in favor of the jurisdiction, the secret cabinets and bureaus of every subject in this kingdom will be thrown open to the search and inspection of a messenger, whenever the secretary of state shall think fit to charge, or even to suspect, a person to be the author, printer, or publisher of a seditious libel." Because of these decisions and the popular feeling they aroused, Parliament was influenced to act against general warrants.[11] Leading the attack was William Pitt, whose eloquent remarks will never

---

[8]N. Lasson, The History and Development of the Fourth Amendment to the United States Constitution 38–39 (1937).

[9]19 Howell's State Trials 1153 (1763). In Amar, Fourth Amendment First Principles, 107 Harv.L.Rev. 757 (1994), the author of this provocative article relies heavily on *Wilkes* to question three mainstays of contemporary Fourth Amendment jurisprudence: the warrant requirement; the probable cause requirement; and the exclusionary rule. That use of *Wilkes* is vigorously questioned in Bandes, "We the People" and Our Enduring Values, 96 Mich.L.Rev. 1376 (1998); Davies, 98 Mich.L.Rev. 547 (1999) (noting, e.g., at 576 that Amar and also Taylor, Two Studies in Constitutional Interpretation (1969), "offered little evidence for their central historical claims—that the Framers broadly approved of warrantless intrusions and that the Framers viewed 'the warrant' as 'an enemy,'" and that "both ignored salient features of the history that are not easily reconciled with their claims"); Dripps, Akhil Amar on Criminal Procedure and Constitutional Law: "Here I Go Down That Wrong Road Again," 74 N.C.L.Rev. 1559 (1996) (Amar's general approach is "historically and theoretically barren"); Maclin, The Complexity of the Fourth Amendment: A Historical Review, 77 B.U.L.Rev. 925 (1997) (relying on scholarship later published in W. Cuddihy, The Fourth Amendment: Origins and Original Meaning, 602–1791 (2009), he

"explains why judges and lawyers should not rely on Amar's theories when interpreting the Amendment"); Maclin, When the Cure for the Fourth Amendment is Worse Than the Disease, 68 So.Cal.L.Rev. 1 (1994); Steiker, Second Thoughts About First Principles, 107 Harv.L.Rev. 820 (1994); Steinberg, An Original Misunderstanding: Akhil Amar and Fourth Amendment History, 42 San Diego L.Rev. 227 (2005). A rebuttal to Maclin appears in Amar, The Fourth Amendment, Boston, and the Writs of Assistance, 30 Suffolk U.L.Rev. 53 (1996).

Consistent with Amar are Arcila, The Death of Suspicion, 51 Wm. & Mary L.Rev. 1275 (2010); Arcila, The Framers' Search Power: The Misunderstood Statutory History of Suspicion and Probable Cause, 50 B.C.L.Rev. 363 (2009); Arcila, In the Trenches: Searches and the Misunderstood Common-Law History of Suspicion and Probable Cause, 10 U.Pa.J. Const.L. 1 (2007). A rebuttal to Arcila appears in Steinberg, Probable Cause, Reasonableness, and the Importance of Fourth Amendment History: A Response to Professor Arcila, 10 U.Pa.J.Const.L. 1211 (2008), answered in Arcila, A Reponse to Professor Steinberg's Fourth Amendment Chutzpah, 10 U.Pa.J.Const.L. 1229 (2008).

[10]19 Howell's State Trials 1029 (1765).

[11]N. Lasson, The History and Development of the Fourth Amendment to the United States Constitution 49 (1937).

cease to be quoted:

> The poorest man may, in his cottage, bid defiance to all the force of
> the Crown. It may be frail; its roof may shake; the wind may blow
> through it; the storm may enter; the rain may enter; but the King
> of England may not enter; all his force dares not cross the thresh-
> old of the ruined tenement.[12]

While this struggle was going on in England, there were
important developments on this side of the Atlantic. The writ of
assistance, seldom used in England,[13] was utilized by customs officers to enter and search buildings for smuggled goods.[14] In 1761,
James Otis, Jr., representing 63 Boston merchants, opposed in
court the issuance of new writs. He did not prevail, but this does
not detract from the impact of Otis' oratory. As John Adams, a
youthful spectator, was later to recall: "[H]e was a flame of fire!
* * * Every man of a crowded audience appeared to me to go
away, as I did, ready to take arms against writs of assistance.
* * * Then and there the Child Independence was born. In fifteen
years, namely in 1776, he grew up to manhood, and declared
himself free."[15] Controversy over the writs continued up to the
Revolutionary War, although curiously no specific mention of
them is to be found in the list of grievances in the Declaration of
Independence.[16]

The Constitutional Convention, meeting in 1787 in Philadelphia, did not include a bill of rights in its draft constitution, an
omission that was the cause of considerable opposition to
ratification. One of the points emphasized in the ratification
debates was the need for a provision dealing with searches.[17]
Because of this national criticism, President Washington urged
the addition of a bill of rights,[18] and James Madison assumed the
role as sponsor of this effort in the Congress. Madison proposed a
clause reading: "The rights of the people to be secured in their
persons, their houses, their papers, and their other property,
from all unreasonable searches and seizures, shall not be violated
by warrants issued without probable cause, supported by oath or
affirmation, or not particularly describing the places to be

---

[12]N. Lasson, The History and
Development of the Fourth Amendment to the United States Constitution 49–50 (1937).

[13]1 H. Hockett, The Constitutional
History of the United States,
1776-1826, 74 (1939).

[14]See N. Lasson, The History and
Development of the Fourth Amendment to the United States Constitution ch. 2 (1937).

[15]10 C. Adams, The Life and
Works of John Adams 247–48 (1856).

[16]It has been noted, however, that

the grievance was possibly intended to
be comprehended within the complaint
that the King had "sent hither swarms
of Officers to harass our people." N.
Lasson, The History and Development
of the Fourth Amendment to the United
States Constitution 80 n. 7 (1937).

[17]N. Lasson, The History and
Development of the Fourth Amendment to the United States Constitution 92–96 (1937), quoting the arguments of Patrick Henry in the Virginia
ratification proceedings.

[18]The Presidents Speak 5 (D.Lott
ed.1961).

searched, or the persons or things to be seized."[19] This provision
was altered in committee to read: "The right of the people to be
secured in their persons, houses, papers, and effects, shall not be
violated by warrants issuing without probable cause, supported
by oath or affirmation, and not particularly describing the place
to be searched and the persons or things to be seized."[20] The committee draft was corrected by replacing the word "secured" with
"secure" and by adding the inadvertently omitted phrase "unreasonable searches and seizures," but Representative Benson's proposal to use stronger language ("no warrant shall issue") was
voted down by a substantial majority.[21] However, Benson, chairman of the committee to arrange the amendments as passed,
reported out his own version; this apparently went unnoticed in
the House, and the amendment was agreed to in the Senate in
this form:

> The right of the people to be secure in their persons, houses,
> papers, and effects, against unreasonable searches and seizures,
> shall not be violated, and no Warrants shall issue, but upon prob-
> able cause, supported by Oath or affirmation, and particularly
> describing the place to be searched, and the persons or things to be
> seized.

The Fourth Amendment, it has been aptly noted, has "both the
virtue of brevity and the vice of ambiguity."[22] It does not define
the critical word "unreasonable,"[23] nor does it indicate what the
relationship is between that part prohibiting unreasonable
searches and that part setting forth the conditions under which

---

[19] 1 Annals of Cong. 452 (1789) [1789–90].

[20] 1 Annals of Cong. 783 (1789) [1789–90].

[21] 1 Annals of Cong. 783 (1789) [1789–90].

[22] J. Landynski, Search and Seizure and the Supreme Court 42 (1966).

[23] Hence "reasonableness analysis employed by the Supreme Court has repeatedly changed and each new case seems to modify the Court's view of what constitutes a reasonable search or seizure. The Court chooses from at least five principal models to measure reasonableness: the warrant prefer- ence model, the individualized suspi- cion model, the totality of the circum- stances test, the balancing test, and a hybrid model that gives dispositive weight to the common law. Because the Court has done little to establish a meaningful hierarchy among the mod- els, in any situation the Court may choose whichever model it sees fit to apply. Thus, cases decided within weeks of each other have had funda- mentally different—and irreconcil- able—approaches to measuring the permissibility of an intrusion. * * * The Court has, from time to time, at- tempted to harmonize its analysis by announcing the primacy—or the de- mise—of a particular model. None of those efforts has been enduring." Clancy, The Fourth Amendment's Concept of Reasonableness, 2004 Utah L. Rev. 977, 978, 1022. See also Colb, the Qualitative Dimensions of Fourth Amendment "Reasonableness," 98 Colum.L.Rev. 1642 (1998); Lee, Reasonableness With Teeth: The Future of Fourth Amendment Reasonableness Analysis, 81 Miss.L.J. 1133 (2012).

warrants may issue.[24] And, unlike the self-incrimination protection in the Fifth Amendment, no mention is made of barring from evidence the fruits of a violation of the proscription.

Especially because of those ambiguities, it might be thought that this Treatise should begin with a much more ambitious recitation of the Fourth Amendment's history. But I have not followed such a course, for the focus of this Treatise is instead upon the contemporary meaning of the Fourth Amendment. This is not to suggest that history is irrelevant to the fundamental question of what the scope and content of the Fourth Amendment is and should be in the present day. (It surely is relevant,[25] and thus this history is further taken into account at various points in the material that follows.) Rather, it is to suggest—notwithstanding the efforts of some scholars[26] and judges[27] to follow the "intent of the Framers" in ascertaining the Amendment's present day application—that such reliance on history is of limited utility. For one thing, it is often difficult if not impossible to determine just what that intent was.[28] As Prof. Cloud put it in reviewing the most comprehensive and objective history written of the Fourth Amendment, the author's "greatest contribution may be that he confirms that the complexity of the Amendment's history defies the simple generalizations—whether glib or thoughtful—that lawyers, judges, and legal scholars have made about the lessons history teaches about the meaning of the Fourth Amendment."[29] But the overriding consideration here (as it has been so well

---

[24]See Amar, Fourth Amendment First Principles, 107 Harv.L.Rev. 757, 762–81 (1994); Bacigal, Dodging a Bullet, but Opening Old Wounds in Fourth Amendment Jurisprudence, 16 Seton Hall L.Rev. 597 (1986); Cloud, Searching Through History; Searching for History, 63 U.Chi.L.Rev. 1707, 1721–31 (1996); Grayson, The Warrant Clause in Historical Context, 14 Am.J.Crim.L. 107 (1987); Luna, Sovereignty and Suspicion, 1999 Duke L.J. 789, 790–98; Wasserstrom, The Fourth Amendment's Two Clauses, 26 Am.Crim.L.Rev. 1389 (1989).

[25]The Supreme Court has frequently taken such history into account in resolving Fourth Amendment issues. See cases discussed in Schroeder, Warrantless Misdemeanor Arrests and the Fourth Amendment, 58 Mo.L.Rev. 771, 808–11 (1993).

[26]E.g., Posner, Rethinking the Fourth Amendment, 1981 Sup.Ct.Rev. 49; Steinberg, Restoring the Fourth Amendment: The Original

Understanding Revisited, 33 Hastings Const.L.Q. 47 (2005); Steinberg, The Original Understanding of Unreasonable Searches and Seizures, 56 Fla.L. Rev. 1051 (2004); Wilson, The Fourth Amendment as More Than a Form of Words: The View from the Founding, in The Bill of Rights: Original Meaning and Current Understanding 151 (Hickok, ed.1991).

[27]E.g., Scalia, J., in California v. Acevedo, 500 U.S. 565, 111 S.Ct. 1982, 114 L.Ed.2d 619 (1991).

[28]See Brest, The Misconceived Quest for the Original Understanding, 60 B.U.L.Rev. 204 (1980); Fallon, A Constructivist Coherence Theory of Constitutional Interpretation, 100 Harv.L.Rev. 1189 (1987); Kamisar, The Writings of John Barker Waite and Thomas Davies on the Search and Seizure Exclusionary Rule, 100 Mich.L. Rev. 1821 (2002).

[29]Cloud, Searching Through History; Searching for History, 63 U.Chi.L.Rev. 1707, 1746 (1996).

expressed by Professor Steiker) is that

almost no one * * * believes that we should be bound for all time by the specific intentions or expectations of the Framers about, say, precisely what kinds of searches are "reasonable" ones or precisely what sorts of remedies are required for violations of the Fourth Amendment. At some point, all but the most absolutist originalists formulate notions of the Framers' intent at some higher level of abstraction, a move that necessarily renders less significant even highly persuasive historical claims about the more specific intentions. Moreover, the Fourth Amendment, more than many other parts of the Constitution, appears to require a fairly high level of abstraction of purpose; its use of the term "reasonable" (actually, "unreasonable") positively invites constructions that change with changing circumstances.[30]

If we accept this proposition—that the construction of the Fourth Amendment's "reasonableness" clause should properly change over time to accommodate constitutional purposes more general than the Framers' specific intentions—* * * focus on colonial history to support a disjunctive reading of the "reasonableness" clause and the Warrant Clause and to attack the exclusionary rule seems short-sighted. Such a focus ignores at least two crucial changes between colonial times and the present that must inform our current readings of the Fourth Amendment as a whole. First, at the time of the drafting and ratifying of the Fourth Amendment, nothing even remotely resembling modern law enforcement existed. The invention in the nineteenth century of armed, quasi-military, professional police forces, whose form, function, and daily presence differ dramatically from that of the colonial constabulary, requires that modern-day judges and scholars rethink both the relationship between "reasonableness" and "warrants" and the nature of Fourth Amendment remedies. Second, the intensification of inter-racial conflict in our society during the Civil War and Reconstruction, and the myriad ways in which this conflict has intersected with law enforcement, likewise necessitate new constructions of the Fourth Amendment. It is no accident that the modern pillars of Fourth Amendment law * * * were significantly fortified during the 1960s at the same time that the Supreme Court and the rest of the country began to address systematically our legacy of racial discrimination.[31]

Of particular concern is the manner in which the Supreme

---

[30]But consider Marceau, The Fourth Amendment At a Three-Way Stop, 62 Ala.L.Rev. 687, 691 (2011): "But if the living constitutionalists have won some of the substantive battles, they appear poised to lose the Fourth Amendment interpretation war. Recent procedural developments, including a more robust practice of severing the Fourth Amendment right from the exclusionary remedy and the sanctioning of substantive avoidance through the relaxation of order of decision-making rules, all but guarantee that the Fourth Amendment will be substantially less dynamic and responsive to changing conditions. By exploring the viability of announcing new rules of constitutional criminal procedure in each of the three main forums for such litigation-habeas proceedings, civil and injunctive litigation under § 1983, and direct review of exclusionary rule litigation-this Article predicts the tortured death by a thousand procedures of the living Fourth Amendment."

[31]Steiker, Second Thoughts About First Principles, 107 Harv.L.Rev. 820, 823–24 (1994).

Court has recently been utilizing history, namely, by making the principal criterion for identifying violations of the Fourth Amendment "whether a particular governmental action * * * was regarded as an unlawful search or seizure under the common law when the Amendment was framed."[32] This approach has been aptly described and critiqued as follows in an excellent article on the subject by Prof. Sklansky:

> [T]he new Fourth Amendment originalism really is new. It departs dramatically from the largely ahistorical approach the Court has taken to the Fourth Amendment for most of the past thirty years, and it differs significantly from the use of history in earlier search-and-seizure opinions, stretching back to the nineteenth century. The Court has a long and celebrated tradition of looking to the background of the Fourth Amendment for the paradigmatic abuses that prompted its adoption, and then generalizing from those specific practices to the broader evils against which the Amendment offers protection. This is a far cry from saying, as the Court now has, that the first task in assessing a Fourth Amendment claim is determining whether the challenged action would have been condemned by common law in 1791.
>
> Unfortunately, the Court's new approach is not only innovative, it is also unjustified. It finds support neither in the constitutional text, nor in what we know of the intentions of the "Framers," however that term is understood. And the new Fourth Amendment originalism will do little to make search-and-seizure doctrine more principled or predictable. Indeed that goal may be better served by drawing from the common law what constitutional law has always drawn from it: not a set of substantive rules, but a centuries-old jurisprudential method, rooted in stare decisis and the practice of reasoned elaboration. That method ultimately may give judges no more leeway than the new Fourth Amendment originalism. It does, however, make the leeway more visible. This transparency is among the method's great virtues, not least because it makes clear what the Court's new approach tends to obscure: that the Fourth Amendment places on courts a burden of judgement, and that the burden cannot be relieved by the common law's sporadic, contradictory, and necessarily time-bound rules of search and seizure.[33]

Moreover, as Prof. Dripps has pointed out,

---

[32] Wyoming v. Houghton, 526 U.S. 295, 119 S.Ct. 1297, 143 L.Ed.2d 408 (1999). See also United States v. Jones, __ U.S. __, 132 S.Ct. 945, 181 L.Ed.2d 911 (2012); Atwater v. City of Lago Vista, 532 U.S. 318, 121 S.Ct. 1536, 149 L.Ed.2d 549 (2001); Florida v. White, 526 U.S. 559, 119 S.Ct. 1555, 143 L.Ed.2d 748 (1999); Wilson v. Arkansas, 514 U.S. 927, 115 S.Ct. 1914, 131 L.Ed.2d 976 (1995).

[33] Sklansky, The Fourth Amendment and Common Law, 100 Colum.L. Rev. 1739, 1813–14 (2000). An additional problem is that the Court sometimes gets the history wrong. See, e.g., Davies, Correcting Search-and-Seizure History: Now-Forgotten Common-Law Warrantless Arrest Standards and the Original Understanding of "Due Process of Law," 77 Miss.L.J. 1 (2007); Davies, The Fictional Character of Law-and-Order Originalism: A Case Study of the Distortions and Evasions of Framing-Era Arrest Doctrine in Atwater v. Lago Vista, 37 Wake Forest L.Rev. 239 (2002); Maclin, Let Sleeping Dogs Lie: Why the Supreme Court Should Leave Fourth Amendment History Unchanged, 82 B.U.L.Rev. 895

deriving specific rules from specific common-law practices detaches common-law practice from its context. Perhaps worse, identifying the rule by reference to how the common-law judges understood the police practice at issue detaches the contemporary rule announced by the Court from its context—a web of other court-made Fourth Amendment rules, each with its own arbitrary margins. To adopt an evolutionary simile, transplanting selected common-law practices into the current constitutional criminal-procedure regime is like doing a skin graft from a zebra to a horse.[34]

§ 1.1(b) The *Boyd* case

The Fourth Amendment "remained for almost a century a largely unexplored territory."[35] Then, in 1886, came *Boyd v. United States*,[36] later characterized by the Court as "the leading case on the subject of search and seizure."[37] In proceedings brought by the federal government for the forfeiture of certain goods alleged to have been illegally imported, the district judge on motion of the government ordered George and Edward Boyd, New York merchants, to produce an invoice showing the quantity and value of a part of these goods. The Boyds complied under protest, after which the jury found for the government and the goods were declared forfeited.

If the Boyds were to prevail on Fourth Amendment grounds, several issues had to be resolved in their favor: (i) whether the forced production of papers was a search within the meaning of the Fourth Amendment; (ii) whether the protections of the Fourth

---

(2002).

[34]Dripps, The Fourth Amendment and the Fallacy of Composition: Determinacy Versus Legitimacy in a Regime of Bright-Line Rules, 74 Miss.L.J. 341, 346 (2004).

Dripps later cautioned again that "[a]n originalist approach to the Fourth Amendment based on specific founding-era practice is illogical and unwise," in part because a "search or seizure in 1791 took place in an institutional context so different from ours that it simply is not the same search or seizure it was then," but then added that "[d]escriptive balance-of-advantage approaches," exemplified by Kyllo v. United States, 533 U.S. 27, 121 S.Ct. 2038, 150 L.Ed.2d 94 (2001), discussed in § 2.2(e), "at least asks the right question about Fourth Amendment cases: Is the search or seizure at issue consistent with the balance of public security and individual freedom the founders hoped our society would achieve?" Dripps, Responding to the Challenges of Contextual Change and

Legal Dynamism in Interpreting the Fourth Amendment, 81 Miss.L.J. 1085, 1131 (2012). As to the latter approach, consider also Kerr, An Equilibrium-Adjustment Theory of the Fourth Amendment, 125 Harv.L.Rev. 476, 480 (2011), offering an explanation/justification for "the patchwork of Fourth Amendment rules," namely, "equilibrium-adjustment": "When new tools and new practices threaten to extend or contract police powers a significant way, courts adjust the level of Fourth Amendment protection to try to restore the prior equilibrium."

[Section 1.1(b)]

[35]J. Landynski, Search and Seizure and the Supreme Court 49 (1966).

[36]Boyd v. United States, 116 U.S. 616, 6 S.Ct. 524, 29 L.Ed. 746 (1886).

[37]E.g., One 1958 Plymouth Sedan v. Pennsylvania, 380 U.S. 693, 85 S.Ct. 1246, 14 L.Ed.2d 170 (1965); Carroll v. United States, 267 U.S. 132, 45 S.Ct. 280, 69 L.Ed. 543 (1925).

Amendment extended to forfeiture proceedings; (iii) whether competent but illegally obtained evidence must be excluded. The Court, per Justice Bradley, held that the forced production was a search because it "effects the sole object and purpose of search and seizure," that the search was unreasonable because it was directed toward mere evidence of crime,[38] and that Fourth Amendment protections were applicable because the proceeding was of a "quasi-criminal nature." But most significant for our present purposes is Justice Bradley's treatment of the third issue, "the most creative, and most controversial, feature of his opinion,"[39] wherein he linked together the Fourth and Fifth Amendments:

> They throw great light on each other. For the "unreasonable searches and seizures" condemned in the fourth amendment are almost always made for the purpose of compelling a man to give evidence against himself, which in criminal cases is condemned in the fifth amendment; and compelling a man "in a criminal case to be a witness against himself," which is condemned in the fifth amendment, throws light on the question as to what is an "unreasonable search and seizure" within the meaning of the fourth amendment. And we have been unable to perceive that the seizure of a man's private books and papers to be used in evidence against him is substantially different from compelling him to be a witness against himself.

He thus concluded "that the notice to produce the invoice * * * and the law which authorized the order, were unconstitutional and void, and that the inspection by the district attorney of said invoice, when produced in obedience to said notice, and its admission in evidence by the court, were erroneous and unconstitutional proceedings."

Justice Miller, joined by the Chief Justice, concurred on the ground that it was "quite clear" the proceedings below had violated the Boyds' privilege against self-incrimination. They thus deemed it inappropriate for the Court to "assume that the action of the court below, in requiring a party to produce certain papers as evidence on the trial, authorizes an unreasonable search or seizure of the house, papers, or effects of that party." Upon this and other grounds, many commentators were critical of the *Boyd* decision,[40] and not entirely without reason. But there is no denying the fact that *Boyd* "was part of the process by which the Fourth Amendment * * * has become more than a dead let-

---

[38]On the demise of the mere evidence rule, see § 2.6(d).

[39]J. Landynski, Search and Seizure and the Supreme Court 53 (1966). See, e.g., Pardo, Disentangling the Fourth Amendment and the Self–Incrimination Clause, 90 Iowa L.Rev. 1857 (2005), and sources cited therein.

[40]Corwin, The Supreme Court's Construction of the Self-Incrimination Clause, 29 Mich.L.Rev. 1, 191 (1930); Nelson, Search and Seizure: Boyd v. United States, 9 A.B.A.J. 773 (1923); Wigmore, Using Evidence Obtained by Illegal Search and Seizure, 8 A.B.A.J. 479 (1922).

ter in the federal courts."[41]

§ 1.1(c) The *Weeks* case

The continued vitality of *Boyd* was cast into doubt some years later in *Adams v. New York*,[42] where state officers executing a warrant for policy slips also seized other papers, which were admitted at trial to identify Adams' handwriting on the policy slips. While the Court might have held, as it did a few years later,[43] that the Constitution did not prohibit unreasonable searches under state authority, it instead declared that "the weight of authority as well as reason" supported the common-law rule that courts will not inquire into the means by which evidence otherwise admissible was acquired. *Boyd* was distinguished on the questionable ground that it was limited to that situation in which a positive act was required on the part of the defendant.

Then, in 1914, the Court decided *Weeks v. United States*,[44] concerning a conviction in the federal courts for using the mails to transmit lottery tickets. Weeks' home had been searched by local police, who turned certain evidence over to the U.S. marshal, and the marshal later that day participated in a second warrantless search of the house by the police. Upon Weeks' pretrial motion for return of the property seized, the court ordered the return of all of the property except that which the prosecutor wished to introduce into evidence. Before the Supreme Court, Weeks contended that the seizure of his private papers violated the Fourth and Fifth Amendments, but Justice Day (who had also written the *Adams* decision), for a unanimous Court, dealt only with the Fourth Amendment. The Court had no doubt but that, given Weeks' timely motion for return of the illegally seized evidence, a conviction based upon that evidence could not stand:

> The effect of the 4th Amendment is to put the courts of the United States and Federal officials, in the exercise of their power and authority, under limitations and restraints as to the exercise of such power and authority * * *. This protection reaches all alike, whether accused of crime or not, and the duty of giving to it force and effect is obligatory upon all intrusted under our Federal system with the enforcement of the laws. The tendency of those who execute the criminal laws of the country to obtain conviction by means of unlawful seizures * * * should find no sanction in the judgments of the courts, which are charged at all times with the support of the

---

[41]Abel v. United States, 362 U.S. 217, 80 S.Ct. 683, 4 L.Ed.2d 668 (1960) (Brennan, J., dissenting).

[Section 1.1(c)]

[42]Adams v. New York, 192 U.S. 585, 24 S.Ct. 372, 48 L.Ed. 575 (1904).

[43]National Safe Deposit Co. v. Stead, 232 U.S. 58, 34 S.Ct. 209, 58 L.Ed. 504 (1914).

[44]Weeks v. United States, 232 U.S. 383, 34 S.Ct. 341, 58 L.Ed. 652 (1914). For an exhaustive analysis of *Weeks* and an argument as to how it should be read in the context of contemporary debate on the underpinnings of the exclusionary rule, see Bradley, Present at the Creation? A Critical Guide to Weeks v. United States and Its Progeny, 30 St.Louis U.L.J. 1031 (1986).

Constitution, and to which people of all conditions have a right to appeal for the maintenance of such fundamental rights.

* * * To sanction [unlawful invasion of the sanctity of his home by officers of the law] would be to affirm by judicial decision a manifest neglect, if not an open defiance, of the prohibitions of the Constitution, intended for the protection of the people against such unauthorized action.

But, the government countered, what of the *Adams* case, where just ten years earlier a unanimous Court had held that it was no valid objection to the use of papers in evidence that they had been illegally seized and that courts would not interrupt a trial to make a determination of that question? *Adams,* Justice Day responded, had as its underlying principle the notion that a court engaged in a criminal trial should not have to get into the collateral issue of the source of competent evidence, and thus it had no application here, as Weeks had petitioned for return of the property before trial. Hence the Court concluded it was necessary to reverse the judgment because of prejudicial error in holding and permitting use at trial of those papers that had been seized by the marshal. The same result was not required as to the fruits of the first search, conducted by state officers, "as the 4th Amendment is not directed to individual misconduct of such officials."

While the *Weeks* Court thus saw no constitutional impediment to admitting in a federal trial the fruits of a state search, it was later necessary for the Court to give this matter closer attention. In two 1927 cases, the Supreme Court concluded otherwise as to state searches with either federal participation or a federal purpose. In *Byars v. United States,*[45] state officers executing a state search warrant, defective by federal standards, were accompanied by a federal agent, who participated in the search. Because "the search in substance and effect was a joint operation of the local and federal officers," the Court concluded that the fruits were inadmissible in the federal courts. But the Court emphasized that the rule was still otherwise as to "evidence improperly seized by state officers operating entirely upon their own account." As Justice Frankfurter was later to state the *Byars* doctrine, "a search is a search by a Federal official if he had a hand in it; it is not a search by a federal official if evidence secured by state authorities is turned over to the federal authorities on a silver platter."[46] But, it is otherwise if the platter was in readiness at the time of the search, the Court concluded in

---

[45]Byars v. United States, 273 U.S. 28, 47 S.Ct. 248, 71 L.Ed. 520 (1927).

[46]Lustig v. United States, 338 U.S. 74, 69 S.Ct. 1372, 93 L.Ed. 1819 (1949), which "marked the first serious challenge of the doctrine by members of the Court." J. Landynski, Search and Seizure and the Supreme Court 73 (1966). *Lustig* is discussed later in this section because of its relationship to Wolf v. Colorado, 338 U.S. 25, 69 S.Ct. 1359, 93 L.Ed. 1782 (1949).

Gambino v. United States.[47] There, though federal agents had neither directed nor participated in a search by state officers of a car suspected to contain illegal liquor, the Court found that "the wrongful arrest, search and seizure were made solely on behalf of the United States." Why? Because the state's prohibition law had been repealed, the national prohibition act contemplated federal-state cooperation, and the governor of the state had directed his officers to proceed as they had prior to repeal of the state law but to turn offenders over to federal authorities.

§ 1.1(d) The *Wolf* case

Because the Bill of Rights was designed as a limitation on the federal government only,[48] it was settled very early that the Fourth Amendment "has no application to state process."[49] With the adoption in 1868 of the Fourteenth Amendment, forbidding the states to "deprive any person of life, liberty, or property, without due process of law," however, there arose the difficult question of the relation of the limitation of that Amendment upon the states to the limitations upon federal action in the first eight Amendments. Commencing with *Hurtado v. California*[50] in 1884, a majority of the Court utilized the so-called fundamental rights interpretation of the due process clause. But it was not until the 1930's, when the Court began to display increasing interest in state criminal procedure, that the Court held that elements of several rights guaranteed by the first eight Amendments were also fundamental rights protected by the Fourteenth Amendment. Illustrative is *Powell v. Alabama*,[51] where the Court held that appointed counsel for an indigent criminal defendant, an element of the Sixth Amendment right to counsel, was fundamental as applied to certain types of state cases. In rejecting the claim that certain guarantees were fundamental, the Court would often limit its holding to the particular problem before it; for example, in *Palko v. Connecticut*,[52] holding that due process did not bar a state appeal on a question of law following acquittal, the Court intimated that other forms of double jeopardy might well violate the Fourteenth Amendment. It is also important to note that the fundamental rights approach was by no means accepted by all members of the Court. Indeed, by 1947 Justice Black was able to muster four votes in support of his position that the due process clause guarantees, as against the

---

[47]Gambino v. United States, 275 U.S. 310, 48 S.Ct. 137, 72 L.Ed. 293 (1927).

[Section 1.1(d)]

[48]Barron v. Baltimore, 32 U.S. (7 Pet.) 243, 8 L.Ed. 672 (1833).

[49]Smith v. Maryland, 59 U.S. (18 How.) 71, 15 L.Ed. 269 (1855).

[50]Hurtado v. California, 110 U.S. 516, 4 S.Ct. 111, 28 L.Ed. 232 (1884).

[51]Powell v. Alabama, 287 U.S. 45, 53 S.Ct. 55, 77 L.Ed. 158 (1932).

[52]Palko v. Connecticut, 302 U.S. 319, 58 S.Ct. 149, 82 L.Ed. 288 (1937).

states, "the complete protection of the Bill of Rights."[53]

The stage was thus set for the Supreme Court to consider the question that was framed by Justice Frankfurter in *Wolf v. Colorado*[54] as follows: "Does a conviction by a State court for a State offense deny the 'due process of law' required by the Fourteenth Amendment, solely because evidence that was admitted at the trial was obtained under circumstances which would have rendered it inadmissible in a prosecution for violation of a federal law in a court of the United States because there deemed to be an infraction of the Fourth Amendment as applied in *Weeks v. United States* * * *?" His answer, for a majority of the Court, was as follows:

> The security of one's privacy against arbitrary intrusion by the police—which is at the core of the Fourth Amendment—is basic to a free society. It is therefore implicit in "the concept of ordered liberty" and as such enforceable against the States through the Due Process Clause. * * *

> Accordingly, we have no hesitation in saying that were a State affirmatively to sanction such police incursion into privacy it would run counter to the guaranty of the Fourteenth Amendment. But the ways of enforcing such a basic right raise questions of a different order. * * *

> [*Weeks*] was not derived from the explicit requirements of the Fourth Amendment; it was not based on legislation expressing Congressional policy in the enforcement of the Constitution. The decision was a matter of judicial implication.[55] Since then it has been frequently applied and we stoutly adhere to it. But the immediate question is whether the basic right to protection against arbitrary intrusion by the police demands the exclusion of logically relevant evidence obtained by an unreasonable search and seizure because, in a federal prosecution for a federal crime, it would be excluded. As a matter of inherent reason, one would suppose this to be an issue as to which men with complete devotion to the protection of the right of privacy might give different answers. When we find that in fact most of the English-speaking world does not regard as vital to such protection the exclusion of evidence thus obtained,[56] we must hesitate to treat this remedy as an essential ingredient of the right.

---

[53]Adamson v. California, 332 U.S. 46, 67 S.Ct. 1672, 91 L.Ed. 1903 (1947).

[54]Wolf v. Colorado, 338 U.S. 25, 69 S.Ct. 1359, 93 L.Ed. 1782 (1949).

[55]More recently, in United States v. Williams, 504 U.S. 36, 112 S.Ct. 1735, 118 L.Ed.2d 352 (1992), a majority of the Court characterized the *Weeks* exclusionary rule as an instance of the Supreme Court utilizing its "supervisory power."

[56]A more recent comparative analysis concludes that "two fundamental concepts are nearly uniform in foreign legal systems": illegally obtained evidence is admitted if it is reliable and probative, and the most widely used method of handling official procedural deviations is internal discipline. Comment, 57 Tul.L.Rev. 648, 680 (1983).

But see Bradley, Reconceiving the Fourth Amendment and the Exclusionary Rule, 73 Law & Contemp. Probs. 211 (Summer 2010) (re exclusionary rule in Canada, England and Wales, France, and Germany); Bradley, Mapp Goes Abroad, 52 Case W.Res.L. Rev. 375, 399 (2001) (noting that in many foreign countries the "illegality

The contrariety of views of the States is particularly impressive in view of the careful reconsideration which they have given the problem in the light of the *Weeks* decision.
Noting that 30 states had rejected the *Weeks* rule, while only 17 were in agreement with it, the Court concluded it was not "a departure from basic standards" to leave the victims of illegal state searches "to the remedies of private action and such protection as the internal discipline of the police, under the eyes of an alert public opinion, may afford."[57]

Justice Black, while not departing from his total incorporation position, concurred on the ground that "the federal exclusionary rule is not a command of the Fourth Amendment but is a judicially created rule of evidence which Congress might negate." Justice Rutledge, one of the three dissenters, objected that without the exclusionary rule the Fourth Amendment, as stated in *Weeks,* "might as well be stricken from the Constitution." Justice Murphy, after cataloguing the reasons why criminal prosecution and civil actions against those who violate the Amendment are ineffective, found the conclusion "inescapable that but one remedy exists to deter violations of the search and seizure clause," namely, "the rule which excludes illegally obtained evidence." Similarly, Justice Douglas concluded that evidence obtained in violation of the Fourth Amendment "must be excluded in state prosecutions as well as in federal prosecutions, since in

---

of the search or seizure of evidence is now a relevant consideration in determining its admissibility," so in that "respect, *Mapp* has been largely adopted," while "the second component of *Mapp* has been universally rejected," namely, "that once a violation of search and seizure rules has been found, evidence must be excluded"); Bradley, The Exclusionary Rule in Germany, 96 Harv.L.Rev. 1032, 1066 (1983) (the "existence of a detailed system of exclusionary rules in Germany suggests that the *Weeks* rule is neither a bizarre aberration nor the only form that a viable exclusionary rule can take"); Chen, One Problem, Two Paths: A Taiwanese Perspective on the Exclusionary Rule in China, 43 N.Y.U.J.Int'l L. & Pol. 713, 723–24 (2011) (in Taiwan, where "Supreme Court's 1998 decision * * * authorized a court to suppress illegally obtained physical evidence on the basis of fairness and justice" and legislation enacted in 2001 and 2002 accords "the courts discretion to exclude physical evidence seized in a search that later proves to be unauthorized," trial courts

"have continued to demonstrate great reluctance to exclude physical evidence"); MacDougall, The Exclusionary Rule and Its Alternatives, Remedies for Constitutional Violations in Canada and the United States, 76 J.Crim.L. & Criminology 608 (1985), and Comment, 4 Can.-Am.L.J. 57 (1988) (both discussing § 24 of the 1982 Canadian Constitution, which says evidence obtained in violation of the Constitution "shall be excluded if it is established that, having regard to all the circumstances, the admission of it in the proceedings would bring the administration of justice into disrepute").

[57] In this connection, the Court perceived a difference between local and national law enforcement: "The public opinion of a community can far more effectively be exerted against oppressive conduct on the part of police directly responsible to the community itself than can local opinion, sporadically aroused, be brought to bear upon remote authority pervasively exerted throughout the country."

absence of that rule of evidence the Amendment would have no effective sanction."

Any thought that *Wolf* meant state courts were permitted to admit all unconstitutionally seized evidence, regardless of how outrageous or offensive the police methods employed, was dispelled three years later in *Rochin v. California.*[58] In *Rochin,* state officers broke into the defendant's home, used force in an unsuccessful attempt to retrieve capsules the defendant put in his mouth, and then took the defendant to a hospital where they directed a doctor to force an emetic solution into defendant's stomach, compelling him to vomit up the capsules he had swallowed. Relying upon the coerced confession cases for the proposition that "convictions cannot be brought about by methods that offend 'a sense of justice,'" the Court, per Justice Frankfurter, held that the capsules must be excluded because they were obtained by "conduct that shocks the conscience." "It would be a stultification of the responsibility which the course of constitutional history has cast upon this Court," Justice Frankfurter declared, "to hold that in order to convict a man the police cannot extract by force what is in his mind but can extract what is in his stomach."[59]

It soon became apparent, however, that the *Rochin* exclusionary rule would not encompass all serious Fourth Amendment violations. In a 5-4 decision, the Court held in *Irvine v. California*[60] that the repeated illegal entries into petitioner's home to install and relocate a secret microphone and the listening to the conversations of the occupants for over a month did not require exclusion of the fruits of such conduct. Justice Jackson, who announced the judgment of the Court, noted that "few police measures have come to our attention that more flagrantly, deliberately, and persistently violated the fundamental principle declared by the Fourth Amendment," but he nonetheless concluded that *Rochin* was inapplicable because "the facts in the case before us * * * do not involve coercion, violence or brutality to the person."[61] And in *Breithaupt v. Abram,*[62] the majority deemed *Rochin* not controlling where the police took a blood

---

[58]Rochin v. California, 342 U.S. 165, 72 S.Ct. 205, 96 L.Ed. 183 (1952).

[59]Justices Black and Douglas, concurring separately, contended that the decision should be grounded upon the Fifth Amendment privilege against self-incrimination, which they argued was applicable to the states.

[60]Irvine v. California, 347 U.S. 128, 74 S.Ct. 381, 98 L.Ed. 561 (1954).

[61]Frankfurter, J., joined by Burton, J., maintained that *Rochin* was controlling. Black, J., joined by Doug-

las, J., argued that the defendant had been convicted on the basis of evidence "extorted" from him in violation of the Fifth Amendment privilege against self-incrimination, which they again argued was applicable to the states. In a separate dissent, Douglas, J., also protested against the use in state prosecutions of evidence seized in violation of the Fourth Amendment.

[62]Breithaupt v. Abram, 352 U.S. 432, 77 S.Ct. 408, 1 L.Ed.2d 448 (1957).

sample "under the protective eye of a physician" from an unconscious person who had been involved in a fatal automobile collision.[63]

The other post-*Wolf* development that merits attention here is the demise of the so-called "silver platter" doctrine, whereby evidence of a federal crime seized by state police in the course of an illegal search while investigating a state crime could be turned over to federal authorities and used in a federal prosecution so long as federal agents had not participated in the illegal search but had simply received the evidence on a "silver platter." In rejecting the doctrine in *Elkins v. United States*,[64] Justice Stewart, for the majority, pointed out that the determination in *Wolf* that Fourteenth Amendment due process prohibited illegal searches and seizures by state officers, marked the "removal of the doctrinal underpinning" for the admissibility of state-seized evidence in federal prosecutions. He continued:

> The very essence of a healthy federalism depends upon the avoidance of needless conflict between state and federal courts. Yet when a federal court sitting in an exclusionary state admits evidence lawlessly seized by state agents, it not only frustrates state policy, but frustrates that policy in a particularly inappropriate and ironic way. For by admitting the unlawfully seized evidence the federal court serves to defeat the state's effort to assure obedience to the Federal Constitution. In states which have not adopted the exclusionary rule, on the other hand, it would work no conflict with local policy for a federal court to decline to receive evidence unlawfully seized by state officers. The question with which we deal today affects not at all the freedom of the states to develop and apply their own sanctions in their own way.

But the author of *Wolf*, Justice Frankfurter, was among the dis-

---

[63]Dissenting Chief Justice Warren, joined by Black and Douglas, JJ., contended that *Rochin* was controlling: "Only personal reaction to the stomach pump and the blood test can distinguish [the two cases]."

Nine years later, even though in the meantime the Court had held in Mapp v. Ohio, 367 U.S. 643, 81 S.Ct. 1684, 6 L.Ed.2d 1081 (1961), that the federal exclusionary rule in search and seizure cases was binding on the states, and in Malloy v. Hogan, 378 U.S. 1, 84 S.Ct. 1489, 12 L.Ed.2d 653 (1964), that the Fifth Amendment protection against compelled self-incrimination was likewise applicable to the states, the Court still upheld the taking by a physician, at police direction, of a blood sample from an injured person over his objection. Schmerber v. California, 384 U.S. 757, 86 S.Ct. 1826, 16 L.Ed.2d 908 (1966). A 5-4 majority, per Brennan, J., held: (1) that the practice did not offend that "sense of justice" of which the Court spoke in *Rochin;* (2) that the privilege against self-incrimination had not been violated, for it covers only "evidence of a testimonial or communicative nature"; and (3) that there had been no unreasonable search, as there was probable cause, not time to get a warrant first, and the test "was a reasonable one * * * performed in a reasonable manner."

[64]Elkins v. United States, 364 U.S. 206, 80 S.Ct. 1437, 4 L.Ed.2d 1669 (1960).

senters[65] in *Elkins*. He deemed it "a complete misconception of the *Wolf* case to assume, as the Court does as the basis for its innovating rule, that every finding by this Court of a technical lack of a search warrant, thereby making a search unreasonable under the Fourth Amendment, constitutes an 'arbitrary intrusion' of privacy so as to make the same conduct on the part of state officials a violation of the Fourteenth Amendment."

As for the reverse of the situation presented in *Elkins,* that is, the turning over to state authorities of evidence acquired in an unconstitutional federal search, the Court had earlier held in *Rea v. United States*[66] that a federal official could be enjoined from turning over such evidence and from giving testimony in a state prosecution concerning the evidence.[67] Significantly, the Court stressed that it was "not asked to enjoin state officials nor in any way to interfere with state agencies in enforcement of state law," and that the case raised "not a constitutional question but one concerning our supervisory powers over federal law enforcement agencies." *Rea* was thus distinguishable from *Stefanelli v. Minard*,[68] where the Court declined to do indirectly what it was unwilling to do directly in *Wolf,* and thus held that federal injunctive relief was not available to bar the use in a state prosecution of evidence obtained in an illegal state search.[69]

§ 1.1(e) The *Mapp* decision

In *Mapp v. Ohio*,[70] the majority, as Justice Harlan complained in his dissent, "simply 'reached out' to overrule *Wolf*." Miss

---

[65]Also dissenting were Clark, Harlan, and Whittaker, JJ.

[66]Rea v. United States, 350 U.S. 214, 76 S.Ct. 292, 100 L.Ed. 233 (1956).

[67]But later, in Wilson v. Schnettler, 365 U.S. 381, 81 S.Ct. 632, 5 L.Ed.2d 620 (1961), a plea for injunctive relief was denied by the Court. *Rea* was distinguished on the curious ground that in that case there had been a prior federal court proceeding where the evidence was ordered suppressed. As one commentator noted, *Wilson* was "one of the most unconvincing and hairsplitting * * * to come from the Court in decades." Broeder, The Decline and Fall of Wolf v. Colorado, 41 Neb.L.Rev. 185, 193 (1961).

[68]Stefanelli v. Minard, 342 U.S. 117, 72 S.Ct. 118, 96 L.Ed. 138 (1951).

[69]*Stefanelli* was followed, and *Rea* distinguished, in Cleary v. Bolger, 371 U.S. 392, 83 S.Ct. 385, 9 L.Ed.2d 390

(1963), denying a federal injunction against a state official from giving evidence in pending state criminal and administrative proceedings even though the official had observed the illegal federal activities as a representative of the bi-state Waterfront Commission. Justice Goldberg, concurring, pointed out that in light of Mapp v. Ohio, 367 U.S. 643, 81 S.Ct. 1684, 6 L.Ed.2d 1081 (1961), holding the Fourth Amendment exclusionary rule applicable to the states, there was no need to grant injunctive relief because of the substantial likelihood that illegally obtained evidence would be excluded in the state proceedings.

[Section 1.1(e)]

[70]Mapp v. Ohio, 367 U.S. 643, 81 S.Ct. 1684, 6 L.Ed.2d 1081 (1961). For detailed accounts and assessments of *Mapp,* see C. Long, Mapp v. Ohio: Guarding Against Unreasonable Searches and Seizures (2006); L. Stevens, Trespass! (1977).

Dollree Mapp was convicted of having in her possession certain obscene books, pictures and photographs, which the police had found in an illegal search of her home. The state supreme court upheld the obscenity statute under which she was convicted and also declined to depart from the state's common-law rule of admissibility of illegally seized evidence. At no time did Miss Mapp's counsel ask the Supreme Court to overrule *Wolf*; he did not even cite the case in his brief, and on oral argument he expressly disavowed that he was seeking to have the *Wolf* case overturned. Rather, he pursued what Justice Clark,[71] for the majority, noted "may have appeared to be the surer ground for favorable disposition," namely, the question of whether one could constitutionally be convicted for the mere knowing possession of obscene materials. Only the American Civil Liberties Union, in a concluding paragraph of its amicus brief, urged that *Wolf* be overruled.

In holding "that all evidence obtained by searches and seizures in violation of the Constitution is, by that same authority, inadmissible in a state court," the Court in *Mapp* reasoned:

> Since the Fourth Amendment's right of privacy has been declared enforceable against the States through the Due Process Clause of the Fourteenth, it is enforceable against them by the same sanction of exclusion as is used against the Federal Government. Were it otherwise then just as without the *Weeks* rule the assurance against unreasonable federal searches and seizures would be "a form of words," valueless and undeserving of mention in a perpetual charter of inestimable human liberties, so too, without that rule the freedom from state invasions of privacy would be so ephemeral and so neatly severed from its conceptual nexus with the freedom from all brutish means of coercing evidence as not to merit this Court's high regard as a freedom "implicit in the concept of ordered liberty."

As for *Wolf,* the majority in *Mapp* found that case to be "bottomed on factual considerations" which were without "current validity." While it was said in *Wolf* that "the contrariety of views of the States" on adoption of the exclusionary rule was "particularly impressive," then supportable by the fact that almost two-thirds of the states were opposed to the use of the exclusionary rule, "more than half of those since passing upon it, by their own legislative or judicial decision, have wholly or partly adopted or adhered to the *Weeks* rule." Similarly, the observation in *Wolf* that "other means of protection" were afforded "the right to privacy" was rebutted by the experience in California and other states "that such other remedies have been worthless and futile." And as for what *Wolf* called the "weighty testimony" of *People v.*

---

[71]For an inside look at Justice Clark's role in *Mapp*, see Dorin, Marshaling Mapp: Justice Tom Clark's Role in Mapp v. Ohio's Extension of the Exclusionary Rule to State Searches and Seizures, 52 Case W.Res. L.Rev. 401 (2001). For another fascinating inside look, see Price, Mapp v. Ohio Revisited: A Law Clerk's Diary, 35 J.Sup.Ct.Hist. 54 (2010).

Defore,[72] characterizing the federal rule as "either too strict or too lax," the *Mapp* majority found that "the force of that reasoning has been largely vitiated by later decisions of this Court."[73]

In an oft-quoted passage, Justice Clark went on to say:

> Moreover, our holding * * * is not only the logical dictate of prior cases but it also makes very good sense. There is no war between the Constitution and common sense. Presently, a federal prosecutor may make no use of evidence illegally seized, but a State's attorney across the street may, although he supposedly is operating under the enforceable prohibitions of the same Amendment. Thus the State, by admitting evidence unlawfully seized, serves to encourage disobedience to the Federal Constitution which it is bound to uphold.

Justice Black, concurring, declared that he was "still not persuaded that the Fourth Amendment, standing alone, would be enough" to support exclusion, but he concluded "that when the Fourth Amendment's ban against unreasonable searches and seizures is considered together with the Fifth Amendment's ban against compelled self-incrimination, a constitutional basis emerges which not only justifies but actually requires the exclusionary rule." In his concurring opinion, Justice Douglas responded to the objection of the three dissenters[74] that the instant case was not "an appropriate occasion for re-examining *Wolf*," noting that the Court had said a year earlier that all the arguments pro and con on this issue were well known.

Justice Harlan, joined by Justices Frankfurter and Whittaker, after stating their objection to reaching the Fourth Amendment issue, turned to the merits. They found the majority's reasoning to rest on an "unsound premise," namely, that "whatever configurations of the Fourth Amendment have been developed in the particularizing federal precedents are likewise * * * enforceable against the States." This is not the case, they declared, for *Wolf* did not hold "that the Fourth Amendment *as such* is enforceable against the States," but rather only "the principle of privacy 'which is at the core of the Fourth Amendment.'" That "core" does not include the exclusionary rule, for each state, "considering the totality of its legal picture," can best conclude what remedies are needed. Thus, the *Mapp* dissenters urged, "this Court should continue to forbear from fettering the States with an adamant rule which may embarrass them in coping with their own peculiar problems in criminal law enforcement."

---

[72]People v. Defore, 242 N.Y. 13, 150 N.E. 585 (1926).

[73]The Court referred to the discarding of the "silver platter" doctrine in *Elkins,* the use of federal injunctive relief against the reverse "silver platter" in *Rea,* and the relaxation of the standing requirements in Jones v. United States, 362 U.S. 257, 80 S.Ct. 725, 4 L.Ed.2d 697 (1960).

[74]Which was shared by Justice Stewart, who by separate memorandum indicated he would reverse the judgment on the ground that the Ohio obscenity statute was unconstitutional.

§ 1.1(f) Purposes

Although not explicitly mentioned in the early cases, such as *Boyd* and *Weeks,* it is fair to say that the deterrence of unreasonable searches and seizures is a major purpose of the exclusionary rule. This was acknowledged even in *Wolf,* declining to apply the exclusionary rule to the states, for it was there noted that while "the exclusion of evidence may be an effective way of deterring unreasonable searches," the states were to be allowed to rely "upon other methods which, if consistently enforced, would be equally effective." And in *Elkins v. United States,*[75] in the course of striking down the "silver platter" doctrine, the Court emphasized: "The rule is calculated to prevent, not to repair. Its purpose is to deter—to compel respect for the constitutional guaranty in the only effectively available way—by removing the incentive to disregard it." This language from *Elkins* was quoted with approval in *Mapp,* where the Court characterized the exclusionary rule as a "deterrent safeguard without insistence upon which the Fourth Amendment would have been reduced to 'a form of words.'" *Elkins* was again quoted in *Linkletter v. Walker,*[76] where it was observed that "all of the cases since *Wolf* requiring the exclusion of illegal evidence have been based on the necessity for an effective deterrent to illegal police action," a purpose that would not "be advanced by making the rule retrospective." More recently, in *Terry v. Ohio,*[77] the Court stressed that the exclusionary rule's "major thrust is a deterrent one."

But, while it may be fair to say that deterrence is the "major thrust" of the exclusionary rule,[78] the rule does serve other purposes as well. There is, for example, what the *Elkins* Court referred to as "the imperative of judicial integrity," namely, that the courts not become "accomplices in the willful disobedience of a Constitution they are sworn to uphold." This language from

---

[Section 1.1(f)]

[75]Elkins v. United States, 364 U.S. 206, 80 S.Ct. 1437, 4 L.Ed.2d 1669 (1960).

[76]Linkletter v. Walker, 381 U.S. 618, 85 S.Ct. 1731, 14 L.Ed.2d 601 (1965).

[77]Terry v. Ohio, 392 U.S. 1, 88 S.Ct. 1868, 20 L.Ed.2d 889 (1968).

[78]Despite occasional claims to the contrary, the conduct to be deterred is not merely avoidance of the search warrant requirement. See Mazepink v. State, 336 Ark. 171, 987 S.W.2d 648 (1999) (rejecting out of hand state's claim "that because the purpose of the exclusionary rule is to deter police misconduct, it would be inappropriate to exclude the evidence in this case because the decision to act illegally (not to knock and announce before forcing entry) was not motivated by a desire to gather evidence by any means other than a search warrant issued on probable cause").

However, the Supreme Court on somewhat different reasoning has concluded that the exclusionary rule is ordinarily inapplicable to violation of the knock-and-announce requirement. See Hudson v. Michigan, 547 U.S. 586, 126 S.Ct. 2159, 165 L.Ed.2d 56 (2006), discussed at § 1.2, text at note 54; § 1.6(h); and § 11.4, text at notes 42 and 107.

Elkins was also relied upon in *Mapp* and again in *Terry,* where the Court explained:

> Courts which sit under our Constitution cannot and will not be made party to lawless invasions of the constitutional rights of citizens by permitting unhindered governmental use of the fruits of such invasions. Thus in our system evidentiary rulings provide the context in which the judicial process of inclusion and exclusion approves some conduct as comporting with constitutional guarantees and disapproves other actions by state agents. A ruling admitting evidence in a criminal trial, we recognize, has the necessary effect of legitimizing the conduct which produced the evidence, while an application of the exclusionary rule withholds the constitutional imprimatur.[79]

A third purpose of the exclusionary rule, as more recently stated most clearly by some members of the Court, is that "of assuring the people—all potential victims of unlawful government conduct—that the government would not profit from its lawless behavior, thus minimizing the risk of seriously undermining popular trust in government."[80] While at first blush this may appear to be merely a statement of the deterrent function, this is not the case, for the focus is on the effect of exclusion upon the public rather than the police. This purpose also has solid credentials in the cases. As early as *Weeks,* the Court declared:

> The tendency of those who execute the criminal laws of the country to obtain conviction by means of unlawful seizures * * * should find no sanction in the judgments of the courts, which are charged at all times with the support of the Constitution, and to which people of all conditions have a right to appeal for the maintenance of such fundamental rights.
>
> * * * To sanction such proceedings would be to affirm by judicial decision a manifest neglect, if not an open defiance, of the prohibition of the Constitution, intended for the protection of the people against such unauthorized action.

The same notion is implicit in the *Mapp* declaration that "no man is to be convicted on unconstitutional evidence."[81]

This brief exploration of the purposes of the exclusionary rule

---

[79]Consider Bilz, Dirty Hands or Deterrence? An Experimental Examination of the Exclusionary Rule, 9 J. Empirical Legal Stud. 149 (2012) (discussing empirical studies indicating substantial public "support for the integrity rationale," and then suggesting "the possibility that reinvigorating the integrity justification would serve the end of the rule better than current doctrine does"); Bloom & Fentin, "A More Majestic Conception": The Importance of Judicial Integrity in Preserving the Exclusionary Rule, 13 U.Pa.J.Const.L. 47 (2010) (urging "that the exclusionary rule be returned to its previous prominence by reinstating judicial integrity as its primary purpose"); Cicchini, An Economics Perspective on the Exclusionary Rule and Deterrence, 75 Mo.L.Rev. 459, 461 (2010) (even if exclusionary rule "does not, and cannot, deter police misconduct," it should not be limited, as it serves other concerns, such as the integrity of the judiciary).

[80]United States v. Calandra, 414 U.S. 338, 94 S.Ct. 613, 38 L.Ed.2d 561 (1974) (dissent).

[81]One commentator has forcefully argued for yet another purpose. Schroeder, Restoring the Status Quo

is of more than academic concern, for the Court's perception of these purposes has determined the scope of the exclusionary rule and, ultimately, could well determine its fate. The Court's focus in recent years has been almost exclusively upon the deterrence function,[82] as is illustrated by *United States v. Calandra.*[83] The majority held that a witness summoned to appear and testify before a grand jury may not refuse to answer questions on the ground that they are based on evidence obtained from an unlawful search, stressing that any "incremental deterrent effect which might be achieved by extending the rule to grand jury proceedings is uncertain at best." The three dissenters,[84] on the other hand, concentrated upon the other two functions and relegated deterrence to "at best only a hoped for effect of the exclusionary rule."

More recently, the *Calandra* approach was followed in such cases as *United States v. Janis,*[85] *Stone v. Powell,*[86] *I.N.S. v. Lopez-Mendoza,*[87] and *United States v. Leon,*[88] as well as *Herring v. United States*[89] and *Davis v. United States.*[90] In *Janis,* the majority concluded that "the 'prime purpose' of the rule, if not the sole one, 'is to deter future unlawful police conduct,'" and then held that this purpose would not be served by utilizing the exclusionary rule to exclude from federal civil tax proceedings evidence

---

Ante: The Fourth Amendment Exclusionary Rule as a Compensating Device, 51 Geo.Wash.L.Rev. 633, 636 (1983), "asserts that the Supreme Court's preoccupation with the exclusionary rule's deterrent function is misplaced, and posits that the principal role of the exclusionary rule should be to restore victims of those unconstitutional searches and seizures that yield incriminating evidence to the position they were in before the illegality occurred." See also Norton, the Exclusionary Rule Reconsidered—Restoring the Status Quo Ante, 33 Wake Forest L.Rev. 261, 262 (1998) ("the exclusionary rule is a just one because it puts both the State and the accused in the positions they would have been in had the Constitution not been violated—neither better nor worse").

[82]For an interesting account of how this came about, see Sundby & Ricca, The Majestic and the Mundane: Two Creation Stories of the Exclusionary Rule, 43 Tex. Tech L.Rev. 391 (2010).

[83]United States v. Calandra, 414 U.S. 338, 94 S.Ct. 613, 38 L.Ed.2d 561 (1974). See Schrock & Welsh, Up From Calandra: The Exclusionary Rule as a Constitutional Requirement, 59 Minn.L.Rev. 251 (1974).

[84]Brennan, Douglas, and Marshall, JJ.

[85]United States v. Janis, 428 U.S. 433, 96 S.Ct. 3021, 49 L.Ed.2d 1046 (1976).

[86]Stone v. Powell, 428 U.S. 465, 96 S.Ct. 3037, 49 L.Ed.2d 1067 (1976).

[87]I.N.S. v. Lopez-Mendoza, 468 U.S. 1032, 104 S.Ct. 3479, 82 L.Ed.2d 778 (1984).

[88]United States v. Leon, 468 U.S. 897, 104 S.Ct. 3405, 82 L.Ed.2d 677 (1984).

[89]Herring v. United States, 555 U.S. 135, 129 S.Ct. 695, 172 L.Ed.2d 496 (2009).

[90]Davis v. United States, __ U.S. __, 131 S.Ct. 2419, 180 L.Ed.2d 285 (2011).

obtained by a state law enforcement officer.[91] In *Stone,* the Court again declared deterrence to be the "primary justification" for the exclusionary rule, which led to the holding that a state prisoner cannot ordinarily[92] obtain habeas corpus relief in federal court on Fourth Amendment grounds because the "additional incremental deterrent effect" of exclusion at that stage would be minimal.[93] The holding in *Lopez-Mendoza* that the exclusionary rule is inapplicable in a deportation proceeding was grounded in part on the majority's supposition that several factors "significantly reduce the likely deterrent value of the exclusionary rule" in that setting. And in *Leon,* recognizing a "good faith" exception to the rule in with-warrant cases, the Court stressed that in situations falling within the exception there was "no basis * * * for believing that exclusion of evidence" would "have a significant deterrent effect." As for *Herring*, a 5–4 decision, the majority was all deterrence function, holding that exclusion in the interest of deterrence was unnecessary in response to "isolated negligence attenuated from the arrest," but it is noteworthy that all four dissenters embraced the "other important purposes" described above. And in *Davis*, the Court held that "[b]ecause suppression would do nothing to deter police misconduct in these circumstances, and because it would come at a high cost to both the truth and the public safety, * * * searches conducted in objectively reasonable reliance on binding appellate precedent are not subject to the exclusionary rule." (Though such uses of the deterrence theory have contributed to a disavowal of it in some quarters, it is well to note that there is "no inevitable connection between the deterrent theory and a narrow scope for the exclusionary rule; the deterrent theory could equally well be invoked by a different Court to reach results far more protective of individual rights."[94] That is, it is a mistake to assume "that there is anything inherently antilibertar-

---

[91]The Court had this to say in a footnote about the judicial integrity rationale:

The primary meaning of "judicial integrity" in the context of evidentiary rules is that the courts must not commit or encourage violations of the Constitution. In the Fourth Amendment area, however, the evidence is unquestionably accurate, and the violation is complete by the time the evidence is presented to the court. * * * The focus therefore must be on the question whether the admission of the evidence encourages violations of Fourth Amendment rights. As the Court has noted in recent cases, this inquiry is essentially the same as the inquiry into whether exclusion would serve a deterrent purpose.

[92]The exception noted by the Court is where the state has failed to provide an opportunity for full and fair litigation of a Fourth Amendment claim. See § 11.7(g).

[93]As for the judicial integrity rationale, the Court in *Stone* asserted: "While courts, of course, must ever be concerned with preserving the integrity of the judicial process, this concern has limited force as a justification for the exclusion of highly probative evidence. The force of this justification becomes minimal where federal habeas corpus relief is sought by a prisoner who previously has been afforded the opportunity for full and fair consideration of his search-and-seizure claim at trial and on direct review."

[94]Meltzer, Deterring Constitutional Violations by Law

ian about an emphasis on deterrence."[95])

Calandra is also noteworthy in another respect. In *Mapp,* the exclusionary rule was declared to be "part and parcel of the Fourth Amendment's limitation upon [governmental] encroachment of individual privacy," and "an essential part of both the Fourth and Fourteenth Amendments." But the *Calandra* majority, looking only to the deterrence function, characterized the rule as "a judicially-created remedy designed to safeguard Fourth Amendment rights generally through its deterrent effect, rather than a personal constitutional right of the party aggrieved." What that language (also relied upon in such later cases as *Stone* and *Leon*) may bode for the future is unclear, but the alarm sounded by the *Calandra* dissenters is not without substance.[96] As Justice Brennan stated, "I am left with the uneasy feeling that today's decision may signal that a majority of my colleagues have positioned themselves to reopen the door still further and abandon altogether the exclusionary rule in search and seizure cases."[97]

These developments have in recent years led to an intense debate as to the precise constitutional status of the exclusionary rule and, in particular, whether Congress could place significant limitations upon the rule or even abolish it entirely by providing some other remedy in its place.[98] Some of the reasoning on the affirmative side borders on the absurd, such as the argument that

---

Enforcement Officials: Plaintiffs and Defendants as Private Attorneys General, 88 Colum.L.Rev. 247, 269 (1988), adding at 268–69 that the deterrent view "is not popular with many academic commentators, particularly those who strongly support the exclusionary rule. Yet I believe the deterrent view's lack of academic popularity has less to do with its inherent defects than with the Burger Court's having followed it while cutting back the scope of the rule. * * * The battle lines have, however, been drawn, so that 'liberals' now espouse the view that the remedy redresses injury to the rights of the defendant himself, while 'conservatives' assert that the remedy's only value is to deter future misconduct.

"I believe, nonetheless, that the deterrent rationale is the most persuasive explanation for the exclusionary remedy."

[95]Meltzer, 88 Colum.L.Rev. 247, 274 (1988).

[96]See White, Forgotten Points in the "Exclusionary Rule" Debate, 81 Mich.L.Rev. 1273, 1281 (1983), noting that the Court's emphasis upon the deterrence function exclusively has had several "unfortunate consequences," especially that it "generates an enormous pressure for reduction of the scope of the rule" through a cost-benefit type of analysis.

[97]But in both *Stone* and *Janis,* the majority indicated its willingness to continue to assume, despite the absence of supportive empirical evidence, that the immediate effect of exclusion in criminal trials is to deter future violations.

[98]Compare the views of Yale Kamisar and Stephen H. Sachs with those of Judge Malcolm Wilkey and Frank G. Carrington in Symposium: The Exclusionary Rule, 1 Criminal Justice Ethics 4 (Summer/Fall, 1982). See also the various views in The Exclusionary Rule Bills: Hearings Before the Subcommittee on Criminal Law of the Senate Comm. on the Judiciary, 97th Cong., 1st & 2d Sess.

because the Fourth Amendment does not expressly declare an exclusionary remedy and because the Court has characterized it as "judicially-created" it has no constitutional foundation.[99] That is hardly a forceful argument—"not, at least, unless someone can name one Supreme Court decision or doctrine that is not 'a matter of judicial implication.' "[100] More difficult is the contention that the Fourth Amendment merely requires *some* effective remedy and that therefore the exclusion sanction may be replaced by any other device having a comparable or greater "deterrent effect." Putting aside for the moment the serious question of whether some of the alternatives commonly suggested, such as a damages action, would be effective,[101] this latter contention lacks merit unless it can fairly be concluded that the exclusionary rule is nothing more than an optional remedy tied exclusively to the function of deterrence.[102]

Some of the Court's more recent pronouncements may lend a modicum of support to such a characterization. Yet it certainly is *not* correct to assert that "the rule was adopted because until recently there was no alternative sanction for violations of the fourth amendment that did not cause severe underdeterrence."[103] The fact of the matter is that "nowhere in *Weeks* is the exclusionary rule called a 'remedy',"[104] and the Court's opinion in that case "contains no language that expressly justifies the rule by reference to a supposed deterrent effect on police officials."[105] (But to

---

(1982); and the articles cited in note 1 of § 1.2.

[99]In testifying before the Attorney General's Task Force on Violent Crime, Judge Wilkey said: "This rule of evidence did not come from on high. It's man-made, not God-given. * * * It's not even in the Constitution." Quoted in Mathias, The Exclusionary Rule Revisited, 28 Loy.L.Rev. 1, 7 (1982).

[100]Kamisar, Does (Did) (Should) the Exclusionary Rule Rest on a "Principled Basis" Rather than an "Empirical Proposition"?, 16 Creighton L.Rev. 565, 581 (1983).

[101]See § 1.2(c).

[102]This conclusion appears to have been rejected in Sanchez–Llamas v. Oregon, 548 U.S. 331, 126 S.Ct. 2669, 165 L.Ed.2d 557 (2006), where the Court's opinion by Chief Justice Roberts says "that the Constitution requires the exclusion of evidence obtained by certain violations of the Fourth Amendment," and in United

States v. Grubbs, 547 U.S. 90, 126 S.Ct. 1494, 164 L.Ed.2d 195 (2006), where the Court's opinion by Justice Scalia asserts without qualification that the "Constitution protected property owners * * * by providing, ex post, a right to suppress evidence improperly obtained and a cause of action for damages."

[103]Posner, Excessive Sanctions for Governmental Misconduct in Criminal Cases, 57 Wash.L.Rev. 635, 638 (1982). See also Posner, Rethinking the Fourth Amendment, 1981 Sup.Ct.Rev. 49.

[104]Kamisar, 16 Creighton L.Rev. 565, 598 (1983).

[105]Allen, The Judicial Quest for Penal Justice: The Warren Court and the Criminal Cases, 1975 U.Ill.L.F. 518, 536 n. 90. See also Hirsch, Big Bill Haywood's Revenge: The Original Intent of the Exclusionary Rule, 22 St. Thomas L.Rev. 35, 85 (2009) ("the exclusionary rule is not, and was never intended to be, a matter of deterrence"); LeFrancois, On Exorcising the Exclusionary Demons: An Essay on

say, as some have,[106] that a personal right to exclusion is to be found in *Weeks,* is likewise a proposition seriously questioned by other commentators.[107]) As for *Mapp,* it briefly discredits the "other means" of enforcing the Amendment discussed in *Wolf,*[108] but the main thrust of the opinion is considerably broader. Justice Clark declared that "no man is to be convicted on unconstitutional evidence," and to that end announced "our holding that the exclusionary rule is an essential part of both the Fourth and Fourteenth Amendments."[109]

Rhetoric, Principle and the Exclusionary Rule, 53 U.Cin.L.Rev. 49 (1984); Morris, The Exclusionary Rule, Deterrence and Posner's Economic Analysis of Law, 57 Wash.L.Rev. 647, 649 (1982); Oakes, The Proper Role of the Federal Courts in Enforcing the Bill of Rights, 54 N.Y.U.L.Rev. 911, 935–36 (1979); Schrock & Welsh, Up From Calandra: The Exclusionary Rule as a Constitutional Requirement, 59 Minn.L.Rev. 251, 281–82, 296–307 (1974); Sunderland, The Exclusionary Rule: A Requirement of Constitutional Principle, 69 J.Crim.L., C. & P.S. 141, 143 (1978); White, Forgotten Points in the "Exclusionary Rule" Debate, 81 Mich.L.Rev. 1273 (1983).

[106]See Heffernan, On Justifying Fourth Amendment Exclusion, 1989 Wis.L.Rev. 1193, 1226 ("One can make sense of Justice Day's conclusions, then, only by reasoning in terms of an implied fourth amendment right to the pretrial return of legally held property that has been illegally seized. Moreover, this implied right can be said to exist in a *Weeks*-type setting only if one reasons in terms of a further implied right available to defendants to prevent the government from proving the pertinence of documents by resort to a privacy wrong committed during the course of unlawful possession of those documents."); Kamisar, 16 Creighton L.Rev. 565 (1983); Schrock & Welsh, 59 Minn.L.Rev. 251 (1974).

[107]See Bradley, Present at the Creation? A Critical Guide to Weeks v. United States and Its Progeny, 30 St. Louis U.L.J. 1031 (1986); Dripps, Living with Leon, 95 Yale L.J. 906, 918–22 (1986).

[108]"In this part [of his opinion in *Mapp*] Justice Clark, as have others, yielded to the temptation to meet the author of the *Wolf* opinion on the latter's own battleground. Clark maintained that the 'factual considerations' asserted in support of the *Wolf* result—one of which was that 'other means of protection' have been afforded 'the right to privacy'—were no longer persuasive. But he stated at the outset of his discussion of the continuing validity of these factual considerations that 'they are *not basically relevant* to a decision that the exclusionary rule is *an essential ingredient* of the Fourth Amendment as the right it embodies is vouchsafed against the States by the Due Process Clause.'" Kamisar, 16 Creighton L.Rev. 565, 625 (1983).

Compare Stewart, The Road to Mapp v. Ohio and Beyond: The Origins, Development and Future of the Exclusionary Rule in Search and Seizure Cases, 83 Colum.L.Rev. 1365, 1380–89 (1983), rejecting the argument that exclusion is required by the Fourth Amendment itself but concluding that exclusion is constitutionally required as the only effective way to remove the incentive to violate it.

[109]This is not to suggest that a Fourth Amendment violation occurs only if the fruits of an illegal search or seizure are admitted at trial. As stated in United States v. Verdugo-Urquidez, 494 U.S. 259, 110 S.Ct. 1056, 108 L.Ed.2d 222 (1990), the Fourth Amendment "operates in a different manner than the Fifth Amendment, which is not at issue in this case. The privilege against self-incrimination guaranteed by the Fifth Amendment is a funda-

§ 1.2 The exclusionary rule under attack

§ 1.2(a)   Clearing the underbrush
§ 1.2(b)   The matter of deterrence
§ 1.2(c)   Replacing the exclusionary rule
§ 1.2(d)   Limiting the exclusionary rule to "substantial" or other
             than "good faith" violations
§ 1.2(e)   Limiting the exclusionary rule to other than "serious
             cases"
§ 1.2(f)   Limiting the exclusionary rule to institutional failures

Research References

West's Key Number Digest
Criminal Law ⊙→394

Legal Encyclopedias
C.J.S., Criminal Law §§ 770 to 798

Introduction

For well over half a century now, the validity and efficacy of the Fourth Amendment exclusionary rule have been vigorously debated by legal commentators.[1] In the following discussion, an

mental trial right of criminal defendants. * * * Although conduct by law enforcement officials prior to trial may ultimately impair that right, a constitutional violation occurs only at trial. * * * The Fourth Amendment functions differently. It prohibits 'unreasonable searches and seizures' whether or not the evidence is sought to be used in a criminal trial, and a violation of the Amendment is 'fully accomplished' at the time of an unreasonable governmental intrusion."

[Section 1.2]

[1]For a useful survey of this literature, see Comment, 65 J.Crim.L. & C. 373 (1974). More recent commentary includes S. Schlesinger, Exclusionary Injustice (1977); Calabresi, The Exclusionary Rule, 26 Harv.J.L. & Pub.Pol'y 111 (2003); Geller, Is the Evidence in on the Exclusionary Rule, 67 A.B.A.J. 1642 (1981); Caldwell, Fixing the Constable's Blunder: Can One Trial Judge in One County in One State Nudge a Nation Beyond the Exclusionary Rule?, 2006 BYU L.Rev. 1; Dripps, The "New" Exclusionary Rule Debate: From "Still Preoccupied with 1985" to "Virtual Deterrence," 37

Fordham Urb.L.J. 743 (2010); Geller, Enforcing the Fourth Amendment: The Exclusionary Rule and Its Alternatives, 1975 Wash.U.L.Q. 621; Kamisar, In Defense of the Search and Seizure Exclusionary Rule, 26 Harv.J.L & Pub.Pol'y 119 (2003); Kamisar, A Defense of the Exclusionary Rule, 15 Crim.L.Bull. 5 (1979); Loewenthal, Evaluating the Exclusionary Rule in Search and Seizure, 49 U.Mo.K.C.L. Rev. 24 (1980); Lynch, In Defense of the Exclusionary Rule, 23 Harv.J.L. & Pub. Pol'y 711 (2000); Miles, Decline of the Fourth Amendment: Time to Overrule Mapp v. Ohio, 27 Cath.U.L. Rev. 9 (1977); Milhizer, The Exclusionary Rule Lottery Revisited, 59 Cath.U. L.Rev. 747 (2010); Milhizer, The Exclusionary Rule Lottery, 39 U.Tol. L.Rev. 755 (2008); Pettys, Instrumentalizing Jurors: An Argument Against the Exclusionary Rule, 37 Fordham Urb.L.J. 837 (2010); Sunderland, Liberals, Conservatives and the Exclusionary Rule, 71 J.Crim.L. & Criminology 343 (1980); Tinsley, Kinsella and Block, In Defense of Evidence and Against the Exclusionary Rule: A Libertarian Approach, 32 S.U.L.Rev. 63 (2004); Weinreb, The Exclusionary Rule

effort has been made initially to set aside those anti-exclusionary rule arguments that are clearly without substance or are misdirected at the suppression doctrine rather than other aspects of the criminal justice system. This makes it possible to focus more clearly upon the question of deterrence, the most frequent arena of debate on the exclusionary rule. There then follows an assessment of extant proposals for replacing or limiting the Fourth Amendment exclusionary sanction.

§ 1.2(a) Clearing the underbrush

Professor Allen has aptly noted that debate on the exclusionary rule is "more remarkable for its volume than its cogency."[2] This is true to no small extent because extraneous matters have often been brought into the debate. It is well, then, to begin by identifying and putting aside those arguments that do not contribute to resolution of the ultimate question whether the exclusionary rule should be either abandoned or modified.

One such contention, which was very much in vogue immediately after the *Mapp* decision, is that the exclusionary rule "handcuffs" the police in the enforcement of the criminal law. Totally apart from the fact that evidence offered to support this conclusion, namely, statistics of "crime waves" following adoption of the exclusionary rule, cannot really be taken to establish the fact that use of the exclusionary rule results in more crime,[3] this argument is misdirected. The fallacy of this argument was clearly established many years before the *Mapp* decision by then Senator Robert F. Wagner:

> Finally, I have no fear that the exclusionary rule will handicap the detection or prosecution of crime. All the arguments that have been made on that score seem to me properly directed not against the exclusionary rule but against the substantive guarantee itself. The exclusion of the evidence is only the sanction which makes the rule effective. It is the rule, not the sanction, which imposes limits on the operation of the police. If the rule is obeyed as it should be,

Redux—Again, 37 Fordham Urb.L.J. 873 (2010).

See also the debate carried on in the following series of articles, listed in the order of their appearance: Kamisar, Is the Exclusionary Rule an "Illogical" or "Unnatural" Interpretation of the Fourth Amendment, 62 Judicature 66 (1978); Wilkey, The Exclusionary Rule: Why Suppress Valid Evidence?, 62 Judicature 214 (1978); Kamisar, The Exclusionary Rule in Historical Perspective, 62 Judicature 337 (1979); Wilkey, A Call for Alternatives to the Exclusionary Rule, 62 Judicature 357 (1979); Canon, The Exclusionary Rule: Have Critics Proven That it Doesn't Deter Police?,

62 Judicature 398 (1979); Schlesinger, The Exclusionary Rule: Have Proponents Proven That it is a Deterrent to Police?, 62 Judicature 404 (1979); Canon & Schlesinger, A Postscript on Empirical Studies and the Exclusionary Rule, 62 Judicature 455 (1979).

[Section 1.2(a)]

[2]Allen, Federalism and the Fourth Amendment: A Requiem for Wolf, 1961 Sup.Ct.Rev. 1, 33.

[3]The "crime wave" statistics are effectively demolished in Kamisar, Public Safety v. Individual Liberties: Some "Facts" and "Theories," 53 J.Crim.L.C. & P.S. 171 (1962).

and as we declare it should be, there will be no illegally obtained evidence to be excluded by the operation of the sanction.

It seems to me inconsistent to challenge the exclusionary rule on the ground that it will hamper the police, while making no challenge to the fundamental rules to which the police are required to conform. If those rules, defining the scope of the search which may be made without a warrant and the scope of a search under a warrant are sound, there is no reason why they should be violated or why a prosecuting attorney should seek to avail himself of the fruits of their violation. If those fundamental rules are open to challenge * * *, the burden is on those who challenge them to specify the modifications they deem to be desirable. I think that is a far better course than to object to * * * the one sanction which will give the constitutional provision, however it is defined, genuine meaning.[4]

The nature of the exclusionary rule is such that it makes the cost of honoring the Fourth Amendment apparent. As Professor Kaplan has observed, "by definition, it operates only after incriminating evidence has already been obtained" and thus "flaunts before us the costs we must pay for fourth amendment guarantees."[5] But it is not correct that the cost (much lower, in any event, than is commonly assumed[6]) is attributable to the exclusionary rule. Those who drafted the Fourth Amendment

---

[4]Record of the N.Y. State Const'l Convention 559-60 (1938), quoted in Allen, The Wolf Case: Search and Seizure, Federalism, and the Civil Liberties, 45 Ill.L.Rev. 1, 19 n. 56 (1950).

[5]Kaplan, The Limits of the Exclusionary Rule, 26 Stan.L.Rev. 1027, 1037 (1974).

[6]In Impact of the Exclusionary Rule on Federal Criminal Prosecutions (Report of the Comptroller General, April 19, 1979), an empirical study of cases handled in 38 U.S. Attorneys' offices from July 1-August 31, 1978, it was found that of 2,804 charged defendants only 30% involved a search or seizure and only 11% filed a motion to suppress on Fourth Amendment grounds. These motions were denied in the "overwhelming majority" of cases, so that in only 1.3% of the 2,804 defendant cases was evidence excluded as a result of a Fourth Amendment suppression motion. Moreover, over half of the defendants whose motions were granted in total or in part were convicted nonetheless. As for the cases during the sample period that the U.S. Attorneys declined to prosecute, in only 0.4% of them was a search and seizure problem the primary reason.

Similarly, in Brosi, A Cross-City Comparison of Felony Case Processing 18–20 (1979), an LEAA-sponsored empirical study of state felony cases in various jurisdictions, it was found that "due process related reasons accounted for only a small portion of the rejections at [prosecutor] screening— from 1 to 9 percent." The rate ranged from 13 to 42% in drug cases, but in "felony cases other than drugs, less than 2 percent of the rejections in each city involved abrogations of due process." As for post-filing dismissals and nolles, "due process problems again accounted for little of the attrition, and again most of the due process problems were accounted for by the drug cases." And in Nardulli, Societal Costs of the Exclusionary Rule: An Empirical Assessment, 1983 A.B.F.Res.J. 585, a study of 9 medium-sized counties in Illinois, Michigan, and Pennsylvania, it is reported that motions to suppress were filed in 4.6% of the cases, were granted 14.6% of the time (i.e., in 0.69% of all cases), and when granted resulted in conviction nonetheless in 21.6% of those cases (i.e., lost convictions as a total of all cases was 0.56%). Moreover, most of the "lost cases"

may not have specifically contemplated the exclusionary sanction, but surely they expected the commands of the Amendment to be adhered to. "To the extent that the police obey the constitutional commands, the community foregoes such advantages as it might enjoy from evidence that can only be obtained illegally."[7] It may fairly be said, then, as Justice Traynor once observed, that the cost argument was rejected when the Fourth Amendment was adopted.[8] As the Supreme Court has put it, "there is nothing new in the realization that the Constitution sometimes insulates the criminality of a few in order to protect the privacy of us all."[9]

Another complaint lodged against the exclusionary rule is that it only comes to the aid of the guilty and does nothing to protect

---

involved first offenders, usually charged with possession of drugs or possession of a weapon.

But in National Institute of Justice, The Effects of the Exclusionary Rule: A Study in California 10 (1982), it is reported that 4.8% of the felony cases rejected for prosecution by California district attorneys during 1976–79 were rejected primarily for search and seizure problems. In contrast to the federal study summarized in the preceding paragraph, this was said to establish "a major impact of the exclusionary rule on state proceedings." Id. at 2. However, it should be noted that these cases amount to less than 8/10ths of one per cent of the total number of felony complaints referred to California district attorneys during this period. See Davies, A Hard Look at What We Know (And Still Need to Learn) About the "Costs" of the Exclusionary Rule: The NIJ Study and Other Studies of "Lost" Arrests, 1983 A.B.F.Res.J. 611, 617 (also noting at 619 that "the NIJ study suffers from the use of inappropriate samples, from the omission of readily available and highly pertinent data, and from a variety of analytical choices that produce a slanted interpretation of the data"); Fyfe, Enforcement Workshop: The NIJ Study of the Exclusionary Rule, 19 Crim.L.Bull. 253, 254 (1983) (speculating that the unique situation in California, especially the high frequency of drug traffic, may well mean "the study's findings might not hold in other states," and generally viewing the impact

shown by that report not to be substantial).

See also Canon, The Exclusionary Rule: A Conservative Argument for its Retention, 23 So.Tex.L.J. 559, 560 (1982) ("A growing body of data, however, indicates that few persons arrested are able to use the rule to escape conviction"); Davies, supra, at 622, 679–80 (noting that all available evidence "consistently indicates that *the general level of the rule's effects on criminal prosecutions is marginal at most*," specifically: that prosecutors screen out between 0.2% and 0.8% of felony arrests because of illegal searches; that the cumulative loss by such screening plus police releases and court dismissals for illegal searches is from 0.6% to 2.35%; that except for drugs and weapon possession felonies the cumulative loss is between 0.3% and 0.7%; that for drug cases the cumulative loss is from 2.8% to 7.1%; that suppression rarely results in acquittal; and that fewer than 7% of those released because of an illegal search are rearrested for violent crimes); Nardulli, The Societal Costs of the Exclusionary Rule Revisited, 1987 U.Ill.L.Rev. 223, 239 (empirical data shows in Chicago "the exclusionary rule accounts for only a minor portion of case attrition," namely, 1.77%).

[7]Allen, 1961 Sup.Ct.Rev. 1, 34.

[8]People v. Cahan, 44 Cal.2d 434, 282 P.2d 905 (1955).

[9]Arizona v. Hicks, 480 U.S. 321, 107 S.Ct. 1149, 94 L.Ed.2d 347 (1987).

the Fourth Amendment rights of the innocent.[10] The Fourth
Amendment exclusionary rule, it has been said, is "more vulnerable" to this complaint than exclusionary rules concerning confessions or eyewitness identification, for "physical evidence is no less
reliable when illegally obtained," while the other exclusionary
rules concern evidence "of doubtful reliability."[11] But, even apart
from the erroneous assumption that all of those who have occasion to move for the suppression of evidence are "guilty," this
argument misperceives the function of the exclusionary rule.
While the most immediate and direct consequence of exclusion
may be to benefit an individual defendant who might otherwise
have been convicted, this is hardly the ultimate goal of the
exclusionary rule. As the Supreme Court noted in *Elkins v.
United States*,[12] "The rule is calculated to prevent, not to repair."
Or, as Justice Traynor put it: "The objective of the exclusionary
rule is certainly not to compensate the defendant for the past
wrong done to him any more than it is to penalize the officer for
the past wrong he has done. The emphasis is forward."[13] Thus, as
one commentator has noted:

> The critics forget that neither the rule nor the fourth amendment
> exists to protect the criminal in whose case the rule is applied. Both
> exist to protect society—all those citizens who never break laws
> more serious than those prohibiting overtime parking. * * * Nar-
> rowly viewed, the exclusionary rule is very unattractive, because in
> the vast majority of cases in which it is applied the immediate
> result is to free an obviously guilty person. But the guilty defen-
> dant is freed to protect the rest of us from unlawful police invasions
> of our security and to maintain the integrity of our institutions.
> Thus to suggest that the exclusionary rule fails to aid the innocent
> or that society rather than the policeman suffers for the policeman's
> transgression is nonsense. The innocent and society are the
> principal beneficiaries of the exclusionary rule.[14]

The only-protects-the-guilty argument has also been thought-
fully challenged in a somewhat different way, taking full account
of the substance of the Fourth Amendment's protections. As one
commentator has put it,

> the occasional benefits that compliance with the Fourth Amend-
> ment confers upon the guilty should be understood as an incidental

---

[10]Plumb, Illegal Enforcement of
the Law, 24 Cornell L.Q. 337, 371
(1939); Taft, Protecting the Public
From Mapp v. Ohio Without Amend-
ing the Constitution, 50 A.B.A.J. 815,
816 (1964).

[11]Oaks, Studying the Exclusion-
ary Rule in Search and Seizure, 37
U.Chi.L.Rev. 665, 737–38 (1970). The
Oaks study, cited repeatedly herein,
remains of great value even today. See
Alschuler, Studying the Exclusionary
Rule: An Empirical Classic, 75 U.Chi.

L.Rev. 1365 (2008).

[12]Elkins v. United States, 364
U.S. 206, 80 S.Ct. 1437, 4 L.Ed.2d
1669 (1960).

[13]Traynor, Mapp v. Ohio at Large
in the Fifty States, 1962 Duke L.J.
319, 335.

[14]Dworkin, Fact Style Adjudication and the Fourth Amendment: The
Limits of Lawyering, 48 Ind.L.J. 329,
330–31 (1973).

burden imposed on society by our lack of perfect searching tools rather than as an intended consequence of the Fourth Amendment. From the perspective of the Fourth Amendment, it is a harm whenever an innocent person is searched, and it is costly whenever a guilty person harboring evidence is not searched. These are the substantive values that animate the Fourth Amendment.

Viewed *ex ante* through the eyes of a government lacking perfect information, however, the guilty are on the same plane as the innocent. Every person has a right not to be targeted without justification. The Fourth Amendment includes not only the rights of the innocent to be secure in their persons, houses, papers and effects, but the right of all people to be treated fairly and hence to be searched and perhaps punished because the government knows (to some set level of certainty) that they deserve to be searched and punished.[15]

To say that the "emphasis is forward," of course, is merely to stress the deterrence function of the exclusionary rule. The significance of the question that many have raised as to whether the exclusionary rule does in fact deter will be considered momentarily. Here, however, it will suffice to note the irrelevance to the exclusionary rule debate of one particular facet of the no-deterrence argument, namely, that which focuses upon police ignorance of the procedures that must be followed in order to comply with the Fourth Amendment. The contention under consideration here has been stated thusly by Professor Oaks:

> To be an effective general deterrent the sanction and the reasons for the sanction must be communicated to the target population. There is reason to believe that the channels of communication between police and courts and prosecutors are such as to minimize the deterrent effect of the rule. * * * The deterrent effectiveness of the exclusionary rule is also dependent upon whether the arrest and search and seizure rules that it is supposed to enforce are stated with sufficient clarity that they can be understood and followed by common ordinary police officers. * * * Though undoubtedly clear in some areas of police behavior, the rules are notoriously complex in others.[16]

Though the problem may have been overstated,[17] I do not question for a moment that Fourth Amendment standards are

---

[15]Colb, Innocence, Privacy, and Targeting in Fourth Amendment Jurisprudence, 96 Colum.L.Rev. 1456, 1525 (1996).

[16]Oaks, 37 U.Chi.L.Rev. 665, 730–31 (1970). See also Burger, Who Will Watch the Watchman?, 14 Am.U.L.Rev. 1, 9–11 (1956); Wright, Must the Criminal Go Free if the Constable Blunders?, 50 Tex.L.Rev. 736, 737 (1972).

[17]See Comment, 49 Emory L.J. 295, 297 (2000), concluding that "the

data collected here illustrates that the exclusionary rule, which requires courts to exclude evidence obtained as a result of illegal police actions, has the potential to have a stronger deterrent effect on police illegality than many recent critics of the rule acknowledge. Contrary to the assertions of commentators critical of the exclusionary rule, the data collected here shows that the law of criminal procedure is not so hopelessly complex that police departments abandon efforts to comply with it. Further, to the extent

sometimes lacking in clarity and that sometimes they have not been effectively communicated to the police. I have noted elsewhere, as have others, that this is justifiably a matter of concern and that consequently there is a need for courts to state Fourth Amendment requirements more simply and clearly and for more effective lines of communication to the police to be established.[18] But, to say that "the law of search and seizure and the law of arrest are filled with technicalities and inconsistencies * * * goes to the content of the rules rather than to the remedy."[19] Similarly, to say that more is required in terms of police education is to state a need that would exist whether or not there were an exclusionary rule. That is, the desire for greater clarity in the rules and for more effective communication of the rules to the police can only be explained on the ground that we wish to minimize the risks of inadvertent and unintentional police violations of the commands of the Fourth Amendment. To suggest that this objective would somehow vanish if the exclusionary rule were abandoned is to concede the force of the warning in *Mapp v. Ohio*[20] that without the suppression doctrine the Fourth Amendment would be no more than "a form of words."

§ 1.2(b) The matter of deterrence

Chief Justice Burger, dissenting in *Bivens v. Six Unknown Named Agents,*[21] asserted that the hope that the Fourth Amendment could be enforced "by the exclusion of reliable evidence from criminal trials was hardly more than a wistful dream." In concluding that the suppression doctrine "is both conceptually sterile and practically ineffective in accomplishing its stated objective" of deterrence, he relied heavily upon the conclusion that "there is no empirical evidence to support the claim that the rule actually deters illegal conduct of law enforcement officials." In support of the latter conclusion, the Chief Justice made reference to a very thorough and useful study conducted by Professor Oaks, in which he subjected to critical examination "the largest

---

that the law is ambiguous, police academies generally err on the side of over-cautious interpretations of the law. Therefore, to the extent police departments are concerned about the possible exclusion of evidence, the data collected here shows that police departments are well able to minimize the possibility of exclusion through careful construction of workable standards for their recruits to follow."

[18]Dworkin, 48 Ind.L.J. 329 (1973); LaFave & Remington, Controlling the Police: The Judge's Role in Making and Reviewing Law Enforcement Decisions, 63 Mich.L.Rev. 987 (1965); LaFave, Improving Police Performance Through the Exclusionary Rule—Part I: Current Police and Local Court Practices, 30 Mo.L.Rev. 391 (1965); LaFave, Improving Police Performance Through the Exclusionary Rule—Part II: Defining the Norms and Training the Police, 30 Mo.L.Rev. 566 (1965).

[19]Paulsen, The Exclusionary Rule and Misconduct by the Police, 52 J.Crim.L.C. & P.S. 255, 256 (1961).

[20]Mapp v. Ohio, 367 U.S. 643, 81 S.Ct. 1684, 6 L.Ed.2d 1081 (1961).

[Section 1.2(b)]

[21]Bivens v. Six Unknown Named Agents, 403 U.S. 388, 91 S.Ct. 1999, 29 L.Ed.2d 619 (1971).

fund of information yet assembled on the effect of the exclusionary rule."[22] However, it is well to note that the characterization by the Chief Justice of Oaks' conclusion is less than complete; Oaks reached the conclusion that these data "fall short of an empirical substantiation *or* refutation of the deterrent effect of the exclusionary rule."[23] That is, it has not been clearly established that the exclusionary rule does deter, or that it does not.

It is more precise, perhaps, to say that we do not have an "effective quantitative measure of the rule's deterrent efficacy,"[24] for there is some evidence available as to when the exclusionary rule does not deter and also some evidence indicating that it sometimes does deter. As to the former, there exists hard evidence, based upon empirical research into police practices,[25] which clearly demonstrates the correctness of the observation in *Terry v. Ohio*[26] that the exclusionary rule "is powerless to deter invasions of constitutionally guaranteed rights where the police either have no interest in prosecuting or are willing to forego successful prosecution in the interest of serving some other goal." Illustrative are "arrest or confiscation as a punitive sanction (common in gambling and liquor law violations), arrest for the purpose of controlling prostitutes and transvestites, arrest of an intoxicated person for his own safety, search for the purpose of recovering stolen property, arrest and search and seizure for the purpose of 'keeping the lid on' in a high crime area or of satisfying public outcry for visible enforcement, search for the purpose of removing weapons or contraband such as narcotics from circulation, and search for weapons that might be used against the searching officer."[27]

The evidence tending to show that the exclusionary rule does deter is, by comparison, of a "softer" variety, but most likely this is inevitably so. As Professor Wright has noted: "With the Exclusionary Rule, as with capital punishment, the occasions on which the deterrent effect has failed are easy to see. It is more difficult to measure the occasions on which the deterrent has been successful."[28] That the exclusionary rule has had a deterrent effect upon the police is certainly suggested by such post-

---

[22] Oaks, 37 U.Chi.L.Rev. 665, 709 (1970).

[23] Oaks, 37 U.Chi.L.Rev. 665, 709 (1970) (emphasis added).

[24] Allen, 1961 Sup.Ct.Rev. 34.

[25] W. LaFave, Arrest chs. 21–25 (1965); J. Skolnick, Justice Without Trial ch. 10 (1966); L. Tiffany, D. McIntyre & D. Rotenberg, Detection of Crime ch. 13 (1967); Harcourt, Unconstitutional Police Searches and Collective Responsibility, 3 Crim. & Pub.Pol'y 363 (2004) (study of 115 police searches found that the "majority of the unconstitutional searches—31 out of 34—were invisible to the courts, having resulted in no arrest, charge, or citation"); LaFave & Remington, 63 Mich.L.Rev. 987 (1965); LaFave, 30 Mo.L.Rev. 391 (1965).

[26] Terry v. Ohio, 392 U.S. 1, 88 S.Ct. 1868, 20 L.Ed.2d 889 (1968).

[27] Oaks, 37 U.Chi.L.Rev. 665, 721–22 (1970).

[28] Wright, 50 Tex.L.Rev. 736, 739 (1972).

exclusionary rule occurrences as the dramatic increase in the use of search warrants where virtually none had been used before,[29] stepped-up efforts to educate the police on the law of search and seizure where such training had before been virtually nonexistent,[30] and the creation and development of working relationships between police and prosecutors to ensure the obtaining of evidence by means that would not result in its suppression.[31] Moreover, if the assertions of police spokesmen, stated by way of complaint, that the police have been "handcuffed" by the exclusionary rule are taken seriously, they can only be taken as an acknowledgment that the police are deterred by the exclusionary sanction.[32] "There would be little reason to complain of the substantive rules unless the exclusionary rule made them relevant to police action."[33]

Despite the lack of hard evidence proving deterrence and of a sound quantitative measure of the extent of deterrence, it is not irresponsible to suggest (i) that the hard evidence the rule does not deter under certain circumstances fails to "demonstrate the absence of all deterrent potential"[34]; and (ii) that a significant amount of deterrence may be assumed from the fact that "conviction of offenders remains obviously an important objective of police activity."[35] But the Chief Justice does not concede even this much in *Bivens*. Although lacking empirical evidence on his side

---

[29]See Milner, Supreme Court Effectiveness and the Police Organization, 36 Law & Contemp.Prob. 467, 475 (1971); Orfield, Deterrence, Perjury, and the Heater Factor: An Exclusionary Rule in the Chicago Criminal Courts, 63 U.Colo.L.Rev. 75, 124 (1992) (judges, prosecutors and public defenders note "increased use of search warrants"); Comment, 54 U.Chi.L.Rev. 1016, 1077 (1987) (empirical study of effects of exclusionary rule on Chicago narcotics officers, concluding their "experience has caused them to use warrants more often").

[30]See Kamisar, 53 J.Crim.L., C. & P.S. 171, 179–82 (1962); Sachs, The Exclusionary Rule: A Prosecutor's Defense, 1 Crim.J.Ethics 28, 31 (1982) ("the rule is at work because of the enormous increases in police training and education about constitutional rights directly attributable to the exclusion sanction").

[31]Kamisar, 53 J.Crim.L., C. & P.S. 171, 179–82 (1962); Orfield, Deterrence, Perjury, and the Heater Factor: An Exclusionary Rule in the Chicago

Criminal Courts, 63 U.Colo.L.Rev. 75, 82 (1992) (judges, prosecutors and public defenders believe "the exclusionary rule fosters a close working relationship between prosecutors and police"); Comment, 54 U.Chi.L.Rev. 1016, 1026–27 (1987) (noting various ways in which Chicago prosecutors work with police on Fourth Amendment matters).

[32]Kamisar, Wolf and Lustig Ten Years Later: Illegal State Evidence in State and Federal Courts, 43 Minn.L. Rev. 1083, 1156–57 (1959).

[33]Paulsen, 52 J.Crim.L., C. & P.S. 255, 262 (1961).

[34]Allen, 1961 Sup.Ct.Rev. 1, 39.

See also Orfield, Deterrence, Perjury, and the Heater Factor: An Exclusionary Rule in the Chicago Criminal Courts, 63 U.Colo.L.Rev. 75, 82 (1992) (judges, prosecutors and public defenders conclude "the exclusionary rule's deterrent effect is greater when officers are working on big or important cases").

[35]Allen, 1961 Sup.Ct.Rev. 1, 39. As one long-time prosecutor put it: "What I can offer, however, is my

of the issue, he finds evidence of nondeterrence in the nature of the exclusionary rule—the fact that it "does not apply any direct sanction to the individual official whose illegal conduct results in the exclusion of evidence."[36] And should this evidence not be deemed convincing, it is of no consequence, for in light of the "high price" that the exclusionary rule extracts[37] the burden is on its proponents to make a "clear demonstration" of its efficacy.[38]

The latter point has been effectively answered by Professor Dworkin:

> Obviously, the assignment of the burden of proof on an issue where evidence does not exist and cannot be obtained[39] is outcome determinative. The Chief Justice's assignment of the burden is merely a way of announcing a predetermined conclusion. * * * The deterrent efficacy of the exclusionary rule can be evaluated without resort to the notion of burdens of proof. If all laws which are justified wholly or partly on the ground that they deter undesirable conduct had to be justified by showing that they actually do deter, very little of the criminal law, at least, could meet the test. Deterrence is partly a matter of logic and psychology, largely a matter of faith. The question is never whether laws do deter, but rather whether conduct ought to be deterred * * *.[40]

Moreover, the Chief Justice's notion that there can be no deterrence absent a "direction sanction to the individual officer" is in error. No one, Professor Amsterdam has noted,

has ever urged that the exclusionary rule is supportable on this

testimony that I have watched the rule deter, routinely, throughout my years as a prosecutor." Sachs, 1 Crim.J. Ethics 28, 30 (1982). See also Orfield, Deterrence, Perjury, and the Heater Factor: An Exclusionary Rule in the Chicago Criminal Courts, 63 U.Colo.L. Rev. 75, 82 (1992) (judges, prosecutors and public defenders "uniformly believe that officers care about convictions and experience adverse personal reactions when they lose evidence"); Comment, 54 U.Chi.L.Rev. 1016, 1042 (1987) (noting Chicago narcotics officers said suppression "perceived as a personal sanction").

[36]Consider also Cicchini, An Economics Perspective on the Exclusionary Rule and Deterrence, 75 Mo.L.Rev. 459, 461 (2010), asserting that the "economic theory of criminal sanctions" shows that "the exclusionary rule does not, and cannot, deter police misconduct."

[37]Again, this "high price" is a fiction. See note 6 supra.

[38]To the same effect is Wright, 50 Tex.L.Rev. 736, 742 (1972).

[39]Allen, 1961 Sup.Ct.Rev. 1, 34, notes that it is not "an easy matter to devise methods to produce a persuasive empirical demonstration" on this issue. And despite the useful suggestions for empirical research set out in Oaks, 37 U.Chi.L.Rev. 665 (1970), it is to be doubted whether a truly "quantitative measure" is possible. See also Canon, The Exclusionary Rule: A Conservative Argument for its Retention, 23 So.Tex.L.J. 559, 560 (1982) (explaining why "neither side can satisfy any very demanding standard of proof that the rule does or does not have a deterrent effect"); Morris, The Exclusionary Rule, Deterrence and Posner's Economic Analysis of Law, 57 Wash.L.Rev. 647, 653 (1982) (explaining why "no conclusively sound social science study of the exclusionary rule's deterrent effect will actually be produced").

[40]Dworkin, 48 Ind.L.J. 329, 332–33 (1973).

principle of "deterrence." It is not supposed to "deter" in the fashion of the law of larceny, for example, by threatening punishment to him who steals a television set—a theory of deterrence, by the way, whose lack of empirical justification makes the exclusionary rule look as solid by comparison as the law of gravity.

Rather, the exclusionary rule is designed to operate in the manner of the procedure now being used in some appliance stores with the encouragement of police authorities; branding the social security number of the purchaser into the chassis of new television sets in order to make them less attractive as objects of larceny by diminishing their resale value in the hands of anyone but the true owner. Of course a branded television set may nonetheless be stolen by someone who does not notice it is branded, or who thinks that he can sell it even with the brand, or who simply wants to watch the Superbowl on it. But at least the effort to depreciate its worth makes it less of an incitement than it might be. A criminal court system functioning without an exclusionary rule, on the other hand, is the equivalent of a government purchasing agent paying premium prices for evidence branded with the stamp of unconstitutionality.[41]

For these reasons, the argument that the "exclusionary rule should be abandoned"[42] for want of proof of its deterrent efficacy deserves to be rejected. This conclusion is also supported by other considerations. For one thing, the exclusionary rule "assures a great deal of judicial attention"[43] to questions concerning police practices, which is essential to a comprehensive and clear statement of Fourth Amendment standards. If an appellate court receives but a few cases, "the bits or slices or splinters which are cast up may be too fragmentary to yield a proper picture or to allow the shaping and joining of complementary hubs and spokes and rims to form a doctrinal wheel."[44] But if the court receives "a related group of cases in a series," then "the court will see more, learn more from the series; the court will begin to see in the round rather than the flat, and to gain some understanding of the whole in action."[45] Experience has shown that the exclusionary rule has provided an essential stimulus to the judicial elaboration of Fourth Amendment requirements.[46] This task could not be effectively continued if the exclusionary rule were abandoned.[47]

It is also worth noting that the usual focus regarding the deter-

---

[41]Amsterdam, Perspectives on the Fourth Amendment, 58 Minn.L.Rev. 349, 431–32 (1974).

[42]As made in the State of California's brief at p. 42 in California v. Krivda, 409 U.S. 33, 93 S.Ct. 32, 34 L.Ed.2d 45 (1972).

[43]Paulsen, 52 J.Crim.L., C. & P.S. 255, 260 (1961).

[44]K. Llewellyn, The Common Law Tradition, Deciding Appeals 263

(1960).

[45]K. Llewellyn, The Common Law Tradition, Deciding Appeals 263 (1960).

[46]As to the California experience, see Traynor, 1962 Duke L.J. 319, 323; as to the Illinois experience, see LaFave, 30 Mo.L.Rev. 566, 580–81 n. 63 (1965).

[47]The situation would then be like that which existed prior to *Mapp* in

rence debate "is far too narrow * * * because it overlooks one of the most beneficial effects of *Mapp*—the educational effects of the suppression hearing itself. * * * By making suppression hearings necessary, * * * the exclusionary rule provided a forum through which the importance and substance of the Fourth Amendment is reaffirmed on a daily basis in city and county courthouses across the nation," so that "suppression hearings act much like a morality play for those involved in the nitty gritty of law enforcement."[48]

Finally, it is well to keep in mind Professor Tiffany's caution that in considering the question of whether the exclusionary rule should be abandoned, it is

> important to distinguish between the functional and symbolic impact of a rule designed to control behavior. From a functional perspective, the *Mapp* rule may be a failure. It need not follow that the rule should be changed if one can find in it sufficient symbolic worth. The question may be put this way: would reversal of the rule place us in a position that is substantially status quo ante? * * * It has been traditional when discussing the exclusionary rule to [ask]: Does the rule work? But at this point that may be the wrong question. Instead, the central question may now be this: how would the police react if the Supreme Court overruled *Mapp v. Ohio*?[49]

The point did not escape Chief Justice Burger, for in his *Bivens* dissent he warned against overruling *Mapp* in the absence of some "meaningful alternative" lest "law enforcement officials were suddenly to gain the impression, however erroneous, that all constitutional restraints on police had somehow been

---

those jurisdictions which had not adopted the exclusionary rule on their own, where appellate courts received arrest and search issues "only when an appeal was taken from a tort action against a police officer. The many barriers to recovery have severely limited the number of appeals, and the defenses available are such that an explicit statement of arrest and search norms is seldom required. Moreover, the civil suit context of the case may divert the appellate court from the question of whether the police conduct was proper to that of whether it is fair to subject the errant officer to personal liability." LaFave, 30 Mo.L.Rev. 566, 581 (1965).

[48]Sundby, Mapp v. Ohio's Unsung Hero: The Suppression Hearing as Morality Play, 85 Chi.-Kent L.Rev. 255, 257 (2010).

[49]Tiffany, Judicial Attempts to Control the Police, Current History, July, 1971, pp. 13, 52. See also Loewenthal, Evaluating the Exclusion-

ary Rule in Search and Seizure, 49 U.Mo.K.C.L.Rev. 24 (1980), concluding from interviews with police that they would conclude the Fourth Amendment had no meaning if the exclusionary rule were withdrawn.

Canon, 23 So.Tex.L.J. 559, 560 (1982), states: "The true conservative position—and my own—is that the rule should be preserved because of its symbolic reassurance to the public that the government is committed to the basic values of privacy, the rule of law and fairness. Such symbolic commitments are valuable because they enhance support for the courts and the criminal justice system. Moreover, if the rule has as little adverse impact on the operation of the criminal justice system or the courts as it appears to, this support is obtained at little practical cost in controlling or punishing crime. This is an accomplishment which ought to appeal to conservatives."

removed—that an open season on 'criminals' had been declared."[50]

A majority of the Supreme Court has declined to abandon the exclusionary rule on the no-deterrence theory, stating in *Stone v. Powell*:[51]

> Despite the absence of supportive empirical evidence,[52] we have assumed that the immediate effect of exclusion will be to discourage law enforcement officials from violating the Fourth Amendment by removing the incentive to disregard it. More importantly, over the long term, this demonstration that our society attaches serious consequences to violation of constitutional rights is thought to encourage those who formulate law enforcement policies, and the officers who implement them, to incorporate Fourth Amendment ideals into their value system.
>
> We adhere to the view that these considerations support the implementation of the exclusionary rule at trial and its enforcement on direct appeal of state court convictions.[53]

However, the majority opinion in *Hudson v. Michigan*,[54] holding that violation of the "knock-and-announce" rule when execut-

---

[50]But later, concurring in Stone v. Powell, 428 U.S. 465, 96 S.Ct. 3037, 49 L.Ed.2d 1067 (1976), the Chief Justice indicated otherwise: "With the passage of time, it now appears that the continued existence of the rule, as presently implemented, inhibits the development of rational alternatives."

[51]Stone v. Powell, 428 U.S. 465, 96 S.Ct. 3037, 49 L.Ed.2d 1067 (1976).

[52]In the immediately preceding case, United States v. Janis, 428 U.S. 433, 96 S.Ct. 3021, 49 L.Ed.2d 1046 (1976), the Court noted that "although scholars have attempted to determine whether the exclusionary rule in fact does have any deterrent effect, each empirical study on the subject, in its own way appears to be flawed. It would not be appropriate to fault those who have attempted empirical studies for their lack of convincing data. The number of variables is substantial, and many cannot be measured or subjected to effective controls. Record-keeping before *Mapp* was spotty at best, and thus severely hampers before-and-after studies. Since *Mapp*, of course, all possibility of broad-scale controlled or even semi-controlled comparison studies has been eliminated. 'Response' studies are hampered by the presence of the respondents' interests. And extrapolation studies are rendered highly inconclu- sive by the changes in legal doctrines and police-citizen relationships that have taken place in the 15 years since *Mapp* was decided."

[53]But the Court, holding that Fourth Amendment claims of state prisoners could not ordinarily be reviewed on federal habeas corpus, refused to accept "the dubious assumption that law enforcement authorities would fear that federal habeas review might reveal flaws in a search or seizure that went undetected at trial and on appeal."

[54]Hudson v. Michigan, 547 U.S. 586, 126 S.Ct. 2159, 165 L.Ed.2d 56 (2006), discussed in Alschuler, The Exclusionary Rule and Causation: Hudson v. Michigan and Its Ancestors, 93 Iowa L.Rev. 1741 (2008); Blair, Hudson v. Michigan: the Supreme Court Knocks and Announced the Demise of the Exclusionary Rule, 42 Tulsa L.Rev. 751 (2007); Castiglione, Hudson and Samson: The Roberts Court Confronts Privacy, Dignity and the Fourth Amendment, 68 La.L.Rev. 63 (2007); Dery, A False Mirror: Hudson v. Michigan's Distortion of the Exclusionary Rule in Knock-and-Announce Litigation, 76 UMKC L.Rev. 67 (2007); Frakt, Fruitless Poisonous Trees in a Parallel Universe: Hudson v. Michigan, Knock-and-Announce, and the Exclusionary Rule, 34 Fla.St.

ing search warrants does not require suppression of evidence found in execution of the search warrant,[55] questioned the continued vitality of the *Mapp* conclusion that an exclusionary rule—said to "always" have been the remedy of "last resort"[56]—was needed to deter Fourth Amendment violations because other remedies would not suffice:

> We cannot assume that exclusion in this context is necessary deterrence simply because we found that it was necessary deterrence in different contexts and long ago. That would be forcing the public today to pay for the sins and inadequacies of a legal regime that existed almost half a century ago. Dollree Mapp could not turn to 42 U.S.C. § 1983 for meaningful relief; *Monroe v. Pape*,[57] which began the slow but steady expansion of that remedy, was decided the same Term as *Mapp*. It would be another 17 years before the § 1983 remedy was extended to reach the deep pocket of municipalities.[58] Citizens whose Fourth Amendment rights were violated by federal officers could not bring suit until 10 years after *Mapp*, with this Court's decision in *Bivens v. Six Unknown Fed. Narcotics Agents*.[59]

> Hudson complains that "it would be very hard to find a lawyer to take a case such as this," but 42 U.S.C. § 1988(b) answers this objection. Since some civil-rights violations would yield damages too small to justify the expense of litigation, Congress has authorized attorney's fees for civil-rights plaintiffs. * * *

Another development over the past half-century that deters civil-

---

U.L.Rev. 659 (2007); Grey, Revisiting the Application of the Exclusionary Rule to the Good Faith Exceptions in Light of Hudson v. Michigan, 42 U.S.F. L.Rev. 621 (2008); Hilton, Alternatives to the Exclusionary Rule After Hudson v. Michigan: Preventing and Remedying Police Conduct, 53 Vill.L.Rev. 47 (2008); Moran, Waiting for the Other Shoe: Hudson and the Precarious State of Mapp, 93 Iowa L.Rev. 1725 (2008); Summers, The Constable Blunders But Isn't Punished: Does Hudson v. Michigan's Abolition of the Exclusionary Rule Extend Beyond Knock-and-Announce Violations?, 10 Barry L.Rev. 25 (2008); Tomkovicz, Hudson v. Michigan and the Future of Fourth Amendment Exclusion, 93 Iowa L.Rev. 1819 (2008); Comments, 2007 BYU L.Rev. 451; 59 Fla.L.Rev. 465 & 475 (2007); 34 Ohio N.U.L.Rev. 217 (2008); 112 Penn.St.L.Rev. 261 (2007); Notes, 44 Am.Crim.L.Rev. 1239 (2007); 73 Brook. L.Rev. 1209 (2008); 21 BYU J.Pub.L. 433 (2007); 37 Cumb.L.Rev. 327 (2007); 30 Hamline L.Rev. 409 (2007); 58 Mercer L.Rev. 779 (2007); 27 Miss.C. L.Rev. 435 (2007); 27 Pace L.Rev. 503 (2007); 32 S.Ill.U.L.J. 447 (2008); 29

Whittier L.Rev. 183 (2007); Recent Decision, 30 Harv.J.L. & Pub. Pol'y 417 (2006).

[55] For discussion of other aspects of *Hudson*, see § 1.6(h), and § 11.4(a), text at notes 42 and 107.

[56] As noted in Davies & Scanlon, Katz in the Age of Hudson v. Michigan: Some Thoughts on "Suppression as a Last Resort," 41 U.C.Davis L.Rev. 1035, 1043 (2008), "Justice Scalia's unadorned claim in *Hudson* that the Court has "always" applied the suppression remedy as a "last resort" so defies historical truth that a review of the controversial penalty's journey through time appears necessary to correct the record."

[57] Monroe v. Pape, 365 U.S. 167, 81 S.Ct. 473, 5 L.Ed.2d 492 (1961).

[58] Citing Monell v. Department of Social Services of City of New York, 436 U.S. 658, 98 S.Ct. 2108, 56 L.Ed.2d 611 (1978).

[59] Bivens v. Six Unknown Named Agents, 403 U.S. 388, 91 S.Ct. 1999, 29 L.Ed.2d 619 (1971).

rights violations is the increasing professionalism of police forces, including a new emphasis on internal police discipline.

Those comments, as the *Hudson* dissenters pointed out, are "an argument against the Fourth Amendment's exclusionary principle itself." (This is not to suggest that the *Hudson* Court is prepared to overrule *Mapp*. The majority's fifth vote was supplied by Justice Kennedy, who curiously joined that part of the Court's opinion but asserted in his concurring opinion that "the continued operation of the exclusionary rule, as settled and defined by our precedents, is not in doubt."[60]) And thus, "[w]ithout further signs that Justice Kennedy is so inclined (or a change in Court membership), judges should hesitate to extend *Hudson*'s cost-benefit exception to other Fourth Amendment realms."[61]

The undocumented assumption[62] of the *Hudson* majority that other remedies alone now supply sufficient deterrence seems unwarranted. The fact of the matter is that "five decades of post-*Weeks* 'freedom' from the inhibiting effect of the federal exclusionary rule failed to produce any meaningful alternative to the exclusionary rule in any jurisdiction," and there is no evidence that "times have changed" in the post-*Mapp* era.[63] It is still true, for example, as the *Hudson* dissenters point out, that the deterrent effect of damage actions "can hardly be said to be great," as such actions are "expensive, time-consuming, not readily available, and rarely successful."[64] As for the matter of police professionalism/self-discipline, certainly much of the improvement in this regard is *because of* the exclusionary rule, and once the rule is eliminated as to specified violations there would doubt-

---

[60]For further discussion of why *Hudson* should not be read as marking the end of the exclusionary rule, see Tomkovicz, 93 Iowa L.Rev. 1819, 1844–49 (2008).

[61]Tomkovicz, 93 Iowa L.Rev. 1819, 1881 (2008).

[62]As noted in Tomkovicz, 93 Iowa L.Rev. 1819, 1881 (2008), "the declaration that civil remedies, lawyers' fees, and increased professionalism provide ample deterrent forces is nothing more than say-so, unsupported by any empirical evidence." And, as noted in Harris, How Accountability-Based Policing Can Reinforce—or Replace—the Fourth Amendment Exclusionary Rule, 7 Ohio St.J.Crim.L. 149, 154 (2009), that assumption does "not square with reality," as reflected in "new empirical work by two criminologists" showing that "Fourth Amendment violations, some quite egregious, showed up in almost a third of all observed police investigations."

[63]Kamisar, In Defense of the Search and Seizure Exclusionary Rule, 26 Harv.J.L. & Pub.Pol'y 119, 126–29 (2003), quoted by the *Hudson* dissent.

[64]Stewart, The Road to Mapp v. Ohio and Beyond: The Origins, Development and Future of the Exclusionary Rule in Search-and-Seizure Cases, 83 Colum.L.Rev. 1365, 1388 (1983).

Sklansky, Is the Exclusionary Rule Obsolete?, 5 Ohio St.J.Crim.L. 567, 580 (2008), after noting there are about 2,000 section 1983 cases filed each year and about 300,000 instances of evidence suppression because of Fourth Amendment violations, concludes: "When one channel of communication carries more than a hundred times as many messages as a second channel, there is reason to be skeptical that the second can substitute entirely for the first."

less be a considerable degree of backsliding. After all, why bother to punish the offending officer if there has been no "cost" to the system in terms of suppressed evidence?[65]

If what the *Hudson* majority means is that those other remedies are particularly effective with respect to the kinds of Fourth Amendment violations *Hudson* removes from the exclusionary rule, knock-and-announce violations, then it is even further off the mark. It would be hard to find an aspect of police activity heretofore covered by the Fourth Amendment for which the other available remedies are so lacking in deterrence. It is thus not surprising (as the dissenters point out), that while the "cases reporting knock-and-announce violations are legion, * * * the majority, like Michigan and the United States, has failed to cite a single reported case in which a plaintiff has collected more than nominal damages solely as a result of a knock-and-announce violation."[66] One § 1983 case decided shortly before *Hudson,* though involving a different kind of "breaking" violation, tells it all: the plaintiff's "reward" was $1.00 in damages and $1.50 in attorney's fees![67]

---

[65]*Hudson* cites no body of professional opinion supporting its particular "take" on deterrence via professionalism vs. the exclusionary rule. A citation to the work of one respected criminologist appears at that point, but he has publicly repudiated such reliance on his work, noting that its import was "misrepresented" by the Court and that his view was that "[b]etter police work * * * was a consequence of the exclusionary rule rather than a reason to do away with it." Adam Liptak, Supreme Court Edging Closer to Repeal of Evidence Ruling, New York Times, Jan. 31, 2009, p. Al, col. 5. That very point is also made by the dissenters' pithy rebuke in Herring v. United States, 555 U.S. 135, 129 S.Ct. 695, 172 L.Ed.2d 496 (2009): "professionalism is a sign of the exclusionary rule's efficacy—not of its superfluity."

Illustrative is the situation that obtains in California, where there is no exclusionary rule for violation of the state constitution not also violating the Fourth Amendment. As noted in Sklansky, Is the Exclusionary Rule Obsolete?, 5 Ohio St.J.Crim.L. 567, 580–81 (2008), "police in California have pretty much completely ignored the warrant requirement imposed by state constitutional law for garbage searches"; indeed, "California police officers are now trained to ignore it."

[66]In Herring v. United States, 555 U.S. 135, 129 S.Ct. 695, 172 L.Ed.2d 496 (2009), another case that, like *Hudson,* withdrew the exclusionary rule from a particular variety of Fourth Amendment violation, there negligent recordkeeping causing defendant to be arrested pursuant to an arrest warrant recalled months earlier, the majority did not even pretend that other remedies were available. The four dissenters thus observed that the majority had left defendant and others like him "with no remedy for violation of their constitutional rights, as "the arresting officer would be sheltered by qualified immunity," "the police department itself is not liable for the negligent acts of its employees," and "identifying the department employer who committed the error may be impossible."

[67]Robbins v. Chronister, 435 F.3d 1238 (10th Cir.2006). An officer ordered a traffic violator out of his car and, when he did not comply, the officer swung his baton into one of the car's windows, shattering it. Following the driver's conviction for a subsequently attempted assault, he brought

§ 1.2(c) Replacing the exclusionary rule

Finding a "meaningful alternative" for the exclusionary rule is easier said than done. In *Mapp v. Ohio*,[68] it will be recalled, the Court concluded that "other remedies have been worthless and futile," and with this part of *Mapp* "there is little quarrel."[69] And, while it may be true that the argument that nothing else works is hardly sufficient justification for adopting the exclusionary rule,[70] it is good reason for maintaining a healthy skepticism about any proposal to abandon the exclusionary rule in favor of some other supposed remedy.

Consider, for example, the suggestion made by the Chief Justice in *Bivens* that Congress might enact a statute with the following components: (a) a waiver of sovereign immunity as to the illegal acts of law enforcement officials committed in the performance of assigned duties; (b) the creation of a cause of action for damages sustained by any person aggrieved by conduct of governmental agents in violation of the Fourth Amendment or statutes regulating official conduct; (c) the creation of a tribunal, quasi-judicial in nature or perhaps patterned after the United States Court of Claims, to adjudicate all claims under the statute; (d) a provision that this statutory remedy is in lieu of the exclusion of evidence secured for use in criminal cases in violation of the Fourth Amendment; and (e) a provision directing that no evidence, otherwise admissible, shall be excluded from any criminal proceeding because of violation of the Fourth Amendment. He added that states would thereafter "develop their own remedial systems on the federal model."[71]

On what basis should one judge this or any other proposed

---

a § 1983 action; the court found the officer's actions violated the Fourth Amendment and then awarded plaintiff nominal damages of one dollar. A dispute about attorney's fees went to the court of appeals, which held plaintiff was entitled to only $1.50 by virtue of 42 U.S.C. § 1997e(d), as "the statute's plain language imposes a 150% fee cap if (1) the plaintiff was a prisoner at the time he brought the action and (2) the plaintiff was awarded attorney fees under § 1988."

[Section 1.2(c)]

[68]Mapp v. Ohio, 367 U.S. 643, 81 S.Ct. 1684, 6 L.Ed.2d 1081 (1961).

[69]Wright, 50 Tex.L.Rev. 736, 738 (1972).

[70]Kaplan, 26 Stan.L.Rev. 1027, 1032 (1974).

[71]See also Amar, Fourth Amendment First Principles, 107 Harv.L.Rev. 757, 786, 798 (1994) (tort remedies were "clearly the ones presupposed by the Framers of the Fourth Amendment" and "make much more sense"); Barnett, Resolving the Dilemma of the Exclusionary Rule: An Application of Restitutive Principles of Justice, 32 Emory L.J. 937 (1983); Estreicher & Weick, Opting for a Legislative Alternative to the Fourth Amendment Exclusionary Rule, 78 UMKC L.Rev. 949 (2010) (described in note 85 infra); Hirschel, What Can We Learn from the English Approach to the Problem of Illegally Seized Evidence?, 67 Judicature 424 (1984); Kafka, The Exclusionary Rule: An Alternative Perspective, 27 Wm. Mitchell L.Rev. 1895 (2001); Levin, An Alternative to the Exclusionary Rule for Fourth Amendment Violations, 58 Judicature 75 (1974) (proposing a "Joint Liability Plan" whereunder the governmental unit would be liable in tort and the of-

substitute for the exclusionary rule? I find wholly satisfactory the

ficer would be discharged on proof of an intentional violation or subjected to a monetary penalty on proof of a reckless or grossly negligent violation); Posner, Excessive Sanctions for Governmental Misconduct in Criminal Cases, 57 Wash.L.Rev. 635 (1982); Pettys, Instrumentalizing Jurors: An Argument Against the Exclusionary Rule, 37 Fordham Urb.L.J. 837 (2010) (proposing replacement with a more robust tort remedy, by (i) broadening the availability of punitive damages, (ii) increasing municipalities' financial exposure for Fourth Amendment violations by their police, and (iii) increasing the amount of attorney's fees that may be received in § 1983 actions); Rychlak, Replacing the Exclusionary Rule: Fourth Amendment Violations as Direct Criminal Contempt, 85 Chi.-Kent L.Rev. 241 (2010) (proposing "that Fourth Amendment violations be treated like direct criminal contempt," so that in event of "a serious Fourth Amendment violation, the offending officer could be criminally punished"); Standen, The Exclusionary Rule and Damages: An Economic Comparison of Private Remedies for Unconstitutional Police Conduct, 2000 B.Y.U.L.Rev. 1443 (concluding that "damages are at least as good as exclusion" in responding to "the perpetual problem of constraining police behavior"); Wilkey, Constitutional Alternatives to the Exclusionary Rule, 23 So.Tex.L.J. 30 (1982); Note, 47 Am.Crim.L.Rev. 1341, 1359 (2010) (proposing replacement of exclusionary rule with a "liability rule," a scheme of "personal liability on law enforcement agencies" with "minimum statutory damages").

The Amar analysis is questioned in Cloud, Searching Through History; Searching for History, 63 U.Chi.L.Rev. 1707, 1739, 1743 (1996) (Amar "selectively deploys incomplete fragments of the historical record to advance a partisan thesis," and his description of the contents of early statutes is "incomplete and one-sided"); Dripps, Akhil Amar on Criminal Procedure and Constitutional Law: "Here I Go

Down That Wrong Road Again," 74 N.C.L.Rev. 1559, 1616 (1996) ("Since *effective* damage remedies for Fourth Amendment violations will not be adopted by legislatures, and are beyond the institutional capacity of the judiciary, Amar's program is a dead letter"); Roots, The Originalist Case for the Fourth Amendment Exclusionary Rule, 45 Gonz.L.Rev. 1 (2009) (challenging Amar's analysis and concluding "that exclusion is actually an ancient remedy, widely applied by courts in various contexts since the dawn of American history," and that "the basic framework for the exclusionary rule was well established in the regular practices of Founding-era judges and lawyers"); Steiker, Second Thoughts About First Principles, 107 Harv.L.Rev. 820 (1994) (concluding at 851 that "history has shown us again and again that the political process will not create structures that can adequately constrain police misconduct"). The Posner analysis, apparently perceiving the problem as merely one of compensating the illegal search victim for his "cleanup costs," is demolished in Morris, The Exclusionary Rule, Deterrence and Posner's Economic Analysis of Law, 57 Wash.L. Rev. 647 (1982).

Compare with the tort proposals that of Caldwell & Chase, The Unruly Exclusionary Rule: Heeding Justice Blackmun's Call to Examine the Rule in Light of Changing Judicial Understanding About Its Effects Outside the Courtroom, 78 Marq.U.L. Rev. 45 (1994) (proposing that exclusionary rule be abolished but that defendant's "incentive to raise the issue of a Fourth Amendment violation" in criminal prosecution be maintained by requiring a sentence reduction if violation established, and officers found to have violated Fourth Amendment would thereafter be required to attend classes on the subject and would receive punishment where appropriate).

Compare also the more recent administrative remedies proposals in Perrin, Caldwell, Chase & Fagan, If

recommendation of Professor Oaks that

> the exclusionary rule should not be abolished until there is
> something to take its place and perform its two essential functions.
> If constitutional rights are to be anything more than pious
> pronouncements, then some measurable consequence must be at-
> tached to their violation. It would be intolerable if the guarantee
> against unreasonable search and seizure could be violated without
> practical consequence. It is likewise imperative to have a practical
> procedure by which courts can review alleged violations of
> constitutional rights and articulate the meaning of those rights.
> The advantage of the exclusionary rule—entirely apart from any
> direct deterrent effect—is that it provides an occasion for judicial
> review, and it gives credibility to the constitutional guarantees.[72]

Under this test, the proposed statute would hardly be a suitable replacement for the exclusionary rule. This conclusion is
supported by the following considerations:

(1) While abrogation of sovereign immunity and creation of a
fair tribunal arguably might overcome two of the longstanding
impediments to the effectiveness of the tort remedy, in the
absence of a prospect of a significant recovery there would be no
incentive to undertake proceedings to collect damages for violation of Fourth Amendment rights. As one commentator has noted,
the victim of a police violation of Fourth Amendment rights is
likely to lack the "aura of respectability" needed to recover a significant amount for injury to feelings and reputation.[73]

(2) For this reason and others, it will be difficult for a potential
plaintiff to obtain effective legal representation. Professor Amsterdam properly asks: "Where are the lawyers going to come
from to handle these cases for the plaintiffs?"[74] One of the great
virtues of the exclusionary rule is that Fourth Amendment violations are regularly brought to light; the accused "has a motive to
challenge the police overreaching" and he "need not resort to an-

---

It's Broken, Fix It: Moving Beyond the Exclusionary Rule, A New and Extensive Empirical Study of the Exclusionary Rule and a Call for a Civil Administrative Remedy to Partially Replace the Rule, 83 Iowa L.Rev. 669 (1998); Slobogin, Why Liberals Should Chuck the Exclusionary Rule, 1999 U.Ill.L.Rev. 363. The first of these, known as "the Pepperdine proposal," is the subject of a Symposium on Reform of the Exclusionary Rule, 26 Pepp.L.Rev. 789 (1999).

[72]Oaks, 37 U.Chi.L.Rev. 665, 756 (1970).

[73]Comment, 63 J.Crim.L.C. & P.S. 256, 263 (1972). See also Casper,

Benedict & Perry, The Tort Remedy in Search and Seizure Cases: A Case Study in Juror Decision Making, 13 Law & Soc. 279, 281–84 (1988) (tort remedy ineffective, as awards small and officers usually win); Orfield, Deterrence, Perjury, and the Heater Factor: An Exclusionary Rule in the Chicago Criminal Courts, 63 U.Colo.L. Rev. 75, 126 (1992) (questioned judges, prosecutors and public defenders "believed that the legal system would be unsympathetic to victims of unconstitutional searches and/or that such victims would not have the resources to bring actions").

[74]Amsterdam, 58 Minn.L.Rev. 349, 430 (1974).

other proceeding or hire another lawyer."[75] But what "would possess a lawyer to file a claim for damages * * * in an ordinary search-and-seizure case?"[76]

(3) Particularly if the Fourth Amendment tort action is pursued infrequently and does not result in substantial recoveries, there is no reason to believe it will act as an effective deterrent. It was noted earlier that the criticism that the exclusionary rule "does not apply any direct sanction to the individual official" takes too narrow a view of deterrence, as suppression of illegally obtained evidence withdraws an incentive to violate the constitution. But if the exclusionary rule is abandoned, so that the inducement to violate is restored, it is to be doubted that this inducement will be overcome by the prospect of recovery from the governmental unit. It has been argued, of course, that "a community which pays the bill will not long tolerate habitual lawlessness."[77] But as yet there has been "no showing that either enlarged liability or indemnity has realized the expectation that government agencies exposed to this prospect of liability would take steps to minimize their risk by effectively reducing police misbehavior."[78] As one commentator has noted, if "the compartmentalized structure of law enforcement machinery prevented the frustrated prosecutor from putting effective pressure on the police to curb their illegal practices, it seems just as likely that the same compartmentalization will prevent the taxing authorities from putting effective pressure on the police."[79]

(4) The "violate now and pay later"[80] character of the tort remedy makes it ineffective both as a deterrent and a means of giving credibility to Fourth Amendment rights. As Professor Dellinger has observed:

> In essence, by disallowing in all cases the use of the exclusionary rule to suppress evidence gathered in violation of the fourth amendment, the Chief Justice's proposal would permit the government to buy itself out of having to comply with constitutional commands. To abolish the exclusionary rule and replace it with an action for damages against the governmental treasury is to have the law speak with two voices. * * * However one resolves the question of whether

---

[75] Paulsen, 52 J.Crim.L., C. & P.S. 255, 260 (1961).

[76] Amsterdam, 58 Minn.L.Rev. 349, 430 (1974), continuing: "The prospect of a share in the substantial damages to be expected? The chance to earn a reputation as a police-hating lawyer, so that he can no longer count on straight testimony concerning the length of skid marks in his personal injury cases? The gratitude of his client when his filing of the claim causes the prosecutor to refuse a lesser-included-offense plea or to charge priors or to pile on 'cover' charges? The

opportunity to represent his client without fee in these resulting criminal matters?"

[77] Hall, The Law of Arrest in Relation to Contemporary Social Problems, 3 U.Chi.L.Rev. 345, 373 (1936).

[78] Oaks, 37 U.Chi.L.Rev. 665, 673–74 n. 37 (1970).

[79] Comment, 63 J.Crim.L., C. & P.S. 256, 264 (1972).

[80] Paulsen, 52 J.Crim.L., C. & P.S. 255, 261 (1961).

49

a valid contract creates a normative duty or merely presents an option to breach and pay damages, it is inconsistent with a constitutional system to view duties imposed by basic guarantees in the latter way. * * * The fourth amendment does not grant the government the discretion to decide whether the benefits of infringing the public's right to be protected from unreasonable searches and seizures are worth some expenditure of the public's funds; the language of the amendment is an affirmative command. It is therefore doubtful that the substitution of a claim against the government for the exclusionary rule in all cases would provide equally effective vindication of the constitutional interests thus protected, and it is therefore doubtful that such a substitution would be constitutionally valid.[81]

(5) Finally, replacement of the exclusionary rule with a tort remedy to be pursued before a special tribunal would have the unfortunate consequence of effectively withdrawing from the Supreme Court and other appellate courts the important function of spelling out police authority under the Fourth Amendment. One of the virtues of the exclusionary rule, as noted above, is that it provides the higher courts with a sufficiently steady diet of Fourth Amendment issues to make possible a meaningful shaping of constitutional standards governing arrest and search.[82] That process of giving content to the Amendment which occupies "a place second to none in the Bill of Rights"[83] is too important to be shunted off upon a special tribunal in the nature of a court of claims. Moreover, experience has shown that tort litigation is not a meaningful context within which to develop constitutional doctrine on arrest and search.[84]

Mention should also be made here of Prof. Dripps' proposal to utilize the exclusionary rule *or* a tort remedy, at the government's option on a case-by-case basis.[85] He proposes "that courts should begin to experiment with suppression orders that are contingent

---

[81]Dellinger, Of Rights and Remedies: The Constitution as a Sword, 85 Harv.L.Rev. 1532, 1562–63 (1972).

[82]But see § 1.1 note 30 concerning the possible effect of limitations on the exclusionary rule and other remedies in this respect.

[83]Harris v. United States, 331 U.S. 145, 67 S.Ct. 1098, 91 L.Ed. 1399 (1947) (Frankfurter, J., dissenting).

[84]See note 47 supra. This would be less so if the various common law defenses were not available when the objective is recovery from the government rather than personal liability of the arresting or searching officer, but it is unclear that this is a part of the proposal made by the Chief Justice.

For other criticism of the tort remedy alternative, see Morris, The Exclusionary Rule, Deterrence and Posner's Economic Analysis of Law, 57 Wash.L.Rev. 647 (1982); Schlag, Assaults on the Exclusionary Rule: Good Faith Limitations and Damage Remedies, 73 J.Crim.L. & C. 875 (1982).

[85]As distinguished from another proposal under which the option would operate on an agency-by-agency basis. See Estreicher & Weick, Opting for a Legislative Alternative to the Fourth Amendment Exclusionary Rule, 78 UMKC L.Rev. 949, 952 (2010), proposing legislation whereby the Department of Justice could certify particular law enforcement agencies as having an effective alternative reme-

on the failure of the police department to pay damages set by the court," which "for deterrent purposes * * * should be set equal to the expected governmental gain from the violation," so that the damages would "leave the government indifferent between exclusion and damages in the ordinary case, yet free to pay the damages when the illegality turns upon exceptionally culpable or dangerous crime." Dripps reasons that such a system would be better than the current system because it "would encourage honest fact-finding and fair interpretations of the Constitution," and better than the self-contained damages action because, since "the government must waive its objection to the damages to avoid suppression, the courts could assess liquidated or punitive damages, cut through immunity defenses, and impose entity liability—all of the frequently urged, but never tried, prescriptions for effective damage actions."[86] The proposal appears impractical for many reasons, including that judges "trained in the common law method are unlikely to take it upon themselves to adopt such a complex, legislative-type, global solution to a so-far unyielding problem" and "are not likely to be institutionally capable of crafting the discerning solution that Dripps envisions."[87]

§ 1.2(d) Limiting the exclusionary rule to "substantial" or other than "good faith" violations

Yet another objection to the exclusionary rule voiced by the Chief Justice in *Bivens,* which has also been made by other commentators with some frequency,[88] is that it

> has increasingly been characterized by a single, monolithic, and drastic judicial response to all official violations of legal norms. Inadvertent errors of judgment that do not work any grave injustice will inevitably occur under the pressure of police work. These hon-

---

dial system, consisting of a publicly accessible registry of all searches and seizures by that agency, quality and conduct standards for agency personnel, an ombudsman's office to review complaints, and provision of "a legally effective compensation system, waiving all sovereign and official immunity, enabling victims of Fourth Amendment violations by the Agency to bring an individual or class action suit for appropriate injunctive relief and special damages (on a schedule approved by the Department) against the Agency."

[86]Dripps, The Case for the Contingent Exclusionary Rule, 38 Am.Crim.L.Rev. 1, 2–4 (2001).

[87]Thomas, Judges Are Not Economists and Other Reasons to be Skeptical of Contingent Suppression Orders: A Response to Professor

Dripps, 38 Am.Crim.L.Rev. 47, 48–49 (2001).

In Dripps, The "New" Exclusionary Rule Debate: From "Still Preoccupied with 1985" to "Virtual Deterrence," 37 Fordham Urb.L.J. 743, 746 (2010), Dripps appears to have abandoned this proposal because "[a]ssessing the damages * * * is difficult and dangerous," but has replaced it with a "virtual deterrence" proposal, discussed in the text at note 156 infra.

[Section 1.2(d)]

[88]Friendly, The Bill of Rights as a Code of Criminal Procedure, 53 Cal.L. Rev. 929, 951–53 (1965); Wingo, Growing Disillusionment with the Exclusionary Rule, 25 Sw.L.J. 573, 584–85 (1971); Wright, 50 Tex.L.Rev. 736, 743–45 (1972); Comment, 46 Fordham L.Rev. 139 (1977).

est mistakes have been treated in the same way as deliberate and flagrant *Irvine*-type[89] violations of the Fourth Amendment. * * *

I submit that society has at least as much right to expect rationally graded responses from judges in place of the universal "capital punishment" we inflict on all evidence when police error is shown in its acquisition.

He cited by way of illustration a section of the Model Code of Pre-Arraignment Procedure declaring that a motion to suppress should be granted only if the court finds the violation to be "substantial," as determined from consideration of all the circumstances, including:

(a) the extent of deviation from lawful conduct;

(b) the extent to which the violation was willful;

(c) the extent to which privacy was invaded;

(d) the extent to which exclusion will tend to prevent violations of this Code;

(e) whether, but for the violation, the things seized would have been discovered; and

(f) the extent to which the violation prejudiced the moving party's ability to support his motion, or to defend himself in the proceeding in which the things seized are sought to be offered in evidence against him.[90]

Similarly, Justice White, dissenting in *Stone v. Powell*,[91] expressed the view that the exclusionary rule

---

[89]The reference is to Irvine v. California, 347 U.S. 128, 74 S.Ct. 381, 98 L.Ed. 561 (1954), a pre-*Mapp* case in which the Court declined to suppress evidence obtained by repeated illegal entries into petitioner's home, first to install a secret microphone and then to move it into the bedroom, in order to listen to the conversations of the occupants.

[90]Model Code of Pre-Arraignment Procedure § SS 290.2(4) (1975). Another provision, § SS 290.2(2), states that suppression shall also occur "if otherwise required by the Constitution of the United States," which some have read as meaning that the "substantial" violation limitation is not applicable to Fourth Amendment violations; see brief of the American Civil Liberties Union at 16, California v. Krivda, 409 U.S. 33, 93 S.Ct. 32, 34 L.Ed.2d 45 (1972). But this is not the case, for the commentary to this section, at p. 565, asserts that "the constitutional issue itself may be affected by the factor of substantiality."

For an explication and defense of the Model Code position, see Coe, The ALI Substantiality Test: A Flexible Approach to the Exclusionary Sanction, 10 Ga.L.Rev. 1 (1975). Wingo, Rewriting Mapp and Miranda: A Preference for Due Process, 31 U.Kan.L.Rev. 219 (1983), argues that the Supreme Court should adopt a due process approach to exclusionary rules, in which case they could be limited in much the way as is the ALI "substantial violation" test. Others have made somewhat similar proposals contemplating that the exclusionary rule should be discretionary rather than mandatory but that the discretion would be guided by certain designated considerations. See Stribopoulos, Lessons from the Pupil: A Canadian Solution to the American Exclusionary Rule Debate, 22 B.C. Int'l & Comp.L.Rev. 77 (1999); Starr & Maness, Reasonable Remedies and (or) the Exclusionary Rule, 43 Tex. Tech L.Rev. 373 (2010); Comment, 30 McGeorge L.Rev. 1293 (1999).

[91]Stone v. Powell, 428 U.S. 465, 96 S.Ct. 3037, 49 L.Ed.2d 1067 (1976).

should be substantially modified so as to prevent its application in those many circumstances where the evidence at issue was seized by an officer acting in the good-faith belief that his conduct comported with existing law and having reasonable grounds for this belief. These are recurring situations; and recurringly evidence is excluded without any realistic expectation that its exclusion will contribute in the slightest to the purposes of the rule, even though the trial will be seriously affected or the indictment dismissed. * * *

When law enforcement personnel have acted mistakenly, but in good faith and on reasonable grounds, and yet the evidence they have seized is later excluded, the exclusion can have no deterrent effect. The officers, if they do their duty, will act in similar fashion in similar circumstances in the future; and the only consequence of the rule as presently administered is that unimpeachable and probative evidence is kept from the trier of fact and the truth-finding function of proceedings is substantially impaired or a trial totally aborted.

This proposal for a "good faith" exception to the Fourth Amendment exclusionary rule later gained some momentum. Several commentators have viewed with favor such an exception,[92] and in 1981 the Attorney General's Task Force on Violent Crime recommended that "evidence should not be excluded from a criminal proceeding if it has been obtained by an officer acting in the reasonable, good faith belief that it was in conformity to the Fourth Amendment."[93] Legislation to that effect was adopted in a few states,[94] and has been proposed on the federal level,[95] resulting in

---

[92]See Ball, Good Faith and the Fourth Amendment: The "Reasonable" Exception to the Exclusionary Rule, 69 J.Crim.L. & C. 635 (1978); Bernardi, The Exclusionary Rule: Is a Good Faith Standard Needed to Preserve a Liberal Interpretation of the Fourth Amendment?, 30 DePaul L.Rev. 51 (1980); Brown, The Good Faith Exception to the Exclusionary Rule, 23 So.Tex.L.J. 655 (1982); Carrington, Good Faith Mistakes and the Exclusionary Rule, 1 Crim.J.Ethics 35 (Summer/Fall, 1982); Friendly, The Bill of Rights as a Code of Criminal Procedure, 53 Cal.L.Rev. 929, 952 (1965); Jensen & Hart, The Good Faith Restatement of the Exclusionary Rule, 73 J.Crim.L. & C. 916 (1982); Leonard, Good Faith Exception to the Exclusionary Rule: A Reasonable Approach for Criminal Justice, 4 Whittier L.Rev. 33 (1982); Schroeder, Deterring Fourth Amendment Violations: Alternatives to the Exclusionary Rule, 69 Geo.L.J.

1361 (1981); Sunderland, The Exclusionary Rule: A Requirement of Constitutional Principle, 69 J.Crim.L. ,C. & P.S. 141 (1978); Wright, Must the Criminal Go Free if the Constable Blunders?, 50 Tex.L.Rev. 736, 740 (1972); Comments, 70 Ky.L.J. 879 (1982); 51 U.Cin.L.Rev. 83 (1982); Notes, 30 Am.U.L.Rev. 863 (1981); 23 Ariz.L.Rev. 801 (1981); 20 Ariz.L.Rev. 915 (1978).

[93]Attorney General's Task Force on Violent Crime, Final Report 55 (1981).

[94]Ariz.Rev.Stat. § 13-3925 (court not to suppress evidence if it "was seized by a peace officer as a result of a good faith mistake or technical violation," former meaning "a reasonable judgmental error concerning the existence of facts which if true would be sufficient to constitute probable cause" and latter including "a reasonable good faith reliance" upon a statute subsequently ruled unconstitutional

or a "warrant that is later invalidated due to a good faith mistake" or a "controlling court precedent that is later overruled" without a declaration that it is to apply retroactively); Colo.Rev. Stat. § 16-3-308 (similar); former Utah Code Ann. § 77-35-12(g) (trial court may only suppress evidence when it finds a substantial Fourth Amendment violation not made in good faith).

But in People v. Quintero, 657 P.2d 948 (Colo.1983), the court held that because the statutory definition of "good faith mistake" is "a reasonable judgmental error concerning the existence of facts which if true would be sufficient to constitute probable cause," the statute was inapplicable in the instant case. "The mistake in this case does not center upon a misperception of existing fact but upon a mistake in judgment of law, that is, the mistaken judgment by the officer that the facts known to him were sufficient to warrant a full custodial arrest of the defendant." And in People v. Mitchell, 678 P.2d 990 (Colo.1984), where an arrest warrant issued for failure to pay a traffic fine the defendant had actually paid earlier, the court declined to invoke the statute where the record was silent as to the source or character of the mistake, for "there is no basis to conclude that the warrant was issued as the result of some reasonable judgmental error concerning the existence of facts which if true would have constituted probable cause to arrest the defendant." For earlier criticism of the Colorado provision, see Note, 53 U.Colo.L.Rev. 809 (1982).

The Utah provision was held unconstitutional in State v. Mendoza, 748 P.2d 181 (Utah 1987), where the court stated: "Even assuming for the sake of argument that the 'good faith' exception established by Leon applies to the type of search involved in this case, the statutes in question here are still unconstitutional. [The statute] requires defendants to establish a substantial violation of their fourth amendment rights. * * * This threshold requirement is beyond the scope of the 'good faith' exception for two rea-

sons. First, Leon establishes an exception to the applicability of the exclusionary rule. * * * Pursuant to Mapp, if the defendant established a fourth amendment violation, the illegally-seized evidence must be suppressed regardless of the egregiousness of, or the intentions motivating, the police officers' conduct. * * * Because Leon is an exception to the application of the exclusionary rule, the State must prove the necessary elements of the 'good faith' exception. [The statute], however, shifts the burden of proof to the defendant, who must prove the equivalent of police conduct made in bad faith before the court can apply the exclusionary rule."

"Subsections [of the statute] also exceed the bounds of the exception established in Leon because both require less than objectively reasonable conduct in order for [the statute] to provide an exception. Pursuant to the broad reading of Leon, a court will not admit the illegally-seized evidence if it finds the police conduct objectively unreasonable. Conduct that is objectively unreasonable, however, is not equivalent to grossly negligent, willful, or malicious conduct; nor does it always arise from either an intent to harass or pursuant to department policy."

[95]E.g., S. 2231, 97th Cong., 2d Sess. (1982), providing that "evidence which is obtained as a result of a search or seizure and which is otherwise admissible not be excluded in a proceeding in a court of the United States if the search or seizure was undertaken in a reasonable, good faith belief that it was in conformity with the fourth amendment to the Constitution of the United States. A showing that evidence was obtained pursuant to and within the scope of a warrant constitutes prima facie evidence of such a reasonable good faith belief, unless the warrant was obtained through intentional and material misrepresentation." The same language appears in the Exclusionary Rule Application Act of 1982, proposed in Title II of S. 2903, 97th Cong., 2d Sess. (1982).

congressional hearings on the subject.[96]

On the judicial front, the first decision to adopt an across-the-board "good faith" exception to the exclusionary rule was *United States v. Williams,*[97] an en banc decision by the 24 circuit judges then serving on the Fifth Circuit. Ms. Williams, who had been convicted of heroin possession and released pending appeal on the condition she remain in Ohio, was arrested at the Atlanta airport for violation of the travel restriction, which resulted in the discovery that she was carrying heroin. Her motion to suppress was granted by the district court on the ground that she had been illegally arrested, and that ruling was affirmed by a panel of the court of appeals[98] but then reversed upon rehearing en banc. Sixteen judges concluded that Williams had been lawfully arrested for breach of court-imposed travel restrictions even absent any initiating request by the court which imposed them, but thirteen members of the court then joined in another opinion declaring "that evidence is not to be suppressed under the exclusionary rule where it is discovered by officers in the course of actions that are taken in good faith and in the reasonable, though mistaken, belief that they are authorized." They reasoned that "any slight deterrent effect of excluding fruits of good-faith arrests is even less than the small deterrence" the Supreme Court had in certain limited contexts concluded "does not justify the societal harm incurred by suppressing relevant and incriminating evidence." Ten judges, in a concurring opinion, objected that the ruling of the 13 was unnecessary, unprincipled, ambiguous

---

[96]See The Exclusionary Rule Bills: Hearings Before the Subcomm. on Criminal Law of the Senate Comm. on the Judiciary, 97th Cong., 1st & 2d Sess. (1982). The testimony is summarized in 31 Crim.L.Rptr. 2018–20, 2226–27 (1982).

[97]United States v. Williams, 622 F.2d 830 (5th Cir.1980), discussed in Comment, 13 Conn.L.Rev. 737 (1981); Notes, 9 Am.J.Crim.L. 141 (1981); 32 Mercer L.Rev. 1329 (1981); 60 Wash.U. L.Q. 161 (1982); and in the post-*Williams* authorities cited in note 92 supra and note 102 infra.

Williams was followed in United States v. Mahoney, 712 F.2d 956 (5th Cir.1983), where police entered premises to arrest, after the person who opened the door stepped back, pursuant to an arrest warrant for "John Doe, a/k/a Dennis (last name unknown)." The district court had sup-pressed the evidence because there was no consent to entry and the warrant was invalid for lack of particularity. The court of appeals reversed, and in doing so revealed just how large a breach in the Fourth Amendment a loosely applied good faith test would create. "Here, only a sophisticated lawyer could have then known with confidence both that the warrant was defective and that the officer could not step through the open door when the person who opened it stepped back without comment." *Williams* was distinguished in United States v. Whaley, 781 F.2d 417 (5th Cir.1986) ("mistake here was on a basic point of established law," namely, that search warrant ordinarily necessary to come onto private property to seize what observed from without).

[98]United States v. Williams, 594 F.2d 86 (5th Cir.1979).

and unworkable.[99] A few other courts elected to follow the lead of *Williams*,[100] while others expressly declined to do so.[101]

The *Williams* "good faith" exception is unsound.[102] It rests upon the erroneous proposition that a "police officer will not be deterred from an illegal search if he does not know that it is illegal" and that, absent such deterrence of that officer, there is no reason to invoke the exclusionary rule. But if at a suppression hearing it is shown that the arresting or searching police officer acted illegally because of an insufficient understanding of the Fourth Amendment's limits on his power, this is hardly a case for withdrawing the exclusionary sanction on the ground that the policeman was not in a condition to be deterred in this instance. Rather, it is an especially compelling case for applying the exclusionary rule so as to encourage the taking of such additional steps as will enhance police understanding of these limits. And this is true

---

[99]They objected that the rule announced by the 13 was unnecessary because a majority of the court was of the view the arrest was lawful; that no other court had altered the exclusionary rule and that a majority of the Supreme Court had not supported any such qualification; that the change rests upon the mistaken assumption that deterrence is the sole basis of the exclusionary rule; that the change "raises many questions," such as whether it will "shield only errors of fact or both errors of fact and errors of law"; and that if the no-deterrence reasoning of the 13 were sound, then "it appears needless to require the police officer's subjective good faith also be objectively reasonable," as "[a] policeman who is in complete subjective good faith is unlikely to stop to ask himself, 'Am I also reasonable?'"

[100]E.g., United States v. Beck, 729 F.2d 1329 (11th Cir.1984); Donovan v. Federal Clearing Die Casting Co., 695 F.2d 1020 (7th Cir.1982); State v. Mincey, 130 Ariz. 389, 636 P.2d 637 (1981).

[101]E.g., People v. Teresinski, 30 Cal.3d 822, 180 Cal.Rptr. 617, 640 P.2d 753 (1982); People v. David, 119 Mich.App. 289, 326 N.W.2d 485 (1982); People v. Jennings, 54 N.Y.2d 518, 446 N.Y.S.2d 229, 430 N.E.2d 1282 (1981); Abell v. Commonwealth, 221 Va. 607, 272 S.E.2d 204 (1980).

[102]For other criticism of the "good faith" exception, see the most comprehensive and exhaustive treatment in Mertens & Wasserstrom, The Good Faith Exception to the Exclusionary Rule: Deregulating the Police and Derailing the Law, 70 Geo.L.J. 365 (1981); and see also Committee on Criminal Law, Report on the Exclusionary Rule, 37 Record 598 (1982); Fyfe, Enforcement Workshop: In Search of the "Bad Faith" Search, 18 Crim.L. Bull. 346 (1982); Goodpaster, An Essay on Ending the Exclusionary Rule, 33 Hastings L.J. 1065 (1982); Ingber, Defending the Citadel: The Dangerous Attack of "Reasonable Good Faith," 36 Vand.L.Rev. 1511 (1983); Kamisar, Gates, "Probable Cause," "Good Faith," and Beyond, 69 Iowa L.Rev. 551 (1984); LaFave, The Fourth Amendment in an Imperfect World: On Drawing "Bright Lines" and "Good Faith," 43 U.Pitt.L.Rev. 307, 333–59 (1982); Schlag, Assaults on the Exclusionary Rule: Good Faith Limitations and Damage Remedies, 73 J.Crim.L. & Criminology 875 (1982); Stewart, The Road to Mapp v. Ohio and Beyond: The Origins, Development and Future of the Exclusionary Rule in Search and Seizure Cases, 83 Colum.L.Rev. 1365, 1399–1403 (1983); Uviller, The Acquisition of Evidence for Criminal Prosecutions: Some Constitutional Premises and Practices in Transition, 35 Vand.L.Rev. 501 (1982); Comments, 15 Ga.L.Rev. 487 (1981); 35 Mercer L.Rev. 699 (1984); Notes, 57 Notre Dame Law. 112 (1981); 34 Vand.L.Rev. 213 (1981).

even if we are prepared to say that from the limited perspective of the particular officer in the particular case the arrest or search was an understandable or "reasonable" action to take.

The full import of this last statement can best be seen by considering a related body of law, that concerning so-called "constitutional tort" actions undertaken against police by those claiming to be the victims of illegal seizures and searches.[103] In *Pierson v. Ray*,[104] the Supreme Court concluded that if a jury "found that the officers reasonably believed in good faith that the arrest was constitutional, then a verdict for the officers would follow even though the arrest was in fact unconstitutional." The standard later was made purely objective,[105] but in such a way that an officer has a defense if he proves "that he neither knew or should have known of the relevant legal standard."[106] As for what constitutes "good faith" in this tort context, decisions are to be found indicating that an officer may quite properly be held to have acted in "good faith" when his misunderstanding of his Fourth Amendment authority was attributable to misinformation conveyed to him by his department.[107] And it would seem to follow from this that a department's failure to communicate relevant information to an officer concerning the legal restraints on his power also has an important bearing on whether that officer "reasonably should have known" that his conduct was illegal.[108] Such an approach to the question of the officer's personal liability is most sensible.

Proponents of a "good faith" limitation on the exclusionary rule find a perfect analogy between existing law in these "constitutional tort" cases and what they believe the law ought to be in the exclusionary rule context. Thus, Justice White concludes his dissent in *Stone v. Powell* with this assertion: "If the defendant in criminal cases may not recover for a mistaken but good-faith invasion of his privacy, it makes even less sense to exclude the evidence solely on his behalf." Similarly, another commentator reasons that the analogy is sound because of a common purpose of the tort remedy and exclusionary rule: "Both seek to isolate those aspects of the officer's conduct that may justifiably inculpate the officer and reasonably subject him to civil or exclusionary sanctions."[109] But comments such as these reflect a profound misunderstanding of what the exclusionary rule's deterrence function is all about.

---

[103]See § 1.10(a) and (b).

[104]Pierson v. Ray, 386 U.S. 547, 87 S.Ct. 1213, 18 L.Ed.2d 288 (1967).

[105]On this development, see § 1.10(a).

[106]Harlow v. Fitzgerald, 457 U.S. 800, 102 S.Ct. 2727, 73 L.Ed.2d 396 (1982).

[107]See, e.g., Dominguez v. Beame, 603 F.2d 337 (2d Cir.1979); Thompson v. Anderson, 447 F.Supp. 584 (D.Md. 1977).

[108]Stadium Films, Inc. v. Baillargeon, 542 F.2d 577 (1st Cir.1976).

[109]Note, 20 Ariz.L.Rev. 915, 918 (1978).

The tort action, the Supreme Court has stressed, is "intended not only to provide compensation to the victims of past abuses, but to serve as a deterrent against future constitutional deprivations, as well."[110] But in an action by the plaintiff-search victim against the defendant-policeman, how far we believe it is fair to go in the service of these two objectives is governed by some rather traditional tort notions about the relative positions of the parties to a negligence lawsuit. If the defendant has performed reasonably, we leave the cost of the harm on the plaintiff, where the fates placed it, instead of requiring the defendant to assume it; similarly, we are not prepared to make the reasonable defendant respond personally in damages merely in the interest of deterring others.

Consider now the criminal case in which the exclusionary rule issue arises. No longer does it make sense to say that the policeman's "good faith," not unlikely attributable to erroneous or inadequate training by his department, must control so that the officer is not unfairly "mulcted in damages."[111] Contrary to the assertion of the commentator quoted above, exclusion is not a sanction to which the officer is personally subjected, but rather is one imposed upon the system. And, contrary to Justice White's assumption, exclusion of evidence is not a benefit conferred upon the defendant "solely on his behalf" to compensate him for the prior wrong done to him,[112] as might be said of tort damages. The defendant is at best an incidental beneficiary when exclusion occurs for the purpose, as the Supreme Court stated in *Stone v. Powell*,[113] of "removing the incentive" to disregard the Fourth Amendment so that "the frequency of future violations will decrease."

This means that whether the officer who made the challenged arrest or search was sufficiently informed about relevant Fourth Amendment principles so that he could have been deterred is beside the point, for that is not the kind of deterrence we are talking about. "The exclusionary rule is not aimed at special deterrence since it does not impose any direct punishment on a law enforcement official who has broken the rule. * * * The exclusionary rule is aimed at affecting the wider audience of law enforcement officials and society at large. It is meant to discourage violations by individuals who have never experienced any

---

[110]Owen v. City of Independence, Missouri, 445 U.S. 622, 100 S.Ct. 1398, 63 L.Ed.2d 673 (1980).

[111]Pierson v. Ray, 386 U.S. 547, 87 S.Ct. 1213, 18 L.Ed.2d 288 (1967).

[112]"The objective of the exclusionary rule is certainly not to compensate the defendant for the past wrong done

to him any more than it is to penalize the officer for the past wrong he has done. The emphasis is forward." Traynor, Mapp v. Ohio at Large in the Fifty States, 1962 Duke L.J. 319, 335.

[113]Stone v. Powell, 428 U.S. 465, 96 S.Ct. 3037, 49 L.Ed.2d 1067 (1976).

sanction for them."[114] This means that the argument for application of a "good faith" exception is absolutely untenable in the common situation where the officer's violation of the Fourth Amendment in "good faith" is "reasonable" as to him only because he has been insufficiently or incorrectly trained. A failure in such circumstances to apply the exclusionary rule would communicate an unmistakable message to "the wider audience of law enforcement officials and society at large." Society at large and police supervisors would know that there is really no need to expend either the money or the effort required to ensure that police with arrest and search responsibilities are adequately trained as to the extent of their powers in that regard.

Thus, if any kind of general "good faith" exception to the exclusionary rule were ever created, it would of necessity have to be grounded in a uniquely narrow conception of what constitutes the requisite good faith. As stated by the Fifth Circuit in what appears to be an afterthought appended to the *Williams* case,[115] the necessary belief "must be grounded in an objective reasonableness" and "must therefore be based upon articulable premises sufficient to cause a reasonable, and reasonably trained, officer to believe that he was acting lawfully." To apply the exclusionary rule when an individual officer oversteps his bounds but not when the violation of the Fourth Amendment is caused by systemic defects would be to turn the Fourth Amendment on its head.[116]

Whether creating such a narrow "good faith" exception to the exclusionary rule would be worth the candle is a question that quite naturally prompts another inquiry: What kinds of errors falling within this exception are not sufficiently dealt with by existing Fourth Amendment doctrine? One type of error sometimes highlighted by advocates of a "good faith" exception is that which occurs when an officer, acting upon a correct perception of the governing legal principles, makes a mistaken judgment as to the relevant facts. But there is no need to tamper with the exclusionary rule to accommodate such situations, for "the exclusionary rule is already held inapplicable where a policeman makes a reasonable factual mistake."[117] Although this is most apparent as to the Fourth Amendment's probable cause standard,[118] reasonable factual mistakes are also generally tolerated with respect to such other police decisions as whether a warrant or even probable cause is required. As the Court stated in *Illinois v. Rod-*

---

[114]Oaks, Studying the Exclusionary Rule in Search and Seizure, 37 U.Chi.L.Rev. 665, 709–10 (1970).

[115]Because set out in a footnote revealingly labeled "4a."

[116]"Fourth Amendment violations become more, not less, reprehensible when they are the product of Government policy rather than an individual

policeman's errors of judgment." United States v. Peltier, 422 U.S. 531, 95 S.Ct. 2313, 45 L.Ed.2d 374 (1975) (Brennan, J., dissenting).

[117]Kaplan, The Limits of the Exclusionary Rule, 26 Stan.L.Rev. 1027, 1044 (1974).

[118]See § 3.2.

riguez,[119] "in order to satisfy the 'reasonableness' requirement of the Fourth Amendment, what is generally demanded of the many factual determinations that must regularly be made by agents of the government—whether the magistrate issuing a warrant, the police officer executing a warrant, or the police officer conducting a search or seizure under one of the exceptions to the warrant requirement—is not that they always be correct, but that they always be reasonable."

Turning now to mistakes of law, it is not difficult to imagine situations in which such a "good faith" mistake is "reasonable" in the sense that we would not be inclined to criticize the individual officer, the police department or even the criminal justice system at large for the error. Consider, for example, a case where an officer made an arrest for violation of a substantive statute thereafter found unconstitutional. Surely, it might well be argued, it makes no sense to exclude evidence obtained incident to that arrest, for admission of the evidence is hardly an inducement to future wrongdoing. But the Supreme Court has already accommodated that case on another basis. In the 1979 case of *Michigan v. DeFillippo*,[120] the Court held that such an arrest is lawful simply because it falls within the traditional definition of probable cause.[121]

That situation must in turn be distinguished from yet another, where the arresting or searching officer fully complied with extant Fourth Amendment requirements, but a subsequent judicial decision interpreting that Amendment would retroactively make the officer's conduct unconstitutional. Though it might be doubted whether anything would be gained by exclusion in such circumstances, for many years this problem was largely taken care of under the law of retroactivity, specifically, the rule that new Fourth Amendment rules constituting a clear break with the past operate prospectively only.[122] Illustrative was *United States v. Peltier*,[123] involving the stop and search of the defendant's car by a roving border patrol, where the Court held that the defendant could not prevail on the basis of a subsequent Supreme Court decision, "the first roving Border Patrol case to be decided by this Court," which overturned the "uniform [favorable] treatment of roving border patrol searches by the federal judiciary." That result, *Peltier* notes, intruded not the slightest on the exclusionary rule's purpose "to deter unlawful police conduct."

---

[119]Illinois v. Rodriguez, 497 U.S. 177, 110 S.Ct. 2793, 111 L.Ed.2d 148 (1990).

[120]Michigan v. DeFillippo, 443 U.S. 31, 99 S.Ct. 2627, 61 L.Ed.2d 343 (1979).

[121]See § 3.2(f).

Whether the same should be true when the statute later found un-constitutional had to do instead with the police officer's arrest or search authority is a harder question, explored in § 1.3(h).

[122]See § 11.5.

[123]United States v. Peltier, 422 U.S. 531, 95 S.Ct. 2313, 45 L.Ed.2d 374 (1975).

But now new Fourth Amendment rulings are fully retroactive prior to the point of conviction finality,[124] giving rise to the argument that arrests or searches violating the Fourth Amendment only because of such retroactivity should be treated as obvious instances of police "good faith,"[125] accepted by the Supreme Court in *United States v. Davis*.[126]

Yet another situation, one which lends itself to somewhat more persuasive arguments in favor of a "good faith" limitation, is that in which evidence is found in execution of an arrest or search warrant later determined to have been improperly issued by the magistrate. As the Attorney General's Task Force put it, this

> is a particularly compelling example of good faith. A warrant is a judicial mandate to an officer to conduct a search or make an arrest, and the officer has a sworn duty to carry out its provisions. Accordingly, we believe that there should be a rule which states that evidence obtained pursuant to and within the scope of a warrant is prima facie the result of good faith on the part of the officer seizing the evidence.[127]

Essentially such a rule was later adopted by the Supreme Court in the case of *United States v. Leon*.[128] This very important development is given separate attention in the following section.

§ 1.2(e) Limiting the exclusionary rule to other than "serious cases"

Professor Kaplan has offered two proposals, one of which is that the exclusionary rule "not apply in the most serious cases—treason, espionage, murder, armed robbery, and kidnapping by organized groups" except perhaps when "the violation of civil liberties were shocking enough."[129] This limitation is said to be justified by "the political costs of the rule, the possibility of releasing serious and dangerous offenders into the community, and the disproportion between the magnitude of the policeman's constitutional violation and the crime in which the evidence is to be suppressed."[130] Moreover, it is claimed that the result would be the development of more meaningful Fourth Amendment limitations with respect to the investigation of other than serious crimes: "Freed of the concern that the fourth amendment doctrine they announce would later result in the release of people guilty of the most serious crimes, judges would be able to interpret more fully and honestly the commands of the fourth

---

[124]United States v. Johnson, 457 U.S. 537, 102 S.Ct. 2579, 73 L.Ed.2d 202 (1982).

[125]See § 1.3(h).

[126]Davis v. United States, __ U.S. __, 131 S.Ct. 2419, 180 L.Ed.2d 285 (2011).

[127]Attorney General's Task Force on Violent Crime, Final Report 55

(1981).

[128]United States v. Leon, 468 U.S. 897, 104 S.Ct. 3405, 82 L.Ed.2d 677 (1984).

[Section 1.2(e)]

[129]Kaplan, 26 Stan.L.Rev. 1027, 1046 (1974).

[130]Kaplan, 26 Stan.L.Rev. 1027, 1046 (1974).

amendment in all the remaining cases."[131]

The wisdom of this proposal is to be doubted. It would seem odd, indeed, to withdraw the exclusionary rule from those cases in which, as far as can be determined,[132] it has the greatest deterrent effect. Nor does it appear correct to say, as Professor Kaplan assumes, that in the investigation of serious offenses "remedies other than the exclusionary rule may be effective."[133] Certainly the restraint of potential adverse public opinion, which generally plays a small part with respect to searches as compared to other forms of police illegality,[134] is virtually nonexistent when the public believes the police were directing their attention to those suspected of the most serious offenses.[135] Moreover, as Kaplan acknowledges, there is the risk that if the police were "freed from the constraints of the rule in the most serious cases" they "might actively encourage violation of the fourth amendment."[136] This fear is justified by the pre-*Mapp* experience, as reported by Professor Allen:

> Some states sought to avoid the heavy costs involved in complete acceptance or rejection of the exclusionary rule by holding the rule applicable only to certain categories of offenses. The consequences were predictable. The police, being of a pragmatic turn, tended to interpret the withdrawal of the rule in given offense categories as a license to proceed in those areas without legal restraint.[137]

Perhaps emboldened by the Supreme Court's adoption in *Leon* of a "good faith" exception, there has recently occurred a reemergence of what might be called a "comparative reprehensibility"[138] approach to the exclusionary rule. In its current broader form, apparently intended to utilize all possible cost-benefit balancing à la *Leon*, "a court might take a two-level approach, (i)

---

[131]Kaplan, 26 Stan.L.Rev. 1027, 1047 (1974).

[132]"Since in the policeman's hierarchy of values, arrest and subsequent conviction are more important the 'bigger' the 'pinch,' compliance with the exclusionary rule seems contingent upon this factor." J. Skolnick, Justice Without Trial 228 (1966). See also Orfield, Deterrence, Perjury, and the Heater Factor: An Exclusionary Rule in the Chicago Criminal Courts, 63 U.Colo.L.Rev. 75, 82 (1992) (judges, prosecutors and public defenders of the view "the exclusionary rule's deterrent effect is greater when officers are working on big or important cases").

[133]Kaplan, 26 Stan.L.Rev. 1027, 1047 (1974).

[134]This is because "illegal searches are typically less offensive to the dig-

nity of the citizenry and less often characterized by violence and brutality than are illegal interrogatory practices," and thus are "less likely to attract the interest of the press" or "to arouse community opinion." Kamisar, 43 Minn.L.Rev. 1083, 1098 (1959). See also Comment, 47 Nw.U.L.Rev. 493 (1952).

[135]Westley, The Police: A Sociological Study of Law, Custom and Morality 118 (unpublished Ph.D. thesis, Dep't of Sociology, Univ. of Chicago, 1951).

[136]Kaplan, 26 Stan.L.Rev. 1027, 1047 (1974).

[137]Allen, 1961 Sup.Ct.Rev. 1, 36.

[138]Kamisar, "Comparative Reprehensibility" and the Fourth Amendment Exclusionary Rule, 86 Mich.L.Rev. 1, 2 (1987).

never excluding illegally seized evidence in the 'most serious' cases (because the defendant's conduct in such cases will *always* be more reprehensible than the police officer's), and (ii) freely balancing the gravity of the constitutional violation against the gravity of the defendant's crime in other cases."[139] Thus, the concurring opinion in *State v. Bolt*[140] asserts that

> where the criminal conduct involved is more dangerous to society than the police misconduct, it does not make sense to sacrifice the criminal prosecution in order to deter the police.
>
> * * * [T]he gravity of ["serious crimes"] always will by definition exceed the gravity of any Fourth Amendment violation. This is because, the rhetoric of some civil libertarians to the contrary, it *is* worse to be murdered or raped than to have one's house searched without a warrant, no matter how aggravated the latter violation.
>
> * * * [Under the proposed balancing approach to the exclusionary rule, t]he accused will be allowed to invoke the rule only where the illegality committed against him is more grave than the crime he has committed against others. Thus, the accused will be "let off" only where he has suffered more than his purported victims.[141]

This approach is, if anything, even less attractive than the narrower concept earlier proposed by Prof. Kaplan. As Prof. Kamisar has pointed out, among its deficiencies are these: (1) " 'compara-

---

[139]Kamisar, 86 Mich.L.Rev. 1, 3 (1987).

[140]State v. Bolt, 142 Ariz. 260, 689 P.2d 519 (1984).

[141]See also Cameron & Lustiger, the Exclusionary Rule: A Cost-Benefit Analysis, 101 F.R.D. 109, 142–52 (1984); Pizzi, The Need to Overrule Mapp v. Ohio, 82 U.Colo.L.Rev. 679, 680 (2011) (proposing *Mapp* be replaced with an exclusionary rule that "would permit courts to balance a range of factors, including the impact of the violation, the culpability of the officer, and the nature of the crime in deciding whether evidence should be suppressed"); Rychlak, Replacing the Exclusionary Rule: Fourth Amendment Violations as Direct Criminal Contempt, 85 Chi.-Kent L.Rev. 241 (2010) (under proposed "standard, before ruling evidence inadmissible, the court would consider the level of the constitutional violation, the seriousness of the crime, whether the violation casts substantial doubt on the reliability of the evidence, and whether the admission of the evidence would seriously damage the integrity of the proceedings"); Note, 18 N.Y.L. Sch.J.Hum.Rts. 271 (2002) (advocating case-by-case determination whether to apply exclusionary rule by balancing victims' rights and probative value). And see also the troublesome analysis in United States v. Stefonek, 179 F.3d 1030 (7th Cir. 1999), to the effect that the exclusionary rule should not apply when the Fourth Amendment violation "imposed a cost on the criminal that was trivial in relation to the social cost of allowing a guilty criminal to walk." This is not to suggest, however, that the narrower conclusion reached in *Stefonek* is wrong, i.e., that even if the warrant failed to incorporate by reference narrower language in the affidavit as to what could be seized, suppression is not necessary when the executing officers were the affiants, who knew of and complied with the "limited scope of the application," as in such circumstances the search and seizure was "identical" to that which would have occurred by express incorporation. See § 4.6(a).

But the language in *Stefonek* was later put to use in another case, producing most disturbing results. See United States v. Espinoza, 256 F.3d 718 (7th Cir.2001), criticized in § 11.4, text at note 105.

tive reprehensibility' balancing would call for 'especially subjective' determinations" of the respective seriousness of the intent of the defendant and the police and thus "would constitute * * * 'almost an open invitation to nullification [of the exclusionary rule] at the trial court level' ";[142] (2) the message to the police would be that in investigating serious crimes the Fourth Amendment may be ignored;[143] (3) "the pressure to lengthen that short list [of serious crimes] would be enormous and * * * what started out as an exception to the exclusionary rule for 'the relatively small class of the most serious cases' would likely end up as an exception for a rather sizeable class of cases."[144] But the most fundamental defect in the "comparative reprehensibility" approach is that it is grounded in the false assumption that a weighing of the relative seriousness of the defendant's crime and the police transgression of his rights somehow captures the relevant concerns regarding the proper boundaries of the exclusionary rule. That is, it is *not* sensible to assert that the deterrence of the police via the exclusionary rule is worth doing *only* when the police conduct themselves in a more reprehensible fashion than the criminals they are at the time seeking to apprehend or implicate. As Kamisar notes,

> there are other ways to frame the question. For example, is it better to let a few wicked persons go free than to furnish the police an incentive to violate many people's rights? Or, is it better to let an occasional criminal go unpunished than to encourage the police to go about their business without regard to the fourth amendment, thus diminishing privacy and freedom to a degree inconsistent with a free and open society? Or, * * * is it "a less evil that some criminals should escape than that the Government should play an ignoble part"? Balancing expediency against values or principles is not an endeavor that lends itself to cost-benefit analysis. It is not unlike balancing one's need for a new car against "Thou shalt not steal."[145]

Thus, one must take a broader perspective as to the consequences of exclusion and nonexclusion where a Fourth Amendment violation has produced evidence of a serious crime. And in this broader perspective, it is certainly most relevant that nonexclusion in the face of police illegality " 'would positively *encourage*' such illegality,"[146] while on the other hand it is not apparent "how the exclusion of evidence in a particular kidnapping or counterfeiting or narcotics case could operate to promote future acts of kidnapping,

[142]Kamisar, 86 Mich.L.Rev. 1, 16 (1987).

[143]See Kamisar, 86 Mich.L.Rev. 1, 20–23 (1987).

[144]Kamisar, 86 Mich.L.Rev. 1, 26 (1987). See also Milhizer, The Exclusionary Rule Lottery Revisited, 59 Cath.U.L.Rev. 747, 762 (2010), concluding a comparative reprehensibility scheme is "doomed to fail."

[145]Kamisar, 86 Mich.L.Rev. 1, 31 (1987).

[146]Kamisar, 86 Mich.L.Rev. 1, 34 (1987).

counterfeiting, or dope peddling."[147]

§ 1.2(f) Limiting the exclusionary rule to institutional failures

Professor Kaplan's other proposal is "to hold the exclusionary rule inapplicable to cases where the police department in question has taken seriously its responsibility to adhere to the fourth amendment."[148] Procedurally, this would mean that if, on a motion to suppress, the judge found a search and seizure unconstitutional, it would then be open to the prosecution "to ask the judge for a further hearing on the police department's regulations, training programs, and disciplinary history."[149] The prosecution, to escape exclusion of the evidence, would have to show "a set of published regulations giving guidance to police officers as to proper behavior in situations such as the one under litigation, a training program calculated to make violations of fourth amendment rights isolated occurrences, and, perhaps most importantly, a history of taking disciplinary action where such violations are brought to its attention."[150]

This proposal deserves serious attention, for it is directed toward the most desirable objective of prompting law enforcement agencies to engage in careful self-study for the purpose of producing clear and comprehensive rules to govern day-to-day police practices.[151] The difficult question, it would seem, is whether the proposal could be feasibly implemented. While Kaplan asserts

---

[147]Kamisar, 86 Mich.L.Rev. 1, 35 (1987).

[Section 1.2(f)]

[148]Kaplan, 26 Stan.L.Rev. 1027, 1050 (1974).

[149]Kaplan, 26 Stan.L.Rev. 1027, 1051 (1974). See also Thomas & Pollack, Saving Rights from a Remedy: A Societal View of the Fourth Amendment, 73 B.U.L.Rev. 147, 188 (1993) (proposing "a case-by-case suppression decision" in which judge would consider "the presence of repeated violations, the existence of a meaningful mechanism for internal disciplinary actions, and departmental compliance efforts and training policies").

[150]Kaplan, 26 Stan.L.Rev. 1027, 1050–51 (1974).

[151]On the desirability of police rule-making, see K. Davis, Discretionary Justice 52-161 (1969); K. Davis, Police Discretion 98-138 (1975); 1 ABA Standards for Criminal Justice § 1-4.3 (2d ed.1980); President's Comm'n on Law Enforcement and Administration

of Justice, Task Force Report: The Police 18–21 (1967); Report of National Advisory Comm'n on Civil Disorders 164–65 (1968); Amsterdam, The Supreme Court and the Rights of Suspects in Criminal Cases, 45 N.Y.U. L.Rev. 785 (1970); Caplan, The Case for Rulemaking by Law Enforcement Agencies, 36 Law & Contemp.Prob. 500 (1971); Goldstein, Police Policy Formulation: A Proposal for Improving Police Performance, 65 Mich.L. Rev. 1123 (1967); Goldstein, Trial Judges and the Police, 14 Crime & Delinq. 14 (1968); LaFave, Police Rulemaking and the Fourth Amendment: The Role of the Courts, in Discretion in Criminal Justice: The Tension Between Individualization and Uniformity 211–270 (L. Ohlin & F. Remington, eds. 1993); LaFave, Controlling Discretion by Administrative Regulations: The Use, Misuse, and Nonuse of Police Rules and Policies in Fourth Amendment Adjudication, 89 Mich.L.Rev. 442 (1990); LaFave & Remington, 63 Mich.L.Rev. 987 (1965); McGowan, Rule-Making and the Police,

that the additional hearing required "need not be very lengthy,"[152] his other comments seem to belie this, for each case would present a unique question as to whether there was compliance with respect to the particular practice challenged[153] at that particular time.[154] Moreover, it seems likely that the objection Kaplan made to the proposed substantial violation limitation is equally apropos here: "So long as lower court trial judges remain opposed on principle to the sanction they are supposed to be enforcing, the addition of another especially subjective factual determination will constitute almost an open invitation to nullification at the trial court level."[155]

A variation on the Kaplan scheme is Professor Dripps' more recent "virtual deterrence" proposal: "If the court hearing a suppression motion found a violation of the Fourth Amendment, it might be required to consider the specific steps, undertaken by the police department and/or the prosecutor's office, by way of training and/or discipline, to prevent recurrence of the violation. If the court concluded that these measures were adequate and reasonable, it could admit the evidence."[156] The two advantages of virtual deterrence, as he sees it, are (i) "that evidence would not be lost,"[157] and (ii) "[e]vasions and fabrications would no longer be necessary to avoid the escape of the guilty."[158] But Dripps acknowledges that there "are two problems with virtual deterrence."[159] "The first is whether the defense would still have incentives to litigate suppression motions. If the government routinely proposed a standard one-hour retraining session for the officers involved, and this were accepted by the courts, then the effect of the proposal would be to abolish the exclusionary rule de

---

70 Mich.L.Rev. 659 (1972); Quinn, The Effect of Police Rulemaking on the Scope of Fourth Amendment Rights, 52 J.Urb.L. 25 (1974); Walker, Controlling the Cops: A Legislative Approach to Police Rulemaking, 63 U.Detr.L. Rev. 361 (1986); Comments, 72 Nw.U.L.Rev. 595 (1977); 130 U.Pa.L. Rev. 1610 (1982).

[152]Kaplan, 26 Stan.L.Rev. 1027, 1051 (1974).

[153]"For example, the regulations governing on-the-street behavior might be sufficient but not those concerning electronic eavesdropping." Kaplan, 26 Stan.L.Rev. 1027, 1053 (1974).

[154]"[A]t least for the foreseeable future, the requirements upon police departments gradually would be grow-

ing more stringent. In each trial, therefore, the defense attorney would be spurred by the possibility that his case might become the vehicle for a further tightening of the standards." Kaplan, 26 Stan.L.Rev. 1027, 1054 (1974).

[155]Kaplan, 26 Stan.L.Rev. 1027, 1045 (1974).

[156]Dripps, The "New" Exclusionary Rule Debate: From "Still Preoccupied with 1985" to "Virtual Deterrence," 37 Fordham Urb.L.J. 743, 793 (2010).

[157]Dripps, 37 Fordham Urb.L.J. 743, 794 (2010).

[158]Dripps, 37 Fordham Urb.L.J. 743, 795 (2010).

[159]Dripps, 37 Fordham Urb.L.J. 743, 796 (2010).

facto."[160] The second problem

is monitoring compliance. The rules of criminal procedure do not provide for consent decrees! Yet the gist of virtual deterrence is to convert the traditional suppression motion into a kind of institutional reform litigation. Suppose the court finds that the government's proposed remedial steps are adequate. How does the court verify compliance?[161]

While Dripps characterizes these problems as "not entirely insurmountable,"[162] it is to be doubted whether a system in which suppression hearings regularly require judges to pass upon the sufficiently of proposed remedial measures, with adequate follow-up, is feasible.

§ 1.3 The *Leon* "good faith" exception

Research References

West's Key Number Digest
Criminal Law ⬤➔394.4; Searches and Seizures ⬤➔112 to 127

Legal Encyclopedias
C.J.S., Criminal Law §§ 770, 772, 778 to 792; Searches and Seizures §§ 129 to 130, 148 to 174, 189, 204, 236

Introduction

As noted earlier,[1] there has been considerable discussion of whether a so-called "good faith" exception to the exclusionary rule should be recognized. There was, even back in the 1980s, some reason to believe that a majority of the Supreme Court favored such a limitation on the exclusionary rule,[2] and thus such a step seemed imminent when the Court ordered reargu-

---

[160]Dripps, 37 Fordham Urb.L.J. 743, 796 (2010).

[161]Dripps, 37 Fordham Urb.L.J. 743, 796 (2010).

[162]Dripps, 37 Fordham Urb.L.J. 743, 796 (2010).

[Section 1.3]

[1]See § 1.2(d).

[2]In addition to those previously noted in § 1.2(d), the Chief Justice in Bivens v. Six Unknown Named Agents, 403 U.S. 388, 91 S.Ct. 1999, 29 L.Ed.2d 619 (1971) and Justice White in Stone v. Powell, 428 U.S. 465, 96 S.Ct. 3037, 49 L.Ed.2d 1067 (1976), Justice Powell (joined by Justice Rehnquist) stated in Brown v. Illinois, 422 U.S. 590, 95

ment in one case on the additional issue of whether the exclusionary rule "should be modified, so as, for example, not to require the exclusion of evidence obtained in the reasonable belief that the search and seizure at issue was consistent with the Fourth Amendment."[3] But in deciding *Illinois v. Gates,*[4] the Court "with apologies to all" declined to rule on that issue because belated retrospection revealed it "was not presented to the Illinois courts." So matters stood when the Supreme Court decided the case of *United States v. Leon.*[5]

S.Ct. 2254, 45 L.Ed.2d 416 (1975): " 'The deterrent purpose of the exclusionary rule necessarily assumes that the police have engaged in willful, or at the very least negligent, conduct which has deprived the defendant of some right.' In cases in which this underlying premise is lacking, the deterrence rationale of the exclusionary rule does not obtain, and I can see no legitimate justification for depriving the prosecution of reliable and probative evidence." Also noteworthy is the fact that Justice O'Connor, at her confirmation hearing, stated that her experience as a trial judge "had led her to conclude that the exclusionary rule sometimes interfered with the administration of justice by requiring the exclusion of evidence obtained through a technical error." N.Y. Times, Sept. 11, 1981, at 9, col. 3.

[3] Illinois v. Gates, 459 U.S. 1028, 103 S.Ct. 436, 74 L.Ed.2d 595 (1982) (order for reargument).

[4] Illinois v. Gates, 462 U.S. 213, 103 S.Ct. 2317, 76 L.Ed.2d 527 (1983).

[5] United States v. Leon, 468 U.S. 897, 104 S.Ct. 3405, 82 L.Ed.2d 677 (1984), discussed in Alschuler, "Close Enough for Government Work": The Exclusionary Rule After Leon, 1984 Sup.Ct.Rev. 309; Bloom, United States v. Leon and Its Ramifications, 56 U.Colo.L.Rev. 247 (1985); Bradley, The "Good Faith" Exception Cases: Reasonable Exercises in Futility, 60 Ind.L.J. 287 (1985); Dripps, Living With Leon, 95 Yale L.J. 906 (1986); Dripps, More on Search Warrants, Good Faith and Probable Cause, 95 Yale L.J. 1424 (1986); Duke, Making Leon Worse, 95 Yale L.J. 1405 (1986); Finer, Gates, Leon, and the Compromise of Adjudica-

tive Fairness (Part I): A Dialogue on Prejudicial Concurrences, 33 Clev.St. L.Rev. 707 (1985); Finer, Gates, Leon, and the Compromise of Adjudicative Fairness (Part II): Of Aggressive Majoritarianism, Willful Deafness, and the New Exception to the Exclusionary Rule, 34 Clev.St.L.Rev. 199 (1986); Harrie, The Exclusionary Rule and the Good Faith Doctrine in the United States and Canada: A Comparison, 14 Loy.L.A. Int'l & Comp.L.J. 779 (1992); LaFave, "The Seductive Call of Expediency": U.S. v. Leon, Its Rationale and Ramifications, 1984 U.Ill.L.Rev. 895 (1984); Melilli, What Nearly a Quarter Century of Experience Has Taught Us About Leon and "Good Faith," 2008 Utah L.Rev. 519; Misner, Limiting Leon: A Mistake of Law Analogy, 77 J.Crim.L. & C. 507 (1986); Taslitz, The Expressive Fourth Amendment: Rethinking the Good Faith Exception to the Exclusionary Rule, 76 Miss.L.J. 483 (2006); Van de Kamp, The Good Faith Exception to the Exclusionary Rule, A Warning Letter to Prosecutors, 26 So.Tex.L.J. 167 (1985); Vienna & Chema, United States v. Leon: Good Faith and the Military Commander, 25 A.F.L.Rev. 95 (1985); Wald, The Unreasonable Reasonableness Test for Fourth Amendment Searches, 4 Crim.Just.Ethics 2 (Winter/Spring, 1985); Wasserstrom & Mertens, The Exclusionary Rule on the Scaffold: But Was It a Fair Trial?, 22 Am.Crim.L. Rev. 85 (1984); The Supreme Court, 1983 Term, 98 Harv.L.Rev. 87, 108 (1984); and student commentary at 49 Albany L.Rev. 1032 (1985); 52 Brooklyn L.Rev. 799 (1986); 27 B.C.L.Rev. 609 (1986); 18 Creighton L.Rev. 819 (1985); 21 Houston L.Rev. 1027 (1984); 50

§ 1.3(a) The *Leon* decision

In *Leon,* the district court suppressed a quantity of drugs found in execution of a facially valid search warrant, on the ground that the affidavit for the warrant did not establish the existence of probable cause. The court of appeals affirmed that conclusion and, as had the district court, refused the government's invitation to recognize a good faith exception to the exclusionary rule. But the Supreme Court, 6–3, reversed, holding that "the Fourth Amendment exclusionary rule should be modified so as not to bar the use in the prosecution's case-in-chief of evidence obtained by officers acting in reasonable reliance on a search warrant issued by a detached and neutral magistrate but ultimately found to be unsupported by probable cause." Because the affidavit in *Leon* related the results of an extensive investigation and consequently "provided evidence sufficient to create disagreement among thoughtful and competent judges as to the existence of probable cause," the Court concluded that "the officers' reliance on the magistrate's determination of probable cause was objectively reasonable, and application of the extreme sanction of exclusion is inappropriate."[6]

In the companion case of *Massachusetts v. Sheppard,*[7] the *Leon* rule was stated and utilized more broadly. The Court there said that "the exclusionary rule should not be applied when the officer conducting the search[8] acted in objectively reasonable reliance on a warrant issued by a detached and neutral magistrate that

---

Mo.L.Rev. 401 (1985); 5 N.Ill.U.L.Rev. 335 (1985); 30 St. Louis U.L.J. 227 (1985); 30 S.Dak.L.Rev. 169 (1984); 15 Sw.U.L.Rev. 767 (1985); 15 U.Balt.L. Rev. 496 (1986); 53 U.Mo.K.C.L.Rev. 677 (1985); 16 U.Tol.L.Rev. 345 (1984).

[Section 1.3(a)]

[6]*Leon* thus concerns whether the property should be suppressed, not whether it should be returned. Prior to the 1989 amendment of Fed.R.Crim. P.41(e), now Fed.R.Crim.P. 41(g), what is there referred to as a motion for return of property was available only as to excluded evidence, and in such circumstances *Leon* was deemed applicable to rule 41(e) motions. Center Art Galleries-Hawaii, Inc. v. United States, 875 F.2d 747 (9th Cir.1989). But under the current version of the rule, suppression and return of property are separate issues, and returned property can still be admitted into evidence. This being the case, *Leon* no longer applies to motions for return of property. J.B. Manning Corp. v. United States, 86 F.3d 926 (9th Cir.1996); Matter of Search of Kitty's East, 905 F.2d 1367 (10th Cir.1990).

[7]Massachusetts v. Sheppard, 468 U.S. 981, 104 S.Ct. 3424, 82 L.Ed.2d 737 (1984), discussed in Note, 59 Tulane L.Rev. 1100 (1985). On remand, 394 Mass. 381, 476 N.E.2d 541 (1985), the court concluded there were no statutory or state constitutional provisions that required exclusion on these facts.

[8]This language in *Sheppard,* where the affiant and the executing officer were one and the same, should not be taken literally. As the Court stated in *Leon*: "References to 'officer' throughout this opinion should not be read too narrowly. It is necessary to consider the objective reasonableness, not only of the officers who eventually executed a warrant, but also of the officers who originally obtained it or who provided information material to the probable-cause determination. Nothing in our opinion suggests, for example, that an officer could obtain a

subsequently is determined to be invalid." Consequently, the Court concluded in *Sheppard,* the evidence obtained in execution of the warrant in that case was admissible even though the warrant was defective in misstating the items that could be seized, as the affiant had properly set out those items in his affidavit and reasonably relied upon the magistrate's representations that the warrant authorized him to conduct the search he had requested. *Leon* and *Sheppard* together, then, amount to a good faith rule for with-warrant cases.[9]

In justification of the *Leon* holding, Justice White, writing for the majority, first concluded that the exclusionary rule was neither "a necessary corollary of the Fourth Amendment" nor "required by the conjunction of the Fourth and Fifth Amendments." Rather, he stated, under the Court's prior decisions the question of whether the exclusionary sanction is to be imposed in a particular case "must be resolved by weighing the costs and benefits of preventing the use in the prosecution's case-in-chief of inherently trustworthy tangible evidence obtained in reliance on a search warrant issued by a detached and neutral magistrate that ultimately is found to be defective." On the costs side of the equation, the Court referred to the "substantial social costs" of the exclusionary rule in terms of its "interference with the criminal justice system's truth-finding function" and the collateral consequence thereof that "some guilty defendants may go free or receive reduced sentences as a result of favorable plea bargains." On the benefits side, the Court inquired into the amount of deterrence in the kind of case under consideration— where the evidence was "obtained in objectively reasonable reliance on a subsequently invalidated search warrant"—and found it to be "marginal or nonexistent."

One aspect of this latter conclusion involves the notion that in such circumstances there is simply no need to utilize the suppression doctrine for the purpose of deterring magistrates. Justice White explained this proposition as follows:

To the extent that proponents of exclusion rely on its behavioral ef-

---

warrant on the basis of a 'bare bones' affidavit and then rely on colleagues who are ignorant of the circumstances under which the warrant was obtained to conduct the search."

[9]In I.N.S. v. Lopez-Mendoza, 468 U.S. 1032, 104 S.Ct. 3479, 82 L.Ed.2d 778 (1984), decided the same day as *Leon* and *Sheppard,* the Court held the exclusionary rule inapplicable to a civil deportation proceeding. White, J., the author of *Leon* and *Sheppard,* dissented in *Lopez-Mendoza* because he believed "that the conclusion of the majority is based upon an incorrect assessment of the costs and benefits of applying the rule in such proceedings," but also asserted that if the officers making the warrantless arrests and searches were "acting in objective good faith," then under *Leon* the evidence would "not be suppressed even if it is held that their conduct was illegal." Stevens, J., also dissenting, declined to join that portion of the White dissent, noting that as yet the Court had not held that *Leon* "has any application to warrantless searches."

fects on judges and magistrates in these areas, their reliance is misplaced. First, the exclusionary rule is designed to deter police misconduct rather than to punish the errors of judges and magistrates. Second, there exists no evidence suggesting that judges and magistrates are inclined to ignore or subvert the Fourth Amendment or that lawlessness among these actors requires application of the extreme sanction of exclusion.

Third, and most important, we discern no basis, and are offered none, for believing that exclusion of evidence seized pursuant to a warrant will have a significant deterrent effect on the issuing judge or magistrate. Many of the factors that indicate that the exclusionary rule cannot provide an effective "special" or "general" deterrent for individual offending law enforcement officers apply as well to judges or magistrates. And, to the extent that the rule is thought to operate as a "systemic" deterrent on a wider audience, it clearly can have no such effect on individuals empowered to issue search warrants. Judges and magistrates are not adjuncts to the law enforcement team; as neutral judicial officers, they have no stake in the outcome of particular criminal prosecutions. The threat of exclusion thus cannot be expected significantly to deter them. Imposition of the exclusionary sanction is not necessary meaningfully to inform judicial officers of their errors, and we cannot conclude that admitting evidence obtained pursuant to a warrant while at the same time declaring that the warrant was somehow defective will in any way reduce judicial officers' professional incentives to comply with the Fourth Amendment, encourage them to repeat their mistakes, or lead to the granting of all colorable warrant requests.

From this, the Court in *Leon* proceeded to the conclusion that if exclusion of evidence were to have any deterrent effect in the case of a subsequently invalidated warrant, "it must alter the behavior of individual law enforcement officers or the policies of their departments." No such deterrent effect was found to be present. The argument that applying the exclusionary rule in such cases "deters future inadequate presentations or 'magistrate shopping'" was dismissed as "speculative." Rather, concluded the Court:

> In most such cases, there is no police illegality and thus nothing to deter. It is the magistrate's responsibility to determine whether the officer's allegations establish probable cause and, if so, to issue a warrant comporting in form with the requirements of the Fourth Amendment. * * * Penalizing the officer for the magistrate's error, rather than his own, cannot logically contribute to the deterrence of Fourth Amendment violations.

§ 1.3(b) Should "costs" and "benefits" be balanced?

The *Leon* result and reasoning is vulnerable on several different levels and from several different perspectives. For one thing, it may be challenged (as it was by dissenting Justices Brennan and Marshall) as being grounded upon the erroneous premise that the exclusionary rule is merely a "judicially created remedy designed to safeguard Fourth Amendment rights generally through its deterrent effect, rather than a personal constitutional right."[10] Such a conclusion hardly follows from the fact that the Fourth Amendment does not make express provision for the exclusion of evidence, for, as these two *Leon* dissenters quite correctly noted, "many of the Constitution's most vital imperatives are stated in general terms and the task of giving meaning to these precepts is therefore left to subsequent judicial decision-making in the context of concrete cases." As for what meaning the Fourth Amendment should be given, they argued with considerable force:

> Because seizures are executed principally to secure evidence, and because such evidence generally has utility in our legal system only in the context of a trial supervised by a judge, it is apparent that the admission of illegally obtained evidence implicates the same constitutional concerns as the initial seizure of that evidence. Indeed, by admitting unlawfully seized evidence, the judiciary becomes a part of what is in fact a single governmental action prohibited by the terms of the Amendment. * * * The Amendment therefore must be read to condemn not only the initial unconstitutional invasion of privacy—which is done, after all, for the purpose of securing evidence—but also the subsequent use of any evidence so obtained.

It is quite clear that this conception of what the Fourth Amendment is all about is precisely what the Supreme Court had in mind when it formulated the exclusionary rule in *Weeks v. United States*[11] and then elaborated upon it in the early cases.[12] It is equally clear, however, as the previous discussion[13] has shown, that this theory cannot be squared completely with the Court's more recent expressions concerning the exclusionary rule's theoretical underpinnings. But this is not to suggest that the "correctness" of *Leon* turns merely upon whether one accepts the earlier or more recent version of the exclusionary rule's rationale. Rather, the essential point is that the *Leon* decision is unsound even if one concedes the majority's precursory supposition that the exclusionary rule is a judicially-created sanction serving a deterrence function.

The *Leon* majority makes it appear that what the Court has done is simply to take another step comparable to those in such earlier cases as *Stone v. Powell*,[14] *United States v. Calandra*,[15]

[Section 1.3(b)]

[10]As the *Leon* majority put it, quoting from United States v. Calandra, 414 U.S. 338, 94 S.Ct. 613, 38 L.Ed.2d 561 (1974).

[11]Weeks v. United States, 232 U.S. 383, 34 S.Ct. 341, 58 L.Ed. 652 (1914).

[12]See Kamisar, Does (Did) (Should) the Exclusionary Rule Rest On a "Principled Basis" Rather Than an "Empirical Proposition"?, 16 Creighton L.Rev. 565, 598–99 (1983); Mertens & Wasserstrom, The Good Faith Exception to the Exclusionary Rule: Deregulating the Police and Derailing the Law, 70 Geo.L.J. 365, 379–80 (1981).

[13]See § 1.1(f).

[14]Stone v. Powell, 428 U.S. 465, 96 S.Ct. 3037, 49 L.Ed.2d 1067 (1976).

and *United States v. Janis.*[16] But that simply is not so. Those decisions were all grounded in the postulate that the exclusionary rule, applicable in a criminal prosecution when illegally seized evidence is offered, need not also be invoked in certain other contexts where no significant *additional* increment of deterrence is deemed likely.[17] Moreover, as Justice Stevens emphasized in his separate dissent,

> until today every time the police have violated the applicable commands of the Fourth Amendment a court has been prepared to vindicate that Amendment by preventing the use of evidence so obtained in the prosecution's case-in-chief against those whose rights have been violated. Today, for the first time, this Court holds that although the Constitution has been violated, no court should do anything about it at any time and in any proceeding.

Certainly the Supreme Court should not, as Justice Stevens added, "so easily concede the existence of a constitutional violation for which there is no remedy." And most certainly such a concession should not be made when it is based upon nothing more than the kind of cost-benefit analysis engaged in by the *Leon* majority. As correctly noted by Justices Brennan and Marshall, "the language of deterrence and of cost/benefit analysis, if used indiscriminately, can have a narcotic effect. It creates an illusion of technical precision and ineluctability. It suggests that not only constitutional principle but also empirical data supports the majority's result." But the result in *Leon* is *not* supported by any empirical data; rather, it was achieved, as Brennan and Marshall quite properly put it, on the basis "of intuition, hunches, and occasional pieces of partial and often inconclusive data," and also by the self-serving and unprincipled device of "casting the burden of proof upon proponents of the rule." Thus, the *Leon* majority had no hesitation in surmising what are called the "substantial social costs" of the exclusionary rule, but found no benefits in this context because "no evidence" but only "speculative" arguments support the notion of deterrence. Especially since one would think that the burden would lie with those seeking to change the status quo by substantially constricting the exclusionary rule, it is apparent what the majority intended to and did achieve by that reasoning in *Leon*. As one commentator warned some years ago, "the assignment of the burden of proof on an issue where evidence does not exist and cannot be obtained is

---

[15]United States v. Calandra, 414 U.S. 338, 94 S.Ct. 613, 38 L.Ed.2d 561 (1974).

[16]United States v. Janis, 428 U.S. 433, 96 S.Ct. 3021, 49 L.Ed.2d 1046 (1976).

[17]But see Davies, The Penalty of Exclusion, A Price or a Sanction?, 73 S.Cal.L.Rev. 1275, 1337–38 (2000), deeming the good faith exception to be consistent with a sanction theory of the exclusionary rule, while the other exceptions set out in the foregoing cases are not because, "where the police misconduct is intentional, * * * consideration of the 'cost' suffered when the penalty is applied * * * is inappropriate."

outcome determinative. [The] assignment of the burden is merely a way of announcing a predetermined conclusion."[18]

§ 1.3(c) Overstated "costs"

Even assuming that the issue presented in *Leon* is subject to resolution by a fair and cautious balancing of the benefits and costs of the exclusionary rule, that kind of evaluation is not to be found in Justice White's opinion for the Court. As Justices Brennan and Marshall quite accurately put it, "we have not been treated to an honest assessment of the merits of the exclusionary rule, but have instead been drawn into a curious world where the 'costs' of excluding illegally obtained evidence loom to exaggerated heights and where the 'benefits' of such exclusion are made to disappear with a mere wave of the hand."

On the costs side of the equation, the *Leon* majority asserted that they were "substantial" and consisted of "some guilty defendants [going] free or receiv[ing] reduced sentences as a result of favorable plea bargains." But this is nothing less than a multiple distortion of the magnitude of the costs attributable to the particular segment of the exclusionary rule at issue in *Leon*. For one thing, it simply is not so that the exclusionary rule generally imposes high costs in terms of lost convictions. The most careful and balanced assessment conducted to date of all available empirical data shows "that the general level of the rule's effects on criminal prosecutions is marginal at most."[19] Specifically, the cumulative loss in felony cases because of prosecutor screening, police releases and court dismissals attributable to the acquisition of evidence in violation of the Fourth Amendment is from 0.6% to 2.35% (from 0.3% to 0.7% if drug and weapon cases are excluded).[20] This same study points out that the available evidence does not show that defendants gain favorable plea bargains because of the exclusionary rule.[21]

The second point to be made concerning the *Leon* majority's reference to the costs of the exclusionary rule is that, whatever the total costs may be, not all of those costs can be fairly put on the scales in deciding the issue before the Court. Rather, the focus should be upon those particular costs that would be alleviated by the change the Court works in the exclusionary rule. But the Court, as Justices Brennan and Marshall stressed in their dissent,

ignores this distinction and mistakenly weighs the aggregated costs

---

[18]Dworkin, Fact Style Adjudication and the Fourth Amendment: The Limits of Lawyering, 48 Ind.L.J. 329, 332–33 (1973).

[Section 1.3(c)]

[19]Davies, A Hard Look at What We Know (and Still Need to Learn) About the "Costs" of the Exclusionary Rule: The NIJ Study and Other Studies of "Lost" Arrests, 1983 A.B.F.Res.J. 611, 622.

[20]Davies, 1983 A.B.F.Res.J. 611, 621–22, 679–80.

[21]Davies, 1983 A.B.F.Res.J. 611, 668–69.

of exclusion in *all* cases, irrespective of the circumstances that led to exclusion, * * * against the potential benefits associated with only those cases in which evidence is excluded because police reasonably but mistakenly believe that their conduct does not violate the Fourth Amendment * * *. When such faulty scales are used, it is little wonder that the balance tips in favor of restricting the application of the rule.

This is not an insignificant error, for had the Court's "cost" inquiry been properly focused it would have been apparent that the relevant costs are insubstantial. The available empirical data shows "that illegally issued warrants cause the loss of only a negligible proportion of felony arrests," meaning that even a total abandonment of the exclusionary rule in with-warrant cases would "not appear to offer any material benefit in terms of saving lost arrests."[22] Moreover, this data most likely overstates the costs attributable to the cases that will be affected by *Leon,* as immediately before *Leon* it was even less likely than it had previously been that evidence would be suppressed because of a warrant defect. This is because just a year before *Leon* the Supreme Court in *Illinois v. Gates*[23] not only watered down the probable cause standard by abandoning the *Aguilar* two-pronged test in favor of a less demanding "totality of the circumstances" approach,[24] but also called for greater deference at the suppression hearing and appellate review stages to the judgment of the magistrate who made the initial probable cause determination when issuing the warrant. This highlights how precipitate the unnecessary[25] holding of *Leon* really was. If the majority really believed that the issue before it was one which could be resolved only by a process of cost-benefit balancing, then surely the prudent course would have been to await further experience under *Gates* so that a clearer measure of the relevant costs could be made.

The third and final point to be made about the *Leon* majority's treatment of the cost factor is that the Court appears to have embraced the kind of cockeyed characterization previously found almost exclusively in the least sophisticated anti-exclusionary rule diatribes. The majority consistently and repeatedly refers to the costs of the exclusionary rule as if they were somehow a matter quite distinct from the Fourth Amendment itself. But this simply is not the case, as is made categorically clear by these words from former Justice Stewart:

---

[22]Davies, 1983 A.B.F.Res.J. 611, 665.

[23]Illinois v. Gates, 462 U.S. 213, 103 S.Ct. 2317, 76 L.Ed.2d 527 (1983).

[24]See § 3.3(a).

[25]As Justice Stevens, dissenting in *Leon,* noted: "It is probable, though admittedly not certain, that the Court of Appeals would now conclude that the warrant in *Leon* satisfied the Fourth Amendment if it were given the opportunity to reconsider the issue in the light of *Gates.* Adherence to our normal practice following the announcement of a new rule would therefore postpone, and probably obviate, the need for the promulgation of the broad new rule the Court announces today."

Much of the criticism leveled at the exclusionary rule is misdirected; it is more properly directed at the Fourth Amendment itself. It is true that, as many observers have charged, the effect of the rule is to deprive the courts of extremely relevant, often direct evidence of the guilt of the defendant. But these same critics fail to acknowledge that, in many instances, the same extremely relevant evidence would not have been obtained had the police officer complied with the commands of the fourth amendment in the first place. * * *

The exclusionary rule places no limitations on the actions of the police. The fourth amendment does. The inevitable result of the Constitution's prohibition against unreasonable searches and seizures and its requirements that no warrant shall issue but upon probable cause is that police officers who obey its strictures will catch fewer criminals. * * * [T]hat is the price the framers anticipated and were willing to pay to ensure the sanctity of the person, home, and property against unrestrained governmental power.[26]

But it is not a price the *Leon* majority is willing to pay. Rather, use of the exclusionary rule merely "to maintain the status quo that would have prevailed if the constitutional requirement had been obeyed"[27] is deemed intolerable in with-warrant cases.

§ 1.3(d) Understated "benefits"

The *Leon* Court's assessment of the benefits of the exclusionary rule is equally flawed. In looking first at the matter of deterrence of magistrates, the majority sets forth a series of supposedly irrefutable propositions, beginning with the assertion that "the exclusionary rule is designed to deter police misconduct rather than to punish the errors of judges and magistrates." No explanation or even citation of authority is offered in support. If the purpose of this sentence is merely to reflect a distinction between deterrence and punishment, then well and good, for it is quite correct to say that the exclusionary rule imposes no punishment on anyone (and is not intended to do so) and thus is aimed at a form of deterrence other than special deterrence.[28] But if that is *all* the sentence means, then it could just as appropriately be turned around in its other respects to read that "the exclusionary rule is designed to deter misconduct by judges and magistrates rather than to punish the errors of police." I take it the *Leon* majority would not be at all happy with that reformulation, for their version of the sentence is intended also to say that the exclusionary rule has only to do with police and not judges and magistrates.

---

[26]Stewart, The Road to Mapp v. Ohio and Beyond: The Origins, Development and Future of the Exclusionary Rule in Search-and-Seizure Cases, 83 Colum.L.Rev. 1365, 1392–93 (1983).

[27]Dellinger, Of Rights and Remedies: The Constitution as a Sword, 85 Harv.L.Rev. 1532, 1563 (1972).

[Section 1.3(d)]

[28]See Oaks, Studying the Exclusionary Rule in Search and Seizure, 37 U.Chi.L.Rev. 665, 709–10 (1970); Stewart, 83 Colum.L.Rev. 1386, 1400 (1983).

But one would hardly have reached such a conclusion on the basis of the Court's language in the seminal exclusionary rule case of *Weeks v. United States,*[29] where it was emphatically declared that "the Fourth Amendment was intended to secure the citizen in person and property against unlawful invasion of the sanctity of his home by officers of the law acting under legislative or judicial sanction."

The Court's second declaration on this subject is that "there exists no evidence suggesting that judges and magistrates are inclined to ignore or subvert the Fourth Amendment or that lawlessness among these actors requires application of the extreme sanction of exclusion." This, as noted earlier, is a slick bit of burden-shifting, and thus one could about as easily assert that there is no evidence suggesting the contrary. The point is that the matter at issue is not subject to solid empirical verification one way or another. But there is at least some basis for being uneasy about the validity of this assertion by the *Leon* majority and, consequently, about the possible consequences of withdrawing the exclusionary rule from with-warrant cases. Empirical studies have shown that there is "substantial disparity between magistrates as to how much evidence is required to obtain a search warrant"[30] and that "the warrant proceeding generally last[s] only about two minutes," during which time judges typically check the affidavit for routinely used boiler-plate allegations.[31] A leading opponent of the exclusionary rule has expressed "no doubt" that "judges do misconstrue the Fourth Amendment and fudge the standards of probable cause, all in what they consider to be the overall good of justice and the community."[32] If that is so to some extent, then it is difficult to accept the notion that all federal and state judicial officers are protecting Fourth Amendment rights with such great enthusiasm that the threat of exclusion can be withdrawn as an unnecessary

[29]Weeks v. United States, 232 U.S. 383, 34 S.Ct. 341, 58 L.Ed. 652 (1914).

[30]L. Tiffany, D. McIntyre & D. Rotenberg, Detection of Crime 204 (1967).

[31]Davies, 1983 A.B.F.Res.J. 611, 666, reporting the conclusions in R. Van Duizend, L. Sutton & C. Carter, The Search Warrant Process (Review Draft, 1983). As stated in Goldstein, The Search Warrant, the Magistrate, and Judicial Review, 62 N.Y.U.L.Rev. 1173, 1182 (1987): "Most magistrates devote very little time to appraising the affidavit's sufficiency. They assume that the affiant is being honest unless something appears from somewhere to disturb the routine, an allegation insufficient in law, a patently incredible tale, or a departure from custom. They tend to ask no questions and to issue warrants in routine fashion."

[32]Wilkey, A Call for Alternatives to the Exclusionary Rule, 62 Judicature 351, 356 (1979). See also Orfield, Deterrence, Perjury, and the Heater Factor: An Exclusionary Rule in the Chicago Criminal Courts, 63 U.Colo.L.Rev. 75, 76 (1992) ("This study demonstrates that judges in Chicago often knowingly credit police perjury and distort the meaning of the law to prevent the suppression of evidence and assure conviction").

deterrent to improperly issued warrants.[33]

But there is a more fundamental problem with this second declaration by the *Leon* majority on the matter of deterrence at the judicial level. The way the proposition is put, it seems as if the Court is making some kind of comparative judgment of the malevolence level of judges generally versus policemen generally. This comes out most clearly in that part of the statement asseverating there is "no evidence suggesting that judges and magistrates"—as compared, apparently, to police—"are inclined to ignore or subvert the Fourth Amendment." The notion seems to be that calculated and deliberate noncompliance with the Fourth Amendment is unlikely at the judicial level, from which it follows that the exclusionary rule and its deterrence function have no place there. But this is not what the Fourth Amendment exclusionary rule is all about. Surely many more Fourth Amendment violations result from carelessness than from intentional constitutional violations, and just as surely the exclusionary rule is logically directed to those more common violations.[34] As the Court recognized in *Stone v. Powell*,[35] what the exclusionary rule demonstrates is "that our society attaches serious consequences to violation of constitutional rights," which encourages those making critical search and seizure decisions "to incorporate Fourth Amendment ideals into their value system." In other words, the long-standing applicability of the exclusionary rule in with-warrant cases has served not only to deter the occasional ill-spirited magistrate, but more importantly to influence judicial behavior more generally by—as the Court put it in *United States v. Johnson*[36]—creating an "incentive to err on the side of constitutional behavior."

The third assertion by the *Leon* majority on this subject is that there is no basis "for believing that exclusion of evidence seized pursuant to a warrant will have a significant deterrent effect on the issuing judge or magistrate." In support two subsidiary points are offered: (i) that the threat of exclusion cannot deter judicial officers because unlike police they "have no stake in the outcome

---

[33]See Nock, The Point of the Fourth Amendment and the Myth of Magisterial Discretion, 23 Conn.L.Rev. 1, 29 (1990), taking note of the empirical evidence discussed in the text above, and concluding that in light of this the Supreme Court should no longer "base constitutional interpretation on a presumption that magistrates regularly and consistently exercise independent judgment in the issuance of warrants," in which case "*Leon* would be wiped from the books."

[34]Even those with some doubts about the extent to which the exclu-

sionary rule's deterrence function is achieved agree that the exclusionary rule, instead of a direct sanction on the officer, is the appropriate sanction in those frequent instances of carelessness. See Heffernan & Lovely, Evaluating the Fourth Amendment Exclusionary Rule: The Problem of Police Compliance with the Law, 24 U.Mich. J.L.Ref. 311 (1991).

[35]Stone v. Powell, 428 U.S. 465, 96 S.Ct. 3037, 49 L.Ed.2d 1067 (1976).

[36]United States v. Johnson, 457 U.S. 537, 102 S.Ct. 2579, 73 L.Ed.2d 202 (1982).

of particular criminal prosecutions"; and (ii) that it cannot be said "admitting evidence obtained pursuant to a warrant while at the same time declaring that the warrant was somehow defective will in any way reduce judicial officers' professional incentives to comply with the Fourth Amendment." These contentions are no more convincing than those previously discussed.

It is classic Fourth Amendment theory, of course, that the warrant process is preferred because then the critical probable cause decision is made by a "neutral and detached magistrate" rather than a police officer "engaged in the often competitive enterprise of ferreting out crime."[37] But one hardly need question that longstanding doctrine to dispute the first of the two subsidiary points quoted above. Certainly the magistrate is more detached than the police officer. It hardly follows, however, that he is so totally disinterested as not to be fazed by the prospect that an erroneous decision on his part could adversely affect a future criminal prosecution. Indeed, it is precisely that prospect which has served to influence many magistrates to take seriously their warrant-issuing responsibilities. This means, as Justices Brennan and Marshall noted in their dissent, that *Leon* unfortunately conveys

> a clear and unambiguous message to magistrates that their decisions to issue warrants are now insulated from subsequent judicial review. Creation of this new exception for good faith reliance upon a warrant implicitly tells magistrates that they need not take much care in reviewing warrant applications, since their mistakes will from now on have virtually no consequence: If their decision to issue a warrant was correct, the evidence will be admitted; if their decision was incorrect but the police relied in good faith on the warrant, the evidence will also be admitted. Inevitably, the care and attention devoted to such an inconsequential chore will dwindle.

In short, as the dissent puts it, magistrates "need to appreciate that their role is of some moment in order to continue performing the important task of carefully reviewing warrant applications."[38]

The majority's answer to this is contained in the second subsid-

---

[37]Johnson v. United States, 333 U.S. 10, 68 S.Ct. 367, 92 L.Ed. 436 (1948).

[38]On the other hand, where the judge's decision itself has nothing to do with the Fourth Amendment directly, but the judge's decision is the cause of some subsequent routine Fourth Amendment activity by the police, it may plausibly be concluded that exclusion of the evidence cannot be justified in terms of deterring either the judicial or law enforcement actors involved. See State v. Robinson, 165 Vt. 351, 683 A.2d 1005 (1996) (where judge ordered family court litigant jailed for disrupting the proceedings, and at jail inventory search uncovered contraband and contemnor, then charged with possession of that contraband, claimed this was a search incident to illegal arrest because the judge abused his discretion in citing defendant for contempt, "the policies behind the exclusionary rule do not require suppression of evidence found incident to incarceration for summary contempt," just as evidence found during "a post-conviction inventory search" is "not subject to suppression even if the conviction is ultimately overturned on appeal").

iary point, namely, that the magistrates' "professional incentives" will suffice to ensure future compliance whenever a reviewing judge admits the evidence but declares the warrant defective. But this is to be doubted. For one thing, it is highly unlikely that magistrates will be much better than the rest of us at maintaining the legality-admissibility distinction under such circumstances. As the Supreme Court explicated in *Terry v. Ohio*:[39] "A ruling admitting evidence in a criminal trial * * * has the necessary effect of legitimizing the conduct which produced the evidence, while an application of the exclusionary rule withholds the constitutional imprimatur." Moreover, the circumstances assumed by the *Leon* majority—admission of the evidence in conjunction with a declaration that the warrant was improperly issued—are not likely to occur. In response to the dissenters' objection that the *Leon* holding will preclude review of the validity of warrants, the majority asserted there "is no need for courts to adopt the inflexible practice of always deciding whether the officers' conduct manifested objective good faith before turning to the question whether the Fourth Amendment has been violated." But it is unlikely that the merits of the underlying Fourth Amendment issue will often be reached. As the dissenters correctly put it, "it is difficult to believe that busy courts faced with heavy dockets will take the time to render essentially advisory opinions concerning the constitutionality of the magistrate's decision before considering the officer's good faith." And thus the conversion of admissibility into legality of which the Court spoke in *Terry* will become even more certain and pervasive.[40]

The remaining critical point in the majority's rationale for the

---

[39]Terry v. Ohio, 392 U.S. 1, 88 S.Ct. 1868, 20 L.Ed.2d 889 (1968).

[40]On the appellate level, it is not uncommon for the court to go directly to the good faith issue and thus bypass the was-it-legal questions. United States v. Sibley, 448 F.3d 754 (5th Cir. 2006); United States v. Bynum, 293 F.3d 192 (4th Cir.2002); United States v. Cancelmo, 64 F.3d 804 (2d Cir. 1995); People v. Altman, 960 P.2d 1164 (Colo.1998); Polston v. Commonwealth, 255 Va. 500, 498 S.E.2d 924 (1998). Consistent with the cases below, this is sometimes justified on the ground that the probable cause or particularity requirements do *not* "involve 'novel question[s] of law whose resolution is necessary to guide future action by law enforcement offices and magistrates.'" United States v. $92,422.57, 307 F.3d 137 (3d Cir.

2002).

But see United States v. Gray, 669 F.3d 556 (5th Cir.2012) (usual "good-faith-first" approach inappropriate here, as proctoscopy-by-warrant issue should be resolved to guide future action by police and magistrates); United States v. Danhauer, 229 F.3d 1002 (10th Cir.2000) (this a case in which appellate court must look at probable cause issue first, situation identified in *Leon* as when resolution of such issue "necessary to guide future action by law enforcement officers and magistrates"); United States v. Dahlman, 13 F.3d 1391 (10th Cir.1993) ("the preferred sequence is to address the Fourth Amendment issues before turning to the good faith issue unless there is no danger of 'freezing' Fourth Amendment jurisprudence").

Note, 68 N.Y.U.L.Rev. 1305, 1307 (1993), concludes "that the recog-

holding in *Leon* is that generally there is no function of police deterrence to be served when a warrant turns out to be constitutionally defective. The Court rejected the notion that exclusion in such circumstances "deters future inadequate presentations or 'magistrate shopping,'" and asserted that when an officer acting with objective good faith has obtained a warrant there is usually "no police illegality and thus nothing to deter." Here again, however, the majority has examined the exclusionary rule's deterrence function from a somewhat skewed and rather unrealistic perspective. The Court in *Leon* mistakenly assumed that the deterrence function can operate only when the police knew or should have known that their conduct violated the Fourth Amendment. As correctly noted by Justices Brennan and Marshall:

> The flaw in the Court's argument * * * is that its logic captures only one comparatively minor element of the generally acknowledged deterrent purposes of the exclusionary rule. * * * [W]hat the Court overlooks is that the deterrence rationale for the rule is not designed to be, nor should it be thought of as, a form of "punishment" of individual police officers for their failures to obey the restraints imposed by the Fourth Amendment. * * * Instead, the chief deterrent function of the rule is its tendency to promote institutional compliance with Fourth Amendment requirements on the part of law enforcement agencies generally. * * * It is only through such an institution-wide mechanism that information concerning Fourth Amendment standards can be effectively communicated to rank and file officers.

> If the overall educational effect of the exclusionary rule is considered, application of the rule to even those situations in which individual police officers have acted on the basis of a reasonable but mistaken belief that their conduct was authorized can still be expected to have a considerable long-term deterrent effect. If evidence is consistently excluded in these circumstances, police departments will surely be prompted to instruct their officers to devote greater care and attention to providing sufficient information to establish probable cause when applying for a warrant, and to review with some attention the form of the warrant that they have been issued, rather than automatically assuming that whatever document the magistrate has signed will necessarily comport with Fourth Amendment requirements.

The point is simply this: Under the pre-*Leon* version of the exclusionary rule, police had finally come to learn that it was not enough that they had gotten a piece of paper called a warrant. Because that warrant was subject to challenge at the later motion to suppress, it was important to the police that the warrant be properly issued or that the warrant request be turned down at a time when it might be possible to acquire necessary additional information without compromising the investigation. Conse-

---

nition of the good faith exception has not had the effect of freezing fourth amendment law."

quently, there had developed in many localities the very sound practice of going through the warrant-issuing process with the greatest of care, often by having the affidavit reviewed by individuals other than the magistrate. The two cases that were before the Supreme Court were not at all unusual in this respect.[41] In *Leon*, the search warrant application "was reviewed by several Deputy District Attorneys"; in *Sheppard*, the detective-affiant had his affidavit checked over by "the district attorney, the district attorney's first assistant, and a sergeant." But under *Leon* there is no reason to go through such cautious procedures[42] and every reason not to.[43] Why take the risk that some conscientious prosecutor or police supervisor will say the application is insufficient when, if some magistrate can be induced to issue a warrant on the basis of it, the affidavit is thereafter virtually immune from challenge?[44] There is thus no escaping the fact that, as the *Leon* dissenters put it, the "long-run effect" of that case "unquestionably will be to undermine the integrity of the warrant process." Doubtless this is why several state courts have rejected *Leon* as a matter of state law.[45]

---

[41]As one former prosecutor put it: "I have watched the rule deter, routinely, throughout my years as a prosecutor. * * * [P]olice-prosecutors consultation is customary in all our cases when Fourth Amendment concerns arise." Sachs, The Exclusionary Rule: A Prosecutor's Defense, 1 Crim.J. Ethics 28, 30 (1982). See also Comment, 54 U.Chi.L.Rev. 1016, 1026–27 (1987), discussing how the exclusionary rule prompted such consultation in Chicago.

[42]In one sense this is not so, for the fact such procedures were followed is sometimes taken into account in determining that good faith was present. See, e.g., United States v. Merritt, 361 F.3d 1005 (7th Cir.2004) (agent's consultation with assistant U.S. Attorney "supports the finding that his reliance upon the warrant was objectively reasonable"); United States v. Clutchette, 24 F.3d 577 (4th Cir.1994); United States v. Frangenberg, 15 F.3d 100 (8th Cir.1994); Commonwealth v. Litke, 873 S.W.2d 198 (Ky.1994).

[43]Cf. People v. Leftwich, 869 P.2d 1260 (Colo.1994) (officer first took affidavit to prosecutor, who advised officer "that the affidavit presented a close case and that the judge might not sign

it"; court refers to the fact prosecutor and officer thus "doubted whether probable cause existed" in concluding no good faith).

[44]Even those generally favorably disposed toward *Leon* acknowledge that the "real danger of the *Leon* standard is that it might cause police officers to dispense with some of the internal checks that they usually follow to ensure that their warrant applications are well supported." Note, 76 Va.L.Rev. 1213, 1235 (1990).

[45]State v. Marsala, 216 Conn. 150, 579 A.2d 58 (1990) (good faith exception incompatible with state constitution; court relies upon criticisms of *Leon* recited herein); Mason v. State, 534 A.2d 242 (Del.1987) (rejected on statutory grounds); Gary v. State, 262 Ga. 573, 422 S.E.2d 426 (1992) (good faith exception conflicts with "unequivocal language" of state statute); State v. Guzman, 122 Idaho 981, 842 P.2d 660 (1992), reaffirmed in State v. Koivu, __ Idaho __, 272 P.3d 483 (2012) ("the good faith exception * * * is ill-conceived and cannot be reconciled with * * * our state constitution"); State v. Cline, 617 N.W.2d 277 (Iowa 2000) (*Leon* rejected; court disagrees with cost-benefit analysis employed

§ 1.3(e) "Good faith": generally

It is particularly unfortunate that the Court set out on this

therein and rejects its "underlying premise that the exclusionary rule's purpose is to deter police misconduct and that the rule has no laudatory effect on the actors of the judicial and legislative branches," and finds that good faith exception "dilutes the constitutional right to be protected against unreasonable searches and seizures"); State v. Prior, 617 N.W.2d 260 (Iowa 2000) (*Cline*, concerning search pursuant to statute, also applicable to search pursuant to warrant); Commonwealth v. Upton, 394 Mass. 363, 476 N.E.2d 548 (1985) (rejected on statutory grounds); Garza v. State, 632 N.W.2d 633 (Minn.2001) (court refuses to apply *Leon* though it has "no reason to believe police executing the warrant in this case did not act in good faith," in light of court's interpretation of "the requirement in the Minnesota Constitution that persons not be subject to unreasonable searches and seizures to require sufficiently particularized circumstances justifying an unannounced entry"); State v. Canelo, 139 N.H. 376, 653 A.2d 1097 (1995) (good faith exception "is incompatible with and detrimental to our citizens' strong right of privacy inherent" in state constitution); State v. Johnson, 168 N.J. 608, 775 A.2d 1273 (2001) (suppression required notwithstanding police good faith reliance on no-knock authorization in warrant; "to permit a good-faith exception to apply in respect of one element of the warrant * * * but not in respect of other elements would lead ultimately to a patch-work of incongruous case law"); State v. Gutierrez, 116 N.M. 431, 863 P.2d 1052 (1993) (good faith exception incompatible with state constitution, under which the right to be free from unreasonable searches "includes the exclusionary rule"); People v. Bigelow, 66 N.Y.2d 417, 497 N.Y.S.2d 630, 488 N.E.2d 451 (1985) (*Leon* rejected as matter of state constitutional law, as "if the People are permitted to use the seized evidence, the exclusionary rule's purpose is completely frustrated, a premium is placed on the illegal police action and

a positive incentive is provided to others to engage in similar lawless acts in the future"); State v. Carter, 322 N.C. 709, 370 S.E.2d 553 (1988) (though Supreme Court "applied a cost-benefit analysis[,] the basis of our exclusionary rule is not suited to such simplistic resolution of the issue"); Commonwealth v. Edmunds, 526 Pa. 374, 586 A.2d 887 (1991) (*Leon* incompatible with state constitution, under which exclusionary rule "a constitutional mandate" not limited to notion of deterrence); State v. McKnight, 291 S.C. 110, 352 S.E.2d 471 (1987) (rejected on statutory grounds); State v. Oakes, 157 Vt. 171, 598 A.2d 119 (1991) (no "good faith" exception for violation of state constitution; court relies on criticisms of *Leon* stated herein). Cf. State v. Wilson, 618 N.W.2d 513 (S.D.2000) (good faith "cannot be used to create jurisdiction," and thus not relevant where state constitution violation was issuance of search warrant by judge from another circuit).

If the warrant was issued and executed by officials of a state that has rejected *Leon*, but the evidence is offered in *federal* court, the good faith rules can be utilized as a basis for admitting the evidence, as admissibility in federal court is controlled by federal law. United States v. Keele, 589 F.3d 940 (8th Cir.2009); United States v. Clay, 355 F.3d 1281 (11th Cir.2004).

For more on what the states' reaction has been and should be, see Hanson, The Aftermath of Illinois v. Gates and United States v. Leon: A Comprehensive Evaluation of Their Impact Upon the Litigation of Search Warrant Validity, 15 West.St.U.L.Rev. 393 (1988); Uchida, Bynum, Rogan & Murasky, Acting in Good Faith: The Effects of United States v. Leon on the Police and Courts, 30 Ariz.L.Rev. 467 (1988); Comments, 4 Adelphia L.J. 69 (1986); 71 Marq.L.Rev. 166 (1987); 1987 Wis.L.Rev. 377; Notes, 83 U.Det. Mercy L.Rev. 441 (2006); 1987 U.Ill.L. Rev. 311.

course unnecessarily by permitting the government to dictate the issues to be decided. Although, as the *Leon* majority acknowledged, "it undoubtedly is within our power to consider the question whether probable cause existed" under the Court's new *Gates* probable cause test, the Court opted to take on the good faith issue because the probable cause question "has not been briefed or argued." (It is interesting to compare this approach with that taken in *Gates* a year earlier; there it was the issue of probable cause rather than that of good faith which was briefed and argued, but the Court unhesitantly directed new briefs and arguments on the later point.) Especially since the district court and court of appeals in *Leon* did not have the benefit of the *Gates* decision, the most logical course of action for the Court would have been that advocated by Justice Stevens: remand to the court of appeals for reconsideration in light of *Gates*. As for the *Sheppard* case, it appears that there as well decision on a good faith basis was unnecessary. Given the considerable preexisting authority to the effect that a defective or erroneous description in a warrant is cured by a proper description in an affidavit incorporated by reference and attached to the warrant,[46] surely (as Justice Stevens elaborated in his dissent) it would have been possible for the Court to decide that the lack of a specific reference or a staple should not be determinative where, as here, the executing officer was the affiant and acted on the basis of his words in the affidavit rather than the improper words printed on the warrant.[47]

It is disturbing, to say the least, that the Court would adopt a good faith rule for with-warrant situations in two cases where, in all likelihood, there was no Fourth Amendment violation in the first place. "The Court," as Justice Stevens lamented in his dissent, "seems determined to decide these cases on the broadest possible grounds," as has been equally true in several other recent Fourth Amendment decisions.[48] This is unfortunate for several reasons. For one thing, it is simply contrary to long-recognized

---

[Section 1.3(e)]

[46]See § 4.5(a).

[47]But later Justice Stevens, writing for a 5-4 majority of the Court, felt differently about another such situation. In Groh v. Ramirez, 540 U.S. 551, 124 S.Ct. 1284, 157 L.Ed.2d 1068 (2004), discussed in § 1.3(f), the affiant, who was also the executing officer, correctly stated the items to be seized in the search warrant application and the supporting affidavit, but in the search warrant itself mistakenly entered in the space for that specification a description of the place to be searched. That error was not noticed by the magistrate who issued the warrant, and was not noticed by the affiant/executing officer until after the warrant was executed, and he instructed his search team on the basis of the items listed in the application and affidavit. Noting that "in this case the warrant did not incorporate other documents by reference, nor did either the affidavit or the application * * * accompany the warrant," the Court concluded this was not a valid with-warrant search.

[48]See LaFave, Fourth Amendment Vagaries (Of Improbable Cause, Imperceptible Plain View, Notorious Privacy, and Balancing Askew), 74 J.Crim.L. & C. 1171, 1222–23 (1983).

sound appellate practice. As Justice Stevens correctly put it, "such determination is utterly at odds with the Court's traditional practice as well as any principled notion of judicial restraint." Secondly, taking on the good faith issue in such circumstances distorts both the extent of the "problem" being addressed and the potential adverse consequences of the "solution" adopted. As noted earlier, by totally ignoring the likelihood that in *Leon* and many similar cases the warrant would now be upheld by reliance upon *Gates*, the Court created the erroneous impression that suppression of evidence obtained pursuant to a warrant is a contemporary problem of serious proportions. Had the Court instead remanded, then, as Justices Brennan and Marshall aptly noted, it is likely the lower court "would find no violation of the Fourth Amendment, thereby demonstrating that the supposed need for the good faith exception in this context is more apparent than real." Also, adoption and application of this new good faith exception in cases like *Leon* and *Sheppard* creates a false sense that the exception produces sensible results in cases that otherwise would have been resolved in the defendants' favor by application of strict, unbending and unrealistic Fourth Amendment doctrine. That is, a good faith exception is bound to look palatable when applied to make evidence admissible in circumstances where that evidence was not acquired in violation of the Fourth Amendment in the first place!

Still another consequence of the Court's action in adopting an exception to the exclusionary rule in two cases where apparently there was no constitutional violation to start with is that these cases do not clearly reflect the degree of difficulty that might be encountered in ascertaining the applicability of the exception when the Fourth Amendment was not complied with. Thus, it is necessary now to examine more closely the exact dimensions of the exception created by *Leon* and *Sheppard,* particularly with a view of determining—to the extent possible—whether these cases confront trial and appellate courts with new problems no less difficult than those issues that can be circumvented by reliance upon the good faith exception.

In the pre-*Leon* good faith debate, one common objection to any good faith exception was that it would impose an intolerable burden upon suppression judges because they would have to "probe the subjective knowledge"[49] of the officer who made the challenged arrest or search in each and every case in which the exception was relied upon. It would also, so the argument goes, intrude into the suppression process a factual issue on which evidence would be "difficult to come by apart from the officer's self-

---

[49]United States v. Peltier, 422   374 (1975) (Brennan, J., dissenting).
U.S. 531, 95 S.Ct. 2313, 45 L.Ed.2d

serving and generally uncontradicted testimony."[50] Cognizant of
such criticism, the *Leon* majority attempted to solve that particular problem by formulating this new exception to the exclusionary rule in terms not dependent upon the subjective state of
mind of the police involved in the particular case. The Court
stated that "the officer's reliance on the magistrate's probable-
cause determination and on the technical sufficiency of the warrant he issues must be objectively reasonable," and went on to
discuss this point in terms making it quite clear that what the
Court has adopted is a *purely* objective test rather than one having both objective and subjective components. Citing to *Harlow v.
Fitzgerald,*[51] where the same result was reached as to the qualified immunity of public officials in suits seeking damages for alleged deprivations of constitutional rights, the Court declared
that "our good-faith inquiry is confined to the objectively
ascertainable question whether a reasonably well-trained officer
would have known that the search was illegal despite the
magistrate's authorization."[52]

In solving this particular problem in this particular way, the
Leon Court placed this new exclusionary rule exception on an
even shakier foundation. The Court's rationale, as previously
noted, was that a police officer cannot be deterred when he neither knew nor should have known that he was acting illegally,
but now we learn that if the searching officer in the individual
case *actually knew* in advance that his intended search was illegal this is no bar to admitting the evidence so long as "a reasonably well-trained officer" would not have had such knowledge.
Thus, even under the Court's own narrow view of the deterrence
function, *Leon* sometimes permits the admission of evidence
notwithstanding the existence of circumstances in which suppression for purposes of deterrence would be an especially compelling course of action. In other words, what the Court calls a
"good-faith exception" really is not that at all, for it extends to
certain situations in which there was no good faith whatsoever.

It is also well to note in this connection that exactly what falls
into the "subjective component" the *Leon* majority declares may
not be inquired into, and what falls into the "objectively ascertainable question" as to which inquiry is appropriate, is not entirely
clear. As just noted, there is no escaping the fact that *Leon*, by
foreclosing inquiry directly into the officer's state of mind, creates
the possibility of nonsuppression notwithstanding even a deliberate constitutional violation. But, to what extent can there be in-

---

[50]Kaplan, The Limits of the
Exclusionary Rule, 26 Stan.L.Rev.
1027, 1045 (1974).

[51]Harlow v. Fitzgerald, 457 U.S.
800, 102 S.Ct. 2727, 73 L.Ed.2d 396
(1982).

[52]United States v. George, 971
F.2d 1113 (4th Cir.1992) (lower court's
"inquiry into the subjective motivations of the officers was irrelevant to
the applicability of *Leon*").

quiry into this officer's experience, especially that which may have conveyed to him the fact that his intended course of action would be illegal, on the notion that the objective inquiry really is into what a reasonable officer who had this particular officer's experiences would conclude? To take a variation on the situation put above, what if a police officer takes his affidavit to a prosecutor for his judgment and is unequivocally advised by the prosecutor that it is insufficient to show probable cause, but the officer then takes the same affidavit to a magistrate who (mistakenly, it turns out) issues a warrant on it. Is the officer's detour to the prosecutor's office to be ignored on the theory that it bears only upon the subjective state of mind of this officer, or is it to be taken into account because the issue is what "a reasonably well-trained officer" would have concluded in light of that experience? Apparently it is the latter, for the *Leon* majority expressly states that in making the determination of when an officer's reliance upon the warrant is "objectively reasonable," "all of the circumstances—including whether the warrant application had previously been rejected by a different magistrate—may be considered."

But, if that may be considered, then why not any other relevant experience by the particular officer? If it is relevant that this particular officer knew that the same affidavit had been found wanting by another magistrate or by a prosecutor, then why is it not just as relevant that this particular officer knew of its deficiency in some other way, such as by his experience in another case involving essentially the same affidavit or by his reading of police training literature on the subject? Certainly vigorous defense counsel can be expected to undertake inquiry into these various experiences, thus requiring courts to grapple with the question of just what the boundaries of legitimate inquiry are. By eschewing inquiry into subjective beliefs, the Court in *Leon* seems only to have foreclosed direct questioning of the officer about what *his* state of mind was. Inquiry less direct, revealing experiences by that officer doubtless producing the improper type of subjective belief, will at least sometimes be allowed as bearing upon the "objectively ascertainable question" *Leon* says must be resolved. Consequently, there is good reason to doubt the *Leon* majority's claim that the exception it has created is "not be difficult to apply in practice" and does not require "a substantial expenditure of judicial time."

Indeed, it would seem at first blush that the issue to be resolved under *Leon* is rather difficult, even apart from the evidentiary problems just alluded to. The basic question is what kind of error regarding the law of search and seizure would be made by a reasonable officer who had been reasonably trained in that law. As some noted before *Leon* was decided, it is extremely "hard to determine what constitutes a reasonable mistake of law,"[53] requiring as it does "objective extrapolations of existing law" and inquiry into "the inferences from existing law" that the police "should have drawn."[54] (It is no answer to say that the Supreme Court has relied upon reasonable good faith considerations in *Michigan v. DeFillippo*[55] and *United States v. Peltier*,[56] dealing, respectively, with the subsequently invalidated statute and the subsequently overruled precedent. Those cases involve "authoritative pronouncements which establish a reasonable basis for"[57] the mistake of law, but no equivalent benchmark exists for assaying other allegations of good faith.) But in order to gain further insight into just how difficult this determination is under *Leon*, it is necessary now to examine the holding in that case much more closely and to determine just what kinds of police errors are and are not included within it.

§ 1.3(f) Scope of *Leon* exception in warrant cases[58]

It is important to understand that *Leon* does *not* hold that the exclusionary rule is totally inapplicable whenever the search or seizure objected to was in some sense incident to a previously issued warrant. The *Leon* rule has to do with a presumptively invalid[59] warrant,[60] such as one issued on less than probable cause (assumed to be so in *Leon*) or one issued with an insufficient

---

[53]Kaplan, 26 Stan.L.Rev. 1027, 1044 (1974).

[54]United States v. Peltier, 422 U.S. 531, 95 S.Ct. 2313, 45 L.Ed.2d 374 (1975) (Brennan, J. dissenting).

[55]Michigan v. DeFillippo, 443 U.S. 31, 99 S.Ct. 2627, 61 L.Ed.2d 343 (1979).

[56]United States v. Peltier, 422 U.S. 531, 95 S.Ct. 2313, 45 L.Ed.2d 374 (1975).

But, the *Peltier* nonretroactivity rule has given way to that of full retroactivity prior to the point of conviction finality, United States v. Johnson, 457 U.S. 537, 102 S.Ct. 2579, 73 L.Ed.2d 202 (1982), so that "good faith" analysis now becomes important in the overruled precedent cases. See § 1.3(h).

[57]Ball, Good Faith and the Fourth Amendment: The "Reasonable" Exception to the Exclusionary Rule, 69 J.Crim.L. & C. 635, 653 (1978).

[Section 1.3(f)]

[58]For other analyses of problems arising from applying the *Leon* exceptions, see Notes, 89 Mich.L.Rev. 625

(1990) (concluding at 627 that *Leon* is often misapplied by lower courts and that "much of the responsibility for the mistakes must rest with the mislabeled and complex exception crafted in *Leon*"); 28 Wm. & Mary L.Rev. 743 (1987).

[59]United States v. Schroeder, 129 F.3d 439 (8th Cir.1997) (where search warrant, "fairly construed, does not authorize search of Mr. Schroeder's residence," police mistake in searching that place does not fall within the good faith exception, for "a good faith exception to the exclusionary rule exists if the reliance by the officer on an *invalid* search warrant is objectively reasonable," but "the warrant in this case was not invalid").

[60]It is unclear whether the rule extends to a warrant "that was essentially void *ab initio*" because of "the issuing court's lack of jurisdiction to authorize the search in the first instance." United States v. Baker, 894 F.2d 1144 (10th Cir.1990) (acknowledging but not resolving the issue, as in other cases cited therein).

Courts have applied *Leon* to arrest warrants as well as search war-

particularity in description (assumed to be so in *Sheppard*).[61] Fourth Amendment violations relating to *execution* of the warrant are unaffected by *Leon*,[62] as is indicated by the majority's

---

rants. See United States v. Teitloff, 55 F.3d 391 (8th Cir.1995); United States v. Gobey, 12 F.3d 964 (10th Cir.1993); United States v. Fama, 758 F.2d 834 (2d Cir.1985); State v. Hyde, 186 Ariz. 252, 921 P.2d 655 (1996); Abbott v. State, 307 Ark. 278, 819 S.W.2d 694 (1991); People v. Blehm, 983 P.2d 779 (Colo.1999). But, in the arrest warrant context, *Leon* does not apply in the case of a mistaken arrest of a person other than the individual named in the warrant. Eaddy v. State, 63 So.3d 1209 (Miss.2011).

Courts have also utilized the *Leon* doctrine as to defects in warrants under state law. See, e.g., Garner v. State, 307 Ark. 353, 820 S.W.2d 446 (1991) (noncompliance with criminal rules provision on nighttime search warrants); State v. Johnson, 814 So.2d 390 (Fla.2002) (good faith effort to comply with statutory notice requirement regarding subpoena of medical records); State v. Brown, 708 S.W.2d 140 (Mo.1986) (clerk's failure to retain application and supporting affidavits); State v. Welch, 316 N.C. 578, 342 S.E.2d 789 (1986) (use of nontestimonial identification order after arrest, not contemplated by statute); Roth v. State, 735 N.W.2d 882 (N.D.2007) (noncompliance with criminal rule on nighttime search warrants).

There is also authority that the *Leon* good faith exception applies to an eavesdropping search warrant improperly issued under Title III. United States v. Moore, 41 F.3d 370 (8th Cir. 1994); United States v. Malekzadeh, 855 F.2d 1492 (11th Cir.1988). Contra: United States v. Rice, 478 F.3d 704 (6th Cir.2007) (as "under Title III, Congress has already balanced the social costs and benefits and has provided that suppression is the sole remedy for violations of the statute").

Leon has also been applied to a judicial order not constituting a warrant. United States v. Koch, 625 F.3d 470 (8th Cir.2010) (where computer and flash drive lawfully seized pursu-

ant to valid search warrant, but months later officer-custodian, on advise of county attorney, applied to state court judge for disposal of property order, and after such order issued officer was "in the process of following the court's directions about disposal of the property seized" in checking contents of flash drive, revealing child porn, *Leon* applies); State v. Sittingdown, 240 P.3d 714 (Okla.Crim.App. 2010) (*Leon* also "applies to a civil writ or order"). Compare State v. Hayes, 809 N.W.2d 309 (N.D.2012) (*Leon* not applicable to a "bond order" conditioned on defendant's consent to search of person, vehicle and residence at any time, as the "imposition of a warrantless search provision in a bond order is too remote a circumstance to be compared to a probable cause determination resulting in a search warrant").

[61]But, *Leon* also applies to other warrant defects. See, e.g., United States v. Gray, 669 F.3d 556 (5th Cir.2012) (search warrant for "medical procedure search of a specific area of the body" not sufficiently limited as to procedures permitted).

[62]United States v. Angelos, 433 F.3d 738 (10th Cir.2006) (where police failed to comply with search warrant's limitation as to specific part of premises to be searched, "it is apparent that the problem lies in the execution," and thus *Leon* not applicable); United States v. Hitchcock, 286 F.3d 1064 (9th Cir.2002) ("good faith exception has no application here, where there is no dispute about the search warrant's validity but only about whether the agents executed the warrant before it was effective"); United States v. Gantt, 194 F.3d 987 (9th Cir.1999) (*Leon* not applicable regarding failure to give defendant, present at search, a copy of the warrant, as "the good faith exception is not relevant where the violation lies in the *execution* of the warrant, not the validity of the warrant"); Garrison v. State, 303 Md. 385, 494 A.2d 193 (1985) (*Leon* of no help

caution that its discussion "assumes, of course, that the officers properly executed the warrant and searched only those places for those objects that it was reasonable to believe were covered by the warrant." This means that *Leon* cannot be invoked in the prosecution's favor on such issues as whether the warrant was executed[63] (or, perhaps, obtained[64]) in a timely fashion, whether entry without prior notice of authority and purpose to execute the warrant was permissible[65] (when not authorized by the warrant itself[66]), whether certain persons were properly detained or searched incident to execution of the warrant,[67] whether the scope

---

to the prosecution where police searched apartment other than the one named in the warrant, which "precisely and unambiguously described the premises to be searched").

But see Ex parte Morgan, 641 So.2d 840 (Ala.1994) (officer's reliance on out-of-state arrest warrants covered by *Leon*; dissent correctly points out *Leon* concerned with improper issuance of warrant, not, as here, improper execution).

[63]See § 4.7(a).

[64]In United States v. Burgard, 675 F.3d 1029 (7th Cir.2012), after holding the 6-day delay in obtaining a search warrant to search defendant's cell phone following its warrantless seizure was not unreasonable, the court then turned to the district court's alternative holding that, even if the delay in obtaining the warrant was unreasonable, the *Leon* good-faith exception would apply. The court asserted that "removing this sort of police misconduct from the ambit of the exclusionary rule would have significant implications," and that "it would eliminate the rule's deterrent effect on unreasonably long seizures." However, the court then appeared to backtrack a bit, stating it would not "rule out" a *Leon* argument if "the unreasonableness of a delay is a very close call."

[65]See § 4.8.

[66]United States v. Singleton, 441 F.3d 290 (4th Cir.2006) (collecting federal cases in accord, and concluding *Leon* applicable to no-knock search warrant provision notwithstanding fact police obligated to assess the exigent circumstances at time they execute the warrant, as "particularly

with preexisting exigencies (like a violent criminal history) that are unlikely to change between the issuance of a warrant and its execution, no purpose is served by requiring officers to wait until just before a search to determine whether such exigencies support a no-knock entry"); United States v. Nielson, 415 F.3d 1195 (10th Cir.2005) (*Leon* applicable to no-knock warrant, but no good faith here, as warrant showed only presence of firearm, not "potential for violence"); United States v. Tavares, 223 F.3d 911 (8th Cir.2000) (*Leon* applicable, but no good faith reliance on no-knock authority granted contrary to "the no-blanket-exception rule" adopted in Richards v. Wisconsin, 520 U.S. 385, 117 S.Ct. 1416, 137 L.Ed.2d 615 (1997)); United States v. Tisdale, 195 F.3d 70 (2d Cir.1999) (*Leon* applicable, as "regardless of the existence of exigent circumstances, the officers were entitled to rely on the no-knock provision of the warrant in good faith"). See also Annot., 2 A.L.R.6th 169 (2005).

In Davis v. State, 383 Md. 394, 859 A.2d 1112 (2004), collecting other cases in accord, the instant case was distinguished because, while the police relied on the no-knock authorization in the search warrant, "such warrants are not authorized under Maryland law."

[67]See § 4.9. Illustrative is Parks v. Commonwealth, 192 S.W.3d 318 (Ky.2006) (since warrant for premises and owner/occupants authorizes seizure and search of latter only when they at the described premises, seizure of them 5 miles away means only that a valid warrant "was improperly executed," so "good faith" exception not

and intensity and duration of the warrant execution were excessive,[68] and whether certain items not named in the warrant were properly seized.[69]

Moreover, because *Leon* rests upon the notion that the exclusionary rule is not implicated where there is no police misconduct to deter, that case does "not allow law enforcement authorities to rely on an error of their own making,"[70] as when they are at fault in failing to update their own records to show that a validly-issued warrant is no longer in effect.[71] Nor can good faith be conferred upon those officers executing a search warrant by erroneous instructions from a supervisory officer as to what the warrant permits—unless, of course, the latter officer's conclusions also meet the good faith test of *Leon*.[72]

The Court in *Leon* also emphasized it was not suggesting "that exclusion is always inappropriate in cases where an officer has obtained a warrant and abided by its terms," and then declared that exclusion is still called for whenever the officer lacks "reasonable grounds for believing that the warrant was properly

---

applicable).

[68]See § 4.10. But see Landers v. State, 250 Ga. 808, 301 S.E.2d 633 (1983), note 96 infra, where the dissent reasoned that the good faith exception applies to errors in execution attributable to advice given by the magistrate who issued the warrant.

Compare United States v. Potts, 586 F.3d 823 (10th Cir.2009) (while "*Leon* does not apply if the execution of the warrant was improper," even assuming "the warrant failed to satisfy the particularity requirement" there no execution defect, as officers read the warrant "as restricting the search to materials connected to child pornography").

[69]See § 4.11. Illustrative is United States v. Strand, 761 F.2d 449 (8th Cir.1985) (where search warrant for "stolen mail" itself valid, officer's assumption this permitted seizure of certain unpackaged items does not fall within *Leon*).

[70]Commonwealth v. Hecox, 35 Mass.App.Ct. 277, 619 N.E.2d 339 (1993).

That notion was carried to an extreme in Groh v. Ramirez, 540 U.S. 551, 124 S.Ct. 1284, 157 L.Ed.2d 1068 (2004), discussed in § 1.3(f). The affiant, who was also the executing officer, correctly stated the items to be seized in the search warrant application and the supporting affidavit, but in the search warrant itself mistakenly entered in the space for that specification a description of the place to be searched. That error was not noticed by the magistrate who issued the warrant, and was not noticed by the affiant/executing officer until after the warrant was executed, and he instructed his search team on the basis of the items listed in the application and affidavit. While one might think that the clerical error was itself an innocent mistake and that the affiant was justified in assuming the judge had authorized the authority sought in the application, the Court, 5-4, concluded that "because [the affiant] himself prepared the invalid warrant, he may not argue that he reasonably relied on the Magistrate's assurance that the warrant contained an adequate description of the things to be seized and was therefore valid."

[71]Commonwealth v. Hecox, 35 Mass.App.Ct. 277, 619 N.E.2d 339 (1993) (defendant, upon hearing arrest warrant issued, appeared in court of his own accord, but police records not updated and thus defendant arrested on that warrant 5 days later).

[72]United States v. Watkins, 179 F.3d 489 (6th Cir.1999) (such good faith present here).

issued."[73] This encompasses at least[74] four situations. First of all, the Court expressly left untouched the doctrine of *Franks v. Delaware*.[75] It is still true, therefore, that a warrant issued upon a facially sufficient affidavit is invalid if based upon knowingly or recklessly made falsehoods[76] in the officer's affidavit. Standing alone, that constitutes a rather small qualification to *Leon*, for defendants have rarely been successful in overcoming the problems of proof attending a *Franks* attack upon a warrant.[77]

---

[73]*Leon* has been interpreted as placing the burden of proof on the government. "Once the defendants convinced the district court that probable cause was lacking, the government was required to prove that the evidence seized during the search was nevertheless admissible because of the officers' objectively reasonable reliance on the warrant. The issue may be of little significance, however, because the determination of good faith will ordinarily depend on an examination of the affidavit by the reviewing court." United States v. Gant, 759 F.2d 484 (5th Cir.1985).

See also State v. Mendoza, 748 P.2d 181 (Utah 1987) (state statute placing burden of proof on defendant to prove absence of good faith unconstitutional; "Because *Leon* is an exception to the application of the exclusionary rule, the State must prove the necessary elements of the 'good faith' exception").

[74]Goldstein, The Search Warrant, the Magistrate, and Judicial Review, 62 N.Y.U.L.Rev. 1173, 1204–05 (1987), says the "question remains whether exclusion can be used as a remedy in contexts other than those covered by four illustrative categories, particularly where it is the magistrate who has erred." He says the answer is yes, and explains that the Supreme Court in *Leon* referred to generalizations about how magistrates usually act and said at one point that evidence obtained pursuant to a warrant should be suppressed "only on a case-by-case basis and only in those unusual cases in which exclusion will further the purposes of the exclusionary rule. * * *

"This reference to a 'case-by-case' approach, taken together with

the other passages quoted, supports the conclusion that the Court meant to fashion a sliding scale of remedies to be applied in accordance with the nature of the violation of the right. The court also appears to have decided that though it could take judicial notice that exclusion is now necessary to deter certain violations, other situations may emerge 'case-by-case' that will also require the use of the exclusionary rule to effectuate fourth amendment rights."

[75]Franks v. Delaware, 438 U.S. 154, 98 S.Ct. 2674, 57 L.Ed.2d 667 (1978).

This reference to *Franks* in *Leon* does *not* mean that whenever a defendant invokes *Franks* because "the *affidavit* is allegedly defective due to error on the part of the *police*," there is then applicable the broader notions of good faith *Leon* "applies when the *search warrant* is allegedly defective due to an error on the part of the *magistrate*." State v. Rufus, 338 Ark. 305, 993 S.W.2d 490 (1999).

[76]Compare Sims v. State, 333 Ark. 405, 969 S.W.2d 657 (1998) (*Leon* applicable in what was actually an anticipatory warrant situation, though affidavit falsely asserted package had already been delivered to place to be searched, as "judge was not misled" because he "saw the package on his desk when he was reviewing the paperwork," and officers "knew the judge was aware that the package containing the contraband would be delivered and that the warrant would not be executed until delivery was accepted").

[77]See § 4.4(d).

But see State v. Horton, 820 So.2d 556 (La.2002) (good faith claims rejected because "the affiant knowingly made several misrepresentations

LEON "GOOD FAITH" EXCEPTION

But one court has gone beyond the usual *Franks* situation to hold that if the officer lied to the magistrate in other respects, i.e., regarding his true purpose in obtaining the warrant, then such misconduct likewise bars that officer from relying upon the good faith doctrine.[78]

The second specific situation mentioned by the Court as one in which reliance upon the warrant would not be "objectively reasonable" is "where the issuing magistrate wholly abandoned his judicial role." But that language must be read in context, particularly in relation to the Court's immediately following observation that "in such circumstances, no reasonably well-trained officer should rely on the warrant." Thus, the mere fact that the person who issued the warrant did not as a general matter or in the circumstances of the particular case qualify as a neutral and detached magistrate[79] is not itself determinative. Apparently on the assumption that such consequences follow from the conclusion deterrence of magistrates is unnecessary, the majority in *Leon* seems to have concluded that a warrant may not be invalidated merely because it was issued by a person not constitutionally authorized to do so,[80] by a person who knew he was disqualified either generally or in the particular case, or

---

to the issuing magistrate"); State v. Johnson, 256 Neb. 133, 589 N.W.2d 108 (1999) (good faith claim rejected because of misleading affidavit that omitted critical facts that defendant found with only a user's amount of drugs and thus not shown to be a seller), "implicitly overruled," State v. Davidson, 260 Neb. 417, 618 N.W.2d 418 (2000), by State v. Edmonson, 257 Neb. 468, 598 N.W.2d 450 (1999).

[78]United States v. Pope, 452 F.3d 338 (5th Cir.2006) (when officer obtained search warrant seeking evidence of prescription-drug operation later held based on stale information, good faith rule not applicable, given that officer "obtained the warrant by way of (1) a deliberate falsehood, i.e., the statement that the purpose of the search was to uncover evidence of a prescription-drug operation, and (2) a deliberate omission of material fact, i.e., that the actual purpose of the search was to uncover evidence of a meth lab").

[79]See § 4.2.

[80]United States v. Malveaux, 350 F.3d 555 (6th Cir.2003) (even if defendant correct in claim that commissioner appointed by county legislative

body does not so qualify, *Leon* applies because officers "acting in good faith" in relying upon commissioner's "apparent authority").

But see United States v. Lucas, 451 F.3d 492 (8th Cir.2006), vacated on other grounds, 499 F.3d 769 (8th Cir.2007) (rejecting good faith claim because arrest warrant issued by state director of correctional services, "a member of the executive branch" who "is not sufficiently neutral and detached to serve as a magistrate"); United States v. Parker, 373 F.3d 770 (6th Cir.2004) (following *Scott* and distinguishing *Malveaux* because it "did not address *Leon's* application when a judicial officer lacking neutrality or detachment issues a warrant," the case here where trial commissioner deemed not to be neutral and detached from activities of law enforcement, while in *Malveaux* commissioner's appointment deemed inconsistent with other state law provisions); United States v. Scott, 260 F.3d 512 (6th Cir.2001) ("Despite the dearth of case law, we are confident that *Leon* did not contemplate a situation where a warrant is issued by a person lacking the requisite legal authority. *Leon* presupposes that the warrant was is-

even by a person who recklessly or intentionally issued a warrant on insufficient evidence.[81] *Leon* recognizes only deterrence of the police, and that kind of deterrence only where the police acted unreasonably, and this means that the circumstances showing the magistrate has "wholly abandoned his judicial role" must have been known by (or, at least reasonably knowable by) the police.[82]

Assuming that hurdle can be overcome, there remains the question of exactly what circumstances indicate such abandonment of the judicial role. In discussing that situation, the Court in *Leon* makes specific mention of *Lo-Ji Sales, Inc. v. New York.*[83] That was a case in which a magistrate viewed two films purchased at an adult bookstore, concluded they were obscene and issued a warrant to search the store for other copies of those films, and

---

sued by a magistrate or judge clothed in the proper legal authority"); State v. Nunez, 634 A.2d 1167 (R.I.1993) (search warrant issued by retired judge invalid under state law; "even were this court to adopt *Leon*'s good-faith-exception rule, that rule would be inapplicable in this case because, without being signed by a magistrate with either *de jure* or *de facto* authority, the search warrant is void *ab initio*").

[81]But see State v. Hess, 327 Wis.2d 524, 785 N.W.2d 568 (2010), discussed in note 133 infra.

[82]Compare United States v. Rodriguez-Suazo, 346 F.3d 637 (6th Cir.2003) ("exclusion should be ordered only if the police officer knew or should 'be charged with knowledge * * *' * * * that the magistrate abandoned his or her neutral and detached function"); United States v. Czuprynski, 46 F.3d 560 (6th Cir.1995) (even if magistrate biased because of dispute with defendant 13 years earlier, *Leon* still applicable because officer seeking warrant "had no knowledge of any personal feud"); United States v. Breckenridge, 782 F.2d 1317 (5th Cir.1986) (even assuming that judge who issued warrant never read affidavit, it appeared to officer who obtained warrant that magistrate read it; "the purposes of the exclusionary rule, as enunciated in *Leon,* would not be served by suppression by the fruits of the search" in such circumstances); State v. Hyde, 186 Ariz. 252, 921 P.2d 655 (1996) (even if "the magistrate's malfeasance,

misfeasance, or nonfeasance was so egregious as to constitute total disregard for her responsibilities," under *Leon* "a court should suppress evidence only upon a showing that the police knew or should have known that its actions were unconstitutional," and no such showing here); with Stewart v. State, 289 Ark. 272, 711 S.W.2d 787 (1986) (officer aware arrest warrant was presigned by judge and issued by clerk, and thus knew "issuing magistrate wholly abandoned his judicial role"; court opines result otherwise had "the officers known nothing about the warrant when they received it")

But see Ex parte Turner, 792 So.2d 1141 (Ala.2000) (*Leon* good faith exception would not be applied notwithstanding reasonable reliance by police on anticipatory search warrant issued by magistrate, given that issuance of such a warrant was totally "without the authority of a constitutional statute or court rule"); State v. Probst, 247 Kan. 196, 795 P.2d 393 (1990) (suppression judge, who was judge who issued the warrant, admitted that he "wholly abandoned his judicial role" by confusing the information in a single affidavit as it applied to three separate search warrant requests; court says this makes *Leon* inapplicable; no mention of whether or why affiant should have know of this failure).

[83]Lo-Ji Sales, Inc. v. New York, 442 U.S. 319, 99 S.Ct. 2319, 60 L.Ed.2d 920 (1979).

then issued a second warrant for other unspecified items said to have been determined by the magistrate to be illegal, after which the magistrate accompanied the police on the raid of the bookstore and there made item-by-item determinations of what else could be seized. In response to the state's contention that this on-the-scene judicial determination sufficed, the Supreme Court responded this was not so because when the magistrate "allowed himself to become a member, if not the leader of the search party which was essentially a police operation," there had occurred "an erosion of whatever neutral and detached posture existed at the outset." Though it is far from clear exactly what (other than this unusual situation[84]) falls within the police-perceived-abandoned-judicial-role qualification in *Leon*,[85] certainly the most likely possibility is that mentioned by the Court earlier in the *Leon* opinion: where the magistrate serves "merely as a rubber stamp for the police."[86] That being so, it would appear that *Leon* permits (indeed, encourages) examination at the suppression hearing of the officer who obtained the warrant for the purpose of determining whether, to his knowledge, the magistrate signed the warrant without reviewing the affidavit. And, unless such conduct is deemed to constitute abandonment of the judicial role only partially rather than "wholly," it may also be

[84]As noted in United States v. Martin, 297 F.3d 1308 (11th Cir.2002), citing cases in support, "the conduct observed in *Lo-Ji Sales, Inc.* is just one of the ways in which a magistrate judge can fail to act in a neutral and detached manner during the warrant process."

[85]United States v. Hessman, 369 F.3d 1016 (8th Cir.2004) (*Leon* applies because "error in this case," failure to swear affiant-officer, "belonged to the issuing magistrate"); United States v. Moore, 968 F.2d 216 (2d Cir.1992) (judge's "failure to require an oath or affirmation was also an oversight that did not preclude application of the good faith exception"); United States v. Richardson, 943 F.2d 547 (5th Cir.1991) (not "inadvertent" failure to administer oath, as it was "not a departure from his neutral and detached role"); State v. Hyde, 186 Ariz. 252, 921 P.2d 655 (1996) (the "issue with regard to the kind of abandonment mentioned in the fourth *Leon* category is not, as defendant suggests, whether the magistrate's malfeasance, misfeasance, or nonfeasance was so egregious as to constitute total disregard for her responsibilities," for "a magistrate does not 'wholly abandon' his or her judicial role unless there is evidence of systemic or patent partiality"); State v. Davidson, 260 Neb. 417, 618 N.W.2d 418 (2000) (judge's failure to specify in arrest warrant a "personal knowledge" basis for issuance without affidavit from someone else does not constitute abandonment of judicial role).

Compare State v. Tye, 248 Wis.2d 530, 636 N.W.2d 473 (2001) ("The exclusionary rule applies when no oath or affirmation supports a search warrant"; court quotes White's concurrence in *Gates* re application of exclusionary rule when "it is plainly evident that a magistrate or judge had no business issuing a warrant").

[86]United States v. Decker, 956 F.2d 773 (8th Cir.1992) (*Leon* not applicable because "judge failed to act in a detached and neutral manner," as indicated by "warrant's glaring omission of the items to be seized," judge's failure to strike "unlawfully stolen" from a warrant for drugs, and judge's admission "he issued 'the search warrant on the strength of what the officer told me,' as opposed to relying on the written warrant and affidavit").

proper for this officer to be examined for the purpose of determining whether in this case, to his knowledge, the magistrate gave the affidavit such a quick scan that meaningful judicial review of the allegations therein simply could not have occurred.[87] But a "rubber stamp" showing apparently cannot be made out merely on the basis of the substantial inadequacy of the probable cause showing in the affidavit.[88]

Before leaving these first two situations, it is necessary to consider yet another kind of case which, though not precisely like either of them, bears some relationship to both of these exceptions to *Leon*. Assume a case in which a police officer presents to

---

[87]Goldstein, The Search Warrant, the Magistrate, and Judicial Review, 62 N.Y.U.L.Rev. 1173, 1207, 1209–10 (1987), argues that *Leon* should be interpreted to require resort to "a process-oriented standard" whereby if the reviewing judge finds "that the warrant hearing was too summary because the magistrate did not go behind the allegations contained in the police affidavit, either for lack of time or for lack of inclination," then the reviewing "judge should look into the issue of probable cause himself, and scrutinize more closely than usual the question whether reliance on the warrant was in good faith. On the other hand, he may find that the magistrate's hearing was not summary, that the magistrate probed the assertions in the affidavit, asked for additional evidence, and called witnesses when necessary. In that case, the magistrate's decision to issue a warrant deserves reliance from the police and deference from the court. The judge would then play an appellate role, reviewing the record before the magistrate simply to assure that the warrant decision meets the standards laid down in *Leon*."

But see United States v. Martin, 297 F.3d 1308 (11th Cir.2002) (despite judge's testimony that was "troubling" because it suggested the judge "relied upon his past experience with [the affiant] Zimbrick rather than the legal validity of the warrant," court declines to find that judge did "wholly abandon his judicial role," as it appears the judge "at least read the affidavit (or heard what it contained from Zimbrick) before signing it"); United States v. Chambers, 987 F.2d 1331 (8th Cir.1993) (defendant's argument "issuing judge was no more than a 'rubber stamp' for the police" rejected, as he "studied the affidavit and the application for approximately 25 minutes"); United States v. Tagbering, 985 F.2d 946 (8th Cir.1993) (upholding district court's finding there no reason to believe "issuing judge abandoned his neutral and detached position," though defendant argued judge's "five-minute perusal of Detective Scudder's affidavit was no more than a rubber stamp approval").

[88]United States v. Wellman, 663 F.3d 224 (4th Cir.2011) (a "rubber stamp" objection, grounded in purported "grossly insufficient information" in affidavit, "is best analyzed under the third *Leon* exclusion"); United States v. Clark, 638 F.3d 89 (2d Cir.2011) ("legal error by the issuing judge in identifying probable cause does not, by itself, indicate the sort of wholesale abandonment of the judicial role discussed in *Leon*"); United States v. McKneely, 6 F.3d 1447 (10th Cir. 1993); United States v. Cardall, 773 F.2d 1128 (10th Cir.1985); United States v. Sager, 743 F.2d 1261 (8th Cir.1984).

See also United States v. Brown, 832 F.2d 991 (7th Cir.1987) (defendant submitted into evidence hundreds of search warrants issued by this magistrate, claiming they showed magistrate routinely found probable cause based on "form" warrant applications; court of appeals adopted district court's finding that this evidence only showed magistrate had "extraordinary experience in reviewing warrant applications").

a magistrate a search warrant affidavit that merely sets out in some detail certain observations he has made, on the basis of which the magistrate issues a search warrant because he concludes that those observations add up to probable cause. If at the later motion to suppress the defendant wishes to challenge *not* the magistrate's conclusion that those observations constitute probable cause, but rather the theretofore unquestioned assumption that the officer's observations were themselves lawful, may *Leon* be invoked to bar suppression on that basis? That is, does the *Leon* good faith rule even extend to prior warrantless activity by the police when that activity now becomes the predicate for a warrant, so that the defendant will not necessarily prevail by showing that the evidence obtained by executing the warrant was a fruit of an earlier unconstitutional warrantless search by the police? Some courts have answered this question in the affirmative,[89] though there is good reason to doubt whether this is correct. As one commentator, after putting such a case in which the earlier observations were accomplished by unconstitutional eavesdropping, has explained:

> The good faith exception should not preclude consideration of the pre-warrant evidence-gathering techniques of the police. The

---

[89]United States v. McClain, 444 F.3d 556 (6th Cir.2005) (*Leon* applied where warrant obtained on basis of information acquired in prior warrantless entry of premises on insufficient evidence of burglary in progress, as "the facts surrounding the initial warrantless searches were close enough to the line of validity to make the executing officers' belief in the validity of the search warrants objectively reasonable"); United States v. Diehl, 276 F.3d 32 (1st Cir.2002) (*Leon* applied although warrantless search produced facts on which search warrant based, as officers acted in good faith by making "inadvertent mistake" as to whether their surveillance point was within the curtilage); United States v. Fletcher, 91 F.3d 48 (8th Cir.1996) (*Leon* applied to search warrant though it based on dog sniff of defendant's suitcase now held to have been illegally detained without reasonable suspicion); United States v. Teitloff, 55 F.3d 391 (8th Cir.1995) (*Leon* deemed to apply though arrest warrant "was later determined to be supported by evidence that was obtained in violation of Teitloff's Fourth Amendment rights," as arresting officers "did not have any knowledge about the prior unlawful searches"); United States v. Carmona, 858 F.2d 66 (2d Cir.1988) (evidence admissible under *Leon* though warrant defective because based on information from prior illegal warrantless search); United States v. Thomas, 757 F.2d 1359 (2d Cir.1985) (though warrant invalid because based largely upon prior illegal warrantless search, specifically the use of a canine to detect drugs inside of defendant's apartment, evidence admissible nonetheless under *Leon*); United States v. Thornton, 746 F.2d 39 (D.C.Cir.1984) (warrant was based on earlier warrantless search of trash defendant now claims was illegal, but *Leon* good faith rule means no need to reach that issue). For discussion of *McClain* and similar cases re the interaction of the good faith exception with the poisonous fruit doctrine, see Notes, 60 Hastings L.J. 1147 (2009); 15 Widener L.Rev. 301 (2009).

Thomas was distinguished in United States v. Reilly, 76 F.3d 1271 (2d Cir.1996), note 92 infra, on the ground that in the earlier case the police fully revealed the nature of their warrantless activity to the judge in applying for the search warrant.

questioned police activity, the eavesdropping, was not performed
pursuant to a warrant. When the magistrate issued the warrant, he
did not endorse past activity; he only authorized future activity. As
Leon makes clear, the function of the magistrate is to determine
"whether a particular affidavit establishes probable cause," not
whether the methods used to obtain the information in that affidavit were legal. The illegal eavesdrop is a warrantless act which cannot be protected by incorporating the information thus obtained
into a warrant application. Despite the police's good faith belief in
its validity, the warrant is simply the fruit of a (warrantless) poisonous tree and the deterrent purpose of the exclusionary rule
would be advanced by excluding [the evidence]. The Court's recognition that *Leon* does not apply when policeman *X* passes on illegally obtained information to policeman *Y*, who then obtains the
warrant, would seem to govern this case as well.[90]

Such a conclusion certainly squares with the fact, as expressed in
Commonwealth v. D'Onofrio,[91] that "neither this court, nor any
other appellate court of which we are aware, has ever required
an affidavit that sets forth a police officer's personal observations
in support of a search warrant to contain information showing
that the officer made those observations without violating the
defendant's rights guaranteed by the Fourth Amendment." That
is, when the warrant-issuing process leaves totally unresolved
the lawfulness of the prior police activity,[92] then there is no reason why that process should, via *Leon*, shield that activity from

---

[90]Bradley, The "Good Faith Exception" Cases: Reasonable Exercises in
Futility, 60 Ind.L.J. 287, 302 (1985).
See also Note, 68 St. John's L.Rev. 217
(1994). Compare Note, 2007 U.Ill.L.
Rev. 467, suggesting a somewhat different approach.

[91]Commonwealth v. D'Onofrio,
396 Mass. 711, 488 N.E.2d 410 (1986).
See also United States v. Deaner, 1
F.3d 192 (3d Cir.1993) (where part of
information affiant offered to establish
probable cause was defendant's
"household refuse," search warrant not
invalid merely because affiant did not
indicate just where that garbage was
found and who seized it; defendant's
argument, "that every piece of evidence relied on by an affiant must be
shown to have been acquired constitutionally," "would constitute a substantial burden on affiants" and "would
subject probable cause determinations
to a hypertechnical analysis insupport-
able under governing case law";
rather, if defendant wants to question
constitutionality of that earlier evidence acquisition, this to be done via
"a hearing on the veracity of the im-

plicit representation that the evidence
was obtained in a constitutional manner," under the procedures of the
Franks rule, § 4.4(d)).

[92]Compare United States v. Reilly,
76 F.3d 1271 (2d Cir.1996) (finding it
necessary on facts presented to adopt
only an intermediary position, namely
that *Leon* is inapplicable when "the officers never gave [the magistrate] a
full account of what they did," so that
"the data presented to the issuing
judge did not allow him to decide
whether the evidence of wrongdoing
was itself obtained illegality and in
bad faith by the officers seeking the
warrant"); State v. Reno, 260 Kan.
117, 918 P.2d 1235 (1996) (where independent source rule not applicable
to search warrant obtained upon probable cause established by what learned
in prior illegal entry made for purposes
of levying execution on defendant's
property, *Leon* not applicable where
affidavit resulted in "concealment of
the nature of the initial intrusion";
court says result re *Leon* would be
otherwise if "the affiant had revealed
the actual circumstances of the entry").

full scrutiny at the suppression hearing.[93]

Compare *Reilly* and *Reno* with United States v. McClain, 430 F.3d 299 (6th Cir.2005) (court concludes "this is one of those unique cases in which the *Leon* good faith exception should apply despite an earlier Fourth Amendment violation," as the "affidavit fully disclosed to a neutral and detached magistrate the circumstances surrounding the initial warrantless search").

[93]The point is forcefully made in United States v. Vasey, 834 F.2d 782 (9th Cir.1987), holding *Leon* could not save a search warrant issued on an affidavit where it now appears a part of the essential facts showing probable cause came from a prior illegal warrantless search: "The constitutional error was made by the officer in this case, not by the magistrate as in *Leon*. The *Leon* Court made it very clear that the exclusionary rule should apply (i.e. the good faith exception should not apply) if the exclusion of evidence would alter the behavior of individual law enforcement officers or the policies of their department. * * * Officer Jensen's conducting an illegal warrantless search and including evidence found in this search in an affidavit in support of a warrant is an activity that the exclusionary rule was meant to deter.

"Further, we conclude that the magistrate's consideration of the evidence does not sanitize the taint of the illegal warrantless search. A magistrate's role when presented with evidence to support a search warrant is to weigh the evidence to determine whether it gives rise to probable cause. A magistrate evaluating a warrant application based in part on evidence seized in a warrantless search is simply not in a position to evaluate the legality of that search. Typically, warrant applications are requested and authorized under severe time constraints. Moreover, warrant applications are considered without the benefit of an adversarial hearing in which the evidentiary basis of the application might be challenged. Although we encourage magistrates to make all possible attempts to ensure that a warrantless search was legal before relying on the fruits of that search, we are mindful of the limitations on a magistrate's fact-finding ability in this context. We therefore conclude that a magistrate's consideration does not protect from exclusion evidence seized during a search under a warrant if that warrant was based on evidence seized in an unconstitutional search. Accordingly, the good faith exception should not and will not be applied to the facts of this case."

See also United States v. Mowatt, 513 F.3d 395 (4th Cir.2008) (*Leon* not applicable here, as "exclusionary rule operates to penalize the officers for their violation of Mowatt's rights *that preceded the magistrate's involvement*," i.e., the original illegal warrantless search); United States v. McGough, 412 F.3d 1232 (11th Cir.2005) (good faith exception not applicable where warrant issued on basis of evidence obtained in illegal search); United States v. O'Neal, 17 F.3d 239 (8th Cir.1994) (*Leon* not applicable here, where the probable cause based on dog sniff achieved by illegal warrantless seizure of defendant's bag, as "the issue is *police misconduct*, the target of the exclusionary rule as recognized in *Leon*"); United States v. Scales, 903 F.2d 765 (10th Cir.1990) (evidence obtained in execution of search warrant on defendant's suitcase suppressed because of prior unlawful seizure of suitcase pending warrant issuance; "the search of the suitcase *after* the search warrant was issued does not prevent us from evaluating the agents' behavior *prior* to that time," when the police "were not acting pursuant to a warrant"); United States v. Wanless, 882 F.2d 1459 (9th Cir.1989) (following *Vasey*); State v. DeWitt, 184 Ariz. 464, 910 P.2d 9 (1996) ("state cannot set up the good faith exception when, as here, the warrant upon which the police claim they relied in good faith was obtained as a direct result of their own unjustified warrantless entry"); People v. Machupa, 7 Cal.4th

A third situation put by the Court in *Leon,* also on the list of specific circumstances in which reliance on the warrant would not be "objectively reasonable," is where the warrant is "so facially deficient—i.e., in failing to particularize the place to be searched or the things to be seized—that the executing officers cannot reasonably presume it to be valid."[94] That language is followed by a citation directing the reader to compare the *Sheppard* case, which is quite appropriate in that *Sheppard* involved a somewhat different problem. There the affiant-detective made out a proper affidavit seeking a warrant for certain specified evidence of a homicide, but was only able to find a warrant form for controlled substances, which the issuing judge later assured him had been sufficiently revised to conform to the affidavit. This, then,

---

614, 29 Cal.Rptr.2d 775, 872 P.2d 114 (1994) (result and analysis similar to that in *Vasey*); State v. Carter, 69 Ohio St.3d 57, 630 N.E.2d 355 (1994) (search warrant issued on basis of information of drug transportation obtained by illegal stop and search; *Leon* inapplicable, as "good-faith exception does not apply where a search warrant is issued on the basis of evidence obtained as a result of an illegal search"); State v. Boll, 651 N.W.2d 710 (S.D.2002) (*Leon* inapplicable here, where essential information in affidavit obtained in prior illegal search).

[94]For other discussion of the relationship between the *Leon* good faith rule and the Fourth Amendment's particular description requirement, see Notes, 16 Fordham Urb.L.J. 577 (1989); 53 Mo.L.Rev. 355 (1988).

A search warrant may be facially deficient in other respects, where again the question is whether the deficiency should have been appreciated by the police. See, e.g., United States v. Kelley, 140 F.3d 596 (5th Cir.1998) (although magistrate inadvertently failed to date and sign the warrant, per *Sheppard* "the evidence in the instant case was properly admitted because the police conduct was objectively reasonable and largely error-free, and * * * it was the judge and not the police officers who made the mistake"); United States v. Cassity, 807 F.2d 509 (6th Cir.1986) ("beeper" warrant failed to limit duration of interception; *Leon* applicable because when the warrant issued no clearly established requirement of such limi-

tation); United States v. Freitas, 800 F.2d 1451 (9th Cir.1986) (warrant defective because special showing needed for surreptitious entry warrant; *Leon* applicable because agents understandably unaware of special requirement in this unusual situation); White v. State, 842 So.2d 565 (Miss.2003) (where warrant was a telephonic warrant, which officers had obtained before and which prosecutor in training sessions told them was permissible, and court holding otherwise came in instant case, good faith present).

Leon has been deemed to be equally applicable to arrest warrants, and the arrest warrant equivalent of this third situation is one "which fails to particularize or enumerate the crime for which the suspect was arrested." Abbott v. State, 307 Ark. 278, 819 S.W.2d 694 (1991).

Reliance upon a facially insufficient warrant is not justified merely because the review process is more elaborate. United States v. Kow, 58 F.3d 423 (9th Cir.1995) (despite indication in earlier case that "exceptional circumstances" would justify reliance on facially insufficient warrant, such circumstances not shown by fact warrant in instant case reviewed by two assistant U.S. Attorneys and the magistrate). Compare United States v. SDI Future Health, Inc., 568 F.3d 684 (9th Cir.2009) (*Kow*, supra, not applicable here, where search warrant description but not affidavit description deficient, but no showing searching officers actually relied on the affidavit).

was not the usual lack-of-particularity case in which the description is simply ambiguous; rather, the problem was that the warrant referred to items other than those as to which probable cause had been shown in the affidavit. The Court concluded that "the officers reasonably believed that the search they conducted was authorized by a valid warrant," especially in view of the fact that the "officers in this case took every step that could reasonably be expected of them."

Although the Court never said so in *Sheppard,* it seems clear that the detective-affiant, who thereafter led the search party executing the warrant, did not prior to that execution read the warrant and discover that it mistakenly referred to controlled substances. What the Court understandably concluded is that it was reasonable for him not to have done so in light of the special circumstances of the case: the judge had informed the detective he would authorize the warrant as requested and, when the detective then informed the judge of the problem concerning the warrant form, the judge said he would make the necessary changes in the warrant and was observed by the detective changing the warrant. Certainly, as the Court put it, there is no reason why the officer "should be expected to disregard assurances that everything is all right, especially when he has alerted the judge to the potential problems." What *Sheppard* left unclear, however, was whether some such "assurances" are always necessary before an executing officer who was also the affiant may fail to read the warrant on the assumption that it authorizes exactly what he requested. The "assurances" referred to by the Court in *Sheppard* were important precisely because the officer was aware that the warrant in the form he submitted it to the judge was likely incorrect.[95] But in the more typical case, where the warrant form submitted with the affidavit conformed to it (or deviated from it because of circumstances of which the affiant was reasonably unaware), courts applying *Sheppard* have concluded that, at least when the magistrate neither intimates he has made any changes in the warrant nor engages in conduct making it appear he has

---

[95]Assurance may likewise be important when the officer has other doubts about the legality of the contemplated search. See, e.g., United States v. Kurt, 986 F.2d 309 (9th Cir.1993) (*Leon* applied where police, upon learning that search warrant named not defendant's residence, as intended, but residence of defendant's parents, contacted judge who authorized change in warrant to show defendant's address; even if judge erred in failing to place officer under oath in receiving information justifying the change, "the error was the judge's" and the officer relied upon the judge's indication he could now proceed to search defendant's residence); United States v. Freitas, 856 F.2d 1425 (9th Cir.1988) (*Leon* applied to invalid sneak-and-peek warrant, see § 4.12(b), as "the agents in this case not only noticed the potential defect in the warrant, they brought it to the attention of an Assistant U.S. Attorney and the magistrate, who both approved it. *Sheppard* teaches that the agents were not required to disbelieve these experts").

made such changes, the affiant-officer is entitled to assume that what the magistrate approved is precisely what he requested.[96]

---

[96]See, e.g., United States v. Hurd, 499 F.3d 963 (9th Cir.2007) (where circumstances surrounding issuance of search warrant, its contents, and circumstances surrounding execution thereof indicated search of defendant's residence within the scope of the warrant, but judge by minor technical error failed to put initials on appropriate line on search warrant, but gave no indication upon or after issuance of warrant that probable cause supported only part of requested search, *Leon* applies); United States v. Watson, 498 F.3d 429 (6th Cir.2007) (where search warrant, sought for search of premises and 4 persons, gave notice in first paragraph that it issued for search of premises and described the premises in great detail, but by virtue of virtually unnoticeable clerical error premises omitted from warrant's grant-of-authority section, *Leon* applicable); United States v. Ware, 338 F.3d 476 (6th Cir.2003) (good faith where officers sought an anticipatory warrant and treated warrant received as such, though boilerplate language therein purported to authorized "immediate search"); United States v. Thomas, 263 F.3d 805 (8th Cir.2001) (good faith where application and supporting affidavit both contained correct address, warrant was executed by same officer who had prepared affidavit, and judge was responsible for erroneous address in search warrant, but affidavit not incorporated by reference into search warrant); United States v. Watkins, 179 F.3d 489 (6th Cir.1999) (affiant, who gave instructions to executing officers, reasonably concluded that warrant for main house and outbuildings, which mentioned the affidavit, thereby incorporated by reference a second dwelling on same property); United States v. Shugart, 117 F.3d 838 (5th Cir.1997) (good faith where affiant in affidavit asked to search for evidence of drug manufacturing, but warrant used boiler-plate language applicable to drug distribution, and where affiant then briefed search team on "the facts leading to the acquisition of the search warrants"); United States v. Berry, 113 F.3d 121 (8th Cir.1997) (where "Cook not only prepared the affidavit and warrant, with the knowledge that he was seeking authority for a night search of the entire premises, but he also participated in executing the warrant," he reasonably thought he had what he requested, authority for night search of all areas listed in the affidavit, though through clerical error warrant authorized night search for more limited area); United States v. Luk, 859 F.2d 667 (9th Cir.1988) (*Leon* applicable where officer relied on affidavit description of what to be seized, not all carried over to search warrant, and this true though affidavit does not directly cure warrant defect because warrant does not incorporate affidavit by reference); United States v. Anderson, 851 F.2d 384 (D.C.Cir.1988) (officers submitted affidavit that detailed items to be seized, but warrant issued for "the above-described items" without listing them; where investigating officers were also executing officers and apparently acted on basis of what they had listed in affidavit, though it neither attached to nor referred to in warrant, *Sheppard* applies); Ex parte Tyson, 784 So.2d 357 (Ala.2000) (where officer "submitted an affidavit clearly establishing grounds for a nighttime search" and did so after dark and advised magistrate of warrant's "imminent execution," but magistrate failed to check box authorizing nighttime execution of warrant, court applies "same rationale" as *Leon*, as officer in good faith assumed that warrant authorized what was requested).

Even certain "assurances" might be relied upon to justify an interpretation later given the language in the warrant by the executing officer. See the pre-*Leon* case of Landers v. State, 250 Ga. 808, 301 S.E.2d 633 (1983) (search warrant for "brick building" did not cover van in driveway; dissent argues a good faith exception should be applied here to uphold the search of the van in light of the magistrate's advice to the officer that the

Upon similar reasoning, it has been held that where "the same agent who prepared the affidavit and obtained the warrant also oversaw the execution of the warrant," that agent reasonably relied upon the magistrate to incorporate by reference the affidavit's description of the things to be seized.[97]

But then came *Groh v. Ramirez*,[98] involving a *Bivens* action[99] brought as a result of execution of a search warrant later determined to have a major defect regarding particularization of the items to be seized. ATF agent Groh, upon being informed by a concerned citizen that on numerous visits to Ramirez's ranch he had seen a large stock of weaponry, prepared an application for a warrant to search for a variety of described weapons and receipts pertaining to purchase or manufacture of such weapons. Groh also prepared a detailed affidavit indicating the basis for his belief that the listed items were on the ranch, and he also completed a warrant form, which the magistrate signed. After a fruitless execution of the warrant, it was discovered that because of a clerical error by Groh the warrant, at the place for describing

---

warrant allowed him to "search anything on that property").

Compare United States v. Brown, 251 F.3d 286 (1st Cir.2001), where in the search warrant affidavit the officer sought a no-knock warrant, but the complaint did not include any language so indicating, so at the judge's request the officer amended the latter document, after which the judge signed the warrant, which the officer mistakenly assumed included a grant of no-knock authority. The court first concluded that because in the record "there is little indication of what the judge said or did," it could not be concluded that "the state judge actually *did* authorize a no-knock search, notwithstanding the lack of a notation to that effect on the face of the warrant." As for the "alternative argument" that "the officers must be given the benefit of *Leon*, even if we cannot find that the search was actually authorized, because the record demonstrates that the officers believed, in good faith, that authorization had been given," the court concluded "the present record provides an inadequate basis for evaluating the objectively reasonableness of the officers' reliance." But, the court also deemed it "unclear whether *Leon* would apply under the circumstances the government describes," reasoning that "*Leon*

provides the safe harbor of reasonable reliance only when authorization *has* been given but is later determined to have been given in error," meaning it "would therefore plainly extend the law to provide similar protection to police actions undertaken in the mistaken, although reasonable, belief that a particular entry was authorized." The court distinguished *Sheppard* as a case in which the judge had intended to issue a warrant as requested, not shown to be the case here.

[97]United States v. Rosa, 626 F.3d 56 (2d Cir.2010) (where search warrant particularized place to be searched and computer equipment therein to be seized and searched, but failed to incorporate application and affidavit indicating crime for which evidence to be sought, *Leon* applies because officer "familiar with the contemplated limits of the search" was "both the affiant and the officer in charge of executing the search warrant and later searching the digital media seized"); United States v. Maxwell, 920 F.2d 1028 (D.C.Cir.1990) (no incorporation in fact because of lack of specific reference in warrant).

[98]Groh v. Ramirez, 540 U.S. 551, 124 S.Ct. 1284, 157 L.Ed.2d 1068 (2004).

[99]See § 1.10(b).

the things to be seized, instead described the dwelling located on the premises to be searched. In light of the fact that "the warrant did not incorporate other documents by reference, nor did either the affidavit or the application * * * accompany the warrant," the majority in *Groh* first decided that the search was unreasonable under the Fourth Amendment because Groh "did not have in his possession a warrant particularly describing the things he intended to seize."[100]

The *Groh* five-Justice majority then held that Groh was not entitled to qualified immunity (which means that if the search had been fruitful and the case had instead arisen in an exclusionary rule context, the *Leon* "good faith" exception would be inapplicable, for it involves exactly "the same standard of objective reasonableness"[101]). The majority explained:

> Given that the particularity requirement is set forth in the text of the Constitution, no reasonable officer could believe that a warrant that plainly did not comply with that requirement was valid. * * * Moreover, because petitioner himself prepared the invalid warrant, he may not argue that he reasonably relied on the Magistrate's assurance that the warrant contained an adequate description of the things to be seized and was therefore valid. Cf. *Sheppard* * * *. And even a cursory reading of the warrant in this case—perhaps just a simple glance—would have revealed a glaring deficiency that any reasonable police officer would have known was constitutionally fatal. * * *

> Petitioner contends that the search in this case was the product, at worst, of a lack of due care, and that our case law requires more than negligent behavior before depriving an official of qualified immunity. * * * But as we observed in [*Leon*], "a warrant may be so facially deficient—i.e., in failing to particularize the place to be searched or the things to be seized—that the executing officers cannot reasonably presume it to be valid."

Even if one takes a dim view of the *Leon* "good faith" exception generally (which is certainly the position taken herein[102]), given that *Leon* is now the law the above conclusion by the *Groh* majority seems flat-out wrong. The proper analysis of the *Groh* events, it is submitted, consists of the following propositions:[103] (i) The case involves "a straightforward mistake of fact," as "the officer simply made a clerical error when he filled out the proposed warrant." (ii) "Given the sheer number of warrants prepared and executed by officers each year," it "is inevitable that officers acting reasonably and entirely in good faith will occasionally make

---

[100]This branch of the case is discussed in § 4.6(a).

[101]Quoting Malley v. Briggs, 475 U.S. 335, 106 S.Ct. 1092, 89 L.Ed.2d 271 (1986).

[102]See § 1.3(b), (c), (d), (e).

[103]The quoted language following is from one or another of the two dissenting opinions (one by Kennedy joined by the Chief Justice; one by Thomas, joined by Scalia and joined by the Chief Justice as to this aspect of the case), which are in most respects similar as to the qualified immunity issue.

such errors." (iii) The officer's later "failure to recognize his clerical error on a warrant form can be a reasonable mistake," and such was the case here, for "where the officer is already fully aware of the scope of the intended search and the magistrate gives no reason to believe that he has authorized anything other than the requested search," there is nothing unreasonable in the officer's failure "to proofread the warrant." (iv) The majority's reliance upon the *Leon* quote is in error, for it has to do with "a mistake of law"; that is, the "issue in this case is whether an officer can reasonably fail to recognize a clerical error, not whether an officer who recognizes a clerical error can reasonably conclude that a defective warrant is legally valid." In short, as compared with the typical case in which *Leon* is successfully invoked to prevent application of the exclusionary rule, virtually nothing by way of deterrence would be lost by recognizing, in a *Groh*-type case arising in an exclusionary rule context, that the officer acted in "good faith."

Moreover, given the way in which the *Groh* case actually turned out, the line dividing *Groh* and *Leon* is a most uncertain one, which may well cause trouble for lower courts in the days ahead. This is because of the above-quoted comments the majority makes by way of support for its conclusion that, on the facts of *Groh*, "no reasonable officer could believe that a warrant that plainly did not comply with [the particularity] requirement was valid." One such comment is that because Groh "himself prepared the invalid warrant, he may not argue that he reasonably relied on the Magistrate's assurance that the warrant contained an adequate description of the things to be seized and was therefore valid." This suggests the possibility, but not the certainty, that in those cases where it is not the affiant but rather the magistrate or a court clerk who causes the warrant not to conform to the application/affidavit, the officer's assumption without actually reading the warrant that he got what he asked for does not of itself manifest a lack of "good faith." Also, the majority in that language may well have manifested an intention to extend *Sheppard* in the manner earlier suggested, for the assertion that the magistrate in *Groh* gave an "assurance that the warrant contained an adequate description" makes sense only if such assurance is provided merely by signing the warrant, rather than by providing a specific assurance of changes as in *Sheppard*. The *Groh* majority also states that "even a cursory reading of the warrant in this case—perhaps just a simple glance—would have revealed a glaring deficiency that any reasonable police officer would have known was constitutionally fatal." This may well mean that the majority did not, as one of the dissents asserted, "impose a proofreading requirement" upon officers obtaining search warrants, and that failure to notice lesser deviations in the warrant from what was sought in the affidavit/application will not likewise be deemed to show an absence of "good faith."

Assuming now a case falling within *Sheppard* rather than *Groh*, what if the affiant and executing officer are not the same person? The Court in *Sheppard* cautioned it was not deciding that question, but instead was leaving open the issue of what "an officer may be required to do when he executes a warrant without knowing beforehand what items are to be seized." Though the Court did note that ordinarily "when an officer who has not been involved in the application stage receives a warrant, he will read it in order to determine the object of the search," this is immediately followed with the observation that whether such an officer "would be justified in failing to notice a defect like the one in the warrant in this case is an issue we need not decide." One possible situation would be this variation on the *Sheppard* facts: the affiant, after obtaining the warrant, turns it over to another officer for execution, and in doing so recites in great detail all the facts upon which the warrant is based and consequently the particular items he claims may be searched for under the warrant, after which this other officer makes such a search without first reading the warrant and learning it instead purports to authorize a search for controlled substances. In such a case it would be not at all surprising if the *Leon* doctrine were construed to make the exclusionary rule inapplicable because of the reasonableness of the conduct of both the affiant and executing officer.

Another possible situation, albeit an unlikely one, is that an officer totally ignorant of the facts leading up to issuance of a warrant is given the warrant to execute. In such a case, the officer will quite obviously have to consult the warrant in order to determine what to do, and the problem now might be that in acting in strict compliance with the warrant he will make a search in excess of what the magistrate could have authorized in any event. Illustrative would be a variation on the *Sheppard* facts in which the warrant is simply turned over to another officer not previously involved in or aware of the murder investigation background, who proceeds to execute the warrant by searching for controlled substances, resulting in the discovery of contraband during a part of the search that was more intensive than would have been justified had the warrant identified the true objects of the search. In that situation, it would seem that if the officer simply examined those most essential parts of the warrant telling him where to search and what to look for and then acted in literal compliance with those dictates, exclusion of the evidence would not be called for under the *Leon* rule. That is, there is no reason why that officer, simply by virtue of his noninvolvement in the earlier investigation or warrant application, should distrust the specific commands of the warrant. But if this officer did examine other portions of the warrant or the affidavit for that warrant and found other assertions that did not square with either the place or things description, then a different result is called for. In such circumstances, the officer (in the words of *Sheppard*) "has unalleviated concerns about the proper scope of the search," and consequently ought not proceed until this uncertainty is authoritatively resolved.[104]

But these *Sheppard*-type situations in which the problem concerns a disparity between the affidavit and the warrant are unusual, and thus it is appropriate to pursue the third situation put by the Court in *Leon* by considering other, more common particularity-of-description problems. One is that in which the description is simply too broad, as where the warrant authorizes seizure of objects *W, X* and *Y* but the probable cause showing in the affidavit is only as to objects *W* and *X,* or where the warrant authorizes seizure of all objects of *Z* variety but the probable cause showing only covers some such objects (e.g., not all patient records of a doctor suspected of fraud, but only those of patients treated during the time of the suspected fraud). This kind of case, it is submitted, does not fit within the *Leon* third situation, described as a "facially deficient" warrant, as there is nothing inherently wrong with the description when it is viewed in isolation, and the problem is essentially a deficiency in the probable cause showing vis-a-vis certain of the described items. Such a case, then, is analytically most similar to that in which it turns out the warrant is lacking in any probable cause showing,[105] and ought to be resolved in the same way.[106] To be distinguished from such cases is one in which, again, the description in the warrant

---

[104]Cf. United States v. Grubbs, 547 U.S. 90, 126 S.Ct. 1494, 164 L.Ed.2d 195 (2006) (three concurring Justices assert that if an anticipatory search warrant not stating therein the triggering condition giving rise to probable cause "is not executed by the official who applied for it and happens to know the unstated condition," and the executing officer "takes such a warrant on its face and makes the ostensibly authorized search before the unstated condition has been met, the search will be held unreasonable," and in addition good faith will be lacking under *Groh* if the officer knows the search warrant was intended to be an anticipatory warrant and thus "must know or should realize when it omits the condition on which authorization depends," for in such circumstances "the government should * * * be held to the condition despite the unconditional face of the warrant"); United States v. Nelson, 36 F.3d 758 (8th Cir.1994) (where police sought search warrant to search defendant's body cavities but knew they had only a search warrant for defendant's "person," no good faith notwithstanding officers' supervisor said that sufficient, as "the endoscopy exceeded the scope of what any reasonable police officer would believe to be authorized by the search warrant").

[105]Discussed herein in text beginning at note 116 infra.

[106]United States v. King, 227 F.3d 732 (6th Cir.2000) (search warrant for one of two units at specified address did not include basement, as "established law" was that a tenant in apartment building has expectation of privacy in common area not open to general public, and executing officer did not have good faith merely because he had legally searched basements of single family dwellings without specification of basement in warrant); United States v. Kow, 58 F.3d 423 (9th Cir.1995) (where place searched was "legitimate business" so that probable cause only as to some records, no reasonable reliance on warrant that encompassed "essentially all documents on the premises"); State v. Thomas,

was too broad, but now a narrower description appears in the affidavit for that warrant. In some circumstances, of course, the affidavit will be deemed to "save" the warrant if certain conditions are met, e.g., that the warrant sufficiently "incorporated" the affidavit.[107] But if there is some defect with respect to the incorporation, it has been concluded that "good faith" exists (at least in the case where the executing officer "drafted the narrower affidavit and was aware of its limits") if "a reasonable officer in his position would assume that the warrant incorporated

---

540 N.W.2d 658 (Iowa 1995) (no good faith as to search warrant authorizing search of "all persons located inside the premises," as the warrant application is "lacking sufficient indicia of probable cause" to allow a reasonable belief it covered "everyone present in a legally licensed public establishment during normal business hours").

Compare United States v. Clark, 638 F.3d 89 (2d Cir.2011) (no particularity problem, as search warrant "identified the place to be searched" and "the items that could be seized"; as for claim no probable cause as to all of multi-unit named place, there no requirement "that probable cause be stated in the warrant itself," and thus case should be resolved "considering a different *Leon* concern, whether the lack of probable cause was so obvious as to preclude reasonable reliance"); United States v. Potts, 586 F.3d 823 (10th Cir.2009) (good faith present here, as while part of warrant on permissible "techniques" for conducting computer search seemed to authorize inspection of "files" generally, other part of warrant limited entirely to material related to "child pornography," and thus even assuming warrant had a particularly-of-description defect, a reasonable officer would have construed warrant as limited to child pornography); United States v. Otero, 563 F.3d 1127 (10th Cir.2009) (good faith here, as "items to be seized" list was limited by reference to crimes under investigation, but "computer items to be seized" had no such limitation, but a reasonable officer would have read the limitations of the first list as being applicable as well to the second); United States v. $92,422.57, 307 F.3d 137 (3d Cir.2002) (good faith

where search warrant authorized search for records for years 1984–97, but arguably no probable cause for years 1984–93, as "that flaw renders the warrant overly broad, not general," for which "the proper remedy * * * was simply to excise the years for which there was no probable cause"); United States v. Travers, 233 F.3d 1327 (11th Cir.2000) (good faith where search warrant overinclusive as to papers that could be seized, as district court's ruling was a "close call"); State v. Sorensen, 688 N.W.2d 193 (S.D.2004) (good faith regarding "all vehicles" provision in warrant, allowing search of all vehicles found on the named premises, as while some courts say only vehicles of occupants covered, and thus warrant here "arguably overbroad," matter not decided in this state and several states follow broader rule).

The same is true of the special rules against overbreadth applicable to material presumptively protected by the First Amendment. United States v. Hale, 784 F.2d 1465 (9th Cir.1986) (evidence suppressed, as ruling "that the warrant was impermissibly overbroad with respect to any material arguably protected by the First Amendment other than that specifically named rests on well-established current law, and it is not unreasonable to require executing officers to know it"). The court in *Hale* went on to say that it had "serious doubts whether material arguably protected by the First Amendment which is seized pursuant to overbroad provisions of a warrant can ever be admitted through the good faith exception."

[107]See §§ 4.5(a), 4.6(a).

and would be construed with the attached affidavit."[108]

Still another kind of particularity-of-description problem is that in which the description initially seems all right but then is a cause of difficulty when it comes time to decide where to look or what to look for pursuant to the warrant. Illustrative is the situation in which the place to be searched is described in terms of an apartment number and street address and a variety of physical characteristics, but at the scene it is determined that there does not exist any single place to which all of those descriptive factors apply. At least in a literal sense, this is not a "facially deficient" warrant either,[109] for the description is not inherently inadequate, and thus it may well be that this situation is likewise not encompassed within the *Leon* Court's third situation. But this is of little moment, for there exists considerable pre-*Leon* authority that permits such cases to be dealt with in essentially the same way as if they were subjected to a *Leon* type of analysis. That is, these earlier cases simply require the police to make reasonable judgments under the circumstances, such as by logically identifying those parts of the multiple-factor description that may be disregarded because most likely a consequence of typographical or similar error.[110]

But if neither these two situations nor *Sheppard*-type cases fall

---

[108]United States v. Tracey, 597 F.3d 140 (3d Cir.2010). Consider also United States v. Allen, 625 F.3d 830 (5th Cir.2010) (while "the warrant was not sufficiently particularized" and "the attachment detailing the items to be seized was not incorporated by reference," police had good faith belief that warrant was valid; case distinguishable from *Groh*, text at note 98 supra, as "the magistrate judge signed not only the warrant, but also the affidavit, to which the list of items to be seized was attached").

[109]United States v. Ellis, 971 F.2d 701 (11th Cir.1992) (*Leon* not applicable where warrant for "third mobile home" but occupant there said person police sought was in 5th mobile home, which police then searched; neither warrant nor affidavit contained name of suspect, and executing officer had not earlier been to premises; court stresses that the error was by the investigating officer and (unlike *Sheppard* and cases in note 96 supra) "cannot be attributed to a clerical error on the part of the issuing magistrate," and the executing officers "did not rely on the warrant at all" but rather on

the word of the mobile home occupant, or, "if the officers can be said to have relied on the warrant, that reliance surely was not reasonable once the officers discovered that the only information in the warrant was erroneous"); United States v. Gordon, 901 F.2d 48 (5th Cir.1990) (incorrect street name in search warrant not "facially deficient," as "one who looked simply at the warrant, or at both the warrant and the supporting affidavit, would not suspect it invalid"; affiant was executing officer and had earlier been at premises intended, so no risk wrong place would be searched).

[110]See § 4.5(a). But in United States v. Lora-Solano, 330 F.3d 1288 (10th Cir.2003), the court first held the search warrant valid notwithstanding the misdescription of a house number, because there was no house with that number and the officer was able to determine the nature of the clerical error as to the number here because this an anticipatory warrant and informant directed them to the proper house—2051, rather than the listed 2021—and *then* held in the alternative that if the warrant was invalid "the good faith exception of *Leon* * * *

comfortably into *Leon* 's "facially deficient" warrant category,
then what does? Some situations easily come to mind in which
the descriptive words are inherently inadequate to describe the
place to be searched or the things to be seized. Illustrative would
be a warrant to search "an apartment" in a specified multiple-
apartment building or a warrant to search a specified place for
"stolen goods." This is not to suggest, however, that even cases of
this kind inevitably fall outside the *Leon* doctrine. The Court in
that case did *not* say a "facially deficient warrant" may never be
relied upon; rather, the question is whether that warrant is "so
facially deficient * * * that the executing officers cannot reasonably presume it to be valid." One might argue, of course, that a
facially deficient warrant is bad precisely because the description
is not "such that the officer with a search warrant can, with reasonable effort ascertain and identify"[111] the place or thing referred
to, and that whenever the officer finds himself in this predicament he can hardly be reasonably relying upon the warrant.
That is, the lack of particularity in the warrant tells the officer
he has been given insufficient direction, and thus he can hardly
reasonably rely upon that warrant.[112] But *Leon* might not be
given such a narrow reading. Under the Fifth Circuit's pre-*Leon*

---

would apply."

[111]Steele v. United States, 267
U.S. 498, 45 S.Ct. 414, 69 L.Ed. 757
(1925).

[112]See United States v. Williamson,
1 F.3d 1134 (10th Cir.1993) (where
search warrant only gave business
mail box number, which "indicates
nothing about the physical location of
the business premises," but did not
even name the business, *Leon* good
faith test inapplicable, as "no reasonable officer could have concluded that
this warrant, which provides no meaningful description of the premises, was
valid"); United States v. George, 975
F.2d 72 (2d Cir.1992) (a warrant for
evidence of any crime thus "not limited
in scope to *any crime at all* is so unconstitutionally broad that no reasonably
well-trained police officer could believe
otherwise"); United States v. Leary,
846 F.2d 592 (10th Cir.1988) (description of items to be seized as "records"
relating to violation of two specified
statutes insufficient, and because it offers no guidance to the officer there no
basis for claim of reasonable reliance
on that description; court notes other
federal cases with rare exception refuse to use *Leon* to admit evidence

where search warrant description in
such general terms); United States v.
Fuccillo, 808 F.2d 173 (1st Cir.1987)
(stressing warrant for "cartons of
women's clothing" and other generally
described items must have been perceived by executing officers as insufficient, given their wholesale seizures
from the premises); United States v.
Crozier, 777 F.2d 1376 (9th Cir.1985)
(search warrant authorizing seizure of
unspecified "evidence of violation of 21
U.S.C.A. 841, 846"; because warrant
did not describe any particular property, under *Leon* "the agent could not
reasonably rely on the warrant"); Green
v. State, 688 So.2d 301 (Fla.1996) (description limited to "the clothing [de-
fendant] wearing the evening of the
8th day of December, 1992," is overbroad because it does not instruct officer what articles of clothing he empowered to seize, and such facial
invalidity a bar to applying *Leon*);
Crum v. Commonwealth, 223 S.W.3d
109 (Ky.2007) (search warrant for "illegal contraband" is "so lacking in
indicia of reliability that the officer's
good faith reliance cannot be deemed
reasonable").

Compare United States v.
Robertson, 21 F.3d 1030 (10th

"good faith" exception (broader, however, than adopted in *Leon*), it has been held objectively reasonable for officers to believe that a particularity defect clear on the face of the warrant "could be 'cured' by their independent personal knowledge"[113] of what the warrant was intended to describe.

In any event, the line between the "facially deficient" warrant cases and those previously described is not as bold as might be assumed. For example, description merely of "a brown house" on a specified street would seem highly suspect from the outset, but it is sufficient if it turns out there is but one brown house on that street. Perhaps it is of no great moment exactly how that case is classified either, for it would presumably come out the same way under either *Leon* or the pre-*Leon* cases alluded to above. But what then of a warrant to search a residence for "shoes"? It is extremely unlikely that such a description would be specific enough, but yet it cannot literally be characterized as a "facially deficient" description, because given just the right set of facts and the right kind of probable cause showing, this description might pass muster.[114] Viewing such a case from the perspective of the officer executing the warrant, may it be said that the designation simply of "shoes" should create enough doubt about the sufficiency of the warrant that it would be unreasonable to act on that warrant without checking further, so that failure to do so would require suppression of evidence if it turns out this description is in fact inadequate? In the words of the *Sheppard* case, does the officer in these circumstances have such "unalleviated concerns about the proper scope of the search" that his reliance upon the warrant is unreasonable? The answer under *Leon,* I suspect, is that this reliance is *not* unreasonable. Perhaps as a statistical matter the designation "shoes" will not often suffice, but since it sometimes will it would seem the executing officer is entitled to assume—at least absent his awareness of other facts suggesting otherwise—that the magistrate has concluded the instant case is one of those rare instances in which such a generality is adequate.

If that is so, then it may be suggested that warrant defects of the particularity-of-description variety will sometimes require

---

Cir.1994) (good faith present, as "agents reasonably could have thought that authorizing seizure of 'fruits and instrumentalities' of a narrow and simple crime like carjacking was not too broad").

[113]United States v. Mahoney, 712 F.2d 956 (5th Cir.1983), thus upholding an in-premises arrest based on an arrest warrant naming only "John Doe a/k/a/ Dennis LNU." To the same effect is the post-*Leon* case of Toland v.

State, 285 Ark. 415, 688 S.W.2d 718 (1985) (though "the directions given on the warrant in this case were absolutely defective," in that "no person could have followed the directions and ended up at the site where the search was supposed to have been conducted," under *Leon* evidence obtained in execution of warrant admissible, as "the officer executing the warrant knew exactly where he was going").

[114]See § 4.6(a).

suppression in post-*Leon* cases even if they are not of the "facially
deficient" variety. That phrase was used by the Court to refer to
a situation in which perhaps the warrant could not reasonably be
presumed valid by "the executing officers." But the Court in *Leon*
also makes it quite clear that admissibility of illegally seized evidence is not assured merely by the good faith of the officer executing the defective warrant:

> It is necessary to consider the objective reasonableness, not only of
> the officers who eventually executed a warrant, but also of the of-
> ficers who originally obtained it or who provided information mate-
> rial to the probable-cause determination. Nothing in our opinion
> suggests, for example, that an officer could obtain a warrant on the
> basis of a "bare bones" affidavit and then rely on colleagues who are
> ignorant of the circumstances under which the warrant was
> obtained to conduct the search.

If this is so, then surely the same approach must be taken as
to particularity-of-description defects. Thus, the fact the executing officer may reasonably rely upon the "shoes" description is
not the end of the matter. Since in all likelihood the authority to
search for "shoes" was given because requested by the officer-
affiant, it remains to be determined whether that officer, given
his knowledge of the underlying facts set out in the affidavit,
could reasonably believe that such broad search and seizure
authority could be conferred upon such facts.[115]

The fourth specific situation put by the *Leon* majority in
describing when suppression "remains an appropriate remedy" is
where the requisite "objective good faith in relying on a warrant"
is lacking because the warrant is "based on an affidavit 'so lacking in indicia of probable cause as to render official belief in its

---

[115]Illustrative are United States v. Fuccillo, 808 F.2d 173 (1st Cir.1987) (warrants to search warehouse, wholesaler's premises, and retail clothing store for "cartons of women's clothing" did not sufficiently describe items to be seized; *Leon* not applicable, court stresses affiant aware of other facts that would describe what stolen and that description actually tendered obviously not useful given nature of places searched); United States v. Spilotro, 800 F.2d 959 (9th Cir.1986) (*Leon* not applicable where description of "gemstones and other items of jewelry" for search of jewelry store and affidavit did not indicate all jewelry there stolen; description obviously overbroad); United States v. Washington, 797 F.2d 1461 (9th Cir.1986) (parts of warrant authorizing seizure of articles "tending to establish the wealth and financial sta-

tus" of defendant and "evidence of association of Ralph Washington with the following persons, but not limited to them" are "patently overbroad" and thus *Leon* exception not applicable).

Compare the questionable result in United States v. Diaz, 841 F.2d 1 (1st Cir.1988) (warrant description of virtually all business records of company insufficient because "the government should have advised the magistrate of its belief regarding the duration of the suspected scheme" so that magistrate could "reach a reasoned decision as to the first date on which there is probable cause to believe that evidence of criminal acts was recorded in [the] business records," but evidence admissible under *Leon* because "reasonably well trained officer would not necessarily have known" that such a time limitation was necessary here).

existence entirely unreasonable.' "[116] This language should not be taken to mean, on the one hand, that an officer executing a warrant is obligated to obtain and examine the affidavit upon which that warrant is based, or, on the other, that because the executing officer is not so obligated the requisite good faith consequently will be present whenever he does not actually examine the affidavit. As the Court made explicit in the language previously quoted, "objective reasonableness" is also required of the officer who applied for the warrant and knew what was in the affidavit.[117] This means, for one thing, that it is *not* the case "that additional facts, which the government proved were known to the affiant po-

---

[116]Quoting from Brown v. Illinois, 422 U.S. 590, 95 S.Ct. 2254, 45 L.Ed.2d 416 (1975) (Powell, J., concurring).

[117]Cf. United States v. Luong, 470 F.3d 898 (9th Cir.2006) ("where the underlying affidavit is entirely lacking in indicia of probable cause, we reject the government's invitation to look to facts orally conveyed to the magistrate"); Ex parte Green, 15 So. 3d 489 (Ala.2008) (court emphasized executing officer was also affiant, whose affidavit "contained no chronological reference" so that no argument against apparent staleness of information); State v. Anderson, 286 Ark. 58, 688 S.W.2d 947 (1985) (good faith exception inapplicable here, as officer seeking warrant knew it obtained on oral testimony, and "procedure of providing an affidavit when obtaining search warrant is so standard a practice that we cannot consider such a deficiency as falling within the purview of good faith error"); People v. Turnage, 162 Ill.2d 299, 205 Ill.Dec. 118, 642 N.E.2d 1235 (1994) (where record silent as to conduct of those who obtained arrest warrant, it insufficient under *Leon* that executing officer had good faith belief warrant valid where, in fact, it invalid because it was the second warrant issued for the same charges and defendant had been arrested and released on first warrant).

But compare United States v. Doyle, 650 F.3d 460 (4th Cir.2011) (in determining good faith, can consider both contents of affidavit and of unsworn summary of investigation by another officer also submitted to magistrate); United States v. Edwards, 798 F.2d 686 (4th Cir.1986) (understandably concluding that the good faith exception applies where the affiant fully established probable cause in his sworn testimony to the magistrate but the magistrate, who himself prepared the affidavit for the officer's signature, left out the information re the informant's reliability). See also United States v. Perez, 393 F.3d 457 (4th Cir.2004) (in determining good faith of officer, court takes into account not only information in affidavit but also what officer orally stated to magistrate and contents of informant's signed statement supplied to magistrate); United States v. Smith, 63 F.3d 766 (8th Cir.1995) (*Leon* applicable where judge failed to sign the jurat on the affidavit; court stresses that, as in *Sheppard*, "the error was the fault of the judicial officer and not the police officer"); State v. Davidson, 260 Neb. 417, 618 N.W.2d 418 (2000) (officer could in good faith rely upon certified copy of arrest warrant lacking affidavit, even though warrant did not specify basis upon which judge could have issued it upon personal knowledge); State v. Edmonson, 257 Neb. 468, 598 N.W.2d 450 (1999) (although *usually* appellate court considering good faith issue "is limited to the four corners of the affidavit," that not so here, as while affidavit on which search warrant issued so lacking that there could be no good faith as to it, after warrant issued police submitted second affidavit, and good faith police reliance on it suffices, even though it could not resuscitate warrant already issued, as error in not issuing a second warrant "was the result of judicial error, not police error," and thus falls within *Leon*).

lice officer, but not revealed to the magistrate prior to issuance of the search warrant, could be considered in the *Leon* analysis," for allowing such consideration[118] would "undercut Fourth Amendment protections, and be at odds with the very purpose of the *Leon* good faith exception."[119]

Exactly what it takes to bring a case within this fourth category is a most difficult issue, one that continues to be frequently litigated.[120] One way of approaching this issue is to ask to what

---

[118]As in United States v. Fiorito, 640 F.3d 338 (8th Cir.2011); United States v. Martin, 297 F.3d 1308 (11th Cir.2002); Moore v. Commonwealth, 159 S.W.3d 325 (Ky.2005). However, State v. Edmonson, 257 Neb. 468, 598 N.W.2d 450 (1999), described in note 117 supra, does not belong in this category, as there the additional facts *were* revealed to the magistrate in a second, post-issuance affidavit. Adams v. Commonwealth, 275 Va. 260, 657 S.E.2d 87 (2008), while collecting many decisions that "have not confined the good-faith inquiry to the four corners of the search warrant affidavit," is itself more like *Edmonson*, as the additional information deemed properly considered by the officer was that in a criminal complaint executed before the same magistrate who issued the search warrant 19 minutes later.

In any event, such cases as *Martin* certainly do *not* mean that "the Government must present evidence beyond the four corners of the affidavit to demonstrate that [the officer] reasonably relied on the search warrant." United States v. Robinson, 336 F.3d 1293 (11th Cir.2003).

[119]United States v. Bynum, 293 F.3d 192 (4th Cir.2002) (finding it unnecessary to resolve this question, but noting that the dissent "makes a persuasive case" for this position). In accord with that position are United States v. Hove, 848 F.2d 137 (9th Cir. 1988); People v. Miller, 75 P.3d 1108 (Colo.2003) (court applying good faith test is "restricted to the information contained within the four corners of the affidavit"); Crum v. Commonwealth, 223 S.W.3d 109 (Ky.2007) (while "officer did know more, and could have put more information in the warrant," that cannot

save a search warrant that is "facially deficient"); State v. Klosterman, 114 Ohio App.3d 327, 683 N.E.2d 100 (1996); Janis v. Commonwealth, 22 Va.App. 646, 472 S.E.2d 649 (1996).

Compare United States v. McKenzie-Gude, 671 F.3d 452 (4th Cir.2011) (citing cases in accord, court says it does "not believe that a court abandons the objective inquiry required by *Leon* when it considers the uncontroverted *facts known* to the officer, which he has inadvertently failed to disclose to the magistrate"); United States v. McCoy, 483 F.3d 862 (8th Cir.2007) (additional information police officer "disclosed to the magistrate in conversation" but not "under oath" can be taken into account re his good faith belief "that the magistrate relied on that additional information").

[120]See, e.g., United States v. Henderson, 595 F.3d 1198 (10th Cir.2010) (good faith here, where officer's "affidavit was based on a standardized form affidavit, which was used by law enforcement officials throughout Wyoming at the time"); United States v. Quezada-Enriquez, 567 F.3d 1228 (10th Cir.2009) (good faith in relying on informant who provided reliable information in past, though no basis of knowledge or corroboration of information provided this time given); United States v. Prideaux-Wentz, 543 F.3d 954 (7th Cir.2008) (while probable cause deemed "stale" because information re defendant uploading child porn to e-group was 4 years old and there "no new evidence to 'freshen' the stale evidence," good faith present based on "the fact that most child pornographers do not dispose of their collections"); United States v. Hodson, 543 F.3d 286 (6th Cir.2008) (reasonably well-trained officer would have realized that probable

extent, if at all, this facet of *Leon* does anything that had not already been accomplished by the Court a year earlier in *Gates*. Justices Brennan and Marshall, in their *Leon* dissent, answered in this way:

> In *Gates*, the Court held that "the task of an issuing magistrate is simply to make a practical, common-sense decision whether, given all the circumstances set forth in the affidavit before him, . . . there is a fair probability that contraband or evidence of a crime will be found in a particular place." * * * The task of a reviewing court is confined to determining whether "the magistrate had a 'substantial basis' for concluding that probable cause existed." * * * Given such a relaxed standard, it is virtually inconceivable that a reviewing court, when faced with a defendant's motion to suppress, could first find that a warrant was invalid under the new *Gates* standard, but then, at the same time, find that a police officer's reliance on such an invalid warrant was nevertheless "objectively reasonable" under the test announced today. Because the two standards overlap so completely, it is unlikely that a warrant could be found invalid under *Gates* and yet the police reliance upon it could be seen as objectively reasonable; otherwise, we would have to entertain the mind-boggling concept of objectively reasonable reliance upon an objectively unreasonable warrant.

There is some force to this argument.[121] "If, as the *Gates* majority beguiles, probable cause is nothing more than a matter of

---

cause of child molestation did not establish probable cause to search for child pornography); United States v. Frazier, 423 F.3d 526 (6th Cir.2005) (where affidavit stated drugs found in defendant's former apartment just after he moved to present one, officer in good faith inferred defendant thus had drugs in present residence as well); United States v. Laughton, 409 F.3d 744 (6th Cir.2005) (no good faith where search warrant affidavit failed to make any connection between suspected drug trafficker and place to be searched); United States v. Helton, 314 F.3d 812 (6th Cir.2003) (evidence inadmissible under *Leon* where "statements originated from an unknown, untested source; they were the product of multiple layers of hearsay; they were sparse in relevant detail, and, most importantly, they were not corroborated in any meaningful manner"); United States v. McDile, 914 F.2d 1059 (8th Cir.1990) (where affidavit said street seller of drugs went directly after sale to certain address, that not probable cause this his "safe house," but evidence admissible under *Leon*); United States v. Brown, 832 F.2d 991 (7th Cir.1987) (where only probable cause defect was failure to spell out in affidavit support for contention place to be searched was residence of implicated defendant, evidence admissible under *Leon*); People v. Gutierrez, 222 P.3d 925 (Colo.2009) (evidence inadmissible under *Leon*, as affidavit "does not merely fail to establish a 'sufficient nexus' between Gutierrez's tax return and the suspected criminal activity, it fails to establish any connection at all"); State v. Spillers, 847 N.E.2d 949 (Ind.2006) (stressing that court's conclusion informant's statements "were not declarations made against his personal interest was reached only after examining more carefully existing case law on the subject"); State v. Longbine, 257 Kan. 713, 896 P.2d 367 (1995) (evidence inadmissible notwithstanding *Leon* where no facts stated in search warrant affidavit to show that the drug in defendant's residence, and affidavit only provides "impression" of such because defendant "a drug dealer with an established network").

[121] But consider United States v. Bynum, 293 F.3d 192 (4th Cir.2002)

'practical, common-sense' decisionmaking, then it would seem that a probable cause determination which is erroneous and thus lacking this sagaciousness is undeserving of either the appellation 'good faith' or the sympathetic reception which a 'good faith' qualification would allow."[122] Moreover, to try to pile the *Leon* standard on top of the *Gates* test, whereunder a warrant is to be upheld upon review if there was a "substantial basis" for a "fair probability" (or, "substantial chance") that criminal activity exists or that evidence of crime would be found, would seem a form of incomprehensible double counting. "To say that evidence obtained pursuant to a warrant should be admissible even though the police *lacked* a 'substantial basis' for a 'substantial chance' of criminal activity *as long as they had a reasonable belief* that they had a 'substantial basis' for a 'substantial chance' would be to promulgate an almost mind-boggling standard."[123]

Although it is generally risky to rely upon a dissenting opinion as marking the true dimensions of a doctrine enunciated by the majority, it is fair to say that the majority opinion in *Leon* lends some support to the Brennan-Marshall thesis. The Court declared that the officer who obtained the search warrant in *Leon* was acting in good faith because the warrant "clearly was supported by much more than a 'bare bones' affidavit,"[124] was grounded in an

---

(lower court erred in concluding that "the good faith exception* * * does not apply" when the affidavit fails to provide "a substantial basis for determining the existence of probable cause").

[122]LaFave, Fourth Amendment Vagaries (Of Improbable Cause, Imperceptible Plain View, Notorious Privacy, and Balancing Askew), 74 J.Crim.L. & C. 1171, 1199 (1983).

[123]Kamisar, Gates, "Probable Cause," "Good Faith," and Beyond, 69 Iowa L.Rev. 551, 589 (1984).

[124]Thus, *Leon* surely cannot be relied upon by the prosecution when the affidavit does not rise at all above the bare-bones level. Virgin Islands v. John, 654 F.3d 412 (3d Cir.2011) ("the catalog of the affidavit's 'indicia of probable cause' with respect to child pornography is completely empty," as while there an assertion defendant, a teacher, fondled students at school, affidavit never alleged any assault/ pornography connection, "let alone any evidentiary reason to believe in it"); United States v. Doyle, 650 F.3d 460 (4th Cir.2011) (no good faith, as where undated reference to pictures of nude

children, "nothing indicated when or if child pornography allegedly existed in Doyle's home"); United States v. West, 520 F.3d 604 (6th Cir.2008) (affidavit "was so bare bones as to preclude any reasonable belief in the validity of the search warrant," as no evidence of nexus between crimes and places searched); United States v. Herron, 215 F.3d 812 (8th Cir.2000) (no good faith probable cause to search defendant's premises for drugs where affidavit revealed no evidence illegal activity there or evidence that defendant involved with known marijuana cultivation elsewhere, but only that defendant had prior marijuana convictions and had familial relation to person who owned place of cultivation); United States v. Jackson, 818 F.2d 345 (5th Cir.1987) (affidavit for *arrest* warrant said police had sworn statement from person saying he burglarized premises and that stolen goods unloaded at defendant's apartment; no showing of reliability because no indication informant knew consequence of false swearing and admission against interest was unrelated to statement about defendant, and no

affidavit that "related the results of an extensive investigation,"[125]

basis of knowledge because no indication why informant believed defendant knew the goods were stolen; thus "the affidavit is totally lacking in indicia of reliability and basis of knowledge, and is therefore a bare bones affidavit"); Campbell v. State, 2009 Ark. 540, 354 S.W.3d 41 (2009) (no good faith where search warrant affidavit set out *no* "facts tending to show that the items to be seized are in the place to be searched," instead relying solely on fact defendant possessed drug paraphernalia when arrested elsewhere); People v. Pacheco, 175 P.3d 91 (Colo. 2006) (where affidavit contained stale information from anonymous informants with "bare assertions of knowledge," this a bare bones affidavit); Agurs v. State, 415 Md. 62, 998 A.2d 868 (2010) (affidavit, though "lengthy and detailed," had a "bare bones" aspect, as it "lack[ed] any indicia of probable cause that the nexus requirement [between crime and place] was satisfied"); State v. Lunde, 752 N.W.2d 630 (N.D.2008) (no good faith here, as affidavit supplied only tenuous and conclusory suggestion defendant involved in criminal activity, based on stale information from uncorroborated informant); State v. Weston, 329 S.C. 287, 494 S.E.2d 801 (1997) (no good faith where 4-sentence affidavit "provided information linking Weston to his car at the time of the incident" but "offered nothing to link Weston or the Datsun to the Crumlin crime itself"); State v. Belmontes, 615 N.W.2d 634 (S.D.2000) (where no mention of informant's credibility or reliability in affidavit and trial court "in essence" found "this was a 'bare bones' affidavit," no good faith); State v. Hlavacek, 185 W.Va. 371, 407 S.E.2d 375 (1991) (conclusory statement by anonymous informant re defendant's trip to get marijuana, with slight corroboration that defendant seen on the highway, treated as essentially a bare-bones affidavit).

[125]Compare United States v. Miller, 673 F.3d 688 (7th Cir.2012) (sufficient that "affidavit included enough detail," which was "recent" albeit "generic");

United States v. Evers, 669 F.3d 645 (6th Cir.2012) (affidavit not "bare bone," as it listed "underlying factual circumstances" and listed items subject to seizure); United States v. Patten, 664 F.3d 247 (8th Cir.2011) (while affidavit did not identify source of information re defendant's sexual abuse of minor, there good faith because it indicated that affiant interviewed source "in person, and thus * * * had a greater opportunity to assess [her] credibility," and that source "had first-hand knowledge of the sexual abuse" and existing photographic evidence thereof); United States v. Wellman, 663 F.3d 224 (4th Cir.2011) ("the affidavit was not a hastily-assembled document based on a single tip, but was the product of a six-week investigation"); United States v. Clark, 638 F.3d 89 (2d Cir.2011) (stressing warrant "was not completely bare bones" and relied upon defendant's supposed control over entire multi-family dwelling to establish probable cause as to entirety, and "need to support an allegation of control with descriptive facts was not previously established in precedent"); United States v. Dismuke, 593 F.3d 582 (7th Cir.2010) (stressing this "not a case where the probable cause determination rested on little more than a 'bare-bones' affidavit"); United States v. Harrison, 566 F.3d 1254 (10th Cir.2009) ("affidavit contains much more than a 'bare bones' statement"); United States v. Crews, 502 F.3d 1130 (9th Cir.2007) (stressing details in affidavit tending to show "reasonable nexus" between crime and place searched); United States v. Pope, 467 F.3d 912 (5th Cir.2006) (officer's "affidavit was based on his direct participation in the illegal drug transaction" with defendant "and his continuing investigation of such activity" was "not a 'bare bones' affidavit"); Jackson v. State, 908 N.E.2d 1140 (Ind.2009) (search warrant not of "bare bones" variety, as affidavit related affiant's relationship with informant and public complaints consistent with informant's information); State v. Long, 884 So.2d 1176 (La.2004) (no absence of good faith re conclusory information from

and consequently was issued upon "evidence sufficient to create disagreement among thoughtful and competent judges as to the existence of probable cause."[126] This is remarkably similar to the assertions in *Gates* that the new rule adopted there applied "beyond the 'bare bones' affidavits" situations, that the affidavit there was sufficient because it contained many facts "obtained through the independent investigation" by the police, and that a warrant should be upheld on review if the magistrate drew "reasonable inferences" notwithstanding the fact that on the same affidavit another magistrate would have been free "to refuse to draw them if he [was] so minded." But it is well to emphasize once again that precisely because the good faith doctrine was unnecessarily relied upon in *Leon,* that case itself leaves unresolved the important question of whether on a probable cause challenge *Leon* sometimes makes admissible certain evidence that could not have been admitted on the authority of *Gates.*

The supposition that it does might be based on the very fact that *Leon* was decided as it was: surely the Court would not have gone to the bother of adopting this new and controversial doctrine if it merely gave courts an alternative basis for reaching a conclusion already available to them under *Gates.* But this assumption is hardly beyond challenge.[127] For one thing, the new rule adopted in *Leon* is broader than *Gates* in the sense of applying to issues other than probable cause. Thus, for example, the decision in the companion *Sheppard* case quite obviously could not have been reached on the basis of *Gates,* for *Sheppard* had to do with a particularity-of-description problem. Secondly, at least

---

confidential informant where affidavit included affiant's statement informant's knowledge consistent with what officer knew about defendant's drug-smuggling activities from two independent sources, and that affiant had seized marijuana and marijuana packaging from defendant's garage); Marshall v. State, 415 Md. 399, 2 A.3d 360 (2010) ("affidavit was not 'bare bones,' nor was it composed of wholly conclusory statements"); with United States v. Leake, 998 F.2d 1359 (6th Cir.1993) (no good faith even though affidavit not of "bare bones" variety, as follow-up investigation after anonymous tip, despite absence of any "time exigencies," was limited to a 2-hour surveillance of premises revealing nothing); Figert v. State, 686 N.E.2d 827 (Ind.1997) (no good faith where "warrant here was issued based solely on the officer's opinion" rather than on facts gathered by investigation); Crum v. Commonwealth, 223 S.W.3d 109 (Ky.2007) (no good faith here, as "the officer's reason for believing the informant to be reliable is not stated," and purported corroboration is "information" but "without stating the nature of the information").

[126]Especially significant in this respect is the case in which a federal circuit court, rather than resolve an issue about the legality of the search warrant unsettled in that circuit, applies the *Leon* rule because the warrant would pass muster under decisions in several other circuits. See, e.g., United States v. Nolan, 199 F.3d 1180 (10th Cir.1999).

[127]See, e.g., People v. Leftwich, 869 P.2d 1260 (Colo.1994) ("in the vast majority of cases, if a court applies *Gates* and ascertains that a substantial basis for determining probable cause did not exist, the court will reach the conclusion that the officer unnecessarily relied on the affidavit").

some members of the *Leon* majority[128] appeared to view the decision in that case as merely a convenient stepping-stone to a broader good-faith test applicable even in without-warrant cases. Because the *Gates* watering down of probable cause may not be fully applicable in such cases,[129] *Leon* could thus be seen as ultimately serving a purpose even if it produced no different immediate results in with-warrant probable cause disputes.

Nonetheless, it seems that *Leon* sometimes benefits the prosecution more than *Gates* even as to with-warrant cases involving a probable cause challenge. That is, the effect of *Leon* is that courts will from time to time declare evidence admissible because of the good faith of the police, despite the fact that these same courts in identical circumstances would feel compelled to suppress if only the *Gates* doctrine was available.[130] This effect would appear to be an almost inevitable consequence of the difference in the focus called for under *Gates* and *Leon*, respectively.

The Court in *Gates* abandoned the *Aguilar-Spinelli* test in favor of a totality-of-the-circumstances probable cause approach because the latter was deemed "more consistent with our traditional deference to the probable cause determination of magistrates." *Gates,* in other words, has to do with an approach or attitude that is to govern when the warrant-issuing magistrate's decision is later challenged before a trial or appellate court. That court still must pass upon the *magistrate's* earlier decision, but in doing so is to give considerable leeway to the magistrate's decision that there was probable cause in all "doubtful or marginal cases."[131] The underlying notion is that there does not exist (and never will exist) a "bright line" marking the exact boundaries of probable cause, so that a warrant should be upheld when the initial judgment of the magistrate could conceivably

---

[128]Most certainly Justice White. See note 9 supra.

[129]But see the discussion of *Gates* in § 3.1(c).

[130]Sometimes it will be unclear whether this is happening, as where a court moves directly to the *Leon* rationale without testing the affidavit under *Gates*. United States v. Owens, 167 F.3d 739 (1st Cir.1999); United States v. Weeks, 160 F.3d 1210 (8th Cir.1998); United States v. Cisneros, 112 F.3d 1272 (5th Cir.1997); McDonald v. State, 347 Md. 452, 701 A.2d 675 (1997). This is most apparent where the court specifically states that the "substantial basis" test under *Gates* is not equally applicable in a *Leon* case. See, e.g., United States v. Laughton, 409 F.3d 744 (6th Cir.2005); United States v. Bynum, 293 F.3d 192 (4th Cir.2002); United States v. Danhauer, 229 F.3d 1002 (10th Cir. 2000); State v. Hoeck, 284 Kan. 441, 163 P.3d 252 (2007); Patterson v. State, 401 Md. 76, 930 A.2d 348 (2007).

Unique in this respect is United States v. Chaar, 137 F.3d 359 (6th Cir. 1998), where the court found it would be very difficult to pursue a straightforward probable cause analysis because the magistrate failed to record a telephonic search warrant request, so that "the only source of evidence we have is an affidavit written nineteen months after the fact." A strong dissent argued that such "facts simply do not provide the reviewing courts with sufficient evidence to apply *Leon*."

[131]United States v. Ventresca, 380 U.S. 102, 85 S.Ct. 741, 13 L.Ed.2d 684 (1965).

have gone either way.

By contrast, as we have seen, under *Leon* the focus is not at all upon the magistrate's decision but instead only upon the police decision to seek and then execute a certain warrant.[132] Because of the Court's conclusion that the exclusionary rule is an inappropriate device for deterring magistrates, the magistrate's decision is not examined even for the limited purpose of determining whether it was made in good faith.[133] Rather, *Leon* instructs that only the good faith of the police is at issue and that such good faith is a usual concomitant of opting for the warrant process because, as the Court put it, "an officer cannot be expected to question the magistrate's probable-cause determination." That is, it is rather easy to read *Leon* as supporting the proposition that the police, having turned the probable cause decision over to another person (the neutral and detached magistrate who by longstanding Fourth Amendment doctrine is viewed as the preferred decisionmaker on the probable cause issue), are generally entitled to presume that the magistrate[134] knows what he is

---

[132]This means that circumstances in which an officer might have good faith are not limited to when "the affidavit presents enough evidence to create disagreement among reasonable jurists as to the existence of probable cause." United States v. Taxacher, 902 F.2d 867 (11th Cir.1990) (noting, however, that this test is used by some courts in applying *Leon*). See also State v. Edmonson, 257 Neb. 468, 598 N.W.2d 450 (1999) (following *Taxacher*, rather than earlier state decision to the contrary, and then concluding reasonable officer could not be expected to know that post-issuance affidavit submitted to judge could not cure defect in original affidavit).

[133]Except perhaps in extreme circumstances. In State v. Hess, 327 Wis.2d 524, 785 N.W.2d 568 (2010), the court concluded it could not "reasonably attribute fault to the law enforcement officer who executed the warrant," yet declined to apply *Leon* where "the civil arrest warrant issued by a circuit judge was void *ab initio* because (a) it did not comply with any statute authorizing the court to issue a warrant; and (b) it was not supported by an oath or affirmation," as such action was "necessary to preserve the integrity of the judicial process." As for *Leon*, the court stated: "The

Court's statement in *Leon* that judicial integrity is not implicated when police rely in good faith on a warrant, 'absent unusual circumstances,' preserves judicial integrity as a secondary consideration when applying the exclusionary rule."

[134]Or, sometimes, the magistrate and prosecutor. See, e.g., United States v. Patten, 664 F.3d 247 (8th Cir.2011) (stressing officer "consulted with the assistant county attorney in drawing up the application"); United States v. Tracey, 597 F.3d 140 (3d Cir.2010) ("reasonable officer would also have confidence in the validity of the warrant after presenting it and having it approved by a district attorney"); United States v. Pappas, 592 F.3d 799 (7th Cir.2010) (stressing that prior to seeking warrant, federal agent "consulted with an Assistant United States Attorney"); United States v. Otero, 563 F.3d 1127 (10th Cir.2009) (stressing that officer "sought the assistance of the Assistant United States Attorney, who ensured him that [the affidavit] satisfied legal requirements"); United States v. Capozzi, 347 F.3d 327 (1st Cir.2003) (stressing officer also "sought a legal opinion" from an assistant district attorney re existence of probable cause); United States v. Mendonsa, 989 F.2d 366 (9th Cir.1993)

doing.[135]

Thus, notwithstanding some language in *Gates* arguably inconsistent with such a conclusion,[136] at least some courts in the post-*Leon* era are understandably attracted to the view that the occasions when a policeman will be reasonably ignorant of the magistrate's mistaken probable cause determination will occur much more frequently than those in which the magistrate himself should have known he had passed beyond the "doubtful or marginal" case contemplated by *Gates*. In other words, the degree of police deference to the magistrate that is perceived by courts as reasonable under *Leon* exceeds significantly[137] the "great deference" owed the magistrate by reviewing courts under *Gates*.[138]

It is important to note, however, that the Supreme Court may

(stressing that officer "sought advice from county attorneys concerning the substantive completeness of the affidavit before he submitted it to the magistrate" and was told "that the affidavit seemed complete"); State v. Eason, 245 Wis.2d 206, 629 N.W.2d 625 (2001) (under state version of good faith exception, state must "also show that the process used in obtaining the search warrant included a significant investigation and review by either a police officer trained and knowledgeable in the requirements of probable cause and reasonable suspicion, or a knowledgeable government attorney").

Consider also Messerschmidt v. Millender, __ U.S. __, 132 S.Ct. 1235, 182 L.Ed.2d 47 (2012), where the Court, in a § 1983 context, stated that "the fact that the officers sought and obtained approval of the warrant application from a superior and a deputy district attorney before submitting it to the magistrate provides further support for the conclusion that an officer could reasonably have believed that the scope of the warrant was supported by probable cause."

[135]See United States v. Gibson, 928 F.2d 250 (8th Cir.1991) (no probable cause under *Gates*, as here information from anonymous informant and corroboration only of "several innocent details," but good faith under *Leon*, as "ordinarily, a police officer cannot be expected to question a judge's probable cause determination"); United States v. Gant, 759 F.2d 484 (5th Cir.1985) (rejecting the district court's finding of no good faith

because the district court erroneously asked what the magistrate should have concluded, while actually the test "is whether it was entirely unreasonable for these officers to accept the magistrate's belief that, based on this affidavit, cocaine was probably located in Gant's house").

[136]Though the cases expressing a preference for warrants have typically assumed that a magistrate is generally in a better position than a policeman to make the probable cause decision correctly, in *Gates* the Court justified its action in part by asserting that "search and arrest warrants long have been issued by persons who are neither lawyers nor judges, and who certainly do not remain abreast of each judicial refinement of the nature of 'probable cause.'"

[137]As one federal judge has noted: "By ignoring the question of whether the police would have had probable cause on the facts of *Leon* under the new totality test of *Gates,* the Court failed to give lower courts any guidance about the margin between the *Gates* standard of reasonableness and the *Leon* standard of reasonableness." Wald, The Unreasonable Reasonableness Test for Fourth Amendment Searches, 4 Crim.J. Ethics 2 (Spring 1985).

[138]The temptation will be to uphold as objectively reasonable even that deference occurring when the officer's affidavit, albeit not of the bare bones variety, is fatally defective in a very substantial way as to some critical aspect of probable cause. Consider in

have signalled a retreat of sorts from the more expansive reading

this regard People v. Deitchman, 695 P.2d 1146 (Colo.1985), where a search warrant issued for 3300 West Ohio Avenue, but by oversight the affiant failed to include in the affidavit *any information whatsoever* indicating or even suggesting that the suspect resided there, as he in fact did, and the affidavit gave a totally different address for the suspect of 1755 South Pecos Street. Three members of the court voted to affirm on a harmless error theory, but one of them went on to address the good faith issue under *Leon,* concluding that the instant case did not fall within *Leon*: "Uncommunicated knowledge of facts never brought to the attention of the judge issuing the warrant neither mitigates the facial deficiency of the affidavit nor provides any discernible indicia that might arguably support an objectively reasonable reliance on the validity of the warrant." However, one other member of the court concluded the instant case came within *Leon* because the affiant mistakenly but "clearly believed that he had provided the magistrate with all the information he himself had collected," while two others thought the instant case was like *Leon* 's companion case, *Sheppard,* in that "the error asserted in both cases involved a 'facial' defect that a reasonably prudent police officer could not be expected to detect."

See also United States v. Loy, 191 F.3d 360 (3d Cir.1999) (notwithstanding probable cause defect in anticipatory search warrant re whether package to be delivered to post office box would be taken by defendant to his home, officers had good faith, as warrant execution was not allowed or made until package in fact taken there by defendant); United States v. Rowland, 145 F.3d 1194 (10th Cir.1998) (*Leon* applicable, as this case "closely analogous" to *Sheppard,* as affiant submitted sufficient description to make it clear that search warrant was to cover abandoned truck parked on the premises, and it was issuing judge who put the truck outside the warrant by using the general

qualifier "occupied by Robert R. Vance" in describing the area to be searched); United States v. Procopio, 88 F.3d 21 (1st Cir.1996) (where new search warrant obtained when street number in first found to be in error, but affidavit for second warrant merely asserted it was defendant's address, *Leon* applies to failure to explain how agent knew, as "it is easy to understand how both the officer applying for the warrant and the magistrate might overlook a lack of detail on a point often established by the telephone book or the name on a mailbox"); People v. Gall, 30 P.3d 145 (Colo.2001) (although affidavit silent as to source of information that identified apartment as belonging to defendant, and this "arguably failed to provide a substantial basis for the issuing magistrate's action," *Leon* applicable, as "a number of courts have found it easy to understand how an officer, and even an issuing magistrate, might overlook a lack of detail on a point that is so common or public that it can often be established by the telephone book or the name on a mailbox"); State v. Varnado, 675 So.2d 268 (La.1996) (where defendant, arrested at girl friend's home because he had been identified as perpetrator of a series of rapes and robberies, stated where he lived and police went there and confirmed that was defendant's residence and even obtained defendant's father's permission to search there but, as an added precaution, obtained a search warrant, case falls within *Leon* notwithstanding fact affidavit and warrant failed to mention that address listed was defendant's residence, where probable cause of items being there required that connection, as affiant was executing officer and any officer in his position "either would not have noticed the defect or would not have failed to correct it immediately if the magistrate had brought the error to his attention").

Compare United States v. Nielson, 415 F.3d 1195 (10th Cir.2005) (no good faith here as to reliance on no-knock warrant based only on showing of presence of gun and no evidence

of *Leon* just discussed. To talk of *Leon* in terms of deference to the magistrate by the police is to suggest that in judging the good faith of the police it is inevitably necessary to take into account the fact that a magistrate, to the knowledge of the police, acted favorably on their warrant request by finding there was probable cause and issuing a warrant. Resort to such a hindsight type of assessment is certainly suggested by much of the language in *Leon,* particularly the majority's assertion that the question to be resolved is "whether a reasonably well-trained officer would have known that the search was illegal despite the magistrate's authorization." But, as noted earlier, *Leon* also requires "objective reasonableness * * * of the officers who originally obtained [the warrant] or who provided information material to the probable-cause determination." As to them, the Court now seems

---

at all re "potential for violence," as in such instance issuing judge's decision was not "borderline," but rather, as suppression judge concluded, was not "a close call"); United States v. Gonzales, 399 F.3d 1225 (10th Cir.2005) (good faith lacking, as there were "no facts" in the affidavit "explaining how the address was linked to Mr. Gonzales, the vehicles, or the suspected criminal activity"); United States v. Zimmerman, 277 F.3d 426 (3d Cir.2002) (no good faith here, as probable cause as to presence of pornography was acutely stale, based on single video clip located on defendant's computer at least 6 months ago, and thus no "colorable showing" of probable cause); United States v. Hove, 848 F.2d 137 (9th Cir.1988) (where information providing nexus to place to be searched was known to police but not included in affidavit, it "was so deficient that any official belief in the existence of probable cause must be considered unreasonable," as "the affidavit offers no hint as to why the police wanted to search this residence," and "facts known only to an officer and not presented to a magistrate" cannot be taken into account under *Leon*);Nelms v. State, 568 So.2d 384 (Ala.Crim.App.1990) (following *Hove*, court concludes *Leon* "good faith" rule not applicable where search warrant affidavit totally lacking any indication of time when informant saw drugs; fact affiant knew the time but did not convey it irrelevant); People v. Miller, 75 P.3d 1108 (Colo.2003) (in "vast majority of cases where a substantial basis does not exist, the police cannot rely on the good faith exception"; such the case here, where affidavit "bereft of current information about illegal activity at Miller's house," and other information known by police may not be considered, as court applying good faith test is "restricted to the information contained within the four corners of the affidavit"); State v. Jamison, 482 N.W.2d 409 (Iowa 1992) (no good faith where "the quantum of evidence offered in the search warrant application to show a nexus between criminal activity or evidence of crime and defendant's automobile or person was zero"); State v. Probst, 247 Kan. 196, 795 P.2d 393 (1990) (*Leon* not applicable here, given extent to which probable cause lacking re defendant's home, in that affidavit merely said defendant's employer at used car lot took drugs from a car parked on street near defendant's residence); State v. Sprunger, 283 Neb. 531, 811 N.W.2d 235 (2012) (no good faith here, re purported probable cause defendant's computer contained child porn, as the police "knew-or certainly should have known-that the only fact showing any connection to child pornography was of their own making"); State v. Lewis, 527 N.W.2d 658 (N.D.1995) (no good faith where probable cause defendant growing something inside his dwelling, as other information about upcoming harvest from a marijuana grow room operation not connected at all to defendant).

to have concluded in *Malley v. Briggs,*[139] this question of reasonableness is to be judged as of the time of warrant application and thus without consideration of the fact that the magistrate thereafter[140] acted favorably upon the affidavit presented.[141]

Malley arose not in an exclusionary rule context but rather out of a section 1983 damages action brought against a state trooper alleging the officer violated the plaintiffs' Fourth Amendment rights in applying for arrest warrants thereafter issued and executed. The trooper claimed that the qualified immunity available to him in such a case meant that "he is entitled to rely on the judgment of a judicial officer in finding that probable cause exists and hence issuing the warrant." The Court responded that this was not so because the question was "whether a reasonably well-trained officer in petitioner's position would have known that his affidavit failed to establish probable cause and that he should not have applied for the warrant." That is, "if no officer of reasonable competence would have requested the warrant, i.e., his request is outside the range of professional competence expected of an officer,"[142] then that officer can hardly rely upon the fact the magistrate issued the requested warrant. As the

---

[139]Malley v. Briggs, 475 U.S. 335, 106 S.Ct. 1092, 89 L.Ed.2d 271 (1986).

[140]Events *prior* to the application, such as rejection by another magistrate, expressly listed as a consideration in fn. 23 of *Leon,* or review by a prosecutor or similar legal advisor, United States v. Brown, 951 F.2d 999 (9th Cir.1991); Ortiz v. Van Auken, 887 F.2d 1366 (9th Cir.1989); United States v. Luk, 859 F.2d 667 (9th Cir. 1988); United States v. Freitas, 856 F.2d 1425 (9th Cir.1988), are of course most relevant.

[141]People v. Camarella, 54 Cal.3d 592, 286 Cal.Rptr. 780, 818 P.2d 63 (1991) ("in determining whether a case is within the third *Leon* situation, the fact that the warrant issued is of no significance").

Some pre-*Malley* commentators, not sharing my degree of pessimism, had already interpreted *Leon* in this way. See, e.g., Bradley, The "Good Faith Exception" Cases: Reasonable Exercises in Futility, 60 Ind.L.J. 287, 297 (1985), asserting "a critical point about *Leon*. That is, when the Court speaks of the good faith of the police, it is talking about their good faith *before going* to the magistrate and not about their good faith *after* they have

received the warrant. * * * If [the latter] were the test, even the most patently defective warrant would escape exclusionary censure. Given the pains that the Court took in *Leon* to insure that truly bad warrants may still be subject to attack, it would make no sense to allow the fact of the issuance of the warrant to paper over reservations that the police had, or should have had, as to its validity."

[142]In making this judgment, one court has concluded, a relevant factor "is the time pressure under which the Officer was operating when he prepared the warrant application." United States v. Weber, 923 F.2d 1338 (9th Cir.1990) (because this a controlled delivery warrant re a package in official custody, no need for "hurried judgment" Court spoke of in *Leon*). See also United States v. Luong, 470 F.3d 898 (9th Cir.2006) (no good faith here, as "the facts here do not favor application of an exception based on exigency"); United States v. Gourde, 382 F.3d 1003 (9th Cir.2004), on rehearing en banc, 440 F.3d 1065 (9th Cir.2006), (no good faith, as "the officers felt little or no time pressure," and in fact waited 4 months to apply for warrant, "ample opportunity" for them to have taken further steps to try to connect

Court put it in *Malley,* in such circumstances the officer "cannot excuse his own default by pointing to the greater incompetence of the magistrate." This holding would seem equally applicable in an exclusionary rule setting,[143] for the *Malley* Court expressly declared that it was following "the same standard of objective reasonableness that we applied in the context of a suppression hearing in *Leon.*"[144] *Malley* thus lends considerable support to those lower courts that have refused to accept the notion that an officer, by providing an affidavit significantly above the "bare bones" level but yet with substantial gaps, may reasonably assume the warrant was valid because the defects got by the magistrate.[145] As one court aptly put it, the mere fact the officer-affiant "added fat to the affidavit, but certainly no muscle," is not

---

defendant with child pornography); United States v. Ramos, 923 F.2d 1346 (9th Cir.1991) (*Leon* good faith requirement met here; *Weber* distinguished, as here the officers "generated a nine-page affidavit and executed the warrant in a matter of hours").

[143]As courts have assumed. See, e.g., United States v. Vigeant, 176 F.3d 565 (1st Cir.1999); Minor v. State, 334 Md. 707, 641 A.2d 214 (1994).

[144]Thus, the question in an exclusionary rule setting is whether at the time of application for the warrant "a well-trained officer reasonably could have believed that the affidavit presented a close or debatable question on the issue of probable cause." People v. Camarella, 54 Cal.3d 592, 286 Cal.Rptr. 780, 818 P.2d 63 (1991).

[145]United States v. Ricciardelli, 998 F.2d 8 (1st Cir.1993) (no good faith as to probable cause lack re anticipatory warrant, in sense that precondition for search not precise enough to ensure contraband would be at place to be searched at time of search, as shortcomings attributable to "the inspectors' omissions in the warrant-application process"); United States v. Jackson, 818 F.2d 345 (5th Cir.1987) (described in note 124 supra); Herrington v. State, 287 Ark. 228, 697 S.W.2d 899 (1985) (affidavit details informant's information, but nothing said on time of events); State v. Thompson, 369 N.W.2d 363 (N.D.1985) (though affidavit detailed what informant said and what officer corroborated, yet "the affidavit in the instant case does not supply anything more than a most tenuous and conclusory suggestion that the Thompsons were involved in criminal activity"). State v. Huft, 106 Wash.2d 206, 720 P.2d 838 (1986) (no indication of informant's track record or basis of knowledge, but limited corroborating information; court nonetheless characterized this as "no more than a 'bare bones' affidavit"). Compare People v. Camarella, 54 Cal.3d 592, 286 Cal.Rptr. 780, 818 P.2d 63 (1991) (court agrees with this position, but concludes instant case different because officer had "obtained substantial corroborating information that, although stale, was sufficient to make the probable cause determination a close question").

See also United States v. Baker, 894 F.2d 1144 (10th Cir.1990) (even assuming *Leon* applicable to warrant issued by court without jurisdiction, no good faith here; government's argument that officer passed on facts putting jurisdiction in question to magistrate and thus properly relied on him rejected; court, citing *Malley,* says that while "the Supreme Court has made it clear that, while more expertise in this regard may be expected of a judicial official, where, as we have already held here, a reasonably well-trained law enforcement officer should himself have been aware that a proposed search would be illegal, a judicial official's concurrence in the improper activity does not serve to bring it within the rule of *Leon* and *Sheppard*").

a basis for finding he acted in good faith.[146] But even after *Malley,*
some courts feel that if an officer takes a " 'close call' to a neutral
and detached judge for review" and the record clearly discloses a
most careful process of review, then the "judge's probable cause
finding is not only a relevant factor, but a significant one as well,
in the good-faith equation."[147] And some apparently deem *Malley*
to be inapplicable in a suppression context where the executing
officer is not the affiant, as they examine good faith *solely* from
the standpoint of the executing officer and not with respect to the
affiant.[148]

But whether or not *Malley* applies in an exclusionary rule
context, there is one situation in which it is quite clear—and, unquestionably, quite appropriate—that the officer's good faith
should prevail even though the warrant is definitely invalid:
where the invalidity is grounded in a court decision handed down
after the warrant was issued. As discussed elsewhere herein,[149] it
is no longer the case that Fourth Amendment rulings are prospective only. But as for with-warrant cases, situations covered

---

[146]United States v. Weber, 923
F.2d 1338 (9th Cir.1990) (where details in the affidavit were "foundation-
less expert testimony," no good faith).

[147]United States v. Corral-Corral,
899 F.2d 927 (10th Cir.1990) (stressing that the officer "was questioned by
an experienced state judge, and that
certain changes were made to the affidavit as a result of that questioning,"
and that "the affiant spent over one
hour with the state judge reviewing
the sufficiency of the warrant").

[148]United States v. Dickerson, 975
F.2d 1245 (7th Cir.1992) (court, without any mention of *Malley,* concludes
it sufficient executing officers acted in
good faith in that they aware of information constituting probable cause
and "did not know that all this information had not been passed on to the
judge who issued the warrant; they did
not see the probable cause affidavit").

Whatever one thinks of *Dickerson,* it would seem that with respect
to the *affiant's* good faith only that information supplied by the affiant to
the judge may be taken into account,
as some courts have held, e.g., United
States v. Hython, 443 F.3d 480 (6th
Cir.2006); United States v. Koerth,
312 F.3d 862 (7th Cir.2002); United
States v. Laughton, 409 F.3d 744 (6th
Cir.2005), discussed in Note, 74 U.Cin.
L.Rev. 1525 (2006); United States v.

Hove, 848 F.2d 137 (9th Cir.1988). But
consider the unique circumstances in
United States v. Hallam, 407 F.3d 942
(8th Cir.2005), considering facts
known by the officer and reported to
the prosecutor who prepared the written affidavit for the officer.

Other cases are collected in
Taylor, Using Suppression Hearing
Testimony to Prove Good Faith Under
United States v. Leon, 54 U.Kan.L.
Rev. 155, 156, (2005), where it is noted
that "[m]ost courts that have explicitly
addressed this question have adopted
bright-line rules, holding either that
information known to the officer but
not communicated to the magistrate
can always be used to establish good
faith or that it never can," and then is
concluded "that an intermediate approach is more faithful to *Leon* and to
the policies that underlie the Fourth
Amendment's warrant requirement,"
namely that "information known to
the affiant officer but never presented
to the magistrate can establish the officer's good faith only where the omission resulted from a reasonable mistake in preparing the warrant
application and the officer's knowledge
of the information at the time of the
warrant application is proven by clear
and convincing evidence").

[149]See § 11.5.

by the earlier nonretroactivity doctrine (and others as well, i.e., where under the prior view the ruling was not sufficiently "new" to be nonretroactive) can now be dealt with in *Leon* terms. Illustrative is *United States v. Skinner*,[150] involving a warrant issued upon information from an informant plus certain corroborating facts, where the trial judge first held the warrant was valid but then upon reconsideration held otherwise, relying on the post-warrant case of *Alabama v. White*[151] for the proposition that anonymous tipsters must accurately predict future behavior that is not generally observable by members of the public. However, the trial judge then applied *Leon* and found good faith sufficient to bar suppression of the evidence. In affirming that decision, the court of appeals agreed with the trial judge's

> conclusion, which was central to his ultimate finding that the officers in the present case acted in good faith, that until *Alabama v. White* was decided, the question of precisely what was required in the way of corroboration of an anonymous tipster's factual assertions was unsettled.[152]

A broader rule, not limited to with-warrant cases, but requiring that the officer in question acted "in objectively reasonable reli-

---

[150]United States v. Skinner, 972 F.2d 171 (7th Cir.1992).

[151]Alabama v. White, 496 U.S. 325, 110 S.Ct. 2412, 110 L.Ed.2d 301 (1990).

[152]See also United States v. Syphers, 426 F.3d 461 (1st Cir.2005) (where 2001 affidavit for child pornography did not include copies or descriptions of the alleged pornographic images so as to show that images depicted actual rather than virtual children or young-looking adults, as required by 2002 Supreme Court decision, officer acted in good faith); United States v. Real Property at 15324 County Highway E, 332 F.3d 1070 (7th Cir.2003) (under *Leon,* "evidence seized by law enforcement agents acting in objectively reasonable reliance upon a validly issued search warrant that, through no misconduct on the part of the agents, rests on a constitutionally flawed probable cause finding owing to a subsequent change in controlling judicial precedent," here, the Supreme Court's *Kyllo* decision re thermal imaging, "is not subject to the exclusionary rule"); United States v. Tuter, 240 F.3d 1292 (10th Cir.2001) (stressing that at time of search neither Supreme Court case nor circuit case most or point had been issued); United States v. Adames, 56 F.3d 737

(7th Cir.1995) (*Leon* applied where Supreme Court decision making warrant invalid "was not decided until more than a year later" and theretofore "most courts" had taken contrary position); People v. Carlson, 185 Ill.2d 546, 236 Ill.Dec. 786, 708 N.E.2d 372 (1999) (good faith, as court decision holding anticipatory search warrants not permitted, based on statute theretofore subject to "evenly plausible but divergent interpretations," came after execution of warrant); State v. Nuss, 279 Neb. 648, 781 N.W.2d 60 (2010) (court holds for first time in this case that general reference in affidavit to "child pornography" not sufficient, unlike decisions re federal statute, as state law different in not using that term; good faith rule applies here, as "we cannot expect that a state trooper executing an affidavit in 2007 would have anticipated this distinction"); State v. Van Beek, 591 N.W.2d 112 (N.D.1999) (good faith here, as Supreme Court and state court decision that probable cause for drug warrant not alone a basis for no-knock authorization came after warrant executed).

Compare State v. Ward, 231 Wis.2d 723, 604 N.W.2d 517 (2000), text at note 190 infra, instead relying by analogy on the *Krull* doctrine.

ance on binding appellate precedent" later overruled, was adopted by the Supreme Court in *Davis v. United States*.[153]

§ 1.3(g) "Good faith" in without warrant cases

Although the holding in both *Sheppard* and *Leon* is limited to with-warrant cases,[154] the possibility that these decisions will serve as stepping stones to a more comprehensive good faith exception to the Fourth Amendment exclusionary rule cannot be discounted. Certainly the author of those two decisions, Justice White, was prepared to go farther, as he clearly indicated prior to[155] and contemporaneously with[156] the rulings in those two cases, and some current members of the Court may be equally prepared to take such a step. If they are, much of the reasoning in *Leon* will offer support for such an extension of that case beyond the with-warrant situation. Particularly noteworthy is the *Leon* majority's broad assertion that whenever the police officer's conduct was objectively reasonable the deterrence function of the exclusionary rule is not served and that "when law enforcement officers have acted in objective good faith or their transgressions have been minor, the magnitude of the benefit conferred on such guilty defendants offends basic concepts of the criminal justice system." Consequently, there is cause for the pessimism expressed by Justice Brennan:

> I am not at all confident that the exception unleashed today will remain so confined. Indeed, the full impact of the Court's regretta-ble decision will not be felt until the Court attempts to extend this rule to situations in which the police have conducted a warrantless search solely on the basis of their own judgment about the exis-

---

[153]Davis v. United States, __ U.S. __, 131 S.Ct. 2419, 180 L.Ed.2d 285(2011), discussed infra at note 199.

[Section 1.3(g)]

[154]United States v. Cos, 498 F.3d 1115 (10th Cir.2007) (good faith reliance on consent given by guest lacking actual or apparent authority not covered by *Leon*); United States v. Herrera, 444 F.3d 1238 (10th Cir.2006) (*Leon*, even as expanded by *Evans*, not applicable here, where it was "state trooper's own factual mistakes" that led to unjustified warrantless administrative inspection); United States v. Scales, 903 F.2d 765 (10th Cir.1990) (*Leon* not applicable where police "were not acting in reliance on a search warrant"); United States v. Curzi, 867 F.2d 36 (1st Cir.1989) (where illegal warrantless search, "the good-faith exception is not available"); United States v. Winsor, 846 F.2d 1569 (9th Cir.1988) ("We decline to

extend *Leon*'s good faith exception to searches not conducted in reliance on a warrant"); King v. Commonwealth, 302 S.W.3d 649 (Ky.2010), rev'd on other grounds, Kentucky v. King, __, U.S. __, 131 S.Ct. 1849, 179 L.Ed.2d 865 (2011) (*Leon* not applicable to this "warrantless entry"); Tomlin v. State, 869 P.2d 334 (Okl.Crim.App.1994) (*Leon* makes no exception "to the rule excluding illegally-obtained evidence for warrantless misdemeanor arrests").

However, the Fifth Circuit has persisted in its pre-*Leon* view that the good faith exception also applies in without warrant cases. United States v. De Leon-Reyna, 930 F.2d 396 (5th Cir.1991).

[155]See, e.g., his concurring opinion in Illinois v. Gates, 462 U.S. 213, 103 S.Ct. 2317, 76 L.Ed.2d 527 (1983).

[156]See note 9 supra.

tence of probable cause and exigent circumstances. When that question is finally posed, I for one will not be surprised if my colleagues decide once again that we simply cannot afford to protect Fourth Amendment rights.

In one sense, what Justice Brennan feared would happen has come to pass. The Supreme Court has now applied *Leon*-type reasoning to instances in which there was police reliance on legislative and clerical action or inaction, and as a consequence has held admissible on "good faith" grounds evidence obtained in warrantless police activity. Thus in *Illinois v. Krull*,[157] involving a warrantless search of an auto junkyard pursuant to an administrative inspection statute later held unconstitutional, the Court held that "a good-faith exception to the Fourth Amendment exclusionary rule applies when an officer's reliance on the constitutionality of a statute is objectively reasonable." And then, in *Arizona v. Evans*,[158] where police made what was in fact an illegal warrantless arrest and incidental search in reliance on a computer record of an outstanding arrest warrant, a record that was in error because of a court clerk's failure to advise law enforcement authorities the warrant had been quashed, the Court held "the reasoning of *Leon*" made the exclusionary rule inapplicable on such facts.[159] (Later, in *Herring v. United States*,[160] the Court in effect superseded *Evans* via a broader and different holding not grounded in the employment status of the person responsible for the error.[161]) These rather special situations are assayed elsewhere herein, and thus will not be considered further at this juncture. Rather, the present concern is with whether good faith claims should be more generally allowed when police have acted without a warrant.

Such a broader good faith exception is neither a desirable nor a necessary step beyond *Leon* and *Sheppard*.[162] The reasoning that was critical to the decisions in those two cases—especially that in

---

[157]Illinois v. Krull, 480 U.S. 340, 107 S.Ct. 1160, 94 L.Ed.2d 364 (1987), discussed in § 1.3(h).

[158]Arizona v. Evans, 514 U.S. 1, 115 S.Ct. 1185, 131 L.Ed.2d 34 (1995), discussed in § 1.8(e).

[159]Lower courts, in the main, viewed *Evans* as applicable only when such errors were by a person not in the employ of a police agency. See, e.g., United States v. Shareef, 100 F.3d 1491 (10th Cir.1996); Hoay v. State, 348 Ark. 80, 71 S.W.3d 573 (2002); People v. Willis, 28 Cal.4th 22, 120 Cal.Rptr.2d 105, 46 P.3d 898 (2002); State v. White, 660 So.2d 664 (Fla. 1995); State v. Allen, 269 Neb. 69, 690 N.W.2d 582 (2005).

[160]Herring v. United States, 555 U.S. 135, 129 S.Ct. 695, 172 L.Ed.2d 496 (2009), discussed in § 1.6(i).

[161]In *Herring*, involving an error by a police clerk, the Court held that suppression in the interest of deterrence was unnecessary whenever "the error was the result of isolated negligence attenuated from the arrest."

[162]See Bradley, The "Good Faith Exception" Cases: Reasonable Exercise in Futility, 60 Ind.L.J. 287, 298–99 (1985); Dripps, Living With Leon, 95 Yale L.J. 906, 944–47 (1986); Fleissner, Glide Path to an "Inclusionary Rule": How Expansion of the Good Faith Exception Threatens to Fundamentally Change the Exclusion-

with-warrant cases there is no need to deter the magistrate and usually no need to discourage the executing officer from relying upon the magistrate's judgment and actions—does not carry over to the without warrant situation.[163] Moreover, to extend *Leon* and *Sheppard* to such situations would deprive those decisions of their one clear incidental benefit: if good faith suffices only when the police had a warrant, then the exception would "give law enforcement officers some solid encouragement to employ the warrant process for all searches and arrests which are not made on an emergency basis."[164]

Extension of the good faith exception beyond warrant cases would also impose upon suppression judges the heavy burden— indeed, the intolerable burden—of frequently making exceedingly difficult decisions about what constitutes (as it was put in *Leon*) "an objectively reasonable belief in the existence of probable cause." *Leon* takes the view that the "objectively reasonable belief" requirement is a purely objective one, so that there is no need for a court to engage in the particularly difficult speculation of what was actually going on in the mind of the searching or arresting officer. Rather, the inquiry is limited to what "a reasonably well-trained officer would have known," and certainly the same limitation ought to obtain if *Leon* were extended to without warrant cases. Even with this limitation, however, it is exceedingly difficult to ascertain which mistaken judgments about Fourth Amendment probable cause and exigent circumstances are reasonable for a reasonably trained officer to make. Once again, the essential point is that it is extremely "hard to

---

ary Rule, 48 Mercer L.Rev. 1023 (1997); Greenhalgh, The Warrantless Good Faith Exception: Unprecedented, Indefensible, and Devoid of Necessity, 26 So.Tex.L.J. 129 (1985); Misner, Limiting Leon: A Mistake of Law Analogy, 77 J.Crim.L. & C. 507, 508 (1986); Note, 40 Baylor L.Rev. 151 (1988).

For a contrary view, see Oliver, Toward a Better Categorical Balance of the Costs and Benefits of the Exclusionary Rule, 9 Buff.Crim.L.Rev. 201 (2005); Note, 38 B.C.L.Rev. 205 (1996).

[163]United States v. Clarkson, 551 F.3d 1196 (10th Cir.2009) (rejecting lower court's recognition of good-faith exception with regard to one officer's reliance on another officer's erroneous representation that narcotics dog was qualified, court says: "Were the good faith exception to apply in this circum-

stance, the improper police conduct of conducting a search with an untrained or unreliable dog would not be effectively deterred").

[164]P. Johnson, New Approaches to Enforcing the Fourth Amendment 10 (Working Paper, Sept. 1978). See also Bradley, 60 Ind.L.J. 287, 292 (1985), asserting that "since these opinions will probably increase warrant use by the police, they will enhance the most important aspect of the warrant: that is, that it forces the police to stop, think, write down their evidence, and submit it to someone else for approval. Aside from the obvious salutary effect that those requirements have in curbing police impetuosity, they also make it more difficult for the police to fabricate probable cause on the basis of what was found instead of what was actually known in advance."

determine what constitutes a reasonable mistake of law,"[165] requiring as it does "objective extrapolations of existing law" and inquiry into "the inferences from existing law" that various persons "should have drawn."[166]

A natural and likely consequence of making the suppression decision even in the more numerous without-warrant cases ride upon such an amorphous standard, involving exceedingly complex and largely unresolvable issues, is a distinct anti-Fourth Amendment bias in suppression rulings. As with the open-ended and unstructured concept of reasonableness entertained by the Supreme Court in an earlier day, an across-the-board good faith exception would mean in practice "that appellate courts defer to trial courts and trial courts defer to the police."[167] Reviewing courts could not be expected to set matters straight, for the elusive good faith exception would "add a factor of discretion to the operation of the exclusionary rule impossible for the appellate courts effectively to control."[168]

Moreover, and perhaps of ultimate importance, there is the fact that a broader good faith exception, applicable even when the police conduct did not have the prior approval of a magistrate, would be perceived and treated by the police as a license to engage in the same conduct in the future. That is, the risk in such tampering with the exclusionary rule "is that police officers may feel that they have been unleashed"[169] and consequently may govern their future conduct by what passed the good faith test in court on a particular occasion rather than on the traditional Fourth Amendment standards of probable cause, exigent circumstances, and the like. Even Professor Steven Schlesinger, a staunch opponent of the exclusionary rule,[170] has concluded that the good faith exception "provides little or no deterrence for violations deemed by the courts to be in good faith" because it fosters "a careless attitude toward detail on the part of law enforcement officials" and encourages "police to see what can be gotten away with."[171]

The essential point was made in *Terry v. Ohio*,[172] where the Court stated: "a ruling admitting evidence in a criminal trial * * * has the necessary effect of legitimizing the conduct which

---

[165]Kaplan, The Limits of the Exclusionary Rule, 26 Stan.L.Rev. 1027, 1044 (1974).

[166]United States v. Peltier, 422 U.S. 531, 95 S.Ct. 2313, 45 L.Ed.2d 374 (1975) (Brennan, J., dissenting).

[167]Amsterdam, Perspectives on the Fourth Amendment, 58 Minn.L.Rev. 349, 394 (1974).

[168]United States v. Peltier, 422 U.S. 531, 95 S.Ct. 2313, 45 L.Ed.2d 374 (1975) (Brennan, J., dissenting).

[169]Wishman, Evidence Illegally Obtained by Police, New York Times, Sept. 21, 1981, at 21, col. 3.

[170]See generally S. Schlesinger, Exclusionary Injustice: The Problem of Illegally Obtained Evidence (1977).

[171]Schlesinger, It is Time to Abolish the Exclusionary Rule, Wall Street Journal, Sept. 10, 1981, at 24, col. 4.

[172]Terry v. Ohio, 392 U.S. 1, 88 S.Ct. 1868, 20 L.Ed.2d 889 (1968).

produced the evidence, while an application of the exclusionary rule withholds the constitutional imprimatur."[173] The notion therefore is not that the police are inherently evil, but rather that because they are "engaged in the often competitive enterprise of ferreting out crime,"[174] they are no less likely than the rest of us to equate admissibility with legality. If illegally seized evidence is not excluded, "it is difficult for the citizenry to believe that the government truly meant to forbid the conduct in the first place."[175] It is thus not at all surprising that an empirical survey of police attitudes found that "to police, the imposition of the exclusionary rule is a prerequisite for the imposition of a legal obligation."[176]

§ 1.3(h) "Good faith" and unconstitutional legislation or overruled precedents

For a good many years the Supreme Court maintained a most important substantive-procedural distinction regarding the effect of a statute, subsequently determined to be unconstitutional, upon efforts by a defendant to suppress evidence obtained by police reliance upon that statute. On the one hand, concluded the Court in *Michigan v. DeFillippo,*[177] if a police officer makes his probable cause determination by assessing the facts at hand against a particular substantive provision and the facts show a sufficient probability that the proscribed conduct has occurred, the officer may lawfully proceed under this "presumptively valid" statutory definition of criminality. His conduct does not thereafter become ab initio unlawful upon a determination that the substantive provision is constitutionally defective. Except for some possible concern with the manner in which the *DeFillippo* Court drew the substantive-procedural line,[178] this was an

---

[173]In Davies, The Penalty of Exclusion, A Price or a Sanction, 73 S.Cal. L.Rev. 1275, 1337 (2000), the author looks at the exclusionary rule from the standpoint of price and sanction theory and concludes that "the cost-benefit analysis currently used by the Court to determine when the benefits of applying the sanction justify its costs skews the sanction's normative message. The Court's failure to emphasize the prohibited nature of official constitutional violations in cases in which it has retreated from the penalty has resulted in a state of confusion about the mandatory nature of the constitutional requirements."

[174]Johnson v. United States, 333 U.S. 10, 68 S.Ct. 367, 92 L.Ed. 436 (1948). And thus understandably will "push to the limit" any authority they are given by the courts. Brinegar v. United States, 338 U.S. 160, 69 S.Ct. 1302, 93 L.Ed. 1879 (1949) (Jackson, J., dissenting).

[175]Paulsen, The Exclusionary Rule and Misconduct by the Police, 52 J.Crim.L.C. & P.S. 255, 258 (1961).

[176]Loewenthal, Evaluating the Exclusionary Rule in Search and Seizure, 49 U.M.K.C.L.Rev. 24, 29 (1980).

[Section 1.3(h)]

[177]Michigan v. DeFillippo, 443 U.S. 31, 99 S.Ct. 2627, 61 L.Ed.2d 343 (1979).

[178]See § 3.2(f).

eminently sound result.[179] Just as sound were the many decisions of the Court both before and after *DeFillippo* adhering to the principle that police conduct undertaken pursuant to an unconstitutional legislative conferral of search or seizure authority is unlawful and a basis for suppression under the *Mapp* exclusionary rule.[180] But this latter line of authority was jettisoned in the *Leon*-based decision of *Illinois v. Krull*.[181] Confronted with a search of an auto junkyard pursuant to an administrative inspection statute later held unconstitutional because it vested inspectors with too much discretion,[182] the Court held that "a good-faith exception to the Fourth Amendment exclusionary rule applies when an officer's reliance[183] on the constitutionality of a statute is objectively reasonable, but the statute is subsequently declared unconstitutional."[184]

---

[179]Such a result is sometimes reached today simply by reliance upon the "good faith" concept in *Krull*, discussed infra. See, e.g., United States v. Meek, 366 F.3d 705 (9th Cir.2004); United States v. Vanness, 342 F.3d 1093 (10th Cir.2003).

Relying directly on *DeFillippo*: United States v. Cardenas-Alatorre, 485 F.3d 1111 (10th Cir.2007) (here, as in *DeFillippo*, it cannot be said that the law in question, here regarding license plate obstruction, was "so grossly and flagrantly unconstitutional that any person of reasonable prudence would be bound to see its flaws").

[180]See, e.g., Ybarra v. Illinois, 444 U.S. 85, 100 S.Ct. 338, 62 L.Ed.2d 238 (1979); Torres v. Puerto Rico, 442 U.S. 465, 99 S.Ct. 2425, 61 L.Ed.2d 1 (1979); Almeida-Sanchez v. United States, 413 U.S. 266, 93 S.Ct. 2535, 37 L.Ed.2d 596 (1973); Coolidge v. New Hampshire, 403 U.S. 443, 91 S.Ct. 2022, 29 L.Ed.2d 564 (1971); Berger v. New York, 388 U.S. 41, 87 S.Ct. 1873, 18 L.Ed.2d 1040 (1967).

[181]Illinois v. Krull, 480 U.S. 340, 107 S.Ct. 1160, 94 L.Ed.2d 364 (1987), discussed in Comment, 63 Tul.L.Rev. 335 (1988); Notes, 66 N.C.L.Rev. 781 (1988); 1993 U.Ill.L.Rev. 411. For other discussion of *Krull*, see Wasserstrom & Seidman, The Fourth Amendment as Constitutional Theory, 77 Geo.L.J. 19, 39 (1988).

[182]See § 10.2 on these limits.

[183]In *Krull*, the Court said the of-ficer was "simply fulfill[ing] his responsibility to enforce the statute as written." Perhaps the responsibilities of certain other officials are different in this respect, so that *Krull* would not be applicable to them. See State v. Thompson, 810 P.2d 415 (Utah 1991) (*Krull* not applicable to attorney general; "As the state's highest law enforcement officer, the attorney general is expected to perform his discretionary functions within constitutional bounds").

[184]For application of *Krull*, see United States v. Duka, 671 F.3d 329 (3d Cir.2011) (even assuming FISA statute, as amended, unconstitutional, evidence obtained in search pursuant to that statute admissible under *Krull*); United States v. Warshak, 631 F.3d 266 (6th Cir.2010) (while government agents violated defendant's Fourth Amendment rights by compelling ISP to turn over e-mails without obtaining a warrant, under *Krull* exclusionary rule not applicable because agents relied on Stored Communications Act, 18 U.S.C.A. §§ 2701 et seq., which not "conspicuously unconstitutional"); United States v. Steed, 548 F.3d 961 (11th Cir.2008) (*Krull* applies here if state statute authorizing safety inspection of commercial trucks fell short re *Burger* requirement that "time, place, and scope" of inspections be sufficiently limited); United States v. Johnson, 408 F.3d 1313 (10th Cir.2005) (*Krull* applies here, re warrantless administrative search of auto

The majority in *Krull* concluded the "approach used in *Leon* is equally applicable to the present case," and thus looked for and found the equivalent of the three factors that were determinative in *Leon*: (1) "The application of the exclusionary rule to suppress evidence obtained by an officer acting in objectively reasonable reliance on a statute would have as little deterrent effect on the officer's actions as would the exclusion of evidence when an officer acts in objectively reasonable reliance on a warrant." (2) Moreover, "legislators, like judicial officers, are not the focus of the rule," for like judges they are not inclined to act contrary to the Fourth Amendment. (3) "There is nothing to indicate that applying the exclusionary rule to evidence seized pursuant to the statute prior to the declaration of its invalidity will act as a significant, additional deterrent" on legislators enacting such statutes. Further following *Leon,* the *Krull* majority next adopted "similar constraints" to those in the earlier holding. Thus, a

> statute cannot support objectively reasonable reliance if, in passing the statute, the legislature wholly abandoned its responsibility to enact constitutional laws. Nor can a law enforcement officer be said to have acted in good-faith reliance upon a statute if its provisions are such that a reasonable officer should have known that the statute was unconstitutional.

The Court then concluded there was good-faith reliance in the instant case, as "the additional restrictions on discretion that might have been necessary are not so obvious that an objectively reasonable police officer would have realized the statute was unconstitutional without them."

The decision in *Krull* is a most unfortunate one. To the extent

---

salvage yard conducted pursuant to state statutes, where statutes not clearly unconstitutional and had been upheld as constitutional by state courts); United States v. Gambrell, 178 F.3d 927 (7th Cir.1999) (following *Stowe*); United States v. Stowe, 100 F.3d 494 (7th Cir.1996) (*Krull* applied to challenge to Illinois no-knock statute; court says that because a judge is not required to issue such a warrant whenever the facts fall within the arguably too broad statutory categories, "the statute is capable of a constitutional interpretation" and thus "is not 'clearly unconstitutional' "); United States v. Ross, 32 F.3d 1411 (9th Cir.1994) (reliance on *Krull* rejected where ticket agent who x-rayed luggage knew no sign posted warning passengers of same, where government regulation explicitly stated x-ray not permitted absent such sign); Starr v. State, 297 Ark. 26, 759 S.W.2d 535 (1988) (though after trial in this case a federal court and then state supreme court held a clerk of court may not on his own issue an arrest warrant, the reliance on a warrant so issued was reasonable here because that was a common practice authorized by a state rule of criminal procedure); State v. Daniel, 291 Kan. 490, 242 P.3d 1186 (2010) (*Krull* applied to pre-*Gant* reliance upon state statute authorizing vehicle search incident to arrest); State v. De La Cruz, 158 N.H. 564, 969 A.2d 413 (2009) ("suppression of evidence obtained as a result of an officer's objectively reasonable reliance upon a presumptively constitutional ordinance would not be consistent with the purposes of the exclusionary rule," and this true under state constitution as well notwithstanding fact state has "rejected a general good faith exception to the exclusionary rule").

that it relies upon and broadens the *Leon* doctrine, it is subject to the many criticisms heretofore directed at that earlier decision. More significantly, even if one accepts the result and reasoning in *Leon* (as does Justice O'Connor, writing for the four dissenters in *Krull*), the *Krull* ruling is nonetheless most objectionable.[185] That is, the dissenters are quite correct in concluding that "application of *Leon*'s stated rationales leads to a contrary result in this case." For one thing, there is "a powerful historical basis for the exclusion of evidence gathered pursuant to a search authorized by an unconstitutional statute," as such statutes "were the core concern of the Framers of the Fourth Amendment." This is why the exclusionary rule has "been regularly applied to evidence gathered under statutes that authorized unreasonable searches," and why the Court in *Leon* could say that these decisions "are fully consistent with our holding here."

For another, this history illustrates that the "distinction drawn between the legislator and the judicial officer is sound."

> A judicial officer's unreasonable authorization of a search affects one person at a time; a legislature's unreasonable authorization of searches may affect thousands or millions and will almost always affect more than one. Certainly the latter poses a greater threat to liberty.
>
> Moreover, * * * [l]egislators by virtue of their political role are more often subjected to the political pressures that may threaten Fourth Amendment values than are judicial officers.[186]

Lastly, nonapplication of the exclusionary rule in *Krull*-type

---

[185]Thus in People v. Krueger, 175 Ill.2d 60, 221 Ill.Dec. 409, 675 N.E.2d 604 (1996), criticized in Comment, 22 S.Ill.U.L.J. 181 (1997), and followed in People v. Wright, 183 Ill.2d 16, 231 Ill.Dec. 908, 697 N.E.2d 693 (1998), the court noted that "one can fully accept the rationale and result in *Leon* while rejecting the rationale and result in *Krull*," and then proceeded to reject *Krull* under the state constitution without disturbing its earlier acceptance of *Leon*.

The court in *Krueger* also noted that "one cannot reject *Leon*'s good-faith exception and accept *Krull*'s extension of that exception," and thus concluded that "several state courts of last resort presumably will reject *Krull*'s extension of the good-faith exception based on their determination that the *Leon* good-faith exception violates their respective state constitutions." See, e.g., State v. Scott, 619 N.W.2d 371 (Iowa 2000). For state cases taking that view of *Leon*, see

note 45 supra.

[186]Some take a somewhat different view of the legislature, at least as to certain types of legislation related to the Fourth Amendment. See Worf, The Case for Rational Basis Review of General Suspicionless Searches and Seizures, 23 Touro L.Rev. 93 (2007) (arguing "that when a legislature has authorized a group search or seizure, courts should generally apply rational basis review," as "the Fourth Amendment guarantees only reasonableness or cost-effectiveness, which legislatures are particularly competent at determining and are normally trusted to do," and "the legislative process, if anything, exhibits a bias in favor of too few general searches and seizures: the costs of general searches and seizures are relatively concentrated and visible, while the benefits to law enforcement are diffuse and invisible, which means that advocates of more privacy should have an organizational advantage"). Consider also Slobogin,

cases "creates a positive incentive to promulgate unconstitutional laws," for *Krull* provides "a grace period during which police may freely perform unreasonable searches." Indeed, *Krull* virtually assures that the grace period will be substantial, for it removes much of the incentive for a person aggrieved by a search or seizure conducted pursuant to a statute to bring the legislation into question. As the dissenters accurately point out, under *Krull* "no effective remedy is to be provided in the very case in which the statute at issue was held unconstitutional." Surely the limited exceptions to the *Krull* good-faith rule are unlikely to encourage any effort by an aggrieved defendant to take on the statute.[187] Establishing that a reasonable policeman should have known the legislature had overstepped its bounds seems virtually impossible, and certainly, as the dissent recognizes, "under what circumstances a legislature can be said to have 'wholly abandoned' its obligation to pass constitutional laws is," to put it mildly, "not apparent on the face of the Court's opinion."

Krull is inapplicable when the officer merely claims that he made a reasonable but mistaken interpretation of the scope of his search authority under a certain statute.[188] As explained in *People v. Madison*,[189] rejecting such an extension of *Krull*,

> to adopt the extension of the good-faith exception proposed by the State would essentially eviscerate the exclusionary rule as it is currently enforced. Police officers would be encouraged to defy the plain language of statutes as written in favor of their own interpretations in conducting searches and seizures. Such a proposal, giving the police unlimited authority to conduct searches and seizures until specifically restricted by the legislature or the courts, is fundamentally at odds with the central purpose of deterring police misconduct which underlies the exclusionary rule.[190]

If under *Krull* the good faith exception ordinarily applies when

---

Government Dragnets, 73 Law & Contemp.Probs. 107, 136 (Summer 2010) ("Political-process theory has much to recommend it in the Fourth Amendment setting. While leaving courts in control of search and seizure law in individual cases, it reinforces democratic values (and avoids charges of Lochnerism) when the search or seizure is of a group, by presuming that legislation authorizing such actions is 'reasonable' ").

[187]The *Krull* majority noted that a statute might be challenged in a non-exclusionary rule context (e.g., by declaratory judgment or injunction proceeding), but surely that is unlikely as to many types of potentially vulnerable statutes, especially those not directed at lawful business operations.

[188]Indeed, as noted in United States v. Warshak, 631 F.3d 266 (6th Cir.2010), dictum in *Krull* "hinted that the good-faith exception does not apply if the government acted 'outside the scope of the statute.' " *Warshak* agrees with this position (noting: "Once the officer steps outside the scope of an unconstitutional statute, the mistake is no longer the legislature's, but the officer's"), but concluded the statutory violations in the instant case were different because they "had no bearing on the constitutional violations."

[189]People v. Madison, 121 Ill.2d 195, 117 Ill.Dec. 213, 520 N.E.2d 374 (1988).

[190]See also Williams v. Commonwealth, 213 S.W.3d 671

the police officer reasonably relies upon a statute subsequently held unconstitutional, then is it likewise true that it applies when the reliance was instead upon judicial precedent subsequently overturned so as to place the officer's conduct outside rather than inside the range of permissible Fourth Amendment conduct? That was the issue considered in *State v. Ward*,[191] where police executed a no-knock search warrant issued on the thesis that the necessary exigent circumstances are always present in execution of a warrant involving felonious drug delivery, a thesis theretofore embraced by the state supreme court but rejected on a later occasion in the Supreme Court's *Richards* decision.[192] The court in *Ward*, as other courts have done,[193] could have easily held the evidence obtained in execution of that warrant admissible under the *Leon* good faith rule on the theory that the executing officer had reasonably relied upon the no-knock authority granted to him by the judge issuing the warrant. But the Court instead took another approach, just as it more logically might have if the executing officer had himself made the no-knock decision in reliance upon the existing state precedent, by drawing an analogy not to *Leon* but to *Krull*. The court asserted that "the officers in this case did not comply with the rule of announcement" later set out in *Richards*, but that this was "not due to negligence, a mistake of law, or willful or malicious misconduct by the officers," but rather because they "relied upon a rule set forth" in state supreme court decisions. Such "good faith reliance upon the pronouncements of this court," the *Ward* majority opined, were on a par with the "good faith reliance upon an apparently valid statute" in *Krull*, for here as there "excluding the evidence seized by the police [would not] serve any remedial objective."

(Ky.2006) (where statute only gave agents of specified administrative agency authority to conduct warrantless search of physicians' offices, other state agents, e.g., investigators from Attorney General's office, could not reasonably rely on statute); State v. Thompson, 810 P.2d 415 (Utah 1991) (*Krull* not applicable where attorney general, who issued illegal subpoenas, claims reliance on ambiguous subpoena statute defining extent of subpoena authority in terms of "the judgment of the attorney general"; "to shield his conduct behind the vagueness of a legislative grant of authority would be tantamount to a grant of immunity to act unconstitutionally").

[191]State v. Ward, 231 Wis.2d 723, 604 N.W.2d 517 (2000).

See also United States v. Jackson, 825 F.2d 853 (5th Cir.1987) (circuit narrowed its long-time broad view of what constitutes a "functional equivalent of the border" and then deprived the defendant who caused this change in the law of any benefit, stating: "The reasoning of *Leon* fully applies to the case at hand. Panels of this court have upheld searches at the Sierra Blanca checkpoint numerous times, and appellants do not suggest that this court is 'inclined to ignore or subvert the Fourth Amendment'").

Compare the cases in note 152 supra applying *Leon* where warrant invalidity is attributable to the retroactive application of a post-warrant court decision making the warrant invalid.

[192]Richards v. Wisconsin, 520 U.S. 385, 117 S.Ct. 1416, 137 L.Ed.2d 615 (1997), discussed in § 4.8(d).

[193]See note 66 supra.

How one feels about *Krull* may well determine one's attitude toward the *Ward* decision as well. On the one hand, both cases might be viewed as especially appealing good faith claims because in both instances there existed "authoritative pronouncements which established a reasonable basis for"[194] the mistaken-by-hindsight judgment made by the officers. On the other hand, some might view both *Krull* and *Ward* as less appealing than *Leon* because the bad-by-hindsight statute or judicial precedent is likely to have accounted for violation of the Fourth Amendment rights of a good many people. But it does seem that in one significant respect *Ward* is less objectionable than *Krull*, considering the cogent observation by the *Krull* dissenters that "[l]egislators by virtue of their political role are more often subjected to the political pressures that may threaten Fourth Amendment values than are judicial officers." That is, *Krull* and *Ward* may be alike when viewed in deterrence-of-police terms, but not when analyzed from the perspective of the relative needs for deterrence of legislators versus deterrence of appellate judiciary.

Assuming for the moment that *Ward* is otherwise unobjectionable because a logical extension of *Leon* and *Krull*, one complicating question is whether the result should be affected by the fact that the case-law precedent relied upon by the police officer was, subsequent to the search in question, rejected by the United States Supreme Court. This precise question soon confronted several courts following the Supreme Court's decision in *Arizona v. Gant*,[195] giving a narrow interpretation to its earlier decision in *New York v. Belton*,[196] although up until that time most lower courts had (quite understandably, given the majority's approach in *Belton*[197]) read that decision as creating a bright-line rule allowing search of a vehicle incident to arrest of an occupant even when the occupant had already been removed from the vehicle and secured. While a majority of the post-*Gant* decisions on this point concluded a *Ward*-style holding was also appropriate in such circumstances,[198] a healthy minority took the contrary

---

[194]Ball, Good Faith and the Fourth Amendment: The "Reasonable" Exception to the Exclusionary Rule, 69 J.Crim.L. & C. 635, 653 (1978), discussing the overruled precedent under the old nonretroactivity rule.

[195]Arizona v. Gant, 556 U.S. 332, 129 S.Ct. 1710, 173 L.Ed.2d 485 (2009).

[196]New York v. Belton, 453 U.S. 454, 101 S.Ct. 2860, 69 L.Ed.2d 768 (1981).

[197]See § 7.1(b).

[198]United States v. Curtis, 635

F.3d 704 (5th Cir.2011); United States v. Davis, 598 F.3d 1259 (11th Cir. 2010); United States v. Davis, 590 F.3d 847 (10th Cir.2009); United States v. McCane, 573 F.3d 1037 (10th Cir. 2009); Kelly v. State, 149 Idaho 517, 236 P.3d 1277 (2010) (accepting view "that retroactivity rules do not preclude application of the good faith exception when an officer relies on case law," but state does not prevail because of failure to show police conformed to preexisting *Thornton* limitation on *Belton* re when initial contact with arrestee is outside the vehicle); State v. Baker, 229 P.3d 650 (Utah

view.[199] Then the Supreme Court weighed in with *Davis v. United States*.[200]

Davis involved a police search of a vehicle that complied with existing circuit precedent broadly interpreting *Belton*, but was unconstitutional under *Gant*, decided while Davis's appeal on Fourth Amendment grounds was pending. The Supreme Court concluded:

> The question here is whether to apply [the exclusionary] sanction when the police conduct a search in compliance with binding precedent that is later overruled. Because suppression would do nothing to deter police misconduct in these circumstances, and because it would come at a high cost to both the truth and the public safety, we hold that searches conducted in objectively reasonable reliance on binding appellate precedent are not subject to the exclusionary rule.

> [I]n 27 years of practice under *Leon*'s good-faith exception, we have "never applied" the exclusionary rule to suppress evidence obtained as a result of nonculpable, innocent police conduct. If the police in this case had reasonably relied on a warrant in conducting their search, see *Leon* * * *, the exclusionary rule would not apply. And if Congress or the Alabama Legislature had enacted a statute codifying the precise holding of the [circuit precedent], we would swiftly conclude that " '[p]enalizing the officer for the legislature's error . . . cannot logically contribute to the deterrence of Fourth Amendment violations.' " See *Krull*. The same should be true of Davis's attempt here to " '[p]enaliz[e] the officer for the [appellate judges'] error.' "

If this is all there is to the problem here under discussion, then it might well be concluded that *Davis* qualifies as a "no-brainer." But some questions exist with respect to either the result or the

---

2010); State v. Dearborn, 327 Wis.2d 252, 786 N.W.2d 97 (2010).

[199]United States v. Gonzalez, 578 F.3d 1130 (9th Cir.2009) ("case should be controlled by long-standing precedent governing the applicability of a new rule announced by the Supreme Court while a case is on direct review"); People v. McCarty, 229 P.3d 1041 (Colo.2010) (citing *Gonzalez* in concluding that a "good-faith exception for reliance upon subsequently overruled Supreme Court decisions would therefore appear to be in 'untenable tension' with its retroactivity precedent"); Baxter v. State, 238 P.3d 934 (Okla.Crim.App.2010) (*Griffith* retroactivity rule not trumped by claim application of exclusionary rule would have no deterrent effect, as application "will confirm to law enforcement officers in Okla. the change in the law and serve as an example and an explanation of the reason law enforcement

agencies must adopt their vehicle search practices"); State v. Afana, 169 Wash.2d 169, 233 P.3d 879 (2010) (state's limited "good faith" exception deemed inapplicable to this situation).

[200]Davis v. United States, __ U.S. __, 131 S.Ct. 2419, 180 L.Ed.2d 285 (2011), discussed in Kerr, Fourth Amendment Remedies and Developments of the Law: A Comment on Camreta v. Greene and Davis v. United States, 2011 Cato Sup.Ct.Rev. 237; Maclin & Rader, No More Chipping Away: The Roberts Court Uses an Axe to Take Out the Fourth Amendment Exclusionary Rule, 81 Miss.L.J. 1183 (2012); Moran, Hanging on by a Thread: The Exclusionary Rule (Or What is Left of It) Lives for Another Day, 9 Ohio St.J.Crim.L. 363 (2011); Tomkovicz, Davis v. United States: The Exclusion Revolution Continues, 9 Ohio St.J.Crim.L. 381 (2011).

majority's reasoning that might give one pause.

For one thing, *Davis* appears to be quite different from *Leon* and *Krull* and, indeed, the other relevant decisions requiring "reasonable reliance." In all of these other cases, the facts indicate that the officer whose conduct was drawn into question was *actually* aware of the thing or circumstance that caused him reasonably to conclude that his conduct conformed to the requirements of the Fourth Amendment. Thus, *Leon* was grounded in the officer's actual "reliance on the magistrate's determination of probable cause"; *Krull* upon the officer's actual "reliance on the Illinois statute"; and *Arizona v. Evans*[201] and *Herring v. United States*[202] each upon the officer's actual reliance upon a database indicating the existence of an arrest warrant. It thus is hardly surprising that, apparently in an effort to bring *Davis* within those precedents, the Court sounds the "reasonable reliance" theme over and over again in the *Davis* opinion. In stating the question presented in the case, in twice stating the holding in the case, as well as on several other occasions, it is repeatedly asserted that for the exclusionary rule not to apply the police must have acted "in objectively reasonable reliance on binding appellate precedent."[203] But nowhere in the Supreme Court's opinion, or for that matter in the court of appeals' decision in *Davis*,[204] does there appear an assertion or even a suggestion that the officer who conducted the search was aware that the Eleventh Circuit Court of Appeals had 15 years earlier, in *United States v. Gonzalez*,[205] held that police could search an arrestee's car even after the arrestee no longer had access to it. Nor is there any particular reason to assume that the officer was proceeding in reliance upon such authority (assuming he was aware of it) at the time he acted, for he was a city police officer in Greenville, Ala-

---

[201]Arizona v. Evans, 514 U.S. 1, 115 S.Ct. 1185, 131 L.Ed.2d 34 (1995).

[202]Herring v. United States, 555 U.S. 135, 129 S.Ct. 695, 172 L.Ed.2d 496 (2009).

[203]While the assumption in the discussion following is that the phrase "objectively reasonable reliance" in *Davis* refers to reliance in fact that is objectively reasonable, one lower court has given *Davis* a different interpretation. In State v. Johnson, 354 S.W.3d 627 (Mo.2011), in response to defendant's objection that "the searching officer did not testify that he was relying on *Belton* or *Harvey* [, a state case broadly construing *Belton*,] during the search," the court asserted defendant's argument had no merit because the "test in *Davis* is clearly an objective one, and the officer's subjective reli-

ance on case law is not considered in that analysis." Even assuming *Johnson* to be correct, asking what the objectively reasonable officer would have relied upon would not appear to produce a different conclusion in the analysis following in the text.

[204]In United States v. Davis, 598 F.3d 1259 (11th Cir.2010), the court asserted that "[r]elying on a court of appeals' well-settled and unequivocal precedent is analogous to relying on a statute . . . or a facially sufficient warrant," but at no point suggested that the city police officer searching incident to arrest for state offenses had any awareness of the 11th Circuit decision broadly construing *Belton*.

[205]United States v. Gonzalez, 969 F.2d 999 (11th Cir.1992).

bama, who had arrested the vehicle occupants for the state offenses of driving under the influence and providing false identity, and thus at the time of his search had no reason to believe the case would ultimately end up in the federal courts. It is only by virtue of the case ending up there, of course, that *Gonzalez* can be said to be (in the words of *Davis*) "binding appellate precedent," for state courts are not obligated to conform their own interpretation of the Fourth Amendment to the views of the federal circuit in which they are located.[206]

It so happens, however, that the *state* appellate precedent in Alabama also broadly construed *Belton*,[207] and thus it is possible that the officer in *Davis* was acting in reliance upon that authority, but the Supreme Court never even mentions that possibility, and thus apparently believes it to be of no significance. (Also, an equivalent basis for reliance at both the federal and state level is not inevitable, meaning the *Davis* approach can produce added mischief. Illustrative is the pre-*Davis* decision in *United States v. McCane*,[208] where (just as in *Davis*) the search was by a local police officer (a member of the Oklahoma City police department) for violation of state law. At the time of the search, the state appellate courts had discussed *Belton* in only a single case, and only for the limited purpose of supporting by analogy the notion that a vehicle search made on probable cause could extend to a package in the vehicle.[209] Because the officer found a gun and McCane was a convicted felon, the case ended up in federal court, which curiously seemed to change everything. The *McCane* court said nothing about the Oklahoma precedents, but instead upheld the good-faith claim, *Davis*-style, because of the "settled circuit precedent" in the 10th Circuit.)

Once it is considered that the *Davis* decision is based only upon either fantasized reliance or conclusively-presumed reliance, and that the law supposedly being relied upon can only be ascertained by virtue of events occurring *after* the search in question, *Davis* loses much of its luster. The *Leon-Krull-Evans-Herring* quartet no longer provide solid support, nor does the *Davis* Court's reliance upon a no-culpability ergo no-exclusion thesis. Especially in a case like *McCane*, "nonculpable" doesn't seem like the best adjective to describe the searching officer—at least as compared to "lucky." It thus must be asked what *Davis* is *really* all about. Two possibilities suggest themselves, the first being that a more honest statement of the holding in that case would simply be (in language the *Davis* Court uses on a few occasions) that the

---

[206]Commonwealth v. James, 12 A.3d 388 (Pa.Super.2010); People v. Chowdhury, 285 Mich.App. 509, 775 N.W.2d 845 (2009); State v. Thompson, 284 Kan. 763, 166 P.3d 1015 (2007); People v. Stansberry, 47 Ill.2d 541, 268 N.E.2d 431 (1971).

[207]E.g., State v. Skaggs, 903 So.2d 180 (Ala.Crim.2004).

[208]United States v. McCane, 573 F.3d 1037 (10th Cir.2009).

[209]Nealy v. State, 636 P.2d 378 (Okla.Crim.App.1981).

exclusionary rule does not apply "when the police conduct a search in compliance with binding precedent"[210] in the jurisdiction of ultimate prosecution. In other words, reliance is actually out of the picture, and the mere fact that the jurisdiction of prosecution, at the time of the search, viewed the search as permissible under the Fourth Amendment alone carries the day. But this is an odd rule, even more disconnected from any measurement of the searching officer's culpability. If the officer in *Davis*, instead of locating a gun, had found the fruits of a burglary committed in Arizona, and those fruits were offered in an Arizona prosecution, the exclusionary rule *would* apply because, at the time of the search, Arizona already adopted the narrow interpretation of *Belton* the Supreme Court later embraced in *Gant*.[211] And if, on the other hand, the drugs found by the officer in the *Gant* case, obtained contrary to the state law interpretation of *Belton*, had instead been offered in a federal prosecution, then the exclusionary rule would *not* apply because of the more expansive view of *Belton* taken in the Ninth Circuit.[212] If this is *really* what *Davis* is all about, then the Court has some explaining to do.

Yet another possible interpretation of what *Davis* is *really* all about is that there must actually be reliance in fact but that, despite the unfortunate asserted need for "binding judicial precedent," this reliance need not be tied to any particular holding in any particular jurisdiction, given the widespread and generally shared view by police pre-*Gant* as to what *Belton* permitted.[213] After all, as the *Gant* majority says, *Belton* "has been widely understood to allow a vehicle search incident to the arrest of a recent occupant even if there is no possibility the arrestee could gain access to the vehicle at the time of the search," and, as the *Gant* dissenters note, the "*Belton* rule has been taught to police

<hr/>

[210]But, as to whether that precedent must embrace *Belton* only in general terms or inh specific terms including the type of intrusion at issue in the instant case, see note 211 infra.

[211]State v. Gant, 202 Ariz. 240, 43 P.3d 188 (Ct. App. Div. 2 2002), opinion vacated, 540 U.S. 963, 124 S. Ct. 461, 157 L. Ed. 2d 308 (2003).

[212]United States v. McLaughlin, 170 F.3d 889 (9th Cir.1999); United States v. Moorehead, 57 F.3d 875 (9th Cir.1995).

[213]Even if this alternative position is not accepted, it may be that the general interpretation of *Belton* elsewhere will be deemed to carry the day in the jurisdiction of prosecution, which had generally embraced *Belton* but had never specifically adopted a particular interpretation of *Belton* that would encompass the police conduct in the instant case. See, e.g., Briscoe v. State, 422 Md. 384, 30 A.3d 870 (2011) (after valid traffic stop, it determined defendant's license was suspended and that there an open arrest warrant for him, so he arrested and removed from vehicle, after which handgun found within locked glove compartment; *Davis* deemed applicable nowithtanding absence of any in-state ruling re validity of search of *locked* glove compartment under *Belton*, as it sufficient that the jurisdiction "had adopted the bright-line rule of *Belton*" and that courts in many other jurisdictions "seemingly have been untroubled by *Belton* searches of locked containers").

officers for more than a quarter century." It is thus at least *possible* that this is the unstated rationale accounting for the result in *Davis*. This would explain the question put by the dissenters in *Davis* as to how that case would apply regarding "a rule that all other jurisdictions, but not the defendant's jurisdiction, had previously accepted." It also squares with the approach in Justice Sotomayor's concurring opinion, where she concludes that *Davis* itself is an easy case considering that the "binding appellate precedent" onto which the majority latches is "in accord with the holdings of nearly every other court in the country," and then cogently asserts that "when the law governing the constitutionality of a particular search is unsettled" then there might well be a basis for applying the exclusionary rule notwithstanding the fact that "the officer's conduct could be characterized as nonculpable."[214] But here again it is not obvious that such a characterization of *Davis* makes it any more palatable. For one thing, it would appear to produce the curious result that even Mr. Gant himself could not benefit from the exclusionary rule though he resided in one of the few jurisdictions prescient regarding the fate of *Belton*.[215]

Other questions regarding *Davis* relate in one way or another to the Court's longstanding view regarding the applicability of a new rule[216] announced by the Supreme Court to another case on direct review,[217] namely, that "a decision of this Court construing the Fourth Amendment is to be applied retroactively to all convictions that were not yet final at the time the decision was rendered."[218] All members of the Court agree that *Gant* thus applies in *Davis*, but do not agree as to what this means. The majority's position is that the Court's "retroactivity jurisprudence

---

[214]Importantly, the Justice noted in this regard: "We have never refused to apply the exclusionary rule where its application would appreciably deter Fourth Amendment violations on the mere ground that the officer's conduct could be characterized as nonculpable."

[215]Unless the *Davis* majority were to act on its suggestion that "in a future case, we could, if necessary, recognize a limited exception to the good-faith exception for a defendant who obtains a judgment overruling one of our Fourth Amendment precedents."

[216]As for whether *Gant* even is a new rule, consider the explanation offered by the *Davis* majority, namely, that while four of the Justices in the *Gant* majority simply claimed that the prevailing interpretation of *Belton* was in error and thus they supplied the

correct interpretation of *Belton* but did not overrule it, the four dissenters thought the new limitation on *Belton* "was to overrule the decision's clear holding," while Justice Scalia, providing the fifth vote to affirm "agreed with the dissenters' understanding of *Belton*'s holding" and "favored a more explicit and complete overruling of *Belton*" but "joined what became the majority opinion to avoid 'a 4-to-1-to-4 disposition.'"

[217]See § 11.5(b).

[218]United States v. Johnson, 457 U.S. 537, 102 S.Ct. 2579, 73 L.Ed.2d 202 (1982), expanded in Griffith v. Kentucky, 479 U.S. 314, 107 S.Ct. 708, 93 L.Ed.2d 649 (1987) (concluding that even decisions constituting a "clear break" with past precedents have retroactive application).

is concerned with whether, as a categorical matter, a new rule is available on direct review as a *potential* ground for relief," so that "[r]etroactive application does not * * * determine what 'appropriate remedy' (if any) the defendant should obtain"; the two dissenters, on the other hand, claim that "the Court's distinction between (1) retroactive application of a new rule and (2) availability of a remedy is highly artificial." In support of the latter position, it might be said, as another court put it, that in *Gant* "the Supreme Court upheld in full the decision of the Arizona Supreme Court, which not only found the search at issue unconstitutional, but ordered the suppression of the evidence found as a result of the unconstitutional search."[219] But, while that statement is true, it seems highly misleading from the standpoint of articulating exactly what it is the Supreme Court has done that brings the retroactivity doctrine into play. Neither the Supreme Court decision in *Gant* nor the state court decision it upheld[220] (nor for that matter any of the other state appellate decisions involving this same case)[221] ever considered or even mentioned in passing the question of whether some exception to the exclusionary rule might be applicable in the case;[222] the entirety of the discussion is directed at the constitutional validity of the search.

As the *Davis* dissenters elaborate, the current version of the Supreme Court's retroactivity doctrine is largely attributable to a desire to treat defendants in all pending cases equally, rather than confer a benefit only upon the one defendant who, perhaps by chance, has his case "fish[ed] from the stream of appellate review." They thus contend that the *Davis* decision contains the very evil that retroactivity was intended to prevent; *Davis*, they say, creates a "problem" of "fairness" by "treat[ing] the defendant in a case announcing a new rule one way while treating similarly situated defendants whose cases are pending on appeal in a different way." But one wonders whether Mr. Gant and Mr. Davis may fairly be characterized as "similarly situated" when only the latter defendant was involved in a case in which the prosecution invoked a good faith claim. Indeed, it would appear that Mr. Gant was not even "potentially similarly situated," as (i) *Gant*

---

[219]United States v. Gonzalez, 578 F.3d 1130 (9th Cir.2009).

[220]State v. Gant, 216 Ariz. 1, 162 P.3d 640 (2007), aff'd, 556 U.S. 332, 129 S. Ct. 1710, 173 L. Ed. 2d 485 (2009).

[221]State v. Gant, 213 Ariz. 446, 143 P.3d 379 (App.2006); State v. Dean, 206 Ariz. 158, 76 P.3d 429 (2003).

[222]However, the four dissenters in *Gant* appear to have assumed that no exception to the exclusionary rule

would come into play, for they complained that the "Court's decision will cause the suppression of evidence gathered in many searches carried out in good-faith reliance on well-settled case law." It is also worth noting that the *Gant* majority, in rejecting the notion "that consideration of police reliance interests requires a different result," dropped a footnote mentioning that "the doctrine of qualified immunity will shield officers from liability" but not suggesting any relief in the suppression context.

involved a state search and a state prosecution, (ii) the defendant consistently prevailed on the search issue in the state appellate courts, and (iii) from those several opinions it appears that the courts in ruling in his favor were not rejecting any prior Arizona precedents to the contrary, meaning the officer in *Gant* would have had neither "reliance" nor "compliance" in his favor had the prosecution made a good-faith claim on his behalf. Of course, the fairness argument might carry more weight if (1) Gant had *lost* below because the state instead followed the then-prevailing view of *Belton*, (2) the Supreme Court gave him the benefit of the new interpretation of *Belton* plus the remedy of exclusion, but then (3) Davis got the rule but not the remedy. Further consideration of that possibility, however, requires examination of yet another question about the *Davis* result.

It might be argued that the Court in *Davis* got the cost-benefit balancing wrong. A very thoughtful pre-*Davis* article spelled out a quite different analysis, arguing

> that an exclusionary rule for new law is essential to deterring constitutional violations. The exclusionary rule for changing law provides the litigation incentives needed to help courts weigh constitutional interests accurately and thus adopt accurate Fourth Amendment rules. The availability of a suppression remedy gives criminal defendants an incentive to argue for changes in the law by allowing them to benefit if they successfully persuade courts to overturn adverse precedents. Recognizing a good faith exception for changing law would mean that defendants could not benefit from arguments to change that law. Defendants would no longer make such arguments, substantially impairing the adversarial process that the Supreme Court needs to analyze constitutional interests accurately. Recognizing a good faith exception for overturned law would introduce a systemic bias into Fourth Amendment litigation: it would encourage the prosecution to argue for changes in the law in its favor but discourage the same argument from the defense. The result would be a systematic skewing of constitutional arguments in the government's favor which would ensure the retention of erroneous precedents that allow practices that should be recognized as unconstitutional.[223]

The *Davis* majority acknowledged the argument "that applying the good-faith exception to searches conducted in reliance on binding precedent will stunt the development of Fourth Amendment law," but then rejected it. One reason given was that because "the *sole* purpose of the exclusionary rule is to deter misconduct by law enforcement," "facilitating the overruling of precedent" cannot be deemed "a relevant consideration in an exclusionary rule case." But it is odd, to say the least, to rely upon the deterrence function to support a system that substantially limits the opportunities for meaningful appellate review of the critical question of exactly what it is that needs to be deterred.

---

[223]Kerr, Good Faith, New Law, and the Scope of the Exclusionary Rule, 99 Geo.L.J. 1077, 1082 (2011).

Beyond this, the *Davis* majority concluded that it sufficed that a stimulus to seek appellate review (i.e., at least a chance of benefit via evidence suppression) is available to defendants in jurisdictions where a particular Fourth Amendment issue "remains open," i.e., where there was no "binding appellate precedent" supporting the challenged police conduct. Of course, the number of such defendants is zero when the precedent is a Supreme Court decision, which may be why the *Davis* majority was moved to acknowledge the *possibility* that "in a future case, we could, if necessary, recognize a limited exception to the good-faith exception for a defendant who obtains a judgment overruling one of our Fourth Amendment precedents."[224]

Even assuming the *result* in *Davis* is correct, there is still good reason to be concerned about that decision. The majority's cost/benefit analysis and no culpability/no exclusion thesis draws heavily upon the Court's earlier opinion in *Herring v. United States*,[225] which (as elaborated elsewhere herein)[226] is seriously flawed. And thus *Davis* (which even appears to expand the breadth of *Herring*)[227] shares with that decision a most troubling aspect: it looks much like a recipe for total abandonment of the Fourth Amendment exclusionary rule. As the two *Davis* dissenters put it, "if the Court means what it now says, if it would place determinative weight upon the culpability of an individual officer's conduct, and if it would apply the exclusionary rule only where a Fourth Amendment violation was 'deliberate, reckless, or grossly negligent,' then the 'good faith' exception will swallow the exclusionary rule."

§ 1.3(i) "Good faith" and unconstitutional police regulations

Does it follow from *Leon* and *Krull* that a "good-faith" exception to the exclusionary rule should also be recognized in those cases in which the officer who conducted the seizure or search now determined to be illegal reasonably relied upon some police rule or policy? From the standpoint of deterring the officer who made the search or seizure, one can argue that suppression where the officer relied upon a police regulation makes no more sense than where the officer relied upon a statute or a warrant. Moreover, it can be contended that such an extension of the "good-faith" exception would have the added advantage of providing po-

---

[224]The dissenters in *Davis* were understandably astonished at the majority's indications that, as things now stand, the Court apparently would "refus[e] to apply the exclusionary rule even to the defendant in the very case in which it announces a 'new rule.'"

[225]Herring v. United States, 555

U.S. 135, 129 S.Ct. 695, 172 L.Ed.2d 496 (2009).

[226]See § 1.6(i).

[227]The *Davis* majority's "restatement" of the *Herring* rule omits its most significant limitation, namely, that "negligent" conduct by police supports a good-faith claim only if the negligence was "attenuated."

lice departments with strong encouragement to engage in careful self-study to produce clear and comprehensive rules governing day-to-day police practices.[228] So the argument goes, this would in fact *advance* the cause of deterrence: "Police will be most effectively deterred from unconstitutional conduct if police departments respond institutionally to search and seizure decisions by continually promulgating field regulations reflective of developing fourth amendment law, and by training officers to follow such regulations."[229] In addition, this argument proceeds, this also would focus the exclusionary rule on instances in which there were institutional failures to protect Fourth Amendment rights, for (assuming the individual officer complied with the existing policy) the costs of evidence suppression would quite properly not be imposed where "the police department in question has taken seriously its responsibility to adhere to the fourth amendment."[230] So focused, the exclusionary rule might be said to have a much more solid grounding, for it would "be based upon an institutional, or systemic, view of deterrence."[231]

Although these are rather compelling arguments, it is nonetheless doubtful whether such use of police regulations in Fourth Amendment adjudication is desirable. The Supreme Court in *Leon* and *Krull* asserted that the Fourth Amendment exclusionary rule has no application to judges and legislators, unlike police; these distinctions were critical to the Court's analysis and to the result reached in these two cases. But it cannot as plausibly be asserted that the exclusionary rule is not directed to those upper-level police officials who are responsible for formulating law enforcement policies touching upon Fourth Amendment rights. It may be true that police administrators, as compared to officers on the beat, are not directly "engaged in the often competitive enterprise of ferreting out crime"[232] and thus are less tempted to cut corners. Yet there is no apparent empirical basis for concluding that law enforcement personnel at the policymaking level are so intensely committed to Fourth Amendment values that they can always be trusted to draft regulations that sufficiently respect those values. As a result, one can hardly be sanguine about the prospects of such draftsmanship if those officials knew (which would be the message of a "good-faith" exception operating in this area) that even if a regulation does not satisfy the requirements of the Amendment, it will nonetheless

---

[Section 1.3(i)]

[228]Comment, 130 U.Pa.L.Rev. 1610, 1618–19 (1982).

[229]Comment, 130 U.Pa.L.Rev. 1610, 1618 (1982).

[230]Kaplan, the Limits of the Exclusionary Rule, 26 Stan.L.Rev. 1027, 1050 (1974).

[231]Comment, 130 U.Pa.L.Rev. 1610, 1619 (1982). For a useful discussion of why that view of deterrence is a more sensible one, see id. at 1627–31.

[232]Johnson v. United States, 333 U.S. 10, 68 S.Ct. 367, 92 L.Ed. 436 (1948).

provide "a grace period during which the police may freely perform unreasonable searches."[233]

This is not to suggest that some judgment must be made about the malevolence level of police administrators as compared to, on the one hand, judges and legislators and, on the other, beat patrolmen. The Fourth Amendment is not concerned merely with calculated and deliberate noncompliance with the Amendment's proscriptions, and thus the exclusionary rule also applies to the more common Fourth Amendment violations resulting from carelessness. That is, the exclusionary rule serves not only to deter the occasional ill-spirited officer but, more importantly, to influence police behavior more generally by creating an "incentive to err on the side of constitutional behavior."[234]

There are many other ways, without such an extension of the "good-faith" exception, in which police regulations in fact are and potentially might be brought to bear in a meaningful way upon the adjudication of Fourth Amendment issues.[235] Thus, it is especially important that those officers responsible for preparing and promulgating these regulations do "incorporate Fourth Amendment ideals into their value system"[236] and, when in doubt, "err on the side of constitutional behavior." The importance of such a frame of reference is further highlighted by the much greater potential for harm an ill-drafted regulation carries as compared to the single mistake by an officer in the field, which ordinarily affects but one person. In this and other ways, "Fourth Amendment violations become more, not less, reprehensible when they are the product of Government policy rather than an individual policeman's errors of judgment."[237] That explains why "any rule intended to prevent fourth Amendment violations must operate not only upon individual law enforcement officers but also upon those who set policy for them."[238] On balance, grounding a "good-faith" exception to the exclusionary rule in reliance upon police regulations is undesirable.[239]

---

[233]Illinois v. Krull, 480 U.S. 340, 107 S.Ct. 1160, 94 L.Ed.2d 364 (1987) (O'Connor, J., dissenting). This grace period might well be substantial, for if the very existence of the police regulation presents a barrier to application of the exclusionary rule, a defendant would have no incentive to bring that regulation into question.

[234]United States v. Johnson, 457 U.S. 537, 102 S.Ct. 2579, 73 L.Ed.2d 202 (1982).

[235]See LaFave, Controlling Discretion by Administrative Regulations: The Use, Misuse, and Nonuse of Police Rules and Policies in Fourth Amendment Adjudication, 89 Mich.L.Rev. 442 (1990).

[236]Stone v. Powell, 428 U.S. 465, 96 S.Ct. 3037, 49 L.Ed.2d 1067 (1976).

[237]United States v. Peltier, 422 U.S. 531, 95 S.Ct. 2313, 45 L.Ed.2d 374 (1975) (Brennan, J., dissenting).

[238]United States v. Peltier, 422 U.S. 531, 95 S.Ct. 2313, 45 L.Ed.2d 374 (1975) (Brennan, J., dissenting).

[239]This conclusion does not call into question those decisions holding that when a police officer is a defendant in a § 1983 action, his good faith

§ 1.4 The *Scott* "bad faith" doctrine

Research References

West's Key Number Digest

Arrest ☞63.4, 63.5; Automobiles ☞349(2.1), 349.5(3); Criminal Law ☞394.4; Searches and Seizures ☞40.1, 82, 112

Legal Encyclopedias

C.J.S., Arrest §§ 19 to 42; Criminal Law §§ 770, 772, 778 to 792; Motor Vehicles §§ 1321 to 1335; Searches and Seizures §§ 13, 36, 38, 48 to 53, 56, 109 to 110, 148

Introduction

If it is sometimes the case, as discussed in the preceding section, that conduct in violation of the Fourth Amendment need not result in suppression because of the "good faith" of the police, what then of a situation somewhat the reverse of that? That is, if the conduct is, at least under some extant theory, the kind of action that *could* be constitutionally engaged in under the existing circumstances, must the evidence nonetheless be suppressed because of what might be characterized (somewhat inaccurately) as the "bad faith" of the police? More precisely, the question here is whether a "bad" intent or motivation by the searching or seizing police officer should be taken into account so as to bring about the exclusion of evidence that otherwise would be deemed admissible. Some of the manifestations of this problem concern not the scope of the exclusionary rule as much as the Fourth Amendment right itself, as dealt with at various later points in this Treatise.[1] But the general subject is appropriately undertaken here because it also involves consideration of the deter-

---

can be established by the officer's reliance upon information conveyed to him by his department concerning the extent of his Fourth Amendment authority, see e.g., Dominguez v. Beame, 603 F.2d 337 (2d Cir.1979); Thompson v. Anderson, 447 F.Supp. 584 (D.Md. 1977). The considerations in that context are very different; see § 1.2(d).

[Section 1.4]

[1]See, e.g., §§ 3.2(b) (on whether probable cause both subjective and objective test), 4.11(f) (subterfuge searches by execution of search warrant), 5.1(e) (significance of booking, including officer declaring arrest for offense other than that for which probable cause actually exists), 5.2(e) (pretext arrests to search the person), 6.7(d) (subterfuge entry of premises without warrant), 7.5(e) (search of vehicles and pretext arrest, detention, impoundment or inventory), 9.2(e) (significance of police officer's mistake as to whether arrest or only a stop called for), 9.6(f) (subterfuge in frisk context), 10.6(h) (subterfuge in airport searches), 10.8(a)

rence rationale and because the Supreme Court, in *Scott v. United States*[2] and later in *Whren v. United States*,[3] has focused attention on the broad issue.[4]

§ 1.4(a) The *Scott* case

In *Scott,* federal agents initiated with judicial authorization a wiretap on a woman's phone because they had reason to believe certain other persons were using her phone in a conspiracy to import and distribute narcotics. Though by statute such surveillance is to be "conducted in such a way as to minimize the interception of communications not otherwise subject to interception,"[5] a requirement that certainly has its foundations in the Fourth Amendment,[6] the surveilling agents made no attempt to minimize their interception of conversations occurring via that telephone. The Supreme Court, per Rehnquist, J., found that the agents' conduct in intercepting all calls was reasonable on the facts of the case in that the calls occurred in circumstances in which the agents could "hardly be expected to know that the calls are not pertinent prior to their termination." But that left unresolved the petitioners' "principal contention," namely, that suppression was required because of "the failure to make good-faith efforts to comply with the minimization requirement," to which the government responded that "subjective intent alone * * * does not make otherwise lawful conduct illegal or unconstitutional." As to this, Justice Rehnquist declared:

We think the Government's position, which also served as the

(subterfuge in vehicle use regulation), 10.10(e) (police purpose and search of parolees and probationers).

[2]Scott v. United States, 436 U.S. 128, 98 S.Ct. 1717, 56 L.Ed.2d 168 (1978). Relying on the *Scott* principle, the Court held in Maryland v. Macon, 472 U.S. 463, 105 S.Ct. 2778, 86 L.Ed.2d 370 (1985), that an officer's intention to retrieve the money with which he purchased an obscene magazine did not make the purchase a Fourth Amendment seizure. "Objectively viewed, the transaction was a sale in the ordinary course of business. The sale is not retrospectively transformed into a warrantless seizure by virtue of the officer's subjective intent to retrieve the purchase money to use as evidence."

[3]Whren v. United States, 517 U.S. 806, 116 S.Ct. 1769, 135 L.Ed.2d 89 (1996), discussed in § 1.4(f).

[4]For another perspective on this topic, questioning some of the conclusions reached herein, see Burkoff, The

Pretext Search Doctrine Returns After Never Leaving, 66 U.Detroit L.Rev. 363 (1989); Burkoff, The Pretext Search Doctrine: Now You See It, Now You Don't, 17 U.Mich.J.L.Ref. 523 (1984); Burkoff, Bad Faith Searches, 57 N.Y.U. L.Rev. 70 (1982). The differing views are assessed in Note, 63 B.U.L.Rev. 223 (1983); and are critically examined in Haddad, Pretextual Fourth Amendment Activity: Another Viewpoint, 18 U.Mich.J.L.Ref. 639 (1985), responded to in Burkoff, Rejoinder: Truth, Justice and the American Way—Or Professor Haddad's "Hard Choices," 18 U.Mich. J.L.Ref. 695 (1985). See also Butterfoss, Solving the Pretext Puzzle: The Importance of Ulterior Motives and Fabrications in the Supreme Court's Fourth Amendment Pretext Doctrine, 79 Ky.L.J. 1 (1990).

[Section 1.4(a)]

[5]18 U.S.C.A. § 2518(5).

[6]Berger v. New York, 388 U.S. 41, 87 S.Ct. 1873, 18 L.Ed.2d 1040 (1967).

basis for decision in the Court of Appeals, embodies the proper approach for evaluating compliance with the minimization requirement. Although we have not examined this exact question at great length in any of our prior opinions, almost without exception in evaluating alleged violations of the Fourth Amendment the Court has first undertaken an objective assessment of an officer's actions in light of the facts and circumstances then known to him. * * *

We have since held that the fact that the officer does not have the state of mind which is hypothecated by the reasons which provide the legal justification for the officer's action does not invalidate the action taken as long as the circumstances, viewed objectively, justify that action. * * * The Courts of Appeals which have considered the matter have likewise generally followed these principles, first examining the challenged searches under a standard of objective reasonableness without regard to the underlying intent or motivation of the officers involved.[7]

Justice Rehnquist is certainly correct in stating that the Court has "not examined this exact question at great length in any of our prior opinions," but it may nonetheless be fairly said that he has presented a somewhat skewed picture of what the Court has had to say on this subject. In support of the statement in the first paragraph set out above, he quoted from *Terry v. Ohio*[8] the proposition that in judging Fourth Amendment reasonableness the facts must "be judged against an objective standard; would the facts available to the officer at the moment of the seizure or the search 'warrant a man of reasonable caution in the belief' that the action taken was appropriate." But the point being made in *Terry* at that juncture was that "subjective good faith alone" does not establish compliance with the Fourth Amendment, a sound proposition hardly dictating (unless symmetry is a governing consideration) what position should be taken as to the *absence* of good faith. In support of the first statement in the second paragraph quoted above, Justice Rehnquist relied upon the assertion in *United States v. Robinson*[9] that in a search incident to arrest case "it is of no moment that [the officer] did not indicate any subjective fear of the respondent or that he did not himself suspect that respondent was armed." But such an assertion is not at all surprising in that particular context, for the holding in *Robinson* was that the search of a person incident to his custodial arrest is justified as a standardized procedure without regard to the probability in the particular case that the arrestee is armed

---

[7] The Court cited at this point United States v. Bugarin-Casas, 484 F.2d 853 (9th Cir.1973); Dodd v. Beto, 435 F.2d 868 (5th Cir.1970); Klingler v. United States, 409 F.2d 299 (8th Cir.1969); Green v. United States, 386 F.2d 953 (10th Cir.1967); Sirimarco v. United States, 315 F.2d 699 (10th Cir. 1963), and then cautioned: "As is our usual custom, we do not in citing these or other cases intend to approve any particular language or holding in them."

[8] Terry v. Ohio, 392 U.S. 1, 88 S.Ct. 1868, 20 L.Ed.2d 889 (1968).

[9] United States v. Robinson, 414 U.S. 218, 94 S.Ct. 467, 38 L.Ed.2d 427 (1973).

or possesses evidence of the crime.[10]

Moreover, *Robinson* hardly supports the proposition that "the underlying intent or motivation" is never relevant, for in that case Justice Rehnquist cautioned that the Court would "leave for another day questions which would arise" upon a showing a police officer "used the subsequent traffic violation arrest as a mere pretext for a narcotics search." And in other cases the Court has upheld certain routine noncriminal searches only after emphasizing that there was "no suggestion whatever that this standard procedure * * * was a pretext concealing an investigatory police motive."[11] Finally, Justice Rehnquist also failed to mention in *Scott* that the Court had previously held that police activity undertaken for one purpose cannot be upheld on the ground that the same intrusion would have been permissible on the facts in the hands of the police had they only acted for a different purpose.[12] Thus, while the alarm that was sounded[13] concerning the quoted language from *Scott* is understandable, that case can hardly be read as a definitive analysis settling that in *all* circumstances Fourth Amendment suppression issues are to be resolved without assaying "the underlying intent or motivation of the officers involved." However, the thesis of the discussion following is that this is precisely what the rule ought to be and that certain other developments in Fourth Amendment doctrine are necessary to ensure that the *Scott* rule persists in such unqualified form.

§ 1.4(b) Unexecuted intent to act unlawfully

One kind of "bad intent" case is that in which, though facts supporting the arrest or search came to light before that action was taken, the police had previously made the subjective determination to act without such facts or without regard to whether such facts were forthcoming. Illustrative is *Massachusetts v. Painten,*[14] where the relevant facts were as follows:

> Two police officers, having a suspicion that respondent had committed felonies but not having probable cause to believe that he had committed them, went to the door of respondent's apartment. Their motive, the courts below found, was to arrest and search, whether or not their investigation provided the probable cause that would

---

[10]See § 5.2.

[11]South Dakota v. Opperman, 428 U.S. 364, 96 S.Ct. 3092, 49 L.Ed.2d 1000 (1976) (inventory of impounded vehicle), noting this was also the case in Cady v. Dombrowski, 413 U.S. 433, 93 S.Ct. 2523, 37 L.Ed.2d 706 (1973). A similar disclaimer was made in the post-*Scott* inventory case of Colorado v. Bertine, 479 U.S. 367, 107 S.Ct. 738, 93 L.Ed.2d 739 (1987).

[12]Jones v. United States, 357 U.S. 493, 78 S.Ct. 1253, 2 L.Ed.2d 1514

(1958), discussed in text at note 42 infra.

[13]Burkoff, The Court that Devoured the Fourth Amendment: The Triumph of an Inconsistent Exclusionary Doctrine, 58 Ore.L.Rev. 151, 181–90 (1979).

[Section 1.4(b)]

[14]Massachusetts v. Painten, 368 F.2d 142 (1st Cir.1966).

make an arrest and search constitutional. This plan was not communicated to respondent, who when he came to the door was led to believe the officers wished only to speak to him. Told no more than that the officers wished to ask questions, respondent asked them to wait a minute, closed the door, tossed a paper bag onto a fire escape, returned, and let the officers enter. The officers did nothing to respondent but ask questions; while doing that another officer, posted below, who had seen the bag drop, walked through the apartment and out onto the fire escape, where he found guns and bullets in the bag. The officers arrested respondent, and undertook a complete search of the apartment incident to the arrest.[15]

The court of appeals suppressed the evidence, reasoning that what transpired *after* the police knocked on the door was irrelevant because at the time of the knock "the police purpose was to arrest petitioner, although they had no warrant or ground for obtaining one."[16] Though the Supreme Court dismissed the writ as improvidently granted,[17] this appropriate action does not detract from[18] the force of the three dissenters'[19] analysis concerning the relevance of a "bad" intent in a case of this kind:

> The position of the courts below must rest on a view that a policemen's intention to offend the Constitution if he can achieve his goal in no other way contaminates all of his later behavior. In the case before us the syllogism must be that although the policeman's words requested entry for the purpose of asking respondent questions, and the policeman—on being allowed to enter—did nothing to respondent but ask questions, the "fruits" of the policeman's otherwise lawful request to enter and question—the bag tossed out the window and into a place where it could be seen from the street—should not be usable by the State. This is because the policeman was willing, had his lawful conduct not developed probable cause justifying respondent's arrest, to search respondent's apartment unlawfully in the hope of finding evidence of a crime.
>
> That such a rule makes no sense is apparent when one sees it in the context of an abstruse application of the exclusionary rule,

---

[15]As summarized by Justice White when the case reached the Supreme Court, Massachusetts v. Painten, 389 U.S. 560, 88 S.Ct. 660, 19 L.Ed.2d 770 (1968).

[16]Coffin, J. concurring, thought it critical that the items on the fire escape were obtained by using the apartment "as a conduit" by an officer other than those who had been voluntarily admitted to the apartment, which might well be a sound basis for not reaching the issue here under discussion. He then continued:

> What troubles me about the opinion of my brothers is their reasoning that, since the officers harbored an improper purpose, their knocking on the door and identifying themselves was also 'improper' and immunized from use

any objects jettisoned into public view and beyond petitioner's premises. I would not go so far as to say that such preliminaries could shield evidence later discovered if it were obtained without going on the premises of a suspect.

[17]Massachusetts v. Painten, 389 U.S. 560, 88 S.Ct. 660, 19 L.Ed.2d 770 (1968).

[18]Fortas, J., concurring, while agreeing with dismissal "because the record is not adequate for disposition of the case in terms of its constitutional problems," stressed he did not "disagree with the position stated in the dissent."

[19]White, J., joined by Harlan and Stewart, JJ.

imposed on the States as the only available way to encourage compliance by state police officers with the commands of the Fourth Amendment. * * * Because we wish to deter policemen from searching without a warrant, we would bar admission of evidence Officer McNamara discovered by ransacking respondent's apartment without a warrant or a basis for warrantless search. The expanded exclusionary rule applied in the opinions below would be defensible only if we felt it important to deter policemen from acting lawfully but with the plan—the attitude of mind—of going further and acting unlawfully if the lawful conduct produces insufficient results. We might wish that policemen would not act with impure plots in mind, but I do not believe that wish a sufficient basis for excluding, in the supposed service of the Fourth Amendment, probative evidence obtained by actions—if not thoughts—entirely in accord with the Fourth Amendment and all other constitutional requirements. In addition, sending state and federal courts on an expedition into the minds of police officers would produce grave and fruitless misallocation of judicial resources.

That reasoning is eminently sound, and has been employed by the Supreme Court[20] and other courts[21] when confronted with cases of this particular type. These cases, of course, must be

---

[20]United States v. Hensley, 469 U.S. 221, 105 S.Ct. 675, 83 L.Ed.2d 604 (1985) (even if police officer was intending to arrest or to hold the person for a substantial period of time in response to a "wanted flyer" from another police department asking that defendant be picked up and held for them, the officer's conduct was a lawful *Terry* stop when the detention was in fact very brief, until a gun was seen, justifying an arrest on probable cause at that point, and there was a reasonable suspicion justifying a *Terry* stop at the source of the flyer).

[21]United States v. Roberts, 986 F.2d 1026 (6th Cir.1993) (though officers responding to call that defendant drunk and disorderly, upon finding defendant not home and his car gone, "decided they would stop any cars they saw to ascertain if defendant was the driver," court "must test the stop against the objective facts that relate to it, namely the erratic driving [the officers witnessed before the stop], not against what the officers may have intended to do even if there had been no erratic driving"); United States v. Frank, 864 F.2d 992 (3d Cir.1988) (where vehicle inventory without standard procedures valid because of defendant's request for return of personal property in rented car, it makes

no difference intent to inventory preceded that request, as evidence "may be suppressed only for constitutional violations, not for bad intentions"); United States v. Rambo, 789 F.2d 1289 (8th Cir.1986) (in presence misdemeanor arrest properly based on conduct of defendant when he answered police knock on door of his motel room, though police testified they knocked on door with intent of making what would have been an illegal arrest for an earlier misdemeanor not in their presence); United States v. Pirolli, 673 F.2d 1200 (11th Cir.1982) (abandonment not product of police misconduct where defendant removed goods from house as police approached it, even though approach may have been for purpose of making illegal search of house); Blair v. United States, 665 F.2d 500 (4th Cir.1981) (stopping of vessel on reasonable suspicion, resulting in obtaining facts amounting to probable cause, lawful even if, as defendants claim, the officers intended from the very outset to conduct more than a brief investigatory stop); United States v. Bugarin-Casas, 484 F.2d 853 (9th Cir.1973) (border patrol agent stopped car on reasonable suspicion but not probable cause for search with intent of searching it, after stop kilos of marijuana seen in car, so car searched; held, evidence admissible,

distinguished from those in which the words or actions of the police would actually communicate to a reasonable person an intention presently to make an illegal search or seizure.[22] In such a case, it would seem that the abandoned effects should be viewed as a suppressible fruit of the poisonous tree, but (as discussed elsewhere herein[23]) the Supreme Court has now foreclosed even that result by concluding that such a communicated intention is not Fourth Amendment activity.[24]

§ 1.4(c) Mistaken belief grounds for action lacking

If "impure plots" not acted upon are insufficient to justify use of the exclusionary rule in the name of deterrence, what then if the officer *does* act on his "bad" state of mind in the sense that he engages in Fourth Amendment activity despite his *mistaken* belief that he is lacking the necessary grounds for such action? Illustra-

---

as "the fact that the agents were intending at the time they stopped the car to search it in any event, generally the sort of search held unconstitutional in *Almeida-Sanchez v. United States*, does not render the search, supported by independent probable cause, invalid"); People v. Sosbe, 789 P.2d 1113 (Colo.1990) (officer's intent to stop defendant on insufficient suspicion of drug transaction irrelevant where defendant engaged in speeding before the stop undertaken); Jones v. State, 409 N.E.2d 1254 (Ind.App.1980) (narcotics thrown out window of motel room after police knocked on door are admissible, for "whatever intent or purpose may have been in their minds, no improper or unlawful act of any kind was committed"); State v. Byrd, 32 Ohio St.3d 79, 512 N.E.2d 611 (1987) (officer's intent to stop vehicle, existing prior to time vehicle pulled into parking lot and stopped, does not require that *Terry* standard be applied to confrontation that followed); Matter of Herrera, 393 N.W.2d 793 (S.D.1986) (even if officer decided to stop car on basis of driving by defendant not amounting to a traffic violation, it sufficient that before acting on that intent other activity by the driver amounting to a traffic violation had occurred); State v. Ashe, 745 P.2d 1255 (Utah 1987) (entry of premises to arrest without warrant lawful because of exigent circumstances; whether police

had already decided to enter without warrant before events creating exigent circumstances irrelevant, as "mere mental decision making (without action) by police officers does not violate a defendant's fourth amendment rights"). Cf. State v. Stafford, 1992 OK CR 47, 845 P.2d 894 (Okla. Crim. App. 1992) (given "the purpose of the exclusionary rule," suppression not required where search warrant without requisite showing authorized execution in nighttime but warrant in fact executed in daytime).

[22] Of course, just when there has been such communication can be a difficult issue. See, e.g., United States v. Acosta, 965 F.2d 1248 (3d Cir.1992) (where officer knocked on apartment door and said, "This is the police. Open the door. Let me in. I have a warrant," but the arrest warrant would not have authorized entry of that apartment, this not deemed deception; defendant's "bad faith intent" theory as to such conduct, which prompted occupant to throw drugs out window, rejected).

[23] See § 9.4(d).

[24] California v. Hodari D., 499 U.S. 621, 111 S.Ct. 1547, 113 L.Ed.2d 690 (1991). The *Hodari D.* analysis, which concerns a manifested intention to make a seizure, has also been used with respect to a manifested intention to make a search. State v. Rawlings, 121 Idaho 930, 829 P.2d 520 (1992).

tive is *United States v. Rowell,*[25] where the police captain who sent officers to arrest the defendant because of information he received from one Pecarro later "testified that after his first [and only] meeting with Pecarro he did not think there were sufficient facts to obtain a warrant." In this situation, it might be argued that exclusion for purposes of deterrence is called for, because suppression in such a case will impress upon the officer that in the future he should not arrest when he believes probable cause is lacking—a desirable result in that if he so believes, often probable cause will actually be lacking. *Rowell* did not go this route, but instead declared in upholding the arrest that the police officer is no more the judge of the insufficiency of his facts than of their sufficiency, the position consistently taken by other courts.[26] Similarly, it has been held that an officer's belief he lacks the reasonable suspicion necessary to make or continue a *Terry* stop is not controlling.[27]

This is a correct result. Here again, as Justice White put it in *Painten,* the evidence was "obtained by actions—if not thoughts— entirely in accord with the Fourth Amendment." That being so, the desired communication to the arresting officer is that he *does* have grounds to arrest on such facts, a message which would be muddled at best if the arrest in that case were deemed to necessitate exclusion of evidence. Moreover, there is something to the adage that actions speak louder than words; the fact that the captain in *Rowell* did order his men to arrest defendant is more convincing evidence of what he then perceived his authority to be than any unfortunately-framed comments elicited from him later concerning his understanding of the legal significance[28] of the information on which he acted.

§ 1.4(d) Wrong legal theory relied upon

The *Rowell*-type situation must be distinguished from yet another in which again the question is whether the officer's "underlying intent or motivation" is relevant, illustrated by *Klingler v. United States.*[29] Police were told by radio that a man with a green jacket and needing a shave had held up a gas station and was now believed to be occupying a 1955 or 1956 white and brown Pontiac with a Minnesota license and two construction helmets visible through the rear window. Later they saw a man in an olive jacket with a few days growth of beard in a 1957 salmon and coral Pontiac with a South Dakota license and two such helmets

---

[Section 1.4(c)]

[25]United States v. Rowell, 612 F.2d 1176 (7th Cir.1980).

[26]See cases collected in § 3.2(b).

[27]State v. Vento, 604 N.W.2d 468 (S.D.1999).

[28]More difficult is the question of whether the same is true of a purely factual interpretation. See DiPasquale v. State, 43 Md.App. 574, 406 A.2d 665 (1979), discussed in § 3.2(b) note 75.

[Section 1.4(d)]

[29]Klingler v. United States, 409 F.2d 299 (8th Cir.1969).

visible from the rear, so they arrested him for *vagrancy*. The court, after concluding there were not grounds to arrest for vagrancy but were grounds to arrest for robbery, held the arrest lawful "notwithstanding the officer's mistaken statement of grounds." Many other courts have reached the same result,[30]

---

[30]See cases collected in § 5.1(e); and Howards v. McLaughlin, 634 F.3d 1131 (10th Cir.2011), aff'd on other grounds., -- U.S. --, 132 S.Ct. 1497, 182 L.Ed.2d 593 (2012); United States v. Perdoma, 621 F.3d 745 (8th Cir.2010); United States v. Hughes, 606 F.3d 311 (6th Cir.2010); Edgerly v. City and County of San Francisco, 599 F.3d 946 (9th Cir.2010); United States v. Vinton, 594 F.3d 14 (D.C.Cir.2010); Lee v. Ferraro, 284 F.3d 1188 (11th Cir. 2002); United States v. Bookhardt, 277 F.3d 558 (D.C.Cir.2002); State v. Julian, 129 Idaho 133, 922 P.2d 1059 (1996); Murrell v. State, 421 N.E.2d 638 (Ind.1981); State v. Frosch, 816 So.2d 269 (La.2002); State v. Currier, 521 A.2d 295 (Me.1987); People v. Arterberry, 431 Mich. 381, 429 N.W.2d 574 (1988); State v. Ortega, 770 N.W.2d 145 (Minn.2009); State v. Klevgaard, 306 N.W.2d 185 (N.D.1981); State v. Retford, 276 S.C. 657, 281 S.E.2d 471 (1981); State v. Robinson, 622 S.W.2d 62 (Tenn.Crim.App.1980). But, the new theory must be based on facts known by the officer at the time of arrest. See, e.g., State v. Martin, 232 Neb. 385, 440 N.W.2d 676 (1989) (arrest without warrant for disturbing the peace not validated by later discovery of outstanding arrest warrant on defendant for a traffic violation; an "arrest which occurs without probable cause cannot be made lawful by events which occur afterward"). As for those decisions with a "reasonably related" limitation, see text at note 33 infra.

Similarly, if an officer arrests for an offense as to which there is sufficient evidence of its commission by defendant but by law only a citation is permitted for that offense, the arrest is nonetheless lawful if the police also had probable cause to arrest for some other offense not requiring the citation alternative. Scott v. United States, 878 A.2d 486 (D.C.App.2005); State v. Sassen, 240 Neb. 773, 484 N.W.2d 469 (1992).

By like reasoning, if a police officer arrests on the erroneous assumption that a valid arrest warrant has been issued for the person but he actually has probable cause to support a warrantless arrest, the arrest is valid. Ex parte Hamm, 564 So.2d 469 (Ala. 1990); Commonwealth v. Williams, 309 Pa.Super. 63, 454 A.2d 1083 (1982), order aff'd, 504 Pa. 511, 475 A.2d 1283.

Likewise, if a police officer makes a temporary detention on one basis, later determined to be insufficient, the stop may be upheld on another basis shown by the facts known to the officer. United States v. Wallace, 213 F.3d 1216 (9th Cir.2000) (traffic stop upheld though on mistaken belief that *any* tinting of front windows illegal, as this tinting illegal because twice as dark as law allows); United States v. Arzaga, 9 F.3d 91 (10th Cir.1993) (defendant's claim stop for tailgating a pretext rejected, as stop motivated by suspicion of drug trafficking sufficient to support the stop); United States v. Lowe, 9 F.3d 43 (8th Cir.1993) (even if no basis for stopping defendant for driving wrong way on one-way street, purported basis of stop, stop upheld because defendant had failed to signal for turn); United States v. Cardona-Rivera, 904 F.2d 1149 (7th Cir.1990) (where officers' testimony they stopped defendant for traffic violation "not worthy of belief," stop upheld because reasonable suspicion of drug trafficking); United States v. Hawkins, 811 F.2d 210 (3d Cir.1987) (though officer said stop was for traffic violation, Supreme Court's analysis "suggests that the legality of a stop must be judged by the objective facts known to the seizing officers rather than the justifications articulated by them," so stop upheld on reasonable suspicion of involvement in drug transaction); Marbury v. United States, 540 A.2d 114 (D.C.App.1985) (stop on sus-

which is as it should be.[31] Exclusion in the interest of deterrence is unjustified here, especially because such situations are often attributable to complicated legal distinctions between offenses or an officer's failure to record all the bases or the strongest basis upon which the arrest was made.[32]

One way of characterizing *Klingler* is to say that the officer's "underlying intent or motivation" simply reflects that he picked the wrong legal theory—claiming the arrest was for offense *A*, as to which probable cause was lacking, instead of offense *B*, as to

---

picion of drug activity upheld as arrest for traffic violation even though officer testified he had not pulled defendant over for traffic violation); State v. Bolosan, 78 Haw. 86, 890 P.2d 673 (1995) ("an investigative stop can be justified based on an objectively reasonable suspicion of any offense, provided that the offense for which reasonable suspicion exists is related to the offense articulated by the officer"); State v. Trombley, 327 Mont. 507, 116 P.3d 771 (2005) (even if stop for illegal U-turn based upon error of law as to what constitutes such violation, stop valid because officer testified he "observed other erratic driving," which he specified);Zimmerman v. North Dakota Dep't of Transportation Director, 543 N.W.2d 479 (N.D.1996) (stop lawful where officer observed moving traffic violation, notwithstanding fact officer testified that reason for stop was directive from another officer); State v. Baudhuin, 141 Wis.2d 642, 416 N.W.2d 60 (1987) (officer stopped car to see if driver needed assistance; stop upheld because of traffic violation). Contra: State v. Bailey, 452 N.W.2d 181 (Iowa 1990) (where officer stopped car upon radio report of officer in another department, stop cannot now be upheld on basis of stopping officer's observation of how vehicle being operated, as that would mean "uphold[ing] the stop based on an officer's exercise of judgment that in fact never occurred").

Similarly, if after a stop an officer frisks to find evidence, the frisk is still lawful if under "the standard of objective reasonableness" there were grounds for a frisk for the legitimate purpose of self-protection. People v. Ratcliff, 778 P.2d 1371 (Colo.1989).

[31]Compare Dix, Subjective "Intent" as a Component of Fourth Amendment Reasonableness, 76 Miss.L.J. 373, 467 (2006), arguing that this conclusion "ignores the potential value of Fourth Amendment law in stimulating proper analysis of situations by law enforcement officers themselves," in that "the lack of a subjective component to Fourth Amendment standards may to some extent contribute to a general attitude on the part of law enforcement that Fourth Amendment law is so uncertain, unrealistic, and perhaps even illegitimate that it can with reasonable confidence simply be disregarded."

[32]"Any other rule would force police officers to routinely charge every citizen taken into custody with every offense they thought he could be held for in order to increase the chances that at least one charge would survive the test for probable cause." United States v. Atkinson, 450 F.2d 835 (5th Cir.1971). This reasoning was endorsed in United States v. Bookhardt, 277 F.3d 558 (D.C.Cir.2002).

The court in *Klingler*, as have some others, see § 5.1(e), went on to stress that the "case fails to show bad faith on the part of the officers in making the arrest for vagrancy." That is, "the circumstances do not give rise to the inference that the arrest was effected for the purpose of creating an excuse to search, which would make both the arrest and search illegal." However, for reasons elaborated later in this discussion, see text at notes 72–85 infra, the more fruitful approach is not to inquire into "bad faith" in terms of the underlying motives of the police but instead to determine whether the action taken was in accordance with established standards for that department.

which grounds for arrest were present.

But just how far apart can offenses *A* and *B* be from one another to justify the *Klinger* result? While some courts had taken the view that the two offenses must be "closely" or "reasonably" related,[33] the Supreme Court rejected any such limitation in *Devenpeck v. Alford*,[34] where the lower court had concluded that an arrest purported to be for violation of the state's privacy statute could not later be upheld because there was probable cause to arrest for impersonating and for obstructing a law enforcement officer. Such a conclusion, a unanimous Supreme Court agreed, was inconsistent with the Court's precedents, especially *Whren v. United States*,[35] wherein it was explained that "the fact that the officer does not have the state of mind which is hypothecated by the reasons which provide the legal justification for the officer's action does not invalidate the action taken as long as the circumstances, viewed objectively, justify that action."[36] Moreover, the Court continued,

> the "closely related offense" rule is condemned by its perverse consequences. While it is assuredly good police practice to inform a person of the reason for his arrest at the time he is taken into custody, we have never held that to be constitutionally required. Hence, the predictable consequence of a rule limiting the probable-cause inquiry to offenses closely related to (and supported by the same facts as) those identified by the arresting officer is not * * * that officers will cease making sham arrests on the hope that such arrests will later be validated, but rather than officers will cease providing reasons for arrest. And even if this option were to be foreclosed by adoption of a statutory or constitutional requirement, officers would simply give every reason for which probable cause could conceivably exist.

Sometimes the gap between the relied upon but unavailing theory and the availing but unrelied upon theory is greater, as where it is not merely a matter of different offense categories but rather of quite different purposes or objectives. Here as well, as

---

[33] See Alford v. Haner, 333 F.3d 972 (9th Cir.2003); State v. Hollis, 161 Vt. 87, 633 A.2d 1362 (1993), and cases cited therein.

[34] Devenpeck v. Alford, 543 U.S. 146, 125 S.Ct. 588, 160 L.Ed.2d 537 (2004).

[35] Whren v. United States, 517 U.S. 806, 116 S.Ct. 1769, 135 L.Ed.2d 89 (1996).

[36] Quoting Scott v. United States, 436 U.S. 128, 98 S.Ct. 1717, 56 L.Ed.2d 168 (1978).

Compare Rosenbaum v. Washoe County, 654 F.3d 1001 (9th Cir.2011): "It cannot be that probable cause for a warrantless arrest exists so long as the facts may arguably give rise to probable cause under *any* criminal statute on the books-even if the crime is buried deep in a dust-covered tomb and never charged or prosecuted. If it were so, officers could arrest without a warrant under virtually any set of facts and later search the legal archives for a statute that might arguably justify it. Such a approach would be inconsistent with the Fourth Amendment's fundamental requirement that searches be cabined by the requirement of reasonableness."

reflected by *State v. Ercolano*,[37] there is presented the issue of whether the evidence must be suppressed because of "the underlying intent or motivation of the officers involved." The defendant was arrested in an apartment on a bookmaking charge, after which his automobile, parked on a nearby street, was subjected to impoundment and subsequent inventory, resulting in the discovery of incriminating evidence. Viewed solely as an impoundment-inventory situation, the car search was deemed unlawful because defendant was not given a reasonable opportunity to make other arrangements for disposition of the car,[38] and thus the question arose whether the search could now be upheld on a theory apparently not contemplated by the police—that there was probable cause to search the car and justification for proceeding without a search warrant. The majority in *Ercolano* answered in the negative, reasoning that a contrary result would be "inconsistent with the rationale of the exclusionary rule":

> It is indisputable that the exclusionary rule, to which the states are bound under *Mapp v. Ohio,* * * * was devised to deter the police from unconstitutional searches and seizures because other remedies were deemed ineffective. * * * It follows from this that if in the present case the police were *intending* only a safekeeping impoundment of the Ercolano vehicle, which as a matter of constitutional law was invalid * * *, the rationale of deterrence of unconstitutional police conduct compels exclusion of the evidence here seized. Saving the validity of the police action on a *court-devised* theory of justification would not deter future unconstitutional impoundments of vehicles or investigatory entries into vehicles without lawful warrant.[39]

Ercolano, however, appears to be a minority view. The Second

---

[37]State v. Ercolano, 79 N.J. 25, 397 A.2d 1062 (1979).

[38]See § 7.3(c).

[39]Schreiber, J., dissenting, stated: "To contend that exclusion of such evidence will act as a deterrent to police action even though defendant's constitutional rights have not been violated is incomprehensible."

See also State v. Jamison, 482 N.W.2d 409 (Iowa 1992) (where officers testifying about stop of car said it pursuant to search warrant, it cannot now be claimed stop valid under *Terry;* "in determining the validity of an investigatory stop police officers are bound by the real reasons for their actions," and "stop may not be upheld based on reasons that might have existed but in fact did not"); Dennis v. State, 342 Md. 196, 674 A.2d 928 (1996) (though from passenger's flight from stopped car "a police officer reasonably and objectively could entertain a suspicion that he was an active and willing participant with the driver" in attempting to elude the police, here "that suspicion was not what prompted the officer to detain the petitioner," as detention "was solely because the officer felt he would be safer if the petitioner were detained," which not the case, and thus no lawful *Terry* stop, and the "prosecution's articulation of a reasonable suspicion * * * is unavailing because no *Terry* investigative stop was intended"); State v. Garcia, 138 N.M. 1, 116 P.3d 72 (2005) (where officer erred in relying upon plain-view doctrine, search of vehicle upheld because there present the exigent circumstances for warrantless search required by state law); Wilson v. State, 874 P.2d 215 (Wyo.1994) (where purported basis of stop, to inquire into driver's condition, would not allow a warrant check, as would a stop on rea-

Circuit has reached the opposite result in essentially the same situation, that is, where again the probable cause theory was substituted for the inventory theory that apparently motivated the police search,[40] and other courts have likewise disregarded "the underlying intent or motivation of the officers involved" in favor of some other purpose on which the police action could have been lawfully grounded.[41] Supreme Court cases exist on both

---

sonable suspicion of criminal conduct, officer's testimony no such suspicion deemed controlling notwithstanding fact officer "could have possessed reasonable suspicion at the time," as court may not "construct after the fact justifications of police conduct").

[40]United States v. Ochs, 595 F.2d 1247 (2d Cir.1979). Two men were lawfully arrested while seated in a car, and the car was then lawfully impounded and was later inventoried, resulting in the discovery of certain incriminating papers. The district court upheld the search as an inventory, but the court of appeals feared that perhaps the examination of papers inside a briefcase could not be justified on that basis and thus affirmed on the ground that what had occurred was a valid *Chambers* search on probable cause. Of significance here is the fact that the court then added: "It is of no importance that the police may have thought their only power was to make an inventory; the test is what could lawfully be done, not what the policemen thought the source of their power to be."

[41]United States v. Brown, 374 F.3d 1326 (D.C.Cir.2004) (though officer wrong in thinking he could search trunk of car incident to driver's arrest, search upheld because there in fact was probable cause for a search); United States v. Cervantes, 19 F.3d 1151 (7th Cir.1994) (where police claimed search of car was incident to arrest for illegal possession of gun purportedly seen therein in plain view, but in fact no grounds for such arrest, search of car can be upheld if probable cause it contained drug proceeds); United States v. Bowman, 907 F.2d 63 (8th Cir.1990) ("fact the agents thought they were making an investigatory stop did not foreclose the government from proving probable cause"); United States v. Roy, 869 F.2d 1427 (11th Cir.1989) (officer viewed search of vessel as safety inspection; court upholds it as a search on probable cause); Sirimarco v. United States, 315 F.2d 699 (10th Cir.1963) (some time after state officers arrested defendant for counterfeiting and seized his car, a federal agent searched the car; though he purported to be making a search incident to the state arrest, a theory rejected by this court, the court then concluded the search could be upheld because as a matter of federal statutory law the agent *could have* impounded the car for forfeiture and then conducted a search of the impounded vehicle; as for the fact this latter course of action apparently never occurred to the federal agent, the court stated "the legality of his actions are not affected by his subjective beliefs"); People v. Hughes, 767 P.2d 1201 (Colo.1989) (though pat-down of defendant done in belief by police they could search anyone in apartment for cocaine incident to execution of warrant for such contraband, it upheld because a basis existed for self-protective frisk; "officer's subjective intent is not critical"); Padron v. State, 449 So.2d 811 (Fla.1984) (search of car upheld on search incident to arrest theory though officer viewed it as an inventory); Grimes v. State, 274 Ind. 378, 412 N.E.2d 75 (1980) (though officer had defendant accompany him and surrender gun because he thought defendant consenting to both, action upheld because there were grounds for arrest and search incident, and it "is of no consequence that officer Snow may not have known that he had probable cause to arrest"); Herod v. State, 311 Md. 288, 534 A.2d 362 (1987) (officer viewed car search as a search for self-protection incident to a *Terry* stop;

sides of the fence. In *Jones v. United States*,[42] where police entered premises for the purpose of executing a search warrant, a defective procedure because the entry was at night and the warrant permitted only daytime execution, the majority declined to uphold the entry and discovery of objects in plain view on the ground that the police *could* have lawfully made an intrusion of that magnitude for the purpose of arresting the petitioner, because the "testimony of the federal officers makes clear beyond dispute that their purpose in entering was to search for distilling equipment, not to arrest petitioner."[43] But in *Peters v. New York*,[44] where it appears the officer viewed his action in seizing an apparent prowler in his apartment house and conducting a search of his person revealing burglar's tools as only a stop-and-frisk, the

court upholds search as search made on probable cause); State v. Speak, 339 N.W.2d 741 (Minn.1983) (though officers without making probable cause determination took defendant in for breathalyzer test pursuant to invalid policy requiring testing of any driver involved in accident resulting in a fatality, test results admissible because probable cause actually existed in this case); State v. Sidebottom, 753 S.W.2d 915 (Mo.1988) (detention at station upheld as arrest made on probable cause though police view had been defendant appeared voluntarily); Nickerson v. State, 645 S.W.2d 888 (Tex.App.1983), judgment aff'd, 660 S.W.2d 825 (search of car upheld as search on probable cause though officer viewed it as an inventory).

[42] Jones v. United States, 357 U.S. 493, 78 S.Ct. 1253, 2 L.Ed.2d 1514 (1958).

[43] The Court may have been influenced to so limit its assessment of the police conduct because, as it acknowledged, discussion of the entry as an arrest entry would "confront us with a grave constitutional question, namely, whether the forceful nighttime entry into a dwelling to arrest a person reasonably believed within, upon probable cause that he had committed a felony, under circumstances where no reason appears why an arrest warrant could not have been sought is, consistent with the Fourth Amendment," an issue the Court did not resolve until over 20 years later. See § 6.1(b).

Clark, J., joined by Burton, J., dissenting in *Jones*, interpreted the

district court's findings as indicating "that the officers, not believing the statement of petitioner's wife that he was not there, entered the house to find and arrest petitioner," and thus did not directly dispute the majority view that only the officers' purpose could be considered. *Jones* thus might be viewed as actually involving an issue quite different from that under consideration here, namely, whether it is proper for a reviewing court to uphold a search on a theory not considered by the trial court. See § 11.7(d).

[44] Peters v. New York, 392 U.S. 40, 88 S.Ct. 1889, 20 L.Ed.2d 917 (1968). *Peters* was relied upon by the plurality in Florida v. Royer, 460 U.S. 491, 103 S.Ct. 1319, 75 L.Ed.2d 229 (1983), declaring that "the fact that the officers did not believe there was probable cause and proceeded on a consensual or *Terry*-stop rationale would not foreclose the State from justifying Royer's custody by proving probable cause and hence removing any barrier to relying on Royer's consent to search."

See also State v. Schwarz, 133 Idaho 463, 988 P.2d 689 (1999) (though police officer testified that he had not arrested the defendant, but only made a traffic stop and then a frisk based on his suspicion defendant was armed and dangerous, court upholds the search as a search incident to arrest because the officer had probable cause to arrest defendant on basis of defendant's prior admission that there was an outstanding warrant for his arrest).

Court (to avoid the difficult issue of whether the search had been sufficiently limited in scope under that theory) proceeded without hesitation to characterize the officer's conduct as a lawful arrest and search incident thereto.[45]

Even in an *Ercolano* type of case, Justice Rehnquist's *Scott* rule produces the better result. For one thing, it is to be strongly doubted that the *Ercolano* majority is correct in asserting that exclusion in that situation is compelled by "the rationale of deterrence." Suppression for police reliance on the wrong theory even when there exists an alternative valid theory would prevent unconstitutional searches only if, absent such an extension of the exclusionary rule, it may be assumed police will conduct arrests and searches on grounds they know or suspect to be insufficient in the hope that their actions will later be upheld on some other grounds of which they are presently unaware. That assumption seems fanciful. Moreover, exclusion in an *Ercolano* kind of case has a "Catch-22" quality to it, for then an erroneous legal characterization by a policeman somehow makes his conduct illegal even though but for that mistake the officer would likely have proceeded to the alternative correct legal characterization. In *Ercolano*, for example, it seems highly probable that had the officer not mistakenly concluded the search fell within the *Opperman* inventory rule, he would then have deemed it necessary to consider the probable cause and exigent circumstances issues and would have resolved them so as to proceed with the search under the *Chambers* car search rule. In the face of that, it is especially apparent that *Ercolano* erects an unduly rigid standard by insisting "that policemen act on necessary spurs of the moment with all the knowledge and acuity of constitutional lawyers."[46] Thus, cases like *Ercolano* press the exclusionary rule into service in such extreme situations that they afford ammunition to those who seek total abolition of the exclusionary rule.

---

[45]*Jones* and *Peters* might be distinguished in that in the former case the effort resisted by the Court was to shift from a broader power to a narrower one (i.e., from entry to search for evidence, to entry to arrest), while in the latter case what was permitted was a shift from a narrower power to a broader power (i.e., from a temporary stop and limited frisk to a full custodial arrest and full search of the person). A court could hardly be expected to uphold certain police action on the ground that something *less* would have been lawful. But that does not explain away *Jones*, for the government's contention (never refuted by the Court) was that the intrusion actually made did not exceed that which *would* have occurred had the agents entered to arrest the defendant and had looked for him.

Consider also that "reverse twists" on *Peters* are to be found. See, e.g., United States v. Reed, 733 F.2d 492 (8th Cir.1984); United States v. Vargas, 633 F.2d 891 (1st Cir.1980); United States v. Blair, 493 F.Supp. 398 (D.Md.1980), aff'd, 665 F.2d 500 (4th Cir.); People v. Stevens, 183 Colo. 399, 517 P.2d 1336 (1973) (officer's intent was to arrest, conduct nonetheless upheld as stop-and-frisk where intrusion did not exceed that permissible under latter theory). See § 9.2(e).

[46]Hall, J., in State v. Romeo, 43 N.J. 188, 203 A.2d 23 (1964).

§ 1.4(e) "Pretext" arrests and searches before *Whren*

There remains for consideration yet another group of cases, those often given the "pretext" characterization.[47] It is the possible impact of *Scott* on these cases that has prompted the greatest concern. Thus, Professor Burkoff states:

> The result of the *Scott* decision is a substantial neutralization of whatever deterrent disincentives the exclusionary rule currently produces, because any colorable legal construct that accounts for the conduct of officers as objectively viewed vitiates at law the consequences of their improper motives. This implies, for example, that if vice squad officers stop a car to search an individual for narcotics without the requisite probable cause or *Terry v. Ohio* reasonable suspicion, the fact that the search was unlawfully motivated is irrelevant to the question of the existence of a remediable fourth amendment violation as long as a court can point to other "objectively reasonable" grounds for stopping the car, such as a minor traffic violation.[48]

> *Scott* also undermines the long established rule that "[a]n arrest may not be used as a pretext to search for evidence," since fourth amendment violations cannot now be established by demonstrating the unlawful motives of the arresting officers. * * * If subjective intent is an inadmissible consideration on the issue whether or not there has been a substantive fourth amendment violation, what other way is there to explore police officers' deterrable motivations for making a stop, an arrest, or a search?[49]

Exactly what constitutes a "pretext" under the "long established rule" referred to by Professor Burkoff? The case from which he quotes, *United States v. Lefkowitz*,[50] turns out upon close inspection to be of no help in answering this question. The warrantless search in *Lefkowitz* of the premises where defendant was arrested was for evidence of the crime for which he was arrested and not for some other purpose, and the Court was actually

---

[Section 1.4(e)]

[47]See, e.g., Comments, 41 Baylor L.Rev. 495 (1989); Notes, 70 B.U.L. Rev. 111 (1990); 50 La.L.Rev. 181 (1989); 1991 Wis.L.Rev. 325 (1991); 12 W.N.Engl.L.Rev. 105 (1990).

To be distinguished from the plain view doctrine requirement of the plurality in Coolidge v. New Hampshire, 403 U.S. 443, 91 S.Ct. 2022, 29 L.Ed.2d 564 (1971), that there must have been an "inadvertent discovery" of the item for its warrantless seizure to be lawful. That requirement was rejected in Horton v. California, 496 U.S. 128, 110 S.Ct. 2301, 110 L.Ed.2d 112 (1990), in part because the Court preferred "application of objective standards of conduct, rather than standards that depend upon the subjective state of mind of the officer,"

a point also relevant in the present context. The two *Horton* dissenters opined "this decision should have only a limited impact, for the Court is not confronted today with what lower courts have described as a 'pretextual' search."

[48]Burkoff drops a footnote at this point citing several cases reaching a contrary result. For these cases, see § 5.2(e).

[49]Burkoff, The Court that Devoured the Fourth Amendment: The Triumph of an Inconsistent Exclusionary Doctrine, 58 Ore.L.Rev. 151, 189–90 (1979).

[50]United States v. Lefkowitz, 285 U.S. 452, 52 S.Ct. 420, 76 L.Ed. 877 (1932).

concerned with the interplay of the since-repudiated[51] "mere evidence" rule and the pre-*Chimel*[52] rule that seemed to allow a full warrantless search of defendant's premises merely because of his arrest there.

But the case next cited by Burkoff, *Abel v. United States*,[53] is another matter. There Immigration and Naturalization Service officers, acting pursuant to an administrative warrant for deportation, placed Russian spy Colonel Abel under arrest, incident to which evidence of espionage was uncovered. Abel sought to suppress that evidence in his criminal prosecution on the ground that the government had "resorted to a subterfuge" because the "true purpose in arresting him" was not to determine his deportability but rather to obtain evidence for a criminal espionage prosecution. As to this, Justice Frankfurter declared for the Court:

> Were this claim justified by the record, it would indeed reveal a serious misconduct by law-enforcing officers. The deliberate use by the Government of an administrative warrant for the purpose of gathering evidence in a criminal case must meet stern resistance by the courts. The preliminary stages of a criminal prosecution must be pursued in strict obedience to the safeguards and restrictions of the Constitution and laws of the United States. A finding of bad faith is, however, not open to us on this record. What the motive was of the I.N.S. officials who determined to arrest petitioner, and whether the I.N.S. in doing so was not exercising its powers in the lawful discharge of its own responsibilities but was serving as a tool for the F.B.I. in building a criminal prosecution against petitioner, were issues fully canvassed in both courts below. The crucial facts were found against the petitioner.

An understanding of what the "crucial facts" were in *Abel* requires some elaboration of the facts then set out by the Court: though a defected spy told the FBI Abel worked with him, the FBI then lacked sufficient evidence for a criminal prosecution; Abel's illegal residence in the country was brought to the attention of the INS by the FBI; the FBI promptly supplied additional information requested by the INS; INS agents met with FBI agents before initiating Abel's arrest; FBI agents accompanied INS agents to the hotel where the arrest was to be made; INS agents delayed the arrest until FBI agents had interviewed Abel and unsuccessfully sought his cooperation; FBI agents were present when the INS agents then arrested Abel and searched his room; and FBI agents searched the room further after Abel checked out. From all of this, it is apparent there was very close cooperation between the two agencies and that the "strongest" government interest in Abel (as well it should have been) was because of his activity as a spy. Yet the Court in *Abel* rejected his

---

[51]See § 2.6(d).

[52]See § 6.3(b).

[53]Abel v. United States, 362 U.S. 217, 80 S.Ct. 683, 4 L.Ed.2d 668 (1960).

"subterfuge" claim because one additional critical fact was deemed fully supported by the evidence. That fact, as stated in the findings of the district court, is

> that while the first information that came to them concerning [Abel] * * * was furnished by the F.B.I.—which cannot be an unusual happening—the proceedings taken by the Department differed in no respect from what would have been done in the case of an individual concerning whom no such information was known to exist.[54]

Abel, then, represents yet another situation in which "the underlying intent or motivation of the officers involved"—to utilize the *Scott* phrase once again—does not require suppression: where, even assuming that intent or motivation was the dominant one in the particular case, the Fourth Amendment activity undertaken is precisely the same as would have occurred had that intent or motivation been entirely absent from the case. This means, for example, that if the police arrest X for crime A, as they would have in any event, in the anticipation or hope of thereby finding evidence of crime B on X's person, the latter "underlying intent or motivation" does not make their action illegal.[55] Likewise, if the police stop X's car for minor offense A, and they "subjectively hoped to discover contraband during the

---

[54]United States v. Abel, 155 F.Supp. 8 (E.D.N.Y.1957).

[55]United States v. D'Antoni, 856 F.2d 975 (7th Cir.1988) (drug suspect arrested when record check showed he wanted for failure to pay $738.40 on traffic conviction; lawful, as reasonable officer would have made the arrest absent motive to search); United States v. Wilson, 853 F.2d 869 (11th Cir.1988) (custodial arrest and search of person driving on suspended license upheld, though officer may have suspected drugs; court answers in affirmative question: "Would a reasonable police officer have arrested Wilson for driving with a suspended license absent a motive to conduct an unrelated search for narcotics not supported by probable cause"); Hines v. State, 289 Ark. 50, 709 S.W.2d 65 (1986) (arrest for criminal mischief not improper pretext notwithstanding desire to investigate defendant for murder-robbery; "Where the police have a dual motive in making an arrest, what might be termed a covert motive is not tainted by the overt motive, even though the covert motive may be dominant, so long as the arrest would have been carried out had the covert motive been absent"; such the case here, as criminal mis-

chief arrested based on substantial evidence from private citizen who made complaint without police encouragement); State v. Vann, 230 Neb. 601, 432 N.W.2d 810 (1988) (defendant's arrest for theft of $360 worth of videotapes not pretextual, though officers accompanied by narcotics agents who were conducting independent investigation of defendant's violation of drug laws); State v. Jones, 127 N.H. 515, 503 A.2d 802 (1985) (though police suspected defendant of rape, arrest of him on bench warrant for failure to pay fine lawful; court emphasizes officers investigating the rape did not obtain the bench warrant and that it was already on file and presumably subject to execution by any officer who knew of it); State v. Gerald, 113 N.J. 40, 549 A.2d 792 (1988) (execution of arrest warrants for failure to appear re traffic violations upheld notwithstanding desire to question about homicide, as conduct was objectively reasonable); Lyons v. State, 787 P.2d 460 (Okl.Crim.App.1989) (where in connection with investigation of tip defendant growing marijuana in his basement police ran record check and learned there was an outstanding municipal warrant on defendant, arrest of him at home not pretextual, as of-

stop" so as to establish serious offense B, the stop is nonetheless lawful if "a reasonable officer *would* have made the stop in the absence of the invalid purpose."[56] Or, if police obtain a search warrant to search X 's premises for evidence of crime A, which

---

ficers "testified that it was the duty of any Tulsa Police Officer, regardless of their particular division, to serve any outstanding warrants that come to their attention"); State v. Archuleta, 850 P.2d 1232 (Utah 1993) (parole hold arrest lawful even if police desired to question defendant about murder, as arrest would have been made in any event, as shown by fact police were trying to make the arrest even before they knew about the murder); Horne v. Commonwealth, 230 Va. 512, 339 S.E.2d 186 (1986) (though police suspected defendant of murder, his arrest on 2 outstanding misdemeanor warrants lawful; court stresses the warrants predated the murder investigation and that earlier efforts to execute them had been made; "Had there been no murder investigation, Horne would still have been arrested if he could have been found").

Similarly, where the defendant's bag would have been x-rayed during airport screening and, because of the unidentified mass disclosed by the x-ray, would have been inspected further in any event, this screening process was lawful even though the defendant was suspected to be carrying narcotics. United States v. Smith, 643 F.2d 942 (2d Cir.1981).

[56]United States v. Guzman, 864 F.2d 1512 (10th Cir.1988), holding the lower court erred in applying a subjective intent-of-officer test. *Guzman* was overruled in United States v. Botero-Ospina, 71 F.3d 783 (10th Cir.1995) (adopting "could" test, discussed in text, infra, instead).

See also United States v. Dirden, 38 F.3d 1131 (10th Cir.1994) (traffic stop no pretext, as "reasonable officer, similarly situated, would have made the stop in the absence of an invalid purpose," for "operation of the vehicle suggested that the driver was intoxicated or falling asleep"); United States v. Cannon, 29 F.3d 472 (9th Cir.1994) (no illegal pretext where vehicle stopped for driving on suspended li-

cense, "a serious offense for which any reasonable officer would stop a driver"); United States v. Mans, 999 F.2d 966 (6th Cir.1993) (traffic stop no pretext to seek drugs, as officer knew defendant's license had been revoked and thus in any event "would have stopped defendant, rather than allowing him to continue to drive illegally"); United States v. Valdez, 931 F.2d 1448 (11th Cir.1991) (illegal pretext stop, as absent instructions from narcotics unit traffic officer would not stop for this traffic violation); Mings v. State, 318 Ark. 201, 884 S.W.2d 596 (1994) (no pretext stop despite suspicion of criminal activity, as absent same officer would nonetheless stop weaving motor home); Kehoe v. State, 521 So.2d 1094 (Fla.1988) (stop for license tag violation not pretextual even if police suspicion of other more serious criminality, provided "a reasonable officer would have stopped the vehicle absent an additional invalid purpose"); State v. Guy, 242 Kan. 840, 752 P.2d 119 (1988) (stop for speeding lawful notwithstanding surveillance was for narcotics activity; court implies this because these officers, though not traffic officers, could be expected in any event to stop car going at speed of 100 m.p.h., the case here); State v. Izzo, 623 A.2d 1277 (Me.1993) (questioning standard appearing in above text, court rejects defendant's claim traffic stop an illegal "excuse to investigate for other criminal activity," as officer "testified that he routinely stops vehicles that have a broken tail lens or an inoperable plate light"); Commonwealth v. Santana, 420 Mass. 205, 649 N.E.2d 717 (1995) (even if trooper hoped to find evidence of illegal drug activity, stop not pretextual here, as "a reasonable police officer would have stopped the defendant's automobile even in the absence of an ulterior motive," for court below found that "the stop of a vehicle for defective equipment was a matter of routine standard police procedure").

again they would have done in any event, the search is not illegal merely because the police suspect they might find evidence of crime B.[57] Similarly, if X's car is searched in the hope or expectation of finding therein evidence of crime B, but the search was an inventory that would have been made in any event[58] or a search for evidence of crime A that would have been made in any event,[59] again the evidence is admissible. Though some contrary authority is to be found,[60] this is a sound result. When the action would have been taken against X even absent the "underlying intent or motivation,"[61] there is no *conduct* that ought to have been deterred and thus no reason to bring the Fourth Amendment exclusionary rule into play for purposes of deterrence.

There remains, then, the case in which the Fourth Amendment activity would not have been undertaken *but for* the "underlying intent or motivation" that, standing alone, could not supply a lawful basis for the police conduct.[62] The driver of an automobile suspected of unlawful drug activity is placed under custodial arrest for a traffic violation and then searched, though the arrest

---

[57]State v. Riedinger, 374 N.W.2d 866 (N.D.1985).

[58]In re One 1965 Econoline, 109 Ariz. 433, 511 P.2d 168 (1973); State v. Rodewald, 376 N.W.2d 416 (Minn. 1985). See other cases in accord in note 72 of § 7.5.

Cf. United States v. Bowhay, 992 F.2d 229 (9th Cir.1993) (notwithstanding investigative motive, inventory of arrestee's satchel lawful, as department's policy was to inventory everything, and thus conduct would have been same absent that motive).

[59]People v. Hill, 12 Cal.3d 731, 117 Cal.Rptr. 393, 528 P.2d 1 (1974). See also State v. Oliver, 341 N.W.2d 744 (Iowa 1983) (citing *Scott*, court holds it irrelevant whether in execution of search warrant for T-shirt police picked up rug to look for magazine, as T-shirt could have been there and thus conduct within scope of that authorized by warrant).

[60]See cases in § 7.5(d) invalidating routine vehicle inventories merely because the police anticipated finding evidence of crime, and cases in § 4.11(f) holding execution of a search warrant invalid because the police hoped to find something other than the evidence for which the warrant issued. The cases in the first category, it is submitted, are in error. As for those in

the second category, they almost always reflect an additional legitimate concern, namely, that the execution of the warrant was likely more intensive than would have been the case had the authorities only been interested in the items named in the search warrant.

[61]One might argue, of course, that what the police *would* have done absent the "underlying intent or motivation" is a matter so difficult to prove that it should not be the determining factor. But, the question is whether the answer to that problem is exclusion in a broader range of cases or, instead, as suggested in the later text at note 82 infra, the establishment of standard procedures against which to test the conduct of the police in the particular case.

[62]On the other hand, if the underlying motivation *is* by itself a lawful basis for the activity, then it is irrelevant whether the purported basis of the activity would not also have prompted such action. See, e.g., United States v. Arzaga, 9 F.3d 91 (10th Cir.1993) (pretextual stop contention rejected without regard to whether police otherwise stop for violation of city ordinance on tailgating, as there was a reasonable suspicion of drug trafficking, which apparently motivated the stop). See § 1.4(d).

was not "one which would have been made by a traffic officer on routine patrol against any citizen driving in the same manner."[63] A person suspected of drug activity is arrested late at night inside the premises of another by state police holding city arrest warrants for two minor traffic violations, hardly the usual practice in dealing with outstanding traffic warrants.[64] An arrestee's car is impounded and then inventoried "contrary to the usual procedure followed in traffic cases."[65] Such situations as these involve what the Supreme Court in *Abel* properly characterized as "serious misconduct by law-enforcing officers," and in the pre-*Whren* era resulted in suppression of evidence so acquired.[66]

So, it would seem that at long last we have encountered a situation proving the error of Justice Rehnquist's declaration for the Court in *Scott* that searches are to be examined "under a standard of objective reasonableness without regard to the underlying intent or motivation of the officers involved." But, it is submitted, this is not the case. The illustrative fact situations in the preceding paragraph and others like them involve "serious misconduct" *in spite of* rather than *because of* the "underlying intent or motivation" of the police. That is, the proper basis of concern is not with

---

[63]Diggs v. State, 345 So.2d 815 (Fla.App.1977). See also United States v. Ferguson, 989 F.2d 202 (6th Cir.1993) (stop for lack of visible license plate a pretext, as absent invalid purpose no such stop would have occurred, as is indicated by fact officer after stop "made no inquiry or investigation whatsoever concerning the absence of a visible license plate"); United States v. Miller, 821 F.2d 546 (11th Cir.1987) (drug suspect illegally stopped where stop for traffic violation of right wheels crossing over lane marker about 4" for 6½ seconds, as "a reasonable officer would not have stopped Miller absent some other motive"); State v. Haskell, 645 A.2d 619 (Me.1994) (where "officer deviated from normal practice" by stopping defendant for driving 59 m.p.h. in 55 m.p.h. zone, stop pretextual and illegal); Black v. State, 739 S.W.2d 240 (Tex.Crim.App.1987) (arrest by homicide detectives of murder suspect for several minor traffic violations, e.g., no light over license plate, was pretextual and unlawful; court stresses no showing "they were in the habit of enforcing traffic laws or writing traffic tickets"); State v. Arroyo, 796 P.2d 684 (Utah 1990) (stop a pretext, as "a reasonable officer would not have stopped

Arroyo and cited him for 'following too closely' except for some unarticulated suspicion of more serious criminal activity").

Such pretext analysis has sometimes been used in instances in which the suspected conduct in fact does not constitute a traffic violation, e.g., United States v. Hernandez, 55 F.3d 443 (9th Cir.1995); United States v. Millan, 36 F.3d 886 (9th Cir.1994), though in such circumstances it would be simpler merely to conclude that because (as stated in *Hernandez*) "a reasonable officer knows the law he is charged with enforcing," the requisite probable cause or reasonable suspicion is lacking. See § 3.2, note 277; § 9.5, note 91.

[64]Harding v. State, 301 So.2d 513 (Fla.App.1974).

[65]State v. Volk, 291 So.2d 643 (Fla.App.1974).

[66]E.g., United States v. Prim, 698 F.2d 972 (9th Cir.1983) (federal drug agents cannot validate their detention of suspected drug courier because they were aware of state nonsupport warrant, on which they otherwise would not act). See also cases cited at notes 63–65 supra and other cases in §§ 5.2(e), 6.7(d), 7.5(e).

why the officer deviated from the usual practice in this case but simply that he *did* deviate.[67] It is the *fact* of the departure from the accepted way of handling such cases that makes the officer's conduct arbitrary, and it is the arbitrariness that in this context constitutes the Fourth Amendment violation; "a paramount purpose of the fourth amendment is to prohibit arbitrary searches and seizures as well as unjustified searches and seizures."[68] In terms of the language of *Scott*, then, it may be said that searches of the kind here under discussion do not pass the "standard of objective reasonableness."

Unfortunately, several poorly reasoned decisions reached precisely the contrary conclusion,[69] and in the process conferred

---

[67]Under this approach, one question is what constitutes a deviation. For example, it may be asked whether the assignment of the particular officer should be taken into account. See, e.g., United States v. Robles-Alvarez, 75 F.3d 559 (9th Cir.1996) (traffic stop not pretextual where "reasonable officer would stop the suspect for violation of a specified law" and "it was within the detaining officer's scope of responsibility to enforce that law"; no need for court to explore "the more specific question of whether a reasonable officer assigned to the particular duties of the detaining officer [here, assignment to unit that gathers information on gang members] would stop the suspect").

[68]Amsterdam, Perspectives on the Fourth Amendment, 58 Minn.L.Rev. 349, 417 (1974). See also Maclin, What Can Fourth Amendment Doctrine Learn From Vagueness Doctrine?, 3 U.Pa.J.Const.L. 398, 454 (2001) (concluding that "the privilege against arbitrary and capricious police intrusion embodied in the Fourth Amendment" is insufficiently protected under the Court's recent decisions and that it is necessary for search and seizure law to "adopt an essential feature of vagueness law: controlling police discretion").

[69]E.g., United States v. Botero-Ospina, 71 F.3d 783 (10th Cir.1995) (traffic stop for brief lane straddling lawful; it "irrelevant whether a reasonable officer would have stopped Mr. Botero-Spina under these circumstances" and "irrelevant that Deputy

Barney may have harbored a secret hope of finding evidence of drug trafficking"); United States v. Flores, 63 F.3d 1342 (5th Cir.1995) (under *Roberson*, discussed in text following, stop lawful where officers investigating drug activity had trooper in marked car stop defendant for speeding, as defendant was actually speeding); United States v. Johnson, 63 F.3d 242 (3d Cir.1995) (even if stopping of vehicle for having air freshener hanging from rear-view mirror was motivated by desire to find drugs, stop lawful because "a reasonable police officer could have made the stop" anyway); United States v. Willis, 61 F.3d 526 (7th Cir.1995) (defendant's claim "that Trooper Hartman, a member of a drug interdiction team, not a traffic officer, selectively operated his radar on out-of-state vehicles, looking for drugs, and that his stop of Mr. Willis' vehicle was merely a pretext to facilitate a drug search" need not be considered, for stop was "objectively reasonable" because defendant in fact speeding); United States v. Scopo, 19 F.3d 777 (2d Cir.1994) (where suspected mobster stopped for failing to signal lane change, it makes no difference whether officer "would" have otherwise made such a stop; "the fact that an officer may be engaged in an arrest which would not usually be affected in the course of the officer's normal duties does not negate the validity of the arrest," only requirement is that there be probable cause); United States v. Harvey, 16 F.3d 109 (6th Cir.1994) (officer stopped car of suspected drug courier because it slightly exceeded

upon the police virtual *carte blanche* to stop people because of the color of their skin or for any other arbitrary reason.[70] One il-

---

speed limit; stop lawful even if defendant correct in asserting "that no reasonable police officer would have stopped the car for those violations absent some other motive"); United States v. Stapleton, 10 F.3d 582 (8th Cir.1993) (police received anonymous tip car carrying drugs, so they followed car and stopped it when it traveled 70–75 in 65 m.p.h. zone; stop lawful without regard to fact "the officers ordinarily may not have stopped a car exceeding the speed limit by five to ten miles per hour"); United States v. Hassan El, 5 F.3d 726 (4th Cir.1993) (traffic stop by narcotics officers who did not even have ticket books; rejecting view that investigative stop will be deemed invalid if it represents a departure from routine police practice, court upholds stop here even if "officer would not have made the stop but for some hunch"); Ex parte Scarbrough, 621 So.2d 1006 (Ala.1993) (when defendant arrested for unpaid traffic tickets because of desire to question him about a murder, arrest lawful because officer doing "what is objectively authorized and legally permitted," and officer's "subjective intent in doing so is irrelevant"); State v. Hofmann, 537 N.W.2d 767 (Iowa 1995) (in response to defendant's claim execution of prior arrest warrants by drug investigators was pretextual, court opts for "an objective or 'could' assessment of the officers' conduct"); State v. Olson, 482 N.W.2d 212 (Minn.1992) (only necessary that there be "an objective legal basis" for the arrest); State v. Mease, 842 S.W.2d 98 (Mo.1992) (sufficient that police "do no more than they are objectively authorized and legally permitted to do," presumably without regard to what usual practice would be, though no showing or allegation as to usual practice re felony nonsupport and carrying concealed weapon bases of arrest); Skelly v. State, 1994 OK CR 55, 880 P.2d 401 (Okla. Crim. App. 1994 (no pretext where stop for license light out, as there was probable cause and "by definition a pretextual stop lacks probable

cause"); Crittenden v. State, 899 S.W.2d 668 (Tex.Crim.App.1995) ("a seizing officer's subjective motivation in effectuating a seizure is deemed irrelevant to the determination of whether the seizure was reasonable," a position acknowledged to be "nothing more than the complete abandonment of any sort of pretext doctrine"); State v. Lopez, 873 P.2d 1127 (Utah 1994) (pretext doctrine rejected on bizarre reasoning that it "offends equal protection by conferring upon suspected citizens greater Fourth Amendment protection against unreasonable searches and seizures than that enjoyed by nonsuspected citizens").

[70] As one distinguished federal judge has noted, when police are given such a broad grant of authority the inherent risk is "that some police officers will use the pretext of traffic violations or other minor infractions to harass members of groups identified by factors that are totally impermissible as a basis for law enforcement activity—factors such as race or ethnic origin, or simply appearances that some police officers do not like, such as young men with long hair, heavy jewelry, and flashy clothing." United States v. Scopo, 19 F.3d 777 (2d Cir.1994) (Newman, C.J., concurring).

Despite this observation, the judge concurred in a majority opinion conforming to the *Roberson* approach in the text following, reasoning that there was no reason to deal with the pretext arrest situation under the Fourth Amendment because "the Equal Protection Clause has sufficient vitality to curb most of the abuses that the appellee apprehends," and that officers "who misuse the authority we approve today may expect to be defendants in civil suits seeking substantial damages for discriminatory enforcement of the law." But there is no reason to believe that this is so, as evidenced by the experience concerning other equal protection challenges to enforcement policy. See 4 W. LaFave, J. Israel, N. King & O. Kerr, Criminal Procedure § 13.4 (3d ed.2007). A major

lustration, *United States v. Roberson,*[71] should suffice: A Texas state trooper passed a van and noted it had out-of-state plates and four black occupants, so he pulled off onto the shoulder after cresting a hill, turned his lights off, and then observed the van change lanes to provide more distance between it and the vehicle on the shoulder. The lane change was unaccompanied by a signal, which hardly seems remarkable in view of the fact that the van was "the only moving vehicle on that stretch of road," but the trooper "obviously regarded this as a serious traffic offense," for he pulled the van over, but he then questioned the van's occupants on unrelated matters and finally exacted a consent to search the vehicle resulting in the discovery of drugs. Despite the court's familiarity with this trooper's "propensity for patrolling the fourth amendment's outer frontier" and his "remarkable record" of turning traffic stops into drug arrests on 250 prior occasions, the defendants in *Roberson* were deemed to be without any basis to challenge the stop because, after all, the trooper had "observed a traffic infraction before stopping the vehicle"!

Such decisions as *Roberson* cannot be squared with the fundamental point that arbitrary action is unreasonable under the Fourth Amendment, as previously recognized by the Supreme Court in a variety of circumstances. Under *Camara v. Municipal Court,*[72] so as not to "leave the occupant subject to the discretion of the official in the field," warrants for housing inspections must show that "reasonable legislative or administrative standards for conducting an area inspection are satisfied with respect to a particular dwelling." Similarly, *Marshall v. Barlow's, Inc.*[73] ordinarily requires a warrant showing a business inspection "is pursuant to an administrative plan containing specific neutral criteria," as the "authority to make warrantless searches devolves almost unbridled discretion upon executive and administrative officers." Absent reasonable suspicion cars may not be stopped by roving patrols seeking illegal aliens,[74] but pursuant to *United States v. Martinez-Fuerte*[75] fixed checkpoints may be operated for that purpose because in such a situation there is not "a grave danger that * * * unreviewable discretion would be abused by some of-

---

difficulty, which as noted in the text following is also a principle reason for not grounding a pretext arrest doctrine in police motivation, is that courts cannot with any degree of regularity determine when there existed an improper motive that influenced the police conduct.

[71]United States v. Roberson, 6 F.3d 1088 (5th Cir.1993).

[72]Camara v. Municipal Court, 387 U.S. 523, 87 S.Ct. 1727, 18 L.Ed.2d 930 (1967).

[73]Marshall v. Barlow's, Inc., 436 U.S. 307, 98 S.Ct. 1816, 56 L.Ed.2d 305 (1978).

[74]United States v. Brignoni-Ponce, 422 U.S. 873, 95 S.Ct. 2574, 45 L.Ed.2d 607 (1975).

[75]United States v. Martinez-Fuerte, 428 U.S. 543, 96 S.Ct. 3074, 49 L.Ed.2d 1116 (1976).

ficers in the field." And more recently, in *Delaware v. Prouse*,[76] the random stopping of vehicles without reasonable suspicion to check for drivers' licenses and vehicle registrations was held unreasonable under the Fourth Amendment, but it was suggested that checkpoints operated for such purposes would be permissible because then "persons in automobiles on public roadways [would] not for that reason alone have their travel and privacy interfered with at the unbridled discretion of police officers." In all of these cases, of course, the need for a meaningful prohibition of arbitrary action was highlighted by the fact that the enforcement activity in question was being permitted without probable cause focusing upon a particular individual or place. In that sense, they are different from the kind of situation presently under discussion, where the arrest or search *is* on probable cause but that probable cause goes to an offense for which an arrest or search would not ordinarily be made. But given the pervasiveness of such minor offenses and the ease with which law enforcement agents may uncover them in the conduct of virtually everyone, that difference hardly matters, for here as well there exists "a power that places the liberty of every man in the hands of every petty officer,"[77] precisely the kind of arbitrary authority that gave rise to the Fourth Amendment.

To the extent that lower court cases using the "would" (rather than "could") formulation have tended, in the course of suppressing evidence on Fourth Amendment grounds, to stress the ulterior motives of the police, they may appear to run contrary to the *Scott* principle. But the inquiry in these cases into "the underlying intent or motivation of the officers involved," it would seem, has ordinarily been prompted by an inability of the courts to ascertain in a more direct fashion whether the police in the particular case had departed from their usual practice. This is not to suggest, however, that inquiry into motivation is either a desirable or an accurate means of resolving that issue. For one thing, there is hardly a perfect correlation between motivation and deviation. Presence of an ulterior motive may show why an officer might want to depart from the usual procedure but does not show that he has done so,[78] and even in the absence of an ulterior motive the officer may have by inadvertence failed to conform to

---

[76]Delaware v. Prouse, 440 U.S. 648, 99 S.Ct. 1391, 59 L.Ed.2d 660 (1979).

[77]2 L. Wroth & H. Zobel, Legal Papers of John Adams 141–42 (1965), setting out Adams' abstract of the argument of James Otis against the writs of assistance.

[78]Thus in United States v. Smith, 799 F.2d 704 (11th Cir.1986), recognizing that improper motivation is not alone sufficient under *Scott,* the court wisely held that a traffic stop probably motivated by a desire to investigate a suspected drug courier was illegal, where based on one instance of weaving over the white line 6 inches into the emergency lane, only because it failed an objective test; "the proper inquiry, again, is not whether the officer could validly have made the stop but whether in the same circumstances a reasonable officer would have made

the usual practice. Secondly, and perhaps more important, there is no reason to believe that courts can with any degree of success determine in which instances the police had an ulterior motive. As Professor Amsterdam has quite persuasively noted:

> But surely the catch is not worth the trouble of the hunt when courts set out to bag the secret motivations of police in this context. A subjective purpose to do something that the applicable legal rules say there is sufficient objective cause to do can be fabricated all too easily and undetectably. Motivation is, in any event, a self-generating phenomenon: if a purpose to search for heroin can legally be accomplished only when accompanied by a purpose to search for a weapon, knowledgeable officers will seldom experience the first desire without a simultaneous onrush of the second.[79]

Underlying the *Scott* rule, then, is the sound notion (expressed earlier by three members of the Court in *Massachusetts v. Painten*[80]) that "sending state and federal courts on an expedition into the minds of police officers would produce a grave and fruitless misallocation of judicial resources."

What this means, then, is that the *Scott* approach of disregarding "the underlying intent or motivation of the officers involved" is correct even in the situation now under discussion, *provided* there are more reliable and feasible means of determining in a particular case whether or not the challenged arrest or search was arbitrary. This could best be accomplished by more widespread application of the requirement utilized by the Supreme Court in *South Dakota v. Opperman*,[81] namely, that the Fourth Amendment activity "was carried out in accordance with *standard procedures* in the local police department."[82] Were the Court to make broader use of that check upon arbitrariness, which unfortunately it has failed to do in circumstances quite obviously calling for that kind of a restriction,[83] there then would be no reason to question the proposition put forward by the Court in *Scott*.

---

the stop in the absence of the invalid purpose."

[79] Amsterdam, 58 Minn.L.Rev. 349, 436–37 (1974).

[80] Massachusetts v. Painten, 368 F.2d 142 (1st Cir.1966).

[81] South Dakota v. Opperman, 428 U.S. 364, 96 S.Ct. 3092, 49 L.Ed.2d 1000 (1976).

[82] Remarkably, it is sometimes assumed that the line of cases in note 69 supra represents the better view precisely because it does *not* require police to follow the policies of their own department! See United States v. Ferguson, 8 F.3d 385 (6th Cir.1993) (by following that view, "we ensure that the validity of such stops is not subject to the vagaries of police departments' policies and procedures concerning the kinds of traffic offenses of which they ordinarily do or do not take note").

[83] Amsterdam, 58 Minn.L.Rev. 349, 415–16 (1974), notes: "Six weeks ago, the Supreme Court handed down decisions holding that a police officer who arrests a motorist for a traffic violation may make a full-scale body search incident to the arrest. The holdings were delivered in two cases. In the first case, both the decision of the officer to make a 'full custody arrest' rather than to issue a citation and his decision to conduct a full 'field type search' in connection with arrests for the particular vehicle code violation in

There would then exist standards[84] against which to examine the police conduct in individual cases; in keeping with the philosophy underlying the *Camara-Prouse* line of cases, decisions of whether to arrest and search when probable cause is present would not be left entirely to officers in the field, and the conduct of individual officers could realistically be judged by resort to those standards.[85]

---

question were apparently dictated by local police regulations. In the second case, both decisions were left entirely to the discretion of the officer. If the Court had distinguished the two cases on this ground, it would, in my judgment, have made by far the greatest contribution to the jurisprudence of the fourth amendment since James Otis argued against the writs of assistance in 1761 and 'the child Independence was born.' But it did not. Without evident appreciation of the significance of the issue or the opportunity within its grasp to fashion a solution to a wide array of fourth amendment problems that would otherwise bedevil it forever, the Court kicked the chance away. It thereby held that whether you and I get arrested and subjected to a full-scale body search or are sent upon our respective ways with a pink multi-form and a disapproving cluck when we happen to go for a drive and to leave our operator's licenses on the dressing table depends upon the state of the digestion of any officer who stops us, or, more likely, upon our obsequiousness, the price of our automobiles, the formality of our dress, the shortness of our hair or the color of our skin." See also § 5.2(g).

[84]For this approach "to work, courts must be willing to evaluate the particular [police] regulations under the fourth amendment, and to require that the regulations effectively restrict the officer's exercise of discretion," but as yet the Supreme Court has "declined that role." Salken, The General Warrant of the Twentieth Century? A Fourth Amendment Solution to Unchecked Discretion to Arrest for Traffic Offenses, 62 Temple L.Rev. 221, 249 (1989). See also LaFave, Controlling Discretion by Administrative Regulations: The Use, Misuse, and Nonuse of Police Rules and Policies

in Fourth Amendment Adjudication, 89 Mich.L.Rev. 442 (1990).

Curiously, it is sometimes asserted that the absence of such standards is *instead* a reason *for* following the *Scott* approach disregarding motivation. See Garcia v. State, 827 S.W.2d 937 (Tex.Crim.App.1992), where, in following a totally objective approach, the court stressed: "Thus, a practical flaw in the limited objective test is that there may not be an easily discernable 'standard' or procedure against which to analyze an individual officer's actions, because of the variety of situations in which traffic and similar offenses occur. Unlike a standard policy for inventory searches, situations concerning stops and arrests are not so readily standardized."

[85]But some courts have utilized the *Scott* theory even when considerable discretion exists. Illustrative are the cases holding motivation irrelevant notwithstanding the fact that Coast Guard officers have vast discretion as to which vessels to stop for a safety and documentation inspection. United States v. Arra, 630 F.2d 836 (1st Cir.1980); State v. Richards, 388 So.2d 573 (Fla.App.1980).

Consider also State v. Bruzzese, 94 N.J. 210, 463 A.2d 320 (1983), where defendant claimed a pretext arrest on an outstanding contempt of court warrant had been made because the officer's true intention was to find evidence of a burglary of which defendant was suspected. The court first rejected defendant's proposed subjective rule, which would "require the court to engage in a costly and time-consuming expedition of the state of mind of the searching officer," and then also refused to assess the officer's actions in terms of a departure from established procedures: "We do not endorse the rule that a search shall be deemed unreasonable merely because

§ 1.4(f) More on "pretext": the effects of *Whren*

But the approach suggested above has not been embraced. Rather, in *Whren v. United States*,[86] the Supreme Court headed

---

a police officer deviates from his department's standard operating procedure. * * * The adoption of such a rule would discourage police officers from thinking and from exercising initiative. There are numerous situations that arise in law enforcement that are unique and call for a special response. It is impossible for a police department to envision and to develop standard operating procedures for all such situations. In many police departments, the standard procedures are more the result of budget constraints than what the departments believe to be ideal operating procedures. To hold that a policeman's conduct is unreasonable because it deviates from standard procedure would penalize the best officers and discourage imaginative police investigative work. For these reasons, we do not hold that a search should be deemed unreasonable per se if the police officer deviates from a standard operating procedure, but rather adopt the rule that a deviation from standard operating procedure should be examined on its merits to determine whether it constitutes an unreasonable act." The court thus concluded that even if it was true that usually a defendant wanted on an outstanding contempt warrant would simply be telephoned to come in, the deviation in this case was proper because such a call might have alerted the defendant that the authorities suspected him of burglary and might have resulted in his flight.

[Section 1.4(f)]

[86]Whren v. United States, 517 U.S. 806, 116 S.Ct. 1769, 135 L.Ed.2d 89 (1996). For other discussion of *Whren*, see Darmer, Teaching Whren to White Kids, 15 Mich.J.Race & L. 109 (2009); Dobson, The Police, Pretextual Investigatory Activity, and the Fourth Amendment: What Hath Whren Wrought?, 9 St. Thomas L.Rev. 707 (1997); Harris, Car Wars; The Fourth Amendment's Death on the Highway, 66 Geo.Wash.L.Rev. 556 (1998); Harris,

"Driving While Black" and All Other Traffic Offenses: The Supreme Court and Pretextual Traffic Stops, 87 J.Crim.L. & C. 554 (1997); Levit, Pretextual Stops: United States v. Whren and the Death of Terry v. Ohio, 28 Loy.U.Chi.L.J. 145 (1996); Johnson, The Story of Whren v. United States: The Song Remains the Same, in Race and Law Stories (Carbado & Moran, eds.2006); Lawton, The Road to Whren and Beyond: Does the "Would Have" Test Work?, 57 DePaul L.Rev. 917 (2008); Maclin, United States v. Whren: The Fourth Amendment Problem with Pretextual Traffic Stops, in M. Avery (ed.), We Dissent: Talking Back to the Rehnquist Court 90-130 (2009); Maclin, Race and the Fourth Amendment, 51 Vand.L.Rev. 333 (1998); O'Neill, Beyond Privacy, Beyond Probable Cause, Beyond the Fourth Amendment: New Strategies for Fighting Pretext Arrests, 69 U.Colo.L.Rev. 693 (1998); Sklansky, Traffic Stops, Minority Motorists, and the Future of the Fourth Amendment, 1997 Sup.Ct.Rev. 271; Notes, 24 Am.J.Crim.L. 627 (1997); 50 Fla.L.Rev. 385 (1998); 6 J.L. & Pol'y 291 (1997); 58 La.L.Rev. 369 (1997); 49 Maine L.Rev. 207 (1997); 76 Texas L.Rev. 1083 (1998); 116 Yale L.J. 1072 (2007).

Compare State v. Sullivan, 348 Ark. 647, 74 S.W.3d 215 (2002) (under state constitution, "pretext arrests—arrests that would not have occurred but for an ulterior investigative motive—are unreasonable police conduct warranting application of the exclusionary rule"); State v. Heath, 929 A.2d 390 (Del.Super.2006) ("purely pretextual stops run afoul" of state constitution); Baldwin v. Reagan, 715 N.E.2d 332 (Ind.1999) (discussing state legislation "intended to provide motorists with protection from the pretextual seat belt searches and seizures that *Whren* authorizes"); State v. Gonzales, 150 N.M. 74, 257 P.3d 894 (2011) (applying without reconsideration, holding in State v. Ochoa, 146 N.M. 32, 206 P.3d 143 (App.2008),

in exactly the opposite direction, for there a *unanimous* holding produced these startling conclusions: (1) The *Scott* rule applies so as to bar a finding of pretext based upon the subjective motivations of the officers involved, even in those cases where the motivation produced a Fourth Amendment intrusion that otherwise would not have occurred. (2) A showing of a departure from usual practice, again producing a Fourth Amendment intrusion that a reasonable police officer "would" not have made, also does not constitute a Fourth Amendment violation. (3) This is so even when, as in *Whren*, the departure is shown because there was a deviation from an existing police regulation regarding the circumstances in which certain Fourth Amendment intrusions were permissible. The effect of *Whren*, then, is that (with limited exceptions, discussed below) the pretext doctrine has disappeared from Fourth Amendment jurisprudence, thus leaving citizens without adequate protection against arbitrary seizures and searches,[87] This is especially apparent when one considers the impact of *Whren* with the other legs of "the Supreme Court's Iron

---

interpreted to mean that if defendant shows pretext then "the State must prove that the totality of the circumstances supports the conclusion that the officer who made the stop would have done so even without the unrelated motive" or else that "the real reason for the stop is supported by objective evidence of reasonable suspicion"); State v. Ladson, 138 Wash.2d 343, 979 P.2d 833 (1999) (rejecting *Whren* as a matter of state constitutional law); Note, 55 Hastings L.J. 1309 (2004) (re Alaska constitution). However, the *Whren* approach has been accepted in most states; see, e.g., State v. Griffin, 691 N.W.2d 734 (Iowa 2005); People v. Robinson, 97 N.Y.2d 341, 741 N.Y.S.2d 147, 767 N.E.2d 638 (2001) (collecting in appendix citations to cases in other jurisdictions); Fertig v. State, 146 P.3d 492 (Wyo.2006). Where *Whren* has been followed, it is applied also where evidence would otherwise be excluded because of violation of a State statute relating to Fourth Amendment interests. See, e.g., State v. Utvick, 675 N.W.2d 387 (N.D.2004). Where *Whren* is not followed, the defendant may not prevail if he grounds his claim only in the Fourth Amendment and not in state law. Nelson v. State, 365 Ark. 314, 229 S.W.3d 35 (2006).

[87]See, e.g., United States v. Chavez, 660 F.3d 1215 (10th Cir.2011)

(claim "the DWI arrest was just a ruse to justify a drug investigation" summarily rejected); Bazzi v. City of Dearborn, 658 F.3d 598 (6th Cir.2011) (officer's observation of speeding and running stop sign provided probable cause "even if Bazzi's traffic violations were merely a pretext for the stop"); United States v. Taylor, 596 F.3d 373 (7th Cir.2010) (*Whren* bars defendant's argument "that the traffic stop was a pretext for a drug investigation"); United States v. Arciniega, 569 F.3d 394 (8th Cir.2009) (where traffic stop on probable cause, under *Whren* it makes no difference that officer "would not have initiated the stop had he not believed that a drug deal was in progress"); United States v. Kellam, 568 F.3d 125 (4th Cir.2009) (under "objective test" for pretext claim, stop that "would not have [been] made * * * but for some hunch" lawful if reasonable suspicion of traffic violation in fact); United States v. Washington, 559 F.3d 573 (D.C.Cir.2009) (per *Whren*, it irrelevant that officers "were not interested in enforcing the traffic laws" but used "aggressive traffic patrol" as a means of finding narcotics and guns); United States v. Harris, 526 F.3d 1334 (11th Cir.2008) (stop of cab on seeing it turn without signally lawful even if motivated by suspicion passenger a drug trafficker); United States v. Stevens, 487 F.3d 232 (5th Cir.2007)

Triangle,"[88] *Atwater v. LagoVista*[89] (allowing full custody arrest on probable cause for any offense, no matter how minor) and *New York v. Belton*[90] (allowing full search of passenger compartment of vehicle permissible upon arrest of occupant, which however has been ameliorated somewhat by the narrowing of *Belton* in *Arizona v. Gant*).[91]

Although the earlier discussion in this section criticizing the

---

(because illegal lane change did occur, traffic stop lawful notwithstanding agent's purpose was to obtain consent of driver to search suspected stash house he just left); United States v. Ibarra, 345 F.3d 711 (9th Cir.2003) (rejecting defendant's argument that reference in *Whren* to rule there applying in "the run-of-the-mill case" means *Whren* inapplicable "when there is extraordinary evidence of pretext," court applies *Whren* in instant case, where officer's stopping of defendant's car for speeding and immediate approach with drug dog "had been planned hours in advance in coordination with DEA agents"); State v. Mancia-Sandoval, 2010 Ark. 134, 361 S.W.3d 835 (2010) (given *Whren*, stop for traffic violation upheld notwithstanding fact "State admitted that the stop was pretextual"); State v. Kalie, 699 So.2d 879 (La.1997) (under *Whren*, it not relevant that officer making traffic stop "was conducting a drug interdiction patrol"); State v. Dallmann, 260 Neb. 937, 621 N.W.2d 86 (2000) (per *Whren*, stop lawful even if "the investigators had decided * * * to follow and stop him before he left the convenience store and that * * * stop based on his failure to turn on his headlights was a pretext to obtain consent to search the vehicle"); People v. Edwards, 14 N.Y.3d 741, 898 N.Y.S.2d 538, 925 N.E.2d 576 (2010) (traffic stop on probable cause not unreasonable because of "officers' subjective motivation to investigate possible drug activity"); State v. Bartelson, 704 N.W.2d 824 (N.D.2005) (even if officer stopped vehicle for tinted windows violation knowing that another officer had stopped same vehicle for same violation earlier that evening, and even if officer would not have made such a stop except for suspicion vehicle contained drugs, under *Whren* stop

not objectionable); Johnson v. State, 272 P.3d 720 (Okla.Crim.App.2012) (given *Whren*, arrest on outstanding traffic warrants not "illegal because it was solely a pretext to hold him for questioning about the homicides"); State v. Overbey, 790 N.W.2d 35 (S.D.2010) (fact officer had "pretextual reason" for traffic stop "was irrelevant"); State v. Vineyard, 958 S.W.2d 730 (Tenn.1997) (under *Whren*, it irrelevant that officer who stopped traffic violator was assigned to "drug interdiction" and "uses a 'courier profile' for selecting the vehicles to be stopped"); State v. Rutter, 2011 Vt. 13, 15 A.3d 132 (2011) (vehicle stop for violation of "trivial" sections of motor vehicle code to check for driving under influence not objectionable); Yoeuth v. State, 206 P.3d 1278 (Wyo.2009) (officer "who observes a traffic violation has probable cause to make a stop regardless of the officer's subjective motivation").

[88]Dripps, The Fourth Amendment and the Fallacy of Composition: Determinacy Versus Legitimacy in a Regime of Bright-Line Rules, 74 Miss.L.J. 341, 392 (2004).

[89]Atwater v. City of Lago Vista, 532 U.S. 318, 121 S.Ct. 1536, 149 L.Ed.2d 549 (2001).

[90]New York v. Belton, 453 U.S. 454, 101 S.Ct. 2860, 69 L.Ed.2d 768 (1981).

[91]Arizona v. Gant, 556 U.S. 332, 129 S.Ct. 1710, 173 L.Ed.2d 485 (2009), discussed in § 7.1(c), (d), interpreting *Belton* as applicable only where (i) the vehicle was "within reaching distance * * * at the time of the search" or (ii) there was reason to believe that evidence of the crime of arrest might be found within.

pre-*Whren* lower court authority to the same effect[92] applies with equal force to *Whren*, a closer look at that decision is nonetheless appropriate. Plainclothes vice-squad officers of the District of Columbia Metropolitan Police Department patrolling a "high drug area" in an unmarked car had their suspicions aroused when they passed a truck with temporary license plates and youthful occupants at a stop sign and noticed that the driver was looking into the lap of a passenger to his right (Whren) and remained stopped for more than 20 seconds. When the police car made a U-turn and headed back toward the truck, the driver of that vehicle turned right without signalling and then sped off at an "unreasonable" speed. The police overtook the truck while it was stopped behind other traffic at a red light, and one officer approached on foot, identified himself as a police officer, directed the driver to put the vehicle in park, and "immediately observed two large plastic bags of what appeared to be crack cocaine in petitioner Whren's hands." Whren and driver Brown were then arrested, and various types of illegal drugs were found inside the car. Although on these facts it might be questioned whether any stop had occurred before the sighting of the bags[93] and, if there was a stop, whether the observations providing the probable cause for arrest and search were a fruit thereof,[94] the district court focussed upon the defendant's claim of a pretextual stop and concluded, notwithstanding the officers' noncompliance with a police department regulation prohibiting stops for minor traffic violations by plainclothes police in unmarked cars, that there "was nothing to really demonstrate that the actions of the officers were contrary to a normal traffic stop." The court of appeals affirmed,[95] and the Supreme Court granted certiorari and then answered in the negative the question, as stated by the Court,

> whether the temporary detention of a motorist who the police have probable cause to believe has committed a civil traffic violation is inconsistent with the Fourth Amendment's prohibition against unreasonable seizures unless a reasonable officer would have been motivated to stop the car by a desire to enforce the traffic laws.

Much of the Court's analysis in *Whren* is expended in attempting to show that the Court's prior decisions do not lend support to a pretext-type argument in the instant case. For example, the Court begins by attempting to distinguish away statements in *Florida v. Wells*,[96] *Colorado v. Bertine*,[97] and *New York v. Burger*[98] seemingly recognizing that pretextual activity sometimes violates

---

[92]Text at notes 62–85 supra.

[93]See § 9.4(d).

[94]See § 11.4(a).

[95]United States v. Whren, 53 F.3d 371 (D.C.Cir.1995).

[96]Florida v. Wells, 495 U.S. 1, 110 S.Ct. 1632, 109 L.Ed.2d 1 (1990),

where the Court stated that "an inventory search must not be used as a ruse for a general rummaging in order to discover incriminating evidence."

[97]Colorado v. Bertine, 479 U.S. 367, 107 S.Ct. 738, 93 L.Ed.2d 739 (1987), where the Court thought it significant that there had been "no show-

the Fourth Amendment. In these cases, the Court now says, "we were addressing the validity of a search conducted in the absence of probable cause. Our quoted statements simply explain that the exemption from the need for probable cause (and warrant), which is accorded to searches made for the purpose of inventory or administrative regulation, is not accorded to searches that are not made for those purposes." But that hardly explains why it is essential that the purported purpose be the real purpose only in the case of inventories and administrative searches, given that well-established Fourth Amendment doctrine requires a "substitute," if you will, for traditional probable cause in both of those situations. Significantly, this substitute is stated in terms of regularity and not motive in both instances; vehicle inventories require "standardized procedures,"[99] while administrative searches of buildings must conform to "reasonable legislative or administrative standards."[100]

Indeed, the Court's basis for distinguishing *Wells*, *Bertine*, and *Burger* virtually overlooks the very core of the petitioner's argument in *Whren*, earlier stated quite accurately by the Court as being that

"in the unique context of civil traffic regulations" probable cause is not enough. Since * * * the use of automobiles is so heavily and minutely regulated that total compliance with traffic and safety rules is nearly impossible, a police officer will almost invariably be able to catch any given motorist in a technical violation. This creates the temptation to use traffic stops as a means of investigating other law violations, as to which no probable cause or even articulable suspicion exists. * * * To avoid this danger, * * * the Fourth Amendment test for traffic stops should be, not the normal one * * * of whether probable cause existed to justify the stop; but rather, whether a police officer, acting reasonably, would have made the stop for the reason given.

The fundamental point in that argument, of course, is that probable cause as to a minor traffic violation can be so easily come by that its existence provides no general assurance against arbitrary police action. Because that is so, the situation addressed by the petitioners in *Whren* is more like that in *Wells*, *Bertine* and *Burger* than it is like seizures and searches on probable cause for more substantial criminal conduct. Indeed, it is likely true that the probable cause requirement in the minor traffic offenses context provides considerably *less* protection against arbitrariness than

---

ing that the police, who were following standard procedures, acted in bad faith or for the sole purpose of investigation."

[98]New York v. Burger, 482 U.S. 691, 107 S.Ct. 2636, 96 L.Ed.2d 601 (1987), where the Court noted the warrantless administrative inspection upheld did not appear to be "a 'pretext' for obtaining evidence of * * * violation of * * * penal laws."

[99]Colorado v. Bertine, 479 U.S. 367, 107 S.Ct. 738, 93 L.Ed.2d 739 (1987).

[100]Camara v. Municipal Court, 387 U.S. 523, 87 S.Ct. 1727, 18 L.Ed.2d 930 (1967).

do the "standardized procedures" and "reasonable legislative or administrative standards" requirements for inventories and administrative inspections, respectively.

As for the petitioners' reliance on the statement in *Colorado v. Bannister*,[101] another traffic stop case, that "there was no evidence whatsoever that the officer's presence to issue a traffic citation was a pretext to confirm any other previous suspicion about the occupants" of the car, the *Whren* Court says that this dictum shows only that in *Bannister* the Court "found no need to inquire into the question now under discussion." Fair enough. But the Court in *Whren* is not satisfied with that, and goes on to say:

> Petitioner's difficulty is not simply a lack of affirmative support for their position. Not only have we never held, outside the context of inventory search or administrative inspection * * *, that an officer's motive invalidates objectively justifiable behavior under the Fourth Amendment; but we have repeatedly held and asserted the contrary.

Note the sleight of hand here. The petitioners' "position" is said to be that "an officer's motive invalidates objectively justifiable behavior," but that is untrue. The petitioners' position is grounded in deviation from usual practice, which of course means that improper motivation unaccompanied by such deviation is not asserted to be "unreasonable" under the Fourth Amendment.

Once that is understood, it is apparent that the four cases the *Whren* Court relies upon to show "we have repeatedly held and asserted the contrary" are as readily distinguishable as is *Bannister* on the other side. In *United States v. Villamonte-Marquez*,[102] where, the Court says in *Whren*, "[w]e flatly dismissed the idea that an ulterior motive might serve to strip the agents of their legal justification," the facts did not present the kind of issue raised by the *Whren* petitioners, and notwithstanding reliance on *Scott* (discussed below), the point of the Court's brief discussion is the unremarkable proposition that the Coast Guard's power to stop vessels without any suspicion to check the manifest and other documents may be used against a vessel even more likely to have insufficient documents because it is suspected of involvement in smuggling.[103] In the second case, *United States v. Robinson*,[104] where, as the Court put it in *Whren*, "we held that a traffic violation arrest (of the sort here) would not be rendered invalid

---

[101] Colorado v. Bannister, 449 U.S. 1, 101 S.Ct. 42, 66 L.Ed.2d 1 (1980).

[102] United States v. Villamonte-Marquez, 462 U.S. 579, 103 S.Ct. 2573, 77 L.Ed.2d 22 (1983).

[103] And thus the Court stated: "Acceptance of respondents' argument would lead to the incongruous result criticized by Judge Campbell in his opinion in United States v. Arra, 630 F.2d 836 (1st Cir.1980): 'We would see little logic in sanctioning such examinations of ordinary, unsuspect vessels but forbidding them in the case of suspected smugglers.'"

[104] United States v. Robinson, 414 U.S. 218, 94 S.Ct. 467, 38 L.Ed.2d 427 (1973).

by the fact that it was 'a mere pretext for a narcotics search,'"
that in fact was *not* the holding of the Court but only a paraphras-
ing of the respondent's argument in the lower court. Rather,
what *Robinson* says on this subject is that respondent has no
complaint because the custodial arrest "was not a departure from
established police department practice,"[105] which is in no sense
inconsistent with the petitioners' claim in *Whren* that they should
prevail because the arrest *was* such a departure.[106] The third case
cited in *Whren* as "contrary" to the petitioner's argument is the
companion case to *Robinson*, *Gustafson v. Florida*.[107] However,
the truth of the matter is that the majority opinion in *Gustafson*
never discusses the significance of *either* ulterior motive *or*
departure from usual practice, hardly surprising in light of the
fact (as noted by Justice Stewart in his concurrence) that "the
petitioner has fully conceded the constitutional validity of his
custodial arrest." The fourth case, of course, is *Scott v. United
States*,[108] where, the Court reminds us in *Whren*, it was said that
"[s]ubjective intent alone * * * does not make otherwise lawful
conduct illegal or unconstitutional." But that language is hardly
contrary to the stance of the *Whren* petitioners, who grounded
their claim not in bad thoughts but in disparate treatment. And
the quoted language in *Scott* would appear to not even settle the
issue whether bad motive is at all relevant in a pretext context,
for *Scott* itself was not a pretext case.[109]

What all this adds up to is simply this: A fair characterization

---

[105]The *Whren* Court later acknowledged that this is what the Court said
earlier in *Robinson*. It is interesting to
note that while the Court's misstatement re what *Robinson* has to say on
the subject of pretext is called a holding, what the Court actually said there
is characterized as "not even dictum
that purports to provide an answer,
but merely one that leaves the question open."

[106]The Court in *Whren*, however,
makes every effort to keep these two
propositions separate. In Abel v. United
States, 362 U.S. 217, 80 S.Ct. 683, 4
L.Ed.2d 668 (1960), the Court said
petitioner's claim he had been arrested
by the INS on pretextual grounds to
enable the FBI to search his hotel
room was an allegation of "serious
misconduct" which, however, the Court
did not have to pursue because the
court below had found that the INS
procedures did not deviate from what
would have been done had there been
no FBI investigation. After taking note
of *Abel*, the Court in *Whren* attempts

to explain it away with this language:
"But it is a long leap from the proposition that following regular procedures
is some evidence of lack of pretext to
the proposition that failure to follow
regular procedures proves (or is an
operational substitute for) pretext."
But, the Court never explains just why
this is such a "long leap" for, for that
matter, why there could have been any
need to show "lack of pretext" in *Abel*
if the Court is now correct in asserting
that it is and has always been the law
that neither bad faith nor disparity in
practice invalidates a seizure or search
made on probable cause (as was the
arrest in *Abel*, where the administrative warrant issued upon a showing of
"a prima facie case of deportability").

[107]Gustafson v. Florida, 414 U.S.
260, 94 S.Ct. 488, 38 L.Ed.2d 456
(1973).

[108]Scott v. United States, 436 U.S.
128, 98 S.Ct. 1717, 56 L.Ed.2d 168
(1978).

[109]The question in *Scott* was
whether the agents had made reason-

of *Villamonte-Marquez, Robinson, Gustafson* and *Scott* would be
that in each case (to use the language employed in *Whren* to
distinguish away *Bannister*) the Court "found no need to inquire
into the question now under discussion." And thus by this reckless use of its own precedents, the Court in *Whren* makes it appear that the issue raised by the petitioners was already settled,
while in fact it was very much an open question.

This appearance that the issue was already settled perhaps
explains why the Court in *Whren* had so little to say about the
merits of petitioner's claim. And what is said is less than
satisfying. For example, while the petitioners' reasoned that their
test was an "objective" one and thus did not conflict with the
Scott rule, the *Whren* Court answers that the test "is plainly and
indisputably driven by subjective considerations" because it asks
"whether (based on general police practices) it is plausible to
believe that the officer had the proper state of mind." But surely
this is not the case, as the petitioners' test would only identify
arbitrariness in the disparate-treatment sense, which can occur
with or without bad thoughts, just as bad thoughts might (but do
not inevitably) produce disparity.

The Court in *Whren* next asserts that the petitioners' reliance
upon material deviation from usual police practices instead of
actual police motivation "might make sense" if (as previously
suggested herein) *Scott* et al. "were based only upon the evidentiary difficulty of establishing subjective intent." But, says the
Court, those cases "were not based only upon that, or indeed even
principally upon that," for their "principal basis" is "simply that
the Fourth Amendment's concern with 'reasonableness' allows
certain actions to be taken in certain circumstances, whatever
the subjective intent." In other words, the reason we ordinarily
bar inquiry into subjective intent is *not* because it is too difficult
to ascertain,[110] but rather because it is simply irrelevant. But
why is it irrelevant? All the Court has to offer at that point is the
following quotation from *Robinson*: "Since it is the fact of
custodial arrest which gives rise to the authority to search, it is
of no moment that [the officer] did not indicate any subjective
fear of the [arrestee] or that he did not himself suspect that [the
arrestee] was armed."

But this is mixing apples and oranges. The context of the just-

---

able efforts at minimizing the calls
they intercepted, but significantly the
agents did not exceed the statutory
minimization constraints even though
they apparently intended to do so.
Scott, therefore, "merely held that
improper intent that is not acted upon
does not render unconstitutional an
otherwise constitutional search."
Burkoff, Bad Faith Searches, 57 N.Y.U.

L.Rev. 70, 83–84 (1982).

[110]And thus *Whren* is not inapplicable in those cases where no such
difficulty exists because the officers
"frankly stated" that they did not rely
on the traffic violation now used as a
justification for the stop. United States
v. Dhinsa, 171 F.3d 721 (2d Cir.1998),
followed in United States v. Harrell,
268 F.3d 141 (2d Cir.2001).

quoted excerpt from *Robinson* makes it apparent that the question there was *not* whether subjective intent should be taken into account, but rather whether the right to search incident to arrest depends upon "the probability in a particular arrest situation that weapons or evidence would in fact be found upon the person of the suspect." The Court in *Robinson* answered that in the negative, and thus opted for the pragmatic, bright-line rule that "a lawful custodial arrest" carries with it a right to make "a full search of the person." That is a different matter entirely! The fact that "a lawful custodial arrest" permits such a full search without a case-by-case showing of need or the officer's thoughts about that need says nothing about whether the taking of custody should itself be deemed lawful even when it is pretextual (a matter not even at issue in *Robinson*). To put it another way, the search in *Robinson* is like the plain view in *Whren*: neither requires any justification apart from the custodial arrest (in *Robinson*) or detention (in *Whren*) making them possible, but that fact hardly dictates the result as to the quite different question of whether the essential antecedent in each case is conclusively reasonable if grounded in probable cause.

The Court in *Whren* next asserts that even if the concern underlying the *Scott* rule "had been only an evidentiary one," it would exist in spades under the approach of the petitioners, for "it seems to us somewhat easier to figure out the intent of an individual officer than to plumb the collective consciences of law enforcement in order to determine whether a 'reasonable officer' would have been moved to act upon the traffic violation." But, while it cannot be denied that the *Whren* petitioners' "would" test does present some difficulties of this kind, the Court makes the situation appear much worse than it actually is. The Court acknowledges that "police manuals and standard procedures may sometimes provide objective assistance," but then appears to dismiss these manuals and procedures because they "vary from place to place and from time to time." Specifically, the Court declares that it could not "accept that the search and seizure protections of the Fourth Amendment are so variable" that the "basis of invalidation [in one jurisdiction] would not apply in jurisdictions that had a different practice." But because, as discussed earlier, pretext claims are grounded in a concern about arbitrariness—the lack of substantial consistency within a particular law enforcement agency—it would seem that it is this consistency, rather than complete consistency from jurisdiction to jurisdiction, which counts the most. Nor can it be said that the Fourth Amendment means exactly the same thing in all jurisdictions; for example, an inventory search or administrative search that violates the Fourth Amendment because it does not conform to "standard procedures" or existing "reasonable legislative or administrative standards" in one jurisdiction may readily pass muster in another jurisdiction precisely because those procedures or standards exist or are different there.

In the concluding portion of its opinion in *Whren*, the Court takes on the petitioners' argument "that the balancing inherent in any Fourth Amendment inquiry requires us to weigh the governmental and individual interests implicated in a traffic stop such as we have here." The Court responds that while it is "true that in principle every Fourth Amendment case, since it turns upon a 'reasonableness' determination, involves a balancing of all relevant factors," it is nonetheless the case that with "rare exceptions * * * the result of that balancing is not in doubt when the search or seizure is based on probable cause." As for those exceptions, the Court elaborated:

> Where probable cause has existed, the only cases in which we have found it necessary actually to perform the "balancing" analysis involved searches or seizures conducted in an extraordinary manner, unusually harmful to an individual's privacy or even physical interests[111]—such as, for example, seizure by means of deadly force,[112] unannounced entry into a home,[113] entry into a home without a warrant,[114] or physical penetration of the body.[115] The making of a traffic stop out-of-uniform does not remotely qualify as such an extreme practice, and so is governed by the usual rule that probable cause to believe the law has been broken "outbalances" private interest in avoiding police contact.[116]

Such characterization substantially misrepresents the essence of the problem presented to the Court in *Whren*. True, making an arrest while out of uniform is not an "extreme practice" per se, and thus that fact standing alone hardly can make a traffic stop unreasonable. But that is not what was at issue. The fact the traffic stop was by plainclothes officers in an unmarked car is relevant because a police department regulation prohibited such

---

[111]Elsewhere in *Whren* it is said that the rule in that case applies in "the run-of-the-mill case." The argument that this means *Whren* is inapplicable "when there is extraordinary evidence of pretext" has been rejected on the ground that such language in *Whren* refers to the special situations described in the language quoted here. United States v. Ibarra, 345 F.3d 711 (9th Cir.2003).

[112]Citing Tennessee v. Garner, 471 U.S. 1, 105 S.Ct. 1694, 85 L.Ed.2d 1 (1985).

[113]Citing Wilson v. Arkansas, 514 U.S. 927, 115 S.Ct. 1914, 131 L.Ed.2d 976 (1995).

[114]Citing Welsh v. Wisconsin, 466 U.S. 740, 104 S.Ct. 2091, 80 L.Ed.2d 732 (1984).

[115]Citing Winston v. Lee, 470 U.S. 753, 105 S.Ct. 1611, 84 L.Ed.2d 662 (1985).

[116]Compare Colb, The Qualitative Dimension of Fourth Amendment "Reasonableness," 98 Colum.L.Rev. 1642 (1998), presenting the most intriguing proposal that in determining whether a particular intrusion is reasonable under the Fourth Amendment, that *in addition to* the probable cause requirement "Fourth Amendment doctrine should explicitly consider the costs to privacy of various ordinary, routine intrusions, along with the relative strength of the government interests at stake in enforcing a given set of criminal statutes through a challenged investigative technique," and suggesting that such analysis would produce a different result in *Whren*.

stops except in circumstances apparently not present in *Whren*,[117] so that the petitioners' real complaint was about the arbitrariness in subjecting them to a traffic stop contrary to general practice. And surely arbitrary intrusions upon liberty are just as "extreme" as those actions mentioned by the Court in *Whren*; indeed, it would seem ludicrous to contend otherwise given the Court's frequent assertions that the "core,"[118] "basic purpose"[119] and "central concern"[120] of the Fourth Amendment have to do with protecting liberty and privacy against arbitrary governmental interference.

The apparent assumption of the Court in *Whren*, that no significant problem of police arbitrariness can exist as to actions taken with probable cause, blinks at reality. As the Supreme Court was advised in the briefs of the petitioners and amici, the tactic at issue in *Whren* is one that has been commonly employed by police in recent years in their "war against drugs." Both in urban areas and on the interstates, police are on the watch for "suspicious" travellers, and once one is spotted it is only a matter of time before some technical or trivial offense produces the necessary excuse for pulling him over.[121] Perhaps because the offenses are so often insignificant, the driver is typically told at the

---

[117]Metropolitan Police Dep't,Washington, D.C., General Order 303, pt. 1, Objectives and Policies (A)(2)(4) (Apr. 30, 1992), permits plainclothes officers in unmarked vehicles to enforce traffic laws "only in the case of a violation that is so grave as to pose an immediate threat to the safety of others."

[118]Wolf v. Colorado, 338 U.S. 25, 69 S.Ct. 1359, 93 L.Ed. 1782 (1949).

[119]Camara v. Municipal Court, 387 U.S. 523, 87 S.Ct. 1727, 18 L.Ed.2d 930 (1967).

[120]United States v. Ortiz, 422 U.S. 891, 95 S.Ct. 2585, 45 L.Ed.2d 623 (1975).

[121]A few illustrations from the many reported cases of this genre reveal how little it takes to supply grounds for a traffic stop acceptable to the courts. See United States v. Herrera Martinez, 354 F.3d 932 (8th Cir.2004) (officer noticed Hispanic passenger in vehicle and then turned around and followed vehicle until right tires crossed fog line and then made stop; dissent objects if that "sufficient to constitute a violation," then "practically every driver of a vehicle travelling on a South Dakota roadway could

be stopped"); United States v. Akram, 165 F.3d 452 (6th Cir.1999) (majority characterizes case as "an example of the very questionable police conduct that is permitted by *Whren*"; dissent explains this because police ordinarily "do not stop vehicles on interstate highways for speeding when they are only exceeding the speed limit by two miles per hour"); United States v. Lee, 73 F.3d 1034 (10th Cir.1996) (when Utah deputy patrolling Interstate 70 saw an automobile driven by a black man straddle the center line for about one second before proceeding to the other lane of traffic, officer had sufficient suspicion the operator was driving while impaired to support stop); United States v. Roberson, 6 F.3d 1088 (5th Cir.1993) (discussed in text at note 71 supra); State v. Waters, 780 So.2d 1053 (La.2001) (one-time "contact" with fog line without crossing it sufficient basis for stop for improper lane use; court dismisses defendant's claim "that this 'almost violation' marks the *de minimis* point at which *Whren*'s objective approach no longer provides a workable rule for determining the reasonableness of vehicular stops").

outset that he will merely be given a warning. But then things often turn ugly. The driver and passengers are usually closely questioned about their identities, the reason for their travels, their intended destination, and the like. The subject of drugs comes up, and often the driver is induced to "consent" to a full search of the vehicle and all effects therein for drugs.[122] If such consent is not forthcoming, another police vehicle with a drug-sniffing dog may appear on the scene.[123]

Illustrative of that tactic is *United States v. Roberson*,[124] discussed earlier,[125] where the court took note of the trooper's "remarkable record" of turning traffic stops into drug arrests on 250 prior occasions. While one can only speculate as to how many innocent people were subjected to roadside indignities to produce that record, no speculation is required to figure out who—in all likelihood—many of those persons were, for race is often a factor in the otherwise amorphous drug courier profile.[126] As one distinguished black educator has wryly noted, "there's a moving

---

[122]See State v. George, 557 N.W.2d 575 (Minn.1997), noting this practice and concluding that in light of *Whren* it is necessary to "subject[ ] claims of voluntary consent in this context [i.e., traffic stops] to careful appellate review."

[123]See, e.g., United States v. Mesa, 62 F.3d 159 (6th Cir.1995); State v. Dominguez-Martinez, 321 Or. 206, 895 P.2d 306 (1995).

[124]United States v. Roberson, 6 F.3d 1088 (5th Cir.1993).

[125]See text at note 71 supra.

[126]The literature supporting this conclusion is collected in Washington v. Lambert, 98 F.3d 1181 (9th Cir. 1996). For illustrative situations, see, e.g., United States v. Harvey, 16 F.3d 109 (6th Cir.1994); Washington v. Vogel, 880 F.Supp. 1534 (M.D.Fla. 1995); Lowery v. Commonwealth, 9 Va.App. 314, 388 S.E.2d 265 (1990). For other evidence and additional discussion of racial profiling, see D. Harris, Profiles in Injustice: Why Racial Profiling Cannot Work (2002); Abramovsky & Edelstein, Pretext Stops and Racial Profiling After Whren v. United States: The New York and New Jersey Responses Compared, 63 Alb.L. Rev. 725 (2000); Banks, Race-Based Suspect Selection & Colorblind Equal Protection Doctrine and Discourse, 48 UCLA L.Rev. 1075 (2001); Beck &

Daly, State Constitutional Analysis of Pretext Stops: Racial Profiling and Public Policy Concerns, 72 Temp.L. Rev. 597 (1999); Brady, A Failure of Judicial Review of Racial Discrimination Claims in Criminal Cases, 52 Syrac.L.Rev. 735 (2002); Capers, Rethinking the Fourth Amendment: Race, Citizenship, and the Equality Principle, 46 Harv.C.R.-C.L.L.Rev. 1, 14–29 (2011); Carbado, (E)racing the Fourth Amendment, 100 Mich.L.Rev. 946 (2002); Chon & Arzt, Walking While Muslim, 68 Law & Contemp. Probs. 215 (2005); Cloud, Quakers, Slaves and the Founders: Profiling to Save the Union, 73 Miss.L.J. 369 (2003); Colb, Profiling With Apologies, 1 Ohio St.J.Crim.L. 611 (2004); Colb, Stopping a Moving Target, 3 Rutgers Race & L.Rev. 191 (2001); Davis, Race, Cops, and Traffic Stops, 51 U.Miami L.Rev. 425 (1997); Etienne, Making Sense of the Ethnic Profiling Debate, 80 Miss.L.J. 1523 (2011); Fox, The Second Generation of Racial Profiling, 38 Am.J.Crim.L. 49 (2010); Geisinger, Rethinking Profiling: A Cognitive Model of Bias and Its Legal Implications, 86 Or.L.Rev. 657 (2007); Gross & Barnes, Road Work: Racial Profiling and Drug Interdiction on the Highway, 101 Mich.L.Rev. 651 (2002); Gross & Livingston, Racial Profiling Under Attack, 102 Colum.L.Rev. 1413 (2002); Harcourt & Meares, Randomization and the Fourth Amendment, 78 U.Chi.

violation that many African-Americans know as D.W.B.: Driving While Black."[127]

The appropriate judicial response to these circumstances, it is submitted, is that of Tenth Circuit Chief Judge Seymour, who, in

L.Rev. 809, 854–59 (2011); Harcourt, Rethinking Racial Profiling: A Critique of the Economics, Civil Liberties, and Constitutional Literature, and Criminal Profiling More Generally, 71 U.Chi. L.Rev. 1275 (2004); Harris, When Success Breeds Attack: The Coming Backlash Against Racial Profiling Studies, 6 Mich.J.Race & L. 237 (2001); Harris, Addressing Racial Profiling in the States: A Case Study of the "New Federalism" in Constitutional Criminal Procedure, 3 U.Pa.J.Const.L. 367 (2001); Harris, The Stories, the Statistics, and the Law: Why "Driving While Black" Matters, 84 Minn.L.Rev. 265 (1999); Harris, "Driving While Black" and All Other Traffic Offenses: The Supreme Court and Pretextual Traffic Stops, 87 J.Crim.L. & C. 554 (1997); Johnson, How Racial Profiling in America Became the Law of the Land: United States v. Brignoni-Ponce and Whren v. United States and the Need for Truly Rebellious Lawyering, 98 Geo.L.J. 1005 (2010); Johnson, "A Menace to Society": The Use of Criminal Profiles and Its Effects on Black Males, 38 How.L.J. 629 (1995); Maclin, "Voluntary" Interviews and Airport Searches of Middle Eastern Men: The Fourth Amendment in a Time of Terror, 73 Miss.L.J. 471 (2003); Maclin, The Fourth Amendment on the Freeway, 3 Rutgers Race & L.Rev. 117 (2001); Maclin, Race and the Fourth Amendment, 51 Vand.L.Rev. 333 (1998); Michelson, Driving While Black: A Skeptical Note, 44 Jurimetrics 161 (2004); Oliver, With an Evil Eye and an Unequal Hand: Pretextual Stops and Doctrinal Remedies to Racial Profiling, 74 Tul.L.Rev. 1409 (2000); Paris, A Primer in Profiling: The Merger of Civil Rights and Criminal Defense, 15 Criminal Justice 4 (Fall 2000); Rudovsky, Law Enforcement by Stereotypes and Serendipity: Racial Profiling and Stops and Searches Without Cause, 3 U.Pa.J.Const.L. 296

(2001); Russell, "Driving While Black": Corollary Phenomena and Collateral Consequences, 40 B.C.L.Rev. 717 (1999); Sklansky, Some Cautious Optimism About the Problem of Racial Profiling, 3 Rutgers Race & L.Rev. 293 (2001); Taslitz, Stories of Fourth Amendment Disrespect: From Elian to the Internment, 70 Fordham L.Rev. 2257 (2002); Thompson, Stopping the Usual Suspects: Race and the Fourth Amendment, 74 NYU L.Rev. 956 (1999); Walker, Racial Profiling-Separate and Unequal Keeping the Minorities in Line-The Role of Law Enforcement in America, 23 St.Thomas L.Rev. 576 (2011); Wang, "Suitable Targets"? Parallels and Connections Between "Hate" Crimes and "Driving While Black," 6 Mich.J.Race & L. 209 (2001); Weatherspoon, Racial Profiling of African-American Males: Stopped, Searched, and Stripped of Constitutional Protection, 38 J.Marshall L.Rev. 439 (2004); Weeden, Criminal Procedure and the Racial Profiling Issue for Professor Gates and Sergeant Crowley, 17 Wash. & Lee J.C.R & Soc.Just. 305 (2011); Zoubek & Susswein, On the Toll Road to Reform: One State's Efforts to Put the Brakes on Racial Profiling, 3 Rutgers Race & L.Rev. 223 (2001); Comments, 47 How.L.J. 989 (2004); 7 J.L.Soc'y 220 (2006); 71 U.Colo.L.Rev. 255 (2000); Note, 21 B.C. Third World L.J. 243 (2001); 50 Duke L.J. 331 (2000); 6 J.L. & Pol'y 291 (1997); 27 Wm. Mitchell L.Rev. 2031 (2001).

Similarly, it has been reported that when traffic laws are used to stop drivers to search for weapons, those stopped are "overwhelmingly black." Schwartz, "Just Take Away Their Guns": The Hidden Racism of Terry v. Ohio, 23 Fordham Urb.L.J. 317, 319 (1996).

[127] Gates, Thirteen Ways of Looking at a Black Man, The New Yorker 56, 59 (Oct. 23, 1995).

dissenting from a pre-*Whren* decision[128] similar to *Whren*, stated:

> In addition to producing the intrusion any individual experiences when subjected to a traffic stop, the majority's standard frees a police officer to target members of minority communities for the selective enforcement of otherwise unenforced statutes. The Supreme Court recognized in *Terry [v. Ohio]*[129] that the harassment of minority groups by certain elements of the police population does occur, and that "the degree of community resentment aroused by particular practices is clearly relevant to an assessment of the quality of the intrusion upon reasonable expectations of personal security caused by those practices." By refusing to examine either the arbitrariness with which a particular statute is enforced or the motivation underlying its enforcement in a particular case, the majority standard does nothing to curb the ugly reality that minority groups are sometimes targeted for selective enforcement. As a result, the majority standard adds the onus of discrimination and resentment to the already significant burden imposed by traffic stops generally. * * *

> The Supreme Court held in *Terry* that to justify a particular intrusion, a "police officer must be able to point to specific and articulable facts which, taken together with the rational inferences from those facts, reasonably warrant that intrusion." It is difficult to justify a stop as reasonable, even if supported by an observed violation, if the undisputed facts indicate that the violation does not ordinarily result in a stop. Moreover, the Court in *Terry* described in detail the appropriate reasonableness inquiry in language that is utterly irreconcilable with the majority standard. The Court stated that in assessing the reasonableness of a particular stop "it is imperative that the facts be judged against an objective standard: would the facts available to the officer at the moment of the seizure or the search 'warrant a man of reasonable caution in the belief' that the action taken was appropriate?" It would hardly seem necessary to point out that the Court's mandate to determine what a reasonable officer would do in the circumstances cannot be fulfilled by merely ascertaining in a vacuum what a particular officer could do under state law.

> Given the "multitude of applicable traffic and equipment regulations" in any jurisdiction, upholding a stop on the basis of a regulation seldom enforced opens the door to the arbitrary exercise of police discretion condemned in *Terry* and its progeny. "Anything less [than the reasonable officer standard] would invite intrusions upon constitutionally guaranteed rights based on nothing more substantial than inarticulate hunches, a result this Court has consistently refused to sanction."

The petitioners in *Whren* were black, and they put before the Court the fact that selective traffic enforcement of the type described above not infrequently is influenced by the race of the vehicle's occupants. To this, the Court responded that it "agree[d] with petitioners that the Constitution prohibits selective enforcement of the law based on considerations such as race," though

---

[128]United States v. Botero-Ospina, 71 F.3d 783 (10th Cir.1995).

[129]Terry v. Ohio, 392 U.S. 1, 88 S.Ct. 1868, 20 L.Ed.2d 889 (1968).

"the constitutional basis for objecting to intentionally discriminatory application of laws is the Equal Protection Clause, not the Fourth Amendment." But it is difficult to believe that an equal protection challenge would be effective in this context,[130] especially if existing law regarding selective prosecution challenges is followed here.[131] Police agencies take considerable pains to keep secret all training materials, directives and instructions that

[130]"In theory there is no problem with relying on the Equal Protection Clause to protect against racial unfairness in law enforcement. The problem is that equal protection doctrine, precisely because it attempts to address all constitutional claims of inequity, has developed in ways that poorly equip it to address the problems of discriminatory police conduct. Equal protection doctrine treats claims of inequitable policing the same as any other claim of inequity; it gives no recognition to the special reasons to insist on evenhanded law enforcement, or to the distinctive concerns with arbitrariness underlying the fourth Amendment. As a result, challenges to discriminatory policy practices will fail without proof of conscious racial animus on the part of the police. For reasons discussed earlier, this amounts to saying that they will almost always fail." Sklansky, Traffic Stops, Minority Motorists, and the Future of the Fourth Amendment, 1997 Sup.Ct.Rev. 271, 326.

See also Aviram & Portman, Inequitable Enforcement: Introducing the Concept of Equity Into Constitutional Review of Law Enforcement, 61 Hastings L.J. 413, 418 (2009), noting the Equal Protection Clause's "inability to address underlying narratives and hidden intentions," discussed therein at 435–41).

[131]Thus it has been suggested that Whren makes necessary a different approach as to equal protection claims, at least in this context. See Aviram & Portman, 61 Hastings L.J. 413, 418 (2009) (proposing "a multivariate matrix of considerations" that could be "used to modify Equal Protection litigation"); Capers, 46 Harv.C.R.-C.L.L. Rev. 1, 38 (2011) (proposing we "reinterpret the Fourth Amendment to permit stop-and-frisks where articulable suspicion is present, but only so long as such suspicion is free of racial bias or prejudice"); Comment, 71 U.Colo.L.Rev. 255, 289 (2000) (proposing "a departure from cases like McClesky v. Kemp, which declined to recognize impact discrimination based on statistical evidence," and an approach "resembl[ing] the Supreme Court's analysis in Batson"); Note, 6 J.L. & Pol'y 291, 295–96 (1997) ("argues that courts should adopt a new equal protection test for analyzing consideration of race by police in detaining motorists for traffic violations. One possible solution is for courts to adopt the test laid out in Batson v. Kentucky, where the Supreme Court lessened the burden of establishing an equal protection violation with respect to the use of race as a factor in making peremptory challenges during jury selection. Another solution is to re-evaluate the discriminatory intent requirement in the equal protection test"); Note, 76 Texas L.Rev. 1083, 1086–87 (1998) ("courts must draw a distinction between selective enforcement and selective prosecution" by recognizing "that the rationale behind each is substantially different and that the policy behind the Armstrong Court's decision will not be advanced by expanding its rule to include selective enforcement claims. [specifically, it is necessary] that motions for discovery on claims of selective enforcement of traffic laws be analyzed under a Fourth Amendment standard of reasonableness that incorporates equal protection principles, thereby allowing courts to consider the racial impact of police decisions in ruling on admissibility of evidence [and] that courts set aside the similarly situated test for the threshold determination of whether defendants may obtain discovery of information about traffic enforcement patterns and practices"). However, the courts have gen-

might reflect the basis upon which selective traffic stops for drug enforcement purposes are undertaken.[132] And under the requirements announced by the Supreme Court just weeks before *Whren* was decided, the defendant's chances of even obtaining discovery are slight, for it is necessary that he first "produce some evidence that similarly situated defendants of other races could have been prosecuted, but were not."[133] Moreover, "[o]nly in rare cases will a statistical pattern of discriminatory impact conclusively demonstrate a constitutional violation."[134] Even if a defendant were to clear those hurdles, it is still less than certain that meaningful relief would be forthcoming. Absent recognition of an equal protection exclusionary rule that would require suppression of drugs found because of a traffic stop denying equal protection,[135]

---

erally held that "claims of racially discriminatory traffic stops and arrests should be held to a * * * high standard" like that utilized as to claims of equal protection violations by a prosecutor. Marshall v. Columbia Lea Regional Hospital, 345 F.3d 1157 (10th Cir.2003) (collecting cases in accord).

[132]See, e.g., People v. Perez, 258 Ill.App.3d 465, 197 Ill.Dec. 237, 631 N.E.2d 240 (1994).

[133]United States v. Armstrong, 517 U.S. 456, 116 S.Ct. 1480, 134 L.Ed.2d 687 (1996). See, e.g., United States v. Frazier, 408 F.3d 1102 (8th Cir.2005) (re stop of black traveler, defendant's "attack on the officer's credibility" by showing "that the stated indicators and disclaimers identified by the investigators were highly consistent with innocent behavior by many law-abiding motorists and may not have been sufficient to raise a reasonable articulable suspicion" not sufficient to show racial motive); United States v. Bullock, 94 F.3d 896 (4th Cir.1996) (black defendant who claims his traffic stop "was motivated by a race-based drug courier profile" does not prevail, as he "has failed to meet the vigorous standard for proving such a violation" imposed by *Armstrong*); United States v. Bell, 86 F.3d 820 (8th Cir.1996) (black bicyclist stopped for lack of headlamp "showed the only people arrested for violating the statute during a certain month were black" and that "there are no lights on 98% of all bicycles in the Des Moines area, which is populated predominantly by white

people," did not meet his *Armstrong* burden, as he "presented no evidence about the number of white bicyclists who ride their bicycles between sunset and sunrise," though police admitted they had "targeted" a high-crime area "populated primarily by minorities").

[134]United States v. Avery, 137 F.3d 343 (6th Cir.1997) (*Avery*, though concerned not with traffic stops but rather with contacts and questioning of air travelers regarding drug transportation, illustrates the point. Even assuming that 53% of the contacts were of blacks but that only 5% of air travelers are black, the court asserted such "statistics simply are not persuasive"). Consider also United States v. Woods, 213 F.3d 1021 (8th Cir.2000) (defendant's claim his consensual encounter resulting in his consent to search was "motivated solely by racial considerations" rejected, as evidence that he the only person approached at bus terminal and that a Minn. Task Force Study found "race is equated with the likelihood of ongoing criminal activity in the minds of many police officers" doesn't come "close to establishing that the officers' decision to approach Woods was motivated by race").

[135]United States v. Nichols, 512 F.3d 789 (6th Cir.2008) (while "checking individuals for outstanding warrants in an intentionally racially discriminatory manner may violate the Equal Protection Clause," court emphasizes "we are aware of no court that has ever applied the exclusionary rule for a violation of [that] Clause,

it may be that defendant's relief would not extend beyond barring prosecution of the *traffic* charge.[136]

The Court in *Whren* concludes its analysis by referring to a couple of problems that would attend acceptance of the approach urged by the petitioners. For one thing, said the Court, even if it is true that a high potential for arbitrariness exists when regulation is so extensive and detailed "that virtually everyone is guilty of a violation," there appears to be "no principle that would allow us to decide at what point a code of law becomes so expansive and so commonly violated that infraction itself can no longer be the ordinary measure of the lawfulness of enforcement." There is

---

and we decline Nichol's invitation to do so here").

But see Commonwealth v. Lora, 451 Mass. 425, 886 N.E.2d 688 (2008) (concluding that racial profiling could be deterred by expanding the scope of the exclusionary rule to permit suppression of contraband seized in the course of a traffic stop made for discriminatory reasons); State v. Segars, 172 N.J. 481, 799 A.2d 541 (2002) (while computer check of moving vehicles' license plates no search and thus does not require even reasonable suspicion, such checks "must not be based on impermissible motives such as race," and "once it has been established" that selective enforcement has occurred" the fruits thereof "will be suppressed" in the interest of "deterrence of impermissible investigatory behavior and maintenance of the integrity of the judicial system"); State v. Maryland, 167 N.J. 471, 771 A.2d 1220 (2001) (one version of evidence was that "police officers approached defendant only because he was one of three young black males the officers had seen at the train station a week earlier," which if true "would establish an irrebuttable inference of invidious and selective law enforcement" and thus "State was required to have established a non-discriminatory basis for the officers to conduct a [nonseizure] field inquiry," and because such not established here the field inquiry tainted subsequent events that otherwise would have supported a frisk, and thus evidence suppressed); State v. Soto, 324 N.J.Super. 66, 734 A.2d 350 (1996) (evidence suppressed because statistical evidence established "an of-

ficially sanctioned or de facto policy of targeting minorities for investigation and arrest").

See also Alschuler, Racial Profiling and the Constitution, 2002 U.Chi. Legal F. 163, 254 ("Police violations of the Equal Protection Clause warrant an effective remedy no less than police violations of the Fourth Amendment. To say that the Supreme Court would have no principled basis for refusing to exclude evidence obtained in violation of the Equal Protection Clause, however, is not to predict that the Court would exclude it"); Holland, Racial Profiling and a Punitive Exclusionary Rule, 20 Temp.Pol. & Civ.Rts.L.Rev. 29 (2010) (grounding argument for equal protection exclusionary rule on "the Supreme Court's recent exclusionary rule jurisprudence"); Holland, Safeguarding Equal Protection Rights: The Search for an Exclusionary Rule Under the Equal Protection Clause, 37 Crim.L.Rev. 1107, 1110 (2001) (re "a sound and workable doctrine for an equal protection exclusionary rule"); Note, 42 Washburn L.J. 657 (2003) (arguing for exclusionary rule for equal protection violations).

[136]But, as noted in Jones v. Sterling, 210 Ariz. 308, 110 P.3d 1271 (2005), citing cases, "numerous decisions after *Whren* have treated selective enforcement of facially neutral traffic laws as a potential defense to non-traffic criminal charges arising from a traffic stop." The court thus rejected the state's claim "that a § 1983 claim is the sole remedy for selective enforcement."

no denying that the necessity of making this judgment would present courts with some degree of difficulty. Yet, it is by no means apparent that such decisions are more complex than others the Supreme Court has imposed upon lower courts in the Fourth Amendment area, such as that of deciding which offenses are so insignificant that they do not permit a warrantless entry of premises to arrest even in the face of exigent circumstances.[137] The Court's second concern, that "we do not know by what standard * * * we would decide * * * which particular provisions are sufficiently important to merit enforcement," misses the mark by an even wider margin. Under the petitioners' approach, police agencies would decide which minor violations do and do not "merit enforcement," and the courts would merely insist that there not be arbitrary deviations from such policies.

The Court's analysis in *Whren* is, to put it mildly, quite disappointing. By misstating its own precedents and mischaracterizing the petitioners' central claim, the Court managed to trivialize what in fact is an exceedingly important issue regarding a pervasive law enforcement practice. Certainly one would have expected more from an opinion that drew neither a dissent nor a cautionary concurrence from any member of the Court. It can only be hoped that state courts, applying their own constitutions, statutes and common law, will find it possible to deal with pretextual stops, arrests and searches in a more meaningful fashion.[138]

Absent relief under state law, there remains the question of just how far *Whren* goes in slamming the door on any sort of pretext claim regarding the Fourth Amendment activities of po-

---

[137]See Welsh v. Wisconsin, 466 U.S. 740, 104 S.Ct. 2091, 80 L.Ed.2d 732 (1984), discussed in § 6.1(f).

[138]As in State v. Sullivan, 348 Ark. 647, 74 S.W.3d 215 (2002), discussed in Note, 64 Ark.L.Rev. 479 (2011); State v. Heath, 929 A.2d 390 (Del.Super. 2006); State v. Ochoa, 146 N.M. 32, 206 P.3d 143 (App.2008); State v. Ladson, 138 Wash.2d 343, 979 P.2d 833 (1999).

But, as noted in People v. Robinson, 97 N.Y.2d 341, 741 N.Y.S.2d 147, 767 N.E.2d 638 (2001), collecting cases, most state courts follow *Whren* as a matter of state constitutional law. Consider, e.g., the analysis and result in Gama v. State, 112 Nev. 833, 920 P.2d 1010 (1996), where defendant was traveling 73 m.p.h. in a 65 m.p.h. zone, the trooper admitted it is "not common practice to stop for such a violation"; and though defendant was also observed going 56 m.p.h. in a 45 m.p.h. construction zone, "other driver's travelled through the forty-five-miles-per-hour construction zone at fifty-six miles-per-hour [but] were neither stopped nor cited." The court noted that it had previously adopted the "would have" test because of "concerns * * * regarding the use of minor traffic infractions as a general law enforcement tool for investigating serious crimes" and the "fear that the practice may result in substantial inconvenience and annoyance for many otherwise law-abiding Nevadans." Yet the court followed *Whren* and thus declined to find that the state constitution provided any greater protection, "at least in the area of pretextual traffic stops," so that "Nevada motorists must look * * * to the Nevada Legislature if they desire to afford themselves greater protection against pretextual traffic stops."

lice and other government agents. For example, since *Whren* concerned a traffic stop made on probable cause, it might be questioned whether the same result should obtain in a case involving a custodial arrest made on probable cause. In *Atwater v. City of Lago Vista*,[139] the four dissenters made a compelling argument that the answer ought to be "no" in light of the fact that a custodial arrest, as compared to a temporary stop, is a very serious intrusion upon one's privacy and liberty.[140] The *Atwater* majority assumed an affirmative answer, and just a few weeks later, in *Arkansas v. Sullivan*,[141] the Court unequivocally concluded, albeit without any meaningful discussion of the point: "That *Whren* involved a traffic stop, rather than a custodial arrest, is of no particular moment."

Another question is whether *Whren* leaves open the possibility of a pretext challenge as to activity based upon individualized suspicion falling short of probable cause, as where a traffic stop is made on reasonable suspicion. While the Court intimated at one point in *Whren* that the existence of reasonable suspicion likewise "ensure[s] that police discretion is sufficiently constrained," any remaining doubts were removed by *Ashcroft v. al-Kidd*.[142] *Ashcroft* involved a *Bivens* action brought by al-Kidd alleging his Fourth Amendment rights were violated by a pretextual detention policy whereby, after 9/11, then Attorney General Ashcroft authorized federal officials to use the federal material witness law[143] to detain terrorist suspects. While all eight participating Justices agreed that Ashcroft was entitled to qualified immunity because the purported right to nonpretextual application of the statute was not "clearly established" at the time of the challenged conduct, the 5-Justice majority then appeared to address the merits of the Fourth Amendment claim. As for al-Kidd's contention "that *Whren* establishes that we ignore subjective intent only when there exists 'probable cause to believe that a violation of law has occurred,'" the Court responded that the reference to probable cause in *Whren* merely reflected it "was the legitimating factor in the case at hand," and that "the opinion swept broadly to reject inquiries into motive generally." Characterizing the instant case as one involving "a validly obtained warrant" that was "based on individualized suspicion" (purportedly conceded by al-Kidd), it was thus deemed to be outside the "two limited exception[s]" to

---

[139]Atwater v. City of Lago Vista, 532 U.S. 318, 121 S.Ct. 1536, 149 L.Ed.2d 549 (2001).

[140]See discussion of this point in § 5.1(i) at note 493.

[141]Arkansas v. Sullivan, 532 U.S. 769, 121 S.Ct. 1876, 149 L.Ed.2d 994 (2001). On remand, the state supreme court held as a matter of state law that

the arrest was unlawful because pretextual. State v. Sullivan, 348 Ark. 647, 74 S.W.3d 215 (2002).

[142]Ashcroft v. al-Kidd, __ U.S. __, 131 S.Ct. 2074, 179 L.Ed.2d 1149 (2011), discussed in Comment, 45 Loy.L.A.L.Rev. 569 (2012); Recent Decision, 81 Miss.L.J. 621 (2012).

[143]18 U.S.C.A. § 3144.

Whren, i.e., "special-needs and administrative-search cases." That is, "subjective intent" comes into play only in the case of warrantless action not based upon individualized suspicion.[144]

If that is so, then one might wonder about the boundaries of *Whren* when there is an arrest on probable cause followed by a search lacking even reasonable suspicion, such as an inventory search of a vehicle following arrest of the occupant. If *Bertine* leaves open the pretext issue, as the Court in *Whren* says, then does it not follow that the defendant should be able to question not only whether there was pretext in the decision to conduct the inventory but also whether there was a pretext in making the arrest in the first place in order get custody of the car so as to have a basis for the inventory? Since the inventory search is itself without reasonable suspicion, it would seem that the answer should be yes, and at least one lower court reached that conclusion, expressing an unwillingness "to sanction conduct where a police officer can trail a targeted vehicle with a driver merely suspected of criminal activity, wait for the driver to exceed the speed limit by one mile per hour, arrest the driver for speeding, and conduct a full-blown inventory search of the vehicle with impunity."[145] But in *Arkansas v. Sullivan*,[146] the Supreme Court granted certiorari and then immediately and summarily reversed that decision, albeit without specifically addressing the issue raised above, as the Court was miffed by the Arkansas court's improper assertion that it could "interpret[ ] the U.S. Constitution more broadly than the United States Supreme Court." But the four concurring Justices in *Sullivan* may have unnecessarily conceded a broader scope to *Whren* than was necessary when they said that while the concern expressed in the above quotation from the state court opinion showed the "Arkansas Supreme Court was moved by a concern rooted in the Fourth Amendment," the Supreme Court in *Whren* had already "held that such exercises of official discretion are unlimited by the Fourth Amendment." In any event, the Court's later language in *Brigham*

---

[144]The other three Justices, concurring in the judgment, objected (1) "to the Court's disposition of al-Kidd's Fourth Amendment claim on the merits"; (2) to the "validly obtained warrant" assumption, in that "omissions and misrepresentations" in the affidavit could mean it was vulnerable under *Franks*, see § 4.4; (3) to the "individualized suspicion" assumption, because the "Court's decisions, until today, have uniformly used the term . . . to mean individualized suspicion *of wrongdoing*"; and (4) that *Whren* did not settle "whether an official's subjective intent matters" in the "novel context" of the instant case, involving

"prolonged detention of an individual without probable cause to believe he had committed any criminal offense."

[145]State v. Sullivan, 340 Ark. 315, 16 S.W.3d 551 (2000). *Sullivan* lives on as a state court decision notwithstanding its fate before the Supreme Court discussed herein, but is inapplicable if the pretext arrest was to investigate another offense for which, as it turns out, there was probable cause. Romes v. State, 356 Ark. 26, 144 S.W.3d 750 (2004).

[146]Arkansas v. Sullivan, 532 U.S. 769, 121 S.Ct. 1876, 149 L.Ed.2d 994 (2001).

City v. Stuart[147] can easily be read as suggesting that vehicle inventories are simply another variety of "programmatic searches" as to which the permitted inquiry into purpose "is directed at ensuring that the purpose behind the *program* is not 'ultimately indistinguishable from the general interest in crime control,'" and "has nothing to do with discerning what is in the mind of the individual officer conducting the search."

The significance of the just-quoted language is best elaborated by considering a post-*Whren* case in which the Supreme Court was dealing with a search clearly *not* grounded in individualized suspicion (one of the "special-needs and administrative-search cases," as it was put in *Ashcroft*),[148] as to which some lower courts after *Whren* have been inclined to take into account pretextual motivation.[149] In *City of Indianapolis v. Edmond*,[150] where the Court held a drug detection checkpoint violated the Fourth

---

[147]Brigham City, Utah v. Stuart, 547 U.S. 398, 126 S. Ct. 1943, 164 L. Ed. 2d 650 (U.S. 2006).

[148]See generally Ch. 10.

[149]See, e.g., United States v. Maldonado, 356 F.3d 130 (1st Cir.2004) (court finds "a patina of plausibility" to defendant's claim inspection of commercial carrier invalid if motivated by intent to search for drugs, given *Whren*'s suggestion "that the exemption from the warrant requirement afforded to an administrative search only extends to searches actually made for administrative purposes," but need not decide that issue because no such intent proved); Anobile v. Pelligrino, 303 F.3d 107 (2d Cir.2002) (district court's statement re inspection of harness racing track that subjective motives of inspector are irrelevant is in error, as "this was an administrative search, and not an 'ordinary' search based on either individualized suspicion or probable cause"); United States v. Cervantes, 219 F.3d 882 (9th Cir.2000) (in determining whether warrantless search justified under the "emergency doctrine," see § 6.6, motivation of officer a relevant consideration notwithstanding *Whren*, which "distinguished cases where probable cause is present from inventory and administrative search cases where a government actor's pretextual motivation for a search or seizure is a viable claim"); United States v. Woodrum, 202 F.3d 1 (1st Cir.2000) (where under

Boston's cabdriver safety program officers could stop cabs bearing decal indicting police could stop cab at any time to check on driver's safety, resulting stopping of passenger justified on basis of third-party consent, but since such stops without probable cause and justified by the special purpose for which such consent given, lower court erred in concluding that *Whren* barred inquiry here into the stopping officer's subjective motives); State v. Holmes, 569 N.W.2d 181 (Minn.1997) (court relies upon distinction drawn in *Whren* in concluding lower court "incorrectly adopted the state's assertion that the subjective motivation of a police officer conducting an alleged inventory search is 'entirely irrelevant'"); People v. Johnson, 1 N.Y.3d 252, 771 N.Y.S.2d 64, 803 N.E.2d 385 (2003) (lower court erred in applying *Whren* to inventory search); State v. Hicks, 55 S.W.3d 515 (Tenn.2001) ("because roadblocks are operated without the protections provided by the probable cause requirement, courts must assume a special role in ensuring that constitutional safeguards are not eroded by subterfuge or pretext"); State v. Mountford, 171 Vt. 487, 769 A.2d 639 (2000) (because "distinguishing feature of community caretaking and emergency assistance searches is that . . ., as is the case with administrative and inventory searches, police are not required to demonstrate probable cause to believe that a crime has taken place," *Whren* not applicable in that context);

Amendment because "the primary purpose" of the checkpoint was "to uncover evidence of ordinary criminal wrongdoing," the petitioners argued that any inquiry into purpose was precluded by *Whren*. The Court answered that "our cases dealing with intrusions that occur pursuant to a general scheme absent individualized suspicion have often required an inquiry into purpose at the programmatic level," and then cautioned "that the purpose inquiry in this context is to be conducted only at the programmatic level and is not an invitation to probe the minds of individual officers acting at the scene."[151] This appears to mean, as it was put in *United States v. McCarty*,[152] that

> as long as (1) the search was undertaken pursuant to a legitimate administrative search scheme; (2) the searcher's actions are cabined to the scope of the permissible administrative search; and (3) there was no impermissible programmatic secondary motive for the search, the development of a second, subjective motive to verify the presence of contraband is irrelevant to the Fourth Amendment analysis.

If so, *Edmond* is unobjectionable, as it squares with the conclusion stated earlier herein[153]—as put by the *McCarty* court, that "an unlawful secondary search purpose" does not "invalidate the otherwise lawful administrative * * * search because the searching officers actions would have been the same regardless of his true 'motivation.'" But, as *McCarty* also recognizes, there is no basis for making the latter judgment if the officer's administrative search authority is not sufficiently and clearly circumscribed. And thus, as that court acknowledged, an officer's "unlawful secondary purpose" can hardly be ignored if he "had unfettered

---

State v. Kramer, 315 Wis.2d 414, 759 N.W.2d 598 (2009) ("a court may consider an officer's subjective intent in evaluating whether the officer was acting as a bona fide community caretaker," as this a situation where "a search or seizure is not supported by probable cause or reasonable suspicion").

Compare United States v. Castro, 166 F.3d 728 (5th Cir.1999) (on rehearing en banc, court holds that where driver and passenger arrested for seat belt violations, after which vehicle impounded and brought to station, where drug dog alerted to it, after which it searched, uncovering drugs, defendant's claim of pretextual impoundment rejected on ground "that the reasonableness inquiry under the Fourth Amendment is an objective one"; dissent objects that Supreme Court "has repeatedly indicated for

discerning readers that improper ulterior motives will invalidate police conduct in the context of inventory searches").

[150]City of Indianapolis v. Edmond, 531 U.S. 32, 121 S.Ct. 447, 148 L.Ed.2d 333 (2000).

[151]Citing *Edmond* in support, the Court likewise looked to "the programmatic purpose" in Ferguson v. City of Charleston, 532 U.S. 67, 121 S.Ct. 1281, 149 L.Ed.2d 205 (2001), holding that a hospital-police developed program to conduct urine test of pregnant patients violated the Fourth Amendment.

[152]United States v. McCarty, 648 F.3d 820 (9th Cir.2011), further discussed in § 10.6, text at note 181.

[153]See § 1.4(e).

discretion in determining which bags or containers to search."[154]

While the Court in *Ashcroft* referred to *Whren* as having "two limited exception[s]," there was yet another exception articulated in *Whren*, i.e., where a balancing analysis is necessary notwithstanding the existence of probable cause because the search or seizure at issue was "conducted in an extraordinary manner, unusually harmful to an individual's privacy or even physical interests." The Court gave some examples,[155] thereby leaving open the question of whether there are others. Illustrative of the questions which can arise as a result is that confronted in *United States v. Hudson*,[156] where defendant claimed his in-premises "arrest under a state warrant was a mere pretext to search his house for evidence to support federal charges." The defendant claimed that the case fell within the *Whren* "extraordinary manner" exception, but the court concluded otherwise because the police entry of the premises was in other respects unobjectionable (the police did knock and announce their authority and were justified in not awaiting a response).[157] But a dissent in *Hudson* objected that the *Whren* dictum compels no such result. Understood in a manner consistent with precedent, an "extraordinary" search of seizure, in the sense in which the Court used that term in *Whren*, is simply one that is "out of the ordinary"—such as an armed assault on a family home in the middle of the night in order to arrest someone for a sixty-dollar drug sale that had occurred over four months earlier at a different location.

In the *Atwater* case, rejecting a claim that custodial arrest for a no-fine offense without any plausible claim that there was a need for custody was unreasonable, the Court rejected the argument that the case fell within the *Whren* exception:

As our citations in *Whren* make clear, the question whether a search or seizure is

"extraordinary" turns, above all else, on the manner in which the search or seizure is executed. * * * Atwater's arrest was surely "humiliating," as she says in her brief, but it was no more "harmful to * * * privacy or * * * physical interests" than the normal custodial arrest. She was handcuffed, placed in a squad car, and taken to the local police station, where officers asked her to remove her shoes, jewelry, and glasses, and to empty her pockets. They

---

[154]Citing as illustrative United States v. Bulacan, 156 F.3d 963 (9th Cir.1998).

[155]See text at note 103 supra and following.

[156]United States v. Hudson, 100 F.3d 1409 (9th Cir.1996), discussed in Note, 66 U.Cin.L.Rev. 1045 (1998).

[157]See also Ricci v. Arlington Heights, 116 F.3d 288 (7th Cir.1997) (where defendant subjected to custodial arrest, terminated promptly, for fine-only violation that could result in very substantial fine, the arrest,

"which was based on probable cause, is not one of those extraordinary cases that requires us to conduct a balancing analysis" under *Whren*); Holland v. State, 696 So.2d 757 (Fla.1997) (though court does not find the list of exceptions to the rule of *Whren* to be exhaustive, other instances must involve "harm to the same degree," which not the case here, where circumstances relied upon by defendant is that plainclothes officer in unmarked car made traffic stop in dangerous part of town where, officer admitted, "a person would be stupid to stop").

then took her photograph and placed her in a cell, alone, for about an hour, after which she was taken before a magistrate, and released on $310 bond. The arrest and booking were inconvenient and embarrassing to Atwater, but not so extraordinary as to violate the Fourth Amendment.[158]

That is a convenient way to dispose of the *Whren* exception if one is disposed, as was the *Atwater* majority, to deny relief to Mrs. Atwater, but surely it is not the only way to look at that exception. Since the matter at issue in *Atwater* was a "custodial arrest," a special subset of the broader category of "arrest" that did not exist until created in *United States v. Robinson*,[159] one might well wonder why the "custodial" character of a particular arrest is not unquestionably the "manner" by which an arrest is made, just as (as the Court admits) the use of force has to do with the "manner" of arrest. And then it might be asked why the making of a custodial arrest for a fine-only case without a shred of justification, in terms of need for custody, is not "extraordinary," given the *Atwater* majority's claim that there is a "dearth" of such cases.

§ 1.5 Federal vs. state standards; constitutional vs. other violations

§ 1.5(a) Federal vs. state standards
§ 1.5(b) Violation of state constitution, state or federal statute, court rule, or administrative regulation
§ 1.5(c) The remaining "silver platter"

Research References

West's Key Number Digest
Constitutional Law ⬅266(5); Criminal Law ⬅394.1(3), 394.2(2), 394.4; Federal Courts ⬅404

Legal Encyclopedias
C.J.S., Constitutional Law §§ 992, 1026, 1031, 1035; Criminal Law §§ 770 to 792

Introduction

Throughout this Treatise, reference is frequently made to "illegal" or "unlawful" searches and seizures. Except when the context

---

[158]In Chortek v. City of Milwaukee, 356 F.3d 740 (7th Cir.2004), the plaintiffs argued for the inapplicability of *Whren* because "they faced 'much worse' treatment than did the plaintiff in *Atwater*," but since the "differences, they emphasize, relate primarily to the length of time spent handcuffed in a police vehicle, the thoroughness of the body searches, their inability to make phone calls and the fact that they had to share a holding cell with other prisoners," the court concluded it could not say this treatment was "unusually harmful" within the meaning of *Whren*.

[159]United States v. Robinson, 414 U.S. 218, 94 S.Ct. 467, 38 L.Ed.2d 427 (1973).

indicates otherwise, this may be taken to be a shorthand albeit imprecise reference to those searches and seizures that violate the Fourth Amendment. But, while this Treatise is by and large limited to a discussion of the Fourth Amendment, it must be noted that a particular search or seizure may not offend the federal Constitution but may yet be unlawful or illegal in the sense that it is contrary to a state constitutional provision or to some statute, rule of court, or administrative regulation. A search or seizure violating the law only in this latter sense[1] is sometimes (but not always) treated by the courts as requiring exclusion of the fruits thereof.

§ 1.5(a) Federal vs. state standards

In *Wolf v. Colorado*,[2] the Court, although then unwilling to impose the exclusionary rule upon the states, did say that the "security of one's privacy against arbitrary intrusion by the police—which is at the core of the Fourth Amendment—is basic to a free society * * * and as such enforceable against the States through the Due Process Clause." As the author of *Wolf,* Justice Frankfurter, was later to note in his dissent in *Elkins v. United States*,[3] this was not intended to mean that every search which, if conducted on the federal level, would be "unreasonable under the Fourth Amendment" is likewise "an 'arbitrary intrusion' of privacy so as to make the same conduct on the part of state officials a violation of the Fourteenth Amendment." In other words, the Fourteenth Amendment incorporates the "core" but not all of the Fourth Amendment, so that state and local police are under somewhat lesser constitutional restraints than federal law enforcement agents.

[Section 1.5]

[1]A violation of state law, even of constitutional dimensions, on the subject of search and seizure does not by virtue of that fact become a Fourth Amendment violation. As the Court stated in California v. Greenwood, 486 U.S. 35, 108 S.Ct. 1625, 100 L.Ed.2d 30 (1988): "Individual States may surely construe their own constitutions as imposing more stringent constraints on police conduct than does the Federal Constitution. We have never intimated, however, that whether or not a search is reasonable within the meaning of the Fourth Amendment depends on the law of the particular State in which the search occurs. * * * Respondent's argument is no less than a suggestion that concepts of privacy under the laws of each State are to determine the reach of the Fourth Amendment. We do not accept this submission." See, e.g., Doe v. Burnham, 6 F.3d 476 (7th Cir.1993) (in § 1983 action, trial judge erred in instructing jury it relevant that strip search violated state statutory provision limiting such action to certain situations).

So too, there is "no authority for the proposition that the existence of [federal] statutory protection renders a search *per se* unreasonable" under the Fourth Amendment. City of Ontario v. Quon, __ U.S. __, 130 S.Ct. 2619, 177 L.Ed.2d 216 (2010).

[Section 1.5(a)]

[2]Wolf v. Colorado, 338 U.S. 25, 69 S.Ct. 1359, 93 L.Ed. 1782 (1949).

[3]Elkins v. United States, 364 U.S. 206, 80 S.Ct. 1437, 4 L.Ed.2d 1669 (1960).

When the *Wolf* holding that the states need not employ the exclusionary rule was ultimately rejected in *Mapp v. Ohio*,[4] the Court did not address itself specifically to the question of what standards would be applied at the state level. Although Justice Clark, for the majority, did say that federal and state officers would be obligated to respect "the same fundamental criteria," this cryptic phrase could be taken to mean either that the Fourth Amendment applied in toto to the states or that the "fundamental fairness" core of the Amendment applied. *Elkins,* abolishing the "silver platter" doctrine, seemed to make sense only if the state and federal standards were the same, but this was not generally taken to be conclusive evidence that the Fourth Amendment and due process standards were equivalents.[5] The uncertainty was finally put to rest in *Ker v. California*,[6] where the Court held that "the standard of reasonableness is the same under the Fourth and Fourteenth Amendments." As later became apparent in decisions of the Court concerning incorporation of other provisions of the Bill of Rights into the Fourteenth Amendment due process clause, *Ker* was illustrative of the broader proposition that when a Bill of Rights provision is so incorporated, it is incorporated in its entirety.[7]

Strong opposition to this approach to Fourteenth Amendment due process was consistently voiced by Justice Harlan.[8] As he said in his concurring opinion in *Coolidge v. New Hampshire*[9]:

> *Mapp* and *Ker* have been primarily responsible for bringing about serious distortions and incongruities in this field of constitutional law. * * * First, the States have been put in a federal mold with respect to this aspect of criminal law enforcement, thus depriving the country of the opportunity to observe the effects of different procedures in similar settings. * * * Second, in order to leave some room for the States to cope with their own diverse problems, there has been generated a tendency to relax federal requirements under the Fourth Amendment, which now govern state procedures as well.

---

[4]Mapp v. Ohio, 367 U.S. 643, 81 S.Ct. 1684, 6 L.Ed.2d 1081 (1961).

[5]Collings, Toward Workable Rules of Search and Seizure, An Amicus Curiae Brief, 50 Cal.L.Rev. 421 (1962); Traynor, Mapp v. Ohio at Large in the Fifty States, 1962 Duke L.J. 319.

[6]Ker v. California, 374 U.S. 23, 83 S.Ct. 1623, 10 L.Ed.2d 726 (1963).

[7]E.g., Benton v. Maryland, 395 U.S. 784, 89 S.Ct. 2056, 23 L.Ed.2d 707 (1969) (double jeopardy); Duncan v. Louisiana, 391 U.S. 145, 88 S.Ct. 1444, 20 L.Ed.2d 491 (1968) (jury trial); Malloy v. Hogan, 378 U.S. 1, 84 S.Ct. 1489, 12 L.Ed.2d 653 (1964) (self-incrimination).

[8]See, e.g., his dissents in *Benton, Duncan,* and *Malloy,* all supra note 7. Justice Powell followed the Harlan approach; see his concurring opinion in the companion cases of Apodaca v. Oregon, 406 U.S. 404, 92 S.Ct. 1628, 32 L.Ed.2d 184 (1972); and Johnson v. Louisiana, 406 U.S. 356, 92 S.Ct. 1620, 32 L.Ed.2d 152 (1972), and later gained the support of Rehnquist, J., and the Chief Justice. See Ballew v. Georgia, 435 U.S. 223, 98 S.Ct. 1029, 55 L.Ed.2d 234 (1978).

[9]Coolidge v. New Hampshire, 403 U.S. 443, 91 S.Ct. 2022, 29 L.Ed.2d 564 (1971).

Although the Harlan view, whatever its merits, has not prevailed, it is important to note that in one sense at least the constitutional standards governing state and local officers may sometimes be different from those governing their federal counterparts. This is not because only a watered-down version of the Fourth Amendment is being applied to the states,[10] but rather because what was referred to in *Ker* as "the standard of reasonableness" requires consideration of the nature of the law enforcement responsibilities being carried out in connection with the challenged search or seizure. Thus, in *Cady v. Dombrowski*,[11] Justice Rehnquist, in the course of upholding an inventory by local police of a car that had been involved in an accident, stressed that local police, unlike federal officers, "have much more contact with vehicles for reasons related to the operation of vehicles themselves," not only because "the officer may believe the operator has violated a criminal statute" but also because he may "frequently investigate vehicle accidents in which there is no claim of criminal liability and engage in what, for want of a better term, may be described as community caretaking functions, totally divorced from the detection, investigation, or acquisition of evidence relating to the violation of a criminal statute."[12]

But while, except in the sense noted in *Cady*, the constitutional standards for federal and state searches are the same, this is not to say that all of the federal search and seizure holdings are applicable to the states. As the Court noted in *Ker*, "the demands of our federal system compel us to distinguish between evidence held inadmissible because of our supervisory powers over federal courts and that held inadmissible because prohibited by the United States Constitution." The difficulty, however, is in distinguishing between these two categories. Sometimes courts are less than precise in stating whether or not the Fourth Amendment is the basis of exclusion, and even when it is reasonably apparent that exclusion has resulted from failure to comply with a

---

[10]Except in the sense discussed in Miller & Wright, Leaky Floors: State Law Below Federal Constitutional Limits, 50 Ariz. L.Rev. 227 (2008), noting, and citing several examples from the law of search and seizure, that while there is a "widely accepted" notion that the federal constitution and interpretation thereof by the Supreme Court "set a 'floor' for personal liberties" below which state courts and legislatures "cannot properly go," states sometimes find it possible to take positions below the federal standards, especially when those standards are expressed as multi-factor or "totality of the circumstances" rules.

[11]Cady v. Dombrowski, 413 U.S. 433, 93 S.Ct. 2523, 37 L.Ed.2d 706 (1973).

[12]Similarly, in United States v. Martinez-Fuerte, 428 U.S. 543, 96 S.Ct. 3074, 49 L.Ed.2d 1116 (1976); United States v. Brignoni-Ponce, 422 U.S. 873, 95 S.Ct. 2574, 45 L.Ed.2d 607 (1975); and United States v. Ortiz, 422 U.S. 891, 95 S.Ct. 2585, 45 L.Ed.2d 623 (1975), the Court emphasized that the limits upon vehicle stops by federal agents were not necessarily applicable to local officers responsible for enforcing laws relating to drivers' licenses, safety requirements, weight limits, and such matters.

statute or court rule there will often remain the uncertainty of whether the rule or statute itself states a constitutional requirement so that—in the last analysis—the violation may be said to be of constitutional dimension.

Ker is illustrative of the problem. The opinion of the Court by Justice Clark, upholding the unannounced entry by state officers, did not deem the Court's prior decision in *Miller v. United States*[13] to be controlling. The four dissenters, on the other hand, while conceding that *Miller* "did not rest upon constitutional doctrine but rather upon an exercise of this Court's supervisory powers," concluded that nothing said in *Miller* "implied that the same result was not compelled by the Fourth Amendment." Similarly, in *Aguilar v. Texas*[14] the majority relied heavily upon *Giordenello v. United States*[15] in holding that a state search warrant affidavit violated the Fourth Amendment because it was based upon "mere conclusions," to which the three dissenters responded that in *Giordenello* the evidence had been suppressed because of a failure to comply with Rule 4 of the Federal Rules of Criminal Procedure.

Just as federal courts may suppress improperly obtained evidence upon other than constitutional grounds in federal prosecutions, state courts may likewise require suppression merely because the search or seizure failed to comply with state law. State requirements extending beyond those of the Fourth Amendment, dealing with such matters as when arrests may be made, when arrestees must be released, when and how entry of premises may be made for purposes of arrest or search, and how a search warrant must be obtained, executed, and returned, are not uncommon. Although the several jurisdictions have by no means given uniform treatment to the question of when exclusion should be deemed an appropriate sanction for violation of such provisions, some generalizations are possible.

Prior to that discussion,[16] however, it is necessary to ask a different question: whether exclusion of evidence obtained in violation of state or local law is sometimes necessary because that violation makes the conduct at issue also a violation of the Fourth Amendment itself. In various settings, the Supreme Court has answered that question in the negative. Indeed, a violation of state law on search and seizure, even of constitutional dimensions, has been deemed not, because of that fact, a violation of the Fourth Amendment as well. As the Court stated in *California*

---

[13]Miller v. United States, 357 U.S. 301, 78 S.Ct. 1190, 2 L.Ed.2d 1332 (1958).

[14]Aguilar v. Texas, 378 U.S. 108, 84 S.Ct. 1509, 12 L.Ed.2d 723 (1964).

[15]Giordenello v. United States, 357 U.S. 480, 78 S.Ct. 1245, 2 L.Ed.2d 1503 (1958).

[16]Which appears in § 1.5(b).

v. Greenwood[17]:

Individual States may surely construe their own constitutions as imposing more stringent constraints on police conduct than does the Federal Constitution. We have never intimated, however, that whether or not a search is reasonable within the meaning of the Fourth Amendment depends on the law of the particular State in which the search occurs. * * * Respondent's argument is no less than a suggestion that concepts of privacy under the laws of each State are to determine the reach of the Fourth Amendment. We do not accept this submission.

The Court has reached the same result with respect to violation of other state and local law.[18] Particularly noteworthy is *Virginia v. Moore*,[19] where the state court suppressed on Fourth Amendment grounds[20] evidence seized in a search incident to an arrest for driving on a suspended license because state law required use of a summons in lieu of arrest in such circumstances. Finding "no historical indication that those who ratified the Fourth Amendment understood it as a redundant guarantee of whatever limits on search and seizure legislatures might have enacted," the Supreme Court next noted that "traditional standards of reasonableness" had consistently led the Court to the conclusion "that when an officer has probable cause to believe a person committed even a minor crime in his presence, the balancing of private and public interests is not in doubt."[21] The Court understandably could find no reason for "changing this calculus when a State chooses to protect privacy beyond the level that the Fourth Amendment requires." A contrary conclusion, the Court

---

[17]California v. Greenwood, 486 U.S. 35, 108 S.Ct. 1625, 100 L.Ed.2d 30 (1988).

[18]Whren v. United States, 517 U.S. 806, 116 S.Ct. 1769, 135 L.Ed.2d 89 (1996) (police stop of vehicle lawful under Fourth Amendment though in violation of local regulations limiting authority of plainclothes officers in unmarked vehicles); Cooper v. California, 386 U.S. 58, 87 S.Ct. 788, 17 L.Ed.2d 730 (1967) (search of seized vehicle lawful under Fourth Amendment even though not specifically authorized by state law).

The point has been made by lower courts as well. See, e.g., Doe v. Burnham, 6 F.3d 476 (7th Cir.1993) (in § 1983 action, trial judge erred in instructing jury it relevant that strip search violated state statutory provision limiting such action to certain situations).

[19]Virginia v. Moore, 553 U.S. 164, 128 S.Ct. 1598, 170 L.Ed.2d 559 (2008), discussed in Kincheloe, Virginia v. Moore: The Supreme Court Delivers Another Blow to Fourth Amendment Protections, 36 W.St.U.L.Rev. 187 (2009); Loya, Judicial Supremacy and Federalism: A Closer Look at Danforth and Moore, 2008 Cato Sup.Ct.Rev. 161; Taslitz, Fourth Amendment Federalism and the Silencing of the American Poor, 85 Chi.-Kent L.Rev. 277 (2010).

[20]The state had no exclusionary rule of its own, of the kind discussed in § 1.5(b), for violation of the statute in question. See note 22 infra.

[21]Citing Devenpeck v. Alford, 543 U.S. 146, 125 S.Ct. 588, 160 L.Ed.2d 537 (2004); Atwater v. City of Lago Vista, 532 U.S. 318, 121 S.Ct. 1536, 149 L.Ed.2d 549 (2001); Gerstein v. Pugh, 420 U.S. 103, 95 S.Ct. 854, 43 L.Ed.2d 54 (1975); Brinegar v. United States, 338 U.S. 160, 69 S.Ct. 1302, 93 L.Ed. 1879 (1949).

emphasized, "would often frustrate rather than further state policy,"[22] and "would produce a constitutional regime" that was "vague and unpredictable" and would "vary from place to place and from time to time."[23]

Particularly in light of those last comments, it might be thought that state and local law can *never* be relevant to the question of whether the Fourth Amendment has been violated. It is to be doubted, however, that the *Greenwood-Moore* line of cases goes quite that far, as sometimes how one comes out under the applicable Fourth Amendment standard will of necessity depend upon the contours of state or local law. Consider: (1) Whether the Fourth Amendment requirement in *Colorado v. Bertine*[24] that the vehicle impoundment/inventory process be conducted pursuant to "standardized criteria" has been met will sometimes require consideration of the content of state law concerning when such activities may be undertaken.[25] (2) Whether the Fourth Amendment requirement in *United States v. Biswell*[26] that warrantless business inspections be "carefully limited in time, place and scope" has been met will often depend upon the content of state

---

[22]As the Court elaborated: "Virginia chooses to protect individual privacy and dignity more than the Fourth Amendment requires, but it also chooses not to attach to violations of its arrest rules the potent remedies that federal courts have applied to Fourth Amendment violations. Virginia does not, for example, ordinarily exclude from criminal trials evidence obtained in violation of its statutes. * * * Moore would allow Virginia to accord enhanced protection against arrest only on pain of accompanying that protection with federal remedies for Fourth Amendment violations, which often include the exclusionary rule. States unwilling to lose control over the remedy would have to abandon restrictions on arrest altogether. This is an odd consequence of a provision designed to protect against searches and seizures."

[23]*Moore* has been taken to mean that police conduct illegal under state law because occurring outside the officer's geographical jurisdiction does not violate the Fourth Amendment, United States v. Sed, 601 F.3d 224 (3d Cir.2010); United States v. Gonzales, 535 F.3d 1174 (10th Cir.2008); Devega v. State, 286 Ga. 448, 689 S.E.2d 293 (2010); Commonwealth v. Hernandez,

456 Mass. 528, 924 N.E.2d 709 (2010) (but court follows earlier cases requiring exclusion instead "based on the application of State legal principles"), and that even if state law prohibits state police from arresting for a federal offense or a particular state offense, that does not make such arrest a violation of the Fourth Amendment, Edgerly v. City and County of San Francisco, 599 F.3d 946 (9th Cir.2010) (state law prohibits arrest for offense punishable only as infraction); United States v. Burtton, 599 F.3d 823 (8th Cir.2010) (state law prohibits arrest for traffic offense of violating open container law); United States v. Turner, 553 F.3d 1337 (10th Cir.2009) (federal offense); State v. Harker, 240 P.3d 780 (Utah 2010) (state law requires offense occur in officer's presence, lacking here). See also § 5.1 note 82.

[24]Colorado v. Bertine, 479 U.S. 367, 107 S.Ct. 738, 93 L.Ed.2d 739 (1987).

[25]See, e.g., United States v. Rios, 88 F.3d 867 (10th Cir.1996) (relying on state statute authorizing impoundment of improperly registered vehicle).

[26]United States v. Biswell, 406 U.S. 311, 92 S.Ct. 1593, 32 L.Ed.2d 87 (1972).

statutes.[27] (3) Whether the Fourth Amendment requirement in *Shadwick v. City of Tampa*[28] that warrants be issued by a "neutral and detached magistrate" who is "lawfully vested" with warrant-issuing authority will often depend upon state statutes regulating such authority.[29] On the other hand, as concluded in *State v. Slayton*,[30] *Moore* is applicable to statutes limiting which state agents may make a *Terry* stop, meaning the stop by an unauthorized agent will pass Fourth Amendment muster if made on reasonable suspicion.

§ 1.5(b) Violation of state constitution, state or federal statute, court rule, or administrative regulation

When (as occurs with some frequency[31]) a state court finds that a certain arrest or search passes muster under the Fourth

---

[27]See. e.g., Bionic Auto Parts and Sales, Inc. v. Fahner, 721 F.2d 1072 (7th Cir.1983) (in overturning injunction barring warrantless inspection of auto parts dealers, court emphasizes recent change in statute from allowing inspection "at any reasonable time during the night or day" to allowing inspections only during normal business hours).

[28]Shadwick v. City of Tampa, 407 U.S. 345, 92 S.Ct. 2119, 32 L.Ed.2d 783 (1972).

[29]See, e.g., United States v. Master, 614 F.3d 236 (6th Cir.2010) (Fourth Amendment violated where judge issued search warrant for premises outside his county, contrary to state law; court notes *Shadwick* "is highly solicitous of state and local authority" and makes it clear that "more is required under the Fourth Amendment for an individual to be qualified and thus authorized to serve as a magistrate" than being neutral and detached, "and the requisite qualifications are determined by state law"); United States v. Scott, 260 F.3d 512 (6th Cir.2001) (Fourth Amendment violated here where state search warrant issued by retired judge when regular judge sitting and present, as state statute specifically states such a judge may act only when active general sessions judge unavailable); State v. Hess, 327 Wis.2d 524, 785 N.W.2d 568 (2010) (relying on *Scott*, court holds that Fourth Amendment violated and evidence must be suppressed where judge issued civil bench warrant but

"(1) the circuit court did not have statutory authority to issue a warrant for failure to meet with a PSI investigator; and (2) the warrant was not supported by an oath or affirmation" and thus was "void *ab initio*").

[30]State v. Slayton, 147 N.M. 340, 223 P.3d 337 (2009).

[Section 1.5(b)]

[31]As noted in Wilkes, More on the New Federalism in Criminal Procedure, 63 Ky.L.J. 873 (1975), a number of state courts "greeted the Burger Court's retreat from activism not with submission, but with a stubborn independence that displays determination to keep alive the Warren Court's philosophical commitment to protection of the criminal suspect." See also Latzer, State Constitutional Criminal Law chs. 2 to 3 (1995); Abrahamson, Criminal Law and State Constitutions: The Emergence of State Constitutional Law, 63 Texas L.Rev. 1141 (1985); Dawson, State-Created Exclusionary Rules in Search and Seizure: A Study of the Texas Experience, 59 Texas L.Rev. 191 (1981); Dix, Nonconstitutional Exclusionary Rules in Criminal Procedure, 27 Am.Crim.L.Rev. 53 (1989); Dix, Exclusionary Rule Issues as Matters of State Law, 11 Am.J.Crim.L. 109 (1983); Hancock, State Court Activism and Searches Incident to Arrest, 68 Va.L.Rev. 1085 (1982); Latzer, The Hidden Conservatism of the State Court "Revolution," 74 Judicature 191 (1991) (in state high court criminal procedure cases based upon state constitutional law over

about 20-year period, U.S. Supreme Court doctrine rejected 32% of the time); Henderson, Beyond the (Current) Fourth Amendment: Protecting Third-Party Information, Third Parties, and the Rest of Us Too, 34 Pepp.L.Rev. 975 (2007); Henderson, Learning From All Fifty States: How to Apply the Fourth Amendment and Its State Analogs to Protect Third Party Information From Unreasonable Searches, 55 Cath.U.L.Rev. 373 (2006); Landau, The Search for the Meaning of Oregon's Search and Seizure Clause, 87 Or.L.Rev. 819 (2008); Marcus, State Constitutional Protection for Defendants in Criminal Prosecutions, 20 Ariz.St.L.J. 151 (1988); Smith & Gordon, Police Encounters with Citizens and the Fourth Amendment: Similarities and Differences Between Federal and State Law, 68 Temple L.Rev. 1317 (1995); Symposium, Independent State Grounds: Should State Courts Depart from the Fourth Amendment in Construing Their Own Constitutions, and if So, on What Basis Beyond Simply Disagreement with the United States Supreme Court's Result, 77 Miss. L.J. i (2007) (articles at 1, 225, 265, 315, 345, 369, 401, 417); Urbonya, Fourth Amendment Federalism? The Court's Vacillating Mistrust and Trust of State Search and Seizure Laws, 35 Seton Hall L.Rev. 911 (2005) (generally discussing how Supreme Court has "selectively invoked" these state provisions, and noting at 913–14 that "twenty-eight States have rejected a particular Fourth Amendment doctrine and have declared a broader protection under state law"); Walinski & Tucker, Expectations of Privacy: Fourth Amendment Legitimacy Through State Law, 16 Harv.Civ.Rts.-Civ.Lib.L.Rev. 1 (1981); Wigdor, What's in a Word? A Comparative Analysis of Article 1, Section 12 of the New York State Constitution and the Fourth Amendment to the United States Constitution, 14 Touro L.Rev. 757 (1998); Wilkes, The New Federalism in Criminal Procedure: State Court Evasion of the Burger Court, 62 Ky.L.J. 421 (1974); Note, 48 Temple L.Q. 780

(1975); the helpful discussion of this trend in State v. Ochoa, 792 N.W.2d 260 (Iowa 2010); State v. Hunt, 91 N.J. 338, 450 A.2d 952 (1982); the thoughtful concurring opinion of Linde, J., in State v. Greene, 285 Or. 337, 591 P.2d 1362 (1979), reasoning that states by legislation and localities by rule should deal with search and seizure questions more than they have, given the fact the constitutional limits are often uncertain and, after all, only set the outer limits on police authority; and the dissenting opinion of Urbigkit, J., in Saldana v. State, 846 P.2d 604 (Wyo.1993), containing an exhaustive analysis of these developments and a complete listing of the relevant literature.

Illustrative of this trend are: State v. Guzman, 122 Idaho 981, 842 P.2d 660 (1992), rejecting the good-faith exception of United States v. Leon, 468 U.S. 897, 104 S.Ct. 3405, 82 L.Ed.2d 677 (1984); State v. Ochoa, 792 N.W.2d 260 (Iowa 2010), declining to follow Samson v. California, 547 U.S. 843, 126 S.Ct. 2193, 165 L.Ed.2d 250 (2006); State v. Reid, 194 N.J. 386, 945 A.2d 26 (2008), rejecting *Miller-Smith* rule re lack of privacy for information exposed to third parties; State v. Johnson, 68 N.J. 349, 346 A.2d 66 (1975), declining to follow Schneckloth v. Bustamonte, 412 U.S. 218, 93 S.Ct. 2041, 36 L.Ed.2d 854 (1973), regarding consent searches; State v. Opperman, 247 N.W.2d 673 (S.D.1976), declining to follow South Dakota v. Opperman, 428 U.S. 364, 96 S.Ct. 3092, 49 L.Ed.2d 1000 (1976), regarding inventory of impounded automobiles; Autran v. State, 887 S.W.2d 31 (Tex.Crim.App.1994), regarding inventory search; State v. Jackson, 102 Wash.2d 432, 688 P.2d 136 (1984), declining to follow Illinois v. Gates, 462 U.S. 213, 103 S.Ct. 2317, 76 L.Ed.2d 527 (1983), regarding the probable cause test.

This movement has been facilitated in those jurisdictions having express right-to-privacy provisions in their constitutions. See State v. Forrester, 343 S.C. 637, 541 S.E.2d 837 (2001) (citing to the 10 state con-

Amendment but that it violates the comparable provision of the state constitution, there does not appear to be any dissent[32] from the conclusion that the fruits thereof must be suppressed from evidence.[33] The rationale for such a result is seldom stated in the

---

stitutions having such provisions, 6 of them within the provision prohibiting unreasonable searches and seizures). However, it has sometimes occurred as well where the state constitutional provision "appears to have been derived from the Fourth Amendment and shares the same language." State v. Bulington, 802 N.E.2d 435 (Ind. 2004). See, e.g., State v. Woods, 866 So.2d 422 (Miss.2003).

In a few jurisdictions this movement has been thwarted by constitutional amendment. See, e.g., In re Lance W., 37 Cal.3d 873, 210 Cal.Rptr. 631, 694 P.2d 744 (1985) (discussing an amendment reading "except as provided by statute hereinafter enacted by a two-thirds vote of the membership in each house of the Legislature, relevant evidence shall not be excluded in any criminal proceeding," which court says "has abrogated * * * a defendant's right to object to and suppress evidence seized in violation of the California, but not the federal, Constitution"); and State v. Lavazzoli, 434 So.2d 321 (Fla.1983) (discussing an amendment reading "This right shall be construed in conformity with the Fourth Amendment to the United States Constitution, as interpreted by the United States Supreme Court," which goes on to say that evidence is not admissible "if such articles or information would be inadmissible under the decisions of the United States Supreme Court construing the Fourth Amendment to the United States Constitution"). Also, in at least one jurisdiction such involvement has been deemed inconsistent with the intent of the drafters of the state's constitution. People v. Caballes, 221 Ill.2d 282, 303 Ill.Dec. 128, 851 N.E.2d 26 (2006) (the "interstitial approach," under which state court may diverge from federal precedent because of flawed federal analysis, structural differences between state and federal government, or distinctive state characteristics,

rejected in favor of "limited lockstep doctrine," deemed consistent with intent of drafters of 1970 state constitution).

[32]Except perhaps Maryland; see Fitzgerald v. State, 384 Md. 484, 864 A.2d 1006 (2004).

[33]E.g., State v. Kaluna, 55 Haw. 361, 520 P.2d 51 (1974); State v. Larocco, 794 P.2d 460 (Utah 1990). A state court may also hold that certain evidence was obtained in violation of the Fourth Amendment and the equivalent provision of the state constitution, in which case the holding would rest upon an independent nonfederal ground and would not be overturned by the Supreme Court. See People v. Krivda, 5 Cal.3d 357, 96 Cal.Rptr. 62, 486 P.2d 1262 (1971), vacated, California v. Krivda, 409 U.S. 33, 93 S.Ct. 32, 34 L.Ed.2d 45 (1972).

However, in Michigan v. Long, 463 U.S. 1032, 103 S.Ct. 3469, 77 L.Ed.2d 1201 (1983), the Court held that "when, as in this case, a state court decision fairly appears to rest primarily on federal law, or to be interwoven with the federal law, and when the adequacy and independence of any possible state law ground is not clear from the face of the opinion, we will accept as the most reasonable explanation that the state court decided the case the way it did because it believed that federal law required it to do so. If a state court chooses merely to rely on federal precedents as it would on the precedents of all other jurisdictions, then it need only make clear by a plain statement in its judgment or opinion that the federal cases are being used only for the purpose of guidance, and do not themselves compel the result that the court has reached. * * * If the state court decision indicates clearly and expressly that it is alternatively based on bona fide separate, adequate, and independent grounds, we, of course, will not undertake to review the decision." See

cases,[34] but exclusion in these circumstances may be explained on the ground that a violation of the fundamental law of the state constitutes such a substantial intrusion upon the defendant's rights that the exclusionary remedy is just as appropriate as when the Fourth Amendment is violated.[35] That state courts do not even pause to consider the matter in these circumstances is perhaps not too surprising, for in those relatively uncommon situations in which a court interprets the state equivalent of the Fourth Amendment to forbid some practice the Supreme Court has not deemed a violation of the Fourth, it is clear the court views the practice as constituting a very serious intrusion.[36]

This is not to suggest that as a matter of federal constitutional law the states are *obligated* to utilize an exclusionary rule for state-constitution expansions upon Fourth Amendment protections. The Supreme Court rejected such a claim in *California v. Greenwood*,[37] where the defendant urged "that the California constitutional amendment eliminating the exclusionary rule for evidence seized in violation of state but not federal law[38] violates the Due Process Clause of the Fourteenth Amendment." After noting that even as to Fourth Amendment violations the

---

Adams, Applying More Restrictive Search and Seizure Requirements Under State Constitutional Law in Federal Courts Using Michigan v. Long and Erie v. Tompkins, 14 Temp.Pol. & Civ.Rts.L.Rev. 201 (2004). For another application of the *Long* principle in a Fourth Amendment context, see Pennsylvania v. Labron, 518 U.S. 938, 116 S.Ct. 2485, 135 L.Ed.2d 1031 (1996).

[34]As noted in Maltz, False Prophet—Justice Brennan and the Theory of State Constitutional Law, 15 Hastings Const.L.Q. 429, 447 (1988), state courts "generally have assumed, without discussion, that the exclusionary rule should be applied to state constitutional violations as well as their federal counterparts."

Of course, it does not follow that the fruits of a *state* constitutional violation must be suppressed in a *federal* prosecution. See, e.g., United States v. Vite-Espinoza, 342 F.3d 462 (6th Cir.2003).

[35]For a contrary view, see Cassell, the Mysterious Creation of Search and Seizure Exclusionary Rules Under State Constitutions: The Utah Example, 1993 Utah L.Rev. 751.

[36]See, e.g., State v. Kaluna, 55 Haw. 361, 520 P.2d 51 (1974) (court strongly disagrees with Supreme Court's holding in *Robinson* that there is an unqualified right to search a person following his custodial arrest); Commonwealth v. Upton, 394 Mass. 363, 476 N.E.2d 548 (1985) (suppressing evidence because state constitution deemed not to permit the watered-down version of probable cause allowed by the Supreme Court's *Gates* decision); State v. Boland, 115 Wash.2d 571, 800 P.2d 1112 (1990) (suppressing evidence because state constitution doesn't permit the no-privacy-in-garbage approach in Supreme Court's *Greenwood* case). See also cases cited in note 33 supra.

But, the same result has been reached when the state constitutional provision violated is other than the state's counterpart to the Fourth Amendment. See, e.g., State v. Wilson, 618 N.W.2d 513 (S.D.2000) (state constitutional provision on jurisdiction of judges, violated here when judge issuing warrant no longer assigned to that circuit).

[37]California v. Greenwood, 486 U.S. 35, 108 S.Ct. 1625, 100 L.Ed.2d 30 (1988).

[38]See note 33.

application of the exclusionary rule has often depended upon a cost-benefits balancing, the Court held:

> The States are not foreclosed by the Due Process Clause from using a similar balancing approach to delineate the scope of their own exclusionary rules. Hence, the people of California could permissibly conclude that the benefits of excluding relevant evidence of criminal activity do not outweigh the costs when the police conduct at issue does not violate federal law.[39]

As for violation of a statutory provision dealing with some aspect of arrest or search,[40] the enacting legislature sometimes resolves the issue by expressly providing for exclusion. An illustration on the federal level is the statute on wiretapping and electronic surveillance, which provides that the fruits of violations of that act (including some that do not also violate the Fourth Amendment, such as failure to obtain a warrant authorization from the Attorney General[41]) must be excluded from evidence.[42] Similar exclusionary rule requirements also are to be found in some state statutes.[43] On the other hand, the legislature may indicate that it does *not* want the exclusionary rule to oper-

---

[39]See State v. Rodriguez, 317 Or. 27, 854 P.2d 399 (1993) (per *Greenwood,* where, as here, arrest violated state constitution but not Fourth Amendment itself, evidence obtained incident to arrest not "subject to suppression under the Fourth Amendment as the 'fruit' of a prior illegality").

[40]In recent years there has been a significant increase in such legislation, especially on the federal level and especially with respect to new technologies. This has given rise to a dispute as to whether legislators or courts are more capable of making the rules in this area. See Kerr, Searches and Seizures in a Digital World, 119 Harv.L.Rev. 531 (2005), responded to in Solove, Fourth Amendment Codification and Professor Kerr's Misguided Call for Judicial Deference, 74 Fordham L.Rev. 747 (2005), responded to in turn in Kerr, Congress, Courts, and the New Technologies: A Response to Professor Solove, 74 Fordham L.Rev. 779 (2005).

[41]See United States v. Giordano, 416 U.S. 505, 94 S.Ct. 1820, 40 L.Ed.2d 341 (1974), in which the Court, in response to the government's argument that the statute did not require suppression where the authorization was by the Attorney General's executive

assistant rather than the Attorney General himself or a person specially designated by him, concluded the "Congress intended to require suppression where there is failure to satisfy any of those statutory requirements that directly and substantially implement the congressional intention to limit the use of intercept procedures to those situations clearly calling for the employment of this extraordinary investigative device."

Compare United States v. Chavez, 416 U.S. 562, 94 S.Ct. 1849, 40 L.Ed.2d 380 (1974), where a 5-4 majority concluded that mere failure to correctly identify the authorizing official, though in violation of the statute, did not require suppression. This was because the provisions here in question were not "meant, by themselves, to occupy a central, or even functional, role in guarding against unwarranted use of wiretapping or electronic surveillance." See also United States v. Donovan, 429 U.S. 413, 97 S.Ct. 658, 50 L.Ed.2d 652 (1977).

[42]18 U.S.C.A. § 2515.

[43]E.g., Ill.C.S.A. ch. 720, § 5/14-5 (declaring inadmissible "any evidence" obtained in violation of state eavesdropping law, which makes criminal various forms of eavesdropping not

ate with respect to certain statutory violations.[44] This is most likely to occur with respect to statutory provisions concerning the issuance, execution and return of search warrants, which frequently contain many rather technical requirements. The legislature may either enumerate the types of illegality calling for suppression of evidence obtained by warrant[45] or may provide that exclusion shall not occur "because of technical irregularities not affecting the substantial rights of the defendant."[46] Or, as with the federal Right to Financial Privacy Act, legislation on a

---

proscribed by the Constitution or federal law).

Consider also Wilson v. State, 311 S.W.3d 452 (Tex.Crim.App.2010) (noting that Texas Code Crim.P. art. 38.23, declaring inadmissible evidence obtained in violation of "any * * * laws of the State of Texas," "imposes what is probably the broadest state exclusionary rule requirement of any American jurisdiction," although the statute "may not be invoked for statutory violations unrelated to the purpose of the exclusionary rule or to the prevention of the illegal procurement of evidence of crime"); State v. Popenhagen, 309 Wis.2d 601, 749 N.W.2d 611 (2008) (violation of statute requiring probable cause for issuance of subpoena for documents a basis for exclusion of evidence, as statute says "Motions to the court, including but not limited to, motions to quash or limit the subpoena, shall be addressed to the court which issued the subpoena").

But consider Miles v. State, 241 S.W.3d 28 (Tex.Crim.App.2007) (that statute does not cover violation of traffic law by private citizen while making citizen's arrest, as an officer in like circumstances would be justified in violating such law to make arrest).

[44]E.g., State v. Thompkin, 341 Or. 368, 143 P.3d 530 (2006) (evidence obtained in violation of statute on permissible scope of traffic stops not subject to suppression, as per Ore.Rev. Stat. § 136.432 "the legislature had determined that such statutory violations do not provide a sufficient basis to exclude challenged evidence").

Or, the state constitution may bar use of an exclusionary rule absent a violation of the federal Constitution.

See People v. Robinson, 47 Cal.4th 1104, 104 Cal.Rptr.3d 727, 224 P.3d 55 (2010), discussed in Note, 99 Cal.L. Rev. 885 (2011) (post-conviction taking of DNA sample for offense not within statutory list does not require suppression under state constitution provision limiting exclusion to when mandated by federal constitution); People v. McKay, 27 Cal.4th 601, 117 Cal.Rptr.2d 236, 41 P.3d 59 (2002) (since violation of state law re use of citation in lieu of arrest does not make the arrest a violation of the Fourth Amendment, such state constitutional provision bars exclusion of evidence obtained by such violation).

[45]E.g., Ill.C.S.A. ch. 725, § 5/114-12(a)(2): "The search and seizure with a warrant was illegal because the warrant is insufficient on its face; the evidence seized is not that described in the warrant; there was not probable cause for the issuance of the warrant; or, the warrant was illegally executed." Consider also Martinez v. State, 17 S.W.3d 677 (Tex.Crim.App. 2000) (because statute requires exclusion of evidence "obtained" by violation of statute, exclusion not necessary when after evidence lawfully obtained it removed from county in violation of statute).

[46]E.g., Ill.C.S.A. ch. 725, § 5/108-14; Wis.Stat.Ann. § 968.22. Consider also State v. Richardson, 295 N.C. 309, 245 S.E.2d 754 (1978) (where statute says evidence "obtained as a result" of violation of statutory provisions must be suppressed, suppression not required for noncompliance with statutory requirement that list of items seized be given to person consenting to search, as items were not obtained as a result of that violation).

particular subject may specifically assert that "the only authorized" remedy is something other than the exclusion of evidence.[47]

If the statute in question does not explicitly state the legislature's view of the matter, counsel is well advised to consider whatever legislative history may be available. Illustrative of the way in which such history may be utilized to resolve the issue is *People v. Brannon*.[48] The defendant in a drunk driving prosecution sought to exclude the results of a breathalyzer test taken by an officer who failed to comply with a statutory requirement that the defendant be given his choice among blood, breath or urine tests. In holding that exclusion was not required, the court noted that the statutory provision was derived from a bill from which the legislature had stricken language to the effect that the results of a test were inadmissible unless the arresting officer advised the person of his choice.

Often, of course, not even that amount of guidance is available to the court. In such circumstances, perhaps the most that the court can do with respect to a violation of a statute or rule of court is to determine whether "the violation significantly affected * * * the defendant's substantial rights."[49] Although this test is of necessity somewhat ambiguous, it does seem fair to say that

---

[47]Because the RFPA says that civil penalties are "the only authorized" remedy for its violation, 12 U.S.C.A. § 3417(d), courts have been unwilling to imply a suppression remedy as well. United States v. Daccarett, 6 F.3d 37 (2d Cir.1993); United States v. Frazin, 780 F.2d 1461 (9th Cir.1986).

Consider also Jenkins v. State, 978 So.2d 116 (Fla.2008) (since strip-search statute refers only to remedies that "are civil and injunctive in nature," this means "exclusionary rule is not a remedy * * * unless a constitutional violation has also occurred"); State v. Mubita, 145 Idaho 925, 188 P.3d 867 (2008) (no suppression for violation of state Health Insurance Portability and Accountability Act, as it "expressly provides for monetary fine in the event of a violation"); State v. Swiek, 955 A.2d 255 (Me.2008) (violation of statutory requirement that officer making a traffic stop be "in uniform" not basis for exclusion of evidence found thereafter, as statutory remedy is bar to convicting defendant for failing or refusing to stop).

[48]People v. Brannon, 32 Cal.App.3d 971, 108 Cal.Rptr. 620

(1973), noted in 7 Loyola L.A.L.Rev. 201 (1974).

Similarly, because the Electronic Communications Privacy Act says that only the legislatively-declared "remedies and sanctions" are available, 18 U.S.C.A. § 2708, "violations of the ECPA do not warrant exclusion of evidence." United States v. Perrine, 518 F.3d 1196 (10th Cir. 2008).

[49]Unif.R.Crim.P. 461(a), 10 U.L.A. 127 (2001). Compare Model Code of Pre-Arraignment Procedure § 290.2(2) (1975), which provides: "A motion to suppress evidence * * * shall be granted only if the court finds that the violation upon which it is based was substantial, or if otherwise required by the Constitution of the United States or of this State." Another provision, § 290.2(4), states: "In determining whether a violation is substantial the court shall consider all the circumstances, including:

"(a) the extent of deviation from lawful conduct;

"(b) the extent to which the violation was willful;

"(c) the extent to which privacy was invaded;

the need for the remedy of exclusion can best be determined by taking into account the significance of the right involved and the degree of infringement. And in assessing the significance of the right, it is certainly appropriate to consider the relationship between the requirement of the relevant rule or statute and the protections of the Fourth Amendment.[50] In *Brannon,* for example,

"(d) the extent to which exclusion will tend to prevent violations of this Code;

"(e) whether, but for the violation, the things seized would have been discovered; and

"(f) the extent to which the violation prejudiced the moving party's ability to support his motion, or to defend himself in the proceeding in which the things seized are sought to be offered in evidence against him."

These provisions, which would also encompass violations of the Constitution as well as of the Code, have been severely criticized. See American Law Institute, Proceedings of 48th Annual Meeting 376–90 (1971).

[50] See United States v. Forrester, 512 F.3d 500 (9th Cir.2008) (following *Thompson*, infra); United States v. German, 486 F.3d 849 (5th Cir.2007) (non-content surveillance of pen register, a violation of pen-trap statute with criminal penalties for knowing violation, not a violation of Fourth Amendment and thus suppression remedy not available); United States v. Becerra-Garcia, 397 F.3d 1167 (9th Cir.2005) (while Fourth Amendment does not directly apply to Indian tribes, United States v. Manuel, 706 F.2d 908 (9th Cir.1983), Indian Civil Rights Act imposes an "identical limitation" on tribal government conduct as the Fourth Amendment, 25 U.S.C.A. § 1302(2), and it assumed that suppression of evidence in a federal proceeding would be appropriate if the tribal officer's conduct violated ICRA); United States v. Thompson, 936 F.2d 1249 (11th Cir.1991) (legislation regulating use of pen registers enacted after Supreme Court held such use not covered by Fourth Amendment and, in contrast to wiretapping law, carrying only criminal sanctions, not to be enforced by exclusionary rule); United

States v. Benevento, 836 F.2d 60 (2d Cir.1987) (exclusionary rule not applicable to statutory reasonable suspicion requirement for search of effects leaving country, as Fourth Amendment requires no suspicion and "there is nothing in the legislative history of section 5317(b) indicating that Congress intended an exclusionary remedy for violations of the statute"); United States v. Blue Diamond Coal Co., 667 F.2d 510 (6th Cir.1981) (no suppression required for failure to obtain consent or administrative warrant required by statute for seizure of lawfully inspected records; no Fourth Amendment violation); Moore v. State, 303 Ark. 514, 798 S.W.2d 87 (1990) (though statute says action is "invalid" if taken by officer who does not meet state standards and qualifications, no exclusionary rule applied in such a case, as the statute "deals with standards for employment" and not "police conduct"); People v. Wolf, 635 P.2d 213 (Colo.1981) (exclusion not required for violation of statute prohibiting police from arresting outside territorial limits of employing agency); State v. Garrow, 480 N.W.2d 256 (Iowa 1992) (no exclusionary rule sanction for violation of court rule against using probationers in undercover work, as that policy not connected with Fourth Amendment concerns and, indeed, was not even intended for benefit of those under investigation); State v. Rideout, 761 A.2d 288 (Me.2000) (arrest on probable cause, but violation of statute on arresting outside territorial limits of employing agency); State v. Smith, 367 N.W.2d 497 (Minn.1985) (suppression not required for violation of statute declaring welfare information to be revealed only by court order, as any constitutional right "that a person has to informational privacy clearly does not extend to his address"); State v. Geraldo, 68 Ohio

213

assuming an absence of the aforementioned legislative history, the court could have reached the same result on the ground that the statutory provision concerning giving the defendant his choice of tests is not related in any direct way to any constitutional limitation upon the taking of breathalyzer tests.[51] *Brannon* is in that respect distinguishable from *People v. Foulger*,[52] excluding the results of a breathalyzer test because of failure to comply with a statutory provision requiring such tests to be performed in accordance with regulations adopted by the state board of health. *Foulger* might well be explained (as noted in *Brannon*) on the ground that the statutory provision in question is directly related to the constitutional requirement that tests of this kind be conducted in a medically approved fashion.[53]

Perhaps the best example of the substantial rights approach is provided by the treatment given to statutes and rules concerning search warrants. On the one hand, provisions to the effect that only certain officials may seek a warrant,[54] that the affidavit must

---

St.2d 120, 429 N.E.2d 141 (1981) (exclusionary rule not applicable for violation of state statute requiring warrant for consensual eavesdropping permitted by Fourth Amendment); State v. Britton, 772 N.W.2d 899 (S.D.2009) (while state statute on certification of drug dogs intended to prevent searches in "false indication of controlled substances by unqualified canine teams," suggesting exclusion would often be appropriate where statute violated, that not so in this case where trooper and dog had passed the required test but the paperwork not yet completed); State v. Valdobinos, 122 Wash.2d 270, 858 P.2d 199 (1993) (collecting cases in accord, court holds exclusionary rule not applicable to a search in violation of the posse commitatus act).

[51]Clearly easier than *Brannon* is People v. Shinaut, 940 P.2d 380 (Colo. 1997), where defendant had the chutzpah to claim that because the governing statute did not permit a motorist to change his election between a blood test and a breath test to determine intoxication, the results of his blood test should be suppressed because the officer had allowed him to change from his original election of a breath test.

[52]People v. Foulger, 26 Cal.App.3d Supp. 1, 103 Cal.Rptr. 156 (1972). See also United States v. Soto-Soto, 598 F.2d 545 (9th Cir.1979) (evidence obtained by FBI agent in border search suppressed because statutory authority to conduct such searches limited to certain officials not including FBI agents; court stresses that "important statutory limitations which protect the balance between sovereign power and constitutional rights were violated here," the point being that this special and extraordinary search power should be limited to officials having the special responsibilities justifying that power).

[53]Cf. Schmerber v. California, 384 U.S. 757, 86 S.Ct. 1826, 16 L.Ed.2d 908 (1966).

But in People v. Rawlings, 42 Cal.App.3d 952, 117 Cal.Rptr. 651 (1974), *Foulger* was disapproved on the ground that "only the mechanical circumstances of [the test's] administration" were involved.

[54]United States v. Bowling, 619 F.3d 1175 (10th Cir.2010), following Bowling v. Rector, 584 F.3d 956 (10th Cir.2009) (fruits of search warrant need not be suppressed because of state law violation where search warrant for investigation of mortgage fraud obtained by ranger, a limited-authority officer without jurisdiction to investigate such offense); United States v. Weiland, 420 F.3d 1062 (9th Cir.2005) (even assuming state police

be sworn before a judge,[55] that a telephonic search warrant application must be recorded,[56] that the warrant must state the affiant's name,[57] that grounds for a nighttime search must be shown in the affidavit,[58] that the warrant must be directed at a specific

---

officer's deputation as U.S. marshal did not make him a "federal law enforcement officer" for purposes of rule 41, suppression not required, as no Fourth Amendment violation and defendant not prejudiced because officer could have gotten a state search warrant); United States v. Freeman, 897 F.2d 346 (8th Cir.1990) (suppression not required re search warrant obtained by special agent for Department of Revenue, not a "peace officer" authorized to seek search warrants); United States v. Luk, 859 F.2d 667 (9th Cir.1988) (person seeking warrant was agent of Department of Commerce who, though acting under supervision of assistant U.S. attorney, not authorized to seek warrant under Fed.R. Crim.P. 41; suppression not required where no prejudice to defendant or deliberate disregard of the rule); State v. West, 291 Mont. 435, 968 P.2d 289 (1998) (person seeking search warrant was prosecutor in another county; this "did not affect West's substantial rights").

[55]People v. Fournier, 793 P.2d 1176 (Colo.1990); State v. Bicknell, 140 Idaho 201, 91 P.3d 1105 (2004).

Consider also United States v. Harris, 566 F.3d 422 (5th Cir.2009) (violation of the "more demanding" standard of federal recusal statute not basis for suppression on ground magistrate not "neutral and detached").

[56]State v. Dominguez, 2011 Utah 11, 248 P.3d 473 (2011) (no Fourth Amendment violation, and no need for suppression otherwise, as violation of court rule requiring retention of supporting materials for electronic warrant "does not affect substantial rights" and was an error of magistrate and not police, so "no basis for imposing the strong remedy of suppression"); State v. Raflik, 248 Wis.2d 593, 636 N.W.2d 690 (2001) (no Fourth Amendment violation, as application promptly reconstructed, and thus no

exclusion for violation of statute unless "a statute specifically provides for the suppression remedy," not the case here).

[57]People v. McKinstry, 843 P.2d 18 (Colo.1993) (purposes behind this requirement in rule and statute, to apprise defendant of who takes responsibility for facts underlying warrant and to facilitate defendant's challenge of warrant, "are not necessarily protected by a strict application of the affiant's name requirement," citing in support many federal cases so holding as to pre-1972 federal requirement).

[58]United States v. Berry, 113 F.3d 121 (8th Cir.1997) (where though nighttime search warrant obtained under 21 U.S.C.A. § 879 failed to specifically authorize nighttime search of total area covered by warrant, suppression not required absent prejudice to defendant or reckless disregard of proper procedure); United States v. Tedford, 875 F.2d 446 (5th Cir.1989) (where federal involvement made the search warrant obtained in state court a federal warrant, and grounds for nighttime search existed but no finding thereof by issuing judge as required by rule 41(c)(1), derivative evidence exclusionary rule deemed inapplicable); United States v. Schoenheit, 856 F.2d 74 (8th Cir.1988) (where warrant obtained from state judge had sufficient federal involvement that Fed.R.Crim.P. 41 applied, noncompliance with nighttime search provision does not require suppression where no prejudice to defendant and no deliberate disregard); Commonwealth v. Grimshaw, 413 Mass. 73, 595 N.E.2d 302 (1992) (violation of bar on nighttime search except when "the warrant so directs" does not require suppression "in this case," where there was a "technical violation * * * that infringed no substantive right of the defendant"); State v. Brock, 294 Or. 15, 653 P.2d 543 (1982) (exclusionary rule

---

peace officer,[59] that a police officer must execute the search warrant or at least oversee its execution,[60] that the warrant must be executed by an officer who is within his territorial jurisdiction,[61] that the warrant must be exhibited upon execution,[62] that a copy of the affidavit supporting the warrant must be supplied,[63] that a receipt must be given for property taken,[64] or that a prompt return of an executed warrant be made[65] or that after return all relevant papers be forwarded to the appropriate court[66] are not generally viewed as being important enough to merit enforce-

---

not applicable to violation of statute re need to show magistrate specific circumstances for nighttime search; violation "purely statutory" as no constitutional requirement warrant be executed at particular time); Commonwealth v. Johnson, 315 Pa.Super. 579, 462 A.2d 743 (1983) (affidavit insufficient under state law because it failed to show cause for nighttime search; law not "a codification of Fourth Amendment requirements" but instead "goes beyond the requirements of the Fourth Amendment" and thus exclusion not required).

   Compare Garner v. State, 307 Ark. 353, 820 S.W.2d 446 (1991) (such failure "was a substantial violation," as "the privacy of the citizens in their homes, secure from nighttime intrusions, is a right of vast importance as attested not only by our Rules but also by our state and federal constitutions"); State v. Jordan, 742 N.W.2d 149 (Minn.2007) (court concludes "suppression is required" under the statute, but goes on "to conclude that, under the present facts, the statutory violation reaches constitutional dimensions"); State v. Santiago, 148 N.M. 144, 231 P.3d 600 (2010) (in case where court rule on nighttime search warrants *not* violated, court says in any case where rule is violated "the fruits of those searches will be suppressed"; concurring opinion objects suppression necessary only if "the violation significantly affected * * * the defendant's substantial rights").

   [59]State v. Pipkin, 289 Mont. 240, 961 P.2d 733 (1998) (applying statutory provision that a search is not to be held illegal because of "any irregularity" that "has no effect on the substantial rights of the accused," court concludes no such effect here, as "[d]espite technical noncompliance with the statute, the information the statute was intended to provide was otherwise available to the person who was subject to the warrant").

   [60]State v. Card, 137 Idaho 182, 45 P.3d 838 (2002) (collecting cases, including Morris v. State, 622 So.2d 67 (Fla.App.1993), quoted re important fact that only police "take appropriate oaths to carry out the provisions of the federal and state constitutions and the laws of the state and nation," and "are specially charged and trained to see that the search is carried out properly, lawfully, and in accord with the provisions of the warrant").

   [61]People v. Martinez, 898 P.2d 28 (Colo. 1995) (but suggesting contrary result if execution of warrants outside officers' territorial jurisdiction were to be "willful and recurrent"); Commonwealth v. Mason, 507 Pa. 396, 490 A.2d 421 (1985). Contra: State v. Sodders, 255 Kan. 79, 872 P.2d 736 (1994).

   [62]See § 4.12(a).

   [63]People v. Sobczak-Obetts, 463 Mich. 687, 625 N.W.2d 764 (2001) (stressing such requirements "are ministerial in nature, and do not in any way lead to the acquisition of evidence; rather, these requirements come into play only *after* evidence has been seized pursuant to a valid search warrant").

   [64]See § 4.12(b).

   [65]See § 4.12(c).

   [66]Commonwealth v. Rucci, 543 Pa. 261, 670 A.2d 1129 (1996).

ment through the exclusionary rule.[67] Even more obviously, violation of a local court rule requiring that search warrants be obtained from a particular court does not require exclusion, for such a provision is merely "designed for the convenience of judges."[68] In contrast, suppression is used as a remedy where the provision concerns the quality of evidence needed for issuance of the warrant,[69] that a record be kept of that evidence,[70] the time at which the warrant was issued[71] or within which the warrant must be executed[72] or the manner in which entry is to be gained in order to execute the warrant,[73] which are provisions more directly related to Fourth Amendment protections, typically

---

[67]Of course, even if an exclusionary rule is utilized, it may be made subject to a *Leon*-type good faith exception. See, e.g., State v. Fitch, 255 Neb. 108, 582 N.W.2d 342 (1998) (*Leon* exception applicable to statutory requirements re nighttime execution of a search warrant, but no good faith here, where "no factual basis supports the issuance of a warrant for a nighttime search," citing other cases reaching same result).

[68]People v. Mordell, 55 Mich.App. 462, 223 N.W.2d 10 (1974). See also United States v. Martinez-Zayas, 857 F.2d 122 (3d Cir.1988) (even if state officer not the kind authorized to issue federal warrant under Fed.R.Crim.P. 41, suppression not required where violation not of constitutional magnitude, no prejudice to defendant and no intentional or deliberate disregard).

[69]People v. Sherbine, 421 Mich. 502, 364 N.W.2d 658 (1984) (statute codifying *Aguilar* test, noncompliance requires suppression notwithstanding fact *Aguilar* itself rejected by Supreme Court in *Gates*). But *Sherbine* was overruled in People v. Hawkins, 468 Mich. 488, 668 N.W.2d 602 (2003), taking the strict view that only "plain language" in the applicable statute providing a "sound basis" for concluding the legislature intended the exclusionary rule to apply would suffice.

[70]People v. Taylor, 73 N.Y.2d 683, 543 N.Y.S.2d 357, 541 N.E.2d 386 (1989) (suppression required for violation of contemporaneous record requirement, as though "not itself a constitutional right, compliance is indispensable to the determination

whether the constitutional requirements for a valid search and seizure have been met").

But see State v. Barrilleaux, 620 So.2d 1317 (La.1993) (using a good faith analysis, suppression not required on facts of this case where police officer, for seeming good reason reported to magistrate, gave some of facts to magistrate orally rather than by written affidavit).

[71]State v. Bobadilla, 181 S.W.3d 641 (Tenn.2005) (stressing court rule says "failure to endorse thereon the date and time of issuance * * * should make any search conducted under said search warrant an illegal search").

[72]See § 4.7, noting however that some courts do *not* suppress if, notwithstanding the delay, probable cause is still present.

[73]See § 4.8. See, e.g., Commonwealth v. Means, 531 Pa. 504, 614 A.2d 220 (1992) (knock-announce court rule "implicates the fundamental constitutional concern of the prohibition against unreasonable search and seizure").

Compare State v. McCloud, 257 Kan. 1, 891 P.2d 324 (1995) (after erroneously concluding manner of entry not a Fourth Amendment issue, court concludes exclusionary rule not applicable to violation of state statute on entry, reasoning that "the right to bring a civil action against an officer is usually a sufficient deterrent to an officer's use of unreasonable force"; court may have been more influenced by defendant's failure to raise the manner-of-entry issue in the lower court).

without concern for whether the rule or statute exceeds the requirements of the Fourth Amendment. But even in this latter area, it sometimes happens that a court disenchanted with the exclusionary rule will decline to apply it with respect to such violations.[74]

A particularly difficult problem is presented with respect to state provisions concerning the circumstances in which an arrest may lawfully be made. While it would appear to be constitutionally permissible to provide, as some states have,[75] that a warrantless arrest may be made for any offense upon probable cause,[76] some states by statute or rule follow the view that a warrantless misdemeanor arrest may be made only if the offense occurred in the arresting officer's presence.[77] Moreover, the prevailing view in these jurisdictions is that if a warrantless misdemeanor arrest is made upon probable cause but not for an offense in the presence of the officer, then the fruits of a search of the person incident to that arrest must be suppressed.[78] Somewhat unique is *State v.*

---

[74]People v. Hawkins, 468 Mich. 488, 668 N.W.2d 602 (2003) (violation of statute codifying *Aguilar* requirements, since rejected by Supreme Court in *Gates*, does not require exclusion, as only "plain language" in the applicable statute providing a "sound basis" for concluding the legislature intended the exclusionary rule to apply would suffice); People v. Stevens, 460 Mich. 626, 597 N.W.2d 53 (1999) (exclusionary rule not applicable to state's knock-and-announce statute, as purpose of statute is "to allow a defendant a brief opportunity to put his personal affairs in order before the police enter," not "to allow the defendant the time to destroy the evidence"); State v. Valentine, 264 Or. 54, 504 P.2d 84 (1972), holding that evidence obtained in violation of the state knock and announce statute is not to be excluded, and expressing doubt that "the exclusionary rule has accomplished its purpose" and "whether the cost brought about by excluding good evidence was worth the goal."

Valentine was distinguished in State v. Valdez, 277 Or. 621, 561 P.2d 1006 (1977), where the exclusionary rule was applied to a violation of the state stop-and-frisk statute because "the purpose of the present statute is to protect interests of the kinds which are protected by the Fourth Amend-

ment."

[75]See § 5.1(b).

[76]Fields v. City of South Houston, 922 F.2d 1183 (5th Cir.1991) ("The United States Constitution does not require a warrant for misdemeanors not occurring in the presence of the arresting officer"); Street v. Surdyka, 492 F.2d 368 (4th Cir.1974).

[77]See § 5.1(c).

[78]E.g., T.L.M. v. State, 371 So.2d 688 (Fla.App.1979); Commonwealth v. Conway, 2 Mass.App.Ct. 547, 316 N.E.2d 757 (1974); State v. Haigh, 112 R.I. 740, 315 A.2d 431 (1974); Hernandez v. State, 600 S.W.2d 793 (Tex.Crim.App.1980) (stressing, however, that this result was dictated by a state statute declaring the exclusionary rule applicable even where a state law is violated); State v. Laflin, 160 Vt. 198, 627 A.2d 344 (1993).

See also State v. Brady, 118 Wis.2d 154, 345 N.W.2d 533 (App.1984) (arrest of material witness without warrant in context of a John Doe proceeding illegal as not provided for by state statute, court says it also an unreasonable seizure under the Fourth Amendment).

By contrast, if the illegality attending the arrest is merely a failure to comply with a court rule requiring the officer to state the offense charged,

Eubanks,[79] holding that "nothing in our law requires the exclusion of evidence obtained following an arrest which is constitutionally valid but illegal for failure to first obtain an arrest warrant."[80]

---

then "the officer's conduct did not implicate a sufficiently substantive right to warrant exclusion." Murray v. State, 855 P.2d 350 (Wyo.1993).

[79]State v. Eubanks, 283 N.C. 556, 196 S.E.2d 706 (1973). See also People v. Burdo, 56 Mich.App. 48, 223 N.W.2d 358 (1974) (same result as *Eubanks* on almost identical facts); State v. Allen, 2 Ohio App.3d 441, 442 N.E.2d 784 (1981) (no exclusion where misdemeanor arrest on probable cause but not in presence as required by state law, as exclusion "not required for violations of statutory provisions by law enforcement officers that fall short of constitutional violations, unless specifically required by the legislature").

[80]Consider also those cases holding that exclusion is not called for as to other types of illegality regarding the making of the arrest. United States v. Abdi, 463 F.3d 547 (6th Cir.2006) (where arrest in public place on probable cause lawful under Fourth Amendment, no exclusionary rule applicable re violation of 18 U.S.C.A. § 1357(a)(2), requiring arrest warrant where no reason to believe alien likely to escape); United States v. Becerra-Garcia, 397 F.3d 1167 (9th Cir.2005) (fact that stop of vehicle by tribal rangers on Indian reservation not allowed under tribal law irrelevant to Fourth Amendment issue; tribal law treated like state law in this respect); United States v. Janik, 723 F.2d 537 (7th Cir.1983) (defendant's claim state police lacked statutory authority to arrest for federal offense does not require suppression of fruits of arrest, as "even if the arrest was invalid under state law, the action of the state officers in arresting Janik was not an 'unreasonable' seizure under the Fourth Amendment"); State v. Sundberg, 611 P.2d 44 (Alaska 1980), noted in 10 U.C.L.A.-Alaska L.Rev. 85 (1980) (exclusionary rule not utilized where the officer used excessive force, in violation of state law, in making the arrest; use of force not likely to be specifically directed toward the purpose of obtaining evidence, so "that the imposition of an additional exclusionary deterrent would at best achieve only a marginal deterrent effect"); People v. McKay, 27 Cal.4th 601, 117 Cal.Rptr.2d 236, 41 P.3d 59 (2002) (violation of statute re use of citation where defendant provides sufficient identification not a basis for suppression of evidence, as no Fourth Amendment violation); People v. Vigil, 729 P.2d 360 (Colo. 1986) (arrest by officer outside his jurisdiction does not require suppression unless "so egregious as to violate the protections against unreasonable searches and seizures guaranteed by our state constitution"); State v. Jolin, 639 A.2d 1062 (Me.1994) (officer's exceeding territorial authority and violation of fresh pursuit statute does not require suppression of evidence obtained incident to arrest made on probable cause); Commonwealth v. Lyons, 397 Mass. 644, 492 N.E.2d 1142 (1986) (violation of state law re certain misdemeanors for which process for arrest not to issue until defendant given opportunity to be heard; no suppression as statute is "not closely affiliated with any constitutional guarantee"); People v. Hamilton, 465 Mich. 526, 638 N.W.2d 92 (2002) (exclusionary rule not applicable re arrest on probable cause by officer outside his territorial jurisdiction, as no showing legislature "intended to apply the drastic remedy of exclusion of evidence" to such violations); State v. Smith, 154 N.H. 113, 908 A.2d 786 (2006) (where officer made "constitutionally valid traffic stop," evidence not to be excluded merely because of violation of statute re territorial jurisdiction of officer); State v. Weideman, 94 Ohio St.3d 501, 764 N.E.2d 997 (2002) (where stop was on probable cause but outside officer's territorial jurisdiction, this statutory violation did not require suppression of evidence); State v. Droste, 83 Ohio St.3d 36, 697 N.E.2d 620 (1998) (where after defendant

Some would doubt the correctness of the *Eubanks* decision. It has been said, citing *United States v. Di Re*[81] in support, that under "the Fourth Amendment, evidence obtained from a search incident to an unlawful arrest must be suppressed even though the illegality of the arrest itself stems from a violation of state law rather than the Fourth Amendment."[82] But, while the issue was—until recently[83]—not free from doubt,[84] a close inspection of the *Di Re* decision indicates that the use of state law there was "based on nonconstitutional considerations."[85] Di Re was convicted in federal court of possessing counterfeit gasoline coupons found on his person following his arrest. The arrest was made by a state detective, who was accompanied by a federal OPA investigator, for violation of federal law. The Court declared that because "no act of Congress lays down a general federal rule for arrest without warrant for federal offenses," the rule is that "the law of the state where an arrest without warrant takes place determines

stopped at stoplight a liquor control officer questioned him and then placed him under arrest, immediately after which police officer appeared and arrested defendant for driving under the influence, court concludes there no Fourth Amendment violation and that liquor control officer's violation of statute, in that he without authority to stop a driver for violating traffic laws, "does not invoke the exclusionary rule"); State v. Westlund, 302 Or. 225, 729 P.2d 541 (1986) (violation of statute on taking intoxicated person into *civil* custody does not require suppression, as statutory purpose "is something other than protection of privacy or property rights").

On the other hand, statutory limits upon the seizure of persons that are essentially Fourth Amendment requirements will, of course, be enforced by exclusion of evidence. See, e.g., State v. Toevs, 327 Or. 525, 964 P.2d 1007 (1998) (suppression required as to fruits of violation of statute which, in effect, "prohibits an officer from continuing to detain a person stopped for a traffic infraction after completing the investigation reasonably related to the infraction unless the officer has some other reason, separable from the traffic stop, for doing so").

[81]United States v. Di Re, 332 U.S. 581, 68 S.Ct. 222, 92 L.Ed. 210 (1948).

[82]Uniform Rules of Criminal Procedure 198 (Approved Draft, 1974).

[83]See text at note 88 infra.

[84]See Dix, Fourth Amendment Federalism: The Potential Requirement of State Law Authorization for Law Enforcement Activity, 14 Am.J.Crim.L. 1, 44 (1987), characterizing the "unresolved nature of this basic federalism issue, when, if ever, is affirmative state law authorization essential to the fourth amendment validity of state law enforcement conduct."

[85]Street v. Surdyka, 492 F.2d 368 (4th Cir.1974). Accord: United States v. Laville, 480 F.3d 187 (3d Cir.2007) ("state or local law does not dictate the reasonableness of an arrest for purposes of a Fourth Amendment probable cause analysis," and thus in this federal prosecution based on a state arrest for a misdemeanor not occurring in the officer's presence, state statutory requirement that misdemeanor must occur in officer's presence irrelevant); People v. McKay, 27 Cal.4th 601, 117 Cal.Rptr.2d 236, 41 P.3d 59 (2002) (collecting other cases so holding, and reasoning: "Constitutionalizing the myriad of technical state procedures that govern arrests would not only trivialize Fourth Amendment protections but would discourage states from ever enacting such rules").

its validity."[86] Consequently the Court looked to New York arrest law, including the warrant requirement for misdemeanors out of the presence. Particularly in light of the fact that the Court looked to state law only after finding no applicable federal law, it would appear that the *Di Re* Court viewed the occurrence as truly a federal (rather than a state) arrest, as indeed it was. True, the arrest was by a city detective, but it was for a federal crime, there is no indication that the detective was pursuing any state interest, and quite obviously he was acting on behalf of the federal investigator who accompanied him but who could not so act on his own behalf because he "had no power of arrest." So interpreted, *Di Re* is simply an instance of the court utilizing its supervisory power to exclude from a federal prosecution evidence obtained pursuant to an illegal but constitutional federal arrest.[87] More recently, in *Virginia v. Moore*,[88] the Court made it perfectly clear that the *DiRe* language "was plainly not a rule we derived from the Constitution."[89]

This means that the Fourth Amendment does not stand in the way of the result reached in *Eubanks*. Whether *Eubanks* represents sound policy is, of course, another matter. It certainly might be argued that the state provision for a before-the-fact judicial determination of the grounds for arrest when it involves a misdemeanor not directly witnessed by the officer is an expression of a substantial right.[90] It may well be, however, though not explicitly stated by the court, that the result was influenced by the fact that the misdemeanor warrant requirement is impracticable under some circumstances. In this connection, it is certainly relevant that the defendant in that case was arrested by an officer who came to the scene of an auto accident in which the de-

---

[86]For a criticism of this holding, see Note, 62 Cornell L.Rev. 364, 373–76 (1977).

[87]"If that is so, United States v. Payner, 447 U.S. 727, 100 S.Ct. 2439, 65 L.Ed.2d 468 (1980), makes clear that the Court is no longer interested in using its supervisory power to exclude evidence obtained unlawfully but under circumstances not violative of the Fourth Amendment." United States v. Walker, 960 F.2d 409 (5th Cir.1992). See also United States v. Janik, 723 F.2d 537(7th Cir.1983), discussed in note 80 supra.

Moreover, the statute relied upon in *Di Re*, 18 U.S.C.A. § 591 (1940 ed.), which says federal arrests "must be agreeabl[e] to the usual mode of process against offenders in such State," has been amended to eliminate that requirement, 18 U.S.C.A. § 3041.

That is, "that statute no longer retains the principle relied on by the *Di Re* Court." United States v. Wright, 16 F.3d 1429 (6th Cir.1994).

[88]Virginia v. Moore, 553 U.S. 164, 128 S.Ct. 1598, 170 L.Ed.2d 559 (2008), discussed in § 1.5(a).

[89]See also United States v. Brobst, 558 F.3d 982 (9th Cir.2009) (concluding that by so treating *DiRe*, the same could now be said of language in Ker v. California, 374 U.S. 23, 83 S.Ct. 1623, 10 L.Ed.2d 726 (1963), to the effect that courts should determine the lawfulness of arrests by reference to state law).

[90]See, e.g., State v. Laflin, 160 Vt. 198, 627 A.2d 344 (1993) (provision deemed to express a substantial right, as it "designed to codify or enhance protections conferred by the Fourth Amendment").

fendant had been involved and who had a basis for seeking a chemical test to confirm his belief that the defendant was intoxicated, an investigative process that might well prove useless if delayed until a warrant could be obtained.[91]

Somewhat similar to the situation just discussed is that involving statutes and rules bearing upon a defendant's right to prompt release following arrest. In a number of cases in recent years, courts have suppressed evidence obtained in the course of an inventory search preparatory to placing an arrestee in detention where it was shown that the defendant had not been afforded his right, set forth in court rule or legislation, to post a fixed amount of bail or otherwise gain his immediate release.[92] Given the Supreme Court's refusal to recognize that the reasonableness requirement of the Fourth Amendment compels a showing of need for custody beyond probable cause,[93] it would seem (for essentially the reasons set out above) that the suppression issue in this context is not of constitutional dimension. This is not to question, however, the proposition that a right to release created by the legislature or court is substantial in nature and thus should be enforced by use of the exclusionary rule.[94]

As noted earlier,[95] there are certain Fourth Amendment issues, such as those where the Amendment is deemed violated absent "standardized procedures"[96] or "reasonable legislative or administrative standards,"[97] where state law can be highly relevant in determining whether the Fourth Amendment has been violated. Search incident to arrest might be looked at in much the same way; it is also a "standardized procedure" rather than a probable cause variety of Fourth Amendment activity,[98] as the Supreme Court held in *United States v. Robinson*[99] that a person may be searched incident to his arrest, without regard to the probability in the individual case that weapons or evidence will be found, *if*

---

[91]Cf. Schmerber v. California, 384 U.S. 757, 86 S.Ct. 1826, 16 L.Ed.2d 908 (1966), noting, with respect to the taking of a blood sample to determine intoxication, that the lack of a search warrant was not objectionable because "the delay necessary to obtain a warrant, under the circumstances, threatened 'the destruction of evidence.'"

[92]E.g., United States v. Mills, 472 F.2d 1231 (D.C.Cir.1972); Carpio v. Superior Court, 19 Cal.App.3d 790, 97 Cal.Rptr. 186 (1971); People v. Greenwood, 174 Colo. 500, 484 P.2d 1217 (1971).

[93]The Supreme Court has expressly reached the contrary conclusion. Atwater v. City of Lago Vista, 532 U.S. 318, 121 S.Ct. 1536, 149 L.Ed.2d 549 (2001).

[94]The same issue will arise with respect to the making of the arrest in the first instance as statutes and rules begin to direct the use of a summons or notice to appear in certain circumstances.

[95]See text at note 23 supra.

[96]Colorado v. Bertine, 479 U.S. 367, 107 S.Ct. 738, 93 L.Ed.2d 739 (1987).

[97]Camara v. Municipal Court, 387 U.S. 523, 87 S.Ct. 1727, 18 L.Ed.2d 930 (1967).

[98]See § 5.2.

[99]United States v. Robinson, 414 U.S. 218, 94 S.Ct. 467, 38 L.Ed.2d 427 (1973).

the search occurs "incident to a lawful custodial arrest." That being so, it might seem that state law is highly relevant on the issue of when a search is constitutional under *Robinson*. Such was the conclusion in *United States v. Mota*,[100] where state officers found counterfeit money in the search of two brothers incident to their custodial arrest for the municipal ordinance violation of operating a food cart without a license. Because a state statute required that such violators merely be given a citation, the court ruled the Fourth Amendment required suppression of the money. The *Mota* result might be explained on either of two grounds: (i) that the *arrest* was itself contrary to the Fourth Amendment because of the statutory violation; or (ii) that the *search* was contrary to the Fourth Amendment because the preceding arrest, albeit constitutional, was in violation of the state statute. But the Supreme Court ruled otherwise in the highly similar case of *Virginia v. Moore*,[101] where the state court had excluded evidence obtained in a search incident to arrest *on Fourth Amendment grounds* albeit because the arrest violated a state statute requiring use of a summons in lieu of arrest in that case, involving the misdemeanor of driving on a suspended license. For the reasons discussed earlier,[102] the Court in *Moore* first concluded that a state's additional limitations on the power to arrest "do not alter the Fourth Amendment's protection." As for *Mota*'s second proposition, also urged in *Moore*, the Court rather summarily (and correctly) concluded that "our constitutional decision in *Robinson* used 'lawful' as shorthand for compliance with constitutional constraints."

As for violation of administrative regulations, it would seem that much the same considerations are involved. Thus, one begins with the proposition that the Fourth Amendment does not compel the exclusion of evidence merely because it was obtained by such a violation.[103] And again, it would seem useful to inquire whether the regulation in question creates rights stemming from though

---

[100]United States v. Mota, 982 F.2d 1384 (9th Cir.1993). See also Bingham v. City of Manhattan Beach, 341 F.3d 939 (9th Cir.2003) (per *Mota*, state law relevant in § 1983 action in determining reasonableness of state action); United States v. Shephard, 21 F.3d 933 (9th Cir.1994) (relying on *Mota*, court concludes that fruits of arrest, illegal under state law because no written request from probation officer, must be suppressed).

[101]Virginia v. Moore, 553 U.S. 164, 128 S.Ct. 1598, 170 L.Ed.2d 559 (2008).

[102]See text at note 19 supra.

[103]People v. Kosoff, 34 Cal.App.3d 920, 110 Cal.Rptr. 391 (1973), rejecting the argument that violation of an administrative regulation becomes a violation of the Fourth Amendment as well because the regulation creates an expectation of privacy under Katz v. United States, 389 U.S. 347, 88 S.Ct. 507, 19 L.Ed.2d 576 (1967).

Similarly, it has been held that the exclusionary rule is inapplicable where the police violated a court order re entry of a tavern during business hours, done without violating the Fourth Amendment. Birkenshaw v. City of Detroit, 110 Mich.App. 500, 313 N.W.2d 334 (1981).

not required by some constitutional provision,[104] that is, whether it is "not merely directive, intended to promote some agency efficiency goal, but [is instead] fashioned to secure the beneficiary's right of privacy."[105] But even in the latter circumstance, courts have been reluctant to exclude evidence where the regulation violated is seen as unduly limiting a long-honored investigative technique.[106]

The Supreme Court addressed this issue in *United States v. Caceres*,[107] where the evidence in question was obtained in violation of regulations in the IRS Manual prohibiting "consensual electronic surveillance" between taxpayers and IRS agents unless certain prior authorization was obtained. The Court, after concluding "the IRS was not required by the Constitution to adopt these regulations,"[108] rejected respondent's claim that they "are of such importance in safeguarding the privacy of the citizenry that

---

[104]Illustrative are the I.R.S. regulations concerning the questioning of taxpayers, enforced by exclusion in United States v. Leahey, 434 F.2d 7 (1st Cir.1970); United States v. Heffner, 420 F.2d 809 (4th Cir.1969).

[105]United States v. McDaniels, 355 F.Supp. 1082 (E.D.La.1973).

[106]Thus in United States v. Sohnen, 298 F.Supp. 51 (E.D.N.Y.1969), the court declined to exclude evidence obtained in violation of postal regulations concerning the obtaining of authorization from the addressee before opening a package, asserting: "Even if they were intended to protect recipients of mail from abroad, in light of the historical basis for customs searches * * *, we cannot say that they rise to the level of national policy so as to require a *per se* rule of exclusion." See also People v. Kosoff, 34 Cal.App.3d 920, 110 Cal.Rptr. 391 (1973), supra note 103, and cases cited therein.

[107]United States v. Caceres, 440 U.S. 741, 99 S.Ct. 1465, 59 L.Ed.2d 733 (1979), assessed in Comment, 46 Brooklyn L.Rev. 147 (1979); Note, 85 Dick.L.Rev. 183 (1980).

See also United States v. Leveto, 540 F.3d 200 (3d Cir.2008) (per *Caceres*, a Tax Division Directive "does not provide any substantive right" to defendant); United States v. Hinton, 222 F.3d 664 (9th Cir.2000) (relying on *Caceres*, court holds that violation of

agency regulation as to use of "mail covers" not basis for use of exclusionary rule); United States v. Ani, 138 F.3d 390 (9th Cir.1998) (relying on *Caceres*, court finds no evidence that Customs Service "intended the exclusionary rule to be a remedy for violation of * * * 19 C.F.R. 145.1 *et seq.*," dealing with international mail, or that Congress so intended in enacting 19 U.S.C.A. § 1582 requiring adoption of regulations on that subject); Pennsylvania Steel Foundry & Machine Co. v. Secretary of Labor, 831 F.2d 1211 (3d Cir.1987) (relying on *Caceres*, court holds exclusionary rule not applicable to violation of OSHA regulation barring resort to ex parte search warrant procedure); United States v. Hensel, 699 F.2d 18 (1st Cir.1983) (*Caceres* relied upon in holding that suppression not required for a violation of international law, as to which defendant lacks standing in any event because international law declares rights of nations rather than rights of individuals); United States v. Choate, 619 F.2d 21 (9th Cir.1980) (*Caceres* relied upon in holding suppression not required for violation of postal regulations on procedures for obtaining approval of a mail cover); McFarlin v. State, 409 Md. 391, 975 A.2d 862 (2009) (violation of prison regulation re seizing inmate's letter not a basis for application of exclusionary rule).

[108]See § 2.2(f).

a rigid exclusionary rule should be applied to all evidence obtained in violation of any of their provisions":

> Regulations governing the conduct of criminal investigations are generally considered desirable, and may well provide more valuable protection to the public at large than the deterrence flowing from the occasional exclusion of items of evidence in criminal trials. Although we do not suggest that a suppression order in this case would cause the Internal Revenue Service to abandon or modify its electronic surveillance regulations, we cannot ignore the possibility that a rigid application of an exclusionary rule to every regulatory violation could have a serious deterrent impact on the formulation of additional standards to govern prosecutorial and police procedures. Here, the Executive itself has provided for internal sanctions in cases of knowing violations of the electronic surveillance regulations. To go beyond that, and require exclusion in every case, would take away from the Executive Department the primary responsibility for fashioning the appropriate remedy for the violation of its regulations. But since the content, and indeed the existence, of the regulations would remain within the Executive's sole authority, the result might well be fewer and less protective regulations. In the long run, it is far better to have rules like those contained in the IRS Manual, and to tolerate occasional erroneous administration of the kind displayed by this record, than either to have no rules except those mandated by statute, or to have them framed in a mere precatory form.[109]

To be distinguished from all of the foregoing situations is the case in which there *has* been a Fourth Amendment violation, albeit one as to which the defendant in the criminal case has no standing,[110] so the defendant seeks to have the evidence excluded through the court's exercise of its supervisory power. In *United States v. Payner*,[111] the Supreme Court held that the district court's use of a "supervisory power" exclusionary rule in such circumstances, even though the evidence was obtained in a violation of state criminal law also amounting to an intentional and most serious violation of the Fourth Amendment rights of another person, was improper. The Court, per Powell, J., reasoned:

> Our Fourth Amendment decisions have established beyond any

---

[109]The Court went on to reject respondent's further claim "that even without a rigid rule of exclusion, his is a case in which evidence secured in violation of the agency regulation should be excluded on the basis of a more limited, individualized approach."

Marshall and Brennan, JJ., dissenting, contended (1) that the IRS's failure to comply with its own mandatory regulations violated due process, and for that reason required exclusion; and (2) that, in any event, the Court under its supervisory power should exclude the evidence, especially "where, as here, agency regulations were designed to stand in the place of legislative action."

[110]On standing requirements, see § 11.3.

[111]United States v. Payner, 447 U.S. 727, 100 S.Ct. 2439, 65 L.Ed.2d 468 (1980); discussed in Comments, 59 Denver L.J. 133 (1981); 83 W.Va.L. Rev. 565 (1981); Notes, 22 B.C.L.Rev. 567 (1981); 14 J.Marshall L.Rev. 569 (1981); 12 Sw.U.L.Rev. 449 (1981); 42 U.Pitt.L.Rev. 709 (1981).

doubt that the interest in deterring illegal searches does not justify the exclusion of tainted evidence at the instance of a party who was not the victim of the challenged practices. * * * The values assigned to the competing interests do not change because a court has elected to analyze the question under the supervisory power instead of the Fourth Amendment. In either case, the need to deter the underlying conduct and the detrimental impact of excluding the evidence remain precisely the same.[112]

Though this may be so as an abstract proposition, the *Payner* case points up the inadequacy of current Fourth Amendment standing doctrine and how it can be readily manipulated by law enforcement agents to their advantage.[113]

§ 1.5(c) The remaining "silver platter"

In *Elkins v. United States*,[114] the Court abolished the so-called "silver platter" doctrine, whereby it was previously permissible for federal courts to receive into evidence items obtained in a state search by means that, if engaged in by federal officers, would constitute a violation of the Fourth Amendment. The *Elkins* Court noted that the "foundation upon which the admissibility of state-seized evidence in a federal trial originally rested—that unreasonable state searches did not violate the Federal Constitution—[had] disappeared in 1949" with the holding in *Wolf v. Colorado*.[115] But, while that assertion may have been subject to question at the time,[116] certainly since *Mapp v. Ohio*,[117] holding that "all evidence obtained by searches and seizures in violation of the Constitution is, by that same authority, inadmissible," *Elkins* rests upon a sound constitutional foundation. Moreover, since *Mapp* it is clear that exclusion is required by the Constitution, and not merely "the Court's supervisory power over the administration of criminal justice in the federal courts," which was invoked in *Elkins*. Thus, there does not currently appear to be any dispute that evidence obtained in violation of the Constitution must be suppressed: (i) when the search was by state of-

---

[112]Marshall, J., joined by Brennan and Blackmun, JJ., dissenting, objected that the majority's holding "effectively turns the standing rules created by this Court for assertions of Fourth Amendment violations into a sword to be used by the Government to permit it deliberately to invade one person's Fourth Amendment rights in order to obtain evidence against another person."

[113]For more on this point, see § 11.3(h).

[Section 1.5(c)]

[114]Elkins v. United States, 364 U.S. 206, 80 S.Ct. 1437, 4 L.Ed.2d 1669 (1960).

[115]Wolf v. Colorado, 338 U.S. 25, 69 S.Ct. 1359, 93 L.Ed. 1782 (1949).

[116]Frankfurter, J., the author of *Wolf*, objected that it did not make every violation of the Fourth Amendment an "arbitrary intrusion" of privacy so as to also constitute a violation of the Fourteenth Amendment.

[117]Mapp v. Ohio, 367 U.S. 643, 81 S.Ct. 1684, 6 L.Ed.2d 1081 (1961).

ficers and the evidence is offered in a federal prosecution[118]; (ii) when the search was by federal officers and the evidence is offered in a state prosecution[119]; and (iii) when the search was by officers in one state and the evidence is offered in a prosecution in another state.[120]

But, what if the search in question, if judged by the law in the jurisdiction where it occurred, was illegal only in the sense that it violated some statute or court rule in that jurisdiction or even some state constitutional provision?[121] Take, for example, the situation in *Burge v. State*,[122] where the defendant was charged in Texas with the offense of burglary with intent to rape. The prosecution offered in evidence a sweater belonging to the defendant, from which a patch had been torn in the struggle with the victim, that was obtained from his Oklahoma residence with the consent of his wife. The Oklahoma rule was that a wife's consent is ineffective against her husband, but the law in Texas was otherwise and not in conflict with the Fourth Amendment.[123] The *Burge* court held the evidence admissible on the ground that "in such instances the law of the forum (Texas in this case) governs as to procedure and rules of evidence."[124] A somewhat more extended analysis of this conflict-of-laws approach is to be found in *People*

---

[118]United States v. Self, 410 F.2d 984 (10th Cir.1969); Sablowski v. United States, 403 F.2d 347 (10th Cir. 1968).

[119]United States ex rel. Coffey v. Fay, 344 F.2d 625 (2d Cir.1965); People v. Smith, 5 Ill.App.3d 341, 275 N.E.2d 480 (1971); State v. Harms, 233 Neb. 882, 449 N.W.2d 1 (1989).

[120]United States ex rel. Krogness v. Gladden, 242 F.Supp. 499 (D.Or. 1965); State v. Krogness, 238 Or. 135, 388 P.2d 120 (1963).

[121]For additional discussion of this issue, see Corr, Criminal Procedure and the Conflict of Laws, 73 Geo.L.J. 1217 (1985); Latzer, The New Judicial Federalism and Criminal Justice: Two Problems and a Response, 22 Rutgers L.J. 863 (1991); Morrison, Choice of Law for Unlawful Searches, 41 Okla.L. Rev. 579 (1988); Theis, Choice of Law and the Administration of the Exclusionary Rule in Criminal Cases, 44 Tenn.L.Rev. 1043 (1977); Tullis & Ludlow, Admissibility of Evidence Seized in Another Jurisdiction: Choice of Law and the Exclusionary Rule, 10 U.S.F.L.Rev. 67 (1975); Comment, 20 Ariz.St.L.J. 285 (1988).

[122]Burge v. State, 443 S.W.2d 720 (Tex.Crim.App.1969).

[123]See § 8.4(a).

[124]See also People v. Orlosky, 40 Cal.App.3d 935, 115 Cal.Rptr. 598 (1974) (reaching the same result as *Burge* on essentially the same facts); State v. Lynch, 292 Mont. 144, 969 P.2d 920 (1998) (evidence from lawful wiretapping in Nev. by Nev. officials excluded in Mont, where, because legislature never adopted statute conforming to Title III requirements, nonconsensual wiretapping not allowed; "by application of conflicts of law principles," "questions concerning evidence admissibility and exclusion typically involve procedural considerations which are determined by the law of the forum"); People v. Price, 54 N.Y.2d 557, 446 N.Y.S.2d 906, 431 N.E.2d 267 (1981) (use of trained narcotics detection dog in Los Angeles, results reported to New York police who obtained search warrant on that basis; if use of dog violated California law, that irrelevant, as question is "whether or not the use of the dog is proscribed by either Federal or New York law, constitutional or statutory").

v. Saiken,[125] concerning the admissibility in an Illinois murder prosecution of evidence found in the execution of an Indiana search warrant upon an affidavit that did not comply with a unique Indiana rule barring reliance upon hearsay. The court held:

> If the problem here presented is considered from the procedural-substance viewpoint the evidence was properly admitted. * * * Evidentiary questions are generally governed by the laws of the forum. If the conflict concerning the choice of law encompassed the preliminary issue of whether the evidence was wrongfully obtained, a substantive matter, then from the viewpoint of "significant relationship" or "center of gravity" rules, the significant contacts were with Illinois. The crime was committed in Illinois; it was being prosecuted there; the defendant was a resident and citizen of Illinois; the great majority of the witnesses, who would testify at the trial, were Illinois residents; Indiana had no vital contact with the crime; and the application of Illinois evidentiary law would not offend the comity of interstate relationships between Indiana and Illinois.

Before taking a closer look at the *Burge-Saiken* approach, it is well to note that unquestionably there is no constitutional requirement that evidence obtained in another jurisdiction be suppressed merely because the process of acquisition offended some local law. The argument that "local rules * * * will have constitutional sanction, for whatever action is illegal is perforce unreasonable,"[126] has not prevailed. While a "more strict local rule may serve as a deterrent to lawless action," it does not follow, as a federal court commented in upholding the *Burge* decision, "that Oklahoma's choice of a deterrent must be imposed upon the State of Texas to trigger application of the exclusionary rule via a nexus of federal constitutional law."[127] So too, if either

---

[125]People v. Saiken, 49 Ill.2d 504, 275 N.E.2d 381 (1971); followed in People v. DeMorrow, 59 Ill.2d 352, 320 N.E.2d 1 (1974). See also State v. Briggs, 756 A.2d 731 (R.I.2000) (using a 5-factor "interest weighing approach" with analysis very similar to that in *Saiken*, and thus subject to same criticism as *Saiken*).

[126]Traynor, Mapp v. Ohio at Large in the Fifty States, 1962 Duke L.J. 319, 328.

[127]Burge v. Estelle, 496 F.2d 1177 (5th Cir.1974). See also People v. Galan, 229 Ill.2d 484, 323 Ill.Dec. 325, 893 N.E.2d 597 (2008) (where police from Ill., acting on their common law right to undertake "hot pursuit" of defendant into neighboring state and arrest him there, subsequent violation of

that state's statutory requirement that such arrestee be presented to magistrate in that state does not mandate exclusion of evidence in Ill., as that statute "does not involve a fundamental right of defendant"); State v. Dentler, 742 N.W.2d 84 (Iowa 2007) (exclusionary rule not applicable to violation of statutory provision like that in *Galan*, as violation was "a statutory violation that does not involve fundamental rights, constitutional overtones or false representations of law or other similar police misconduct"); Helm v. Commonwealth, 813 S.W.2d 816 (Ky.1991) (Ohio search need not comply with Kentucky law in order for fruits to be admissible in Kentucky, as "state constitution in this situation has no extraterritorial effect"); State v. Lucas, 372 N.W.2d

federal[128] or state[129] officers conduct a search that is illegal under

731 (Minn.1985) (Minn. police engaged in telephone eavesdropping with consent of one party in Wis.; though evidence would be suppressed in Wis., it can be admitted in Minn.); State v. Ferrell, 218 Neb. 463, 356 N.W.2d 868 (1984) (exclusionary rule not applicable where violation of statute like that in *Galan*, as such statutory violation did not affect validity of the arrest or amount to a due process violation); State v. Evers, 175 N.J. 355, 815 A.2d 432 (2003) ("None of New Jersey's interests ordinarily advanced by the exclusionary rule would be vindicated in this case by suppressing the evidence gathered out-of-state" in violation of that state's law when "gathered by law enforcement officers of another jurisdiction over which our state has no control or authority"); State v. Bonds, 98 Wash.2d 1, 653 P.2d 1024 (1982) (police of this state arrested on probable cause in neighboring state, where they acted only as private citizens and thus by statute could only arrest on in presence basis; violation of that statute does not require suppression).

    Moreover, it makes no difference that the search in question had actually been declared illegal and the fruits thereof suppressed in the state of the search. United States v. Bedford, 519 F.2d 650 (3d Cir.1975); Patterson v. Lash, 452 F.2d 150 (7th Cir.1971).

[128]United States v. Martin, 372 F.2d 63 (7th Cir.1967), noting that in Lee v. United States, 343 U.S. 747, 72 S.Ct. 967, 96 L.Ed. 1270 (1952), the Court emphasized that a "violation of state law, even had it been shown here, as it was not, would not render the evidence obtained inadmissible in federal courts." *Martin* involved conduct by federal agents of a kind proscribed by the strict Illinois eavesdropping statute, for which the legislature had provided both criminal penalties and an exclusionary rule. See also United States v. Dela Espriella, 781 F.2d 1432 (9th Cir.1986); United States v. Keen, 508 F.2d 986 (9th Cir.1974); United States v. Infelice, 506 F.2d 1358 (7th Cir.1974); United States v. Teller, 412 F.2d 374 (7th Cir.1969); United States v. Jones, 369 F.2d 217 (7th Cir.1966).

[129]United States v. Brewer, 588 F.3d 1165 (8th Cir.2009) (no suppression in federal court merely "because *state* law was violated"); United States v. Brobst, 558 F.3d 982 (9th Cir.2009) (more restrictive Montana law not applicable); United States v. Gonzales, 535 F.3d 1174 (10th Cir.2008) (traffic stop outside officer's jurisdiction violated state law only, so fruits admissible in federal court); United States v. Chirino, 483 F.3d 141 (2d Cir.2007) (search need not be found unreasonable in federal prosecution just because search exceeded scope of state probation order and state law); United States v. Cordero, 465 F.3d 626 (5th Cir.2006) (evidence obtained by search warrant admissible even assuming violation of state law); United States v. Simms, 385 F.3d 1347 (11th Cir.2004) (evidence admissible notwithstanding claim search tainted by use of tracking device that "violated Texas state law"); United States v. Vite-Espinoza, 342 F.3d 462 (6th Cir.2003) (where "there may have been a violation of a state constitution, the appropriate remedy is a civil action in state court, not evidentiary exclusion in federal court"); United States v. Quintanilla, 218 F.3d 674 (7th Cir.2000) (federal standards control in federal prosecution "even though the evidence was seized by state officials"); United States v. Van Metre, 150 F.3d 339 (4th Cir.1998) ("evidence admissible under federal law cannot be excluded because it would be inadmissible under state law"); United States v. Stiver, 9 F.3d 298 (3d Cir.1993); United States v. Soule, 908 F.2d 1032 (1st Cir.1990) ("state court search warrant * * * resulting in a federal prosecution is evaluated under federal standards"). Cf. United States v. Hornbeck, 118 F.3d 615 (8th Cir.1997) (relying on cases involving state officers, court holds that a search by tribal authorities that violated tribal law but did not "violate[ ] the Consti-

the law of the state where undertaken, the fruits thereof are not constitutionally[130] barred from evidence in the federal courts.[131] As the Supreme Court declared in *Elkins:* "The test is one of federal law,[132] neither enlarged by what one state court may have countenanced, nor diminished by what another may have colorably suppressed."[133]

---

tution or other federal law" does not require suppression in federal court).

But see United States v. Robinson, 650 F.2d 537 (5th Cir.1981) (without discussion, court rules evidence inadmissible in federal court because obtained incident to illegal arrest by state officer, though illegality was simply failure to have arrest warrant in possession at time of arrest in circumstances where Fourth Amendment requires no warrant at all).

Dicta in some cases "implies only that in an extreme case of flagrant abuse of the law by state officials" the federal court "might choose to exercise its supervisory powers by excluding ill-gotten evidence," but no cases have "actually found circumstances supporting an exception," and the trend now is toward disapproval of such prior dicta. United States v. Sutherland, 929 F.2d 765 (1st Cir.1991).

[130]But, a federal *statute* may nonetheless bar the evidence. See United States v. McNulty, 729 F.2d 1243 (10th Cir.1983) (because federal wiretapping law provides for suppression if evidence "unlawfully intercepted," that federal law covers evidence obtained by state officers in violation of an applicable *state* wiretapping law). Compare State v. Minter, 116 N.J. 269, 561 A.2d 570 (1989) (same not true of conduct by federal officer, as state "cannot make illegal what federal law makes legal for federal agents").

[131]There is not agreement as to whether this is a desirable state of affairs. Compare Melilli, Exclusion of Evidence in Federal Prosecutions on the Basis of State Law, 22 Ga.L.Rev. 667, 739 (1988) ("the interest of maintaining the control of federal institutions over their own destinies mandates * * * the disregard of state law as a condition of admissibility in federal criminal cases"); with Note, 45

Wash. & Lee L.Rev. 1499, 1526 (1988) (federal courts "should respect state sovereignty and established principles of federalism by excluding evidence that state officials obtained in violation of a state constitution"). Consider also concurring opinion of Newman, J., in United States v. Santa, 180 F.3d 20 (2d Cir.1999), "questioning the wisdom of using the federal forum to enable state officials to avoid state law restrictions" in a case (possession of 3 grams of cocaine) "developed solely by local police officers" that "would have been left for state court prosecution were it not for the fact that state law arrest restrictions barred a state, but not a federal, prosecution."

[132]Actually, if there is a violation of federal *statutory* law applicable only to federal officers, then the federal law does not govern. See United States v. Moore, 956 F.2d 843 (8th Cir.1992) (collecting other cases in accord and distinguishing the few cases contra, court holds that when state officers without federal involvement made a no-knock entry to execute a warrant lawful under the Fourth Amendment and state statutes, exclusion in federal court not required merely because federal statutes applicable to federal officers would produce different result).

[133]See also Preston v. United States, 376 U.S. 364, 84 S.Ct. 881, 11 L.Ed.2d 777 (1964) ("The question whether evidence obtained by state officers and used against a defendant in a federal trial was obtained by unreasonable search and seizure is to be judged as if the search and seizure had been made by federal officers"); Rios v. United States, 364 U.S. 253, 80 S.Ct. 1431, 4 L.Ed.2d 1688 (1960) (remand to trial court for determination of lawfulness of state officer's conduct under Fourth Amendment although evidence obtained by that conduct earlier suppressed in state prosecu-

The issue in *Burge* and *Saiken*, then, is best viewed simply as one of whether, as a matter of policy, it would be sound to exclude the fruits of a violation of local law occurring in a jurisdiction other than that in which the prosecution is pending. Stated differently, one might ask whether, given the tendency of jurisdictions to enforce many of their own local search and seizure requirements by exclusion (as noted in the preceding subsection), the same respect should be afforded local requirements elsewhere. That is a question of some difficulty, but it is submitted that the *Burge-Saiken* conflicts analysis unduly confuses the issue.[134]

The summary disposition in *Burge* on the ground that the law of the forum controls on matters of procedure has been justly criticized for its imprecision. As one commentator has noted, the issue of admissibility "could only become relevant" if it is first determined that the seizure was unlawful, an issue that "bore no substantial relationship to the manner in which the judicial business of the forum was conducted, and hence fell outside the scope of permissible procedural characterization."[135] That criticism cannot be leveled at *Saiken*, for it states that under a "significant relationship" or "center of gravity" test the lawfulness-of-the-search issue is also governed by the law of the forum rather than the place of the search. But that conclusion is surely in error. If, to take the matter in issue in *Saiken*, the law of Indiana says that search warrants may not issue upon hearsay affidavits, then certainly that is the law governing an Indiana search by Indiana police, without regard to whether the search is undertaken to aid in the investigation of an Illinois crime.[136] Thus, if in that search the police had inadvertently come upon evidence of an Indiana crime, one would hardly expect an Indiana court to admit the evidence on the ground that there was an Illinois "significant relationship" connected to the search and that such a search would be lawful if conducted within Illinois. The absurdity of the *Saiken*

---

tion); United States v. Garrett, 565 F.2d 1065 (9th Cir.1977) (it still true that federal courts to make independent inquiry into constitutional validity of state search).

[134]See State v. Lucas, 372 N.W.2d 731 (Minn.1985) (concluding "that it is preferable to use an exclusionary rule analysis rather than a traditional conflicts of law approach to determine the admissibility of evidence obtained from another state"); State v. Evers, 175 N.J. 355, 815 A.2d 432 (2003) (following *Lucas* approach).

[135]Note, 23 Vand.L.Rev. 425, 428–29 (1970).

[136]See, e.g., D'Antorio v. State, 926 P.2d 1158 (Alaska 1996) (where Ohio police officer made traffic stop and then arrested defendant and impounded and inventoried his car upon learning of outstanding Alaska arrest warrant, law of Ohio, "where the search occurred," governs the inventory search, at least absent any "ongoing or concerted effort" between Alaska and Ohio).

Or, for that matter, without regard to whether the search was for an Indiana crime but evidence of an Illinois crime was inadvertently discovered. This is another common type of "silver platter" situation; see, e.g., Patterson v. Lash, 452 F.2d 150 (7th Cir.1971); People v. Orlosky, 40 Cal.App.3d 935, 115 Cal.Rptr. 598 (1974).

position, however, is best pointed up by considering a hypothetical differing from *Saiken* only in that it is the law of Illinois rather than Indiana that forbids the use of hearsay affidavits. It is beyond belief that the Illinois court would have directed suppression under these circumstances on the ground that Illinois law governed on the question of whether the search was lawful.[137]

---

[137]See, e.g., United States v. Shields, 978 F.2d 943 (6th Cir.1992) (where state officer obtained state search warrant but evidence offered in federal trial, written affidavit then required by Fed.R.Crim.P. 41(c) not required by Fourth Amendment is not applicable); United States v. Moore, 956 F.2d 843 (8th Cir.1992) (collecting other cases in accord and distinguishing the few cases contra, court holds that when state officers without federal involvement made a no-knock entry to execute a warrant lawful under the Fourth Amendment and state statutes, exclusion in federal court not required merely because federal statutes applicable to federal officers would produce different result); United States v. Piver, 899 F.2d 881 (9th Cir.1990) (search by state officers in compliance with state law and Fourth Amendment admissible in federal court even if not in compliance with Fed.R.Crim.P. 41); United States v. Millar, 543 F.2d 1280 (10th Cir.1976) (though manner in which state search warrant obtained, while constitutional and in compliance with state law, would not suffice under federal law, evidence obtained thereby is nonetheless admissible in federal prosecution); D'Antorio v. State, 837 P.2d 727 (Alaska App.1992) (stricter forum law not applicable to search by Ohio officers in Ohio); People v. Blair, 25 Cal.3d 640, 159 Cal.Rptr. 818, 602 P.2d 738 (1979) (evidence obtained in seizure by federal officers in Philadelphia of telephone records is admissible in California, notwithstanding such a seizure in that state would violate California law, as the seizure was constitutional and did not violate Pennsylvania law, and thus the deterrence objective of the exclusionary rule would not be served by exclusion); State v. Boyd, 295 Conn. 707, 992 A.2d 1071 (2010) (collecting cases in accord, court holds fruits of constitutional search in another state need not be suppressed because that search would have been unlawful in forum state; "because the primary justification for the exclusionary rule is to deter illegal police conduct, no valid purpose is served by excluding evidence that has been obtained legally"; court adds, citing cases going both ways, that it need not decide if forum law would apply if the police of another state acted at the request of forum police); Echols v. State, 484 So.2d 568 (Fla.1985) (defendant prosecuted in Fla. for murder seeks exclusion of evidence obtained in Indiana by wired-for-sound informant, a practice lawful under federal and Indiana law but not Fla. law; exclusion would not "have any discernible effect on police officers of other states who conduct investigations in accordance with the laws of their state"; "we do not believe that the interest of Florida is served by imperially attempting to require that out-of-state police officials follow Florida law, and not the law of the situs, when they are requested to cooperate with Florida officials in investigating crimes committed in Florida"); People v. Barrow, 133 Ill.2d 226, 139 Ill.Dec. 728, 549 N.E.2d 240 (1989) (fruits of eavesdropping done within Maryland with consent of only one of the parties, lawful in Maryland but illegal in Illinois, are admissible in Illinois; essential point is that the evidence was "legally obtained * * * within the borders of another State"); State v. Davis, 679 N.W.2d 651 (Iowa 2004) (where in Iowa prosecution Mo. search warrant found defective as a matter of Mo. state law, but evidence would be admissible in Mo. under good faith exception, but Iowa rejects such exception, the Mo. good faith exception applies, as there "no reason to give greater protection to the integrity of the Missouri statute than the Missouri

If Indiana police[138] do not mysteriously become subject to more

courts do under similar circumstances"); State v. Rivers, 420 So.2d 1128 (La.1982) (evidence obtained in search of car in Alabama admissible if search constitutional, without regard to whether it lawful under Louisiana constitution or statute); Commonwealth v. Banville, 457 Mass. 530, 931 N.E.2d 457 (2010) (noting "trend is" to uphold search warrant "based on the validity of the warrant in the State where it was issued," though no need to "decide the conflict of law question" here as higher probable cause requirement in forum state also met); State v. Palmer, 210 Neb. 206, 313 N.W.2d 648 (1981) (it sufficient that arrest in Texas lawful under law of that state; but court asserts broader proposition that "the legality of an arrest is, within constitutional limits, governed by the law of the state where the arrest takes place"); Commonwealth v. Sanchez, 552 Pa. 570, 716 A.2d 1221 (1998) (where Pa. search warrant obtained on basis of dog sniff occurring in Cal., deemed a nonsearch under Cal. law but a search under Pa. law, at issue is a substantive right rather than a procedural point, as to which "California possessed the greatest interest" because the "canine sniff took place in California and involved a package shipped by California residents," and thus "[n]o Pennsylvania state interest would be advanced by analyzing the propriety of the canine sniff under Pennsylvania law"); State v. Cauley, 863 S.W.2d 411 (Tenn.1993) (where Tenn. officer was affiant for Ky. search warrant to search premises in Ky. to get evidence of Tenn. crime and Tenn. officers participated in execution of that warrant, higher standards of Tenn. law—resulting from rejection of *Gates* in that state—apply, as in such circumstances purpose of deterring Tenn. police deemed to be served, notwithstanding acknowledged fact that magistrates in other states would not be aware of and, in any event, would not follow Tenn. law); State v. Fowler, 157 Wash.2d 387, 139 P.3d 342 (2006) (recording of conversations

inside Ore. at instigation of Ore. police involving Ore. crime admissible in Wash., where Ore. but not Wash. permits such recording on consent of only one of the parties, as occurred here).

Contra: State v. Davis, 313 Or. 246, 834 P.2d 1008 (1992) (special search and seizure requirements of Oregon constitution apply in Oregon prosecution even though the search was in Mississippi by Mississippi officers, yet court concedes: "It may fairly be argued that the rule means that otherwise probative evidence will be unavailable to Oregon courts and juries because of the actions of out-of-state law enforcement authorities, actions that such authorities almost certainly will have taken without knowing (and without even having any practical way to find out) what the Oregon constitutional rules may be").

The federal decisions suppressing in a federal prosecution evidence obtained under a warrant issued by a state court because the warrant does not comply with the requirements for federal warrants, see § 4.2(f), cannot be said to support the rule that forum law controls on the question of the legality of the search, for those cases concern federal use of state process, as authorized by Fed.R.Crim.P. 41, and thus the searches were actually of federal rather than state origin. Even in that setting, courts are increasingly reluctant to exclude because all aspects of federal warrant practice were not followed. See, e.g., United States v. $22,287.00, United States Currency, 709 F.2d 442 (6th Cir.1983); United States v. Harrington, 504 F.2d 130 (7th Cir.1974). Whether there was sufficient federal involvement has become "immaterial" in some cases because of more recent recognition that certain federal requirements are also Fourth Amendment requirements. See, e.g., United States v. Scroggins, 361 F.3d 1075 (8th Cir.2004).

[138]As compared to Illinois police engaged in search activity in Indiana. See D'Antorio v. State, 837 P.2d 727 (Alaska App.1992) (Alaska officer's ex-

onerous Illinois standards when they are investigating[139] (or inadvertently discover) Illinois criminality, then certainly they are not freed from the more strict Indiana standards on the same basis merely because those standards are not followed in Illinois.

Thus, the question in *Burge* and *Saiken* is not whether the searches are to be declared legal (under forum law) or illegal (under place-of-the-search law), but rather whether, given their illegality where performed, the result should be exclusion of the fruits in another jurisdiction. *Burge* and *Saiken* indicate that this is an evidentiary question as to which the law of the forum should prevail. But, this inevitably leads to some uncertainty as to exactly in what dimension the forum law should be viewed. Defense counsel might assert that because it is already established that the search is illegal because of a defect in the affidavit, then the evidentiary question is simply whether it is the forum's practice to exclude evidence obtained by in-state searches where there is some defect under state law in the affidavit. Under this approach, the fact that the forum would not characterize the use of hearsay as a defect under its own law is not relevant; rather, the fact the forum enforces its own rules on what must be done to obtain a warrant is seen as establishing the "forum law" on exclusion when a warrant is obtained upon a defective affidavit. Given the general practice (noted in the preceding section) of using the exclusionary rule for substantial violations of state law, the defendant could be expected to prevail. On the other hand, the prosecution would contend that the evidentiary question is whether the forum excludes evidence obtained in this particular way. But this is nothing more than a restatement of the legality-of-the-search question;[140] if the forum state would not characterize the search as illegal, using its own law, then quite obviously the forum state would not exclude the fruits thereof.

Both approaches are in error. The defense position is incorrect,

---

amination of impounded effects in Ohio subject to Alaska law, as "Alaska has the most significant relationship to and governmental interest in Sergeant Stauber's activities in Ohio"), reversed on further appeal, 926 P.2d 1158 (Alaska 1996), but because of a different interpretation of Alaska precedents.

[139]In Gambino v. United States, 275 U.S. 310, 48 S.Ct. 137, 72 L.Ed. 293 (1927), where New York police made a warrantless search without probable cause to find liquor possessed in violation of federal law (there was no state prohibition at the time), the Court declined to follow the "silver platter" rule because, though federal agents had not directed or participated

in the search, "the wrongful arrest, search and seizure were made solely on behalf of the United States." But, the fact that in *Gambino* exclusion was thus required for failure to meet Fourth Amendment standards hardly suggests that any time officers conduct a search on behalf of another jurisdiction that the latter jurisdiction's laws of search and seizure are applicable.

[140]Except in the rare situation in which both jurisdictions would view the practice in question as illegal under local law, but the forum state, unlike the state where the search occurred, does not view the violation as substantial enough to call for exclusion.

for it removes from consideration entirely the fact that a foreign rather than a domestic search is involved. That is, it assumes that the policy reasons underlying use of an exclusionary rule for violations of forum law on obtaining warrants inevitably apply with the same force with respect to violations of the law of another state on obtaining warrants. This is not necessarily the case. The purposes for using the exclusionary rule for violations of state law, it would seem, are essentially the same as those that have been given for suppression where the Fourth Amendment is violated: deterrence of the police; the imperative of judicial integrity; and assuring the people that the government will not profit from its lawless behavior.[141] It is certainly understandable that a state which, for one or more of these reasons, is prepared to suppress evidence obtained by its own police in violation of its own laws, even at the cost of a possibly guilty person escaping conviction, might not be equally prepared to suppress because of out-of-state violations by other police.[142] The prospect of deterrence is more remote, as is the judicial taint from acceptance of the evidence, and there has been no profit from its own wrongdoing by the convicting jurisdiction.[143]

---

[141]See § 1.1(f).

[142]As compared to the forum state's own police. See D'Antorio v. State, 837 P.2d 727 (Alaska App.1992) (Alaska officer's examination of impounded effects in Ohio subject to Alaska law, as "Alaska has the most significant relationship to and governmental interest in Sergeant Stauber's activities in Ohio"), reversed on further appeal, 926 P.2d 1158 (Alaska 1996), but because of a different interpretation of Alaska precedents; State v. Cauley, 863 S.W.2d 411 (Tenn.1993) (where Tenn. officer was affiant for Ky. search warrant to search premises in Ky. to get evidence of Tenn. crime and Tenn. officers participated in execution of that warrant, higher standards of Tenn. law, resulting from rejection of Gates in that state, apply, as in such circumstances purpose of deterring Tenn. police deemed to be served, notwithstanding acknowledged fact that magistrates in other states would not be aware of in and, in any event, would not follow Tenn. law).

When the question is one of the jurisdiction of the forum's police to act outside the state, then it is of course understandable that the forum's police must find their authority in the law of the other state, as in "fresh pursuit" cases. See, e.g., People v. Jacobs, 67 Ill.App.3d 447, 24 Ill.Dec. 370, 385 N.E.2d 137 (1979) (suppressing evidence where Ill. police failed to take defendant before Iowa magistrate as required by Iowa's Uniform Fresh Pursuit Law); Commonwealth v. Sadvari, 561 Pa. 588, 752 A.2d 393 (2000) (evidence suppressed where Pa. police failed to take defendant before Del. magistrate as required by Del. Uniform Fresh Pursuit Law). However, Jacobs and Sadvari represent a minority view. See the cases collected in note 127 supra, especially Galan, Dentler, Ferrell, and Bonds. In the main, these decisions emphasize that the "hot pursuit" arrest was itself lawful and that the subsequent failure to take the arrestee before a magistrate of the neighboring state was a mere statutory violation not involving fundamental rights of the defendant, especially since the defendant received a prompt appearance when taken by police back to their state.

[143]People v. Orlosky, 40 Cal.App.3d 935, 115 Cal.Rptr. 598 (1974) (holding admissible evidence obtained by Indiana police in violation of an Indiana rule that a wife cannot effectively consent to a search without the concur-

As for the other possible position set out above, namely that the question is whether the forum excludes evidence obtained within the state in precisely the same way, it is likewise unsatisfactory because it also diverts attention away from the more fundamental question of whether the benefits to be derived from exclusion outweigh the costs. Whether or not the forum also forbids the practice in question is largely irrelevant to that fundamental issue. Thus, if in *Saiken* it had been the law in Illinois as well that a warrant could not be obtained there upon a hearsay affidavit, it would not inevitably follow from that fact that exclusion is required for violation of a comparable Indiana proscription. This hardly bears upon the question of whether the Illinois courts should attempt to deter Indiana police, nor does it enhance the degree of taint or profit involved in receiving evidence obtained in violation of Indiana law.

Finally, consideration must be given to the question of whether items seized in violation of local law only, or, indeed, even items lawfully seized in all respects, may be subject to suppression when offered in evidence in another jurisdiction on the ground that the "silver platter" process—the transfer to agents in the other jurisdiction—is itself constitutionally objectionable. Consider, for example, *United States v. Birrell*,[144] where New York police, in the course of a homicide investigation, seized certain papers from the victim's apartment. Shortly after Birrell had notified the police that some of these papers belonged to him and had demanded their return, they were turned over to federal authorities as evidence that Birrell had committed perjury in prior federal proceedings. The court held that on these facts, though the initial seizure of the documents was lawful, they must be suppressed because the subsequent federal acquisition was another intrusion into defendant's privacy for which a warrant was required. "While the police were justified in retaining the papers for a reasonable time to discover whether they afforded any clues with respect to the homicide, Birrell had sufficiently manifested his claim that a search by law enforcement officers of

---

rence of her husband; "the concept of 'dirty business'—i.e., that the state should not avail itself of illegal acts by its officers—obviously would lead to admissibility of the evidence herein in issue, since California does not regard the police conduct as being improper"; moreover, "[t]his state should not be impeded, in a local prosecution for a local crime by barring evidence which California law regards as legitimately procured under a doctrine that recognizes modern concepts of the husband-wife relation, merely to add a wrist slap to a foreign police officer whose

personal interest in a California prosecution must be relatively remote"); State v. Lucas, 372 N.W.2d 731 (Minn. 1985) (tape recording of telephone conversation would not be admissible in Wis., where it obtained by cooperative efforts of Wis. and Minn. authorities, but such conduct proper in Minn.; held, evidence admissible, as "exclusion of the tapes would not serve to deter misconduct by police officers of either Minnesota or Wisconsin").

[144]United States v. Birrell, 470 F.2d 113 (2d Cir.1972).

another sovereign for a different purpose could not be made without a warrant."

The exact rationale of the *Birrell* decision is uncertain. Judge Friendly asserted at one point:

> We fail to see how the taking into custody by the city police, proper though we have held this to be, relieves federal authorities from a requirement that would have existed if Birrell's papers had been left where they were. The propriety of the first intrusion into Birrell's privacy does not automatically sanction a second. Even when a "major" intrusion falls within a recognized exception to the Fourth Amendment, the warrant requirement as to a further "minor" intrusion is not abrogated.

That language, if taken seriously, would seem to render constitutionally invalid every "silver platter" situation in which the receiving jurisdiction did not obtain the items by a search warrant, for it views the receipt by that jurisdiction in terms of what would be required by the Fourth Amendment if the objects had not previously been lawfully seized by other authorities. But, the case relied upon by Judge Friendly, *Coolidge v. New Hampshire*,[145] hardly supports such a proposition, as the discussion therein to which reference was made concerns the fact that a lawful entry of premises to arrest does not make lawful the added intrusion of search of the place of arrest. As Judge Anderson noted in his *Birrell* concurrence, it certainly does not follow that "evidence which is legitimately in the hands of one state or federal police department cannot be made available to other state or federal law enforcement agencies without a warrant, even if it is to be used for a different purpose."

Judge Friendly confined his holding to the facts of the case, stressing that whatever the rule might be in other circumstances the Fourth Amendment was violated here because: (i) Birrell had requested return of his papers four days before the federal "search"; (ii) this was *not* an instance where "the city police * * * had on their own initiative delivered" the items to federal authorities; and (iii) the federal authorities wanted the items for a totally different purpose. Other courts have thus declined to follow *Birrell* where the turnover was attributable to a common state-federal interest in the suppression of the narcotics traffic,[146] where the turnover occurred before rather than after the demand for return,[147] and where the turnover was initiated by state officials.[148]

The Supreme Court has held that "in determining whether [a]

---

[145]Coolidge v. New Hampshire, 403 U.S. 443, 91 S.Ct. 2022, 29 L.Ed.2d 564 (1971).

[146]United States v. DeBerry, 487 F.2d 448 (2d Cir.1973).

[147]United States v. Gargotto, 476 F.2d 1009 (6th Cir.1973).

But in United States v. Lewis, 504 F.2d 92 (6th Cir.1974), the evidence had been used in two state prosecutions, the defendant had filed a motion for return after the first state trial, and thereafter the evidence was given to the federal authorities. Though purporting to rely on *Gargotto*,

seizure and search were 'unreasonable' our inquiry is a dual one—whether the officer's action was justified at its inception, and whether it was reasonably related in scope to the circumstances which justified the interference in the first place."[149] Thus, it is not fanciful to suggest (without regard to whether *Birrell* is such a case) that the continuing custody of objects lawfully seized but later found not to be of evidentiary value becomes, at some point, unreasonable under the Fourth Amendment. If this is so, then it is not correct to say that it inevitably takes a demand for return to trigger the Fourth Amendment violation,[150] nor would it be particularly relevant that the turnover was instigated by state rather than federal authorities or that the federal interest was similar to that of the state.[151]

But in all of these situations, it would seem that *if* the continuing possession of the objects by the seizing jurisdiction has not yet become unreasonable in a Fourth Amendment sense,[152] then certainly (as occurred in *Birrell*) it is no search for a law enforcement agent of another jurisdiction to scrutinize the property—at least to the extent it has already been examined.[153] The apt anal-

---

the court held: "The fact that a motion has been filed for the return of the evidence has no bearing on the rule that one police agency need not get a warrant prior to obtaining evidence from another police agency."

[148]United States v. Andrews, 22 F.3d 1328 (5th Cir.1994); United States v. Joseph, 829 F.2d 724 (9th Cir.1987); United States v. Gargotto, 476 F.2d 1009 (6th Cir.1973).

[149]Terry v. Ohio, 392 U.S. 1, 88 S.Ct. 1868, 20 L.Ed.2d 889 (1968).

[150]While the demand may have been significant in *Birrell* because the police were theretofore unaware of the defendant's ownership of the papers, often the ownership will be apparent from other facts. See, e.g., United States v. Gargotto, 476 F.2d 1009 (6th Cir.1973), where the papers had been seized from the defendant's premises but *Birrell* was not followed because the federal inspection of them preceded the demand.

[151]If the continuing custody were itself a violation of the Fourth Amendment, it would hardly be relevant that there was no "federal search" in the acquisition. As for the similarity of the federal interest, this would not appear significant *if* the period of reasonable

state custody had run, but the fact that the items, by their nature, obviously relate to some federal enforcement interest might have a bearing on the question of how long the custody would be reasonable pending federal inquiry.

[152]Just when this point is reached has not received close attention from the Supreme Court. In United States v. Johns, 469 U.S. 478, 105 S.Ct. 881, 83 L.Ed.2d 890 (1985), the Court commented that the police may not "indefinitely retain possession of a vehicle and its contents before they complete a vehicle search," but concluded that the delay in the instant case had not adversely affected a possessory interest, as the defendant had not in the interim "sought return of the property."

[153]Of course, the issue may not simply be whether the continued possession was reasonable under the Fourth Amendment. It has been persuasively argued that existing Fourth Amendment doctrine provides "two principal justifications for placing use restrictions on the information and property obtained by law enforcement authorities. First, once the Supreme Court discarded the property paradigm for the Fourth Amendment, no

ogy is to *United States v. Jacobsen*,[154] holding it "infringed no legitimate expectation of privacy and hence was not a 'search' within the meaning of the Fourth Amendment" for police to scrutinize a container and its contents to the same extent as had theretofore been done by the private person then having custody of the container and who called the police. And if by such examination or otherwise it is now determined that there is probable cause this material has evidentiary value to this other jurisdiction, then it would seem that the mere act of interjurisdictional transfer of it is not the kind of law enforcement activity for which a search warrant is required. "Evidence legally obtained by one police agency may be made available to other such agencies without a warrant, even for a use different from that for which it was originally taken."[155]

A variation on *Birrell* was presented in *State v. Mollica*,[156] where a federal officer acting within that state obtained evidence without violating the Constitution or federal law but in a manner that would have constituted a violation of the state constitution if utilized by a state officer. The question presented was whether, after the federal officer gave that evidence to state authorities, suppression in the state courts would be appropriate. The court first concluded that the federal officer's in-state acquisition of the evidence was lawful notwithstanding the state constitution: "Because federal officers necessarily act in the various states, but in the exercise of federal jurisdictional power, pursuant to federal authority and in accordance with federal standards, state courts treat such officers as officers from another jurisdiction."[157] As the *Mollica* court explained, this approach makes good sense, as "the

---

rationale remained for freezing the reasonableness inquiry to the moment of the search or seizure. Because the government does not enjoy a superior possessory interest in the seized items or information, the reasonableness of a seizure hinges upon the government's intended use of the items acquired. Second, imposition of use restrictions recognizes that what government officials do with seized information and items may affect an individual's privacy and property rights as much as the seizure itself. Taken together, the two justifications suggest that governmental authorities must use seized information and property in a manner consistent with the reasonableness requirement in the Fourth Amendment." Krent, Of Diaries and Data Banks: Use Restrictions Under the Fourth Amendment, 74 Texas L.Rev. 49 (1995). However, it is

also suggested there that use of the type discussed here is not unreasonable. Id. at 91.

[154]United States v. Jacobsen, 466 U.S. 109, 104 S.Ct. 1652, 80 L.Ed.2d 85 (1984).

[155]United States v. Lester, 647 F.2d 869 (8th Cir.1981). See also United States v. Thompson, 837 F.2d 673 (5th Cir.1988); Jabara v. Webster, 691 F.2d 272 (6th Cir.1982); United States v. Gargotto, 476 F.2d 1009 (6th Cir. 1973); State v. Jackson, 304 Conn. 383, 40 A.3d 290 (2012); State v. Motley, 153 N.C.App. 701, 571 S.E.2d 269 (2002); State v. Coburn, 165 Vt. 318, 683 A.2d 1343 (1996).

[156]State v. Mollica, 114 N.J. 329, 554 A.2d 1315 (1989).

[157]In support, the court cited Morales v. State, 407 So.2d 321 (Fla. App.1981); State v. Dreibelbis, 147 Vt.

application of the state constitution to the officers of another jurisdiction would disserve the principles of federalism and comity, without properly advancing legitimate state interests." That being the case, and considering also the fact that there "was no federal restriction against such a transfer," the court concluded it followed this evidence would be admissible in state court once turned over to state authorities. But, quite understandably the court added a proviso, a "vital, significant condition" necessary to ensure that such turnover was not a consequence of efforts by state officers to circumvent the state constitution: the federal officer must not have been acting as an agent of the state at the time he acquired the evidence.

§ 1.6 The exclusionary rule in criminal proceedings

98, 511 A.2d 307 (1986); State v. Bradley, 105 Wash.2d 898, 719 P.2d 546 (1986). See also Commonwealth v. Brown, 456 Mass. 708, 925 N.E.2d 845 (2010) (applying statutory provision that state wiretap limits not applicable to actions of federal officers pursuant to federal laws, and also holding that state constitutional provision "does not constrain Federal authorities unless they operate as part of an 'essentially' State investigation," not the case here); Dillon v. State, 844 S.W.2d 139 (Tenn.1992) (following *Mollica*, but reserving judgment on case where, unlike instant case, federal officer made search within the state).

Contra:State v. Torres, 125 Haw. 382, 252 P.3d 1229 (2011) ("where evidence sought to be admitted in state court is the product of acts that occurred on federal property or in another state, by Hawaii law enforcement officials or officers of another jurisdiction, due consideration * * * must be given to the Hawaii Constitution and applicable case law": court's bizarre reasoning is "that if state courts admitted evidence in a state prosecution that was obtained in a manner that would be unlawful under our constitution, our courts would necessarily be placing their imprimatur of approval on evidence that would otherwise be deemed illegal, thus compromising the integrity of our courts"); State v. Cardenas-Alvarez, 130 N.M. 386, 25 P.3d 225 (2001) (actions of federal border agents within state subjected to more demanding state constitutional standards when evidence obtained thereafter offered in state prosecutions); State v. Davis, 313 Or. 246, 834 P.2d 1008 (1992) (more demanding state constitutional provisions apply in state prosecution regardless of "where that evidence was obtained (in-state or out-of-state) or what government entity (local, state or federal, or out-of-state) obtained it"). The *Cardenas-Alvarez* decision is severely criticized in Note, 32 N.M.L. Rev. 531 (2002).

§ 1.6(i) Deterrence/cost balancing as to specific kinds of violations: the *Herring* approach

---

Research References

West's Key Number Digest
Bail ☞49(3); Criminal Law ☞219; Extradition and Detainers ☞39; Grand Jury ☞36.4; Indictment and Information ☞10.2; Pardon and Parole ☞90; Sentencing and Punishment ☞321, 972, 2019; Witnesses ☞16

Legal Encyclopedias
C.J.S., Bail; Release and Detention Pending Proceedings §§ 18, 54 to 59, 64; Criminal Law §§ 334, 1460, 1472, 1479, 1492, 1527, 1530, 1564; Indictments and Informations § 20; Pardon and Parole §§ 71, 85; Witnesses §§ 2, 21, 32 to 52

Introduction

In the typical case, the impact of the Fourth Amendment exclusionary rule is to bar from use *at trial* evidence obtained by an unreasonable search or seizure. That is, if the defendant has standing to object,[1] he may by undertaking the appropriate procedural steps[2] obtain a ruling as to whether certain evidence constitutes the fruit[3] of a violation of the Fourth Amendment, and if it is determined that the evidence is of this character then the prosecution may not introduce it at the defendant's trial, at least in its case in chief.[4] The concern in this section is with (1) the possible application of the exclusionary rule at other stages of the criminal process (those proceedings occurring either in advance of or subsequent to the trial itself); and (2) the possible nonapplication of the exclusionary rule at the trial itself as a result of deterrence-cost balancing.

§ 1.6(a) Subpoena to testify before grand jury

In *United States v. Calandra*,[5] the Supreme Court was confronted with the question whether a witness summoned to ap-

---

[Section 1.6]

[1] See § 11.3.

[2] See § 11.1.

[3] See § 11.4.

[4] The exclusionary rule applies to all of the prosecution's case in chief, including evidence of other offenses admitted under Fed.R.Evid. 404(b) to prove defendant's mental state, "at least where there is some nexus between the initial search and seizure and the subsequent charged offense," when "the alleged unlawfully obtained evidence is being used to prove an essential element of a charged offense." United States v. Hill, 60 F.3d 672 (10th Cir.1995) (nexus here, as earlier drug crimes were "just a few months" before crime charged, and "it is well known that drug investigations, in particular, can go on for a long time and involve many different transactions and even many police encounters before a subsequent drug charge is brought"). For more on the situation in which the fruits of the unlawful search are to be offered to prove a post-search crime, see § 11.6(c). As to introduction for impeachment purposes, see § 11.6(a).

[Section 1.6(a)]

[5] United States v. Calandra, 414 U.S. 338, 94 S.Ct. 613, 38 L.Ed.2d 561 (1974), noted in 51 Chi.-Kent L.Rev. 212 (1974); 9 Harv.C.R.-C.L.L.Rev.

pear and testify before a grand jury may refuse to answer questions on the ground that they are based on evidence obtained from an unlawful search and seizure. In late 1970, federal agents executed a search warrant for gambling paraphernalia at Calandra's place of business; they did not find any such paraphernalia, but did discover and seize certain papers that appeared to relate to loansharking activities. In March of 1971 a grand jury was convened to investigate these activities, and Calandra was subpoenaed to appear in order that he might be questioned based on the evidence seized in the search. Upon Calandra's motion to suppress, the court ruled that the search had been unlawful and that consequently the evidence must be suppressed and returned to him and that he need not answer any of the grand jury's questions based on the suppressed evidence. The Court of Appeals affirmed,[6] but the Supreme Court reversed.

The Court, in an opinion by Justice Powell, after declaring that the exclusionary rule "is a judicially created remedy designed to safeguard Fourth Amendment rights generally through its deterrent effect, rather than a personal constitutional right of the party aggrieved," went on to say:

> In deciding whether to extend the exclusionary rule to grand jury proceedings, we must weigh the potential injury to the historic role and functions of the grand jury against the potential benefits of the rule as applied in this context. It is evident that this extension of the exclusionary rule would seriously impede the grand jury. Because the grand jury does not finally adjudicate guilt or innocence, it has traditionally been allowed to pursue its investigative and accusatorial functions unimpeded by the evidentiary and procedural restrictions applicable to a criminal trial. Permitting witnesses to invoke the exclusionary rule before a grand jury would precipitate adjudication of issues hitherto reserved for the trial on the merits and would delay and disrupt grand jury proceedings. Suppression hearings would halt the orderly progress of an investigation and might necessitate extended litigation of issues only tangentially related to the grand jury's primary objective. The probable result would be "protracted interruption of grand jury proceedings," * * * effectively transforming them into preliminary trials on the merits. In some cases the delay might be fatal to the enforcement of the criminal law. * * *

> Against this potential damage to the role and functions of the grand jury, we must weigh the benefits to be derived from this proposed extension of the exclusionary rule. Suppression of the use of illegally seized evidence against the search victim in a criminal trial is thought to be an important method of effectuating the Fourth Amendment. But it does not follow that the Fourth Amendment requires adoption of every proposal that might deter police misconduct. * * *

Any incremental deterrent effect which might be achieved by

---

598 (1974); 1 Hastings Const.L.Q. 179 (1974); 5 Seton Hall L.Rev. 917 (1974); 27 Vand.L.Rev. 560 (1974).

[6] United States v. Calandra, 465 F.2d 1218 (6th Cir.1972).

extending the rule to grand jury proceedings is uncertain at best. Whatever deterrence of police misconduct may result from the exclusion of illegally seized evidence from criminal trials, it is unrealistic to assume that application of the rule to grand jury proceedings would significantly further that goal. Such an extension would deter only police investigation consciously directed toward the discovery of evidence solely for use in a grand jury investigation. The incentive to disregard the requirement of the Fourth Amendment solely to obtain an indictment from a grand jury is substantially negated by the inadmissibility of the illegally seized evidence in a subsequent criminal prosecution of the search victim. For the most part, a prosecutor would be unlikely to request an indictment where a conviction could not be obtained. We therefore decline to embrace a view that would achieve a speculative and undoubtedly minimal advance in the deterrence of police misconduct at the expense of substantially impeding the role of the grand jury.

As for the argument that "each and every question based on evidence obtained from an illegal search and seizure constitutes a fresh and independent violation of the witness' constitutional rights," the Court responded that the Fourth Amendment wrong in the instant case was "fully accomplished by the original search without probable cause," so that the questions based thereon constituted only "a derivative use of the product of a past unlawful search and seizure." The Court's prior conclusion was thus deemed to control "both the fruits of an unlawful search and seizure and any question or evidence derived therefrom," as the "same considerations of logic and policy apply to both."

The three *Calandra* dissenters[7] objected that the majority had erred in focusing upon the deterrent effect of the exclusionary rule, in that "uppermost in the minds of the framers of the rule" were "the twin goals of enabling the judiciary to avoid the taint of partnership in official lawlessness and of assuring the people * * * that the government would not profit from its lawless behavior, thus minimizing the risk of seriously undermining popular trust in government." As for the majority's assertion that the Fourth Amendment rights of a grand jury witness are sufficiently protected by the inadmissibility of the illegally-seized evidence in a subsequent prosecution of the search victim, the dissenters responded:

> This, of course, is no alternative for Calandra, since he was granted transactional immunity and cannot be criminally prosecuted. But the fundamental flaw of the alternative is that to compel Calandra to testify in the first place under penalty of contempt necessarily "thwarts" his Fourth Amendment protection and "entangle[s] the courts in the illegal acts of Government agents."

The issue before the Court in *Calandra* is clearly a most difficult one, and it is not at all surprising that it produced a sharp

---

[7]Justices Brennan, Douglas and Marshall.

division of views by the Justices. It is fair to say, however, that neither the majority opinion nor the dissenting opinion adequately explores that issue. The majority's concentration upon the deterrence function of the exclusionary rule makes quite plausible the dissenters' reading of the holding to mean "that the application of the exclusionary rule depends solely upon whether its invocation in a particular type of proceeding will significantly further the goal of deterrence." Such a proposition is not sound, for—as pointed out in the earlier discussion in this Chapter[8]— there is more to the exclusionary rule than this. Yet, the dissenters are no more correct, in terms of setting forth a proposition that may be squared with the Court's prior holdings, in asserting that "the vital function of the rule [is] to insure that the judiciary avoids even the slightest appearance of sanctioning illegal government conduct." The Court's decisions on the question of who has standing to invoke the exclusionary rule[9] quite clearly cannot be explained on this basis.

Indeed, it is not inappropriate to suggest that the standing doctrine does greater violence to the goals emphasized by the *Calandra* dissenters than does the *Calandra* holding. As for the judiciary avoiding "the taint of partnership in official lawlessness," this taint is much more apparent when a judge receives illegally seized evidence at a criminal trial because only the rights of a nondefendant were violated, than when such evidence is received by a grand jury before whom (as noted in *Calandra*) "no judge presides to monitor its proceedings." And as for the concern that the government "not profit from its unlawful behavior," that profit seems significantly greater when illegally seized evidence is used to obtain a conviction than when it plays a part in a grand jury investigation, which in any event "is not fully carried out until every available clue has been run down and all witnesses examined in every proper way to find if a crime has been committed."[10]

Of course, to say that the *Calandra* holding intrudes less upon Fourth Amendment interests than the Court's prior rulings on the standing issue is not to say that *Calandra* is correctly decided, particularly in light of the criticism the Court's approach to standing has engendered.[11] But that is not the point of the comparison. Despite the apparent reluctance of the *Calandra* dissenters to take into account the general desirability of barring litigious interference with grand jury proceedings, it does seem appropriate to weigh that objective against *all* of the objectives of the exclusionary rule. The *Calandra* majority, perhaps because of its

---

[8]See § 1.1(f).

[9]See § 11.3.

[10]United States v. Stone, 429 F.2d 138 (2d Cir.1970), quoted with approval in Branzburg v. Hayes, 408 U.S. 665, 92 S.Ct. 2646, 33 L.Ed.2d 626 (1972).

[11]See § 11.3.

failure to carefully weigh all of the latter objectives,[12] neglects to give adequate attention to the fact that no one but witness Calandra could effectively call the police to task for their prior conduct. In short, the true villain may be the standing doctrine. The *Calandra* result would be much more palatable, and the majority's concern with avoiding undue interference with the grand jury's duties much more understandable, if it would later be open to the indicted defendant to challenge evidence offered against him derived from the violation of anyone's Fourth Amendment rights.

In the pre-*Calandra* case of *Gelbard v. United States*,[13] the Supreme Court held that a grand jury witness could defend against a contempt charge, brought against him for his refusal to answer questions, on the ground that the questions were based upon information unlawfully intercepted through wiretapping and electronic surveillance. *Gelbard* is not inconsistent with *Calandra* in the constitutional sense, for it was based upon the conclusion that the Congress had provided the witness with this remedy in the Omnibus Crime Control and Safe Streets Act of 1968.[14]

It must be emphasized that *Calandra* and *Gelbard* are concerned with the subpoenaing of a witness to answer questions based upon a prior invasion of the rights of that witness. This is quite different from the claim that the subpoenaing of a witness to appear and testify before the grand jury is itself an unreasonable search and seizure, which has been rejected on the merits. In *United States v. Dionisio*,[15] the Court held:

> It is clear that a subpoena to appear before a grand jury is not a "seizure" in the Fourth Amendment sense, even though that summons may be inconvenient or burdensome. Last Term we again acknowledged what has long been recognized, that "[c]itizens generally are not constitutionally immune from grand jury subpoenas . . . ." * * *

> The compulsion exerted by a grand jury subpoena differs from the seizure effected by an arrest or even an investigative "stop" in more than civic obligation. For, as Judge Friendly wrote for the Court of Appeals for the Second Circuit:

> The latter is abrupt, it is effected with force or the threat of it

---

[12]The objectives other than deterrence are not completely ignored by the majority in *Calandra,* but are dealt with only summarily in footnote 11 of the opinion.

[13]Gelbard v. United States, 408 U.S. 41, 92 S.Ct. 2357, 33 L.Ed.2d 179 (1972).

[14]A 5-4 majority, per Brennan, J., held that such testimony would constitute "evidence derived" from violations of Title III of the Crime Control Act, whose use in grand jury proceedings is prohibited by § 2515, which provides that where a communication has been illegally intercepted "no part of the contents of such communication and no evidence derived therefrom" may be received "in any trial, hearing, or other proceeding in or before any * * * grand jury."

[15]United States v. Dionisio, 410 U.S. 1, 93 S.Ct. 764, 35 L.Ed.2d 67 (1973).

and often in demeaning circumstances, and, in the case of arrest, results in a record involving social stigma. A subpoena is served in the same manner as other legal process; it involves no stigma whatever; if the time for appearance is inconvenient, this can generally be altered; and it remains at all times under the control and supervision of a court. * * *

Thus the Court of Appeals for the Seventh Circuit recognized in a case subsequent to the one now before us, that a "grand jury subpoena to testify is not that kind of governmental intrusion on privacy against which the Fourth Amendment affords protection once the Fifth Amendment is satisfied.[16]

But, if the summoning is not a seizure under the Fourth Amendment, is the subsequent questioning a search? The answer, as one court has emphatically put it, is that "compelled grand jury testimony is neither a search for, nor a seizure of, oral statements in the sense envisioned by the Fourth Amendment."[17] True, the Supreme Court in an earlier time intimated that there might be limits upon how far the grand jury could intrude into the privacy of the witness; it was said in *Hale v. Henkel*[18] that it would be an abuse of the grand jury's power "if the object of the inquiry were merely to pry into the details of domestic or business life" of the witness, and in *Blair v. United States*[19] that "for special reasons a witness may be excused from telling all that he knows." But objections of this kind not also based on some recognized evidentiary privilege, such as the attorney-client privilege, have been consistently rejected by the courts,[20] which have stressed the need for unrestrained investigations by grand juries and the impracticality of justifying to a particular witness a basis for the line of inquiry being followed.

---

[16]The *Dionisio* Court also held that requiring the grand jury witness to give voice exemplars does not violate the Fourth Amendment, as "[t]he physical characteristics of a person's voice, its tone and manner, as opposed to the content of a specific conversation, are constantly exposed to the public," so that "[n]o person can have a reasonable expectation that others will not know the sound of his voice." In the companion case of United States v. Mara, 410 U.S. 19, 93 S.Ct. 774, 35 L.Ed.2d 99 (1973), the Court reached the same result as to the subpoenaing of a witness to give handwriting exemplars. See § 2.6(a).

[17]Fraser v. United States, 452 F.2d 616 (7th Cir.1971). So too, requiring a person to answer questions in other circumstances is likewise activity governed by the Fifth rather than the Fourth Amendment. Nelson v. National Aeronautics and Space Administration, 530 F.3d 865 (9th Cir.2008) (questions about drug use or counseling for drug problems by government contract employees); Greenawalt v. Indiana Dept. of Corrections, 397 F.3d 587 (7th Cir.2005), rev'd and remanded on other grounds, 131 S. Ct. 746, 178 L. Ed. 2d 667 (2011) (psychological examination required for continued government employment).

[18]Hale v. Henkel, 201 U.S. 43, 26 S.Ct. 370, 50 L.Ed. 652 (1906).

[19]Blair v. United States, 250 U.S. 273, 39 S.Ct. 468, 63 L.Ed. 979 (1919).

[20]United States v. Doe (Popkin), 460 F.2d 328 (1st Cir.1972); United States v. Weinberg, 439 F.2d 743 (9th Cir.1971).

§ 1.6(b) Grand jury subpoena duces tecum

The 1920 case of *Silverthorne Lumber Co. v. United States*[21] presented a factual situation that might be deemed the subpoena duces tecum counterpart of *Calandra*. Federal agents unlawfully seized papers belonging to the Silverthornes and their corporation, and presented them to a grand jury that had already indicted them. After the documents were returned upon order of the district court, the grand jury attempted to recoup them by issuance of a subpoena duces tecum. Contempt convictions followed refusal to comply with the subpoena. The Supreme Court, per Holmes, J., reversed, stating that "the essence of a provision forbidding the acquisition of evidence in a certain way is that not merely evidence so acquired shall not be used before the Court but that it shall not be used at all."

Does this mean, then, that a grand jury witness may invoke the Fourth Amendment exclusionary rule in order to justify noncompliance with a subpoena duces tecum for objects that would be the fruits of a prior illegal search? Most likely not, it must be said since the *Calandra* decision. Precisely what part of *Silverthorne* has survived is less than clear, for the *Calandra* majority distinguished the earlier case on several grounds: (1) that the subpoenaed parties "had previously been indicted by the grand jury and thus could invoke the exclusionary rule on the basis of their status as criminal defendants"; (2) that because an indictment had already been issued it could not be said that "the grand jury needed the documents to perform its investigative or accusatorial functions"; and (3) that the illegality of the prior search had been adjudicated before the subpoenas were issued, so that there was no "interruption of grand jury proceedings." But, given the *Calandra* holding, it would seem that *Silverthorne* has been virtually distinguished out of existence.

However, it has long been recognized that an individual ordered to respond to a grand jury subpoena duces tecum may object that it is "far too sweeping in its terms to be regarded as reasonable" under the Fourth Amendment.[22] *Calandra* does not change this, for the Court there emphasized: "Judicial supervision is properly exercised in such cases to prevent the wrong before it occurs." But this is not to say that when the merits of the issue are reached, the person subpoenaed will prevail by showing an absence of those limitations attending the issuance of a search warrant. As one court observed:

> It is now clear that this is not so, and that what is "unreasonable" in the case of search and seizure is not the measure of what is "unreasonable" in the case of a subpoena duces tecum; that the "probable cause" required for a search or arrest warrant is very different

[Section 1.6(b)]

[21]Silverthorne Lumber Co. v. United States, 251 U.S. 385, 40 S.Ct.

182, 64 L.Ed. 319 (1920).

[22]Hale v. Henkel, 201 U.S. 43, 26 S.Ct. 370, 50 L.Ed. 652 (1906).

from the "probable cause" required to support the subpoena; and
that the specificity required of a search warrant is not applicable to
it.[23]

Thus, it may be said that there is no requirement that the
grand jury have probable cause to support the subpoena; a grand
jury "does not depend on a case or controversy for power to get
evidence but can investigate merely on suspicion that the law is
being violated, or even just because it wants assurance that it is
not."[24] Nor does the grand jury have to have some clear basis for
determining that the objects sought will in fact constitute evidence of the activity under investigation.[25] As for the permissible
breadth of a subpoena, courts have considered such factors as (1)
the capacity of the grand jury to be more selective in light of the
subject matter of their inquiry; (2) the volume of records
subpoenaed; (3) the time period over which the records were assembled; (4) the disruptive impact of production upon the
subpoenaed party's continuing operations; and (5) the relation of
that party to the activities under investigation.[26] The Fourth
Amendment limits on subpoenas duces tecum, such as they are,
are discussed in more detail later in this Treatise.[27]

§ 1.6(c) Challenge of indictment

What if an indicted defendant moves to quash the indictment
against him on the ground that some of the evidence received by
the grand jury was obtained as a consequence of a violation of his
Fourth Amendment rights? Must the exclusionary rule be applied in this setting, in the sense that the indictment will be allowed to stand only if based upon sufficient evidence apart from
that obtained by illegal search? Although the Supreme Court has
not answered this precise question, there is little doubt from the
manner in which the Court has dealt with very similar issues
that the answer is no.

In *Costello v. United States*,[28] the question was whether a defendant may be required to stand trial where only hearsay evidence was presented to the grand jury indicting him. The Court
concluded that "neither the Fifth Amendment nor any other
constitutional provision prescribes the kind of evidence upon
which grand juries must act," noting:

If indictments were to be held open to challenge on the ground that

---

[23]In re Addonizio, 53 N.J. 107,
248 A.2d 531 (1968).

[24]United States v. Morton Salt
Co., 338 U.S. 632, 70 S.Ct. 357, 94
L.Ed. 401 (1950).

[25]People v. Dorr, 47 Ill.2d 458,
265 N.E.2d 601 (1970); People v. Allen,
410 Ill. 508, 103 N.E.2d 92 (1951).
Compare People v. Lurie, 39 Ill.2d 331,
235 N.E.2d 637 (1968).

[26]In re Grand Jury Subpoena
Duces Tecum Addressed to Provision
Salesmen and Distributors Union,
Local 627, 203 F.Supp. 575 (S.D.N.Y.
1961).

[27]See § 4.13.

[Section 1.6(c)]

[28]Costello v. United States, 350
U.S. 359, 76 S.Ct. 406, 100 L.Ed. 397
(1956).

there was inadequate or incompetent evidence before the grand jury, the resulting delay would be great indeed. The result of such a rule would be that before trial on the merits a defendant could always insist on a kind of preliminary trial to determine the competency and adequacy of the evidence before the grand jury. This is not required by the Fifth Amendment. An indictment returned by a legally constituted and unbiased grand jury, like an information drawn by the prosecutor, if valid on its face, is enough to call for trial of the charge on the merits.

Except for the disinclination of the Court to permit the delay that would occur from inquiring into the sufficiency of evidence heard by the grand jury, it could be said that *Costello* standing alone is not very persuasive on the issue being considered here. For one thing, *Costello* was a net worth tax prosecution in which the alternative to permitting hearsay was the calling of over a hundred witnesses before the grand jury.[29] For another, it could be said that the receipt of hearsay evidence by the grand jury is properly viewed differently than the receipt of illegally obtained evidence, for the former unlike the latter "may be translated into competent evidence by the time of trial if the originator or primary source of the hearsay testifies in court."[30]

However, in *Lawn v. United States*,[31] where the defendants had moved to dismiss the indictment against them and had sought (i) a hearing to determine whether the government had used evidence obtained in violation of their privilege against self-incrimination, and (ii) leave to inspect the minutes of the grand jury, a unanimous Court affirmed the district court's ruling for the government. While the Court emphasized that the defendants "had no reason, beyond suspicion, to believe" that the grand jury had used such material and that they "laid no foundation for the holding of a protracted preliminary hearing * * * to determine whether there was any substance to their suspicion," the Court went on seemingly to indicate that even if a foundation had been laid the result would be the same. In support, the Court quoted the language from *Costello* set out above. Similarly, in *United States v. Blue*[32] the Court reversed the district court's dismissal of an indictment on the ground that the government, in other proceedings, had compelled defendant to incriminate himself, stating that if the government had acquired evidence in violation of the Fifth Amendment, the defendant would at most be entitled

---

[29] See 24 Moore's Federal Practice § 606.04[1] (3d ed.1997), noting that the Court could have "rel[ied] on the peculiar nature of a net-worth prosecution, in which witnesses whose credibility is rarely in question are used primarily to identify documents, or emphasiz[ed] the impracticability of bringing a hundred or more witnesses before the grand jury."

[30] Comment, 43 N.Y.U.L.Rev. 578, 581 (1968).

[31] Lawn v. United States, 355 U.S. 339, 78 S.Ct. 311, 2 L.Ed.2d 321 (1958).

[32] United States v. Blue, 384 U.S. 251, 86 S.Ct. 1416, 16 L.Ed.2d 510 (1966).

to suppress that evidence and the fruits thereof if they were offered against him at trial. Citing *Costello* and *Lawn*, the Court observed in a footnote: "It does not seem to be contended that tainted evidence was presented to the grand jury; but in any event our precedents indicate this would not be a basis for abating the prosecution pending a new indictment, let alone barring it altogether." And more recently in *United States v. Calandra*,[33] discussed in detail earlier in this section, the Court made some observations bearing more directly upon the issue under consideration here than the issue that confronted the Court:[34]

> Such an extension [of the exclusionary rule] would deter only police investigation consciously directed toward the discovery of evidence solely for use in a grand jury investigation. The incentive to disregard the requirement of the Fourth Amendment solely to obtain an indictment from a grand jury is substantially negated by the inadmissibility of the illegally seized evidence in a subsequent criminal prosecution of the search victim. For the most part, a prosecutor would be unlikely to request an indictment where a conviction could not be obtained.

Relying upon *Costello, Lawn* and *Blue*, the federal courts have in the main refused to quash indictments where it was claimed that evidence before the grand jury was obtained in violation of the Fourth Amendment.[35] Illustrative is *West v. United States*:[36]

> The exclusionary rule * * * finds its purpose in the desire to curb illegal police practices. It is our opinion that the judicial policy which brought about the exclusionary rule would not be advanced in any significant degree by extending its application to grand jury

---

[33]United States v. Calandra, 414 U.S. 338, 94 S.Ct. 613, 38 L.Ed.2d 561 (1974).

[34]In *Calandra,* the search had been directed at the witness, so it could not correctly be said that the evidence could later be suppressed by the defendant or that the prosecutor would be unlikely to use illegally seized evidence to indict because that evidence could not be used to convict.

[35]United States v. Greve, 490 F.3d 566 (7th Cir.2007); United States v. Kenny, 462 F.2d 1205 (3d Cir.1972); Truchinski v. United States, 393 F.2d 627 (8th Cir.1968); United States v. Lawson, 502 F.Supp. 158 (D.Md.1980); United States v. Wolfson, 294 F.Supp. 267 (D.Del.1968); United States v. Birrell, 242 F.Supp. 191 (S.D.N.Y. 1965).

But consider United States v. Busk, 730 F.2d 129 (3d Cir.1984) (suggesting that if "following the grant of a suppression motion, a federal prosecutor were to present the same evidence to a grand jury," it might be proper to dismiss the indictment for prosecutorial misconduct under the supervisory power rule of United States v. Serubo, 604 F.2d 807 (3d Cir.1979)); United States v. Huberts, 637 F.2d 630 (9th Cir.1980) (previously suppressed evidence cannot be presented to grand jury to secure an indictment and would require dismissal of indictment). Compare United States v. Puglia, 8 F.3d 478 (7th Cir.1993) (relying on United States v. Williams, 504 U.S. 36, 112 S.Ct. 1735, 118 L.Ed.2d 352 (1992), limiting the circumstances in which a district court may use its supervisory powers to dismiss a grand jury indictment, court holds indictment not subject to dismissal because of grand jury's use of previously-suppressed evidence).

[36]West v. United States, 359 F.2d 50 (8th Cir.1966).

proceedings. Illegally seized evidence is already kept from the trier of fact. Extension to grand jury activities would probably have no laudatory effect on police practices that have not already been accomplished by the law as it now stands. * * *

Furthermore, as a practical matter, the United States District Attorney is the only person with free access to a grand jury. In such a situation the accused has no practical opportunity to object to evidence before it is presented to the grand jury. Likewise, since a judge is not presiding, it would be difficult, if not impossible, at this point in the litigation to have a final and binding determination of the legality of offered evidence. If we adopted appellant's position we would be faced with two alternatives. We could leave the essential nature of the grand jury proceeding unchanged. The government would then be forced to make an ex parte determination of the legality of the offered evidence without the guidance of opposition or ruling from judicial authority. The penalty for a mistake in judgment would be the striking down of the entire grand jury proceeding. We could, on the other hand, change the nature of the grand jury investigation, making it into an adversary system. The exclusionary rule could then be enforced by a case-by-case judicial determination. Such a change, however, would add an additional burden to judicial time, completely alter our judicial system, and seriously cripple the supposedly investigative purpose of the grand jury. We do not believe such a move is warranted or wise and consequently hold that the exclusionary rule does not apply to grand jury proceedings.

This is generally the position also taken by state courts.[37] Although several states by statute direct grand juries to receive only such evidence as would be admissible at trial, these provisions are usually viewed as "admonitory in character only, not mandatory."[38] Even when the *Costello* rule (that an indictment "sufficient on its face" is beyond challenge) has been rejected, it has been held that it "is not required that the evidence be the kind that would not fall within one of the exclusionary rules of evidence."[39] While New York courts have long recognized an "inherent right" of a defendant to quash an indictment not supported by sufficient "legal evidence,"[40] to obtain a dismissal on the ground that the indictment is based upon evidence obtained in violation of the Fourth Amendment the unconstitutionality of the acquisition of the evidence must either have been determined in a separate proceeding or be clearly established on the face of the record before the grand jury.[41] It is seldom the case that the il-

---

[37]See 4 W. LaFave, J. Israel, N. King & O. Kerr, Criminal Procedure § 15.5(c) (3d ed.2007).

[38]State v. McDonald, 231 Or. 24, 361 P.2d 1001 (1961). But see State v. Terrell, 283 N.W.2d 529 (Minn.1979), noting that as a matter of state law a person may challenge an indictment on the ground that it is based upon evidence obtained by an illegal search.

[39]State v. Parks, 437 P.2d 642 (Alaska 1968).

[40]People v. Nitzberg, 289 N.Y. 523, 47 N.E.2d 37 (1943).

[41]People v. Chalfa, 50 Misc.2d 845, 271 N.Y.S.2d 881 (1966).

legality of a search will appear on the face of the record.[42]

The question of whether a defendant should be allowed to invoke the Fourth Amendment exclusionary rule for purposes of quashing an indictment against him is a difficult one, for there are various relevant considerations pointing in opposite directions. On one level, it may be asked whether application of the rule would be consistent with the function of the indictment process. It has sometimes been said that the function of the grand jury is the "protection of the *innocent* against oppression and unjust prosecution,"[43] and if that is correct then it may be forcefully contended that this function would not be served by barring from the grand jury room illegally obtained but highly reliable evidence of the defendant's guilt. But it is to be doubted whether that is a correct characterization; as the Supreme Court has emphasized, the grand jury is also "a protector of citizens against arbitrary and oppressive governmental action."[44] Thus, if it may fairly be said that grand jury screening is intended to insure that the burdens of a trial are not "imposed upon a defendant when the likelihood of his conviction is small,"[45] this points in the direction of applying the exclusionary rule at the grand jury stage.

On another level, it may be asked whether use of the rule at this stage would significantly serve the purposes of the exclusionary rule. As for the deterrence objective, the language quoted above from *Calandra* and *West* is rather persuasive on the point that little if any added deterrence would be gained. This leaves the two goals stressed by the *Calandra* dissenters, "enabling the judiciary to avoid the taint of partnership in official lawlessness" and "assuring the people * * * that the government would not profit from its lawless behavior." Given the fact that "no judge presides to monitor its proceedings,"[46] the taint on the judiciary is rather remote. As for the "profit" of obtaining an indictment by the use of illegally seized evidence, one's assessment of this is bound to be influenced by attitudes concerning the significance of the grand jury screening process. It has been noted that the "increasing reluctance on the part of the courts to examine the sufficiency of the evidence before the grand jury" is tied directly to an "increasing feeling * * * that the grand jury was an inefficient 'rubber stamp' for the prosecutor."[47]

As in *Calandra*, the benefits of applying the exclusionary rule must be balanced against the costs. Unlike the situation in

---

[42]See cases collected in Annot., 20 A.L.R.3d 7 (1968).

[43]State v. Parks, 437 P.2d 642 (Alaska 1968) (concurring opinion) (emphasis added).

[44]United States v. Calandra, 414 U.S. 338, 94 S.Ct. 613, 38 L.Ed.2d 561 (1974).

[45]Note, 1963 Wash.U.L.Q. 102, 120.

[46]United States v. Calandra, 414 U.S. 338, 94 S.Ct. 613, 38 L.Ed.2d 561 (1974).

[47]Goldstein, The State and The Accused: Balance of Advantage in Criminal Procedure, 69 Yale L.J. 1149, 1171 (1960).

Calandra, a post-indictment challenge by the defendant would not "halt the orderly progress of an investigation." As for the concern expressed in *Costello* about the delay which would result from a "preliminary trial to determine the competency and adequacy of the evidence before the grand jury," some have questioned whether such delay need occur when the challenge is based upon the Fourth Amendment. It has been noted that the hearing on the pretrial motion to suppress evidence at trial "could be employed to entertain motions to suppress indictments secured by the use of unconstitutional evidence."[48] While this may be true, it does not follow that the hearing would not be any more complicated as a result. Unless the mere fact that some of the evidence before the grand jury was illegally obtained is to be deemed a basis for quashing the indictment, which apparently no court has held,[49] more would be required than a determination that certain evidence was illegally obtained and put before the grand jury. It would be necessary for the judge to assess all of the other evidence put before the grand jury to see if it establishes probable cause[50] or to determine if the illegal and competent evidence is "so intertwined that the court is unable to say * * * that the grand jury did not in fact return the indictment primarily influenced by the illicit evidence."[51] Given this added burden and the fact, as pointed out in *West*, that the "penalty for a mistake in judgment would be the striking down of the entire grand jury proceeding," it would seem on balance that the prevailing rule is sound.

§ 1.6(d) Preliminary hearing; extradition hearing

It is the prevailing view that at a preliminary hearing to determine whether there is probable cause to believe that the defendant committed the crime charged, the magistrate may take into account evidence offered by the prosecution without regard to whether that evidence was obtained by an illegal search. This has been so in the federal system at least since *Giordenello v. United States*,[52] where the Court declared that "the Commissioner here had no authority to adjudicate the admissibility" of heroin taken from defendant's person, and the matter is now

---

[48]Comment, 43 N.Y.U.L.Rev. 578, 581 (1968). See also Note, 111 U.Pa.L. Rev. 1154, 1170 (1963).

[49]In United States v. Remington, 208 F.2d 567 (2d Cir.1953), Hand, J., dissenting, noted that "in those not very numerous instances in which courts have considered the admission of incompetent evidence before a grand jury, they have held pretty generally * * * that the indictment will stand, provided that the jury had before it

other adequate competent evidence to support the charge."

[50]People v. Leary, 305 N.Y. 793, 113 N.E.2d 303 (1953).

[51]United States v. Laughlin, 226 F.Supp. 112 (D.D.C.1964).

[Section 1.6(d)]

[52]Giordenello v. United States, 357 U.S. 480, 78 S.Ct. 1245, 2 L.Ed.2d 1503 (1958).

dealt with explicitly in the federal rules.[53] In the absence of a statute or rule of court providing otherwise, to be found in a few states, the states permit suppression motions to be made only at the trial court level.[54]

The question of whether, as a matter of sound Fourth Amendment policy, illegally seized evidence should be received at a preliminary hearing, is in many respects similar to the question of whether such evidence should be subject to consideration by the grand jury, although this is not to say that the same conclusion must inevitably be reached on both issues. Here again it may be asked, on one level, whether exclusion of unconstitutionally obtained evidence would be consistent with the purpose of the proceeding. This depends upon whether the purpose of the probable cause determination at the preliminary is "to insure that persons who are clearly innocent do not have to undergo the burdens of a long, public trial" or "to insure that these same burdens will not be imposed upon a defendant when the likelihood of his conviction is small"?[55] The latter is certainly the better view, and it comports with the traditional statement of the reasons for preliminary examination.[56] It is thus fair to conclude, then, that one major objective[57] of the preliminary hearing would be served by not permitting bindover upon evidence that may not be received against the defendant at trial.

Considering the issue in terms of the purposes of the exclusionary rule, it seems doubtful whether any significant added deter-

---

[53]Fed.R.Crim.P. 5.1(e) provides that at the preliminary hearing the defendant "may not object to evidence on the ground that it was unlawfully acquired."

[54]State v. Earley, 192 Kan. 167, 386 P.2d 189 (1963). For discussion of other cases, see Comment, 15 Kan.L. Rev. 374, 384–86 (1967); Notes, 66 J.Crim.L. & Crimin. 135 (1975); 1963 Wash.U.L.Q. 102, 116–18.

Compare State v. Wilson, 55 Haw. 314, 519 P.2d 228 (1974), holding that while the district court (the preliminary hearing court) could not entertain a motion to suppress in a felony case because of the statutory requirement that a motion to suppress be made before "the court having jurisdiction to try the offense," it was nonetheless required that the district court, in conducting preliminary hearings, "adhere to the general rules of evidence which include objections to the admissibility of unconstitutionally seized evidence." Accord: State v. Mitchell, 42 Ohio St.2d 447, 329 N.E.2d 682 (1975).

[55]Note, 1963 Wash.U.L.Q. 102, 120.

[56]"The object or purpose of the preliminary investigation is to prevent hasty, malicious, improvident, and oppressive prosecutions, to protect the person charged from open and public accusations of crime, to avoid both for the defendant and the public the expense of a public trial, and to save the defendant from the humiliation and anxiety involved in public prosecution, and to discover whether or not there are substantial grounds upon which a prosecution may be based." Thies v. State, 178 Wis. 98, 189 N.W. 539 (1922).

[57]Incidental functions of the preliminary hearing are discovery and perpetuation of testimony and, in some jurisdictions, review of the prior bail decision. See Coleman v. Alabama, 399 U.S. 1, 90 S.Ct. 1999, 26 L.Ed.2d 387 (1970).

rence would be achieved by earlier application of the exclusionary rule, although it has been argued that under present law "in difficult cases the police might actually feel encouraged to violate constitutional rights in order to prevent the escape of the accused and gain additional time for investigation."[58] As for the judiciary avoiding what the *Calandra* dissenters called "the taint of partnership in official lawlessness," quite clearly the taint is stronger here than when illegally seized evidence is received by a grand jury. Finally, with respect to the goal of ensuring the public that the government will not profit from its lawless behavior, it may of course be argued that there is a "profit" of sorts in obtaining a probable cause finding at a preliminary hearing. However, some would doubtless respond that this profit is insignificant in light of the fact that in most jurisdictions the prosecutor may avoid the necessity of such a finding by the magistrate by the simple device of obtaining a grand jury indictment.[59]

Under the *Calandra* approach, these "potential benefits" must be weighed against the "potential damage" that might result from application of the exclusionary rule at the preliminary hearing. One legitimate matter of concern is that "increasing the procedural and evidentiary requirements applicable to the preliminary examination" will "add to the administrative pressure to avoid the preliminary examination" by proceeding directly to grand jury indictment.[60] Such avoidance, it has been noted, could have adverse consequences for the defendant by depriving him of "an opportunity for some early discovery of the nature of the case against him" and "the occasion to create and preserve evidence for later use."[61] But, this problem could be dealt with by doing away with the rule that a preliminary hearing may be mooted by a prior indictment, a change some commentators believe has merit for other reasons.[62]

Another practical objection is that "allowing objections to evidence on the ground that evidence has been illegally obtained

---

[58]Comment, 15 Kan.L.Rev. 374, 385–86 (1967).

[59]United States v. Gilchrist, 347 F.2d 715 (2d Cir.1965); Burke v. Superior Court, 3 Ariz.App. 576, 416 P.2d 997 (1966).

[60]Fed.R.Crim.P. 5.1, Advisory Committee Note (1972).

[61]State v. Wilson, 55 Haw. 314, 519 P.2d 228 (1974) (dissent).

[62]See Blue v. United States, 342 F.2d 894 (D.C.Cir.1964), questioning whether the defendant's right to a preliminary hearing "should depend upon the outcome of a race between counsel * * * and the grand jury acting upon the charge." Model Code of Pre-Arraignment Procedure § 330.1 (1975), rejects the prevailing rule, with this explanation in the commentary: "Because of the importance the Code puts on the screening function of the preliminary hearing and because of the value of the preliminary hearing as a discovery method in a system that does not provide for depositions in criminal cases * * * the grand jury indictment is not an adequate or fair substitute for a preliminary hearing."

would require two determinations of admissibility,"[63] one by the magistrate for purposes of the preliminary hearing and one by the trial judge for purposes of the trial. That is the pattern in jurisdictions permitting objections to evidence on Fourth Amendment grounds at the preliminary hearing.[64] It has been suggested, however, that this problem could be obviated by generally providing that "a defendant who has had a hearing on such a motion [at the preliminary hearing] is not entitled to a later hearing for suppression of the same evidence on the same basis."[65] The feasibility of this solution may depend in large part upon whether it is felt that committing magistrates are equipped to make rulings which would ordinarily be final in their effect upon what may often be complex constitutional issues.[66] Judgments on that point are bound to vary from jurisdiction to jurisdiction, depending upon the legal qualifications for the office of magistrate and the quality of the persons holding that office.

On occasion the question is raised as to whether illegally obtained evidence is admissible in an extradition hearing in the asylum jurisdiction. Because probable cause is ordinarily taken to be conclusively established by the documents received from the jurisdiction seeking extradition,[67] this question is likely to arise only when the evidence challenged, such as fingerprints or witness identification, is claimed to be the fruit of an illegal arrest and is utilized to establish that the defendant is the person sought. In both international[68] and interstate[69] rendition proceedings, courts have refused to utilize the exclusionary rule in such circumstances. By way of explanation, it is said that such "proceedings are summary in nature and the accused is not entitled to all of the procedural protections of a criminal trial,"[70] and that the deterrent effect of suppressing such evidence in the criminal case "would not be enhanced to any significant degree

---

[63]Fed.R.Crim.P. 5.1, Advisory Committee Note (1972). See also State v. Wilson, 55 Haw. 314, 519 P.2d 228 (1974) (dissent).

[64]But see People v. Taylor, 50 Ill.2d 136, 277 N.E.2d 878 (1971), holding that a ruling by the preliminary hearing judge against the prosecution was appealable and thus binding upon the trial court if the prosecution failed to appeal. See further discussion in § 11.2(f).

[65]Model Code of Pre-Arraignment Procedure § 330.3 (1975), also recognizing exceptions where "the trial court determines that there are substantial grounds for such a motion of which the defendant was not aware at the time of the prior hearing or that for some other reason it would be manifestly unfair to deny such a later motion."

[66]Weinberg & Weinberg, The Congressional Invitation to Avoid the Preliminary Hearing: An Analysis of Section 303 of the Federal Magistrates Act of 1968, 67 Mich.L.Rev. 1361, 1399 (1969).

[67]See § 1.9(c).

[68]Simmons v. Braun, 627 F.2d 635 (2d Cir.1980).

[69]Holland v. Hargar, 274 Ind. 156, 409 N.E.2d 604 (1980).

[70]Holland v. Hargar, 274 Ind. 156, 409 N.E.2d 604 (1980).

by also excluding that evidence from extradition proceedings."[71]

§ 1.6(e) Bail hearing

Generally, it may be said that information offered at a pretrial hearing concerning the terms and conditions of defendant's release need not conform to the rules of evidence.[72] In general, this is a salutary rule; it is desirable that the bail-setting magistrate have all available information concerning such matters as the defendant's residential, employment, and family ties without regard to whether that information comes to him via hearsay.

But, assume the prosecution wishes to put before the magistrate, to support an argument for high bail, information concerning the nature and circumstances of the offense charged or the weight of the evidence against the defendant.[73] Or, assume that in a capital case the prosecution wishes to prove that "the proof is evident, or the presumption great," which under the constitutions of most states would justify denial of bail.[74] In either instance, should the defendant be entitled to object to the receipt of evidence on the ground that it was obtained in violation of his Fourth Amendment rights? This question has very seldom reached the appellate courts. In *Steigler v. Superior Court*,[75] concerning a hearing at which defendant was denied bail pending his trial on a capital offense, the court appeared to answer in the affirmative. Although eschewing bail hearing procedures that would give "even the appearance of a determination of ultimate guilt or innocence," the court upheld the denial of bail notwithstanding the fact the court below considered "other evidence subsequently found to be inadmissible," but only because "there was sufficient admissible evidence" supporting the conclusion of that court.

The considerations bearing upon the issue under discussion here are in many respects similar to those set out above with respect to application of the exclusionary rule at the preliminary hearing. Once again, it may be said that exclusion of evidence not

---

[71]Simmons v. Braun, 627 F.2d 635 (2d Cir.1980). But in that case the arrest was not made with extradition in mind, so the court could say that it was "totally unrealistic to think that agents will unlawfully arrest people on the off chance that they may be wanted by [another] government." If the arrest *was* made with extradition in mind, suppression *would* be justified for purposes of deterrence.

[Section 1.6(e)]

[72]Thus, the federal Bail Reform Act of 1984 provides: "The rules concerning admissibility of evidence in criminal trials do not apply to the pre-

sentation and consideration of information at the [detention] hearing." 18 U.S.C.A. § 3142(f).

[73]Such information is generally deemed relevant on the question of bail. See 18 U.S.C.A. § 3142(g); ABA Standards for Criminal Justice § 10-5.4(e) (2d ed. rev. 1985).

[74]Such constitutional provisions are to be found in about 40 states, and under the better view the burden of proof is on the prosecution to make the necessary showing. State v. Engel, 99 N.J. 453, 493 A.2d 1217 (1985).

[75]Steigler v. Superior Court, 252 A.2d 300 (Del.1969).

usable at trial is consistent with the purposes of the hearing; whether evidence of the offense is offered as relevant on the amount of bail to be required[76] or on the question of whether release on bail is to be denied,[77] the purpose is not to determine the probability of guilt but rather the likelihood of conviction. As for the goals of the exclusionary rule, it may once again be said that little by way of added deterrence would be gained, but that the other two goals discussed earlier would be advanced by excluding illegally obtained evidence at bail hearings. And again, these benefits must be weighed against the "cost" of unduly complicating pretrial proceedings[78] and of permitting multiple suppression motions with respect to the same evidence. Because nonapplication of the exclusionary rule at bail hearings permits the government to "profit from its lawless behavior"[79] by making highly probable or certain incarceration of the defendant pending trial and the debilitating effects of that incarceration,[80] a "profit" not unlike that which would be gained if the exclusionary rule did not apply at trial, it would seem that the arguments in favor of applying the exclusionary rule at the bail hearing are more persuasive than as to the other proceedings discussed earlier in this section.

§ 1.6(f) Sentencing

Turning to the post-trial setting, it may be asked whether the Fourth Amendment exclusionary rule should be applicable at the time of sentencing. That is, should the defendant be entitled to have excluded from consideration at the time of sentencing illegally seized evidence that was suppressed at trial or would have been suppressed had it been offered at the trial? Utilizing the approach employed by the Supreme Court in *United States v.*

---

[76]ABA Standards for Criminal Justice § 10-5.4(e) (2d ed. rev.1985), provides that it is appropriate to inquire into "the nature of the current charge, the apparent probability of conviction, and the likely sentence."

[77]Thus, it is noted in State v. Konigsberg, 33 N.J. 367, 164 A.2d 740 (1960), that "guilt or innocence is not the issue" and that bail should only "be denied when the circumstances disclosed indicate a fair likelihood that the defendant is in danger of a jury verdict of first degree murder. For only in instances where such likelihood exists is his life in jeopardy and the well recognized urge to abscond present."

[78]In State v. Tucker, 101 N.J.Super. 380, 244 A.2d 353 (1968), where defendant objected that the court below had denied bail by taking into account a statement obtained

from him in violation of *Miranda,* the court sought to accommodate the conflicting concerns in this way: "Considering the preliminary nature of this application for bail, the liberal use of evidence in hearings in connection therewith and the policy against fragmenting the trial by a pretrial hearing on the admissibility of the statement, all the state need do is demonstrate by prima facie proof that the requirements of *Miranda,* were met before the defendant signed the statement."

[79]United States v. Calandra, 414 U.S. 338, 94 S.Ct. 613, 38 L.Ed.2d 561 (1974).

[80]See D. Freed & P. Wald, Bail in the United States: 1964 ch. 4 (1964); Report of the Attorney General's Committee on Poverty and the Administration of Criminal Justice 68–72 (1963).

Calandra,[81] this question may be more precisely stated in terms of whether "the potential benefits of the rule as applied in this context" outweigh the "potential injury."

A pre-*Calandra* case following this approach is *United States v. Schipani.*[82] As in *Calandra,* the *Schipani* court commenced with the assumption that the purpose of the exclusionary rule is deterrence, and, having done so, then concluded that "no appreciable increment in deterrence would result from applying a second exclusion at sentencing after the rule has been applied at the trial itself." On the "potential injury" side of the ledger, the court stressed "the necessity for unfettered access to information by the sentencing judge."[83] As another court more recently put it: "The desirability of reaching an appropriate decision in sentencing outweighs what little deterrent effect may be present."[84]

In assessing the *Schipani* approach, it is useful to begin by considering more carefully the deterrence objective. The *Schipani* court was not as absolute on the question of deterrence as the above quotation would suggest, for it was recognized that in "some special situation," such as that present in the earlier case of *Verdugo v. United States,*[85] the deterrence objective would point toward exclusion. In *Verdugo,* the search producing the evidence considered at the time of sentencing was conducted outside the course of the regular criminal investigation and was undertaken not to obtain evidence to support an indictment and conviction, but to recover contraband and thus enhance the possibility of a heavier sentence after the basic investigation had been completed. *Schipani* acknowledges that on those facts the *Verdugo* court properly held that the seized evidence could not be considered at the time of sentencing, for were it otherwise "law

---

[Section 1.6(f)]

[81]United States v. Calandra, 414 U.S. 338, 94 S.Ct. 613, 38 L.Ed.2d 561 (1974).

[82]United States v. Schipani, 315 F.Supp. 253 (E.D.N.Y.1970), aff'd, 435 F.2d 26 (2d Cir.1970), noted in 71 Colum.L.Rev. 1102 (1971); 66 Nw.U.L. Rev. 698 (1971); 40 U.Cin.L.Rev. 172 (1971); 57 Va.L.Rev. 1255, 1269 (1971).

[83]Consider also that in the Organized Crime Control Act of 1970, 18 U.S.C.A. § 3577, Congress provided: "No limitation shall be placed on the information concerning the background, character, and conduct of a person convicted of an offense which a court of the United States may receive and consider for the purpose of imposing an appropriate sentence." For a discussion of the legislative history of this provision, now 18 U.S.C.A. § 3661, which shows the intention was to bar use of the exclusionary rule at sentencing, see Note, 57 Va.L.Rev. 1255, 1256 n. 5, 1277 n. 129 (1971), also questioning the constitutionality of the provision.

Certain legislation may be deemed to have decided the issue the other way. See, e.g., People v. Belleci, 24 Cal.3d 879, 157 Cal.Rptr. 503, 598 P.2d 473 (1979) (statute making suppressed evidence inadmissible "at any trial or other hearing" covers sentencing).

[84]United States v. Torres, 926 F.2d 321 (3d Cir.1991).

[85]Verdugo v. United States, 402 F.2d 599 (9th Cir.1968), distinguished in United States v. Vandemark, 522 F.2d 1019 (9th Cir.1975).

enforcement officials would have little to lose, but much to gain, in violating the Fourth Amendment." But *Verdugo* was deemed not controlling in *Schipani* because in the latter case the evidence excluded at trial but used at the time of sentencing was not gathered "for any purpose other than the indictment and conviction of the defendant."

It is fair to say, then, that *Calandra* does not bring into question the *Verdugo* position that where "the use of illegally seized evidence at sentencing would provide a substantial incentive for unconstitutional searches and seizures, that evidence should be disregarded by the sentencing judge."[86] (Unfortunately, it might be argued that *Pennsylvania Board of Probation and Parole v.*

[86]The point is frequently stressed in the cases. See, e.g., United States v. Ryan, 236 F.3d 1268 (10th Cir.2001) (use of illegally seized evidence at sentencing not error "unless there is evidence that the officer's actions in violating Ryan's rights were done with the intent to secure an increased sentence"); United States v. Brimah, 214 F.3d 854 (7th Cir.2000) (leaving open question of whether exclusionary rule applies when police intentionally act illegally in order to enhance defendant's sentence); United States v. Tejada, 956 F.2d 1256 (2d Cir.1992) ("Absent a showing that officers obtained evidence expressly to enhance a sentence, a district judge may not refuse to consider relevant evidence at sentencing, even if that evidence has been seized in violation of the Fourth Amendment"); United States v. McCrory, 930 F.2d 63 (D.C.Cir.1991) (suppression not required here, as "no showing of a violation of the Fourth Amendment purposefully designed to obtain evidence to increase a defendant's base offense level at sentencing"); United States v. Torres, 926 F.2d 321 (3d Cir.1991) (stressing *Verdugo* "issue is not before the Court"); United States v. Butler, 680 F.2d 1055 (5th Cir.1982) (what is needed is a "case-by-case weighing of the potential deterrent effect on police misconduct"); Elson v. State, 659 P.2d 1195 (Alaska 1983) ("where the State is able to prove (1) that the illegal evidence is reliable, (2) that the police did not obtain the evidence as a result of gross or shocking misconduct, and (3) that the evidence was not obtained for purposes of influencing the sentencing court, the illegally seized evidence may be considered by the sentencing court in fashioning a defendant's sentence"); State v. Swartz, 278 N.W.2d 22 (Iowa 1979) (exclusion not required "absent some showing that the evidence in question was gathered in violation of the defendant's constitutional rights and for the express purpose of influencing the sentencing court"); Pellegrini v. State, 104 Nev. 625, 764 P.2d 484 (1988) (stressing search occurred in the investigation of "a completely different crime, committed nearly one year before Pellegrini's penalty hearing," and that the searchers "had no idea that the information they gained would become useful in the murder trial"); State v. Banks, 157 N.J.Super. 442, 384 A.2d 1164 (1978) (holding the exclusionary rule not applicable at sentencing on the facts there presented, but recognizing two exceptions: "(1) where police are assembling a dossier to be offered to a sentencing judge should the subject ever be convicted of an offense, and (2) where police have accumulated sufficient evidence to convict and then seize additional evidence unlawfully solely to affect the sentence"); State v. Campbell, 43 Or.App. 979, 607 P.2d 745 (1979) (admitting the evidence only after stressing the evidence was not seized to enhance defendant's sentence); State v. Habbena, 372 N.W.2d 450 (S.D.1985) (evidence need not be suppressed unless it gathered for express purpose of influencing the sentencing judge, which not so here).

Scott,[87] discussed herein,[88] does bring *Verdugo* into question, as a majority of the Court there was not moved to apply the exclusionary rule at a parole revocation hearing despite a showing of a similar substantial incentive.) What is less clear is whether *Verdugo* has identified the only situation in which that "substantial incentive" is present, namely where the search in question occurred after the basic investigation was completed.[89] Apart from the difficulty in determining precisely when that point is reached, there is reason to believe the incentive may exist in other circumstances. As one commentator has observed:

> If courts limit the exclusionary rule to only these circumstances it would be easy for police officers to institute an illegal search during the course of the basic investigation and then lodge a single charge against the defendant. * * * Thus, through the simple expedient of limiting the indictment to a single count the police would leave themselves free to introduce the evidence at the subsequent sentencing.[90]

This comment is especially compelling in the context of a guidelines sentencing system such as now exists at the federal level. Although illegally seized evidence is accepted to determine

---

[87]Pennsylvania Bd. of Probation and Parole v. Scott, 524 U.S. 357, 118 S.Ct. 2014, 141 L.Ed.2d 344 (1998).

[88]See § 1.6(g).

[89]Actually, *Verdugo* has sometimes been interpreted as not inevitably extending to all such searches. See United States v. Kim, 25 F.3d 1426 (9th Cir.1994) (while, "as in *Verdugo*, before embarking on a warrantless quest for additional contraband, the agents in the instant case already had enough evidence to support the single charge of which the defendant was later convicted," exclusionary rule still not applicable "because the marginal deterrent value of applying the exclusionary rule to sentencing in these circumstances would be slight," as the later seizure of defendant and search for additional contraband was prompted by (i) "a fleeting opportunity to interdict a potentially substantial shipment of narcotics," and (ii) a desire to seize a defendant they reasonably believed was trying to evade capture). Consider also United States v. Ryan, 236 F.3d 1268 (10th Cir.2001), stressing *both* that there "was no case pending" and no "situation where the officers egregiously violated [defendant's] rights," distinguishing United States v. Gilmer, 811 F.Supp.

578 (D.Colo.1993), suppressing the evidence where the police, who knew defendant had already been indicted, ransacked his house.

[90]Note, 66 Nw.U.L.Rev. 698, 711–12 (1971). Consider also Note, 57 Va.L.Rev. 1255, 1275–76 (1971):

> One problem with the *Schipani* rationale is that it views the case in retrospect, resorting only to considerations of *time* and *motive* in determining whether the deterrence policy of the rule will be served. But the fact that officers searched Verdugo's home after they had bought narcotics from him merely clarified the motive of the search. As to the motive itself, the *Schipani* court quoted approvingly a footnote in *Verdugo* which said that exclusion of evidence obtained purely for conviction purposes, but not necessary for the conviction in question, would have little deterrent effect. The *Schipani* court, however, misread the footnote, because the illegally seized evidence discussed there was evidence "of the same offense" as that for which the defendant was tried and convicted. On the other hand, the evidence considered in *Schipani,* while possibly disclosing certain undeclared income, was in fact used to convince the sentencing judge that defendant was a "professional criminal," not to establish the nature of the defendant's tax evasion.

the sentence under the guidelines,[91] it is open to question whether this is necessarily a proper result, as the balancing of the beneficial (i.e., deterrent) and detrimental effects of exclusion is not the same in that context. Consider *United States v. McCrory*,[92] where an undercover officer bought a small quantity of cocaine from defendant, shortly after which a team of officers made an illegal entry and search of the apartment where the sale had occurred and recovered therefrom weapons and about a kilo and a half of cocaine. If the defendant could have been tried and convicted on the additional drug-trafficking and weapons offenses that the illegally seized evidence established, he would have received a sentence under the guidelines ranging from 248 to 295 months. Such prosecution, of course, was barred because that evidence was inadmissible to prove guilt, so the defendant was charged only with the drug distribution crime supported by the evidence lawfully acquired by the undercover agent. That offense, unadorned, carried a sentence of 27 to 33 months under the guidelines, but taking into account the weapons and additional drugs it was possible to raise the base offense level such as to reach a sentencing range of 235–293 months! The judge sentenced defendant to 235 months. Under such a sentencing scheme, as one member of the *McCrory* court aptly noted, an incentive to make illegal searches exists whenever "the prosecution has more than enough evidence to convict the defendant on a lesser charge *before* they conduct the illegal search," even if that search is not (as in *Verdugo*) outside the course of the regular criminal investigation.[93] To follow the *Schipani* rule in such circumstances, that judge noted sadly, involves "taking a big bite out of the

---

[91]United States v. Ryan, 236 F.3d 1268 (10th Cir.2001); United States v. Brimah, 214 F.3d 854 (7th Cir.2000); United States v. Tauil-Hernandez, 88 F.3d 576 (8th Cir.1996); United States v. Raposa, 84 F.3d 502 (1st Cir.1996); United States v. Montoya-Ortiz, 7 F.3d 1171 (5th Cir.1993); United States v. Jenkins, 4 F.3d 1338 (6th Cir.1993); United States v. Lynch, 934 F.2d 1226 (11th Cir.1991); United States v. Kim, 25 F.3d 1426 (9th Cir.1994); United States v. Tejada, 956 F.2d 1256 (2d Cir.1992) (*Schipani* reaffirmed as to sentencing under new federal sentencing guidelines despite court's acknowledgment: "Because the Guidelines remove a great deal of judicial discretion and the consideration of illegally seized evidence at sentencing is likely to result in increased penalties, the consideration of such evidence at sentencing now takes on greater significance"); United States v.

McCrory, 930 F.2d 63 (D.C.Cir.1991); United States v. Torres, 926 F.2d 321 (3d Cir.1991). See Bader & Douglas, Where to Draw the Guidelines: Factoring the Fruits of Illegal Searches into Sentencing Guidelines Calculations, 7 Touro L.Rev. 1 (1990); Comment, 59 U.Chi.L.Rev. 1209 (1992); Note, 34 Wm. & Mary L.Rev. 241 (1992).

[92]United States v. McCrory, 930 F.2d 63 (D.C.Cir.1991).

[93]This concurring opinion in *McCrory* continues: "If the police and prosecution know beforehand that they can get a conviction on a relatively minor offense which has a broad statutory sentencing range and that they can guarantee a sentence near the maximum by seizing other evidence illegally and introducing it at sentencing, there is nothing to deter them from seizing the evidence immediately without obtaining a warrant, especially when a conviction on a

exclusionary rule."[94]

Especially noteworthy in this connection is *United States v. Nichols,*[95] where the court concluded "that the exclusionary rule bars a sentencing court's reliance on evidence illegally seized during the investigation or arrest of a defendant for the crime of conviction[96] in determining the defendant's sentence under the sentencing guidelines." In reaching this conclusion, the court emphasized that "under pre-guidelines practice, * * * there was no guarantee that evidence not relied upon at trial would play a significant role in the district court's determination of a defendant's sentence," so that police "had little incentive to seize evidence illegally." However, the sentencing guidelines "dramatically changed the calculus of costs and benefits underlying the exclusionary rule," as

> officers now have the somewhat perverse incentive to rely more heavily on sentencing than trial to establish facts that may be of overriding importance in determining a defendant's length of imprisonment—for example, the total amount of drugs involved in a criminal scheme. As a result, sentencing has to a significant extent replaced trial as the principal forum for establishing the existence of certain criminal conduct. It therefore follows that excluding illegally seized evidence from trial but permitting its use at

---

'greater' crime would lead to a similar sentence." For similar criticisms, see United States v. Kim, 25 F.3d 1426 (9th Cir.1994) (Schroeder, J., dissenting); United States v. Jewel, 947 F.2d 224 (7th Cir.1991) (Easterbrook, J., concurring).

[94] Yet that judge did not dissent, observing that the "Supreme Court in recent years has been extremely hesitant to extend the exclusionary rule," and would not likely extend it in this instance given the declaration of Congress in 18 U.S.C.A. § 3661 that "no limitation" shall be placed on the evidence a sentencing judge may consider. See also United States v. Tejada, 956 F.2d 1256 (2d Cir.1992), relying upon that statute and also Guideline § 6A1.3(a) ("the court may consider relevant information without regard to its admissibility").

[95] United States v. Nichols, 979 F.2d 402 (6th Cir.1992).

[96] The court decided the present case was different because the illegally obtained evidence "involved conduct unrelated to that for which Nichols was convicted in this case," that is, activity "so remote as to not fall within the sentencing guidelines' relevant conduct provisions. * * * Application of the exclusionary rule to the facts of this case would necessarily require the inference that, absent the rule, police would have an incentive to seize evidence illegally *solely* on the expectation that the evidence might be used in sentencing the defendant for a subsequent crime. Given the prophylactic purpose of the exclusionary rule, as well as the Supreme Court's overly restrictive interpretation of the rule, we find ourselves obliged to conclude that such an inference is simply too frail to support application of the exclusionary rule in this instance. Although we are troubled that the result we reach today may give insufficient weight to the valuable rights enshrined in the Fourth Amendment, we nevertheless feel compelled to hold that, where evidence is illegally seized in relation to conduct that does not fall within the relevant conduct provisions of the sentencing guidelines, and the district court does not otherwise rely on the evidence in determining the defendant's sentence, the court may consider such evidence in determining where to sentence the defendant within the recommended guideline range."

sentencing will result in a corresponding decrease in the deterrent effect of the exclusionary rule on unconstitutional law-enforcement practices.

Broader use of the exclusionary rule at sentencing is also supported by other recognized bases for the rule. If evidence obtained in violation of the defendant's Fourth Amendment rights is accepted by the sentencing judge and used by him to enhance the defendant's sentence, it is unquestionably true that the government has profited from its lawless behavior and that the judge bears the taint of partnership in official lawlessness.[97]

Turning to the "potential injury" side of the ledger, as to which *Schipani* emphasizes the desirability of the sentencing judge having access to all relevant information, this is to be sure an important consideration. As the Supreme Court stressed in *Williams v. New York*,[98] holding there was no right of confrontation and cross-examination at sentencing:

> Highly relevant—if not essential—to [the sentencing judge's] selection of an appropriate sentence is the possession of the fullest information possible concerning the defendant's life and characteristics. And modern concepts individualizing punishment have made it all the more necessary that a sentencing judge not be denied an opportunity to obtain pertinent information by a requirement of rigid adherence to restrictive rules of evidence properly applicable to the trial.

But the *Williams* language is not as persuasive in this context as might first appear. For one thing, as stressed in *Verdugo*, "the use of illegally seized evidence at sentencing cannot always be justified by this simple generality," for "whenever it is held that the deterrent value of the exclusionary rule justifies the release of a guilty man, courts necessarily also surrender the opportunity of imposing sentence upon him," and "the loss of this opportunity is not regarded as too great a price for insuring observance of Fourth Amendment restraints by law enforcement officers." Secondly, it is not correct to say that the purpose of the sentencing hearing is to obtain all relevant information about the defendant at whatever cost. In the longer view, the purpose of the hearing is to provide for a disposition most likely to accomplish the rehabilitative and other goals of the criminal justice process. And thus the Supreme Court's "requirement of fair play"[99] at sentencing is particularly important, for a defendant who perceives that he was not treated fairly will be resistant to correctional treatment.[100] A defendant who receives an enhanced sentence as a consequence of the fact that the police illegally

---

[97]See the concurring opinion of Browning, J., in Verdugo v. United States, 402 F.2d 599 (9th Cir.1968).

[98]Williams v. New York, 337 U.S. 241, 69 S.Ct. 1079, 93 L.Ed. 1337 (1949).

[99]Townsend v. Burke, 334 U.S. 736, 68 S.Ct. 1252, 92 L.Ed. 1690 (1948). See also Mempa v. Rhay, 389 U.S. 128, 88 S.Ct. 254, 19 L.Ed.2d 336 (1967).

[100]3 ABA Standards for Criminal

ransacked his home or tapped his telephone is hardly a prime candidate for rehabilitation.[101]

Finally, note must be taken of certain "practical considerations" set out in *Schipani*. One is that it "would be almost impossible for a district judge, who has screened proffered evidence on the motion to suppress, to banish it entirely from his mind at sentencing." But this argument has not been deemed persuasive at the guilt-determining stage, for the judicial system has traditionally reposed "confidence in a trial judge's ability to rule on questions of admissibility of evidence and to then assume the role of trier of fact without having carried over to his factual deliberations a prejudice on the matters contained in the evidence which he may have excluded."[102] The analogy may be thought imperfect because the sentencing process involves the judge's discretion to a greater degree, which accounts for the complaint in *Schipani* that a "seriously enforced requirement that the exclusionary rule be applied in sentencing would require the judge to explain the basis of his decision." But, totally apart from the exclusionary rule issue, that would appear to be a desirable reform.[103]

§ 1.6(g) Revocation of conditional release

Courts have held that the exclusionary rule need not be applied in proceedings to revoke a suspended sentence,[104] probation,[105] or parole,[106] or supervised release.[107] Although many of the

---

Justice § 18-6.4, commentary (2d ed.1980); 4 ABA Standards for Criminal Justice § 20-1.2, commentary (2d ed.1980); President's Comm'n on Law Enforcement and Administration of Justice, Task Force Report: The Courts 23 (1967).

[101]Similar considerations are relevant on the question of whether illegally obtained evidence may be considered by the prosecutor in determining whether the defendant is ineligible for a statutory diversion program. See People v. Dyas, 100 Cal.App.3d 464, 161 Cal.Rptr. 39 (1979), concluding that as a matter of state law evidence previously suppressed was improperly considered in denying diversion.

[102]State v. Hutchinson, 260 Md. 227, 271 A.2d 641 (1970). See also State v. Cleveland, 50 Wis.2d 666, 184 N.W.2d 899 (1971).

[103]ABA Standards for Criminal Justice § 18-5.19(b) (3d ed.1994);

NCCD Model Sentencing Act § 10 and commentary thereto at 29; S. Rubin, Law of Criminal Correction 173 to 74 (2d ed.1973).

[Section 1.6(g)]

[104]Sherman v. State, 2009 Ark. 275, 308 S.W.3d 614 (2009) ("unless the defendant demonstrates that the officers conducting the search acted in bad faith," not the case here, as no evidence officers knew defendant "was subject to a term of suspended imposition of sentence" or "conducted the search for the purpose of harassment"); Stone v. Shea, 113 N.H. 174, 304 A.2d 647 (1973).

[105]United States v. Bazzano, 712 F.2d 826 (3d Cir.1983); United States v. Frederickson, 581 F.2d 711 (8th Cir. 1978); United States v. Wiygul, 578 F.2d 577 (5th Cir.1978); United States v. Vandemark, 522 F.2d 1019 (9th Cir. 1975); United States v. Farmer, 512 F.2d 160 (6th Cir.1975); Ex parte Caffie, 516 So.2d 831 (Ala.1987); State

decisions predate *United States v. Calandra*,[108] the typical analysis is not unlike that used in that decision. In weighing the benefits of exclusion in this setting against the costs, the only purpose underlying the exclusionary rule given serious attention

---

v. Sears, 553 P.2d 907 (Alaska 1976); State v. Alfaro, 127 Ariz. 578, 623 P.2d 8 (1980); People v. Wilkerson, 189 Colo. 448, 541 P.2d 896 (1975); Payne v. Robinson, 207 Conn. 565, 541 A.2d 504 (1988); State v. Thackston, 289 Ga. 412, 716 S.E.2d 517 (2011); People v. Dowery, 62 Ill.2d 200, 340 N.E.2d 529 (1975); Dulin v. State, 169 Ind.App. 211, 346 N.E.2d 746 (1976); Kain v. State, 378 N.W.2d 900 (Iowa 1985); State v. Davis, 375 So.2d 69 (La.1979); State v. Foisy, 384 A.2d 42 (Me.1978); Chase v. State, 309 Md. 224, 522 A.2d 1348 (1987); Commonwealth v. Olsen, 405 Mass. 491, 541 N.E.2d 1003 (1989); State v. Thorsness, 165 Mont. 321, 528 P.2d 692 (1974); State v. Field, 132 N.H. 760, 571 A.2d 1276 (1990); State v. Spratt, 120 R.I. 192, 386 A.2d 1094 (1978); Anderson v. Commonwealth, 251 Va. 437, 470 S.E.2d 862 (1996); State v. Kuhn, 7 Wash.App. 190, 499 P.2d 49 (1972); Panesenko v. State, 706 P.2d 273 (Wyo.1985). See also cases collected in Annots., 30 A.L.R.Fed. 824 (1976) (federal); 77 A.L.R.3d 636 (1977) (state).

Contra: United States v. Workman, 585 F.2d 1205 (4th Cir. 1978); State v. Dodd, 419 So.2d 333 (Fla.1982) (under state constitution-);State ex rel. Juvenile Dept. v. Rogers, 314 Or. 114, 839 P.2d 127 (1992) (under state constitution); Wilson v. State, 621 S.W.2d 799 (Tex.Crim.App.1981).

Some of the no-exclusion cases, however, intimate a contrary result would be reached if the violation were serious enough. Illustrative are People v. Atencio, 186 Colo. 76, 525 P.2d 461 (1974), stating that "where the unreasonable search or seizure is such as to shock the conscience of the court, the court will not permit such conduct to be the basis of a state-imposed sanction," and Anderson v. Commonwealth, 251 Va. 437, 470 S.E.2d 862 (1996), holding the exclusionary rule inapplicable "in a probation revocation proceeding absent a showing of bad

faith on the part of the police." Logan v. Commonwealth, 276 Va. 533, 666 S.E.2d 346 (2008), held that the bad faith exception of *Anderson* survived *Scott*, discussed in text following, as the latter case had to do with a parolee rather than a probationer and with an administrative rather than a judicial proceeding.

For other discussion of this line of cases, see Crowe, The Exclusionary Rule in Probation Revocation Proceedings, 13 Loy.U.L.J. 373 (1982).

[106]United States ex rel. Sperling v. Fitzpatrick, 426 F.2d 1161 (2d Cir. 1970); In re Martinez, 1 Cal.3d 641, 83 Cal.Rptr. 382, 463 P.2d 734 (1970); State ex rel. Wright v. Ohio Adult Parole Authority, 75 Ohio St.3d 82, 661 N.E.2d 728 (1996).

Contra: People ex rel. Piccarillo v. New York State Bd. of Parole, 48 N.Y.2d 76, 421 N.Y.S.2d 842, 397 N.E.2d 354 (1979).

[107]United States v. Armstrong, 187 F.3d 392 (4th Cir.1999) ("For purposes of the rule established in *Scott* [text at note 111 infra] * * *, parole and supervised release are not just analogous, but virtually indistinguishable," as "the costs and benefits of applying the exclusionary rule to revocation proceedings are almost identical in the parole and supervised release contexts"); United States v. Montez, 952 F.2d 854 (5th Cir.1992) (well-established rule that exclusionary rule not applicable at probation revocation proceedings also applicable to supervised release under 18 U.S.C.A. § 3583(e) (3), as contemplated by that statutory provision that court to proceed pursuant to provisions "applicable to probation revocation").

For other discussion of this line of cases, see Note, 17 Memphis St.U.L. Rev. 555 (1987).

[108]United States v. Calandra, 414 U.S. 338, 94 S.Ct. 613, 38 L.Ed.2d 561 (1974).

is that of deterrence. It is said that "the bungling police officer is not likely to be halted by the thought that his unlawful conduct will prevent the termination"[109] of the conditional release. On the matter of costs, the contention is that "an agency whose delicate duty is to decide when a convicted offender can be safely allowed to return to and remain in society"[110] needs all of the relevant facts.

The Supreme Court did not decide a case specifically falling within this category until 1998, when, in *Pennsylvania Board of Probation and Parole v. Scott*,[111] a 5-4 majority concluded, on the general issue of whether the exclusionary rule should apply at parole revocation hearings, that application of the rule in that context "would provide only minimal deterrence benefits," which "would not outweigh" the costs, namely, that "the exclusionary rule would both hinder the functioning of state parole systems and alter the traditionally flexible, administrative nature of parole revocation proceedings." On the deterrence side of the scales, the Court's most convincing showing of minimal deterrence was as to

> an officer who is unaware that the subject of his search is a parolee.[112] In that situation, the officer will likely be searching for evidence of criminal conduct with an eye toward the introduction of the evidence at a criminal trial. The likelihood that illegally obtained evidence will be excluded from trial provides deterrence against Fourth Amendment violations, and the remote possibility that the subject is a parolee and that the evidence may be admitted at a parole revocation proceeding surely has little, if any, effect on the officer's incentives.

As for the first of the costs stated above, the *Scott* majority emphasized the "overwhelming interest" of the state "in ensuring that a parolee complies with [his parole] requirement and is returned to prison if he fails to do so," and that interference with those interests by evidence exclusion is "compounded by the fact that parolees * * * are more likely to commit future criminal offenses than are average citizens." As for the second of the previously-stated costs, the Court noted that most states "have adopted informal, administrative parole revocation procedures in

---

[109]In re Martinez, 1 Cal.3d 641, 83 Cal.Rptr. 382, 463 P.2d 734 (1970).

[110]In re Martinez, 1 Cal.3d 641, 83 Cal.Rptr. 382, 463 P.2d 734 (1970).

[111]Pennsylvania Bd. of Probation and Parole v. Scott, 524 U.S. 357, 118 S.Ct. 2014, 141 L.Ed.2d 344 (1998), discussed in Binnall, Deterrence is Down and Social Costs Are Up: A Parolee Revisits Pennsylvania Board of Probation and Parole v. Scott, 32 Vt.L.Rev. 199 (2007), and noted in 52 Ark.L.Rev. 639 (1999); 51 Baylor L.Rev.

1115 (1999); 31 Conn.L.Rev. 1179 (1999); 23 Hamline L.Rev. 249 (1999); 89 J.Crim.L. & Criminology 1047 (1999); 31 Loy.U.Chi.L.J. 69 (1999); 10 Seton Hall Const.L.J. 215 (1999); 73 Tem.L.Rev. 451 (2000); 9 Temp.Pol. & Civ.Rts.L.Rev. 189 (1999); 33 U.Rich. L.Rev. 631 (1999).

[112]But, as discussed in the text following, the search in *Scott* was not of that type at all, but instead was a search by parole officers of a parolee's dwelling.

order to accommodate the large number of parole proceedings," and asserted that application of the exclusionary rule "would significantly alter this process" in light of the fact that such proceedings are "not conducted by judges," are not bound by "traditional rules of evidence," and are not "entirely adversarial." (Because this last array of costs is only to a lesser extent present as to conditional release revocation proceedings occurring before a judicial officer, the *Scott* holding cannot be taken to have settled the applicability of the exclusionary rule in such circumstances.[113])

Looking more closely at the matter of deterrence, it is well to note that in line with the *Verdugo* case, discussed above, there can be special circumstances in which failure to apply the exclusionary rule would quite obviously run contrary to the deterrence function. If the search is made by a person who is particularly responsible for the individual on conditional release, such as his probation officer or parole officer, then it is clear that there is a need to deter, for such persons will be primarily interested in the question of whether the individuals under their supervision will have their conditional release revoked rather than whether they will be convicted of a new offense.[114] Similarly, if the search is made by a regular law enforcement officer who is aware of the unique status of the victim of the search, there is again a special need to be concerned about deterrence, for the officer will know "that an independent prosecution and revocation under an old conviction are often interchangeable."[115] It is particularly noteworthy that virtually all of the pre-*Scott* appellate decisions holding the exclusionary rule inapplicable in revocation proceedings have stressed that the search in question was made by an official who was *not* aware of the defendant's unique status. If the person making the search were so aware, then the compelling reasoning of *Verdugo v. United States*[116] would govern, and (as many pre-*Scott* appellate cases recognize[117]) the exclusion-

---

[113]But see United States v. Armstrong, 187 F.3d 392 (4th Cir.1999) ("Although supervised release revocation proceedings, unlike parole revocation proceedings, do take place before a judge, they are characterized by the same 'flexibility' that the Supreme Court found significant in *Scott*," and thus *Scott* applies nonetheless).

[114]White, The Fourth Amendment Rights of Parolees and Probationers, 31 U.Pitt.L.Rev. 167, 201 (1969). See also Comment, 1979 Brigham Young L.Rev. 161.

[115]United States v. Hill, 447 F.2d 817 (7th Cir.1971) (Fairchild, J., dissenting); Sherman v. State, 2009 Ark. 275, 308 S.W.3d 614 (2009) (bad faith exception not applicable here as no evidence officers knew defendant "was subject to a term of suspended imposition of sentence"). See also Comment, 1979 Brigham Young L.Rev. 161.

[116]Verdugo v. United States, 402 F.2d 599 (9th Cir.1968).

[117]United States v. Rea, 678 F.2d 382 (2d Cir.1982) (exclusionary rule applicable where evidence illegally obtained by probation officer, as "a probation officer who seeks to discover and seize evidence for use in a probation revocation hearing is very likely to be deterred from proceeding without a warrant if the officer knows that ev-

ary rule should definitely be applied,[118] at least as to warrantless Fourth Amendment activity.[119] It is to be doubted whether this

---

idence so seized is apt to be excluded from the very proceeding with which he is concerned"); United States v. Vandemark, 522 F.2d 1019 (9th Cir.1975) (stating the evidence is admissible if "the law enforcement officers did not know or have reason to believe that the suspect was on probation"); Ex parte Caffie, 516 So.2d 831 (Ala.1987) ("where illegal acts of the police were directed specifically at a probationer," not so here, then need to exclude for deterrence); State v. Sears, 553 P.2d 907 (Alaska 1976) (cautioning that in "the event the lawless arrest and search or seizure is carried out by enforcement personnel with knowledge or reason to believe the suspect was a probationer, we would then apply the exclusionary rule in the probation revocation proceeding"); State v. Shirley, 117 Ariz. 105, 570 P.2d 1278 (1977) (exclusion where officer knew defendant was a probationer); Payne v. Robinson, 207 Conn. 565, 541 A.2d 504 (1988) (suggesting exclusion would be proper "when a police officer who had conducted the search was aware or had reason to be aware of the suspect's probationary status"); Thompson v. United States, 444 A.2d 972 (D.C.App.1982) (exclusion not required here, but result would be otherwise if "illegal acts of a government agent were directed specifically at a probationer"); People v. Watson, 69 Ill.App.3d 497, 26 Ill.Dec. 19, 387 N.E.2d 849 (1979) (court below acted properly in not holding evidentiary hearing on motion to suppress, but only because probationer's motion did not allege "that the arresting officers were aware of defendant's status at the time of the search"); Kain v. State, 378 N.W.2d 900 (Iowa 1985) (exception to admissibility "believed to exist where the evidence in question was gathered for the express purpose of influencing the revocation of probation"); State v. Turner, 19 Kan.App.2d 535, 873 P.2d 208 (1994) (exclusionary rule applied because searching officer knew victim of search was a probationer); State v. Davis, 375 So.2d 69

(La.1979) (exclusion required if search "was conducted in bad faith and was consciously and purposely directed at a probationer with knowledge of his status as such"); Chase v. State, 309 Md. 224, 522 A.2d 1348 (1987) (probationer should have opportunity "to establish that the officer * * * acted in bad faith," not so here as no indication officer aware defendant on probation); Commonwealth v. Olsen, 405 Mass. 491, 541 N.E.2d 1003 (1989) (exclusionary rule not applicable where, as here, there is no "police officer's knowledge of the probationer's status"); State v. Lombardo, 306 N.C. 594, 295 S.E.2d 399 (1982) (exclusion not required only "so long as the enforcement officer does not know that the defendant is on probation"); Richardson v. State, 841 P.2d 603 (Okl.Crim.App.1992) (exclusion would be necessary "where illegal acts of the police were directed specifically at a probationer"); State v. Nettles, 287 Or. 131, 597 P.2d 1243 (1979) (exclusion required if "the officer is securing the evidence of a crime for the purpose of probation revocation").

[118]Assuming a Fourth Amendment violation, which may depend on whether the search was by a police officer or a probation or parole officer, as the latter officials generally have greater search authority; see § 10.10. That question of what search authority should exist vis-a-vis probationers and parolees ordinarily has nothing to do with the special focus of the present discussion re the offering of evidence at a revocation hearing instead of at a criminal prosecution. But see the unique position discussed in Soca v. State, 673 So.2d 24 (Fla.1996) (where broader search authority of probation supervisors relied upon evidence is admissible in revocation proceedings but not in a separate criminal proceeding).

[119]It was concluded in State v. Jacobs, 229 Conn. 385, 641 A.2d 1351 (1994), that "even if police officers know or have reason to know that the target of their search is on probation,

interest in deterrence is sufficiently served by the lesser step of applying the exclusionary rule where such knowledge existed only if *in addition* harassment is actually shown.[120]

But the Supreme Court's *Scott* decision is to the contrary, at least as to parole revocation proceedings, for there the applicability of the exclusionary rule had been raised because of an apparently illegal[121] search of parolee Scott's residence by parole officers fully aware of Scott's status. And the Court was directly confronted by the distinction drawn in the preceding paragraph, as it had been the basis of the state court decision under review—to its extant per se bar against application of the exclusionary rule in parole revocation hearings,[122] that court had carved out an exception for cases in which the searching officer was aware of the parolee's status.[123] But the *Scott* majority saw

---

the presence of a warrant sufficiently guards against the risk that, unless the exclusionary rule applies, the officers will not be deterred from performing an illegal search." The court added that it need not then decide "whether the exclusionary rule would nonetheless apply if the search were performed pursuant to a warrant that was so patently defective that no reasonable police officer would have requested it and no reasonable judge would have issued it."

[120]But that lesser step was approved in United States v. Montez, 952 F.2d 854 (5th Cir.1992), reasoning "that the value to society of safely reintegrating former prisoners clearly outweighs whatever marginal benefit which might accrue from extending the exclusionary rule to supervised release revocation hearings which do not involve harassment." *Montez* is troubling because (i) Fourth Amendment shortcuts not rising to the level of "harassment" are left undeterred; and (ii) many instances of actual harassment are likely to remain unknown to the courts, despite the *Montez* caution that "where the agents knew that the one to be searched was on supervised release, the court must carefully review the agents' conduct to determine if harassment was involved."

In apparent accord with the *Montez* approach are People v. Ressin, 620 P.2d 717 (Colo.1980) ("If it is demonstrated that law enforcement of-

ficers knowingly engaged in a pretext arrest and exploratory search of the defendant because of his probationary status, * * * suppression of the fruits of that government activity would be both appropriate as a deterrent * * * and necessary in the interest of judicial integrity"); State v. Turner, 257 Kan. 19, 891 P.2d 317 (1995) (exclusion might be required where officer's acts "so egregious that the need for their deterrence outweighs the court's need for information," but "mere knowledge that the subject of an illegal search was a probationer is not enough"); Hughes v. Gwinn, 170 W.Va. 87, 290 S.E.2d 5 (1982) (exclusionary rule not applicable at probation revocation proceedings unless "there is evidence of police harassment").

[121]The state court concluded that the parolee's right against unreasonable searches and seizures was "unaffected" by his signing of a parole agreement giving parole officers permission to conduct warrantless searches, and that the search in question was unreasonable because it was supported only by "mere speculation" rather than a "reasonable suspicion" of a parole violation. Scott v. Pennsylvania Board of Probation and Parole, 548 Pa. 418, 698 A.2d 32 (1997).

[122]Commonwealth v. Kates, 452 Pa. 102, 305 A.2d 701 (1973).

[123]Scott v. Pennsylvania Board of Probation and Parole, 548 Pa. 418, 698 A.2d 32 (1997) (where, as here, "the suspect's parole/probation officer or a

no need for such a distinction, reasoning that even in cases falling within the exception—i.e., search by a police officer who knows the subject of his search is a parolee, or search by a parole officer—the deterrence would be "minimal" and "marginal" and at the expense of "an additional layer of collateral litigation regarding the officer's knowledge of the parolee's status."

There then appears in the *Scott* majority opinion this remarkable passage regarding search by a police officer:

> In any event, any additional deterrence from the Pennsylvania Supreme Court's rule would be minimal. Where the person conducting the search is a police officer, the officer's focus is not upon ensuring compliance with parole conditions or obtaining evidence for introduction at administrative proceedings, but upon obtaining convictions of those who commit crimes. The non-criminal parole proceeding "falls outside the offending officer's zone of primary interest." * * * Thus, even when the officer knows that the subject of his search is a parolee, the officer will be deterred from violating Fourth Amendment rights by the application of the exclusionary rule to criminal trials.

The degree of naiveté reflected in that passage is truly astonishing. That paragraph, as the *Scott* dissenters charitably put it, "rests on erroneous views of the roles of regular police * * * in relation to revocation proceedings," for the truth of the matter is that

> the police have reason for concern with the outcome of a parole revocation proceeding, which is just as foreseeable as the criminal trial and at least as likely to be held. Police officers, especially those employed by the same sovereign that runs the parole system, therefore have every incentive not to jeopardize a recommitment by rendering evidence inadmissible. [Indeed,] the actual likelihood of trial is often far less than the probability of a petition for parole revocation, with the consequence that the revocation hearing will be the only forum in which the evidence will ever be offered. [This is not merely because] parole revocation is the government's consolation prize when, for whatever reason, it cannot obtain a further criminal conviction, though that will sometimes be true. * * * What is at least equally telling is that parole revocation will frequently be pursued instead of prosecution as the course of choice, a fact recognized a quarter of a century ago when we observed in *Morrissey v. Brewer*[124] that a parole revocation proceeding "is often preferred to a new prosecution because of the procedural ease of recommitting the individual on the basis of a lesser showing by the State."[125]

Given those facts, the claim by the *Scott* majority that the pa-

___

police officer aware of the parolee's status engages in the misconduct, * * * there is a need to apply the exclusionary rule to the revocation process since otherwise there is nothing to deter a parole agent from conducting an illegal search or engaging in other illegal activity to obtain evi-

dence").

[124]Morrissey v. Brewer, 408 U.S. 471, 92 S.Ct. 2593, 33 L.Ed.2d 484 (1972).

[125]As the dissenters elaborated: "The reasons for this tendency to skip any new prosecution are obvious. If

role revocation proceeding "falls outside the offending officer's zone of primary interest" is, if anything, even less convincing than the comparable assertion in *United States v. Janis*,[126] from which those words were taken. In *Janis,* the Court reached the dubious conclusion that where a Los Angeles police officer illegally seized $4,940 in cash and gambling records from a bookmaker and then informed the IRS of that fact (just as he had previously notified the IRS whenever he uncovered a gambling operation involving a substantial sum of money), and thereafter worked with an IRS agent to establish that Janis's activities made him liable for $89,026.09 in unpaid taxes, that officer would not have been significantly deterred by the risk of suppression in the civil tax proceeding because it was not in his "zone of primary interest." If anything can top that, it is surely the conclusion in *Scott* that an officer investigating a known parolee would be significantly deterred by the threat of exclusion at a criminal trial but not significantly deterred by the threat of exclusion at a revocation proceeding. That simply is not so, for the reasons the Scott dissenters state so well: "the actual likelihood of trial is often far less than the probability of a petition for parole revocation," meaning that "there will be nothing incremental about the significance of evidence offered in the administrative tribunal, and nothing 'marginal' about the deterrence provided by an exclusionary rule operating there."

As for searches conducted by a parole officer rather than a policeman, the *Scott* case takes the position that again

> the deterrence benefits of the exclusionary rule remain limited. Parole agents, in contrast to police officers, are not "engaged in the often competitive enterprise of ferreting out crime" * * *; instead, their primary concern is whether their parolees should remain free on parole. Thus, their relationship with parolees is more supervisory than adversarial. It is thus "unfair to assume that the parole officer bears hostility against the parolee that destroys his neutrality; realistically the failure of the parolee is in a sense a failure for his supervising officer." * * * Although this relationship does not prevent parole officers from ever violating the Fourth Amendment rights of their parolees, it does mean that the harsh deterrent of exclusion is unwarranted, given such other deterrents as departmental training and discipline and the threat of damages actions. Moreover, although in some instances parole officers may act like police officers and seek to uncover evidence of illegal activity, they

---

the conduct in question is a crime in its own right, the odds of revocation are very high. Since time on the street before revocation is not subtracted from the balance of the sentence to be served on revocation, * * * the balance may well be long enough to render recommitment the practical equivalent of a new sentence for a separate crime. And all of this may be accomplished without shouldering the burden of proof beyond a reasonable doubt; hence the obvious popularity of revocation in place of new prosecution."

[126]United States v. Janis, 428 U.S. 433, 96 S.Ct. 3021, 49 L.Ed.2d 1046 (1976).

(like police officers) are undoubtedly aware that any unconstitutionally seized evidence that could lead to an indictment could be suppressed in a criminal trial.

This line of reasoning is also unconvincing. As for the very last assertion, it is covered by the earlier discussion; once again, the essential point is when parole revocation is the most likely disposition, the risk of evidence suppression should there be a criminal trial is unlikely to act as a sufficient deterrent. As for the purported neutrality of parole officers, that view, as the *Scott* dissenters put it, "suffers * * * from its selectiveness," for the truth of the matter is that parole officers "wear several hats; while they are indeed the parolees' counselors and social workers, they also 'often serve as both prosecutors and law enforcement officials in their relationship with probationers and parolees.' "[127] Moreover, because "state parole agents are considered police officers with respect to the offenders under their jurisdiction,"[128] they can no more than other police be thought to be adequately deterred by the risk of departmental discipline or the threat of damages actions. Indeed, as the dissenters put it, the majority's claim to the contrary "sounds hollow" because it is unaccompanied by any evidence of departmental training directed at ensuring compliance with the Fourth Amendment, the disciplining of parole officers for making illegal searches, or of damages actions being brought by parolees against their parole officers for illegal searches. All this supports the dissenters' conclusion that "if the police need the deterrence of an exclusionary rule to offset the temptations to forget the Fourth Amendment, parole officers need it quite as much."

The essential point, then, as to both the police and the parole officer situations previously discussed, is that absence of an exclusionary rule at the proceedings most likely to occur if a search uncovers incriminating evidence against a parolee, serves to encourage those officials to violate the Fourth Amendment rights of parolees in the interest of what is characterized in *Scott* as the "overwhelming interest" in returning parole violators to prison. This is tantamount to saying that parolees have no Fourth Amendment rights, which is hardly justified in order to avoid what the *Scott* majority sees as the costs of permitting the exclusionary rule to be utilized in revocation hearings. And this is so even without considering, as discussed later herein, that these purported costs are not quite what they are made out to be.

Somewhat more difficult is the question of whether, even excluding from consideration functions of the exclusionary rule

---

[127]Cohen & Gobert, Law of Probation and Parole § 11.04, p. 533 (1983).

[128]Wile, Pennsylvania Law of Probation and Parole § 5.12, at 89 (1993).

other than deterrence,[129] it is correct to say that exclusion in the interest of deterrence is justified only when the searching official was aware of the defendant's status. However, there is considerable force to the argument, accepted by some courts[130] prior to *Scott*, that revocation of conditional release is a sufficiently common consequence of a policeman's activities that a broader use of the exclusionary rule is warranted. As explained by Justice Peters in *In re Martinez*,[131] if the exclusionary rule is deemed inapplicable at parole revocation proceedings, then

> a law enforcement official is encouraged to engage in unconstitutional law enforcement methods in the hope that the evidence thereby secured may be profitably used should it subsequently appear that the victim of such conduct was a parolee.
>
> * * * Investigations of parole violations and new criminal offenses are very often cooperative efforts; police and parole officers frequently work together to reimprison the parolee suspected of criminal activity.* * *
>
> Thus the similarity of the results of conviction and parole revocation and the ongoing participation of general law enforcement officials in parole violation cases support the conclusion that the consequences of potential parole revocation are within the general police officer's train of thought.[132]

Of course, after the *Scott* decision this position cannot prevail as a Fourth Amendment matter, though the Court in that case

---

[129]If, unlike the approach of the *Calandra* majority, the other functions of the exclusionary rule were also taken into account, the case for application of the exclusionary rule would be stronger. These other functions are stressed in the dissents in Stone v. Shea, 113 N.H. 174, 304 A.2d 647 (1973); and In re Martinez, 1 Cal.3d 641, 83 Cal.Rptr. 382, 463 P.2d 734 (1970). Compare the post-*Calandra* case of People v. Dowery, 62 Ill.2d 200, 340 N.E.2d 529 (1975), relying upon *Calandra* for the proposition that only the deterrence function need be taken into account.

[130]United States v. Workman, 585 F.2d 1205 (4th Cir.1978) (in applying exclusionary rule to *all* probation revocation proceedings, court stresses that the Supreme Court "has never exempted from the operation of the exclusionary rule any adjudicative proceeding in which the government offers unconstitutionally seized evidence in direct support of a charge that may subject the victim of a search to imprisonment," and also that it

"frequently happens" that a federal probation revocation proceeding is used as "an alternative to federal trial on the new charges"); People ex rel. Piccarillo v. New York State Bd. of Parole, 48 N.Y.2d 76, 421 N.Y.S.2d 842, 397 N.E.2d 354 (1979); State v. Burkholder, 12 Ohio St.3d 205, 466 N.E.2d 176 (1984) (exclusionary rule applicable to *all* probation revocation proceedings, as police "have ready access to criminal records, and they know of the high probability that any suspect in a new crime may also be a probationer or parolee").

[131]In re Martinez, 1 Cal.3d 641, 83 Cal.Rptr. 382, 463 P.2d 734 (1970) (dissent).

[132]Moreover, it may be argued that the more limited *Verdugo* exception is difficult to administer. Note, 54 Texas L.Rev. 1115, 1125 (1976), questions "whether any exclusionary standard that relies on proof of police motive, inferences of police incentives, or evidence of actual police knowledge at the time of a particular search could provide workable guidance to judges."

might be said to have supplied an additional reason for favoring an across-the-board exclusionary rule for parole revocation hearings over one limited to with-knowledge cases: that the latter "would add an additional layer of collateral litigation regarding the officer's knowledge of the parolee's status."[133]

Turning to the cost side of the ledger, the courts have quite consistently asserted that application of the exclusionary rule to revocation proceedings would be undesirable because of the strong public interest in incarcerating those convicted offenders who have violated the terms their release. Upon closer inspection, this reasoning is unpersuasive. This cost is "equally a result of applying the rule to court proceedings," where "the result will sometimes be that the government will be unable to act against criminals,"[134] but yet the exclusionary rule has been deemed worth that price. In *Scott*, of course, the claim is made that there is an "overwhelming interest" in incarcerating parole violators because parolees "are more likely to commit future criminal offenses than are average citizens." But it will not do to argue in response that society's interests are greater with respect to recidivist crimes; "society's interest in protecting itself from the crimes of ex-convicts and parolees is identical," but "yet ex-convicts are protected by the exclusionary rule."[135]

Sometimes the cost argument is stated somewhat differently. It is said that the "possible unavailability of relevant evidence at the probation revocation proceeding might also result in a hesitancy to initially sentence to probation, which would be manifestly unfair to offenders and to society and might seriously interfere with the rehabilitative purposes of the criminal justice system."[136] In a similar vein, it is contended that probation and parole officers would have to spend too much time gathering proof

---

[133]It is less than clear where the *Scott* dissenters stand on the issue under discussion here. Because they "would affirm the decision of the Supreme Court of Pennsylvania," it was unnecessary for them to go any further than did the state court, which had made an exception to their general no-exclusionary-rule position in cases where the parolee's status was known. But the dissenters do at another point state without qualification that they "would apply the exclusionary rule to evidence offered in revocation hearings," and certainly the across-the-board approach draws some support from the analysis in the dissent, especially the observation there that "the police very likely do know a parolee's status when they go after him" because "local police know the lo-

cal felons, criminal history information is instantly available nationally, and police and parole officers routinely cooperate."

[134]In re Martinez, 1 Cal.3d 641, 83 Cal.Rptr. 382, 463 P.2d 734 (1970) (dissent). See also United States v. Workman, 585 F.2d 1205 (4th Cir.1978) (in applying exclusionary rule to *all* probation revocation proceedings, court stresses that the costs in this context "are neither significantly more nor less than in other adjudicative proceedings").

[135]Comment, 45 N.Y.U.L.Rev. 1111, 1114 (1970).

[136]People v. Dowery, 20 Ill.App.3d 738, 312 N.E.2d 682 (1974), aff'd, 62 Ill.2d 200, 340 N.E.2d 529 (1975).

of violations, to the detriment of their other charges, if they were deprived of the information gained by illegal police searches.[137] But surely the probation and parole systems are not so weak that it must be assumed that only through police illegality can they effectively function. It is to be doubted that judges will make greater use of probation only if it is known that probationers are fair game for illegal searches. This is not to say that certain convicted defendants may not present a sufficient risk of recidivism that release would be inappropriate unless they may be placed under a regime of supervision involving intrusions into privacy beyond that to which the general public may be subjected. But this question is better dealt with more directly, that is, by considering whether release may be conditioned upon an agreement that the probationer or parolee must submit to periodic inspection.[138]

Finally, it is argued that bringing the exclusionary rule into the revocation process will make those proceedings more adversary and formal, to the detriment of the rehabilitative objective.[139] And thus the contention by the *Scott* majority that though "States could adapt their parole revocation proceedings to accommodate [exclusionary rule] litigation, such a change would transform those proceedings from a 'predictive and discretionary' effort to promote the best interests of both parolees and society into trial-like proceedings 'less attuned' to the interests of the parolee." But, as the dissenters there noted, "Any revocation hearing is adversary to a degree: counsel must now be provided whenever the complexity of fact issues so warrant." The point is that this kind of argument has certainly lost much of its force since *Morrissey v. Brewer*[140] and *Gagnon v. Scarpelli*,[141] holding that probationers and parolees must be afforded due process in the revocation process.[142] Indeed, it may well be that using the fruits of police illegality in this way is itself detrimental to rehabilitation.

---

[137]United States v. Winsett, 518 F.2d 51 (9th Cir.1975); United States ex rel. Sperling v. Fitzpatrick, 426 F.2d 1161 (2d Cir.1970) (Lumbard, J., concurring).

[138]United States ex rel. Sperling v. Fitzpatrick, 426 F.2d 1161 (2d Cir.1970) (Kaufman, J., concurring). See § 10.10.

[139]United States ex rel. Sperling v. Fitzpatrick, 426 F.2d 1161 (2d Cir. 1970); United States v. Allen, 349 F.Supp. 749 (N.D.Cal.1972).

[140]Morrissey v. Brewer, 408 U.S. 471, 92 S.Ct. 2593, 33 L.Ed.2d 484 (1972).

[141]Gagnon v. Scarpelli, 411 U.S.

778, 93 S.Ct. 1756, 36 L.Ed.2d 656 (1973).

[142]However, neither of the cases passes directly on the issue under consideration here. In *Morrissey*, concerning parole revocation, the Court did say that it was permissible "to consider evidence including letters and affidavits, and other material that would not be admissible in an adversary criminal trial," but made no specific mention of evidence obtained in violation of the Fourth Amendment. In *Gagnon*, concerning probation revocation, the Court concluded that the defendant might be entitled to counsel because he claimed that the confession used against him was coerced, but this

"Society's sending a probationer or parolee to prison for his subsequent illegal activity through the use of equally illegal police activities can only instill bitterness and hostility that the individual will carry back into society upon completing his sentence."[143]

§ 1.6(h) Deterrence/cost balancing as to specific kinds of violations: the *Hudson* approach

Whatever else might be said about the limitations upon the exclusionary rule in criminal proceedings discussed in this section up to this point, at least none of the limitations discussed restrict the operation of the exclusionary rule at the most critical time in those proceedings: when the fruits of an illegal search or seizure are offered into evidence at a criminal trial on the matter of guilt or innocence.[144] Of a totally different order is *Hudson v. Michigan*,[145] where a bare majority of the Court took the shocking step of holding that sometimes the exclusionary rule is inap-

---

recognition of the necessity for procedures to exclude unreliable evidence does not of necessity extend to evidence which is reliable but was obtained in violation of the Fourth Amendment.

[143]Note, 54 Texas L.Rev. 1115, 1126 (1976).

[Section 1.6(h)]

[144]Assuming a fruits relationship, the exclusionary rule applies at that point except in very limited circumstances where "appreciable deterrence" would not be achieved because the police acted in "good faith," e.g., United States v. Leon, 468 U.S. 897, 104 S.Ct. 3405, 82 L.Ed.2d 677 (1984), or because the evidence is offered only for impeachment purposes, e.g., Walder v. United States, 347 U.S. 62, 74 S.Ct. 354, 98 L.Ed. 503 (1954).

[145]Hudson v. Michigan, 547 U.S. 586, 126 S.Ct. 2159, 165 L.Ed.2d 56 (2006), discussed in Alschuler, The Exclusionary Rule and Causation: Hudson v. Michigan and Its Ancestors, 93 Iowa L.Rev. 1741 (2008); Blair, Hudson v. Michigan: the Supreme Court Knocks and Announced the Demise of the Exclusionary Rule, 42 Tulsa L.Rev. 751 (2007); Castiglione, Hudson and Samson: The Roberts Court Confronts Privacy, Dignity and the Fourth Amendment, 68 La.L.Rev. 63 (2007); Dery, A False Mirror: Hudson v. Michigan's Distortion of the Exclusionary Rule in Knock-and-Announce Litigation, 76 UMKC L.Rev. 67 (2007); Frakt, Fruitless Poisonous Trees in a Parallel Universe: Hudson v Michigan, Knock-and-Announce, and the Exclusionary Rule, 34 Fla.St.U.L. Rev. 659 (2007); Grey, Revisiting the Application of the Exclusionary Rule to the Good Faith Exceptions in Light of Hudson v. Michigan, 42 U.S.F.L. Rev. 621 (2008); Hilton, Alternatives to the Exclusionary Rule After Hudson v. Michigan: Preventing and Remedying Police Conduct, 53 Vill.L.Rev. 47 (2008); Maclin & Rader, No More Chipping Away: The Roberts Court Uses an Axe to Take Out the Fourth Amendment Exclusionary Rule, 81 Miss.L.J. 1183 (2012); Moran, Waiting for the Other Shoe: Hudson and the Precarious State of Mapp, 93 Iowa L.Rev. 1725 (2008); Summers, The Constable Blunders But Isn't Punished: Does Hudson v. Michigan's Abolition of the Exclusionary Rule Extend Beyond Knock-and-Announce Violations?, 10 Barry L.Rev. 25 (2008); Tomkovicz, Hudson v. Michigan and the Future of Fourth Amendment Exclusion, 93 Iowa L.Rev. 1819 (2008); Comments, 2007 BYU L.Rev. 451; 59 Fla.L.Rev. 465 & 475 (2007); 34 Ohio N.U.L.Rev. 217 (2008); 112 Penn.St.L. Rev. 261 (2007); Notes, 44 Am.Crim.L. Rev. 1239 (2007); 73 Brook.L.Rev. 1209 (2008); 21 BYU J.Pub.L. 433 (2007); 37 Cumb.L.Rev. 327 (2007); 30 Hamline L.Rev. 409 (2007); 58 Mercer

plicable at that critical stage as well. Relying upon the notion, as stated in *Pennsylvania Board of Probation and Parole v. Scott*,[146] that the exclusionary rule is applicable only "where its deterrence benefits outweigh its 'substantial social costs,' " the Court in *Hudson* held the exclusionary rule inapplicable to evidence obtained in execution of a search warrant[147] whenever the Fourth Amendment violation[148] was a failure to comply with the "knock-and-announce" doctrine[149] upon entry of the premises to be searched. And thus in *Hudson* the drugs and a firearm found during the subsequent execution of the warrant in Hudson's house were deemed admissible notwithstanding a Fourth Amendment violation conceded by the state, that after announcing their presence, the police "waited only a short time—perhaps 'three to five seconds.' " While the Michigan court had held the evidence admissible on fruit-of-the-poisonous tree grounds, the majority in *Hudson* (perhaps recognizing the weakness of each of its contentions) opted to affirm on two highly dubious propositions: (i) that the drugs and gun were not the fruit of the violation;[150] and (ii) that in any event the social costs of exclusion outweighed the

---

L.Rev. 779 (2007); 27 Miss.C.L.Rev. 435 (2007); 27 Pace L.Rev. 503 (2007); 32 S.Ill.U.L.J. 447 (2008); 29 Whittier L.Rev. 183 (2007); Recent Decision, 30 Harv.J.L. & Pub. Pol'y 417 (2006).

[146]Pennsylvania Bd. of Probation and Parole v. Scott, 524 U.S. 357, 118 S.Ct. 2014, 141 L.Ed.2d 344 (1998).

[147]However, it has been held that "*Hudson* applies with equal force in the context of an arrest warrant." United States v. Pelletier, 469 F.3d 194 (1st Cir.2006). Accord: United States v. Acosta, 502 F.3d 54 (2d Cir. 2007); United States v. Bruno, 487 F.3d 304 (5th Cir.2007). So too, *Hudson* is "not confined to situations in which the officers violate the knock-and-announce rule after obtaining a warrant as opposed to situations, like this one, where they allegedly violate the rule when they need not obtain a warrant." United States v. Smith, 526 F.3d 306 (6th Cir.2008).

And in the case of a search warrant, *Hudson* applies notwithstanding defendant's claim that the search was in one sense "warrantless" because the police could have but did not obtain a no-knock warrant. United States v. Ankeny, 502 F.3d 829 (9th Cir.2007). Also, *Hudson* applies even when the no-knock entry to execute a search warrant involved "shock-and-awe tac-

tics" or "aggressive and violent tactics." United States v. Garcia-Hernandez, 659 F.3d 108 (1st Cir.2011) (claiming that even in the instant case, involving police use of an armored vehicle, battering ram, and noise-flash devices, "police misconduct could be effectively deterred through civil suits").

[148]In an attempt to avoid the impact of *Hudson*, federal defendants have sometimes grounded their claim not in the Fourth Amendment but rather in the knock-and-announce statute, 18 U.S.C.A. § 3109. This tactic has been rejected on the ground "that § 3109 and the Fourth Amendment have merged both in the standards governing entries into the home and in the remedy for violations of those standards." United States v. Southerland, 466 F.3d 1083 (D.C.Cir.2006). But a *state* defendant might prevail in state court because of a violation of the state knock-and-announce statute. See, e.g., State v. Cable, 51 So.3d 434 (Fla.2010) (concluding *Hudson* "does not mandate" rejection of existing statute exclusionary policy re state statute).

[149]See § 4.8.

[150]On this branch of the case, see § 11.4(a), text at notes 42, 107 supra.

deterrence benefits. Just as two wrongs do not make a right, two weak arguments do not add up to one strong argument.

Of concern here is the second of these propositions, the "unprecedented" use of cost-benefit analysis "as a self-sufficient ground for placing an entire category of Fourth Amendment violation beyond the reach of the suppression remedy."[151] The *Hudson* majority first described what it saw as the "costs" of applying the exclusionary rule with respect to this kind of Fourth Amendment violation.[152] These costs are not only (i) the "grave adverse consequences" that exclusion "always entails (viz., the risk of releasing dangerous criminals into society)," but also (ii) the frequency of motions relating to such violations ("a constant flood of alleged failures to observe the [knock-and-announce] rule,[153] and claims that any asserted * * * justification for a no-knock entry * * * had inadequate support," made by defendants seeking the coveted "get-out-of-jail free card"—previously known as the exclusionary rule!); (iii) the difficulty presented by such motions ("what constituted a 'reasonable wait time' in a particular case (or, for that matter, how many seconds the police in fact waited), or whether there was 'reasonable suspicion' of the sort that would invoke the * * * exceptions, is difficult for the trial court to determine and even more difficult for an appellate court to review"); and (iv) the resulting effect upon the police, i.e., "police officers' refraining from timely entry after knocking and announcing," thus "producing preventable violence against officers in some cases, and the destruction of evidence in many others."[154]

As for the "deterrence benefits" side of the ledger regarding

---

[151]Tomkovicz, 93 Iowa L.Rev. 1819, 1832 (2008). Consider Dripps, The "New" Exclusionary Rule Debate: From "Still Preoccupied with 1985" to "Virtual Deterrence," 37 Fordham Urb.L.J. 743, 763 (2010): "Loose references to lost evidence as a 'cost,' made without reference to the constitutional judgment that the better course is *not* to gather all possible evidence of crime, should be banished from the law and from the literature as the veiled attacks on the Constitution that they are."

[152]On the error in thus assuming that the public interest is in all respects on the side of nonexclusion, see Reiner, Public Interest(s) and Fourth Amendment Enforcement, 2010 U.Ill. L.Rev. 1461.

[153]Consider Alschuler, 93 Iowa L.Rev. 1741, 1767 (2008): "When lawyers throughout the United States had been making no-knock challenges for

a half century or more, the Supreme Court's statement that a contrary ruling in *Hudson* would generate suppression hearings 'as never before' revealed a Court that had lost perspective."

[154]As to this fourth "cost," Alschuler, 93 Iowa L.Rev. 1741, 1765–66 (2008), cogently notes: "Although the Supreme Court had previously restricted the scope of the exclusionary rule by questioning its deterrent efficacy in many contexts, the *Hudson* majority apparently was convinced of the rule's power. The rule's transformation was so remarkable that it now overdeterred, inhibiting even lawful and valuable police conduct. Presumably the Court thought civil remedies less able to influence police behavior, for it did not suggest that they might have the same unfortunate effect. As the Court recognized, it had held that the Fourth Amendment allows officers to enter

knock-and-announce violations, the *Hudson* majority concluded that "the incentive to such violations is minimal to begin with, and the extant deterrences against them are substantial—incomparably greater than the factors deterring warrantless entries when *Mapp* was decided." On the incentive point, the majority declared that "deterrence of knock-and-announce violations is not worth a lot," as while violation of the warrant requirement "sometimes produces incriminating evidence that could not otherwise be obtained," by contrast "ignoring knock-and-announce can realistically be expected to achieve absolutely nothing except the prevention of destruction of evidence and the avoidance of life-threatening resistance by occupants of the premises—dangers which, if there is even 'reasonable suspicion' of their existence, *suspend the knock-and-announce requirement anyway.*" Next, the majority rejected the deterrence analysis in *Mapp* on the ground of purported changes in the intervening 45 years: the "slow but steady expansion" of the § 1983 remedy, later "extended to reach the deep pocket of municipalities,"[155] and made more available by virtue of the fact that "Congress has authorized attorney's fees for civil-rights plaintiffs,"[156] plus "the increasing professionalism of police forces, including a new emphasis on internal police discipline."

Neither half of the tortured reasoning of the *Hudson* majority in finding knock-and-announce violations a "special" case in which the deterrent effect is outweighed by the social costs can withstand close analysis. On the costs side, the fact of the matter is, as the dissenters cogently noted, that the only costs mentioned by the majority

> are those that typically accompany *any* use of the Fourth Amendment's exclusionary principle: (1) that where the constable blunders, a guilty defendant may be set free * * * (2) that defendants may assert claims where Fourth Amendment rights are uncertain * * *, and (3) that sometimes it is difficult to decide the merits of those uncertain claims.[157] In fact, the "no-knock" warrants that are provided by many States, by diminishing uncertainty, may make

---

without knocking whenever they have even a reasonable suspicion that giving notice might lead to the destruction of evidence or to violence. Having given the police the benefit of every reasonable doubt, the *Hudson* majority decided that they needed more."

Similarly, Dripps, The "New" Exclusionary Rule Debate: From "Still Preoccupied with 1985" to "Virtual Deterrence," 37 Fordham Urb.L.J. 743, 753 (2010), cogently notes: "*Any* effective remedy for Fourth Amendment violations will carry those same 'substantial social costs.' Justice Scalia seems to be in a celebratory mood in writing about damage actions and police professionalism, as if searches that don't take place because of the threat of tort liability or departmental discipline are somehow different from searches that don't take place because of the threat of exclusion."

[155] Monell v. Department of Social Services of City of New York, 436 U.S. 658, 98 S.Ct. 2108, 56 L.Ed.2d 611 (1978).

[156] 42 U.S.C.A. § 1988(b).

[157] As noted in Tomkovicz, 93 Iowa L.Rev. 1819, 1877 (2008): "The Court did suggest that the opportunities to make colorable claims and the com-

application of the knock-and-announce principle less "cost[ly]" on the whole than application of comparable Fourth Amendment principles, such as determining whether a particular warrantless search was justified by exigency. The majority's "substantial social costs" argument is an argument against the Fourth Amendment's exclusionary principle itself. And it is an argument that this Court, until now, has consistently rejected.[158]

This means not only that *Hudson* is dead wrong, but also that it has the capacity to metastasize into a much broader limitation upon the suppression doctrine. This is because the costs recited by the *Hudson* majority can easily be found to exist with respect to other varieties of Fourth Amendment violations.[159] For example, consider the two-pronged "protective sweep" doctrine of *Maryland v. Buie*.[160] Given the frequency with which police are confronted with *Buie* issues, the "difficult" nature of the multitude of issues presented under *Buie* (How far may the police search without reasonable suspicion? How far may they search with reasonable suspicion? Was there reasonable suspicion in the instant case?), and the possibility that police reluctance to make a search even when one would be allowed under *Buie* would "produc[e] preventable violence against officers in some cases," this branch of the *Hudson* case looks like a perfect fit.

The deterrence side of the *Hudson* majority's analysis is no more compelling. The majority's claim that increased police professionalism and self-discipline have changed things[161] overlooks the fact that such changes have come about largely

---

plexities of the litigation were unique in the knock-and-announce context due to the ambiguity and amorphousness of the governing standards. In truth, however, many Fourth Amendment rules are equally ambiguous and amorphous, and determining whether officers have complied could be just as difficult and time-consuming. Put simply, the premises that led the Court to predict costly, burdensome litigation over knock-and-announce compliance could be readily discovered in a host of other Fourth Amendment areas."

Tomkovicz goes on to note that while the "final cost of suppression for knock-and-announce violations—the risk of violence against officers and lost evidence—was tied specifically to the knock-and-announce context," here again "other rules have similar—even equal—ambiguities that could produce comparable uncertainty and reluctance to exercise constitutionally legitimate authority. The results would sometimes be unnecessary increases

in violence and would often be losses of valuable evidence." Id. at 1877–78.

[158]See also Gross, Dangerous Criminals, the Search for the Truth and Effective Law Enforcement: How the Supreme Court Overestimates the Social Costs of the Exclusionary Rule, 51 Santa Clara L.Rev. 545, 547 (2011), which "explore[s] the underlying assumptions that the Court makes in order to come to the conclusion that the rule imposes these social costs and demonstrate[s] why these assumptions are false."

[159]See Tomkovicz, 93 Iowa L.Rev. 1819, 1875–80 (2008).

[160]Maryland v. Buie, 494 U.S. 325, 110 S.Ct. 1093, 108 L.Ed.2d 276 (1990).

[161]As noted in Miller, Putting the Practice Into Theory, 7 Ohio St.J.Crim.L. 31, 67 (2009), "the Court rejects exclusion because it has only an indirect deterrent effect, whereas self-regulation by the police and law-

because of the exclusionary rule. Once the exclusionary rule is removed from knock-and-announce violations, what reason is there to believe that any police department in the country would be prepared to discipline an officer for premature entry unaccompanied by physical injury to an occupant or at least substantial damage to the premises? And while the majority says it may be "assumed" that "civil liability is an effective deterrent," this (as the dissent points out) is only "a support-free assumption that *Mapp* and subsequent cases make clear does not embody the Court's normal approach to difficult questions of Fourth Amendment law." As for the touted § 1983 action and its promise of money damages and attorney's fees in the particular context of knock-and-announce violations, what promise does it provide to a potential plaintiff like Hudson, who can show an intrusion into his constitutionally-protected privacy under the Fourth Amendment but no accompanying injury to property or person? A case decided a few months before *Hudson, Robbins v. Chronister,*[162] while involving a somewhat different kind of "breaking" in violation of the Fourth Amendment, is instructive. An officer ordered a traffic violator out of his car and, when he did not comply, the officer swung his baton into one of the car's windows, shattering it. Following the driver's conviction for a subsequent attempted assault, he brought a § 1983 action; the court found the officer's actions violated the Fourth Amendment and then awarded plaintiff nominal damages of one dollar. A dispute about attorney's fees went to the court of appeals, which held plaintiff was entitled to only $1.50 by virtue of 42 U.S.C. § 1997e(d), as "the statute's plain language imposes a 150% fee cap if (1) the plaintiff was a prisoner at the time he brought the action and (2) the plaintiff was awarded attorney fees under § 1988."

Whatever one might think of *Hudson's* fruit-of-the-poisonous-tree holding, the majority's quite unnecessary alternate[163] deterrence/costs holding is especially unfortunate, for it is open to broader application to other varieties of Fourth Amendment violations[164] (and, indeed, perhaps even as to knock-and-announce

suits or civilian review boards purportedly have a more direct deterrent effect. Yet if the Court has no idea whether police training is done in an effective manner, then there is no reason to assume that training regimes are more effective than (the admittedly marginally deterrent) exclusionary rule."

[162]Robbins v. Chronister, 435 F.3d 1238 (10th Cir.2006).

[163]The *Hudson* majority first ruled against the defendant via a fruit-of-the-poisonous-tree analysis, and then went on to say that "[q]uite apart" from that holding the exclusionary rule would not apply because "the massive remedy of suppressing evidence of guilt is unjustified" in the knock-and-announce context, considering the deterrence/costs balance.

[164]See, e.g., United States v. Lopez-Garcia, 565 F.3d 1306 (11th Cir.2009) (following *Farias-Gonzalez*, infra, on similar facts); United States v. Farias-Gonzalez, 556 F.3d 1181 (11th Cir.2009) (relying on *Hudson* in con-

violations[165]). The *Hudson* majority (as the dissenters conclude) has "destroy[ed] the strongest legal incentive to comply with the Constitution's knock-and-announce requirement," and has done so even absent "precedent that might offer the majority support for its contrary conclusion," for the Court's previous decisions declining to apply the exclusionary rule have been "in proceedings other than criminal trials" or else in circumstances where "appreciable deterrence"[166] would not have been gained, typically because of the absence of fault in the police agency. True, the fifth vote in *Hudson* was provided by Justice Kennedy, who cautions in his separate concurrence that "the continued operation of the exclusionary rule * * * is not in doubt," but this provides little solace when it is considered how many other types of Fourth Amendment violations could easily be encompassed within a comparably slipshod deterrence/costs balancing. This branch of *Hudson* should be confined to its particular facts, if not promptly overruled, lest it "let a kind of computer virus loose in the Fourth Amendment."[167]

But even if the cost-benefit ruling in *Hudson* is hereafter ap-

---

cluding that fingerprints and photographs taken of defendant after his illegal seizure should not be suppressed in defendant's prosecution for reentering U.S. after deportation, as the "social cost" of the government not knowing defendant's identity deemed too high and lost deterrence benefits minimal because "police can obtain both photographs and fingerprints without conducting a search under the Fourth Amendment"!!!); United States v. Hector, 474 F.3d 1150 (9th Cir. 2007), discussed in § 4.12(a), text at note 24 (*Hudson* applied to possible Fourth Amendment violation of failure to serve a copy of the warrant); Davies & Scanlon, Katz in the Age of Hudson v. Michigan: Some Thoughts on "Suppression as a Last Resort," 41 U.C.Davis L.Rev. 1035, 1043 (2008) ("Our examination of *Hudson*'s progeny shows that the new anti-suppression analysis will not be confined to the knock-and-announce context, but will be applied to other constitutional missteps by the police as well"); Summers, The Constable Blunders But Isn't Punished: Does Hudson v. Michigan's Abolition of the Exclusionary Rule Extend Beyond Knock-and-Announce Violations?, 10 Barry L.Rev. 25 (2008); Comment, 2007 B.Y.U.L.Rev. 451 (2007) (arguing

Hudson applicable to unauthorized nighttime searches).

[165]Applying only a fruits analysis, it would seem that notwithstanding *Hudson* there would be instances in which items not named in the warrant would be deemed the fruit of a premature entry or an entry without notice because absent that violation the evidence would not have been discovered. See the discussion of *Hudson* in § 11.4(a), text at note 116 supra. But, as noted there, it is to be doubted that it could likewise be said that there is a greater need for deterrence of those knock-and-announce violations that serendipitously produce such evidence.

[166]United States v. Janis, 428 U.S. 433, 96 S.Ct. 3021, 49 L.Ed.2d 1046 (1976).

[167]Comment of Justice Breyer, htt p://www.supremecourtus.gov/oral_arg uments/argument_transcripts/4-1360 b.pdf, p. 50.

Indeed, as noted in Dripps, The Fourth Amendment, the Exclusionary Rule, and the Roberts Court: Normative and Empirical Dimensions of the Over-Deterrence Hypothesis, 85 Chi.-Kent L.Rev. 209 (2010), one might read *Hudson* as a substantial step toward ultimate total abandonment of the Fourth Amendment exclusionary

plied only in instances of knock-and-announce violations, it is still a most unfortunate one, with significant undesirable consequences. As Prof. Alschuler has aptly noted,

> the exclusionary rule works primarily by giving courts the opportunity to articulate Fourth Amendment standards in decisions with enough bite to be taken seriously. If this perception of the rule's operation is accurate, *Hudson*'s virtual elimination of litigation concerning the validity of no-knock searches is a cost rather than a benefit. Knock-and-announce questions arise so rarely in civil litigation that, after *Hudson*, courts will almost never have occasion to address them. *Hudson* will bring judicial development of the law of no-knock searches to a halt.[168]

§ 1.6(i) Deterrence/cost balancing as to specific kinds of violations: the *Herring* approach

Just two and a half years after *Hudson v. Michigan*,[169] the Supreme Court in *Herring v. United States*[170] took another slice out of the exclusionary rule, once again finding that a particular

---

rule, though he predicts this will *not* come to pass because (i) a majority of the Court does not appear to believe that "the current remedial mix is * * * over-deterring Fourth Amendment violations," and (ii) the Court would not want to make such a "radical change" and thereby "curtail its own institutional power in the process."

[168]Alschuler, 93 Iowa L.Rev. 1741, 1767 (2008).

Consider also the thoughtful concurring opinion in United States v. Garcia-Hernandez, 659 F.3d 108 (1st Cir.2011), emphasizing "that the influence of the rule we announce today [see note 147 supra] and the prevailing methodological approach to the resolution of qualified immunity issues raises the significant possibility that conscientious law enforcement officers will be deprived of needed judicial guidance concerning the manner in which warrants must be executed."

[Section 1.6(i)]

[169]Hudson v. Michigan, 547 U.S. 586, 126 S.Ct. 2159, 165 L.Ed.2d 56 (2006).

[170]Herring v. United States, 555 U.S. 135, 129 S.Ct. 695, 172 L.Ed.2d 496 (2009), discussed in Alschuler, Herring v. United States: A Minnow or Shark?, 7 Ohio St.J.Crim.L. 463 (2009); Aviram, Seymour & Leo, Moving Targets: Placing the Good Faith Doctrine in the Context of

Fragmented Policing, 37 Fordham Urb.L.J. 709 (2010); Clancy, The Irrelevancy of the Fourth Amendment in the Roberts Court, 85 Chi.-Kent L.Rev. 191 (1010); Debevoise, Reflections Upon Herring v. United States: The Dangers of Narrowing Protections of Civil Rights in the Pressure Cooker Environment in Which We Live, 61 Rutgers L.Rev. 855 (2009); Dery, Good Enough for Government Work: The Court's Dangerous Decision in Herring v. United States, to Limit the Exclusionary Rule to Only the Most Culpable Police Behavior, 20 Geo.Mason U.Civ.Rts.L.J. 1 (2009); Josephson, To Exclude or Not to Exclude: The Future of the Exclusionary Rule After Herring v. United States, 43 Creighton L.Rev. 175 (2009); LaFave, The Smell of Herring: A Critique of the Supreme Court's Latest Assault on the Exclusionary Rule, 99 J.Crim.L. & Criminology 757 (2009); Laurin, Trawling for Herring: Lessons in Doctrinal Borrowing and Convergence, 111 Colum.L.Rev. 670 (2011); Maclin & Rader, No More Chipping Away: The Roberts Court Uses an Axe to Take Out the Fourth Amendment Exclusionary Rule, 81 Miss.L.J. 1183 (2012); Nolasco, del Carmen & Vaughn, What Herring Hath Wrought: An Analysis of Post-Herring Cases in the Federal Courts, 38 Am.J.Crim.L. 221, 252 (2011); Perrine, Speirs & Horwitz, Fusion Centers and the Fourth Amend-

species of Fourth Amendment violation was not deserving of the suppression remedy. In *Herring,* an investigator, apparently suspicious of defendant because he "was no stranger to law enforcement" and was seeking "to retrieve something from his impounded truck," ran a warrant check on him and was advised that the computer database in the sheriff's department of a neighboring county showed "an active arrest warrant for [his] failure to appear on a felony charge." On the basis of that information, the investigator arrested defendant and, in a search incident to the arrest, found drugs and a pistol on his person, ultimately leading to federal prosecution. It was subsequently determined that the computer record was in error and that actually the warrant had been recalled five months earlier. The court of appeals assumed that whoever failed to update the sheriff's records "was also a law enforcement official,"[171] but nonetheless affirmed the district court's denial of defendant's motion to suppress because "the conduct in question [wa]s a negligent failure to act, not a deliberate or tactical choice to act." The Supreme Court, in a 5-4 decision, while "accept[ing] the parties' assumption that there was a Fourth Amendment violation" in arresting defendant on a nonexistent warrant, concluded the exclusionary rule was not applicable in a case such as this, namely, where "the error was the result of isolated negligence attenuated from the arrest." The *Herring* majority reached this conclusion by application of the seemingly broader proposition that "[t]o trigger the exclusionary rule, police conduct must be sufficiently deliberate that exclusion can meaningfully deter it, and sufficiently culpable that such deterrence is worth the price paid by the justice system."

The holding in *Herring,* it is submitted, is flat-out wrong, and finds little support in the Chief Justice's opinion for the majority, which perhaps accurately reflects his apparent longstanding opposition to the exclusionary rule,[172] but is totally unconvincing and in many respects irrelevant and disingenuous. The *Herring* majority gets off to a bad start by hanging its collective hat on

---

ment: Application of the Exclusionary Rule in the Post-9/11 Age of Information Sharing, 38 Cap.U.L.Rev. 721 (2010) (re application of *Herring* generally where reliance on information from other agencies); Vitiello, Herring v. United States: Mapp's "Artless" Overruling?, 10 Nev.L.J. 164 (2009); Zarr, The Supreme Court's Long and Perhaps Unnecessary Struggle to Find a Standard of Culpability to Regulate the Federal Exclusionary Remedy for Fourth/Fourteenth Amendment Violations, 62 Me.L.Rev. 265 (2010); Comments, 62 Stan.L.Rev. 563 (2010); 43 Suffolk U.L.Rev. 265 (2009); 44 Val.U.L.Rev. 747 (2010); Notes, 37 Hofstra L.Rev. 839 (2009); 61 Mercer L.Rev. 663 (2010); 77 Tenn.L.Rev. 233 (2009).

[171]United States v. Herring, 492 F.3d 1212 (11th Cir.2007).

[172]See Liptak, Supreme Court Edging Closer to Repeal of Evidence Ruling, New York Times, Jan. 31, 2009, p. Al, col. 5 (noting that back in 1983, as a lawyer in the Reagan White House, Roberts "was hard at work on what he called in a memorandum 'the campaign to amend or abolish the exclusionary rule' ").

Justice Scalia's bald assertion in *Hudson* that suppression "has always been our last resort, not our first impulse," a declaration which, as two thoughtful scholars have recently documented, "defies historical truth."[173] Next, the *Herring* Five describes the Fourth Amendment exclusionary rule solely in terms of its deterrence function, rather than as encompassing the other two purposes also recognized in earlier decisions of the Supreme Court,[174] which at least can be said to be unremarkable[175] in light of the Court's tendency for some years now to view the suppression sanction with an equally narrow focus.

Following this comes the announcement of the general principle, without any stated restriction or limitation, that "the benefits of deterrence must outweigh the costs."[176] Put in such bold terms, it is made to appear that this cost/benefits balancing process is a routine part of the assessment as to when the Fourth Amendment exclusionary rule should be applied, but nothing could be farther from the truth. This is manifested by the cases then primarily relied upon by the *Herring* Court in its further discussion of this balancing concept: *United States v. Leon*,[177] *Illinois v. Krull*,[178] *Arizona v. Evans*,[179] *United States v. Calandra*,[180]

---

[173]Davies & Scanlon, Katz in the Age of Hudson v. Michigan: Some Thoughts on "Suppression as a Last Resort," 41 U.C.Davis L.Rev. 1035, 1043 (2008).

[174]See § 1.1(f).

[175]At least as compared to the embrace of those other functions by all four dissenters. As noted in McAdams, Herring and the Exclusionary Rule, appearing at http://uchicagolaw.typep ad.com/faculty/2009/01/herring-and-th e-exclusionary-rule.html: "The four dissenters say something equally interesting for the future direction of the exclusionary rule, given some possibility that the new administration might replace one of the Justices in the *Herring* majority. For some time, the Court has appeared to agree that there is no rationale for the exclusionary rule other than the deterrence of future Fourth Amendment violations. But the four dissenters appear to revive the other rationale for the rule, stated in *Mapp* but fallen from favor: that exclusion preserves the integrity of the judiciary by avoiding complicity in the constitutional violation. One more vote for this proposition would

not only reverse *Herring*, but might actually re-invigorate the exclusionary rule to a degree not seen since before the Rehnquist Court."

[176]"Chief Justice Roberts does not explain why 'the benefits of deterrence must outweigh the costs.' If police violate the Constitution, why must a court engage in cost-benefit analysis at all? What makes the Fourth Amendment so different in this respect from the First Amendment, under which the Court does not weigh the cost and benefits of content-based censorship? These are difficult questions the majority's analysis fails to address." Crocker, The Political Fourth Amendment, 88 Wash.U.L.Rev. 303, 333 (2010).

[177]United States v. Leon, 468 U.S. 897, 104 S.Ct. 3405, 82 L.Ed.2d 677 (1984).

[178]Illinois v. Krull, 480 U.S. 340, 107 S.Ct. 1160, 94 L.Ed.2d 364 (1987).

[179]Arizona v. Evans, 514 U.S. 1, 115 S.Ct. 1185, 131 L.Ed.2d 34 (1995).

[180]United States v. Calandra, 414 U.S. 338, 94 S.Ct. 613, 38 L.Ed.2d 561 (1974).

Stone v. Powell,[181] and *Pennsylvania Board of Probation and Parole v. Scott*.[182] The last three decisions, as well as several other Supreme Court cases of like kind,[183] all represent instances in which the Court has concluded that application of the exclusionary rule at the criminal trial itself suffices to provide the necessary deterrence, so that suppression at certain other proceedings as well (e.g., before the grand jury, on habeas corpus, and at a parole revocation hearing, in *Calandra*, *Stone* and *Scott*, respectively) in the interest of still more deterrence is not worth the candle. Thus, those cases are clearly distinguishable from the action taken in *Herring*.

The same is true of the first three cases in the above listing. The two "good faith" cases, *Leon* and *Krull*, represent instances where cost/benefit balancing was deemed appropriate because of another kind of special circumstance: the person primarily responsible for the Fourth Amendment violation was not a law enforcement official but rather a judge (in *Leon*) and legislators (in *Krull*), a very significant fact deemed to change the dynamics of the deterrence analysis. The same is true of *Evans*, which deserves special attention here because the nature of the Fourth Amendment violation was identical to that in *Herring* except for the fact that the offending clerk was in the employ of the judiciary. As acknowledged by the *Herring* majority, *Evans* decided that exclusion in the interest of deterrence was not called for in such circumstance "for three reasons": (i) the exclusionary rule was crafted to curb police rather than judicial misconduct; (ii) court employees were unlikely to try to subvert the Fourth Amendment; and (iii) there was no reason to believe that application of the exclusionary rule in such a case would have a significant effect in deterring errors by court employees.

Obviously, none of these reasons is present in *Herring*, where the misconduct *was* by a law enforcement official. Yet the Court would have us believe that *Herring* matches up with these decisions, especially *Leon*, by offering the non sequitur that if under *Leon* it is not necessary to suppress "evidence obtained in objectively reasonable reliance on a subsequently invalidated search warrant," then the "same is true when evidence is obtained in objectively reasonable reliance on a subsequently recalled warrant." Not so, as these are apples and oranges.

Thus, on the preliminary question of whether *Herring* is the kind of case in which some sort of cost/benefit balancing process might be appropriately pursued, the many precedents cited by the Court do not support any such undertaking. Rather, of the Court's prior decisions the precedent for pursuing such an inquiry even as to exclusion at a criminal trial for a Fourth Amend-

---

[181]Stone v. Powell, 428 U.S. 465, 96 S.Ct. 3037, 49 L.Ed.2d 1067 (1976).

[182]Pennsylvania Bd. of Probation

and Parole v. Scott, 524 U.S. 357, 118 S.Ct. 2014, 141 L.Ed.2d 344 (1998).

[183]See § 1.6 generally.

ment violation by police is reduced to a list of one: the previously discussed[184] *Hudson* decision, where the Court's cost/benefit balancing was not even essential to the decision given the Court's added reliance upon the fruit-of-the-poisonous tree doctrine. But even if we pass by all of this and simply concentrate upon how the balancing act was performed in *Herring*, the Court's decision still does not pass muster.

On the cost side of the equation, the *Herring* majority makes no claim that the cost of exclusion in this particular case would be especially high, and rightly so, as any claim otherwise would invoke the discredited "comparative reprehensibility"approach to the exclusionary rule.[185] The "principal cost of applying the rule" in this case, just as in all others where exclusion occurs, says the Court, is "letting guilty and possibly dangerous defendants go free." But, while this is not an insignificant cost, this matter of cost ought to be kept in perspective.[186] As discussed elsewhere herein,[187] the essential point is that the cost is imposed not by the exclusionary rule but by the Fourth Amendment itself. If the exclusionary rule *was* applied to Mr. Herring's benefit, he would then not have been convicted in the federal court for illegally possessing the gun and drugs found on his person. But by like token, if the law enforcement officials had not violated the Fourth Amendment in such a way as to cause Mr. Herring's arrest on a nonexistent warrant, then once again he would have escaped conviction for those crimes on that occasion.

Whatever weight is assigned to the cost factor must be outdone by the potential for deterrence in that particular situation, for, as *Herring* instructs, "the benefits of deterrence must outweigh the costs."[188] (Defendants, apparently, lose all ties.) Assaying the magnitude of those benefits has proved to be a daunting task in the kinds of cases the Court has most often dealt with in the past, where it is at least possible to think about the need for and/or possibility of deterrence via exclusion regarding various

---

[184]See § 1.6(h).

[185]See § 1.2(e).

[186]Consider Gross, Dangerous Criminals, the Search for the Truth and Effective Law Enforcement: How the Supreme Court Overestimates the Social Costs of the Exclusionary Rule, 51 Santa Clara L.Rev. 545, 547 (2011), which "explore[s] the underlying assumptions that the Court makes in order to come to the conclusion that the rule imposes these social costs and demonstrate[s] why these assumptions are false."

[187]See § 1.3(c).

[188]The *Herring* majority in a footnote acknowledged that exclusion in the instant case would have *some* deterrent effect, but then asserted that "here exclusion is not worth the cost." Dripps, The "New" Exclusionary Rule Debate: From "Still Preoccupied with 1985" to "Virtual Deterrence," 37 Fordham Urb.L.J. 743, 755 (2010), cogently notes: "In this revealing passage, the majority agrees that suppression would prevent future violations of the Constitution, but characterizes prevention of constitutional violations as not worth the loss of a single case against a hoodlum so dysfunctional that he cannot drive to the impound lot without his contraband."

kinds of nonpolice actors or with respect to settings other than the criminal trial itself. But how does one go about this task when, as *Herring* contemplates, the question is whether the exclusionary rule is to be applied at a trial in light of a Fourth Amendment violation by a law enforcement official? The answer of the *Herring* majority is that the deterrence benefit derived from exclusion "varies with the culpability of the law enforcement conduct." Hence one important-probably the most important-characteristic of the class of Fourth Amendment violations now declared to be outside the reach of the exclusionary rule is said to be that the error constitutes only "isolated negligence," as distinguished from "deliberate, reckless, or grossly negligent conduct, or in some circumstances recurring or systemic negligence."

But where does the *Herring* Court find this "culpability" test for determining the scope of the exclusionary rule? It is set out as if a foregone conclusion, and is immediately followed with quotations from *Leon* and *Krull*, suggesting that the notion is well-grounded in existing jurisprudence on the exclusionary rule. The quote from *Leon*, which seems rather compelling, is that "an assessment of the flagrancy of the police misconduct constitutes an important step in the calculus" of applying the exclusionary rule. But that brief excerpt has been taken completely out of context by the *Herring* majority, as the "calculus" the Court was talking about at that point in *Leon* regards the "dissipation of the taint" of the fruit of the poisonous tree doctrine, the notion that the connection between the Fourth Amendment violation and the evidence sought to be suppressed can sometimes be so tenuous that the exclusionary rule need not be applied to that evidence. The *Leon* case cites *Dunaway v. New York*[189] in support of the proposition quoted in *Herring*, and then, significantly, offers this quote from *Dunaway*: "Where there is a close causal connection between the illegal seizure and the confession, not only is exclusion of the evidence more likely to deter similar police misconduct in the future, but use of the evidence is more likely to compromise the integrity of the courts." This makes it even more apparent that the quote extracted from *Leon* has absolutely nothing to do with the issue in *Herring*. In *Herring*, the connection between the negligent omission causing the records of the sheriff's office to render a false report on the date defendant was arrested and the arrest itself is indeed "close," and thus there is no occasion in a *Herring* kind of case to engage in the sort of "assessment of flagrancy" the Court talked about in *Leon*.

As for the other quote put forward by the *Herring* majority, from *Krull*, it says that "evidence should be suppressed 'only if it can be said that the law enforcement officer had knowledge, or

---

[189]Dunaway v. New York, 442 U.S. (1979).
200, 99 S.Ct. 2248, 60 L.Ed.2d 824

may properly be charged with knowledge, that the search was unconstitutional under the Fourth Amendment.'" But here again the context of the quotation indicates that its meaning is other than as represented in *Herring. Krull* presented the question of whether the exclusionary rule should apply when an officer acted pursuant to authority set forth in a statute that itself is subsequently found to violate the Fourth Amendment, and the discussion in the case where the above quotation appears is directed toward making the point that such a situation should be dealt with in essentially the same fashion as in *Leon*. Both cases involved situations having two common ingredients: (i) the officer in each instance had acted in reliance upon an authoritative nonpolice source (a judge who issued the warrant at issue in *Leon*, the legislators who enacted the statute at issue in *Krull*); and (ii) exclusion merely to deter the nonpolice source was deemed unnecessary. By the above quoted language the *Krull* Court was making the point that because in both instances we would ordinarily expect the police officer to act according to the directive received from the judge and legislature, respectively, it also makes no sense to exclude the evidence in the interest police deterrence where he neither knew or should have known that the directive received from an authoritative nonpolice source would later turn out not to square with the protections of the Fourth Amendment. That notion has no counterpart in a case like *Herring*, where the arresting/searching officer was prompted to act as he did by an error of Fourth Amendment magnitude made within the law enforcement system itself.

Since neither *Leon* nor *Krull* supports the *Herring* majority's magnitude-of-culpability approach, it is not surprising that the Court went on to seek other underpinnings for it, one being an assertion by Judge Friendly in an article nearly 45 years ago that "[t]he beneficent aim of the exclusionary rule to deter police conduct can be sufficiently accomplished by a practice . . . outlawing evidence obtained by flagrant or deliberate violation of rights."[190] The Friendly piece seems an odd choice, at best, if one is seeking to determine the proper limits of the Fourth Amendment exclusionary rule, for, as the *Herring* dissenters point out, the Friendly article argues that the rule should not apply just because the police have "blundered," thus aligning Friendly with the oft-quoted position of Justice (then Judge) Cardozo, who "distilled in a single * * * sentence"[191] the case against the exclusionary rule: "The criminal is to go free because the constable has blundered."[192] But this "misleading epigram"[193] has *never* been an ingredient in the pre-*Herring* exclusionary rule; it was

---

[190]Friendly, The Bill of Rights as a Code of Criminal Procedure, 53 Calif. L.Rev. 929, 953 (1965).

[191]Elkins v. United States, 364

U.S. 206, 80 S.Ct. 1437, 4 L.Ed.2d 1669 (1960).

[192]People v. Defore, 242 N.Y. 13, 150 N.E. 585 (1926).

quoted but then rejected by the Supreme Court in Fourth Amendment cases on more than one occasion.[194]

The *Herring* majority attempts to rehabilitate Friendly because of his prescience, characterizing his above-quoted words as "[a]nticipating the good-faith exception to the exclusionary rule." Not so! As discussed above, the main thrust of such cases as *Leon* and *Krull* is that the Fourth Amendment violation was brought about by an authoritative agency or individual outside law enforcement who is neither in need of deterrence or likely to be deterred by suppression of the fruits of that violation. There is in these cases, to be sure, recognition that there must also be some inquiry to ensure that the police should not have appreciated the subsequently-declared defect in the directive they received from the judiciary or legislature, thus assuring that there is no police deterrence function to be served. But that is a far cry from an across-the-board limitation of the exclusionary rule to instances of "flagrant or deliberate" violations of the Fourth Amendment. And in any event, *Leon* and *Krull* do not represent instances in which, even in the special circumstances obtaining in those cases, police conduct that is merely "negligent" is an occasion for nonsuppression. As the Court explained in *Krull* regarding the rule applicable in both of those cases, for the police to be acting "in objective good faith," so that the fruits of the Fourth Amendment violation need not be suppressed, it is essential to show that the officer acted "in objective reasonable reliance" upon the judge's warrant or the legislature's statute.

The *Herring* majority also contends that the Friendly position is on target because the conduct he would remove from the exclusionary sanction, and, indeed, the conduct that *Herring* does remove from that sanction, is "far removed from the core concerns that led us to adopt the rule in the first place." The reference, of course, is to *Weeks v. United States*[195] and *Mapp v. Ohio*,[196] where, it is emphasized in *Herring*, "flagrant conduct" was involved- search of a home without a warrant and without probable cause in *Weeks*, and search of a home on a false warrant in *Mapp*. But since in neither of these cases was the Supreme Court's adoption

---

[193]United States v. Leon, 468 U.S. 897, 104 S.Ct. 3405, 82 L.Ed.2d 677 (1984) (Brennan and Marshall, JJ., dissenting).

[194]As in Elkins v. United States, 364 U.S. 206, 80 S.Ct. 1437, 4 L.Ed.2d 1669 (1960); and Mapp v. Ohio, 367 U.S. 643, 81 S.Ct. 1684, 6 L.Ed.2d 1081 (1961).

On the other hand, Cardozo's language was most frequently embraced in the concurring and dissenting opinions of Chief Justice Burger.

See United States v. Payner, 447 U.S. 727, 100 S.Ct. 2439, 65 L.Ed.2d 468 (1980); Brewer v. Williams, 430 U.S. 387, 97 S.Ct. 1232, 51 L.Ed.2d 424 (1977); Bivens v. Six Unknown Named Agents of Federal Bureau of Narcotics, 403 U.S. 388, 91 S.Ct. 1999, 29 L.Ed.2d 619 (1971).

[195]Weeks v. United States, 232 U.S. 383, 34 S.Ct. 341, 58 L.Ed. 652 (1914).

[196]Mapp v. Ohio, 367 U.S. 643, 81 S.Ct. 1684, 6 L.Ed.2d 1081 (1961).

of an exclusionary rule, in the federal system and in the states, respectively, a we-hold-on-these-facts type of ruling, the claim that it was the flagrancy of the acts in *Weeks* and *Mapp* that led to adoption of the exclusionary rule is, at best, pure speculation. The opinion in *Weeks* described the flagrant conduct in some detail, but there is no suggestion of a degree-of-culpability limitation in the Court's ruling, which instead declares the absolute that "unlawful seizures * * * should find no sanction in the judgments of the courts." *Mapp* is, if anything, even more certain on this point, as while there again the flagrant acts are described in the case, the Court's ultimate holding could not be clearer: "all evidence obtained by searches and seizures in violation of the Constitution is, by that same authority, inadmissible in a state court."

The *Herring* majority's next line of attack, which has a bit more substance to it, is an argument by analogy to the Court's decision in *Franks v. Delaware.*[197] At issue in *Franks* was whether a defendant in a criminal case ever has a right, subsequent to the ex parte issuance of a search warrant, to challenge the affidavit upon which the warrant issued notwithstanding its facial sufficiency. The Court answered that in the affirmative, but limited somewhat the circumstances in which a hearing upon such a challenge must be held: the allegedly false statements had to be critical to the prior probable-cause finding, and there had to be "allegations of deliberate falsehood or of reckless disregard for the truth," as "[a]llegations of negligence or innocent mistake are insufficient." Hence the *Herring* majority concluded:

> Both this case and *Franks* concern false information provided by police. Under *Franks*, negligent police miscommunications in the course of acquiring a warrant do not provide a basis to rescind a warrant and render a search or arrest invalid. Here, the miscommunications occurred in a different context-after the warrant had been issued and recalled-but that fact should not require excluding the evidence obtained.

But, just as there can be "false information," there can be false analogies, and thus before this reasoning is accepted as providing a useful analogy to the step taken in *Herring*, it would seem that two questions deserve to be answered: (1) What is the reason underlying the Court's drawing of the negligent vs. intentional/reckless distinction in *Franks*? (2) Does that reason carry over to the different issue presented in *Herring*?

Unfortunately, the answer to the first of these questions is not to be found in *Franks*, for, notwithstanding the pre-*Franks* existence in some jurisdictions of an affidavit-impeaching process

---

[197]Franks v. Delaware, 438 U.S.   (1978).
154, 98 S.Ct. 2674, 57 L.Ed.2d 667

that extended even to negligent misrepresentations,[198] nothing is said in *Franks* as to precisely why the line was drawn as it was, except for the general observation that this balance was struck in light of the competing interests involved. But in asserting that "a flat ban on impeachment of veracity" was unjustified, it appears that the *Franks* Court wished to open the door, but not too far, thus leaving what is now referred to as a *Franks* hearing as somewhat of a disfavored procedure. This is understandable, as under the pre-*Franks* "four-corners" approach, followed in many jurisdictions, a challenge to the probable cause finding in a search warrant case was confined to the four-corners of the affidavit itself, meaning no evidentiary hearing was required. On the other hand, if impeachment of the affidavit is permitted, this can result in a lengthy time-consuming evidentiary hearing.[199] Holding, as *Franks* does, that no hearing need be held unless the defendant makes a preliminary showing of subjective fault in the affiant, significantly limits the number of cases in which such hearing must be held. Moreover, drawing the line as the Court did in *Franks* avoids the difficult question[200] of whether a factual assertion in an affidavit subsequently shown to be false (or, especially, a true fact not included in the affidavit) was included (or omitted) innocently or negligently. Beyond this, the *Franks* Court may have been influenced by the teaching of *United States v. Ventresca*[201] that a "grudging or negative attitude by reviewing courts toward warrants will tend to discourage police officers from submitting their evidence to a judicial office before acting." In any event, it is clear that *none* of these considerations are at play in *Herring*. Indeed, the *Herring* rule cuts in exactly the opposite direction by intruding a new and often difficult issue into many suppression hearings, as the *Herring* dissenters properly noted.[202]

There is good reason to be highly critical of the majority opinion in the *Herring* case. One reason is because, as explained above, much of what the majority has to say in support of its result has a bogus quality to it. But another reason, perhaps even more compelling, concerns what is missing from that opinion. Since the Court's holding rests upon the conclusion that Fourth Amendment violations of the negligence variety (or, as discussed below, at least some of them) are different from more culpable violations because the "benefits of deterrence" are significantly lower in

[198]See, e.g., Theodor v. Superior Court, 8 Cal.3d 77, 104 Cal.Rptr. 226, 501 P.2d 234 (1972).

[199]See, e.g., United States v. Averell, 296 F.Supp. 1004 (E.D.N.Y. 1969), where the hearing in which challenge of the truth of the affidavit was made took 12 days.

[200]See United States v. Carmichael, 489 F.2d 983 (7th Cir.1973).

[201]United States v. Ventresca, 380 U.S. 102, 85 S.Ct. 741, 13 L.Ed.2d 684 (1965).

[202]As the dissenters note, the majority in *Herring* "has imposed a considerable administrative burden on courts and law enforcement."

such circumstances, one would think that somewhere in the *Herring* case there would appear a direct statement as to precisely why this is so. But no such statement by the *Herring* majority is to be found. This is a shocking omission, but is in a sense understandable, as it is far from apparent that any halfway plausible case for that proposition can be made.

The first argument that comes to mind in that regard is that the "benefits of deterrence" are low in negligence cases because negligent acts are not subject to meaningful deterrence. While this point is certainly implied in the opinion of the Chief Justice, nothing is offered by way of establishing that this is so. It would seem that it is not so, for, as pointed out by the four *Herring* dissenters, such a

> suggestion runs counter to a foundational premise of tort law-that liability for negligence, i.e., lack of due care, creates an incentive to act with greater care. The Government so acknowledges. * * *
>
> That the mistake here involved the failure to make a computer entry hardly means that application of the exclusionary rule would have minimal value. "Just as the risk of *respondeat superior* liability encourages employers to supervise . . . their employees' conduct [more carefully], so the risk of exclusion encourages policymakers and systems managers to monitor the performance of the systems they install and the personnel employed to operate those systems."

Remarkably, the majority's only response to this point is a footnote objection that they "do not suggest" exclusion in such cases "could have *no* deterrent effect," apparently a backhanded way of saying that in negligence cases there is significantly less deterrent effect, although once again nothing at all is offered to support that conclusion. Nor is it apparent what might have been offered. If the "benefits of deterrence" would have been sufficiently weighty if the bad recordkeeping had been attributable to intentional or reckless conduct of an employee of the sheriff's office, presumably because the suppression would have prompted the sheriff to take appropriate corrective measures, why is it less likely the sheriff would so act in response to the suppression where the more probable event[203] of an employee's negligence brought about equally serious consequences?

And, because the consequences are equally serious whatever the degree of culpability of the sheriff's employee, it is apparent

---

[203] As noted in Murphy, Databases, Doctrine and Constitutional Criminal Procedure, 37 Fordham Urb.L.J. 803, 835 (2010), "regulation of databases require constitutional criminal procedure to focus less upon deliberate or intentional abuses of power than upon unintentional omissions, or mere benign neglect. There is always the risk that a malfeasant actor will corrupt or exploit a database system, to be sure. But constitutional regulation of databases aimed at ferreting out intentional harms will be very thin indeed; it is far easier to do harm, and far greater harm can be done, through mere benign neglect of database systems than through intentional manipulation."

that no distinction can be drawn in terms of just what *results* need to be deterred. For five months Herring was at risk of being arrested on a withdrawn warrant, a risk that ended only after he was in fact arrested (apparently the only event likely to have corrected the records error and thus to have ended the risk for the future[204]), but this was so whether the records error was attributable to intentional, reckless or negligent conduct. Nor can it plausibly be argued that negligent violations of the Fourth Amendment, as a class, are not sufficiently harmful to be an appropriate subject of the exclusionary doctrine. As any habitual reader of Fourth Amendment appellate opinions can attest, many more violations of the Fourth Amendment are the result of carelessness than are attributable to deliberate misconduct. Application of the exclusionary rule, the Supreme Court instructs, demonstrates "that our society attaches serious consequences to violations of constitutional rights,"[205] and provides "an incentive to err on the side of constitutional behavior."[206] There is nothing about the volume or nature of negligent violations of the Fourth Amendment that makes such demonstration unnecessary, and providing an incentive to do things right is no less important when the wrongdoing was simply failing to pay attention.

While the negligent character of the actor's conduct appears to be the principle feature of the category excluded by *Herring*, the line the Court draws is actually narrower than this, as the Court's holding only covers such negligence as is "attenuated" from the subsequent search or seizure-in *Herring* itself the defendant's arrest on the nonexistent warrant. This means that the analysis up to this point is in a sense incomplete, as any critique of *Herring* must take into account this "attenuated" qualifier. It is well to note, however, that *Herring* is a "scary" decision in the same sense that *Hudson* is, in that both cases involve "analysis" that far outruns the holding. In *Hudson* the holding has to do only with a particular kind of Fourth Amendment violation, unjustified no-knock entries, but language in the opinion seems to claim that the Fourth Amendment's exclusionary rule has more generally become obsolete. In *Herring*, the holding is limited to such negligence as is "attenuated" (whatever that means, about which more below), but the reasoning seems directed at an across-by-board embrace of Judge Friendly's thesis, under which only "flagrant or deliberate" violations of the Fourth Amendment count when it comes to the exclusionary rule. That is, both *Hudson* and *Herring* seem to be setting the table for a more ominous holding on some future occasion. In a sense, *Herring* is more scary than *Hudson* because it is somewhat easier to anticipate the Court

---

[204]As the *Herring* dissenters note, the "record reflects no routine practice of checking the database for accuracy."

[205]Stone v. Powell, 428 U.S. 465,

96 S.Ct. 3037, 49 L.Ed.2d 1067 (1976).

[206]United States v. Johnson, 457 U.S. 537, 102 S.Ct. 2579, 73 L.Ed.2d 202 (1982).

later taking a bigger bite out of the exclusionary rule than abandoning it entirely.[207] It is thus understandable that some have responded to the *Herring* decision with alarm precisely because they believe that the "attenuated" qualifier in that case will soon evaporate,[208] a step some lower courts appear more than willing to take.[209] As the preceding discussion demonstrates, there does not exist a legitimate basis for excising all negligence cases from the exclusionary rule.

With that out of the way, it is possible to return to the *Herring* holding itself and ask (i) just how broad the *holding* in the case actually is, considering the "attenuated" qualifier; and (ii) whether there is something about this status of attenuation that actually lessens the "deterrent effect" of evidence exclusion, so that it is legitimate to remove all such cases from the reach of the exclusionary rule. Such inquiry, it would seem, must begin by asking exactly what the word "attenuated" means as used in *Herring*. The word pops up only one other time in the *Herring* majority opinion, but neither there nor earlier is any effort made to describe the sense in which that word is being employed. (That this is so would seem to reinforce the speculation that the Chief Justice's opinion was originally drafted to free *all* forms of negligence from the exclusionary rule, and that the "attenuated" qualification became a necessary add-on to garner the needed fifth vote.[210])

While something is attenuated when it becomes diluted, lessened or weakened, it is far from clear in what sense that can that be said to be true on the facts of *Herring*, especially since the negligent bookkeeping carried as much force on the date the defendant was arrested as it did when made. The word "attenuated" in *Herring* conceivably refers to any number of things: (i)

---

[207]As for why total abandonment is unlikely, see note 167 supra.

[208]Consider McAdams, Herring and the Exclusionary Rule, appearing at http://uchicagolaw.typepad.com/faculty/2009/01/herring-and-the-exclusionary-rule.html ("But if 'attenuated from the arrest' turns out not to mean much and not to limit the exception, then courts will refuse exclusion whenever the defendant fails to prove the police violation was recurring or more than negligent. The effect here would be to create a strong presumption *against* exclusion."); Goldstein, The Surpassing Significance of Herring, http://www.scotusblog.com/wp/the-surpassing-significance-of-herring/ ("The one limitation on the Court's opinion—and it will be the key to determining whether it reworks Fourth Amend-

ment jurisprudence very significantly—is the Court's statement that its rule applies to police conduct 'attenuated from the arrest.' Those statements constrain today's holding largely to the bounds of existing law. But the logic of the decision spans far more broadly, and the next logical step—which I predict is 2 years away—is abandoning the 'attenuation' reference altogether.")

[209]See note 267 infra.

[210]"The reason for this * * * is, I strongly suspect, due to the refusal of Justice Anthony Kennedy to go along with the broad reworking of the exclusionary rule desired by the other four justices in the majority of this 5-4 decision." Bradley, Red Herring or the Death of the Exclusionary Rule?, 45 Trial 52, 53 (Apr.2009).

that the negligence was by someone other than the officer who made the arrest;[211] (ii) that the negligence was an omission rather than an act;[212] (iii) that the negligence occurred five months prior to the arrest;[213] (iv) that the negligence was by a person in a different jurisdiction than the locale of arrest and/or prosecution, who for that reason is not as amenable to deterrence;[214] (v) that the negligence had to do with the maintenance of police records, a subset of police activity not prone to error or in need of deterrence;[215] or (vi) that while the negligence was by a law enforcement employee, that employee, by virtue of his or her assignment, is less in need of deterrence than the typical policeman.[216] As to each of these alternatives, it must be asked (a) how likely it is that this is the *Herring* majority's perception of the qualifier "attenuated," and (b) whether it can be said that such a perception of "attenuated" actually describes a class of conduct as to which the critical consequence of reduced "benefits of deterrence" actually exists.

Under an option (i) interpretation of *Herring*, all "second-hand" Fourth Amendment negligence, that is, negligence committed by someone other than the arresting/searching officer and not known by that officer, would no longer be subject to the exclusionary rule. There is some suggestion in *Herring* that this is what the majority is thinking, especially in their attempt to match the instant case up with *Leon*. It is claimed that since that case does not require suppression of "evidence obtained in objectively reasonable reliance on a subsequently invalidated search warrant," then the "same is true when evidence is obtained in objectively reasonable reliance on a subsequently recalled warrant." By thus equating reliance on a warrant later invalidated with reliance on a warrant that doesn't even exist, the *Herring* Court seems to be

---

[211]As pointed out by the *Herring* majority, this proposition was emphasized by the court of appeals, which noted that the arresting officers "were entirely innocent of any wrongdoing or carelessness."

[212]The *Herring* majority observed that the lower court characterized the clerk's conduct as "a negligent failure to act."

[213]It has been suggested that the "attenuated" language in *Herring* "appears to refer to the fact that the clerical error was made five months before the arrest." McAdams, Herring and the Exclusionary Rule, appearing at http://uchicagolaw.typepad.com/faculty/2009/01/herring-and-the-exclusionary-rule.html.

[214]It has been said of *Herring* that "it is unclear whether the fact that these were police from a different county is significant or not." Bradley, 45 Trial 52, 53 (Apr.2009).

[215]McAdams, Herring and the Exclusionary Rule, appearing at http://uchicagolaw.typepad.com/faculty/2009/01/herring-and-the-exclusionary-rule.html, speculates that the Court might later "distinguish errors that do not involve record-keeping."

[216]Such an interpretation would be consistent with Orin Kerr's conclusion that *Herring* "is a minor case," as stated at http://volokh.com/posts/123196.1926.shtml, one that is "almost a replay" of Arizona v. Evans, 514 U.S. 1, 115 S.Ct. 1185, 131 L.Ed.2d 34 (1995), as stated at http://groups.yaho o.com/group/Lex_Rex/message/1885.

saying that the matter must be viewed solely from the perspective of the arresting/searching officer, so that if he as an individual is not at fault then the exclusionary rule is inapplicable. Yet there also exists in the *Herring* majority opinion other language reflected that those Justices fully appreciate that such a broad view of the "attenuated" concept cannot be squared with the Court's prior holdings on the scope of the exclusionary rule. Quoting important language from the very same *Leon* case,[217] the Court quite correctly asserts than in "analyzing the applicability of the rule * * * we must consider the action of all the police officers involved." That word "all" obviously includes those members of law enforcement who communicate information to others who then are prompted to act by making a seizure or search.[218]

But one is not totally reassured by the inclusion of this latter language in *Herring*, given comments by many of the same Justices in *Arizona v. Evans*[219] regarding *Whiteley v. Warden*.[220] *Whiteley* held that where an officer makes an arrest on reasonable reliance upon a radio bulletin, the Fourth Amendment still requires suppression of the evidence obtained thereby if that bulletin was not in fact grounded in probable cause. But *Whiteley* was summarily dismissed in *Evans* on the basis that it was grounded in the now-rejected approach under which "the Court treated identification of a Fourth Amendment violation as synonymous with application of the exclusionary rule to evidence secured incident to that violation." *Whiteley* is an exceedingly important Fourth Amendment decision, for without it an officer lacking grounds to search or seize could avoid any risk of suppression by merely passing the job on to another officer. Especially in light of the frequency with which police are prompted to make seizures and searches based upon communications with other police,[221] it would be unconscionable if *Whiteley* were, in effect, largely nullified by construing all *Whiteley* situations as fitting with *Herring*'s attenuation principle. If that is what *Herring*

---

[217]"It is necessary to consider the objective reasonableness, not only of the officers who eventually executed a warrant, but also of the officers who originally obtained it or who provided information material to the probable-cause determination."

[218]State v. Handy, 206 N.J. 39, 18 A.3d 179 (2011) (where officer in the field arrested defendant upon being advised by dispatcher that there an outstanding arrest warrant for defendant, but the dispatcher acted on the basis of a 10-year-old warrant for a California resident with a slightly different name and a different birth date, *Herring* does not apply to such "con-duct by the dispatcher, an integral link in the law enforcement chain," as "[a]ttenuation is not a part of the factual calculus before us," and thus here "suppressing the evidence garnered from this illegal search would have important deterrent value, would underscore the need for training officers and dispatchers to focus on detail").

[219]Arizona v. Evans, 514 U.S. 1, 115 S.Ct. 1185, 131 L.Ed.2d 34 (1995).

[220]Whiteley v. Warden, Wyo. State Penitentiary, 401 U.S. 560, 91 S.Ct. 1031, 28 L.Ed.2d 306 (1971).

[221]See § 3.5.

contemplates, then the day has arrived when the Fourth Amendment is truly nothing more than "a form of words."[222]

Precisely because an option (i) interpretation of "attenuated-"would cut such a wide swath through the exclusionary rule, any of the other five possibilities may seem relatively benign by comparison. However, each of the other interpretations has its own difficulties. Option (ii) seems the least likely, for no plausible reason is apparent as to why the "deterrent effect" of the exclusionary rule could be said to be different depending upon whether the Fourth Amendment violation was of the omission rather than commission variety. That is, if the bookkeeping error had been the mistaken and negligent entry of defendant's name as being the person for whom a warrant had issued, it is difficult to see why that situation should be treated any differently than the actual facts of *Herring*.

As for option (iii), as noted earlier, it is of course true that in another branch of exclusionary rule jurisprudence, that having to do with the "fruit of the poisonous tree," a temporal span between the "tree," that is the occasion of the underlying Fourth Amendment violation, and the "fruit," the evidence the defendant now seeks to suppress, is of some relevance. But the fact that time is a relevant consideration in working out the matter of causation hardly suggests that it is likewise relevant as to the issue presented by *Herring*. If one were to assume a case like *Herring* except that the failure to strike the withdrawn warrant had occurred five days earlier instead of five months earlier, that would hardly seem to make any difference, as in both instances the erroneous record was in place at the time it was consulted, and thus in a quite direct way caused an arrest of the defendant despite the absence of any actual basis for it. In short, whatever one's view of the concept of "deterrent effect," it is difficult to see how that effect would somehow diminish with the passage of time.[223]

Consider then option (iv), the notion that attenuation existed in *Herring* because the mistake occurred in a different county than the resulting arrest and/or prosecution. The *Herring* majority did not specifically embrace such a reading of its "attenuated" qualifier, but it is noteworthy that the Court at one point did emphasize that "somebody in Dale County" was responsible for the error in the records there and that the "Coffee County officers did nothing improper." Moreover, in affirming the decision of the court of appeals, it is noted that the lower court's decision was

---

[222]Mapp v. Ohio, 367 U.S. 643, 81 S.Ct. 1684, 6 L.Ed.2d 1081 (1961).

[223]Indeed, there is a sense in which the passage of time makes the circumstances more egregious and thus more in need of deterrence. As noted in another case with facts similar to those in *Herring*, the defendant "was a 'marked man' for the five months prior to his arrest." United States v. Mackey, 387 F.Supp. 1121 (D.Nev.1975).

grounded in a finding that the negligence in the instant case was in fact "attenuated," so it is worth noting here an important aspect of the court of appeals' analysis. That court stated:

> There is also the unique circumstance here that the exclusionary sanction would be levied not in a case brought by officers of the department that was guilty of the negligent record keeping, but instead it would scuttle a case brought by officers of a different department in another county, one whose officers and personnel were entirely innocent of any wrongdoing or carelessness. We do not mean to suggest that Dale County law enforcement agencies are not interested in the successful prosecution of crime throughout the state, but their primary responsibility and interest lies in their own cases. Hoping to gain a beneficial deterrent effect on Dale County personnel by excluding evidence in a case brought by Coffee County officers would be like telling a student that if he skips school one of his classmates will be punished. The student may not exactly relish the prospect of causing another to suffer, but human nature being what it is, he is unlikely to fear that prospect as much as he would his own suffering. For all of these reasons, we are convinced that this is one of those situations where "[a]ny incremental deterrent effect which might be achieved by extending the rule . . . is uncertain at best," * * * where the benefits of suppression would be "marginal or nonexistent," and where the exclusionary rule would not "pay its way by deterring official lawlessness."[224]

This notion that the Fourth Amendment exclusionary rule stops at the county line is an odd one indeed, especially when it is recognized that the argument set out in the above quotation has not to do simply with the fact that the *arrest* was made by an officer in another county but that also the case was "brought" in the neighboring county,[225] so that application of the exclusionary rule would "scuttle a case" brought other than in the county where the record error occurred. But that assertion-the notion that the deterrence effect of the exclusionary rule is significantly diminished when the much-trumpeted "cost" (loss of a conviction that doubtless would not have been obtained anyway had the Fourth Amendment been complied with) occurs in another jurisdiction, so that the rule should not apply in such circumstances-runs contrary to longstanding and well-accepted Fourth Amendment doctrine. The fact that the exclusionary rule is applicable even when the jurisdiction of the offending individual and the jurisdiction that would lose the fruits via suppression are different was settled even before *Mapp v. Ohio*,[226] when the Supreme Court in *Elkins v. United States*[227] abolished the so-called "silver platter" doctrine. Ever since *Elkins*, it has been clear that evidence

---

[224]United States v. Herring, 492 F.3d 1212 (11th Cir.2007).

[225]The court of appeals was not strictly correct in this respect, of course, as the case was "brought," in the sense of being prosecuted, in fed-

eral court for violations of federal law.

[226]Mapp v. Ohio, 367 U.S. 643, 81 S.Ct. 1684, 6 L.Ed.2d 1081 (1961).

[227]Elkins v. United States, 364 U.S. 206, 80 S.Ct. 1437, 4 L.Ed.2d 1669 (1960).

obtained in violation of the Fourth Amendment must be suppressed (1) when the error was by state officers and the evidence is offered in a federal prosecution,[228] (2) when the error was by federal officers and the evidence is offered in a state prosecution,[229] (3) when the error was by officers in one state and the evidence is offered in a prosecution in another state,[230] and, most certainly, (4) when the error was by officers in one county and the evidence is offered in a prosecution in another county of that state.[231] Although *Elkins* pre-dates *Mapp*, it is directly relevant to the matter under issue here, for the Court in that case grounded its decision in the proposition that the exclusionary rule's "purpose is to deter-to compel respect for the constitutional guaranty in the only effectively available way–by removing the incentive to disregard it." Such purpose was served in the instant case, the Court reasoned, in light of the extent of "federal-state cooperation in criminal investigation." Considering that the most common form of cooperation between jurisdictions is that involving the exchange of information, such as about outstanding warrants, the firmly established *Elkins* doctrine stands as a most effective rebuttal of the argument made by the court of appeals in *Herring*.

Of course, in the typical *Elkins* situation the search was conducted by an officer in one jurisdiction and the fruits are being offered in another jurisdiction, while *Herring* is a bit more complex in that the police error producing the constitutional violation occurred in one county, the illegal-arrest consequence was then innocently brought about by an officer of another county, and then finally the fruits were tendered in a federal prosecution. But if under *Elkins* the jurisdiction-of-prosecution difference is of no significance, it is hard to see how it is that the jurisdiction-of-arrest difference should matter. The contrary has sometimes been asserted; for example, in *Hoay v. State*,[232] a case quite similar to *Herring*, the dissenting justices argued that the exclusionary rule should not apply where "the arresting officer from one county relied in good faith upon the information from another county." But their explanation for this conclusion was that "there was nothing the arresting officer could have done except ignore the outstanding warrant, and that would have been a clear dereliction of his duty." Quite obviously, that reasoning gives no support to a county-line limitation on the exclusionary rule, for had

---

[228]E.g., United States v. Self, 410 F.2d 984 (10th Cir.1969); Sablowski v. United States, 403 F.2d 347 (10th Cir. 1968).

[229]E.g., United States ex rel. Coffey, v. Fay, 344 F.2d 625 (2d Cir.1965); State v. Harms, 233 Neb. 882, 449 N.W.2d 1 (1989).

[230]E.g., United States ex rel. Krogness v. Gladden, 242 F.Supp. 499 (D.Or.1965); State v. Krogness, 238 Or. 135, 388 P.2d 120 (1963).

[231]E.g., Hoay v. State, 348 Ark. 80, 71 S.W.3d 573 (2002).

[232]Hoay v. State, 348 Ark. 80, 71 S.W.3d 573 (2002).

the officer making the arrest in *Herring* been an officer in the department where the error was made he would have been in precisely the same predicament. And because the arresting officer himself was in no sense at fault, so that neither the officer personally nor his employing jurisdiction could be held liable to pay damages,[233] there is no reason to believe that if the arrest in *Herring* had been by a same-county officer, then that officer's actions would have had a more profound impact upon that sheriff's department in a deterrence sense.

In short, since it was the negligent maintenance of the records rather than the conduct of the arresting/searching officer that produced the Fourth Amendment violation in *Herring*, the location of the arresting officer should make no difference. As the point was put by the *Hoay* majority, if the "fault" there regarding the unconstitutional arrest was not in the arresting officer but rather in the police records in another county, it "would fly in the face of the *Leon* principle * * * were this court to refuse to suppress," as *Leon* "makes clear" that "the touchstone of the exclusionary rule is deterrence of police misconduct," and thus "that rule should apply equally to" such "defective recordkeeping." Indeed, there is one sense in which arrests based upon out-of-jurisdiction bogus records are a more serious matter; in *Herring*, for example, it meant that the defendant was at risk of being illegally arrested on the false Dale County records even when he was outside that county.[234] (However, some lower court cases applying *Herring* have placed special emphasis upon the multi-jurisdiction circumstances present.)[235]

What then of option (v), under which the requisite attenuation is deemed to occur only through a process of a mistaken entry into a law enforcement recordkeeping system and the subsequent extraction and reliance upon that misinformation to justify an arrest or search? That this is what the *Herring* majority meant by

---

[233]As noted by the *Herring* dissenters, in such a case the "arresting officer would be sheltered by qualified immunity, * * * and the police department itself is not liable for the negligent acts of its employees."

[234]Although this was apparently not the case in *Herring* itself, in a great many instances the erroneous police record will haunt the defendant wherever he goes. See, e.g., United States v. Mackey, 387 F.Supp. 1121 (D.Nev.1975), noting that once misinformation was introduced into the NCIC computer, defendant could have been falsely arrested "anywhere in the United States where law enforcement officers had access to NCIC information."

[235]See, e.g., Shotts v. State, 925 N.E.2d 719 (Ind.2010) (where Ind. police arrested upon NCIC-verified existence of Ala. felony arrest warrant for defendant, then even if warrant issued on bare bones affidavit, so that *Leon* inapplicable, per *Herring* result should not be exclusion in Ind. "where the Indiana authorities behaved reasonably and responsibly," as exclusion in Ind. "would not deter the Alabama officer who applied for the Alabama warrant"; court asserts case for exclusion here less compelling than in *Herring*, which involved "failed communication between two counties," as here "any flaw in the warrant was not attributable to Indiana at all").

the "attenuated" limitation on its holding is not apparent, but there is a suggestion at least that this is so because of the majority's reliance upon *Arizona v. Evans*,[236] another erroneous-records case (albeit involving judicial records), leading to the declaration that the error in the instant case was of a lesser magnitude than in *Evans* because such errors in the *Evans* warrant records were slightly less rare.[237] But even if it thus might be concluded that *Herring* involves "only a slight change from *Arizona v. Evans*,"[238] this hardly means that the *Herring* case, so construed, can simply be dismissed because of its benign character, for (as discussed further below) in the broad view of things the problem of Fourth Amendment violations resulting from bad recordkeeping can hardly be dismissed as insignificant.

Assuming that the "attenuated" limitation in *Herring* is directed specifically at bookkeeping errors in police records, it is once again necessary to ask the question put earlier as to other aspects and other possible readings of that case: exactly what is there about this particular variety of Fourth Amendment violation that produces the necessary reduced "benefits of deterrence"? While not even a clue is to be found in the *Herring* majority opinion, it might be thought that the answer lies in making a calculation similar to that in *Hudson v. Michigan*,[239] purportedly showing that the particular kind of violation there at issue (noncompliance with the knock-and-announce requirement) wasn't in need of more deterrence via the exclusionary rule. The contention in *Hudson* was that "the incentive to such violations is minimal to begin with" because the only thing to be gained by unannounced entry is "prevention of destruction of evidence and the avoidance of life-threatening resistance by occupants of the premises," the very risks that make the knock-and-announce procedures inapplicable in particular cases.

Actually, the government in *Herring* did make a no-more-deterrence-needed type of argument; as noted by the dissenters, the government contended "that police forces already possess sufficient incentives to maintain up-to-date records," as "the police have no desire to send officers out on arrests unnecessarily, because arrests consume resources and place officers in danger." But the facts of *Herring* belie that assertion. As the four dissenters aptly note: "The facts of this case do not fit that description of police motivation. Here the officer wanted to arrest Herring and consulted the Department's records to legitimate his

---

[236] Arizona v. Evans, 514 U.S. 1, 115 S.Ct. 1185, 131 L.Ed.2d 34 (1995).

[237] The *Herring* Court noted that in the instant case testimony of the record clerk was that she could "remember no similar miscommunication ever happening on their watch," touted as "even less error" than in *Evans*, where the testimony was as to a similar error "every three or four years."

[238] Bradley, 45 Trial 52, 53 (Apr. 2009).

[239] Hudson v. Michigan, 547 U.S. 586, 126 S.Ct. 2159, 165 L.Ed.2d 56 (2006).

predisposition." Nor is there any reason to believe that this aspect of *Herring* is anything out of the ordinary. During the course of *Terry* stops on reasonable suspicion of criminal activity, it is very common for the officer to obtain the suspect's identity and then run a warrant check.[240] And during a traffic stop, even for the most petty of infractions, it has become part of the "routine" to run a warrant check not only on the driver, but also on all the passengers.[241]

Given the pervasiveness and utility of the warrant check in current practice, certainly a higher level of illegal arrests because of clerical errors is likely to appear advantageous rather than disadvantageous if there is no risk that windfall evidence acquired by arrest on a nonexistent warrant will be suppressed. This is especially the case since the nature of the illegality is such that the arresting officers in these instances cannot be faulted for having made the arrests. Indeed, after *Herring* police are unlikely to be troubled by the fact that these windfalls are being gained only at the cost of violating the constitutional rights of citizens; as *Terry v. Ohio*[242] teaches, "admitting evidence in a criminal trial * * * has the necessary effect of legitimizing the conduct which produced the evidence."

A somewhat different claim of the requisite reduced "benefits of deterrence" might be grounded in the supposed infrequency of errors in police records. That the *Herring* Court may have been thinking along these lines is suggested by the fact that the majority emphasized that in the sheriff's department involved, witnesses "testified that they could remember no similar miscommunication ever happening on their watch." Thus, the thinking might be that since such a mistake had never been made before, it was unlikely ever to occur again, and thus suppression in the interest of prompting closer supervision of that records system would hardly be necessary. But viewing the problem nationwide and not merely as to the record system at issue in *Herring*, there is every reason to believe that illegal arrests attributable to record error is no small problem. For one thing, through a process of data aggregation and data mining,[243] greatly facilitated by modern technology, law enforcement agencies now have available a volume of information in their records far exceeding that maintained in the past. This data is not limited simply to such matters as outstanding warrants, but includes a broad range of information that could be accepted as factually accurate and then used in total or partial justification of a seizure or search. Also, computers have facilitated information sharing, so that much of this data is now available to other law enforcement agencies. In short, as the four *Herring* dissenters put it: "Electronic databases

---

[240]See cases collected in § 9.2 note 208.

[241]See § 9.3(c).

[242]Terry v. Ohio, 392 U.S. 1, 88 S.Ct. 1868, 20 L.Ed.2d 889 (1968).

[243]See § 2.7(e).

form the nervous system of contemporary criminal justice operations."

There is no basis for concluding that the amount of error in this vast array of data is at some tolerable or irreducible minimum. Government reports indicate "that law enforcement databases are insufficiently monitored and often out of date."[244] And the appellate cases discussed elsewhere herein[245] make it apparent that illegal arrests and searches attributable to error in police records is no small problem. (Those cases, of course, reflect only a part of the problem, considering "that there are many unlawful searches * * * of innocent people which turn up nothing incriminating * * * about which courts do nothing, and about which we never hear."[246]) Moreover, as mentioned earlier, bad recordkeeping such as that in *Herring*, representing that there is an outstanding arrest warrant on a person when there is not, has a ticking time bomb character to it, and in that sense is a more serious matter than many other sorts of Fourth Amendment violations. When at a particular time and place a particular police officer unreasonably interprets the observed circumstances and makes an arrest that ought not have been made, this is bad enough, but at least it is a single event with rather narrow time-place-occasion dimensions. But a mistake of the kind at issue in *Herring* is quite a different matter; "computerization greatly amplifies an error's effect," as "inaccurate data can infect not only one agency, but the many agencies that share access to the database."[247] Such errors can result in the object of the erroneous information being arrested repeatedly,[248] and make that individual a "marked man" subject to illegal arrest "anywhere," "at any time," and "into the indefinite future."[249]

Finally, there is option (vi) regarding the possible interpretation of the word "attenuated" as used in *Herring*, one that finds the requisite reduced "benefits of deterrence" in the nature of the job held by the individual whose negligent act led to the illegal arrest. Under this view of *Herring*, it could be said that the Court

---

[244]As it was put by the *Herring* dissenters, citing several government reports.

[245]See § 3.5(d).

[246]Brinegar v. United States, 338 U.S. 160, 69 S.Ct. 1302, 93 L.Ed. 1879 (1949) (Jackson, J., dissenting).

[247]As stated in Justice Ginsburg's dissent in Arizona v. Evans, 514 U.S. 1, 115 S.Ct. 1185, 131 L.Ed.2d 34 (1995), noting, for example, that NCIC records are available to about 71,000 federal, state and local agencies, so that "any mistake entered into the NCIC spreads nationwide in an instant."

[248]See, e.g., Finch v. Chapman, 785 F.Supp. 1277 (N.D.Ill.1992) (misinformation long retained in NCIC records resulted in plaintiff being arrested and detained twice); Rogan v. Los Angeles, 668 F.Supp. 1384 (C.D.Cal.1987) (as a result of misinformation in computer records, plaintiff arrested four times, three times at gunpoint).

[249]United States v. Mackey, 387 F.Supp. 1121 (D.Nev.1975).

has merely taken the reasoning in *Arizona v. Evans*[250] and extended it to what was believed to be a very closely analogous situation, where again the error is not attributable to a "front line" or "on the street" police officer but rather someone performing clerical tasks. *Evans* is a case much like *Herring*, except that the mistake was attributable to a clerk who worked in the judicial branch. In holding the exclusionary rule inapplicable in those circumstances, the Court relied largely upon the proposition that there was no basis for concluding that "court employees are inclined to ignore or subvert the Fourth Amendment." The implication is that these court employees (who, the *Evans* Court reminds us, are not "engaged in the competitive enterprise of ferreting out crime") are hardly motivated to undertake calculated intrusions upon Fourth Amendment interests, and consequently are unworthy objects of the exclusionary rule and its deterrence function. Thus it might be concluded that the "attenuated" test is met in *Herring* precisely because that is an apt description of clerks generally, without regard to whether they are located in the courthouse or the police station.

Whether this is the unstated underpinning of *Herring* is not clear, although the possibility that this is the case is suggested by the majority's disclaimer that *Evans* "was entirely 'premised on a distinction between judicial errors and police errors,'" as well as the majority's game of "gotcha" with the dissenters-dismissing Justice Breyer's reliance on a judicial errors/police errors distinction by noting that in *Evans* Justice Ginsburg had characterized such a distinction as "artificial." Perhaps the reason the *Herring* majority said no more along these lines was because it was not possible on the record in that case to determine the precise status of the person whose negligence left the warrant notice outstanding in the sheriff's department's records. But, while the court below merely "assume[d] * * * that the negligent actor, who is unidentified in the record, is an adjunct to law enforcement,"[251] it appears likely that the offender was either a person holding the position of "warrant clerk" or someone under her supervision.[252] In support of *Herring*, therefore, it might be asserted that a warrant clerk in the sheriff's department needs no more deterrence than the warrant clerk over in the courthouse.

With *Evans* on the books, this interpretation of the *Herring* "attenuated" requirement certainly has more appeal than any of the others previously considered. (For one thing, such an interpretation would ensure that *Herring* is limited in same fashion as *Evans*, producing the most desirable result that if there is a

---

[250]Arizona v. Evans, 514 U.S. 1, 115 S.Ct. 1185, 131 L.Ed.2d 34 (1995).

[251]United States v. Herring, 492 F.3d 1212 (11th Cir.2007).

[252]The Court in *Herring* says that this is the person who "[n]ormally * * * enters the information in the sheriff's computer database" when a warrant is recalled.

mistake in a police record, computer or otherwise, but the mistake was not that of the recordkeepers but of detectives and other police officials who supplied information for the records, the defendant would prevail.[253]) There is still reason to be concerned about *Herring*, however, even if it is ameliorated by such a limited reading. Given that the *Herring* exception to the exclusionary rule covers only instances of "isolated negligence attenuated from the arrest," there is something odd about the conclusion that only some negligence is being exempted, namely that by clerical personnel, and that the reason is because such persons are not motivated to engage in *deliberate* violations of the Fourth Amendment. As noted earlier, the central concern is with negligently maintained records, which is a current problem of considerable magnitude, and consequently the criticisms stated earlier with respect to the option (v) interpretation of "attenuated" would appear to be largely applicable to option (vi) as well.

Moreover, in terms of minimizing the risk of erroneous records leading to arrests and searches in violation of the Fourth Amendment, it does not necessarily follow from the fact that *Evans* exempts the errors of judicial clerks that the same result should obtain as to police clerks. When the clerk is also a member of the police department, whether civilian employee or uniformed officer, the police agency is in a better position to remedy the situation and might well do so if the exclusionary rule were there to remove the incentive to do otherwise. Finally, this option (vi) reading of *Herring* has less going for it than the view of the dissenters in that case for yet another reason: the *Evans* distinction between police errors and nonpolice errors presents a clear line, but once it is concluded that police employees must be sorted out on the basis of their assignment, the temptation will be to extend the exemption to others, such as dispatchers,[254] whose conduct has traditionally and rightly been viewed as within the exclusionary rule's purview.[255]

While the foregoing extended discussion of *Herring* would indicate that the decision is more to be regretted than praised, it is now a part of our Fourth Amendment jurisprudence, and hence it is necessary to consider how trial and appellate courts should go about interpreting and applying the case whenever presented with a fact situation not on all fours with *Herring*. That will sometimes be a daunting task, given the fact that *Herring*

---

[253]People v. Willis, 28 Cal.4th 22, 120 Cal.Rptr.2d 105, 46 P.3d 898 (2002).

[254]As in United States v. Groves, 559 F.3d 637 (7th Cir.2009), deeming *Herring* applicable "whether the bulletin was mistakenly entered into the department's system as a warrant or whether the dispatcher mistook it for a warrant when communicating with officers in the field after the 911 call."

[255]United States v. Shareef, 100 F.3d 1491 (10th Cir.1996) ("the exclusionary rule should be applied when a *dispatcher*'s error leads to a violation of the Fourth Amendment"); State v. Trenidad, 23 Wash.App. 418, 595 P.2d 957 (1979).

requires what two of the dissenters aptly referred to an a "multifactored inquiry"-yet another reason to have doubts about the wisdom of *Herring*.[256] For one thing, courts will need to determine what variety of Fourth Amendment violation, in a culpability sense, will bring the case within the *Herring* exception, and then will have to determine whether that is the degree of culpability existing in the instant case. Quite clearly intentional and reckless wrongdoing will not qualify,[257] but negligence will, at least sometimes.[258] It is important to note that the first branch of the "circumstances" incorporated into *Herring*'s "We hold" sentence is stated not merely as any negligence, but rather as "isolated negligence," referred to elsewhere in the opinion as "nonrecurring" negligence and later distinguished from "routine or widespread" negligence. This strongly suggests that in a case

---

[256]As concluded in Nolasco, del Carmen & Vaughn, What Herring Hath Wrought: An Analysis of Post-Herring Cases in the Federal Courts, 8 Am.J.Crim.L. 221, 253 (Spring 2011), based upon an analysis of all the post-*Herring* federal cases making reference to that decision: "This study shows that federal courts have applied the *Herring* good-faith exception to police searches and seizures that involved facts substantially dissimilar from those in *Herring*.This likely stems from the absence of clear guidelines for lower courts to follows. Words such as 'isolated,' 'systemic,' 'reckless,' or 'attenuated,' are inherently susceptible to varying interpretations by lower court judges."

However, from the details given in the article, especially at 238–49, what seems even more apparent is that *Herring* is being most often cited unnecessarily as if the case somehow lends support to decisions otherwise properly grounded in either the "good faith" cases discussed in § 1.3 herein (that is, *Leon, Krull* and *Davis*) or the various "fruit-of-the-poisonous tree" doctrines discussed in § 11.4 herein.

[257]The Court in *Herring* stated: "If the police have been shown to be reckless in maintaining a warrant system, or to have knowingly made false entries to lay the groundwork for future false arrests, exclusion would certainly be justified under our cases should such misconduct cause a Fourth Amendment violation."

But, United States v. Noster,

573 F.3d 664 (9th Cir.2009), suggests a problem here: that lower courts may be tempted by *Herring* to characterize as only negligent what in fact may be even deliberate misrepresentations. A close reading of *Noster* suggests the dissent there is correct in concluding that an officer acted in a "deliberate and culpable" manner in "caus[ing] a knowingly false entry," i.e., that a vehicle was "stolen" when there was only a "payment delinquency—a civil matter." The *Noster* majority invoked *Herring*, unnecessarily it would seem, given their take on the evidence, by which they concluded the officer filing the report had probable cause, which then under the *Hensley* principle would have validated the subsequent actions of other officers who relied on the report. Fortunately, the above-referenced opinion was later amended and superseded to eliminate any reliance on *Herring*. United States v. Noster, 590 F.3d 624 (9th Cir.2009).

[258]United States v. Lazar, 604 F.3d 230 (6th Cir.2010) (*Herring* "does not purport to alter that aspect of the exclusionary rule which applies to warrants that are facially deficient warrants *ab initio*," and thus does not broaden the *Leon* rule); United States v. Song Ja Cha, 597 F.3d 995 (9th Cir.2010) (*Herring*, where the "police officers made a mistake of fact," deemed not applicable here, where officer made "a mistake of law," as "mistakes of law can and should be deterred").

somewhat like *Herring* in which the record failed to show[259] that such mistakes were occurring in the use of this particular records system only rarely, then the *Herring* exception to the exclusionary rule would not apply.

Later on the Court seems to identify two other varieties of negligence that are probably not encompassed with the *Herring* exception, for the majority declares that the "exclusionary rule serves to deter * * * grossly negligent conduct, or in some circumstances * * * systemic negligence." The Court offers no definition or illustration of either of these two categories. As for the term gross negligence, it is, as the Supreme Court has itself observed, one of those "elusive terms" that has "left the finest scholars puzzled,"[260] and hence it can fairly be said that the term's use in *Herring* is itself somewhat puzzling. On yet another occasion the Court observed that "the term is a 'nebulous' one, in practice typically meaning little different from recklessness."[261] But since the "grossly negligent conduct" term is used in *Herring* to fill out a list into which the term "reckless" had already been placed, presumably the term is not being used merely as a synonym for recklessness. This suggests that perhaps the reference is to that version of gross negligence involving only objective fault but a greater departure from the reasonable man standard,[262] in which case an otherwise "isolated" instance of negligence would not qualify for the *Herring* treatment if it involved such a greater deviation.

As for "systemic negligence," a term never before used by the Supreme Court,[263] it presumably refers to a variety of negligence that has an effect upon an entire recordkeeping system. Such is the case, it has been noted, as to "an environment in which negligent management and oversight created conditions" permitting the specific error to occur.[264] Thus it would seem that if a false entry in law enforcement records or failure to discover same is fairly attributable to a lack of sufficient management or oversight, then the case would not fall within the *Herring*

---

[259] The proposition is put this way because, as discussed later herein, the burden of proof of proving facts justifying application of the *Herring* exception properly is placed upon the prosecution.

[260] Daniels v. Williams, 474 U.S. 327, 106 S.Ct. 662, 88 L.Ed.2d 662 (1986).

[261] Farmer v. Brennan, 511 U.S. 825, 114 S.Ct. 1970, 128 L.Ed.2d 811 (1970).

[262] See 1 LaFave, Substantive Criminal Law § 3.7(b) (2d ed.2003).

[263] As compared to the term "systemic deterrence," sometimes used in discussion of the exclusionary rule, e.g., United States v. Leon, 468 U.S. 897, 104 S.Ct. 3405, 82 L.Ed.2d 677 (1984), which may be what is lost if there is no suppression in the case of "systemic negligence."

[264] D. Fairgrieve & S. Green, Child Abuse Tort Claims Against Public Bodies: A Comparative Law View 165 (2004).

exception.[265] The same would appear to be true if either the making of the error or the failure to detect it is related to some other "systemic" problem, such as the manner in which the recordkeeping system at issue has been structured. But just what is necessary to show what the Court referred to as "systemic error" at another point in *Herring* is far from clear. Certainly the reoccurrence of the same kind error for some time without any effective response would seem highly relevant, and perhaps the length of time that a specific error remained uncorrected is also significant[266]—although *Herring* indicates that length of time must exceed five months!

But while the first task of a lower court in applying the *Herring* case is to distinguish so-called "isolated" negligence from all other forms of culpability (intent, recklessness, and negligence of a gross or systemic nature), that is the beginning but by no means the end of that court's responsibility. While it is true that a fair amount of the *discussion* in *Herring* has to do only with that distinction, the *holding* in the case requires that *in addition* the requisite form of negligence can also be said to be "attenuated," in the sense of manifesting a situation where the "benefits of deterrence" are less than would otherwise be the case. Especially since, as noted earlier, the "attenuated" qualification in the Court's holding appears to have been added because it was necessary to garner the requisite five votes, it would be a serious mistake for a lower court to pretend that the "attenuated" element of *Herring* did not exist[267] or to interpret that element so broadly as to render much of the exclusionary rule inoperable.

---

[265]Cf. United States v. Song Ja Cha, 597 F.3d 995 (9th Cir.2010) (police delay of 26.5 hours in obtaining search warrant after premises seized without a warrant was a "systemic" error, as "there was no departmental training or protocol instructing the officers that a warrant must be secured reasonably quickly after a premises had been seized").

[266]As stated by the three concurring Justices in Arizona v. Evans, 514 U.S. 1, 115 S.Ct. 1185, 131 L.Ed.2d 34 (1995): "Surely it would not be reasonable for the police to rely, say, on a recordkeeping system, their own or some other agency's, that has no mechanism to ensure its accuracy over time and that routinely lead to false arrests, even years after the probable cause for any such arrest has ceased to exist (if it ever existed)."

[267]But precisely such a mistake was made in People v. Robinson, 47

Cal.4th 1104, 104 Cal.Rptr.3d 727, 224 P.3d 55 (2010), discussed in Kay, Unraveling the Exclusionary Rule: From Leon to Herring to Robinson-and Back?, 58 UCLA L.Rev. Discourse 207 (2011); Note, 99 Cal.L.Rev. 885 (2011), claiming "that the Supreme Court's general holding regarding what conduct triggers the exclusionary rule does not focus on the issue of attenuation," and thus "that issue has no relevance to our analysis in this particular case." See also United States v. Master, 614 F.3d 236 (6th Cir.2010) (where police erred in obtaining search warrant for defendant's residence in wrong county, so Fourth Amendment violated because judge without authority to issue the warrant, and error attributable to defendant's earlier misstatement of his county of residence, court asserts *Herring* requires "that in order for a court to suppress evidence following the finding of a Fourth Amendment violation, 'the benefits of

While surely *Herring* does not apply when the error regarding police records occurred at the other end (that is, at the time when those records were consulted by the arresting/searching officer),[268] the mere fact that the arresting/searching officer was not personally at fault in relying upon the information supplied to him by other police sources is not alone a basis for finding that the "attenuated" requirement of *Herring* has been satisfied. As noted earlier, such a ham-handed application of *Herring* is totally without justification, and would have the unfortunate result of withdrawing the protections of the Fourth Amendment from all cases governed by the principle of *Whiteley v. Warden*,[269] namely, that a good faith arrest by an officer relying upon a police source is still a constitutional violation if the requisite grounds for that arrest did not exist at the source.

This is not to suggest that lower courts should deem the "attenuated" requisite to be unmet except upon a case factually on all fours with *Herring*; as explained earlier, it does not seem that the attenuation in *Herring* itself is attributable to either the fact that the negligence was of the omission variety, the fact that it occurred five months prior to the defendant's arrest, or the fact that it occurred in a different county. On the other hand, what was characterized earlier as options (v) and (vi) to interpreting *Herring*, finding attenuation, respectively, in the fact that a mistake in police records was involved and that the mistake was made by clerical personnel, would seem-especially if viewed collectively-to capture what the attenuation element of *Herring* is all about. Lower courts are thus well-advised to apply *Herring* accordingly.

---

deterrence must outweigh the costs,'" and so remand for application of *Herring*); United States v. Julius, 610 F.3d 60 (2d Cir.2010) (remanding for lower court consideration of relevance of *Herring*, notwithstanding fact that "[u]nlike in *Herring*, in which the alleged error was attenuated from the search, the error here was made by the searching officer," as "*Herring* recognizes careful consideration by district courts of whether the goal of deterring violations of the Fourth Amendment outweighs the costs to truth-seeking and law enforcement objective in each case"!); United States v. Tracey, 597 F.3d 140 (3d Cir.2010) (asserts *Herring* means that "isolated negligent acts on the part of the police do not warrant application of the exclusionary rule"); Delker v. State, 50 So.3d 300 (Miss.2011) (court applies *Herring* to a "mistake" by the seizing officer that, as the dissent emphasizes, "was

not attenuated from his illegal pursuit" of defendant).

Indeed, even the Supreme Court itself has ignored the "attenuated" limitation in characterizing the holding in *Herring*. Davis v. United States, ___ U.S. ___, 131 S.Ct. 2419, 180 L.Ed.2d 285 (2011).

[268]Cf. Phelan v. Village of Lyons, 531 F.3d 484 (7th Cir.2008) (where officer ran routine license plate check on Cadillac with plate number 1020 and computer reported back that vehicle with that plate was stolen, but officer failed to read next line on the screen indicating that vehicle was a motorcycle, significant in that same numbers used for car and cycle licenses, though plates for latter smaller, "there was no probable cause").

[269]Whiteley v. Warden, Wyo. State Penitentiary, 401 U.S. 560, 91 S.Ct. 1031, 28 L.Ed.2d 306 (1971).

Yet another factor that lower courts, especially trial courts, will have to take into account in any future cases in which a *Herring* claim is made concerns matters of proof. One important question is that of which party has the burden of proof on the issue of whether or not there exists culpability beyond "isolated negligence" and whether such negligence is "attenuated," which can well depend upon a careful assessment of the facts in the particular case. (As the dissenters in *Herring* note, the majority's "focus on deliberate conduct" makes the problems of proof uniquely difficult, for as a general proposition "application of the exclusionary rule does not require inquiry into the mental state of the police.") Though nothing is said about this in *Herring*, it would seem that the burden of proof must be on the prosecution. As for the generality that the burden of proof is on the defendant in warrant cases,[270] surely it has no application in a case like *Herring*, where it turns out that in fact there was no warrant.

Moreover, since *Herring*, like *Evans*, is simply an extension of the "good faith" doctrine, the controlling consideration is the fact that in the past courts have consistently ruled "that the government has the burden to prove facts warranting application of the good faith exception."[271] That conclusion is especially appropriate in *Herring*-type cases, for in such instances placing the burden on the prosecution squares with the general policy of placing the burden on the party who has the greatest access to the relevant facts.[272] It also squares with the policy of placing the burden on the party seeking an exception to a general rule,[273] which is certainly what a *Herring* claim amounts to. Of course, from *Herring*'s quotation of the *Hudson* assertion that exclusion "has always been our last resort, not our first impulse," it might seem that another general policy, that of handicapping disfavored contentions,[274] would support placing the burden on the defendant,[275] but even apart from the fact that the *Hudson* contention "defies historical truth,"[276] surely this proposition does not trump the several others referenced above pointing the opposite direction.

Also worthy of note in this connection is the fact that proving

---

[270]See § 11.2(b).

[271]People v. Willis, 28 Cal.4th 22, 120 Cal.Rptr.2d 105, 46 P.3d 898 (2002).

[272]See § 11.2(b).

[273]See § 11.2(b).

[274]See § 11.2(b).

[275]Certainly if the defendant *does* have the burden of proof, then, as the *Herring* dissenters noted, it would seem, as acknowledged at oral argument, "that a defendant is entitled to discovery (and, if necessary, an audit of police databases)," meaning the

Court has "imposed a considerable administrative burden on courts and law enforcement." Of course, discovery can be most important to a defendant in connection with a suppression hearing even when he does not have the burden of proof. See United States v. Salsedo, 477 F.Supp. 1235 (E.D.Cal. 1979), quoted in § 11.2(d) at note 221.

[276]Davies & Scanlon, Katz in the Age of Hudson v. Michigan: Some Thoughts on "Suppression as a Last Resort," 41 U.C.Davis L.Rev. 1035, 1043 (2008).

the unreliability of a law enforcement database *and* that any defects are attributable to the kind of misconduct *Herring* requires are exceedingly difficult tasks. As to the former,

> the faulty products of a database can go entirely unnoticed under current doctrine even when they are common and recurring. Consider the debate in *Herring* itself: the majority demanded evidence that the database routinely produced bad information, refusing to consider the absence of quality control mechanisms itself a sufficient "harm." Yet a database that generates bad information— say, that falsely reports arrest warrants—may produce many arrests, but little record of those arrests. Unless the arrested person sues civilly, or is found in violation of contraband (as in the case of *Herring*), no formal record of the error may be made. And even if formal suits are filed, it may be difficult to link them to one another as the product of a faulty database. The only proof of the reliability of the database in *Herring* itself were the statements of its keepers—hardly disinterested parties—and yet, even those were contested factually.[277]

As to the latter,

> Databases are rarely the product of one individual's action, and rarely contain easily separable individual information. Instead, they tend to be the product of numerous actors and inputs and collate numerous tiers of information. Think about *Herring*: an anonymous person put in the erroneous information, or else failed to remove it; then the information was accessed by one clerk and transmitted to another who failed to undertake any steps to verify it. It is difficult, and maybe impossible, to identify the moment the error occurred or the individual who perpetrated it.[278]

§ 1.7 The exclusionary rule in quasi-criminal, civil and administrative proceedings

§ 1.7(a)   Forfeiture proceedings
§ 1.7(b)   Juvenile delinquency proceedings
§ 1.7(c)   Commitment and related proceedings
§ 1.7(d)   Civil tax proceedings
§ 1.7(e)   Child protection proceedings
§ 1.7(f)   Administrative hearings
§ 1.7(g)   Legislative hearings
§ 1.7(h)   Private litigation

Research References

West's Key Number Digest
Administrative Law and Procedure ⬤54.1(3), 461; Evidence ⬤154; Forfeitures ⬤5; Infants ⬤173.1; Mental Health ⬤135; United States ⬤23(4)

Legal Encyclopedias
C.J.S., Rico (racketeer Influenced and Corrupt Organizations) § 30; Aliens §§ 53,

---

[277]Murphy, Databases, Doctrine and Constitutional Criminal Procedure, 37 Fordham Urb.L.J. 803, 823 (2010).

[278]Murphy, 37 Fordham Urb.L.J. 803, 827 (2010).

124, 172, 201; Evidence §§ 252 to 258; Infants § 58; Public Administrative Law and Procedure §§ 124 to 125; United States §§ 36, 39

Introduction

The Fourth Amendment exclusionary rule is most frequently applied in the context of a criminal proceeding brought against the victim of the search. However, as noted in the immediately preceding section, the courts have been most reluctant to apply the exclusionary rule in criminal cases except to bar from use *at trial* evidence obtained by an unreasonable search or seizure. The reason most often given is that no appreciable added deterrence would be gained by application of the exclusionary rule at other points in the criminal process. As discussed below, somewhat the same reasoning has been used to support nonapplication of the exclusionary rule in civil litigation between private parties, but this rationale has generally not been deemed persuasive as to civil proceedings in which a governmental unit is a party.[1]

§ 1.7(a) Forfeiture proceedings

In *One 1958 Plymouth Sedan v. Pennsylvania,*[2] the Supreme Court had occasion to consider the earlier holding of the Pennsylvania Supreme Court that the exclusionary rule was not applicable in a forfeiture[3] proceeding which that court characterized as civil in nature. Specifically, the Pennsylvania court had held that in proceedings for the forfeiture of an automobile to the state on the ground that it had been used in the illegal transportation of liquor, the illegal use could be proved by the admission

---

[Section 1.7]

[1]See also Annot., 105 A.L.R.5th 1 (2003).

[Section 1.7(a)]

[2]One 1958 Plymouth Sedan v. Pennsylvania, 380 U.S. 693, 85 S.Ct. 1246, 14 L.Ed.2d 170 (1965).

In United States v. James Daniel Good Real Property, 510 U.S. 43, 114 S.Ct. 492, 126 L.Ed.2d 490 (1993), the Court concluded that "it does not follow [from *Plymouth Sedan*] that the Fourth Amendment is the sole constitutional provision in question when the Government seizes property subject to forfeiture," and went on to hold that in the absence of exigent circumstances the due process clause of the Fifth Amendment prohibits the government in a civil forfeiture case from seizing real property without first affording the owner notice and an opportunity to be heard.

Applying *Good*, it was held in

United States v. Bowman, 341 F.3d 1228 (11th Cir.2003), "that the remedy for an illegal ex parte seizure based on the Government's failure to establish exigent circumstances, where the Government is able to establish probable cause to believe the property is connected to crime at the post-seizure adversarial hearing, is a recovery by the real property owner of rents or lost profits during the period of illegal seizure, with the Government retaining possession of the property until the forfeiture action is decided on the merits."

[3]Forfeiture is "a permanent governmental taking of title and all rights to and in property that has been condemned for its role in a criminal violation," and is to be distinguished from an impoundment, "the temporary taking of tangible, personal property." City of Hollywood v. Mulligan, 934 So.2d 1238 (Fla.2006).

into evidence of liquor taken from the car in an unconstitutional search. A unanimous Supreme Court[4] reversed.

The Court, per Goldberg, J., noted that one of the early and leading cases on the subject of search and seizure, *Boyd v. United States,*[5] had been a forfeiture case, and that it "would seem to be dispositive of this case." Pennsylvania argued that *Boyd* had been undermined by statements in *United States v. Jeffers*[6] and *Trupiano v. United States,*[7] both criminal cases, to the effect that the exclusion of the contraband (illegally imported narcotics in *Jeffers,* an unregistered still, alcohol and mash in *Trupiano*) in those cases would not mean that the government was required to return those items. The Court distinguished those cases by noting that they "concerned objects the possession of which, without more, constitutes a crime," so that the "repossession of such *per se* contraband by Jeffers and Trupiano would have subjected them to criminal penalties" and the "return of the contraband would clearly have frustrated the express public policy against the possession of such objects." By contrast, in the instant case there "is nothing even remotely criminal in possessing an automobile"; it is merely "derivative contraband" by virtue of its prior illegal use, and "the return of the automobile to the owner would not subject him to any possible criminal penalties for possession or frustrate any public policy concerning automobiles, as automobiles."

As for the Pennsylvania court's characterization of the proceeding as civil, the Supreme Court responded that it was "quasi-criminal in character" because its object was "to penalize for the commission of an offense against the law." Indeed, given the fact that the auto in question was worth approximately $1,000 and that for a criminal conviction for the offense involved the defendant could have received no more than a $500 fine, the Court noted it "would be anomalous indeed, under these circumstances, to hold that in the criminal proceeding the illegally seized evidence is excludable, while in the forfeiture proceeding, requiring the determination that the criminal law has been violated, the same evidence would be admissible."

While *Plymouth Sedan* would thus appear to foreclose any argument that the exclusionary rule is never applicable in forfeiture proceedings,[8] it is important to understand precisely what type of situation that decision covers. For one thing, the Court

---

[4]Black, J., restated in a concurring opinion his view that exclusion was required by the Fifth rather than the Fourth Amendment.

[5]Boyd v. United States, 116 U.S. 616, 6 S.Ct. 524, 29 L.Ed. 746 (1886).

[6]United States v. Jeffers, 342 U.S. 48, 72 S.Ct. 93, 96 L.Ed. 59 (1951).

[7]Trupiano v. United States, 334 U.S. 699, 68 S.Ct. 1229, 92 L.Ed. 1663 (1948).

[8]United States v. $186,416.00 in U.S. Currency, 583 F.3d 1220 (9th Cir.2009) (exclusionary rule applied here, as evidence that would show probable cause for forfeiture was "tainted"); United States v. $291,828.00

was concerned with use of the exclusionary rule in essentially the same way it is used in a criminal prosecution—to suppress evidence obtained by an illegal search or seizure from the proceedings to prove the criminal violation. Thus, it has quite properly been held[9] that *Plymouth Sedan* does not draw into question the prior holdings of the Supreme Court[10] and other courts[11] to the effect that if the contraband character of the object to be forfeited is proved by lawfully obtained evidence, it is no defense that the

in U.S. Currency, 536 F.3d 1234 (11th Cir.2008) ("exclusionary rule applies to civil forfeiture actions"); United States v. Taylor, 13 F.3d 786 (4th Cir.1994) (exclusionary rule applicable in in rem civil forfeiture action against money and land allegedly connected with illegal gambling); United States v. $7,850.00 in U.S. Currency, 7 F.3d 1355 (8th Cir.1993) (in proceedings to forfeit money, "government must show with untainted evidence that probable cause to forfeit exists"); United States v. $53,082.00 in U.S. Currency, 985 F.2d 245 (6th Cir.1993) (exclusionary rule applicable in forfeiture proceeding directed at money involved in drug transactions); United States v. $149,442.43 in U.S. Currency, 965 F.2d 868 (10th Cir.1992) (exclusionary rule applicable in forfeiture proceeding directed at vehicles and money with nexus to drug trafficking and tax evasion); Vance v. United States, 676 F.2d 183 (5th Cir.1982) (exclusionary rule applies in vehicle forfeiture proceeding); Nicaud v. State ex rel. Hendrix, 401 So.2d 43 (Ala.1981) (exclusionary rule applicable in proceeding for forfeiture of boat and trucks used in transporting drugs, as statute is "clearly intended to be a deterrent to illegal drug dealings, and to aid the objectives of criminal law enforcement"), Kaiser v. State, 296 Ark. 125, 752 S.W.2d 271 (1988) (exclusionary rule applicable in quasi-criminal action to forfeit pistol and $10,000 found in car with drugs); One 1995 Corvette v. Mayor and City Council of Baltimore, 353 Md. 114, 724 A.2d 680 (1999) (rejecting lower court's conclusion that *Plymouth Sedan* impliedly overruled by United States v. Ursery, 518 U.S. 267, 116 S.Ct. 2135, 135 L.Ed.2d 549 (1996), holding forfeiture procedure not "punishment" for double jeopardy

purposes, and citing cases from 13 federal circuits and 34 states holding *Plymouth Sedan* makes the exclusionary rule applicable to civil in rem forfeiture proceedings); Commonwealth v. Nine Hundred and Ninety-Two Dollars, 383 Mass. 764, 422 N.E.2d 767 (1981) (exclusionary rule applicable in proceeding to forfeit vehicle used in drug traffic); State v. One 1987 Toyota Pickup, 233 Neb. 670, 447 N.W.2d 243 (1989) (exclusionary rule applicable in action for forfeiture of truck carrying drugs); Ohio Dept. of Liquor Control v. FOE Aerie 0456, 99 Ohio App.3d 380, 650 N.E.2d 940 (1994) (exclusionary rule applicable in action seeking forfeiture of gambling devices and gambling proceeds seized in search of private club); Deeter v. Smith, 106 Wash.2d 376, 721 P.2d 519 (1986) (exclusionary rule applicable in auto forfeiture proceedings since their "purpose is to penalize individuals who participate in the illegal transportation of controlled substances").

[9]United States v. $186,416.00 in U.S. Currency, 590 F.3d 942 (9th Cir. 2010); United States v. $7,850.00 in U.S. Currency, 7 F.3d 1355 (8th Cir. 1993); United States v. One 1975 Pontiac Lemans, 621 F.2d 444 (1st Cir. 1980); State v. One Uzi Semi-Automatic 9mm Gun, 589 A.2d 31 (Me.1991). State v. Jones, 181 N.J.Super. 549, 438 A.2d 581 (1981).

[10]Dodge v. United States, 272 U.S. 530, 47 S.Ct. 191, 71 L.Ed. 392 (1926); United States v. One Ford Coupe' Automobile, 272 U.S. 321, 47 S.Ct. 154, 71 L.Ed. 279 (1926), both of which were distinguished in *Plymouth Sedan.*

[11]See cases collected in Annot., 8 A.L.R.3d 473 (1966).

object itself came into the possession of the government by an illegal search or seizure.[12] On the merits, it may be said that the conclusion forfeiture proceedings need not be quashed merely because the government came by the property to be forfeited illegally, is no more harsh than the longstanding rule that jurisdiction over a criminal defendant is not affected by his illegal seizure.[13] Thus, the former rule may be expected to survive as long as the latter one does.[14]

Secondly, the Court in *Plymouth Sedan* clearly recognized that at some point the policies underlying the exclusionary rule must give way to other interests. Thus, while the Court was willing that the party in interest in *Plymouth Sedan* should be able to get his car back, it was made absolutely clear that the same result would not be reached in certain other situations, as where the objects in question were contraband per se (e.g., narcotics). This is because in the latter situation the return of the objects "would clearly have frustrated the express public policy against the possession of such objects." On this basis, it has been held, for example, that *Plymouth Sedan* does not bar the forfeiture of such objects as controlled substances,[15] obscene materials,[16]

---

[12]Despite some authority to the contrary, United States v. $37,780.00 in U.S. Currency, 920 F.2d 159 (2d Cir.1990), it does not follow that the res in a forfeiture proceeding, if itself illegally seized, can also be admitted for its evidentiary value. United States v. $191,910.00 in U.S. Currency, 16 F.3d 1051 (9th Cir.1994) (noting "the majority of circuits to consider the issue" agree). See also United States v. $186,416.00 in U.S. Currency, 590 F.3d 942 (9th Cir.2010) (because "we are precluded from considering how much currency the LAPD illegally seized," government cannot prevail on argument that given the amount the currency seized it must have been connected with marijuana sales); United States v. $493,850.00 in U.S. Currency, 518 F.3d 1159 (9th Cir.2008) (concluding, as to *$191,910.00*, that while court cannot "consider the amount of currency that the government illegally seized," it does not follow that court is "prohibited from considering the fact that the illegally seized property is, in fact, currency"); United States v. $557,933.89, More or Less, in U.S. Funds, 287 F.3d 66 (2d Cir.2002) (noting, as to *$37,780.00*, that "its precise meaning, indeed, even its status as a

holding, * * * is unclear").

See also

[13]Compare Comment, 80 Cal.L. Rev. 1309, 1311 (1992), which "proposes a rule that would bar the forfeiture of any asset seized in violation of the Fourth Amendment," reasoning that the "emphasis of the current Supreme Court on deterrence in framing the exclusionary rule, which has previously justified a narrowing of evidentiary exclusions in criminal trials, requires by its own logic a broadly framed rule that prohibits law enforcement agency retention of unlawfully seized property."

[14]See § 1.9 on the latter rule. The analogy would seem to hold up only if it is acknowledged that the seizure of things rather than a person may also be objected to on the ground that the existence (as opposed to the illegal character) of the things was discovered by an unconstitutional search. Cf. Berkowitz v. United States, 340 F.2d 168 (1st Cir.1965).

[15]Deeter v. Smith, 106 Wash.2d 376, 721 P.2d 519 (1986) ("since public policy expressly forbids Mr. Deeter's possession of such contraband").

gambling paraphernalia,[17] and adulterated food.[18]

As for precisely when other interests must predominate over the exclusionary rule, the *Plymouth Sedan* Court relied upon the "distinction between what has been described as contraband per se and only derivative contraband" in concluding that the exclusionary rule is applicable only when the "property [is] not intrinsically illegal in character." This is generally sound, although it may be suggested that a most difficult situation is presented by the case in which the contraband in question is the *fruit* of illegal activity (e.g., the profits of a gambling operation). While the Court in *Plymouth Sedan* could say that the return of the auto to its owner would not "frustrate any public policy concerning automobiles," it is far less apparent that the return of ill-gotten gains such as gambling profits does not frustrate public policy. It certainly might be argued that just as an illegal search does not require the return of inherently unlawful property, such as narcotics, or property owned by another, such as the fruits of a burglary,[19] it does not require return of the profits of criminal activity. At least in some jurisdictions, this argument could be bolstered by pointing out that certain contraband, such as gambling moneys, are (unlike the auto in *Plymouth Sedan*) subject to mandatory forfeiture and arguably a basis for criminal penalties upon repossession.[20] Yet, the fact remains, which has been deemed determinative by most courts,[21] that gambling money is more like the auto in *Plymouth Sedan* than the narcot-

---

[16]State v. Voshart, 39 Wis.2d 419, 159 N.W.2d 1 (1968).

[17]State v. 192 Coin-Operated Video Game Machines, 338 S.C. 176, 525 S.E.2d 872 (2000) (*Plymouth Sedan* has to do with "derivative contraband," and thus is not applicable here, as "the machines are contraband *per se*"); State v. Lesnick, 84 Wash.2d 940, 530 P.2d 243 (1975) (*Plymouth Sedan* no bar to forfeiture of punch boards and similar gambling devices, though that illegally seized evidence could not be used to prove that merchandise found with those devices were intended as gambling prizes).

[18]United States v. An Article of Food, Etc., 477 F.Supp. 1185 (S.D.N.Y.1979) (exclusionary rule not applicable in proceeding to condemn adulterated food, as returning contaminated food would frustrate the public policy against possession of same).

[19]Warden v. Hayden, 387 U.S. 294, 87 S.Ct. 1642, 18 L.Ed.2d 782 (1967).

[20]As to the situation in Illinois, for example, see LaFave, Search and Seizure: "The Course of True Law . . . Has Not . . . Run Smooth," 1966 U.Ill. L.F. 255, 381.

Consider also United States v. Bagley, 899 F.2d 707 (8th Cir.1990) (convicted felon could not obtain return of guns illegally seized from him but which it unlawful for him to possess; defendant's argument "the weapons should be sold by a third party with the proceeds remitted to Bagley * * * is frivolous," as defendant should not "reap the economic benefit" of illegal ownership).

[21]Silbert v. United States, 289 F.Supp. 318 (D.Md.1968); United States v. $125,882 in U.S. Currency, 286 F.Supp. 643 (S.D.N.Y.1968); People v. Zimmerman, 44 Ill.App.3d 601, 3 Ill.Dec. 317, 358 N.E.2d 715 (1976); State v. Sherry, 46 N.J. 172, 215 A.2d 536 (1965); Reyes v. Rosetti, 47 Misc.2d 517, 262 N.Y.S.2d 845 (1965); Ohio Dept. of Liquor Control v. FOE Aerie 0456, 99 Ohio App.3d 380, 650 N.E.2d

ics in *Jeffers* because it is "not intrinsically illegal in character." In support of applying the exclusionary rule where the forfeiture concerns such items as gambling moneys,[22] it could also be argued that the ability to deprive gamblers of their ill-gotten gains notwithstanding the unconstitutional means used to find the money or determine its character would actually encourage violations of the Fourth Amendment,[23] especially in view of the fact that "[l]aw enforcement agencies today depend, at least in part, on the proceeds of forfeiture actions to finance their activities."[24]

There is another kind of forfeiture action, rather different from the one at issue in *Plymouth Sedan*, where unquestionably the exclusionary rule applies: municipal ordinance forfeiture actions. As one court noted, such an action

> is a quasi-criminal proceeding where the defendant is required as in criminal cases to enter a plea of guilty, not guilty or nolo contendere. The ordinance in many instances is derived from a criminal statute. We perceive no logical reason why a search and seizure cannot be challenged by a motion to suppress.[25]

Similarly, there does not appear to be any doubt but that the *Plymouth Sedan* approach is called for when the government instead brings an action to abate a nuisance and would prove the illegal activity constituting the nuisance by the means of evidence come by through an unconstitutional search.[26]

---

940 (1994).

See also State v. $11,346.00 in U.S. Currency, 777 P.2d 65 (Wyo.1989) (rejecting dissent's argument that money received in sale of drugs is contraband per se and thus outside *Plymouth Sedan* rule).

[22]Even if so applied, consider the exception with respect to impeachment of the defendant's testimony, discussed in § 11.6(a), which is most likely to come into play if a person brings a civil action to force return of money the plaintiff alleges was not connected with gambling activity. See Compton v. United States, 334 F.2d 212 (4th Cir.1964).

[23]See W. LaFave, Arrest ch. 24 (1965).

[24]United States v. $186,416.00 in U.S. Currency, 590 F.3d 942 (9th Cir.2010) (concluding that consequently the exclusionary rule "is particularly well-suited * * * in the context of civil forfeiture proceedings" to advance the goal of deterring police misconduct, and adding that in this context "the exclusion of evidence * * * is without the major societal cost associated with exclusion in criminal cases: setting a criminal free").

[25]City of Milwaukee v. Cohen, 57 Wis.2d 38, 203 N.W.2d 633 (1973). See also State v. Barclay, 398 A.2d 794 (Me.1979) (exclusionary rule applicable in adjudication that defendant committed civil violation by possessing a usable amount of marijuana).

[26]Carlisle v. State ex rel. Trammell, 276 Ala. 436, 163 So.2d 596 (1964); Carson v. State ex rel. Price, 221 Ga. 299, 144 S.E.2d 384 (1965); Jefferson Parish v. Bayou Landing, Limited, Inc., 350 So.2d 158 (La.1977). As Crandley, A Plymouth, a Parolee, and the Police: The Case for the Exclusionary Rule in Civil Forfeiture After Pennsylvania Board of Probation and Parole v. Scott, 65 Alb.L.Rev. 147, 150 (2001), concludes, "the deterrence to police in the context of civil forfeiture is high because of the emphasis on civil forfeiture in modern police work; conversely, the social cost of the rule in civil forfeiture is low because of the formality such proceedings exhibit, and because the only loss the

§ 1.7(b) Juvenile delinquency proceedings[27]

Although the issue has seldom been raised, in recent years those state courts that have had to face the question have consistently held that the Fourth Amendment exclusionary rule is applicable in juvenile delinquency proceedings.[28] The United States

government suffers is the value of a seized asset. [T]his alchemy of high deterrence and low costs makes the exclusionary rule an effective device for civil forfeiture proceedings."

See also Boston Housing Authority v. Guirola, 410 Mass. 820, 575 N.E.2d 1100 (1991) (implying exclusionary rule applicable in proceedings to evict a tenant from public housing because of drug possession; though "its purpose is not punitive but curative, the removal of a nuisance, the statute's impact on the ousted tenant is similar to that of the forfeiture proceeding" in *Plymouth Sedan*); State v. Spoke Committee, University Center, 270 N.W.2d 339 (N.D.1978) (exclusionary rule applicable in civil proceedings to enjoin the future showing of an allegedly obscene film).

Contra: Housing Authority of City of Stamford v. Dawkins, 239 Conn. 793, 686 A.2d 994 (1997) (exclusionary rule not applicable in summary process action brought by city housing authority to recover possession of tenant's premises because illegal drug activity discovered there in search warrant execution, at least where reasonable reliance on warrant); State, ex rel. Rear Door Bookstore v. Tenth District Court of Appeals, 63 Ohio St.3d 354, 588 N.E.2d 116 (1992) (in nuisance action against bookstore as a place of prostitution, court declares "the exclusionary rule has not been applied in civil cases; we see no reason to expand the exclusionary rule to the facts of this case").

[Section 1.7(b)]

[27]See Note, 16 Buff.L.Rev. 462 (1967); Comments, 4 Colum.Human Rts.L.Rev. 417 (1972); 11 J.Fam.Law 753 (1972).

[28]United States v. Doe, 801 F.Supp. 1562 (E.D.Tex.1992); In re Tyrell J., 8 Cal.4th 68, 32 Cal.Rptr.2d 33, 876 P.2d 519 (1994); In re Marsh, 40 Ill.2d 53, 237 N.E.2d 529 (1968); In re Montrail M., 87 Md.App. 420, 589 A.2d 1318 (1991); State in Interest of L.B., 99 N.J.Super. 589, 240 A.2d 709 (1968); State v. Doe, 93 N.M. 143, 597 P.2d 1183 (App.1979); In re Edwin R., 60 Misc.2d 355, 303 N.Y.S.2d 406 (1969); State ex rel. Juvenile Dept. v. Rogers, 314 Or. 114, 839 P.2d 127 (1992); In Interest of Jermaine T.J., 181 Wis.2d 82, 510 N.W.2d 735 (App. 1993). Section 27(b) of the Uniform Juvenile Court Act (1968) provides: "Evidence illegally seized or obtained shall not be received over objection to establish the allegations made against him." The situation is otherwise as to proceedings occurring in juvenile court (or elsewhere) for the purpose of determining whether steps must be taken to protect a juvenile from his or her parents. See § 1.7(e).

This issue must be distinguished from that of whether specific Fourth Amendment safeguards are applicable in the juvenile court process. See, e.g., In re Order Requiring Fingerprinting of a Juvenile, 42 Ohio St.3d 124, 537 N.E.2d 1286 (1989) (reasonable suspicion requirement for fingerprinting of person not arrested applies, as "a juvenile is as entitled as an adult to the constitutional protections of the Fourth Amendment"); Lanes v. State, 767 S.W.2d 789 (Tex.Crim.App.1989) (probable cause requirement for arrest applies in juvenile proceedings, as this Fourth Amendment right consistent with "the purposes and goals of the juvenile system").

In other contexts as well, it has been held that "children are entitled to the same constitutional guarantees as adults, including protection from unnecessary searches and seizures under the fourth amendment." People v. Chard, 808 P.2d 351 (Colo.1991) (right of privacy of child abuse victim re involuntary psychological examina-

Supreme Court has not yet had occasion to deal with this question, and the Court's recent decisions in the juvenile justice area by no means make it certain that the position taken by the lower courts is constitutionally required.

In *In re Gault*,[29] the Court held that in the adjudicatory phase of delinquency proceedings before a juvenile court on charges that may result in incarceration, the juvenile is entitled to notice of the charges against him, counsel, the protection of the privilege against self-incrimination, and the right to confront and cross-examine the witnesses against him. However, the Court emphasized that it was not holding that "the hearing to be held must conform with all of the requirements of a criminal trial or even of the usual administrative hearing," so that *Gault* can hardly be read as inevitably pointing toward application of the Fourth Amendment exclusionary rule in the juvenile courts. It may fairly be said, however, that the Court's treatment of the Fifth Amendment exclusionary rule in *Gault* would support such application. The Court stressed that it was concerned with more than the "danger of unreliability," that arguments that the proceedings were not criminal overlooked the fact that the police would not likely know at the time of interrogation whether a juvenile or criminal disposition would be forthcoming, and that "the child's reaction is likely to be hostile and adverse" if he perceives that he has been dealt with unfairly.

In holding that the beyond a reasonable doubt standard was applicable in juvenile proceedings, the Court emphasized once again in *In re Winship*[30] that "civil labels and good intentions do not themselves obviate the need for criminal due process safeguards in juvenile courts." That this did not signal a departure from the cautionary language in *Gault* was made clear a year later in *McKeiver v. Pennsylvania*,[31] declaring that "the applicable due process standard in juvenile proceedings, as developed by *Gault* and *Winship,* is fundamental fairness," and that under such a standard the Constitution does not require trial by jury in the adjudicative phase of a state juvenile proceeding. In reaching this conclusion, the Court emphasized the cost of jury trial in the juvenile context: it would make the proceedings more adversary and would bring with it the delay, the formality and the clamor of the adversary system; and it would impair the ability of the states to experiment with other procedures. Those concerns hardly support the notion that the exclusionary rule should not be applied, for suppression would occur in a prior hearing and thus would not significantly affect

---

tion).

[29]In re Gault, 387 U.S. 1, 87 S.Ct. 1428, 18 L.Ed.2d 527 (1967).

[30]In re Winship, 397 U.S. 358, 90 S.Ct. 1068, 25 L.Ed.2d 368 (1970).

[31]McKeiver v. Pennsylvania, 403 U.S. 528, 91 S.Ct. 1976, 29 L.Ed.2d 647 (1971).

the character of the adjudicative hearing itself.[32]

Moreover, the purposes of the Fourth Amendment exclusionary rule would be served by its application to juvenile proceedings. This is certainly true of the purpose now receiving primary attention from the Court, deterrence of the police,[33] for it is not to be expected that the police will feel compelled to follow the constraints of the Fourth Amendment in investigating juveniles if they know that there is available an alternative to criminal prosecution involving no exclusion for police misconduct but yet permitting the imposition of substantial sanctions upon those so processed.[34] As for the "twin goals of enabling the judiciary to avoid the taint of partnership in official lawlessness and of assuring the people * * * that the government would not profit from its lawless behavior,"[35] they would seem no less applicable in juvenile proceedings than in criminal proceedings.

In *United States v. Calandra,*[36] the Court weighed the benefits of exclusion against the costs. In the juvenile court context, the cost of the exclusionary rule is that "there will be instances when the state will be forced to return the child to his or her home without aid because the piece of evidence vital to proving his or her delinquency is the product of an illegal search and seizure."[37] But, while this is understandably a matter of concern, it may be said, as the Court intimated in *Gault,* that a juvenile justice system which accepts evidence without regard to the manner in which it was obtained will, perhaps to an even greater degree, fail to fulfill the objectives of the process. As one judge put it:

> Since Family Court judges must be fact finders as well as law interpreters, we would do well to stand solidly in behalf of children before us, to avoid contamination of the fact sources and to see to it that we brook no shabby practices in fact gathering which do not comport with fair play. We must not only be fair; we must convince the child before us that the state is firm but fair and that the judge, a parent image, is careful to ensure those civilized standards of conduct toward the child, which we expect of the child toward organized society.[38]

It has been noted that *Gault* and *Winship* both state that the procedural protections granted therein apply only to the adjudicatory phase of a delinquency proceeding, and that it might likewise be held that the Fourth Amendment exclusionary rule applies to

---

[32]Comment, 4 Colum.Human Rts.L.Rev. 417, 444–46 (1972).

[33]United States v. Calandra, 414 U.S. 338, 94 S.Ct. 613, 38 L.Ed.2d 561 (1974).

[34]Quick, Constitutional Rights in the Juvenile Court, 12 How.L.J. 76, 97 (1966).

[35]United States v. Calandra, 414 U.S. 338, 94 S.Ct. 613, 38 L.Ed.2d 561 (1974) (dissent).

[36]United States v. Calandra, 414 U.S. 338, 94 S.Ct. 613, 38 L.Ed.2d 561 (1974).

[37]Comment, 4 Colum.Human Rts.L.Rev. 417, 446 (1972).

[38]In re Ronny, 40 Misc.2d 194, 242 N.Y.S.2d 844 (1963).

the adjudicatory hearing but not the dispositional hearing.[39] This conclusion is bolstered somewhat by the fact that in criminal cases the prevailing rule is that illegally seized evidence may be considered at sentencing, and it will suffice here to observe that the arguments made against that rule[40] might also be made with respect to the use of unconstitutionally obtained evidence in juvenile disposition hearings.

§ 1.7(c) Commitment and related proceedings

In the main, the considerations discussed above concerning application of the exclusionary rule in delinquency proceedings would seem equally relevant with respect to the question of whether the rule should be applied in a proceeding to commit a narcotics addict. Thus, the California Supreme Court quite properly held, in *People v. Moore*[41]:

> It has been suggested that the narcotic addict proceeding is for the benefit of the addict and that therefore the state does not profit from its wrong when evidence obtained in violation of the Fourth and Fourteenth Amendments is admitted in such a proceeding. Certainly, the proceeding is in part for the benefit of the addict, but this is not determinative. Rehabilitation is one of the prime goals of our penal system, and the fact that the end result of incarceration in jail may be beneficial to the inmate furnishes no ground for the view that the state does not profit by using evidence to obtain criminal convictions. Narcotic addict proceedings involve a loss of liberty, and the proceedings are for the benefit of society as well as the addict. * * * Whatever the label that may be attached to those proceedings, it is apparent that there is a close identity to the aims and objectives of criminal law enforcement * * *, and we are satisfied that to hold unconstitutionally obtained evidence admissible in the proceedings would furnish an incentive to violate the Fourth and Fourteenth Amendments. Accordingly, we hold that the exclusionary rule is applicable to such proceedings.

A much harder case was presented in *Conservatorship of Susan T.*,[42] where the record established "that a government official entered a private home with neither statutory authorization nor a warrant, and in the absence of any demonstrable exigent circumstances, for the sole purpose of photographing the interior of

---

[39]Comment, 4 Colum.Human Rts.L.Rev. 417, 446–47 (1972).

[40]See § 1.6(f).

[Section 1.7(c)]

[41]People v. Moore, 69 Cal.2d 674, 72 Cal.Rptr. 800, 446 P.2d 800 (1968).

Consider also Morse v. Municipal Court, 13 Cal.3d 149, 118 Cal.Rptr. 14, 529 P.2d 46 (1974), holding defendant's consent to a diversionary program afforded to first-time drug offenders was not untimely on the ground that the defendant had already made a pretrial motion to suppress evidence on Fourth Amendment grounds in the pending criminal case. The court reasoned that were it otherwise "[d]iversion could evolve into a procedural device for the prevention of release of defendants who are charged solely upon illegally seized evidence."

[42]Conservatorship of Susan T., 8 Cal.4th 1005, 36 Cal.Rptr.2d 40, 884 P.2d 988 (1994), followed in Matter of Guardianship & Conservatorship of Larson, 530 N.W.2d 348 (N.D.1995).

the home to obtain evidence of the householder's mental disability." Because of this apparent[43] violation of the Fourth Amendment, the court found itself faced with the issue of whether the exclusionary rule applies at a trial to determine whether a person is under a "grave disability" so as to justify the appointment of a conservator. Answering in the negative, the court first sought to distinguish away *Moore*: "Although commitment under the narcotics addict scheme is broadly analogous to involuntary civil commitment for mental disability, the aims and objectives of the two types of proceedings are quite dissimilar. The narcotics addict commitment is essentially in lieu of criminal prosecution for narcotics possession," while imposition "of a conservatorship * * * is not dependent on either a charged or uncharged criminal act." Rather, the "sole state interest" in the latter situation "is the custodial care, diagnosis, treatment, and protection of persons who are unable to take care of themselves and who for their own well being and the safety of others cannot be left adrift in the community."

Having thus concluded that the proceedings in question in *Susan T.* were truly noncriminal, the court then proceeded with an analysis grounded in the Supreme Court's civil proceedings cases, *United States v. Janis*[44] and *I.N.S. v. Lopez-Mendoza*,[45] by undertaking a cost-benefit analysis of the exclusionary rule in this context. As for the benefit, "the extent to which application of the rule would deter the type of misconduct alleged in this case," the court acknowledged that substantial weight might be assigned to this side of the scales under the general principle that "the deterrent effect of the rule is at its greatest when, as is true here, the government agency that effectuated the search is the same agency * * * that seeks to introduce the fruits of its search at trial." But the court then concluded such deterrent effect was nothing "more than theoretical" in the instant setting because the fruits of such searches would often not be put to such use, as under the act "conservatorship proceedings are brought as a last resort, when voluntary treatment has been refused and the temporary involuntary treatment provisions of the act have been exhausted," and if brought can be resolved on the basis of evidence "derived primarily from the patient" instead of from such searches. The deterrent effect, the court thus concluded, is "marginal at best" and clearly outweighed by the "social cost of

---

[43] Although the court stated at one point, with regard to the mental health department's assertion that the search was lawful, that "the department's arguments are not supported by the record," the court only assumed, "without deciding, a search violating the Fourth Amendment occurred," as before the court of appeals the department's "argument assumes the department's conduct violated the Fourth Amendment."

[44] United States v. Janis, 428 U.S. 433, 96 S.Ct. 3021, 49 L.Ed.2d 1046 (1976), discussed in § 1.7(d).

[45] I.N.S. v. Lopez-Mendoza, 468 U.S. 1032, 104 S.Ct. 3479, 82 L.Ed.2d 778 (1984), discussed in § 1.7(f).

applying the exclusionary rule to conservatorship proceedings." The goals of such proceedings, evaluation and treatment of the gravely disabled and the protection of public safety, the court next concluded, "are frustrated if the best and most complete evidence concerning the detainee's mental condition is withheld from the trier of fact."

Although admittedly the determination of when the Fourth Amendment exclusionary rule should apply in various types of noncriminal proceedings is a daunting task, it is difficult to take seriously the analysis of the *Susan T.* majority, for the inconsistencies in that analysis virtually leap off the page at the reader. If the fruits of such illegal searches are indeed "the best and most complete evidence concerning the detainee's mental condition," as the court says in its "social cost" assessment, then how can it be that such evidence would "have little effect on the outcome of the proceeding," as asserted as part of the court's deterrence analysis? Or, to play the inconsistency the other direction, if it really is true that such evidence "would have little effect on the outcome of the proceeding," then how can it seriously be contended that the goals of the proceeding would be "frustrated" if the fruits of illegal searches were not admitted in the first place?

More importantly, the entire cost-benefit analysis in *Susan T.* is badly skewed by the failure of the court to view either from the correct perspective. Why not ask what the results would be in the future if the court *was* to hold the exclusionary rule applicable in such proceedings? On the deterrence side, it would seem apparent that the deterrence would be substantial. Given the fact (as the court admits) that the searches are by employees of the agency which later might seek to use the evidence in a conservatorship proceeding, and given also (as the court asserts) that mental health workers' "first concern" is the well being of the person thought to be gravely disabled, then what would possess a properly trained health worker to bypass the magistrate as did the official intruder in *Susan T.*? On the cost side as well, it can be said that with a modicum of training health workers could be made to understand that evidence-gathering activities involving intrusion into the privacy of homes require a magistrate's approval, so that no significant cost would then be involved—unless what the *Susan T.* majority *really* means is that the social cost must be reduced to virtually zero by giving health workers free reign to do anything short of conduct that would "shock the conscience."[46]

There is thus much to be said for the dissenting opinion of Justice Mosk in *Susan T.*, where he makes three telling points: (i) given the fact that conservatorship proceedings, in which "the state is the defendant's opponent," may result in consequences

---

[46]The court in *Susan T.* emphasized that the presumably illegal conduct did not go this far and thus did "not implicate due process concerns."

"as severe as that faced by a criminal defendant," there is "no principled basis for distinguishing *Moore*"; (ii) "there is no reason to conclude that conservatorship proceedings are so unusual that mental health workers would as a general rule be heedless of the privacy rights of detainees regardless of the exclusionary rule"; and (iii) the social costs "are minimal," as once "aware of the warrant requirement, department employees will have a significant incentive to respect the privacy rights of detainees."

§ 1.7(d) Civil tax proceedings[47]

In *United States v. Janis,*[48] the Supreme Court was confronted with the question whether evidence illegally seized by a state law enforcement officer is admissible in civil tax proceedings by or against the United States. Los Angeles police obtained a warrant directing a search for bookmaking paraphernalia at two specified apartments and on the persons of Janis and another. The police seized $4,940 in cash and certain wagering records from Janis. Soon thereafter, Officer Weissman (who had been the affiant for the warrant) notified the IRS that Janis had been arrested for bookmaking. With Weissman's assistance, an IRS agent analyzed the seized records to determine the volume of Janis' gambling activity for the five days preceding the seizure. Weissman advised that surveillance established Janis had been engaged in bookmaking for a 77-day period, so the IRS made an assessment against him for unpaid taxes in the amount of $89,026.09, plus interest. The IRS then levied on the seized cash in partial satisfaction of the assessment. The local gambling charges against Janis were dropped after he successfully moved to quash the search warrant. Janis then sued in federal court to recoup his $4,940, and the government counterclaimed for the unpaid balance. The district court ruled for Janis on the ground that "substantially all, if not all, of the evidence utilized by the defendants herein in making their assessment * * * was illegally obtained." The court of appeals affirmed, but the Supreme Court reversed on the ground that a contrary ruling would extend the exclusionary rule beyond the point where the deterrent function of the rule would be served. Stated Justice Blackmun for the majority:

> Working, as we must, with the absence of convincing empirical data, common sense dictates that the deterrent effect of the exclusion of relevant evidence is highly attenuated when the "punish-

---

[Section 1.7(d)]

[47]See Comment, 48 N.Y.U.L.Rev. 197 (1973); Notes, 68 Texas L.Rev. 789 (1990); 9 Wake Forest L.Rev. 273 (1973), 19 Wayne L.Rev. 1583 (1973).

[48]United States v. Janis, 428 U.S. 433, 96 S.Ct. 3021, 49 L.Ed.2d 1046 (1976), noted in 1977 Brigham Young U.L.Rev. 211; 6 Cap.U.L.Rev. 489 (1977); 20 How.L.J. 195 (1977); 12 New Engl.L.Rev. 789 (1977); 30 Tax Law. 478 (1977); 12 Tulsa L.J. 357 (1977); 31 U.Miami L.Rev. 721 (1977); 22 Vill.L.Rev. 492 (1977); 13 Wake Forest L.Rev. 161 (1977). See also Note, 51 Fordham L.Rev. 1019 (1983), discussing the experience under *Janis*.

ment" imposed upon the offending criminal enforcement officer is the removal of that evidence from a civil suit by or against a different sovereign. In *Elkins [v. United States*[49]] the Court indicated that the assumed interest of criminal law enforcement officers in the criminal proceedings of another sovereign counter-balanced this attenuation sufficiently to justify an exclusionary rule. Here, however, the attenuation is further augmented by the fact that the proceeding is one to enforce only the civil law[50] of the other sovereign.

This attenuation, coupled with the existing deterrence effected by the denial of use of the evidence by either sovereign in the criminal trials with which the searching officer is concerned,[51] creates a situation in which the imposition of the exclusionary rule sought in this case is unlikely to provide significant, much less substantial, additional deterrence. It falls outside the offending officer's zone of primary interest.[52] The extension of the exclusionary rule, in our view, would be an unjustifiably drastic action by the courts in the pursuit of what is an undesired and undesirable supervisory role over police officers.

The trouble with the *Janis* case is that the majority's deterrence theory points in precisely the opposite direction,[53] as Justice

[49]Elkins v. United States, 364 U.S. 206, 80 S.Ct. 1437, 4 L.Ed.2d 1669 (1960).

[50]In Grimes v. C.I.R., 82 F.3d 286 (9th Cir.1996), the defendant attempted to distinguish *Janis* because the "Tax Court decision here not only assessed a deficiency but also entered penalties against Grimes." The court answered that civil fraud penalties are remedial rather than punitive, so that there was no "punishment" for double jeopardy purposes, and then added that in any event "whether a proceeding results in a 'punishment' for double jeopardy purposes does not determine what is likely to deter officers in the field from violating the Fourth Amendment."

[51]Elsewhere in *Janis,* the Court asserted state law enforcement officers were already "punished" by exclusion of the evidence in the state prosecution. This unfortunate choice of words has prompted the argument that if no state prosecution is undertaken, then there is no such punishment, meaning exclusion in the tax proceeding is called for. But that makes no sense. "The decision not to prosecute because of the police officers' conduct provides deterrence equivalent to the exclusion

of the evidence." Adamson v. C.I.R., 745 F.2d 541 (9th Cir.1984).

[52]Such "zone of primary interest" analysis is also utilized in determining whether evidence must be suppressed when tendered in the prosecution of a crime committed well *after* the acquisition of that evidence. See § 11.6(c).

Efforts to avoid suppression by such "zone of primary interest" analysis in still other circumstances has not succeeded. See, e.g., United States v. Payne, 181 F.3d 781 (6th Cir.1999) (where search at issue "was conducted primarily by parole officers, whose zone of interest is distinct from, but overlaps with, an interest in enforcing the drug laws," exclusionary rule applies in criminal prosecution).

[53]The other purposes of the exclusionary rule, especially in some circumstances, also point in the other direction. In Adamson v. C.I.R., 745 F.2d 541 (9th Cir.1984), the court noted that the Supreme Court "has never abandoned its pronouncement in *Elkins* * * * that in addition to deterrence, the exclusionary rule serves the vital function of preserving judicial integrity," and thus concluded that if the state officer "acted in bad

Stewart stressed in his dissenting opinion.[54] Noting that it was admitted by Officer Weissman that he notified the IRS whenever he uncovered a gambling operation involving a substantial amount of cash, Stewart commented:

> Federal officials responsible for the enforcement of the wagering tax provisions regularly cooperate with federal and local officials responsible for enforcing criminal laws restricting or forbidding wagering. * * * Similarly, federal and local law enforcement personnel regularly provide federal tax officials with information, obtained in criminal investigations, indicating liability under the wagering tax. The pattern is one of mutual cooperation and coordination, with the federal wagering tax provisions buttressing state and federal criminal sanctions.

> Given this pattern, our observation in *Elkins* is directly apposite:

> Free and open cooperation between state and federal law enforcement officers is to be commended and encouraged. Yet that kind of cooperation is hardly promoted by a rule that . . . at least tacitly [invites federal officers] to encourage state officers in the disregard of constitutionally protected freedom. * * *

> To be sure, the *Elkins* case was a federal criminal proceeding and the present case is civil in nature. But our prior decisions make it clear that this difference is irrelevant for Fourth Amendment exclusionary rule purposes where, as here, the civil proceeding serves as an adjunct to the enforcement of the criminal law. See *One 1958 Plymouth Sedan v. Pennsylvania*[55] * * *.

> If state police officials can effectively crack down on gambling law violators by the simple expedient of violating their constitutional rights and turning the illegally seized evidence over to Internal Revenue Service agents on the proverbial "silver platter," then the deterrent purpose of the exclusionary rule is wholly frustrated.

The reasoning of Justice Stewart on this point is unquestionably correct. The *Janis* majority, begrudgingly conceding in a footnote that it might rule otherwise if there were "federal participation" in the search, employed a narrow and artificial concept of deterrence that can hardly be attributed to the "common sense" the Court purported to be relying upon. Rather, common sense teaches that "the exclusionary rule, focused upon general, not specific, deterrence, depends not upon threatening a sanction for lack of compliance but upon removing an *inducement*

---

faith in obtaining the evidence" (not so in the instant case, as "the constitutional questions are close enough that a reasonably competent police officer could have believed that the search was legal"), suppression in the tax proceeding would be necessary because "the integrity of the courts would be implicated."

[54] Brennan and Marshall, JJ., dis-

senting separately, rejected the proposition that deterrence of police misconduct is the only purpose served by the exclusionary rule, but added that even accepting that proposition the Stewart dissent "persuasively demonstrates the error of today's result."

[55] One 1958 Plymouth Sedan v. Pennsylvania, 380 U.S. 693, 85 S.Ct. 1246, 14 L.Ed.2d 170 (1965).

to violate Fourth Amendment rights."[56] This means, as the Court earlier understood in *Elkins,* that federal courts should not admit into evidence the fruits of an illegal state search even if the search was neither prompted by federal authorities nor undertaken by state authorities with the express thought of assisting the federal government, for it is nonetheless true that admission of the evidence would constitute an "inducement to subterfuge and evasion with respect to federal-state cooperation."

One court has extended *Janis* to a case in which the search and the subsequent civil tax proceeding were both federal. In *Tirado v. Commissioner,*[57] the court, though rejecting the notion that the exclusionary rule is never applicable in civil proceedings, also deemed it "unsound to invoke the exclusionary rule on the assumption that officers of one federal agency have such a strong motivating interest in all federal law enforcement concerns that broad application of the rule will achieve significant marginal deterrence."[58] Noting that the narcotics agent who made the search testified he had no pre-existing agreement with the IRS and that there was no general liaison arrangement which would have encouraged this action, the court concluded that on the facts of this case the deterrent purpose of the exclusionary rule would not be served by suppression. In the language of *Janis,* even the federal tax litigation was deemed to be outside the "zone of primary interest" of the federal narcotics agent.[59] Even more remarkably, *Janis* has been applied where the searching police-

[56]United States v. Peltier, 422 U.S. 531, 95 S.Ct. 2313, 45 L.Ed.2d 374 (1975) (Brennan, J., dissenting).

[57]Tirado v. Commissioner, 689 F.2d 307 (2d Cir.1982).

[58]The court added: "The fact that a federal law enforcement officer, attached to an agency and trained to investigate a limited class of unlawful acts, receives his paycheck from the same treasury that pays all other federal agents neither charges him with concern for all the multiple and unrelated law enforcement activities of the federal government, nor warrants the suspicion that his motivations include a desire to help other agencies succeed. If anything, the rivalries and jealousies among many federal law enforcement agencies point to precisely the opposite conclusion."

In Grimes v. C.I.R., 82 F.3d 286 (9th Cir.1996), the court relied on *Tirado* but "limit[ed] our holding to the facts of this case, where Grimes does not allege and the record does not reveal any preexisting agreement, implicit or explicit, between the FBI and the IRS." And in Wolf v. C.I.R., 13 F.3d 189 (6th Cir.1993), the court, while rejecting that part of *Tirado* that reasoned an officer's "primary zone of interest" could be inferred from his expertise and responsibilities, declined to apply the exclusionary rule in the instant civil tax case, as there was "no indication that the criminal narcotics investigation and the secondary civil tax proceeding were initiated by the same agency" and "no indication of an explicit agreement between [the FBI agent] and agents of the IRS."

[59]That unfortunate phrase was later used by a majority of the Court to produce an equally unconvincing conclusion that police officers who know they are searching a parolee would not be significantly deterred by the applicability of the exclusionary rule at parole revocation proceedings. See Pennsylvania Bd. of Probation and Parole v. Scott, 524 U.S. 357, 118 S.Ct. 2014, 141 L.Ed.2d 344 (1998), criti-

man and subsequent civil tax proceeding were of the same state, even though "both police and revenue officers are involved in enforcing" the tax in question, the Controlled Substance Excise Tax, in that "police investigations uncover illegal narcotics, while the Department's revenue officers must collect CSET assessments on those narcotics."[60] To justify that conclusion, the court put forth two dubious assertions: that the "police's primary concern is the enforcement of the State's criminal laws, not its tax code," and that the "cost of lost evidence is even greater in CSET assessments than it is in criminal cases."

Given the tortured reasoning utilized in *Janis* to reach the result, it might be thought that the majority had clearly rejected the notion that the exclusionary rule is *never* applicable in civil tax proceedings. This, however, is not the case. The Court noted that it "never has applied [the exclusionary rule] to exclude evidence from a civil proceeding," that it "need not consider here" that issue, and that if on remand Janis proved federal participation there would remain the question "whether the exclusionary rule is to be applied in a civil proceeding" of this type. However, other courts have held that the Fourth Amendment exclusionary rule is applicable in a civil tax proceeding. The Tax Court reached this result in *Efrian T. Suarez,*[61] as have the federal courts in

---

cized in § 1.6(g).

[60]State, Indiana Dep't of Revenue v. Adams, 762 N.E.2d 728 (Ind.2002).

See also Kivela v. Department of Treasury, 449 Mich. 220, 536 N.W.2d 498 (1995) (relying on *Tirado* and concluding that where the search and tax proceeding were both state, admitting the illegally seized evidence in that proceeding "would not hinder the deterrent effect of the exclusionary rule and would not increase the use of criminal cases as a 'mere' pretext for civil cases" where, as here, "there is no evidence that the law enforcement agents who seized the incriminating financial records were motivated by an unethical desire to illegally assist the Department of Treasury").

[61]Suarez v. Commissioner of Internal Revenue, 58 T.C. 792 (1972). In *Suarez,* the Commissioner's determination that the petitioners owed $713,609.58 in deficient taxes and $35,680.48 in penalties was based upon evidence obtained by state police in an illegal raid. Simpson, J., dissenting, utilizing reasoning similar to that later adopted by the majority in *Janis,*

argued that the facts made it clear that exclusion in the name of deterrence would be inappropriate, as the IRS was merely the beneficiary of a "windfall" because the search had been made by state officers investigating an abortion scheme and the IRS became involved only after the fact when an agent read of the raid in the newspaper. This conclusion is questioned in Baade, Illegally Obtained Evidence in Criminal and Civil Cases: A Comparative Study of a Classic Mismatch II, 52 Texas L.Rev. 621, 650 (1974): "A rereading of the majority opinion, however, discloses that when the special investigator from the State attorney general's office returned to his office with the files *on the day of the raid,* there was already a telephone message for him from the Internal Revenue Service!"

Suarez was criticized in *Janis* because "the court did not distinguish between intersovereign and intrasovereign uses of unconstitutionally seized material," and consequently the Tax Court later concluded, in Guzzetta v. Commissioner, 78 T.C. 173 (1982): "To the extent that *Suarez* is inconsis-

Pizzarello v. United States[62] and *United States v. Blank*.[63]

In assessing this issue, account must be taken of *One 1958 Plymouth Sedan v. Pennsylvania,* discussed earlier in this section. (*Plymouth Sedan,* it will be recalled, held the exclusionary rule applicable in forfeiture proceedings directed at "derivative contraband," such as an auto used in illegal transportation of liquor, on the ground that such proceedings are "quasi-criminal in character" because the object is "to penalize for the commission of an offense against the law.") The *Blank* court deemed *Plymouth Sedan* to be controlling, and this conclusion is correct. True, the Supreme Court has held, in another context not analogous,[64] that civil tax cases are not quasi-criminal in nature because the statutory penalties "are provided primarily as a safeguard for the protection of the revenue and to reimburse the Government for the heavy expense of investigation and the loss resulting from the taxpayers' fraud."[65] But in the same case the Court acknowledged that in "determining whether particular rules of criminal procedure are applicable to civil actions to enforce sanctions, the cases have usually attempted to distinguish between the type of procedural rule involved rather than the kind of sanction being enforced."

In *Plymouth Sedan,* the Court emphasized that the forfeiture proceedings would deprive the owner of a car worth about $1,000, "a higher amount than the maximum fine in the criminal proceeding." It is most significant, therefore, that in *Suarez* the petitioners were subject to a five per cent penalty[66] of nearly thirty-six thousand dollars, while the maximum fine for tax eva-

---

tent with *Janis* with respect to the application of the exclusionary rule, we will no longer follow our prior decision."

[62]Pizzarello v. United States, 408 F.2d 579 (2d Cir.1969).

[63]United States v. Blank, 261 F.Supp. 180 (N.D.Ohio 1966). See also Vander Linden v. United States, 502 F.Supp. 693 (S.D.Iowa 1980) (in civil action for refund of taxes and fraud penalties assessed, government could not use evidence found in criminal tax evasion prosecution to be illegally obtained; *Janis* distinguishable because it an intersovereign situation).

[64]The question was whether a prior acquittal in a criminal tax evasion case would bar the civil tax proceeding, which the court answered in the negative. But, the *Plymouth Sedan* holding that a forfeiture proceeding is "quasi-criminal in character" has not resulted in forfeiture proceedings be-

ing barred by an earlier acquittal in a related criminal case. This is because "the difference in the burden of proof in criminal and civil cases precludes application of the doctrine of collateral estoppel." One Lot Emerald Cut Stones v. United States, 409 U.S. 232, 93 S.Ct. 489, 34 L.Ed.2d 438 (1972).

[65]Helvering v. Mitchell, 303 U.S. 391, 58 S.Ct. 630, 82 L.Ed. 917 (1938).

[66]This was by virtue of 26 U.S.C.A. § 6653(a), which provides that if the underpayment of taxes was due to negligent or intentional disregard of the rules, then there "shall" be added to the tax an amount equal to five percent of the underpayment. If the underpayment were due to fraud, then there "shall" be added an amount equal to fifty percent of the underpayment. These provisions make unconvincing the argument that the "situation might be viewed as a contract between a private party and the government" in which "one contracting

sion is ten thousand dollars.[67] Similarly, in *Blank* the court noted that it was dealing with a civil action "which imposes a penalty upon the citizen commensurate with the criminal sanctions" to which the person would have been exposed but for the illegal search. The *Blank* court also noted that *Plymouth Sedan* asserted it would be "anomalous" to exclude the evidence in a criminal proceeding but not in a forfeiture proceeding "requiring the determination that the criminal law has been violated," and that this reasoning was persuasive on the facts presented because the attempted deficiency assessment also required such a determination. In short, Justice Stewart was correct in stating in *Janis* that the tax proceeding involved there, as with the forfeiture proceeding in *Plymouth Sedan,* "serves as an adjunct to the enforcement of the criminal law."[68]

United States v. Calandra,[69] in which the Court balanced the potential benefits against the potential damage in concluding that the exclusionary rule could not be invoked by a grand jury witness, is not inconsistent with the result reached in *Suarez, Pizzarello* and *Blank*. On the benefits side of the ledger, the *Calandra* majority considered only the deterrence function of the exclusionary rule,[70] and found the possible gain in deterrence insubstantial given the fact that illegally seized evidence could be suppressed "in a subsequent criminal prosecution of the search victim." The same may not be said of civil tax proceedings. It may be true that the usual tax investigation does not give rise to a situation in which there would be occasion for the investigators to violate the Fourth Amendment,[71] but this is not always the case. *Pizzarello,* for example, involved an illegal search made by I.R.S.

---

party is merely attempting to obtain payment for services rendered." Note, 19 Wayne L.Rev. 1583, 1592 (1973). If the underpayment was not even negligent, so that the government were merely collecting the amount of tax otherwise due, then this argument would take on greater force, although the situation would then be comparable to a forfeiture proceeding directed at the profits of an illegal enterprise, as to which the courts have deemed *Plymouth Sedan* controlling. See cases collected in note 8 supra.

[67] Or up to five years imprisonment, or both. 26 U.S.C.A. § 7201.

[68] Compare Turner v. State Department of Revenue, 643 So.2d 568 (Ala.1994) (evidence suppressed in criminal proceeding admissible in civil proceeding on assessment of controlled substantive excise tax, as purpose of tax was economic in nature and thus

tax assessment proceeding, unlike forfeiture action, not quasi-criminal).

[69] United States v. Calandra, 414 U.S. 338, 94 S.Ct. 613, 38 L.Ed.2d 561 (1974), discussed in § 1.4(a).

[70] The dissenters objected that account must also be taken of "the twin goals of enabling the judiciary to avoid the taint of partnership in official lawlessness and of assuring the people * * * that the government would not profit from its lawless behavior," which if taken into consideration, as they were by the *Suarez* court, would also point toward application of the exclusionary rule in civil tax cases.

[71] "An income tax investigation does not involve catching a criminal redhanded or in hot pursuit. Instead it more nearly resembles an archaeological expedition, the digging up and analysis of records several years old. Further, the coercive power to gather

agents, and other cases show that these agents become involved in the making of searches, particularly when organized crime is under investigation.[72]

As for the cost of applying the exclusionary rule in civil tax proceedings, Judge Simpson, dissenting in *Suarez,* argued that in "our self-assessment tax system" application of the rule "raises the prospect of seriously undermining the practice of voluntary compliance with the tax laws." It is to be doubted that this is so, or at least that it is any more true than the proposition that application of the rule in criminal cases undermines the practice of general compliance with the criminal law. Indeed, it may well be said, as stated by the *Suarez* majority, that the "costs to society of applying the exclusionary rule in civil tax cases are substantially less than in the criminal area." This is particularly apparent when one takes into account the fact that the I.R.S. possesses rather substantial enforcement powers.[73]

§ 1.7(e) Child protection proceedings

Although the cases are few in number, it has been consistently held that the Fourth Amendment exclusionary rule is not applicable in proceedings occurring in juvenile court or some other court for the purpose of determining whether transfer of custody or some other steps should be taken for the purpose of ensuring the protection of a juvenile.[74] The leading case is *State ex rel. A.R.*

---

information normally cannot be exercised without an administrative summons which may be challenged in court before enforcement." Comment, 48 N.Y.U.L.Rev. 197, 199 n. 21 (1973). See also Lyon, Government Power and Citizen Rights in a Tax Investigation, 25 Tax Law. 79 (1971).

[72]E.g., United States v. Schipani, 289 F.Supp. 43 (E.D.N.Y.1968).

[73]Thus, Tannenwald, J., concurring in *Suarez,* notes: "The fact of the matter is that [the Commissioner] is afforded many weapons by means of which he can require such persons to pay the taxes they owe. He has the power of subpoena and he has available to him various broad techniques for developing a person's taxable income, e.g., net worth, bank deposits, and cash expenditures." See also Duke, Prosecutions for Attempts to Evade Income Tax: A Discordant View of a Procedural Hybrid, 76 Yale L.J. 1 (1966); Note, 57 Colum.L.Rev. 676 (1957).

[Section 1.7(e)]

[74]In re Mary S., 186 Cal.App.3d 414, 230 Cal.Rptr. 726 (1986) (a "parent at a dependency hearing cannot assert the Fourth Amendment exclusionary rule, since 'the potential harm to children in allowing them to remain in an unhealthy environment out People ex rel. A.E.L., 181 P.3d 1186 (Colo.App.2008) (exclusionary rule not applicable to child protection proceedings, as societal costs of applying the rule would exceed deterrent effect); In re Nicholas R., 92 Conn.App. 316, 884 A.2d 1059 (2005) (exclusionary rule not applicable in child neglect proceedings); Idaho Dept. Of Health & Welfare v. Doe, 150 Idaho 103, 244 P.3d 247 (2010) (exclusionary rule not applicable "in the context of a child protection proceeding," as "application of the rule may thwart the state's interest in protection of children"); In re Corey P., 269 Neb. 925, 697 N.W.2d 647 (2005) ("application of the rule in juvenile proceedings [regarding child protection] may lead to an erroneous conclu-

v. C.R.,[75] where police officers found petitioner's children unattended and then discovered drug and sexual paraphernalia in petitioner's house, leading to the commencement of child protection proceedings in juvenile court, which culminated in the awarding of custody of one child to his natural father. Although the warrantless searches violated petitioner's Fourth Amendment rights, the court deemed the exclusionary rule inapplicable in these circumstances, a conclusion ultimately affirmed by the state supreme court.

Although conceding that the exclusionary rule may well apply in those cases, such as *Plymouth Sedan*, which are quasi-criminal in nature, that court concluded this point was of no benefit to the petitioner here:

> The primary focus of and sole statutory justification for child protection proceedings is to protect the interests of children who are neglected or abused. * * * Although parents may suffer a severe detriment in losing temporary or permanent custody of their children, punishment of the parents is not the purpose of the proceeding. A child is never removed from a home as "punishment" to the parent. Indeed, it is strongly presumed that "it is in the best interest and welfare of a child to be raised under the care and supervision of his [or her] natural parents." * * * In most cases, the primary objective is to effectuate a family treatment plan that will allow children to be returned to their parents.

The court in *C.R.* then proceeded to apply "the principles enunciated in *Calandra* and its progeny," concluding:

> In light of the purpose of the exclusionary rule, as well as the State's interest in protecting children, it is improper to exclude evidence discovered during a warrantless search in subsequent child protection proceedings. State officials confronting the possibility of child abuse or neglect-emergencies that occasionally lead to child protection proceedings-do not ordinarily seek to uncover incriminating evidence during the warrantless searches incidental to these investigations. There is little incentive to violate the Fourth Amendment because these officers do not usually act with the object of obtaining evidence for criminal prosecution.

> There appears to be little likelihood that any substantial deterrent effect on unlawful police intrusion would be achieved by apply-

---

sion that there has been no abuse or neglect, leaving innocent children to remain in unhealthy or compromising circumstances"); State ex rel. Children, Youth & Families Dep't v. Michael T., 143 N.M. 75, 172 P.3d 1287 (App.2007) (exclusionary rule not applicable in child abuse and neglect proceedings, where focus is on health and safety of innocent children); In re Diane P., 110 A.D.2d 354, 494 N.Y.S.2d 881 (1985) ("the State's overwhelming interest in protecting and promoting the best interests and safety of minors in a child protective proceeding far outweighs the rule's deterrent value"); State ex rel. Dep't of Human Services v. W.L.P., 345 Or. 657, 202 P.3d 167 (2009) (neither state nor federal constitution requires application of exclusionary rule in juvenile dependency proceedings); State ex rel. A.R. v. C.R., 982 P.2d 73 (Utah 1999) (discussed in text at note 74 infra).

[75]State ex rel. A.R. v. C.R., 982 P.2d 73 (Utah 1999).

ing the exclusionary rule to child protection proceedings. Whatever deterrent effect there might be is far outweighed by the need to provide for the safety and health of children in peril.

§ 1.7(f) Administrative hearings[76]

The question next to be considered is whether the Fourth Amendment exclusionary rule is applicable with respect to evidence offered in a hearing before a local, state or federal administrative agency. This issue, it must be emphasized at the outset, is a distinct one from that of whether administrative officials may under some circumstances engage in searches on a less restrictive basis than police investigating crime,[77] although an affirmative determination on the latter question sometimes makes unnecessary resolution of the first one.[78] Nor are the two issues inevitably related, for evidence obtained in a so-called administrative search may ultimately be offered in a criminal prosecution.[79]

Courts have held or at least assumed that the exclusionary rule is applicable in a wide variety of administrative proceedings, including FTC hearings to uncover discriminatory pricing practices,[80] SEC proceedings,[81] OSHA proceedings,[82] proceedings before the public utilities commission to terminate phone service

---

[Section 1.7(f)]

[76]See Comment, 2 Conn.L.Rev. 648 (1970); Notes, 54 Geo.Wash.L.Rev. 564 (1986); 37 Hastings L.J. 1133 (1986); 66 Iowa L.Rev. 343 (1981); 40 Okla.L.Rev. 320 (1987).

[77]See ch. 10.

[78]Thus, in Solomon v. Liquor Control Comm'n, 4 Ohio St.2d 31, 212 N.E.2d 595 (1965), because the court concluded that licensed premises were subject to warrantless inspection without probable cause by commission agents, it became "unnecessary to consider and discuss the question of whether the exclusionary rule * * * is applicable to hearings before a public administrative agency."

[79]Camara v. Municipal Court, 387 U.S. 523, 87 S.Ct. 1727, 18 L.Ed.2d 930 (1967) (Court, in discussing administrative inspection for housing violations, notes that "housing codes are enforced by criminal processes"); Abel v. United States, 362 U.S. 217, 80 S.Ct. 683, 4 L.Ed.2d 668 (1960) (evidence seized incident to arrest upon an "administrative" deportation warrant used in criminal espionage prosecution).

[80]Knoll Associates, Inc. v. FTC, 397 F.2d 530 (7th Cir.1968); FTC v. Page, 378 F.Supp. 1052 (N.D.Ga.1974) (distinguishing Supreme Court's ruling in Calandra that exclusionary rule not applicable to grand jury witness, as here "[n]o investigative proceedings will be interrupted by consideration of respondents' Fourth Amendment arguments at this point").

[81]OKC Corp. v. Williams, 461 F.Supp. 540 (N.D.Tex.1978); judgment aff'd, 614 F.2d 58 (5th Cir.).

[82]Savina Home Industries, Inc. v. Secretary of Labor, 594 F.2d 1358 (10th Cir.1979) (noting that the Barlow's case, discussed in § 10.2(a), did not resolve the issue because there no OSHA search had yet taken place). Consider also Weyerhaeuser Co. v. Marshall, 592 F.2d 373 (7th Cir.1979) (company can seek suppression in district court notwithstanding fact OSHA administrative proceedings still pending; exhaustion of administrative remedies not required here, "as counsel for the Secretary informed us at oral argument that the OSHA Review Commission has never ruled on the issue of a warrant's validity"). See also Trant, OSHA and the Exclusionary

because of illegal use,[83] NLRB hearings concerning labor controversies,[84] immigration hearings,[85] hearings to terminate a public
employee's government service,[86] hearings to suspend or revoke a
license to practice a profession[87] or to sell liquor,[88] hearings to
suspend or revoke a driver's license,[89] and hearings to suspend or
expel a student from a public high school[90] or a state university.[91]
However, the cases so holding or assuming, and the several cases

---

Rule: Should the Employer Go Free
Because the Compliance Officer Has
Blundered?, 1981 Duke L.J. 667;
Annot., 67 A.L.R.Fed. 724 (1984);
Comments, 64 Minn.L.Rev. 789 (1980);
19 Wake Forest L.Rev. 819 (1983).

[83]Goldin v. Public Utilities Comm.,
23 Cal.3d 638, 153 Cal.Rptr. 802, 592
P.2d 289 (1979).

[84]NLRB v. Bell Oil & Gas Co., 98
F.2d 870 (5th Cir.1938).

[85]Wong Chung Che v. Immigra-
tion and Naturalization Service, 565
F.2d 166 (1st Cir.1977); Schenck ex
rel. Chow Fook Hong v. Ward, 24
F.Supp. 776 (D.Mass.1938). See Frago-
men, Procedural Aspects of Illegal
Search and Seizure in Deportation
Cases, 14 San Diego L.Rev. 151 (1976);
Annot., 44 A.L.R.Fed. 933 (1979);
Comment, 14 U.C.Davis.L.Rev. 955
(1981); Note, 58 N.Car.L.Rev. 647
(1980). But see text at note 119 infra.

[86]Powell v. Zuckert, 366 F.2d 634
(D.C.Cir.1966); Sullivan v. District Ct.
of Hampshire, 384 Mass. 736, 429
N.E.2d 335 (1981) ("Illegally obtained
evidence may not be used by the government in a Civil Service Commission proceeding to support the discharge of a public employee");
Minnesota State Patrol Troopers Ass'n
v. State, Dep't of Public Safety, 437
N.W.2d 670 (Minn.App.1989); City of
New Brunswick v. Speights, 157
N.J.Super. 9, 384 A.2d 225 (1978).

But see People v. McGrath, 46
N.Y.2d 12, 412 N.Y.S.2d 801, 385
N.E.2d 541 (1978) (under the "length
of the road" part of the fruit-of-the-
poisonous-tree analysis used by the
Supreme Court in the *Ceccolini* case,
discussed in § 11.4(i), the fact the evidence was offered in such a proceedings is relevant because it shows it is
somewhat less likely that suppression
is needed as a deterrent).

[87]Elder v. Board of Medical
Examiners, 241 Cal.App.2d 246, 50
Cal.Rptr. 304 (1966) (questioned in
Pierce v. Board of Nursing Education,
255 Cal.App.2d 463, 63 Cal.Rptr. 107
(1967)); Yarbrough v. Pfeiffer, 370
So.2d 1177 (Fla.App.1979).

[88]Finn's Liquor Shop v. State
Liquor Authority, 24 N.Y.2d 647, 301
N.Y.S.2d 584, 249 N.E.2d 440 (1969);
Leogrande v. State Liquor Authority,
25 A.D.2d 225, 268 N.Y.S.2d 433
(1966); Board of License Comm'rs v.
Pastore, 463 A.2d 161 (R.I.1983).

[89]Whisenhunt v. State, Department of Public Safety, 746 P.2d 1298
(Alaska 1987); Pooler v. Motor Vehicles
Division, 306 Or. 47, 755 P.2d 701
(1988). Cf. State v. Lussier, 171 Vt.
19, 757 A.2d 1017 (2000) (re civil *judicial* action to suspend driver's license,
court concludes "it is appropriate to
apply the exclusionary rule in civil
license suspension proceeding to protect the core value of privacy embraced
in [the state constitution], to promote
the public's trust in the judicial system, and to assure that unlawful police conduct is not encouraged"). See
also Annot., 23 A.L.R.5th 108 (1994).

[90]Jones v. Latexo Independent
School Dist., 499 F.Supp. 223 (E.D.
Tex.1980); Caldwell v. Cannady, 340
F.Supp. 835 (N.D.Tex.1972). Cf. Note,
72 N.Y.U.L.Rev. 1494, 1495 ("argues
that New York courts should apply the
state constitution-based exclusionary
rule to school disciplinary proceedings
and suggests that other states should
do the same with their own exclusionary rules").

[91]Smyth v. Lubbers, 398 F.Supp.
777 (W.D.Mich.1975); Moore v. Student
Affairs Committee of Troy State
University, 284 F.Supp. 725 (M.D.Ala.
1968).

holding to the contrary,[92] are for the most part lacking in careful

[92]Thompson v. Carthage School District, 87 F.3d 979 (8th Cir.1996) (exclusionary rule not applicable in school disciplinary proceedings); Garrett v. Lehman, 751 F.2d 997 (9th Cir.1985) (exclusionary rule not applicable to military administrative discharge proceedings); Webster v. Redmond, 599 F.2d 793 (7th Cir.1979) (school board, in deciding to suspend teacher, may consider illegally seized evidence); NLRB v. South Bay Daily Breeze, 415 F.2d 360 (9th Cir.1969) (exclusionary rule not applied in Board's proceeding because "neither criminal procedures nor sanctions are involved," but alternate ground was that search was by a private party rather than a government agent); Alvarez v. State, Dept. of Admin., Div. of Motor Vehicles, 249 P.3d 286 (Alaska 2011) ("the exclusionary rule does not apply to license suspicion hearings"); Emslie v. State Bar of California, 11 Cal.3d 210, 113 Cal.Rptr. 175, 520 P.2d 991 (1974) (though there was no illegal search, court holds exclusionary rule not applicable in attorney disciplinary proceedings; court stresses police would not be deterred thereby and intimates contrary result would be reached if purpose of search was related to such proceedings); Governing Board of Mountain View School District v. Metcalf, 36 Cal.App.3d 546, 111 Cal.Rptr. 724 (1974) (rule not applied in proceedings to discharge teacher for immoral conduct); Ahart v. Colorado Dept. of Corrections, 964 P.2d 517 (Colo.1998) (exclusionary rule not applicable in administrative hearing to terminate corrections officers for admitted drug use); People v. Harfmann, 638 P.2d 745 (Colo.1981) (exclusionary rule not applicable to disciplinary proceedings against lawyer, as in that context "the court's primary duty is to protect the public and the legal profession from unscrupulous lawyers"); Valdez v. Department of Revenue, 622 So.2d 62 (Fla.App.1993) (not applicable in administrative proceedings challenging civil tax assessment); Grames v. Illinois State Police, 254 Ill.App.3d 191, 192

Ill.Dec. 790, 625 N.E.2d 945 (1993) (exclusionary rule not applicable in state police discharge proceeding); Westendorf v. Iowa Department of Transportation, 400 N.W.2d 553 (Iowa 1987) (not applicable in driver's license revocation proceeding); Chase v. Neth, 269 Neb. 882, 697 N.W.2d 675 (2005) (collecting cases elsewhere in accord, court holds exclusionary rule not applicable in administrative driver's license revocation proceedings; "the marginal deterrent effect of the exclusionary rule is outweighed by the substantial societal cost of losing reliable information used to remove intoxicated drivers from the highways"); Pullin v. Louisiana State Racing Comm'n, 484 So.2d 105 (La.1986) (not applicable to racing commission affirmance of track stewards' suspension of owner and trainer of horses; court says Janis, note 93 infra, and Lopez-Mendoza, note 119 infra, require balancing approach, and reaches bizarre conclusion that those state police who are members of the State Police Investigations Unit would not be deterred by exclusion because they also have criminal law responsibilities); Powell v. Secretary of State, 614 A.2d 1303 (Me.1992) (not applicable in driver's license revocation hearing; court uses Lopez-Mendoza and Janis-style balancing); Sheetz v. Mayor & City Council of Baltimore, 315 Md. 208, 553 A.2d 1281 (1989) (exclusionary rule not applicable to discharge proceedings involving correctional officer); Riche v. Director of Revenue, 987 S.W.2d 331 (Mo.1999) (exclusionary rule not applicable at driver's license suspension hearing, as application "would unnecessarily complicate and burden an administrative process designed to remove drunken drivers from Missouri's roads and highways as quickly as possible"); Martin v. Kansas Dept. of Revenue, 285 Kan. 625, 176 P.3d 938 (2008) (exclusionary rule not applicable in administrative driver's license suspension proceedings, collecting cases in accord); Lopez v. Director, Division of Motor Vehicles, 145 N.H. 222, 761 A.2d 448 (2000) (not applicable in administrative driver's

analysis of the question. Because this is so, and also because the Supreme Court has yet to meet this issue squarely,[93] except in a rather unique context,[94] it is not possible to state with certainty when application of the exclusionary rule in administrative hearings is required. But by reference to Supreme Court decisions on related matters, particularly *One 1958 Plymouth Sedan v. Pennsylvania*[95] and *United States v. Calandra,*[96] it would seem that the exclusionary rule must at least sometimes be utilized in the administrative setting.

Plymouth Sedan tells us that the exclusionary rule is to be applied to proceedings that are "quasi-criminal in character" because their object "is to penalize for the commission of an offense against the law." It is thus fair to conclude that the rule applies in administrative proceedings with that object, as where a state agency responsible for the control of liquor sales is

---

license suspension procedure); Catena v. Seidl, 66 N.J. 32, 327 A.2d 658 (1974) (witness called before state commission investigating organized crime may be required to answer questions based on illegal search; case may be viewed as administrative investigation equivalent of *Calandra* holding that grand jury witness may not invoke exclusionary rule, but court strangely fails to even cite *Calandra*); Boyd v. Constantine, 81 N.Y.2d 189, 597 N.Y.S.2d 605, 613 N.E.2d 511 (1993) (fruits of unlawful search by city police admissible in disciplinary proceeding against state trooper); Holte v. North Dakota State Highway Commissioner, 436 N.W.2d 250 (N.D.1989) (refusing to extend exclusionary rule to license suspension hearing).

But see State v. Taeger, 781 N.W.2d 560 (Iowa 2010) (noting that after *Westendorf*, supra, legislature adopted statute with mandatory exclusionary rule that prevents the introduction of evidence in a civil license proceeding that was suppressed in the parallel criminal proceeding).

[93]The issue was not squarely presented in Camara v. Municipal Court, 387 U.S. 523, 87 S.Ct. 1727, 18 L.Ed.2d 930 (1967), or Abel v. United States, 362 U.S. 217, 80 S.Ct. 683, 4 L.Ed.2d 668 (1960), both supra note 79, or in Wyman v. James, 400 U.S. 309, 91 S.Ct. 381, 27 L.Ed.2d 408 (1971), holding that even if the home visit state statutes and regulations prescribed as a condition for assistance under the

AFDC program possessed some characteristics of a search in the traditional criminal law sense, the visit did not fall within the Fourth Amendment's proscription against unreasonable searches and seizures where the visit was made by a caseworker only during working hours and without forcible entry or snooping. For the reasons explained in. Savina Home Industries, Inc. v. Secretary of Labor, 594 F.2d 1358 (10th Cir.1979), supra note 82, the issue was not squarely presented in *Barlow's* either.

As for United States v. Janis, 428 U.S. 433, 96 S.Ct. 3021, 49 L.Ed.2d 1046 (1976), holding the exclusionary rule inapplicable in federal civil tax proceedings where the illegal search was by a state law enforcement officer, the Court did not reach the broader question of whether the rule is at all applicable in civil proceedings. *Janis* may well be applicable, however, when the evidence is offered in an administrative hearing in a jurisdiction other than that where the search occurred. See note 113 infra.

[94]See I.N.S. v. Lopez-Mendoza, 468 U.S. 1032, 104 S.Ct. 3479, 82 L.Ed.2d 778 (1984), discussed in text at note 119 and following.

[95]One 1958 Plymouth Sedan v. Pennsylvania, 380 U.S. 693, 85 S.Ct. 1246, 14 L.Ed.2d 170 (1965).

[96]United States v. Calandra, 414 U.S. 338, 94 S.Ct. 613, 38 L.Ed.2d 561 (1974), discussed in § 1.4(a).

empowered to impose fines[97] or declare forfeitures on bonds[98] for criminal and other violations by licensees. The Court in *Plymouth Sedan* also noted that the forfeiture proceeding at issue there could "result in even greater punishment than the criminal prosecution" for the underlying conduct. This strongly suggests that a highly relevant (but not necessarily controlling) factor in other cases is the magnitude of the consequences for the individual involved. Thus, the courts in the cases cited earlier have stressed the seriousness of taking away a person's license to practice a profession[99] or to operate an establishment selling liquor,[100] a person's public employment,[101] or a person's opportunity for an education.[102] In each of these instances, the government is attempting to use its coercive power to force the individual to

---

[97]Pennsylvania Liquor Control Bd. v. Leonardziak, 210 Pa.Super. 511, 233 A.2d 606 (1967).

[98]Leogrande v. State Liquor Authority, 25 A.D.2d 225, 268 N.Y.S.2d 433 (1966).

[99]Governing Board of Mountain View School District v. Metcalf, 36 Cal.App.3d 546, 111 Cal.Rptr. 724 (1974) (noting that "a proceeding to dismiss a member of his profession from his position is punitive in character," particularly "where the proceeding before us forms the basis for a subsequent revocation of Metcalf's teaching credential"); Elder v. Board of Medical Examiners, 241 Cal.App.2d 246, 50 Cal.Rptr. 304 (1966) (noting that a license to practice medicine "is recognized as a property right").

[100]Leogrande v. State Liquor Authority, 25 A.D.2d 225, 268 N.Y.S.2d 433 (1966) (noting that liquor licensee was "subject to loss of his valuable liquor license").

[101]Powell v. Zuckert, 366 F.2d 634 (D.C.Cir.1966) (noting that the Supreme Court, in considering proceedings to discharge a public employee, "has analogized to proceedings that 'involve the imposition of criminal sanctions * * * ','" citing Peters v. Hobby, 349 U.S. 331, 75 S.Ct. 790, 99 L.Ed. 1129 (1955)); Governing Board of Mountain View School District v. Metcalf, 36 Cal.App.3d 546, 111 Cal.Rptr. 724 (1974) (noting proceeding to discharge teacher "is punitive in character"); Ahart v. Colorado Dept. of Corrections, 964 P.2d 517 (Colo.1998)

(a factor here is that "discharge proceedings do exact a penalty from the employee involved, the loss of employment"); City of New Brunswick v. Speights, 157 N.J.Super. 9, 384 A.2d 225 (1978) (noting "that the loss of a police officer's position with a city is sufficiently severe and carries with it such penal and quasi-criminal overtones as may require the consideration by a court" of the exclusionary rule).

[102]Smyth v. Lubbers, 398 F.Supp. 777 (W.D.Mich.1975) (noting that "the punishment in fact imposed by the College," expulsion, "is more severe than that likely to be imposed by any state or federal court for the same offense" of marijuana possession); Caldwell v. Cannady, 340 F.Supp. 835 (N.D.Tex.1972) (noting that "a student loses none of his constitutional rights by virtue of his status as a student," citing Tinker v. Des Moines Independent School Dist., 393 U.S. 503, 89 S.Ct. 733, 21 L.Ed.2d 731 (1969)). See also Notes, 37 Hastings L.J. 1133 (1986) (reasoning that the exclusionary rule should apply in administrative proceedings against a student only if the proposed sanction is 10 days or more out of school); 77 Mich.L. Rev. 1540, 1554–65 (1979) (concluding "that college disciplinary proceedings impose sufficient quasi-criminal deprivations to warrant application of the exclusionary rule").

Compare Thompson v. Carthage School District, 87 F.3d 979 (8th Cir.1996) (relationship of school officials to school discipline deemed to be unlike that of police to criminal

refrain from activity of considerable importance to that individual. By contrast, if the administrative process merely provides a special procedure for resolving what are essentially private disputes, then the *Plymouth Sedan* analogy fails. Thus, it would seem that there is no more reason to apply the exclusionary rule in workmen's compensation proceedings[103] than in the purely private litigation discussed later in this section. This is not to say, however, with respect to the *Plymouth Sedan* reference to the "commission of an offense," that the exclusionary rule should not be applied in administrative proceedings unless the search in question was undertaken for the purpose of uncovering criminal conduct. As the Supreme Court has observed in a related context, it "is surely anomalous to say that the individual and his private property are fully protected by the Fourth Amendment only when the individual is suspected of criminal behavior."[104]

In *Calandra,* the approach of the Court was to balance the potential benefits of applying the exclusionary rule, namely the added deterrence, against the potential damage from such application. This would suggest that a second important consideration in determining when exclusion is required in administrative proceedings is the extent to which exclusion would deter (or, more properly, the extent to which non-exclusion would encourage) illegal searches and seizures. On this basis, the argument for exclusion is most compelling when the administrative agency in question has an investigative function and investigative personnel of that agency participated in the illegal activity for the purpose of providing information to support administrative proceedings against the suspect.[105] The benefit of exclusion in terms of deterrence is just as strong when the search was by a

---

prosecution, as school officials "do not have an adversarial relationship with students").

[103]Cf. Thanhauser v. Milprint, Inc., 9 A.D.2d 833, 192 N.Y.S.2d 911 (1959); Neff v. Franklinville Roofing Co., 283 A.D. 903, 130 N.Y.S.2d 101 (1954) (both declining to exclude illegally obtained statement).

[104]Camara v. Municipal Court, 387 U.S. 523, 87 S.Ct. 1727, 18 L.Ed.2d 930 (1967).

[105]Illustrative are Savina Home Industries, Inc. v. Secretary of Labor, 594 F.2d 1358 (10th Cir.1979) (OSHA proceeding; court stresses objectives of exclusionary rule "do not become inconsequential simply because an illegal search is conducted by the Department of Labor instead of by the Department of Justice"); Knoll Associ-

ates, Inc. v. FTC, 397 F.2d 530 (7th Cir.1968) (FTC counsel did not deny he encouraged search by private person);Jones v. Latexo Independent School Dist., 499 F.Supp. 223 (E.D.Tex. 1980) (search of high school students by school officials; "failure to apply the corollary of the exclusionary rule in this context would leave school officials free to trench upon the constitutional rights of students in their charge without meaningful restraint"); OKC Corp. v. Williams, 461 F.Supp. 540 (N.D.Tex.1978) judgment aff'd, 614 F.2d 58 (5th Cir.) (SEC proceedings; court notes need for deterrence here, where search was by officers and employees of SEC); Moore v. Student Affairs Committee of Troy State University, 284 F.Supp. 725 (M.D.Ala. 1968) (dean of men participated in search of student's quarters); Schenck

police officer specifically assigned to the investigation of the kinds of wrongdoing handled by the administrative agency, but by unjustified reliance upon the Supreme Court's ill-considered *Janis* decision[106] some courts have reached the mistaken conclusion that no significant deterrent benefit would exist in such circumstances.[107] When the administrative agency is merely the recipient of the fruits of an illegal search or seizure by some government agent[108] not employed by or otherwise serving the agency, then a closer look at the circumstances is required. If it may be said that the special status of the person subjected to the

---

ex rel. Chow Fook Hong v. Ward, 24 F.Supp. 776 (D.Mass.1938) (search by immigration authorities); Elder v. Board of Medical Examiners, 241 Cal.App.2d 246, 50 Cal.Rptr. 304 (1966) (search by agents of licensing authority);Finn's Liquor Shop v. State Liquor Authority, 24 N.Y.2d 647, 301 N.Y.S.2d 584, 249 N.E.2d 440 (1969) (search by agents of licensing authority).

But see Thompson v. Carthage School District, 87 F.3d 979 (8th Cir.1996) (court admits that application of exclusionary rule in school disciplinary proceedings "would likely have a strong deterrent effect" where, as here, "school officials both conducted the search and imposed the student discipline," but deems that consideration to be outweighed by others, see notes 92, 102); Ahart v. Colorado Dept. of Corrections, 964 P.2d 517 (Colo. 1998) (applying exclusionary rule "would increase the likelihood of deterring unlawful behavior," as the "same DOC officials who violated Ahart and McWhirter's Fourth Amendment rights later sought to use the illegally seized evidence in their discharge proceedings," but that consideration outweighed by another, see note 103).

[106]Discussed in text at note 48 supra.

[107]Pullin v. Louisiana State Racing Comm'n, 484 So.2d 105 (La.1986) (court rules applying exclusionary rule before racing commission to evidence obtained by members of the State Police Racing Investigations Unit "is not likely to provide significant additional deterrence due to the interagency nature of the violation"; court stresses that SPRIU is a component of the State Police, in turn within the Department of Public Safety, while the

Racing Commission is in the Department of Commerce; one of the dissenters correctly asserts that "since the Louisiana State Police Racing Investigations Unit was at least affiliated with the Louisiana State Racing Commission, the opposite result obtains," especially where, as here,"the primary purpose of the illegal search of Pullin's barn was for use in the license revocation proceeding"); Powell v. Secretary of State, 614 A.2d 1303 (Me.1992) (court assumes because evidence not admissible in criminal prosecution for a violation calling for license suspension or revocation, "there is little additional deterrent effect on police" by using the exclusionary rule in driver's license revocation hearing).

Compare Turner v. City of Lawton, 733 P.2d 375 (Okla.1986) (distinguishing *Janis* and also relying upon exclusionary rule of *state* constitution, court holds, re illegal search of city employee who then fired on basis of evidence so obtained, that such evidence should have been excluded in the "civil administrative proceeding" resulting in the employee's termination, as if "the evidence can be used to discharge Turner from his job, even though the criminal charges were dismissed, there would still be a substantial incentive to the city's police officers to engage in further unlawful searches especially when municipal employees are the targets thereof").

[108]In NLRB v. South Bay Daily Breeze, 415 F.2d 360 (9th Cir.1969), an alternative ground for the decision was that the search had been made by a private person who was not an agent of the government. On such "private" searches, see § 1.8.

---

search, making him amenable to administrative action, was known in advance by the agent conducting the search, then exclusion in the name of deterrence is certainly sound.[109] But even if there was no question but that the government agent making the search never contemplated the possibility of administrative sanctions flowing from the search, exclusion for purposes of deterrence would be justified if admission of the evidence in the instant case could be expected to encourage future illegal searches by such agents because of their expectation that in any event the evidence would be usable in the administrative process.

For these reasons, it is certainly appropriate to apply the exclusionary rule in administrative proceedings when, for example, the police have searched premises known to be licensed for the sale of liquor and turned the fruits over to the administrative agency empowered to revoke the license,[110] or Air Force OSI agents have participated in the illegal search of the home of one known to be an Air Force civilian employee and then turned the evidence over to the agency empowered to discharge the employee.[111] By contrast, the exclusion-for-deterrence argument is relatively weak where a school board, empowered to discharge teachers for immoral conduct, has been the recipient of evidence that a teacher was one of the persons the police discovered, by illegal means, engaged in unlawful sexual activity in the restroom of a department store.[112] In that situation, there are two significant considerations: (i) the investigation was not directed at persons known to be teachers, so there is no basis for saying the illegality was prompted by an expectation that the evidence obtained would be usable in dismissal proceedings; and (ii) admission of the evidence is unlikely to result in the police singling out teachers for illegal searches in the future, as (unlike the tavern licensee case) investigative activities are not normally directed toward teachers as a class.[113]

As for the cost factor in the *Calandra* equation, this will

---

[109]Unfortunately, in the context of another sort of administrative hearing, a parole revocation hearing, a majority of the Supreme Court failed to recognize the significance of this knowledge-of-status circumstance in terms of a showing of the need for deterrence, which could be realized by applying the exclusionary rule at the administrative hearing. See Pennsylvania Bd. of Probation and Parole v. Scott, 524 U.S. 357, 118 S.Ct. 2014, 141 L.Ed.2d 344 (1998), criticized in § 1.6(g).

[110]See cases cited in note 88 supra.

[111]Powell v. Zuckert, 366 F.2d 634 (D.C.Cir.1966).

[112]Governing Board of Mountain View School District v. Metcalf, 36 Cal.App.3d 546, 111 Cal.Rptr. 724 (1974).

[113]In this situation, the reasoning of the Supreme Court in United States v. Janis, 428 U.S. 433, 96 S.Ct. 3021, 49 L.Ed.2d 1046 (1976), supra note 113, that exclusion will not deter because the proceeding in which the evidence is offered "falls outside the offending officer's zone of primary interest" is much more persuasive than it was on the facts of *Janis*. See also Sheetz v. Mayor & City Council of Baltimore, 315 Md. 208, 553 A.2d 1281 (1989) (evidence would be inadmissible in civil discharge proceedings if defen-

likewise vary in administrative proceedings cases, depending upon the circumstances. Thus in *Governing Board of Mountain View School District v. Metcalf,*[114] concerning the question of whether the exclusionary rule should be applied in school board proceedings to discharge a sixth grade teacher for immoral conduct, namely, an act of oral copulation in a public restroom in a department store, the court stated:

> We recognize that like the criminal law generally a proceeding to dismiss a member of his profession from his position is punitive in character. * * * But we are also mindful that the primary purpose of the proceeding before us is to protect Metcalf's pupils and other school children. Accordingly, we hold that the exclusionary rule does not apply to this proceeding. * * *
>
> In so holding we do not intimate whether the rule should be applied in a proceeding to discipline a member of the teaching profession on non-moral grounds or to proceedings to discipline members of professions generally.[115]

This type of reasoning has sometimes been questioned. It has

---

dant established police improperly motivated to illegally seize evidence to benefit those proceedings); Boyd v. Constantine, 81 N.Y.2d 189, 597 N.Y.S.2d 605, 613 N.E.2d 511 (1993) (evidence admissible; court stresses that city police "did not know, prior to the search, that defendant was a State Trooper" and thus "could not have foreseen" before the search that any fruits would be offered in a disciplinary proceeding against a state trooper).

Even closer to *Janis,* in the sense that two different sovereigns are involved, is Emslie v. State Bar of California, 11 Cal.3d 210, 113 Cal.Rptr. 175, 520 P.2d 991 (1974). The court held the exclusionary rule inapplicable in attorney disciplinary proceedings, reasoning that "the officer [making the illegal search] might not even know that the suspect was an attorney and might not even contemplate the consequences of an arrest or conviction upon professional disciplinary proceedings." Doubtless the court was influenced by the fact that the search at issue had been conducted by law enforcement officers in Nevada who apparently did not even know Emslie was an attorney. The court indicated that the need for exclusion must be determined on a case-by-case basis, thus intimating that under other circumstances there may be a greater need to exclude so as

not to encourage Fourth Amendment violations.

Compare City of New Brunswick v. Speights, 157 N.J.Super. 9, 384 A.2d 225 (1978), concerning the question of whether the exclusionary rule should be applicable in proceedings to discharge a city police officer where the search was apparently made by federal agents for purposes of a federal prosecution for illegal possession of an unregistered sawed-off shotgun, in which the court noted that the "foreseeability of a subsequent disciplinary hearing directed at a police officer charged with criminal violations may be logically apparent at the time of the search and seizure."

[114]Governing Board of Mountain View School District v. Metcalf, 36 Cal.App.3d 546, 111 Cal.Rptr. 724 (1974).

[115]See Thompson v. Carthage School District, 87 F.3d 979 (8th Cir.1996) (exclusionary rule not applicable in school disciplinary proceedings, as the "societal costs of applying the rule in school disciplinary proceedings are very high," as when exclusion prevents imposition of discipline "it frustrates the critical governmental function of educating and protecting children"); Garrett v. Lehman, 751 F.2d 997 (9th Cir.1985) (exclusionary rule not applicable in military administrative discharge proceedings, as

been asserted, for example, that it "is extremely doubtful that the public interest in the granting or revocation of a license to practice medicine or law is greater than the similar public interest in the conviction of criminals."[116] In the context of the *Metcalf* case, the argument would be that the public interest in removing a sexual deviant from the public school system is hardly greater than the public interest, which may be thwarted by the exclusionary rule in a criminal case, in incarcerating a rapist or murderer. But there are two answers to this. For one thing, the administrative process may reflect a stronger public interest because it is designed to deprive the offender of a special opportunity to do further harm; it is one thing to acquit a person who has recklessly shot and killed another, but quite different to fail to revoke the license of a doctor who has recklessly killed a patient.[117] Secondly, it must be remembered that the *Calandra* cost factor is

---

damage to military discipline outweighs benefits); Ahart v. Colorado Dept. of Corrections, 964 P.2d 517 (Colo.1998) (exclusionary rule not applicable in discharge proceeding regarding corrections officers, as "[a]pplying the exclusionary rule here would ensure the continued employment of individuals whose drug use would negatively affect their ability to perform as corrections officers," which "threatens the integrity of the state corrections system"); Grames v. Illinois State Police, 254 Ill.App.3d 191, 192 Ill.Dec. 790, 625 N.E.2d 945 (1993) (exclusionary rule not applicable in state police discharge proceeding; "damage to the operation of an effective State police force would far outweigh any benefit"); Martin v. Kansas Dept. of Revenue, 285 Kan. 625, 176 P.3d 938 (2008) ("Public interest demands that alcohol and/or drug-impaired drivers be removed from the road"); Riche v. Director of Revenue, 987 S.W.2d 331 (Mo.1999) (deterrent benefits of applying exclusionary rule at hearing to suspend driver's license outweighed by cost in terms of "allow-[ing] many drivers to remain on the road who would otherwise lose their licenses"); Chase v. Neth, 269 Neb. 882, 697 N.W.2d 675 (2005) (exclusionary rule not applicable in administrative driver's license revocation proceedings, as "the marginal deterrent effect of the exclusionary rule is outweighed by the substantial societal cost of losing reliable information used

to remove intoxicated drivers from the highways").

[116]Comment, 2 Conn.L.Rev. 648, 658–59 (1970).

[117]Cf. Pierce v. Board of Nursing Education, 255 Cal.App.2d 463, 63 Cal.Rptr. 107 (1967) (observing: "We do not wish to intimate a belief that these rules apply in administrative proceedings, especially in one involving fitness of a person to be licensed in a healing art where the welfare of sick and helpless persons depends on his integrity, fidelity and skill"); People v. Harfmann, 638 P.2d 745 (Colo.1981) (exclusionary rule not applicable to disciplinary proceedings against lawyer, as in that context "the court's primary duty is to protect the public and the legal profession from unscrupulous lawyers"); Powell v. Secretary of State, 614 A.2d 1303 (Me.1992) (even if conviction of drunk driving not possible, the "costs to society" of excluding evidence in license revocation proceeding and thus permitting that person to continue to drive "would be substantial"); Boyd v. Constantine, 81 N.Y.2d 189, 597 N.Y.S.2d 605, 613 N.E.2d 511 (1993) ("the benefit to be gained from precluding police officers, who unlawfully possess controlled substances, from making arrests, including arrests for drug-related offenses, clearly outweighs any deterrent effect that may arise from applying the exclusionary rule").

simply a part of the formula, to be weighed against the deterrence objective, so that the question is not whether there is a public interest greater than that present in criminal cases. That is, even assuming the public interest identified in *Metcalf* is not greater than that ordinarily present in criminal cases, this alone is not determinative, for that interest must only outweigh the deterrence factor, which in that case was significantly less than in criminal cases.[118]

An extreme and fundamentally unsound cost-benefit analysis was utilized by the majority in *I.N.S. v. Lopez-Mendoza,*[119] where the Court, per O'Connor, J., held 5-4[120] that the exclusionary rule is inapplicable in a civil deportation hearing.[121] The deterrent value of the exclusionary rule in this context was deemed to be

---

[118]Thus, it is significant that the court in *Metcalf* also noted: "The police in making investigations of suspected criminal activity are, we surmise, generally completely unaware of any consequences of success in their investigative efforts other than the subsequent criminal prosecution of the suspected offender."

[119]I.N.S. v. Lopez-Mendoza, 468 U.S. 1032, 104 S.Ct. 3479, 82 L.Ed.2d 778 (1984), discussed in Notes, 54 Geo.Wash.L.Rev. 564 (1986); 31 Loyola L.Rev. 193 (1985); 20 U.S.F.L.Rev. 143 (1985).

[120]There were separate dissents by Brennan, White, Marshall and Stevens, JJ. The others shared the views of Justice White set out in the text following.

[121]The Court limited its holding to situations that do not involve "egregious violations of Fourth Amendment or other liberties that might transgress notions of fundamental fairness and undermine the probative value of the evidence obtained." On suppressing the defendant's identity at the deportation proceedings because of the egregious conduct of the police, see Annot., 40 A.L.R.Fed.2d 489 (2009); Notes, 28 Colum.Hum.Rts.L.Rev. 431 (1997); 50 Stan.L.Rev. 139 (1997).

This language is rather ambiguous. For one interpretation, see Gonzalez-Rivera v. I.N.S., 22 F.3d 1441 (9th Cir.1994) (this "egregious violations" exception is not limited to physical brutality, but includes all bad faith Fourth Amendment violations, and "a fundamentally unfair Fourth Amendment violation is considered egregious regardless of the probative value of the evidence obtained"). See also Martinez-Medina v. Holder, 673 F.3d 1029 (9th Cir.2011)(applying *Gonzalez-Rivera*, violation here not egregious, as the "law was unclear as to whether an alien's admission to being illegally present in the United States created probable cause to seize the alien"); Luevano v. Holder, 660 F.3d 1207 (10th Cir.2011) (no "egregious circumstances" shown here, where defendant claims prolonged detention, after lawful traffic stop, because of unspecified suspicion passengers were illegal aliens); Garcia-Torres v. Holder, 660 F.3d 333 (8th Cir.2011) ("mere garden-variety error" such as "warrantless entry of business premises and arrest," not "egregious"); Lopez-Gabriel v. Holder, 653 F.3d 683 (8th Cir.2011) (expressing doubt whether egregious violation by state or local officers would suffice); Puc-Ruiz v. Holder, 629 F.3d 771 (8th Cir.2010) (no "egregious" violation here, as defendant claimed only lack of probable cause; court emphasizes this not a case where police acted "with *no* articulable suspicion" or based on "race or appearance" or "employed an unreasonable show or use of force"); Gutierrez-Berdin v. Holder, 618 F.3d 647 (7th Cir.2010) ("very minor physical abuse coupled with aggressive questioning" not egregious); Lopez-Rodriguez v. Mukasey, 536 F.3d 1012 (9th Cir.2008), discussed in Note, 2010 BYU L.Rev. 51 (applying *Gonzalez-Rivera* to find violation "egregious" where "reasonable

reduced because (i) "deportation will still be possible when evidence not derived directly from the arrest is sufficient to support deportation," (ii) INS agents know "that it is highly unlikely that any particular arrestee will end up challenging the lawfulness of his arrest," (iii) "the INS has its own comprehensive scheme for deterring Fourth Amendment violations" by training and discipline, and (iv) "alternative remedies" including the "possibility of declaratory relief" are available for institutional practices violating the Fourth Amendment. On the cost side, the Court continued, are these factors: (i) that application of the exclusionary rule "in proceedings that are intended not to punish past transgressions but to prevent their continuance or renewal would require courts to close their eyes to ongoing violations of the law," (ii) that invocation of the exclusionary rule at deportation hearings, where "neither the hearing officers nor the attorneys * * * are likely to be well versed in the intricacies of Fourth Amendment law," "might significantly change and complicate the character of these proceedings,"[122] and (iii) that because many INS arrests "occur in crowded and confused circumstances," application of the exclusionary rule "might well result in the suppression of large amounts of information that had been obtained entirely lawfully."[123]

Such bizarre reasoning was even too much for Justice White, who had authored the "good faith" decision in *United States v. Leon*,[124] handed down the very same day. Although he set out a point-by-point rebuttal of each one of the assertions summarized above, some of his responses are of special relevance and deserve noting here. For one thing, Justice White quite correctly pointed out that prior cases, involving illegal acquisition of evidence for

officers should have known that they were violating the Fourth Amendment in entering Gastelum's and Lopez's home without a warrant, consent, or exigent circumstances"); Orhorhaghe v. I.N.S., 38 F.3d 488 (9th Cir.1994) (applying the *Gonzalez-Rivera* interpretation). For criticism of *Gonzalez-Rivera*, see Comment, 9 Geo.Immigr. L.J. 855 (1995); Note, 40 Vill.L.Rev. 1133 (1995). For further discussion of the "egregious violations" exception, see Scharf, The Exclusionary Rule in Immigration Proceedings: Where It Was, Where It Is, Where It May be Going, 12 San Diego Int'l L.J. 53 (2010); Treadwell, Fugitive Operations and the Fourth Amendment: Representing Immigrants Arrested in Warrantless Home Raids, 89 N.C.L. Rev. 507 (2011).

[122]Some later cases have relied on this point. See, e.g., Powell v. Secretary of State, 614 A.2d 1303 (Me.1992) (exclusionary rule not applicable at driver's license suspension hearing, as "requiring hearing examiners to apply the exclusionary rule would unnecessarily complicate and burden an administrative proceeding designed to focus on the single issue of whether a person was operating a vehicle with excessive alcohol in his blood").

[123]As later noted in United States v. Verdugo-Urquidez, 494 U.S. 259, 110 S.Ct. 1056, 108 L.Ed.2d 222 (1990), the Court in *Lopez-Mendoza* assumed but did not decide "whether the protections of the Fourth Amendment extend to illegal aliens in this country."

[124]United States v. Leon, 468 U.S. 897, 104 S.Ct. 3405, 82 L.Ed.2d 677 (1984).

criminal prosecution, had ruled that this evidence is inadmissible in the prosecution's case in chief, but that otherwise the exclusionary rule was "applicable only when the likelihood of deterring the unwanted conduct outweighs the societal costs imposed by exclusion of relevant evidence." But, he continued, those cases, such as *United States v. Janis,*[125] *Stone v. Powell,*[126] and *United States v. Calandra,*[127] did not establish the principle that the exclusionary rule applies fully only in criminal prosecutions. Rather, "in all of these cases it was unquestioned that the illegally seized evidence would not be admissible in the case-in-chief of the proceeding for which the evidence was gathered; only its collateral use was permitted." In the instant case the civil deportation proceedings were in no sense collateral, as they were the primary objective of the INS agents whose actions were being challenged. In the language of *Janis,* these proceedings fall within "the offending officer's zone of primary interest," and thus exclusion to serve the objective of deterrence was unquestionably called for.

Justice White went on to conclude quite correctly "that the costs and benefits of applying the exclusionary rule in civil deportation proceedings do not differ in any significant way from the costs and benefits of applying the rule in ordinary criminal proceedings." The majority's claim that the deterrent effect of exclusion was diminished in deportation proceedings because often deportation would be possible anyway is hardly a basis of distinction, for a great many criminal prosecutions are successful notwithstanding the suppression of illegally obtained evidence.[128] As for the fact the INS has a "comprehensive scheme" for deterring Fourth Amendment violations, this shows (as Justice White put it) "that the exclusionary rule has created incentives for the agency to ensure that its officers follow the dictates of the Constitution." The *Lopez-Mendoza* majority's assertion that hearing officers should defer to INS agents on matters concerning the Fourth Amendment is, as Justice White properly noted, "startling indeed." But perhaps the most outrageous aspect of the decision in this case is the contention that the exclusionary rule cannot be utilized without excessive costs in this context because of the confusion typically attendant the arrest of illegal aliens. Again Justice White: "The Court may be willing to throw up its hands in dismay because it is administratively inconvenient to determine whether constitutional rights have been violated, but we neglect our duty when we subordinate constitutional rights to expediency in such a manner."

---

[125]United States v. Janis, 428 U.S. 433, 96 S.Ct. 3021, 49 L.Ed.2d 1046 (1976).

[126]Stone v. Powell, 428 U.S. 465, 96 S.Ct. 3037, 49 L.Ed.2d 1067 (1976).

[127]United States v. Calandra, 414 U.S. 338, 94 S.Ct. 613, 38 L.Ed.2d 561 (1974).

[128]See § 1.2 note 3.

Just what the impact of *Lopez-Mendoza* ultimately will be on the general issue surveyed herein, application of the exclusionary rule in administrative hearings, or indeed upon the broader question of the applicability of the rule in a great variety of circumstances other than the prosecution's case-in-chief in a criminal prosecution, is unclear.[129] It is to be hoped, however, that it will be limited to its facts and will not influence other Fourth Amendment decisions by the Supreme Court or the lower courts. Such a fate is certainly deserved for a decision such as this, for rarely has an opinion joined by a majority of the Court been so lacking in substance and so unfaithful to the precedents upon which it purports to rely.[130]

§ 1.7(g) Legislative hearings

The Supreme Court has asserted that the "Bill of Rights is applicable to [Congressional] investigations as to all forms of governmental action" and that consequently witnesses "cannot be subjected to unreasonable search and seizure."[131] However, the Court has not had occasion to consider the precise question of whether the exclusionary rule applies in legislative hearings, at least under some circumstances. By analogy to the more numerous cases concerning the summoning of witnesses before a grand jury,[132] it would seem clear that: (i) a person subpoenaed to testify before a legislative committee cannot object on Fourth Amendment grounds, as neither the compelled appearance nor the testimony is a search or seizure[133]; and (ii) a person subpoenaed to produce documents to a legislative committee may challenge

---

[129]Not particularly encouraging is Pullin v. Louisiana State Racing Comm'n, 484 So.2d 105 (La.1986), discussed in note 107 supra, where the court also relied upon *Lopez-Mendoza* though, as one of the dissenters noted, there the Court stressed the INS had its own scheme for deterring Fourth Amendment violations, while there was no comparable showing here.

[130]See also Chacon, A Diversion of Attenuation? Immigration Courts and the Adjudication of Fourth and Fifth Amendment Rights, 59 Duke L.J. 1563, 1642 (2010) (concluding that "the evidence of increasing constitutional violations by immigration enforcement officials" and "a growing number of violations" by "state and local law enforcement agencies" now assisting in immigration enforcement "requires the application of the exclusionary rule in immigration proceedings"); Slobogin, The Poverty Exception to the Fourth Amendment, 55 Fla.L.Rev.

391, 394–95 (2003) (noting that "*Lopez-Mendoza* allowed the introduction of illegally seized evidence even though neither the good faith nor secondary proceeding rationales apply," and that because "it departs from the Supreme Court's normal explanations for rejecting the exclusionary remedy, * * * evidences particular hostility toward search and seizure claims that are raised by illegal aliens"); Note, 82 St.John's L.Rev. 1157, 1160 (2008) (arguing "that vast changes in the immigration laws since 1984 necessitate an examination of *Lopez-Mendoza*'s cost-benefit analysis, leading to the readoption of the exclusionary rule in removal proceedings").

[Section 1.7(g)]

[131]Watkins v. United States, 354 U.S. 178, 77 S.Ct. 1173, 1 L.Ed.2d 1273 (1957).

[132]See § 1.6(a).

[133]As for objections based on the

the subpoena duces tecum on Fourth Amendment grounds,[134] although here as in the grand jury context the subpoena power is not confined to the same degree as the search warrant power.[135]

What has very seldom been raised in appellate cases, perhaps because of the infrequency of circumstances for doing so,[136] is the question whether either testimony or physical evidence may be suppressed from a legislative hearing because it is the fruit of a prior illegal search by a committee investigator or some government agent not connected with the legislature. Unique is *United States v. McSurely*,[137] which involved the following facts. Kentucky law enforcement officials obtained and executed a search warrant for the McSurelys' premises to search for seditious matter, and certain documents seized in that search were turned over to the prosecutor, who indicted them for sedition. Prosecution was then enjoined by a federal court on the ground that the state sedition statute was unconstitutional; the court ordered the prosecutor to hold the seized documents in safekeeping until the case was finally disposed of by appeal or otherwise. Thereafter, an investigator for the Permanent Subcommittee on Investigations of the United States Senate Committee on Government Operation inspected these documents and made copies of many of them prior to their court-ordered return to the McSurelys, which served as the basis of subpoenas to them to testify before the Subcommittee and to bring certain records with them. They appeared but refused to produce the subpoenaed records, and on this basis were convicted of contempt, after which they appealed.

The majority in *McSurely* first scrutinized the events leading up to the issuance of the subpoenas. Significantly, the court not only found that the state officials had come by the documents by an illegal search (the warrant affidavit did not set forth sufficient underlying facts, and the warrant did not particularly describe the objects to be seized), but also concluded that the Subcommittee investigator's subsequent examination of the documents was

scope of the inquiry and the pertinency of the questions asked, see Note, 52 Minn.L.Rev. 665, 673–77 (1968).

[134]It is noted in United States v. Fort, 443 F.2d 670 (D.C.Cir.1970), that "an unreasonable search and seizure is no less illegal if conducted pursuant to a subpoena of a congressional subcommittee than if conducted by a law enforcement official."

[135]See Note, 52 Minn.L.Rev. 665, 684–87 (1968). For more on the Fourth Amendment limits on use of the subpoena duces tecum, see § 4.13.

[136]But consider this observation in Williams v. Williams, 8 Ohio Misc. 156, 221 N.E.2d 622 (1966): "According to recent newspaper reports, in connection with the Senator Dodd hearing before the Senate Ethics Committee, it was ruled that documents illegally seized at 'great risk' by his former aid, James Boyd, were not admissible in evidence."

Of course, if an agent of the legislative branch makes an illegal search, the fruits thereof are not admissible in a criminal trial. Nelson v. United States, 208 F.2d 505 (D.C.Cir. 1953).

[137]United States v. McSurely, 473 F.2d 1178 (D.C.Cir.1972).

also an illegal search. The court then concluded that there "is nothing in logic nor in the history of the 'exclusionary rule' to support its inapplicability to legislative subpoenas framed upon information derived by the Government through a previous unconstitutional search," and thus held that the contempt convictions could not stand because the subpoenas introduced at trial were the fruit of a prior Fourth Amendment violation.

Putting aside the serious procedural questions raised by this decision, particularly whether the subpoenas are themselves properly characterized as the fruits of an illegal search and whether the defendants should not have instead tendered and then moved to suppress the subpoenaed documents,[138] it is appropriate to inquire whether *McSurely* has been undercut by the more recent Supreme Court decision in *United States v. Calandra*.[139] Because the *Calandra* Court declined to permit a grand jury witness to invoke the exclusionary rule so as to justify his refusal to answer questions based upon evidence obtained by a prior illegal search of his premises, it might be thought that the same result could now be expected on the *McSurely* facts. It is submitted, however, that this is not the case. *Calandra* calls for a balancing of the potential benefits of exclusion in terms of deterrence against the potential damage. While the Court could say in that case that deterrence would be minimal, given the improbability of "police investigation consciously directed toward the discovery of evidence solely for use in a grand jury investigation,"[140] the same cannot be said about the *McSurely* facts, for a legislative investigator did make an illegal search[141] for the express purpose of obtaining evidence solely for use in a legislative investigation.[142]

However, *Calandra* does not support the conclusion that the

---

[138]These matters are discussed by Wilkey, J., concurring on other grounds in *McSurely*.

[139]United States v. Calandra, 414 U.S. 338, 94 S.Ct. 613, 38 L.Ed.2d 561 (1974).

[140]As noted elsewhere, see § 1.6(a), this observation is very questionable, as a police officer might well search a person other than the suspect, in which case the evidence would not be usable solely before the grand jury, as the defendant would lack standing to suppress the evidence at trial.

[141]Wilkey, J., concurring in *McSurely* on other grounds, acknowledged that "some degree of *active* participation by the Subcommittee's investigator in a violation of the McSurelys' Fourth Amendment rights

* * * might justify refusal to enforce the subpoenas," but he deemed incorrect the majority's conclusion that the investigator's inspection of the documents in the possession of the state prosecutor was an illegal search.

[142]The McSurelys also commenced an action against the Chairman, General Counsel, Chief Counsel, and Investigator of the Subcommittee and the Kentucky Commonwealth Attorney, seeking compensatory and punitive damages. In McSurely v. McClellan, 553 F.2d 1277 (D.C.Cir.1976), the court, en banc, (i) reversed the district court's failure to grant the motion of the federal defendants to dismiss that part of the complaint relating to the original taking of the McSurelys' books and papers by the Kentucky authorities; (ii) reversed with directions to

exclusionary rule must always be applied in legislative hearings, for under some circumstances the deterrent benefit will be slight compared to the cost. Specifically, if a legislative committee is the recipient by a windfall of evidence illegally seized by a government agent who was in no sense an agent of the committee, it would seem that admission of that evidence would not encourage future illegal searches for the purpose of aiding the legislative process.[143] As Judge Wilkey, concurring[144] in *McSurely,* observed, in such a situation the cost of "enforced legislative ignorance" in "the determination of national policy" surely outweighs the "remote" prospect that "the 'cop on the beat'" will alter his

---

grant summary judgment to appellants on those parts of the complaint that complained of the alleged use made of the documents within Congress, since such use is protected by the Speech or Debate Clause; (iii) affirmed the district court on the claim as to alleged dissemination of some of the documents outside of Congress; and (iv) affirmed the district court's denial of summary judgment on the allegations concerning the action of subcommittee investigator Brick in inspecting the documents and transporting copies of some of them to Washington prior to issuance of a subcommittee subpoena. Leaventhal, J., writing for a majority of the court, had this to say about *Calandra*:

> Without determining whether *Calandra* applies with full force to the legislative context, we find maintenance of the present action wholly congruent with *Calandra*. In *Calandra* the government agent had taken custody and authorized delivery of the seized materials to the grand jury before there was any judicial determination of illegality and ruling restricting access to the materials. Here prior to Subcommittee access a court had intervened and declared the state search and seizure without legal justification because the operative statute was unconstitutional. Through the 'safekeeping' directive the court asserted control over the seized documents, and did not authorize delivery to the Subcommittee. In Fourth Amendment terms, *Calandra* involved a single search and seizure by federal agents and mere 'derivative use' by the grand jury, whereas two separate, independent searches and seizures took place here. When *Calandra* refused to apply the exclusionary rule, it noted the availability of an action for damages for the unlawful taking by government agents. To raise *Calandra* as a bar to this action is to extend that decision beyond its rationale and express limitations, to the effect that there is no action for any constitutional wrong by federal defendants, with the McSurelys 'necessarily left remediless in the face of an unlawful search and seizure.' * * * *Calandra* does not bar plaintiffs' action against Brick, and any federal defendants who acted in concert with him, for acting outside of judicial channels in inspecting the materials in court safekeeping and transporting copies back to Washington.

Five dissenters objected:

> In sum, it would appear under *Calandra* that a Congressional committee should enjoy at least the same prerogative as a grand jury to use material which has been unlawfully seized. As with the grand jury, the Congressional committee may not be privileged to utilize such information if its agents have actively participated in the original unlawful seizure. Outside of that circumstance, however, a committee commits no new Fourth Amendment wrong by examining and copying documents originally unlawfully secured.

[143] The reasoning in United States v. Janis, 428 U.S. 433, 96 S.Ct. 3021, 49 L.Ed.2d 1046 (1976), that exclusion will not deter when the evidence is offered in a proceeding which "falls outside the offending officer's zone of primary interest," is more persuasive in this context than it was on the facts of *Janis*.

[144] On the separate ground of "the failure of the Government to establish one of the necessary elements of its case: pertinency of its demands to the valid subject of the legislative inquiry."

conduct if the exclusionary rule is applied to Congressional hearings.[145]

§ 1.7(h) Private litigation[146]

Finally, it must be asked whether the Fourth Amendment exclusionary rule is applicable in purely private litigation, that is, a civil action in which a governmental unit or representative is not a party.[147] One way in which this issue might arise, although such situations are found only rarely in the appellate decisions, is when the fruits of an illegal governmental search are later made available to a private litigant. One illustration is provided by *Kassner v. Fremont Mutual Insurance Co.,*[148] where evidence of arson illegally obtained by state fire marshals was tendered by the insurer in defense of an action to collect on an insurance policy. Another is found in an earlier Michigan case, *Lebel v. Swincicki,*[149] where the plaintiff in a wrongful death action tendered proof of the defendant's intoxication based upon a blood sample illegally taken from the defendant, apparently at police direction,[150] while he was unconscious. The holding in both cases, based upon the state constitution counterpart to the Fourth Amendment, was that the evidence must be suppressed.

---

[145]It must be emphasized that this conclusion is consistent only with the formula used by the *Calandra* majority. The dissenters emphasized the "twin goals of enabling the judiciary to avoid the taint of partnership in official lawlessness and of assuring the people * * * that the government would not profit from its lawless behavior." How the *Calandra* dissenters would view the situation now under discussion is unclear. Perhaps it is equally desirable that the legislative branch "avoid the taint of partnership in official lawlessness," although the "profit" to the government is less apparent here.

[Section 1.7(h)]

[146]See Baade, Illegally Obtained Evidence in Criminal and Civil Cases: A Comparative Study of a Classic Mismatch, 51 Tex.L.Rev. 1325 (1973), and Baade, Illegally Obtained Evidence in Criminal and Civil Cases: A Comparative Study of a Classic Mismatch II, 52 Tex.L.Rev. 621 (1974); Sutherland, Use of Illegally Seized Evidence in Non-Criminal Proceedings, 4 Crim.L.Bull. 215 (1968); Notes, 46 Minn.L.Rev. 1119 (1962), 55 Va.L.Rev. 1484 (1969); Annot., 5 A.L.R.3d 670 (1966).

[147]As compared with a civil action with a government party, as in State v. Lussier, 171 Vt. 19, 757 A.2d 1017 (2000), note 89 supra.

[148]Kassner v. Fremont Mut. Ins. Co., 47 Mich.App. 264, 209 N.W.2d 490 (1973).

[149]Lebel v. Swincicki, 354 Mich. 427, 93 N.W.2d 281 (1958), followed in Gilbert v. Leach, 62 Mich.App. 722, 233 N.W.2d 840 (1975). Compare Diener v. Mid-American Coaches, Inc., 378 S.W.2d 509 (Mo.1964), admitting evidence based upon a blood test taken from a dead body by a pathologist representing the county coroner, on the ground that the objecting party did not have standing to complain about the search of the deceased.

[150]The court never specifically states that the sample was taken at police direction, but intimates that this was the case by noting that the sample was not taken for purposes of the defendant's treatment and that it was promptly forwarded on to the police. See also Kuzmiak v. Flowers, 580 S.W.2d 226 (Ky.1979) (blood sample was taken at policeman's request; court assumes exclusionary rule applies in wrongful death action but finds search lawful).

There is no reason to believe that such a conclusion is compelled under current Fourth Amendment theory, as reflected in *United States v. Calandra.*[151] *Calandra,* again, requires a balancing of the potential benefit in terms of deterrence against the potential damage. On the damage side of the ledger, it may be true that in one sense there is no great public interest threatened, in that society "has little direct concern * * * in the actual outcome of individual lawsuits between private parties."[152] But in another sense, society does have an interest in whether, for example, the surviving children of a deceased recover for a tortious killing, and in any event the personal interest of the litigants is substantial and deserving of consideration. More significant, under the *Calandra* formula, is the fact that there would not likely be any gain in deterrence. "The police in making investigations of suspected criminal activity are * * * generally completely unaware of any consequences of success in their investigative efforts other than the subsequent criminal prosecution of the suspected offender."[153] It is doubtful that even the

---

[151]United States v. Calandra, 414 U.S. 338, 94 S.Ct. 613, 38 L.Ed.2d 561 (1974). In Honeycutt v. Aetna Insurance Co., 510 F.2d 340 (7th Cir.1975), the court relied on *Calandra* in holding that evidence illegally obtained by state and local fire investigators was admissible on behalf of the defendant insurance company in a civil action to collect an insurance claim. Relying upon and following *Honeycutt* are Winterland Concessions v. Trela, 735 F.2d 257 (7th Cir.1984); Midwest Growers Co-op Corp. v. Kirkemo, 533 F.2d 455 (9th Cir.1976); Elliott v. Mid-Century Ins. Co., 701 S.W.2d 462 (Mo.App.1985).

[152]Baade, 51 Tex.L.Rev. 1325 (1973).

[153]Governing Board of Mountain View School District v. Metcalf, 36 Cal.App.3d 546, 111 Cal.Rptr. 724 (1974).

The reasoning in United States v. Janis, 428 U.S. 433, 96 S.Ct. 3021, 49 L.Ed.2d 1046 (1976), that there is no gain in deterrence when the proceeding in which the evidence is offered "falls outside the offending officer's zone of primary interest," is more persuasive here than on the facts of *Janis. Janis* was relied upon in Wren v. Towe, 130 F.3d 1154 (5th Cir.1997) (despite expression of "grave reserva-

tions about whether, as a matter of law, police officers who illegally obtain evidence may use that evidence to establish a good-faith defense to a Section 1983 action," in Jonas v. City of Atlanta, 647 F.2d 580 (5th Cir.1981), court concludes evidence found in illegal search of truck can be used to show truck was properly seized, as application of exclusionary rule in this § 1983 case "would be inappropriate"); Youssef v. United Management Co., 683 A.2d 152 (D.C.App.1996) (even if Fourth Amendment violated when police and fire officials entered apartment of defendant, in this civil action by a landlord to evict tenants evidence obtained thereby is nonetheless admissible; "[a]bsent a showing of complicity and benefit to government officers flowing from the litigation, exclusion of evidence in a *private* civil dispute * * * is not called for because exclusion would not have the deterrent effect of preventing future Fourth Amendment violations by government officers"); Lamartiniere v. Department of Employment Sec., 372 So.2d 690 (La.App.1979) (employer may defend an unemployment compensation claim with illegally seized evidence showing the employee had been properly discharged for work-related misconduct); Tucker v. Pahkala, 268 N.W.2d 728 (Minn.1978) (evidence from noncon-

Calandra dissenters would so extend the exclusionary rule, for of the two goals they stressed, "enabling the judiciary to avoid the taint of partnership in official lawlessness" and "assuring the people * * * that the government would not profit from its lawless behavior," only the first is arguably relevant.

One commentator has suggested that the deterrence question may deserve closer attention. As for the *Lebel* situation, it has been suggested that perhaps "police reports are a staple element in civil drunken-driver litigation," in which case utilization of these reports "as staple evidence in civil drunken-driver litigation, free of the exclusionary rule's proscriptions, would provide an avenue for the indirect enforcement of criminal drunken-driver statutes with illegally obtained evidence."[154] Similarly, it is said that the *Kassner* result "might be justified if successful resistance by insurers to fire insurance claims on the strength of official fire department reports constitutes an established pattern for the indirect enforcement of fire safety law—civil enforcement through evidence inadmissible in a criminal prosecution."[155] While it is doubted that there do exist such established relationships between law enforcement and certain types of civil litigation, it is fair to say that if they did exist the deterrence factor would take on much greater significance in this context.

The more common situation is that in which the evidence tendered in private litigation was obtained in a search conducted by or on behalf of one of the parties to the litigation. As discussed elsewhere in this Treatise,[156] the prevailing view is that evidence obtained by such a "private" search, conducted by a person who was not a government official and who was not acting at the instigation of a government official, is admissible in a criminal prosecution. It is not too surprising, therefore, that in the private search-private litigation cases, the courts have usually focused upon the character of the search in holding the evidence admissible. The leading case is *Sackler v. Sackler,*[157] where a husband seeking a divorce was permitted to establish adultery by evidence secured by a forced entry into his wife's separately maintained apartment. The court held that the Fourth Amendment exclusionary rule "is of course not controlling here or even applicable since its impact is on governmental seizures only and not on evidence illegally gathered by private persons." Other

---

sensual blood alcohol test need not be excluded in civil trial); Simpkins v. Snow, 139 N.H. 735, 661 A.2d 772 (1995) (fruits of illegal search may be admitted by defense in civil defamation action against chief of police, as at time of search "it is unlikely that Chief Snow contemplated the use of the evidence in defense of a later defamation action").

[154] Baade, 52 Tex.L.Rev. 621, 652 (1974).

[155] Baade, 52 Tex.L.Rev. 621, 653 (1974).

[156] See § 1.8.

[157] Sackler v. Sackler, 15 N.Y.2d 40, 255 N.Y.S.2d 83, 203 N.E.2d 481 (1964).

courts have reached the same conclusion,[158] the lone exception being *Williams v. Williams,*[159] where the Fourth Amendment exclusionary rule was held applicable on the ground that "certainly no individual has a greater power than the government itself."

It could be argued, of course, that the policies permitting acceptance of the fruits of a private search in a criminal case do not carry over to the situation where those fruits are used in private litigation involving the person who made or caused the search. In the first instance, it may generally be said that exclusion would gain nothing by way of deterrence. But as to the latter situation, one commentator has argued that

> an exclusionary rule barring the admission of illegally obtained evidence in civil litigation, at least when it was procured by the deliberate illegality of a party seeking selfish advantage, has much to say for it. The transgressor would be deprived of the fruits of his own wrong; others in his position would be deterred from resorting to lawless conduct; violence would be discouraged; and there would be an enhanced incentive to comply with carefully drawn procedural rules for the discovery of evidence from adverse parties.[160]

This position, only rarely reflected in the decided cases,[161] has considerable merit. However, it must be emphasized that while

---

[158]See cases collected in Annot., 5 A.L.R.3d 670 (1966).

[159]Williams v. Williams, 8 Ohio Misc. 156, 221 N.E.2d 622 (1966). In Del Presto v. Del Presto, 97 N.J.Super. 446, 235 A.2d 240 (1967), rev'g 92 N.J.Super. 305, 223 A.2d 217 (1966), the court, in accepting the prevailing view, noted that it has been consistently held, except in *Williams,* that "the Fourth Amendment proscribes only unreasonable searches by the sovereign."

[160]Baade, 52 Tex.L.Rev. 621, 700 (1974).

[161]In Day & Zimmermann, Inc. v. Strickland, 483 S.W.2d 541 (Tex.Civ. App.1972), an action against an insurer under a homeowner's policy for damages to a house from an explosion, the court held that the trial judge properly excluded testimony based upon a trespass into the damaged house by an architect sent by the insurer. The court noted that there existed a rule of court whereby a court order for such a viewing could be obtained, and emphasized that the purpose of the rule was "to protect a party from undue annoyance, embar-rassment, oppression or expense." Compare Honeycutt v. Aetna Insurance Co., 510 F.2d 340 (7th Cir.1975), holding admissible evidence obtained in an illegal entry by an investigator for the insurance company; noting that the circumstances "may well have led [investigator] Leahy to the honest but incorrect belief that his intrusion was authorized," the court concluded "that the district court did not abuse its discretion in refusing to discipline or punish Daniel Leahy and his client, Aetna."

Under certain facts, the deterrence theory will be inapplicable. In Drew v. International Brotherhood of Sulphite and Paper Mill Workers, 37 F.R.D. 446 (D.D.C.1965), a suit claiming improper discharge of an employee, the defense was disloyalty of the employee as shown in a letter from that employee obtained by an illegal private search before such litigation was contemplated. The court rejected the analogy to the Fourth Amendment exclusionary rule: "The most obvious distinction is that the assumed wrongful conduct in this case was not undertaken with a view to furthering a claim in litigation. Accordingly, the

this position might be supported by drawing an analogy to the deterrence function of the Fourth Amendment exclusionary rule, there is no basis for saying that such a result is constitutionally compelled. This is because the Supreme Court has interpreted the Fourth[162] and Fourteenth[163] Amendments as limiting the actions of governments and their agents rather than private individuals. A dissenting judge in *Sackler* found such governmental action in the fact that "[w]hen evidence illegally obtained is offered in evidence in court, that is done for the purpose of inducing official action by the courts," and it has sometimes been argued that this conclusion is supported by the concept of state action developed by the Supreme Court in *Shelley v. Kraemer*.[164] But this is not so, for while

> the Court did hold in *Shelley* that it was violative of the fourteenth amendment for a state court to compel a private citizen to perform a contract which required racial discrimination in the sale of real estate, the facts in that case are hardly analogous to those in the [*Sackler*] case. In *Shelley* the lower court was asked to compel a private citizen to do an act which would be unconstitutional for the state to perform, whereas in [*Sackler*] the court was merely asked to give evidentiary status to illegally seized information.[165]

The distinction drawn in that quotation suggests that a much harder case is that in which, in the context of civil litigation involving only private parties, one party seeks a form of discovery against the other party that, at least if done directly by a government actor, would be a search subject to Fourth Amendment limitations. Illustrative is *Doe v. Senechal*,[166] where a former patient at an institution for mentally ill adolescents sued the owner of the facility and several employees, alleging that a staff person had engaged in sexual contact with her. On plaintiff's motion, the judge ordered that this staff person submit to a physical examination to determine paternity of the plaintiff's child. As for the staff persons's effort to quash the subpoena on Fourth Amendment grounds, the court dismissed the claim rather summarily: "The civil litigation here concerns private litigants and Senechal

---

desired deterrent effect which an exclusionary rule is designed to foster would be of dubious efficacy."

[162]See Burdeau v. McDowell, 256 U.S. 465, 41 S.Ct. 574, 65 L.Ed. 1048 (1921), noting that the "origin and history" of the Fourth Amendment "clearly show that it was intended as a restraint upon the activities of sovereign authority, and was not intended to be a limitation upon other than governmental agencies."

[163]See Civil Rights Cases, 109 U.S. 3, 3 S.Ct. 18, 27 L.Ed. 835 (1883), noting that the Amendment says that "no

state" shall deprive a person of due process, and concluding: "It is state action of a particular character that is prohibited. Individual invasion of individual rights is not the subject-matter of the amendment."

[164]Shelley v. Kraemer, 334 U.S. 1, 68 S.Ct. 836, 92 L.Ed. 1161 (1948). See Sutherland, 4 Crim.L.Bull. 215, 223 (1968).

[165]Note, 46 Minn.L.Rev. 1119, 1124–25 (1962).

[166]Doe v. Senechal, 431 Mass. 78, 725 N.E.2d 225 (2000).

points to no authority for his proposition that the Fourth Amendment has any application in this context."[167] But the court cautiously went on to conclude that in any event "the physical examination ordered here-the buccal swab paternity test-would meet the standard of reasonableness" under the Fourth Amendment.[168]

§ 1.8 The exclusionary rule and "private" or nonpolice searches

§ 1.8(a) The *Burdeau* rule
§ 1.8(b) Government participation or specific instigation
§ 1.8(c) Other pre-search government encouragement
§ 1.8(d) The "public function" approach
§ 1.8(e) Applicability of exclusionary rule to nonprivate-nonpolice actors
§ 1.8(f) The "ratified intent" approach
§ 1.8(g) The "judicial action" approach
§ 1.8(h) Foreign police and the international "silver platter"

Research References

West's Key Number Digest
Criminal Law ☞394.2; Searches and Seizures ☞33, 35, 73

Legal Encyclopedias
C.J.S., Criminal Law §§ 770, 776; Searches and Seizures §§ 18, 23, 43, 78, 102

Introduction

[167]The court relied upon the observation in Bowerman v. MacDonald, 431 Mich. 1, 427 N.W.2d 477 (1988), that there apparently were no "cases in which otherwise properly constituted discovery in a civil action has been held to constitute a violation of the Fourth Amendment," and upon the fact that the Supreme Court, in Schlagenhauf v. Holder, 379 U.S. 104, 85 S.Ct. 234, 13 L.Ed.2d 152 (1964), made no mention of a possible Fourth Amendment constraint in holding that "Rule 35 * * * is free of constitutional difficulty."

The holding in *Senechal* was relied upon in In re Jansen, 444 Mass. 112, 826 N.E.2d 186 (2005), criticized in § 5.4(d), text at note 132, where one Lampron, charged with rape, obtained a court order requiring a third party not charged with any offense to provide a buccal swab for DNA analysis. Notwithstanding the court order, it was concluded that because Lampron, "acting in a private capacity, is furthering his own ends by attempting to secure all favorable proofs in advance of trial," which was *opposed* by the prosecution, "there simply has been no government involvement." By footnote, the court cautioned it was not deciding "whether the buccal swab obtained by Lampron could, at some later date, be turned over to the Commonwealth for use in a future criminal prosecution without implicating Jansen's constitutional rights."

[168]The court in *Doe* noted that there "are a scattering of reported decisions where courts have declined to decide whether the Fourth Amendment applies to civil discovery orders among private litigants, but have nevertheless considered the 'reasonableness' of the discovery order." See United States v. International Business Machines Corp., 83 F.R.D. 97 (S.D.N.Y.1979); Ambassador College v. Goetzke, 244 Ga. 322, 260 S.E.2d 27 (1979); Bowerman v. MacDonald, 431 Mich. 1, 427 N.W.2d 477 (1988).

In *Burdeau v. McDowell*,[1] the Supreme Court held that the Fourth Amendment is a limitation upon the government[2] only and that consequently evidence secured by private illegal searches need not be excluded from a criminal trial. Although this is still the law today, the issue of precisely what it takes to put a search outside the "private" category is frequently litigated in a wide variety of settings.

To illustrate the kinds of questions that are raised, it is useful to assume a hypothetical case in which the dormitory room of a student at a private college is searched by a security officer of the college, resulting in the discovery of narcotics.[3] Because this is not a public educational institution and because, it may be further assumed, the officer has not been deputized or otherwise been formally given regular law enforcement authority by the state, the search is in at least that respect private. But, what other facts would make this search other than private? Would the receipt of the narcotics into evidence in a criminal prosecution of the student constitute tacit governmental approval of the search, thereby turning it into a governmental search? Or, is the search other than private if the security officer's motivation was to find evidence that could be used in a criminal trial? Would it be significant that there existed an understanding between the college and the local police department that the college would assume responsibility for detection of criminal law violations occurring on campus? What if the local police had alerted college authorities to the increasing on-campus narcotics traffic and had urged those authorities to take effective action against it? Or, what if the police had specifically asked the security agent to search this student's room? These are the kinds of issues considered herein.

While the concern here is primarily with the *Burdeau* rule, regarding when the Fourth Amendment has *no* applicability because of the nature of the party making the search or seizure, the scope of this section is somewhat broader. It also considers when certain arrests or searches that are not really "private," meaning the Fourth Amendment *is* applicable to them, are nonetheless inappropriate occasions for invocation of the exclusionary

---

[Section 1.8]

[1]Burdeau v. McDowell, 256 U.S. 465, 41 S.Ct. 574, 65 L.Ed. 1048 (1921).

[2]However, the Fourth Amendment does not directly apply to Indian tribes, United States v. Manuel, 706 F.2d 908 (9th Cir.1983), although the Indian Civil Rights Act imposes an "identical limitation" on tribal government conduct as the Fourth Amendment, 25 U.S.C.A. § 1302(2), United States v. Schmidt, 403 F.3d 1009 (8th Cir.2005); United States v. Clifford, 664 F.2d 1090 (8th Cir.1981), and it has been assumed that suppression of evidence in a federal proceeding would be appropriate if the tribal officer's conduct violated ICRA. United States v. Becerra-Garcia, 397 F.3d 1167 (9th Cir.2005).

[3]For a useful discussion of this type of problem, see Note, 56 Cornell L.Rev. 507 (1971).

rule because they were made or caused by nonpolice public officials deemed less in need of the exclusionary rule's deterrent force. It is clear since the Supreme Court's decision in *Arizona v. Evans*[4] that such a result must obtain in at least some circumstances.

§ 1.8(a) The *Burdeau* rule

In the *Burdeau* case, petitioner McDowell sought the return of certain books, papers and other materials that he alleged would be submitted to a grand jury for use against him in charging him with fraudulent use of the mails. The items in question had been taken from McDowell's office by private detectives, which the district judge characterized as a gross violation of the Fourth Amendment when he directed the return of the items to McDowell. The Supreme Court reversed:

> The Fourth Amendment gives protection against unlawful searches and seizures, and as shown in the previous cases, its protection applies to governmental action. Its origin and history clearly show that it was intended as a restraint upon the activities of sovereign authority, and was not intended to be a limitation upon other than governmental agencies; as against such authority it was the purpose of the Fourth Amendment to secure the citizen in the right of unmolested occupation of his dwelling and the possession of his property, subject to the right of seizure of process duly issued.

> In the present case the record clearly shows that no official of the federal government had anything to do with the wrongful seizure of the petitioner's property, or any knowledge thereof until several months after the property had been taken from him * * *. It is manifest that there was no invasion of the security afforded by the Fourth Amendment against unreasonable search and seizure, as whatever wrong was done was the act of individuals in taking the property of another. A portion of the property so taken and held was turned over to the prosecuting officers of the federal government. We assume that petitioner has an unquestionable right of redress against those who illegally and wrongfully took his private property under the circumstances herein disclosed, but with such remedies we are not now concerned.

Although much has happened in the realm of Fourth Amendment jurisprudence since the time of the *Burdeau* decision, the holding set out above seems not to have been disturbed by subsequent developments. While it has occasionally been sug-

---

[4] *Arizona v. Evans*, 514 U.S. 1, 115 S.Ct. 1185, 131 L.Ed.2d 34 (1995). While *Evans* was in a sense superseded by a broader rule in Herring v. United States, 555 U.S. 135, 129 S.Ct. 695, 172 L.Ed.2d 496 (2009), discussed in § 1.6(i), namely that the exclusionary rule is inapplicable to "isolated negligence attenuated from the arrest," *Evans* has continuing independent significance as to arrests or searches *by* nonpolice.

gested that *Elkins v. United States,*[5] overturning the so-called "silver platter" doctrine whereby federal authorities were theretofore permitted to receive and use evidence unlawfully acquired by state officers, casts doubt upon the continued vitality of *Burdeau,*[6] that is not the case.[7] *Elkins* never mentioned *Burdeau,* and the reasoning employed in *Elkins* was specifically directed to searches by state officials.[8] Likewise, it can hardly be said that *Mapp v. Ohio*[9] put *Burdeau* in doubt at the state level, for *Mapp* applied the Fourth Amendment to the states via the Fourteenth Amendment, which itself encompasses only state action.[10] And, despite an assertion to the contrary by one court,[11] it is not correct to say that the substantial redefinition of Fourth Amendment coverage in *Katz v. United States*[12] affects the *Burdeau* rule. Notwithstanding the emphasis in *Katz* upon the Amendment's protection of privacy, the Court carefully noted that the Fourth Amendment cannot be translated into a general right of privacy and that the general right is left to the law of the states. It is not surprising, therefore, that the Supreme Court continues to view the *Burdeau* rule as being very much alive.[13]

On another plane, it may be said that the consequences of

[Section 1.8(a)]

[5]Elkins v. United States, 364 U.S. 206, 80 S.Ct. 1437, 4 L.Ed.2d 1669 (1960).

[6]United States v. Williams, 314 F.2d 795 (6th Cir.1963); Williams v. United States, 282 F.2d 940 (6th Cir. 1960).

[7]The *Elkins* argument was specifically rejected in United States v. McGuire, 381 F.2d 306 (2d Cir.1967); United States v. Goldberg, 330 F.2d 30 (3d Cir.1964); People v. Horman, 22 N.Y.2d 378, 292 N.Y.S.2d 874, 239 N.E.2d 625 (1968).

[8]The Court pointed out in *Elkins* that the determination in Wolf v. Colorado, 338 U.S. 25, 69 S.Ct. 1359, 93 L.Ed. 1782 (1949), that Fourteenth Amendment due process prohibited illegal searches and seizures by state officers, marked the "removal of the doctrinal underpinning" for the admissibility of state-seized evidence in federal prosecutions.

[9]Mapp v. Ohio, 367 U.S. 643, 81 S.Ct. 1684, 6 L.Ed.2d 1081 (1961).

[10]Civil Rights Cases, 109 U.S. 3, 3 S.Ct. 18, 27 L.Ed. 835 (1883).

[11]State v. Brecht, 157 Mont. 264, 485 P.2d 47 (1971).

In State v. Coburn, 165 Mont. 488, 530 P.2d 442 (1974), the "state and amicus argue that *Brecht* was improvident and against the weight of authority." The court declined to overrule the decision, which it said "rested only in part on the Fourth Amendment," but repeated its reliance on *Katz* to justify the *Brecht* rule. The *Brecht* rule later came to be grounded only in the state constitution, but ultimately was rejected altogether. State v. Long, 216 Mont. 65, 700 P.2d 153 (1985).

The question reserved in *Long,* whether private felonious conduct requires exclusion under the state constitution, was answered in the negative in State v. Christensen, 244 Mont. 312, 797 P.2d 893 (1990) ("The prospect of serving time along with their victims should be enough to discourage private citizens from conducting felonious searches").

[12]Katz v. United States, 389 U.S. 347, 88 S.Ct. 507, 19 L.Ed.2d 576 (1967).

[13]In Coolidge v. New Hampshire, 403 U.S. 443, 91 S.Ct. 2022, 29 L.Ed.2d 564 (1971), for example, *Burdeau* was cited as supporting the proposition that had "Mrs. Coolidge, wholly on her own initiative, sought out her hus-

Burdeau do not offend the more modern rationale of the Fourth Amendment exclusionary rule. Exclusion of the fruits of police illegality is most often explained on grounds of deterrence. However, extension of the exclusionary rule to all private illegal searches for purposes of deterrence would be difficult to justify.[14] For one thing, civil and criminal action against the person making the illegal search are more likely when that person is not a police officer.[15] More important, however, is the fact that the exclusionary rule would not likely deter the private searcher, who is often motivated by reasons independent of a desire to secure criminal conviction and who seldom engages in searches upon a sufficiently regular basis to be affected by the exclusionary sanction. As for another explanation sometimes given for the exclusionary rule, namely, that the government should not profit from its own wrongdoing, it quite obviously has no application where the wrongdoing was private in nature. Finally, there is the "imperative of judicial integrity" mentioned in *Elkins,* whereby courts are not to become "accomplices" in violation of the Constitution by admitting evidence and thus legitimizing the conduct that produced it. It arguably is of some relevance in the private search context, although it would seem that where the conduct in question is by private individuals rather than the police "the courts do not, by using this evidence, condone the actions of the individual."[16]

Virtually all courts continue to follow the *Burdeau* rule.[17] Thus, courts have deemed evidence obtained in a search[18] admissible where, without government instigation or participation, a landlord searched his tenant's possessions,[19] a crime victim

---

band's guns and clothing and then taken them to the police station to be used as evidence against him, there can be no doubt under existing law that the articles would later have been admissible in evidence."

[14]The point is frequently made by courts following *Burdeau.* See, e.g., People v. Botts, 250 Cal.App.2d 478, 58 Cal.Rptr. 412 (1967); People v. Johnson, 153 Cal.App.2d 870, 315 P.2d 468 (1957).

[15]Note, 63 Colum.L.Rev. 168, 173 (1963).

[16]State v. Rice, 110 Ariz. 210, 516 P.2d 1222 (1973).

[17]See cases collected in Annot., 36 A.L.R.3d 553 (1971). But see State v. Eisfeldt, 163 Wash.2d 628, 185 P.3d 580 (2008) (holding private search doctrine contrary to state constitution's

protection against invasion of private affairs or home without authority of law).

[18]If the private person's intrusion was not into an area as to which there existed a justified expectation of privacy, then the case can be resolved on no-search grounds without determining whether the private person was an agent of the government. See, e.g., United States v. Welliver, 976 F.2d 1148 (8th Cir.1992) (defendant's employee took business records and turned them over to government agency to which defendant by statute obligated to provide access).

[19]United States v. Ramirez, 810 F.2d 1338 (5th Cir.1987); United States v. Beasley, 485 F.2d 60 (10th Cir. 1973); People v. Brewer, 690 P.2d 860 (Colo.1984); People v. Nash, 418 Mich. 196, 341 N.W.2d 439 (1983);

searched for property taken from him,[20] a burglar discovered evidence of his victim's criminality and sent it to the police,[21] a telephone company monitored calls to discover theft of services,[22] an internet service provider scanned a customer's e-mails,[23] a computer repairman accessed files while diagnosing problems with a computer,[24] an airline or freight company employee opened a freight shipment,[25] or an airline employee searched an unclaimed bag[26] or all bags for a flight as to which a bomb threat had been received,[27] and in similar circumstances.[28] So too, evidence obtained as a result of a seizure of a person is likewise

---

Commonwealth v. Cosby, 234 Pa.Super. 1, 335 A.2d 531 (1975); Simmons v. State, 491 S.W.2d 633 (Tenn.Crim.App.1972). See also State v. Zagorski, 701 S.W.2d 808 (Tenn. 1985) (landlord put tenant's possessions into street).

[20]United States v. Miller, 688 F.2d 652 (9th Cir.1982); State v. Hutchinson, 349 So.2d 1252 (La.1977); State v. Carr, 20 N.C.App. 619, 202 S.E.2d 289 (1974).

[21]State v. Christensen, 244 Mont. 312, 797 P.2d 893 (1990); Torres v. State, 442 N.E.2d 1021 (Ind.1982).

[22]United States v. Manning, 542 F.2d 685 (6th Cir.1976); United States v. Harvey, 540 F.2d 1345 (8th Cir. 1976); United States v. Auler, 539 F.2d 642 (7th Cir.1976); United States v. Goldstein, 532 F.2d 1305 (9th Cir. 1976).

See also von Lusch v. State, 39 Md.App. 517, 387 A.2d 306 (1978) (private search where telephone company placed pen register in response to complaint of subscriber).

[23]United States v. Richardson, 607 F.3d 357 (4th Cir.2010).

[24]United States v. Grimes, 244 F.3d 375 (5th Cir.2001); United States v. Hall, 142 F.3d 988 (7th Cir.1998). For a discussion of situations of this kind, see Note, 96 Va.L.Rev. 677 (2010).

[25]United States v. Young, 153 F.3d 1079 (9th Cir.1998); United States v. Livesay, 983 F.2d 135 (8th Cir. 1993); United States v. Pierce, 893 F.2d 669 (5th Cir.1990); United States v. Koenig, 856 F.2d 843 (7th Cir.1988); United States v. Crabtree, 545 F.2d 884 (4th Cir.1976); United States v.

DeBerry, 487 F.2d 448 (2d Cir.1973); Whittemore v. State, 617 P.2d 1 (Alaska 1980); Commonwealth v. Varney, 391 Mass. 34, 461 N.E.2d 177 (1984); Golden v. State, 95 Nev. 481, 596 P.2d 495 (Nev.1979); Commonwealth v. Kozak, 233 Pa.Super. 348, 336 A.2d 387 (1975).

[26]United States v. Walsh, 791 F.2d 811 (10th Cir.1986); United States v. Blanton, 479 F.2d 327 (5th Cir. 1973); State v. Bookout, 281 So.2d 215 (Fla.App.1973). See also State v. Loyd, 126 Ariz. 364, 616 P.2d 39 (1980) (personnel of bus company opened trunk left in restroom of bus terminal); Hill v. State, 764 P.2d 210 (Okl.Crim. App.1988) (airline baggage handler dropped bag, causing it to break open).

[27]State v. Fellows, 109 Ariz. 454, 511 P.2d 636 (1973).

[28]United States v. Muhlenbruch, 634 F.3d 987 (8th Cir.2011) (when defendant's wife asked a friend, "a private citizen," to search defendant's computer's hard drive for porn, search was private); United States v. Poe, 556 F.3d 1113 (10th Cir.2009), discussed in Comment, 49 Washburn L.J. 201 (2009) (bounty hunters entered and searched home where defendant apprehended); United States v. Seldon, 479 F.3d 340 (4th Cir.2007) (service technicians advised police they found two hidden compartments in vehicle, one within gas tank and one near gas tank, while accessing tank to service fuel pump); United States v. Steiger, 318 F.3d 1039 (11th Cir.2003) ("anonymous source had hacked into Steiger's computer" to obtain information about child pornography, and such information "acquired *before* making *any* contact" with police);

United States v. Papajohn, 212 F.3d 1112 (8th Cir.2000) (insurance company investigators collected evidence of arson at fire scene); United States v. Paige, 136 F.3d 1012 (5th Cir.1998) (roofers discovered drugs in attic over garage while looking for extra siding to repair inadvertent damage to house); United States v. Mithun, 933 F.2d 631 (8th Cir.1991) (hotel employees searched car parked on hotel ramp); United States v. Jackson, 578 F.2d 1162 (5th Cir.1978) (defendant's business records taken by his ex-spouse and turned over to IRS); Bruce v. State, 367 Ark. 497, 241 S.W.3d 728 (2006) (wife not a state actor when she searched her husband's belongings and then summoned police and "handed over" child pornography); People v. Pilkington, 156 P.3d 477 (Colo.2007) (insurance investigator turned over fruits of his investigation of fire in insured premises); State v. Betts, 286 Conn. 88, 942 A.2d 364 (2008) (defendant's fiancé not state agent where, at police request, she obtained letter from bedroom she shared with defendant, after she summoned police); State v. Lasaga, 269 Conn. 454, 848 A.2d 1149 (2004) (where computer specialist Gluhosky, employed by private university, downloaded professor's files after being told professor had downloaded child pornography, and "the police did not seek out Gluhosky and were not involved in his decision to obtain information regarding the defendant," and "Gluhosky had no previous affiliation with the police and was not rewarded monetarily or promised any favors in return for his cooperation," search was private); Limpuangthip v. United States, 932 A.2d 1137 (D.C.App.2007) (community director at private university searched student's dorm room); Pruitt v. State, 258 Ga. 583, 373 S.E.2d 192 (1988) (private persons searching for missing child saw defendant within his trailer in bloody shirt, entered and took the shirt); Williams v. State, 257 Ga. 788, 364 S.E.2d 569 (1988) (hospital employees who removed bullet from defendant turned it over to police pursuant to established hospital policy); Gajdos v. State, 462 N.E.2d 1017 (Ind.1984) (mother of defendant's girl friend turned over to police letters written by defendant to girl friend while he was in jail); State v. Barrett, 401 N.W.2d 184 (Iowa 1987) (restaurant employees read and turned over to police personal journal left behind by customer and indicating intent to kill people); State v. Andrei, 574 A.2d 295 (Me.1990) (defendant's husband turned her incriminating diary over to arson investigators); Commonwealth v. Considine, 448 Mass. 295, 860 N.E.2d 673 (2007) (search of student's hotel rooms by officials of Catholic high school while students on school-sponsored trip); Commonwealth v. Robinson, 399 Mass. 209, 503 N.E.2d 654 (1987) (doctor trying to determine cause of hospitalized child's critical illness had baby's formula tested); State v. Nelson, 283 Mont. 231, 941 P.2d 441 (1997) (doctor's action at medical center in drawing blood from accident victim not state action, as he not "acting at the direction or request of the State"); State v. Berosik, 352 Mont. 16, 214 P.3d 776 (2009) (private search where defendant's wife seized sexually explicit materials, removed them from home, and later at police request turned them over to police); State v. Davis, 161 N.H. 292, 12 A.3d 1271 (2010) (withdrawal and testing of blood by hospital "for medical purposes"); State v. Nemser, 148 N.H. 453, 807 A.2d 1289 (2002) (where police of private college had adopted policy to simply destroy small quantities of drugs found on campus and turn over to city police large quantities, search by campus police in which large quantity found was still a private search, as "the college acted for its own purposes in enforcing its own policy against drug possession by students," and city police did not induce college policy but only manifested "grudging acceptance" of it); State v. Kornegay, 313 N.C. 1, 326 S.E.2d 881 (1985) (secretary of law firm, noting what appeared to be dishonest transactions and not wanting to be implicated, copied records and took them home and later turned them over to police);

admissible where the seizure, though it "may have assisted the government," was made by a private person and "there is no suggestion that the government initiated or participated in the citizen action."[29] The few holdings to the contrary are not carefully reasoned, and typically rest upon the mistaken assumption that if *Burdeau* is followed it will mean that an "individual has a greater power than the government."[30] A few commentators have expressed displeasure with the *Burdeau* rule, but typically because of a misunderstanding of its foundations.[31]

Before undertaking a closer examination of how the *Burdeau* rule has been applied by the lower courts in order to determine

---

Rawlings v. State, 740 P.2d 153 (Okl.Crim.App.1987) (defendant's mother found gun and other suspicious items in son's suitcase and turned them over to police). Commonwealth v. Johnson, 556 Pa. 216, 727 A.2d 1089 (1999) ("where a medical professional has made an independent decision that removal of the bullet was in the best interests of the patient, and where there was no antecedent direction from the authorities to do so," no "governmental action"); State v. Barkmeyer, 949 A.2d 984 (R.I.2008) (discovery of rope by child's grandfather while cleaning closet in room occupied by child's stepfather a private search); State v. Guido, 698 A.2d 729 (R.I.1997) (where "blood tests were performed as a result of hospital protocol rather than at the command of law enforcement," "the private hospital's activity triggered no Fourth Amendment concern"); Cobb v. State, 85 S.W.3d 258 (Tex.Crim.App.2002) (defendant's father entered apartment, shared by defendant and his girl friend, at girl friend's request and while there seized several knives and turned them over to police); State v. Eisfeldt, 163 Wash.2d 628, 185 P.3d 580 (2008) (contractor making repairs in defendant's home looked in garbage bag and saw marijuana, which he reported to police).

[29]United States v. Mendez-de Jesus, 85 F.3d 1 (1st Cir.1996).

[30]Williams v. Williams, 8 Ohio Misc. 156, 221 N.E.2d 622 (1966), holding that consequently the court should not grant a new trial in a divorce action on the basis of newly discovered evidence that the former husband illegally took from his ex-wife's car. While the court's criticism of *Burdeau* is in error, this is not to suggest that it would necessarily be inappropriate for a court to adopt a rule of evidence to the effect that a civil litigant may not introduce evidence obtained by his illegal acts. Nor is it inappropriate for a legislature to decide that the fruits of certain illegal conduct should be inadmissible, without regard to the character of the person engaging in the conduct. See, e.g., 18 U.S.C.A. § 2515; Ill.C.S.A. ch. 720, § 5/14-5 (violations of eavesdropping law); Texas Code Crim.P. art. 38. 23, discussed in Comment, 36 St. Mary's L.J. 195 (2004) (providing that if a private citizen seized evidence in violation of law (e.g., by theft), then such evidence is subject to exclusion).

[31]See, e.g., Comment, 16 Am.U.L. Rev. 403, 404 (1967), which misperceives the issue: "The paramount question, therefore, is why should unconstitutionally obtained evidence be admissible in a court of law when it is the product of a private search and inadmissible when the product of a governmental search?"

The soundest anti-*Burdeau* argument is that presented in Note, 63 Colum.L.Rev. 168, 174–75 (1963), namely, that "the grave danger exists that the general admissibility of such evidence may create an atmosphere encouraging government officials to act in clandestine concert with private persons; while concerted activity would undoubtedly taint such evidence and require its exclusion in a criminal action, the problems of proof are obvious."

when a search may be deemed "private" (i.e., no search at all under the Fourth Amendment) despite some government participation, specific instigation or general encouragement, it must first be considered where the line is to be drawn between such nonsearches and a particular kind of Fourth Amendment search that also has a very significant involvement by a private person: searches by consent, which are lawful if that consent was voluntary and the person giving it had or reasonably appeared to have authority to give such consent.[32] (While the precise location of this line may be of little practical significance when the evidence would obviously be admissible or inadmissible under either approach, it becomes important when, e.g., the consent search alternative is foreclosed because of the invalidity of the consent[33] or appears less attractive because of the difficult issues that would need to be resolved by the court under that theory.[34]) Consider these two situations. *Number 1*: While defendant was in custody for investigation of a murder apparently committed with a handgun, police went to his home to question his wife; she invited them in, and during the course of their questioning was asked if he owned any guns; she replied in the affirmative and said she would get them from the bedroom; the officers said they would accompany her, and when the group reached the bedroom the wife took four guns out of the closet and then also retrieved clothing her husband had been wearing on the night in question, and stated the police could take those items to the station. *Number 2*: Police responding to a call of a domestic dispute were told by defendant's wife that he was a user of cocaine and that there were "items of drug evidence" in their house; when defendant refused to consent to a search of the premises, the wife gave her consent and then led one officer to an upstairs bedroom where the officer saw a section of a drinking straw containing what appeared to be cocaine residue; that information was the basis for issuance of a search warrant for the premises, pursuant to which further evidence of drug use was seized. While these two situations are similar in many respects, the Supreme Court dealt with them quite differently

Situation #1 is from *Coolidge v. New Hampshire*,[35] where the Supreme Court, perhaps to circumvent defendant's claim that his wife's purported consent was insufficient to waive his Fourth Amendment protection against unreasonable search and seizure, chose to treat those facts as manifesting a *Burdeau* nonsearch. The Court began by hypothesizing a somewhat different set of facts that would beyond dispute come within *Burdeau*: "Had Mrs. Coolidge, wholly on her own initiative, sought out her husband's

---

[32]See Chapter 8.

[33]As in the *Randolph* case, discussed in the text following.

[34]As in the *Coolidge* case, dis-

cussed in the text following.

[35]Coolidge v. New Hampshire, 403 U.S. 443, 91 S.Ct. 2022, 29 L.Ed.2d 564 (1971).

guns and clothing and then taken them to the police station to be
used as evidence against him, there can be do doubt under existing law that the articles would later have been admissible in
evidence."³⁶ Asking whether "the conduct of the police officers at
the Coolidge house" necessitated a different conclusion, the Court
answered in the negative, relying upon the general proposition
that "it is no part of the policy underlying the Fourth and
Fourteenth Amendments to discourage citizens from aiding to
the utmost in their ability in the apprehension of criminals." It
thus followed (i) that the police were acting "normally and
properly" when they asked about the guns and clothing; (ii) that
once the wife "of her own accord produced the guns and clothes
for inspection, * * * it was not incumbent on the police to stop
her or avert their eyes"; and (iii) that the police could then seize
these items when the wife said they could do so.

Situation #2 is from *Georgia v. Randolph,*³⁷ where there was, if
anything, even greater reason than in *Coolidge* to characterize
the situation as a private nonsearch rather than a consent search
if the circumstances permitted, for in that way the Court could
have avoided the very contentious issue of whether the husband's
refusal to consent somehow trumped the wife's subsequent
consent to search of the residence.³⁸ Yet seven of the eight Justices participating struggled mightily with this latter issue
without any hint that *Coolidge* might provide an easier way to
resolve the case.³⁹ Only Justice Thomas, dissenting separately in
Randolph, concluded that the police "entry into the Randolph's
home at the invitation of Mrs. Randolph to be shown evidence of
respondent's cocaine use does not constitute a Fourth Amendment search" under the "principle in *Coolidge* * * * that when a
citizen leads police officers into a home shared with her spouse to
show them evidence relevant to their investigation into a crime,
that citizen is not acting as an agent of the police, and thus no
Fourth Amendment search has occurred."

<hr/>

³⁶See, e.g., United States v. Wiest,
596 F.3d 906 (8th Cir.2010) (defendant
had spent night at home of his girl
friend's stepmother; following defendant's arrest there stepmother, "un-
prompted, turned Wiest's clothes over
to police because she didn't want them
left in her home"); United States v.
Starr, 533 F.3d 985 (8th Cir.2008)
(wife took husband's photo albums,
photo prints and videotapes to police
station because she concerned they
contained child pornography; this a
private search situation).

³⁷Georgia v. Randolph, 547 U.S.
103, 126 S.Ct. 1515, 164 L.Ed.2d 208
(2006).

³⁸For discussion of this branch of
Randolph, see § 8.3(d).

³⁹The majority cited *Coolidge* for
the proposition that a co-tenant "may
be able to deliver evidence to the police" but then appeared to misstate the
facts of *Coolidge* in summarizing the
case as one where defendant's wife
"retrieved his guns *from* the couple's
house and turned them over to the police" (emphasis added). Two of the dissenters, in support of the notion that
"our privacy can be compromised by
those with whom we share common
living space," gave as one example
where co-occupants "deliver the contraband to the police" as in *Coolidge.*

To what extent do the various factors relied upon by the Court in *Coolidge* serve to distinguish that case from *Randolph*? One point of emphasis in *Coolidge* was that when the officers went to the residence, "they were not motivated by a desire to find the murder weapon," but *Randolph* is not different in that respect, for it can be said with even greater confidence that the police in that case did not go to the residence to find evidence of drug use, as they were merely responding to a domestic abuse complaint and knew nothing of defendant's use of cocaine. So too, while the *Coolidge* Court stressed that it "cannot be said that the police should have obtained a warrant for the guns and clothing before they set out to visit Mrs. Coolidge," it is again even more apparent that there is no basis for asserting the officers in *Randolph* should have first obtained a search warrant for the drug evidence of which they were unaware. In *Coolidge,* the Court deemed it significant that the police acted "normally and properly" in asking about the guns and clothing, but in *Randolph* the police never asked about the drug evidence at all; the information was volunteered by defendant's wife, and in that respect at least it thus appears that the wife in *Randolph* was, if anything, less of an "instrumentality" of the police than the spouse in *Coolidge.* In *Coolidge,* it is said that the wife "of her own accord produced the guns and the clothes for inspection," but that act simply put those items within the plain view of the officers who had followed her into the bedroom without any express invitation to do so from the wife; in that sense, the situation seems not significantly different from *Randolph,* where the wife "led the officer" into the bedroom where it was unnecessary for the wife to produce any items because the straw with cocaine residue was in plain view to start with. Of course, that officer, unlike the officers in *Coolidge,* was apparently acting with the intention of making a general search of the premises, but—so Justice Thomas concludes—that fact "is inconsequential, as he ultimately did not do so; he viewed only those items shown to him by Mrs. Randolph."

Even assuming the two cases are thus indistinguishable on any of the above bases, there remains one fact emphasized in *Coolidge* that clearly was not present in *Randolph*: in rejecting the claim that "this course of conduct amounted to a search and seizure," the *Coolidge* Court declared that it was "well to keep in mind that Mrs. Coolidge described her own motive as that of clearing her husband," and then went on to assert that finding a search and seizure in such circumstances "would be to hold, in effect, that a criminal suspect has constitutional protection against the adverse consequences of a spontaneous good-faith effort by his wife to clear him of suspicion." Is this fact standing alone sufficient to distinguish *Coolidge* from *Randolph*? Justice Thomas doesn't think so, for he dropped a footnote stating: "Nor is it relevant that, while Mrs. Coolidge intended to aid the police in apprehending a criminal because she believed doing so would

367

exonerate her husband, Mrs. Randolph believed aiding the police
would implicate her husband." But he offers no explanation whatsoever in support of that conclusion.

One thing is certain: a benign motive is not a immutable prerequisite to bringing a case within the *Burdeau* rule. Such a motive was not present in the *Burdeau* case itself, and is also lacking in the great majority of the cases later discussed herein.
Indeed, the Court in *Coolidge* made it apparent that no such motive is always essential, for in describing the quintessential
private person nonsearch situation that served as the starting
point for the analysis in that case, the Court said: "Had Mrs.
Coolidge, wholly on her own initiative, sought out her husband's
guns and clothing and then taken them to the police station *to be
used as evidence against him*, there can be no doubt under existing law that the articles would later have been admissible in evidence" (emphasis added). But having said that, it must be
acknowledged that courts sometimes rely upon the fact that the
private person's motive was other than aiding law enforcement.
In those cases where the police were on the scene at the time
that a private party exposed to or transferred to the police some
incriminating object and it appears that such conduct was either
acquiesced in or encouraged by the police, courts deeming such
situations to fall within *Burdeau* have often stressed that the
private person's motives differed from those of the police.[40]
Coolidge was precisely such a case, and thus it may well be that
the only necessary difference between *Coolidge* and *Randolph* is
the matter of motive.

Some might doubt whether the line between private person
nonsearches and searches based upon consent by a private person
can be drawn on the basis of that factor standing alone, and thus
might be inclined to believe that Justice Thomas was correct in
concluding that the imbroglio engaged in by the other Justices in
Randolph was totally unnecessary. But a closer look at *Coolidge*
and *Randolph* suggests that there are certain other differences
between those cases which—at least when considered with the
difference in motives—serve to explain why *Randolph* could not
have been dealt with other than as a consent search case. These
other differences concern the troublesome police presence in the
bedroom in each of the two cases. That presence is troublesome
in *Coolidge* because the police decided on their own to accompany
Mrs. Coolidge to that location absent any express consent by her
to their movement about the premises in such a fashion. But that
movement was in no sense critical or essential to the weapons
falling into the hands of the police, for Mrs. Coolidge had already
announced her intention to retrieve them for the police.[41] Except
for the fact that the Court did not get around to embracing the

---

[40]See the cases summarized in
notes 72, 73 and 113 infra.

[41]It was probably not essential to
the obtaining of defendant's clothing

about-to-be impounded vehicle,[53] and where a customs agent asked an airline transportation agent to open a package placed with the airline for shipment.[54] While it is often said that under these circumstances the private person becomes the "agent" of the government official,[55] it should not be presumed from this that the agent inevitably has no more authority than his principal. To take the most obvious case, it is lawful for the agent to conduct a warrantless search of areas under his proper control even though the requesting officer could not do so on his own.[56] But this is not to say that the official request has no bearing

---

[53]State v. Tucker, 330 Or. 85, 997 P.2d 182 (2000).

[54]Corngold v. United States, 367 F.2d 1 (9th Cir.1966).

[55]Where the private person's authority is limited by the fact of this agency (as compared with the situations discussed in the text following), courts sometimes refer to certain limitations. In United States v. Sparks, 265 F.3d 825 (9th Cir.2001), where an officer accompanied by a burglary victim stopped a suspect and, while searching the defendant, asked the victim to search the defendant's car, the court in holding this was proper set out "certain general principles that can be used to test whether a warrantless search by a civilian aiding the police comports with the Fourth Amendment. First, the civilian's role must be to aid the efforts of the police. In other words, civilians cannot be present simply to further their own goals. * * * Second, the officer must be in need of assistance. Police cannot invite civilians to perform searches on a whim; there must be some reason why a law enforcement officer cannot himself conduct the search and some reason to believe that postponing the search until an officer is available might raise a safety risk. Third, the civilians must be limited to doing what the police had authority to do."

[56]United States v. West, 453 F.2d 1351 (3d Cir.1972), reversing the district court's holding that one Trott violated the Fourth Amendment when he searched his own car. "The mere fact that an agency relationship might have arisen between Trott and the police could not encroach upon the right of Trott to enter and search his own

car any more than it could suspend Trott's right to enter and search his own house." See also United States v. Wiest, 596 F.3d 906 (8th Cir.2010) (while court also says defendant's girl friend's stepmother's turning over defendant's clothing to police was "unsolicited act," it also stresses that it was "not intrusive for her to take clothes out of her own washer and dryer"); United States v. Bruce, 396 F.3d 697 (6th Cir.2005) (where police asked hotel cleaning staff to keep separate trash removed from defendant's rooms and they did so, there no police search, as cleaning staff had "the distinct and independent intent * * * to clean these rooms and empty their trash, just as they would do with any other room in the hotel," and by request that defendant's trash be kept separate "the cleaning staff were not asked to *search* for evidence, but merely to *preserve* any possible evidence); United States v. Jenkins, 46 F.3d 447 (5th Cir.1995) (defendant's employee, who by virtue of employment entitled to receive and open packages of videotapes arriving in Memphis, could still do so even if he a government agent for Fourth Amendment purposes, as such "does not terminate one's right to engage in conduct which was authorized prior to entering the agency relationship"); People v. Wharton, 53 Cal.3d 522, 280 Cal.Rptr. 631, 809 P.2d 290 (1991) (where hammer found in apartment of murder victim by administrator of her estate while accounting for her belongings, it not objectionable that police earlier told him of their interest in such an item); People v. Heflin, 71 Ill.2d 525, 17 Ill.Dec. 786, 376 N.E.2d 1367 (1978) (man could turn his broth-

upon the legality of the agent's conduct, for the agent's authority over certain property may be limited by the purposes for which he is acting. For example, even assuming that postal authorities may be authorized to open packages to see if the proper rate of postage was paid, it does not follow that it is lawful for those authorities to open a package upon request of a state police officer for the purpose of finding evidence of crime.[57] Likewise, although a shipper may have authority pursuant to the contract of carriage to open a package to see that the proper rate was charged, this does not mean that the shipper's employees may lawfully open a package placed with the shipper at the instigation of a customs agent who is seeking evidence of criminal conduct.[58]

A search will also be deemed subject to Fourth Amendment restrictions if it is a "joint endeavor,"[59] involving both a private person and a government official, as where a detective and a victim of a theft together enter a suspect's apartment to retrieve the stolen goods.[60] It is not essential that the government official be involved in the endeavor at the very outset; cases in this area

---

er's letters over to police at their request, where it was brother and not the police who caused the letters to come into his possession); State v. Mata, 266 Neb. 668, 668 N.W.2d 448 (2003) (where at police request when they executing search warrant defendant's sister removed from residence she shared with defendant a dog belonging to her son, she not thereby an agent of law enforcement, as there "a difference between acting as an agent of law enforcement and simply cooperating with a reasonable request made by law enforcement," and "even if an agency relationship had been established," where one has a "right to search in a particular place or seize certain property by virtue of his or her own personal relationship to the premises or property in question, that right is not diminished by the individual's relationship with law enforcement"); State v. James, 638 S.W.2d 848 (Tenn. Crim.App.1982) (proper for officer to tell informant to go back to defendant's premises to make more current observations therein, as informant a person with free access to that place).

Thus, there is a relationship between this problem and the law that has developed concerning third-party concept searches. See § 8.3.

[57]Commonwealth v. Dembo, 451

Pa. 1, 301 A.2d 689 (1973). Likewise, while it is a private search for a telephone company to install a pen register for its own purposes, see note 22 supra, such a search is governmental when requested by police investigating harassing phone calls. People of City of Dearborn Heights v. Hayes, 82 Mich.App. 253, 266 N.W.2d 778 (1978).

[58]Corngold v. United States, 367 F.2d 1 (9th Cir.1966). See also United States v. Souza, 223 F.3d 1197 (10th Cir.2000) ("While companies such as UPS have legitimate reasons to search packages independent of any motivation to assist police," here search was governmental, as officers who had witnessed drug dog alert to package twice encouraged UPS clerk to open package and then assisted her in doing so).

[59]Corngold v. United States, 367 F.2d 1 (9th Cir.1966).

[60]State v. Scrotsky, 39 N.J. 410, 189 A.2d 23 (1963). See also People v. Aguilar, 897 P.2d 84 (Colo.1995) (governmental search where officer and tow truck operator "were acting together in determining the existence of anything suspicious" in impounded vehicle); State v. Collins, 367 Md. 700, 790 A.2d 660 (2002) (where "the bail bond persons had utilized the services of the officer to knock on the door, and

often apply the rule from *Lustig v. United States*[61] that it is "immaterial" whether the government official "originated the idea or joined in it while the search was in progress" and that it is sufficient that the official "was in it before the object of the search was completely accomplished."[62] (A striking example of this point is provided by *United States v. Knoll*,[63] where apparently private persons burglarized an attorney's office and took boxes of documents, examined some of the documents and turned them over to the prosecutor, and then when the prosecutor, knowing of the burglary and that it had produced even more documents, expressed a need for more information, the private persons examined more documents from the same burglary and gave them to the prosecutor. Applying the *Lustig* principle, the court concluded that upon such facts the government's involvement after the burglary but before the examination of the second set of documents made the search of them governmental.) Nor is it necessary that the government official directly participate in the illegal entry. The courts have found sufficient government involvement where the officer was standing by giving tacit approval to the entry made by a private person.[64]

A useful illustration of what will suffice in terms of government

---

to inform Collins that they desired to enter to search for a 'wanted' person; yet neither the officer nor the bail bond persons had informed Collins of the private nature of the request and the officer included the bail bond person in his generic use of the word 'we' when seeking entry," "the actions of the officer and the bail bond persons in the present case were, from the beginning and almost to the point of arrest, so intertwined with each other, that the entire action from its inception took on the characteristics of 'State action'"); State v. Smith, 279 Neb. 918, 782 N.W.2d 913 (2010) (while search of night club patron was by private security guard, police officer with him told patron to keep his hands up and placed his arm under patron's wrist, and thus the search "was a joint venture"); State v. Payano-Roman, 290 Wis.2d 380, 714 N.W.2d 548 (2006) (search was a governmental search here, where "officers and medical personnel were engaged in a joint endeavor to speed the passage of the baggie of drugs through [defendant's] system"; medical personnel decided on laxative, but it administered at hospital by police who had arrested defendant after he swallowed bag of drugs,

and defendant required by police to use portable toilet to facilitate drug recovery).

[61]Lustig v. United States, 338 U.S. 74, 69 S.Ct. 1372, 93 L.Ed. 1819 (1949).

[62]United States v. Ogden, 485 F.2d 536 (9th Cir.1973).

[63]United States v. Knoll, 16 F.3d 1313 (2d Cir.1994).

[64]Moody v. United States, 163 A.2d 337 (D.C.App.1960); State v. Becich, 13 Or.App. 415, 509 P.2d 1232 (1973). See also Commonwealth v. Borecky, 277 Pa.Super. 244, 419 A.2d 753 (1980) (notwithstanding lower court's finding that officer did not instruct informer to search home for drugs, where officer searched informer before he did so and planned to meet informer upon his completion of the search, the officer's "admitted prior knowledge of the warrantless search, and acquiescence therein" was sufficient to make the search governmental).

Compare Atamian v. Hawk, 842 A.2d 654 (Del.2003) ("Mere presence of a police officer, without more, is insufficient to implicate Fourth Amendment concerns. If a government agent

participation is provided by *Stapleton v. Superior Court.*[65] Police and special agents of credit card companies together went to the defendant's residence for the purpose of arresting him for credit card fraud. They together engaged in a search of the defendant's house, and at some point one of the credit card agents, Bradford, took car keys from the table and went outside and searched defendant's car, resulting in the discovery of incriminating evidence in the trunk. The court held:

> The search of petitioner's car was clearly part of a joint operation by police and the credit card agents aimed at arresting petitioner and obtaining evidence against him. This official participation in the planning and implementation of the overall operation is sufficient without more to taint with state action the subsequent acts of such credit card agents. * * *
>
> * * * Bradford joined the operation and entered petitioner's house at the request and as an agent of the police. The agency did not end nor Bradford revert to private status when as part of that operation, although without a specific instruction from the police, Bradford searched petitioner's car. * * *
>
> In the instant case the Highland Park police, by allowing Bradford to join in the search and arrest operation, put Bradford in a position which gave him access to the car keys and thus to the trunk of petitioner's car. Thereafter the police stood silently by while Bradford made the obviously illegal search. Contrary to the assumption of the respondent court, the police need not have requested or directed the search in order to be guilty of "standing idly by"; knowledge of the illegal search coupled with a failure to protect the petitioner's rights against such a search suffices.

With respect to the very last point made in *Stapleton,* this has been interpreted to mean that a search is private if it is undertaken without police knowledge[66] or if, notwithstanding the presence of the police, it is undertaken in direct contravention of po-

---

'is involved "merely as a witness," the requisite governmental action implicating Fourth Amendment concerns is absent' "); State v. Jolitz, 231 Neb. 254, 435 N.W.2d 907 (1989) (distinguishing *Moody, Becich* and *Borecky,* court notes that here hitchhiker Hart entered defendant's premises to get marijuana after being driven there by off-duty officer who waited in the car, but Hart didn't know he was an officer, getting marijuana was Hart's only motivation, Hart identified defendant as his friend who supplied him with marijuana, officer never suggested Hart should enter and, though he knew defendant was not at home, did not know whether Hart was authorized to enter or possibly gained entry by use of a key; all this means this not an instance of the officer "giving tacit approval").

[65]Stapleton v. Superior Court, 70 Cal.2d 97, 73 Cal.Rptr. 575, 447 P.2d 967 (1968).

[66]*Stapleton* was distinguished in People v. North, 29 Cal.3d 509, 174 Cal.Rptr. 511, 629 P.2d 19 (1981) (victim, suspecting defendant of burglary, tried to look into defendant's car at night and then summoned officer who shined light into car and saw liquor bottles similar to those taken in burglary; officer said that not probable cause for search, victim said perhaps car was stolen, so officer went to his squad car to make a radio check, and during his absence victim entered car and searched it; held, private search, as no "police foreknowledge or simultaneous awareness of a citizen entry").

Also compare United States v.

Day, 591 F.3d 679 (4th Cir.2010) (arrests by private security officer at apartment complex not state action, as "no law enforcement agency had ever given him any directives concerning his work"); United States v. Poe, 556 F.3d 1113 (10th Cir.2009), discussed in Comment, 49 Washburn L.J. 201 (2009) (bounty hunters' search of residence for defendant, who had jumped bail, was a private search, as defendant "cannot assert that the government 'knew of or acquiesced in' the bounty hunters' entry and search"); United States v. Silva, 554 F.3d 13 (1st Cir.2009) (defendant's brother Norman told police he had found evidence of identity theft, including traffic tickets and medical bills in Norman's name, in defendant's bedroom in the family home; while officer asked Norman "to bring the items to the station," he assumed Norman had already seized those items and thus Norman's second search of defendant's bedroom was private); United States v. Connors, 441 F.3d 527 (7th Cir.2006) (while defendant's ex-wife was "exploiting his misplaced trust in her," perhaps "at the behest of the government," her search through his "private files for incriminating documents" is a governmental search only if the government agent "directed or acquiesced in it," but evidence here was that he "did not know of any illegal rummaging"); United States v. Humphrey, 208 F.3d 1190 (10th Cir.2000) (notwithstanding fact that private person had earlier given police tip with respect to drug conspiracy involving her acquaintances, who were then arrested, did not require court to draw inference that this person was a police agent with respect to her actions a month later in examining the contents of a purse belonging to one of the conspirators); United States v. Pervaz, 118 F.3d 1 (1st Cir.1997) (where secret service agent advised employees of cellular phone company that company's customers being defrauded and asked if they had equipment to locate source of cloned calls, company's later use of such equipment not a government search, as no evidence secret service agent "authorized the search or even knew about it"); United States v. Snowadzki, 723 F.2d 1427 (9th Cir.1984) (where defendant's fellow employee called IRS agent to say defendant had unreported income and asked if copies of defendant's records would be helpful, to which agent answered in affirmative, and that person then took records from defendant's desk, that a private search, as no showing government agents "knew of or encouraged [the] seizure of his records"); State v. Zarick, 227 Conn. 207, 630 A.2d 565 (1993) (photo lab's seizure of customer's photos not state action, as policy initiated by lab, decision to turn over specific photos entirely up to lab's manager, and no police supervision or instructions re that policy); Commonwealth v. Ghee, 414 Mass. 313, 607 N.E.2d 1005 (1993) (police called private towing company to tow away car on interstate after arrest of operator, no police inventory process applicable in such a case, and trunk thereafter opened by towing company operator because of smell; private search); State v. Buswell, 460 N.W.2d 614 (Minn.1990) (race track security guard's activity in searching vehicles at track not governmental notwithstanding "antecedent contact" between them and police, as contact regarded arrest procedures, and nothing in record indicates police encouraged or even knew of practice of searching vehicles without consent); State v. Berosik, 352 Mont. 16, 214 P.3d 776 (2009) (where defendant's wife seized sexually explicit materials and removed them from home, and thereafter contacted police, who asked her to bring items in, wife's subsequent search of home and vehicle was also private, as police "did not ask her to seize more items"); State v. Santiago, 147 N.M. 76, 217 P.3d 89 (2009) (mere fact police aware mall security guards "were performing protective searches' does not show "an agency relationship"; situation might be different if police had encouraged the guards "to obtain evidence for use by the state" or if police knew guards "routinely exceeded the permissible scope

lice instructions.[67] But, when are the police obligated to give such instructions or otherwise take steps to prevent a private search? Although the issue is not well developed in the decided cases, some pertinent observations may be made. For one thing, the reference in *Stapleton* is to an "illegal search," and thus it may be said that the police need not attempt to prevent a search the private party may lawfully make merely because such a search could not be undertaken by the officer himself.[68] Secondly, it

---

of protective searches * * * and condoned or participated in it, or even failed to discourage it").

[67]United States v. Maxwell, 484 F.2d 1350 (5th Cir.1973). See also United States v. Bennett, 729 F.2d 923 (2d Cir.1984) (where federal "agents had given the informant specific instructions against the illegal search, and the informant committed the illegal acts 'in direct contravention of his instructions,'" the search was private); United States v. Mekjian, 505 F.2d 1320 (5th Cir.1975) (nurse gave FBI documents showing doctor was defrauding government, FBI agents told her not to copy any more records, but she did so anyway; held, private search); State v. Smith, 110 Wash.2d 658, 756 P.2d 722 (1988) (detective told informant prosecutor refused warrant on basis of information informant provided so far, but detective had earlier repeatedly discouraged informant from going onto property in question without legitimate reason and told him he should not trespass; when informant later without police knowledge entered the property and reported back seeing marijuana, this a private search).

[68]See United States v. Cleaveland, 38 F.3d 1092 (9th Cir.1994) (mere fact police in area to ensure safety of power company inspector, who went onto defendant's property and checked meter for illegal hookup, as authorized by Customer Service Agreement, did not make inspector's conduct state action where, as here, one of inspector's motives was to protect his employer's interests); United States v. Ramirez, 810 F.2d 1338 (5th Cir.1987) (mere fact federal agents who arrested defendant "probably understood" but "had no specific

knowledge" that the manager of the hotel where defendant had been staying would examine defendant's luggage when his rental term expired did not make manager's action governmental); United States v. Coleman, 628 F.2d 961 (6th Cir.1980) (mere fact police standing by in case of trouble did not make private person's repossession of truck pursuant to statute state action); Clark v. State, 562 N.E.2d 11 (Ind.1990) (after defendant, a fireman, hospitalized for burns, defendant's father, who had the keys thereto, searched defendant's car; this a private search though another fireman "was present at this search" but "did not initiate it"); State v. Ware, 219 Neb. 594, 365 N.W.2d 418 (1985) (police indicated they would get search warrant for defendant's room at Boys' Town, but teacher then said it was their policy to search boys' rooms when they were in trouble and police said if that was their policy they could do so if they wanted to; teacher's search not governmental); State v. Patch, 142 N.H. 453, 702 A.2d 1278 (1997) (where police served restraining order on woman, requiring her to leave apartment she had shared with defendant, and order did not prohibit her "from retrieving her personal belongings," police had no duty to prevent her from retrieving defendant's drugs from cabinets and other areas and handing them to an officer); State v. Grant, 67 Ohio St.3d 465, 620 N.E.2d 50 (1993) (entry of private insurance agent into burned premises "for private purposes without official instigation" not state action merely because police officers then "present as a courtesy"); Kalmas v. Wagner, 133 Wash.2d 210, 943 P.2d 1369 (1997) (where police were present "to keep the peace and prevent any kind of

would appear to be of some significance that in *Stapleton* the police put the agent into the situation where he was in a position to make the search.[69] If, on the other hand, police have been called to the scene and are thus present while a private person retrieves evidence of a crime he had uncovered before contacting the police, and the private person's authority to make the search is not obviously nonexistent, courts do not appear to be concerned about the failure of the police to prevent the search.[70] Indeed, as is

confrontation between the parties," and at tenant's request the officer entered with property manager, who by statute had a right to enter to exhibit the premises to a prospective tenant or purchaser, no Fourth Amendment violation).

Police encouragement of such action, however, is another matter. See, e.g., United States v. Souza, 223 F.3d 1197 (10th Cir.2000).

[69]See also State v. Abdouch, 230 Neb. 929, 434 N.W.2d 317 (1989) (where decedent's divorced wife obtained assistance of sheriff's office in securing decedent's effects in premises decedent now shared with defendant, and during that operation officer was looking in barn while wife and son looking in home, discovery of drug paraphernalia by son was a Fourth Amendment search because of the government participation, as the private citizens "entered the premises with police assistance and approval, and officers who, in effect, provided the 'key' to enter the premises through a display of government authority").

But see Buonocore v. Chesapeake & Potomac Telephone Co., 254 Va. 469, 492 S.E.2d 439 (1997) (where deputy was told Buonocore possessed illegal firearm and also property taken from Chesapeake, and deputy obtained warrant only for firearm but invited Chesapeake security officer to come along, when latter official searched cabinets in home "on his own initiative" that search private and thus not covered by Fourth Amendment).

[70]United States v. Crowley, 285 F.3d 553 (7th Cir.2002) (where UPS driver had earlier opened suspicious package and then called police, and in presence of police proceeded to open the package again without encourage-

ment from police, second search also private); United States v. Kinney, 953 F.2d 863 (4th Cir.1992) (defendant's girl friend, having told police she had found guns in closet of apartment where she lived with him, entered closet a second time after police arrived; "more than the mere presence of a police officer is necessary to constitute the government action required"); United States v. Coleman, 628 F.2d 961 (6th Cir.1980) (man police knew had repossessed truck met with police and then retrieved from truck and briefcase therein weapons he had found earlier); United States v. Bulgier, 618 F.2d 472 (7th Cir.1980) (airline agent opened bag to find identity of owner but found drugs, federal agent summoned and airline employee then reopened envelope in bag to expose drugs to officer); State v. Lee, 32 Conn.App. 84, 628 A.2d 1318 (1993) (self-employed auto recovery agent repossessed car for Ford Motor Co. and then, at police station and in presence of police officer, inventoried contents); State v. Araki, 82 Haw. 474, 923 P.2d 891 (1996) (minor's mother called police, played for them a video rented by her son, and then turned the tape over to the police); State v. Oldaker, 172 W.Va. 258, 304 S.E.2d 843 (1983) (landlord of auto upholstery shop gave police statement re stolen truck in shop, and when they took him back to shop he said they could look inside but police said they could not do so without a warrant, so landlord said he would look himself and police said they could not stop him; landlord's search private).

The same is true where the private person's actions appear to have some other lawful purpose. See, e.g., Pepper v. Village of Oak Park, 430 F.3d 805 (7th Cir.2005) (where police

sometimes important in other contexts as well,[71] even if the police were present before any search began and again "knew of and acquiesced in the intrusive conduct" of the private person, the matter may ultimately be resolved by determining whether that person "intended to assist law enforcement efforts or further his own ends";[72] courts have generally viewed the activity as a private search if a private purpose was being served.[73]

---

officer sent to residence to be "escort" while owner's estranged husband removed his personal property from the residence, this not a public search notwithstanding officer's failure to stop the husband where nothing in the circumstances indicated husband not entitled to enter or that he did not own TV set he removed).

[71]See text at note 133 infra.

[72]United States v. Miller, 688 F.2d 652 (9th Cir.1982). See, e.g., United States v. Dahlstrom, 180 F.3d 677 (5th Cir.1999) (where sheriff was present when a group of corporate employees entered an associate's office and removed corporate property, but employees "conceived the plan on their own and solely for their own benefit" and sheriff's "presence was merely requested to keep the peace," court deems this a private search notwithstanding claim sheriff's present "gave the unauthorized act an air of legality and that this inhibited [defendants'] attempts to retain control of the documents"); United States v. Reed, 15 F.3d 928 (9th Cir.1994) (motel manager summoned police because he suspected a guest was using room for drug activities; officer stood in doorway while manager searched room and effects; held, not a private search, as searcher must have "had a legitimate motive *other than crime prevention,*" and purported private purpose of ensuring hotel property not damaged rejected because manager "did not stop searching after he had learned the room was in good condition"); Virdin v. State, 780 A.2d 1024 (Del.2001) (where action of missing woman's mother, in using her key to search daughter's apartment, "was motivated by an urgent concern for her daughter's safety, and was not related to assisting with police investigation," and

she "requested that the police accompany [her and her husband during search] because of concern about a confrontation with the defendant," daughter's husband, parents were not state agents, and role of police whose presence "was not for any investigative purpose but * * * only to keep the peace," did not transform the private search into a police search); State v. Jorgensen, 660 N.W.2d 127 (Minn. 2003) (where woman's family learned man she lived with gave false reason for her absence, and woman's sister went there and met police, who said they could not enter because it appeared no one home, and sister then declared she was going to break in because of her concern for her sister's safety and attempted to do so while police standing by, but door partially blocked by object then seen to be missing woman's body, sister not agent of police, as evidence showed she "was planning to break into the house long before the police arrived"); State v. Burroughs, 926 S.W.2d 243 (Tenn. 1996) (where dorm supervisor at private college entered defendant's dorm room and found white powdery substance and then summoned police officer who identified substance as cocaine, after which dorm supervisor removed the substance from defendant's room and turned it over to police, this was a private search because conducted by "a college official whose purpose and actions were in furtherance of college policy, not state policy").

[73]United States v. Day, 591 F.3d 679 (4th Cir.2010) (lower court's conclusion private security officers intended to assist law enforcement rejected with observation that "the objective of 'deterring crime' is entirely consistent with [their] responsibility to protect the tenants or property" of employing apartment complex); United

States v. Poe, 556 F.3d 1113 (10th Cir.2009) (bounty hunters' search of residence for defendant, who had jumped bail, was private, as they primarily "intended . . . to further [their] own ends'-the financial stake in Poe's bail-rather than to assist state officials"); United States v. Silva, 554 F.3d 13 (1st Cir.2009) (Norman, defendant's brother, told police of evidence of identity theft he found in defendant's bedroom in the family home, traffic tickets and medical bills in Norman's name; Norman's later retrieval of those items at police request, involving a second search of defendant's bedroom, was a private search, as he was "motivated by his desire to clear his name"); United States v. Robinson, 390 F.3d 853 (6th Cir.2004) (where DEA officers who received information from California police that drug dog had alerted to UPS package informed UPS security representative that the package would be arriving at his facility the next morning, and while DEA officer preparing to obtain a search warrant security representative opened the package in accordance with UPS policy and without request or encouragement of DEA officer, this a private search); United States v. Smith, 383 F.3d 700 (8th Cir.2004) (manager of courier service facility did not act as government agent when he opened package suspected by police to contain drugs, even though police present and acquiesced, as no indication manager motivated solely or even primarily by intent to aid police rather than because of desire to ensure company not being used as vehicle in drug trade); United States v. Smythe, 84 F.3d 1240 (10th Cir.1996) (where bus station manager called police, who witnessed his opening of suspicious package, and manager testified "the decision to open the package was entirely his" and "that he would have opened the package regardless of whether the police responded to his call," this a private search; manager's actions had an independent motivation, i.e., "his concern for the passengers on the bus," and police "need not discourage private citizens from doing that which is not unlawful"); State v. Betts, 286 Conn. 88, 942 A.2d 364 (2008) (where defendant's fiancé summoned police and then retrieved letter from bedroom she shared with defendant, after officer asked her to "see if [you] can find" the letter she had told police about, this nonetheless a private search, as she "had acted on her own because she and [her daughter, victim of sexual assault by defendant,] wanted the police to know about the letter"); Atamian v. Hawk, 842 A.2d 654 (Del.2003) (though police officer present during part of search by private hospital's security guard, this a private search, as guard "had an independent motivation * * * for searching the bags to ensure the safety of the hospital and staff in the vicinity"); Commonwealth v. Richmond, 379 Mass. 557, 399 N.E.2d 1069 (1980) (private search where mother called police chief to ask if she could open letter to her 16-year-old daughter from prisoner in jail as murder suspect, chief said she could if she thought it in her daughter's interest to do so, and mother testified she would have opened the letter in any event "in the interest of her daughter"); State v. Brockman, 339 S.C. 57, 528 S.E.2d 661 (2000) (where police summoned to domestic disturbance witnessed defendant's mother break into his moped and uncover cocaine, that a private search because mother had "a legitimate, independent justification for conducting the search," i.e., a desire "to avoid any future altercation with her son"); State v. Bembenek, 111 Wis.2d 617, 331 N.W.2d 616 (App.1983) (search of defendant's locker by defendant's superior at private university, where defendant employed, was private notwithstanding presence of police, as purpose was to see if defendant had any of university's property).

Compare United States v. Souza, 223 F.3d 1197 (10th Cir.2000), note 58 supra (distinguishing *Smythe* and *Leffall*); United States v. Newton, 510 F.2d 1149 (7th Cir.1975) (search of suitcase arriving on later flight than passenger, in presence of drug agent, not private; "the airline employees did

Somewhat related to this problem is the notion from *Lustig,* noted earlier, that a search is governmental if an official of the government joined in "before the object of the search was completely accomplished." Under this approach, it may be said that if an agent of a shipper were to open a package and find contraband and then summon the police and display the open package to them, there is no governmental search but rather a plain view situation.[74] But, what if the agent closed the package again before the police arrived upon the scene? If the reopening

---

not need to search the luggage to find out to whom it belonged," as "[t]hey already knew").

In State v. Kahoonei, 83 Haw. 124, 925 P.2d 294 (1996), decided under the *state* constitution, the court rejected the common approach of considering the private person's motivation, and concluded the focus should be exclusively "on the actions of the police officers," so that a private person "may be a government agent even if he or she is acting for personal reasons," just as "private individuals may be acting on their own even if they erroneously believe they are acting as an agent of the police." The court thus concluded that even assuming defendant's wife's "motivation in retrieving the gun was out of concern that the firearm might injure a member of her household," the search was still governmental because idea of searching originated with the police, who told defendant's wife that a search warrant "could be gotten to search the house" and that a search "would be done anyway" if she did not turn over the evidence.

[74]United States v. Pierce, 893 F.2d 669 (5th Cir.1990); United States v. Rodriguez, 596 F.2d 169 (6th Cir. 1979); United States v. Sherwin, 539 F.2d 1 (9th Cir.1976); United States v. Ford, 525 F.2d 1308 (10th Cir.1975); United States v. DeBerry, 487 F.2d 448 (2d Cir.1973); State v. Stump, 547 P.2d 305 (Alaska 1976); State v. Pontier, 103 Idaho 91, 645 P.2d 325 (1982); State v. Rode, 456 N.W.2d 769 (N.D.1990).

Compare United States v. Kelly, 529 F.2d 1365 (8th Cir.1976), where the items were suspected obscene literature, which the court concluded required a different result. The "plain view" reasoning was rejected on the ground that under Roaden v. Kentucky, 413 U.S. 496, 93 S.Ct. 2796, 37 L.Ed.2d 757 (1973), the government must obtain a search warrant before seizing materials presumptively protected by the First Amendment, even if they are in plain view. In *Sherwin,* involving similar facts, the court declined to follow *Kelly.* See Comment, 90 Harv.L. Rev. 463, 466, 471–72 (1976), noting that *Sherwin,* supra, "seems more consistent with current fourth amendment analysis," which tends "to focus primarily on the right of privacy," but preferring the *Kelly* approach because "property interests in first amendment materials should be presumed legitimate in the absence of a judicial determination to the contrary." *Kelly* was also rejected in United States v. Sanders, 592 F.2d 788 (5th Cir.1979), upholding FBI receipt of obscene films found in a private search by employees of a corporation to which they were missent, in that "neither we nor the Supreme Court have ever held that government acceptance of those articles constitutes a seizure requiring compliance with the warrant requirement, even in cases where no exception to that requirement would have covered the Government's action." *Sanders* was reversed by the Supreme Court in *Walter v. United States* (discussed in text at note 78 infra), but without specific mention of the *Kelly* rationale; the Stevens opinion says in a footnote: "For purposes of decision, we accept the Government's argument that the delivery of the films to the FBI by a third party was not a 'seizure' subject to the warrant requirement of the Fourth Amendment."

is done by the private person without a police request or police assistance, then the search is deemed to be private.[75] But where the subsequent reopening of the package was by the police[76] or by the agent at police request,[77] lower courts for a time were inclined to treat this as a governmental search. When that issue reached the Supreme Court, however, it was resolved somewhat differently.

In *Walter v. United States*,[78] an interstate shipment of several securely sealed packages containing films was mistakenly delivered to a party other than the consignee. Employees of that party opened the packages and found individual film boxes with suggestive drawings and explicit descriptions of the contents on the outsides. The packages were turned over to FBI agents, who by a warrantless screening of the films determined they were obscene. Noting that under the *Sanders* rule[79] "an officer's authority to possess a package is distinct from his authority to examine its contents," so that ordinarily a search warrant would be needed in such an instance, Justice Stevens (announcing the judgment of the Court in an opinion joined only by Justice Stewart[80]) then turned to the significance of the earlier private search:

> Nor does the fact that the packages and one or more of the boxes had been opened by a private party before they were acquired by the FBI excuse the failure to obtain a search warrant. * * * In this case there was nothing wrongful about the Government's acquisition of the packages or its examination of their contents to the

<hr/>

[75]Stange v. State, 559 P.2d 650 (Alaska 1977); State v. Edwards, 197 Neb. 354, 248 N.W.2d 775 (1977); Commonwealth v. Kozak, 233 Pa.Super. 348, 336 A.2d 387 (1975). Consider also People v. Clements, 80 Ill.App.3d 821, 36 Ill.Dec. 63, 400 N.E.2d 483 (1980) (where nurse called police and said they had discovered marijuana in patient's bag, and officer came to hospital and asked nurse for the bag, which she then retrieved from patient's room, this not a police request for a search, as officer "did not go there to conduct a search but merely to pick up the fruits of a purely private search").

[76]E.g., United States v. Haes, 551 F.2d 767 (8th Cir.1977) (carrier opened package, but turned films over to FBI without first examining them); Cash v. Williams, 455 F.2d 1227 (6th Cir.1972) (wrecker operator found bag containing what appeared to be marijuana in car, replaced bag, and then summoned police, who aided in second search of car for bag); People v.

Robinson, 41 Cal.App.3d 658, 116 Cal.Rptr. 455 (1974) (landlady summoned police and told officer she found gun in pocket of tenant's coat, which she had placed in porch with his other effects, officer removed gun from pocket).

[77]E.g., United States v. Ogden, 485 F.2d 536 (9th Cir.1973) (airline agent pried open edge of suitcase and saw marijuana, police then summoned, agent asked officer if he would like bag opened, officer responded, "If you had it opened, yes").

[78]Walter v. United States, 447 U.S. 649, 100 S.Ct. 2395, 65 L.Ed.2d 410 (1980). For other discussion of *Walter,* see Comment, 52 U.Cin.L.Rev. 172 (1983).

[79]See § 5.5(c).

[80]Blackmun, J., joined by the Chief Justice and by Powell and Rehnquist, JJ., dissented. White, J., joined by Brennan, J., concurred in part and in the judgment. Marshall, J., concurred in the judgment.

extent that they had already been examined by third parties. Since that examination had uncovered the labels, and since the labels established probable cause to believe the films were obscene, the Government argues that the limited private search justified an unlimited official search. That argument must fail, whether we view the official search as an expansion of the private search or as an independent search supported by its own probable cause.

* * * Even though some circumstances—for example, if the results of the private search are in plain view when materials are turned over to the Government—may justify the Government's re-examination of the materials,[81] surely the Government may not exceed the scope of the private search unless it has the right to make an independent search. In this case, the private party had not actually viewed the films. Prior to the Government screening, one could only draw inferences about what was on the films. The projection of the films was a significant expansion of the search that had been conducted previously by a private party and therefore must be characterized as a separate search. That separate search was not supported by any exigency, or by a warrant even though one could have easily been obtained.

* * * The fact that the cartons were unexpectedly opened by a third party before the shipment was delivered to its intended consignee does not alter the consignor's legitimate expectation of privacy. The private search merely frustrated that expectation in part. It did not simply strip the remaining unfrustrated portion of that expectation of all Fourth Amendment protection.

The four dissenters in *Walter* concluded that because the FBI agents received the packages after they had been opened and after the films' labels were revealed, the "viewing of the movies on a projector did not 'change the nature of the search' and was not an additional search subject to the warrant requirement." Especially because that view did not prevail, it is clear from *Walter* that a private search does not permit a later government search significantly more intrusive or extensive than the earlier private search.[82]

---

[81]See, e.g., State v. Andrei, 574 A.2d 295 (Me.1990) (distinguishing *Walter,* as here, when defendant's husband directed officer's attention to open page of defendant's diary, officer's "pause to read the indicated passage * * * was not an additional search beyond the scope of that already conducted by the third party").

[82]Consider in this regard United States v. Donnes, 947 F.2d 1430 (10th Cir.1991) (where private person picked up glove in another's premises and found syringe inside and then handed glove to officer, who removed and opened camera lens case inside and found drugs, that a government

search; here as well, fn. 13 of *Sanders,* discussed in § 5.5(f), inapplicable as no plain view); United States v. Miller, 769 F.2d 554 (9th Cir.1985) (much like *Jacobsen,* in text following, except that field test negative, which prompted agent to then break through inner bag to reach other powder, which tested positive; court held latter action a government search; government's reliance on fn. 13 of *Sanders* rejected, as bag itself "did not, by its outward appearance, announce to the observer that it contained a controlled substance"); State v. Ressler, 701 N.W.2d 915 (N.D.2005) (full police search of contents of package illegal where employee of private shipper examined

Before examining that limitation more closely,[83] it is first necessary to consider another question, which is whether the government is even free to do later *all* of what was done earlier by the private party. This issue, of importance when the government receives the goods from the searching private party in a less exposed condition than they were during the earlier search, reached the Supreme Court in *United States v. Jacobsen.*[84] The facts there, as assumed by the majority,[85] were that a Federal Express employee opened a damaged package and found several plastic bags of white powder inside a closed 10-inch tube wrapped in several pieces of crumpled newspaper. A federal drug agent was summoned, but before his arrival the bags had been put back into the tube and the tube and newspapers back into the box, so that apparently when the agent examined the box the powder was not visible to him until he removed the tube from the box. The majority in *Jacobsen,* per Justice Stevens, proceeded to utilize what was now seen as the "standard * * * adopted by a majority of the Court in *Walter,*" namely, that the "additional invasions of respondent's privacy by the government agent must be tested by the degree to which they exceeded the scope of the private search." Thus, since "the removal of the plastic bags from the tube and the agent's visual inspection of their contents enabled the agent to learn nothing that had not previously been learned during the private search,"[86] the Court held it "infringed no legitimate expectation of privacy and hence was not a 'search' within

---

only some of contents, so that defendant "still maintained a legitimate expectation of privacy in the contents * * * not inspected during the private-party search").

[83]See text at note 99 infra.

[84]United States v. Jacobsen, 466 U.S. 109, 104 S.Ct. 1652, 80 L.Ed.2d 85 (1984), discussed in Junker, The Structure of the Fourth Amendment: The Scope of the Protection, 79 J.Crim.L. & C. 1105, 1136–47 (1989).

[85]White, J., concurring, felt "the case should be judged on the basis of the Magistrate's finding that, when the first DEA agent arrived, the 'tube was in plain view in the box and the bags of white powder were visible from the end of the tube.'" Brennan and Marshall, JJ., dissenting, stated: "Because the record in this case is unclear on the question of whether the contents of respondent's package were plainly visible when the Federal Express employee showed the package to the DEA officer, I would remand the

case for further factfinding on this central issue."

[86]See also United States v. Bowers, 594 F.3d 522 (6th Cir.2010) (where defendant's housemate and her boyfriend looked through album belonging to defendant and discovered child porn and then summoned police, who likewise examined album, that viewing did not violate Fourth Amendment, as per *Jacobsen* the police "learn[ed] nothing that had not previously been learned during the private search"); United States v. Starr, 533 F.3d 985 (8th Cir.2008) (where wife took husband's photo albums, photo prints and videotapes to police station because she concerned they contained child pornography, police warrantless examination of these items lawful, as "i[n] her private search prior to contacting law enforcement, Mrs. Starr examined all of the evidence that she subsequently brought to police"); United States v. Grimes, 244 F.3d 375 (5th Cir.2001) (computer repairman found child pornography and sum-

moned police, and repairman then showed them "only the previously-found images," and thus police viewing was "within the scope of the original private-party search"); United States v. Bowman, 215 F.3d 951 (9th Cir.2000) (where manager of storage lockers facility, upon defendant's failure to pay rental, opened defendant's locker and then opened footlockers therein with intent to sell contents and then found suspicious items and summoned ATF agent, agent's warrantless search of lockers after taking possession of them permissible "to the extent that it mimicked the private search conducted by the manager"); United States v. Knoll, 16 F.3d 1313 (2d Cir.1994) (where private persons stole boxes of papers from attorney's office and then searched through some of the papers and turned them over to prosecutor, prosecutor's examination of them no search; but if other papers later turned over from same burglary had not been examined by private persons until prosecutor, knowing of burglary and that it included other documents, expressed need for more information, then that examination was not private and thus *Walter* rather than *Jacobsen* applies); People v. Clendenin, 238 Ill.2d 302, 345 Ill.Dec. 467, 939 N.E.2d 310 (2010) (police search did not exceed private search, as private party took defendant's computer disc to her own home and "in addition to viewing a video file containing apparent child pornography, she also searched the disc widely enough to discover several file names * * * suggestive of child pornography," and police looked at other files but did not "search[ ] anywhere on the disc that by its file name likely would not contain child pornography"); People v. Phillips, 215 Ill.2d 554, 294 Ill.Dec. 624, 831 N.E.2d 574 (2005) (where computer repairman opened a.mpg file and found child pornography and then summoned police and showed them same file, fact the police thereby "learn[ed] with more precision what the video depicted did not take them beyond the scope of [the repairman's] search"); State v. Gentry, 462 So.2d 624 (La.1985) (no search where police reopened package agents of private shipping company had previously opened); State v. Rivera, 148 N.M. 659, 241 P.3d 1099 (2010) (where private citizen opened "a sealed container that contained a toolbox holding several opaque bundles" but "did not open any of the opaque bundles," officer aware of private search reopened the container and then cut open an opaque bundle, this deemed within *Jacobsen*, a "de minimis" expansion of the private search "in light of the certainty of the contents," but contrary result then reached as matter of state constitutional law); Hill v. State, 764 P.2d 210 (Okl.Crim.App. 1988) (where airline employee removed from luggage accidentally broken open a small amount of a suspicious substance, turning it over to DEA agent no search, as agent "did not exceed the scope of the 'antecedent private search' "); State v. Luman, 347 Or. 487, 223 P.3d 1041 (2009) (where employees of defendant, restaurant owner, played his videotape showing he taped activity in women's restroom, and then turned tape over to police, police viewing unobjectionable, as "private parties, not state actors, first viewed the videotape and then, on their own initiative, brought it to the sheriff's office"); State v. Thunder, 777 N.W.2d 373 (S.D.2010) (where defendant's family members viewed child porn on cell phone defendant left behind on moving out and then turned the phone over to police, under *Jacobsen* police viewing of same pictures unobjectionable).

Compare United States v. Rouse, 148 F.3d 1040 (8th Cir.1998) (where airline employee opened bag and found number of identification cards and blank social security cards and then called police, who searched same bag and found those items plus a laminating machine and material for laminating cards, latter items were discovered in a government search, as there "no evidence that these items were in plain view when the officers arrived or that [the airline employee] had discovered them prior to that time").

the meaning of the Fourth Amendment." (The Court added that there *had* been a seizure of the package when the agent asserted dominion and control over it, but this was deemed a reasonable seizure given the fact that "it was apparent that the tube and plastic bags contained contraband and little else.")

Especially because three members of the Court rejected Justice Stevens' no-search conclusion, reasoning instead that if "the evidence or contraband is not in plain view and not in a container that clearly announces its contents at the end of a private search,[87] the government's subsequent examination of the previously searched object necessarily constitutes an independent, governmental search that infringes Fourth Amendment privacy interests,"[88] it is necessary to look more closely at the majority's reasoning. Justice Stevens asserted that the majority's

> standard follows from the analysis applicable when private parties reveal other kinds of private information to the authorities. It is well-settled that when an individual reveals private information to another, he assumes the risk that his confidant will reveal that information to the authorities, and if that occurs the Fourth Amendment does not prohibit governmental use of that information. Once frustration of the original expectation of privacy occurs, the Fourth Amendment does not prohibit governmental use of the now-nonprivate information * * *.[89]

But this analogy is less than perfect. As Justice White pointed out, the line of authority referred to merely allows police to make use of confidences revealed to them by third parties, and the Court has "never intimated until now that an individual who

---

[87] If the evidence *is* in such a container, this will provide a basis for the government agent doing more than the private searcher earlier did. See, e.g., United States v. Bowman, 907 F.2d 63 (8th Cir.1990) (private search into suitcase uncovered 5 identical bundles, first of which was opened, revealing white powder; federal agent, upon determining this was cocaine, could open the other 4 bundles without a warrant, as the "presence of the cocaine in the exposed bundle' 'spoke volumes as to [the] contents [of the remaining bundles]' ").

[88] White, J., concurring. Brennan and Marshall, JJ., dissenting, agreed with Justice White "that the Court has expanded the reach of the private-search doctrine far beyond its logical bounds."

[89] Of course, the defendant may sometimes not have any "original expectation of privacy" in the object to start with, in which case the police may examine it to a greater extent than did the private person who turned it over to the police. See United States v. Felton, 753 F.2d 256 (3d Cir.1985) (where one member of conspiracy taped his conversations with others and a private person took the tapes from the first individual and turned them over to police, under *Jacobsen* the police needed no warrant to listen to the tapes, as the other participants in the tape recording, the defendants here, had no expectation of privacy in them); State v. Flynn, 360 N.W.2d 762 (Iowa 1985) (when defendant left tapes under tarpaulin on peat moss pile at country club and private person took them and turned them over to police, police could play the tapes without a warrant, as defendant's "choice of the peat moss pile as the temporary location for his records, gave rise to no constitutionally protected privacy right").

reveals that he stores contraband in a particular container or location to an acquaintance who later betrays his confidence has no expectation of privacy in that container or location and that the police may thus search it without a warrant." If, he added, a person could lose his expectation of privacy in the contents of a container in the instant circumstances, then it would seem to follow that the same would be true when the police are told of the contents by one who was present when contraband was placed in the container, when contraband was exposed when yet another person opened the container, or when the owner stated the container had contraband in it.[90]

Most certainly those and similar circumstances should not be characterized as situations in which there exists no legitimate expectation of privacy in the contents of the container, and thus one might doubt whether *Jacobsen* was rightly decided. But Justice Stevens clearly did not intend such a broad rule, as is reflected by his assertion that the instant case is distinguishable "from one in which the police simply learn from a private party that a container contains contraband, seize it from its owner, and conduct a warrantless search." The present case is different, he added, because "the Federal Express employees who were lawfully in possession of the package invited the agent to examine its contents; the governmental conduct was made possible only because private parties had compromised the integrity of this container."[91]

Exactly why it is different is not easy to articulate, which perhaps is why the *Jacobsen* analysis is somewhat unsettling and hard to judge. Justice White is certainly correct in saying that the Court's conclusion "cannot rest on the proposition that the owner no longer has a subjective expectation of privacy since a person's expectation of privacy cannot be altered by subsequent events of which he was unaware." For precisely this reason,

---

[90]Consider United States v. Martin, 157 F.3d 46 (2d Cir.1998) (where person told police defendant was shipping him stolen goods via UPS and government claims warrantless inspection of that package would be justified under *Jacobsen*, court says because "UPS did not open the package or invite the police to examine its contents," "we are aware of no case that would extend *Jacobsen* to justify a warrantless search under these circumstances," but because there was a valid search warrant court "need not decide" that point).

[91]The *dissent* in United States v. Oliver, 630 F.3d 397 (5th Cir.2011), relied upon that language in concluding that, "under *Jacobsen*, the private search doctrine applies only when a private search is followed by an individual's disclosures to police about that search." The majority, on the other hand, upheld under *Jacobsen* a search of defendant's cardboard box, which he had left with his girl friend, who turned it over to police, even though the police were unaware of her previous search of that box. The majority concluded "that the initial private search, which was reasonably foreseeable, and the searcher's act, later that day, of voluntarily giving authorities the box, in which no reasonable expectation of privacy remained, rendered the subsequent police search permissible."

Justice Stevens' use of "assumption of risk" terminology here is not particularly helpful. But in determining whether a Fourth Amendment search has occurred, the more fundamental question is whether there has been an intrusion upon a privacy expectation "that society is prepared to recognize as 'reasonable.' "[92] It just may be that society is *not* prepared to so recognize the expectation existing in a *Jacobsen*-type situation. After all, if the private searcher had simply left the container unwrapped, then the police scrutiny would have implicated no Fourth Amendment interests. Similarly, if the private person had first opened (or reopened) the container while the police were standing by, then again as a general matter it may be said that there is no Fourth Amendment interest infringed by police observation of that process.[93] Because the private person *could* have done either of these, and most certainly *would* have done so had he had any inkling this would be necessary to ensure that his efforts to report criminal activity could be promptly acted upon by the police, it would seem strange if a different result were required as a Fourth Amendment matter simply because the private person happened to do some repackaging before the appearance of the police.

Given the fact that the private person had already breached the privacy of the package under circumstances where Fourth Amendment restraints are not applicable, and given also the other essential fact in Justice Stevens' rule—that the private person had "invited the agent to examine its contents," it is difficult to accept that person's repackaging as somehow restoring an aura of privacy to the contents of the package when, as Justice Stevens also requires, that person is still "lawfully in possession of the package." At the nub of *Jacobsen,* then, may be the feeling, as revealed in a footnote in the majority opinion, that cases of this kind ought not "turn on the fortuity" of whether and to what extent the private person put the contents back into the container before the police appeared. But this is not to suggest that any police activity to recover what a private searcher earlier discovered falls outside the Fourth Amendment merely because the private person *could* have—but, perhaps by a fortuity, didn't—simply seize the evidence and hand it over to the police. For example, it is to be doubted that if a private person searched the premises of another and then reported to police what he had found (instead of removing the evidence and handing it over to the police), that the police could then make a warrantless entry of those premises and seize the named evidence,[94] but there is authority to the

---

[92]See § 2.1(d).

[93]See cases in note 73 supra.

[94]United States v. Young, 573 F.3d 711 (9th Cir.2009) (following *Allen*, infra, in refusing "to expand *Ja-* *cobsen*'s decision to warrantless searches of private residences," especially since here "neither the hotel room nor the backpack" previously searched by hotel employees "con-

contrary.[95]

___

tained only contraband"); United States v. Williams, 354 F.3d 497 (6th Cir.2003) (*Allen*, infra, correct; court there "not obliged to adhere to [earlier] dicta," considering earlier decision's "failure to make any real distinction between a federal express package and a home, which is entitled to significantly more protection"); United States v. Allen, 106 F.3d 695 (6th Cir.1997) (court rejects government's argument "that the police officer's warrantless search of Allen's motel room was not illegal because it did not exceed in scope the initial private search conducted by the motel manager," stating it "is unwilling to extend the holding in *Jacobsen* to cases involving private searches of residences"); People v. Brewer, 690 P.2d 860 (Colo.1984) (landlord found marijuana in apartment and summoned police into apartment, where they seized marijuana; State's reliance on *Jacobsen* rejected, as notwithstanding the landlord's earlier discovery the expectation of privacy in the apartment remained); State v. Miggler, 419 N.W.2d 81 (Minn. App.1988) (*Jacobsen* distinguished on grounds that police entered house of suspect to reenact search conducted by private individual); State v. Barkmeyer, 949 A.2d 984 (R.I.2008) (where child's grandfather found rope in closet of child's stepfather, so "the rope was found during a private search," subsequent entry by police to recover the rope "requires analysis beyond the law of private search," but was lawful because of householder's consent); State v. Eisfeldt, 163 Wash.2d 628, 185 P.3d 580 (2008) (notwithstanding fact private contractor doing work in defendant's home looked in garbage bag therein and found marijuana, police entry to retrieve same a government search, unlawful because contractor without authority to consent to such entry). Indeed, even if the first viewing had been by the police themselves during lawful entry, there is "no general rule that officials can then reenter without a warrant simply to seize contraband or evidence that was seen in plain view during the orig-

inal entry." Bilida v. McCleod, 211 F.3d 166 (1st Cir.2000).

A more limited approach was taken in United States v. Roberts, 644 F.2d 683 (8th Cir.1980). Employees of a company that rented out storage units found units at two separate locations unlocked with broken padlocks nearby, so they entered and found marijuana, and then closed the units and summoned police, who entered the units and seized the marijuana. The court held that at the location where the company's employees had not secured the premises with the purpose of preventing access by the lessee, the seizure was by the police and was unlawful because without a warrant; but at the location where the employees had kept the premises guarded until the police arrived the court concluded "that the drugs stored [there] had been seized privately before the arrival of the officers, and that the district court erred in suppressing evidence based on that seizure." Three of the 7 judges dissented, noting that if this distinction made sense then if a hotel guest left his key with the desk clerk and the clerk then decided to hold the key until the police could be admitted to the room, that action would constitute a private seizure shielding the later police action.

[95]Some pre-*Jacobsen* cases applied to premises searches the notion that "a police view subsequent to a search conducted by private citizens does not constitute a 'search' within the meaning of the Fourth Amendment so long as the view is confined to the scope and product of the initial search." It was utilized in United States v. Bomengo, 580 F.2d 173 (5th Cir.1978), to support the questionable conclusion that no governmental search has occurred when a police officer was called into an apartment to view evidence of crime discovered by the chief engineer of the apartment complex, who had entered earlier to locate the source of a water leak. Similar to *Bomengo* is Lucas v. State, 381 So.2d 140 (Miss.1980) (victim of burglary obtained consent to search neigh-

Another branch of the *Jacobsen* case has to do with the agent's actions after reopening the package in subjecting the white powder to a field test revealing it was in fact cocaine. All members of the Court agreed that, assuming lawful access to the powder, this testing was lawful, but there was not agreement as to why this was so. Seven Justices took the view that this was no search either because a "chemical test that merely discloses whether or not a particular substance is cocaine does not compromise any legitimate interest in privacy." This conclusion, the Court added, was dictated by the holding a year earlier in *United States v.*

bor's apartment and found his property there, after which he summoned officer who accompanied him on second search with consent; held: "Even if Hooker was acting as an agent for the police on the second visit, that search could not constitute a 'search' within the meaning of the Fourth Amendment, so long as the view was confined to the scope and product of the first search").

See also the post-*Jacobsen* cases of United States v. Jones, 421 F.3d 359 (5th Cir.2005) (where manager of apartment building lawfully entered unit with pest exterminator and, upon seeing what appeared to be drug paraphernalia, left and then asked policeman to accompany her upon her reentry, where officer observed same objects, officer's actions upheld under *Jacobsen*, but court in footnote also notes district court emphasized that policeman entered "in the company of a private citizen who had the right to enter"); United States v. Miller, 152 F.3d 813 (8th Cir.1998) (when supervisor entered defendant's apartment at halfway house for adults with mental diseases and saw evidence of drug activity and then changed lock to keep defendant out and called and admitted police, court concludes that "application of *Jacobsen*'s private search rule here is as straightforward as the rule itself" and that consequently there was no search; without either adopting or rejecting *Paige* limitation, court concludes that police entry proper here because, in the language of *Paige*, "the private party's intrusion was reasonably foreseeable"); United States v. Paige, 136 F.3d 1012 (5th Cir.1998) (court says it agrees with the

decision in *Allen*, note 94 supra, "not to extend *Jacobsen*'s holding to cases involving private searches of residences," but then tries to accommodate that conclusion with its prior *Bomengo* decision, supra, by then holding that a subsequent police entry is no search if the prior private person entry was "reasonably foreseeable"); United States v. Clutter, 914 F.2d 775 (6th Cir.1990) (though court rightly concludes valid third party consent to search, court then unwisely states as "an alternative theory" the notion that because private persons cooperating with the police had searched the bedroom of another in their home and found marijuana, which they reported to the police, that a police search in that bedroom was no search under *Jacobsen* because the officer "learned nothing as the result of his own conduct that he had not already heard about as a result of the private search"); State v. Miller, 110 Nev. 690, 877 P.2d 1044 (1994) (where babysitter found what she thought was illegal drugs and police then entered and followed her to bedroom and found the drugs there, this treated as only a private search under *Jacobsen*, strong dissent objects that "any time a private citizen fortuitously discovers evidence of contraband at another's home, they are not free to invite police in for a romp around the connubial bed"); Peters v. State, 302 S.C. 59, 393 S.E.2d 387 (1990) (private person told police she saw LSD in sister's house and then, at police request, returned there and conducted a "re-search of the area" and "retrieval of a small amount of LSD," latter deemed lawful on a *Jacobsen*-style theory).

Place[96] that a canine sniff is no search. (The Court added that this testing did not broaden the earlier seizure to an unreasonable extent,[97] given that it was "virtually certain that the substance tested was in fact contraband" and that "only a trace" of the substance was consumed in the test.[98]) The other two

---

[96]United States v. Place, 462 U.S. 696, 103 S.Ct. 2637, 77 L.Ed.2d 110 (1983), discussed in § 2.2(g).

[97]See also United States v. Kinney, 953 F.2d 863 (4th Cir.1992) (private party revealed guns in closet to police, who checked serial numbers and determined one stolen; court holds there "no analytically significant reason to view the recording of gun serial numbers in the present case any differently from the drug field test in *Jacobsen*," as it only determined "whether the guns were contraband"); United States v. Duchi, 906 F.2d 1278 (8th Cir.1990) (officers' removal of substance for testing "did not materially exceed the scope of the private search"; court stresses that in *Jacobsen* "that removal was arguably even more intrusive: there a plastic bag was opened to reach the suspicious substance, here once the clear outer layers of wrapping were removed, an existing tear in the inner wrapping allowed the officers access to the substance"); State v. Rode, 456 N.W.2d 769 (N.D.1990) (although the white powder contents of the open package were taken to another location for testing as cocaine, *Jacobsen* rather than *VonBulow* and *Mulder* governs, as neither "the complexity of the test [n]or any delays in the process significantly expanded the scope of the private search"); Commonwealth v. Harris, 572 Pa. 489, 817 A.2d 1033 (2002) (where Mathias opened letters to his sister, sent by defendant, and then photocopied them before forwarding letters to sister and gave photocopies to police, police reading of same "was not an unlawful warrantless search under *Walter* and *Jacobsen*," as "far from exceeding the scope of the antecedent private search here, the reading of the copies of the letters was less intrusive than Mathias' conduct in opening the letters addressed to his sister and copying them");

State v. Loveland, 2005 SD 48, 696 N.W.2d 164 (S.D. 2005) (where sample of bodily fluids was lawfully acquired for one purpose, also testing it for cocaine is no search, as there was no exposure of noncontraband items); State v. Price, 270 P.3d 527 (Utah 2012) (following *Loveland*, supra, on similar facts).

[98]Compare the celebrated case of State v. von Bulow, 475 A.2d 995 (R.I. 1984), where without a warrant police subjected to substantial laboratory testing certain pills turned over to them by private persons. The court, in holding this was an illegal search, distinguished *Jacobsen* on these grounds: (i) the testing "occurred, not in the field immediately following a lawful private search, but rather in the state toxicology laboratory one week after its delivery to the State Police"; (ii) the "tests positively identified the exact chemical composition of a myriad of substances whose identities were previously unknown to the state"; (iii) the substances were "clearly not discovered in such a condition * * * as would make it a virtual certainty 'that [they] contained nothing but contraband'"; and (iv) there "is no evidence in the record to indicate that the State Police knew that these substances were unlawfully in the possession of defendant prior to the time that they were delivered to the State Police."

Compare also United States v. Paige, 136 F.3d 1012 (5th Cir.1998) (after nonsearch discovery of packages of marijuana in attic of defendant's garage, police "seized to haul away" the marijuana; such action not authorized by *Jacobsen*, as the seizure there "was designed only to be a temporary one for the purpose of investigating, seizing, and testing the package's contents," while "in the instant case was intended to be the permanent seizure from the outset"; seizure then upheld

members of the Court,[99] understandably fearful the now-expanding *Place* principle—"that a surveillance technique does not constitute a search if it reveals only whether or not an individual possesses contraband"—could result in wholesale and random use of dogs and other such surveillance techniques, took a different approach. They reasoned that because it was "inconceivable that a legal substance would be packaged in this manner for transport by a common carrier," there was such "virtual certainty" of the powder's identity that "it was essentially as though the chemical identity of the powder was plainly visible," and thus there existed "no reasonable expectation of privacy in the identity of the powder."[100]

If the police action in *Jacobsen* was lawful because it did not significantly exceed the scope of the private search, then what other investigative actions deserve a like characterization? That was the question explored in *United States v. Runyan,*[101] where a most interesting set of facts necessitated a careful examination of that issue, as to which the court found "a remarkable dearth of federal jurisprudence." Runyan's estranged wife entered his ranch with friends in his absence to remove her personal effects. One friend dismantled a desktop computer she claimed as hers, and in removing it also took several CDs, ZIP disks and floppy disks found lying nearby. When the computer was reassembled at the wife's current residence, that friend viewed approximately 20 CDs and floppy disks and found that they contained images of child pornography. That friend then turned over to the sheriff's office 22 CDs, 10 ZIP files, and 11 floppy disks, the contents of which were thereafter examined by the authorities. The *Runyan*

---

under plain view doctrine, as here "a further search of the packages to verify their contents was unnecessary"); United States v. Mulder, 808 F.2d 1346 (9th Cir.1987) (involving private search of defendant's luggage uncovering plastic bags apparently containing drugs, which were turned over to federal agents who sent the material to a lab for testing; court concluded "facts here are sufficiently different from those in *Jacobsen* that we do not believe its 'field test' exception to the warrant requirement can be extended to the case at bar. First of all, this case does not involve a field test, but a series of tests conducted in a toxicology laboratory several days after the tablets were seized. Secondly, the chemical testing in this case was not a field test which could merely disclose whether or not the substance was a particular substance, but was a series of tests designed to reveal the molecular structure of a substance and indicate precisely what it is. Because of the greater sophistication of these tests, they could have revealed an arguably private fact"). *Mulder* was distinguished in United States v. Pierce, 893 F.2d 669 (5th Cir.1990) (field test identifying substance as cocaine, conducted before a small sample was then sent on for further analysis; because "agents had already identified the substance as cocaine * * * Pierce no longer had a protectable privacy interest in the identity of the substance when it was sent for in-depth testing").

[99] Brennan and Marshall, JJ.

[100] For more on this "virtual certainty" approach, see § 7.2(d).

[101] United States v. Runyan, 275 F.3d 449 (5th Cir.2001).

court thus found it necessary to address two questions:

"(1) whether a police search exceeds the scope of a private search when private searchers examine selected items from a collection of similar closed containers and police searchers subsequently examine the entire collection." Noting that under the analysis in *Jacobsen* it appears that "confirmation of prior knowledge does not constitute exceeding the scope of a private search," the *Runyan* court quite correctly concluded that the guideline that emerges as to this situation "is that the police exceed the scope of a prior private search when they examine a closed container that was not opened by the private searchers unless the police are already substantially certain of what is inside that container based on the statements of the private searchers, their replication of the private search, and their expertise." Thus where an airline employee opened an unclaimed suitcase and found five identical bundles therein, opened one and summoned a federal narcotics agent who identified the contents as a kilo brick of cocaine and then proceeded to open the other bundles, the agent acted lawfully because the presence of cocaine in the exposed bundle " 'spoke volumes as to [the] contents [of the remaining bundles], particularly to the trained eye of the officer.' "[102] By comparison, in the instant case the police examination of disks the private party had not earlier examined was not lawful, for the mere fact those disks had also been found in Runyan's residence was "insufficient to establish with substantial certainty that all of the storage media in question contained child pornography."

"(2) whether a police search exceeds the scope of the private search when the police examine more items within a particular container than did the private searchers." The court in *Runyan* answered this question in the negative, and thus held that the police in that case did not exceed the scope of the private search when they examined more files on each of the disks than did the private searchers. It is certainly open to question whether the *Runyan* court was correct on this branch of the case.[103] The court claimed that it had "adopted the logic" of *United States v. Simp-*

---

[102]United States v. Bowman, 907 F.2d 63 (8th Cir.1990), quoting *Jacobsen*. Consider also United States v. Garcia-Bercovich, 582 F.3d 1234 (11th Cir.2009) (where 13 boxes "were shrink-wrapped together on a single pallet and covered by a single shipping manifest," this properly deemed "all one package," so that "once one box was permissibly opened [by private party], the other boxes could also be searched as part of that same 'pack-

age' ").

[103]For other telling criticism of this aspect of *Runyan* and other discussion of this kind of issue in computer search cases, see Clancy, The Fourth Amendment Aspects of Computer Searches and Seizures: A Perspective and a Primer, 75 Miss.L.J. 193, 236–43 (2005); Kerr, Searches and Seizures in a Digital World, 119 Harv.L.Rev. 531, 554–56 (2005).

son,[104] said to be "that the police do not exceed the scope of a prior private search when they examine the same materials that were examined by the police private searchers, but they examine these materials more thoroughly than did the private parties." The facts of *Simpson* are that FedEx investigators opened a box, determined that the magazines therein contained child pornography, and then played four of the tapes therein and determined that they appeared also to involve child pornography, after which an FBI agent and assistant U.S. attorney viewed *the very same* magazines and videotapes, and the court's holding in that case was that the latter viewing "did not exceed the scope of the prior private searches for Fourth Amendment purposes simply because they took more time and were more thorough than the Federal Express agents." But the police in *Runyan* opened up files on privately-examined disks that the private searcher had not even opened, which seems quite unlike the situation in *Simpson* and more analogous to *United States v. Rouse*.[105] In *Rouse*, an airline employee opened a bag, found a number of identification cards and blank social security cards, and thus summoned a police officer, who searched the bag further and found a laminating machine and material for laminating cards. These latter items were subject to suppression, the court concluded, because they were neither in "plain view" of the officer nor discovered in the prior private search, and thus it could not be said (in the language of *Jacobsen*) that defendant's expectation of privacy had "already been frustrated." Such analysis is especially compelling, and the *Runyan* rule is most clearly inadequate, in those cases where the "container" in question (e.g., a computer or a filing cabinet) is filled with many items, only a few of which the private searcher examined.[106]

Before leaving *Walter* and *Jacobsen,* it must be emphasized that the issues in those cases concerning what the police may do with materials to which their attention has been directed by private individuals are difficult ones precisely because of the private parties' limited connection with the materials in those cases—*Walter,* again, concerned the recipient of a mistaken delivery; *Jacobsen,* a common carrier. Thus, those decisions cast

---

[104]United States v. Simpson, 904 F.2d 607 (11th Cir.1990).

[105]United States v. Rouse, 148 F.3d 1040 (8th Cir.1998).

[106]Nonetheless, this second holding in *Runyan* was specifically relied upon in United States v. Slanina, 283 F.3d 670 (5th Cir.2002), where the earlier nonpolice search by one Keller was of a "computer and the zip disk," and the later FBI search was "of the same materials even though the FBI may have looked at more files than Keller."

Compare also United States v. Oliver, 630 F.3d 397 (5th Cir.2011) (where prior private search of defendant's cardboard box did not extend to notebook therein, police search of notebook upheld on theory that "the notebook's contents were obvious" given the writing on the cover and a piece of paper with fraud victim's name protruding from side of notebook).

no doubt upon the proposition that police may examine materials received from private parties well beyond what the private parties themselves have theretofore done when the person handing over those materials has lawfully consented to such examination. Illustrative is *Ex parte Hilley,*[107] where, after suspicion developed that defendant might have been responsible for the arsenic poisoning of her husband and daughter, the husband's sister took to police certain effects belonging to the defendant which had been left in the sister's basement and at another location under the partial control of the sister. The police tested the substances found in these effects and discovered some of it was arsenic, but defendant challenged the admissibility of that analysis under the *Walter* rule. The court responded: "In the present case, [the sister] had the authority to possess and control the items and could rightfully consent to a complete scientific analysis, whereas, the third party in *Walter* never had rightful possession or control of the pornographic films involved in that case and could not properly consent to an expansive search of them." In other words, when one subjects her property to the joint or exclusive control of another, she has thereby assumed the risk that the other person will turn that property over to the police and will allow the police to examine it further.[108] (It is also true that the *Walter-Jacobsen* limitation on testing is inapplicable where no private person is involved and the police themselves initially made a lawful intrusion upon the privacy interests of the owner of the effects in question.[109])

The potential reach of the general rule that police participation

---

[107]Ex parte Hilley, 484 So.2d 485 (Ala.1985).

[108]See also United States v. Jenkins, 46 F.3d 447 (5th Cir.1995) (*Walter* limitations not applicable in instant case, as there "FBI obtained the films from a third party who had no actual or apparent authority over the packages," while here "the government obtained the videotapes from Boyd, a third party who not only had lawful possession of the packages, but who had the actual authority to open the boxes, and, at minimum, apparent authority to view the films," and thus police could play the tapes without a warrant because of Boyd's consent); Lee v. State, 849 N.E.2d 602 (Ind.2006) (where defendant and his fiancé lived together in house and she viewed 2 or 3 tapes in box and then turned over 16 tapes to police, police viewing of other tapes no violation of *Walter-Jacobsen*, as she had authority to

consent as to all the tapes).

But see State v. von Bulow, 475 A.2d 995 (R.I.1984), discussed in note 98 supra, which the court in *Hilley* deemed not controlling.

[109]Illustrative is State v. Moretti, 521 A.2d 1003 (R.I.1987), involving laboratory testing of carpet samples and similar items lawfully seized in a post-fire inspection of burned premises. The court reasoned that the two Supreme Court decisions "recognize that a remaining interest in privacy can exist when objects are seized during private searches and then given to law enforcement officials. We do not, however, recognize remaining privacy interests in objects seized pursuant to a validly executed warrant, nor do we see reason to recognize remaining privacy interests in objects seized during a warrantless search that is completely valid because of some recognized exception to the warrant

in the search makes the search governmental is illustrated by *Corngold v. United States*.[110] After holding that the search of a package placed with TWA could not be justified on the ground of the airline's authority to inspect packages to insure that the proper rate was charged, given the fact that the airline agent had testified that his only reason for opening the package was the request of a customs' agent, the court then set forth an alternative ground:

> But the evidence would be excludable in the present case even if the TWA employee had not acted solely to satisfy the government's interest in viewing the contents of the package, but instead had initiated and participated in the search for reasons contemplated by the inspection clause in TWA's tariff. The customs agents joined actively in the search. They held open the flaps of the large package; removed, opened, and inspected the contents of the small boxes which it contained; and marked the small boxes for future identification. Thus, at the very least, the search of appellant's package was a joint operation of the customs agents and the TWA employee. When a federal agent participates in such a joint endeavor, "the effect is the same as though he had engaged in the undertaking as one exclusively his own."[111]

Corngold appears to stand for the proposition, then, that participation by a government agent makes the search governmental in nature, so as to bring the Fourth Amendment into play, without regard to the purpose for which the search was undertaken.[112] But, should this necessarily be so? What, for example, if the private person had already determined to make a search for a lawful purpose, but then summoned the police for assistance? Such was the situation in *United States v. Capra*,[113] where a baggage agent at a railroad terminal, concerned about a suitcase that had not been claimed for about a week (contrary to

---

requirement. * * * No principle of constitutional law requires any law enforcement official to obtain a warrant prior to testing any item seized during a valid search. To hold otherwise in this case would be effectively to neutralize the power of the governmental fire inspector, who was expected by his or her employer to determine the cause and origin of fires occurring within the inspector's area of responsibility and to prevent them in the future."

[110]Corngold v. United States, 367 F.2d 1 (9th Cir.1966).

[111]The language quoted at the end is from Byars v. United States, 273 U.S. 28, 47 S.Ct. 248, 71 L.Ed. 520 (1927), a pre-*Elkins* case declining to apply the "silver platter" doctrine where federal agents participated in a state search, a situation which does not necessarily provide a perfect analogy to that under discussion here.

[112]Which, of course makes it critical to determine what amounts to participation. Compare State v. Blackshear, 14 Or.App. 247, 511 P.2d 1272 (1973), where an airline agent summoned a member of the airport police (rather than his supervisor, who was busy) to act as a witness during search of luggage, which was held to be a private search because "the officer had no part in the search of the luggage except observing it."

[113]United States v. Capra, 372 F.Supp. 603 (S.D.N.Y.1973), aff'd on ground defendant lacked standing, 501 F.2d 267 (2d Cir.1974).

the usual practice of checking luggage for just a few hours), sought police assistance in opening the case after his own efforts were unsuccessful. Given the fact that the search "was undertaken by private persons acting upon private suspicions touching legitimate concerns of their own and their employer," and that the occasion for police presence "was primarily service to those who had enlisted their aid rather than the pursuit or detection of criminals," the court concluded that this was a private search notwithstanding the possibility the police "were prepared to be interested in evidence of criminal misconduct."[114] It is interesting to note that the *Capra* court relied upon *Cady v. Dombrowski*,[115] where the Supreme Court indicates that in assessing the reasonableness of the conduct of local police, account must be taken of the fact that they must perform functions "totally divorced from the detection, investigation, or acquisition of evidence relating to the violation of a criminal statute." This would suggest that the *Capra* court may have reached the proper result, but upon somewhat faulty reasoning. Instead of struggling to

---

[114]See also United States v. Howard, 752 F.2d 220 (6th Cir.1985), reasoning adopted en banc 770 F.2d 57 (6th Cir.1985) (where "insurance company investigator was rightfully on the property to determine the liability of the insurance company," and "there is no question that the government had knowledge of, and even participated in the search," evidence found by the investigator rather than police admissible, as he not an agent of police when lawfully on the property pursuing a legitimate private purpose); United States v. Gomez, 614 F.2d 643 (9th Cir.1979) (officer was present when airline supervisor opened suitcase that fell off conveyor and was without identification, and officer tapped lock to release it for supervisor; held, "we are not inclined to hold that this slight 'participation' by the officer converted the clearly private search into a governmental one" where the supervisor's motivation was to identify the owner of the luggage); United States v. Pryba, 502 F.2d 391 (D.C.Cir.1974) (FBI agent supplied projector with which air freight employee viewed shipped films; held, this "limited role in the airport inspection of the box in question did not activate the Fourth Amendment"); Maciejack v. State, 273 Ind. 408, 404 N.E.2d 7 (1980) (fire insurance company investigator Kramer called on police and fire

department before visiting the burned premises and was accompanied there by representatives of the departments; this still a private search, as "there is nothing to indicate that it was their investigation, as opposed to his" and it "was logical" for him to begin with the public authorities who had completed their investigation and to "want the police to know who he was and why he was on the premises of another"); State v. Miesbauer, 232 Kan. 291, 654 P.2d 934 (1982) (while sheriff present outside missing woman's home at time foul play not suspected, concerned relative entered the home with help of locksmith summoned by sheriff); State v. Kumpula, 355 N.W.2d 697 (Minn. 1984) (where frightened caretaker had policeman accompany him as he exercised his right under the lease to inspect premises, no governmental search except to extent that officer, once present, did some searching on his own).

Again, such cases are to be distinguished from those in which there was government assistance and, in addition, government instigation, as in United States v. Souza, 223 F.3d 1197 (10th Cir.2000), note 58 supra.

[115]Cady v. Dombrowski, 413 U.S. 433, 93 S.Ct. 2523, 37 L.Ed.2d 706 (1973).

find a basis for saying that a police detective's actions in picking a suitcase lock was not government conduct, it would be better to conclude that there *was* a government search, albeit one that was reasonable in light of the purposes for which it was undertaken, as in *Cady*.[116]

§ 1.8(c) Other pre-search government encouragement

Generally, it may be said that other pre-search contacts between a government official and private citizen, whether or not apparently intended by the former to prompt the latter to render some type of assistance, are not deemed sufficient to make a search by the private citizen other than a "private" search.[117] There are a few exceptions, most significantly when the contacts have been similar to those that occur when a particular policeman asks a particular individual to conduct a search. Thus, where the police have made a general appeal to the public at large to make a citizen's arrest of a specified person for murder, the arrest and incidental search conducted by a group of private citizens in response to this appeal is quite properly deemed to be governmental.[118] Likewise, where the government actually requires[119] that private parties conduct searches under certain specified circumstances, as with the pre-9/11 hijacker detection

---

[116]State v. Morris, 42 Ohio St.2d 307, 329 N.E.2d 85 (1975), involved the very same search. Although this court also concluded that "the search in question was a private search," much of the court's reasoning is instead directed to the conclusion, by analogy to *Cady*, that the search was a reasonable one because it "amounted to what has been described as a community caretaking function."

[Section 1.8(c)]

[117]See, e.g., State v. Wall, 154 N.H. 237, 910 A.2d 1253 (2006) ("A conclusion that an agency relationship existed between the government and a private individual requires proof of an affirmative act by a state official prior to the search or seizure that can reasonably be seen to have induced the search or seizure by the private party," not so here as to taking of blood sample by hospital staff, as officer did not request that sample be taken and did no more than direct ambulance driver to take defendant to that hospital).

[118]Thacker v. Commonwealth, 310 Ky. 702, 221 S.W.2d 682 (1949).

[119]Compare United States v.

Young, 153 F.3d 1079 (9th Cir.1998) (though 14 C.F.R. § 109 requires carriers to adopt a security program, it "does not require carriers to search packages" and does not involve "extensive federal involvement in the design, development and implementation of an elaborate security program," and there "no evidence in this record of federal involvement in the design, development and implementation of the FedEx security program"); United States v. Gumerlock, 590 F.2d 794 (9th Cir.1979) (panel decision that airline search of freight governmental under Air Transportation Security Act rejected, as Act and accompanying regulations do not require carriers to adopt any particular procedure with respect to cargo and does not require inspection of cargo, it not shown airline adopted any security procedures because of the Act, and searching agent said he searched pursuant to tariff provision allowing but not requiring inspection). To the same effect are United States v. Andrews, 618 F.2d 646 (10th Cir.1980); United States v. Rodriguez, 596 F.2d 169 (6th Cir. 1979).

Also compare Gilmore v. Enogex, Inc., 878 P.2d 360 (Okl.1994) (drug

system, and a search is undertaken pursuant to those government regulations rather than for some private purpose,[120] it is again correct to characterize the search as being governmental in character.[121] On the other hand, the fact that statutes or govern-

---

testing of employees by regulated monopoly not state action, as its "involvement with the state and federal government is confined to the area of rate regulation and to matters directly related to the operation of its pipelines"); Ohio Domestic Violence Network v. Public Utilities Comm'n, 70 Ohio St.3d 311, 638 N.E.2d 1012 (1994) (commission's approval of caller identification service sought by telephone company not sufficient to make such service state action, as "mere approval of or acquiescence in the initiatives of a private party is not sufficient to justify holding the state responsible for those initiatives").

[120]United States v. Ogden, 485 F.2d 536 (9th Cir.1973) (distinguishing the *Davis* case, note 120 infra, in that the search in the instant case extended beyond that contemplated by the government-regulated hijacker detection system); Snyder v. State, 585 P.2d 229 (Alaska 1978) (Air Transportation Security Act did not make airline search of freight governmental; "there is no indication that Powledge's search was for weapons, explosives, or other destructive substances, and we do not believe the statutory authority to search for such substances automatically causes searches for other airline purposes to be governmental activity"); State v. Pohle, 166 N.J.Super. 504, 400 A.2d 109 (1979).

[121]United States v. Davis, 482 F.2d 893 (9th Cir.1973), holding a search of carry-on luggage to be governmental because it was "part of a nationwide anti-hijacking program conceived, directed, and implemented by federal officials in cooperation with air carriers." The court noted that the government had "significantly involved itself" in airport searches by developing a hijacker detection profile and a system using the profile and magnetometer, by the 1971 FAA requirement that all carriers submit a screening program for approval, by the 1972 FAA direc-

tive that no airline was to permit any person meeting the profile to board a plane unless his carry-on luggage was searched, and by the later FAA order that searches of all carry-on items and magnetometer screening of all passengers be instituted. It was thus deemed "entirely clear * * * that throughout the period since late 1968 the government's participation in the development and implementation of the airport search program has been of such significance as to bring any search conducted pursuant to that program within the reach of the Fourth Amendment." See also United States v. Ross, 32 F.3d 1411 (9th Cir.1994); United States v. Fannon, 556 F.2d 961 (9th Cir.1977); United States v. Canada, 527 F.2d 1374 (9th Cir.1975), following *Davis*; and Cassidy v. Chertoff, 471 F.3d 67 (2d Cir.2006) (ferry company's search of passengers and vehicles not private, as company "implemented its security policy in order to satisfy the requirements imposed" by the Maritime Transportation Security Act of 2002).. Consider also United States v. Barry, 673 F.2d 912 (6th Cir.1982) (notwithstanding company memo prepared with assistance of DEA requesting cooperation in efforts to detect illegal drugs, search here not governmental, as package was diverted for inspection for private reasons; court suggests result would be otherwise if "carrier opened packages randomly or perhaps because they matched the criteria of a drug profile").

Compare United States v. Burton, 475 F.2d 469 (8th Cir.1973) (search of *checked* luggage because person fit hijacker profile and because of unusual weight distribution in one of the bags; court rejected defendant's claim this was a governmental search because of FAA's authority over the airlines, noting that the "directives relied upon are not cited to us and our independent research has disclosed none warranting the conclusion as-

ment regulations specify or clarify the power of certain private persons or groups to act in a certain way for their own protection does not alone make such actions governmental.[122] Indeed, even

serted"); United States v. Echols, 477 F.2d 37 (8th Cir.1973) (defendant not permitted to board because he fit hijacker profile and could not furnish identification, checked bag left with plane and was opened at destination because it unclaimed; held, private search); United States v. Wilkerson, 478 F.2d 813 (8th Cir.1973) (woman who partially fit profile checked bag but failed to board plane; plane recalled and bag searched because of airline regulation that passenger must accompany his luggage; held, private search). These three cases are distinguishable from *Davis* in that, while use of the government-supplied profile played a part, the searches themselves apparently were not specifically related to FAA security requirements.

[122]United States v. Poe, 556 F.3d 1113 (10th Cir.2009), discussed in Comments, 87 Denv.U.L.Rev. 789 (2010); 49 Washburn L.J. 201 (2009) (bounty hunters' search of residence for defendant, who had jumped bail, was private notwithstanding extensive state regulation of the bail bond industry, coupled with conferral of powers of arrest); United States v. Momoh, 427 F.3d 137 (1st Cir.2005) (notwithstanding fact FAA regulation provided that package sent overseas by person not registered with FAA subject to opening and inspection, inspection by employee of private shipping company in such circumstances not governmental where, as here, it was to further company's "interest in ensuring that its services were not being used for illegal purposes" and was *not* "undertaken primarily to further the interests of the government"); United States v. Garlock, 19 F.3d 441 (8th Cir.1994) (fact federal regulations require banks to designate a security officer whose duties include developing a program to help identify persons committing crimes within the bank did not make that officer's conduct other than private where "government exercised absolutely no control over the manner

in which [bank] maintained its internal security," and mere fact bank "engages in a heavily regulated business does not create the required nexus"); United States v. Edwards, 602 F.2d 458 (1st Cir.1979) (CAB regulations "did not expand upon or require the exercise of [the] common law right to conduct the search"); United States v. Harvey, 540 F.2d 1345 (8th Cir.1976) (telephone company's use of device to detect use of blue box was private notwithstanding fact 18 U.S.C.A. § 2511(2)(a)(i) extends wire interception authority to communications carriers in certain instances); United States v. Goldstein, 532 F.2d 1305 (9th Cir.1976) (same); United States v. Pryba, 502 F.2d 391 (D.C.Cir.1974) (fact CAB regulation provides that "[a]ll shipments are subject to inspection by the carrier" does not turn such inspections "into a search under the aegis of the Federal Government," as the regulation is nothing more than "bare recognition" that air carriers have the same rights other carriers possess as a matter of common law rule); Akins v. United States, 679 A.2d 1017 (D.C.App.1996) ("bondsmen are not subject to the Fourth Amendment as it regards the seizure of personal effects," for while "18 U.S.C.A. § 3149 entitles bondsmen to arrest individuals where they have failed to appear in court, D.C. Code § 23-582(b) also confers on private citizens the power to arrest for certain offenses"); United States v. Lima, 424 A.2d 113 (D.C.App. 1980) (an arrest by a private citizen is not governmental simply because the common law power of a citizen to arrest has been codified); District Attorney v. Coffey, 386 Mass. 218, 434 N.E.2d 1276 (1982) (telephone company's installation of on-line trapping system to detect source of annoying calls to subscriber not governmental merely because company a public utility subject to state regulation); State v. Sanders, 185 N.J.Super. 258, 448 A.2d 481 (1982) (activity of casino security guards is private when they act

the fact that certain persons have been designated as "special policemen" is not enough either if in fact the individual in question only has very limited powers.[123]

This is not to suggest, however, that only those government regulations actually mandating private parties to make searches will make the activity undertaken pursuant thereto governmental. The issue was addressed by the Supreme Court in *Skinner v. Railway Labor Executives' Ass'n*,[124] concerning two sets of Federal Railroad Administration regulations: the Subpart C regulations, which *required* railroads to see that blood and urine tests of covered employees are conducted following certain major train accidents or incidents; and the Subpart D regulations, *authorizing* but not requiring railroads to administer

---

on "a private matter between defendant and Caesar's," notwithstanding fact state legislation requires certain security procedures and permits detention of persons by casino agents in specified circumstances); State v. Edwards, 50 Ohio App.2d 63, 361 N.E.2d 1083 (1976) (statute defining when merchant may detain suspected shoplifter does not make such detentions governmental, as statute merely intended to clarify extent of merchant's tort liability).

Likewise, if the challenged activity was beyond that required by government regulations or was not specifically required by the government regulations, this increases the chances that it will be found to be private. See United States v. Bloom, 450 F.Supp. 323 (E.D.Pa.1978) (brokerage firm's search of discharged employees' desks a private search notwithstanding SEC requirement of self-policing by such firms, as the "laws and regulations do not specify the means for accomplishing brokerage self-policing"); Commonwealth v. Storella, 6 Mass.App.Ct. 310, 375 N.E.2d 348 (1978) (doctor's action in turning over bullet from patient not state action, as it went beyond statutory requirement that police be notified whenever a bullet wound treated).

[123]As stated in Payton v. Rush-Presbyterian-St.Luke's Medical Center, 184 F.3d 623 (7th Cir.1999), while "no legal difference exists between a privately employed special officer *with full police powers* and a regular Chicago police officer," the

situation is otherwise when the special officers are not "entrusted with all powers possessed by police." Compare Johnson v. Larabida Children's Hospital, 372 F.3d 894 (7th Cir.2004) (where hospital security guard was a special policeman, but did not and was not authorized to carry firearms, was not expected or authorized to carry out functions of police officer, was merely responsible for routine security duties and had to call police in order to have persons removed from hospital, guard not a state actor); Wade v. Byles, 83 F.3d 902 (7th Cir.1996) (CHA security guard not a state actor, as guard only permitted to detain trespassers pending arrival of police); Limpuangthip v. United States, 932 A.2d 1137 (D.C.App. 2007) (special police officers, appointed by mayor to protect property on premises of their employer, here a private university, are state agents if using their arrest powers, broader than those of ordinary citizens, but not otherwise, as here, where they merely present at time of search of dorm room by university administrator); with United States v. Hoffman, 498 F.2d 879 (7th Cir.1974) (Chicago special police officers who privately employed as railroad policemen were state actors, as they "authorized on a continuing and full-time basis to search actively for criminals" and "to use the powers of the state when their search [was] successful").

[124]Skinner v. Railway Labor Executives' Ass'n, 489 U.S. 602, 109 S.Ct. 1402, 103 L.Ed.2d 639 (1989).

breath and urine tests to covered employees who violate certain safety rules. Because a "railroad that complied with the provisions of Subpart C of the regulations does so by compulsion of sovereign authority," the Court readily concluded those regulations were controlled by the Fourth Amendment. The Court then held the Subpart D regulations were also so controlled, as "the Government did more than adopt a passive position toward the underlying private conduct." The regulations preempted state laws and superseded collective bargaining agreements, conferred a right upon the FRA to receive test results, and required that employees refusing to submit to such tests be withdrawn from covered service, thus making "plain not only [the government's] strong preference for testing, but also its desire to share the fruits of such intrusions."[125]

Other government encouragement of a more general nature has not been deemed sufficient to turn a private-person search into "governmental action." It is not enough, for example, that it is established government policy to pay an informer's fee for information concerning certain forms of criminal conduct.[126] And in

---

[125]See alsoState ex rel. Ohio AFL-CIO v. Bureau of Workers' Comp., 97 Ohio St.3d 504, 780 N.E.2d 981 (2002) (where statute permits warrantless drug and alcohol testing of any workers injured on the job and makes refusal a basis for denying workers' compensation benefits, the testing by private employers constitutes state action, as there is "a complete entanglement of private and state action").

Compare United States v. Richardson, 607 F.3d 357 (4th Cir.2010) (distinguishing *Skinner*, where law enforcement agents did not know of or request internet service provider to scan defendant's e-mails, court holds that mere fact that 42 U.S.C.A. § 13032 required provider to report any knowledge it had regarding child pornography did not make search governmental, as that statute "neither directed AOL to actively seek evidence of child pornography in certain circumstances nor prescribed the procedures for doing so"); City of Pasco v. Shaw, 161 Wash.2d 450, 166 P.3d 1157 (2007) (over compelling dissent, court holds that city ordinance providing landlords lose their required license without a certification after passing inspection re health, safety and building code

violations of all their rental units every two years by a private, city-approved inspector, "does not require state action").

[126]United States v. Snowadzki, 723 F.2d 1427 (9th Cir.1984) (mere fact person acted in part out of hope of reward in searching co-employee's desk for tax records does not make search governmental); Meister v. Commissioner, 504 F.2d 505 (3d Cir. 1974); Bertolotti v. State, 476 So.2d 130 (Fla.1985) (search was private though private person received $1,000 reward upon notifying police-operated Crime Watch program, as a "community-wide, regularly advertised program which rewards any citizen who provides information useful to the police in their criminal investigations is not tantamount to recruiting police agents"). Cf. United States v. Lambert, 771 F.2d 83 (6th Cir.1985) (search private notwithstanding fact housekeeper had provided information in past and had been paid expense money over period of time). But see State v. Boynton, 58 Haw. 530, 574 P.2d 1330 (1978), holding that when the officer approached an informant, requested drug information and offered to pay for same, this "recruitment imposed upon the informant the constitutional

United States v. Valen,[127] where an employee of an air freight company searched two suitcases placed with the company for shipment, the court concluded that there was no governmental participation notwithstanding the fact that the employee had received $375.00 for information previously supplied customs authorities, that he had been asked to notify customs officials if he came across anything suspicious in the future, and that he was ultimately paid $100.00 for the information in the instant case.[128] The court stressed that the employee "was requested to do no more than report suspicious parcels" and that his act of opening the suitcases was undertaken "in order to protect himself and his employer."[129] Indeed, even where an officer went so far as

---

requirement that is imposed upon the officer's searches."

[127]United States v. Valen, 479 F.2d 467 (3d Cir.1973).

[128]See also Snyder v. State, 585 P.2d 229 (Alaska 1978) (though concluding that "the facts of this case approach the outer limits of permissible police involvement," airline agent's act in opening suspicious package not governmental notwithstanding fact police had asked to be notified if drugs discovered, this employee had found drugs on 12 prior occasions as a result of which he had testified at several drug trials and had received a commendation from the city for his efforts); McConnell v. State, 595 P.2d 147 (Alaska 1979) (same result as to same employee as in *Snyder*; Rabinowitz, C.J., dissenting, objects the employee "had a substantial financial motive, since in 'a significant number of cases' he was able to 'cash in' airline tickets, paid for by states where he was to testify * * * because as an airline employee he could fly free on an airline 'pass'").

Compare United States v. Walther, 652 F.2d 788 (9th Cir.1981) (where airline employee had relationship with DEA whereby he reported persons fitting drug profile and over 4-year period had received $800 for giving information, his search governmental where "the only reason why he opened the case was his suspicion that it contained illegal drugs" and he "opened the case with the expectation of probable reward from the DEA").

[129]Consider also United States v.

Simpson, 904 F.2d 607 (11th Cir.1990) (search by Federal Express for "sole purpose of determining where to deliver the parcel" not governmental merely because of prior "training by Government law enforcement officers on when to contact Government agents after contraband had been discovered"); United States v. Feffer, 831 F.2d 734 (7th Cir.1987) (no government action where woman employed by corporation repeatedly turned over corporate documents to IRS agents; court stresses she originally made the contact because of concern she might be held responsible for signing false documents); United States v. Bazan, 807 F.2d 1200 (5th Cir.1986) (neighbor's entry of nearby ranch not governmental, notwithstanding two prior meetings with federal agent re activity there, as agent merely told neighbor "to call 'if he saw something strange'" and "had no reason to predict that [the neighbor] would enter the ranch"); United States v. Lambert, 771 F.2d 83 (6th Cir.1985) (acts of defendant's housekeeper in bringing drugs from defendant's house to FBI were private, notwithstanding she had contacted FBI on 25 prior occasions re activities there, as she acted because of concern about use of drugs by young people, and "the record shows that she was told on several occasions that she should not take items from the house"); United States v. Ford, 765 F.2d 1088 (11th Cir.1985) (defendant lived with brother, who first agreed to but then would not allow police to bring drug dog into house, after which he broke into defendant's room himself

to tell uncompensated citizen informers what type of evidence he would like to receive from them, their theft of such items while at a "pot" party was held not to be governmental because the officer had not known they would be attending that particular party and they "were not under his specific direction at the time of this party."[130] Other courts have held that a search is not governmental

---

because of concern about safety of his wife and child; this a private search, as no showing "that the government had any preknowledge of the search nor that the agents openly encouraged or cooperated in it"); State v. Coy, 397 N.W.2d 730 (Iowa 1986) (after 2 girls sexually assaulted in backyard tent, officer asked father and neighbor to check adjacent yards for certain items, but they instead searched inside suspect's home; no agency, as officer neither encouraged that search nor knew it likely to occur); State v. Cohen, 305 S.C. 432, 409 S.E.2d 383 (1991) (UPS employee's search of package not governmental, as police had merely requested that they be notified if another package arrived for defendant); State v. Watts, 750 P.2d 1219 (Utah 1988) (private search where informant offered dismissal of charges for information but "he was not given specific directions and the police did not exercise control over his activities").

[130]Herbert v. State, 10 Md.App. 279, 269 A.2d 430 (1970). See also United States v. Jarrett, 338 F.3d 339 (4th Cir.2003) (where, after anonymous computer hacker supplied information to FBI re one person's possession of child pornography computer files, FBI agent e-mailed hacker with "perfunctory expressions of gratitude" and "a vague offer of availability to receive more information in the future," but "did not actively discourage [future] illicit hacking," that did "not suffice to create an agency relationship" re the hacker's later search into defendant's computer; moreover, even if e-mail exchange *after* latter search sufficient to "create a agency relationship going forward," such "after-the-fact conduct cannot serve to transform the prior relationship * * * into an agency relationship"); United States v. Malbrough, 922 F.2d 458 (8th Cir.1990) (Kelley's entry of defendant's land and discovery of marijuana plants in greenhouse private, as "the police directed Kelley to do nothing more than participate in narcotics purchases" and "no evidence exists that the police asked Kelley to seek out manufacturers of marijuana or even knew of Kelley's entry of Malbrough's property until after it occurred"); United States v. Feffer, 831 F.2d 734 (7th Cir.1987) (employee of corporation gave documents to IRS agents and then later provided additional documents; later events not governmental as IRS agent "never requested any documents," and it not sufficient he "knew, or should have known, that [the employee] would be producing additional documents"); State v. Locquiao, 100 Haw. 195, 58 P.3d 1242 (2002) (where Kim, operator of pool hall, searched and detained defendant, suspected of illegal drug activity in rest room there, those actions private in nature because unrelated to Kim's earlier participation with police in drug investigations as part of his plea agreement); State v. Sardeson, 231 Neb. 586, 437 N.W.2d 473 (1989) (person who told police he possessed stolen property was encouraged by police to turn it in, and following day he acquired some of the property from defendant's residence; he not then acting as police agent, as he "was not expressly recruited by police investigators to act as their agent for purposes of conducting a warrantless search"); Stoker v. State, 788 S.W.2d 1 (Tex.Crim.App.1989) (drug informant Todd told officer that defendant had a .22 caliber weapon, and officer responded he'd like to see weapon if Todd ever obtained it; Todd's later action in acquiring weapon from defendant was private, as "the government did not instruct Todd on how to obtain the weapon, or even that he should obtain it").

merely because the private party was alerted by the police to be on the lookout for certain forms of suspicious conduct,[131] or merely because citizen volunteers were advised by police that the information previously supplied by them was not sufficient to justify police intervention.[132]

---

[131]United States v. Crowley, 285 F.3d 553 (7th Cir.2002) (where police merely warned UPS agency "to watch for suspicious packages and contact authorities," UPS driver's action in opening suspicious package only a private search); United States v. Jennings, 653 F.2d 107 (4th Cir.1981) (no governmental search notwithstanding fact federal drug agents passed on to airline security anonymous tip that certain woman sending illegal drugs from Chicago to D.C., and 6 weeks later airline security agents as a result searched package shipped by that woman); Smith v. State, 267 Ark. 1138, 594 S.W.2d 255 (App.1980) (burglary victim's arrest of defendant at gunpoint when he seen with fruits of burglary was private notwithstanding fact police told victim that defendant was a suspect and that police should be contacted if victim discovered leads; "it would strain logic to the breaking point to hold that a police officer could instruct the victim of a theft to get back in touch with him if he had any leads or heard anything and by so doing invoke an agency by which the police were bound, in whatever fashion the private citizen subsequently chose to act"); State v. Sanders, 327 N.C. 319, 395 S.E.2d 412 (1990) (where detective's recruitment of private person Gardin "was to advise him that defendant was under suspicion, describe certain evidence that might link defendant to the crime, and to ask Gardin if he could gain entry into defendant's house or locate defendant and talk with him," and Gardin later responded "he would visit defendant's home and ask for a recipe," even if Gardin a police agent in making such entry same not true of his later "ruse to gain entry into defendant's bedroom by lying to defendant's sister about defendant's criminal liability," conduct by Gardin of which the police were ignorant); State v. Blackshear, 14

Or.App. 247, 511 P.2d 1272 (1973) (airline agent search of luggage placed for shipment by two black men not governmental where police alerted airlines that unknown blacks were shipping stolen clothing to other cities); Duarte v. Commonwealth, 12 Va.App. 1023, 407 S.E.2d 41 (1991) (dean of students' search of college student's dorm room private though police earlier informed him that student a burglary suspect, as when dean indicated she would probably search defendant's room, the officer "responded by specifically asking her to refrain" from doing so).

Compare State v. Sheppard, 325 N.W.2d 911 (Iowa App.1982) (activity was governmental where hospital employees turned over to police effects of shooting victim, as this a routine procedure in such cases, "part of an overall plan enacted with police cooperation, advice and planning").

[132]Gundlach v. Janing, 401 F.Supp. 1089 (D.Neb.1975) (employee's landlady asked employer if he missing any inventory because she suspicious of items in garage employee rented; employer notified police, who said they could not act without complaint and suggested employer establish if property was missing from his inventory; employer instead went to garage and with landlady's assistance examined items; held, private search); Collins v. State, 9 Ark.App. 23, 658 S.W.2d 881 (1983), rev'd on other gnds. 280 Ark. 453, 658 S.W.2d 877, (officer's statement that informant's information was stale did not make informant's reentry to determine if marijuana plants still there a governmental search); People v. Cohn, 30 Cal.App.3d 738, 106 Cal.Rptr. 579 (1973) (woman called police and reported suspicious activity in garage near her residence; police came to scene but saw nothing suspicious and departed; woman then entered garage and obtained packet of mari-

Even where the government encouragement was rather strong and specific, but yet short of an explicit request for a search, courts have been inclined to declare the search private nonetheless if there was in addition a legitimate private purpose behind the search. Illustrative is *Gold v. United States,*[133] where FBI agents advised a customer service manager of United Air Lines that they had reason to believe that the contents of cartons placed with the airline for shipment were not electronic controls, as indicated on the way bill, and that the address of the shipper was nonexistent. The FBI agents, who did not indicate what they believed the true contents of the packages to be, then departed. Sometime thereafter, the manager opened the packages and found obscene films within, which he reported to the FBI agents, who then obtained a warrant for seizure of the packages. The court held:

> We conclude that the initial search of the packages by the airline's employee was not a federal search, but was an independent investigation by the carrier for its own purposes. * * * [H]ere the agents did not request that the package be opened, and they were not present when it was opened. The agents had the same right as any citizen to point out what they suspected to be a mislabeled shipping document, and they exercised no control over what followed. What did follow was the discretionary action of the airline's manager and was not so connected with government participation or influence as to be fairly characterized * * * as "a federal search cast in the form of a carrier inspection."

While it might be expected that the carrier would not ignore the packages after being advised of the mislabelling by government agents who obviously had more than a citizen's interest in the shipment, the carrier had sufficient reasons of its own for pursuing the investigation. The manager testified that packages suspected of containing something other than what was described on the air waybill were sometimes opened so that the airline would know what was being carried on its airplanes, and so that it could assess proper charges. Despite the manager's inquiry, the government

---

juana; held, private search); People v. Sellars, 93 Ill.App.3d 744, 49 Ill.Dec. 187, 417 N.E.2d 877 (1981) (where 2 men approached officer and told him defendant admitted burglary and officer said if they saw stolen radio in defendant's apartment to "let me know," later break-in by the 2 men to get radio not governmental, as "they were instructed to try to be invited in by defendant"); Wolf v. State, 281 So.2d 445 (Miss.1973) (man told police he thought plants on neighbors land were marijuana; police responded warrant could not be obtained in the absence of further information; man then entered the property and seized some plants and delivered same to po-

lice; held, private search); State v. Malkuch, 336 Mont. 219, 154 P.3d 558 (2007) (where defendant's teen-age son told police she using drugs and asked if police could do something about it, and officer said police would need evidence, and son then entered defendant's home, where he no longer living, and picked up vial of drugs and delivered same to police, that a private search, as "the police did not know of or acquiesce in the search until after it occurred"); State v. Gundlach, 192 Neb. 692, 224 N.W.2d 167 (1974) (same facts as *Gundlach v. Janing,* supra; held, private search).

[133]Gold v. United States, 378 F.2d 588 (9th Cir.1967).

agents did not reveal what they suspected the true contents of the packages to be. His suspicions aroused, the manager had no way to determine whether the contents of the packages were fit for carriage and properly classified except by opening them. This the carrier had the right to do under its tariffs.[134]

One commentator has questioned the manner in which courts have dealt with cases where the police have extended to private persons general requests for assistance short of an explicit request to make a search. Noting that, unlike the situation in *Burdeau,* "police bulletins may motivate private persons to take steps to aid the police in gathering information" and "the police expect bulletins to induce individuals to obtain information in the future," it is recommended that the balance "be struck between private and police activity by attributing the private citizen's acts to the police whenever the acts, other than the mere calling of the police, would not have occurred but for the police request."[135] Thus, were the police, suspecting that drugs are being stored in subway rental lockers, to ask the locker inspector to call them if he found any drugs in the course of his inspections, his continuation of his regular locker inspections at the usual pace and intensity would be private conduct.[136] On the other hand, were the inspector, desiring to aid the police in discovering drugs,

---

[134]The usefulness of this technique apparently has not gone unnoticed by the FBI. See United States v. Cangiano, 464 F.2d 320 (2d Cir.1972), where the facts are remarkably similar to those in *Gold,* reaching the same result.

See also United States v. Aldridge, 642 F.3d 537 (7th Cir.2011) (where former corporate secretary to suspected corporation, also wife of present director, turned incriminating records over to SEC after being told "to keep a lookout for suspicious materials," her actions private, as she "had a number of reasons why it was in her personal interest to help the government investigate" the corporation, including desire "to exonerate herself"); United States v. Ellyson, 326 F.3d 522 (4th Cir.2003) (where defendant arrested in his trailer for possession of child pornography police found there, and police told woman living with him there that she would be well-advised to turn in anything illegal in the trailer lest she be held liable for it, and later without police encouragement she went to visit defendant at jail, and he then asked her to dispose of certain computer disks in the trailer, which she later handed over to

police, woman not a police agent, as district court found her "actions were not motivated by a desire to aid the police in building their case," but by a desire to preclude "law enforcement from holding her responsible for any items subsequently discovered in the trailer"); United States v. Pervaz, 118 F.3d 1 (1st Cir.1997) (where secret service agent advised employees of cellular phone company that company's customers being defrauded and asked if they had equipment to locate source of cloned calls, company's later use of such equipment not a government search, as company "had a legitimate independent motivation for its search: to prevent a fraud from being perpetrated on its customers"); State v. Cohen, 305 S.C. 432, 409 S.E.2d 383 (1991) (despite earlier police request for assistance, UPS search of package private, as it "was not motivated to assist law enforcement * * * but appears to have been motivated by a concern that it was delivering contraband").

[135]Comment, 119 U.Pa.L.Rev. 163, 167 (1970).

[136]As held in United States v. Small, 297 F.Supp. 582 (D.Mass.1969).

to depart from his usual practices and conduct more frequent or more thorough searches, then the searches would be governmental. However, this commentator would qualify the test by holding the police "accountable only for acts—even if not specifically requested—which they might reasonably have foreseen as a result of their request."[137] This is because "[d]eterrence of improper police conduct will not be achieved by excluding evidence in cases in which it is unlikely that the private action taken could have been anticipated by the police."[138] Thus, notwithstanding the police bulletin, if the inspector undertook to search some subway patrons in the hope of finding drugs, this would constitute a private search.

This approach has considerable appeal. It certainly would produce more rational results in those cases where the assumption seems to be that a police request is operative only if explicit and specific rather than implicit and general. It is preferable, for example, to the holding in *Herbert v. State*[139] that where a narcotics officer enlisted the assistance of two private citizens and encouraged them to gather evidence, such as marijuana pipes, while attending pot parties, their seizure of pipes at a particular party was private action only because the officer had been unaware that the two would be attending that particular party and had given them no specific instructions concerning that event. More troublesome is the question of whether this theory should compel a different result in a case like *Gold*. True, the search would not have been made but for the FBI communication, and certainly the search was foreseeable by the FBI agents, but what of the fact that the search had a legitimate private objective?[140] If, as concluded earlier,[141] a search by a police agent may be lawful even though the same search could not lawfully have been undertaken by the police themselves, perhaps it may be concluded that in a situation of the *Gold* type there is sufficient police encouragement to bring the search within the restrictions of the Fourth Amendment, at which point its reasonableness may be determined by reference to the private purpose being served.[142]

Also illustrating this point is Craft v. Commonwealth, 221 Va. 258, 269 S.E.2d 797 (1980), holding that fact officer told surgeon he wanted bullet in defendant did not make operation a governmental search, as the "fact that the police wanted the bullet * * * was not the reason the operation took place."

[137]Comment, 119 U.Pa.L.Rev. 163, 170 (1970).

[138]Comment, 119 U.Pa.L.Rev. 163, 170 (1970).

[139]Herbert v. State, 10 Md.App. 279, 269 A.2d 430 (1970).

[140]Comment, 119 U.Pa.L.Rev. 163, 114 (1970), never speaks to this point specifically, although it is asserted that in *Gold* "the court missed the crucial point that the police knew the bags would be opened and anticipated the finding of contraband." Id. at 170 n. 30.

[141]See text at note 56 supra.

[142]Thus, *Gold* is distinguishable from Corngold v. United States, 367

§ 1.8(d) The "public function" approach

The courts have not hesitated to admit into evidence under the *Burdeau* rule the fruits of illegal searches conducted by persons who, while not employed by the government,[143] have as their responsibility the prevention and detection of criminal conduct.[144] Included within this category are store detectives,[145] security of-

---

F.2d 1 (9th Cir.1966), where customs agents told the airline employee that the packages placed for shipment were thought to contain watches rather than, as stated on the waybill, furniture, as there was nothing "in the record which would indicate that the package was in fact opened for any purpose of the carrier, it does not appear, for example, that the rate for carrying furniture and watches differed."

[Section 1.8(d)]

[143]On the other hand, if a private investigator is employed by a public agency, searches conducted by him in the course of his employment are governmental searches, without regard to whether the searches in question were specifically ordered by his superiors. Hajdu v. State, 189 So.2d 230 (Fla.App.1966); State ex rel. Sadler v. District Court, 70 Mont. 378, 225 P. 1000 (1924).

Likewise, where tribal rangers on an Indian reservation stop cars, an activity beyond their legal authority, their actions are not for that reason those of private persons, considering that they "intended to assist law enforcement" and "two different government entities * * * acknowledged and endorsed the patrol activities of the rangers." United States v. Becerra-Garcia, 397 F.3d 1167 (9th Cir.2005). And similarly, where a police service aid, an employee of the police department, makes a seizure, that conduct may not be deemed private merely because the employee lacked the statutory authority to take the challenged action. State v. Slayton, 147 N.M. 340, 223 P.3d 337 (2009).

[144]See Sklansky, The Private Police, 46 UCLA.L.Rev. 1165 (1999) (considering "not only the problems that private policing presents for the

concept of state action, but also the lessons it may offer"); Annot., 36 A.L.R.3d 553 (1971). In such circumstances it makes no difference that the private employer's objectives in keeping the business operation free of criminal activity coincides with the government interest in law enforcement. As stated in United States v. Koenig, 856 F.2d 843 (7th Cir.1988), "it should come as no surprise when the goals of private individuals or organizations coincide with those of the government. However, this happy coincidence does not make a private actor an arm of the government." See, e.g., United States v. Pierce, 893 F.2d 669 (5th Cir.1990) (private search pursuant to American Airlines' " 'valid reasonable policy' of exercising caution with and opening suspicious packages").

[145]Boykin v. Van Buren Township, 479 F.3d 444 (6th Cir.2007); People v. Moreno, 64 Cal.App.3d Supp. 23, 135 Cal.Rptr. 340 (1976); United States v. Lima, 424 A.2d 113 (D.C.App.1980) (provided security guard at store not commissioned or deputized as a special police officer, who would have "powers beyond that of an ordinary citizen"); People v. Toliver, 60 Ill.App.3d 650, 18 Ill.Dec. 54, 377 N.E.2d 207 (1978); Sizemore v. State, 483 N.E.2d 56 (Ind. 1985); People v. Holloway, 82 Mich.App. 629, 267 N.W.2d 454 (1978) (but a lengthy concurring opinion argues to the contrary); State v. Allen, 599 S.W.2d 782 (Mo.App.1980); State v. Keyser, 117 N.H. 45, 369 A.2d 224 (1977); People v. Horman, 22 N.Y.2d 378, 292 N.Y.S.2d 874, 239 N.E.2d 625 (1968); State v. Edwards, 50 Ohio App.2d 63, 361 N.E.2d 1083 (1976); Stanfield v. State, 666 P.2d 1294 (Okl. Crim.App.1983); Commonwealth v. Corley, 507 Pa. 540, 491 A.2d 829 (1985) (stressing that the "sole connection between the conduct of the secu-

ficers at shopping malls,[146] hotels,[147] banks,[148] casinos,[149] race tracks,[150] and amusement parks,[151] insurance investigators,[152] corporation security investigators,[153] industrial security guards,[154] and airline security agents.[155] However, in *Stapleton v. Superior Court*,[156] involving a search by an investigator for a credit card corporation investigating credit card fraud, the court, although holding this was a government search because of the participation in the total venture by local police, dropped this interesting footnote:

> We are not called upon to decide whether searches by private investigators and private police forces should be held subject per se to the commands of the Fourth Amendment on the ground that one of their basic purposes is the enforcement of the law. * * * Searches by such well financed and highly trained organizations involve a particularly serious threat to privacy.[157]

---

rity guard in this case and state law is the privilege which if properly established might shield him from liability for false arrest/false imprisonment"); Gillett v. State, 588 S.W.2d 361 (Tex. Crim.App.1979); State v. Gonzales, 24 Wash.App. 437, 604 P.2d 168 (1979).

[146]United States v. Shahid, 117 F.3d 322 (7th Cir.1997); State v. Santiago, 147 N.M. 76, 217 P.3d 89 (2009).

[147]Commonwealth v. Considine, 448 Mass. 295, 860 N.E.2d 673 (2007).

[148]United States v. Garlock, 19 F.3d 441 (8th Cir.1994).

[149]State v. Sanders, 185 N.J.Super. 258, 448 A.2d 481 (1982) (even though state law requires casino to establish security procedures).

[150]State v. Buswell, 460 N.W.2d 614 (Minn.1990).

[151]United States v. Francoeur, 547 F.2d 891 (5th Cir.1977).

[152]Romano v. Home Ins. Co., 490 F.Supp. 191 (N.D.Ga.1980); State v. Hughes, 8 Ariz.App. 366, 446 P.2d 472 (1968); People v. Mangiefico, 25 Cal.App.3d 1041, 102 Cal.Rptr. 449 (1972); Lester v. State, 145 Ga.App. 847, 244 S.E.2d 880 (1978); Stone v. Commonwealth, 418 S.W.2d 646 (Ky. 1967).

[153]United States v. Dzialak, 441 F.2d 212 (2d Cir.1971).

[154]State v. Robinson, 86 N.J.Super. 308, 206 A.2d 779 (1965); State v. Hutson, 649 S.W.2d 6 (Tenn.Crim.

App.1982) ("unless the security guard has powers akin to that of a regular police officer and is appointed by a governmental official").

Compare State v. Roccasecca, 130 N.J.Super. 585, 328 A.2d 35 (1974) (where police lieutenant made search at factory where he a part-time security consultant, this not a private search, as he was investigating lottery activities, which was not shown to be within his responsibilities as security consultant).

[155]People v. Trimarco, 41 Misc.2d 775, 245 N.Y.S.2d 795 (1963).

[156]Stapleton v. Superior Court, 70 Cal.2d 97, 73 Cal.Rptr. 575, 447 P.2d 967 (1968).

[157]In People v. Zelinski, 24 Cal.3d 357, 155 Cal.Rptr. 575, 594 P.2d 1000 (1979), the court found it necessary to answer the question left open in *Stapleton* and *Dyas,* at least as a matter of state constitutional law, and held "that in any case where private security personnel assert the power of the state to make an arrest or detain another person for transfer to custody of the state, the state involvement is sufficient for the court to enforce the proper exercise of that power * * * by excluding the fruits of illegal abuse thereof."

Consider also Dobyns v. E-Systems, Inc., 667 F.2d 1219 (5th Cir.1982) (state action where employees of corporation had their personal effects searched by corporate represen-

The situation has become, if anything, more acute in the intervening years. As one careful study of private policing has recently concluded, today "private police participate in much of the police work that their public counterparts do," and "state action exists as a matter of degree in most cases."[158] A number of commentators, generally looking with favor upon the suggestion that private investigators and private police be held subject to the requirements of the Fourth Amendment,[159] have noted that the Supreme Court has provided a basis for such a holding by its reasoning in *Marsh v. Alabama.*[160] In *Marsh,* overturning the conviction of a person who undertook to distribute religious literature on the premises of a company-owned town contrary to the wishes of the town's management, the Court, after noting that the town (owned by a shipbuilding company) had "all the characteristics of any other American town," concluded that the limitation of appellant's access had amounted to state action because the town's "operation is essentially a public function."[161] So the argument goes, *Marsh* and its progeny[162] supply a basis for holding that private investigators and private police are subject to the Fourth Amendment because they are with some regularity engaged in the "public function" of law enforcement.

The *Marsh* argument has considerable appeal, although it is fair to say that its application in this area requires more careful attention to precisely what it is that various private police and investigators do and why they do it. Such attention is necessary not only to determine whether they are truly engaged in a "public function," but also to assess whether application of the exclusion-

---

tatives, as corporation had contracted with federal government to provide personnel, materials and transportation for Sinai field mission to construct and operate an early warning surveillance system, and thus corporation's role "was that of a peace keeper, a function which undoubtedly is 'traditionally exclusively reserved to the State'").

[158]Joh, The Paradox of Private Policing, 95 Nw.U.L.Rev. 49, 51, 125 (2004). For other concerns about the privatization of policing, see Sklansky, Private Police and Democracy, 43 Am.Crim.L.Rev. 89 (2006).

[159]Euller, Private Security and the Exclusionary Rule, 15 Harv.C.R.-C.L. L.Rev. 649 (1980); Comments, 1972 Law & Soc.Order 585, 599; 38 U.Chi. L.Rev. 555, 581–82 (1971); Notes, 59 Duke L.J. 519 (2009); 48 Geo.Wash.L. Rev. 433 (1980); 40 S.Cal.L.Rev. 540, 548–49 (1967); 19 Stan.L.Rev. 608, 615 (1967).

[160]Marsh v. Alabama, 326 U.S. 501, 66 S.Ct. 276, 90 L.Ed. 265 (1946).

[161]Relying on *Marsh*, the court in Watchtower Bible and Tract Society of New York, Inc. v. Sagardia De Jesus, 634 F.3d 3 (1st Cir.2011), held that where a law permitted local entities organized by the community to control street access within areas, such control could be questioned on Fourth Amendment grounds, as " '[r]egulating access to and controlling behavior on public streets and property is a classic government function."

[162]Particularly, Amalgamated Food Employees Union v. Logan Valley Plaza, 391 U.S. 308, 88 S.Ct. 1601, 20 L.Ed.2d 603 (1968), extending *Marsh* to a shopping center that "serves as the community business block 'and is freely accessible and open to the people in the area and those passing through.' "

ary rule to their conduct is warranted in the name of deterrence. As one commentator has aptly noted, exclusion can be an effective deterrent only if two conditions are met: (i) "the searcher must have a strong interest in obtaining convictions"; and (ii) "the searcher must commit searches and seizures regularly in order to be familiar enough with the rules to adapt his methods to conform to them."[163] The complexity of the problem is exposed by *People v. Houle,*[164] where the question was whether a bondsman's conduct in the course of apprehending a defendant who had failed to appear in court as required was state action. It could be argued that the apprehending of absconded defendants is certainly a "public function," engaged in by bondsmen with some regularity, so that the bondsman's conduct should be tested by the requirements of the Fourth Amendment.[165] However, the *Houle* court concluded otherwise. The bondsman was found to be "acting to protect his own private financial interest and not to vindicate the interest of the state"; hence there was no public function and hence exclusion would not act as an effective deterrent.[166]

The extent to which the same may be said of the actions of

---

[163]Note, 19 Stan.L.Rev. 608, 614–15 (1967).

[164]People v. Houle, 13 Cal.App.3d 892, 91 Cal.Rptr. 874 (1970). Compare Maynard v. Kear, 474 F.Supp. 794 (N.D.Ohio 1979) (in § 1983 context, bondsman engaged in state action where he possessed a bench warrant and "acted or purported to act pursuant to the authority of the bench warrant in seizing Maynard").

[165]Cf. Comment, 65 U.Cin.L.Rev. 665 (1997) (concluding that in some circumstances bounty hunters should be deemed to be state actors). Compare Notes, 1998 U.Ill.L.Rev. 1175; 52 Vand.L.Rev. 171 (1999), both concluding bounty hunters should not be deemed state actors, but are in need of greater regulation by statute. See also Notes, 47 Drake L.Rev. 877 (1999); 32 Ind.L.Rev. 1413 (1999).

[166]See also Akins v. United States, 679 A.2d 1017 (D.C.App.1996) ("neither a bail bondsman nor his bounty hunter agent is bound by the constraints of the Fourth Amendment," as exclusionary rule "will not deter a bondsman from achieving his goal or, for that matter, from taking things that are not related to it," for "a bondsman's motivation to recover evidence of a crime is no greater than that of any private citizen"); State v. Collins, 367 Md. 700, 790 A.2d 660 (2002) ("Bail bond agents, who are licensed and regulated by the State, do not have police powers by statute and are not, generally, State agents. Therefore, bail bond agents are generally not State actors for Fourth Amendment suppression purposes").

Somewhat similar analysis was used in State v. Bryant, 325 So.2d 255 (La.1975). After defendant was arrested, police called a towing company, next on the list of companies used by the police for this purpose, to impound defendant's car. After the car was towed to a service station, it was then inventoried. While this action might be said to be governmental in the sense that it is identical to that which in many jurisdictions is done by the police themselves, see § 7.4(a), the court held it was private, stressing that the station owner "testified that he conducted the search for his own protection against liability which would arise if it were claimed that articles in the car were missing while it was stored under his care."

In any event, the mere fact the private person or his employer holds a state business license, Bowers v. State, 298 Md. 115, 468 A.2d 101 (1983), or a government contract for non-law en-

private police and investigators is unclear. Some have contended that private police are "concerned primarily with protection of property and personnel,"[167] which, if true, weighs strongly against both the *Marsh* analogy and the notion that exclusion would deter. But it is doubtful that this is a correct characterization of all private police undertakings. Where private police actually supplant the public police[168] or deal regularly with the general public,[169] particularly if it may be said they are not disinterested in criminal convictions as an aid to the private objectives of their employer,[170] it would be sound as a matter of law and policy to hold those police subject to the commands of the Fourth

---

forcement activities, State v. Hutson, 649 S.W.2d 6 (Tenn.Crim.App.1982), hardly makes his search governmental.

[167]Comment, 38 U.Chi.L.Rev. 555, 572 (1971). See also United States v. Shahid, 117 F.3d 322 (7th Cir.1997) (mall security officers "acted to ensure the safety and security of the mall in order to further private purposes, such as satisfying their employer and the mall's retailers"); United States v. Garlock, 19 F.3d 441 (8th Cir.1994) (bank security personnel "were pursuing legitimate private ends unrelated to the pursuit of a criminal conviction," as indicated by fact their investigation resulted in discharge of embezzling employee); Waters v. State, 320 Md. 52, 575 A.2d 1244 (1990) (security guards' "private status is not altered because their interest in protecting property coincides with the public's interest in preventing crime generally"); State v. Buswell, 460 N.W.2d 614 (Minn.1990) (stressing purpose of race track security officers was "private," "to prevent people from entering the raceway without first paying admission" and "to prevent illegal drugs," etc., "from entering the raceway in order to minimize disruptive behavior"); State v. Santiago, 147 N.M. 76, 217 P.3d 89 (2009) (where mall security guard not "also a commissioned law enforcement officer" and not "delegated police powers," their "actions can reasonably be construed to serve the interests of their private employer," so "public function doctrine" not applicable).

[168]See Comment, 38 U.Chi.L.Rev. 555, 555–57 (1971). Compare United

States v. Shahid, 117 F.3d 322 (7th Cir.1997) (*Marsh* argument unavailing here, as it not shown mall security agency was "the de facto or de jure law enforcement agency for the Castleton Square Mall").

[169]See Comment, 38 U.Chi.L.Rev. 555, 582 (1971), noting, as an example, that "state action may be present in the activity of a security guard employed by a privately owned shopping center," and citing in support the *Logan Valley* case, note 162 supra.

[170]Note, 19 Stan.L.Rev. 608, 615 (1967) argues that "in situations where the investigations focus on members of the general public, institutionalized private searchers have a strong enough interest in acquiring criminal convictions to be expected to change their investigatory methods if the exclusionary rule were applied to them. Store detectives searching for evidence of shoplifting by customers fall within this category. Although the store owner's basic interest is in recovering stolen goods, he also has a strong interest in seeking criminal convictions. * * * Security guards in transportation industries charged with discovery of passengers with fraudulently obtained tickets have similar interests in obtaining convictions to protect their employers against freeloaders and unfounded false imprisonment charges."

In People v. Zelinski, 24 Cal.3d 357, 155 Cal.Rptr. 575, 594 P.2d 1000 (1979), discussed in note 157 supra, the court stressed that the store security personnel "were utilizing the coercive power of the state to further a state interest. Had the security guards

Amendment.[171] But an even easier case is that in which state law confers "general police powers" on officers of some private entity, such as a private educational institution, for a "private entity is deemed a state actor when the state delegates to it a traditional public function."[172]

This situation must be distinguished from yet another, and that is where a person who is employed as a police officer for a governmental unit also works at some other time as a security guard or the like for a private individual or organization. Although there is some disagreement in the cases,[173] the better view is that the Fourth Amendment applies when the person,

---

sought only the vindication of the merchant's private interest they would have simply exercised self-help and demanded the return of the stolen merchandise. Upon satisfaction of the merchant's interest, the offender would have been released. By holding defendant for criminal process and searching her, they went beyond their employer's private interest."

[171]Even courts declining to so hold sometimes concede that the reason for not applying the exclusionary rule to private persons, "that the rule will not deter private individuals," is "less compelling when it is applied to the actions of private investigators and security officers whose primary goal is often to obtain evidence of crimes, who often possess professional knowledge and skill and who conduct searches and seizures on a regular and institutionalized basis." State v. Keyser, 117 N.H. 45, 369 A.2d 224 (1977). See also Comment, 63 U.Cin.L.Rev. 1807, 1811 (1995) ("advocating extension of the Fourth Amendment exclusionary rule to unreasonable searches and seizures undertaken by those engaged in private security"); Note, 40 N.Y.L.Sch.L. Rev. 225 (1995) (argues need for exclusionary rule for private police is great, and that statutes so providing should be enacted); and other authorities collected in note 159 supra.

But one commentator responds: "Whether or not the evidence gathered by private security forces is admissible in the public courts might not matter much to the private police, nor to the individuals, organizations, and companies that hire them, nor even to the suspects that the private police apprehend. This is because as often as not, those who employ private police decide to opt out of the public criminal justice system altogether and merely take their own private action against the alleged perpetrator. Thus, the entire incentive system upon which the jurisprudence of the Fourth, Fifth, and Sixth Amendment relies—excluding evidence from court if it was improperly obtained—is ineffective with regard to the private police." Simmons, Private Criminal Justice, 42 Wake Forest L.Rev. 911, 931 (2007).

[172]Finger v. State, 799 N.E.2d 528 (Ind.2003) (police at Butler University). See also Romanski v. Detroit Entertainment, 428 F.3d 629 (6th Cir.2005) (where "private security guards are endowed by law with plenary police powers such that they are *de facto* police officers, they may qualify as state actors"); Rodriguez v. Smithfield Packing Co., 338 F.3d 348 (4th Cir.2003) (plant security official was state actor, as he "invested with the full panoply of powers afforded to full-time deputies, including the power to arrest").

Compare United States v. Day, 591 F.3d 679 (4th Cir.2010) (private security officers working at apartment complex not state actors under public function test, as their statutory arrest power was "more circumscribed than that of police officers" and was "essentially the same as that of any private citizen").

[173]Compare Traver v. Meshriy, 627 F.2d 934 (9th Cir.1980) (off-duty officer working in bank as "security teller" acted "under color of state law" when he detained bank customer in

even during his private employment, has some special authority under state law. But, it was noted in *Commonwealth v. Leone*,[174]

response to fellow employee's call for help, as he responded to the situation as a police officer, use of officers by bank part of police department's secondary hiring program, and department selected officers for program); Ex parte Kennedy, 486 So.2d 493 (Ala.1986) (where off-duty police officer employed as exterminator took leaf from plant and sent it to lab for determination as marijuana, this state action, as officer "stepped out of his exterminator role" in taking those steps); State v. Wilkerson, 367 So.2d 319 (La.1979) (deputy sheriff, when engaged in private employment as security guard at apartment complex, still subject to Fourth Amendment, as he "remains at all times a member of the law enforcement agency, charged with greater knowledge and responsibility in criminal affairs"); In re Albert S., 106 Md.App. 376, 664 A.2d 476 (1995) (state action where off-duty officer working as security guard for group of rental townhouses, as he "was driving a marked police cruiser at the time" and thus "was acting under color of police authority"); State v. Woods, 790 S.W.2d 253 (Mo.App.1990) (off-duty officer acting as caretaker of properties saw marijuana cigarette and then searched cabin, latter activity state action, as officer "proceeded beyond his duties as a watchman or caretaker by searching areas he was not otherwise authorized to enter"); State v. Smith, 279 Neb. 918, 782 N.W.2d 913 (2010) (where police officer was "off duty and employed by" night club, but was "in full police uniform and was carrying a firearm," he "was acting in his official capacity as a police officer"); State v. Graham, 130 Wash.2d 711, 927 P.2d 227 (1996) (where "off-duty police officers employed as private security guards," "if any off-duty officer conducts a search or performs an arrest pursuant to his or her authority as a police officer, then officer would be acting on behalf of the state and would, therefore, be required to comply with the constitution"); with United States v. McGreevy,

652 F.2d 849 (9th Cir.1981) (the "security consultant" for Federal Express, working for them 6 hours a week, also a police officer; his search of package, a private search, as he did not hold position because he was a police officer and he carefully separated the two jobs); State v. Buswell, 460 N.W.2d 614 (Minn.1990) (searches by racetrack security officers private though agency headed by police officer, as "he had only the power to make a citizen's arrest because he was outside the jurisdiction in which he had any authority as a licensed public officer"); State v. McDaniel, 44 Ohio App.2d 163, 337 N.E.2d 173 (1975) (where a store detective commissioned as a special deputy sheriff, detective's activities were private, as there "is no statutory authority for a sheriff to commission special deputy sheriffs" and "there is no indication herein that the sheriff exercises any control whatsoever over the activities of such security employees"), criticized in Comment, 2 U.Dayton L.Rev. 275 (1977).

Consider also Alston v. United States, 518 A.2d 439 (D.C.App.1986) (security officers of department store who are licensed but only have arrest powers of private citizen are not thereby involved in governmental action, while special police officers employed by the store but appointed by a public official and having arrest powers of police are involved in governmental action; but when former acts at direction of latter, this enough to bring the Fourth Amendment into play, for otherwise "store security personnel could continually evade the Fourth Amendment by 'circuitous means'"); Waters v. State, 320 Md. 52, 575 A.2d 1244 (1990) (action by "special police officers," who have powers of police while on their private employer's premises, is state action, but same not true of actions by "security guards" who "are not vested with arrest or other police powers").

[174]Commonwealth v. Leone, 386 Mass. 329, 435 N.E.2d 1036 (1982).

this does not mean that the bounds of permissible conduct are the same for the privately employed special officer as they would be for the ordinary police officer. The guard's private function adds a new aspect to his activities, which we believe is relevant to the proper application of the Fourth Amendment. The action he takes on behalf of his employer may be a lawful and necessary means of protecting the employer's property, although it would be impermissible if taken on behalf of the State in pursuit of evidence. * * * When the guard's conduct is justified by his legitimate private duties, it should not be treated as lawless, or "unreasonable," search and seizure. * * *

For these reasons, we conclude that an investigation by a special police officer privately employed as a security guard does not violate the Fourth Amendment when it is conducted on behalf of the private employer, in a manner that is reasonable and necessary for protection of the employer's property. If, on the other hand, the officer steps out of this sphere of legitimate private action, the exclusionary rule applies as it would to any State officer.[175]

In the context of the foregoing discussion, it might well appear that the phrase "public function" is the equivalent of "law enforcement function," for the principal inquiry has been whether private police perform functions essentially the same as their public counterparts. But quite clearly the two terms are not synonymous, as evidenced by the fact that many employees of local, state and national government are engaged in the carrying out of public functions which do not strictly speaking fall within the realm of law enforcement. Is the conduct of such employees, carried out in the course of their employment, covered by the Fourth Amendment?

---

[175]For the more lenient standard to apply, the court cautioned in *Leone,* several requirements must be met:

First, the guard must have acted under the control of his private employer. * * * If the investigation exceeds his private duties or authorization, he must be considered to have acted in his official capacity. Similarly, if the guard has received instructions from State authority, on a regular basis or in regard to the particular investigation at issue, his conduct is not protected by his private role.

Second, the guard's actions must be clearly related to his employer's private purposes. An investigation that goes beyond the employer's needs cannot be justified as an incident of the guard's private function. If, for example, none of the General Electric property to which the defendant had access could have been concealed in a travel bag or sleeping compartment, Vousboukis was not entitled to search these areas.

Third, the investigation must be a legitimate means of protecting the employer's property, and so must be reasonable in light of the circumstances surrounding it. * * * Reasonableness depends in part on the expectations engendered by the particular setting. If the employer has maintained the private character of his property, those who use it must anticipate and accept supervision. But if the employer has exposed his premises and chattels to semi-public use, the sense of private prerogative to control its users is much diminished. Custom or advance warning may bear upon the propriety of an investigation, but should not be determinative. * * * Finally, the judge should consider the methods chosen and the manner in which they are carried out. Failure to employ available, less intrusive alternatives may suggest that the methods employed were unwarranted, and an offense to individual dignity is impermissible in almost any circumstances.

See also State v. Murillo, 113 N.M. 186, 824 P.2d 326 (App.1991) (remand for application of the four *Leone* factors).

A number of courts have assumed or held that the answer is no. One way in which this conclusion emerges is when a court holds the Fourth Amendment applicable to a search conducted by an employee of a public agency other than a police department only upon a showing that the employee in question has been assigned law enforcement responsibilities.[176] But its acceptance has the greatest significance when a court holds that a public employee is governed by no Fourth Amendment restraints at all because his job description does not encompass activities directed to the prevention or detection of crime.[177] In a number of cases the *Burdeau* rule has been extended to searches conducted by a principal or similar official of a public school.[178] Also illustrative

---

[176]Bell v. State, 519 P.2d 804 (Alaska 1974) (airport security officer, though employee of Department of Public Works rather than Department of Public Safety, was an agent of the state for Fourth Amendment purposes, as the "controlling principle" depends "on the nature of the duties performed," and his duties were to assure physical security in the airport); Dyas v. Superior Court, 11 Cal.3d 628, 114 Cal.Rptr. 114, 522 P.2d 674 (1974) (uniformed patrolman of Los Angeles Housing Authority was agent of the state for Fourth Amendment purposes; "[m]erely because the 'primary' mission of a governmental agency is not law enforcement does not provide its employees with authority to violate with impunity the privacy of citizens"); People v. Bowers, 72 Misc.2d 800, 339 N.Y.S.2d 783 (1973) (high school uniformed service officer, while not a peace officer as defined by state law, was an agent of the state for Fourth Amendment purposes, as he "was employed by the Board of Education, a governmental agency, in a position involving law enforcement and security"); State v. Boggess, 115 Wis.2d 443, 340 N.W.2d 516 (1983) (entry by social worker with county department of social services was governmental, as that agency authorized to investigate reports of child abuse).

[177]E.g., Roberts v. State, 443 So.2d 1082 (Fla.App.1984) (search by employees of state university alumni office not governmental, as their "jobs and announced motives were unconnected with law enforcement purposes").

It is noteworthy, however, that the cases so holding, cited below, typically set forth as an alternative ground of decision the conclusion that even if the Fourth Amendment were applicable the search would not be held unreasonable, given the unique responsibilities of the employee in question.

[178]D.R.C. v. State, 646 P.2d 252 (Alaska App.1982); In re Donaldson, 269 Cal.App.2d 509, 75 Cal.Rptr. 220 (1969); People v. Stewart, 63 Misc.2d 601, 313 N.Y.S.2d 253 (1970); Commonwealth v. Dingfelt, 227 Pa.Super. 380, 323 A.2d 145 (1974); R.C.M. v. State, 660 S.W.2d 552 (Tex. App.1983). For other cases, see Annot., 31 A.L.R.5th 229 (1995). See also State v. Kappes, 26 Ariz.App. 567, 550 P.2d 121 (1976) (search by student resident advisors in dorm at state university was a private search); State v. Wingerd, 40 Ohio App.2d 236, 318 N.E.2d 866 (1974) (search of public university dorm room by university employee in charge of dorm was a private search).

Contra: Doe ex rel. Doe v. State of Hawaii Dept. Of Education, 334 F.3d 906 (9th Cir.2003) (seizure of student by teacher); In Interest of J.A., 85 Ill.App.3d 567, 40 Ill.Dec. 755, 406 N.E.2d 958 (1980); State v. Mora, 307 So.2d 317 (La.1975); Commonwealth v. Carey, 407 Mass. 528, 554 N.E.2d 1199 (1990); In re Dominic W., 48 Md.App. 236, 426 A.2d 432 (1981); People v. Ward, 62 Mich.App. 46, 233 N.W.2d 180 (1975); People v. D., 34 N.Y.2d 483, 358 N.Y.S.2d 403, 315 N.E.2d 466 (1974); State v. Walker, 19

of this position is *United States v. Coles,*[179] holding a search by an administrative officer at a job corps center of the suitcase of an incoming job corps student to be a private search under *Burdeau.*[180]

But these cases are wrongly decided,[181] as the Supreme Court concluded in *New Jersey v. T.L.O.,*[182] involving search of a student by a public[183] high school administrator. In response to the state's argument "that the history of the Fourth Amendment indicates

---

Or.App. 420, 528 P.2d 113 (1974); Kuehn v. Renton School District, 103 Wash.2d 594, 694 P.2d 1078 (1985); In the Interest of Isiah B., 176 Wis.2d 639, 500 N.W.2d 637 (1993).

[179]United States v. Coles, 302 F.Supp. 99 (D.Me.1969).

[180]See also J.M.A. v. State, 542 P.2d 170 (Alaska 1975) (search by a foster parent in a foster home licensed by the state and receiving a monthly allowance from the state; foster parent's activities "involved both her state duties and her private functions" as manager of her home, but Fourth Amendment was inapplicable because her duties were not "related to law enforcement"; court on more solid ground in asserting that in any event the searches were reasonable, given the fact that the child had been found delinquent and was subject to close supervision similar to that permissible in a correctional institution); Commonwealth v. Cote, 15 Mass.App. Ct. 229, 444 N.E.2d 1282 (1983) (search by meter reader for municipally-owned gas company not governmental, as he "not even occasionally engaged in a law enforcement capacity or in the administration of a local code"); State v. Keadle, 51 N.C.App. 660, 277 S.E.2d 456 (1981) (dorm advisor at state university looked in student's room and found state property; not governmental search; "advisor, motivated by reasons independent of a desire to secure evidence to be used in a criminal conviction would be under no disciplinary compulsion to obey the exclusionary rule").

[181]Gates v. Texas Dept. of Protective and Regulatory Services, 537 F.3d 404 (5th Cir.2008) ("the Fourth Amendment regulates social workers' civil investigations"); Jacob v. Township of West Bloomfield, 531 F.3d 385 (6th Cir.2008) (Fourth Amendment applicable to inspection by code enforcement officer, as "a government official does not have to carry a badge and gun to be subject to the Fourth Amendment"); United States v. Rohrig, 98 F.3d 1506 (6th Cir.1996) (Fourth Amendment not inapplicable "simply because the official conducting the search wears the uniform of a firefighter rather than a policeman"); Dubbs v. Head Start, Inc., 336 F.3d 1194 (10th Cir.2003) ("contention that the Fourth Amendment does not apply in the 'noncriminal' and 'noninvestigatory' context is without foundation," and there "is no 'social worker' exception to the Fourth Amendment"); Doe v. Heck, 327 F.3d 492 (7th Cir.2003) ("the strictures of the Fourth Amendment apply to child welfare workers, as well as all other governmental employees"); State v. Doe, 93 N.M. 143, 597 P.2d 1183 (App.1979) (search by doctor at juvenile detention home covered by Fourth Amendment and exclusionary rule, as doctor was exercising government authority); State v. Okeke, 304 Or. 367, 745 P.2d 418 (1987) (inventory of intoxicated person's effects by employee of private nonprofit agency operating treatment facility under contract with county is governed by Fourth Amendment). See also cases in paragraph 2, note 178.

[182]New Jersey v. T.L.O., 469 U.S. 325, 105 S.Ct. 733, 83 L.Ed.2d 720 (1985).

[183]The question of whether, in the event of school privatization via a government-sponsored voucher program, teachers and administrators would still be government agents is discussed in Comment, 34 U.Miami Inter-Am.L.Rev. 315 (2003).

that the Amendment was intended to regulate only searches and seizures carried out by law enforcement officers," the Court stated:

> It may well be true that the evil toward which the Fourth Amendment was primarily directed was the resurrection of the pre-Revolutionary practice of using general warrants or "writs of assistance" to authorize searches for contraband by officers of the Crown. * * * But this Court has never limited the Amendment's prohibition on unreasonable searches and seizures to operations conducted by the police. Rather, the Court has long spoken of the Fourth Amendment's strictures as restraints imposed upon "governmental action"—that is, "upon the activities of sovereign authority." * * * Accordingly, we have held the Fourth Amendment applicable to the activities of civil as well as criminal authorities: building inspectors, * * * OSHA inspectors, * * * and even firemen entering privately owned premises to battle a fire,[184] * * * are all subject to the restraints imposed by the Fourth Amendment. As we observed in *Camara v. Municipal Court*, * * * "[t]he basic purpose of this Amendment, as recognized in countless decisions of this Court, is to safeguard the privacy and security of individuals against arbitrary invasions by governmental officials." * * * Because the individual's interest in privacy and personal security "suffers whether the government's motivation is to investigate violations of criminal laws or breaches of other statutory or regulatory standards," * * * it would be "anomalous to say that the individual and his private property are fully protected by the Fourth Amendment only when the individual is suspected of criminal behavior."[185]

This reasoning in *T.L.O.* leaves room for the argument, accepted in *United States v. Attson*,[186] that there are still some governmental employees whose activities do not constitute Fourth Amendment "searches and seizures." The defendant in *Attson*, who was involved in an auto accident in which his passenger was killed, was taken to a hospital for emergency medical treatment, where a doctor ordered a blood alcohol test run on defendant

---

[184]This includes volunteer firemen, who "receive state sponsored training" and "typically depend upon a local taxing district for their source of financial support." Rose v. State, 586 So.2d 746 (Miss.1991).

[185]Quoting this language from *T.L.O.*, the Court in O'Connor v. Ortega, 480 U.S. 709, 107 S.Ct. 1492, 94 L.Ed.2d 714 (1987), held: "Searches and seizures by government employers or supervisors of the private property of their employees, therefore, are subject to the restraints of the Fourth Amendment." At issue in *O'Connor* was the search of a doctor's office at a state hospital ordered by the hospital's executive director.

The Court went on in *T.L.O.* to reject the state's argument that a contrary result was called for under the so-called in loco parentis doctrine: "In carrying out searches and other disciplinary functions pursuant to such policies, school officials act as representatives of the State, not merely as surrogates for the parents, and they cannot claim the parents' immunity from the strictures of the Fourth Amendment."

And in Ferguson v. City of Charleston, 532 U.S. 67, 121 S.Ct. 1281, 149 L.Ed.2d 205 (2001), the Court cited *T.L.O.* in holding, in connection with urine tests conducted by staff members at a state hospital, that they "are government actors, subject to the strictures of the Fourth Amendment."

[186]United States v. Attson, 900 F.2d 1427 (9th Cir.1990).

purely for medical purposes—intoxication could mask symptoms of serious pain or make certain medications inappropriate. The report was not divulged to the police, but was later obtained by the government via subpoena.[187] Because the doctor was a federal employee, the defendant claimed his action in drawing and analyzing the blood was subject to Fourth Amendment restraints. The court rejected that contention, holding that "for the conduct of a governmental party to be subject to the fourth amendment, the governmental party engaging in that conduct must have acted with the intent to assist the government in its investigatory or administrative purposes and not for an independent purpose."[188] This approach, rather than one patterned after the Fourteenth Amendment "state action" cases, was proper, the court reasoned, for the latter alternative could not be incorporated here "without greatly distorting the standards governing [the fourth] amendment's application."[189]

Somewhat the reverse of the issue discussed earlier is the question of whether a person who *is* a law enforcement officer for a public agency may, under certain circumstances when he is not on duty,[190] be deemed to have made a purely private search because he was not at that time performing a governmental

---

[187]As for whether the patient has an expectation of privacy in this medical report, see § 2.7(d).

[188]See also United States v. Inman, 558 F.3d 742 (8th Cir.2009) (while employees of county ambulance service opened fellow employee's laptop, which was already turned on and sitting on table, and saw icons suggesting child porn and then clicked them and saw child porn, Fourth Amendment inapplicable, as these employees acted "to satisfy their curiosity" and "did not act with the intent to assist the government in its investigatory or administrative purposes").

[189]See also United States v. Chukwubike, 956 F.2d 209 (9th Cir.1992) (balloons removed from defendant's body by various medical procedures no search; court cites Attson for proposition that "invasions of the body by doctors for medical purposes are neither a search nor a seizure"); People v. Perlos, 436 Mich. 305, 462 N.W.2d 310 (1990) ("the Fourth Amendment was not implicated when defendants had their blood withdrawn for medical treatment" because "blood was drawn for medical reasons, by medical personnel, and not

in connection with any police investigation"). The *Perlos* court cited in support: Nelson v. Alaska, 650 P.2d 426 (Alaska App.1982); Turner v. State, 258 Ark. 425, 527 S.W.2d 580 (1975); State v. Johnston, 108 N.M. 778, 779 P.2d 556 (1989); State v. Enoch, 21 Or.App. 652, 536 P.2d 460 (1975); Commonwealth v. Gordon, 431 Pa. 512, 246 A.2d 325 (1968).

Compare Dubbs v. Head Start, Inc., 336 F.3d 1194 (10th Cir.2003) (in present context, where parents of preschool children enrolled in Head Start program complained that their children were subjected to intrusive physical exams, including genital exams and blood tests, on school premises without parental notice or consent, *Attison* properly distinguished, as here "the plaintiffs contend that the medical examination itself was performed without consent," and here action taken *was* for "administrative purposes and not for an independent purpose").

[190]The term "not on duty," it must be emphasized, requires something more than that the officer was not involved in law enforcement activities at the time. See Soldal v. Cook County, 506 U.S. 56, 113 S.Ct. 538, 121 L.Ed.2d

function. Generally, the courts have responded that such a search is private if the off-duty officer was at that time acting as a private individual rather than as a policeman.[191] Illustrative is

---

450 (1992) (Fourth Amendment applicable to police conduct in helping landlord evict tenant by having tenant's house trailer towed off property); Cochran v. Gilliam, 656 F.3d 300 (6th Cir.2011) (Fourth Amendment applicable to police conduct in assisting landlord to evict tenant by seizing tenant's personal property).

[191]United States v. Ginglen, 467 F.3d 1071 (7th Cir.2006) (where defendant's three sons, one of who a policeman, entered family home, where they had been raised, after identifying their father as person depicted as bank robber in internet surveillance photo, observation of evidence within not state action, as the brothers' "actions in entering the home are consistent with concerned sons attempting to prevent a misguided father from engaging in continued destructive behavior," and officer-son "did not attempt to collect evidence while inside"); People v. Wachter, 58 Cal.App.3d 911, 130 Cal.Rptr. 279 (1976) (off-duty deputy sheriff went fishing with friend, friend then went to home of acquaintance to show deputy a barn with distinctive features, deputy while on property saw marijuana growing; held, private search); People v. Topp, 40 Cal.App.3d 372, 114 Cal.Rptr. 856 (1974) (off-duty police officer accompanied friend to friend's home that friend shared with another, remained in living room while friend searched bedroom of other occupant and found drugs; held, "there was no state action involved and the evidence was properly admissible"); State v. Andrews, 33 Conn.App. 590, 637 A.2d 787 (1994) (off-duty auxiliary police officer was "functioning in his private capacity," as he then driving home from work in his personal vehicle, when he stopped reckless driver, and he thereafter "conducted himself" as a private person, as he merely asked defendant to await the police); State v. Castillo, 108 Idaho 205, 697 P.2d 1219 (App.1985) (off-duty officer who inadvertently discovered marijuana in letter addressed to his brother-in-law was not acting as government official when he opened the envelope); Stevenson v. State, 43 Md.App. 120, 403 A.2d 812 (1979), judgment aff'd, 287 Md. 504, 413 A.2d 1340 (Maryland officers were not in uniform, not in marked car, and were not engaged in investigation on behalf of either Md. or D.C. when they arrested robbers in D.C.); Commonwealth v. Considine, 448 Mass. 295, 860 N.E.2d 673 (2007) (search by hotel's head of security private notwithstanding fact he a part-time police officer, as "he was not acting in that capacity at the time of the incident, and, in any case, he was outside his jurisdiction"); State v. Walker, 236 Neb. 155, 459 N.W.2d 527 (1990) (despite fact officer-landlord had been told by neighbor that narcotics activity occurring at his house, his visit to house was private because it concerned needed repairs, late security deposit and late rent; court stresses that had he wished to search for narcotics activity he would not have given tenant advance notice as he did and would not have limited entry to one room in which repairs were to be made); State v. Young, 2010 Vt. 97, 12 A.3d 510 (2010) (where off-duty police officer activated garage door opener as he approached his home, at which another car drove all the way up his driveway, court concludes officer in encountering driver "was initially acting as a concerned homeowner, and not as a police officer," as officer's "actions are consistent with the behavior of a concerned homeowner"). Compare State v. Roccasecca, 130 N.J.Super. 585, 328 A.2d 35 (1974) (off-duty police lieutenant employed part-time as security consultant at factory searched for evidence of gambling there; held, this a police search, as there was "no evidence that the investigation of lottery activities came within the scope of his employment" at the factory); Moore v. State, 562 S.W.2d 484 (Tex.Crim.App.1978)

People v. Wolder,[192] where a Los Angeles police officer learned that his daughter and her roommate were being evicted from their apartment. He called on the landlord to ascertain the reason, and during the course of the discussion the landlord said that the daughter had stored in the garage boxes she said contained items given to her by her grandmother. The officer responded that his daughter had no grandmother and asked to see the items. The landlord opened the garage, and the officer discovered stolen property. The court understandably concluded that this was a private search because the officer had been acting in the role of a concerned parent and was theretofore unaware of his daughter's involvement in a burglary.

Although the *Wolder* result is not troublesome given the strong evidence of private purpose, it may be suggested that courts should be more demanding than they sometimes are with respect to a showing that there was such a purpose. Consider, for example, the situation in *Commonwealth v. Eshelman.*[193] Decker, an off-duty auxiliary policeman, went into a wooded area looking for a friend who was training hunting dogs. While in the area he saw a car that was obviously abandoned because grass and weeds had grown up around it. He looked in the car and saw rolls of newspaper which, from his police training, he suspected were packages of marijuana being dried. He retrieved one of the packages and took it to the sheriff, who determined that the substance inside was marijuana. The court held "that an off duty auxiliary police officer is a private citizen and as such is not bound by the restrictions of the fourth amendment insofar as they apply to a search." A dissenting judge, stressing that Decker was "relying on skills and training acquired while in state employment," concluded the Fourth Amendment was applicable; otherwise, he objected, "we permit a class of state-trained police officers to ferret out crime unconstrained by important constitutional guarantees." *Eshelman,* it is submitted, was wrongly decided. Decker's approach of the car and, particularly, his decision to

---

(neighbor of off-duty officer asked him to search van parked in front of her house; held, a police search, as "an officer is for many purposes on duty 24 hours a day").

Just because the police were out of their own bailiwick and thus only had the arrest power of private citizens is not alone a reason to view their actions as private. State v. Phoenix, 428 So.2d 262 (Fla.App.1982), decision approved and remanded 455 So.2d 1024; Commonwealth v. Gullick, 386 Mass. 278, 435 N.E.2d 348 (1982). Nor is an officer's action private merely because he acted outside his particular area of enforcement responsibility. State v.

Longlois, 374 So.2d 1208 (La.1979) (though agent of Dep't of Wildlife and Fisheries was not authorized to arrest for marijuana possession, that arrest "was made by a special police officer purporting to act under authority of law" and thus exclusionary rule must apply "to discourage police officers * * * from unreasonably exceeding their lawful authority").

[192] People v. Wolder, 4 Cal.App.3d 984, 84 Cal.Rptr. 788 (1970).

[193] Commonwealth v. Eshelman, 236 Pa.Super. 223, 345 A.2d 286 (1975).

take the package had nothing whatsoever to do with his private purpose of seeking out his friend, but rather was prompted by his suspicion of criminal activity.[194]

Courts are understandably more ready to find a private purpose when the conduct is by a governmental employee without law enforcement responsibilities, as in *State v. Smith*.[195] There, one Smee, whose duties were to collect trash from trash barrels at a state park, heard an odd hissing sound while on his rounds and then entered the defendants' open trailer and turned off a leaking hose he found and then saw marijuana. The defendants claimed this was a government search because it occurred in the course of Smee's duties as a state employee. The court acknowledged that under *T.L.O.* the Fourth Amendment applies to nonpolice government employees, but then continued:

> One common thread runs through the cases in which the Supreme Court has held that a warrantless search is unreasonable and within the protections afforded by the Fourth Amendment. In every case, the search has been conducted or sought by government "officials" or "agents" as part of their regular duties of employment and were conducted within the scope of that employment. No case has been cited by counsel, and our research has found none, in which the sole basis for invoking the Fourth Amendment protections was the mere fact that the person who discovered the incriminating evidence happened to be a government employee as opposed to a private citizen. In every case the search or proposed search has furthered the government's objectives as they relate to the duties of the government employee.
>
> In the present case, Smee's duties were limited to the collection of trash. In that position he happened to be a State employee. His

---

[194]As was decided upon further appeal, Commonwealth v. Eshelman, 477 Pa. 93, 383 A.2d 838 (1978). Decker's training makes it more apparent that such was his purpose. This is not to suggest, however, that if police training comes into play at any point the search must be deemed governmental. In *Wolder*, for example, it is likely that the officer's training and experience as a policeman may have aided in his determination that the goods were stolen, but this does not affect the private characterization of the preceding search. See also Smith v. State, 623 So.2d 382 (Ala.Crim.App.1993) (off-duty police officer who saw suspicious activity in his apartment complex identified himself as an officer to suspect and stopped suspect and investigated; not private, as officer "conducted himself as an on-duty police officer would have" and was "engaged in normal police business"); State v. LeGassey, 456 A.2d 366 (Me.1983) (off-duty park ranger came upon vehicle stuck in snow and with other passersby pulled it out, he then radioed state police and put defendant in marked ranger's truck and told him to stay there; held, this not a purely private seizure, for though the ranger's original actions were like those of a good samaritan private citizen, his act of detaining the defendant put him in the role of policeman); Commonwealth v. Price, 543 Pa. 403, 672 A.2d 280 (1996) (FBI agent who stopped vehicle for state traffic violation engaged in state action, given his use of lights and siren and display of badge, as his "obvious display of authority * * * imbued his actions with an official aura").

[195]State v. Smith, 243 Kan. 715, 763 P.2d 632 (1988).

illegal entry into the Smiths' property had no connection with his duties of collecting trash and no connection with the objectives of the governmental entity which employed him. As stated by the trial court, his actions were nothing more than those of "a good neighbor." Under such circumstances his actions were tantamount to those of a private citizen with no different status than that of an employee of an independent privately owned trash service. * * * Smee, when he entered the Smiths' property for absolutely no purpose connected with his employment, had the same status of any private citizen acting under similar circumstances.

This is not to suggest, however, that the absence of law enforcement responsibilities itself settles the matter, for such a conclusion would be inconsistent with *T.L.O.* Rather, a very significant consideration in such cases as *Attson* and *Smith* is that the actor whose conduct was in question just happened to be a government employee but was performing tasks equivalent to those performed by his or her privately-employed counterparts. Such was the case as to the doctor in *Attson*, just as in *Smith* the park employee's "actions were tantamount to those of a private citizen with no different status than that of an employee of an independent privately owned trash service." Those cases, then, as with several others,[196] lend support to the proposition "that the Fourth Amendment does not constrain the activities of persons acting in an essentially private capacity merely because they happen to be government employees."[197]

The difference between that approach and a law-enforcement-purpose approach is best illustrated by considering the instance of a tax assessor's entry upon the curtilage of a private residence to examine closely the nature and size of a building addition, during which activity marijuana is seen or smelled. Under a pure law-enforcement-purpose approach, a court would likely reach the erroneous result that the Fourth Amendment has no application to such officials,[198] while under the "private capacity" approach suggested above a court would likely conclude that the assessors *are* covered by the Fourth Amendment (albeit possibly to

---

[196]E.g., United States v. Soderstrand, 412 F.3d 1146 (10th Cir.2005) (where clerical employee at public university looked inside safe in department supply room, employee "was not a state actor" where no showing she "conducted her search pursuant to any * * * governmental objective," as she "simply became curious about the safe and its contents"); Commonwealth v. Cote, 15 Mass.App. 229, 444 N.E.2d 1282 (1983) (actions of meter reader for municipally-owned public utility did not implicate Fourth Amendment, as they furthered only the "proprietary functions of utility companies without

regard to their public or private ownership"); State v. Ellingsworth, 966 P.2d 1220 (Utah App.1998) (actions of workers' compensation adjuster employed by quasi-governmental corporations in examining defendant's medical records did not implicate Fourth Amendment, as the adjuster "was acting like any other private insurer").

[197]State v. Schofner, 174 Vt. 430, 800 A.2d 1072 (2002) (Johnson, J., dissenting).

[198]The result reached in State v. Schofner, 174 Vt. 430, 800 A.2d 1072 (2002).

a different extent than as to police officers).[199]

§ 1.8(e) Applicability of exclusionary rule to nonprivate-nonpolice actors

Up to this point (and in later subsections of this section as well), the primary concern is with the *Burdeau* rule on what persons' conduct is subject to the proscriptions of the Fourth Amendment. As we have seen, *Burdeau* itself holds that private persons are not covered, while *New Jersey v. T.L.O.*[200] unequivocally establishes that public employees other than law enforcement officers *are* covered. But as to this latter group, still another question must be asked: even if such persons are subject to the Fourth Amendment, does it follow that the exclusionary rule is an appropriate sanction when they violate the Fourth Amendment?

For many years, this question very rarely surfaced in the appellate cases, most likely because its very existence seemed to be denied by the Supreme Court, which in the main "treated identification of a Fourth Amendment violation as synonymous with application of the exclusionary rule to evidence secured incident to that violation."[201] But the *T.L.O.* case made it abundantly clear that the question of whether the Fourth Amendment is applicable to certain non-police governmental activity and the question of whether the Fourth Amendment's *exclusionary rule* is applicable to that conduct are not one and the same and might not inevitably be answered in the same way. The Court gave a clear affirmative answer to the first question but, because the search was then found to be reasonable, carefully avoided expressing any opinion on the second question in the school context,[202] though that issue prompted the original grant of certiorari.

That certain nonpolice government actors are not in such need of deterrence as to be appropriate objects of the exclusionary sanction was a critical assumption by the Supreme Court in

---

[199]The result reached in State v. Vonhof, 51 Wash.App. 33, 751 P.2d 1221 (1988), later cited in Matter of Maxfield, 133 Wash.2d 332, 945 P.2d 196 (1997), for the proposition that an inspection by a tax appraiser implicates constitutional privacy rights.

[Section 1.8(e)]

[200]New Jersey v. T.L.O., 469 U.S. 325, 105 S.Ct. 733, 83 L.Ed.2d 720 (1985).

[201]Arizona v. Evans, 514 U.S. 1, 115 S.Ct. 1185, 131 L.Ed.2d 34 (1995), referring specifically to the Court's ap-

proach in Whiteley v. Warden, Wyo. State Penitentiary, 401 U.S. 560, 91 S.Ct. 1031, 28 L.Ed.2d 306 (1971).

[202]In a footnote the Court stated that by its holding it did "not implicitly determine that the exclusionary rule applies to the fruits of unlawful searches conducted by school authorities," so that the decision in *T.L.O.* "implies no particular resolution of the question of the applicability of the exclusionary rule." The specific question not decided in *T.L.O.* is discussed in Note, 2011 B.Y.U.Edu. & L.J. 667.

developing the "good faith" exception to the exclusionary rule.[203] In *United States v. Leon*,[204] holding admissible evidence obtained in execution of a facially valid search warrant grounded in an affidavit later found to be lacking probable cause, the Court ruled "the extreme sanction of exclusion" was "inappropriate."[205] There was no need to deter the police where, as here, they had in good faith relied upon the warrant, and there was also no need to deter the warrant-issuing judiciary, for "there exists no evidence suggesting that judges and magistrates are inclined to ignore or subvert the Fourth Amendment." By similar reasoning, the Court later held in *Illinois v. Krull*[206] that exclusion was unnecessary when police searched in reasonable reliance upon statutory authorization; this time, the Court stressed that there was "nothing to indicate that applying the exclusionary rule to evidence seized pursuant to the statute prior to the declaration of its invalidity will act as a significant, additional deterrent" on legislators enacting such statutes. This "*Leon* framework," as the Court put it, was next used in the case deserving principal attention here: *Arizona v. Evans*,[207] where again the actual search was by the police but the assumed Fourth Amendment violation[208] was attributable to the conduct of a court clerk.

In *Evans*, a police officer stopped Evans in January of 1991 for a traffic violation and then entered his name into a computer data terminal located in his patrol car. The computer indicated there was an outstanding misdemeanor warrant for Evans' arrest, so the officer then placed him under arrest and incident thereto found a bag of marijuana in the car. Testimony at the suppression hearing established that an arrest warrant had issued on December 13 because Evans had failed to appear to answer for several traffic violations, but that on December 19th a justice of the peace ordered the warrant quashed when Evans

---

[203]See § 1.3.

[204]United States v. Leon, 468 U.S. 897, 104 S.Ct. 3405, 82 L.Ed.2d 677 (1984), discussed in § 1.3.

[205]Lower courts have sometimes used similar analysis in somewhat different situations. See, e.g., United States v. Chaar, 137 F.3d 359 (6th Cir.1998) (where noncompliance with Fed.R.CrimP. 41(c)(2)(D) requirement of a record of probable cause information when telephonic search warrant obtained, this not a basis for suppression of evidence obtained in execution of the warrant; "exclusion is an inapt remedy," as it was the magistrate and not the police officer "that deprived us of both tape and transcript").

[206]Illinois v. Krull, 480 U.S. 340, 107 S.Ct. 1160, 94 L.Ed.2d 364 (1987),

discussed in § 1.3(h).

[207]Arizona v. Evans, 514 U.S. 1, 115 S.Ct. 1185, 131 L.Ed.2d 34 (1995), discussed in Notes, 25 Cap.U.L.Rev. 705 (1996); 29 Creighton L.Rev. 903 (1996); 34 Duq.L.Rev. 231 (1995); 55 Md.L.Rev. 265 (1996); 26 Seton Hall L.Rev. 866 (1996); 26 Sw.U.L.Rev. 1183 (1997).

[208]The state conceded that Evans' arrest violated the Fourth Amendment, so the Court "declined to review that determination," namely, that an arrest is unreasonable when made in response to a computer entry of an outstanding warrant that is in error because a court clerk failed to communicate the quashing of that warrant to the law enforcement authorities.

then appeared in court. The standard procedure in such a case was for a justice court clerk to inform the sheriff's office that the warrant had been quashed, so that the sheriff's office could then remove the warrant from its computer records, but that apparently did not happen in Evans' case.[209] The trial court granted Evans' motion to suppress because the state had been at fault in failing to quash the warrant; the court of appeals reversed on the ground that the exclusionary rule was inapplicable to public employees "not directly associated with the arresting officers or the arresting officers' police department"; and the state supreme court in turn reversed that decision.

Then it was the Supreme Court's turn. After surveying earlier decisions of the Court supporting the proposition that the exclusionary rule's application is "restricted to those instances where its remedial objectives are thought most efficaciously served," the Evans majority said this:

> Applying the reasoning of Leon to the facts of this case, we conclude that the decision of the Arizona Supreme court must be reversed. The Arizona Supreme Court determined that it could not "support the distinction drawn . . . between clerical errors committed by law enforcement personnel and similar mistakes by court employees," and that "even assuming . . . that responsibility for the error rested with the justice court, it does not follow that the exclusionary rule should be inapplicable to these facts."
>
> This holding is contrary to the reasoning of Leon * * * and Krull. If court employees were responsible for the erroneous computer record, the exclusion of evidence at trial would not sufficiently deter future errors so as to warrant such a severe sanction.[210] First, as we noted in Leon, the exclusionary rule was historically designed as a

[209]As the Supreme Court noted, "there was no indication in respondent's file that a clerk had called and notified the Sheriff's Office," and "the Sheriff's Office had no record of a telephone call informing it that respondent's arrest warrant had been quashed."

[210]See also United States v. Santa, 180 F.3d 20 (2d Cir.1999) (because Evans "did not turn on the particular type or magnitude of the error, but on the identity of the individuals responsible for the error," it applies here notwithstanding the presence of "repeated errors," as they were all by court personnel); People v. Blehm, 983 P.2d 779 (Colo.1999) (Evans applicable here, where "as a result of clerical errors by court employees, the fact that the warrant had been vacated was not communicated to the police"); Commonwealth v. Wilkerson, 436 Mass. 137, 763 N.E.2d 508 (2002) (where arrest based on erroneous information from state registry of motor vehicles that defendant's driver's license had been revoked, the "interest in deterring unlawful police conduct, which is the foundation of the exclusionary rule, is not implicated"); State v. Jesfjeld, 1997 N.D. 23, 559 N.W.2d 543 (1997) (juvenile probation office secretary's mistake in reporting to police officer that defendant was on probation with curfew restrictions, leading to defendant's arrest, not covered by exclusionary rule, as "the juvenile probation office is a part of the judicial branch and not part of the 'law enforcement team'").

Also noteworthy, although there is no specific reliance upon Evans, is United States v. Lowe, 516 F.3d 580 (7th Cir.2008), involving a Franks falsity-in-affidavit problem. The court concluded that because "the inaccura-

means of deterring police misconduct, not mistakes by court employees. * * * Second, respondent offers no evidence that court employees are inclined to ignore or subvert the Fourth Amendment or that lawlessness among these actors requires application of the extreme sanction of exclusion. * * *

Finally, and most important, there is no basis for believing that application of the exclusionary rule in these circumstances will have a significant effect on court employees responsible for informing the police that a warrant has been quashed. Because court clerks are not adjuncts to the law enforcement team engaged in the often competitive enterprise of ferreting out crime, * * * they have no stake in the outcome of particular criminal prosecutions. * * * The threat of exclusion of evidence could not be expected to deter such individuals from failing to inform police officials that a warrant had been quashed. * * *

If it were indeed a court clerk who was responsible for the erroneous entry on the police computer, application of the exclusionary rule also could not be expected to alter the behavior of the arresting officer. As the trial court in this case stated: "I think the police officer [was] bound to arrest. I think he would [have been] derelict in his duty if he failed to arrest." * * * There is no indication that the arresting officer was not acting objectively reasonable when he relied upon the police computer record.[211]

As detailed elsewhere in this Treatise,[212] the reasoning in the *Leon* case is extremely vulnerable on several different levels and from several different perspectives. Because *Evans* purports to follow that reasoning, certainly the rationale of *Evans* is no less shaky. Indeed, the *Evans* case, if anything, has even less going for it than *Leon*; one could even fully accept the holding in *Leon* and still conclude that the *Evans* decision is dead wrong. As the matter was put by Justice Stevens in his *Evans* dissent:

> The *Leon* Court's exemption of judges and magistrates from the deterrent ambit of the exclusionary rule rested, consistently with the emphasis on the warrant requirement, on those officials' constitutionally determined role in issuing warrants. * * * Taken on its own terms, *Leon*'s logic does not extend to the time after the warrant has issued; nor does it extend to court clerks and functionar-

---

cies contained in the affidavit solely arose from poor editing on the part of the District Attorney's Office," there was no "police misconduct" and thus "the purposes of the exclusionary rule" were not "even implicated in this case."

[211]This quotation is from the majority opinion of the Chief Justice. O'Connor, Souter and Breyer, JJ., concurring, opined that in cases such as this it could still be questioned whether the police "acted reasonably in their reliance on the recordkeeping system itself." Souter and Breyer, JJ., in another concurrence, emphasized

the Court had not yet determined whether, at least in this context, "our very concept of deterrence by exclusion of evidence should extend to the government as a whole, not merely the police." Stevens, J., dissenting, disagreed generally on the merits. Ginsburg and Stevens, JJ., in another dissent, focused primarily on the question of whether there was a basis for the Court to assert jurisdiction in this case, but also questioned the majority's assumptions about what effect exclusion would have in this kind of case.

[212]See § 1.3.

ies, some of whom work in the same building with police officers and may have more regular and direct contact with police than with judges or magistrates.

This distinction was appreciated by the state supreme court, which cogently noted that while "it may be inappropriate to invoke the exclusionary rule where a magistrate has issued a facially valid warrant (a discretionary judicial function) * * *, it is useful and proper to do so where negligent record keeping (a purely clerical function) results in an unlawful arrest."[213] By comparison, the Rehnquist opinion in *Evans* unequivocally asserts that it would not be "useful and proper" to exclude the evidence in that case because exclusion would (i) neither deter clerks from such errors (ii) nor alter the behavior of arresting officers. Closer analysis of the latter two assertions and the assumptions apparently underlying them serves to further demonstrate what is wrong with the *Evans* rationale:

(1) The *Evans* majority seems to say that exclusion is not necessary to deter clerks because there is nothing to deter. Why? Because there is no basis for concluding that "court employees are inclined to ignore or subvert the Fourth Amendment." If, as seems the case, the word "inclined" is being used here in its usual sense as reflecting one's state of mind, the Court's reasoning seems to include the notion that deterrence cannot operate upon instances of inaction by inadvertence. But this is not so. As the Ginsburg opinion in *Evans* put it, the suggestion "that an exclusionary rule cannot deter carelessness, but can affect only intentional or reckless misconduct[,] runs counter to a premise underlying all of negligence law—that imposing liability for negligence, i.e., lack of due care, creates an incentive to act with greater care."

Nor is the Court's assumption correct as a matter of Fourth Amendment theory. In stating that "court employees" (in contrast, apparently, to the police) are not "inclined to ignore or subvert the Fourth Amendment," the implication is that these court employees (who, the Court reminds us, are not "engaged in the often competitive enterprise of ferreting out crime") are hardly motivated to undertake calculated intrusions upon Fourth Amendment interests, and consequently are unworthy objects of the exclusionary rule and its deterrence function. But surely the exclusionary rule should not be so limited,[214] as certainly many more violations of the Fourth Amendment are the result of carelessness than of deliberate misconduct. And just as surely the exclusionary rule is logically directed at those more common

---

[213]State v. Evans, 177 Ariz. 201, 866 P.2d 869 (1994).

[214]But see Herring v. United States, 555 U.S. 135, 129 S.Ct. 695, 172 L.Ed.2d 496 (2009), discussed at note 232 infra and criticized in detail in § 1.6(i).

types of violations; as it was put in *Stone v. Powell*,[215] the exclusionary rule demonstrates "that our society attaches serious consequences to violation of constitutional rights," and thereby encourages public officers whose actions bear on the making of searches and seizures "to incorporate Fourth Amendment ideals into their value system." To put the proposition another way, if the exclusionary rule (as stated in *United States v. Johnson*[216]) provides an "incentive to err on the side of constitutional behavior," then it is an appropriate tool for preventing carelessness by court clerks.

(2) In asserting that exclusion of evidence on the facts of *Evans* "would not sufficiently deter future errors" of the same kind, a part of the Court's thinking in this regard seems to be that future errors will be so infrequent that there is virtually nothing to deter. This is highlighted by the fact that in the very same paragraph the Court sets out the testimony of the chief clerk to the effect that "this type of error occurred once every three or four years." But the relevance and accuracy of the Court's assumption are certainly open to question. For one thing, it is curious at best to explain withdrawal of the exclusionary rule in terms of the expected infrequency of its application; as Justice Stevens pointed out in his dissent, "even if errors in computer records of warrants were rare, that would merely minimize the cost of enforcing the exclusionary rule in cases like this." For another, it is by no means apparent that such errors are so rare that their reoccurrence need not be deterred. As Justice Stevens also noted, the chief clerk "promptly contradicted herself" and admitted that three other errors of the same kind occurred the very same day that Evans' warrant notice was not cancelled. This means, he cogently added, that there was thus "slim evidence on which to base a conclusion that computer error poses no appreciable threat to Fourth Amendment interests." From a broader perspective— nationwide, and not the "particular court" about which the chief clerk testified—there is reason to believe that illegal arrests attributable to computer error is no small problem. As documented elsewhere in this Treatise,[217] cases of this genre are reaching the appellate courts with increasing frequency. And that is doubtless only the tip of the iceberg; surely there are many more evidence-producing illegal arrests caused by erroneous computer records that are disposed of at the trial level. Even that does not reflect the total dimensions of the problem, for certainly in this context the supposition of Justice Jackson is especially apt—"that there are many unlawful searches * * * of innocent people which turn up nothing incriminating * * * about which courts do nothing,

---

[215]Stone v. Powell, 428 U.S. 465, 96 S.Ct. 3037, 49 L.Ed.2d 1067 (1976).

[216]United States v. Johnson, 457 U.S. 537, 102 S.Ct. 2579, 73 L.Ed.2d 202 (1982).

[217]See § 3.5(d).

and about which we never hear."[218] It is thus fair to conclude, as did Justice Ginsburg, that "Evans' case is not idiosyncratic."

The *Evans* majority's reliance upon the supposed insignificant number of such computer errors is objectionable for another reason: it fails also to take into account the dimensions of the risk to Fourth Amendment values that even a single such error creates. When at a particular time and place a particular police officer unreasonably interprets the observed circumstances and makes an arrest that ought not have been made, this is bad enough, but at least it is a single event with rather narrow time-place-occasion dimensions. But a mistake of the kind at issue in *Evans* is quite a different matter; "computerization greatly amplifies an error's effect," as "inaccurate data can infect not only one agency, but the many agencies that share access to the database."[219] Such errors can result in the object of the erroneous information being arrested repeatedly,[220] and make that individual a "marked man" subject to illegal arrest "anywhere," "at any time," and "into the indefinite future."[221]

The *Evans* majority ignores all this, and as a consequence misses a compelling reason why this is an inauspicious occasion for withdrawing the exclusionary sanction. Given "the advent of powerful, computer-based recordkeeping systems that facilitate arrests in ways that have never before been possible," the "benefits of more efficient law enforcement mechanisms" carry with them a "burden of corresponding constitutional responsibili-

---

[218]Brinegar v. United States, 338 U.S. 160, 69 S.Ct. 1302, 93 L.Ed. 1879 (1949) (dissenting opinion).

[219]As stated by Justice Ginsburg, dissenting, who went on to point out: "The computerized databases of the FBI's National Crime Information Center (NCIC), to take a conspicuous example, contain over 23 million records, identifying, among other things, persons and vehicles sought by law enforcement agencies nationwide. * * * NCIC information is available to approximately 71,000 federal, state, and local agencies. * * * Thus, any mistake entered into the NCIC spreads nationwide in an instant."

[220]See, e.g., Finch v. Chapman, 785 F.Supp. 1277 (N.D.Ill.1992) (misinformation long retained in NCIC records resulted in plaintiff being arrested and detained twice); Rogan v. Los Angeles, 668 F.Supp. 1384 (C.D.Cal.1987) (as a result of misinformation in computer records, plaintiff arrested four times, three times at

gunpoint, after traffic stops in Michigan and Oklahoma).

[221]In United States v. Mackey, 387 F.Supp. 1121 (D.Nev.1975), discussed in Note, 28 Hastings L.J. 509 (1976), the court stated: "Because of the inaccurate listing in the NCIC computer, defendant was a 'marked man' for the five months prior to his arrest, and, had this particular identification check not occurred, he would have continued in this status into the indefinite future. At any time, * * * a routine check by the police could well result in defendant's arrest, booking, search and detention. * * * Moreover, this could happen anywhere in the United States where law enforcement officers had access to NCIC information. Defendant was subject to being deprived of his liberty at any time and without any legal basis." See also United States v. Santa, 180 F.3d 20 (2d Cir.1999) (misdirected order to vacate arrest warrant occurred Nov. '95, defendant arrested in April '97).

ties"[222] that ought not be trivialized by withdrawal of the exclusionary rule. The Arizona Supreme Court had it right: "As automation increasingly invades modern life, the potential for Orwellian mischief grows. Under such circumstances, the exclusionary rule is a 'cost' we cannot afford to be without."[223]

(3) Yet another aspect of the *Evans* majority's no-deterrence-of-clerks theme is the notion that such officials simply are not deterrable, at least by this kind of sanction. The point, as they put it, is that the "threat of exclusion of evidence could not be expected to deter such individuals" because "they have no stake in the outcome of particular criminal prosecutions." If this rationale sounds familiar, it is because the Court has used it before, most notably in *Leon* as to warrant-issuing judges. It made no sense there, for the characterization of such a judge as a "neutral and detached magistrate" hardly means that he is so disinterested in his responsibilities as to not be fazed by the prospect that an erroneous decision on his part could adversely affect a future criminal prosecution.[224] Much the same point can be made here. It is doubtless true that there are some public employees whose duties are so far removed from the criminal justice system and so seldom an occasion for uncovering evidence of criminal conduct that the risk of evidence suppression will never have occasion to influence their conduct.[225] But surely a court clerk whose responsibilities include ensuring that law enforcement records are kept current is not so situated. Such an individual is a part of the criminal justice system, and as such can hardly be totally disinterested in how that system works—including whether his own derelictions might cause evidence to be suppressed and perpetrators to be released.

But there is another sense (never mentioned by the *Evans* majority) in which the warrant-issuing magistrate and recordkeeping clerk may legitimately be viewed as somewhat different in this regard. In the case of the magistrate considering a warrant application in pre-*Leon* days, there was a genuine risk that mistakes by the judge would result in the loss of evidence that otherwise could have been lawfully obtained. For example, if instead of issuing a warrant on an affidavit falling a bit below the probable cause line, the magistrate were to tell the applicant that the affidavit was insufficient, then the police might be able to solve the problem immediately by revising the affidavit to include other facts then known, or they might be able to solve it by additional investigation so that again the evidence could be obtained by a valid warrant. Similarly, a magistrate who failed to ensure that the particularity of description requirements had been met

---

[222]O'Connor, J., concurring in *Evans*.

[223]State v. Evans, 177 Ariz. 201, 866 P.2d 869 (1994).

[224]The point is elaborated in § 1.3(d).

[225]See, e.g., the cases discussed in note 238 infra.

would often cause the suppression of evidence that could have been lawfully obtained had he been a bit more demanding. Precisely because judges knew that how they performed would make this difference, the risk of exclusion provided a motivation for them to carry out their warrant-issuing responsibilities correctly.

It could be argued, however, that there is no comparable threat to court clerks concerning their responsibility to advise law enforcement agencies about quashed warrants, for they will not have reason to believe that how they perform will likely make any difference in evidence-acquisition terms. That is, a failure to update computer records is unlikely to be seen as causing suppression of evidence the police were otherwise likely to obtain by lawful means. If they *do* report the quashed warrant, then the person named therein will not be arrested and searched; if they do not, then that person might be illegally arrested, but the earlier satisfaction of the warrant makes him no more likely a possessor of evidence of crime than a person stopped and searched at random. That being so, the occasions when such evidence is found by serendipity after the illegal arrest cannot be characterized an instances in which, had the police known there was no warrant, the suppressed evidence might otherwise have been lawfully obtained.

But even if there is a reduced level of deterrence in this sense, it hardly follows that *Evans* was rightly decided. For one thing (as will be elaborated a bit latter, because it relates most directly to the *Evans* majority's most egregious error in analysis), such lack of deterrence is hardly determinative, as the proper focus is upon systemic deterrence rather than deterrence of a particular actor in the criminal justice system. For another, as important as deterrence is, it should not be the exclusive determinant of the exclusionary rule's dimensions. Exclusion also serves as a means "of assuring the people—all potential victims of unlawful government conduct—that the government would not profit from its lawless behavior."[226] Put another way, it may be said that exclusion is appropriate precisely because it places the government in the same position as if it had not conducted the illegal search and seizure in the first place.[227] Such return to the status quo ante is especially compelling in the present situation, where the actual facts known within the criminal justice system prior to the arrest and search make it apparent that there did not exist even a remotely arguable justification for those actions, meaning that the acquisition of evidence of the arrestee's criminality cannot be

---

[226]United States v. Calandra, 414 U.S. 338, 94 S.Ct. 613, 38 L.Ed.2d 561 (1974) (dissent).

[227]See Stewart, The Road to Mapp v. Ohio and Beyond: The Origins, Development and Future of the Exclusionary Rule in Search-and-Seizure Cases, 83 Colum.L.Rev. 1365, 1400 (1983).

characterized as anything but a complete windfall. Even if the exclusionary rule must be trimmed at the edges à la *Leon*, so that the prosecution rather than the defendant wins in certain instances of close-case illegality (e.g., where the search warrant affidavit is sufficiently close to showing probable cause that the police were justified in relying on the magistrate's mistaken conclusion probable cause was present), it hardly follows that the defendant should also lose in cases like *Evans*, where the quashed warrant totally deprives the arrest and search of any legitimacy.

(4) Even if none of the foregoing criticisms of *Evans* are thought to be compelling, there remains one more characteristic of the majority opinion in that case that alone demonstrates the error of the Court's holding. This fundamental defect is that the *Evans* majority confines the exclusionary rule's deterrence function within much too narrow a compass. The Court looks only at the deterrence of "court clerks" and "the arresting officer," and then concludes there is no deterrence to be had on the facts of *Evans*, when instead the Court ought to have occupied itself with the matter of systemic deterrence: whether exclusion could be expected to influence changes in the criminal justice system that would eliminate or greatly reduce future illegal arrests on phantom warrants.

One consequence of the *Evans* majority's narrow focus is that the Court has drawn a rather bold line between the police and nonpolice actors in the system, when in real life no such line exists. As a general matter, it is fair to say that our processes of criminal justice are best understood if viewed as they actually are: as a system of interlocking stages and agencies, rather than as discrete bits and pieces.[228] This is particularly true as to the matters here under consideration, as Justice Ginsburg's dissent in *Evans* so aptly illustrates:

> In this electronic age, particularly with respect to recordkeeping, court personnel and police officers are not neatly compartmentalized actors. Instead, they serve together to carry out the State's information-gathering objectives. Whether particular records are maintained by the police or the courts should not be dispositive where a single computer database can answer all calls. Not only is it artificial to distinguish between court clerk and police clerk slips; in practice, it may be difficult to pinpoint whether one official, e.g., a court employee, or another, e.g., a police officer, caused the error to exist or persist. Applying an exclusionary rule as the Arizona court did may well supply a powerful incentive to the State to promote the prompt updating of computer records.

Moreover, if such an artificial distinction is avoided, then it becomes more apparent that the necessary incentive need not come from the court clerks themselves, or even from their imme-

---

[228] See Ohlin, Surveying Discretion by Criminal Justice Decision Makers, in Discretion in Criminal Justice 1, 9–12 (L. Ohlin & F. Remington, eds. 1993).

diate judicial or administrative supervisors. It might just as logically, if not more logically, come from the police. Justice Stevens had it right, then, when he suggested in his dissent: "We should reasonably presume that law enforcement officials, who stand in the best position to monitor such errors as occurred here, can influence mundane communication procedure in order to prevent those errors."

If the police *can* do so, the next question is whether the application or nonapplication of the exclusionary rule in *Evans*-type situations (i.e., where a warrant check is run incident to a traffic stop, an arrest is made because the computer indicates there is an outstanding warrant, but it is later learned that is not the case) has anything to do with whether they *will* do so. The answer is yes, as can been seen by assessing the competing incentives upon the police regarding the timely and accurate updating of their computer records. While Justice Ginsburg's analysis quoted above speaks of the exclusionary rule as providing an incentive to prevent such illegal arrests, that is not quite correct. Rather, it is properly said (as the Court put it in *Elkins v. United States*[229]) that the exclusionary rule deters Fourth Amendment violations by "removing the incentive to disregard it." Thus, if we want to identify an incentive on the police department to seek greater accuracy in their computer records and thus fewer illegal arrests, it would be more appropriate to focus upon certain pragmatic considerations, such as that the police can best conserve their scarce patrol resources if officers do not spend their time (including all the post-arrest processing ordinarily required) making unnecessary arrests pursuant to nonexistent warrants.

Although that might not seem like a powerful incentive, it probably is good enough if there is not a more compelling incentive pulling in the direction of *not* doing anything to minimize the chances of such illegal arrests occurring. If (and only if) the exclusionary rule is inapplicable here, there is likely to be such a countervailing incentive: such an illegal arrest will sometimes provide a substantial windfall in the form of evidence of ongoing criminality by the arrestee, just as happened in *Evans*. Though it might be contended that the chance of occasional windfalls of this kind would not be enough to make the police disinterested in greater oversight of the clerks to keep the records straight, I doubt it. Those doubts are strengthened by the fact that the potential for similar windfalls has already had a profound influence upon police policymaking. Police agencies all across the country have adopted the tactic of using traffic stops (sometimes for the most insignificant of violations) as a device for seeking out drugs and weapons whenever possible, such as when the detained driver can be induced to consent to a vehicle search or when a

[229]Elkins v. United States, 364   1669 (1960).
U.S. 206, 80 S.Ct. 1437, 4 L.Ed.2d

record check provides an apparent basis for arrest and an incidental search.[230] In the context of such programs, a higher level of illegal arrests because of clerical errors is likely to appear advantageous rather than disadvantageous if there is no risk that the windfall evidence will be suppressed, especially since the nature of the illegality will be such that the arresting officer cannot be faulted for having made those arrests. Indeed, after *Evans* the police will in no sense be troubled by the thought that these windfalls are being gained only at the cost of violating the constitutional rights of citizens, for arrests made upon false computer records will no longer be viewed as illegal arrests. This is because, as the Supreme Court fully recognized in *Terry v. Ohio*,[231] "admitting evidence in a criminal trial * * * has the necessary effect of legitimizing the conduct which produced the evidence." No wonder, then, that after *Evans* there is little likelihood that police agencies will aggressively seek better recordkeeping about outstanding warrants.

Fourteen years after *Evans*, the Supreme Court in *Herring v. United States*[232] decided another "negligent bookkeeping error" case, this time involving a mistake made by an unspecified law enforcement official in failing to revise the sheriff's department computer records to show that an arrest warrant for defendant had been withdrawn five months before he was arrested on the basis of the supposed warrant. The Court concluded the exclusionary rule was inapplicable in those circumstances as well, now relying upon the broader proposition that suppression in the interest of deterrence is unnecessary whenever "the error was the result of isolated negligence attenuated from the arrest." Because of *Herring*'s broader holding, it has in a sense displaced the *Evans* decision. (Given its broader theoretical basis, it discussed elsewhere herein;[233] suffice it to note here that the criticisms leveled at *Evans* in the preceding pages are applicable in spades to the unfortunate *Herring* decision.) However, the *Evans* decision continues to have independent and primary relevance to the question of the exclusionary rule's applicability when illegal searches and seizures are actually *made* by nonpolice. If the point of *Evans*, *Leon* and *Krull* is that when an arresting or searching officer violates the Fourth Amendment but the fault lies with public officials having clerical, judicial or legislative functions, there is no point to evidence exclusion because those latter officials need not be or would not be deterred, then it certainly may be contended that seizures and searches by nonpolice should be treated likewise because once again those persons (unlike the po-

---

[230]See § 1.4(e), (f); LaFave, The Present and Future Fourth Amendment, 1995 U.Ill.L.Rev. 111.

[231]Terry v. Ohio, 392 U.S. 1, 88 S.Ct. 1868, 20 L.Ed.2d 889 (1968).

[232]Herring v. United States, 555 U.S. 135, 129 S.Ct. 695, 172 L.Ed.2d 496 (2009).

[233]See § 1.6(i).

lice themselves) are not appropriate objects of the exclusionary rule's deterrent function. And this brings us back to where we started, namely, *New Jersey v. T.L.O.*,[234] where the Court, noting it had previously "held the Fourth Amendment applicable to the activities of civil as well as criminal authorities: building inspectors, * * * OSHA inspectors, * * * and even firemen entering privately owned premises to battle a fire," ruled that the Amendment was likewise applicable to the search of a student by a high school administrator. But the Court in *T.L.O.* cautioned it did "not implicitly determine that the exclusionary rule applies to the fruits of unlawful searches conducted by school authorities," which highlights that this question (as well as its counterpart for a variety of other nonpolice searches and seizures) is ripe for assessment (or reassessment) in this post-*Evans* era.

As for the kinds of nonpolice mentioned in the above *T.L.O.* quote—building inspectors, OSHA inspectors, firemen—nothing in *Evans*, *Leon* or *Krull* casts serious doubt upon the applicability of *both* the Fourth Amendment and its exclusionary rule to their investigative activities. After all, they *are* on a fairly regular basis engaged in the competitive enterprise of ferreting out crime (or at least quasi-criminal violations), and thus even the somewhat narrower conception of the deterrence function accepted in the aforementioned three Supreme Court decisions has meaning with respect to the actions of those officials. By like reasoning, it seems clear that probation and parole officers are likewise covered by the Fourth Amendment *and* its exclusionary rule.[235] The result may be less obvious as to school officials, which perhaps accounts for the fact that even in pre-*Evans* days there was a split of authority on the question of whether the fruits of the school teacher's and principal's illegal searches should be suppressed in the interest of deterrence.[236]

However, it would seem, as Justice Stevens indicated in his

---

[234]New Jersey v. T.L.O., 469 U.S. 325, 105 S.Ct. 733, 83 L.Ed.2d 720 (1985).

[235]People v. Willis, 28 Cal.4th 22, 120 Cal.Rptr.2d 105, 46 P.3d 898 (2002) (parole agents are "adjuncts to the law enforcement team" within the meaning of *Evans*, as they work hand-in-hand with police and may make arrests and searches, and serve a "law enforcement function" and have a "general law enforcement character"; court notes its conclusion supported by declaration in Pennsylvania Bd. of Probation and Parole v. Scott, 524 U.S. 357, 118 S.Ct. 2014, 141 L.Ed.2d 344 (1998), that when parole officers "act like police officers and seek to uncover evidence of illegal activity, they (like police officers) are undoubtedly aware that any unconstitutionally seized evidence that could lead to an indictment could be suppressed in a criminal trial"; collecting cases in accord, court also notes "that both before and after *Evans*, courts have uniformly held that the exclusionary rule applies in a criminal proceeding where a parole officer obtains evidence during an unconstitutional search").

[236]Compare In re William G., 40 Cal.3d 550, 221 Cal.Rptr. 118, 709 P.2d 1287 (1985) (where illegal school search, evidence not admissible in juvenile court; "the exclusionary rule is the only appropriate remedy");In Interest of J.A., 85 Ill.App.3d 567, 40 Ill.Dec.

dissenting opinion in *T.L.O.*, that the "simple and correct answer to the question" would be that the exclusionary rule *does* apply in criminal or juvenile court proceedings to searches by school personnel. For one thing, such a conclusion squares with the deterrent function of the exclusionary rule. As noted in *State v. Baccino*,[237] the notion that public employees outside law enforcement, like truly private individuals, would not be deterred by an exclusionary rule "may be true in the case of isolated private searches," but "it is inapposite to the situation of a school principal who has a duty to investigate unlawful activity." Also, as Justice Stevens pointed out:

> In the case of evidence obtained in school searches, the "overall educative effect" of the exclusionary rule adds important symbolic force to this utilitarian judgment.
>
> * * *
>
> Schools are places where we inculcate the values essential to the meaningful exercise of rights and responsibilities by a self-governing citizenry. If the Nation's students can be convicted through the use of arbitrary methods destructive of personal liberty, they cannot help but feel that they have been dealt with unfairly. The application of the exclusionary rule in criminal proceedings arising from illegal school searches makes an important statement to young people that "our society attaches serious consequences to a violation of constitutional rights," and that this is a principle of "liberty and justice for all."

As is suggested by the fact the *Baccino* court deemed it necessary to distinguish "isolated private searches" from the case before it, there are admittedly fact situations where the arguments for the exclusionary rule are less compelling than they are with respect to searches conducted by school authorities. Specifi-

---

755, 406 N.E.2d 958 (1980) (even where search by school officials, juveniles in delinquency proceedings entitled to "all constitutional protections against unlawful searches and seizures, * * *, and * * * the exclusionary rule is also applicable"); State v. Mora, 307 So.2d 317 (La.1975), judgment vacated on other grounds, 423 U.S. 809, 96 S.Ct. 20, 46 L.Ed.2d 29 (1975), on remand, 330 So.2d 900 (La.1976) (where illegal school search, "the fruits of such a search may not be used by the State prosecutorial agency as the basis for criminal proceedings"); with D.R.C. v. State, 646 P.2d 252 (Alaska App.1982) (though search by school officials "state action" subject to constitutional limitations, no suppression required given "the purpose served by the exclusionary rule," as "enforcement of school regulations

* * * provide substantial incentives to 'search' that would not be lessened by the suppression of evidence at a subsequent delinquency proceeding"); State v. Young, 234 Ga. 488, 216 S.E.2d 586 (1975) (though "public school officials are state officers acting under color of law, whose action is therefore state action which must comport with the Fourth Amendment," exclusionary rule not applicable "to searches by non-law enforcement persons").

This issue must be distinguished from that of whether the evidence, whoever the searching party was, should be admissible in noncriminal disciplinary proceedings against the student. See § 1.7(f).

[237] State v. Baccino, 282 A.2d 869 (Del.Super.1971).

cally, when the public official is not a police officer, is not otherwise a part of the criminal justice system in the broad sense of that phrase, and does not have responsibilities involving (except perhaps upon the rarest of occasions) investigation of activities that might later be a proper subject of criminal prosecution or similar proceedings, then it just may be that the prospect of exclusion bringing about any deterrence in like future situations is so remote that the *Evans* rule would properly be applied. Although the point has rarely been litigated, some pre-*Evans* authority to that effect is to be found.[238]

§ 1.8(f) The "ratified intent" approach

In *Knoll Associates, Inc. v. Federal Trade Comm'n*,[239] the corporation sought review of an FTC order that it desist from discriminatory pricing practices, contending that the Commission improperly admitted into evidence documents stolen by one Prosser, an employee of the corporation's sales representative. While Prosser had communicated by telephone with an attorney for the Commission at about the time of the theft, a witness who overheard Prosser's end of the conversation testified that he indicated he already had incriminating documents he would provide to the Commission. There was no evidence indicating that the theft had been requested or suggested by the Commission attorney. But the court of appeals ruled that the stolen documents should have been suppressed, reasoning:

> The action of the Commission in utilizing the fruits of the misconduct of Prosser violated rights of petitioner protected by the fourth amendment to the federal constitution. The undisputed evidence shows that Prosser stole the documents for the purpose of assisting the Commission counsel in the prosecution of the proceeding then pending, and the record shows that the Commission by its use of the documents knowingly gave its approval to Prosser's unlawful act.

Knoll, then, appears to stand for the proposition "that where the evidence is taken to aid the Government, and when the Government uses the evidence, the taint of that illegal action is

---

[238]People v. Scott, 43 Cal.App.3d 723, 117 Cal.Rptr. 925 (1974) (exclusionary rule not applicable where airport manager, while looking in car illegally parked by plane for the ignition key or registration certificate, found marijuana; court stresses that while one of his duties was to supervise enforcement of safety regulations at the airport, actual enforcement always left to law officers, and manager did not himself issue citations or otherwise engage in criminal investigations, and was not seeking evidence of crime at time he looked into the car); Roberts v. State, 443 So.2d 1082 (Fla.App.1984) (following *Scott*, court concludes exclusionary rule not applicable where membership clerk in Alumni Office of Florida State University looked in desk of fellow employee after receiving several complaints from membership applicants).

[Section 1.8(f)]

[239]Knoll Associates, Inc. v. FTC, 397 F.2d 530 (7th Cir.1968).

transferred to the Government so as to make the use unlawful."[240] In short, it is a "ratified intent" approach.[241]

Knoll cites *Gambino v. United States*[242] in support of its holding. *Gambino* was a "silver platter" case predating *Elkins v. United States*,[243] and it involved a situation in which New York troopers, at a time following repeal of the state prohibition law, arrested and searched persons suspected of transporting liquor and then turned them and the evidence over to federal authorities for prosecution under the National Prohibition Act. The Court held the evidence inadmissible. While "the troopers were not shown to have acted under the directions of the federal officials in making the arrest and seizure," the fact remained that the "wrongful arrest, search, and seizure were made solely on behalf of the United States" and that the federal prosecution "was, as conducted, in effect a ratification of the arrest, search, and seizure made by the troopers on behalf of the United States." Although not cited in *Knoll,* it has been suggested that the result reached there might also be based upon *Marsh v. Alabama*,[244] in that any searches undertaken "to assist criminal prosecutions may be * * * an inherently governmental task."[245] However, the *Knoll* "ratified intent" approach is a decidedly minority view, for most courts unhesitatingly apply the *Burdeau* rule notwithstanding the fact that the victim of a crime or some other private person engaged in a search and seizure for the purpose of obtaining evidence of crime.[246]

It is not evident that the "ratified intent" theory would consti-

---

[240]Comment, 44 N.Y.U.L.Rev. 206, 209 (1969).

[241]Comment, 44 N.Y.U.L.Rev. 206, 209 (1969).

[242]Gambino v. United States, 275 U.S. 310, 48 S.Ct. 137, 72 L.Ed. 293 (1927).

[243]Elkins v. United States, 364 U.S. 206, 80 S.Ct. 1437, 4 L.Ed.2d 1669 (1960).

[244]Marsh v. Alabama, 326 U.S. 501, 66 S.Ct. 276, 90 L.Ed. 265 (1946), discussed in text at note 160 supra.

[245]Stapleton v. Superior Court, 70 Cal.2d 97, 73 Cal.Rptr. 575, 447 P.2d 967 (1968).

[246]E.g., United States v. Huber, 404 F.3d 1047 (8th Cir.2005) (where detective talked with defendant's bookkeeper but did not ask her to take any action, defendant's claim she later engaged in illegal search or seizure of records rejected, as mere fact that bookkeeper "may have been motivated, to some extent, by an urge to help the government * * * is not enough to make her a government agent"); United States v. Veatch, 674 F.2d 1217 (9th Cir.1981) (actions "purely private" though person turned over defendant's effects to FBI upon learning FBI investigating defendant); United States v. Ziperstein, 601 F.2d 281 (7th Cir.1979) (pharmacist contacted FBI agent *after* he had possession of employer's records showing wrongdoing); United States v. Gumerlock, 590 F.2d 794 (9th Cir.1979) (airline employee's tariff inspection of freight private even if "motivated in whole or in part by a unilateral desire to aid in the enforcement of the law"); United States v. Mekjian, 505 F.2d 1320 (5th Cir.1975) (nurse, employed by doctor who was submitting false claims under medicare program, initiated contact with FBI agent and supplied him with records of the fraud); McConnell v. State, 595 P.2d 147 (Alaska 1979) (exclusionary rule not applicable even if airline employee had "some partial motive to enforce the law," as he did not act "in

tute a desirable corollary to the *Burdeau* rule. While it has been suggested that the "application of the exclusionary rule to such 'private' searches is more likely to deter unlawful searches than it would in other cases,"[247] it is doubtful that this is true to any appreciable extent. Private citizens, even when acting for the purpose of supplying evidence to the authorities, are unlikely to be aware of the risk of suppression or of precisely how to avoid that risk. And while, as suggested earlier, doubts about deterrence should not serve as a basis for concluding that the Fourth Amendment applies to only some government officials, contrary to the intention of the framers,[248] it is another matter when it is suggested that the reach of the Amendment be extended beyond that originally contemplated. And certainly the "ratified intent" theory cannot be justified on the ground that somehow government agents will be deterred from illegal conduct. "To impute motive to the Government, focusing on its ratification of the taker's intent, wrongly assumes that the Government has some control over the taker's intent."[249] Finally, it is appropriate to note that neither *Gambino*[250] nor *Marsh*[251] lends firm support to the "ratified intent" concept.

---

conjunction with or at the direction of the police"); Gasaway v. State, 137 Ga.App. 653, 224 S.E.2d 772 (1976) (bookkeeper for investment partnership, upon discovery that partnership's account had been depleted by defendant, took partnership records to the district attorney); State v. Christensen, 244 Mont. 312, 797 P.2d 893 (1990) ("Even if the burglars had taken the marijuana with the intention of turning it over to state prosecutors, the exclusionary rule would still not apply"); State v. Kornegay, 313 N.C. 1, 326 S.E.2d 881 (1985) (secretary for law firm copied records of dishonest transactions and then turned them over to police); Commonwealth v. Corley, 507 Pa. 540, 491 A.2d 829 (1985) (store security guard seized suspect in shooting-robbery); State v. Sweet, 23 Wash.App. 97, 596 P.2d 1080 (1979) (mere purpose to aid government by airline employee's search of luggage); State v. Heiner, 683 P.2d 629 (Wyo.1984) (even if private insurance investigator gathering evidence for criminal prosecution, that alone did not make the search governmental). See also cases collected in Annot., 36 A.L.R.3d 553 (1971).

Compare State v. Coburn, 165 Mont. 488, 530 P.2d 442 (1974), other aspects of which are discussed in note 11 supra, holding a private search subject to the Fourth Amendment, and stressing that the instant case "is not the example used in argument of an innocent assist to the government with no conviction motive."

[247] Stapleton v. Superior Court, 70 Cal.2d 97, 73 Cal.Rptr. 575, 447 P.2d 967 (1968).

[248] "History also makes it clear that the searches to be controlled were of the kind which had constituted abuse of the asserted rights of the colonists, those carried out under public authority, in the name of the law, not those made by private persons not acting under color of law." J. Landynski, Search and Seizure and the Supreme Court 44 (1966).

[249] Comment, 44 N.Y.U.L.Rev. 206, 210 (1969). Compare Note, 51 B.U.L. Rev. 464 (1971).

[250] For one thing, notwithstanding the broad language in the *Gambino* opinion re after-the-fact ratification, it appears that the state police were doing precisely what they had been asked to do by federal authorities. The Court dropped a footnote stating: "Immediately after the repeal of the [state prohibition law] the federal prohibi-

This is not to suggest, however, that evidence of the private person's motive is never relevant on the question of whether a particular search is to be classified as governmental in nature. As noted earlier,[252] many of the cases take an unduly limited view of what will suffice as the requisite government encouragement. Where it is shown that there was some pre-search contact between the private party making the search and a potentially interested government official, particularly when the government has been less than helpful in establishing the precise nature of that contact, it is quite appropriate to view the private party's intention as quite relevant evidence on the government encouragement issue.[253] Indeed, the *Knoll* decision may itself be explained in these terms, for it was never clearly established whether Prosser was asked to seize the papers by the Commission attorney, as the attorney refused to take the stand and testify on the matter.

§ 1.8(g) The "judicial action" approach

One step beyond the "ratified intent" theory discussed above is the position taken by a dissenting judge in the case of *Sackler v. Sackler,*[254] where the majority held admissible in a civil divorce action evidence obtained by means of an illegal forcible entry into the wife's home by the husband and several private investigators employed by him.[255] Judge Van Voorhis stated in his dissent:

When evidence illegally obtained is offered in evidence in court,

---

tion director in New York City announced that he would call upon the superintendent of state troopers, the sheriff of each county, and every chief of police to aid in arresting violators of the national Prohibition Act. In February, 1924, he attended a conference of state and federal enforcement agencies at Albany, where he reiterated the need for co-operation." In addition, it is not correct to assume that concepts employed in pre-*Wolf, Elkins* and *Mapp* cases to deal with the troublesome problem of the state-federal "silver platter" are necessarily applicable to the distinct question of when a search is governmental rather than private.

[251]In *Marsh* the "public function" was not based upon one isolated act with a governmental purpose, but rather the ongoing existence of a town with "all the characteristics of any other American town."

[252]See text at note 134 supra.

[253]Illustrative is United States v. Issod, 370 F.Supp. 1110 (E.D.Wis.

1974), where an airline employee searched a trunk only after he discussed the situation with a narcotics officer. Noting that the "Government has made no effort to show that this conversation did not influence the employee's decision to open the trunks," the court concluded that "where a private seizure is preceded by contacts with government officers, influence may be inferred," especially when "a search has no other purpose than to further a government investigation." See also State v. Anonymous, 34 Conn.Sup. 104, 379 A.2d 946 (1977), applying the "ratified intent" theory where the searching informant had been asked by the police to furnish information about the defendant.

[Section 1.8(g)]

[254]Sackler v. Sackler, 15 N.Y.2d 40, 255 N.Y.S.2d 83, 203 N.E.2d 481 (1964).

[255]Although the two issues are sometimes confused, *Sackler* also presented the distinct question of whether the exclusionary rule should be ap-

that is done for the purpose of inducing official action by the courts, which appears to be contrary to the purpose served by the adjudication in *Mapp v. Ohio*. In either instance the product of the search cannot legally be utilized by the courts as an official branch of the State.

The assumption, which of course is contrary to *Burdeau* and the host of cases decided thereunder, is that the action of the judicial branch in receiving the fruits of private illegality into evidence is, standing alone, sufficient governmental involvement to bring the Fourth Amendment into play.

Some commentators, approving of the position taken in the *Sackler* dissent,[256] have suggested that it finds support in the Supreme Court decision in *Shelley v. Kraemer*.[257] In *Shelley*, the question was whether the equal protection clause inhibits judicial enforcement by state courts of restrictive covenants based on race or color. The respondents, who had successfully sued in state court to enjoin black purchasers from taking possession of property subject to such covenants, argued that the covenants themselves constituted only private action and that judicial enforcement of a private agreement does not amount to state action. The Court disagreed:

> We have no doubt that there has been state action in these cases in the full and complete sense of the phrase. The undisputed facts disclose that petitioners were willing purchasers of properties upon which they desired to establish homes. The owners of the properties were willing sellers; and contracts of sale were accordingly consummated. It is clear that but for the active intervention of the state courts, supported by the full panoply of state power, petitioners would have been free to occupy the properties in question without restraint.

> These are not cases, as has been suggested, in which the States have merely abstained from action, leaving private individuals free to impose such discriminations as they see fit. Rather, these are cases in which the States have made available to such individuals the full coercive power of government to deny to petitioners, on the grounds of race or color, the enjoyment of property rights in premises which petitioners are willing and financially able to

---

plicable in civil proceedings. See § 1.5(g).

[256]Comments, 16 Am.U.L.Rev. 403, 406–07 (1967); 5 Land & Water L.Rev. 653, 659–60 (1970). See also Burkoff, Not So Private Searches and the Constitution, 66 Cornell L.Rev. 627, 666 (1981), concluding: "When the State affirmatively accepts illegally seized evidence in its criminal justice system, thereby authorizing or encouraging actions by private parties that would be unconstitutional if performed by governmental officials, it ignores reality to then assert that there is no 'sufficiently close nexus between the State and the challenged action.' The State accepts the illegally seized evidence; the State encourages its use through the lack of deterrent disincentives; and the State tries and punishes the criminal defendant on the basis of the evidence so received. Whichever strand of the state action doctrine is invoked, many private searches therefore bear the unmistakable imprimatur of the State."

[257]Shelley v. Kraemer, 334 U.S. 1, 68 S.Ct. 836, 92 L.Ed. 1161 (1948).

acquire and which the grantors are willing to sell.

A close reading of the above passage compels the conclusion that the continued vitality of *Burdeau* has not been put in doubt by *Shelley*. "In *Shelley* the lower court was asked to compel a private citizen to do an act which would be unconstitutional for the state to perform, whereas in [*Sackler*] the court was merely asked to give evidentiary status to illegally seized information."[258] Moreover, in *Shelley* the challenged "racial discrimination could not have occurred unless the court enforced the discriminatory restrictive covenant," while in "the case of a search by a private party the invasion of privacy has taken place before the court is called on to admit the evidence."[259] Notwithstanding such earlier invasions, it is not correct to say that subsequent judicial decisions to admit the fruits thereof "somehow constitute distinct violations of * * * Fourth Amendment rights."[260]

It has also been held that the fact that a judge, even in the context of a criminal case,[261] has entered an order requiring a third party not charged with any offense to provide a buccal swab for DNA analysis, does not make the obtaining of the swab governmental where the judge's order was in response to the defendant, "acting in a private capacity [to] further[ ] his own ends by attempting to secure all favorable proofs in advance of trial."[262] But as considered later,[263] this case seems much closer to *Shelley* than the situations previously discussed here.

§ 1.8(h) Foreign police and the international "silver platter"

With an increase in the cooperative efforts of police on the international level, particularly with respect to narcotics enforcement[264] and (more recently) counterterrorism,[265] the heretofore uncommon event of evidence seized by police of a foreign country being offered in a criminal prosecution in a federal or state court

---

[258]Note, 46 Minn.L.Rev. 1119, 1124–25 (1962). See also Note, 37 Mo.L.Rev. 545, 549 (1972).

[259]Note, 19 Stan.L.Rev. 608, 614 (1967).

[260]United States v. Calandra, 414 U.S. 338, 94 S.Ct. 613, 38 L.Ed.2d 561 (1974).

[261]Regarding similar situations arising in the context of a civil action, see § 1.7(h).

[262]In re Jansen, 444 Mass. 112, 826 N.E.2d 186 (2005). By footnote, the court cautioned it was not deciding "whether the buccal swab obtained by Lampron could, at some later date, be turned over to the Commonwealth for use in a future criminal prosecu-

tion without implicating Jansen's constitutional rights."

[263]See § 5.4(d), text at note 132.

[Section 1.8(h)]

[264]See Mueller, International Judicial Assistance in Criminal Matters, in International Criminal Law 429 (G. Mueller & E. Wise ed. 1965).

[265]See Note, 49 Colum.J.Transnat'l L. 411 (2011) (concluding "that the rise of international terrorism and heightened transnational law enforcement cooperation demands to some extent a broad international silver platter doctrine and a narrow joint venture exception").

is now occurring with greater frequency. Searches undertaken by the police of another country can hardly be called private searches. Yet, there is certainly a similarity between the private person "silver platter" and what might be called the international "silver platter." As with the private citizen in this country, the foreign policeman is not directly subject to the restraints of the Fourth Amendment. But federal and state officers are, and these restraints do not inevitably vanish merely because the acts that these officers have brought about occurred outside the boundaries of the United States.[266]

Prior to examining the various relationships that might exist with respect to foreign police and American officials, it is necessary to consider first the fundamental question of whether the Constitution (and, particularly, the Fourth Amendment) *ever* has *any* application outside the United States. At one time it was deemed settled law that the Constitution applies "only to citizens and others within the United States, * * *, and not to residents or temporary sojourners abroad."[267] But this is no longer true with respect to an American citizen abroad. As stated in *Reid v. Covert*.[268] "When the government reaches out to punish a citizen who is abroad, the shield which the Bill of Rights and other parts of the Constitution provide to protect his life and liberty should not be stripped away just because he happens to be in another country." This means, assuming a sufficient American nexus or involvement with a foreign search (about which more later), that an American citizen in another country can invoke the protections of the Fourth Amendment with respect to search activity occurring there.[269]

But, does the Fourth Amendment likewise have some application to a foreign search of a foreign national's residence? The Supreme Court confronted this issue in *United States v. Verdugo-*

---

[266]Powell v. Zuckert, 366 F.2d 634 (D.C.Cir.1966).

[267]Ross v. McIntyre, 140 U.S. 453, 11 S.Ct. 897, 35 L.Ed. 581 (1891).

[268]Reid v. Covert, 354 U.S. 1, 77 S.Ct. 1222, 1 L.Ed.2d 1148 (1957).

[269]United States v. Conroy, 589 F.2d 1258 (5th Cir.1979); United States v. Rose, 570 F.2d 1358 (9th Cir.1978).

But see In re Directives Pursuant to Section 105B of Foreign Intelligence Surveillance Act, 551 F.3d 1004 (For.Intel.Surv.Rev.2008) ("a foreign intelligence exception to the Fourth Amendment's warrant requirement exists when surveillance is conducted to obtain foreign intelligence for national security purposes and is directed against foreign powers or agents of foreign powers reasonably believed to be located outside the United States"); United States v. Bin Laden, 126 F.Supp.2d 264 (S.D.N.Y. 2000), criticized in Comments, 82 B.U.L.Rev. 555 (2002); 69 U.Chi.L. Rev. 403 (2002), but favorably viewed in Note, 55 Duke L.J. 1059 (2006) (no warrant required for a search by United States government of an American citizen living abroad when the search is for foreign intelligence purposes, as such search falls within a "foreign intelligence exception" to the Fourth Amendment's warrant clause); Note, 23 Rev.Litig. 209 (2004). For the statutory limits on physical searches for foreign intelligence purposes, see 50 U.S.C.A. §§ 1821 to 1829.

Urquidez,[270] a review of a Ninth Circuit holding that when U.S. Drug Enforcement Agency agents, working in concert with Mexican Federal Judicial Police, made a search of the Mexican home of defendant, a Mexican citizen and resident, they violated the Fourth Amendment because they lacked a search warrant, requiring suppression of the fruits of that search in an U.S. prosecution. The Supreme Court, per Rehnquist, C.J., reversed, declaring

> that the text of the Fourth Amendment, its history, and our cases discussing the application of the Constitution to aliens and extraterritorially require rejection of respondent's claim. At the time of the search, he was a citizen and resident of Mexico with no voluntary attachment to the United States, and the place searched was located in Mexico. Under these circumstances, the Fourth Amendment has no application.[271]

As for the text of the Fourth Amendment, the Court reasoned that the phrase "the people," used therein and also in the First,

---

[270]United States v. Verdugo-Urquidez, 494 U.S. 259, 110 S.Ct. 1056, 108 L.Ed.2d 222 (1990), discussed in Bentley, Toward an International Fourth Amendment: Rethinking Searches and Seizures Abroad After Verdugo-Urquidez, 27 Vand.J.Trans.L. 329 (1994); Freiwald, Electronic Surveillance at the Virtual Border, 78 Miss.L.J. 329 (2008); Comments, 10 Mich.Telecom. & Tech.L.Rev. 139 (2003); 15 Suffolk Transnat'l L.J. 339 (1991); 41 Cath.U. L.Rev. 289 (1991); Notes, 23 Ariz.St. L.J. 261 (1991); 20 Cal.W.Int'l L.J. 355 (1990); 20 Cap.U.L.Rev. 521 (1991); 25 Colum.Hum.Rts.L.Rev. 435 (1994); 34 Colum.J.Transnat'l L. 705 (1996); 41 Duke L.J. 907 (1992); 14 Fordham Int'l L.J. 267 (1990); 32 Harv.Int'l L.J. 295 (1991); 52 La.L.Rev. 455 (1991); 64 St. John's L.Rev. 629 (1990); 36 S.D.L. Rev. 120 (1991); 22 U.Tol.L.Rev. 1153 (1991).

[271]See also United States v. Emmanuel, 565 F.3d 1324 (11th Cir.2009) (under *Verdugo-Urquidez*, the "Fourth Amendment exclusionary rule does not apply to the interception of wire communications in the Bahamas of a Bahamian resident," and thus it irrelevant whether Bahamian officials acted as U.S. agents); United States v. Bravo, 480 F.3d 88 (1st Cir.2007) ("the Fourth Amendment does not apply to activities of the United States against aliens in international waters"); United States v. Zakharov, 468 F.3d 1171 (9th Cir.2006) (re delay in obtaining judicial review of warrantless arrest of alien, since "delay took place outside of the United States in international waters" *Verdugo-Urquidez* applies); United States v. Aikins, 946 F.2d 608 (9th Cir. 1990). ("The Fourth Amendment does not apply to the search of non-resident aliens on a ship in international waters"); United States v. Davis, 905 F.2d 245 (9th Cir.1990) ("Although *Verdugo-Urquidez* only held that the fourth amendment does not apply to searches and seizures of nonresident aliens in foreign countries, the analysis and language adopted by the Court creates no exception for searches of nonresident aliens on the high seas").

Kennedy, J., concurring, asserted that "all would agree" that the Fifth Amendment due process clause does protect "persons in the position of the respondent," but then added that "nothing approaching a violation of due process has occurred in this case." See also United States v. Inigo, 925 F.2d 641 (3d Cir.1991) (defendant's "conclusory statement that the FBI's cooperation with the Swiss police who seized the documents was not in conformity with the general principles of fairness and privacy" does not show violation of due process).

Second, Ninth and Tenth Amendments, "refers to a class of persons who are part of a national community or who have otherwise developed sufficient connection with this country to be considered part of that community."[272] This conclusion, the Court explained, squares with the history of the Fourth Amendment, which shows its purpose "was to protect the people of the United States against arbitrary action by their own Government"; with the understanding of the Framers' contemporaries, who authorized action against aliens in foreign territory or international waters without Fourth Amendment limits; and with earlier decisions of the Court, including both the *Insular Cases,* holding not every constitutional provision applies to government activity even where the United States has sovereign power, and also cases rejecting the claim that aliens are entitled to all due process rights outside the sovereign territory of the United States. (The three dissenters took issue with all these conclusions and agreed on the broader proposition "that when a foreign national is held accountable for purported violations of the United States criminal laws, he has effectively been treated as one of 'the governed' and therefore is entitled to Fourth Amendment protections."[273])

But, just who are "the people" within the meaning of the Fourth Amendment? In the view of Justice Stevens, concurring, this phrase at least includes any alien then "lawfully present in the United States," which would cover the defendant in *Verdugo-Urquidez,* for prior to the search he had been arrested by Mexican officials and turned over to U.S. authorities, who moved him to a correctional center in San Diego. To this, Chief Justice Rehnquist responded for the majority:

> But this sort of presence—lawful but involuntary—is not of the sort to indicate any substantial connection with our country.[274] The extent to which respondent might claim the protection of the Fourth

---

[272]Some have suggested that this view, central to the holding in *Verdugo-Urquidez,* cannot be squared with the Court's later holding in Boumediene v. Bush, 553 U.S. 723, 128 S.Ct. 2229, 171 L.Ed.2d 41 (2008), that aliens detained as enemy combatants are entitled to the privilege of habeas corpus to challenge the legality of their detention. See Neuman, The Extraterritorial Constitution After Boumediene v. Bush, 82 S.Cal.L.Rev. 259 (2008); Podgor, Welcome to the Other Side of the Railroad Tracks: A Meaningless Exclusionary Rule, 16 Sw.J.Int'l L. 299 (2010).

[273]Blackmun, J., dissenting, stating he agrees with that much of the Brennan-Marshall dissent.

[274]Martinez-Aguero v. Gonzalez, 459 F.3d 618 (5th Cir.2006), discussed in Comment, 22 Emory Int'l L.Rev. 247 (2008) (Mexican national's "regular and lawful entry of the United States pursuant to a valid border-crossing card and her acquiescence in the U.S. system of immigration constitute * * * 'substantial connections' "); Riechmann v. State, 581 So.2d 133 (Fla.1991) (German citizen on trial for murder committed in U.S. while he voluntarily here objected to search in Germany; his "claim is not controlled by *Verdugo-Urquidez* because Riechmann did have a voluntary attachment to the United States and thus had greater entitlement to fourth amendment protection, having assumed the benefits and burdens of

Amendment if the duration of his stay in the United States were to be prolonged—by a prison sentence, for example—we need not decide. When the search of his house in Mexico took place, he had been present in the United States for only a matter of days. We do not think the applicability of the Fourth Amendment to the search of premises in Mexico should turn on the fortuitous circumstance of whether the custodian of its nonresident alien owner had or had not transported him to the United States at the time the search was made.[275]

To this were added the observations that the applicability of the Fourth Amendment to illegal aliens when searched *inside* the United States was still an open question,[276] and that even if it was then applicable this would be because they, unlike the defen-

American law when he chose to come to this country").

Compare United States v. Barona, 56 F.3d 1087 (9th Cir.1995) (it "yet to be decided * * * whether a resident alien * * * to be considered one of 'the People of the United States' even when he or she steps outside the territorial borders of the United States").

[275]See also United States v. Valencia-Trujillo, 573 F.3d 1171 (11th Cir.2009) (alien defendant, extradited from Columbia, sought to make a *Franks* challenge of an FBI affidavit providing the sole factual foundation for all documents submitted with extradition request; while defendant claims he was invoking the Fourth Amendment in the United States and not in Columbia, court responds that *Verdugo-Urquidez* applied because the "allegedly improper seizure * * * occurred in Columbia"); United States v. Vilches-Navarrete, 523 F.3d 1 (1st Cir.2008) (defendant, a Chilean not residing in U.S., captain of vessel approached by US. Coast Guard in international waters and brought to San Juan for search, likewise "had 'no previous significant voluntary connection to the United States,'" as he "brought to the United States for the sole purpose of conducting a safe search of the vessel he captained").

[276]Noting that I.N.S. v. Lopez-Mendoza, 468 U.S. 1032, 104 S.Ct. 3479, 82 L.Ed.2d 778 (1984), discussed in § 1.7(f), assumed but did not decide "whether the protections of the Fourth Amendment extend to illegal aliens in this country." See Connell & Valla-

dares, Search and Seizure Protections for Undocumented Aliens: the Territoriality and Voluntary Presence Principles in Fourth Amendment Law, 34 Am.Crim.L.Rev. 1293, 1295 (1997) ("courts have cited *Verdugo-Urquidez* for the proposition that the Fourth Amendment does not automatically protect undocumented aliens even if the challenged search and seizure took place in this country"); Medina, Exploring the Use of the Word "Citizen" in Writings on the Fourth Amendment, 83 Ind.L.J. 1557, 1559 (2008) (while government has argued in a number of cases "that undocumented non-citizens are not entitled to Fourth Amendment protections" even while within the U.S., courts "have resisted adoption" of such a rule); Nunez, Inside the Border, Outside the Law: Undocumented immigrants and the Fourth Amendment, 85 S.Cal.L.Rev. 85 (2011) ("Lower courts have relied on *Verdugo*'s holding to categorically deny Fourth Amendment rights to certain classes of undocumented immigrants"); Romero, The Domestic Fourth Amendment Rights of Undocumented Immigrants: On Gutierrez and the Tort Law/Immigration Law Parallel, 35 Harv.C.R.-C.L.Rev. 57 (2000); Scaperlanda, The Domestic Fourth Amendment Rights of Aliens: To What Extent Do They Survive United States v. Verdugo-Urquidez?, 56 Mo.L.Rev. 213 (1991); Slobogin, The Poverty Exception to the Fourth Amendment, 55 Fla.L.Rev. 391, 396 (2003) ("The practical consequences, if not the intent, of *Lopez-Mendoza* [discussed herein in § 1.7(f)] and *Verdugo-Urquidez* is the creation of an illegal

dant in this case, had entered the country "voluntarily and presumably had accepted some societal obligations."

Given *Verdugo-Urquidez,* it might understandably be thought that the issue discussed herein—when, if ever, a United States connection with a search in a foreign country is substantial enough to make the Fourth Amendment and its exclusionary rule applicable—is of no relevance whenever that search is directed at an alien not then in the United States. But, an examination of the positions of the two concurring and three dissenting Justices suggests otherwise. The dissenters, as previously noted, are of the view that if the foreign search is properly characterized as United States activity (as it presumably was in *Verdugo-Urquidez* because DEA agents were directly involved in the search itself), then the Fourth Amendment applies if the defendant is being subjected to U.S. criminal prosecution. Justice Kennedy, concurring, subscribed to a narrower proposition: "The absence of local judges or magistrates available to issue warrants, the differing and perhaps unascertainable conceptions of reasonableness and privacy that prevail abroad, and the need to cooperate with foreign officials all indicate that the Fourth Amendment's warrant requirement should not apply in Mexico as it does in this country." Similarly, Justice Stevens explained his concurrence as follows: "I do not believe the Warrant Clause has any application to searches of noncitizens' homes in foreign jurisdictions because American magistrates have no power to authorize such searches."[277] Thus, the *most* that can be definitely concluded from *Verdugo-Urquidez* is that the Fourth Amendment's warrant clause is inapplicable to a search conducted under the circumstances present in that case.[278]

Turning now to the "silver platter" issue, and taking the easi-

---

alien exception to the Fourth Amendment").

[277]Blackmun, J., dissenting, agreed "that an American magistrate's lack of power to authorize a search abroad renders the Warrant Clause inapplicable to the search of a noncitizen's residence outside this country," but (unlike Justice Stevens) believed remand was necessary to establish the reasonableness of the search (i.e., whether probable cause existed).

[278]Beyond that, much depends upon the exact positions of the two concurring Justices. Kennedy, again, says the warrant clause is inapplicable and that the instant case is not one in which "the full protections of the Fourth Amendment would apply." He also finds much fault with the majori-

ty's analysis (e.g., reliance on the phrase "the people" in the Fourth Amendment), yet says without further explanation that there are "other persuasive justifications stated by the Court." This, it would seem, leaves it less than certain how he would come out, e.g., as to a foreign search clearly lacking in probable cause and directed at a nonresident alien.

Stevens also says the warrant clause is inapplicable "to searches of noncitizens' homes in foreign jurisdictions," and in addition asserts that "aliens who are lawfully present in the United States are among those 'people' who are entitled to the protection of the Bill of Rights." He never suggests that other aliens are not also protected.*Verdugo-Urquidez* was later relied upon in In re Terrorist Bombings

est situation first, assume a case in which the police of a foreign country,[279] acting for the purpose of enforcing their own law and without any instigation by American officials, conduct a search that would not meet the requirements of the Fourth Amendment if conducted by police in the United States. Assume further that the fruits of this search are thereafter determined to constitute evidence of criminal conduct within the jurisdiction of a court in this country, and that consequently these fruits are handed over to American authorities and offered into evidence in a criminal trial. The courts are in agreement that this evidence is not subject to suppression on constitutional grounds.[280] This is because the Fourth Amendment is not "directed at foreign police, and no purpose would be served by applying the exclusionary rule, since what we do will not alter the search and seizure policies of the foreign nation."[281]

Surprisingly, some commentators have questioned this result and have asserted that Fourth Amendment standards should be applied to *all* foreign searches that produce evidence offered in an American court.[282] Such a rule, it is contended, "will place all nations on notice of the high regard of our courts for individuals' rights, and will relieve the courts of the problem of applying different standards according to the place where the search occurred."[283] Just why it is necessary to "place all nations on notice," particularly when the search was conducted for local

---

of U.S. Embassies in East Africa, 552 F.3d 157 (2d Cir.2008), discussed in § 4.1(b), holding that the Fourth Amendment warrant requirement does not apply in foreign countries, even as to searches directed at U.S. citizens.

[279]This does not include, for example, police of the Commonwealth of Puerto Rico. See Torres v. Puerto Rico, 442 U.S. 465, 99 S.Ct. 2425, 61 L.Ed.2d 1 (1979), holding "that the constitutional requirements of the Fourth Amendment apply to the Commonwealth."

[280]United States v. Mitro, 880 F.2d 1480 (1st Cir.1989); United States v. LaChapelle, 869 F.2d 488 (9th Cir. 1989); United States v. Rosenthal, 793 F.2d 1214 (11th Cir.1986) (citing "doubtful deterrent effect on foreign police practices that will follow"); United States v. Mount, 757 F.2d 1315 (D.C.Cir.1985) (as "United States courts cannot be expected to police law enforcement practices around the world, let alone to conform such practices to Fourth Amendment standards

by means of deterrence"); Stowe v. Devoy, 588 F.2d 336 (2d Cir.1978) (noting, however, that "if the circumstances of the foreign search and seizure are so extreme that they 'shock the judicial conscience', a federal court in the exercise of its supervisory powers can require exclusion of the evidence so seized"); United States v. Callaway, 446 F.2d 753 (3d Cir.1971); Thomas v. State, 274 Ga. 156, 549 S.E.2d 359 (2001); Commonwealth v. Wallace, 356 Mass. 92, 248 N.E.2d 246 (1969).

[281]Commonwealth v. Wallace, 356 Mass. 92, 248 N.E.2d 246 (1969).

[282]Notes, 53 Cornell L.Rev. 886, 898 (1968); 2 N.Y.U.J.Int'l L. & Pol. 280, 304 (1969). For other commentary on this subject, see Annot., 33 A.L.R. Fed. 342 (1977); Notes, 102 Harv.L. Rev. 1672 (1989); 25 San Diego L.Rev. 609 (1988); 34 Wash. & Lee L.Rev. 263 (1977); 25 Wm. & Mary L.Rev. 161 (1983).

[283]Note, 53 Cornell L.Rev. 886, 898 (1968).

purposes and when the search might comply fully with the law of jurisdiction where conducted,[284] is not made clear. Nor is it apparent why applying different standards "according to the place where the search occurred" is any more of a problem than applying different standards when a domestic search is conducted by a private person. The argument that suppression is required because admission of the evidence is itself a violation of the defendant's right of privacy[285] is in error,[286] and the same may be said[287] of the contention that use of the evidence to obtain a conviction is itself a sufficient involvement by officials of this country to bring the situation within the restraints of the Fourth Amendment.[288]

What then if the assumed case is changed in but one respect: the foreign official conducted the search, at least in part, with the intention of finding evidence that could be turned over to American authorities? Here too the courts have concluded that suppression is not required merely because the foreign search was below Fourth Amendment standards. Thus, in *Johnson v. United States*,[289] where Cuban police searched defendant's hotel room pursuant to a consent that arguably would not pass Fourth Amendment voluntariness requirements, the jewelry found was held admissible even though the search and seizure was "accomplished by the Cuban police, apparently in an effort to assist the Miami police in recovering the jewelry and bringing about appellant's capture on the State charge." Utilization of the "ratified intent" theory, discussed earlier,[290] would produce a contrary result, but for the reason set forth in that earlier discussion it may be said that this theory is unsound. As for its apparent use in *Gambino v. United States*,[291] it is well to note again that the facts of that case show a continuing course of state-federal cooperation resulting from federal encouragement.[292] Moreover, *Gambino* stressed that the wrongful searches "were made solely on behalf of the United States," an unlikely occurrence when foreign police are involved.[293] And even if the "ratified intent" approach were thought to have some merit as to domestic searches

---

[284]Note, 2 N.Y.U.J.Int'l L. & Pol. 280, 310 (1969), acknowledges that a "search may be unreasonable under fourth amendment standards, but may be legal under foreign law. A suspect's dwelling, for example, may be searched on the basis of suspicion in Germany and without a warrant in France when a felony has been discovered during the commission of the very act or has just been committed. Exclusion of the evidence thereby obtained from a Federal court will not alter these policies."

[285]Note, 2 N.Y.U.J.Int'l L. & Pol.

280, 305 (1969).

[286]See text at note 260 supra.

[287]See text at note 258 supra.

[288]Note, Note, 2 N.Y.U.J.Int'l L. & Pol. 280, 305 (1969).

[289]Johnson v. United States, 207 F.2d 314 (5th Cir.1953).

[290]See text at note 239 supra.

[291]Gambino v. United States, 275 U.S. 310, 48 S.Ct. 137, 72 L.Ed. 293 (1927).

[292]See note 250 supra.

[293]In *Johnson*, for example, the

by private parties or pre-*Elkins* searches by state police, perhaps on the notion that those who set out to assist federal authorities should comply with the law governing those authorities, it is less apparent that a foreign police officer, merely because he knows his investigative efforts may also prove beneficial to authorities in our country, should be expected to somehow discover and apply a rather complicated body of law from another country.[294]

If the assumed case is changed in yet another respect, so that it may be said the foreign officer is aware of the potential benefit to American authorities of his investigation because those authorities supplied him with information, the result is no different. It has been held upon such facts that the evidence is admissible in an American court without regard to whether the search would pass muster under the Fourth Amendment if performed in this country.[295] This is none too surprising, for the pre-*Elkins* state-federal "silver platter" cases did not deem the mere giving of information to state officials by federal authorities sufficient to make a resulting search subject to the exclusionary rule.[296] And while it has been argued herein that the courts have been somewhat overgenerous in permitting the private person "silver platter" where the police made an implicit request for a search,[297] police requests to foreign officials need not be viewed with the same jaundiced eye. It is one thing for a police officer to encourage a domestic search by a private person, where it may

---

Cubans were interested in deporting an undesirable alien. Similarly, in United States v. Marzano, 537 F.2d 257 (7th Cir.1976), refusing to follow the "ratified intent" theory, the court noted: "The defendants violated Grand Cayman law, according to [foreign officer] Tricker, and that is the reason for which he arrested them. That he might also have intended to help the United States is not a sufficient reason to treat his actions as those of the United States agents." But there are exceptions; see, for example, Powell v. Zuckert, 366 F.2d 634 (D.C.Cir.1966), summarized in text at note 305 infra.

[294]"It would be just as unrealistic to expect Senegalese police officers to receive general instruction in Federal law, as it would be to expect New York City police officers to receive general instructions in Senegalese law." Note, 2 N.Y.U.J.Int'l L. & Pol. 280, 311 (1969).

[295]United States v. Behety, 32 F.3d 503 (11th Cir.1994) (DEA agent's communication to Guatemalan authorities regarding arrival of U.S. vessel in

Guatemala to pick up cocaine for export did not trigger exclusionary rule re search of vessel by Guatemala officials); United States v. Maturo, 982 F.2d 57 (2d Cir.1992) (Turkish wiretap not subject to Fourth Amendment restraints though undertaken after DEA requested information re certain Turkish telephone numbers and "no evidence that the DEA was, in any way, involved in the decision to seek a wiretap"); United States v. Hawkins, 661 F.2d 436 (5th Cir.1981) (exclusionary rule not applicable to search of plane in Panama, as "American involvement was limited to notifying Panamanian authorities that a plane suspected of carrying drugs had made a crash landing in their country"); United States v. Rose, 570 F.2d 1358 (9th Cir.1978); United States v. Marzano, 537 F.2d 257 (7th Cir.1976).

[296]Shurman v. United States, 219 F.2d 282 (5th Cir.1955); Sloane v. United States, 47 F.2d 889 (10th Cir. 1931).

[297]See text at note 135 supra.

often be said that the officer would proceed to make the search himself except for his knowledge that he could not constitutionally do so. It is quite another for an officer to enlist the assistance of law enforcement officials in another country without making certain that these officials will follow the dictates of their own law or, when it is more demanding, of the Fourth Amendment.[298]

What then if American authorities have actually requested or even participated in a foreign search? In response to this question, one commentator states: "Since foreign officers occupy the same position as did state officers during the silver platter era prior to 1960, and since searches by foreign officers present problems similar to those created by state searches during this era, the standards developed and applied to state searches prior to 1960, at least logically, should apply equally to searches by foreign officers."[299] But, although the decided cases are few in number, this does not appear to have occurred. In the pre-*Elkins* state-federal "silver platter" case of *Lustig v. United States*,[300] the Court held that the search was federal because a federal officer "had a hand in it" in the limited sense that state officers conducting the search summoned him to the search scene before all of the evidence had been selected; it was enough that the federal agent "was in it before the object of the search was completely accomplished." By comparison, somewhat similar involvement in foreign searches has not been deemed sufficient to bring those searches within the restraints of the Fourth Amendment.[301]

This failure to slavishly follow *Lustig* and other cases dealing

---

[298]As stated in United States v. Maturo, 982 F.2d 57 (2d Cir.1992), quoting United States v. Paternina-Vergara, 749 F.2d 993 (2d Cir.1984): "The investigation of crime increasingly requires the cooperation of foreign and United States law enforcement officials, but there is no reason to think that Congress expected that such cooperation would constitute the foreign officials as agents of the United States."

[299]Note, 2 N.Y.U.J.Int'l L. & Pol. 280, 282–83 (1969).

[300]Lustig v. United States, 338 U.S. 74, 69 S.Ct. 1372, 93 L.Ed. 1819 (1949).

[301]United States v. Behety, 32 F.3d 503 (11th Cir.1994) (DEA agent's presence at and videotaping of search of U.S. vessel by Guatemala officials did not trigger exclusionary rule); United States v. Rosenthal, 793 F.2d 1214 (11th Cir.1986) (no improper joint venture where decision to arrest was

by Columbian authorities and American agents present at time of arrest and search at request of Columbian authorities); United States v. Benedict, 647 F.2d 928 (9th Cir.1981) (no improper joint venture where U.S. agents played "a passive role" and were summoned to search by Thai authorities who initiated the investigation); United States v. Maher, 645 F.2d 780 (9th Cir.1981) (no improper joint venture where "investigation of Maher was initiated and controlled by Canadian police, with only limited support and assistance from American officials on this side of the border"); Government of the Canal Zone v. Sierra, 594 F.2d 60 (5th Cir.1979) (asserting that "Fourth Amendment rights are generally inapplicable to an action by a foreign sovereign in its own territory in enforcing its own laws, even though American officials are present and cooperate in some degree"); Stowe v. Devoy, 588 F.2d 336 (2d Cir.1978) (noting that Canadian authorities fol-

with the federal-state relationship, it is submitted, is not inappropriate. The dynamics of the state-federal "silver platter" problem, finally put to rest in *Elkins v. United States*,[302] are significantly different from those relating to foreign searches. As to the former, the dominant concern of the Court was "to prevent violations of the Constitution by circuitous and indirect methods,"[303] that is, to prevent federal officers from avoiding Fourth Amendment restraints by the simple technique of having state officers conduct those searches the federal authorities would doubtless conduct themselves but for the exclusionary rule. Quite understandably, that concern was met by a series of holdings that made it apparent that federal officers could not accomplish by indirection, through request of or participation with state officials, that which they could not constitutionally do themselves. But, while a "Federal officer in the United States has the authority to make searches without any assistance from state officers," in a foreign country "the Federal officer ordinarily has no authority to conduct searches and seizures on his own initiative; he must depend on cooperation from the local authorities."[304] The fact he has sought such assistance, therefore, should not be inherently suspect.

This is not to say that all foreign searches, no matter how offensive in nature and no matter how deep the involvement of American officials, should be immune from Fourth Amendment

---

lowed their own law and did not engage in shocking conduct, and that there "exists no case, so far as we are aware, which suppresses evidence obtained in a foreign country under such conditions, regardless of whether the foreign officers failed to follow American constitutional procedures or of the extent to which American agents may have been involved in their activities"); United States v. Marzano, 537 F.2d 257 (7th Cir.1976) (FBI agents were present when foreign police officer conducted investigation and searches, "but there is no evidence that they took an active part in interrogating or searching the suspects or in selecting evidence to seize"); Stonehill v. United States, 405 F.2d 738 (9th Cir.1968) (IRS agent sent informer to Phillipines official, went to warehouse where search had been made and assisted in selection of relevant documents); Birdsell v. United States, 346 F.2d 775 (5th Cir.1965) (a Texas deputy sheriff, in Mexico concerning other matters, acted as interpreter in questioning that led to search); State v. Barajas, 195 Neb. 502, 238 N.W.2d 913 (1976) (held, the "mere request made by Sheriff Schleve to the Mexican police that they search a residence in Juarez, Mexico, for a weapon used in a homicide did not convert the resulting seizure made by the Mexican authorities into a joint venture").

[302]Elkins v. United States, 364 U.S. 206, 80 S.Ct. 1437, 4 L.Ed.2d 1669 (1960).

[303]Byars v. United States, 273 U.S. 28, 47 S.Ct. 248, 71 L.Ed. 520 (1927).

[304]Note, 2 N.Y.U.J.Int'l L. & Pol. 280, 312 (1969).

As stated in United States v. Morrow, 537 F.2d 120 (5th Cir.1976): "The few courts that have considered the question of how much American participation in a foreign search and seizure is required to mandate application of the exclusionary rule have not been unanimous in their choice of the precise test to be applied, though they have as a statistical matter been virtually unanimous in rejecting claims of undue participation."

restraints. In *Powell v. Zuckert*,[305] for example, the court quite properly held that where Air Force investigators joined Japanese officers in the execution of a Japanese warrant at an off-base dwelling of a civilian Air Force employee, the warrant did not particularly describe the items to be seized and in the execution thereof thousands of the employee's private papers were examined, and the warrant was requested by the Air Force investigators and the Japanese authorities had no interest in the search at all except in the sense that by international treaty Japan had agreed to assist American military authorities with their investigations, the Fourth Amendment was applicable.[306] But it is not inconsistent with *Powell* to suggest that the practicalities of international law enforcement cooperation are such that a rigid all-or-nothing approach is not feasible.

In dealing with other types of "silver platter" situations, the courts have either found sufficient government involvement to bring the search within the reach of the Fourth Amendment, at which point *all* the requirements of the Amendment had to be met, or have found the government involvement not sufficient to do so, in which case quite obviously *none* of the Fourth Amendment limitations were applicable. On the international level, however, this black-or-white treatment is neither necessary nor proper. Assuming a significant degree of involvement by American authorities, they should not be permitted to totally disregard the Fourth Amendment, nor should they inevitably be compelled to supervise the resulting foreign law enforcement operations to the degree necessary to ensure that all procedures subsequently undertaken fit the American mold.

For example, if American authorities should go so far as to request an arrest or a search in a foreign country, the fact the request is acted upon in another country by local police is no reason to forego the requirement that the request must be based upon information amounting to probable cause.[307] But if the arrest is made and a search incident thereto extends beyond that

---

[305]Powell v. Zuckert, 366 F.2d 634 (D.C.Cir.1966).

[306]Consider also the possibility that evidence obtained in a foreign search may be deemed the fruit of a prior American search. See United States v. Schnell, 50 C.M.R. 483, 23 U.S.C.M.A. 464, (1975), excluding evidence found in a German search of defendant's civilian room because that search was a consequence of an illegal search of defendant's military quarters by a CID agent, which produced the evidence connecting defendant with the civilian room.

[307]See Riechmann v. State, 581 So.2d 133 (Fla.1991) (evidence seized in Germany admissible, as "German authorities seized the relevant evidence pursuant to search warrants lawfully issued by a German court," for which "probable cause existed"). Cf. Lalmalani, Extraordinary Rendition Meets the U.S. Citizen: United States' Responsibility Under the Fourth Amendment, 5 Conn.Publ.Int.L.J. 1 (2005) (concluding Fourth Amendment applies to such rendition of a U.S. citizen by foreign officials at request of U.S.); Note, 36 Hastings Const.L.Q. 329, 345–49 (2009) (regarding joint ventures respecting wiretaps by foreign governments).

permitted in this country under *Chimel v. California,*[308] perhaps because the foreign law permits what was allowed in the United States for the many years preceding *Chimel,*[309] exclusion of the evidence found would appear inappropriate.[310] To exclude under these circumstances would be to say, in effect, that the requesting authority should have (i) ascertained what the foreign law was on the general subject of arrest and search incident thereto, (ii) educated the foreign authorities as to any Fourth Amendment requirements extending beyond their own law, and (iii) induced the foreign authorities to follow the more restrictive procedures in this particular case.

While there is no litmus-paper test for ascertaining the result in a particular case under the approach suggested, it is possible to identify certain factors that should be taken into account. The general proposition being applied is that use of the exclusionary rule with respect to foreign searches is justifiable only when American authorities may fairly be held accountable for not preventing the particular conduct complained of. This means, for one thing, that the degree of American participation is relevant. When, for example, American authorities actually participate in

---

But see United States v. Barona, 56 F.3d 1087 (9th Cir.1995) (compliance with Danish law all that required as to Danish wiretaps that were a "joint venture" with U.S. officials; strong dissent objects that in addition it must be shown there was probable cause).

[308] Chimel v. California, 395 U.S. 752, 89 S.Ct. 2034, 23 L.Ed.2d 685 (1969).

[309] This is not to suggest that if a foreign search violates foreign law that the fruits thereof should for that reason be suppressed in a prosecution occurring in the United States. Although such a view has been urged, Note, 2 N.Y.U.J.Int'l L. & Pol. 280, 302 (1969), the law is otherwise, United States v. Emmanuel, 565 F.3d 1324 (11th Cir.2009) (while there is a "shocks the judicial conscience" exception, as a matter of supervisory power, to general rule that evidence obtained from foreign officials in their countries is admissible, mere fact multi-level review prior to wiretap does not involve a judge under Bahama law not sufficient for exception to apply); United States v. Morrow, 537 F.2d 120 (5th Cir.1976); Birdsell v. United States, 346 F.2d 775 (5th Cir.1965), which is consistent with the general view that

a mere violation of law in another U.S. jurisdiction is not a basis for exclusion, see § 1.3(c).

But see United States v. Phillips, 479 F.Supp. 423 (M.D.Fla.1979) (though defendant not constitutionally entitled to suppression in U.S. court of eavesdropping evidence obtained by Canadian police in that country after "an innocuous exchange of intelligence information" with U.S. authorities, "considerations of comity" require suppression because the defendants established "that the interception was *unlawful* under Canadian law; that the content of the intercepted conversation could not be used in evidence against them in Canada; and that, had the interception been made in the United States, it would have been equally unlawful and the content of the conversation equally inadmissible").

[310] A somewhat broader proposition, as accepted in United States v. Juda, 46 F.3d 961 (9th Cir.1995), is "that the Fourth Amendment's reasonableness standard applies to United States officials conducting a search affecting a United States citizen in a foreign country" and "that a foreign search is reasonable if it conforms to the requirements of foreign law."

the activities, as in *Powell,* there is obviously a greater opportunity for them to bring about conformance to Fourth Amendment standards. There is a lesser opportunity where they have merely requested or suggested foreign cooperation, and no opportunity (as to prior illegality) where American officials are simply called to the scene of a completed search to share in the evidence discovered. A second factor is the relative interest of the American and foreign governments in the matters under investigation. In *Powell,* where no Japanese interest was being served except compliance with the treaty obligation to assist American military investigators, the American officials could more likely have influenced Japanese authorities to conform to unfamiliar external requirements than in a case where the foreign authorities were vigorously pursuing the investigation for their own purposes. And, while admittedly involving some element of hindsight, the degree of departure from Fourth Amendment requirements should not be ignored.[311]

Yet another consideration, it was concluded in *United States v. Peterson,*[312] is whether the American agents, even if rather substantially involved in the foreign investigation, reasonably believed that the foreign police were complying with local law. In that case there was daily contact between American agents and Philippine police conducting wiretaps which, as it turned out, violated Philippine law. Invoking the *Leon* good faith rule,[313] the court held that it

> applies as well to reliance on foreign law enforcement officers' representations that there has been compliance with their own law. * * * American law enforcement officers were not in an advantageous position to judge whether the search was lawful, as would have been the case in a domestic setting. Holding them to a strict liability standard for failings of their foreign associates would be even more incongruous than holding law enforcement officials to a strict liability standard as to the adequacy of domestic warrants. We conclude that the good faith exception to the exclusionary rule announced in *Leon* applies to the foreign search.
>
> We do not suggest that objectively unreasonable reliance on foreign law officers can cloak the search with immunity from the exclusionary rule. That said, permitting reasonable reliance on representations about foreign law is a rational accommodation to the exigencies of foreign investigations.[314]

---

[311]This is not to say, as intimated in United States v. Morrow, 537 F.2d 120 (5th Cir.1976); Birdsell v. United States, 346 F.2d 775 (5th Cir.1965), supra note 309, that there must be "conduct that shocked the conscience." However, this test may be appropriate where the remedy sought is not exclusion of evidence but challenge of jurisdiction. See United States v. Toscanino,

500 F.2d 267 (2d Cir.1974), discussed in § 1.7.

[312]United States v. Peterson, 812 F.2d 486 (9th Cir.1987).

[313]See § 1.3.

[314]See also United States v. Juda, 46 F.3d 961 (9th Cir.1995) (*Peterson* controls here, as DEA agent told by high official of Australian Federal Po-

§ 1.9 Challenge of jurisdiction

§ 1.9(a)   Illegality in bringing the defendant into the jurisdiction
§ 1.9(b)   Illegal arrest within the jurisdiction
§ 1.9(c)   Extradition proceedings

Research References

West's Key Number Digest
Criminal Law ⬤═99; Extradition and Detainers ⬤═12, 39

Legal Encyclopedias
C.J.S., Criminal Law §§ 167 to 171

Introduction

Unquestionably, an unreasonable seizure of the person—such as an arrest made upon less than probable cause—is of itself a violation of the Fourth and Fourteenth Amendments.[1] But the nature of the exclusionary rule sanction is such that it comes into play only when the police have obtained evidence as a result of an unconstitutional seizure.[2] If no such evidence has been obtained, then it is generally accepted that the illegal arrest does not affect the power of the state to proceed with the prosecution. That is, an illegal arrest does not divest the trial court of jurisdiction over the defendant or otherwise preclude his trial. Indeed, other types of Fourth Amendment violations, even though of a most serious nature, require suppression of the seized evidence but *not* dismissal of the case.[3]

§ 1.9(a) Illegality in bringing the defendant into the jurisdiction

As one might expect, the question whether an illegal taking of custody deprives the trial court of jurisdiction first arose where the illegality actually caused the defendant to be brought into the state where trial was pending from another state or country. The matter first reached the Supreme Court as early as 1886, in *Ker*

---

lice "that no warrant was required under Australian law" for installation of transmitter on vessel).

[Section 1.9]

[1]Terry v. Ohio, 392 U.S. 1, 88 S.Ct. 1868, 20 L.Ed.2d 889 (1968); Henry v. United States, 361 U.S. 98, 80 S.Ct. 168, 4 L.Ed.2d 134 (1959).

[2]E.g., Davis v. Mississippi, 394 U.S. 721, 89 S.Ct. 1394, 22 L.Ed.2d 676 (1969) (fingerprints); Wong Sun v. United States, 371 U.S. 471, 83 S.Ct. 407, 9 L.Ed.2d 441 (1963) (statement).

[3]United States v. Rodriguez, 948 F.2d 914 (5th Cir.1991) (despite defen-dant's claim "that the government engaged in such outrageous conduct in executing a post-indictment search of her former attorney's office," remedy is "exclusion of evidence rather than dis-missal of the indictment"); State v. Marks, 114 Wash.2d 724, 790 P.2d 138 (1990) (notwithstanding "the egregious behavior" of the police in seizing over 600 items in executing warrant for 57 items, "dismissal is an improper rem-edy where the evidence from the ille-gal search has been suppressed, and the violation has no impact on the criminal proceedings").

v. Illinois,[4] where the defendant objected that he had been deprived of due process when he was kidnapped in Peru and forcibly brought back to Illinois to stand trial for larceny and embezzlement. A unanimous Court disagreed:

> The "due process of law" here guarantied is complied with when the party is regularly indicted by the proper grand jury in the state court, has a trial according to the forms and modes prescribed for such trials, and when, in the trial and proceedings, he is deprived of no rights to which he is lawfully entitled. * * * [F]or mere irregularities in the manner in which he may be brought into custody of the law, we do not think he is entitled to say that he should not be tried at all for the crime with which he is charged in a regular indictment. * * * So here, when found within the jurisdiction of the state of Illinois, and liable to answer for a crime against the laws of that state, * * * it is not easy to see how he can say that he is there "without due process of law," within the meaning of the constitutional provision.

Another aspect of *Ker* had to do with the fact that there existed an extradition treaty between Peru and the United States; the Court rejected Ker's argument that he had a right under that treaty to be returned to this country only in accordance with its terms.[5] This branch of *Ker* was revisited in *United States v. Alvarez-Machain,*[6] where a Mexican citizen and resident indicted for the kidnapping and murder of a DEA special agent was forc-

---

[Section 1.9(a)]

[4]Ker v. Illinois, 119 U.S. 436, 7 S.Ct. 225, 30 L.Ed. 421 (1886).

[5]Sometimes the issue is whether a *statute* creates an exception to *Ker*. See, e.g., United States v. Shi, 525 F.3d 709 (9th Cir.2008) (requirement in 18 U.S.C.A. § 2280 that defendant be "later found" in U.S. "does not contain the implicit requirement that the defendant's arrival in the United States be voluntary").

[6]United States v. Alvarez-Machain, 504 U.S. 655, 112 S.Ct. 2188, 119 L.Ed.2d 441 (1992). See Angulo & Reardon, The Apparent Political and Administrative Expediency Exception Established by the Supreme Court in United States v. Humberto Alvarez-Machain to the Rule of Law as Reflected by Recognized Principles of International Law, 16 B.C.Int'l & Comp.L.Rev. 245 (1993); Bush, How Did We Get Here? Foreign Abduction After Alvarez-Machain, 45 Stan.L.Rev. 939 (1993); Iraola, Jurisdiction, Treaties, and Due Process, 59 Buff.L. Rev. 693 (2011); Sanders, In Search of an Alternative Remedy for Violations of Extradition Treaties, 34 Sw.U.L. Rev. 1 (2004); Wilske & Schiller, Jurisdiction Over Persons Abducted in Violation of International Law in the Aftermath of United States v. Alvarez-Machain, 5 U.Chi.L.Sch.Roundtable 205 (1998); Comments, 43 Case W.Res. L.Rev. 675 (1993); 17 Fordham Int'l L.J. 126 (1993); 42 UCLA L.Rev. 1397 (1994); 28 Wake Forest L.Rev. 671 (1993); Notes, 47 Ark.L.Rev. 477 (1994); 41 Buff.L.Rev. 627 (1993); 43 DePaul L.Rev. 449 (1994); 31 Duq.L. Rev. 939 (1993); 27 Hous.J. Int'l L. 221 (2004); 20 Pepp.L.Rev. 1503 (1993); 23 Seton Hall L.Rev. 1128 (1993); 48 St. Louis U.L.J. 1373 (2004); 67 S.Cal.L. Rev. 475 (1994); 25 Toledo L.Rev. 297 (1994); 18 U. Dayton L.Rev. 889 (1993).

In a related civil action "which has been litigated in one form or another for more than a decade," it was held "that the DEA had no authority to effect Alvarez's arrest and detention in Mexico, and that he may seek relief in federal court." Alvarez-Machain v. United States, 331 F.3d 604 (9th Cir. 2003).

ibly abducted from Mexico and brought to the United States for trial. The case differed from *Ker* in two respects: (i) Mexico, unlike Peru, objected to the abduction; and (ii) here, U.S. officials were responsible for the abduction, while *Ker* had been decided on the premise there had been no government involvement. But the Court ruled that nonetheless *Ker* was "fully applicable to this case," as the "Treaty says nothing about the obligations of the [parties] to refrain from forcible abductions of people from the territory of the other nation, or the consequences under the Treaty if such an abduction occurs."[7] On the question of "whether the Treaty should be interpreted so as to include an implied term prohibiting prosecution where the defendant's presence was obtained by means other than those established by the Treaty," the Court answered in the negative.[8] Such a large "inferential leap," the Court concluded, was unjustified "with only the most general of international law principles to support it."[9] The broader due process claim rejected in *Ker* was not reexamined in *Alvarez-Machain*.

In *Mahon v. Justice*,[10] where the objection was to the kidnapping of a person in West Virginia and the subsequent forcible

---

[7]And thus, it was concluded in United States v. Chapa-Garza, 62 F.3d 118 (5th Cir.1995), the "fact that extradition proceedings had been initiated" before the abduction "is irrelevant."

[8]See also United States v. Struckman, 611 F.3d 560 (9th Cir.2010) (defendant's presence from Panama achieved via expulsion, and thus court rejects defendant's argument his extradition not in compliance with treaty; also treaty does not prohibit use of other means); United States v. Valencia-Trujillo, 573 F.3d 1171 (11th Cir.2009) ("It necessarily follows from *Alvarez-Machain* that the United States does not lose the right to prosecute a foreign citizen it obtains by the lesser misconduct of an agent misrepresenting or omitting material facts in the affidavit used to secure extradition"); United States v. Mejia, 448 F.3d 436 (D.C.Cir.2006) ("the U.S.-Panama treaty contains no prohibition against procuring the presence of an individual outside the terms of the treaty"); United States v. Best, 304 F.3d 308 (3d Cir.2002) (U.S. has jurisdiction "in spite of the potential violation of international law" in abducting defendant from Brazil, and district court erroneously relied upon two treaties to which Brazil not a party and a third not ratified by the Senate and also a presidential proclamation purporting not to amend existing law); Kasi v. Angelone, 300 F.3d 487 (4th Cir.2002) (U.S. has jurisdiction where treaty between U.S. and Pakistan "contains no provision that bars forcible abductions" or providing "that, once a request for extradition is made, the procedures outlined in the treaty become the sole means of transferring custody"); Serrano v. State, 64 So.3d 93 (Fla.2011) (state has jurisdiction under *Alvarez-Machain* even if defendant "improperly deported from Ecuador").

[9]The three dissenters, on the other hand, objected that the comprehensive treaty provisions "only make sense if they are understood as requiring each treaty signatory to comply with those procedures whenever it wishes to obtain jurisdiction over an individual who is located in another treaty nation," quoting United States v. Verdugo-Urquidez, 939 F.2d 1341 (9th Cir.1991), cert. granted and judgment vacated 505 U.S. 1201, 112 S.Ct. 2986, 120 L.Ed.2d 864 (1992).

[10]Mahon v. Justice, 127 U.S. 700, 8 S.Ct. 1204, 32 L.Ed. 283 (1888).

taking of him to Kentucky to stand trial for murder, the Court reached the same conclusion as *Ker* on the due process issue, asserting: "The jurisdiction of the court in which the indictment is found is not impaired by the manner in which the accused is brought before it." That issue reached the High Court once again, over sixty years later, in *Frisbie v. Collins*,[11] where the defendant was abducted in Illinois and taken into Michigan for a murder trial, but the Court could see no reason to depart from *Ker*:

> No persuasive reasons are now presented to justify overruling this line of cases. They rest on the sound basis that due process of law is satisfied when one present in court is convicted of crime after having been fairly apprized of the charges against him and after a fair trial in accordance with constitutional procedural safeguards. There is nothing in the Constitution that requires a court to permit a guilty person rightfully convicted to escape justice because he was brought to trial against his will.

Frisbie received a cool reception from many commentators. Given the fact that the Court had decided earlier that Term in *Rochin v. California*[12] that resort to a stomach pump to acquire evidence violated due process because it was "conduct that shocks the conscience," the commentators were understandably critical of the Court for its summary treatment of the issue in *Frisbie* and its unquestioned acceptance of "precedents decided under narrower concepts of due process."[13] And, while *Frisbie* was a pre-*Mapp* decision, the unanimity of the state rulings in accord[14] was seen as inconsistent with the view taken in many of those states that exclusion of evidence was required to deter the police.[15] After

---

[11]Frisbie v. Collins, 342 U.S. 519, 72 S.Ct. 509, 96 L.Ed. 541 (1952).

[12]Rochin v. California, 342 U.S. 165, 72 S.Ct. 205, 96 L.Ed. 183 (1952).

[13]The Supreme Court, 1951 Term, 66 Harv.L.Rev. 89, 127 (1952), also noting that "it is arguable that there should be no constitutional difference between a trial using reliable evidence brutally obtained and a proceeding against a defendant brutally obtained." Similarly, Allen, Due Process and State Criminal Procedures: Another Look, 48 Nw.U.L.Rev. 16, 28 (1953), observes that the practices used in *Frisbie* "represent a threat to life and limb which may be at least as serious as the practices pursued by the police in the *Rochin* case." And Scott, Criminal Jurisdiction of a State Over a Defendant Based Upon Presence Secured by Force or Fraud, 37 Minn.L. Rev. 91, 98 (1953), notes: "The brutal-

ity involved in kidnapping is not far removed in degree from the brutality of the stomach pump. At all events, it is surprising that, in view of the *Rochin* case, all of the members of the Supreme Court so readily concluded that due process was not violated in *Frisbie v. Collins*."

[14]See cases collected in Annot., 165 A.L.R. 947 (1946).

[15]Scott, 37 Minn.L.Rev. 91, 101–02 (1953): "It would seem that the existence of the remedies of civil and criminal actions against policemen who kidnap and abduct are equally inadequate, and that the right to be free from unlawful bodily interference by police officers is at least as important as the right to be free from unlawful search and seizure of property by them; so that the only effective way to deter police from such lawlessness is to say to them, 'We will not try a crim-

Mapp, therefore, it was not surprising to find courts[16] and commentators[17] manifesting serious doubts about the continued vitality of the *Frisbie* holding. Finally, in *United States v. Toscanino,*[18] the Second Circuit declined to follow the *Ker-Frisbie* rule.

Toscanino, appealing from a narcotics conviction, argued (as he had prior to trial) that he could not be tried because his presence within the territorial jurisdiction of the court had been illegally obtained. He offered to prove that by the connivance and participation of U.S. officials he had been kidnapped from his home in Uruguay, detained for three weeks of interrogation accompanied by physical torture in Brazil, and then brought into the United States for trial. After taking note of *Mapp* and other Supreme Court decisions in the Fourth Amendment area, the court asserted:

> In light of these developments we are satisfied that the *"Ker-Frisbie"* rule cannot be reconciled with the Supreme Court's expansion of the concept of due process, which now protects the accused against pretrial illegality by denying to the government the fruits of its exploitation of any deliberate and unnecessary lawlessness on its part. Although the issue in most of the cases forming part of this evolutionary process was whether evidence should have been excluded * * *, it was unnecessary in those cases to invoke any other sanction to insure that an ultimate conviction would not rest on governmental illegality. Where suppression of evidence will not suffice, however, we must be guided by the underlying principle that the government should be denied the right to exploit its own illegal conduct * * *, and when an accused is kidnapped and forcibly brought within the jurisdiction, the court's acquisition of power over his person represents the fruits of the government's exploitation of its own misconduct. Having unlawfully seized the defendant in violation of the Fourth Amendment, * * * the government should as a matter of fundamental fairness be obligated to return him to his *status quo ante.*
>
> * * * [W]e view due process as now requiring a court to divest itself of jurisdiction over the person of a defendant where it has been acquired as the result of the government's deliberate, unnecessary and unreasonable invasion of the accused's constitutional rights. This conclusion represents but an extension of the well-

---

inal whose presence in the state has been thus secured.' "

[16]United States v. Edmons, 432 F.2d 577 (2d Cir.1970); Government of Virgin Islands v. Ortiz, 427 F.2d 1043 (3d Cir.1970).

[17]Pitler, "The Fruit of the Poisonous Tree" Revisited and Shepardized, 56 Cal.L.Rev. 579, 600 (1968): "It is not readily apparent why the exclusion of illegally obtained evidence may be a proper way to deter illicit police activity while the divesting of jurisdiction is not."

[18]United States v. Toscanino, 500 F.2d 267 (2d Cir.1974), commented on in 28 A.L.R.Fed. 685 (1976); 88 Harv.L. Rev. 813 (1975); 50 N.Y.U.L.Rev. 681 (1975); 12 San Diego L.Rev. 865 (1975); 47 U.Colo.L.Rev. 489 (1976); 21 Wayne L.Rev. 1473 (1975). See also Abramovsky & Eagle, United States Policy in Apprehending Alleged Offenders Abroad: Extradition, Abduction or Irregular Rendition, 57 Ore.L.Rev. 51 (1977); Iraola, Jurisdiction, Treaties, and Due Process, 59 Buff.L.Rev. 693 (2011).

recognized power of federal courts in the civil context to decline to exercise jurisdiction over a defendant whose presence has been secured by force or fraud.

The precise impact of *Toscanino* was, at best, uncertain. For one thing, the court also distinguished *Frisbie* on the ground that the instant case was a federal prosecution, permitting exercise of the court of appeal's supervisory power over the district courts, and on the ground that here the abduction had been in violation of international treaties. This would permit *Toscanino* to be read as not applicable to an interstate abduction or to a prosecution in the state courts. Moreover, *Toscanino* did not make it clear whether *any* unconstitutional act in bringing a defendant before the court would suffice to divest the court of jurisdiction. At one point the court said that jurisdiction is divested if the defendant's presence was acquired by a "deliberate, unnecessary and unreasonable invasion" of the defendant's rights, which could be taken to cover any knowing interjurisdiction abduction in lieu of established extradition procedures. On the other hand, the court's repeated reliance upon the *Rochin* test[19] suggested a more narrow holding.

The possibility that *Toscanino* amounted to a total rejection of the *Ker-Frisbie* rule, a position some commentators criticized as too extreme,[20] is no longer a matter of speculation. In *United States ex rel. Lujan v. Gengler*,[21] the defendant, relying on *Toscanino,* claimed the federal court in New York did not have jurisdiction over him because he had been abducted in Bolivia by Bolivian police acting as agents of the United States and placed on a plane bound for New York. In rejecting this contention, the court offered this clarification of *Toscanino:*

> Yet in recognizing that *Ker* and *Frisbie* no longer provided a carte blanche to government agents bringing defendants from abroad to the United States by the use of torture, brutality and similar outrageous conduct, we did not intend to suggest that *any* irregularity in the circumstances of a defendant's arrival in the jurisdiction would

---

[19]The court noted that the continuing force of *Rochin* had been recognized in United States v. Russell, 411 U.S. 423, 93 S.Ct. 1637, 36 L.Ed.2d 366 (1973), and that the instant case fit the *Russell* characterization of "conduct * * * so outrageous that due process principles would absolutely bar the government from invoking judicial processes to obtain a conviction."

[20]Note, 88 Harv.L.Rev. 813, 816 (1975): "Refusing to exercise jurisdiction is far more drastic a step than, say, excluding evidence produced by the illegal arrest; it completely deprives the state of the opportunity to present its case. *Ker* and *Frisbie* reflect a judgment not that due process is limited to the guarantee of a fair trial, but that interstate or international abduction is not misconduct sufficiently egregious to justify releasing the defendant."

Compare Note, 50 N.Y.U.L.Rev. 681, 707 (1975), approving the "*Toscanino* sanction" because it "would not have precluded a subsequent prosecution once personal jurisdiction had been acquired legitimately."

[21]United States ex rel. Lujan v. Gengler, 510 F.2d 62 (2d Cir.1975).

vitiate the proceedings of the criminal court. In holding that *Ker* and *Frisbie* must yield to the extent they were inconsistent with the Supreme Court's more recent pronouncements we scarcely could have meant to eviscerate the *Ker-Frisbie* rule, which the Supreme Court has never felt impelled to disavow. Although we cited other cases in *Toscanino* as evidence of the partial erosion of *Ker* and *Frisbie,* the twin pillars of our holding were *Rochin v. California*[22] * * * and dictum in *United States v. Russell*[23] * * *, both of which dealt with government conduct of a most shocking and outrageous character. * * *

The cruel, inhuman and outrageous treatment allegedly suffered by Toscanino brought his case within the *Rochin* principle * * *.

But the same cannot be said of Lujan. It requires little argument to show that the government conduct of which he complains pales by comparison with that alleged by Toscanino. Lacking from Lujan's petition is any allegation of that complex of shocking governmental conduct sufficient to convert an abduction which is simply illegal into one which sinks to a violation of due process. Unlike Toscanino, Lujan does not allege that a gun blow knocked him unconscious when he was first taken into captivity, nor does he claim that drugs were administered to subdue him for the flight to the United States. Neither is there any assertion that the United States Attorney was aware of his abduction, or of any interrogation. Indeed, Lujan disclaims any acts of torture, terror, or custodial interrogation of any kind.

In sum, but for the charge that the law was violated during the process of transporting him to the United States, Lujan charges no deprivation greater than that which he would have endured through lawful extradition. We scarcely intend to convey approval of illegal government conduct. But we are forced to recognize that, absent a set of incidents like that in *Toscanino,* not every violation by prosecution or police is so egregious that *Rochin* and its progeny requires nullification of the indictment.

The post-*Toscanino* decisions of other courts are generally in accord with *Lujan;* they recognize the continued vitality of the *Ker-Frisbie* rule except perhaps when the abduction is accompanied by conduct that shocks the conscience.[24] But as yet, the Supreme

---

[22]Rochin v. California, 342 U.S. 165, 72 S.Ct. 205, 96 L.Ed. 183 (1952).

[23]United States v. Russell, 411 U.S. 423, 93 S.Ct. 1637, 36 L.Ed.2d 366 (1973).

[24]United States v. Struckman, 611 F.3d 560 (9th Cir.2010) (lies to Panamanian officials that defendant already convicted in U.S. do not meet "shocking and outrageous" test, considering that "the Panamanians had already decided to cooperate with the United States in returning Struckman"); Scrivner v. Tansy, 68 F.3d 1234 (10th Cir.1995) (*Ker-Frisbie* applies even if New Mexico officers arrested defendant in Arizona without a warrant and then transported him to New Mexico for trial); United States v. Chapa-Garza, 62 F.3d 118 (5th Cir.1995) (mere circumvention of pending extradition proceedings insufficient, as *Toscanino* "limited to those situations involving torture, brutality and similar outrageous conduct"); United States v. Matta, 937 F.2d 567 (11th Cir.1991) (even were *Toscanino* exception recognized, alleged misconduct here does "not rise to the level of 'brutal torture and incessant interrogation'"); United States v. Yunis,

Court has not had occasion to pass on this purported exception,[25] and "no court, including the *Toscanino* court which remanded the case for factual findings, has ever found conduct that rises to the level necessary to require the United States to divest itself of jurisdiction."[26] On the basis of *Graham v. Connor*,[27] holding that use of force during arrest (as opposed to during pretrial detention) is properly analyzed under the Fourth Amendment rather than the Fifth Amendment due process clause, it has been held

---

924 F.2d 1086 (D.C.Cir.1991) (deception luring defendant into international waters not outrageous under *Toscanino*); United States v. Wilson, 732 F.2d 404 (5th Cir.1984) (*Toscanino* not applicable where defendant was merely "the victim of a non-violent trick" when he induced to travel to another country where agents willing to turn him over to U.S. officials); United States v. Reed, 639 F.2d 896 (2d Cir.1981) (defendant was seized in the Bahamas pursuant to an arrest warrant and on probable cause and thus the seizure was reasonable for Fourth Amendment purposes even though extradition treaty not followed and excessive force possibly used in holding gun to defendant's head and wrenching his arm); United States v. Herrera, 504 F.2d 859 (5th Cir.1974) (defendant only claimed abduction, court stresses "wide variance" between instant case and *Toscanino*); Jenkins v. State, 260 Ga. 231, 391 S.E.2d 397 (1990) ("even assuming the validity of *Toscanino* and *Lujan,* the circumstances of Jenkins' arrest [in Missouri] do not fit within such a rule"); People v. Galan, 229 Ill.2d 484, 323 Ill.Dec. 325, 893 N.E.2d 597 (2008) ("that Chicago police ignored the extradition process in this case does not constitute a constitutional violation"; "we reaffirm our adherence to the *Ker-Frisbie* doctrine"); Johnson v. State, 271 Ind. 145, 390 N.E.2d 1005 (1979) (following *Ker-Frisbie* notwithstanding illegal arrest in Mo. and transfer to Ind. without formal extradition or waiver thereof); People v. Walls, 35 N.Y.2d 419, 363 N.Y.S.2d 82, 321 N.E.2d 875 (1974) (New York police made arrest in New Jersey but failed to comply with hot pursuit law; *Ker-Frisbie* rule followed). See generally Iraola, A Primer on Legal Issues Surrounding the Extraterritorial Apprehension of Criminals, 29 Am.J.Crim.L. 1 (2001); McNeal, Snatch-and-Grab Ops: Justifying Extraterritorial Abduction, 16 Transnat'l L. & Contemp. Probs. 491 (2007) (concluding at 522, regarding international abduction of terrorists who will not be handed over by their host countries, that "the extraterritorial abduction is still permissible under the doctrine of male captus, bene detentus under customary international law, codified international rules, U.S. jurisprudence, and foreign state decisions"); Annot., 64 A.L.R. Fed. 292 (1983); Note, 23 Vand.J. Transnat'l L. 385 (1990).

Compare Benally v. Marcum, 89 N.M. 463, 553 P.2d 1270 (1976) (police pursued defendant into Navajo Reservation and arrested him there and took him off reservation, which "violated tribal sovereignty because it circumvented and was contrary to the orderly procedure for extradition from the Navajo Reservation provided for in [the] Navajo Tribal Code"; held, "the reasoning of the *Toscanino* case * * * is applicable to the instant case").

[25]In United States v. Alvarez-Machain, 504 U.S. 655, 112 S.Ct. 2188, 119 L.Ed.2d 441 (1992), text at note 6 supra, the majority at one point acknowledged that perhaps defendant's abduction was "shocking," but this hardly seems an expression of a judgment on this purported exception, as the district court had already rejected the defendant's outrageous government conduct claim, which was not then before the Supreme Court.

[26]Matta-Ballesteros v. Henman, 896 F.2d 255 (7th Cir.1990).

[27]Graham v. Connor, 490 U.S. 386, 109 S.Ct. 1865, 104 L.Ed.2d 443 (1989).

that such force of whatever degree is not a basis for divesting jurisdiction.[28]

The Second Circuit also soon had occasion to stress another of *Toscanino*'s limits. In *United States v. Lira,*[29] Mellafe testified that he was arrested by Chilean police, held for several weeks and tortured, and then put on a plane to New York. Affirming his conviction, the court stated:

> Essential to a holding that *Toscanino* applies is a finding that the gross mistreatment leading to the forcible abduction of the defendant was perpetrated by representatives of the United States Government. * * *

> The only suggestion of possible involvement on the part of United States officials comes from Mellafe's testimony that he heard English spoken during the time of his torture in Santiago, that he saw the Special Agents at the Naval Prosecutor's office, and that he was told that his photograph was "for the Americans." However there was no evidence that American agents were present at or privy to his interrogation or that the persons overheard to speak English were Americans, much less Government agents. Agent Cecil, furthermore, testified that he was not at the prosecutor's office or aware of the activities of the Chilean police and that he did not seek Mellafe until he boarded the plane on May 4, 1974. Thus on this record there was no direct evidence of any misconduct on the part of the United States Government.

> Although no direct involvement by the Government in Mellafe's torture could be proven, appellant nevertheless suggests that the Government was "vicariously responsible" for his torture, since the DEA requested Mellafe's arrest and expulsion and thus "placed the matter in motion." This argument must be rejected. Unlike *Toscanino,* where the defendant was kidnapped from Uruguay in defiance of the laws of the country, here the Government merely asked the Chilean Government to arrest and expel Mellafe in accord with its own procedures. This action can hardly be faulted. Agencies such as the DEA presumably must cooperate with many foreign governments in seeking transfer to the United States of violators of the United States law. The DEA can hardly be expected to monitor the conduct of representatives of each foreign government to assure that a request for extradition or expulsion is carried out in accordance with American constitutional standards. Moreover, no purpose would be served by holding the Government responsible for the actions of Chilean police. * * * Hopefully divestiture of jurisdiction over a defendant forcibly abducted by our Government from a foreign jurisdiction would inhibit our Government from engaging in similar unlawful conduct in the future. However, where the United States Government plays no direct or substantial role in the misconduct and the foreign police have acted not as United States agents but merely on behalf of their own government, the imposition of a penalty would only deter United States representatives from making a lawful request for the defendant and would not deter any illegal conduct. Since our Government has no control over

---

[28]Matta-Ballesteros v. Henman, 896 F.2d 255 (7th Cir.1990).

[29]United States v. Lira, 515 F.2d 68 (2d Cir.1975).

the foreign police, extension of *Toscanino* to the present case would serve no purpose.[30]

§ 1.9(b) Illegal arrest within the jurisdiction

In the *Ker* case, discussed above, holding that international abduction did not violate due process, the Court supported its conclusion by reference to what result would obtain if there were a within-the-jurisdiction illegality:

> He may be arrested for a very heinous offense by persons without any warrant, or without any previous complaint, and brought before a proper officer; and this may be, in some sense, said to be "without due process of law." But it would hardly be claimed that, after the case had been investigated and the defendant held by the proper authorities to answer for the crime, he could plead that he was first arrested "without due process of law."

The state[31] and federal[32] courts, often citing *Ker* and its progeny, have held that the unlawfulness of an arrest does not affect

---

[30]Following remand, Toscanino lost on this basis, for he did not submit "any credible evidence which would indicate any participation on the part of United States officials prior to the time the defendant arrived in this country." United States v. Toscanino, 398 F.Supp. 916 (E.D.N.Y.1975). See also United States v. Cordero, 668 F.2d 32 (1st Cir.1981) (United States agents merely identified defendant and had nothing to do with his treatment in Panamanian jail; were our courts to "seek to improve conditions in foreign jails by refusing to try those who are temporarily held there, the result would not be better jails, but the creation of safe havens in foreign lands for those fleeing the reach of American justice").

On the related point that evidence seized by independent action of foreign police is admissible in American courts even if the procedures used would be unconstitutional if employed by our police, see § 1.8(h).

[Section 1.9(b)]

[31]State v. Richardson, 373 Ark. 1, 280 S.W.3d 20 (2008); State v. Johnson, 227 Conn. 534, 630 A.2d 1059 (1993); York v. Jarvis, 248 Ga. 774, 286 S.E.2d 296 (1982); State v. Barros, 131 Idaho 379, 957 P.2d 1095 (1998); Chambers v. State, 478 N.E.2d 1234 (Ind.1985); State v. Hill, 281 Kan. 136, 130 P.3d 1 (2006); Commonwealth v. Jacobsen, 419 Mass. 269, 644 N.E.2d 213 (1995);

People v. Burrill, 391 Mich. 124, 214 N.W.2d 823 (1974); Fleming v. State, 604 So.2d 280 (Miss.1992); State v. Sor-Lokken, 247 Mont. 343, 805 P.2d 1367 (1991); Graves v. State, 112 Nev. 118, 912 P.2d 234 (1996); State ex rel. Jackson v. Brigano, 88 Ohio St.3d 180, 724 N.E.2d 424 (2000); State v. Lee, 763 P.2d 385 (Okl.Crim.App.1988); Primeaux v. Leapley, 502 N.W.2d 265 (S.D.1993); State v. Smith, 787 S.W.2d 34 (Tenn.Crim.App.1989); Stiggers v. State, 506 S.W.2d 609 (Tex.Crim.App. 1974); State v. Beck, 584 P.2d 870 (Utah 1978); State v. Klinker, 85 Wash.2d 509, 537 P.2d 268 (1975); State v. Smith, 131 Wis.2d 220, 388 N.W.2d 601 (1986). For earlier decisions, see Annot., 96 A.L.R. 982 (1935).

Likewise, an illegal detention without a probable cause determination following a warrantless arrest, see § 5.1(g), does not deprive the trial court of jurisdiction. Montoya v. Scott, 65 F.3d 405 (5th Cir.1995).

[32]See Guzman-Flores v. U.S. Immigration & Naturalization Service, 496 F.2d 1245 (7th Cir.1974), citing decisions in accord from other circuits and applying the rule to deportation proceedings as well. See also Luevano v. Holder, 660 F.3d 1207 (10th Cir.2011) (re removal proceedings); United States v. Jeremiah, 493 F.3d 1042 (9th Cir.2007) (even if arrest warrant for convicted defendant on supervised release invalid, court still had jurisdiction to revoke release,

the jurisdiction or power of the trial court to proceed in a criminal case.[33] The Supreme Court in *Gerstein v. Pugh*[34] declined to "retreat from the established rule that illegal arrest or detention does not void a subsequent conviction," and in *I.N.S. v. Lopez-Mendoza*[35] held an illegal arrest has no bearing upon a subsequent civil hearing undertaken for the purpose of deporting the person illegally arrested.[36]

Even if, as concluded above, *Ker* and *Frisbie* are no longer absolute with respect to international and interstate abduction, it does not follow that a divesting of jurisdiction is constitutionally required whenever the defendant is before the court as a consequence of an antecedent illegal arrest.[37] Such a rule would be difficult to administer, and would not likely bring about any appreciable deterrence of illegal arrests. As one commentator highly

---

distinguishing United States v. Vargas-Amaya, 389 F.3d 901 (9th Cir.2004), based on 18 U.S.C.A. § 3583(i) requirement of valid warrant as a condition of jurisdiction when term of supervision has expired); Men Keng Chang v. Jiugni, 669 F.2d 275 (5th Cir.1982); Katris v. Immigration & Naturalization Service, 562 F.2d 866 (2d Cir. 1977).

[33]The same rule applies when the proceeding is a forfeiture action and the illegal seizure was of the property to be declared forfeited. United States v. Daccarett, 6 F.3d 37 (2d Cir.1993); United States v. $277,000.00 U.S. Currency, 941 F.2d 898 (9th Cir.1991); United States v. United States Currency $31,828, 760 F.2d 228 (8th Cir.1985); Matter of Property Seized on January 31, 1983, 362 N.W.2d 565 (Iowa 1985). See § 1.7(a).

Despite some authority to the contrary, United States v. $37,780.00 in U.S. Currency, 920 F.2d 159 (2d Cir.1990), it does not follow that the res in forfeiture proceedings, if itself illegally seized, can also be admitted for its evidentiary value. United States v. $191,910.00 in U.S. Currency, 16 F.3d 1051 (9th Cir.1994) (noting "the majority of circuits to consider the issue" agree).

[34]Gerstein v. Pugh, 420 U.S. 103, 95 S.Ct. 854, 43 L.Ed.2d 54 (1975), discussed in Garcia, The Scope of Police Immunity from Civil Suit Under Title 43 Section 1983 and Bivens: A Realistic Appraisal, 11 Whittier L.Rev. 511 (1989).

[35]I.N.S. v. Lopez-Mendoza, 468 U.S. 1032, 104 S.Ct. 3479, 82 L.Ed.2d 778 (1984).

[36]*Lopez-Mendoza* should not be read "as excepting from the 'fruits' doctrine all evidence that tends to show a defendant's identity," as it only has to do with "cases in which the defendant challenges the jurisdiction of the court," as "is evident simply from looking at the cases the Court cites in support," *Frisbie* and *Gerstein*, and with the manner in which the Court dealt with "the two separate proceedings in that case" re Lopez, who made only a jurisdictional challenge, and Sandoval, who sought suppression of evidence. United States v. Olivares-Rangel, 458 F.3d 1104 (10th Cir.2006). Accord: United States v. Farias-Gonzalez, 556 F.3d 1181 (11th Cir.2009); United States v. Oscar-Torres, 507 F.3d 224 (4th Cir.2007); United States v. Guevara-Martinez, 262 F.3d 751 (8th Cir.2001); State v. Maldonado-Arreaga, 772 N.W.2d 74 (Minn.App.2009); State v. Moscone, 161 N.H. 355, 13 A.3d 137 (2011).

[37]If the arrest is lawful but without a warrant, there is a Fourth Amendment requirement that there be a prompt judicial probable cause determination in order to hold or only conditionally release the defendant pending trial. See § 5.1(g). But violation of such a Fourth Amendment requirement likewise does not deprive the court of jurisdiction. In re Vernon E., 121 N.H. 836, 435 A.2d 833 (1981).

critical of *Frisbie* noted: "If the suspect is forced to go to trial and there is sufficient admissible evidence to convict, it should not be necessary to have a new trial merely because the entire process was commenced by an illegal arrest. Surely it is an exercise in futility to release the defendant and then immediately rearrest him based on evidence unrelated to the first arrest."[38] Of course, some might object to that statement on the ground that the awesome prospect of requiring new trials merely because of an illegal arrest can be avoided by always determining the jurisdiction question (including appeals on that issue) before trial.[39] But such a cumbersome procedure would cause delay without any offsetting benefit. As for deterrence, it is naive to say that release for an illegal arrest followed by a new arrest will result in the police being "taught to respect the law."[40] And, unlike the acceptance of illegally seized evidence by a court, it cannot be said that a trial of a person who was illegally arrested (without an intervening release and lawful arrest) either allows the government to profit from its wrongdoing or makes the judiciary a partner in unconstitutional activity. This conclusion is not inconsistent with *United States v. Toscanino*,[41] qualifying *Ker* and *Frisbie* in the international (and, presumably, interstate) setting, for there the court was concerned with conduct "so outrageous that due process principles would absolutely bar the government from invoking judicial processes to obtain a conviction."[42]

---

[38]Pitler, 56 Cal.L.Rev. 579, 601 (1968). Similarly, in State v. Smith, 131 Wis.2d 220, 388 N.W.2d 601 (1986), the court stated: "After examining the purpose of the illegal arrest/personal jurisdiction rule, this court questions whether treating an illegal arrest as a jurisdictional defect provides substantive protection against unreasonable searches and seizures. The rule merely elevates form over substance; it will not deter illegal arrests per se. The state may simply rearrest a defendant after lack of jurisdiction has been found, and thereby afford a court proper personal jurisdiction over the defendant."

[39]Such is the proposal in Note, 100 U.Pa.L.Rev. 1182, 1215 (1952).

[40]Note, 100 U.Pa.L.Rev. 1182, 1215 (1952).

[41]United States v. Toscanino, 500 F.2d 267 (2d Cir.1974).

[42]Quoting from United States v. Russell, 411 U.S. 423, 93 S.Ct. 1637, 36 L.Ed.2d 366 (1973). In United States

v. Lawrence, 434 F.Supp. 441 (D.D.C. 1977), the court, citing *Toscanino* and *Russell,* said there could be a situation where the arrest was so outrageous as to bar jurisdiction, but concluded the instant case (defendant was shot at close range with unauthorized ammunition at time of arrest) was not such a situation.

In Commonwealth v. Phillips, 413 Mass. 50, 595 N.E.2d 310 (1992), the trial judge apparently believed he was dealing with such an outrageous situation, as he concluded the defendant's arrests were pursuant to "a Boston police department policy to 'search on sight' all young, black persons in Roxbury suspected of being gang members or of being in the company of a gang member," but the appellate court concluded that even if that were so evidence suppression rather than dismissal of indictments was the proper remedy, as "the deterrent effect of dismissal of these indictments would be little, if any, more than the deterrent effect of suppression of the unlawfully obtained evidence."

§ 1.9(c) Extradition proceedings

In *Ker v. Illinois*,[43] discussed above, where the Court held that due process had not been violated by kidnapping the defendant in Peru and bringing him to Illinois for trial, the defendant also objected that there had been certain defects in the extradition proceedings that brought about his transfer from California, where he arrived back into the United States, to Illinois. The Court responded that "it is hardly a proper subject of inquiry on the trial of the case to examine into the details of the proceedings by which the demand was made by the one state, and the manner in which it was responded to by the other."[44] However, the Court cautioned that it was *not* saying that a person seized in an asylum state for extradition was foreclosed to "test the authority by which he was held." Thus, while no effort will be made herein to survey the entire range of legal problems attending the extradition process,[45] it is appropriate to inquire whether the Fourth Amendment offers some protection to the person against whom extradition proceedings are undertaken.[46]

Extradition, or, more precisely, interstate rendition,[47] is specifi-

---

[Section 1.9(c)]

[43]Ker v. Illinois, 119 U.S. 436, 7 S.Ct. 225, 30 L.Ed. 421 (1886).

[44]Consider also United States v. Valencia-Trujillo, 573 F.3d 1171 (11th Cir.2009) ("It necessarily follows from *Alvarez-Machain*," the Supreme Court's *Ker*-based ruling, "that the United States does not lose the right to prosecute a foreign citizen it obtains by the lesser misconduct of an agent misrepresenting or omitting material facts in the affidavit used to secure extradition").

[45]See Council of State Governments, The Handbook on Interstate Crime Control (1977); R. Hurd, Interstate Rendition (2d ed. 1876); M. Bassiouni, International Extradition: United States Law and Practice (5th ed.2007); C. Doyle, Extradition to and from the United States (2008); J. Moore, Extradition and Interstate Rendition (1891); J. Scott, Interstate Rendition (1917); S. Spear, Law of Rendition (3d ed. 1885); Abramson, Extradition in America: Of Uniform Acts and Government Discretion, 33 Baylor L.Rev. 793 (1981); Glander, Practice in Ohio Under the Uniform Criminal Extradition Act, 8 Ohio St.L.J. 255 (1942); Green, Duties of the Asylum State Under the Uniform Criminal Extradition Act, 30 J.Crim.L. & Criminology 295 (1939); Hoague, Extradition Between States, 13 Am.L.Rev. 181 (1879); Horowitz & Steinberg, The Fourteenth Amendment, Its Newly Recognized Impact on the "Scope" of Habeas Corpus in Extradition, 23 S.Cal.L.Rev. 441 (1950); Kopelman, Extradition and Rendition, History, Law, Recommendations, 14 B.U.L.Rev. 596 (1934); Murphy, Revising Domestic Extradition Law, 131 U.Pa.L.Rev. 1063 (1983); Parry, International Extradition, The Rule of Non-Inquiry, and the Problem of Sovereignty, 90 B.U.L.Rev. 1973 (2010); Snow, The Arrest Prior to Extradition of Fugitives from Justice of Another State, 17 Hastings L.J. 767 (1966); Comment, 21 U.Chi.L.Rev. 735 (1954); Note, 74 Yale L.J. 78 (1964) (both on extradition habeas corpus); Note, 66 Yale L.J. 970 (1956) (on executive discretion).

[46]For a more extended discussion of this topic, see Note, 24 Rutgers L.Rev. 551 (1970).

[47]Note, 24 Rutgers L.Rev. 551 (1970), noting that the word extradition is more properly employed to describe the surrender of fugitives between nations.

cally provided for in the United States Constitution.[48] In order to implement the rendition clause, Congress enacted the Federal Rendition Act, which requires that the demanding state produce "a copy of an indictment found or an affidavit made before a magistrate of any State or Territory, charging the person demanded with having committed treason, felony, or other crime, certified as authentic by the governor."[49] While that Act provides no details concerning the procedures to be used in apprehending and returning suspected fugitives, virtually all jurisdictions have adopted the Uniform Criminal Extradition Act.[50] The Uniform Act provides that the demand must be

> accompanied by a copy of an indictment found or by information supported by affidavit in the state having jurisdiction of the crime, or by a copy of an affidavit made before a magistrate there, together with a copy of any warrant which was issued thereupon; or by a copy of a judgment of conviction or of a sentence imposed in execution thereof, together with a statement by the Executive Authority of the demanding state that the person claimed has escaped from confinement or has broken the terms of his bail, probation or parole. The indictment, information, or affidavit made before the magistrate must substantially charge the person demanded with having committed a crime under the law of that state; and the copy of indictment, information, affidavit, judgment of conviction or sentence must be authenticated by the Executive Authority making the demand.[51]

Both Acts, it will be noted, permit the arrest of an individual upon an affidavit alleging that he has committed a crime in the demanding state; and in neither instance is there any specific mention of a requirement that the affidavit set forth underlying facts showing probable cause to believe he has done so. It is none too surprising, therefore, that the traditional view, developed well before the *Mapp* decision or even *Wolf*, was that no such showing was required to justify rendition.[52] But even in more recent times, the courts were inclined to accept as indisputable the propositions that "the question of whether or not the demanding state has sufficient evidence * * * cannot be considered in an extradition proceeding"[53] and that "the sufficiency of the affidavit * * * is not open to inquiry on habeas corpus proceedings to review the issuance of a rendition warrant."[54]

Then, in 1967, the District of Columbia Court of Appeals

[48]U.S. Const. art. IV, § 2: "A Person charged in any State with Treason, Felony, or other Crime, who shall flee from Justice, and be found in another State, shall on Demand of the executive Authority of the State from which he fled, be delivered up, to be removed to the State having Jurisdiction of the Crime."

[49]18 U.S.C.A. § 3182.

[50]See 11 U.L.A. 93 (2003).

[51]Section 3.

[52]See cases collected in Note, 24 Rutgers L.Rev. 551, 560–65 (1970); Annot., 40 A.L.R.2d 1158 (1955).

[53]State v. Limberg, 274 Minn. 31, 142 N.W.2d 563 (1966).

[54]Smith v. State, 89 Idaho 70, 403 P.2d 221 (1965).

decided *Kirkland v. Preston,*[55] a habeas corpus proceeding challenging confinement under an extradition arrest warrant issued upon a Florida affidavit stating in conclusory terms that petitioner had committed the crime of arson in that state. The court held that the affidavit required by statute "does not succeed in 'charging' a crime unless it sets out facts which justify a Fourth Amendment finding of probable cause," reasoning:

There is no reason why the Fourth Amendment, which governs arrests, should not govern extradition arrests. Under its familiar doctrine arrests must be preceded by a finding of probable cause. When an extradition demand is accompanied by an indictment, that document embodies a grand jury's judgment that constitutional probable cause exists. But when the extradition papers rely on a mere affidavit, even where supported by a warrant of arrest, there is no assurance of probable cause unless it is spelled out in the affidavit itself. Thus Fourth Amendment considerations require that before a person can be extradited * * * the authorities in the asylum state must be satisfied that the affidavit shows probable cause.

The law appreciates the hardship which extradition can involve: not only the suspension of one's liberty, but his deportation from the state in which he lives into another jurisdiction which may be hundreds of miles from his home. The law accordingly surrounds the accused with considerable procedural protection to stave off wrongful rendition. It is consistent with this concern for the accused's just treatment to recognize his right to require official confirmation of probable cause in the asylum state before extradition. This right to probable cause confirmation seems especially appropriate in view of the fact that the accused will have no access to an evidentiary preliminary hearing on probable cause until he finally arrives in the accusing jurisdiction.

In addition, the interests of the asylum state are advanced by its own probable cause determination. For it would be highhanded to compel that jurisdiction to lend its coercive authority, and the processes of its law, against even its own citizens in aid of an enterprise the key details of which remain in the dark. If, as here, it turns out that the prosecution against the fugitive is unfounded, the asylum state will have expended its resources and given the legitimizing stamp of its judiciary to a cause which is at best futile, at worst arbitrary.

Recognizing a probable cause requirement * * *, moreover, conflicts with no compelling interests elsewhere in the legal system. If the demanding state does have probable cause data, it will be no real inconvenience to record this evidence in the extradition papers. Documenting probable cause in an affidavit is what the policeman in many jurisdictions * * * must do if he is to secure an ordinary warrant for an arrest or search. And governors, or habeas corpus judges, will hardly be significantly burdened by having to study written submissions for probable cause in extradition cases.

Many other courts thereafter reached essentially the same

---

[55]Kirkland v. Preston, 385 F.2d 670 (D.C.Cir.1967).

conclusion,[56] but some declined to do so.[57]

One argument against *Kirkland* is that the prosecutor's decision is entitled to as much respect as a grand jury indictment; it is presumed "that a public prosecutor, like any other public official, will be true to the duties of his office" and "that he, like the grand jury, will exercise his powers in accordance with the law," meaning that "the issuance of an information" should be afforded "the same degree of sanctity" as "the return of an indictment."[58] But in *Coolidge v. New Hampshire*[59] the Supreme Court held that a prosecutor was not sufficiently "neutral and detached" to be entrusted with the authority to issue search warrants. Even more significant is the fact that in *Gerstein v. Pugh*[60] the Court, in holding that "the Fourth Amendment requires a judicial determination of probable cause as a prerequisite to extended restraint on liberty following arrest" without a warrant, rejected the contention "that the prosecutor's decision to file an information is itself a determination of probable cause that furnishes sufficient reason to detain a defendant pending trial." It may be argued, of course, that the *Coolidge* and *Gerstein* analogies are imperfect in that there is a greater likelihood a prosecutor will exercise restraint when the question is whether public moneys should be expended to bring a person back to the state for purposes of trial. But, while there may be some truth to this,[61] it is not correct to say that prosecutors always make a careful probable cause determination before commencing extradition proceedings. The cases indicate otherwise.[62]

A second objection to the *Kirkland* rule is that an inquiry into

---

[56]Ierardi v. Gunter, 528 F.2d 929 (1st Cir.1976); United States ex rel. Grano v. Anderson, 446 F.2d 272 (3d Cir.1971); Montague v. Smedley, 557 P.2d 774 (Alaska 1976); Renton v. Cronin, 196 Colo. 109, 582 P.2d 677 (1978); Grano v. State, 257 A.2d 768 (Del.Super.1969); Tucker v. Commonwealth, 308 A.2d 783 (D.C. App.1973); Struve v. Wilcox, 99 Idaho 205, 579 P.2d 1188 (1978); Wilbanks v. State, 224 Kan. 66, 579 P.2d 132 (1978); In re Consalvi, 376 Mass. 699, 382 N.E.2d 734 (1978); People v. Doran, 401 Mich. 235, 258 N.W.2d 406 (1977); Sheriff, Clark County v. Thompson, 85 Nev. 211, 452 P.2d 911 (1969); People ex rel. Miller v. Krueger, 35 A.D.2d 743, 316 N.Y.S.2d 246 (1970); Clement v. Cox, 118 N.H. 246, 385 A.2d 841 (1978); State v. Towne, 46 Wis.2d 169, 174 N.W.2d 251 (1970).

[57]People ex rel. Kubala v. Woods, 52 Ill.2d 48, 284 N.E.2d 286 (1972);

Bailey v. Cox, 260 Ind. 448, 296 N.E.2d 422 (1973); In re Ierardi, 366 Mass. 640, 321 N.E.2d 921 (1975); McEwen v. State, 224 So.2d 206 (Miss.1969); Salvail v. Sharkey, 108 R.I. 63, 271 A.2d 814 (1970).

[58]Salvail v. Sharkey, 108 R.I. 63, 271 A.2d 814 (1970).

[59]Coolidge v. New Hampshire, 403 U.S. 443, 91 S.Ct. 2022, 29 L.Ed.2d 564 (1971).

[60]Gerstein v. Pugh, 420 U.S. 103, 95 S.Ct. 854, 43 L.Ed.2d 54 (1975).

[61]However, it overlooks the possibility that the prosecutor may approve an information at a time when it was not known the accused was in another jurisdiction and that he might not thereafter reconsider the matter before the extradition process is commenced.

[62]Thus, in *Kirkland* the court noted that it had turned out "that the

probable cause in the asylum state is, in effect, premature. It is asserted that "no inquiry may be made into the merits of the criminal charge or whether there is probable cause for the initiation of criminal proceedings" because these "are all evidentiary issues to be heard and tried in the demanding state, not in a foreign jurisdiction."[63] Even apart from the fact that this argument appears to ignore that what is required under *Kirkland* is not a "preliminary hearing," but rather a proceeding "akin to an ex parte application for an arrest warrant,"[64] it is unsound.[65] It overlooks the fact that the arrest of the suspect in the asylum state and his subsequent transportation back to the demanding state is itself a seizure, and that it is quite obviously in the interest of the suspect to have the reasonableness of that seizure determined at the outset. "Only a strained interpretation of 'reasonableness' would allow the removal of an unindicted suspect hundreds, perhaps thousands, of miles to another jurisdiction on the strength of an *ex parte* accuser's allegation which is untested for constitutional probable cause."[66] Indeed, it would seem, as was held in *Ierardi v. Gunter*,[67]

> that *Gerstein* requires a judicial determination of probable cause as a prerequisite to interstate extradition. After *Gerstein* such a determination must precede "any significant pretrial restraint of liberty," * * * and we think interstate extradition necessarily involves significant restraint. At best extradition means an extended period of detention, involving custody pending administrative arrangements in two states as well as forced travel in between. At worst it means separation from a familiar jurisdiction and effective denial of the support of family, friends and familiar advisors. If the charge is unsupported, the individual charged has a very substantial interest in having the error brought to light before rendition.

---

prosecution against the fugitive is unfounded," as the court had given the Florida authorities two weeks to correct the defective affidavit, but they had not done so. And in People ex rel. Gatto v. District Attorney, 32 A.D.2d 1053, 303 N.Y.S.2d 726 (1969), when the demanding state attempted to supply the missing underlying facts it was established that the defendant had not committed the crime alleged.

[63]Bailey v. Cox, 260 Ind. 448, 296 N.E.2d 422 (1973).

[64]Grano v. State, 257 A.2d 768 (Del.Super.1969).

[65]The "postponement of inquiry" doctrine, of course, may be traced back to In re Strauss, 197 U.S. 324, 25 S.Ct. 535, 49 L.Ed. 774 (1905), but at "the time *Strauss* was decided, the 'right' being asserted was *not* the right to be free from arrests supported by less

than fourth amendment probable cause, since at the time no such protection existed for state arrestees; rather, a 'substantial charge' contained in an affidavit was sufficient to satisfy the general notion of fourteenth amendment due process." Note, 24 Rutgers L.Rev. 551, 584–85 (1970).

[66]Note, 24 Rutgers L.Rev. 551, 584 (1970). Indeed, as noted therein, under the balancing test of Camara v. Municipal Court, 387 U.S. 523, 87 S.Ct. 1727, 18 L.Ed.2d 930 (1967), and Terry v. Ohio, 392 U.S. 1, 88 S.Ct. 1868, 20 L.Ed.2d 889 (1968), "rendition could arguably demand a *more* stringent determination of probable guilt than that prerequisite to the usual arrest."

[67]Ierardi v. Gunter, 528 F.2d 929 (1st Cir.1976).

Yet another objection to *Kirkland* is that the extradition process "is designed to furnish an expeditious and summary procedure for returning a fugitive to the demanding State."[68] But there is no reason to believe that protection of Fourth Amendment rights will unduly complicate the procedure. The "demanding state's case is usually presented solely by affidavit," and "the requirement is merely one of an affidavit confrontation which can not be disputed beyond the face of the affidavit by the person sought."[69] It is hardly a great burden upon the asylum state to provide for the kind of judicial determination normally made upon application for an arrest warrant, nor is it a great burden upon the demanding state to have to prepare an affidavit that would suffice for an arrest warrant if the suspect were within the state. "The administration of justice will not be frustrated in the slightest by requiring the [demanding] authorities to supply the facts supporting the conclusions in the affidavit, for if they do not have such facts they obviously have no case against" the person.[70] And this is not a case "where declaring the warrant invalid would bring into play the often harsh effects of an exclusionary rule,"[71] for if through an oversight the demanding jurisdiction failed to supply sufficient facts, they may be given a reasonable time to fill the gap without having to commence anew yet another extradition proceeding.[72]

Kirkland has also been objected to on the ground that "principles of comity operate against inquiry into the criminal procedures of the demanding State."[73] The interest of comity in transactions between sister states is a legitimate one, but it is adequately protected so long as the *Kirkland* approach is understood as not depriving the demanding state of its power and responsibilities. As explained in *Ierardi*:

> Respondents seem to assume that if a judicial determination of probable cause must precede extradition, it must be provided by the courts of the asylum state, where the fugitive is held. This is not so. *Gerstein* explicitly rejected the need for adversarial procedures; it required only the neutral and detached judgment of a judicial officer or tribunal, and contemplated that this could be provided before as well as shortly after arrest. Thus nothing in *Gerstein* prevents the demanding state from providing the requisite prerendition determination of probable cause.

With this in mind, we do not believe it compromises the principles

---

[68]People ex rel. Kubala v. Woods, 52 Ill.2d 48, 284 N.E.2d 286 (1972).

[69]Grano v. State, 257 A.2d 768 (Del.Super.1969).

[70]United States ex rel. Grano v. Anderson, 446 F.2d 272 (3d Cir.1971) (Van Dusen, J., dissenting).

[71]United States ex rel. Grano v. Anderson, 446 F.2d 272 (3d Cir.1971)

(Van Dusen, J., dissenting).

[72]In *Kirkland,* the demanding state was given this opportunity. See also Grano v. State, 257 A.2d 768 (Del. Super.1969); People v. McFall, 175 Colo. 151, 486 P.2d 6 (1971), to the same effect.

[73]In re Ierardi, 366 Mass. 640, 321 N.E.2d 921 (1975).

of comity to require a judicial determination of probable cause before rendition. Such a determination is fully consistent with reliance by the asylum state on the regularity of the demanding state's procedures. If, for example, the papers submitted by Florida were to show that a judicial officer or tribunal there had found probable cause, Massachusetts would not need to find probable cause anew, nor would it need to review the adequacy of the Florida determination. Instead, it would be entitled to rely on the official representations of its sister state that the requisite determination had been made; thus in our view Massachusetts may credit an arrest warrant shown to have issued upon a finding of probable cause in Florida just as it would credit a Florida indictment.

This is a sensible approach, provided it is clearly understood that the issuance of an arrest warrant in the demanding jurisdiction does not necessarily mean that there has been a judicial determination of probable cause there.[74]

Although support for the *Kirkland* rule had theretofore been growing,[75] the Supreme Court decision in *Michigan v. Doran*[76] would appear, at a minimum, to have significantly limited its scope. After Doran was arrested in Michigan for possession of a stolen truck he had driven there from Arizona, Arizona authorities were notified, and this led to the filing of a sworn complaint with a justice of the peace in that state charging Doran with theft of the vehicle and the issuance of an arrest warrant stating the justice of the peace had found probable cause Doran committed the offense. Arizona then sought to extradite Doran. Relying on both *Gerstein* and the Extradition Act requirement that an affidavit must "substantially charge" the fugitive with a crime, the Michigan high court held that Doran could not be extradited on the papers submitted, as the complaint and warrant were "both phrased in conclusory language" and the two supporting affidavits "fail to set out facts which could justify a Fourth Amendment finding of probable cause."[77] But the Supreme Court reversed.

Writing for the majority, the Chief Justice characterized "the question" as one of "the power of the courts of an asylum state to review the finding of probable cause made by a judicial officer in the demanding state," which he then dealt with as a matter

---

[74]In Garrison v. Smith, 413 F.Supp. 747 (N.D.Miss.1976), the court claimed that it was following *Ierardi* and *Gerstein* in concluding that Garrison's claim must fail here, since the State of Missouri has found probable cause for his arrest through the issuance of an arrest warrant by a disinterested judicial officer whose duty it is to make an a priori determination of probable cause. However, the court ignored the fact, recited earlier in the opinion, that this warrant had been issued upon a conclusory prosecutor's affidavit providing no facts upon which the magistrate could have made a probable cause determination.

[75]See cases in note 56 supra.

[76]Michigan v. Doran, 439 U.S. 282, 99 S.Ct. 530, 58 L.Ed.2d 521 (1978), assessed in Note, 16 Hous.L. Rev. 975 (1979).

[77]People v. Doran, 401 Mich. 235, 258 N.W.2d 406 (1977).

exclusively concerned with the Extradition Clause.[78] Because it contemplates "a summary and mandatory executive proceeding," the Court in *Doran* concluded that "once the governor has granted extradition,[79] a court considering release on habeas corpus can do no more than decide (a) whether the extradition documents on their face are in order;[80] (b) whether the petitioner has been charged with a crime in the demanding state; (c) whether the petitioner is the person named in the request for extradition; and (d) whether the petitioner is a fugitive."[81] This means, the Court

---

[78]The sole reference to the Fourth Amendment in the majority's analysis in *Doran* is in a footnote asserting it need not be decided "whether the criminal charge on which extradition is requested must recite that it was based on a finding of probable cause."

[79]In Puerto Rico v. Branstad, 483 U.S. 219, 107 S.Ct. 2802, 97 L.Ed.2d 187 (1987), noted at 19 Cumb.L.Rev. 109 (1988), the Court stated and then examined the two propositions of Kentucky v. Dennison, 65 U.S. (24 How.) 66, 16 L.Ed. 717 (1860): "first, that the Extradition Clause creates a mandatory duty to deliver up fugitives upon proper demand; and second, that the federal courts have no authority under the Constitution to compel performance of this ministerial duty of delivery." The Court reaffirmed the first, concluding that the Extradition Clause "afford[s] no discretion to the executive officers or courts of the asylum State." But the Court rejected the second because "there is no justification for distinguishing the duty to deliver fugitives from the many other species of constitutional duty enforceable in the federal courts."

[80]Consider Sonkin v. State, 824 So.2d 564 (Miss.2002) ("a habeas corpus hearing conducted pursuant to a rendition warrant is not intended to be a mere rubber stamp, but instead is intended to afford to a petitioner a true opportunity to rebut the presumption that extradition documents are in order," and thus judge "required to examine the documents to determine not only their correct form and authenticity, but also whether they are proper on their face," not so in instant case because facts alleged in arrest warrant affidavit "contradicted on the face of

six other documents contained in the extradition package introduced at the habeas corpus hearing by the state").

[81]Relying on this language, the Court held in California v. Superior Court, 482 U.S. 400, 107 S.Ct. 2433, 96 L.Ed.2d 332 (1987), that when Smolin was charged with kidnapping under a Louisiana statute covering taking one's own child from a person to whom custody had been granted, the California court erred in barring extradition upon the basis of an earlier California custody decree awarding Smolin sole custody of his children. Because the Louisiana information and related documents "set forth the facts that clearly satisfy each element of the crime of kidnapping as it is defined" by statute, the court in the asylum state may not even inquire into whether the charge would withstand a motion to dismiss in the demanding state.

The two dissenters cogently objected that the Court had often said it must appear the person to be extradited is "substantially charged with a crime," that omission of the word "substantially" in *Doran* "was not intended to modify or eliminate a requirement that this Court had recognized for decades," and that Smolin had not been substantially charged because "there is no reasonable possibility that the charges of simple kidnapping filed * * * in Louisiana are valid."

See also Smith v. State, 284 Ga. 356, 667 S.E.2d 95 (2008) (once court found "the extradition documents were facially valid," it "could not examine the probable cause determination in the demanding state"); Petition of Gay, 406 Mass. 471, 548 N.E.2d 879 (1990) (relying on this language, court holds

held, "that once the governor of the asylum state has acted on a requisition for extradition based on the demanding state's judicial determination that probable cause existed, no further judicial inquiry may be had on that issue in the asylum state." The Michigan court, therefore, had taken a step not open to it under the Extradition Clause[82] in finding the arrest warrant asserting a probable cause finding deficient merely because the factual basis of that finding was not revealed.

Just where *Doran* leaves the Fourth Amendment issue addressed above is less than clear, for the majority refused even to acknowledge its existence.[83] As the three concurring Justices[84] correctly observed, the Chief Justice seems "almost to ignore" the "presence and significance of the Fourth Amendment in the extradition context." However, there is nothing in the *Doran* majority opinion casting the slightest doubt upon the conclusion reached by the concurring Justices (and in the preceding discussion) that *Gerstein v. Pugh*[85] means "that, even in the extradition context, where the demanding State's 'charge' rests upon something less than an indictment, there must be a determination of probable cause by a detached and neutral magistrate, and that the asylum State need not grant extradition unless that determination has been made." This means, *at a bare minimum,* that a person facing extradition is protected by the Fourth Amendment from the "significant restraint on liberty" inevitably involved in forced interstate transportation, when the papers sent to the asylum state by the demanding state include neither a copy of an indictment nor a copy of an arrest warrant asserting that a judicial finding of probable cause has occurred.[86]

If that much is granted, it is then possible to see much more

---

asylum state cannot inquire into defendant's claim that earlier, when defendant a prisoner there, demanding state failed to comply with Interstate Agreement on Detainers' requirement that after demand trial shall be had within 180 days, as even if that so defendant still a "fugitive").

[82]Generally, states may of course give defendants greater protection than is required under the Fourth Amendment. But under the *Doran* reasoning it appears that states are forbidden by the Extradition Clause from being more solicitous in extradition cases.

[83]See note 79 supra.

[84]Blackmun, J., joined by Brennan and Marshall, JJ.

[85]Gerstein v. Pugh, 420 U.S. 103, 95 S.Ct. 854, 43 L.Ed.2d 54 (1975).

[86]The post-*Doran* cases typically stress that such documentation was provided. See, e.g., Johnson v. Cronin, 690 P.2d 1277 (Colo.1984); Fain v. Bourbeau, 195 Conn. 465, 488 A.2d 824 (1985).

Consider also Application of Danko, 240 Kan. 431, 731 P.2d 240 (1987) (warrant that does not itself reflect probable cause determination is sufficient when from a state where courts "are required to make a finding of probable cause before issuing arrest warrants"); State v. Wallace, 240 Neb. 865, 484 N.W.2d 477 (1992) (sufficient that papers included prosecutor's information *and* an affidavit by a magistrate that he found probable cause to support the charges); White v. King County, 109 Wash.2d 777, 748 P.2d 616 (1988) (where papers supporting extradition were a conclusory felony

clearly that which the *Doran* majority apparently did not perceive at all—that the issue presented there was *not,* as the Chief Justice claimed, whether courts in the asylum state can "review the finding of probable cause made by a judicial officer in the demanding state," but rather what it takes for the demanding state (which "has the burden of so demonstrating")[87] to establish that a judicial determination of probable cause actually occurred at all. The Michigan supreme court, after all, did *not* hold that the asylum state is *always* entitled to make its own probable cause determination; rather, it only held that when it has not been shown that there was either an indictment or a judicial determination of probable cause in the demanding state, *then and only then* does there arise "a requirement that the demanding state's affidavit set forth facts which support a determination of probable cause." In other words, the Michigan court did no more than reach the sensible conclusion that *Gerstein* requires a judicial determination of probable cause either in the demanding state or in the asylum state.

As suggested above, this means that the real issue raised by the Michigan court's disposition of the case was what should be required by way of a showing that a judicial determination of probable cause *did* occur in the demanding state. The concurring opinion in *Doran* recognizes this fact, and responds by saying that it "is enough if the papers submitted by the demanding State in support of its request for extradition *facially* show that a neutral magistrate has made a finding of probable cause."[88] But why should that be enough? As far as can be determined, the self-serving declaration in the Arizona warrant that such a finding had been made was printed "boilerplate," hardly entitled to great respect in the face of the fact that appellate opinions[89] and also empirical studies[90] have shown that arrest warrants are not infrequently issued for extradition or charging purposes without any meaningful judicial participation. Moreover, it would seem that the declaration is not entitled to much weight when, as in *Doran,* the warrant refers only to a complaint known to be

---

complaint, an affidavit setting out the facts relating to the theft, and an arrest warrant that did not expressly state a probable cause finding had occurred, this sufficient in light of fact law of requesting state declares a warrant may issue only upon "a judicial determination of probable cause").

[87]As stated in the concurring opinion in *Doran.*

[88]Lower courts have typically applied *Doran* in this way. See, e.g., Fain v. Bourbeau, 195 Conn. 465, 488 A.2d 824 (1985); Scott v. Walker, 253 Ga. 695, 324 S.E.2d 187 (1985); State v.

Wallace, 240 Neb. 865, 484 N.W.2d 477 (1992).

[89]In re Consalvi, 376 Mass. 699, 382 N.E.2d 734 (1978). See also cases cited in note 56 supra. Also, the Michigan court in *Doran* noted that arrest warrants in that state are often issued without a probable cause showing.

[90]F. Miller, Prosecution 51–58 (1970). See also W. LaFave, Arrest 39–40 (1965), re the prosecutor's role in issuance of warrants for extradition purposes, sometimes even when "he is uncertain about prosecution."

conclusory in nature. True, a warrant may constitutionally issue upon sworn oral statements to the magistrate,[91] but this can hardly be characterized as a preferred procedure—especially with respect to such a serious matter as extradition[92]—and in any event should not be assumed to have been utilized absent any reference to it in the extradition papers. Nor does it make sense to assume, as do the *Doran* concurring Justices, that the self-serving boilerplate in the arrest warrant takes on greater credibility because the documents were "certified and approved by two governors," for there is no reason to believe that either governor made independent inquiry into just how the Arizona justice of the peace conducted herself. Thus, one is left with the unsettling feeling that under *Doran* the Fourth Amendment, as a practical matter, offers no protection in the extradition process, provided the demanding state prints up the right kind of form.

What remains to be seen is whether this is literally true or whether there is any way at all that the habeas corpus petitioner in an extradition context can get a judge in the asylum state to seriously entertain his claim that no judicial probable cause determination has occurred in the demanding state. By asserting that the "asylum State should be allowed to scrutinize the charging documents only," even the somewhat more sympathetic concurring Justices in *Doran* seem to hold out little hope. It must be noted, however, that at another point they stress that the majority opinion declares that the governor's grant of extradition "is prima facie evidence that the constitutional and statutory requirements have been met," which they read as "a suggestion that the governor's review and determination effects only a rebuttable presumption that there has been a judicial determination in the demanding State."

That this latter point is of some significance is illustrated by the pre-*Doran* case of *In re Consalvi*.[93] The two petitioners there were arrested pursuant to a demand by the governor of Kansas for their rendition, which was accompanied by conclusory complaints and arrest warrants stating a judicial probable cause determination had been made. The *Consalvi* court held, consistent with *Doran* and other pre-*Doran* cases,[94] that "where an indictment or an arrest warrant accompanies a demand for interstate rendition we will presume that the demanding State has conducted an independent judicial determination of probable

---

[91]See § 4.3(b).

[92]See Amsterdam, Perspectives on the Fourth Amendment, 58 Minn.L. Rev. 349, 392 (1974), suggesting that greater Fourth Amendment protection than is needed for an ordinary arrest might well "be required to rip a man out of the fabric of his life in California and ship him off 3,000 miles to Florida to stand trial upon criminal charges." See also text at note 64 supra.

[93]In re Consalvi, 376 Mass. 699, 382 N.E.2d 734 (1978).

[94]Olson v. Thurston, 393 A.2d 1320 (Me.1978); Commonwealth v. Gedney, 478 Pa. 299, 386 A.2d 942 (1978).

cause." But, the court then very significantly added that

> where a petitioner can show that a demanding State's arrest war-
> rant or indictment procedure does not guarantee the requisite
> judicial finding of probable cause, * * * we will require the demand-
> ing State to provide sufficient documentation or other evidence to
> demonstrate that a constitutionally valid determination of probable
> cause had been made in the demanding State. If such information
> is not forthcoming within a reasonable period of time, rendition
> should be denied.

The court then noted that under Kansas law an arrest warrant
could be issued without a finding of probable cause because only
a complaint setting out the crime in the words of the statute is
required.[95] This being so, the court ruled in the petitioners' favor
because there was

> a substantial probability that the arrest warrant for the petitioners
> could have issued solely on the constitutionally improper basis of
> an informant's conclusions unsupported by personal knowledge or
> reliable information. * * *
>
> * * * Although the Kansas magistrate might well have taken
> oral testimony from the officers supplying this necessary informa-
> tion, no evidence of such colloquies exists in the papers accompany-
> ing the rendition demands.

The *Consalvi* result is certainly sound, and it is to be hoped
that the poorly reasoned *Doran* case will not be read as foreclosing such a result in future cases.[96] But the Supreme Court's
language in one post-*Doran* case, albeit on another point, is not

---

[95]Compare Application of Danko, 240 Kan. 431, 731 P.2d 240 (1987) (demanding state is one in which courts "are required to make a finding of probable cause before issuing arrest warrants," and thus "the fact that a magistrate in the demanding state has issued an arrest warrant conclusively shows, so far as our courts are concerned, that a finding of probable cause has been made").

[96]Supportive is the post-*Doran* case of Zambito v. Blair, 610 F.2d 1192 (4th Cir.1979), where the court asserted it did not read *Doran* as precluding a "court inquiry into the correctness of a statement contained in the demanding papers that a judicial finding of probable cause had been made. * * * [T]he holding in *Doran* applies only 'when a neutral judicial officer of the demanding state had determined that probable cause exists.' * * * The statement in the demanding papers that there has been a finding of probable cause is no more

conclusive than would be an absence of such a statement. It is the actual fact, not the statement or lack of a statement that, in the end, matters."

Zambito, however, involved somewhat the reverse situation, in that the extradition papers included a prosecutor's information and an affidavit of probable cause, but no declaration that there had actually been a judicial probable cause determination in the demanding state. The court concluded "that the fourth amendment, as applied to the states by the fourteenth amendment, requires only that, prior to an extradition, there in fact have been a finding of probable cause by a neutral judicial officer, not that the demanding papers, additionally, must say so." The court then added this was not to suggest "that the circumstances would then preclude the person for whom extradition has been sought from calling attention to the omission in the demanding papers of any assertion that there had been a judicial finding of probable cause, and,

particularly encouraging; the Court asserted that "claims relating to what actually happened in the demanding State [and] the law of the demanding State * * * are issues that must be tried in the courts of that State, and not in those of the asylum State."[97]

It appears less likely that *Doran* should be followed in the international extradition context, where perhaps there is even greater reason not to assume that the probable cause finding has been made in the foreign jurisdiction. In *Caltagirone v. Grant*,[98] when the Italian government became aware that Caltagirone was in the United States the State Department was notified that warrants had issued in Italy and Caltagirone's arrest was requested pending extradition. The U.S. Attorney obtained a warrant upon a complaint merely alleging the existence of the Italian warrants but without a showing of probable cause that Caltagirone had committed a crime in Italy. After holding this procedure was improper under a treaty, the court noted:

> Indeed, the Government, if its view were accepted, could arrest and indefinitely detain American citizens upon no more than an allegation by a foreign government that a warrant for the citizen was outstanding. We doubt that the tenuous relationship between an application for provisional arrest and subsequent request for extradition implicates a sufficiently strong foreign policy interest in the executive to justify such a departure from usual Fourth Amendment protections.

Again with respect to international extradition, it is well to remember that the "Fourth Amendment protects all persons from arbitrary arrests, including persons arrested pursuant to treaties."[99] This means, as illustrated by *Parretti v. United*

---

from obtaining, as here, an independent court inquiry as to whether such a finding had been made." Because the probable cause affidavit "set out sufficient facts to support a judicial finding of probable cause," it was proper to conclude that such a finding had been made in the demanding state.

See also Proctor v. Skinner, 104 Idaho 426, 659 P.2d 779 (App.1982) (court assumes it possible for a defendant to overcome the presumption of regularity, as it stressed the defendant here "made no affirmative showing that the arrest warrant was issued in violation of procedural requirements imposed by Nevada law," determined by the court to include the necessity of a probable cause showing).

[97]New Mexico ex rel. Ortiz v. Reed, 524 U.S. 151, 118 S.Ct. 1860, 141 L.Ed.2d 131 (1998). It would be a mistake, however, to view *Reed* as if it settled the issue discussed in the preceding text. The case did not involve a probable cause issue, and there was no discussion at all of the Fourth Amendment, as the case had to do with whether the asylum state could refuse extradition on the ground that because petitioner had fled under duress he was consequently not a "fugitive," to which the Court unanimously answered in the negative.

[98]Caltagirone v. Grant, 629 F.2d 739 (2d Cir.1980).

[99]Parretti v. United States, 122 F.3d 758 (9th Cir.1997), citing Reid v. Covert, 354 U.S. 1, 77 S.Ct. 1222, 1 L.Ed.2d 1148 (1957) (plurality opinion); In re Aircrash, 684 F.2d 1301 (9th Cir.1982); Plaster v. United States, 720 F.2d 340 (4th Cir.1983).

The cases often state that at the

States,[100] that a person arrested under an extradition treaty may prevail on Fourth Amendment grounds notwithstanding full compliance with that treaty. In *Parretti*, an Italian citizen was "provisionally" arrested in this country pursuant to an arrest warrant, the complaint for which alleged that such action had been requested by France, where a warrant had been issued for specified extraditable offenses. Citing *Doran*, the government first asked the court "to accept the foreign warrant at face value as satisfying the probable cause requirement of the Warrant Clause," but the court quite correctly declined to do so. As the court explained, *Doran*, "grounded in the presumption that the judicial proceedings of every State comport with the requirements of the Constitution," was simply inapplicable in the instant case for the reason that "foreign governments are not bound by the Constitution." The court thus found it necessary to resolve an issue of first impression,[101] whether an exception to the usual Fourth Amendment requirements should be found to exist when, as in the instant case, a treaty allows arrest "based solely on the 'existence of a warrant of arrest' * * * issued by a treaty partner." On this point, the court concluded that the clarity of the Fourth Amendment's warrant clause "allows for no exceptions, regardless whether the government's purpose in making the arrest is to enforce treaties or our own domestic laws." And thus, because the French warrant contained "nothing more than naked allegations," the government had "failed to make the necessary evidentiary showing of probable cause to believe that Parretti had committed an extraditable offense." (The above opinion was later withdrawn under the fugitive disentitlement doctrine in light of Parretti's decision to flee the United States.[102])

Finally, it should be noted that the question of whether there

---

extradition hearing the fugitive may only introduce evidence to explain rather than to contradict the evidence presented by the government. The case law on this "murky" distinction is analyzed in Iraola, Contradictions, Explanations, and the Probable Cause Determination at a Foreign Extradition Hearing, 60 Syrac.L.Rev. 95 (2009).

[100]Parretti v. United States, 122 F.3d 758 (9th Cir.1997), discussed in Wiehl, Extradition Law at the Crossroads: The Trend Toward Extending Greater Constitutional Procedural Protections to Fugitives Fighting Extradition from the United States, 19 Mich.J.Int'l L. 729 (1998); Note, 48 Cath.U.L.Rev. 161 (1998).

[101]In earlier cases, the courts had been able to conclude that the treaty

itself required a full evidentiary showing of probable cause. See, e.g., Sahagian v. United States, 864 F.2d 509 (7th Cir.1988); Caltagirone v. Grant, 629 F.2d 739 (2d Cir.1980).

[102]Parretti v. United States, 143 F.3d 508 (9th Cir. 1998) (en banc). The conclusion reached in the panel decision has been questioned. See Iraola, Foreign Extradition, Provisional Arrest Warrants, and Probable Cause, 43 San Diego L.Rev. 347, 375–76 (2006) ("a determination of probable cause in the provisional arrest context should not be measured in the traditional domestic criminal warrant sense because the purpose of the seizure is not the initiation of a criminal prosecution, but rather, a determination of whether the fugitive should be extradited pursuant to the foreign government's request for his or her extradition," and thus, "at

is probable cause for extradition to the demanding state is different from that of whether there was probable cause for the arrest made of the defendant in the asylum state. A probable cause deficiency in the latter respect should not itself bar extradition. Illustrative is *In re Brown*,[103] where defendant was arrested by Boston police on the unsubstantiated tip that a "wanted" man was at a certain apartment. It was later determined that defendant was under indictment in West Virginia, so an extradition warrant was issued. On appeal of defendant's habeas corpus action questioning the legality of the extradition proceeding, the court quite properly concluded that "what is tested on habeas corpus is the legality of the cause for detention existing at that time, and the extradition warrant, if otherwise valid, supplies sound, present legal cause even though there may have been prior illegality." As the court explained, even if the police in the asylum state violated the defendant's constitutional rights, this does not "justify depriving [the demanding state] of the means of proceeding against [the defendant] for violation of its own laws. To work such a deprivation would be to push an exclusionary rule beyond its proper limits."[104]

§ 1.10 Civil suit; criminal prosecution; disciplinary proceedings

§ 1.10(a)   The "constitutional tort" by state officers
§ 1.10(b)   The "constitutional tort" by federal officers
§ 1.10(c)   Criminal prosecution
§ 1.10(d)   Disciplinary proceedings
§ 1.10(e)   Takings Clause litigation

Research References

West's Key Number Digest
Civil Rights ⬦1088(4), 1344, 1358, 1376; Eminent Domain ⬦2.35 to 2.39; Searches and Seizures ⬦85; United States ⬦50.10(3)

Legal Encyclopedias
C.J.S., Eminent Domain §§ 6 to 9, 82 to 83, 87 to 88, 106 to 107; Searches and Seizures §§ 227 to 234; United States § 70

Introduction

Much has been written concerning those other remedies for po-

---

the provisional arrest stage, the object of the probable cause inquiry should be limited to the existence of a foreign warrant charging an extraditable offense").

[103]In re Brown, 370 Mass. 267, 346 N.E.2d 830 (1976).

[104]Reaching the same result upon the same analysis and relied upon in *Brown* is People ex rel. Taylor v. Johnson, 47 Ill.2d 103, 264 N.E.2d 198 (1970). See also In re Saunders, 138 Vt. 259, 415 A.2d 199 (1980) (in such a case "no deterrent function is served by punishing a demanding state for the wrongful actions of the asylum state").

lice misconduct that involve proceeding directly against the offending officer, such as tort actions for trespass or battery,[1] criminal prosecutions,[2] and disciplinary action.[3] The conclusion
usually reached is that these other remedies are inadequate,
which of course was a point of emphasis in *Mapp v. Ohio*.[4] No effort will be made here to canvass all proceedings of this kind.
Rather, because the focus of this Treatise is upon the Fourth
Amendment, attention will be limited to those remedies of this
nature uniquely directed to the protection of constitutional rights.

§ 1.10(a) The "constitutional tort" by state officers

42 U.S.C.A. § 1983 provides: "Every person who, under color of
any statute, ordinance, regulation, custom, or usage, of any State
or Territory, subjects, or causes to be subjected, any citizen of the
United States or other person within the jurisdiction thereof[5] to
the deprivation of any rights, privileges, or immunities secured

---

[Section 1.10]

[1]See, e.g., Foote, Tort Remedies for Police Violations of Individual Rights, 39 Minn.L.Rev. 493 (1955).

[2]See, e.g., Edwards, Criminal Liability for Unreasonable Search and Seizure, 41 Va.L.Rev. 621 (1955).

[3]There is considerable disagreement as to the current and potential effectiveness of various forms of administrative grievance mechanisms, including civilian, police, and other governmental review boards, in fairly determining whether police have violated the rights of individuals and in imposing significant sanctions. See, e.g., Report of the National Advisory Comm'n on Civil Disorders 162–63 (1968); President's Comm'n on Law Enforcement and Administration of Justice, Task Force Report: The Police 200–05 (1967); W. Gellhorn, When Americans Complain 170–95 (1966); Clarke, Arrested Oversight: A Comparative Analysis and Case Study of How Civilian Oversight of the Police Should Function and How Its Fails, 43 Colum.J.L. & Soc.Probs. 1 (2009); Goldman & Puro, Decertification of Police: An Alternative to Traditional Remedies for Police Misconduct, 15 Hastings Const.L.Q. 45 (1987); Goldstein, Administrative Problems in Controlling the Exercise of Police Authority, 58 J.Crim.L.C. & P.S. 160 (1967); McGowan, Rule-Making and the Police, 70 Mich.L.Rev. 659 (1972);

Perino, Developments in Citizen Oversight of Law Enforcement, 36 Urb.Law. 387 (2004); Schwartz, Complaints Against the Police: Experience of the Community Rights Division of the Philadelphia District Attorney's Office, 118 U.Pa.L.Rev. 1023 (1970); Note, 77 Harv.L.Rev. 499 (1964); Comment, 7 Vill.L.Rev. 656 (1962).

[4]Mapp v. Ohio, 367 U.S. 643, 81 S.Ct. 1684, 6 L.Ed.2d 1081 (1961).

[Section 1.10(a)]

[5]In Inyo County v. Paiute-Shoshone Indians of the Bishop Community, 538 U.S. 701, 123 S.Ct. 1887, 155 L.Ed.2d 933 (2003), where the county district attorney had obtained and executed a search warrant for casino records and was expected to seek one or more additional warrants for the casino, the tribe that owned and operated the casino sought injunctive and declaratory relief and also relief including damages under § 1983. Noting that the claim was *not* that probable cause was lacking or that the warrant was otherwise defective, but rather that the tribe had "sovereign" status giving it immunity from the county's process, the Court held the tribe was not a "person within the jurisdiction" under § 1983, as that statute "was designed to secure private rights against government encroachment, * * * not to advance a sovereign's prerogative to withhold evidence relevant to a criminal investigation."

by the Constitution and laws, shall be liable to the party injured in an action at law, suit in equity, or other proper proceeding for redress." Pursuant to this statute, an action for damages may be brought in a federal court or state court[6] against municipal and state officers[7] (but not those of the federal government,[8] including District of Columbia police[9]) by a plaintiff who sufficiently alleges a violation of his constitutional rights.[10] Although such actions have been undertaken for a wide variety of constitutional violations,[11] "the fourth amendment prohibition against unreasonable searches and seizures has been a popular vehicle for section 1983

---

[6]But not a tribal court, Nevada v. Hicks, 533 U.S. 353, 121 S.Ct. 2304, 150 L.Ed.2d 398 (2001), as while a "state court's jurisdiction is general," tribal courts "cannot be courts of general jurisdiction in this sense, for a tribe's inherent adjudicative jurisdiction over nonmembers is at most only as broad as its legislative jurisdiction."

[7]Sometimes suit is brought not merely against the officers directly causing the harm, but also their supervisors. The appropriate standard for supervisory liability in such cases has been a source of considerable disagreement in the federal courts. See Kinports, The Buck Does Not Stop Here: Supervisory Liability in Section 1983 Cases, 1997 U.Ill.L.Rev. 147.

In Ashcroft v. Iqbal, __ U.S. __, 129 S.Ct. 1937, 173 L.Ed.2d 868 (2009), the Court stated: "In a § 1983 suit or a *Bivens* action-where masters do not answer for the torts of their servants-the term 'supervisory liability' is a misnomer. Absent vicarious liability, each Government official, his or her title notwithstanding, is only liable for his or her own misconduct." On supervisory liability after *Iqbal*, see Blum, Supervisory Liability After Iqbal: Misunderstood But Not Misnamed, 43 Urb.Law. 541 (2011); Comment, 77 U.Chi.L.Rev. 1401 (2010).

[8]But see the immediately following subsection concerning the bringing of an action against federal officers under the *Bivens* rule.

[9]See District of Columbia v. Carter, 409 U.S. 418, 93 S.Ct. 602, 34 L.Ed.2d 613 (1973), holding that section 1983 does not apply to the District of Columbia because it is not a "state or territory" within the meaning of the statute.

[10]Project, Suing the Police in Federal Court, 88 Yale L.J. 781, 782–85 (1979), "uses field research to provide support for the following propositions: (1) juries, the critical decisionmaking bodies in section 1983 suits, are not impartial because many jurors disfavor plaintiffs and favor police defendants in these suits; and (2) adverse verdicts have minimal effect on defendants because police departments and police officers are insulated from the consequences of the suits," in that police are indemnified "by their municipal employers or by the municipality's insurance carrier." See also Emery & Maazel, Why Civil Rights Lawsuits do Not Deter Police Misconduct: The Conundrum of Indemnification and a Proposed Solution, 28 Fordham Urb.L.J. 587 (2000).

Another objection is that the money damages are often insufficient to justify commencing the action. Comment, 129 U.Pa.L.Rev. 192 (1980), favors presumed damages, as "the doctrine should make constitutional tort suits a more consistent and rational means of vindicating society's most important civil rights." Id. at 220.

Consider also Casper, Benedict & Perry, The Tort Remedy in Search and Seizure Cases: A Case Study in Juror Decision Making, 13 Law & Soc. 279 (1988), concluding by use of simulated juries that potential municipal liability did not increase the damage awards, though keeping from jurors the outcome of the challenged search did.

[11]See Nahmod, Section 1983 and the "Background" of Tort Liability, 50 Ind.L.J. 5 (1974); Shapo, Constitutional

claims."[12] Thus, actions have been undertaken with some frequency for illegal arrests,[13] illegal traffic stops,[14] illegal seizures of property,[15] illegal searches,[16] and accompanying use of unreasonable force.[17]

Tort: Monroe v. Pape, and the Frontiers Beyond, 60 Nw.U.L.Rev. 277 (1965).

[12]Shapo, Constitutional Tort: Monroe v. Pape, and the Frontiers Beyond, 60 Nw.U.L.Rev. 277, 323 (1965).

[13]E.g., Albright v. Oliver, 510 U.S. 266, 114 S.Ct. 807, 127 L.Ed.2d 114 (1994). Note, 106 Colum.L.Rev. 643, 678 (2006), noting that *Albright* "left the status of malicious prosecution claims under § 1983 unresolved," argues that this tort "is directly within the sphere of interests protected by the Fourth Amendment," so that "§ 1983 liability is an appropriate remedy."

In Heck v. Humphrey, 512 U.S. 477, 114 S.Ct. 2364, 129 L.Ed.2d 383 (1994), the Court quoted approvingly the proposition that "if there is a false arrest claim, damages for that claim cover the time of detention up until issuance of process or arraignment, but not more." As the matter was put in Gauger v. Hendle, 349 F.3d 354 (7th Cir.2003), citing Hector v. Watt, 235 F.3d 154 (3d Cir.2000), and Townes v. City of New York, 176 F.3d 138 (2d Cir.1999), "the interest in not being prosecuted groundlessly is not an interest that the Fourth Amendment protects."

In light of *Heck*, supra, the Court in Wallace v. Kato, 549 U.S. 384, 127 S.Ct. 1091, 166 L.Ed.2d 973 (2007), held that the statute of limitations upon a § 1983 claim seeking damages for a false arrest in violation of the Fourth Amendment begins to run at the time the claimant becomes detained pursuant to legal process, and not at a subsequent point where he was released from custody as a consequence of the state dropping the charges.

"A critical issue in a § 1983 false arrest case is the presence or absence of probable cause. Circuits are divided on who should bear the burden of proof

on this issue: should the defendant officer be required to prove that probable cause existed, or should the plaintiff be required to prove the absence of probable cause? The debate is complicated by our federal system, in which a preliminary issue is whether federal or state law should be applied to determine the burden of proof. Three circuits apply the parallel state law on false arrest to determine where the burden of proof should be placed. If a federal standard applies, the courts must further decide who bears the burden of proof (production). The nine circuits applying a federal standard are split between assigning the burden to the plaintiff or the defendant." Comment, 73 U.Chi.L.Rev. 347, 348 (2006).

[14]Bingham v. City of Manhattan Beach, 329 F.3d 723 (9th Cir.2003) (noting that Supreme Court "has never held that actions that do violate the Fourth Amendment may result in such little harm that § 1983 is not an available remedy,"court rejects argument that an unlawful traffic stop is a *de minimis* violation that, "without more, cannot serve as the basis of a § 1983 action").

[15]E.g., Soldal v. Cook County, 506 U.S. 56, 113 S.Ct. 538, 121 L.Ed.2d 450 (1992).

[16]E.g., Howlett v. Rose, 496 U.S. 356, 110 S.Ct. 2430, 110 L.Ed.2d 332 (1990).

[17]Use of force is not infrequently an aspect of the litigated cases, see Annot., 1 A.L.R.Fed. 519 (1969), presumably because those cases in which the potential damages make the litigation worth while frequently involve some injury to person or damage to property. But relief is available under § 1983 with respect to an *illegal* arrest that is "de minimis" in the sense that it is unaccompanied by use of force or prolonged detention. Pritchard v. Perry, 508 F.2d 423 (4th Cir.1975).

In order to comprehend the reach of section 1983, one must understand the broad interpretation that has been given to the phrase "under color of any statute, ordinance, regulation, custom, or usage, of any State or Territory." Instructive is the leading case of *Monroe v. Pape*,[18] concerning an action for damages against the City of Chicago and thirteen Chicago police officers, where the complaint alleged that the officers had broken into petitioners' home in the early morning, routed them from bed, made them stand naked in the living room, and ransacked every room in the house, after which Mr. Monroe was taken to the station and interrogated incommunicado about a murder. The defendants contended "that 'under color of' enumerated state authority excludes acts of an official or policeman who can show no authority under state law, state custom, or state usage to do what he did." They claimed that the district court properly dismissed the complaint because "under Illinois law a simple remedy is offered for that violation and * * *, so far as it appears, the courts of Illinois are available to give petitioners that full redress which the common law affords for violence done to a person."

Justice Douglas, for the majority in *Monroe,* concluded from his examination of the legislative history of the statute that it had three aims: "it might, of course, override certain kinds of state laws" and "it provided a remedy where state law was inadequate"; but in addition it "was to provide a federal remedy where the state remedy, though adequate in theory, was not available in practice." He also noted this history indicated that the "under color" language in the statute was to be accorded the same construction as the same language in the statute providing for criminal punishment. The latter statute had been interpreted by the Court as follows: "Misuse of power, possessed by virtue of state law and made possible only because the wrongdoer is clothed with the authority of state law, is action taken 'under color of' state law."[19] Thus, the Court concluded in *Monroe:*

> It is no answer that the State has a law which if enforced would give relief. The federal remedy is supplementary to the state remedy, and the latter need not be first sought and refused before the federal one is invoked. Hence the fact that Illinois by its constitution and laws outlaws unreasonable searches and seizures is no barrier to the present suit in the federal court.[20]

But, does this mean that damages may be collected under sec-

---

[18]Monroe v. Pape, 365 U.S. 167, 81 S.Ct. 473, 5 L.Ed.2d 492 (1961).

[19]United States v. Classic, 313 U.S. 299, 61 S.Ct. 1031, 85 L.Ed. 1368 (1941). See also Screws v. United States, 325 U.S. 91, 65 S.Ct. 1031, 89 L.Ed. 1495 (1945), and Williams v. United States, 341 U.S. 97, 71 S.Ct. 576, 95 L.Ed. 774 (1951), both reaffirming that view.

[20]In a lengthy dissent, Justice Frankfurter argued that Congress "created a civil liability enforceable in the federal courts only in instances of injury for which redress was barred in the state courts because some 'statute,

487

tion 1983 any time an officer[21] engages in conduct, though not affirmatively sanctioned by state law, which is thereafter determined to infringe upon constitutional rights? Certainly it would seem unduly harsh if, for example, a policeman could be subjected to personal liability any time his actions were thereafter found to intrude within the uncertain and ever-changing boundaries of the protections of the Fourth Amendment. One possible limitation, that there must be "a specific intent to deprive a person of a federal right," was rejected in *Monroe*. While this was a requirement under the statute carrying criminal penalties,[22] that statute—unlike section 1983—imposed penalties only for acts "wilfully" done and in any event had to be interpreted to avoid challenge "on the ground of vagueness." As for section 1983, Justice Douglas declared that it "should be read against the background of tort liability that makes a man responsible for the natural consequences of his actions."

That ambiguous statement, which proved a source of considerable difficulty in subsequent litigation,[23] was clarified by the Court in *Pierson v. Ray*.[24] A unanimous Court[25] rejected the court of appeals' interpretation of *Monroe* as meaning that local police who arrested for violation of a criminal statute subsequently held unconstitutional could not interpose a defense[26] of good faith:

[The defendants'] claim is * * * that they should not be liable if

---

ordinance, regulation, custom, or usage' sanctioned the grievance complained of."

[21]In virtually all § 1983 actions involving a claim of a Fourth Amendment violation, the defendant will be a police officer instead of a prosecutor, who generally enjoys absolute immunity from such a suit. But see Kalina v. Fletcher, 522 U.S. 118, 118 S.Ct. 502, 139 L.Ed.2d 471 (1997), noted in 89 J.Crim.L. & Criminology 867 (1999) (while "the prosecutor is fully protected by absolute immunity when performing the traditional functions of an advocate," which includes "the determination that the evidence was sufficiently strong to justify a probable-cause finding," and "the preparation and filing" of an information, a motion for an arrest warrant, and a certification for determination of probable cause, that immunity does not extend to the action of a prosecutor who has "performed the function of a complaining witness" by swearing to the truth of the allegations set out in such certification).

[22]Screws v. United States, 325 U.S. 91, 65 S.Ct. 1031, 89 L.Ed. 1495 (1945).

[23]See Nahmod, Section 1983 and the "Background" of Tort Liability, 50 Ind.L.J. 5 (1974); Shapo, Constitutional Tort: Monroe v. Pape, and the Frontiers Beyond, 60 Nw.U.L.Rev. 277 (1965).

[24]Pierson v. Ray, 386 U.S. 547, 87 S.Ct. 1213, 18 L.Ed.2d 288 (1967).

[25]Douglas, J., dissented, but only as to the Court's other holding that judges are immune from liability for damages for acts committed within their judicial discretion.

[26]Because it is a defense, "the burden of pleading it rests with the defendant," and thus a plaintiff in a § 1983 action need make only two allegations "in order to state a cause of action under that statute. First, the plaintiff must allege that some person has deprived him of a federal right. Second, he must allege that the person who has deprived him of that right acted under color of state or territorial law." Gomez v. Toledo, 446 U.S. 635, 100 S.Ct. 1920, 64 L.Ed.2d 572 (1980).

they acted in good faith and with probable cause in making an arrest under a statute that they believed to be valid. Under the prevailing view in this country a peace officer who arrests someone with probable cause is not liable for false arrest simply because the innocence of the suspect is later proved. * * * A policeman's lot is not so unhappy that he must choose between being charged with dereliction of duty if he does not arrest when he has probable cause, and being mulcted in damages if he does. Although the matter is not entirely free from doubt, the same consideration would seem to require excusing him from liability for acting under a statute that he reasonably believed to be valid but that was later held unconstitutional, on its face or as applied.[27] * * *

We hold that the defense of good faith and probable cause, which the Court of Appeals found available to the officers in the common-law action for false arrest and imprisonment, is also available to them in the action under § 1983. * * * [I]f the jury found that the officers reasonably believed in good faith that the arrest was constitutional, then a verdict for the officers would follow even though the arrest was in fact unconstitutional.

Although for a time the Supreme Court treated this "good faith" defense as having both an objective and a subjective aspect,[28] in *Harlow v. Fitzgerald*[29] the Court concluded that "substantial costs attend the litigation of the subjective good faith of government officials,"[30] necessitating use of a purely objective standard in the future. Thus, government officials are now generally "shielded from liability for civil damages insofar as their conduct does not

---

[27]Relying upon this language, lower courts have excused officers from liability when they relied in good faith on other types of statutes. See, e.g., Mattis v. Schnarr, 502 F.2d 588 (8th Cir.1974) (reliance on statute permitting use of deadly force when necessary to effect arrest for any felony); Huotari v. Vanderport, 380 F.Supp. 645 (D.Minn.1974) (reliance on statute permitting warrantless entry of premises to arrest).

Police likewise need not forecast the overruling of court decisions. See Laverne v. Corning, 522 F.2d 1144 (2d Cir.1975) (warrantless administrative inspection of premises occurring before Supreme Court overturned prior decision allowing same).

[28]Wood v. Strickland, 420 U.S. 308, 95 S.Ct. 992, 43 L.Ed.2d 214 (1975).

[29]Harlow v. Fitzgerald, 457 U.S. 800, 102 S.Ct. 2727, 73 L.Ed.2d 396 (1982). The Court asserted that because the defendants had been federal officers the case "involves no issue concerning the elements of the immunity available to state officials sued for constitutional violations under § 1983." But the Court went on to note that it had previously held it would be untenable to draw a distinction between federal and state officials on matters of this kind, thus indicating the same result would be reached in a § 1983 context.

[30]The Court noted in this regard that when "questions of subjective intent" are involved the matter seldom "can be decided by summary judgment" and "there often is no clear end to the relevant evidence. Judicial inquiry into subjective motivation therefore may entail broad-ranging discovery and the deposing of numerous persons, including an official's professional colleagues. Inquiries of this kind can be peculiarly disruptive of effective government."

violate clearly established[31] statutory or constitutional rights of which a reasonable person would have known." The Court explained:

> Reliance on the objective reasonableness of an official's conduct, as measured by reference to clearly established law, should avoid excessive disruption of government and permit the resolution of many insubstantial claims on summary judgment. On summary judgment, the judge appropriately may determine, not only the currently applicable law, but whether that law was clearly established at the time an action occurred. If the law at that time was not clearly established, an official could not reasonably be expected to anticipate subsequent legal developments, nor could he fairly be said to "know" that the law forbade conduct not previously identified as unlawful. Until this threshold immunity question is resolved, discovery should not be allowed. If the law was clearly established, the immunity defense ordinarily should fail, since a reasonably competent public official should know the law governing his conduct. Nevertheless, if the official pleading the defense claims extraordinary circumstances and can prove that he neither knew or should have known of the relevant legal standard, the defense should be sustained. But again, the defense would turn primarily on objective factors.[32]

---

[31]See, e.g., Safford Unified School District # 1 v. Redding, 557 U.S. 364, 129 S.Ct. 2633, 174 L.Ed.2d 354 (2009) (law regarding strip searches of students at school not clearly established to extent school officials should have known that their conduct in strip searching 13-year-old middle school student in attempt to find contraband prescription-strength pain reliever drugs was unreasonable); Pearson v. Callahan, 555 U.S. 223, 129 S.Ct. 808, 172 L.Ed.2d 565 (2009) (officer's entry into home without warrant to make arrest, based on consent given to informant, did not violate clearly established law; although issue had not been decided in officers' circuit, "consent-once-removed" doctrine had been accepted by three federal courts of appeals and two state supreme courts); Brosseau v. Haugen, 543 U.S. 194, 125 S.Ct. 596, 160 L.Ed.2d 583 (2004) (while Tennessee v. Garner, 471 U.S. 1, 105 S.Ct. 1694, 85 L.Ed.2d 1 (1985), and Graham v. Connor, 490 U.S. 386, 109 S.Ct. 1865, 104 L.Ed.2d 443 (1989), established that claims of excessive force to be judged under Fourth Amendment's "objective reasonableness" standard, those cases "are cast at a high level of generality" and thus are insufficient to show it "clearly established" that defendant was violating plaintiff's Fourth Amendment rights in this case); Wilson v. Layne, 526 U.S. 603, 119 S.Ct. 1692, 143 L.Ed.2d 818 (1999) ("clearly established," under Court's prior decisions, means that the "contours of the right must be sufficiently clear that a reasonable official would understand that what he is doing violates that right," and in that context "the right allegedly violated must be defined at the appropriate level of specificity before a court can determine if it was clearly established," and thus in instant case "the appropriate question is the objective inquiry of whether a reasonable officer could have believed that bringing members of the media into a home during the execution of an arrest warrant was lawful, in light of clearly established law and the information the officers possessed").

[32]For further elaboration of the Harlow standard as it has been applied in the analogous Bivens/federal officer context, see text at note 78 infra. Regarding when a court should proceed directly to the "clearly established" issue, see note 87 infra.

In *Malley v. Briggs*,[33] the plaintiffs brought a section 1983 action against a state trooper, alleging that he violated their Fourth Amendment rights in applying for arrest warrants thereafter issued and executed. In response to the trooper's claim that in this context he should have the same absolute immunity a prosecutor has in deciding to prosecute, the Court, per White, J., responded that

> it is our judgment that the judicial process will on the whole benefit from a rule of qualified rather than absolute immunity. We do not believe that the *Harlow* standard, which gives ample room for mistaken judgments, will frequently deter an officer from submitting an affidavit when probable cause to make an arrest is present. True, an officer who knows that objectively unreasonable decisions will be actionable may be motivated to reflect, before submitting a request for a warrant, whether he has a reasonable basis for believing that his affidavit establishes probable cause. But such reflection is desirable, because it reduces the likelihood that the officer's request for a warrant will be premature. Premature requests for warrants are at best a waste of judicial resources; at worst, they lead to premature arrests, which may injure the innocent or, by giving the basis for a suppression motion, benefit the guilty.

> * * *

> Accordingly we hold that the same standard of objective reasonableness that we applied in the context of a suppression hearing in *Leon* * * * defines the qualified immunity accorded an officer whose request for a warrant allegedly caused an unconstitutional arrest. Only where the warrant application is so lacking in indicia of probable cause as to render official belief in its existence unreasonable * * * will the shield of immunity be lost.

The Court in *Malley* thus rejected the trooper's claim "that he is entitled to rely on the judgment of a judicial officer in finding that probable cause exists and hence issuing the warrant," reasoning that it was more in keeping with *Harlow* and *Leon* to ask "whether a reasonably well-trained officer in petitioner's position would have known that his affidavit failed to establish probable cause and that he should not have applied for the warrant. If such was the case, the officer's application for a warrant was not objectively reasonable, because it created the unnecessary danger of an unlawful arrest." Since the matter is put that way, it would seem *totally* irrelevant in deciding that issue that the magistrate thereafter issued the requested warrant. This prompted Justices Powell and Rehnquist, dissenting in part, to complain that because *Leon* declares that "our good-faith inquiry is confined to the objectively ascertainable question whether a reasonably well-trained officer would have known that the search was illegal despite the magistrate's authorization," meaning the fact of the warrant's issuance *is* relevant there, the Court had now reached the incorrect conclusion that "less weight should be accorded the

---

[33]Malley v. Briggs, 475 U.S. 335,   106 S.Ct. 1092, 89 L.Ed.2d 271 (1986).

magistrate's decision in a § 1983 damages suit against the police officer who applied for the warrant."

Indeed, the Supreme Court later concluded that the doctrine of absolute immunity for prosecutors, invoked in *Malley*, does not inevitably apply when a § 1983 action is brought against a prosecutor for a purported Fourth Amendment violation. As concluded in *Burns v. Reed*,[34] while a state prosecutor's appearance in court in support of an application for a search warrant and presentation of evidence at that hearing are protected by absolute immunity, such immunity does not extend to a state prosecutor's giving of legal advise to police, as there is no "historical or common-law support for extending absolute immunity to such actions," which are not "intimately associated with the judicial phase of the criminal process."[35]

A quite different issue reached the Court in *Haring v. Prosise*,[36] namely, whether a plaintiff in a section 1983 action based on an allegedly unconstitutional search was barred by his earlier guilty plea to the offense uncovered by the challenged search. A unanimous Court answered in the negative. After concluding that no such collateral estoppel effect would exist on these facts as a matter of state law,[37] the Supreme Court declined to "create a special rule of preclusion which nevertheless would bar litigation of his § 1983 claim." In support of that refusal, the Court reasoned that the "guilty plea in no way constituted an admission that the search of his apartment was proper under the Fourth Amendment," that "it is impermissible for a court to assume that a plea of guilty is based on a defendant's determination that he would be unable to prevail on a motion to suppress evidence,"[38] and that a plea of guilty cannot be said to constitute a "waiver" of "any claim involving an antecedent Fourth Amendment violation."[39]

As to one final matter, it is necessary to return to *Monroe v. Pape*,[40] where it will be recalled the plaintiffs also brought suit against the officers' employer, the City of Chicago. Examining the legislative history of the statute, Justice Douglas concluded "that

---

[34]Burns v. Reed, 500 U.S. 478, 111 S.Ct. 1934, 114 L.Ed.2d 547 (1991).

[35]See also Schneyder v. Smith, 653 F.3d 313 (3d Cir.2011) (where practice was for prosecutors to monitor material witnesses, regarding prosecutor's alleged Fourth Amendment violation in not informing judge who had ordered witness incarcerated that the trial date had been pushed back several months, this failure "was an administrative one, lacking any significant discretionary or advocative component," and thus "absolute immunity was inapplicable").

[36]Haring v. Prosise, 462 U.S. 306, 103 S.Ct. 2368, 76 L.Ed.2d 595 (1983).

[37]So as possibly to come within *Allen v. McCurry*, discussed in § 11.2(g).

[38]The Court noted that defendant's decision to plead guilty "may have any number of other motivations," including the prospect of a favorable plea agreement.

[39]On this latter point, see § 11.1(d).

[40]Monroe v. Pape, 365 U.S. 167, 81 S.Ct. 473, 5 L.Ed.2d 492 (1961).

Congress did not undertake to bring municipal corporations within the ambit of" section 1983. Thus, it was unnecessary to reach "the constitutional question whether Congress has the power to make municipalities liable for acts of its officers" or the policy argument that municipal liability is to be preferred "because private remedies against officers for illegal searches and seizures are conspicuously ineffective, and because municipal liability will not only afford plaintiffs responsible defendants but cause those defendants to eradicate abuses that exist at the police level." In *Moor v. County of Alameda*,[41] the Court reached the same result where the municipality was vulnerable to suit under local law.

Then came *Monell v. New York City Dep't of Social Services*,[42] in which the Court, after a "fresh analysis of debate on the Civil Rights Act of 1871," concluded that this legislative history "compels the conclusion that Congress *did* intend municipalities and other local government units to be included among those persons to whom § 1983 applies." The Court thus proceeded to overrule *Monroe v. Pape* "insofar as it holds that local govern-

---

[41]Moor v. County of Alameda, 411 U.S. 693, 93 S.Ct. 1785, 36 L.Ed.2d 596 (1973).

[42]Monell v. Department of Social Services of City of New York, 436 U.S. 658, 98 S.Ct. 2108, 56 L.Ed.2d 611 (1978). Petitioners, female employees of the Department and the Board of Education, brought a § 1983 class action against the Department and its Commissioner, the Board and its Chancellor, and the City of New York and its Mayor, complaining that the Board and Department had as a matter of official policy compelled pregnant employees to take unpaid leaves of absence before such leaves were required for medical reasons. The district court found that their rights had been violated, but held that *Monroe v. Pape* barred recovery of backpay from the Department, the Board and the City., 394 F.Supp. 853 (S.D.N.Y.1975). The court of appeals affirmed on a similar theory. 532 F.2d 259 (2d Cir.1976).

Monell was a 7-2 decision, with the Chief Justice and Rehnquist, J., dissenting. However, Stevens, J., concurring in part, declined to join the part of the opinion quoted below on the ground that those statements "are merely advisory and are not necessary to explain the Court's decision."

For other discussions of *Monell*, see Blum, From Monroe to Monell: Defining the Scope of Municipal Liability in Federal Courts, 51 Temple L.Q. 409 (1978); Day & Jacobs, Opening the Deep Pocket—Sovereign Immunity Under Section 1983, 31 Baylor L.Rev. 389 (1979); Kramer, Section 1983 and Municipal Liability: Selected Issues Two Years After Monell v. Dep't of Social Services, 12 Urban Lawyer 232 (1980); Kushnir, The Impact of Section 1983 After Monell on Municipal Policy Formulation and Implementation, 12 Urban Lawyer 466 (1980); Mead, 42 U.S.C.A. § 1983 Municipal Liability: The Monell Sketch Becomes a Distorted Picture, 65 N.Car.L.Rev. 517 (1987); Morrison, The Defense of Local Governments in Civil Rights Litigation, 4 U.Dayton L.Rev. 1 (1979); Schnapper, Civil Rights Litigation After Monell, 79 Colum.L.Rev. 213 (1979); Comments, 16 Cal.W.L.Rev. 58 (1980); 64 Iowa L.Rev. 1032 (1979), 46 U.Chi.L.Rev. 935 (1978); Notes, 79 B.U.L.Rev. 195 (1999); 8 Cap.U.L.Rev. 103 (1978); 79 Colum.L.Rev. 304 (1979), 28 DePaul L.Rev. 429 (1979), 24 Loyola L.Rev. 761 (1979), 30 Mercer L.Rev. 747 (1979), 53 St. John's L.Rev. 66 (1978), 10 U.Tol.L.Rev. 519 (1979); 12 Whittier L.Rev. 333 (1980).

ments are wholly immune from suit under § 1983."[43] The majority then proceeded to give some guidance on the scope of this new-found municipal liability:

> Local governing bodies, therefore, can be sued directly under § 1983 for monetary, declaratory, or injunctive relief[44] where, as here, the action that is alleged to be unconstitutional implements or executes a policy statement, ordinance, regulation, or decision officially adopted and promulgated by that body's officers. Moreover, although the touchstone of the § 1983 action against a government body is an allegation that official policy is responsible for a deprivation of rights protected by the Constitution, local governments, like every other § 1983 "person," by the very terms of the statute, may be sued for constitutional deprivations visited pursuant to governmental "custom" even though such a custom has not received formal approval through the body's official decisionmaking channels. * * * "Although not authorized by written law, such practices of state officials could well be so permanent and well settled as to constitute a 'custom or usage' with the force of law."

> On the other hand, the language of § 1983, read against the background of the same legislative history, compels the conclusion that Congress did not intend municipalities to be held liable unless action pursuant to official municipal policy of some nature caused a constitutional tort. In particular, we conclude that a municipality cannot be held liable *solely* because it employs a tortfeasor, or, in other words, a municipality cannot be held liable under § 1983 on a *respondeat superior* theory.

> We begin with the language of § 1983 as passed:

>> "[A]*ny person who,* under color of any law, statute, ordinance, regulation, custom, or usage of any State, *shall subject, or cause to be subjected,* any person . . . to the deprivation of any rights, privileges, or immunities secured by the Constitution of the United States, shall, any such law, statute, ordinance, regulation, custom, or usage of the State to the contrary notwithstanding, be liable to the party injured in any action at law, suit in equity, or other proper proceeding for redress . . . ." * * * (emphasis added).

> The italicized language plainly imposes liability on a government that, under color of some official policy, "causes" an employee to violate another's constitutional rights. At the same time, that

---

[43]*Monell* brought into question the continuing vitality of Fitzpatrick v. Bitzer, 427 U.S. 445, 96 S.Ct. 2666, 49 L.Ed.2d 614 (1976), relying on *Monroe v. Pape* in holding § 1983 "could not have been intended to include States as parties defendant." But in Will v. Michigan Dep't of State Police, 491 U.S. 58, 109 S.Ct. 2304, 105 L.Ed.2d 45 (1989), the Court held that a state is not a "person" within the meaning of § 1983, and explained that such a holding is "fully consistent" with *Monell,* as "by the time of the enactment of § 1983, municipalities no longer retained the sovereign immunity they had previously shared with the States."

[44]Thus a lower court position that *Monell*'s "policy or custom" requirement applies only to claims for damages and not to claims for prospective relief such as an injunction or declaratory judgment was rejected in Los Angeles County v. Humphries, ___ U.S. ___, 131 S.Ct. 447, 178 L.Ed.2d 460 (2011).

language cannot be easily read to impose liability vicariously on governing bodies solely on the basis of the existence of an employer-employee relationship with a tortfeasor. Indeed, the fact that Congress did specifically provide that A's tort became B's liability if B "caused" A to subject another to a tort suggests that Congress did not intend § 1983 liability to attach where such causation was absent. * * *

We conclude, therefore, that a local government may not be sued for an injury inflicted solely by its employees or agents. Instead, it is when execution of a government's policy or custom, whether made by its lawmakers or by those whose edicts or acts may fairly be said to represent official policy, inflicts the injury that the government as an entity is responsible under § 1983.[45]

From the language just quoted, it is apparent that not every section 1983 action for a Fourth Amendment violation that could be successfully brought against a police officer will likewise be successful against the employing municipality.[46] It is also apparent that as a result of *Monell* courts will now have to decide the difficult issue of when a Fourth Amendment violation by a police officer may be said to amount to "execution of a government's policy or custom." That case gives rise to such questions as whether a directive in a police department manual[47] or from a po-

---

[45]Prior to *Monell,* there was some authority to the effect that the municipal employer could be sued in federal court without regard to the statute. By analogy to Bivens v. Six Unknown Named Agents, 403 U.S. 388, 91 S.Ct. 1999, 29 L.Ed.2d 619 (1971), discussed in detail in the next subsection, holding the Fourth Amendment provides the basis for a cause of action against federal officers, it was sometimes held that the Fourteenth Amendment provided the basis for suit against an employing city, Williams v. Brown, 398 F.Supp. 155 (N.D.Ill.1975), or county, Clark v. Illinois, 415 F.Supp. 149 (N.D.Ill.1976). But after *Monell* courts rejected the *Williams-Clark* theory when used by plaintiffs in an effort to escape the limits on municipal liability under *Monell*. Turpin v. Mailet, 591 F.2d 426 (2d Cir.1979); Molina v. Richardson, 578 F.2d 846 (9th Cir.1978).

As noted in Kramer, Section 1983 and Municipal Liability: Selected Issues Two Years After Monell v. Dep't of Social Services, 12 Urban Lawyer 232 (1980), "it appears that local government can no longer be sued under a *Bivens* theory, either as an alterna-

tive cause of action to the Section 1983 action, or as a means of avoiding the prohibition against Section 1983 liability based on the theory of respondeat superior." For further discussion of that development, see id. at 233–40.

[46]For a section 1983 suit to be against the municipality, it is not necessary that the municipality itself be specifically named as a defendant in the suit. The Supreme Court concluded in Brandon v. Holt, 469 U.S. 464, 105 S.Ct. 873, 83 L.Ed.2d 878 (1985), "that a judgment against a public servant 'in his official capacity' imposes liability on the entity that he represents provided, of course, the public entity received notice and an opportunity to respond."

[47]Many have urged more comprehensive rulemaking at the police level as one important means of ensuring against Fourth Amendment violations. E.g., 1 ABA Standards for Criminal Justice § 1-4.3 (2d ed.1980); Amsterdam, Perspectives on the Fourth Amendment, 58 Minn.L.Rev. 349, 416–28 (1974); Caplan, The Case for Rulemaking by Law Enforcement Agencies, 36 Law & Contemp.Prob. 500 (1971); Iglebarger & Schubert,

lice supervisor[48] can be said to constitute the requisite "official policy," whether lack of sufficient police training on a particular matter can ever constitute the requisite "official policy,"[49] and whether a "custom" as to certain kinds of Fourth Amendment violations might be established by such facts as a pattern of nondiscipline for such conduct.[50]

Policy Making for the Police, 58 A.B.A.J. 307 (1972); LaFave, Controlling Discretion by Administrative Regulations: The Use, Misuse and Nonuse of Police Rules and Policies in Fourth Amendment Adjudication, 89 Mich.L.Rev. 442 (1990); McGowan, Rule-Making and the Police, 70 Mich.L. Rev. 659 (1972). It would be regrettable if municipalities, in a desire to protect the public treasury after *Monell*, were to move in the other direction in an effort to avoid having the requisite "official policy" that would support a suit against the municipality.

[48]SeeAlexander v. City and County of San Francisco, 29 F.3d 1355 (9th Cir.1994) (no municipal liability, as plaintiff "cites neither facts nor law showing that a San Francisco police commander is an authorized decision-maker for the City and County").

[49]In City of Canton, Ohio v. Harris, 489 U.S. 378, 109 S.Ct. 1197, 103 L.Ed.2d 412 (1989), the Court held "that the inadequacy of police training may serve as the basis of § 1983 liability only where the failure to train amounts to deliberate indifference to the rights of persons with whom the police come into contact. This rule is most consistent with our admonition in *Monell* * * * that a municipality can be liable under § 1983 only where its policies are the 'moving force [behind] the constitutional violation.' * * *

"In resolving the issue of a city's liability, the focus must be on adequacy of the training program in relation to the tasks the particular officers must perform. That a particular officer may be unsatisfactorily trained will not alone suffice to fasten liability on the city, for the officer's shortcomings may have resulted from factors other than a faulty training program."

[50]In Walters v. City of Ocean Springs, 626 F.2d 1317 (5th Cir.1980), the court held summary judgment in favor of the city was justified, as no genuine issue of fact as to the requisite policy under *Monell* was raised by the police officer's deposition that he had believed his conduct met the standards of the police department. In Edmonds v. Dillin, 485 F.Supp. 722 (N.D.Ohio 1980), the court, though dismissing a complaint claiming the city failed to train its police adequately, stated: "If a municipality completely fails to train its police force, or trains its officers in a manner that is in reckless disregard of the need to inform and instruct police officers to perform their duty in conformity with the constitution, and if the municipality might reasonably foresee that unconstitutional actions of its police officers might be committed by reason of the municipality's failure or reckless disregard, then the municipality would have implicitly authorized or acquiesced in such future unconstitutional acts." Compare Smith v. Oklahoma City, 696 F.2d 784 (10th Cir.1983) (plaintiff prevails in showing illegal arrest attributable to city policy, which is to issue arrest warrants for parking tickets 2 to 8 months old by a computer check of the *present* owner of the vehicle, defective because in interim car might have been purchased by another).

For additional discussion of the problems in this area, see Day & Jacobs, 31 Baylor L.Rev. 389, 400 (1979); Gilles, Breaking the Code of Silence: Rediscovering "Custom" in Section 1983 Municipal Liability, 89 B.U.L.Rev. 17, 91–92 (2000) (concluding "that § 1983's 'custom' language, largely forgotten by lawyers, courts and commentators, holds the promise of reinvigorating modern civil rights litigation" by which "we should be able

Often the question arises as to whether the plaintiff's complaint sufficiently alleges the requisite official policy or custom. The problem is helpfully discussed in *Powe v. City of Chicago*[51]:

> In *Monell,* since the plaintiff explicitly attacked the municipal department's official policy of forcing pregnant women to take unpaid leaves of absence, the Supreme Court had no occasion to consider when an official policy or custom should be inferred from a complaint's allegations. Cases following *Monell,* however, have considered this question, and these cases suggest that, normally, the mere allegation of a single act of unconstitutional conduct by a municipal employee will not support the inference that such conduct was pursuant to official policies.[52] On the other hand, where the plaintiff alleges a pattern or a series of incidents of unconstitutional conduct, then the courts have found an allegation of policy sufficient to withstand a dismissal motion. * * *

> In the present case, Powe has alleged that he was the victim of a series of unlawful arrests, each arrest based on the same, allegedly invalid, warrant. In our view, his allegations are sufficient to raise the inference that the municipal defendants are responsible for the challenged arrests. The complaint indicates that the challenged probation-violation warrant was prepared, promulgated, and executed by various employees of separate departments of the defendants' law enforcement agencies. Assuming the warrant was invalid, its invalidity would lie * * * in the failure of the municipal authorities to include in the warrant an adequate description of the person sought. This failure to describe the arrestee was repeated four times. We find it reasonable to infer that the inadequacy of the description in the warrant was systemic in nature, that is, that it resulted from the procedures followed by the defendants' law enforcement agencies in issuing warrants of the type involved here. Given this reasonable inference, we must conclude that Powe is entitled to maintain his suit against the defendant municipalities.

Consistent with that analysis, the court in *Powe* went on to hold there was no basis for an action against those municipalities on defendant's other contention that on one occasion he had been detained an excessive period of time after his arrest. This is a sensible way of looking at actions taken at the police officer level, and is not inconsistent with the Supreme Court's later pronounce-

---

to develop a theory of civil rights liability that meaningfully addresses common constitutional deprivations caused by police in urban America today"); Schnapper, 79 Colum.L.Rev. 213, 215–240 (1979); Note, 79 Colum. L.Rev. 304 (1979). The Schnapper article helpfully considers "which city employees should be regarded as 'policymakers' in various circumstances," "the role of 'custom' in section 1983 litigation," and "whether a city's liability should be affected if it adopts rules forbidding unconstitutional conduct."

[51] Powe v. City of Chicago, 664 F.2d 639 (7th Cir.1981).

[52] In City of Oklahoma City v. Tuttle, 471 U.S. 808, 105 S.Ct. 2427, 85 L.Ed.2d 791 (1985), the Court so concluded. As expressed by the four-Justice plurality: "Proof of a single incident of unconstitutional activity is not sufficient to impose liability under *Monell,* unless proof of the incident includes proof that it was caused by an existing, unconstitutional municipal policy, which policy can be attributed to a municipal policymaker."

THE EXCLUSIONARY RULE

ment in *Pembaur v. City of Cincinnati*[53] that "where action is directed by those who establish governmental policy, the municipality is equally responsible whether the action is to be taken only once or to be taken repeatedly." It was thus properly concluded in *Pembaur* that a claim against the county was improperly dismissed where it was grounded in the prosecutor's action in directing deputy sheriffs on one occasion to forcibly enter premises to serve capiases.

In *Board of County Commissioners v. Brown*,[54] the plaintiff (who alleged that a county police officer used excessive force in arresting her and that the county was liable because the sheriff, admittedly the policymaker for the sheriff's department, had hired that officer without adequately reviewing his background) relied on *Pembaur* for the proposition that a single act by a decisionmaker with final authority in the relevant area constitutes a "policy" attributable to the municipality sufficient to trigger municipal liability. But the majority in *Brown*[55] distinguished *Pembaur*, a case in which the "county's final decisionmaker * * * had specifically directed the action resulting in the deprivation of petitioner's rights," from the instant case, where plaintiff's claim instead was that "a single facially lawful hiring decision can launch a series of events that ultimately cause a violation of federal rights." The distinction, "between § 1983 cases that present no difficult questions of fault and causation and those that do," meant that the plaintiff here faced "much more difficult problems of proof," and thus the plaintiff here could not prevail because she had failed to show that the sheriff's decision "reflected a conscious disregard for a high risk that [the arresting officer] would use excessive force in violation of respondent's federally protected right."[56]

The Court in *Monell* cautioned that "[s]ince the question

[53]Pembaur v. City of Cincinnati, 475 U.S. 469, 106 S.Ct. 1292, 89 L.Ed.2d 452 (1986).

[54]Board of County Commissioners v. Brown, 520 U.S. 397, 117 S.Ct. 1382, 137 L.Ed.2d 626 (1997).

[55]A total of four Justices dissented. One dissenting opinion in which three Justices joined objected to the Court holding "as a matter of law that the sheriff's act could not be thought to reflect deliberate indifference to the risk that his subordinate would violate the Constitution by using excessive force." Another dissenting opinion in which three Justices joined expressed the view that it was necessary to "ask for further argument that would focus upon the continued

viability of *Monell's* distinction between vicarious liability and municipal liability based upon policy and custom." On that point, see Symposium, 31 Urb.Law. 393 (1999).

[56]As for plaintiff's reliance on City of Canton, Ohio v. Harris, 489 U.S. 378, 109 S.Ct. 1197, 103 L.Ed.2d 412 (1989), discussed in note 49 supra, the *Brown* majority responded that she "ignores the fact that predicting the consequences of a single hiring decision, even one based on an inadequate assessment of a record, is far more difficult than predicting what might flow from the failure to train a single law enforcement officer as to a specific skill necessary to the discharge of his duties. * * * Unlike the risk from a particular glaring omission in a train-

whether local government bodies should be afforded some form of official immunity was not presented as a question to be decided on this petition and was not briefed by the parties nor addressed by the courts below, we express no views on the scope of any municipal immunity beyond holding that municipal bodies sued under § 1983 cannot be entitled to an absolute immunity." But in *Owen v. City of Independence, Missouri,*[57] the Supreme Court held that a municipality has no immunity from liability under section 1983 flowing from its constitutional violations and may not assert the good faith of its officers as a defense to such liability. The majority, per Brennan, J., reasoned: (i) that the broad language and legislative history of section 1983 reflects that it "creates a species of tort liability that on its face admits of no immunities"; (ii) that, while section 1983 has been construed to incorporate well established common law immunities compatible with its purpose, there is no tradition of immunity for municipal corporations; (iii) that the doctrines a municipality is immune with respect to "governmental" functions and for "discretionary" activities were not intended to be applicable, as there is no discretion to violate the Constitution and governmental immunity is clearly abrogated by section 1983; and (iv) that the result is also compelled "by considerations of public policy," as "owing to the qualified immunity enjoyed by most government officials, * * * many victims of municipal malfeasance would be left remediless if the city were also allowed to assert a good-faith defense." Moreover, absence of a defense of good faith "should create an incentive for officials who may harbor doubts about the lawfulness of their intended actions to err on the side of protecting citizens' constitutional rights" and "encourage those in a policymaking position to institute internal rules and programs designed to minimize the likelihood of unintentional infringements on constitutional rights." Finally, the majority in *Owen* concluded that the reasons for immunizing the employee did not carry over to the municipality. While it would be unjust to make the employee respond in damages in the absence of bad faith, "even where some constitutional development could not have been foreseen by municipal officials, it is fairer to allocate any resulting financial loss to the inevitable costs of government borne by all the taxpayers, than to allow its impact to be felt solely by those whose rights, albeit newly recognized, have been violated." As for the concern that the threat of liability would unduly inhibit vigorous exercise of official authority, the *Owen* majority reasoned that this "inhibiting effect is significantly reduced, if not eliminated, * * * when the threat of personal liability is

---

ing regimen, the risk from a single instance of inadequate screening of an applicant's background is not 'obvious' in the abstract; rather, it depends upon the background of the applicant."

[57] Owen v. City of Independence, Missouri, 445 U.S. 622, 100 S.Ct. 1398, 63 L.Ed.2d 673 (1980), noted in 30 DePaul L.Rev. 243 (1980).

removed," and added that "consideration of the *municipality's* liability for constitutional violations is quite properly the concern of its elected or appointed officials."[58]

When a § 1983 plaintiff was convicted following the police activity about which the plaintiff now complains, a further problem is presented. As the Supreme Court put it in *Heck v. Humphrey*,[59] a "district court must consider whether a judgment in favor of the plaintiff would necessarily imply the invalidity of his conviction or sentence; if it would,[60] the complaint must be dismissed unless the plaintiff can demonstrate that the conviction or sentence has already been invalidated."[61] But the Court in *Heck* then dropped a footnote describing the type of action that, "even if successful, will *not* demonstrate the invalidity of any outstanding criminal judgment against the plaintiff," reading as follows:

> For example, a suit for damages attributable to an allegedly unreasonable search may lie even if the challenged search produced evidence that was introduced in a state criminal trial resulting in the § 1983 plaintiff's still-outstanding conviction. Because of doctrines like independent source and inevitable discovery, and especially harmless error, such a § 1983 action, even if successful, would not *necessarily* imply that the plaintiff's conviction was unlawful.

Although this footnote "is a bit unclear" because it could be interpreted to mean either (i) that only *some* Fourth Amendment claims would not necessarily be barred, e.g., where the circumstances show the tainted evidence would nonetheless be admissible under a theory of inevitable discovery, or (ii) that *all* Fourth Amendment claims may go forward because such claims, as a class, do not imply a conviction is invalid, the latter interpretation appears to be the correct one.[62] On the other hand, by virtue

---

[58]Powell, J., joined by the Chief Justice and Stewart and Rehnquist, JJ., dissenting, argued that the Court's decision "conflicts with the apparent intent of the drafters of the statute, with the common law of municipal tort liability, and with the current state law of municipal liability," and that it "subjects local governments to damages judgments for actions that were reasonable when performed."

[59]Heck v. Humphrey, 512 U.S. 477, 114 S.Ct. 2364, 129 L.Ed.2d 383 (1994).

[60]Compare Lockett v. Ericson, 656 F.3d 892 (9th Cir.2011) (where after Lockett's motion to suppress denied he pled nolo contendere, this means validity of his conviction in no way depended upon legality of the search, and thus *Heck* does not bar his § 1983

claim); Schreiber v. Moe, 596 F.3d 323 (6th Cir.2010) (where the alleged Fourth Amendment violation is the use of excessive force, plaintiff's claim does not challenge his earlier conviction for resisting arrest unless lack of excessive force is an element of the crime or excessive force is an affirmative defense to the crime).

[61]See, e.g., Barnes v. Wright, 449 F.3d 709 (6th Cir.2006) (under *Heck* rule, notwithstanding plaintiff's acquittal of second charge of interfering with officers' duties, plaintiff's action for false arrest barred by his conviction of wanton endangerment by pointing firearm at conservation officers).

[62]Copus v. City of Edgerton, 151 F.3d 646 (7th Cir.1998), noting that circuit had opted for alternative (ii) in Antonelli v. Foster, 104 F.3d 899 (7th

of the earlier ruling in *Allen v. McCurry*[63] to the effect that collateral estoppel, or issue preclusion, may apply when a § 1983 plaintiff attempts to relitigate in federal court issues decided against him in state criminal proceedings, it is possible that the § 1983 action may be barred even though the plaintiff was *acquitted* in the criminal proceeding.[64]

Despite the aforementioned roadblocks, it has been asserted that "[t]oday, § 1983 is an important avenue for private impact litigators," such as the ACLU and NAACP, "to seek reform of police practices."[65] Such lawsuits (as well as those brought against police departments by the U.S. Attorney General under 18 U.S.C. § 14141[66]), while "formal avenues of litigation," are said to have "their greatest utility" in "bringing expert parties together to bargain for reform."[67] As one commentator has noted:

> What is striking is that many of the key reforms forged by settlement stipulations, agreements, and consent decrees generate data to penetrate the opacity of police discretion through information-reporting, collection, and dissemination. Many of the reforms in cases involving recurrent problems such as excessive force or racial targeting call for police to report uses of force, demographic information, and bases for investigative stops and searches. The methods of regulation and remedies are shifting to information and data-driven surveillance of police practices.[68]

Cir.1997). See also Sanford v. Motts, 258 F.3d 1117 (9th Cir.2001) (defendant's *Heck* claim that when plaintiff "convicted of resisting this arrest, the lawfulness of [officer] Motts' action was conceded" erroneously accepted by district court; plaintiff's allegations of excessive force by officer do not " 'necessarily imply the invalidity' of her conviction" because it may be that "Motts used excessive force subsequent to the time that Sanford interfered with his duty").

[63]Allen v. McCurry, 449 U.S. 90, 101 S.Ct. 411, 66 L.Ed.2d 308 (1980).

[64]See, e.g., Crumley v. City of St. Paul, 324 F.3d 1003 (8th Cir.2003) (§ 1983 plaintiff's contention her arrest without probable cause barred notwithstanding her acquittal, which "is irrelevant to this discussion" considering that before acquittal there had been a finding of probable cause for the arrest).

[65]Fan, Panopticism for Police: Structural Reform Bargaining and Police Regulation by Data-Driven Surveillance, 87 Wash.L.Rev. 93, 115

(2012).

[66]Conferring standing on the Attorney General to seek civil injunctive relief against police departments exhibiting a pattern or practice of violating federal civil rights.

[67]Fan, 87 Wash.L.Rev. 93, 116 (2012).

[68]Fan, 87 Wash.L.Rev. 93, 127 (2012), adding: "The benefits of data collection and dissemination for public deliberation and oversight concerning police tactics are demonstrated by the New York City Police Department's collection of data on *Terry* stops and frisks. After mass protests erupted in New York over the fatal shooting of Amadou Diallou, an unarmed West African immigrant in the Bronx, by four police officers in 1999, the Center for Constitutional Rights sued the city for data. The resulting data-gathering measures have documented the disparate impact of *Terry* stops, showing, for example, that Black and Latino people were nine times more likely to be stopped than Whites in 2009."

§ 1.10(b) The "constitutional tort" by federal officers

The Congress has not enacted a statute comparable to section 1983, discussed above, applicable to constitutional violations by federal officials. That gap was filled, at least with respect to Fourth Amendment violations, by the Supreme Court in *Bivens v. Six Unknown Named Agents.*[69] The plaintiff's action against several Federal Bureau of Narcotics agents to collect damages for an alleged illegal arrest and search was dismissed by the federal district court on the ground that it failed to state a cause of action,[70] and the court of appeals affirmed on that basis.[71] But the Supreme Court held that the plaintiff's "complaint states a cause of action under the Fourth Amendment" and that consequently he was "entitled to recover money damages for any injuries he has suffered as a result of the agents' violation of the Amendment."[72]

The respondent agents took the position that it was sufficient that Bivens could bring an action in tort in the state courts, wherein "the Fourth Amendment would serve merely to limit the extent to which the agents could defend the state law tort suit by asserting that their actions were a valid exercise of federal power: if the agents were shown to have violated the Fourth Amendment, such a defense would be lost to them and they would stand

[Section 1.10(b)]

[69]Bivens v. Six Unknown Named Agents, 403 U.S. 388, 91 S.Ct. 1999, 29 L.Ed.2d 619 (1971). For discussions of *Bivens,* see Berch, Money Damages for Fourth Amendment Violations by Federal Officials: An Explanation of Bivens v. Six Unknown Named Agents of Federal Bureau of Narcotics, 1971 Law & Soc. Order 43; Dellinger, Of Rights and Remedies: The Constitution as a Sword, 85 Harv.L.Rev. 1532 (1972); Lehmann, Bivens and Its Progeny: The Scope of a Constitutional Cause of Action for Torts Committed by Government Officials, 4 Hastings Const.L.Q. 531 (1977); Pfander & Baltmanis, Rethinking Bivens: Legitimacy and Constitutional Adjudication, 98 Geo.L.J. 117 (2009); Reinert, Measuring the Success of Bivens Litigation and Its Consequences for the Individual Liability Model, 62 Stan.L.Rev. 809 (2010); Rosen, The Bivens Constitutional Tort: An Unfulfilled Promise, 67 N.Car.L.Rev. 337 (1989); Comments, 62 SMU L.Rev. 1945 (2009); 1972 Utah L.Rev. 276; Notes, 38 Brook.L.Rev. 522 (1971); 21 DePaul L.Rev. 1135 (1972); 25 U.Miami L.Rev. 785 (1971); 33 U.Pitt.L.Rev. 271 (1971). For an extended analysis of the experience under *Bivens,* see Student Project, 9 Hofstra L.Rev. 943 (1981). For the argument that a statutory cause of action is needed in lieu of *Bivens,* see Note, 37 Fordham Urb.L.J. 1057 (2010).

[70]276 F.Supp. 12 (E.D.N.Y.1967).

[71]409 F.2d 718 (2d Cir.1969), noted at 83 Harv.L.Rev. 684 (1970); 24 Hastings L.J. 987 (1973).

[72]"Drawing to varying degrees on the reasoning of *Bivens,* courts in a number of states have recognized damages remedies under their state constitutions. Many of these courts have utilized the analytical framework adopted by *Bivens* and its progeny, in some cases supplemented by factors not expressly raised in *Bivens*." Binette v. Sabo, 244 Conn. 23, 710 A.2d 688 (1998) (collecting cases to that effect, and noting also, again citing cases, that courts "in some states have rejected a *Bivens*-type action in the cases before them, but expressly or impliedly have left the door open to recognizing such a remedy in other circumstances").

before the state law merely as private individuals." But this position, said Justice Brennan writing for the majority, rests upon "an unduly restrictive view of the Fourth Amendment's protection," for it seeks "to treat the relationship between a citizen and a federal agent unconstitutionally exercising his authority as no different from the relationship between two private citizens." This is not the case, he concluded, for the following three reasons: (1) It is not true that "the Fourth Amendment proscribes only such conduct as would, if engaged in by private persons, be condemned by state law." In several instances, the Court has found the Fourth Amendment to be violated without regard to the apparent legality of the conduct under state law. In *Katz v. United States*,[73] for example, the Court declared that the Fourth Amendment was not tied to the niceties of local trespass laws. (2) The interests protected by state laws and those protected by the Fourth Amendment "may be inconsistent or even hostile." For example, the law of trespass may provide that a private citizen, asserting no authority other than his own, is not liable in trespass if he demands and is granted admission to another's home, on the ground that if the householder objected he could have barred the door or called the police. But these options are effectively closed when the demand for admission rests upon a claim of federal authority. (3) That damages may be obtained for injuries consequent upon a Fourth Amendment violation by federal officers "hardly seem[s] a surprising proposition," for historically "damages have been regarded as the ordinary remedy for an invasion of personal interests in liberty."[74]

Bivens left a number of issues unresolved concerning this new remedy for Fourth Amendment violations. For one thing, because the court of appeals had not considered the matter, the Court did not pass upon the district court's ruling "that in any event respondents were immune from liability by virtue of their official position." Although at least one court has ruled to the contrary,[75] the better view is that taken by the court of appeals on remand, namely, that there is no absolute immunity with respect to the police activity of making arrests and searches.[76] Under *Barr v.*

---

[73]Katz v. United States, 389 U.S. 347, 88 S.Ct. 507, 19 L.Ed.2d 576 (1967).

[74]Harlan, J., concurring, explained why he was "of the opinion that federal courts do have the power to award damages for violation of 'constitutionally protected interests' and * * * that a traditional judicial remedy such as damages is appropriate to the vindication of the personal interests protected by the Fourth

Amendment." Burger, C.J., and Black and Blackmun, JJ., in separate dissents, all argued that it should lie with Congress rather than the Court to create such a cause of action against federal officials.

[75]Davidson v. Kane, 337 F.Supp. 922 (E.D.Va.1972).

[76]Bivens v. Six Unknown Named Agents, 456 F.2d 1339 (2d Cir.1972).

In Apton v. Wilson, 506 F.2d 83 (D.C.Cir.1974), the court held that

Matteo,[77] the court noted, an official is immune if he performs "discretionary acts at those levels of government where the concept of duty encompasses the sound exercise of discretionary authority" and the act complained of was "within the outer perimeter of [the official's] line of duty." The latter requirement was met in *Bivens,* the court of appeals concluded, for "the duties of these defendants include making arrests in cases involving narcotics" and they "were doing just that." As for the "discretionary acts" requirement, the court quite correctly noted that this label is not particularly helpful and that it is more useful to proceed directly to "the real question to be asked," whether "federal officers performing police duties warrant the protection of the immunity defense." The court held that they do not, for laxity in complying with the Fourth Amendment "would only be encouraged by a grant of immunity." Moreover:

> In its decision in this case, the Supreme Court recognized a right of action against federal officers that is roughly analogous to the right of action against state officers that was provided when Congress enacted the Civil Rights Act. It would, we think, be incongruous and confusing, to say the least, if we should rule that under one phase of federal law a police officer had immunity and that under another phase of federal law he had no immunity.

The court of appeals then proceeded to consider another matter left open by the Supreme Court in *Bivens:* the standards by which federal officers' conduct was to be judged in the context of this newly-created action for damages. The court concluded that an officer should not be held liable in every instance in which, upon a motion to suppress, it would be determined by the traditional objective test that an unreasonable search had occurred. Rather, "it is a defense to allege and prove good faith and reasonable belief in the validity of the arrest and search and in the necessity for carrying out the arrest and search in the way the arrest was made and the search was conducted." In *Harlow v. Fitzgerald,*[78] the Court concluded that a purely objective test of liability should be utilized and that consequently federal officials are generally shielded from liability "insofar as their conduct[79] does not violate clearly established statutory or constitutional rights of which a

---

high officials of the Department of Justice did not enjoy absolute immunity from civil liability for their conduct in directing or participating in District of Columbia law enforcement activity allegedly depriving innocent citizens of their Fourth Amendment rights. Relying upon "general principles of tort law [which] provide a cause of action for unlawful arrest against a defendant who 'affirmatively instigated, encouraged, incited, or caused the unlawful arrest,'" it was held in Rodriguez v. Ritchey, 539 F.2d 394 (5th Cir.1976), that a *Bivens*-type action could be brought against investigating officers who did not participate in the actual arrest. But see note 7 supra.

[77] Barr v. Matteo, 360 U.S. 564, 79 S.Ct. 1335, 3 L.Ed.2d 1434 (1959).

[78] Harlow v. Fitzgerald, 457 U.S. 800, 102 S.Ct. 2727, 73 L.Ed.2d 396 (1982).

[79] Under *Bivens,* "Government of-

reasonable person would have known."[80]

The *Harlow* qualified immunity standard was applied by the Supreme Court to a Fourth Amendment *Bivens* suit in *Anderson v. Creighton,*[81] involving an entry for purposes of arrest of plaintiffs' premises by an FBI agent allegedly acting without probable cause and exigent circumstances. The Court there instructed that for the violated right to be "clearly established" the

> contours of the right must be sufficiently clear that a reasonable official would understand that what he is doing violates that right. This is not to say that an official action is protected by qualified immunity unless the very action in question has previously been held unlawful * * *; it is to say that in light of preexisting law the unlawfulness must be apparent.[82]

Thus, the Court continued, even if the plaintiffs' right to be free of a warrantless search of their premises unless probable cause and exigent circumstances are present was itself clearly established, FBI agent Anderson could still argue "that it was *not* clearly established that the circumstances with which Anderson was confronted did not constitute probable cause and exigent circumstances." That is, the question to be considered on remand with respect to Anderson's motion for summary judgment "is the objective (albeit fact-specific) question whether a reasonable officer could have believed Anderson's warrantless search to be lawful, in light of clearly established law and the information the searching officers possessed."[83] In reaching that conclusion, the *Anderson* majority rejected several contentions of the plaintiffs, namely: (i) that a violation of the Fourth Amendment, being an "unreasonable" search or seizure, could never be reasonable under *Harlow;* (ii) that qualified immunity should not be recognized in

---

ficials may not be held liable for the unconstitutional conduct of their subordinates under a theory of *respondeat superior.* [A] plaintiff must plead that each Government official, through the official's own individual actions, has violated the Constitution." Ashcroft v. Iqbal, 556 U.S. 662, 129 S.Ct. 1937, 173 L.Ed.2d 868 (2009).

[80]See further discussion in text at note 28 supra.

[81]Anderson v. Creighton, 483 U.S. 635, 107 S.Ct. 3034, 97 L.Ed.2d 523 (1987), discussed in Garcia, The Scope of Police Immunity from Civil Suit Under Title 43 Section 1983 and Bivens: A Realistic Appraisal, 11 Whittier L.Rev. 511 (1989).

[82]See also Ashcroft v. al-Kidd, __ U.S. __, 131 S.Ct. 2074, 179 L.Ed.2d 1149(2011) (applying the *Anderson*

test, and holding the Attorney General had qualified immunity because "not a single judicial opiion had held that pretext could render an objectively reasonable arrest pursuant to a material-witness warrant unconstitutional"); Wilson v. Layne, 526 U.S. 603, 119 S.Ct. 1692, 143 L.Ed.2d 818 (1999) (involving both state officials under § 1983 and federal officials under *Bivens,* quoting and applying the *Anderson* test).

[83]As the Court later put it in Ashcroft v. al-Kidd, __ U.S. __, 131 S.Ct. 2074, 179 L.Ed.2d 1149 (2011), the court of appeals erred in finding "clearly established law lurking in the broad 'history and purposes of the Fourth Amendment,' " as courts are "not to define clearly established law at a high level of generality."

instances of warrantless searches; and (iii) that qualified immunity should not be applicable to circumstances, such as in the instant case, where a rule of strict liability obtained at common law.[84]

As the Court later noted in *Saucier v. Katz*,[85] *Anderson* thus "rejected the argument that there is no distinction between the reasonableness standard for warrantless searches and the qualified immunity inquiry." But in *Saucier*, a *Bivens* action brought by a protester who was hustled away from an Al Gore speech at a military base when he attempted to unfurl a banner, the Court was confronted with the contention that the same could not be said of claims of excessive force in violation of the Fourth Amendment. The respondents there, the Court explained, contended "that, unlike the qualified immunity analysis applicable in other contexts, the excessive force test [set out in *Graham v. Connor*[86]] already affords latitude for mistaken beliefs as to the amount of force necessary, so that '*Graham* has addressed for the excessive force area most of the concern expressed in *Anderson*.'" The Court disagreed, however, and concluded that the "inquiries for qualified immunity[87] and excessive force remain distinct, even after *Graham*." The latter, the Court explained,

---

[84]The three dissenters objected that neither logic nor the precedents "supports the proposition that a warrantless search should be evaluated under a standard less strict than the constitutional standard of reasonableness."

[85]Saucier v. Katz, 533 U.S. 194, 121 S.Ct. 2151, 150 L.Ed.2d 272 (2001).

[86]Graham v. Connor, 490 U.S. 386, 109 S.Ct. 1865, 104 L.Ed.2d 443 (1989).

[87]While *Saucier* says that courts addressing a qualified immunity claim must first ask whether plaintiff alleged a violation of a constitutional right and second ask whether that right was clearly established at the time, in Pearson v. Callahan, 555 U.S. 223, 129 S.Ct. 808, 172 L.Ed.2d 565 (2009), discussed in Comments, 62 Stan.L.Rev. 563 (2010); 59 UCLA L.Rev. 468 (2011), the Court allowed judges "to exercise their sound discretion in deciding which of the two prongs of the qualified immunity analysis should be addressed first."

But in Camreta v. Greene, __ U.S. __, 131 S.Ct. 2020, 179 L.Ed.2d 1118 (2011), discussed in Kerr, Fourth Amendment Remedies and Developments of the Law: A Comment on Camreta v. Greene and Davis v. United States, 2011 Cato Sup.Ct.Rev. 237, the Supreme Court instructed that courts should proceed directly to, "should address only," and should deny relief exclusively based on the second element in the seven particular circumstances outlined in *Pearson*: when (1) the first constitutional violation question "is so factbound that the decision provides little guidance for future cases"; (2) "it appears that the question will soon be decided by a higher court"; (3) deciding the constitutional question requires "an uncertain interpretation of state law"; (4) "qualified immunity is asserted at the pleading stage" and "the precise factual basis for the * * * claim * * * may be hard to identify"; (5) tackling the first element "may create a risk of bad decisionmaking" due to inadequate briefing; (6) discussing both elements risks "bad decisionmaking" because the court is firmly convinced the law is not clearly established and is thus inclined to give little thought to the existence of the constitutional right; or (7) the doctrine of "constitutional avoidance"

takes into account reasonable mistakes of fact as to the circumstances, such as where "an officer reasonably, but mistakenly, believed that a suspect was likely to fight back," while the "qualified immunity inquiry * * * has a further dimension." That is, the "concern of the immunity inquiry is to acknowledge that reasonable mistakes can be made as to the legal constraints on particular police conduct" because it "is sometimes difficult for an officer to determine how the relevant legal doctrine * * * will be applied to the factual situation the officer confronts."[88]

It is important to note that, notwithstanding the foregoing analogies between the *Bivens*-type cause of action against federal police and the section 1983 action against state and local police, the former is by no means as broad as the latter. The statute deals with the deprivation of constitutional rights generally, while the Court in *Bivens* had occasion to deal only with an action based upon violation of Fourth Amendment rights.[89] This means that counsel who is planning to undertake a *Bivens*-type

---

suggests the wisdom of passing on the first constitutional question because "it is plain that a constitutional right is not clearly established but far from obvious whether in fact there is such a right." On the other hand, as it was put in Kerns v. Bader, 663 F.3d 1173 (10th Cir.2011), the Court in *Camreta* "has told us that courts may 'avoid avoidance'—and so answer the first qualified immunity question before proceeding to the second—in cases involving a recurring fact pattern where guidance on the constitutionality of the challenged conduct is required and the conduct is only likely to be challenged within the qualified immunity regime."

[88]Three Justices, concurring in the judgment, declared: "The two-part test today's decision imposes holds large potential to confuse. Endeavors to bring the Court's abstract instructions down to earth, I suspect, will bear out what lower courts have already observed-paradigmatically, the determination of police misconduct in excessive force cases and the availability of qualified immunity both hinge on the same question: Taking into account the particular circumstances confronting the defendant officer, could a reasonable officer, identically situated, have believed the force employed was lawful?"

[89]Of course, a plaintiff suing a federal officer for some other type of constitutional violation might make a *Bivens*-type claim. But, because "implied causes of action are disfavored, the Court has been reluctant to extent *Bivens* liability 'to any new context or new category of defendants.'" Ashcroft v. Iqbal, 556 U.S. 662, 129 S.Ct. 1937, 173 L.Ed.2d 868 (2009).

But even if the conduct of a government agent *does* intrude upon Fourth Amendment rights, it is possible that a court will hold that, because of the nature and degree of that intrusion, a *Bivens* cause of action is not available. Such was the holding in Seibert v. Baptist, 594 F.2d 423 (5th Cir.1979), concerning a suit by a taxpayer against IRS officers seeking damages based upon alleged abuses of their authority in terminating the plaintiff's taxable period, failing to follow prescribed procedures in making jeopardy assessments of an income tax deficiency, and seizing plaintiff's property. The court ruled, in effect, that it would be inappropriate to recognize an implied Fourth Amendment cause of action in this context, in that to do so would be inconsistent with relevant federal law.

Actually, the court relied upon several factors: (1) that "while in *Bivens* infringement of the plaintiff's fourth amendment rights was clear and direct, in the present case it appears that appropriate notice of termi-

suit may have to give closer attention to the precise constitutional violation involved in the police misconduct being complained of. Illustrative of the problems which may arise is *Davidson v. Kane*,[90] holding that a battery by a federal officer is not actionable under *Bivens* because "it is not a violation of a Fourth Amendment right." It may well be true that not every battery by a policeman constitutes a violation of the Constitution,[91] but it does not follow, as the *Davidson* court seemed to assume, that excessive force must always be characterized in terms of a general due process violation rather than a violation of the Fourth Amendment.[92] Because "*Bivens* actions are quite similar to those brought under § 1983," a "*Bivens* action is governed by the same statute of limitations as would a § 1983 action in that court."[93]

---

nation and notice of seizure were given to the plaintiff at the time his property was taken," so that "the seizure was not so unreasonable as that involved in *Bivens*"; (2) that there has been no congressional activity indicating an attempt to allow such a remedy, and that in fact congressional indications are that there should be no such remedy because the Federal Tort Claims Act excludes claims against the United States if they relate to the assessment or collection of taxes and because the Internal Revenue Code prohibits any suit to restrain the assessment or collection of taxes; (3) that implication of such a remedy would not be consistent with the purposes of the constitutional right asserted, as extensive statutory regulation of internal revenue matters suggests that implication of a private cause of action would be inconsistent with the statutory scheme enacted by Congress; (4) that the implied cause of action would not be an appropriate one for federal law, given the fact that extensive and specific congressional regulation already exists; (5) that a damage action is not indispensable to the effectuation of the constitutional rights asserted as the comprehensive scheme enacted by Congress provides protection against unreasonable searches and seizures.

[90]Davidson v. Kane, 337 F.Supp. 922 (E.D.Va.1972).

[91]See note 17 supra.

[92]Amsterdam, Perspectives on the Fourth Amendment, 58 Minn.L.Rev.

349, 366–67 (1974), notes: "The preconstitutional history of the amendment discloses no specific evidence of a concern against the use of excessive force to effect a search or seizure that could otherwise be properly effected. Yet the Supreme Court has strongly hinted that a search or seizure may be constitutionally unreasonable by virtue of undue brutality alone." The reference is to Schmerber v. California, 384 U.S. 757, 86 S.Ct. 1826, 16 L.Ed.2d 908 (1966).

See James v. United States, 358 F.Supp. 1381 (D.R.I.1973), noting that the cases have variously characterized the application of unreasonable force as a violation of the Fifth Amendment due process clause, the Fourth Amendment protection against unreasonable seizure, and the Eighth Amendment proscription against cruel and unusual punishment. But in Tennessee v. Garner, 471 U.S. 1, 105 S.Ct. 1694, 85 L.Ed.2d 1 (1985), the Court held that "there can be no question that apprehension by the use of deadly force is a seizure subject to the reasonableness requirement of the Fourth Amendment." And in Graham v. Connor, 490 U.S. 386, 109 S.Ct. 1865, 104 L.Ed.2d 443 (1989), the Court ruled that claims of excessive force in the course of an arrest or investigatory stop are to be evaluated under the Fourth Amendment and *not* under "more generalized notions of 'substantive due process.'"

[93]Kelly v. Serna, 87 F.3d 1235 (11th Cir.1996). Accord: Sanchez v. United States, 49 F.3d 1329 (8th Cir.

Finally, there is the question of whether in a *Bivens*-type action the government itself may be held liable for the acts of its police agents. No mention was made of this possibility in *Bivens,* but one commentator has forcefully argued that such a result is a logical extension of that decision.

> An action against the treasury has several potential advantages over an action against the officer as a vehicle for redressing constitutional violations: it would provide a suitable recovery for every damage-causing violation of constitutional rights by law enforcement officers without subjecting individual officers to the burden of being personally liable for mistakes of judgment, and it might be more likely than the individual officer action to produce systemic changes. * * * [T]he Court should consider whether an action for money damages against governmental units might be an appropriate additional mechanism for the implementation of the fourth and fourteenth amendments. *Bivens* may be read as resting upon a premise that constitutional rights have a self-executing force that not only permits but requires the courts to recognize remedies appropriate for their vindication.[94]

Although the argument for government liability is compelling, it appeared doubtful that the Court would itself take this added step. In *Bivens,* even the majority evidenced concern about the role of the Court vis-a-vis the Congress in this matter, and it was hinted that when "the federal purse was involved" the issue is better left to Congress. The lower courts declined to extend *Bivens* so as to impose liability upon the employer-government.[95] Later, the Supreme Court held that a *Bivens* cause of action could not be brought against a federal agency.[96]

However, in 1974 the Congress amended the Federal Tort Claims Act to provide that

> with regard to acts or omissions of investigative or law enforcement officers of the United States Government, the provisions of this chapter and section 1346(b) of this title shall apply to any claim arising, on or after the date of the enactment of this proviso, out of assault, battery, false imprisonment, false arrest, abuse of process, or malicious prosecution. For the purpose of this subsection, "investigative or law enforcement officer" means any officer of the United States who is empowered by law to execute searches, to seize evidence, or to make arrests for violations of Federal law.[97]

As the legislative history states, the "effect of this provision is to

---

1995); Kurinsky v. United States, 33 F.3d 594 (6th Cir.1994); Van Strum v. Lawn, 940 F.2d 406 (9th Cir.1991); Bieneman v. City of Chicago, 864 F.2d 463 (7th Cir.1988); Chin v. Bowen, 833 F.2d 21 (2d Cir.1987).

[94]Dellinger, 85 Harv.L.Rev. 1532, 1556–57 (1972).

[95]Monarch Insurance Company v. District of Columbia, 353 F.Supp. 1249 (D.D.C.1973).

[96]F.D.I.C. v. Meyer, 510 U.S. 471, 114 S.Ct. 996, 127 L.Ed.2d 308 (1994). A unanimous Court there noted that an opposite result would be contrary to the rationale of *Bivens* itself, explainable "in part *because* a direct action against the Government was not actionable," and would create "a potentially enormous financial burden for the Federal Government."

[97]28 U.S.C.A. § 2680(h). For a

deprive the Federal Government of the defense of sovereign immunity in cases * * * [involving] the same kind of conduct that is alleged to have occurred in *Bivens.*"[98]

One issue that has arisen under this legislation, albeit rarely, is whether the United States may assert the same good faith-reasonable belief defense that is available to individual officers. In *Norton v. United States,*[99] the court, although finding the legislative history unclear "with regard to the intended scope of the government's vicarious liability," held "that the liability of the United States under § 2680(h) is coterminous with the liability of its agents under *Bivens.*" The court explained that "there can be little question but that imposition of liability without regard to the individual officer's defenses of good faith and reasonable belief would be a substantial enough departure from general principles of *respondeat superior* and would impose a potentially burdensome enough impact on the federal treasury that it should be supported by a clear expression of legislative intent in either the statute itself or in the accompanying legislative history."[100]

Another issue that has arisen with respect to the FTCA is whether, when a remedy is available under the Act, it is the exclusive remedy, so that a *Bivens* action against the offending officer is impermissible. In *Carlson v. Green,*[101] the Supreme Court answered in the negative. Though recognizing that a *Bivens* cause of action may be defeated "when defendants show that Congress

---

useful discussion of this change, see Boger, Gitenstein & Verkuil, The Federal Tort Claims Act Intentional Torts Amendment: An Interpretative Analysis, 54 N.C.L.Rev. 497 (1976).

While in 28 U.S.C.A. § 2680(h) "the FTCA excludes intentional torts such as false arrest, this exclusion is followed by an important proviso: It does not apply if the intentional tort is committed by an 'investigative or law enforcement officer.'" Alvarez-Machain v. United States, 331 F.3d 604 (9th Cir.2003). Moreover, while the FTCA bars recovery for "[a]ny claim arising in a foreign country," 28 U.S.C.A. § 2680(k), a "claim can still proceed under the headquarters doctrine if harm occurring in a foreign country was proximately caused by acts in the United States," as where the "claim involves federal employees working from offices in the United States to guide and supervise actions in other countries." *Alvarez-Machain v. United States,* supra.

[98]S.Rep. No. 93-588, 93d Cong., 2d Sess., 1974 U.S.Code Cong. & Ad.News 2789, 2791 (1974).

[99]Norton v. United States, 581 F.2d 390 (4th Cir.1978).

[100]But consider Arnsberg v. United States, 739 F.2d 417 (9th Cir.1984), holding that the *Norton* rule applies only when the claim is based upon the Fourth Amendment rather than, as in the instant case, state tort law. The court explained: "The basic purpose of the FTCA is to make the United States liable in instances where private persons acting under like circumstances would have liability. See 28 U.S.C.A. § 2674 (1982). However, the qualified immunity defense which the government requests is inherently a defense which belongs to public officials. It has no private law counterpart. It would thus contravene the central purpose of the FTCA to extend it to the United States."

[101]Carlson v. Green, 446 U.S. 14, 100 S.Ct. 1468, 64 L.Ed.2d 15 (1980).

has provided an alternative remedy which it explicitly declared to be a *substitute* for recovery directly under the Constitution and viewed as equally effective," the Court noted that the legislative history of the aforementioned amendments to the FTCA "made it crystal clear that Congress views FTCA and *Bivens* as parallel, complementary causes of action."[102] Justice Brennan, for the majority,[103] then continued:

> Four additional factors, each suggesting that the *Bivens* remedy is more effective than the FTCA remedy, also support our conclusion that Congress did not intend to limit respondent to an FTCA action. First, the *Bivens* remedy, in addition to compensating victims, serves a deterrent purpose. * * *
>
> Second, our decisions, although not expressly addressing and deciding the question, indicate that punitive damages may be awarded in a *Bivens* suit[, while] punitive damages in an FTCA suit are statutorily prohibited.
>
> Third, a plaintiff cannot opt for a jury in an FTCA action * * * as he may in a *Bivens* suit. * * *
>
> Fourth, an action under FTCA exists only if the State in which the alleged misconduct occurred would permit a cause of action for that misconduct to go forward. * * *

However, the Supreme Court later held that there was no implied private right of action, pursuant to *Bivens*, for damages against private entities that engaged in alleged constitutional deprivations while acting under color of federal law.[104] A contrary result, the majority concluded, would constitute "a marked extension of *Bivens* to contexts that would not advance *Bivens'* core purpose of deterring individual officers from engaging in unconstitutional wrongdoing." But the four dissenters deemed the majority's position inconsistent with the reasoning underlying *Carlson.*[105]

---

[102]That history declares that "after the date of enactment of this measure, innocent individuals who are subjected to raids [like that in *Bivens*] will have a cause of action against the individual Federal agents and the Federal Government." S.Rep. No. 93-588, 93d Cong., 2d Sess., 1974 U.S.Code Cong. & Ad.News 2789, 2791 (1974).

[103]Powell, J., joined by Stewart, J., concurring, expressed the view that if Congress *had* created an adequate alternative avenue of relief, then the plaintiffs would be limited to that remedy without any express declaration by Congress that this should be the case.

The Chief Justice, dissenting,

objected that *Bivens* is "limited to those circumstances in which a civil rights plaintiff had no other effective remedy," and concluded such was not the case here in light of the FTCA amendment.

Rehnquist, J., dissenting, concluded "it is 'an exercise of power that the Constitution does not give us' for this Court to infer a private civil damage remedy from * * * any * * * constitutional provision."

[104]Correctional Services Corp. v. Malesko, 534 U.S. 61, 122 S.Ct. 515, 151 L.Ed.2d 456 (2001).

[105]Specifically, because the majority argued that respondent in the instant case enjoyed alternative remedies against the corporate agent that

§ 1.10(c) Criminal prosecution

There are also federal statutes providing for criminal penalties where Fourth Amendment rights have been violated. Because prosecutions of police under these provisions are relatively infrequent[106] and, in any event, cannot be instituted solely upon the demand of the party whose rights have been violated, these statutes will be given only passing attention here.

18 U.S.C.A. § 242 provides: "Whoever, under color of any law, statute, ordinance, regulation, or custom, willfully subjects any person in any State, Territory, or District to the deprivation of any rights, privileges, or immunities secured or protected by the Constitution or laws of the United States, * * * shall be fined * * * or imprisoned * * *, or both; and [in the described circumstances] may be sentenced to death."

One who "acts under 'color' of law," within the meaning of this statute, "may be a federal officer or a state officer."[107] And it makes no difference that state or federal law does not affirmatively authorize the deprivation that has occurred. As the Supreme Court said in *United States v. Classic*,[108] "Misuse of power, possessed by virtue of state law and made possible only because the wrongdoer is clothed with the authority of state law, is action taken 'under color of' state law." This encompasses, for example, abuses by police in exercising their authority to arrest.[109]

As for the "willfully" requirement in the statute, the Court had occasion to elucidate its meaning in *Screws v. United States*,[110] where the law was challenged on the ground of vagueness. If the "general rule" of criminal liability that finds an intentional violation when a person intentionally adopts certain conduct the law

---

distinguished the case from those encompassed within *Bivens*.

[Section 1.10(c)]

[106]It has been suggested that greater reliance on criminal prosecution, as an alternative to exclusion of evidence, is justified. See Misner, In Partial Praise of Boyd; The Grand Jury as Catalyst for Fourth Amendment Change, 29 Ariz.St.L.J. 805 (1997) (concluding at 807 that the grand jury "should be the first forum for Fourth Amendment issues," as "indictment in response to official misconduct certainly sends a message to law enforcement that is at least as strong a deterrent as is the exclusion of evidence").

[107]Screws v. United States, 325 U.S. 91, 65 S.Ct. 1031, 89 L.Ed. 1495 (1945). However, it is not necessary that the defendant, prosecuted under

this statute, be a state or federal officer; one is acting "under color" of law if he is a willful participant in a joint activity with such a person. United States v. Price, 383 U.S. 787, 86 S.Ct. 1152, 16 L.Ed.2d 267 (1966).

[108]United States v. Classic, 313 U.S. 299, 61 S.Ct. 1031, 85 L.Ed. 1368 (1941).

[109]Screws v. United States, 325 U.S. 91, 65 S.Ct. 1031, 89 L.Ed. 1495 (1945), where state officers arrested one Hall and then beat him, causing his death. Assuming the existence of willfulness, discussed in the text below, an illegal arrest unaccompanied by either threat or violence is a violation of the statute. United States v. Ramey, 336 F.2d 512 (4th Cir.1964).

[110]Screws v. United States, 325 U.S. 91, 65 S.Ct. 1031, 89 L.Ed. 1495 (1945).

proscribes were applied here, the Court noted, this would "cast law enforcement agencies loose at their own risk on a vast uncharted sea," given the "closeness of decisions of this Court interpreting the due process clause." The Court then concluded:

> An analysis of the cases in which "willfully" has been held to connote more than an act which is voluntary or intentional would not prove helpful, as each turns on its own peculiar facts. Those cases, however, make clear that if we construe "willfully" in [the statute] as connoting a purpose to deprive a person of a specific constitutional right, we would introduce no innovation. The Court, indeed, has recognized that the requirement of a specific intent to do a prohibited act may avoid those consequences to the accused which may otherwise render a vague or indefinite statute invalid. * * * We repeat that the presence of a bad purpose or evil intent alone may not be sufficient. We do say that a requirement of a specific intent to deprive a person of a federal right made definite by decision or other rule of law saves the Act from any charge of unconstitutionality on the grounds of vagueness.[111]

It should also be noted that federal officers who abuse their search and seizure authority may under some circumstances be subject to prosecution under other statutes. These statutes make criminal the following: willfully exceeding one's authority or exercising it with unnecessary severity in executing a search warrant[112]; maliciously and without probable cause procuring a search warrant[113]; and, except under specified circumstances,[114] searching an occupied private dwelling without a warrant or maliciously and without reasonable cause searching any other building without a search warrant.[115] These statutes encompass many types of Fourth Amendment violations and perhaps even certain conduct that is not unconstitutional.[116]

---

[111]In United States v. Lanier, 520 U.S. 259, 117 S.Ct. 1219, 137 L.Ed.2d 432 (1997), the lower court "added two glosses to the made-specific standard of fair warning. In its view, a generally phrased constitutional right has been made specific within the meaning of *Screws* only if a prior decision of this Court has declared the right, and then only when the Court has applied its ruling in a case with facts 'fundamentally similar' to the case being prosecuted. None of the considerations advanced in this case, however, persuade us that either a decision of this Court or the extreme level of factual specificity envisioned by the Court of Appeals is necessary in every instance to give fair warning."

[112]18 U.S.C.A. § 2234.

[113]18 U.S.C.A. § 2235.

[114]Namely, where the person is serving a warrant of arrest, or is attempting to arrest a person without a warrant, or is making a search with the consent of the occupant.

[115]18 U.S.C.A. § 2236.

[116]Thus, as noted in United States v. Freeman, 144 F.Supp. 669 (D.D.C. 1956), it does not necessarily follow that a violation of one of these statutes will require exclusion of evidence.

§ 1.10(d) Disciplinary proceedings

As noted earlier,[117] much has been written about the current and potential effectiveness of various forms of administrative grievance mechanisms for dealing with police misconduct. That area will not be explored here. Rather, the focus here is upon the important question of whether, under certain circumstances at least, the Fourth Amendment may be said to require an effective system of police discipline, which in turn raises the delicate question of the extent to which the federal courts[118] may intrude into the operations of a municipal police agency.

In *Council of Organization on Philadelphia Police Accountability and Responsibility v. Rizzo,*[119] the plaintiffs, alleging widespread and systematic violations of the constitutional rights of citizens by the police, sought, in addition to other relief, establishment of appropriate machinery to deal with civilian complaints against police. From the evidence produced before the federal district judge, he found that frequent violations of the legal and constitutional rights of citizens were being committed by a small percentage of the members of the Philadelphia Police Department. These violations included the making of arrests "for investigation" upon insufficient grounds. As for the existing procedures for handling civilian complaints and for enforcement of police discipline related to such complaints, they were found to be "totally inadequate. It is the policy of the department to discourage the filing of such complaints, to avoid or minimize the consequences of proven police misconduct, and to resist disclosure of the final disposition of such complaints."

Noting that "intrusion by the courts into this sensitive area should be limited, and should be directed toward insuring that the police themselves are encouraged to remedy the situation," the district court ordered the defendants "to submit to this Court for its approval a comprehensive program for improving the handling of citizen complaints alleging police misconduct." The court offered the following "guidelines":

(1) Appropriate revision of police manuals and rules of procedure

---

[Section 1.10(d)]

[117]See note 3 supra.

[118]Involvement of the federal courts in a different way than discussed below is suggested in Misner, In Partial Praise of Boyd; The Grand Jury as Catalyst for Fourth Amendment Change, 29 Ariz.St.L.J. 805, 808 (1997), namely, that "the grand jury must be encouraged to return to its historical role as commentator on governmental misconduct and officially report the misconduct to the trial court. If substantiated, the court must decide to whom the report will be published. In this way, the court can fashion a proportional remedy for the Fourth Amendment violation. For example, an inadvertent constitutional violation might warrant placing the grand jury report in the officer's personnel file, while an intentional violation or a pattern of violations might justify making the grand jury report public."

[119]Council of Organization on Philadelphia Police Accountability and Responsibility v. Rizzo, 357 F.Supp. 1289 (E.D.Pa.1973).

spelling out in some detail, in simple language, the "dos and don'ts" of permissible conduct in dealing with civilians (for example, manifestations of racial bias, derogatory remarks, offensive language, etc.; unnecessary damage to property and other unreasonable conduct in executing search warrants; limitations on pursuit of persons charged only with summary offenses; recording and processing of civilian complaints, etc.). (2) Revision of procedures for processing complaints against police, including (a) ready availability of forms for use by civilians in lodging complaints against police officers; (b) a screening procedure for eliminating frivolous complaints; (c) prompt and adequate investigation of complaints; (d) adjudication of non-frivolous complaints by an impartial individual or body, insulated so far as practicable from chain of command pressures, with a fair opportunity afforded the complainant to present his complaint, and to the police officer to present his defense; and (3) prompt notification to the concerned parties, informing them of the outcome.

In contrast to *Rizzo* is *Calvin v. Conlisk*,[120] where the plaintiffs also alleged widespread police misconduct and an ineffective discipline system, and asked the court "to use its equitable powers to order the City of Chicago, the Superintendent of Police and Members of the Police Board to adopt and implement an effective police discipline system." The district court granted the defendants' motion to dismiss, finding that these matters were not justiciable because they would require "the court to inject itself into the management and administration of the police department." In so doing, the court placed considerable reliance upon *Gilligan v. Morgan*,[121] arising out of the Kent State tragedy, which held that there was no justiciable controversy where the plaintiffs asked the district court to establish standards for the training, kind of weapons, scope and kind of orders to control the actions of the Ohio National Guard, and to exercise a continuing judicial surveillance over the Guard to assure compliance with whatever procedures were approved by the court. "It would be difficult," declared the Chief Justice, "to think of a clearer example of the type of governmental action that was intended by the Constitution to be left to the political branches * * *. Moreover, it is difficult to conceive of an area of governmental activity in which the courts have less competence. The complex, subtle, and professional decisions as to the composition, training, equipping, and control of a military force are essentially professional military judgments."

Gilligan does not support the conclusion that federal courts should never act to bring about greater protection of Fourth Amendment rights through improvements in police discipline. For one thing, it is apparent that the relief sought there, which would have involved the district court in the actual development

---

[120]Calvin v. Conlisk, 367 F.Supp. 476 (N.D.Ill.1973).

[121]Gilligan v. Morgan, 413 U.S. 1, 93 S.Ct. 2440, 37 L.Ed.2d 407 (1973).

of standards for training, equipping and controlling a military force, far exceeded that which was sought in *Rizzo*. In *Rizzo*, the court merely directed the police to come up with a better system, a process which appears to have worked successfully[122] and which intrudes the court into the affairs of the department no more than when a court orders a department to clarify its enforcement policies, a practice whose merits have been stated elsewhere in this Chapter.[123] And while it is unquestionably true that a "federal court should avoid unnecessarily dampening the vigor of a police department by becoming too deeply involved in the department's daily operations,"[124] this risk would seem relatively insignificant when a federal court directs a department to put its own house in order, as compared to the more common device of a federal court injunction directed toward all members of the department.[125]

Secondly, the assertion in *Gilligan* that the matters at issue there should be left "to the elective process" is hardly applicable in the *Rizzo* type of situation. The effective protection of Fourth Amendment rights, particularly as to unpopular and minority groups, is hardly a matter of that kind. Courts have served as a means for protecting Fourth Amendment rights by the exclusion of illegally obtained evidence, by permitting the collection of damages from offending officers, and—occasionally at least—by imposing criminal sanctions upon police. The notion that courts might also play a role with respect to another remedy which, in many circumstances, will be more effective than these others[126] is not remarkable.

However, it is not likely that federal courts will in the future be in a position to direct local police departments to improve their disciplinary machinery. When the Philadelphia litigation reached the Supreme Court, it reversed in *Rizzo v. Goode*.[127] For one thing, the Court concluded there was "no occasion for the

---

[122]In the court's later opinion concerning awarding of counsel fees, it is noted: "The required submissions were made, and various conferences have been held, at which the views of all counsel were fully presented. Concurrently with the filing of this Memorandum, I am entering in each case a 'final judgment,' the principal features of which appear to be reasonably acceptable to the parties." Council of Organizations on Philadelphia Police Accountability and Responsibility v. Tate, 60 F.R.D. 615 (E.D.Pa.1973).

[123]See § 1.12(c).

[124]Lewis v. Kugler, 446 F.2d 1343 (3d Cir.1971).

[125]See § 1.12(c), noting the difficulties in drafting a clear and effective injunction that does not also inhibit constitutional enforcement practices.

[126]The exclusionary rule, it was correctly noted in Terry v. Ohio, 392 U.S. 1, 88 S.Ct. 1868, 20 L.Ed.2d 889 (1968), "is powerless to deter invasions of constitutionally guaranteed rights where the police either have no interest in prosecuting or are willing to forego successful prosecution in the interest of serving some other goal." And, as was noted in *Rizzo*, private suits "are expensive, time-consuming, not readily available, and not notably successful," while criminal prosecution is "unlikely" except in extreme cases.

[127]Rizzo v. Goode, 423 U.S. 362, 96 S.Ct. 598, 46 L.Ed.2d 561 (1976).

District Court to grant equitable relief against the petitioners" (the mayor, the city managing director, and the police commissioner) because "none of the petitioners had deprived the respondent classes of any rights secured under the Constitution." This was so because "the responsible authorities had played no affirmative part in depriving any members of the two respondent classes of any constitutional rights." From this, it appears that those persons who could be required to revise disciplinary procedures will be beyond the reach of the federal courts when they have done no more than fail to act to eliminate an existing statistical pattern of constitutional violations by members of their department.[128]

Secondly, and perhaps even more significant, the Court in *Rizzo* concluded that "principles of federalism" made inappropriate the kind of relief the district court had granted:

> When a plaintiff seeks to enjoin the activity of a government agency, even within a unitary court system, his case must contend with "the well-established rule that the Government has traditionally been granted the widest latitude in the 'dispatch of its own internal affairs,' * * *." The District Court's injunctive order here, significantly revising the internal procedures of the Philadelphia police department, was indisputably a sharp limitation on the department's "latitude in the 'dispatch of its own internal affairs.'" * * *

> Contrary to the District Court's flat pronouncement that a federal court's legal power to "supervise the functioning of the police department . . . is firmly established," it is the foregoing cases and principles that must govern consideration of the type of injunctive relief granted here. When it injected itself by injunctive decree into the internal disciplinary affairs of this state agency, the District Court departed from these precepts.[129]

§ 1.10(e) Takings Clause litigation

The Takings Clause of the Fifth Amendment declares "nor shall private property be taken for public use, without just compensa-

---

[128]The *Rizzo* opinion is by no means a model of clarity, and thus it is not at all clear that the Court has held that such officials may never be reached unless they have played an "affirmative part." The Court at another point asserted that "there was no showing that the behavior of the Philadelphia police was different in kind or degree from that which exists elsewhere," and thus the case could be narrowly construed to mean that the supervisory officials of the department have no constitutional duty to act under such circumstances.

[129]This branch of the *Rizzo* opinion is likewise ambiguous. The Court did not make it clear whether it meant that this type of intrusion into "internal disciplinary affairs" would never be proper, or was simply improper on this record, in which "there was no showing that the behavior of the Philadelphia police was different in kind or degree from that which exists elsewhere." Because the Court at another point asserted that such relief should not be given "except in the most extraordinary circumstances," it may be that upon a more extreme set of facts the kind of relief ordered by the district judge would be proper.

tion,"[130] while state constitutions contain similar or identical language guaranteeing protection against takings of private property.[131] (The federal provision, of course, is also applicable against the states via the Fourteenth Amendment.[132]) The question has sometimes arisen as to whether compensation may be awarded under the federal or state provisions because of the police seizure of private property as evidence of crime.[133]

Illustrative is *Eggleston v. Pierce County*,[134] where, pursuant to a search warrant authorizing seizure of various items of evidence relating to a homicide, the police seized a load-bearing wall, thereby leaving the premises unstable and uninhabitable. The owner of the house later brought suit for the destruction and loss of use of her property under several theories, including the state constitutional provision relating to takings. On appeal of the trial court's grant of summary judgment to the county on the takings issue, the court affirmed. The court concluded that "not every government action that takes, damages, or destroys property is a taking," and that it was necessary to distinguish between the police power and the power of eminent domain, which "are essential and distinct powers of government." An exercise of the police power, the court explained, "is not a taking or damaging for the public use," as with eminent domain, "but to conserve the safety, morals, health and general welfare of the public," and consequently the "gathering and preserving of evidence," as in the instant case, "is a police power function, necessary for the safety and general welfare of society" and thus not subject to the takings clause. In reaching that conclusion, the *Eggleston* court emphasized that it was "aware of no case that holds or even supports the proposition that the seizure or preservation of evidence can be a taking." Indeed, there exist several state cases[135] and

[Section 1.10(e)]

[130]U.S.Const. amend V. as explained in Atkinson, The Bilateral Fourth Amendment and the Duties of Law-Abiding Persons, 99 Geo.L.J. 1517 (2011), "the Fourth Amendment (regulating government searches) and the Takings Clause of the Fifth Amendment (regulating government takings) are different types of legal regimes: the Fourth Amendment is analogous to a negligence regime common in torts, while the Takings Clause follows more of a strict liability rule."

[131]D. Dana & T. Merrill, Property: Takings 2 (2002) ("all state constitutions (except North Carolina) include takings clauses").

[132]Chicago, B. & Q. R. Co. v. City

of Chicago, 166 U.S. 226, 17 S.Ct. 581, 41 L.Ed. 979 (1897).

[133]The question may also arise when an instrumentality of a crime is seized for impoundment or forfeiture. See, e.g., Bennis v. Michigan, 516 U.S. 442, 116 S.Ct. 994, 134 L.Ed.2d 68 (1996) (vehicle seized and forfeited because of its use in violation of state indecency law not a "taking" because vehicle seized pursuant to state's police power, not under eminent domain); City of Hollywood v. Mulligan, 934 So.2d 1238 (Fla.2006) (same result re vehicle impounded because used to facilitate act of prostitution).

[134]Eggleston v. Pierce County, 148 Wash.2d 760, 64 P.3d 618 (2003).

[135]McCambridge v. City of Little

also federal authority[136] supporting this branch of *Eggleston*.[137]

The court in *Eggleston* then turned to the "harder question," namely, "whether the destruction of property by police activity other than collecting evidence pursuant to a warrant could ever be a compensable taking." This is an issue on which the courts are divided,[138] as the court explained:

> A clear split on clear grounds exists. Those courts rejecting takings claims based on police destruction of property have relied on the original understanding of the constitutions and the continuing vitality of the separate doctrines of eminent domain and police power. The courts that have found takings have been justifiably outraged by the destruction of real property owned by third parties utterly unconnected with the alleged crime.

The *Eggleston* court then somewhat reluctantly sided with the former group of decisions.[139] While that conclusion may not be beyond dispute, there is something to the court's final assertion

---

Rock, 298 Ark. 219, 766 S.W.2d 909 (1989) (seizure of evidence not a taking); McCoy v. Sanders, 113 Ga.App. 565, 148 S.E.2d 902 (1966) (no taking to drain pond to look for body); Soucy v. New Hampshire, 127 N.H. 451, 506 A.2d 288 (1985) (blocking repair of apartment during arson trial not a taking); Emery v. Oregon, 297 Or. 755, 688 P.2d 72 (1984) (no taking where truck was seized as evidence of a murder and dismantled and then later returned dismantled).

[136]Amerisource Corporation v. United States, 525 F.3d 1149 (Fed.Cir. 2008) ("Property seized and retained pursuant to the police power is not taken for a 'public use' in the context of the Takings Clause," and "[o]nce the government has lawfully seized property to be used as evidence in a criminal prosecution, it has wide discretion to retain it so long as the investigation continues, regardless of the effect on that property," here that legal drugs were retained until they expired); Porter v. United States, 473 F.2d 1329 (5th Cir.1973) (action by widow of Lee Harvey Oswald to recover value of personal property seized in the investigation of the Kennedy assassination; parties agreed there had been a taking, but issue was when the taking took place, since the value of the evidence changed during the course of the investigation; court rejected the argument that the taking occurred when the evidence was seized, and ruled

that the taking occurred when the government declared its intent to acquire the property for its own).

[137]Compare Kelly, The Costs of the Fourth Amendment: Home Searches and Takings Law, 28 Miss.C.L.Rev. 1, 35 (2008) ("there is a sound argument which could be made and supported based on existing legal precedent for allowing home searches to be conceptualized and compensated as physical takings," though "it unlikely a court would sustain a claim brought on the grounds I suggest").

[138]The cases are collected in Cohen, Taking Analysis of Police Destruction on Innocent Owners' Property in the Course of Law Enforcement: The View from Five State Supreme Courts, 34 McGeorge L.Rev. 1 (2002); Neuenhaus, State Constitutional Takings Jurisprudence, 24 Rutgers L.J. 1352 (1993).

[139]See also Johnson v. Manitowoc County, 635 F.3d 331 (7th Cir.2011) (use of jackhammer on floor of plaintiff's garage, seeking blood samples that might have seeped through cracks; "the Takings Clause does not apply when property is retained or damaged as the result of the government's exercise of its authority pursuant to some power other than the power of eminent domain"); Brutsche v. City of Kent, 164 Wash.2d 664, 193 P.3d 110 (2008), distinguishing Loretto v. Teleprompter Manhattan CATV Corp., 458 U.S. 419, 102 S.Ct. 3164,

that there should be "other, more suitable, remedies available" when "law enforcement exceeds its lawful powers."

Assuming circumstances in which a takings claim is otherwise permissible, it is necessary that the claim be sufficiently "ripe." "Under the Takings Clause, a takings claim is not ripe 'until (1) the relevant governmental unit has reached a final decision as to what will be done with the property and (2) the plaintiff has sought compensation through whatever adequate procedures the state provides.' "[140]

§ 1.11 Expungement of arrest records

§ 1.11(a)   Constitutional basis
§ 1.11(b)   Conflicting interests
§ 1.11(c)   Balancing the interests; alternative remedies

Research References

West's Key Number Digest
Constitutional Law ⬦82(7), 257; Criminal Law ⬦1226(3)

Legal Encyclopedias
C.J.S., Constitutional Law §§ 444 to 455, 459 to 460, 471, 476, 511, 584, 619 to 648, 992, 1019, 1023, 1132, 1134; Criminal Law § 1734; Right to Die § 2

Introduction

Over the years, there has been a considerable amount of litigation concerning whether a person who has been arrested is thereafter entitled, either because the arrest was unlawful or because he was not ultimately convicted, to the expungement or restrictions on dissemination of his fingerprints, photographs, or other criminal identification or arrest records.[1] For many years, this litigation could be summed up by saying that most courts summar-

---

73 L.Ed.2d 868 (1982) (as "there simply is no permanent physical occupation of property that occurs when police officers damage property during execution of a search warrant").

[140]Waltman v. Payne, 535 F.3d 342 (5th Cir.2008), quoting Sandy Creek Investors, Ltd. v. City of Jonestown, Tex., 325 F.3d 623 (5th Cir.2003). In any event, The Constitution is not violated "unless just compensation is denied," and thus, "to state a valid taking claim," the plaintiffs are "required to have sought compensation through state law mechanisms, or to prove that such mechanisms were unavailable or inadequate." Estate of Bennett v. Wainwright, 548 F.3d 155 (1st Cir.

2008).

[Section 1.11]
[1]The cases are collected in Annot., 46 A.L.R.3d 900 (1972).

Occasionally an expungement issue arises with respect to an allegedly illegal seizure of effects. See Doe v. United States Air Force, 812 F.2d 738 (D.C.Cir.1987) (plaintiff claims he victim of illegal search while in military and that government made copies of documents before returning them; court holds the action for injunctive relief not moot and declares that "the government's showings on its motion for summary judgment have not conclusively shown that court ordered expungement is not available as a remedy if it be determined that the

ily denied relief. Typically, two grounds were given for the denial:
(i) it is for the legislature, rather than the courts, to determine
what use shall be made of arrest records[2]; and (ii) absent restrictive legislation, the decision to release or retain arrest records is
within the realm of police discretion, for the police must be
granted sufficient authority to determine what records will enable them most effectively and efficiently to discharge their duty
in protecting society.[3]

In more recent times there occurred a substantial upsurge in
the number of cases raising the issue, as well as a flood of law
review commentary on this subject over a relatively brief period
of time.[4] These cases, in the main, have been more sympathetic
to the complainant's plight and reflect a greater willingness to
get the judicial branch involved in the matter, a development applauded almost universally in the literature. This, it has been
suggested, may be attributed to "the advent of the computer age
* * * and the growing concern for the individual's loss of privacy

---

retained copies and information were
unconstitutionally obtained").

[2]E.g., Sterling v. Oakland, 208
Cal.App.2d 1, 24 Cal.Rptr. 696 (1962);
Cissell v. Brostron, 395 S.W.2d 322
(Mo.App.1965); Weisberg v. Police
Dep't, 46 Misc.2d 846, 260 N.Y.S.2d
554 (1965).

[3]E.g., Cissell v. Brostron, 395
S.W.2d 322 (Mo.App.1965); Fernicola
v. Keenan, 136 N.J.Eq. 9, 39 A.2d 851
(1944).

[4]See Alexander & Walz, Arrest
Record Expungement in California, 9
U.S.F.L.Rev. 299 (1974); Booth, The
Expungement Myth, 38 L.A.Bar Bull.
161 (1963); Franklin & Johnsen,
Expunging Criminal Records: Conceal-
ment and Dishonesty in an Open
Society, 9 Hofstra L.Rev. 733 (1981);
Haskel, The Arrest Record and New
York City Public Hiring, 9 Colum.J.L.
& Soc.Prob. 442 (1973); Hess &
LaPoole, Abuse of the Record of Arrest
Not Leading to Conviction, 13 Crime
& Del. 494 (1967); Karabian, Record of
Arrest: The Indelible Stain, 3 Pacific
L.J. 20 (1972); Kogon & Loughery,
Sealing and Expungement of Criminal
Records, the Big Lie, 61 J.Crim.L.C. &
P.C. 378 (1970); Ober, Expungement
of Criminal Arrest Records in
Pennsylvania, 83 Dick.L.Rev. 425
(1979); Raybin, Expungement of Arrest
Records: Erasing the Past, 44 Tenn.B.J.
22 (Mar.2008); Schiavo, Condemned

by the Record, 55 A.B.A.J. 540 (1969);
Steele, A Suggested Legislative Device
for Dealing with Abuses of Criminal
Records, 6 U.Mich.J.L.Ref. 32 (1972);
Comments, 3 Cal.W.L.Rev. 121 (1967);
1 Cal.W.L.Rev. 126 (1965); 23 Clev.St.
L.Rev. 123 (1974); 6 Harv.Civ.Rts.-Civ.
Lib.L.Rev. 165 (1970); 62 Minn.L.Rev.
229 (1978); 44 Miss.L.J. 928 (1973); 46
Notre Dame Law. 825 (1971); 5 Seton
Hall L.Rev. 864 (1974); 17 St. Louis
U.L.J. 263 (1971); 48 Tul.L.Rev. 629
(1974); 19 UCLA L.Rev. 654 (1972); 38
U.Chi.L.Rev. 850 (1971); 1971 Utah
L.Rev. 381; 1970 Wash.U.L.Q. 530;
Notes, 56 Cornell L.Rev. 470 (1971);
59 Iowa L.Rev. 1161 (1974); 8 Loyola
L.A.L.Rev. 238 (1975); 37 Mo.L.Rev.
709 (1972); 49 N.C.L.Rev. 509 (1971);
4 Rutgers-Camden L.J. 378 (1973); 17
Santa Clara L.Rev. 709 (1977); 35
U.Pitt.L.Rev. 205 (1973); 47 Wash.L.
Rev. 659 (1972); 17 Wayne L.Rev. 995
(1971).

A related but different issue is
whether a "privacy right should attach
to arrestees and suspects," so that
"government actors should accordingly
be presumptively required to withhold
the identities of arrestees and suspects
until a judge or a grand jury has found
probable cause of guilt," discussed in
Reza, Privacy and the Criminal
Arrestee or Suspect: In Search of a
Right, In Need of a Rule, 64 Md.L.Rev.
755 (2005).

as a natural by-product of our modern technology"; enhanced "awareness of the economic and personal harm to an individual that results if his arrest becomes known to employers, credit agencies, or even neighbors"; and "the nascent recognition by our courts and legislatures that there exists in the individual a fundamental right of privacy."[5]

This change in attitude has been reflected in many ways. For one thing, some legislatures have adopted statutes concerning the use, dissemination, and expungement of arrest records.[6] Police agencies are taking greater initiative in adopting internal regulations on the subject of when arrest records are to be destroyed or closed.[7] Some courts have granted relief on motion ancillary to a criminal proceeding, calling upon general equity principles or local rules rather than constitutional considerations.[8] And finally, courts have given more attention to whether there is a constitutional right to expungement or similar relief. It is this latter process that is discussed herein.

§ 1.11(a) Constitutional basis

Courts that have struggled with the question of whether expungement or some other relief is constitutionally required have usually[9] considered that question in terms of rights flowing directly or indirectly from the Fourth Amendment. The Fourth Amendment becomes directly involved when it is alleged that the arrest was itself illegal, for then it is likely to be asserted that retention and use of the record of that arrest is "a part of that initial unreasonable intrusion and therefore unjustified."[10] It becomes involved more indirectly when a person who was ar-

---

[5]Davidson v. Dill, 180 Colo. 123, 503 P.2d 157 (1972).

[6]The statutes are collected in Kaye, The Constitutionality of DNA Sampling on Arrest, 10 Cornell J.L. & Pub.Pol'y 455, 499 n. 194 (2001). But see Comment, 23 Clev.St.L.Rev. 123, 127 (1974), questioning the effectiveness of these statutes.

[7]Model Rules for Law Enforcement, Release of Arrest and Conviction Records (rev. 1974).

[8]E.g., United States v. Sumner, 226 F.3d 1005 (9th Cir.2000) ("a district court's ancillary jurisdiction is limited to expunging the record of an unlawful arrest"); Morrow v. District of Columbia, 417 F.2d 728 (D.C.Cir. 1969); Irani v. District of Columbia, 272 A.2d 849 (D.C.App.1971).

The federal courts are not in agreement as to whether district courts have ancillary jurisdiction to expunge arrest records based on equitable considerations where the arrest was lawful. United States v. Coloian, 480 F.3d 47 (1st Cir.2007) (collecting cases in both categories). See also Diehm, Federal Expungement: A Concept in Need of a Definition, 66 St. John's L.Rev. 73 (1992).

[Section 1.11(a)]

[9]But not always. Memorialization of the arrest may be deemed to chill some other constitutional right because the arrest was made to infringe that right. See, e.g., Bilick v. Dudley, 356 F.Supp. 945 (S.D.N.Y. 1973), where an alternate ground of decision was that expungement was required because the arrests at a political gathering had been made in violation of First Amendment rights.

[10]Comment, 38 U.Chi.L.Rev. 850, 859 (1971).

rested (perhaps lawfully) claims that because he was not thereafter convicted the maintenance of the arrest record violates his right to privacy. The constitutional right of privacy, the Supreme Court has declared, is a penumbral right emanating from various specific guarantees in the Bill of Rights, including the Fourth Amendment protection against unreasonable searches and seizures.[11]

Although the right to privacy claim was rejected in the earlier cases,[12] more recent decisions recognize that this constitutional protection extends to the arrest records area. In *Eddy v. Moore,*[13] for example, the court declared that while it is not correct to say that "the right of privacy an acquitted person has in his fingerprints and photographs is an absolute and complete bar to their retention," nonetheless "the requirements of a free society demands the existence of a right of privacy in the fingerprints and photographs of an accused who has been acquitted, to be at least placed in the balance, against the claim of the state for a need for their retention." The same result was reached in *Davidson v. Dill,*[14] quoting extensively from *Eddy,* and other decisions are likewise based on some degree upon the right of privacy.[15]

However, the Supreme Court appears to have rejected the *Eddy* rationale. In *Paul v. Davis,*[16] a police chief distributed a flyer to about 800 merchants warning them about shoplifters; Davis' picture was included in five pages of "mug shot" photos of persons described as "active shoplifters." Davis had previously been arrested for shoplifting, but he had never been prosecuted. He brought an action in federal court under 42 U.S.C.A. § 1983 seeking damages and declaratory and injunctive relief. The district court dismissed the complaint, but the court of appeals reversed. The Supreme Court ruled that the chief's action did not deprive Davis of any "liberty" or "property" rights secured against state deprivation by the due process clause and also that the flyer did not deprive Davis of his constitutional right to privacy. In reach-

---

[11]Griswold v. Connecticut, 381 U.S. 479, 85 S.Ct. 1678, 14 L.Ed.2d 510 (1965).

[12]See Annot., 46 A.L.R.3d 900, § 7 (1972).

[13]Eddy v. Moore, 5 Wash.App. 334, 487 P.2d 211 (1971).

[14]Davidson v. Dill, 180 Colo. 123, 503 P.2d 157 (1972).

[15]United States v. Rosen, 343 F.Supp. 804 (S.D.N.Y.1972) (noting that the "retention of arrest records, fingerprints or photos under certain circumstances may be viewed as an invasion of the right to privacy," but declining to order expungement as to an acquitted person absent a showing of improper use of the records by police or others); United States v. Kalish, 271 F.Supp. 968 (D.P.R.1967) (finding on the facts presented that the "preservation of these records constitutes an unwarranted attack upon his character and reputation and violates his right of privacy"); State v. Pinkney, 33 Ohio Misc. 183, 290 N.E.2d 923 (1972) (where defendant arrested for murder but another later confessed to the crime, expungement required as "a fundamental right of privacy").

[16]Paul v. Davis, 424 U.S. 693, 96 S.Ct. 1155, 47 L.Ed.2d 405 (1976).

ing the latter conclusion, the Court concluded that under its prior decisions the activities protected by the right of privacy

> were ones very different from that for which respondent claims constitutional protection—matters relating to marriage, procreation, contraception, family relationships, and child rearing and education. In these areas it has been held that there are limitations on the State's power to substantially regulate conduct.
>
> Respondent's claim is far afield from this line of decisions. He claims constitutional protection against the disclosure of the fact of his arrest on a shoplifting charge. His claim is based not upon any challenge to the State's ability to restrict his freedom of action in a sphere contended to be "private," but instead on a claim that the State may not publicize a record of an official act such as an arrest. None of our substantive privacy decisions hold this or anything like this, and we decline to enlarge them in this manner.

Paul has been held to foreclose expungement of arrest records on a constitutional right to privacy theory.[17]

As for reliance upon the Fourth Amendment, *Sullivan v. Murphy*[18] is a leading case. *Sullivan* was a class action brought on behalf of all those arrested during the May Day demonstrations in the District of Columbia. Although it was alleged that many arrests had been without probable cause and that consequently expungement of the arrest records was an appropriate remedy, the district court denied this relief. The court of appeals, noting that the federal courts have "authority to use their remedial mechanisms to redress or obviate such constitutional injuries," concluded:

> While some, maybe most, of the persons taken into police custody during the May Day demonstrations may have been engaged in criminal activity, it appears that many others were innocent of any wrongdoing. Yet the arrest procedures used and the subsequent treatment of the arrestees during the course of their detention made it impossible to distinguish between the two classes. * * *
>
> We conclude, in the unusual circumstances presented by the case at bar, that in an action to remedy the denial of a constitutional right, the Federal court's broad and flexible equitable powers call for an order that limits the maintenance and dissemination of the arrest records, and of all materials obtained from persons taken into custody during the May Day protest, in the absence of affirmative evidence produced by the Defendants to demonstrate the existence of probable cause either at the time of the arrest or subsequent

---

[17]Hammons v. Scott, 423 F.Supp. 618 (N.D.Cal.1976); Loder v. Municipal Court, 17 Cal.3d 859, 132 Cal.Rptr. 464, 553 P.2d 624 (1976); State v. Howe, 308 N.W.2d 743 (N.D.1981). Cf. Paul P. v. Verniero, 170 F.3d 396 (3d Cir.1999) (in upholding statute requiring registration and community notification of sex offenders, court notes "that arrest records and related infor-

mation are not protected by a right to privacy"). But see Natwig v. Webster, 562 F.Supp. 225 (D.R.I.1983), opining that *Paul* does not bar a claim grounded in the right to privacy re arrest records "in cases where the arrest itself is challenged as defective or without probable cause."

[18]Sullivan v. Murphy, 478 F.2d 938 (D.C.Cir.1973).

thereto.

Other courts have also alluded to a right based upon the Fourth Amendment, sometimes but not always relying upon the right in reaching a decision.[19] In *Menard v. Mitchell*,[20] for example, a suit to compel removal from FBI files of plaintiff's fingerprints and an accompanying notation regarding his arrest by California authorities, the court, in remanding for a hearing, intimated that the Fourth Amendment would require expungement if the arrest were without probable cause. After the district court upheld the retention of the records by the FBI provided they were not disseminated to other than law enforcement agencies,[21] the case returned to the court of appeals in *Menard v. Saxbe*.[22] The court expressed no doubt but that it could order "the expungement of records of police action taken in flagrant violation of the Fourth Amendment," but decided the case on statutory grounds by holding that once the FBI had learned that Menard's encounter with the police had been "purely fortuitous" and without probable cause it was without authority to retain the record in its criminal files.

That a claim for expungement or other relief against the maintenance or dissemination of arrest records and similar data may be based upon the Constitution is a matter of some significance. For one thing, this means that relief may be granted even though the remedy sought has not been expressly created by the legislature[23] and, indeed, even though the legislature has apparently foreclosed such relief.[24] Moreover, it means that relief may be obtained in the federal courts, not only with respect to federal records,[25] but also as to state records.[26]

But, it should not be assumed that this flurry of cases relying

---

[19]Wilson v. Webster, 467 F.2d 1282 (9th Cir.1972); United States v. Seasholtz, 376 F.Supp. 1288 (N.D.Okl. 1974) (declining to expunge, as arrest not unlawful); Bilick v. Dudley, 356 F.Supp. 945 (S.D.N.Y.1973); United States v. Rosen, 343 F.Supp. 804 (S.D.N.Y.1972) (declining to expunge, as arrest not unlawful); Wheeler v. Goodman, 306 F.Supp. 58 (W.D.N.C. 1969); Hughes v. Rizzo, 282 F.Supp. 881 (E.D.Pa.1968).

[20]Menard v. Mitchell, 430 F.2d 486 (D.C.Cir.1970).

[21]Menard v. Mitchell, 328 F.Supp. 718 (D.D.C.1971).

[22]Menard v. Saxbe, 498 F.2d 1017 (D.C.Cir.1974). On what records may be acquired and retained under 28 U.S.C.A. § 534, directing the Attorney General to acquire and preserve crimi-

nal identification and other records, see Annot., 28 A.L.R.Fed. 266 (1976). On the FBI's duty under that statute to prevent dissemination of inaccurate arrest records, see Tarlton v. Saxbe, 507 F.2d 1116 (D.C.Cir.1974).

[23]Davidson v. Dill, 180 Colo. 123, 503 P.2d 157 (1972).

[24]Sullivan v. Murphy, 478 F.2d 938 (D.C.Cir.1973), rejecting defendant's claim that expungement could not be ordered because destruction of such records is barred by statute.

[25]Sullivan v. Murphy, 478 F.2d 938 (D.C.Cir.1973), relying upon Bivens v. Six Unknown Named Agents, 403 U.S. 388, 91 S.Ct. 1999, 29 L.Ed.2d 619 (1971), where it was held that federal officers could be sued for damages in federal court for Fourth Amendment violations, see § 1.10(b), and

upon either the right of privacy or the Fourth Amendment has settled the question of exactly when a person is constitutionally entitled to expungement or some other relief. *Eddy* and *Davidson* (which, in any event, may have no force since the Supreme Court's decision in *Paul*) do not resolve specifically the scope of relief under the right of privacy; both simply overturned the summary denials of relief that had occurred below and called for a hearing at which all the relevant facts could be considered, and both indicate that the right of privacy does not extend so far as to require expungement of the records of every person who is not convicted. Similarly, in *Sullivan,* involving the Fourth Amendment, the court remanded for a hearing as to precisely what remedy was required. And while dictum in some cases would suggest that an arrest without probable cause is per se a basis for expungement,[27] the decisions do not support that proposition; typically, expungement has occurred or been recognized as potential relief where there has been a Fourth Amendment violation of an egregious character.[28]

What the cases do indicate is that the matter is to be resolved by a process of balancing. In *Sullivan,* the court said: "The Fourth Amendment establishes a principle of reason under which the individual's privacy and freedom from official interference must be weighed against society's need for effective law enforcement. This balancing underlies both judicial evaluation of the circumstances under which an arrest was made and the relief that a court may provide in consequence of a tainted arrest." And in *Davidson,* using the now-suspect right to privacy analysis, it was said that "a court should expunge an arrest record or order its return when the harm to the individual's right of privacy or dangers of unwarranted adverse consequences outweigh the pub-

---

wherein the Court said that "where federally protected rights have been invaded, it has been the rule from the beginning that courts will be alert to adjust their remedies so as to grant the necessary relief."

[26]Wilson v. Webster, 467 F.2d 1282 (9th Cir.1972); Wheeler v. Goodman, 306 F.Supp. 58 (W.D.N.C. 1969); Hughes v. Rizzo, 282 F.Supp. 881 (E.D.Pa.1968), recognizing that a suit for expungement is a "proper proceeding for redress" under 42 U.S.C.A. § 1983, providing a remedy for constitutional violations under color of state law.

[27]Bilick v. Dudley, 356 F.Supp. 945 (S.D.N.Y.1973); United States v. Rosen, 343 F.Supp. 804 (S.D.N.Y. 1972).

[28]Wilson v. Webster, 467 F.2d 1282 (9th Cir.1972) (mass arrest of demonstrators); Sullivan v. Murphy, 478 F.2d 938 (D.C.Cir.1973) (mass arrest of demonstrators and bystanders); Bilick v. Dudley, 356 F.Supp. 945 (S.D.N.Y.1973) (mass arrest of those at political gathering where anti-police views stated); Wheeler v. Goodman, 306 F.Supp. 58 (W.D.N.C.1969) (harassment of "hippies"). And thus expungement was denied in Doe v. Webster, 606 F.2d 1226 (D.C.Cir. 1979), because there was no "serious governmental misbehavior leading to the arrest"; and in State v. Nettles, 375 So.2d 1339 (La.1979), because such circumstances as "mass arrests * * * made without legal justification" or of "unpopular groups * * * solely to harass them" were not present.

lic interest in retaining the records in police files." It is appropriate to turn, therefore, to an assessment of the conflicting interests.

§ 1.11(b) Conflicting interests

The interests on one side of the ledger are relatively simple to state: the individual desires to avoid all of the adverse consequences which may flow from the fact that the record exists. These consequences were concisely stated in *Menard v. Mitchell*[29] in the following terms:

> Information denominated a record of arrest, if it becomes known, may subject an individual to serious difficulties. Even if no direct economic loss is involved, the injury to an individual's reputation may be substantial. Economic losses themselves may be both direct and serious. Opportunities for schooling, employment, or professional licenses may be restricted or nonexistent as a consequence of the mere fact of an arrest, even if followed by acquittal or complete exoneration of the charges involved. An arrest record may be used by the police in determining whether subsequently to arrest the individual concerned, or whether to exercise their discretion to bring formal charges against an individual already arrested. Arrest records have been used in deciding whether to allow a defendant to present his story without impeachment by prior convictions, and as a basis for denying release prior to trial or an appeal; or they may be considered by a judge in determining the sentence to be given a convicted offender.

While the interest of law enforcement has been the traditional reason for denying relief, it is fair to say that "specific reasons for this position are rarely articulated."[30] It would seem, however that a predominant reason for retention of arrest records is their potential future use in crime prevention and the apprehension of offenders. As one commentator notes:

> Neutral identification information contained in the records, such as fingerprints and photographs, can be quite helpful to local police if the individual is ever under investigation again. Positive identification is often essential to link a suspect to a crime or to protect a person who is innocent. Also, imputational information such as the arrest notation can indicate a pattern of conduct that may be the basis for a future arrest or for a decision to press charges. If a rearrest is made, the arrest record may furnish facts concerning prior conduct which, although not sufficient to warrant conviction in the previous case, may still be useful to trained interpreters of records.[31]

But, while there is no basis for questioning that statement, the

---

[Section 1.11(b)]

[29]Menard v. Mitchell, 430 F.2d 486 (D.C.Cir.1970).

[30]Comment, 38 U.Chi.L.Rev. 850, 854 (1971).

[31]Comment, 38 U.Chi.L.Rev. 850, 855 (1971). For judicial statements of this interest, see Morrow v. District of Columbia, 417 F.2d 728 (D.C.Cir.

1969); United States v. Kalish, 271 F.Supp. 968 (D.P.R.1967).

By far the best judicial elaboration of the law enforcement interest appears in Loder v. Municipal Court, 17 Cal.3d 859, 132 Cal.Rptr. 464, 553 P.2d 624 (1976), where it is noted that information derived from an arrest may be used in several ways: (1) Photographs and fingerprints may be used

courts and commentators are not in agreement as to exactly under what circumstances an arrest record has that potential value.

For example, it may well be asked whether that potential exists with respect to the record of any arrest that was unlawful because not based upon probable cause. Some would answer this in the negative:

> The core of the arrest record is the notation of arrest. This notation either memorializes the arresting officer's perception connecting the arrested person with a particular crime or signifies a connection based upon a warrant. For the arrest to be legal, the connection with the crime must be reasonable or the warrant must be based on probable cause. The arrest notation thus becomes the basis for a continuing inference by law enforcement officials that there were reasonable grounds at the time of the arrest for associating the arrested person with the crime. When an arrest is made without probable cause, however, the arresting officer's perception is by definition unreasonable and the continuing inference based on his perception is invalid; the arrest notation thus will not be useful.[32]

"to identify the perpetrator of a subsequent crime." (2) "Often the prior arrest is not an isolated event but one of a series of arrests of the same individual on the same or related charges. This is especially true when the crime in question is typically subject to recidivism, such as the use of addictive drugs, child molesting, indecent exposure, gambling, bookmaking, passing bad checks, confidence frauds, petty theft, receiving stolen goods, and even some forms of burglary and robbery. In these circumstances a pattern may emerge—for example, a distinctive modus operandi—which has independent significance as a basis for suspecting the arrestee if the crime is committed again." (3) "[A]mong the circumstances often taken into account in the exercise of prosecutorial discretion is the arrest record of the defendant. For example, prosecutors have considered that record, or information developed therefrom, in deciding whether to file a formal charge against the defendant, or whether to prosecute as a felony or as a misdemeanor a crime which can be either class of offense, or whether to agree to a bargain for a specified penalty or a plea to a lesser offense." (4) "After the defendant has been appropriately charged,

the court is usually called upon to determine the question of pretrial release. Again arrest records may be relevant. The form by which the defendant applies to be released on his own recognizance or on bail often provides for him to list his prior arrests and their dispositions. * * * These matters may then be considered by the court in conjunction with all other relevant information, in deciding whether to release the defendant on recognizance or in fixing the appropriate amount of bail." (5) "Upon conviction, the case of each eligible felony defendant is referred to the probation officer. That officer must investigate the circumstances of the crime and 'the prior record and history of the person,' and report his finding and recommendations to the court. * * * Any prior arrest record of the defendant is routinely obtained and included in the report as part of his criminal history. * * * And it has also been held that if the defendant is sentenced to prison, the Adult Authority may take his arrest record into account in determining when to release him on parole."

[32]Comment, 38 U.Chi.L.Rev. 850, 856 (1971), noting that where "such neutral identification data as finger-

Apparently on this theory, the court in *Menard v. Mitchell*[33] declared that it could see no reason why a record of an arrest that was not made upon probable cause was any more reliable than a record of an arrest that in fact did not occur.

This view is incorrect. As the district court noted in *Menard,* whether the arrest was "made with or without probable cause is * * * a fact * * * that proves nothing so far as the actual conduct of the person arrested is concerned. An arrest without probable cause may still lead to conviction and one with probable cause may still result in acquittal."[34] Surely, then, if the officer did not have probable cause at the time of the arrest but the arrestee is later convicted on the basis of information developed later, there is no basis for questioning the utility of the arrest record. And just as surely, even if no conviction follows, the arrest record is useful where the arrest was without probable cause but "detention of the person involved is justified by information developed subsequent to the arrest."[35] That is, the "continuing inference" discussed in the paragraph quoted above, in terms of its utility in future investigations, is not diminished because the probable cause existed after rather than before the moment of arrest. Indeed, it may be said that an inference of a lesser degree, but yet sufficiently useful for detection purposes, may exist where there was no probable cause either at the time of arrest or thereafter. For example, if a person is arrested near the scene of a just-committed burglary because of his suspicious conduct (perhaps sufficient to justify a stop[36] but not an arrest), but no fruits or implements of the crime are found on his person and he cannot be identified by the victim, so that he is released without prosecution, logic would suggest that the fact of this arrest is an element that may be considered with other facts in deciding whether this person should be arrested for a later burglary involving the same unique modus operandi.

To this, some would respond that even though some such connection may be made as a matter of logic it cannot be made as a matter of law. Thus, one commentator, analyzing the *Menard* case, states that

> if the arrest was made without probable cause the FBI should be under a duty to return the fingerprints and records which were the

---

prints" are "stored and used in conjunction with the misleading arrest notation, these data lose their neutrality."

[33]Menard v. Mitchell, 430 F.2d 486 (D.C.Cir.1970).

[34]Menard v. Mitchell, 328 F.Supp. 718 (D.D.C.1971).

[35]Sullivan v. Murphy, 478 F.2d 938 (D.C.Cir.1973). See also United States v. Bagley, 899 F.2d 707 (8th Cir.1990) (defendant's arrest record and indictment are "valuable law enforcement records" and need not be expunged merely because post-arrest warrantless search of briefcase was illegal and suppression resulted in dismissal of indictment).

[36]See § 9.5(h).

product of the arrest since such records would be largely useless because inadmissible as evidence. In fact, it is hard to see how any legal use, including that of detection, could be made of such records. Any evidence acquired by using fingerprints obtained through an illegal arrest should be considered what Justice Holmes in *Silverthorne Lumber Co. v. United States*[37] called "the fruit of the poisonous tree."[38] An intimation to this effect is to be found in the court of appeals' initial disposition of *Menard*.[39]

But this argument rests upon a mistaken perception of the reach of the "fruit of the poisonous tree" doctrine. It is true, of course, that fingerprints may be subject to suppression because the fruit of an illegal arrest, as in *Davis v. Mississippi*,[40] where the illegal arrest was made for the purpose of matching the defendant's prints with those found at the crime scene. But it does not follow that those prints are unusable at any time for any purpose. If fingerprints, or photos, or the notation of a prior arrest were never usable in pursuing another investigation, the effect, as Judge Friendly has noted, would be "to grant life-long immunity from investigation and prosecution simply because a violation of the Fourth Amendment first indicated to the police that a man was not the law-abiding citizen he purported to be."[41] The "fruit of the poisonous tree" doctrine does not demand this; rather, as held in *Wong Sun v. United States*,[42] the question is not whether the evidence "would not have come to light but for the legal actions of the police," but rather "whether, granting establishment of the primary illegality, the evidence to which instant objection is made has been come at by exploitation of that illegality or instead by means sufficiently distinguishable to be purged of the primary taint." Under this test, it is not objectionable, for example, that certain identification testimony originated with the witness viewing a photograph of the defendant taken following his illegal arrest for an earlier, unrelated crime, even though it might well be said that "but for" the earlier illegal arrest he would not have been identified in the second case.[43] The essential point, as one court put it, is "that evidence obtained

---

[37]Silverthorne Lumber Co. v. United States, 251 U.S. 385, 40 S.Ct. 182, 64 L.Ed. 319 (1920).

[38]Note, 17 Wayne L.Rev. 995, 1004–05 (1971). See also Note, 49 N.C.L.Rev. 509, 511 (1971).

[39]"There is, to say the least, serious question whether the Constitution can tolerate any adverse use of information or tangible objects obtained as the result of an unconstitutional arrest of the individual concerned." Menard v. Mitchell, 430 F.2d 486 (D.

C.Cir.1970).

[40]Davis v. Mississippi, 394 U.S. 721, 89 S.Ct. 1394, 22 L.Ed.2d 676 (1969).

[41]United States v. Friedland, 441 F.2d 855 (2d Cir.1971).

[42]Wong Sun v. United States, 371 U.S. 471, 83 S.Ct. 407, 9 L.Ed.2d 441 (1963), discussed in detail in § 11.4.

[43]People v. McInnis, 6 Cal.3d 821, 100 Cal.Rptr. 618, 494 P.2d 690 (1972); People v. Pettis, 12 Ill.App.3d 123, 298 N.E.2d 372 (1973).

from searches and seizures that violate the fourth amendment has some legitimate uses," from which it "follows that the records of such acts may be maintained."[44]

It would seem, then, that in assessing the potential value of particular arrest records in future investigations, one must look beyond the arrest itself. Here, as well, considerable confusion exists. For example, in *Eddy v. Moore*,[45] the court stated: "The value of fingerprints and photographs of an arrested person depends upon two factors: An assumption the individual arrested did in fact commit the crime for which he is accused and that his commission of this crime indicates a likelihood that other crimes will be committed. An acquittal seems to negate both premises."[46] But, this is not inevitably true of either an acquittal or (as was actually involved in *Eddy*) a dismissal of charges:

> [T]hese dispositions do not necessarily controvert the usefulness of the record. Acquittal means only that the defendant was not proven guilty beyond a reasonable doubt. Other dispositions can result from the death of an only witness, prosecutorial discretion, or the illegal seizure of evidence. Because of these considerations, the simple fact that a person has not been found guilty should not be sufficient to compel return of the record.[47]

Thus, it may be said that the mere fact that the arrest was not followed by conviction does not show that the arrest records in question are without potential value in future investigations. On the other hand, where it is shown that the defendant's arrest was a case of mistaken identity and that another person committed the crime[48] or that in fact no crime had occurred,[49] this potential value is not present. In the absence of such exoneration,[50] the degree of this potential value will vary depending upon the nature of the suspected criminality. "[S]ome types of crimes may follow a pattern, in which case it would be more reasonable to retain a record of who has been repeatedly arrested in a certain area for such a crime."[51]

As for other interests that militate against expungement, it is

---

[44]Scruggs v. United States, 929 F.2d 305 (7th Cir.1991), where the court added: "The Supreme Court has never understood the exclusionary rule to bar the government from knowing about an illegal arrest or search, even though the Constitution may block particular deployments of that information."

[45]Eddy v. Moore, 5 Wash.App. 334, 487 P.2d 211 (1971).

[46]Similarly, in United States v. Kalish, 271 F.Supp. 968 (D.P.R.1967), it is asserted that "when an accused is acquitted of the crime or when he is discharged without conviction, no pub-

lic good is accomplished by the retention of criminal identification records."

[47]Comment, 38 U.Chi.L.Rev. 850, 857 (1971).

[48]E.g., State v. Pinkney, 33 Ohio Misc. 183, 290 N.E.2d 923 (1972).

[49]E.g., Menard v. Saxbe, 498 F.2d 1017 (D.C.Cir.1974).

[50]Some commentators incorrectly use the word "exoneration" as encompassing everything but the situation in which the arrestee is thereafter convicted. See Comment, 23 Clev.St.L. Rev. 123, 133 (1974).

[51]Morrow v. District of Columbia,

sometimes asserted information on arrests is needed by police superiors and others for the purpose of measuring and evaluating departmental activities and the nature of the crime problem in the community.[52] But, while it is true that such information is needed, it is doubtful that identification of arrestees is essential; "purely statistical data should be sufficient for this purpose."[53] Finally, although the point is often ignored,[54] maintenance of arrest records is important in the event of subsequent litigation against the arresting officer. As noted in *Spock v. District of Columbia*[55]:

> Clearly, law enforcement interests are and must be served by preserving records of arrest if for no other reason than to permit a determination whether and how to defend in the event of an action based on asserted police misconduct. Upon destruction of arrest records in such cases the defense would be left at best with faded recollection by the arresting officer of an event lost in memory because of hundreds of subsequent cases.

Moreover, this particular need is greater, rather than lesser, when the arrest did not lead to conviction or was determined to be without probable cause in an exclusionary rule context.

§ 1.11(c) Balancing the interests; alternative remedies

Much of the current ambiguity concerning the dimensions of the constitutional right to expungement of arrest records may be attributed to the fact, as noted above, that the characterization of the law enforcement interests involved has often been inaccurate or incomplete. But even after the conflicting interests are properly identified, there remains the task of striking a balance between them. This enterprise is inevitably more subjective, involving as it does a weighing of each of these interests. Some comments about the balancing process are nonetheless appropriate, particularly with respect to the relative merits of expungement and the other remedies that have been discussed in the cases and literature, namely: prohibition of dissemination for other than law enforcement purposes; prohibition of use for any purpose except pursuant to court order; and elaboration of the record to indicate subsequent disposition or other facts bearing upon the actual significance of the arrest.

As for expungement, it is an inappropriate remedy whenever there remains open the possibility of future suit against the arresting officer. It would be unconscionable to permit the arrestee

---

417 F.2d 728 (D.C.Cir.1969).

[52]Spock v. District of Columbia, 283 A.2d 14 (D.C.App.1971); Miller v. Gillespie, 196 Mich. 423, 163 N.W. 22 (1917).

[53]Comment, 38 U.Chi.L.Rev. 850, 854 (1971).

[54]E.g., Note, 35 U.Pitt.L.Rev. 205, 216 (1973), listing among the reasons for retention the possibility of a damages action against the police, but then concluding, without further consideration of that reason, that arrest records should not be kept.

[55]Spock v. District of Columbia, 283 A.2d 14 (D.C.App.1971).

to have all the facts concerning the circumstances of his arrest destroyed and then to allow him to proceed against the officer, who at that point would be deprived of information potentially essential to his defense.[56] If this obstacle is overcome, perhaps by a binding commitment not to sue by the person seeking expungement, then expungement is certainly appropriate where the arrest record would have no significance for investigative purposes, as where later events made it clear that another person was guilty of the crime suspected or that the suspected crime did not in fact occur. This is particularly so where the arrest was undertaken for harassment purposes in the first instance.[57] "The arrest record constitutes one aspect of the total punitive effect of an arrest when made solely for the purpose of achieving that effect."[58]

As for the possibility of placing the records under seal and prohibiting any disclosure of their contents, except by further order of the court upon a showing of good cause,[59] this would be an appropriate remedy where the sole justification for denying expungement is the possibility of future tort litigation. Where, on the other hand, there is in addition a basis for viewing the record as potentially useful in subsequent criminal investigations, sealing would appear to be impracticable. The significance of the arrest data in the investigation of future crimes would not be apparent until it was examined, and thus a showing of cause could not be made in advance.

If the record in question does have potential use in later investigations, this of course is no reason for not prohibiting dissemination of the record outside of law enforcement channels.[60] Some commentators have viewed the protection of business interests by, for example, supplying arrest records to employers

---

[Section 1.11(c)]

[56]See testimony of Quinn Tamm, Executive Director, International Association of Chiefs of Police, in Hearings on H.R. 13315 Before a Subcomm. of the House Comm. on the Judiciary, 92d Cong., 2d Sess. 1973 to 1974 (1972).

[57]As in Bilick v. Dudley, 356 F.Supp. 945 (S.D.N.Y.1973); Wheeler v. Goodman, 306 F.Supp. 58 (W.D.N.C.1969); Hughes v. Rizzo, 282 F.Supp. 881 (E.D.Pa.1968).

[58]Note, 49 N.C.L.Rev. 509, 510 (1971).

[59]In Sullivan v. Murphy, 478 F.2d 938 (D.C.Cir.1973), this was seen as "a remedy reasonably equivalent to expungement in terms of protection of plaintiffs' rights."

[60]In United States v. Rosen, 343 F.Supp. 804 (S.D.N.Y.1972), the court declined to expunge the records, but indicated "it might be proper to allow injunctive relief" restraining the use of the records for certain purposes, as "where the person's arrest records are disseminated to potential employers." In Menard v. Mitchell, 328 F.Supp. 718 (D.D.C.1971), this restriction was imposed on statutory grounds. In Loder v. Municipal Court, 17 Cal.3d 859, 132 Cal.Rptr. 464, 553 P.2d 624 (1976), the court declined to order expungement, noting that by statute the authorized dissemination of arrest records was very restricted.

The commentators generally favor restriction of dissemination as a remedy. See Comments, 46 Notre Dame Law. 825, 832–33 (1971); 19 UCLA Rev. 654, 668 (1972); 1970 Wash.U.L.Q. 530, 535.

an insufficient basis for allowing such dissemination.[61] Others have noted, however, that these interests may sometimes be "relevant to law enforcement,"[62] which apparently refers to the fact that law enforcement should be just as interested in preventing crime as in detecting crime and that one means of prevention is to keep certain persons who present certain risks out of those types of employment in which the temptations are great or the potential for harm substantial. The issue is a difficult one, although it may be relevant that the due process limitations existing with respect to use of arrest records in the criminal process "are not present when an arrest record is used for employment purposes, often without the knowledge of the person involved."[63]

Finally, elaboration of the record to indicate that the arrestee was thereafter exonerated or to show other facts concerning later processing in the criminal justice system is hardly inconsistent with any law enforcement interest in maintenance of the records.[64] Indeed, such elaboration would increase the utility of the records. It is to be doubted, however, whether this is a sufficient remedy against misuse outside law enforcement circles. Even with the elaboration, it may well be that the prospective employer still "considers an arrest tantamount to conviction."[65] At best, such a record would not "have a completely neutral effect upon an employer."[66]

---

[61]Note, 49 N.C.L.Rev. 509, 514 (1971).

[62]Comment, 38 U.Chi.L.Rev. 850, 864 (1971).

[63]Menard v. Mitchell, 328 F.Supp. 718 (D.D.C.1971). On the other hand, if the prospective employer asks the applicant if he has an arrest record, he at least has some chance to explain the circumstances. In Spock v. District of Columbia, 283 A.2d 14 (D.C.App. 1971), the plaintiffs asked that the court authorize them to answer in the negative if ever asked on employment or financial applications whether they were ever arrested. The court responded: "No system of law can, with integrity, lend or appear to lend its aid to an unreal denial of the events, particularly as such denials may affect the lawful judgment of other persons who may in the future deal with them." To the same effect is Cissell v. Brostron, 395 S.W.2d 322 (Mo.App.1965). Compare Wheeler v. Goodman, 306 F.Supp. 58 (W.D.N.C. 1969), noting the plaintiffs' claim that "where an arrest is unlawful, the

victim should be entitled equitably to deny that it ever occurred," and speculating: "Whether an unlawful arrest 'occurred' is a question of semantics. One possible viewpoint is that there was never any 'arrest' at all, but that the victim, in reality, was 'falsely imprisoned.'" See also Tatum v. Morton, 562 F.2d 1279 (D.C.Cir.1977), holding illegally arrested persons entitled to expungement of arrest records and to court order declaring that the seizures should not be deemed to have been arrests.

[64]Comment, 38 U.Chi.L.Rev. 850, 858 (1971). See Hammons v. Scott, 423 F.Supp. 618 (N.D.Cal.1976); and Loder v. Municipal Court, 17 Cal.3d 859, 132 Cal.Rptr. 464, 553 P.2d 624 (1976), both declining to order expungement and noting that the records in question indicated the disposition of the charges.

[65]Note, 17 Wayne L.Rev. 995, 1005 (1971).

[66]Note, 49 N.C.L.Rev. 509, 514 (1971).

§ 1.12 Injunction

§ 1.12(a)   Absence of adequate remedy at law
§ 1.12(b)   Threat of imminent harm
§ 1.12(c)   Practical limitations on injunctive remedy

Research References

West's Key Number Digest
Civil Rights ⚷1358, 1454; Federal Courts ⚷13.15; Injunction ⚷75, 77(2)

Legal Encyclopedias
C.J.S., Injunctions §§ 115 to 116, 118, 121 to 122

Introduction

A somewhat different type of remedy, specifically intended to afford preventive relief, is an injunction. Over the years, individuals[1] and groups[2] have with some frequency sought injunctive relief to protect themselves, and often others similarly situated,[3] from illegal searches and seizures by particular policemen[4] or by all members of a particular police agency.[5] The purpose here is to take note of this development, rather than to survey generally the rather complicated body of law that exists concerning the issuance and enforcement of injunctions.[6] Because the cases in the state courts are in the main not too helpful on the particular subject under examination,[7] the emphasis here will be upon the protection of Fourth Amendment rights by federal court

---

[Section 1.12]

[1]Gomez v. Wilson, 477 F.2d 411 (D.C.Cir.1973); Long v. District of Columbia, 469 F.2d 927 (D.C.Cir. 1972).

[2]Lewis v. Kugler, 446 F.2d 1343 (3d Cir.1971); Lankford v. Gelston, 364 F.2d 197 (4th Cir.1966).

[3]Gomez v. Wilson, 477 F.2d 411 (D.C.Cir.1973); Long v. District of Columbia, 469 F.2d 927 (D.C.Cir. 1972); Lewis v. Kugler, 446 F.2d 1343 (3d Cir.1971); Lankford v. Gelston, 364 F.2d 197 (4th Cir.1966).

[4]Wecht v. Marsteller, 363 F.Supp. 1183 (W.D.Pa.1973) (one police officer); Hairston v. Hutzler, 334 F.Supp. 251 (W.D.Pa.1971) (7 police officers).

[5]Gomez v. Wilson, 477 F.2d 411 (D.C.Cir.1973) (District of Columbia police); Long v. District of Columbia, 469 F.2d 927 (D.C.Cir.1972) (same); Lewis v. Kugler, 446 F.2d 1343 (3d Cir.1971) (New Jersey state police); Lankford v. Gelston, 364 F.2d 197 (4th

Cir.1966) (Baltimore police).

[6]See J. Dobbyn, Injunctions in a Nutshell (1974); O. Fiss & D. Rendleman, Injunctions (2d ed.1984); Note, 78 Harv.L.Rev. 994 (1965).

[7]Most of the state cases "concern invasions of business interests, rather than denials of individual liberty. They typically involve such tactics as stationing officers on or near business premises, searching the premises or customers repeatedly, seizing property, or questioning customers excessively, discouraging them, even if unintentionally, from patronizing the plaintiff's business." Comment, 1967 Wash.U.L.Q. 104, 108. But, while it might once have been said that equity is confined to the protection of property rights, that principle "has lost whatever vitality it might previously have had." O. Fiss, Injunctions 2 (1984). As stated in Kenyon v. City of Chicopee, 320 Mass. 528, 70 N.E.2d 241 (1946), where Jehovah's Witnesses obtained injunctive relief against re-

injunction.[8]

§ 1.12(a) Absence of adequate remedy at law

The longstanding principle that equity will not grant relief to a petitioner who has an adequate remedy at law[9] has sometimes been invoked, but without success, against plaintiffs seeking to enjoin repeated or continuing Fourth Amendment violations. For example, in *Gomez v. Layton*,[10] where the plaintiff sought to enjoin the District of Columbia from subjecting him to stopping and questioning when he was on the public streets, one of the bases upon which the district court dismissed the complaint was that plaintiff had an adequate remedy at law. The court of appeals disagreed:

> The court's underlying assumption was that appellant could assert whatever claims he had when he was arrested and tried and that prior to arrest there is no irreparable injury. This assumption is incorrect. Appellant alleges that he is being deprived of constitutional rights regardless of whether he is ever arrested. * * * Recent case law makes clear that courts have the power to enjoin unconstitutional police practices. They are not always required to await criminal trials which may never materialize in order to vindicate crucial constitutional rights.

Unquestionably, the *Gomez* court was correct. The exclusionary rule, after all, "is calculated to prevent, not to repair,"[11] and thus it cannot be said that exclusion of evidence is an adequate remedy. Nor, quite obviously, is acquittal following arrest

---

peated arrests for distributing handbills, "if equity would safeguard their right to sell bananas, it ought to be at least equally solicitous of their personal liberties guaranteed by the Constitution."

The state cases also declare that "he who comes into equity must come with clean hands," Society of Good Neighbors v. Van Antwerp, 324 Mich. 22, 36 N.W.2d 308 (1949), but this should not be taken to mean that a plaintiff must be innocent of criminal conduct before he may obtain an injunction against Fourth Amendment violations. As one court noted, "It may be that the plaintiff is breaking the law; but the law does not confer arbitrary power on the defendant to deal with him. * * * Officials who override the law and do as they please are guilty of a vice more dangerous to society than all the other vices and crimes combined." Hertz v. McDermott, 45 Misc. 28, 90 N.Y.S. 803 (1904).

[8]42 U.S.C.A. § 1983 provides that a person who under color of law subjects a person "to the deprivation of any rights, privileges, or immunities secured by the Constitution and laws, shall be liable to the party injured in [a] suit in equity." See also 28 U.S.C.A. § 1343.

Regarding the negotiated settlement option when such organizations as the ACLU or NAACP seek reform of police practices under § 1983, or when the U.S. Attorney General seeks injunctive relief via 42 U.S.C.A. § 14141, see § 1.10, text at note 66.

[Section 1.12(a)]

[9]See J. Dobbyn, Injunctions in a Nutshell 34 (1974); Note, 78 Harv.L. Rev. 994, 997 (1965).

[10]Gomez v. Layton, 394 F.2d 764 (D.C.Cir.1968).

[11]Elkins v. United States, 364 U.S. 206, 80 S.Ct. 1437, 4 L.Ed.2d 1669 (1960).

adequate.[12] This is particularly apparent when one takes account of the fact that "the police may feel they can best prevent or make more difficult the commission of a crime by searching and arresting a suspect, even though they consider ultimate prosecution and conviction of him unlikely."[13]

What, then, of the alternative of a legal action against the offending police officers for damages? Given the Supreme Court's low regard for this alternative in *Mapp*, it is not surprising that it has likewise not been deemed an adequate remedy in the sense of foreclosing injunctive relief. As stated in *Lankford v. Gelston:*[14]

> There can be little doubt that actions for money damages would not suffice to repair the injury suffered by the victims of the police searches. Neither the personal assets of policemen nor the nominal bonds they furnish afford genuine hope of redress. Nor is there any provision for compensation from public funds. In any event the wrongs inflicted are not readily measurable in terms of dollars and cents. Indeed, the Supreme Court itself has already declared that the prospect of pecuniary redress for the harm suffered is "worthless and futile." Moreover, the lesson of experience is that the remote possibility of money damages serves as no deterrent to future police invasions.[15]

§ 1.12(b) Threat of imminent harm[16]

The plaintiff seeking an injunction must also show "that there is an imminent threat of harm,"[17] and this requirement has sometimes proved to be a barrier to injunctive relief from Fourth Amendment violations because of the plaintiff's inability to show the continuing nature of these violations. Thus, in *Hughes v. Rizzo*,[18] where Philadelphia police had been harassing hippies in a local park and had conducted two mass arrests there, but at a

[12]Easyriders Freedom F.I.G.H.T. v. Hannigan, 92 F.3d 1486 (9th Cir.1996) (re California Highway Patrol citation policy that "violates the Fourth Amendment when used to cite motorcyclists without knowledge of their certified helmet's non-compliance with federal standards, an injunction is appropriate" notwithstanding argument "that none of the motorcyclists is threatened with irreparable injury because the Fourth Amendment lack-of-probable-cause defense would be available at their trials on potential traffic citations," as "the wrong that the Fourth Amendment is designed to prevent is completed when a motorcyclist is cited without probable cause").

[13]Note, 45 U.Colo.L.Rev. 91, 93 (1973).

[14]Lankford v. Gelston, 364 F.2d 197 (4th Cir.1966).

[15]See also National Federation of Federal Employees v. Weinberger, 818 F.2d 935 (D.C.Cir.1987) (injunction action against urinalysis drug testing program not barred by possibility of damage action, as "the awarding of a *Bivens* remedy does not compel the government to alter its policies or practices," while "that is the precise function of prospective injunctive relief"); Siedel, Injunctive Relief for Police Misconduct in the United States, 50 J.Urb.L. 681, 691–93 (1973); Note, 45 U.Colo.L.Rev. 91, 94–97 (1973).

[Section 1.12(b)]

[16]The discussion herein follows closely the very helpful analysis in Note, 45 U.Colo.L.Rev. 91, 107–11 (1973).

[17]O. Fiss, Injunctions 9 (1984).

[18]Hughes v. Rizzo, 282 F.Supp.

pretrial hearing informal arrangements were made for voluntary cessation of that activity and no further harassment occurred thereafter, the court denied injunctive relief. Acknowledging that "if there were any likelihood of further attempts in that direction, an injunction should issue," the court concluded that such a likelihood did not exist. Similarly, in *Wilson v. Webster*,[19] although the police had conducted "a campaign of terror and brutality" against antiwar demonstrators, including illegal arrests and searches, injunctive relief was denied because there was no indication that more demonstrations would be held in the immediate future. The court asserted that injunctions "should not be issued merely to allay fear or apprehension, but only where there is an imminent and threatened injury."[20]

Whatever one might think of these decisions, it is clear that relief is properly denied when the plaintiff does not even establish that there was a pattern of illegality, as opposed to an isolated instance of an illegal search or seizure. Illustrative is *Long v. District of Columbia*,[21] where the court noted that "the complaint is of a single nonrecurring instance of alleged harassment by police officers," namely, that plaintiff had been stopped and frisked by police called to a jewelry store. The *Long* court concluded it had not been shown that "there is a substantial risk that future violations will occur," as there was neither a "clear pattern of harassment" nor (in the police department's published guidelines) a "stated policy of inflicting searches which, when tested, are unlawful."[22]

While in *Long* only one incident was alleged, this is not to say that proof of several instances of unconstitutional conduct by particular officers over a period of time will justify an injunction directed at the entire department or the officers in charge of the department. Instructive in this regard is *Rizzo v. Goode*,[23] which began as two separate actions brought by various individuals and organizations against the mayor, city managing director, and police commissioner of Philadelphia. The plaintiffs alleged a pervasive pattern of unconstitutional treatment of citizens, pri-

---

881 (E.D.Pa.1968).

[19]Wilson v. Webster, 315 F.Supp. 1104 (C.D.Cal.1970).

[20]Compare Gomez v. Wilson, 430 F.2d 495 (D.C.Cir.1970), holding that the case was not moot by virtue of the fact that some but not all of the subsections of the vagrancy statute, upon which the "vagrancy observation" stops were based, had since been held unconstitutional.

[21]Long v. District of Columbia, 469 F.2d 927 (D.C.Cir.1972).

[22]Similarly, in Gomez v. Wilson, 477 F.2d 411 (D.C.Cir.1973), the court held that the stopping and questioning of the plaintiff on two occasions would "hardly generate, simply on their own, a realistic prospect of future repetition," but the court then remanded for a determination of whether there had been other similar incidents involving the plaintiff or others.

[23]Rizzo v. Goode, 423 U.S. 362, 96 S.Ct. 598, 46 L.Ed.2d 561 (1976), noted in 30 Rutgers L.Rev. 103 (1976); 62 Va.L.Rev. 1259 (1976).

marily by two policemen who were not defendants, and that the defendant officials had failed to act so as to prevent recurrence of such abuses. The district court found that constitutional rights were violated by only a small percentage of Philadelphia police, that the violations could not be "dismissed as rare, isolated instances" in that they occurred in an "unacceptably high number of instances," and that while there was no "conscious" departmental policy of violating constitutional rights, it was the "policy of the department to discourage the filing of such complaints, to avoid or minimize the consequences of proven police misconduct, and to resist disclosure of the final disposition of such complaints."[24]

Relying upon the proposition stated in *O'Shea v. Littleton*[25]— that "if none of the named plaintiffs * * * establishes the requisite of a case or controversy with the defendants, none may seek relief on behalf of himself or any other member of the class" they purport to represent—the Supreme Court, per Rehnquist, J., concluded in *Rizzo* that there were "serious doubts whether on the facts as found there was made out the requisite Art. III case or controversy between the individually named respondents and petitioners." This was because "the individual respondents' claim to 'real and immediate' injury rests not upon what the named petitioners might do to them in the future * * * but upon what one of a small, unnamed minority of policemen might do to them in the future because of that unknown policeman's perception of departmental disciplinary procedures." Nor did the Court believe there was a "pattern" of unconstitutional conduct, for

> there was no showing that the behavior of the Philadelphia police was different in kind or degree from that which exists elsewhere; indeed, the District Court found "that the problems disclosed by the record . . . are fairly typical of [those] afflicting police departments in major urban areas."[26]

---

[24]Council of Organization on Philadelphia Police Accountability and Responsibility v. Rizzo, 357 F.Supp. 1289 (E.D.Pa.1973).

[25]O'Shea v. Littleton, 414 U.S. 488, 94 S.Ct. 669, 38 L.Ed.2d 674 (1974).

[26]Blackmun, J., joined by Brennan and Marshall, JJ., dissented. On this point, they said that to the extent "the Court's opinion today indicates that some constitutional violations might be spread so extremely thin as to prevent any individual from showing the requisite case or controversy, I must agree. I do not agree however, with the Court's substitution of its

judgment for that of the District Court on what the evidence here shows."

Commentators have likewise been critical of this part of *Rizzo*. They find it "confusing and uncertain in scope," Note, 62 Va.L.Rev. 1259, 1265 (1976), and likely to unduly limit the availability of injunctive relief: "Given a large group of identifiable people, such as the classes certified in *Rizzo*, and wide-spread instances of police unlawfulness toward such a group, it is unlikely that individual named plaintiffs will be victims of police transgressions multiple times so as to demonstrate the sufficient statistical likelihood of future injury to *themselves* that the Court now appears to

Rizzo and *O'Shea* were followed in *City of Los Angeles v. Lyons*.[27] Respondent's complaint alleged that he was stopped by Los Angeles police officers for a traffic violation and that although he offered no resistance or threat whatsoever the officers applied a chokehold rendering him unconscious and causing damage to his larynx. An injunction against the city barring such holds was sought, and in support it was alleged that the city's police officers, "pursuant to the authorization, instruction and encouragement of defendant City of Los Angeles, regularly and routinely apply these choke holds in innumerable situations where they are not threatened by the use of any deadly force whatsoever," that numerous persons have been injured as the result of the application of the chokeholds, that Lyons and others similarly situated are threatened with irreparable injury in the form of bodily injury and loss of life, and that Lyons "justifiably fears that any contact he has with Los Angeles police officers may result in his being choked and strangled to death without provocation, justification or other legal excuse." The Supreme Court held that the trial court had properly entered judgment for the city.

The Court first concluded that these allegations were insufficient to show an Article III case or controversy, as

> it is no more than conjecture to suggest that in every instance of a traffic stop, arrest, or other encounter between the police and a citizen, the police will act unconstitutionally and inflict injury without provocation or legal excuse. And it is surely no more than speculation to assert either that Lyons himself will again be involved in one of those unfortunate instances, or that he will be arrested in the future and provoke the use of a chokehold by resisting arrest, attempting to escape, or threatening deadly force or serious bodily injury.[28]

Even if Lyons had standing incidental to his pending damages

---

require in order to establish standing to challenge those violations." Note, 30 Rutgers L.Rev. 103, 131–32 (1976).

[27]City of Los Angeles v. Lyons, 461 U.S. 95, 103 S.Ct. 1660, 75 L.Ed.2d 675 (1983), characterized in Amar, Fourth Amendment First Principles, 107 Harv.L.Rev. 757, 816 (1994) as "a sad entry in the annals of the Fourth Amendment."

[28]This language has frequently been relied upon in holding there is no standing because the particular plaintiff failed to make a showing that he would likely be subjected to the allegedly unconstitutional conduct in the future. See, e.g., Warshak v. United States, 532 F.3d 521 (6th Cir.2008) (injunctive relief inappropriate, as question "is whether the government

will conduct another *ex parte* search of his e-mails, a possibility that is exceedingly remote given that the reason the government kept these searches confidential—that they would jeopardize the ongoing investigation—no longer exists") Brown v. Edwards, 721 F.2d 1442 (5th Cir.1984) (plaintiff not entitled to injunction of fee system whereby constable gets $10 for each charge resulting in conviction, as he failed to " 'establish any real and immediate threat' that he will again be injured in such a way"); John Does 1-100 v. Boyd, 613 F.Supp. 1514 (D.Minn.1985) (plaintiffs not entitled to injunction of strip searches of detainees, as they could not "establish a 'credible threat' that they will be arrested again"). Compare National Organization for Reform of Marijuana

action, the Court added, he would still not be entitled to equitable relief because there was no showing of irreparable injury: "Absent a sufficient likelihood that he will again be wronged in a similar way, Lyons is no more entitled to an injunction than any other citizen of Los Angeles; and a federal court may not entertain a claim by any or all citizens who no more than assert that certain practices of law enforcement officers are unconstitutional."

In *Rizzo,* the Court repeatedly emphasized the failure of the plaintiffs to name as defendants the particular police officers who were engaging in repeated unconstitutional conduct.[29] This suggests that it is still true that where the injunction is sought

Laws v. Mullen, 608 F.Supp. 945 (N.D.Cal.1985) (injunctive relief available to persons living near rural marijuana gardens re helicopter surveillance of their premises, as established official policy "virtually ensures" they will be surveilled further "as long as the plaintiffs live in the general vicinity"); Wilkinson v. Forst, 591 F.Supp. 403 (D.Conn.1984) (plaintiff entitled to injunction against stopping and searching persons attending KKK rallies, as his "position as Imperial Wizard of the Klan" and recurrence of the stops shows he "is 'realistically threatened by repetition of his experience' ").

Consider also Lewis v. Tully, 99 F.R.D. 632 (N.D.Ill.1983), where the case had been certified as a class action, and the court reasoned that under Gerstein v. Pugh, 420 U.S. 103, 95 S.Ct. 854, 43 L.Ed.2d 54 (1975), and its progeny, "the existence of probable future harm to the class can satisfy the personal stake requirement of article III even if the named plaintiff(s) do not meet article III's requirements." "Nothing in *Lyons* suggests that the Court intended to overrule *Gerstein,*" the court explained, for "*Lyons* apparently did not involve a class action."

A reverse twist on the *Lewis* situation is that in Easyriders Freedom F.I.G.H.T. v. Hannigan, 92 F.3d 1486 (9th Cir.1996), holding that an injunction limiting the California Highway Patrol's actions in giving helmet citations without probable cause as "against *all* motorists" and not just against the named plaintiffs, even though "there is no class certification,"

is proper because "it is unlikely that law enforcement officials who were not restricted by an injunction governing their treatment of all motorcyclists would inquire before citation into whether a motorcyclist was among the named plaintiffs," and thus "the plaintiffs would not receive the complete relief to which they are entitled without statewide application of the injunction."

Of the *Lyons* requirement of a "real and immediate threat" of future injury, Kerr, The Limits of Fourth Amendment Injunctions, 7 J.Tel. & High Tech.L. 127, 129 (2009), states: "The precise meaning of that requirement remains murky, but it arguably means that a plaintiff must show a real and immediate threat of a highly specific set of facts occurring." He adds, id. at 131: "The basic idea, both in the drug testing and the roadblock cases, is that the fact-sensitivity of Fourth Amendment law does not prohibit injunctive relief so long as the facts can be either stipulated or found at trial or otherwise established with reasonable detail. The court can take the facts of an existing or proposed program and treat it as a past set of facts rather than a current and future one."

[29] The Court, for example, stated that a "central paradox" permeating the lower court's opinion was that "individual police officers *not named as parties* to the action were found to have violated the constitutional rights of particular individuals, only a few of whom were parties plaintiff."

against a particular policeman[30] or a small group of policemen,[31] then it would be sufficient to show that the individual or individuals involved were "guilty of such violations and with such frequency that they cannot be dismissed as simply isolated instances of intemperance."[32]

The case of *Lankford v. Gelston*,[33] a leading case in this area distinguished in *Rizzo,* deserves particular attention here, for it is instructive on the question of what will suffice to show a pattern of Fourth Amendment violations and also a sufficient likelihood of recurrence. Four black families in Baltimore, on behalf of themselves and others similarly situated, sought an injunction in federal court against the police commissioner of that city to prevent further invasions of Fourth Amendment rights. The police, in an attempt to capture two brothers who had killed a policeman, conducted warrantless searches over a 19-day period of over 300 buildings, mostly private dwellings, based in almost every instance upon unverified anonymous tips. Noting that the commissioner had since issued a general order forbidding such searches except on probable cause and that the order had been complied with in later searches for the two men, the district court declined to issue the injunction. The court of appeals "remanded for the entry of a decree enjoining the Police Department from conducting a search of any private house to effect the arrest of any person not known to reside therein, whether with or without an arrest warrant, where the belief that the person is on the premises is based only on an anonymous tip and hence without probable cause."

Unquestionably, a pattern of Fourth Amendment violations was present in *Lankford,* for these searches were made by a special squad established for the express purpose of finding the two wanted men. But, what about the likelihood of recurrence? In addition to compliance with the general order mentioned above, it should be noted that by the time the matter was before the court of appeals the wanted men had been apprehended, and the former commissioner had been replaced by "a new Interim Police Commissioner whose enlightened efforts to foster better relations between the Negro community and the Police Department have been widely applauded by all elements of the community." As for the fact the two wanted men were now in custody, this was not controlling on the issue because the police, in searching for them, "were engaging in a practice which on a smaller scale has routinely attended efforts to apprehend persons accused of serious crime." As for the general order and compliance therewith, the court deemed them insufficient evidence of

---

[30]Wecht v. Marsteller, 363 F.Supp. 1183 (W.D.Pa.1973).

[31]Hairston v. Hutzler, 334 F.Supp. 251 (W.D.Pa.1971).

[32]Wecht v. Marsteller, 363 F.Supp. 1183 (W.D.Pa.1973).

[33]Lankford v. Gelston, 364 F.2d 197 (4th Cir.1966).

reform for several reasons: (i) they may have been "timed to anticipate or to blunt the force of a lawsuit"; (ii) they may only reflect police awareness "of the futility of continuing the searches when it had become manifest" that the two men had made their escape; and (iii) the general order, in merely stating the probable cause requirement, "adds nothing to the general rule with which the rank-and-file policeman should already have been familiar" and "is too vague to provide even a faint warning that searches based only on anonymous tips do not constitute proper police tactics." Finally, and perhaps most significant, the court concluded that an injunction was needed notwithstanding the appointment of a new commissioner for which the court itself had praise. Stressing that the conduct complained of was "the effectuation of a plan conceived by high ranking officials" and had been directed at "those who feel that they have been harassed by reason of their color or their poverty," the court determined that "the clear assurance which the injunction is designed to give is nevertheless still necessary in the interest of public tranquility."

Some commentators view *Lankford* as having "departed from the traditional requirement that an 'imminent threat of harm' exist before an injunction will issue."[34] This may be true. At least, it is clear that *Lankford* may not be completely squared with the more traditional position that injunctions "should not be issued merely to allay fear or apprehension."[35] But this is said in praise rather than in criticism of the *Lankford* decision. Given the unique circumstances present in *Lankford*, the injunction protected in a meaningful way the Fourth Amendment "right of the people to be secure in their persons, houses, papers, and effects." The "clear assurance" given by the injunction made the people "secure" in the true sense of that word.[36]

As a general matter, however, it is fair to conclude that as a result of the *O'Shea-Rizzo-Lyons* line of cases, federal courts are very demanding as to the requisite showing of pending injury to Fourth Amendment rights that will suffice to justify federal injunctive relief against state or local police. Fairly typical is the statement in *Gonzales v. City of Peoria*[37] that because of the principles of equity, comity and federalism stressed in those Supreme Court decisions, "federal courts may not intervene in state enforcement activities absent extraordinary circumstances." The reluctance to intervene is somewhat less when federal law enforcement practices have been challenged, which is explained on the ground that "*Lyons, Rizzo* and *O'Shea* all involved at-

---

[34]Note, 45 U.Colo.L.Rev. 91, 110 (1973). See also Siedel, 50 J.Urb.L. 681, 697 (1973).

[35]Wilson v. Webster, 315 F.Supp. 1104 (C.D.Cal.1970).

[36]"Secure" means to be "free from fear, care, or anxiety." Webster's Third New International Dictionary 2053 (1961).

[37]Gonzales v. City of Peoria, 722 F.2d 468 (9th Cir.1983).

tempts by plaintiffs to 'entangle' federal courts in the operations of state law enforcement and criminal justice systems."[38]

§ 1.12(c) Practical limitations on injunctive remedy

While it is no longer true that courts will decline to enjoin continuing Fourth Amendment violations by unquestioned acceptance of the hoary maxim that "equity will not interfere with criminal law enforcement,"[39] the fact remains that there are certain practical considerations limiting somewhat the utility of the equitable remedy. Even in recent years, courts have declined to issue injunctions against police violations on the grounds that it was impossible to formulate an injunction clearly expressing what was prohibited and what was permitted[40] and that it was not feasible to involve the court in the day-to-day operations of the police department.[41]

The concern is legitimate.[42] As stated in *Lewis v. Kugler*,[43] a "federal court should avoid unnecessarily dampening the vigor of a police department by becoming too deeply involved in the department's daily operations, both because of the vital public interests at stake, and because of the danger that the court could become enmeshed in endless time-consuming bickering and controversy." The problem of drafting a clear injunction is particularly acute in the Fourth Amendment area because of the difficulty in dealing concretely with such concepts as probable cause and unreasonableness. If an injunction were to do no more, in effect, than to command all the officers in a department not to search unreasonably, a particular officer "will either disregard the injunction when he realizes that it fails to give him any indication of how to act in the given situation * * *, or he will react too cautiously and refuse to do anything at all for fear of

---

[38]LaDuke v. Nelson, 762 F.2d 1318 (9th Cir.1985).

[Section 1.12(c)]

[39]See, e.g., Harris v. Commissioner of Police, 274 Mass. 56, 174 N.E. 198 (1931), where the court refused to interfere with the police even though they had searched the defendant's club seventy times without finding any illegal activity.

[40]Wilson v. Webster, 315 F.Supp. 1104 (C.D.Cal.1970).

[41]Hughes v. Rizzo, 282 F.Supp. 881 (E.D.Pa.1968).

[42]Kerr, The Limits of Fourth Amendment Injunctions, 7 J.Tel. & High Tech.L. 127, 129 (2009), argues "that as a matter of normative policy, any ambiguity in the current state of the law should be resolved against imposing broad Fourth Amendment

injunctions. At first blush, it may seem that crafting a broad injunction to avoid Fourth Amendment violations appropriately shapes the remedy to the wrong. But crafting broad injunctive relief forces courts to assume duties that they are not competent to handle. Fourth Amendment doctrine is tremendously fact-specific: every fact pattern is different, and even the exceptions to the exceptions have their own exceptions. Courts are poorly suited to design broad injunctive relief in this setting: They lack the ability to predict how the government may act and the fact patterns that may arise. Courts should therefore decline to craft Fourth Amendment injunctions involving hypothetical facts."

[43]Lewis v. Kugler, 446 F.2d 1343 (3d Cir.1971).

being held in contempt."[44]

But, as suggested in *Lewis,* one way to meet this problem is for the court "to direct appropriate orders to the responsible officials, with a view to having the situation corrected by them internally." This approach has several advantages. Besides freeing the court itself from becoming, in effect, a temporary police chief, it would leave the actual head of the policy agency "free to frame orders to patrolmen and alter enforcement procedures to achieve the desired result with a minimum of adverse effect on the morale and efficiency of his police department."[45] Moreover, proceeding in this way would minimize "the danger that federal injunctive remedies might inhibit constitutional as well as unconstitutional law enforcement practices."[46]

Indeed, if as a result of this kind of approach the head of the police agency were required to formulate and articulate general law enforcement policy and to then justify that policy before the enjoining court, the procedure would be particularly beneficial. As Judge Bazelon has observed:

> The President's 1967 Crime Commission suggested that the courts recognize "the importance of the administrative policy-making function of [the] police" and "take appropriate steps to make this a process which is . . . articulate and responsive to external controls appropriate in a democratic society." Likening the police policymaking function to that of an administrative agency, the Commission called on the courts to develop judicial remedies that would "require the law enforcement agency to articulate its policy and to defend it, and if the challenge is successful to change the policy."[47]

> The American Bar Association has also focused on the need for providing positive guidance to the police, "rather than concentrating solely on penalizing improper police conduct," as by application of the exclusionary rule. The ABA Report specifically approved of "injunctive actions to terminate a pattern of unlawful conduct."[48]

> The class action injunctive suit is one means by which the police can be required to identify, articulate, and defend, as well as be afforded an opportunity to change, their official policies and practices. The class action, by its very nature, focuses on the broad policy rather than the individual incident. Hence, it provides the kind of positive guidance suggested by the ABA and the kind of remedy called for by the Crime Commission.[49]

Unfortunately, however, the Supreme Court's decision in *Rizzo*

---

[44]Note, 45 U.Colo.L.Rev. 91, 99 (1973).

[45]Note, 78 Yale L.J. 143, 149 (1968).

[46]Note, 78 Yale L.J. 143, 153 (1968).

[47]The reference is to The President's Commission on Law Enforcement and the Administration of Justice, Task Force Report: The Police 18, 32 (1967).

[48]The reference is to what is now 1 ABA Standards for Criminal Justice §§ 1-5.2, 1-5.3 (2d ed. 1980).

[49]Gomez v. Wilson, 477 F.2d 411 (D.C.Cir.1973) (Bazelon, C.J., concurring in part and dissenting in part).

v. Goode,[50] has severely limited the availability of this technique when injunctive relief is sought in federal court against a local police department. In *Rizzo*, the district court found that the violation of constitutional rights by a small percentage of Philadelphia police could not be "dismissed as rare, isolated instances," and that, while such acts were not the result of a "conscious" departmental policy of violating constitutional rights, it was department policy to discourage the filing of citizen complaints, to resist disclosure of their final disposition, and "to avoid or minimize the consequences of proven police misconduct." That court directed the defendants—the mayor, city managing director, and police commissioner—to prepare "a comprehensive program" for dealing with the problem, which was to include: (1) revision of police manuals with respect to such matters as "unnecessary damage to property and other unreasonable conduct in executing search warrants" and "limitations on pursuit of persons charged only with summary offenses"; (2) revision of procedures for processing complaints against the police; and (3) prompt notification to concerned parties of the action taken with respect to such complaints. The Supreme Court, per Rehnquist, J., reversed.

The Court in *Rizzo* first concluded that there was no "threshold statutory liability" upon which equitable relief could be granted against the defendants:

> The theory of liability underlying the District Court's opinion, and urged upon us by respondents, is that even without a showing of direct responsibility for the actions of a small percentage of the police force, petitioners' *failure* to act in the face of a statistical pattern is indistinguishable from the active conduct enjoined in *Hague* and *Medrano.*[51] Respondents posit a constitutional "duty" on the part of petitioners (and a corresponding "right" of the citizens of Philadelphia) to "eliminate" future police misconduct; a "default" of that affirmative duty being shown by the statistical pattern, the District Court is empowered to act in petitioners' stead and take whatever preventive measures are necessary, within its discretion, to secure the "right" at issue. Such reasoning, however, blurs accepted usages and meanings in the English language in a way which would be quite inconsistent with the words Congress chose in § 1983. We have never subscribed to these amorphous propositions, and we decline to do so now.

> * * * Here, the District Court found that none of the petitioners had deprived the respondent classes of any rights secured under

---

[50]Rizzo v. Goode, 423 U.S. 362, 96 S.Ct. 598, 46 L.Ed.2d 561 (1976).

[51]The references are to Hague v. Committee for Indus. Organization, 307 U.S. 496, 59 S.Ct. 954, 83 L.Ed. 1423 (1939) (injunctive relief proper where there was a pattern of police misconduct in consequence of deliberate policies of the mayor and police chief directed against the plaintiff's labor organizers); and Allee v. Medrano, 416 U.S. 802, 94 S.Ct. 2191, 40 L.Ed.2d 566 (1974) (injunctive relief proper where there was intentional, concerted and conspiratorial efforts by named Texas Rangers to deprive organizers of their First Amendment rights).

the Constitution. Under the well-established rule that federal "judicial powers may be exercised only on the basis of a constitutional violation," * * * this case presented no occasion for the District Court to grant equitable relief against petitioners.[52]

Next, the *Rizzo* Court noted that the district court's injunctive order, "significantly revising the internal procedures of the Philadelphia police department, was indisputably a sharp limitation on the department's 'latitude in the "dispatch if its own internal affairs.'" " Relying upon the rule that in federal equity cases "the nature of the violation determines the scope of the remedy" and upon "important considerations of federalism," the Court concluded:

> Contrary to the District Court's flat pronouncement that a federal court's legal power to "supervise the functioning of the police department . . . is firmly established," it is the foregoing cases and principles that must govern consideration of the type of injunctive relief granted here. When it injected itself by injunctive decree into the internal disciplinary affairs of this state agency, the District Court departed from these precepts.[53]

As a consequence of *Rizzo,* "persons seeking to attack patterns of police illegality by enjoining police officials now face additional obstacles heretofore not widely anticipated."[54] It remains less than clear "whether high police officials could be proper defendants when the magnitude of the abuses is different in kind or degree, but either no demonstrable policy exists or plaintiffs can only establish one that has evolved *de facto* at lower levels in the police department hierarchy."[55] But it nonetheless appears that this branch of *Rizzo* is unnecessarily broad.

> The Court could have accomplished its aim, however, by requiring only a deliberate policy. Insisting that an enjoinable policy be affirmative as well as deliberate severely restricts the usefulness of Section 1983 for correcting officially-condoned police abuses. Acquiescence in subordinate misconduct is far more prevalent than affirmative departmental policies that require violations of constitutional rights. Under the "affirmative policy" requirement, most "patterns" of police illegality will go unchecked. If only affirmative policies can be enjoined, police officials may relax existing disciplin-

---

[52]Blackmun, J., joined by Brennan and Marshall, JJ., dissented. Relying on Monroe v. Pape, 365 U.S. 167, 81 S.Ct. 473, 5 L.Ed.2d 492 (1961), they concluded it was "clear that an official may be enjoined from consciously permitting his subordinates, in the course of their duties, to violate the constitutional rights of persons with whom they deal. In rejecting the concept that the official may be responsible under § 1983, the Court today casts aside reasoned conclusions to the contrary reached by the courts of appeals of 10 circuits."

[53]The three dissenters objected that the district court's "remedy is carefully delineated, worked out within the administrative structure rather than superimposed by edict upon it, and essentially, and concededly, 'livable.' "

[54]Note, 62 Va.L.Rev. 1259, 1263 (1976).

[55]Note, 62 Va.L.Rev. 1259, 1272 (1976).

ary and complaint accounting procedures and thereby encourage subordinates to continue engaging in abuses.[56]

The scope of the Court's holding regarding federal equitable restraint is likewise unclear, for it "left uncertain the extent to which its holding regarding mandatory relief applies to cases that satisfy *Rizzo*'s standards for liability."[57] It is nonetheless "the most disturbing feature of the *Rizzo* opinion,"[58] for it may bar the type of relief that, for the reasons stated earlier,[59] would often best accommodate the interests of the plaintiffs, the police department, and the enjoining court. As one commentator has noted,

> *Rizzo* may place a disturbing limitation on a district court's ability to fashion even less intrusive relief when police systematically violate individual rights. For example, the district court in *Rizzo* could have stopped short of reorganizing the department's disciplinary apparatus and simply required the Police Commissioner to develop rules to govern the conduct of the individual police malefactors. Such relief has been suggested as desirable in situations where a few policemen employ unconstitutional practices against a large segment of the community. This remedy would not require changes in the regular disciplinary machinery of the department or the nearly 7500 officers who were not involved. If the officers continued their unconstitutional practices, the Court could order that the scope of the rules be broadened. A Commissioner failing to make or enforce the rules could be held in contempt.
>
> The *Rizzo* holdings on Section 1983 liability and equitable restraint combine to render this limited remedy unavailable. The new rules governing equitable restraint prevent the courts from fashioning equitable remedies that tinker with the internal workings of the police department, even when a proper 1983 claim is made out. Where plaintiffs can establish a deliberate, affirmative plan or policy, the logical and appropriate relief would be to enjoin the plan or policy. But where superiors merely acquiesce in statistically significant patterns of misconduct by subordinates, a prohibitory injunction would have no affirmative actions upon which to operate.[60]

In short, what is most disturbing about *Rizzo* "is that, in its haste to reject the relief granted, the Court has erected a barrier to far less intrusive remedies."[61]

---

[56]Note, 62 Va.L.Rev. 1259, 1274–75 (1976).

[57]Note, 62 Va.L.Rev. 1259, 1281 (1976).

[58]Note, 30 Rutgers L.Rev. 103, 143 (1976).

[59]See quotation in text preceding note 59 supra.

[60]Note, 62 Va.L.Rev. 1259, 1279–80 (1976).

[61]Note, 62 Va.L.Rev. 1259, 1283

(1976). See also Meltzer, Deterring Constitutional Violations by Law Enforcement Officials: Plaintiffs and Defendants as Private Attorneys General, 88 Colum.L.Rev. 247, 297 (1988), arguing in favor of broad availability of injunctive relief: "Indeed, if deterrent remedies are appropriate when sought by criminal defendants, there is no reason why they should not also be thought appropriate at the behest of civil plaintiffs."

§ 1.13 Self-help

§ 1.13(a)   Resistance to illegal arrest
§ 1.13(b)   Other forms of self-help

Research References

West's Key Number Digest
Arrest ☞63.4(14); Assault and Battery ☞67; Obstructing Justice ☞3, 7, 8

Legal Encyclopedias
C.J.S., Arrest § 34; Assault and Battery § 87; Obstructing Justice or Governmental Administration §§ 2, 4, 10, 12 to 29, 31 to 32, 38

Introduction

The final possible remedy for Fourth Amendment violations to be discussed here is that of self-help. Particular attention will be given to the question of whether the Amendment necessitates continuing recognition of the right forcibly to resist an unlawful arrest, although other forms of self-help will also be noted.

§ 1.13(a) Resistance to illegal arrest

The right to resist an unlawful arrest was well established at common law. As the Supreme Court stated in *John Bad Elk v. United States:*[1] "If the officer had no right to arrest, the other party might resist the illegal attempt to arrest him, using no more force than was absolutely necessary to repel the assault constituting the attempt to arrest."[2] This is still the law today in several jurisdictions,[3] although the legal commentators have rather consistently criticized the common law rule.[4] (But, even when the common law rule still exists, courts are disinclined to

---

[Section 1.13(a)]

[1] John Bad Elk v. United States, 177 U.S. 529, 20 S.Ct. 729, 44 L.Ed. 874 (1900).

[2] More recently, the Court stated in dictum: "One has an undoubted right to resist an unlawful arrest, and courts will uphold the right of resistance in proper cases." United States v. Di Re, 332 U.S. 581, 68 S.Ct. 222, 92 L.Ed. 210 (1948).

[3] E.g., Telfare v. City of Huntsville, 841 So.2d 1222 (Ala.2002) ("to a limited degree, a party is justified in attempting to resist an unlawful arrest"); State v. Sims, 851 So.2d 1039 (La.2003) ("the doctrine continues to be a part of Louisiana law"); State v. Wiegmann, 350 Md. 585, 714 A.2d 841 (1998) (declining to abolish common law rule because "this change

is best left to the Legislature"). See the post-1956 cases collected in Annot., 44 A.L.R.3d 1078 (1972). One possible limitation is that "a person may not resist an arrest carried out pursuant to a court-issued warrant." Hill v. State, 419 Md. 674, 20 A.3d 780 (2011).

See also State v. Ritter, 472 N.W.2d 444 (N.D.1991) (though illegality of arrest no defense where charge is assault, etc., statutory defense "that the public servant was not acting lawfully" exists to charge of preventing arrest, defined as creating a "substantial risk of bodily injury" to another with intent to prevent an arrest).

[4] Warner, The Uniform Arrest Act, 28 Va.L.Rev. 315, 330–31 (1942); Notes, 7 Nat.Res.J. 119 (1969); 3 Tulsa L.Rev. 40 (1966). Consider also Wright, Resisting Unlawful Arrests; Inviting

recognize a comparable right to resist an illegal stop-and-frisk,[5] often emphasizing policy arguments used elsewhere to support abolition of the common law rule itself.)

It has been noted, however, that there is a strong trend away from the common law position.[6] This movement must be attributed, in large measure, to the influence of the Model Penal Code, which provides that the "use of force is not justifiable * * * to resist an arrest which the actor knows is being made by a peace officer, although the arrest is unlawful."[7] As the draftsmen explained, it "should be possible to provide adequate remedies against illegal arrest, without permitting the arrested person to resort to force, a course of action highly likely to result in greater injury even to himself than the detention."[8] Either by legislation or judicial decree, many jurisdictions have now adopted the Model Penal Code position or some variation thereof.[9] While adoption of this position is obviously of importance in terms of the substan-

---

Anarchy or Protecting Individual Freedom?, 46 Drake L.Rev. 383 (1997) (exploring "the middle ground between the complete abrogation of the right and its continued retention"). But see Comments, 10 Akron L.Rev. 171 (1976); 31 La.L.Rev. 120 (1970).

[5]Graves v. Thomas, 450 F.3d 1215 (10th Cir.2006) (stressing "the most dire consequence of the attempted stop * * * was the possibility of an allegedly unwarranted traffic violation–a matter that is normally and dispassionately addressed in a courtroom"; court adds that in any event defendant's "resistance" by high-speed flight with lights off was excessive under the *Bad Elk* test); State v. Sims, 851 So.2d 1039 (La.2003) ("whether the officer did, in hindsight, possess articulable suspicion to justify the frisk should be resolved in the courtroom rather than in the streets"); Barnhard v. State, 86 Md.App. 518, 587 A.2d 561 (1991), aff'd, 325 Md. 602, 602 A.2d 701 (1992); State v. Hill, 264 Va. 541, 570 S.E.2d 805 (2002).

Compare State v. Bishop, 146 Idaho 804, 203 P.3d 1203 (2009) (defendant was entitled to "peacefully resist" illegal frisk; state's argument said to ignore "the distinction between peaceful and forceful resistance").

[6]State v. Wiegmann, 350 Md. 585, 714 A.2d 841 (1998) (citing cases in 14 states and statutes in 27 other states abolishing the common law

right to resist).

[7]Section 3.04(2)(a) (1962). As the draftsmen emphasize, it is important to note that this provision has no application when the officer uses unnecessary force to make the arrest and reasonable force is used in defense, or when the other person is not known to be a police officer. Model Penal Code § 3.04, Comment (Tent. Draft No. 8, 1958).

[8]Model Penal Code § 3.04, Comment (Tent. Draft No. 8, 1958).

[9]Miller v. State, 462 P.2d 421 (Alaska 1969); People v. Curtis, 70 Cal.2d 347, 74 Cal.Rptr. 713, 450 P.2d 33 (1969); People v. Hess, 687 P.2d 443 (Colo.1984); Claire v. State, 294 A.2d 836 (Del.1972); Marshall v. State, 354 So.2d 107 (Fla.App.1978); State v. Lusby, 146 Idaho 506, 198 P.3d 735 (2008); People v. Gnatz, 8 Ill.App.3d 396, 290 N.E.2d 392 (1972); State v. Dawdy, 533 N.W.2d 551 (Iowa 1995); State v. Austin, 381 A.2d 652 (Me. 1978); Rodgers v. State, 280 Md. 406, 373 A.2d 944 (1977); Commonwealth v. Moreira, 388 Mass. 596, 447 N.E.2d 1224 (1983); State v. Wick, 331 N.W.2d 769 (Minn.1983); State v. Briggs, 435 S.W.2d 361 (Mo.1968); State v. Yeutter, 252 Neb. 857, 566 N.W.2d 387 (1997); State v. Mulvihill, 57 N.J. 151, 270 A.2d 277 (1970); People v. Santiago, 69 Misc.2d 1098, 332 N.Y.S.2d 733 (1972); State v. Ritter, 472 N.W.2d 444 (N.D.1991); City of Columbus v. Fraley,

tive criminal law, it also has an important procedural characteristic: the resistance to the illegal arrest is a new crime for which the police may now make a lawful arrest and a lawful search incident thereto.[10] (It is important to note, however, that the "lawful search" conclusion might well be disconnected from the "new crime" conclusion, as some courts have done.[11] The rather compelling reasoning is this: if the defendant is arrested or otherwise detained on insufficient suspicion of, say, drug possession and the defendant then commits a resistance-of-arrest-or-detention type of offense, the defendant is not immune from prosecution for the latter offense and thus can be arrested for it, but to also uphold the search incident to that arrest for the new crime which uncovers the drugs originally but insufficiently suspected goes too far because it would create a "significant potential for official abuse."[12])

The question as to whether this modern view could be squared with the Fourth Amendment was raised by Justice Douglas, dissenting from the dismissal of certiorari as improvidently granted, in *Wainwright v. New Orleans*.[13] He asserted that one "had the right to offer some resistance to an unconstitutional 'seizure' or 'search'" under "the principle that a citizen can defy an unconstitutional act." Shortly thereafter, precisely such a challenge was made of a provision (§ 834a) in the California penal law forbidding forcible resistance of an arrest made by one known to be a

---

41 Ohio St.2d 173, 324 N.E.2d 735 (1975); State v. Crane, 46 Or.App. 547, 612 P.2d 735 (1980), conviction aff'd, 289 Or. 757, 619 P.2d 217; State v. Ramsdell, 109 R.I. 320, 285 A.2d 399 (1971); State v. Miskimins, 435 N.W.2d 217 (S.D.1989); Barnett v. State, 615 S.W.2d 220 (Tex.Crim.App.1981); State v. Holeman, 103 Wash.2d 426, 693 P.2d 89 (1985); State v. Hobson, 218 Wis.2d 350, 577 N.W.2d 825 (1998)..

See also United States v. Moore, 483 F.2d 1361 (9th Cir.1973) (the right to resist is not available when the arrest "was 'unlawful' only in the exclusionary-rule sense that it was a 'fruit' of the prior unlawful search"); Crossland v. United States, 32 A.3d 1005 (D.C.App.2011) (forceful resistance to illegal *search* prohibited); Clarke v. State, 303 So.2d 35 (Fla.App. 1974) (force may not be used to resist an illegal *search* of the person); Roberts v. State, 711 P.2d 1131 (Wyo.1985) ("a limited departure from the common law view because we only decide that a citizen cannot resist an arrest by a uniformed police officer who is executing a warrant").

[10]United States v. Sledge, 460 F.3d 963 (8th Cir.2006); United States v. Dawdy, 46 F.3d 1427 (8th Cir.1995); State v. Dawdy, 533 N.W.2d 551 (Iowa 1995). For more on the "new crime" principle, see § 11.4(j).

[11]Jones v. State, 745 A.2d 856 (Del.1999); State v. Beauchesne, 151 N.H. 803, 868 A.2d 972 (2005).

[12]Jones v. State, 745 A.2d 856 (Del.1999).

[13]Wainwright v. New Orleans, 392 U.S. 598, 88 S.Ct. 2243, 20 L.Ed.2d 1322 (1968). In White v. Morris, 345 So.2d 461 (La.1977), where the court declined to abandon the common law rule in light of the state legislature's refusal to do so, the Douglas dissent in *Wainwright* was referred to as "respectable judicial * * * authority for the proposition that the right to resist an unlawful arrest is protected as part of the guaranty against unreasonable seizures of the person by the Fourth Amendment to the United States Constitution."

peace officer. In *People v. Curtis*,[14] the court held:

An arrest is a "seizure" and an arrest without a warrant or probable cause is "unreasonable" within the purview of the Fourth Amendment. * * * If section 834a, by eliminating the remedy of self-help, facilitates or sanctions arrests which are by definition unlawful, it could be urged with considerable persuasion that defendant's constitutional rights would be violated by the statute.

While defendant's rights are no doubt violated when he is arrested and detained a matter of days or hours without probable cause, we conclude the state in removing the right to resist does not contribute to or effectuate this deprivation of liberty. In a day when police are armed with lethal and chemical weapons, and possess scientific communication and detection devices readily available for use, it has become highly unlikely that a suspect, using *reasonable* force, can escape from or effectively deter an arrest, whether lawful or unlawful. His accomplishment is generally limited to temporary evasion, merely rendering the officer's task more difficult or prolonged. Thus self-help as a practical remedy is anachronistic, whatever may have been its original justification or efficacy in an era when the common law doctrine permitting resistance evolved. * * * Indeed, self-help not infrequently causes far graver consequences for both the officer and the suspect than does the unlawful arrest itself. Accordingly, the state, in deleting the right to resist, has not actually altered or diminished the remedies available against the illegality of an arrest without probable cause; it has merely required a person to submit peacefully to the inevitable and to pursue his available remedies through the orderly judicial process.

We are not unmindful that under present conditions the available remedies for unlawful arrest—release followed by civil or criminal action against the offending officer—may be deemed inadequate. * * * However, this circumstance does not elevate physical resistance to anything other than the least effective and desirable of all possible remedies; as such its rejection, particularly when balanced against the state's interest in discouraging violence, cannot realistically be considered an affirmative "seizure" or deprivation of liberty.

Thus there is no denial of due process because the deprivation of liberty which an individual suffers upon an unlawful arrest is in no substantial or practical way effectuated, sanctioned or increased by section 834a. There is no constitutional impediment to the state's policy of removing controversies over the legality of an arrest from the streets to the courtroom.[15]

Curtis did not respond specifically to the Douglas contention

---

[14]People v. Curtis, 70 Cal.2d 347, 74 Cal.Rptr. 713, 450 P.2d 33 (1969).

[15]The court went on to note that the same could not be said for use of force in resisting excessive force in making an arrest: "Liberty can be restored through legal processes, but life and limb cannot be repaired in a courtroom. Therefore any rationale, pragmatic or constitutional, for outlawing resistance to unlawful arrests and resolving the dispute over legality in the courts has no determinative application to the right to resist excessive force." See, e.g., State v. Oliphant, 347 Or. 175, 218 P.3d 1281 (2009) (to reconcile self-defense statute with can't-resist-arrest statute, it necessary to distinguish between use of force in resisting arrest and use of force in re-

that the right to resist an unlawful arrest rested upon the same footing as the right, recognized by the Supreme Court, to disobey an unlawful police order. But, as even commentators critical of the *Curtis* rule have acknowledged,[16] the analogy is imperfect. As one court has noted,[17] it is more proper to ask "whether resistance to an unlawful *arrest* more closely resembles refusal to obey an unlawful police order, which is not punishable,[18] than disobedience of a constitutionally defective court order, which the Court has held[19] *is* punishable by contempt." The answer is that it more closely resembles the latter:

> An unlawful arrest, like both a police order and a court order, can result in immediate interference with enjoyment of constitutional rights. It differs, however, from the former and resembles the latter in that an unlawfully arrested person like an unlawfully restrained one has open to him an opportunity to vindicate his rights in court. These rights are not irrevocably compromised by initial compliance as they are in the case of the person who obeys a police order and who, as a result, forever loses his chance to contest it by allowing the policeman the final say. Put otherwise, the arrest and the court order have built into them the potential of submitting the dispute to the impartial determination of the courts of law (including the appellate courts). The unlawful police order, on the other hand, if obeyed, makes the policeman the final arbiter.[20]

sponse to officer's use of excessive force). For other cases on the right to resist excessive force, see Annot., 77 A.L.R.3d 281 (1977).

Because of this right, a broad instruction that defendant cannot respond with force to an arrest by one known to be an officer is in error. United States v. Span, 970 F.2d 573 (9th Cir.1992) (but not plain error here).

[16]Chenen, California Penal Code § 834-a: An Infringement of the Constitutional Right to Resist Unlawful Arrest, 5 U.S.F.L.Rev. 195, 205–08 (1971); Chevigny, The Right to Resist an Unlawful Arrest, 7 Crim.L.Bull. 189, 200 (1971), reprinted from 78 Yale L.J. 1128 (1969).

[17]United States ex rel. Horelick v. Criminal Court, 366 F.Supp. 1140 (S.D.N.Y.1973), rev'd on other grounds, 507 F.2d 37 (2d Cir.1974).

[18]Shuttlesworth v. Birmingham, 382 U.S. 87, 86 S.Ct. 211, 15 L.Ed.2d 176 (1965); Wright v. Georgia, 373 U.S. 284, 83 S.Ct. 1240, 10 L.Ed.2d 349 (1963).

[19]Walker v. Birmingham, 388 U.S. 307, 87 S.Ct. 1824, 18 L.Ed.2d 1210 (1967).

[20]United States ex rel. Horelick v. Criminal Court, 366 F.Supp. 1140 (S.D.N.Y.1973). As noted in Chenen, 5 U.S.F.L.Rev. 195, 207–08 (1971), this distinction is most persuasive where the unlawful police order infringed upon First Amendment rights, as it "is easy to see why it is absolutely necessary to protect the right to speak out at a particular time and place," but is arguably less persuasive where the unlawful police order infringed upon the subjects' right to equal protection (as in Wright v. Georgia, 373 U.S. 284, 83 S.Ct. 1240, 10 L.Ed.2d 349 (1963), where blacks were arrested for refusing to obey a policeman's order to leave a segregated park), as "it would not have been unreasonable, nor in any way have facilitated the deprivation of liberty, to have required of the demonstrator, like the resistor, compliance with the unlawful order and reliance on orderly judicial processes for redress." But, as Chenen notes at 208, "the equal protection cases do not involve the violence element which, by definition, is necessarily present in resistance to unlawful arrest."

As for the conclusion in *Curtis* that the statute does not sanction unlawful arrests, it has been argued that this is incorrect and that the " 'imperative of judicial integrity' requires recognition of the right to resist unlawful arrest" because "punishment for resisting unlawful arrest constitutes judicial validation of unconstitutional conduct."[21] But, even putting aside the apparently diminishing status of the goal "of enabling the judiciary to avoid the taint of partnership in official lawlessness,"[22] this argument is not persuasive. While the "partnership" characterization is understandable when a court receives into evidence objects obtained in violation of the Fourth Amendment, this is not the case when a court imposes sanctions for an unnecessary use of force against a policeman. The fact that the force was unnecessary in the sense that the arrestee's rights could be vindicated in court, rather than unnecessary in the sense that it produced greater injury than was needed to frustrate the arrest, does not manifest any greater degree of "judicial validation."

The conclusion in *Curtis* that the statute does not facilitate illegal arrests has also been challenged. It has been argued that the resistance rule, like the exclusionary rule, should be viewed from the standpoint of deterring future abuses, and it is said: "If resistance to unlawful arrest is punished, it would be to the advantage of police to arrest and search by force because even if

---

Regarding the unlawful arrest/police order distinction, consider also State v. Trane, 57 P.3d 1052 (Utah 2002) (while defendant's conduct was that he "began to physically struggle with the officers to prevent them from * * * arresting him," defendant charged under interfering-with-officer statute covering an "arrested person's refusal to perform any act required by lawful order * * * necessary to effect the arrest * * * made by a peace officer involved in the arrest"; defendant claims right to refuse "to follow an unlawful order," but court responds "there is no right to physically resist either an arrest or an order of the police," for the "law prefers judicial settlement of disputes over street brawls and altercations, even when the lawfulness of police conduct is in question").

[21]Chenen, 5 U.S.F.L.Rev. 195, 214 (1971). But, he apparently qualifies the objection when he notes: "While a court may have no problem overlooking a respectable but unlawful arrest, it may be much more difficult to overlook a clearly abusive one." Id. at 214–15. This relates to the due process argument discussed below.

One court appears to have accepted the argument. In State v. Bradshaw, 541 P.2d 800 (Utah 1975), the court held unconstitutionally vague a statute making it a crime for one to interfere with a person known to be a police officer, seeking to make an arrest of him or another, "regardless of whether there is a legal basis for the arrest." The vagueness holding seems to be based in part upon the conclusion that the statute could not mean what it says, for the court asserts: "If the intention of the legislature was to penalize a law-abiding citizen by incarceration because he did not willingly submit to an unlawful arrest, a statute authorizing the same is in violation of both the Utah and United States Constitutions * * * in that it permits and authorizes an arrest without probable cause and without lawful basis for the arrest."

[22]United States v. Calandra, 414 U.S. 338, 94 S.Ct. 613, 38 L.Ed.2d 561 (1974) (dissent, objecting that majority considered only deterrent function of exclusionary rule).

unlawfully obtained evidence is excluded, the police might nonetheless obtain a valid conviction for the provoked resistance
itself."[23] But to suggest that the typical illegal arrest, based upon
a police misjudgment of the sufficiency of the evidence at hand, is
made in the expectation that the arrestee may resist and
therefore supply a basis for his conviction, seems fanciful. And if
such a consequence is not ordinarily contemplated, then it is
unconvincing to say that the making of illegal arrests can be
deterred by manipulating the rules on the use of defensive force.

This is not to say, however, that the circumstances of all illegal
arrests are so unprovocative that a forcible response should be
deemed unreasonable. As one court noted: "Circumstances are
readily imaginable in which an arrest would be so flagrant an
intrusion on a citizen's rights that his resistance would be virtually inevitable."[24] In such a case, there is certainly merit to the
argument that conviction for the resistance would violate due
process. Put in the language the Supreme Court employed in
United States v. Russell,[25] this would be "a situation in which the
conduct of law enforcement agents is so outrageous that due process principles would absolutely bar the government from invoking judicial processes to obtain a conviction."[26]

§ 1.13(b) Other forms of self-help

Of the various other situations in which self-help has been
employed to prevent or terminate a violation of the Fourth
Amendment, the one coming closest to that discussed above is
when physical resistance is used against an illegal entry of
premises for purposes of making a search or arrest therein. In
United States v. Ferrone,[27] the court utilized analysis similar to
that in *Curtis* (discussed above) in rejecting the defendant's claim

---

[23]Chenen, 5 U.S.F.L.Rev. 195, 211 (1971).

[24]United States ex rel. Horelick v. Criminal Court, 366 F.Supp. 1140 (S. D.N.Y.1973). Similarly, Roberts v. State, 711 P.2d 1131 (Wyo.1985), states: "There may be situations in which police activity is so provocative and resistance so understandable that it can only be concluded that the po-lice were not engaged in the lawful performance of their officials duties," in which case "the resisters cannot be prosecuted under our resisting arrest statute." Thus, Chevigny, 7 Crim.L. LBull. 189, 203 (1971), observes: "The impairment of fourth amendment rights, however, is not enough to jus-tify resistance to an unlawful arrest. The problem is to determine the cir-cumstances under which such a sei-

zure becomes so provocative as to make unfair the imposition of a crimi-nal penalty for resisting it."

[25]United States v. Russell, 411 U.S. 423, 93 S.Ct. 1637, 36 L.Ed.2d 366 (1973).

[26]For a discussion of what circum-stances might be deemed to make the unlawful arrest sufficiently provoca-tive, see Chevigny, 7 Crim.L.Bull. 189 (1971).

[Section 1.13(b)]

[27]United States v. Ferrone, 438 F.2d 381 (3d Cir.1971). See also State v. Hatton, 116 Ariz. 142, 568 P.2d 1040 (1977); State v. Line, 121 Haw. 74, 214 P.3d 613 (2009) (no Fourth Amendment defense to hindering pros-ecution charge where defendant, in resisting police warrantless entry of

that he was entitled to forcibly resist the execution of an invalid search warrant:

> Society has an interest in securing for its members the right to be free from unreasonable searches and seizures. Society also has an interest, however, in the orderly settlement of disputes between citizens and their government; it has an especially strong interest in minimizing the use of violent self-help in the resolution of those disputes. We think a proper accommodation of those interests requires that a person claiming to be aggrieved by a search conducted by a peace officer pursuant to an allegedly invalid warrant test that claim in a court of law and not forcibly resist the execution of the warrant at the place of search. * * * Indeed, since the validity of written process is readily susceptible to judicial review, it is doubtful whether resistance to written process can ever be justified today, absent a showing of transparent invalidity.[28] This argument is particularly forceful when applied to the execution of search warrants, where resistance often leads to violence and physical injury. A public officer supported by written process has a right to expect that citizens will respond peaceable, that neither his life nor those of other parties will be endangered, and that any dispute will be resolved through legal means.

The *Ferrone* result is sound, for essentially the same reasons set out above concerning the *Curtis* rule. It is important to note, however, which is likewise consistent with the earlier discussion, that the *Ferrone* court intimated the result would be otherwise if the circumstances of the search had been so provocative that a

---

her home, "did not merely refuse to unlock her doors; she braced herself into the sliding glass door's opening * * *, blocking the officer's entry"); State v. Hoagland, 270 N.W.2d 778 (Minn.1978) (defendant properly convicted of obstructing legal process by threatening to kill officers who came onto his land to investigate suspected game violations, even if proposed search was illegal); State v. Panarello, 157 N.H. 204, 949 A.2d 732 (2008) (defendant properly convicted of pointing gun at officer who illegally entered his home); State v. Doe, 92 N.M. 100, 583 P.2d 464 (1978) (defendant properly convicted of battery on police officer who searched him after illegal arrest, where there was "no evidence that the booking officers were acting in bad faith or using unreasonable force").

Contra: People v. Stark, 120 Mich.App. 350, 327 N.W.2d 474 (1982) (where police entered without search warrant to arrest another person, "the defendants had a common law privilege to use reasonable force to prevent this search").

[28]The court dropped a footnote at this point saying: "We do not, however, mean to suggest that the 'transparent invalidity' exception applies to the rule we lay down today in connection with the execution of search warrants." But the court then gave the caution concerning searches under provocative circumstances, discussed in the text following.

The "transparent invalidity" qualification may have been added because of the fact that there is considerable authority to the effect that "the service of a writ or process may be resisted, without incurring criminal liability, where the process is issued by a court or officer not having jurisdiction in the premises or where the writ or process is 'void' on its face." See Annot., 10 A.L.R.3d 1146 (1966), also noting that there is considerable confusion in the cases as to precisely what constitutes void process.

reasonable man would resist.[29]

Sometimes defendants in situations resembling that in *Ferrone* have taken a different approach. Instead of, in effect, claiming a defense based upon the Fourth Amendment, they will invoke the exclusionary rule in an effort to exclude from evidence any testimony concerning their act of resistance. This not only permits them to rely upon the doctrine that testimony as to matters observed during an unlawful search is subject to suppression,[30] but also sets up a situation in which if they were to prevail they could escape conviction for resorting to even death-causing force.[31] Because "application of the exclusionary rule in such fashion would in effect give the victims of illegal searches a license to assault and murder,"[32] it is not surprising that the courts have held that an accused "cannot effectively invoke the fourth amendment to suppress evidence of his own unlawful conduct which was in response to police actions in violation of the amendment."[33]

Defendants have been equally unsuccessful in attempting, ei-

---

[29]In doing so, the court referred to Chevigny, 7 Crim.L.Bull. 189 (1971), which develops the argument for such an exception with respect to resistance to illegal arrest. The court also noted it was not deciding whether "a person would, under some circumstances, have a right to resist an unlawful *warrantless* search," although the fact there was no warrant would seem, at most, to bear upon the provocation question.

In State v. Gallagher, 191 Conn. 433, 465 A.2d 323 (1983), the court concluded: "Coupling an unlawful arrest with an unlawful entry adds to the seriousness of the governmental intrusion because of the recognized privacy interest that attaches to a private home. In such circumstances, it is reasonable to view the governmental intrusion as especially provocative and a defendant's resistance to entry and arrest as excusable and therefore privileged." For this reason, the court declined in the instant case to follow the *Curtis* line of cases and instead continued "to adhere to the common law view that there are circumstances where unlawful warrantless intrusion into the home creates a privilege to resist, and that punishment of such resistance is therefore improper."

In a curious decision that appears to intermix and confuse the doctrine discussed in this section with the

"other crimes" exception to the usual fruit-of-the-poisonous-tree rules, see § 11.4(j), the court in State v. Brocuglio, 264 Conn. 778, 826 A.2d 145 (2003), proceeded "to overrule *Gallagher* only to the extent that it conflicts with the new crime exception." That is, the court held "that the common-law privilege to challenge an unlawful entry into one's home still exists to the extent that a person's conduct does not rise to the level of a crime." The court then ruled, apparently on the ground that the change being made was both to the exclusionary rule and to the law regarding privileged resistance, that this change in the common law could not be applied retroactively to defendant's conduct.

[30]See Wong Sun v. United States, 371 U.S. 471, 83 S.Ct. 407, 9 L.Ed.2d 441 (1963), and § 11.4(h).

[31]See State v. Miller, 282 N.C. 633, 194 S.E.2d 353 (1973), where the defendant killed one of the officers executing an invalid search warrant.

[32]State v. Miller, 282 N.C. 633, 194 S.E.2d 353 (1973).

[33]People v. Abrams, 48 Ill.2d 446, 271 N.E.2d 37 (1971). See also State v. Boilard, 488 A.2d 1380 (Me.1985); State v. Kingery, 239 Mont. 160, 779 P.2d 495 (1989); State v. Guevara, 349 N.C. 243, 506 S.E.2d 711 (1998). But

ther by the defense-to-crime route or the exclusionary-rule route, to thwart conviction for other criminal efforts to prevent or terminate an illegal search or seizure. Thus, courts have upheld convictions for destroying evidence sought under an illegal warrant,[34] for eluding a police officer to avoid an illegal arrest,[35] for escape following an illegal seizure,[36] for falsely representing oneself as an American citizen,[37] and for attempting to bribe an

see State v. Hagler, 32 N.C.App. 444, 232 S.E.2d 712 (1977) (if uniformed police officer's entry into motel room was illegal, then defendant who put a gun to officer's stomach when the officer placed him under arrest could not be convicted of assault with a firearm upon a law enforcement officer while the officer was in the performance of his duties).

[34]United States v. Gibbons, 331 F.Supp. 970 (D.Del.1971), where the court relied upon *Ferrone* in holding that a defendant found eating gambling records upon entry of FBI agents executing an allegedly defective search warrant could be convicted of the offense of destroying property "before, during, or after seizure of any property by any person authorized to make searches and seizures, in order to prevent the seizure or securing" of the property.

[35]State v. Berker, 112 R.I. 624, 314 A.2d 11 (1974), noting that the court had previously held in State v. Ramsdell, 109 R.I. 320, 285 A.2d 399 (1971), that the state could make criminal forcible resistance to an illegal arrest, and concluding that "the considerations expressed in *Ramsdell* are equally applicable to the litigation before us and are dispositive of defendant's argument on this point. * * * The motorist seeking to escape the scrutiny of an approaching police officer poses a threat to the public's life, limb or property."

Consider also State v. Alexander, 157 Vt. 60, 595 A.2d 282 (1991) (even if roadblock illegal, defendant could still be convicted of failure to stop when signalled by police officer to do so, which occurred as he passed through that roadblock, as "a defendant who believes he is illegally detained may not resort to self-help");

State v. Mather, 28 Wash.App. 700, 626 P.2d 44 (1981) (where defendant convicted of driving in wanton and willful disregard for lives or property of others while attempting to elude police who had signaled defendant to stop, the statute constitutional even without a requirement that there be a basis for the stop, as "the constitutional right to be free from unreasonable searches and seizures does not create a constitutional right to react unreasonably to an unreasonable detention. The police power, therefore, may lawfully extend to prohibiting flight from an unlawful detention where that flight indicates a wanton and willful disregard for the life and property of others").

[36]Leshore v. State, 755 N.E.2d 164 (Ind.2001) ("just as a citizen may not resist arrest by a police officer even if the arrest later proves to be unlawful, * * * a citizen may not escape from a police officer's detention even if the grounds upon which the detention is based are later determined to be defective"); State v. Crawley, 187 N.J. 440, 901 A.2d 924 (2006) (even assuming "that seizure, which occurred pursuant to an investigatory stop," unreasonable, police officer was "lawfully performing an official function" even if reasonable suspicion lacking, and thus under obstruction of justice statute defendant's flight still an offense).

[37]United States v. Garcia-Jordan, 860 F.2d 159 (5th Cir.1988) (during arguably illegal stop near border, defendant produced false identification misrepresenting self as American citizen; court declares that a "person who is stopped or detained illegally is not immunized from prosecution for crimes committed during his detention period").

officer following an illegal arrest or search by that officer.[38] Illustrative is *Ellison v. State*,[39] upholding a charge of resisting arrest against a defendant who fled when, following an illegal traffic stop, he admitted he had no driver's license and the officer said he was under arrest. The court in *Ellison* rejected defendant's reliance on Supreme Court decisions holding defendants could not be punished for refusing to obey an illegal police order, as in those cases

> that obedience to the police orders would have forever deprived the defendants of their rights to engage in the protected activities and also would have denied them the opportunity to challenge the lawfulness of the police orders. [Those] orders are thus distinguishable from an arrest order since the latter order's propriety will necessarily be subject to subsequent judicial review at the election of the arrestee. Because of this significant distinction, the Court finds the reasoning in another line of cases to be more apposite * * *. These are cases like *Walker v. Birmingham*,[40] which holds that ex parte court injunctions, even if unconstitutional, must be obeyed until overturned or dissolved through proper judicial process. The crucial similarity between court injunctions and police arrest orders is that both are subject to prompt judicial review during which the propriety of such orders is fully open to attack by the aggrieved party. Where society has provided its members with a reasonable means to obtain prompt and impartial review of their legal disputes, the necessity for resort to self-help remedies is radically dissipated and society need no longer tolerate such efforts. Put another way, the State has an overriding interest in assuring that orderly judicial procedures established for the resolution of legal disputes are honored, for respect for the "rule of law" is the keystone to a modern civilized society.

These types of self-help may be less a matter of concern, however, as they do not involve the use of force against the police, and in that sense at least it might be said that the arguments deemed persuasive in *Curtis* and *Ferrone* carry little weight. It is nonetheless useful to ask, as in *Curtis,* whether permitting the conviction would facilitate or sanction Fourth Amendment violations. The question may be, as one commentator has suggested, whether such nonviolent acts of self-help are so infrequent and unpredictable that conviction would not encourage future illegal arrests and searches.[41]

Whatever the result in such circumstances, certainly the

---

[38]Vinyard v. United States, 335 F.2d 176 (8th Cir.1964); United States v. Troop, 235 F.2d 123 (7th Cir.1956); United States v. Perdiz, 256 F.Supp. 805 (S.D.N.Y.1966); People v. Guillory, 178 Cal.App.2d 854, 3 Cal.Rptr. 415 (1960).

[39]Ellison v. State, 410 A.2d 519 (Del.Super.1979).

[40]Walker v. Birmingham, 388 U.S. 307, 87 S.Ct. 1824, 18 L.Ed.2d 1210 (1967).

[41]Note, 8 UCLA L.Rev. 454 (1961). In Ellison v. State, 410 A.2d 519 (Del.Super.1979), the court, after noting that the record was "completely devoid of facts tending to show that the police attempted to harass, provoke or entrap the Appellant into resisting arrest," emphasized: "Flight from the police is not the natural,

Fourth Amendment bars criminal punishment of a mere failure
to surrender rights under that Amendment. Illustrative is *United
States v. Prescott*,[42] overturning the defendant's conviction for assisting a federal offender to hinder or prevent apprehension. The
conviction was based upon the defendant's conduct in not permitting federal agents to enter her apartment without a warrant, after which the agents made a forcible entry and found the fugitive
they were seeking. After concluding that the agents needed a
warrant to enter,[43] the court ruled:

> One cannot be penalized for passively asserting this right, regard-
> less of one's motivation. Just as a criminal suspect may validly
> invoke his Fifth Amendment privilege in an effort to shield himself
> from criminal liability, * * * so one may withhold consent to a war-
> rantless search, even though one's purpose be to conceal evidence of
> wrongdoing.
>
> Plainly [the Federal Tort Claims Act] is not a sufficient protector
> of the citizens' constitutional rights, and without a clear congressio-
> nal mandate we cannot hold that Congress relegated respondent
> exclusively to the FTCA remedy.
>
> Had Prescott forcibly resisted the entry into her apartment, we
> might have a different case. We express no opinion on that question.
> We only hold that her passive refusal to consent to a warrantless
> search is privileged conduct which cannot be considered as evidence
> of criminal wrongdoing. If the government could use such a refusal
> against the citizen, an unfair and impermissible burden would be
> placed upon the assertion of a constitutional right and future
> consents would not be "freely and voluntarily given."[44]

---

predictable or even likely reaction of
the average person who has been unconstitutionally stopped and arrested
for mere traffic offenses."

[42]United States v. Prescott, 581
F.2d 1343 (9th Cir.1978). See also
Freeman v. Gore, 483 F.3d 404 (5th
Cir.2007) ("refusal to consent to a warrantless search of her home cannot
itself provide probable cause to arrest
her for hindering apprehension");
Fletcher v. Town of Clinton, 196 F.3d
41 (1st Cir.1999) (refusal to consent to
warrantless search cannot justify arrest for hindering prosecution).

[43]On this issue, see § 6.1(b).

[44]There are cases, of course,
which appear to fall between the "forcibly resisted" and "passive refusal" categories. See, e.g., Dolson v. United
States, 948 A.2d 1193 (D.C.App.2008)
(where police seek to enter defendant's
premises in violation of Fourth
Amendment, defendant "may refuse to
take down a pre-established barrier,
e.g, to unlock a door," but the permissible "passive resistance or avoidance"
does not include "action that reinforces
an existing barrier, e.g., locking a
closed door, and even creation of a new
barrier, e.g., closing then locking a
door–or a gate"); State v. Pembaur, 9
Ohio St.3d 136, 459 N.E.2d 217 (1984)
(where defendant, doctor at medical
center, closed and barred door leading
from reception area to main office in
order to prevent service of bench warrants on two employees, court by analogy to *Curtis* rule upheld defendant's
conviction for obstructing official business, as "an occupant of business
premises cannot obstruct the officer in
the discharge of his duty, whether or
not the officer's actions are lawful
under the circumstances").

CHAPTER 2

PROTECTED AREAS AND INTERESTS

§ 2.1 The *Katz* expectation of privacy test

Research References

West's Key Number Digest
Arrest ⬥68(4); Searches and Seizures ⬥13 to 26

Legal Encyclopedias
C.J.S., Arrest §§ 3 to 4, 38, 43 to 49, 54; Searches and Seizures §§ 3 to 5, 8 to 16, 18, 20 to 24, 27 to 35, 37 to 38, 41, 47 to 48, 50, 58, 66 to 67, 70 to 76, 78, 102 to 103

Introduction

The Fourth Amendment guarantees "[t]he right of the people[1] to be secure in their persons, houses, papers, and effects, against unreasonable searches and seizures." The words "searches and seizures," as Professor Amsterdam has reminded us, "are terms of limitation. Law enforcement practices are not required by the Fourth Amendment to be reasonable unless they are either 'searches' or 'seizures.'"[2] Central to an understanding of the Fourth Amendment, therefore, is a perception of what police activities, under what circumstances and infringing upon what areas and interests, constitute either a search or a seizure within

---

[Section 2.1]

[1]Regarding whether the Fourth Amendment is best read as protecting the rights of individuals or of the people collectively, see Clancy, The Fourth Amendment as a Collective Right, 43 Tex. Tech L.Rev. 255 (2010).

[2]Amsterdam, Perspectives on the Fourth Amendment, 58 Minn.L.Rev. 349, 356 (1974).

the meaning of that Amendment.[3]

§ 2.1(a) Definition of "searches" and "seizures"

The word "seizures" in the Fourth Amendment has, in the main, not been a source of difficulty. The "act of physically taking and removing tangible personal property is generally a 'seizure.' "[4] Or, as the Supreme Court has put it, a "seizure" of property occurs when "there is some meaningful interference[5] with an

[3]If the police activity *is* a search or a seizure then typically it may be said that it is the Fourth Amendment and *only* the Fourth Amendment which determines the constitutionality of that activity. See Graham v. Connor, 490 U.S. 386, 109 S.Ct. 1865, 104 L.Ed.2d 443 (1989) (claims of excessive force in the course of an arrest or investigatory stop are to be evaluated under the Fourth Amendment, not under the "more generalized notion of 'substantive due process' "); Gerstein v. Pugh, 420 U.S. 103, 95 S.Ct. 854, 43 L.Ed.2d 54 (1975) (Fourth Amendment, rather than due process clause, determines the requisite post-arrest proceedings when defendants are detained on criminal charges).

But in United States v. James Daniel Good Real Property, 510 U.S. 43, 114 S.Ct. 492, 126 L.Ed.2d 490 (1993), the Court cautioned that "neither *Gerstein* nor *Graham* * * * provides support for the proposition that the Fourth Amendment is the beginning and end of the constitutional inquiry whenever a seizure occurs." The Court there went on to hold in this forfeiture proceeding that because the government "seized property not to preserve evidence of wrongdoing but to assert ownership and control of the property itself," a "purpose and effect [going] beyond the traditional meaning of search or seizure," such action "must comply with the Due Process Clauses of the Fifth and Fourteenth Amendments" as well as with the Fourth Amendment, which is not the case as to an ex parte seizure of real property absent exigent circumstances. However, "the remedy for an illegal ex parte seizure based on the Government's failure to establish exigent circumstances, where the Government is able to establish probable

cause to believe the property is connected to crime at the post-seizure adversarial hearing, is a recovery by the real property owner of rents or lost profits during the period of illegal seizure, with the Government retaining possession of the property until the forfeiture action is decided on the merits." United States v. Bowman, 341 F.3d 1228 (11th Cir.2003).

[Section 2.1(a)]

[4]68 Am.Jur.2d Searches and Seizures § 8 (1973). In Hale v. Henkel, 201 U.S. 43, 26 S.Ct. 370, 50 L.Ed. 652 (1906), the Court stated that "a seizure contemplates a forcible dispossession of the owner."

[5]Compare United States v. Ward, 144 F.3d 1024 (7th Cir.1998) (touching and removing bag from luggage compartment of bus no seizure); United States v. Gant, 112 F.3d 239 (6th Cir.1997) (removal of unattended bag from overhead compartment of bus to seat below no search); United States v. Gault, 92 F.3d 990 (10th Cir.1996) (kicking and lifting bag train passenger left unattended, protruding slightly into aisle, no search); United States v. TWP, 17 R 4, 970 F.2d 984 (1st Cir.1992) (issuance of arrest warrant in rem for real property did not result in seizure where marshal merely tacked the warrant on a tree and filed a lis pendens to inform title searches, as no "meaningful interference with an individual's possessory interests" in the property); United States v. Harvey, 961 F.2d 1361 (8th Cir.1992) (where bus stopped for cleaning and refueling and passengers out of bus, movement of luggage from overhead racks to floor so drug dogs could sniff it no seizure, as this not a case where luggage was taken "directly from their custody"; rather, the "lug-

individual's possessory interests[6] in that property."[7] Such is the

gage was moved from one public area * * * to another" and such "temporary removal of the bags caused no delay to appellant's travel," and thus there "was no meaningful interference with appellant's possessory interests in their baggage"); State v. McKinney, 185 Ariz. 567, 917 P.2d 1214 (1996) (where consent search of defendant's home, removal of watches from dresser drawer to top of dresser no seizure, as such movement "did not meaningfully interfere with or deprive Hedlund of any possessory interest in the watches"); Weishapl v. Sowers, 771 A.2d 1014 (D.C.App.2001) (where plaintiff in this § 1983 action, owner of restaurant in financial difficulties, obtained help of one Sowers, actually a con-artist, and Sowers then locked owner out of the business, after which police summoned by owner and asked by him to evict Somers failed to so act and instead recommended that owner leave, knowing the matter was in litigation, there was no seizure by the police, as "it cannot be said that the police * * * interfered with possession"); and consider the cases discussed in §§ 4.11(d), 6.7(b), 7.5(b) on whether an object seen in premises or a vehicle by a lawfully present police officer may, without probable cause, be moved slightly for examination.

But see United States v. Jones, __ U.S. __, 132 S.Ct. 945, 181 L.Ed.2d 911 (2012), discussed in § 2.7(e) (attaching GPS device to undercarriage of vehicle "for the purpose of obtaining information" is a *search*); Bond v. United States, 529 U.S. 334, 120 S.Ct. 1462, 146 L.Ed.2d 365 (2000), discussed in § 2.2(a) (squeezing carry-on luggage in bus a *search*); People v. Ortega, 34 P.3d 986 (Colo.2001) (where during bus stopover police officer removed defendant's suitcase from luggage compartment and subjected it to drug dog sniff, that no seizure, but where officer dressed in Greyhound uniform then boarded bus and asked that owner of bag identify it so new claim tag could be attached, and then officer accompanied by defendant walked back to garage with suitcase

and then questioned defendant, "there was a seizure of Defendant's suitcase because the officer's conduct caused a 'meaningful interference' with Defendant's possessory interest in the suitcase").

[6] And thus a seizure may occur because of an interference with that interest even as to property owned by the searching governmental unit. Lesher v. Reed, 12 F.3d 148 (8th Cir. 1994).

And a seizure may occur without any movement of the property. United States v. Bradley, 644 F.3d 1213 (11th Cir.2011) (where federal agents ordered company employees to "shut down" the company's computer servers, this "was a seizure"); Audio Odyssey, Ltd. v. Brenton First National Bank, 245 F.3d 721 (8th Cir.2001) ("the officers seized Audio Odyssey's premises by entering the store, ordering those inside to leave, arranging for the locks to be changed, and erecting 'No Trespassing' signs, thereby excluding the company's principals from the store's property"); State v. Smith, 327 Or. 366, 963 P.2d 642 (1998) ("the padlocking of defendant's storage unit" was a seizure, as "it deprived defendant of the use of the unit and access to its contents").

However, it has been held that "the Fourth Amendment protects an individual's interest in retaining possession of property but not the interest in regaining possession of property," so that there is no seizure upon a police refusal to return property earlier seized lawfully. Fox v. Van Oosterum, 176 F.3d 342 (6th Cir. 1999). Accord: Lee v. City of Chicago, 330 F.3d 456 (7th Cir.2003); United States v. Jakobetz, 955 F.2d 786 (2d Cir.1992).

[7] United States v. Jacobsen, 466 U.S. 109, 104 S.Ct. 1652, 80 L.Ed.2d 85 (1984).

As noted in Platteville Area Apartment Ass'n v. City of Platteville, 179 F.3d 574 (7th Cir.1999), a statement (such as in *Soldal* and *Jacobsen*) that a "seizure" refers to interference

case where, as in *Soldal v. Cook County*,[8] police assist a landlord in dispossessing a tenant by disconnecting the utilities from a trailer home and towing it off the property; where tenants are forcibly evicted, "even if in a more peaceful or traditional manner than in *Soldal*"[9]; and where significant damage has been caused to property.[10] And such is also the case where, as in *United States v. Jacobsen*,[11] government agents assert dominion and control[12]

with possessory interests apparently "means only that such an interference is actionable even if no invasion of privacy occurs, not that only possessory interests are protected," as a "person has no possessory interest in a telephone conversation" yet such is subject to seizure under the Supreme Court's analysis in Berger v. New York, 388 U.S. 41, 87 S.Ct. 1873, 18 L.Ed.2d 1040 (1967).

[8]Soldal v. Cook County, 506 U.S. 56, 113 S.Ct. 538, 121 L.Ed.2d 450 (1992).

[9]Thomas v. Cohen, 304 F.3d 563 (6th Cir.2002) (noting that *Soldal* "does not require that the 'meaningful interference' by governmental agents actually involve the physical seizure of the property in question"). See also Dixon v. Lowery, 302 F.3d 857 (8th Cir.2002) (where individual seeking fraudulent control of restaurant told police he needed their assistance while he changed locks and secured equipment and police, without questioning his authority, went to scene and stood by to maintain order while locks changed and employees of operator of restaurant ordered to leave and police then remained to guard the premises, facts are "much like those in *Soldal*" as police "helped effectuate the seizure" of the restaurant).

See also Revis v. Meldrum, 489 F.3d 273 (6th Cir.2007) (deputy's "actions in physically taking possession of Revis's house by having the locks changed, retaining a key, and evicting Revis demonstrably effected a seizure within the meaning of the Fourth Amendment").

[10]Maldonado v. Fontanes, 568 F.3d 263 (1st Cir.2009) ("killing a person's pet dog or cat * * * without the person's consent is also a seizure"); Viilo v. Eyre, 547 F.3d 707 (7th Cir.2008) ("the killing of a companion dog constitutes a 'seizure' "); Altman v. City of High Point, 330 F.3d 194 (4th Cir.2003) (animal control officers' actions of killing dog owners' dogs constituted a seizure of the owners' effects); Brown v. Muhlenberg Township, 269 F.3d 205 (3d Cir.2001) ("Destroying property meaningfully interferes with an individual's possessory interest in that property," and thus killing plaintiff's dog a seizure); Bonds v. Cox, 20 F.3d 697 (6th Cir.1994) (under *Soldal*, damage to house, including broken doors, mutilated vinyl siding, broken desks, and holes in walls, rises to the level of "meaningful interference" with one's possessory interests). See also Annot., 98 A.L.R.5th 305 (2002).

[11]United States v. Jacobsen, 466 U.S. 109, 104 S.Ct. 1652, 80 L.Ed.2d 85 (1984).

[12]In United States v. Allen, 644 F.2d 749 (9th Cir.1980), defendant accompanied officers to an airport police station and there refused to consent to search of his briefcase, after which an officer announced his intent to seize the case and to give defendant a receipt for it, and defendant remained while the receipt was prepared and in that interim made incriminating remarks. The court held the seizure occurred when the officer made the announcement, for then "a reasonable person would not have believed that he or she was free to leave the station with the briefcase," and thus the admissions could not be considered in determining if there was probable cause for the seizure.

The analysis in *Allen* must be compared with that in United States v. Letsinger, 93 F.3d 140 (4th Cir. 1996), where federal drug agents, after conversing with a train passenger, told him "they were going to detain his

over a package that was in transit[13] and not then in the immediate custody of the objecting party[14].

By contrast, the Court concluded in *United States v. Karo*,[15] merely placing an electronic tracking device into a container is not a seizure of it, for in such circumstances "it cannot be said that anyone's possessory interest was interfered with in a

---

bag." Neither the passenger nor the agents "took any steps toward the luggage" and the conversation continued until the passenger admitted there was marijuana in the bag, at which the agents searched it. The court rejected defendant's claim a seizure of the bag without reasonable suspicion occurred at the time the agents announced that they were going to detain it. The court reasoned: (i) "because the common law required actual custody," under that test the "bag obviously was not seized upon the officers' mere announcement"; (ii) it is unclear whether the "two exceptions to the general common law requirement of actual custody for seizure" stated in California v. Hodari D., 499 U.S. 621, 111 S.Ct. 1547, 113 L.Ed.2d 690 (1991), namely "a physical touching without control or a complied-with show of authority," may "ultimately be held to extend to objects as well as persons," for on the one hand *Hodari D.* itself noted that "common law seizure of inanimate objects, like common law seizure of even most animate objects, occurred only upon the exercise of physical control over the object," while on the other hand the *Jacobsen* definition of seizure of an object—"meaningful interference with . . . [a] possessory interest"—"follows directly from the parallel definition of the seizure of a person"; (iii) even assuming the *Hodari D.* exceptions also apply in the instant case, there is still no seizure, for (a) there "is no claim that the officers touched or applied any physical force to the bag until they actually took possession," (b) it is "quite possible" the agents' statement "did not constitute a show of authority" because it was "calmly uttered during an ongoing, casual, consensual conversation," "was not phrased as an 'order,'" and was not followed by any movement toward the bag, and (c) in any event

there was not submission to any show of authority, as the defendant "did not hand the officers the bag," "did not step out of the way to allow them access to the bag," and did not "even verbally assent to their detention of it," but instead "continued to try to dissuade the officers yet again from taking the bag."

Also, "there is no seizure within the meaning of the Fourth Amendment when an object discovered in a private search is voluntarily relinquished to the government." United States v. Coleman, 628 F.2d 961 (6th Cir.1980), relying upon Coolidge v. New Hampshire, 403 U.S. 443, 91 S.Ct. 2022, 29 L.Ed.2d 564 (1971). See also State v. Badger, 141 Vt. 430, 450 A.2d 336 (1982) (seizure in instant case because "although the items were physically handed to the police," unlike *Coolidge* the court here "found that the consent to these transfers was involuntary"). But, even if there has been no seizure there remains the question of whether the police may now search that object; see §§ 1.8(b), 5.5(b).

[13]Compare United States v. Clutter, 674 F.3d 980 (8th Cir.2012) (curiously concluding "no Fourth Amendment 'seizure' occurred" here, where police took away defendant's computer with consent of defendant's father, "who was in actual possession," because such action "did not meaningfully interfere with [defendant's] possession," given that he "was in jail at the time).

[14]There is not agreement, however, as to precisely when this is the case. This matter is considered in § 9.8(e).

[15]United States v. Karo, 468 U.S. 705, 104 S.Ct. 3296, 82 L.Ed.2d 530 (1984).

meaningful way."[16] Similarly, the Court declared in *Arizona v. Hicks*,[17] merely recording serial numbers observed on equipment "did not 'meaningfully interfere' with respondent's possessory interest in either the serial numbers or the equipment, and therefore did not amount to a seizure."[18] Likewise, the act of an undercover agent in purchasing obscene magazines offered for sale in a store, the Court concluded in *Maryland v. Macon*,[19] is not a Fourth Amendment seizure, for the seller had thereby "voluntarily transferred any possessory interest he may have had in the magazine to the purchaser upon the receipt of the funds."[20]

---

[16]Stevens, J., joined by Marshall and Brennan, JJ., dissenting in part, disagreed: "The owner of property, of course, has a right to exclude from it all the world, including the Government, and a concomitant right to use it exclusively for his own purposes. When the Government attaches an electronic monitoring device to that property, it infringes that exclusionary right; in a fundamental sense it has converted the property to its own use. Surely such an invasion is an 'interference' with possessory rights; the right to exclude, which attached as soon as the can respondents purchased was delivered, had been infringed. That interference is also 'meaningful'; the character of the property is profoundly different when infected with an electronic bug than when it is entirely germ free."

But in United States v. Jones, ___ U.S. ___, 132 S.Ct. 945, 181 L.Ed.2d 911 (2012), the Court held that attaching a GPS device to the undercarriage of a vehicle "for the purpose of obtaining information" is a *search*. As noted in Priester, Five Answers and Three Questions After United States v. Jones (2012), the Fourth Amendment "GPS case," http://papers.ssrn.com/sol3/papers.cfm?abstract_id=2030390 n. 43 (2012): "By defining a Fourth Amendment 'search' of an enumerated protected category to require both a technical trespass *and* an attempt to obtain information, the Court also resolved what could have ben potentially broad ramifications for civil liability under 42 U.S.C. § 1983," as the Court's precedents "meant that mere trespass * * * was not actionable under § 1983."

[17]Arizona v. Hicks, 480 U.S. 321, 107 S.Ct. 1149, 94 L.Ed.2d 347 (1987).

[18]"By a parallel process of reasoning, it follows that the recording of visual images of a scene by means of photography does not amount to a seizure because it does not 'meaningfully interfere' with any possessory interest." Bills v. Aseltine, 958 F.2d 697 (6th Cir.1992).

The copying of computer records may be another matter. See text in § 2.6 at note 293.

[19]Maryland v. Macon, 472 U.S. 463, 105 S.Ct. 2778, 86 L.Ed.2d 370 (1985).

[20]The Court in *Macon* added that First Amendment interests did not require a contrary result, as the "risk of prior restraint, which is the underlying basis for the special Fourth Amendment protections accorded searches for and seizures of First Amendment materials, does not come into play in such cases." As for defendant's argument that the purchase was a seizure because the undercover officer had intended from the very beginning to retrieve the purchase money upon the seller's arrest, the Court said this was not so under the *Scott* objective test, discussed in § 1.4, as "[o]bjectively viewed, the transaction was a sale in the ordinary course of business." If the retrieval of the money was wrongful, the Court added, then it is the money, not the items purchased with it, that should be suppressed.

Likewise, rental of a videotape is no seizure. State ex rel. Eckstein v. Video Express, 119 Ohio App.3d 261, 695 N.E.2d 38 (1997) (and result not

While such cases as *Katz v. United States*,[21] discussed herein,[22] demonstrate that the Fourth Amendment is only marginally concerned with property rights, this does not mean that the Amendment has no application to a seizure unaccompanied by a search. The Supreme Court expressly rejected such a view in *Soldal v. Cook County*,[23] where police became involved in a landlord's efforts to dispossess his tenant by having the tenant's house trailer towed off the landlord's property, resulting in a § 1983 action against the police. The court of appeals affirmed the trial court's grant of the defendant's motion for summary judgment, reasoning that what had occurred was a seizure in a literal sense but not in the Fourth Amendment sense because the plaintiff's privacy had not been invaded. In rejecting that view, the Supreme Court noted that the court of appeals had provided "no justification for departing from our prior cases,"[24] which "unmistakably hold that the Amendment protects property as well as privacy."[25]

It is less apparent when (or if) intangibles may be said to have been seized, although the Supreme Court has assumed[26]—albeit over strong objection[27]—that eavesdropping upon or recording of

---

different where investigator who rented tapes copied them, as there "no indication that the state violated any express terms of the rental," there "no indication [defendant] holds a copyright over the contents of the videotapes," and "no other compelling explanation of how the state compromised her possessory interest in the videotapes").

[21]Katz v. United States, 389 U.S. 347, 88 S.Ct. 507, 19 L.Ed.2d 576 (1967).

[22]See § 2.1(b).

[23]Soldal v. Cook County, 506 U.S. 56, 113 S.Ct. 538, 121 L.Ed.2d 450 (1992). The significance of *Soldal* is explored in Heffernan, Property, Privacy and the Fourth Amendment, 60 Brook.L.Rev. 633 (1994). For more on the Fourth Amendment and property interests, see Clancy, What Does the Fourth Amendment Protect: Property, Privacy, or Security, 33 Wake Forest L.Rev. 307 (1998); Cloud, The Fourth Amendment During the Lochner Era: Privacy, Property and Liberty in Constitutional Theory, 48 Stan.L.Rev. 555 (1996).

[24]See, e.g., Horton v. California, 496 U.S. 128, 110 S.Ct. 2301, 110 L.Ed.2d 112 (1990); Arizona v. Hicks, 480 U.S. 321, 107 S.Ct. 1149, 94 L.Ed.2d 347 (1987); Maryland v. Macon, 472 U.S. 463, 105 S.Ct. 2778, 86 L.Ed.2d 370 (1985); United States v. Jacobsen, 466 U.S. 109, 104 S.Ct. 1652, 80 L.Ed.2d 85 (1984).

[25]See also Cochran v. Gilliam, 656 F.3d 300 (6th Cir.2011) (seizure of plaintiff's personal property); Lesher v. Reed, 12 F.3d 148 (8th Cir.1994) (police seizure of dog fits "within Fourth Amendment" though no search involved).

[26]See Berger v. New York, 388 U.S. 41, 87 S.Ct. 1873, 18 L.Ed.2d 1040 (1967), declaring that "authorization of eavesdropping for a two month period is the equivalent of a series of intrusions, searches, *and seizures* pursuant to a single showing of probable cause" (emphasis added). Compare Olmstead v. United States, 277 U.S. 438, 48 S.Ct. 564, 72 L.Ed. 944 (1928), concerning wiretapping, where the Court said "[t]here was no seizure" because the "evidence was secured by the use of the sense of hearing and that only."

[27]Namely, Black, J., dissenting in *Berger* ("It simply requires an imaginative transformation of the English

conversations constitutes a seizure of those conversations.[28] As for the seizure of a person, this includes not only full-fledged arrests,[29] but also "investigatory detentions"[30] and any other "detention of the [person] against his will."[31] All that is required, the

---

language to say that conversations can be searched and words seized"); Harlan, J., dissenting in *Berger* ("Just as some exercise of dominion, beyond mere perception, is necessary for the seizure of tangibles, so some use of the conversation beyond the initial listening process is required for the seizure of the spoken word"); White, J., dissenting in *Berger* ("Recording an innocent conversation is no more a 'seizure' than occurs when the policeman personally overhears conversation while conducting a warranted search").

These objections arguably have taken on greater force with the holding in Arizona v. Hicks, 480 U.S. 321, 107 S.Ct. 1149, 94 L.Ed.2d 347 (1987), that making a record of what is *seen* is no seizure.

[28]By analogy to *Berger,* it was held in LeClair v. Hart, 800 F.2d 692 (7th Cir.1986), citing other cases in accord, that dictating verbatim into a recorder the contents of documents amounted to a seizure of those contents.

[29]Henry v. United States, 361 U.S. 98, 80 S.Ct. 168, 4 L.Ed.2d 134 (1959). See also Tennessee v. Garner, 471 U.S. 1, 105 S.Ct. 1694, 85 L.Ed.2d 1 (1985), noting that "there can be no question that apprehension by the use of deadly force is a seizure subject to the reasonableness requirement of the Fourth Amendment."

[30]Davis v. Mississippi, 394 U.S. 721, 89 S.Ct. 1394, 22 L.Ed.2d 676 (1969).

[31]Cupp v. Murphy, 412 U.S. 291, 93 S.Ct. 2000, 36 L.Ed.2d 900 (1973). This includes such detentions even when they are unrelated to enforcement of the criminal law. See, e.g., Pino v. Higgs, 75 F.3d 1461 (10th Cir.1996) (seizure for emergency mental health evaluation).

It has also been held to include pretrial release attended by certain conditions. See Evans v. Ball, 168 F.3d 856 (5th Cir.1999) (following *Gallo,* infra, court holds defendant had been seized when he received a "summons to appear in court, coupled with the requirements that he obtain permission before leaving the state, report regularly to pretrial services, sign a personal recognizance bond, and provide federal officers with financial and identification information"); Gallo v. City of Philadelphia, 161 F.3d 217 (3d Cir.1998) (though a "close question," court concludes defendant had been seized, though never formally arrested, when his "post-indictment liberty was restricted in the following ways: he had to post a $10,000 bond, he had to attend all court hearings including his trial and arraignment, he was required to contact Pretrial Services on a weekly basis, and he was prohibited from traveling outside New Jersey and Pennsylvania"); Murphy v. Lynn, 118 F.3d 938 (2d Cir.1997) ("while a state has the undoubted authority, in connection with a criminal proceeding, to restrict a properly accused citizen's constitutional right to travel outside of the state as a condition of his pretrial release, and may order him to make periodic court appearances, such conditions are appropriately viewed as seizures within the meaning of the Fourth Amendment"). From *Gallo,* supra, it has been concluded "that when a material witness is subjected to constitutionally significant restrictions of her liberty for the purpose of securing her appearance at [another's] trial, those restrictions are governed by the Fourth Amendment." Schneyder v. Smith, 653 F.3d 313 (3d Cir. 2011).

Compare Harrington v. City of Nashua, 610 F.3d 24 (1st Cir.2010) (pretrial release conditions that arrestee notify court of any change of address, refrain from committing crimes, and forebear from consuming controlled substances or excessive quantities of alcohol not a seizure); Nielander v. Board of County Commissioners,

Court declared in *Terry v. Ohio*,[32] is that an "officer, by means of physical force or show of authority,[33] has in some way restrained[34] the liberty of a citizen"[35] (which, when there is no physical force to restrain movement,[36] means the person must have submitted

---

582 F.3d 1155 (10th Cir.2009) (rejecting plaintiff's argument "he was 'seized' because the criminal summons had a legal effect on his freedom of movement" in that "it precluded him from starting his out-of-state job"); Bielanski v. County of Kane, 550 F.3d 632 (7th Cir.2008) (summons requiring appearance in court and court order requiring permission to leave the state did not constitute a seizure); Becker v. Kroll, 494 F.3d 904 (10th Cir.2007) (distinguishing *Evans*, *Gallo* and *Murphy*, court holds "criminal charge" not a seizure when not "coupled with another significant restraint on liberty, such as restrictions on travel"); Shell v. United States, 448 F.3d 951 (7th Cir.2006) (placing bug on prison visitor's badge not a seizure of visitor, who failed to show this "in any way restrained his liberty"); Karam v. City of Burbank, 352 F.3d 1188 (9th Cir.2003) (conditions of pretrial release that plaintiff make court appearances and not depart state without court's permission did not rise to level of seizure); Johnson v. City of Cincinnati, 310 F.3d 484 (6th Cir.2002) (ordinance banning persons arrested for or convicted of drug crime from "drug exclusion zones" for 90 days not a seizure, as it "imposes solely travel restrictions" for period "not bounded by an eventual court appearance"); Nieves v. McSweeney, 241 F.3d 46 (1st Cir.2001) (while imposition here "marginally greater" than that in *Britton*, because arrestee required to appear several times in court, *Evans*, *Gallo* and *Murphy* distinguished because they "involved definitive restrictions on the right to travel"); Britton v. Maloney, 196 F.3d 24 (1st Cir.1999) (no seizure where Britton never arrested but just received summons in the mail, and his "criminal prosecution * * * did not impose any restrictions on his liberty other than the legal obligation to appear in court at a future date"). Cf. Jefferson v. City of

Omaha Police Department, 335 F.3d 804 (8th Cir.2003) (where consensual encounter resulted in issuance of a citation, court doubts there any seizure "during the time that it took to issue the citation"); Williams v. Chai-Hsu Lu, 335 F.3d 807 (8th Cir.2003) ("court's mere acquisition of jurisdiction over a person in a civil case by service of process is not a seizure").

[32] Terry v. Ohio, 392 U.S. 1, 88 S.Ct. 1868, 20 L.Ed.2d 889 (1968).

[33] Where a person, upon learning a warrant has been issued for his arrest, appears at the police station and turns himself in, such "surrender to the State's show of authority constitutes a seizure for purposes of the Fourth Amendment." Albright v. Oliver, 510 U.S. 266, 114 S.Ct. 807, 127 L.Ed.2d 114 (1994) (plurality opinion).

[34] If the person was seized earlier and remains in a state of seizure, police movement of him from one location to another does not constitute a second seizure. Commonwealth v. Bomar, 573 Pa. 426, 826 A.2d 831 (2003).

[35] For further discussion of what it takes to constitute such a restraint, see § 9.4. As explained in § 9.8(a), appearance in response to a subpoena is not a "seizure" of the person.

[36] Compare Acevedo v. Canterbury, 457 F.3d 721 (7th Cir.2006) (distinguishing *McCoy*, infra, as here officer knocked victim "to the ground in a location far away from his home under the general control of the police," causing victim "to black out momentarily"); Carr v. Tatangelo, 338 F.3d 1259 (11th Cir.2003) (where plaintiff struck by bullet from police officer's gun when officer "had shot to kill" but was able to keep running, this was a seizure "when the bullet struck or contacted him" notwithstanding absence of submission); with McCoy v. Harrison, 341 F.3d 600 (7th Cir.2003)

to the assertion of authority[37]). But as the Court later cautioned, "a person has been 'seized' within the meaning of the Fourth Amendment only if, in view of all of the circumstances surrounding the incident, a reasonable person would have believed that he was not free to leave"[38] (except that when a person's "freedom of movement [is] restricted by a factor independent of police

---

(slapping plaintiff's face not a seizure, as "there is no evidence to show he intended to or did acquire physical control over her person").

[37]California v. Hodari D., 499 U.S. 621, 111 S.Ct. 1547, 113 L.Ed.2d 690 (1991), discussed in § 9.4(d) in a stop-and-frisk context. See also Mettler v. Whitledge, 165 F.3d 1197 (8th Cir.1999) (dispatching a police dog to locate person in a garage not a seizure here, as no evidence of physical contact or acquiescence to assertion of police authority); State v. Reynolds, 264 Conn. 1, 836 A.2d 224 (2003) (where police sealed off neighborhood including apartment building within which defendant in bed at time, this not a seizure, as no evidence defendant aware of that police action, so there "nothing in the record to establish either that the defendant believed that he was not free to leave or that he submitted to a show of police force or authority").

[38]United States v. Mendenhall, 446 U.S. 544, 100 S.Ct. 1870, 64 L.Ed.2d 497 (1980) (opinion of Stewart, J., announcing judgment of the Court). This test was adopted by a majority of the Court in Florida v. Royer, 460 U.S. 491, 103 S.Ct. 1319, 75 L.Ed.2d 229 (1983), and is discussed further in § 9.4. See, e.g., American Federation of Labor and Congress of Indus Organizations v. City of Miami, FL, 637 F.3d 1178 (11th Cir.2011) (police response to protesters whereby they "forced off Biscayne Boulevard" no seizure, as protesters "still had the ability to * * * walk away" via a side street); Watchtower Bible and Tract Society of New York, Inc. v. Sagardia De Jesus, 634 F.3d 3 (1st Cir.2011) ("a Jehovah's Witness halted at an urbanization barrier need not answer questions or remain at the barrier; anyone so questioned is free to walk or to drive way," and thus no seizure); Reyes

v. Maschmeier, 446 F.3d 1199 (11th Cir.2006) (where sergeant/supervisor struck sheriff's department employee on back of head with 3-ring binder, no seizure, as no restraint on employee's ability to move, and feeling by employee that she not free to leave was based entirely on supervisor-employee relationship); White v. City of Markham, 310 F.3d 989 (7th Cir.2002) (where "police, by threatening arrest, prevent a current or former resident from remaining on their premises," but "resident was free to travel anywhere else," court finds it need not decide difficult question of whether that was a seizure); Laughlin v. Olszewski, 102 F.3d 190 (5th Cir.1996) (where police officer told plaintiff to leave corporation's premises and plaintiff did leave, no arrest; plaintiff "was not only free to leave; he was told he would be arrested if he did *not* leave"); Sheppard v. Beerman, 18 F.3d 147 (2d Cir.1994) (where fired law clerk escorted from courthouse by court officers, no seizure, as he "was 'free to go anywhere else that he desired,' with the exception of * * * the court house").

Compare Estate of Bennett v. Wainwright, 548 F.3d 155 (1st Cir.2008) (a seizure here, as while occupants of residence "were free to leave," due to police show of authority "they were not free to stay and thus, their liberty interest was impinged upon"); Thames Shipyard & Repair Co. V. United States, 350 F.3d 247 (1st Cir.2003) (Coast Guard's forcible evacuation of a sinking sea vessel constituted a seizure of the persons therein); United States v. Enslin, 327 F.3d 788 (9th Cir.2003) (where man lying in bed under covers was ordered to show his hands, that a seizure because a "reasonable person in Enslin's situation would not have felt free to ignore the request").

conduct," then "the appropriate inquiry is whether a reasonable person would feel free to decline the officers' request or otherwise terminate the encounter"[39]). In addition, however, it is necessary that there have been "a governmental termination of freedom of movement *through means intentionally applied,*" as the Fourth Amendment does not address "the accidental effects of otherwise lawful government conduct."[40]

---

[39]Florida v. Bostick, 501 U.S. 429, 111 S.Ct. 2382, 115 L.Ed.2d 389 (1991). See, e.g., United States v. Reeves, 524 F.3d 1161 (10th Cir.2008) (seizure where police after 2:43 a.m. engaged in "twenty minutes of banging and yelling" at defendant's motel room door); United States v. Jerez, 108 F.3d 684 (7th Cir.1997) (where deputies knocked on motel room door at 11:00 p.m. for 3 minutes, made commands and requests to open the door, knocked for 1½ to 2 minutes on outside of window, and shone flashlight through small opening in window's drapes into face of one defendant as he lay in bed, collectively manifesting "the law enforcement officers refused to take 'no' for an answer," this constituted a seizure under the *Bostick* test); Commonwealth v. Ramos, 430 Mass. 545, 721 N.E.2d 923 (2000) (where police congregated outside defendant's apartment and notified her that they would not leave until she came out of apartment and that, if she continued to refuse, they would have fire department break down door, defendant was seized within meaning of state constitution).

Compare Estate of Bennett v. Wainwright, 548 F.3d 155 (1st Cir.2008) (no seizure from fact that police established a perimeter around the residence, as no showing that occupant "submitted to the restriction imposed by the police perimeter" or, indeed, "even knew that the * * * residence had ben cordoned off").

[40]Brower v. County of Inyo, 489 U.S. 593, 109 S.Ct. 1378, 103 L.Ed.2d 628 (1989), explaining: "Thus, if a parked and unoccupied police car slips its brake and pins a passerby against a wall, it is likely that a tort has occurred, but not a violation of the Fourth Amendment. And the situation would not change if the passerby happened, by lucky chance, to be a serial murderer for whom there was an outstanding arrest warrant—even if, at the time he was thus pinned, he was in the process of running away from two pursuing constables. * * * That is the reason there was no seizure in the hypothetical situation that concerned the Court of Appeals. The pursuing police car sought to stop the suspect only by the show of authority represented by flashing lights and continuing pursuit; and though he was in fact stopped, he was stopped by a different means—his loss of control of his vehicle and the subsequent crash. If, instead of that, the police cruiser had pulled alongside the fleeing car and sideswiped it, producing the crash, then the termination of the suspect's freedom of movement would have been a seizure." So too, as stated in Berg v. County of Allegheny, 219 F.3d 261 (3d Cir.2000), citing cases in support: "[I]f a police officer fires his gun at a fleeing robbery suspect and the bullet inadvertently strikes an innocent bystander, there has been no Fourth Amendment seizure. * * * If, on the other hand, the officer fires his gun directly at the innocent bystander in the mistaken belief that the bystander is the robber, then a Fourth Amendment seizure has occurred."

Compare Eldredge v. Town of Falmouth, Massachusetts, 662 F.3d 100 (1st Cir.2011) (where two police cars speeding to same emergency call and front car suddenly decelerated and was struck by second car, which caromed off lead car and hit pedestrian, there no seizure under *Brower*, as no showing officer driving second car "intended to stop the plaintiff by striking him with his cruiser"); United States v. Al Nasser, 555 F.3d 722 (9th Cir.2009) (where border patrol agent

The meaning of the word "searches," the matter of primary concern in this Chapter, is not as easily captured within any verbal formulation. Under the traditional approach, the term "search" is said to imply

> some exploratory investigation, or an invasion and quest, a looking for or seeking out. The quest may be secret, intrusive, or accomplished by force, and it has been held that a search implies some sort of force, either actual or constructive, much or little. A search implies a prying into hidden places for that which is concealed and that the object searched for has been hidden or intentionally put out of the way. While it has been said that ordinarily searching is a function of sight, it is generally held that the mere looking at that which is open to view is not a "search."[41]

Similar language is to be found in a great many appellate decisions.[42]

The Supreme Court, quite understandably, has never managed to set out a comprehensive definition of the word "searches" as it is used in the Fourth Amendment. Many years ago the Court asserted that "a search ordinarily implies a quest by an officer of

---

had stopped five vehicles on the road at night and, when defendant approached in his vehicle, agent shined his flashlight only to avoid being hit, but defendant then stopped, possibly because he thought agent was signaling him to stop, there no seizure under *Inyo*, as "the means that led him to stop-the lights, stopped vehicles and officer directing traffic-were not 'means intentionally applied' to bring about the stop of Al Nasser's car"); Schultz v. Braga, 455 F.3d 470 (4th Cir.2006) (even if driver of car stopped by FBI agents was target of seizure and it foreseeable by agent who shot passenger that driver could also be injured by that shooting, agent not liable to driver under Fourth Amendment for excessive force used against passenger, since driver not the target of seizure effectuated by excessive force); with Henry v. Purnell, 501 F.3d 374 (4th Cir.2007) ("a seizure surely occurred here where Purnell intended to stop Henry by firing a weapon at him and succeeded in doing so," even though he intended to draw and shoot with his Taser rather than his firearm); Flores v. City of Palacios, 381 F.3d 391 (5th Cir.2004) (where defendant police officer shot at plaintiff's car and hit muffler and plaintiff heard something

hit her car and stopped to investigate, this a seizure because "the termination of her freedom of movement was accomplished by exactly the means he intentionally applied"); Vaughan v. Cox, 343 F.3d 1323 (11th Cir.2003) (under *Brower* rule, it "is not necessary for the means by which a suspect is seized to conform exactly to the means intended by the officer," and thus where officer fired at fleeing truck intending to disable either the vehicle or the driver but the bullet struck passenger, the "means intentionally applied" test met, as officer fired to stop vehicle and all occupants).

[41] C.J.S., Searches and Seizures § 1 (1952).

[42] See, e.g., Doe v. Heck, 327 F.3d 492 (7th Cir.2003) (thus police in coming onto property of private school "for the specific purpose of gathering information" was "an activity that most certainly constitutes a search"); Brown v. State, 372 P.2d 785 (Alaska 1962); People v. Holloway, 230 Cal.App.2d 834, 41 Cal.Rptr. 325 (1964); People v. Exum, 382 Ill. 204, 47 N.E.2d 56 (1943); State v. Coolidge, 106 N.H. 186, 208 A.2d 322 (1965); State v. Smith, 242 N.C. 297, 87 S.E.2d 593 (1955).

the law,"[43] but no one has ever suggested that every "act or instance of seeking"[44] is a search in the Fourth Amendment sense[45] (although the fact the officer was *not* looking for something ordinarily[46] is not alone a basis for concluding there was no search[47]). Indeed, on occasion the Court has held that certain po-

---

[43]Hale v. Henkel, 201 U.S. 43, 26 S.Ct. 370, 50 L.Ed. 652 (1906).

[44]"Quest" is so defined. Webster's Third New International Dictionary 1863 (1961).

[45]Thus, where an officer asked the defendant what he had in his pocket and the defendant handed over the objects, there was no search. Neely v. State, 402 So.2d 477 (Fla.App.1981). Cf. Coolidge v. New Hampshire, 403 U.S. 443, 91 S.Ct. 2022, 29 L.Ed.2d 564 (1971) (where police asked defendant's wife if there were guns in the house and she then produced them and turned them over to the police, Court declined to "hold that the conduct of the police here was a search and seizure"); Janecka v. Cockrell, 301 F.3d 316 (5th Cir.2002) (where woman "handed the gun and the mace to Detective McAnulty voluntarily while he was interviewing her," there was no search).

This is not to suggest than in every case where the physical action revealing the object is by someone other than the police that there has been no search. Compare with the prior cases State v. Naeole, 80 Haw. 419, 910 P.2d 732 (1996) (where defendant removed items from her pants "in response to [officer's] direct order, thus creating an involuntary removal, it constituted a search");In re Anthony F., 163 N.H. 163, 37 A.3d 429 (2012) (collecting cases in accord, court holds that if in response to police claim of right to make warrantless search defendant hands over the sought items, this constitutes a search).

[46]But consider United States v. Jones, _ U.S. _, 132 S.Ct. 945, 181 L.Ed.2d 911 (2012), holding that a trespass, there attaching a GPS device to the undercarriage of a vehicle, is a search if done "for the purpose of obtaining information." As noted in Priester, Five Answers and Three Questions After United States v. Jones (2012), the Fourth Amendment "GPS case," http://papers.ssrn.com/sol3/papers.cfm?abstract_id=2030390 n. 43 (2012): "By defining a Fourth Amendment 'search' of an enumerated protected category to require both a technical trespass *and* an attempt to obtain information, the Court also resolved what could have ben potentially broad ramifications for civil liability under 42 U.S.C. § 1983," as the Court's precedent "meant that mere trespass * * * was not actionable under § 1983."

[47]In United States v. Maple, 334 F.3d 15 (D.C.Cir.2003), an officer securing an automobile in lieu of impounding it saw a cellphone while in the vehicle and decided to put it somewhere out of view of passersby, which was why he opened a console between the seat, revealing a gun. The court noted that in Kyllo v. United States, 533 U.S. 27, 121 S.Ct. 2038, 150 L.Ed.2d 94 (2001), the Court had stated that "when the Fourth Amendment was adopted, as now, to 'search' meant '[t]o look over or through *for the purpose* of finding something; to explore; to examine by inspection; as, to search the house for a book; to search the wood for a thief.'" The court then ruled that because when the officer "opened the console he was not looking for 'something,'" it "follows then that he did not conduct a 'search,'" any more than "if an officer legitimately in a house to interview a witness attempts to leave the house and inadvertently walks into a closet next to an exit door and sees guns and drugs." But upon rehearing, 348 F.3d 260 (D.C.Cir.2003), the *Maple* court concluded otherwise. Quoting language from Bond v. United States, 529 U.S. 334, 120 S.Ct. 1462, 146 L.Ed.2d 365 (2000), the court concluded that " 'the issue is not' the law enforcement officer's 'state of mind'—whether he

lice efforts in seeking out evidence of crime[48] were not Fourth Amendment searches, as in three cases decided during the 1920's. In *Hester v. United States*,[49] the Court asserted that "the special protection accorded by the Fourth Amendment to the people in their 'persons, houses, papers and effects,' is not extended to the open fields," and thus held that revenue officers made no search when, while trespassing on defendant's land, they observed his incriminating conduct. And in *United States v. Lee*,[50] where the boatswain on a Coast Guard patrol boat shined a searchlight on the deck of a motorboat and saw cases of liquor, the Court unhesitantly concluded that "no search on the high seas is shown." A year later, in *Olmstead v. United States*,[51] the Court held that the placing of a tap on telephone wires and thereby eavesdropping upon defendant's telephone conversations "did not amount to a search * * * within the meaning of the Fourth Amendment," for the reason that the "wires are not part of his house or office, any more than are the highways along which they are stretched." What these and other decisions of the Court added up to, as the Supreme Court was later to put it, was that for there to be a Fourth Amendment search the police must have physically intruded into "a constitutionally protected area."[52] These areas were those enumerated in the Fourth Amendment itself: "persons," including the bodies[53] and clothing[54] of individuals; "houses," including apartments,[55] hotel rooms,[56] garages,[57]

---

was intentionally rummaging about for contraband or wished to find something in particular—'but the objective effect of his actions'—whether a reasonable expectation of privacy was infringed." Accord: Commonwealth v. Lopez, 458 Mass. 383, 937 N.E.2d 949 (2010) (rejecting court of appeals' conclusion that officer's entry of motel room no search because he did not enter with the purpose of conducting a search; "inquiry into an officer's intent * * * is not a factor in determining whether a search in the constitutional sense took place").

[48]The claim that there is no "search" under the Fourth Amendment if the purpose is other than a criminal investigation has been rightly rejected. See Nakamoto v. Fasi, 64 Haw. 17, 635 P.2d 946 (1981); Commonwealth v. Ford, 394 Mass. 421, 476 N.E.2d 560 (1985), and discussion in § 10.1(a).

[49]Hester v. United States, 265 U.S. 57, 44 S.Ct. 445, 68 L.Ed. 898 (1924).

[50]United States v. Lee, 274 U.S. 559, 47 S.Ct. 746, 71 L.Ed. 1202 (1927).

[51]Olmstead v. United States, 277 U.S. 438, 48 S.Ct. 564, 72 L.Ed. 944 (1928).

[52]Silverman v. United States, 365 U.S. 505, 81 S.Ct. 679, 5 L.Ed.2d 734 (1961). See also Berger v. New York, 388 U.S. 41, 87 S.Ct. 1873, 18 L.Ed.2d 1040 (1967); Lanza v. New York, 370 U.S. 139, 82 S.Ct. 1218, 8 L.Ed.2d 384 (1962).

[53]Schmerber v. California, 384 U.S. 757, 86 S.Ct. 1826, 16 L.Ed.2d 908 (1966).

[54]Beck v. Ohio, 379 U.S. 89, 85 S.Ct. 223, 13 L.Ed.2d 142 (1964).

[55]Clinton v. Virginia, 377 U.S. 158, 84 S.Ct. 1186, 12 L.Ed.2d 213 (1964).

[56]Stoner v. California, 376 U.S. 483, 84 S.Ct. 889, 11 L.Ed.2d 856 (1964).

[57]Taylor v. United States, 286 U.S. 1, 52 S.Ct. 466, 76 L.Ed. 951

business offices,[58] stores,[59] and warehouses[60]; "papers," such as letters[61]; and "effects," such as automobiles.[62] So things stood when in 1967 the Supreme Court announced the "seminal"[63] and "landmark decision"[64] in *Katz v. United States*.[65]

§ 2.1(b) The *Katz* case

Katz was convicted in federal court on a charge of transmitting wagering information by telephone from Los Angeles to Miami and Boston in violation of federal law. At trial the government was permitted to introduce, over defendant's objection, evidence of his end of telephone conversations, overheard by FBI agents who had attached an electronic listening and recording device to the exterior of a public telephone booth from which Katz habitually placed long-distance calls.

The court of appeals affirmed Katz' conviction,[66] reasoning that the electronic surveillance did not amount to a Fourth Amendment search because the microphone had not penetrated the wall of the telephone booth. In so holding, the court relied upon *Goldman v. United States*,[67] where the Supreme Court, applying *Olmstead,* decided that listening to a conversation in an adjoining room by means of a detectaphone placed against the wall was no search. In the later case of *Silverman v. United States*,[68] the Supreme Court had held that overhearing a conversation through a common wall by means of a spike microphone that penetrated the wall did amount to a Fourth Amendment search, but the court of appeals did not view *Silverman* as controlling. Unlike *Goldman* and the instant case, it had involved a physical intrusion of sorts. Moreover, in *Silverman* the Court declined "to reexamine *Goldman,*" and instead simply "decline[d] to go beyond it, by even a fraction of an inch."

The Supreme Court granted certiorari in order to consider the

---

(1932).

[58]United States v. Lefkowitz, 285 U.S. 452, 52 S.Ct. 420, 76 L.Ed. 877 (1932).

[59]Amos v. United States, 255 U.S. 313, 41 S.Ct. 266, 65 L.Ed. 654 (1921).

[60]See v. City of Seattle, 387 U.S. 541, 87 S.Ct. 1737, 18 L.Ed.2d 943 (1967).

[61]Ex parte Jackson, 96 U.S. (6 Otto) 727, 24 L.Ed. 877 (1877). See Desai, Wiretapping Before the Wires: The Post Office and the Birth of Communications Privacy, 60 Stan.L. Rev. 553 (2007) (discussing *Jackson*'s incorporation of prior post office policy into the Fourth Amendment, the true source of today's "principle of communications privacy").

[62]Preston v. United States, 376 U.S. 364, 84 S.Ct. 881, 11 L.Ed.2d 777 (1964).

[63]Amsterdam, 58 Minn.L.Rev. 349, 383 (1974).

[64]Note, 43 N.Y.U.L.Rev. 968 (1968).

[65]Katz v. United States, 389 U.S. 347, 88 S.Ct. 507, 19 L.Ed.2d 576 (1967).

[Section 2.1(b)]

[66]Katz v. United States, 369 F.2d 130 (9th Cir.1966).

[67]Goldman v. United States, 316 U.S. 129, 62 S.Ct. 993, 86 L.Ed. 1322 (1942).

[68]Silverman v. United States, 365 U.S. 505, 81 S.Ct. 679, 5 L.Ed.2d 734 (1961).

constitutional questions presented, which, as counsel for Katz characterized them, were: (1) Whether a public telephone booth is a constitutionally protected area within which a person has a right of privacy? and (2) Whether a physical penetration of that area is necessary before it may be said that a Fourth Amendment search has occurred? But the Court, per Justice Stewart, declined

to adopt this formulation of the issues. In the first place the correct solution of Fourth Amendment problems is not necessarily promoted by incantation of the phrase "constitutionally protected area." Secondly, the Fourth Amendment cannot be translated into a general constitutional "right to privacy."[69] That Amendment protects individual privacy against certain kinds of governmental intrusion, but its protections go further, and often have nothing to do with privacy at all. Other provisions of the Constitution protect personal privacy from other forms of governmental invasion. But the protection of a person's *general* right to privacy—his right to be let alone by other people—is, like the protection of his property and of his very life, left largely to the law of the individual States.

Because of the misleading way the issues have been formulated, the parties have attached great significance to the characterization of the telephone booth from which the petitioner placed his calls. The petitioner has strenuously argued that the booth was a "constitutionally protected area."[70] The Government has maintained with equal vigor that it was not. But this effort to decide whether or not a given "area," viewed in the abstract, is "constitutionally protected" deflects attention from the problem presented by this case. For the Fourth Amendment protects people, not places. What a person knowingly exposes to the public, even in his own home or office, is not a subject of Fourth Amendment protection. * * * But what he seeks to preserve as private, even in an area accessible to the public, may be constitutionally protected. * * *

The Government stresses the fact that the telephone booth from which the petitioner made his calls was constructed partly of glass, so that he was as visible after he entered as he would have been if he had remained outside. But what he sought to exclude when he entered the booth was not the intruding eye—it was the uninvited

[69]In Greenawalt v. Indiana Dept. of Corrections, 397 F.3d 587 (7th Cir. 2005), rejecting the contention that "subjecting a public employee to a probing psychological examination is a search," the court cautioned that "the Fourth Amendment does not expand accordion-like to fill what may be a gap in the privacy law of a particular state." The court deemed the Supreme Court's conclusion in Schmerber v. California, 384 U.S. 757, 86 S.Ct. 1826, 16 L.Ed.2d 908 (1966), that a lie detector test seeks testimonial rather than physical evidence and thus was governed by the Fifth Amendment rather than the Fourth, to be "even more apropos with respect to inter-rogations that do not involve a physical touching." See also Nelson v. National Aeronautics and Space Administration, 530 F.3d 865 (9th Cir.2008) (relying on *Greenawalt* in holding questioning government contract employees about drug use no search). Compare Covey, Interrogation Warrants, 26 Cardozo L.Rev. 1867 (2005), contending that "police interrogations are a kind of search."

[70]But see Schneider, Katz v. United States: The Untold Story, 40 McGeorge L.Rev. 13 (2009); Winn, Katz and the Origins of the "Reasonable Expectation of Privacy" Test, 40 McGeorge L.Rev. 1 (2009).

ear. He did not shed his right to do so simply because he made his calls from a place where he might be seen. No less than an individual in a business office, in a friend's apartment, or in a taxicab, a person in a telephone booth may rely upon the protection of the Fourth Amendment. One who occupies it, shuts the door behind him, and pays the toll that permits him to place a call is surely entitled to assume that the words he utters into the mouthpiece will not be broadcast to the world. To read the Constitution more narrowly is to ignore the vital role that the public telephone has come to play in private communication.

The Government contends, however, that the activities of its agents in this case should not be tested by Fourth Amendment requirements, for the surveillance technique they employed involved no physical penetration of the telephone booth from which the petitioner placed his calls. It is true that the absence of such penetration was at one time thought to foreclose further Fourth Amendment inquiry * * * , for that Amendment was thought to limit only searches and seizures of tangible property. But "[t]he premise that property interests control the right of the Government to search and seize has been discredited."[71] * * * Thus, although a closely divided Court supposed in *Olmstead* that surveillance without any trespass and without the seizure of any material object fell outside the ambit of the Constitution, we have since departed from the narrow view on which that decision rested. Indeed, we have expressly held that the Fourth Amendment governs not only the seizure of tangible items, but extends as well to the recording of oral statements overheard without any "technical trespass under . . . local property law." * * * Once this much is acknowledged, and once it is recognized that the Fourth Amendment protects people—and not simply "areas"—against unreasonable searches and seizures it becomes clear that the reach of that Amendment cannot turn upon the presence[72] or absence of a physical intrusion into any given enclosure.

We conclude that the underpinnings of *Olmstead* and *Goldman* have been so eroded by our subsequent decisions that the "trespass" doctrine there enunciated can no longer be regarded as controlling. The Government's activities in electronically listening to and recording the petitioner's words violated the privacy[73] upon which he justifiably relied while using the telephone booth and thus consti-

---

[71]Quoting from Warden v. Hayden, 387 U.S. 294, 87 S.Ct. 1642, 18 L.Ed.2d 782 (1967).

[72]See, e.g., Reeves v. Churchich, 484 F.3d 1244 (10th Cir.2007) (pointing rifle at premises occupant, even if end of rifle inserted inside those premises, if it "constituted a common law trespass," nonetheless was "not a Fourth Amendment violation" because "the rifle was incapable of obtaining information").

[73]While in "the law of criminal procedure, two kinds of privacy seem to matter," namely, (1) "keeping infor-

mation and activities secret from the government," and (2) "preventing invasions of dignitary interests, as when a police officer publicly accosts someone and treats him as a suspect," the former "has been preeminent" in Fourth Amendment law and is the focus when, as in *Katz*, the question is whether a search has occurred. Stuntz, Privacy's Problem and the Law of Criminal Procedure, 93 Mich.L.Rev. 1016, 1021 (1995).

Stuntz has also put forward the thesis that this focus upon the former variety of privacy in Fourth Amendment law "makes wealthier suspects

tuted a "search and seizure" within the meaning of the Fourth Amendment. The fact that the electronic device employed to achieve that end did not happen to penetrate the wall of the booth can have no constitutional significance.

The Court then proceeded to hold that the electronic eavesdropping, although apparently undertaken upon a "strong probability" that Katz was using the telephone in violation of federal law, was an unconstitutional search because the agents had not first obtained a search warrant.[74]

In his concurring opinion in *Katz,* Justice Harlan indicated that he "join[ed] the opinion of the Court," but then explained what he took that opinion to mean. Because lower courts attempting to interpret and apply *Katz* quickly came to rely upon the Harlan elaboration,[75] as ultimately did a majority of the Supreme Court,[76] the critical portion deserves to be set out here:

> As the Court's opinion states, "the Fourth Amendment protects people, not places." The question, however is what protection it affords to those people. Generally, as here, the answer to that question requires reference to a "place." My understanding of the rule that has emerged from prior decisions is that there is a twofold requirement, first that a person have exhibited an actual (subjective) expectation of privacy and, second, that the expectation be one that society is prepared to recognize as "reasonable." Thus a man's home is, for most purposes, a place where he expects privacy, but objects, activities, or statements that he exposes to the "plain view" of outsiders are not "protected" because no intention to keep them to himself has been exhibited. On the other hand, conversations in the open would not be protected against being overheard, for the expectation of privacy under the circumstances would be unreasonable.

---

better off than they otherwise would be, and may make poorer suspects worse off." Stuntz, The Distribution of Fourth Amendment Privacy, 67 Geo.Wash.L.Rev. 1265, 1266 (1999), critiqued in Seidman, Making the Best of Fourth Amendment Law: A Comment on The Distribution of Fourth Amendment Privacy, 67 Geo.Wash.L.Rev. 1296 (1999); Slobogin, The Poverty Exception to the Fourth Amendment, 55 Fla.L.Rev. 391, 407–12 (2003); Steiker, "How Much Justice Can You Afford?"—A Response to Stuntz, 67 Geo.Wash.L. Rev. 1290 (1999). See also Note, 39 Hastings Const.L.Q. 297 (2011).

[74]Marshall, J., took no part in the case. White, J., concurring, opined that no search warrant would be necessary in national security cases. Douglas and Brennan, JJ., concurring, expressed their disagreement with White. Harlan, J., concurred separately, as discussed in the text following. Black, J., dissenting, could not "agree with the Court that eavesdropping carried on by electronic means (equivalent to wiretapping) constitutes a 'search' or 'seizure.'"

[75]E.g., United States v. Freie, 545 F.2d 1217 (9th Cir.1976); Government of Virgin Islands v. Berne, 412 F.2d 1055 (3d Cir.1969); People v. Berutko, 71 Cal.2d 84, 77 Cal.Rptr. 217, 453 P.2d 721 (1969).

[76]California v. Ciraolo, 476 U.S. 207, 106 S.Ct. 1809, 90 L.Ed.2d 210 (1986); Smith v. Maryland, 442 U.S. 735, 99 S.Ct. 2577, 61 L.Ed.2d 220 (1979). But, for a defense of the Stewart opinion over the Harlan opinion, see Radsan, The Case for Stewart over Harlan on 24/7 Physical Surveillance, 88 Tex.L.Rev. 1475 (2010).

As it has turned out, the *Katz* decision is not of day-to-day importance with respect to the particular type of police investigative activity there at issue—electronic surveillance. This is because a year later the Congress enacted the Omnibus Crime Control and Safe Streets Act of 1968, Title III of which prohibits all wiretapping and electronic surveillance except pursuant to specified procedures and which requires the suppression of all evidence obtained in violation of those provisions.[77] But this is not to suggest that *Katz* is a case of little significance, for this is most assuredly not so. It

> is important to realize that *Katz* did not merely extend fourth amendment protection to electronic surveillance. By redefining the basis upon which it could be said that a search and seizure had taken place, *Katz* * * * also potentially altered all future applications of fourth amendment rights regarding searches and seizures.[78]

Thus, it is no overstatement to say, as the commentators have asserted, that *Katz* "marks a watershed in fourth amendment jurisprudence"[79] because the Court "purported to clean house on outmoded fourth amendment principles"[80] and moved "toward a redefinition of the scope of the Fourth Amendment."[81]

But, while *Katz* "has rapidly become the basis of a new formula of fourth amendment coverage,"[82] it can hardly be said that the Court produced clarity where theretofore there had been uncertainty. If anything, the exact opposite has occurred. The pre-*Katz* rule, though perhaps "unjust," was "a workable tool for the reasoning of the courts."[83] But the *Katz* rule, which the Court has since—somewhat inaccurately[84]—stated as the "reasonable 'expectation of privacy' "[85] test, is by comparison "difficult to apply."[86] In short, the *Katz* "opinion offers little to fill the void it

---

[77] 18 U.S.C.A. §§ 2510 to 2520.

[78] Note, 23 Clev.St.L.Rev. 63, 66 (1974).

[79] Amsterdam, 58 Minn.L.Rev. 349, 382 (1974).

[80] Note, 43 N.Y.U.L.Rev. 968, 975 (1968).

[81] Kitch, Katz v. United States: The Limits of the Fourth Amendment, 1968 Sup.Ct.Rev. 133.

[82] Amsterdam, 58 Minn.L.Rev. 349, 383 (1974).

[83] Note, 43 N.Y.U.L.Rev. 968 (1968).

[84] See Amsterdam, 58 Minn.L.Rev. 349, 383–86 (1974).

[85] Terry v. Ohio, 392 U.S. 1, 88 S.Ct. 1868, 20 L.Ed.2d 889 (1968).

[86] Kitch, 1968 Sup.Cty.Rev. 133, 135. See also Clancy, What Does the Fourth Amendment Protect: Property, Privacy, or Security?, 33 Wake Forest L.Rev. 307 (1998) (concluding at 308 that "both the property and privacy approaches have proven to be inadequate," and that consequently a "security" approach should be adopted); Penney, Reasonable Expectations of Privacy and Novel Search Technologies: An Economic Approach, 97 J.Crim.L. & Criminology 477 (2007) (because "reasonable expectation of privacy test is notoriously circular, imprecise, and unpredictable," author proposes an "economically-informed approach"); Saleem, The Physics of Fourth Amendment Privacy Rights, 32 T. Marshall L.Rev. 147, 164 (2007) (noting "absence of a bright line as to

has thus created."[87]

This should not be taken as a criticism of the Court's work in *Katz*. That "decision was written to resist captivation in any formula,"[88] and rightly so.[89] "An opinion which sets aside prior formulas with the observation that they cannot 'serve as a talismanic solution to every Fourth Amendment problem' should hardly be read as intended to replace them with a new talisman."[90] Realistically, no more could have been expected of the Court in its first step toward a redefinition of the reach of the Fourth Amendment. As Professor Amsterdam has so wisely pointed out:

> The Supreme Court ordinarily must decide the case before it. It must do so even though it is not prepared to announce the new principle in terms of comparable generality with the old, still less to say how much the old must be displaced and whether or how the old and new can be accommodated. If the Court declines to give birth to the new principle, it will never acquire the experience or the insight to answer these latter questions. If it attempts to answer them at the moment of the new principle's birth, it is not likely to answer them wisely. Clarity and consistency are desirable, certainly, to the extent that they can be achieved. But the temptation to achieve them by ignoring the complex and the unpredictable quality of real problems is fortunately less beguiling to Justices

---

what constitutes an invasion of privacy"); Solove, Fourth Amendment Pragmatism, 51 B.C.L.Rev. 1511 (2010) (arguing "reasonable expectation of privacy test should be abandoned" in favor of pragmatic approach, utilizing broad scope of coverage and concentrating upon the procedural question of how the Fourth Amendment should regulate particular forms of government information gathering); Note, 91 Yale L.J. 313, 328–29 (1981), asserting that the *Katz* rule is "essentially standardless" and that this could be overcome by a "secrecy and solitude" analysis.

[87] Note, 43 N.Y.U.L.Rev. 968, 976 (1968).

[88] Amsterdam, 58 Minn.L.Rev. 349, 385 (1974).

[89] And thus, while in post-*Katz* cases "the Supreme Court has refused to provide a consistent explanation for what makes an expectation of privacy 'reasonable,'" which "has disappointed scholars and frustrated students for four decades," the fact is that "no one test can accurately and consistently distinguish less troublesome police practices that do not require Fourth Amendment oversight from more

troublesome police practices that are reasonable only if the police have a warrant or compelling circumstances," so that the Court has instead recognized "four models of Fourth Amendment protection: a probabilistic model, a private facts model, a positive law model, and a policy model," which "allows the courts to use different approaches in different contexts depending on which approach most accurately and consistently identifies practices that need Fourth Amendment regulation." Kerr, Four Models of Fourth Amendment Protection, 60 Stan.L. Rev. 503 (2007).

In Kerr, An Equilibrium-Adjustment Theory of the Fourth Amendment, 125 Harv.L.Rev. 476, 480 (2011), the author offers another explanation/justification for "the patchwork of Fourth Amendment rules," namely, "equilibrium-adjustment": "When new tools and new practices threaten to extend or contract police powers a significant way, courts adjust the level of Fourth Amendment protection to try to restore the prior equilibrium."

[90] Amsterdam, 58 Minn.L.Rev. 349, 385 (1974).

perennially faced with responsibility for solving those problems than to the Justices' academic critics.[91]

Although *Katz* unquestionably expands the coverage of the Fourth Amendment,[92] even now—despite the intervening years since *Katz* was handed down—it is impossible to state with precision the degree of this expansion.[93] The range of law enforcement practices that fell outside the Fourth Amendment under the pre-*Katz* rule but which at least arguably come within the Amendment under the *Katz* test is substantial. In later sections of this Chapter, the effort is to assess the more common of these practices one by one and to indicate how courts have treated or ought to treat each of them in light of *Katz*. As a prelude to this, it is useful to make some more general inquiries concerning the import of the *Katz* decision.

§ 2.1(c) An "actual (subjective) expectation of privacy"

In his oft-quoted concurring opinion in *Katz,* Justice Harlan stated the rule in terms of a "two fold requirement," the first part of which was "that a person have exhibited an actual (subjective) expectation of privacy." No comparable statement is to be found in the majority opinion. However, the majority did say that the government's conduct directed at Katz "violated the privacy upon which he justifiably relied," which can easily be read as encompassing a subjective element. It is appropriate, therefore, to inquire whether such a subjective expectation is or ought to be a prerequisite to a finding that a Fourth Amendment search has occurred.

There are, to be sure, a great many instances in which it is rather easy to say that the police made no search because the defendant surely did not actually expect privacy. If, for example, a person were openly to engage in criminal conduct in Times Square at high noon and this conduct were observed by a passing patrolman, it could hardly be seriously claimed that this observation constituted a Fourth Amendment search. Any such claim would likely be dismissed with the explanation that the person

---

[91]Amsterdam, 58 Minn.L.Rev. 349, 352 (1974).

[92]Some would view this observation as too generous. See Cloud, A Liberal House Divided: How the Warren Court Dismantled the Fourth Amendment, 3 Ohio St.J.Crim.L. 33, 34 (2005) (*Katz* "typically has been applied in ways that * * * permit government actions to employ technological devices to pry into the lives of the people largely unconstrained by constitutional rules"); Luna, Sovereignty and Suspicion, 1999 Duke L.J. 789, 794 ("But in an ironic twist, *Katz* has been used to constrict Fourth Amendment rights rather than expand them"). See also the discussion in the text at note 127 infra and also the sources cited in that footnote.

[93]As stated in Cloud, Pragmatism, Positivism, and Principles of Fourth Amendment Theory, 41 UCLA L.Rev. 199, 252–53 (1993): "Despite the ubiquity of the *Katz* test, its meaning remains unsettled and controversial" because of "the Justices' use of pragmatic ideas to decide what privacy expectations are reasonable."

observed certainly had no actual expectation of privacy with respect to his conduct at that time and place.[94] But such reasoning
is to be avoided; while it will frequently lead to the correct result,
it distorts and unduly limits the rule of the *Katz* case.

> An actual, subjective expectation of privacy obviously has no place
> in a statement of what *Katz* held or in a theory of what the fourth
> amendment protects.[95] It can neither add to, nor can its absence
> detract from, an individual's claim to fourth amendment protection.
> If it could, the government could diminish each person's subjective
> expectation of privacy merely by announcing half-hourly on televi-
> sion that * * * we were all forthwith being placed under comprehen-
> sive electronic surveillance.[96]

Justice Harlan, it should be noted, ultimately came around to
this position. Analysis under *Katz,* he counseled in his dissenting
opinion in *United States v. White,*[97] "must * * * transcend the
search for subjective expectations," for "[o]ur expectations, and
the risks we assume, are in large part reflections of laws that
translate into rules the customs and values of the past and
present." A majority of the Court, while continuing to utilize the

---

[Section 2.1(c)]

[94]This situation should be distinguished from that in United States v.
Gooch, 6 F.3d 673 (9th Cir.1993),
where the government made a broader
no-subjective-expectation claim: that
because the defendant had committed
a public offense for which he could
have anticipated a police response, he
thus should have expected the police
to intrude into his nearby place of
temporary residence to arrest him. As
the court noted in rejecting this contention, under "this view, no law-
breaker would have a subjective expectation of privacy in any place because
the expectation of arrest is always imminent."

[95]Consider, in this connection, the
observation in Note, 60 N.Y.U.L.Rev.
725, 743–44 (1985): "It should be noted
that in this first part of the test the
inquiry is directed at determining
whether the dweller has *exhibited* a
subjective expectation of privacy
through his conduct, not whether the
dweller in fact had such an expectation."

[96]Amsterdam, 58 Minn.L.Rev.
349, 384 (1974). See also Cloud,
Pragmatism, Postivisim, and
Principles in Fourth Amendment
Theory, 41 UCLA L.Rev. 199, 250
(1993) ("the first prong is perhaps the
most nonsensical premise in fourth

amendment law"); United States v.
Taborda, 635 F.2d 131 (2d Cir.1980)
("a purely subjective criterion is not
appropriate," as by "use of a subjective
test * * * it would be possible for the
government by edict or by known systematic practice to condition the expectations of the populace in such a way
that no one would have any real hope
of privacy").

Some members of the Court are
not as careful with respect to this
point as they should be. Thus, in
Florida v. Riley, 488 U.S. 445, 109
S.Ct. 693, 102 L.Ed.2d 835 (1989), the
4-Justice plurality said that in deciding whether a particular form of aerial
surveillance was a search, it must be
decided whether the defendant "could
not reasonably have expected that his
greenhouse was protected from public
or official observation," thus seemingly
asserting that defendant's expectation
of privacy could be destroyed merely
by the fact of such police surveillance.
But Blackmun, J., dissenting, noted
that a "majority of this Court" agrees
"that the reasonableness of Riley's
expectation depends, in large measure,
on the frequency of *non*-police helicopter flights at an altitude of 400 feet."
(Emphasis added in both instances.)

[97]United States v. White, 401
U.S. 745, 91 S.Ct. 1122, 28 L.Ed.2d
453 (1971).

"actual (subjective) expectation of privacy" formulation, has at least cautioned that in some situations it "would provide an inadequate index of Fourth Amendment protection."[98]

Because "the courts frequently do not distinguish between the two parts of the *Katz* test,"[99] little attention has been given to the independent significance of the first factor or to precisely how it is to be interpreted. Not atypical is *California v. Ciraolo*,[100] where the Supreme Court answered in the negative the question "whether the Fourth Amendment is violated by aerial observation without a warrant from an altitude of 1,000 feet of a fenced-in backyard within the curtilage of a home." The defendant was growing marijuana in a 15 by 25 foot plot in his backyard, surrounded by a 6-foot outer fence and 10-foot inner fence, which apparently prompted the majority to assert: "Clearly—and understandably—respondent has met the test of manifesting his own subjective intent and desire to maintain privacy as to his unlawful agricultural pursuits." Though that seemed an unequivocal acceptance of the fact that the first *Katz* requirement had been met (as the dissenters concluded[101]), the *Ciraolo* Court then backed off with the observation that "we need

---

[98]Smith v. Maryland, 442 U.S. 735, 99 S.Ct. 2577, 61 L.Ed.2d 220 (1979). Although the majority in *Smith,* as explained in § 2.7(b), seems not to have heeded its own warning, it did identify some extreme instances in which it would not follow the subjective approach: "For example, if the Government were suddenly to announce on nationwide television that all homes henceforth would be subject to warrantless entry, individuals thereafter might not in fact entertain any actual expectation of privacy regarding their homes, papers, and effects. Similarly, if a refugee from a totalitarian country, unaware of this Nation's traditions, erroneously assumed that police were continuously monitoring his telephone conversations, a subjective expectation of privacy regarding the contents of his calls might be lacking as well. In such circumstances, when an individual's subjective expectations had been 'conditioned' by influences alien to well-recognized Fourth Amendment freedoms, those subjective expectations obviously could play no meaningful role in ascertaining what the scope of Fourth Amendment protections was. In determining whether a 'legitimate

expectation of privacy' existed in such cases, a normative inquiry would be proper."

In State v. Smith, 279 Neb. 918, 782 N.W.2d 913 (2010), the court, citing *Smith*, rejected the state's argument that, because defendant knew a night club patted down patrons, he lacked a reasonable expectation of privacy in the contents of his pockets, as "whether an expectation of privacy is reasonable does not turn on notice"; the club's only option was "to refuse entry to a person who is unwilling to be searched." Unfortunately, the point is sometimes missed by lower courts. See, e.g., Gillett v. State, 588 S.W.2d 361 (Tex.Crim.App.1979) (over forceful dissent, court holds there was no search by looking into department store fitting room, as trial judge could have found that defendant saw sign warning of such surveillance).

[99]Note, 60 N.Y.U.L.Rev. 725, 744–45 (1985).

[100]California v. Ciraolo, 476 U.S. 207, 106 S.Ct. 1809, 90 L.Ed.2d 210 (1986).

[101]"The Court begins its analysis of the Fourth Amendment issue posed here by deciding that respondent had

not address that issue" because the state had conceded the point. This in turn was followed by the gratuitous observation that because "a 10-foot fence might not shield these plants from the eyes of a citizen or a policeman perched on the top of a truck or a 2-level bus," it "is not entirely clear" whether the defendant "therefore maintained a subjective expectation of privacy from *all* observations of his backyard, or whether instead he manifested merely a hope that no one would observe his unlawful gardening pursuits." The unfortunate implication of this comment is that a defendant cannot even get by the first *Katz* hurdle unless he has taken steps to ensure against all conceivable efforts at scrutiny, and that it is not enough that (as the dissenters put it) "he had taken steps to shield those activities from the view of passersby."

If, as the *Ciraolo* dicta intimates, it is appropriate under the first *Katz* requirement to ponder such hypothetical occurrences as police perched atop double-decker buses, then it would be just as easy to say there was no subjective expectation of privacy in light of the surveillance technique *actually* used, which-after all-was successful. But surely this would be a perversion of *Katz*.[102] As one perceptive commentator has put it:

> The essential focus of the *Katz* analysis is on the *reasonableness* of expectations of privacy; it is thus disingenuous for a court to evade consideration of that issue, under the second part of the *Katz* analysis, by failing to recognize that a dweller exhibited an expectation of privacy because he did not take extraordinary precautions against the specific way in which the state conducted the surveillance.
>
> In *Katz* itself, there was no suggestion that the defendant in the phone booth took any precautions against the wiretapping at issue in that case; he simply closed the door to the phone booth to prevent being overheard by those within earshot. * * * The first part of the *Katz* test requires only that the dweller have exhibited an expectation of privacy—in other words, that his conduct have demonstrated an intention to keep activities and things within the curtilage private, and that he did not knowingly expose them to the open view of the public.[103]

§ 2.1(d) An expectation "that society is prepared to recognize as 'reasonable'"

In his effort to parse the holding in *Katz*, Justice Harlan declared that the second requirement was that "the expectation

---

an expectation of privacy in his backyard. I agree with that conclusion."

[102] As noted in Serr, Great Expectations of Privacy: A New Model for Fourth Amendment Protection, 73 Minn.L.Rev. 583, 627 (1989), what is needed under *Katz* is "an inquiry into the *degree* of public exposure, not simply the *fact* of public exposure, or worse, the mere *possibility* of public exposure."

[103] Note, 60 N.Y.U.L.Rev.725, 753–54 (1985). Regarding the extent to which the taking of precautions has become significant in applying the *Katz* test, and also whether "our precautionary behavior * * * should be protected against undue government interference," see Tien, Doors, Envelopes, and Encryption: The Uncertain Role of Precautions in Fourth Amendment Law, 54 DePaul L.Rev. 873 (2005).

be one that society is prepared to recognize as 'reasonable.'" This was apparently an attempt to give content to the word "justifiably" in the majority's assertion that eavesdropping on Katz was a search because it "violated the privacy upon which he justifiably relied while using the telephone booth." Central to any application of the *Katz* rule, therefore, as the Court later put it in *White,* is a determination of "what expectations of privacy are constitutionally 'justifiable.'" This in turn requires that it be ascertained precisely what the word "justifiable" means in this context.

Sometimes the Court has referred to the *Katz* rule as the "reasonable 'expectation of privacy'" test.[104] From this, it might be assumed that police investigative activity constitutes a search whenever it uncovers incriminating actions or objects the law's hypothetical reasonable man would expect to be private, that is, which as a matter of statistical probability were not likely to be discovered. But this is not really what *Katz* is all about.[105] As one commentator has helpfully put it:

> [I]t is possible that a person could reasonably rely on privacy in a given situation and, in light of all the surrounding circumstances, be unjustified. If two narcotics peddlers were to rely on the privacy of a desolate corner of Central Park in the middle of the night to carry out an illegal transaction, this would be a reasonable expectation of privacy; there would be virtually no risk of discovery. Yet if by extraordinary good luck a patrolman were to illuminate the desolate spot with his flashlight, the criminals would be unable to suppress the officer's testimony as a violation of their rights under the fourth amendment. * * * [I]n order for an expectation to be

---

[Section 2.1(d)]

[104]Terry v. Ohio, 392 U.S. 1, 88 S.Ct. 1868, 20 L.Ed.2d 889 (1968).

[105]As the Court has sometimes noted in later cases. For example, in Oliver v. United States, 466 U.S. 170, 104 S.Ct. 1735, 80 L.Ed.2d 214 (1984), the Court rejected "the suggestion that steps taken to protect privacy establish that expectations of privacy in an open field are legitimate. It is true, of course, that petitioner Oliver and respondent Thornton, in order to conceal their criminal activities, planted the marijuana upon secluded land and erected fences and no trespassing signs around the property. And it may be that because of such precautions, few members of the public stumbled upon the marijuana crops seized by the police. Neither of these suppositions demonstrates, however, that the expectation of privacy was *legitimate* in the sense required by the Fourth Amendment. The test of legitimacy is not whether the individual chooses to conceal assertedly 'private' activity. Rather, the correct inquiry is whether the government's intrusion infringes upon the personal and societal values protected by the Fourth Amendment."

Probability is occasionally important in making a judgment as to whether the place of police surveillance was a "public vantage point," but a place that is on other grounds clearly such a point does not have to be frequently used. Thus in Florida v. Riley, 488 U.S. 445, 109 S.Ct. 693, 102 L.Ed.2d 835 (1989), all members of the Court agreed that whether aerial surveillance at 400 feet was a search depended upon whether such use of helicopters was sufficiently "rare," but several Justices rightly emphasized that as for any surveillance of defendant's residence from an adjoining public road, it would make *no* difference how often travelers used the road.

considered justified it is not sufficient that it be merely reasonable; it must be based on something in addition to a high probability of freedom from intrusion. The premise upon which the hypothetical criminals in Central Park based their activities was realistic and involved little risk, but their expectation was not "justified." Justification, as here used, is intended to be a basis of differentiating those expectations which are merely reasonable from those expectations which are to be constitutionally enforced due to other social considerations.[106]

But if the expectation of those hypothetical criminals was not "justified," precisely why is this so? How can it be determined when reliance upon privacy is "justified"? Justice Harlan points the way in his dissent in *United States v. White*.[107] "This question," he says, "must * * * be answered by assessing the nature of a particular practice and the likely extent of its impact on the individual's sense of security balanced against the utility of the conduct as a technique of law enforcement." Therefore, Harlan concludes, "those more extensive intrusions that significantly jeopardize the sense of security which is the paramount concern of Fourth Amendment liberties" are searches.

For one thing, this means that a judgment must be made about what "sense of security" is important in our society. In forming this judgment, it is necessary to look to "the customs and values of the past and present."[108] "We have to look for the answer to this question in the structure of society, the patterns of interaction, the web of norms and values."[109]

Beginning with Justice Harlan's assertion in *Katz* that the standard should be what "*society* is prepared to recognize as 'reasonable,'" courts, when they have considered the matter, seem to have drawn upon the customs and sensibilities of the populace in determining what expectations of privacy are constitutionally reasonable.[110] Secondly, the realization of privacy is itself very much a product of life in a human community,[111] made possible through the operation of socialization and social controls. The quantity and quality of seclusion available to an individual or group

---

[106]Note, 43 N.Y.U.L.Rev. 968, 983 (1968).

[107]United States v. White, 401 U.S. 745, 91 S.Ct. 1122, 28 L.Ed.2d 453 (1971). See Hancock, Warrants for Wearing a Wire: Fourth Amendment Privacy and Justice Harlan's dissent in United States v. White, 79 Miss.L.J. 35 (2009).

[108]Harlan, J., dissenting in United States v. White, 401 U.S. 745, 91 S.Ct. 1122, 28 L.Ed.2d 453 (1971).

[109]Simmel, Privacy is not an Isolated Freedom, in Nomos XIII: Privacy, at 71, 84 (J. Pennock & J. Chapman eds. 1971).

[110]E.g., United States v. Vilhotti, 323 F.Supp. 425 (S.D.N.Y.1971), noting that a court must take into account "both contemporary norms of social conduct and the imperatives of a viable democratic society."

[111]"Privacy, no less than good reputation or physical safety, is a creature of life in a human community and not the contrivance of a legal system concerned with its protection. We should not be misled, therefore, in speaking of a legally recognized interest in privacy or the rights attending it. Privacy in these contexts does not exist because of such recognition, but depends only upon habits of life." Gross,

are socially and culturally determined, and in that sense society and culture may be said to dictate what sorts of privacy one may reasonably expect, at least in social situations. Thus the appropriate frame of reference is a collective one. The criteria for reasonable expectations must be abstracted from the flow of life, and it is the judge's task to find and articulate those societal standards.[112]

As the Supreme Court noted more recently in *Oliver v. United States*,[113] what is involved here is "our societal understanding" regarding what deserves "protection from government invasion." This means, for example, as the Court went on to conclude in *Oliver*, that the Fourth Amendment does not have the same reach as extant trespass laws, for "the common law of trespass furthers a range of interests that have nothing to do with privacy and that would not be served by applying the strictures of trespass law to public officers."[114] But this proposition cuts both ways, and thus certain police activity violates the Fourth Amendment even when it does *not* violate applicable statutes, especially statutes concerned with matters other than protection of privacy.[115]

Next, it is necessary to make a judgment as to whether the

The Concept of Privacy, 42 N.Y.U.L. Rev. 34, 36 (1967).

[112]Note, 6 U.Mich.J.L.Ref. 154, 179–80 (1972). See also Cloud, Pragmatism, Positivism, and Principles in Fourth Amendment Theory, 41 UCLA L.Rev. 199, 250 (1993) ("by asking whether the expectation in dispute is one society is willing to recognize as reasonable, the test's second prong implicitly encourages decisionmakers to define fundamental constitutional values by referring to contemporary social values, goals, and attitudes"). For another helpful analysis of *Katz*, see Note, 76 Mich.L.Rev. 154 (1977).

[113]Oliver v. United States, 466 U.S. 170, 104 S.Ct. 1735, 80 L.Ed.2d 214 (1984).

[114]Similarly, in Dow Chemical Co. v. United States, 476 U.S. 227, 106 S.Ct. 1819, 90 L.Ed.2d 226 (1986), the Court stated: "Dow nevertheless relies heavily on its claim that trade secret laws protect it from any aerial photography of this industrial complex by its competitors, and that this protection is relevant to our analysis of such photography under the Fourth Amendment. That such photography might be barred by state law with regard to competitors, however, is irrelevant to the questions presented here. State

tort law governing unfair competition does not define the limits of the Fourth Amendment."

See also California v. Greenwood, 486 U.S. 35, 108 S.Ct. 1625, 100 L.Ed.2d 30 (1988), rejecting the defendant's claim "that his expectation of privacy in his garbage should be deemed reasonable as a matter of federal constitutional law because the warrantless search and seizure of his garbage was impermissible as a matter of California law." The Court declared that the "societal understanding" referred to in *Oliver* was not to be determined by the law, even constitutional law, of a particular state.

Compare Yeager, Search, Seizure and the Positive Law: Expectations of Privacy Outside the Fourth Amendment, 84 J.Cr.L. & C. 249, 251 (1993) (arguing that "state property law and other expressions of the positive law are more resilient and useful to Fourth Amendment analysis than the Court's decisions of the past three decades recognize").

[115]In Florida v. Riley, 488 U.S. 445, 109 S.Ct. 693, 102 L.Ed.2d 835 (1989), the 4-Justice plurality held helicopter surveillance from 400 feet was not a search, stressing that "helicopters are not bound by the lower limits of the navigable airspace allowed to other aircraft." But as Black-

particular police investigative practice in question threatens that "sense of security." The issue is not whether the resort to that practice in the particular case at hand, given either the grounds which the police had in advance for engaging in the practice[116] or the hindsight knowledge that the practice was directed toward a person engaged in criminal activity,[117] is particularly offensive. Rather, the matter must be viewed from a much broader perspective. It must be asked whether permitting the police regularly to engage in that type of practice, limited by nothing "more than self-restraint by law enforcement officials,"[118] requires the "people" to which the Fourth Amendment refers to give "up too much freedom as the cost of privacy."[119] That is, the fundamental inquiry is whether that practice, if not subjected to Fourth Amendment restraints, would be intolerable because it would either encroach too much upon the "sense of security" or impose unreasonable burdens upon those who wished to maintain that security.[120] An affirmative answer to the question, *Arizona v. Hicks*[121] teaches, might be given even when the privacy invasion required very little effort by the police and "uncovered nothing of

---

mun, J., pointed out in his dissent, a "majority of this Court" (the four dissenters and one concurring Justice) believe that whether the helicopter surveillance was a search "depends upon whether Riley has a 'reasonable expectation of privacy' that no such surveillance would occur, and does not depend upon the fact that the helicopter was flying at a lawful altitude under FAA regulations."

[116]Courts sometimes misapply the *Katz* test by focusing only upon the fact that the practice was undertaken upon adequate grounds in the instant case, which of course goes to the question of whether the search was reasonable, not whether a search has occurred so as to bring the Fourth Amendment into play. See, e.g., United States v. Bronstein, 521 F.2d 459 (2d Cir.1975), where the question (discussed herein in § 2.2(g)) was whether use of a marijuana-sniffing dog was a search. The court, in answering in the negative, stressed that the dog "was not employed in a dragnet operation directed at all flight passengers but rather on the basis of reliable information that reasonably triggered the surveillance employed here." But if such use of trained dogs is no search, then their use in a "dragnet operation" would likewise be constitutionally permissible.

[117]Thus, in considering whether window-peeping is a search, "[t]he question is not whether you or I must draw the blinds before we commit a crime. It is whether you and I must discipline ourselves to draw the blinds every time we enter a room, under pain of surveillance if we do not." Amsterdam, 58 Minn.L.Rev. 349, 403 (1974). See also McFerguson v. United States, 770 A.2d 66 (D.C.App.2001) (rejecting government's claim that defendant lacked expectation of privacy society prepared to recognize as reasonable in unexposed contents of shopping bag because defendant a burglar and contents were stolen property).

[118]Harlan, J., dissenting in United States v. White, 401 U.S. 745, 91 S.Ct. 1122, 28 L.Ed.2d 453 (1971).

[119]Amsterdam, 58 Minn.L.Rev. 349, 403 (1974).

[120]Thus, "this approach raises the question of how tightly the fourth amendment permits people to be driven back into the recesses of their lives by the risk of surveillance." Amsterdam, 58 Minn.L.Rev. 349, 402 (1974).

[121]Arizona v. Hicks, 480 U.S. 321, 107 S.Ct. 1149, 94 L.Ed.2d 347 (1987).

any great personal value"; thus in that case the Court decided the mere act of moving a piece of stereo equipment to expose its serial number was a Fourth Amendment search.[122]

This means that the "ultimate question," as Professor Amsterdam has emphasized,

> is a value judgment. It is whether, if the particular form of surveillance practiced by the police is permitted to go unregulated by constitutional restraints, the amount of privacy and freedom remaining to citizens would be diminished to a compass inconsistent with the aims of a free and open society. That, in outright terms, is the judgment lurking underneath the Supreme Court's decision in *Katz,* and it seems to me the judgment that the fourth amendment inexorably requires the Court to make.[123]

It may be said, of course, that this merely means that under *Katz* "the fourth amendment protects those interests that may justifiably claim fourth amendment protection,"[124] and that this is nothing more than a tautology. But certainly "it begs the question no more or less than any other theory of fourth amendment coverage that the Court has used."[125] *Katz* presents lower courts with a hard issue, but at least it is the correct issue; by "releas[ing] the Fourth Amendment * * * from the moorings of precedent," the Court has made it possible "to determine its scope by the logic of its central concepts."[126]

Though this is the way that the second *Katz* prong *ought* to be interpreted, it is beyond question that the post-*Katz* decisions of the Supreme Court do not ordinarily or often square with the foregoing analysis.[127] As one perceptive observer aptly put it, while "privacy may have been a promising theory of the Fourth

---

[122]This is not to suggest that such minor contact is a search in all circumstances. In United States v. Lovell, 849 F.2d 910 (5th Cir.1988), holding it was no search for an agent to pick up a suitcase off an airline conveyor belt and squeeze it, *Hicks* was distinguished as being concerned with police activity inside defendant's apartment, where he clearly had a legitimate expectation of privacy, while in the instant case the agent's actions occurred in a semi-public area after defendant had entrusted the handling of his bags to a common carrier and thus at that point had "no reasonable expectation that his luggage would not be moved or handled."

[123]Amsterdam, 58 Minn.L.Rev. 349, 403 (1974).

[124]Amsterdam, 58 Minn.L.Rev. 349, 385 (1974).

[125]Amsterdam, 58 Minn.L.Rev. 349, 385 (1974).

[126]Kitch, 1968 Sup.Ct.Rev. 133.

[127]As noted in Junker, The Structure of the Fourth Amendment: The Scope of the Protection, 79 J.Crim.L. & C. 1105, 1125–26 (1989): "What is remarkable, however, is how little was changed by *Katz*'s abandonment of the 'trespass' standard of *Olmstead v. United States* and *Goldman v. United States.* True, it changed the result in the electronic surveillance cases. However, it did not bring the use of sense enhancing devices within the scope of the amendment as a general proposition. Moreover, *Katz* had no effect on the scope-narrowing doctrines of 'plain view,' 'consensual encounter,' 'voluntary transfer,' consent or abandonment. Indeed, the main function of the expectation of privacy rubric minted in *Katz* seems to have been to provide an additional ground for denying fourth amendment protec-

Amendment at one time, it has now lost much of its luster and

tion by refusing 'legitimacy' to assertions of privacy in, for example, one's voice and handwriting, bank records, open fields or any 'private enclave' visible from public airspace."

See also Benner, Diminishing Expectations of Privacy in the Rehnquist Court, 22 J. Marshall L.Rev. 825 (1989); Berner, The Supreme Court and the Fall of the Fourth Amendment, 25 Val.U.L.Rev. 383 (1991); Colb, What is a Search? Two Conceptual Flaws in Fourth Amendment Doctrine and Some Hints of a Remedy, 55 Stan.L.Rev. 119 (2002); Cunningham, A Linguistic Analysis of the Meaning of "Search" in the Fourth Amendment: A Search for Common Sense, 73 Iowa L.Rev. 541 (1988); Gruber, Garbage Pails and Puppy Dog Tails: Is That What Katz is Made Of?, 40 U.C.Davis L.Rev. 781, 793 (2008) ("After *Katz*, * * * the Court twisted the reasonableness requirement, holding that an individual must assume the risk of government intrusion when she has not taken truly extraordinary and even impossible precautions"); Gutterman, A Formulation of the Value and Means Models of the Fourth Amendment in the Age of Technologically Enhanced Surveillance, 39 Syrac.L. Rev. 647 (1988); Halliburton, How Privacy Killed Katz: A Tale of Cognitive Freedom and the Property of Personhood as Fourth Amendment Norm, 42 Akron L.Rev. 803 (2009); Heffernan, Fourth Amendment Privacy Interests, 92 J.Crim. L. & Crimin. 1, 126 (2001) (criticizing Court's application of *Katz* and arguing "that the privacy conventions of everyday life are best understood in terms of a forbearance model, one that requires individuals seeking privacy to take certain reasonable steps to indicate their desire for it but that then requires restraint on the part of outsiders"); Henderson, Nothing New Under the Sun? A Technologically Rational Doctrine of Fourth Amendment Search, 56 Mercer L.Rev. 507 (2005); Hutchins, The Anatomy of a Search: Intrusiveness and the Fourth Amendment, 44 U.Rich.L.Rev. 1185, 1187 (2010) (*Katz*

should be modified so that "intrusiveness" is the benchmark, "clearly defined to require an examination of two factors: the functionality of a challenged form of surveillance and the potential for disclosure created by the device"); Katz, In Search of a Fourth Amendment for the Twenty-First Century, 65 Ind.L.J. 549 (1990); Kerr, Searches and Seizures in a Digital World, 119 Harv.L.Rev. 531, 585 (2005) ("The new world of computer searches and seizures sheds * * new skepticism * * * on *Katz*'s privacy-based focus," as the "perspective of computer searches and seizures suggests that the deeper role of Fourth Amendment doctrine is regulating the information flow between individuals and the state"); McAninch, Unreasonable Expectations: The Supreme Court and the Fourth Amendment, 20 Stetson L.Rev. 435 (1991); Power, Technology and the Fourth Amendment: A Proposed Formulation for Visual Searches, 80 J.Crim.L. & C. 1 (1989); Serr, Great Expectations of Privacy: A New Model for Fourth Amendment Protection, 73 Minn.L.Rev. 583 (1989); Simon, Katz at Forty: A Sociological Jurisprudence Whose Time Has Come, 41 U.C.Davis L.Rev. 935, 937 (2008) ("*Katz*, in its most promising aspects, was never fully developed by the U.S. Supreme Court"); Slobogin & Schumacher, Reasonable Expectations of Privacy and Autonomy in Fourth Amendment Cases: An Empirical Look at "Understanding Recognized and Permitted by Society," 42 Duke L.J. 727 (1993) (concluding at 774 "that the Supreme Court's conclusions about the scope of the Fourth Amendment are often not in tune with community held attitudes about police investigative techniques"); Steinberg, Making Sense of Sense-Enhanced Searches, 74 Minn.L.Rev. 563 (1990).

But consider Slobogin, The Liberal Assault on the Fourth Amendment, 4 Ohio St.J.Crim.L.603 (2007), arguing that while it "is fashionable to place much of the blame for today's law on the Warren Court's adoption of the malleable expectation of privacy

utility" because of two serious mistakes by the Court in post-*Katz* cases: the Court (1) "has interpreted privacy to be a question of fact rather than a constitutional value" and (2) is apparently "out of touch with society's true expectations of privacy."[128] In particular, as is detailed in the later sections of this Chapter, too often the Court has failed to appreciate that "privacy is not a discrete commodity, possessed absolutely or not at all,"[129] and that there is a dramatic difference, in privacy terms, between revealing bits and pieces of information sporadically to a small and often select group for a limited purpose and a focused police examination of the totality of that information regarding a particular individual. Some hope—modest to be sure, given the outcome of the case—is to be found, however, in *Florida v. Riley*,[130] holding that an officer's naked-eye observation into defendant's residential greenhouse from a helicopter 400 feet off the ground was no search. Significant for present purposes is the observation of Blackmun, J., dissenting, that a "majority of this Court" (the four dissenters and one concurring Justice) believe that the reasonableness of the defendant's expectations "depends, in large measure, on the frequency of nonpolice helicopter flights at an altitude of 400 feet." That is, a majority of the Court does *not* accept "the plurality's exceedingly grudging Fourth Amendment theory, [whereunder] the expectation of privacy is defeated if a single member of the public could conceivably position herself to see into the area in question without doing anything illegal."[131] Also promising are such cases as *Kyllo v. United States*[132] and *Ferguson v. City of Charleston*,[133] as in "addressing heat detection technology and perinatal cocaine testing * * * the Court specifi-

---

concept," it is attributable instead to "the probable-cause forever position, the individualized suspicion mantra, and the obsession with exclusion as a remedy."

[128]Luna, Sovereignty and Suspicion, 1999 Duke L.J. 789, 827. Consider also Fradella, Morrow, Fischer & Ireland, Quantifying Katz: Empirically Measuring "Reasonable Expectations of Privacy" in the Fourth Amendment Context, 38 Am.J.Crim.L. 289 (2011), describing an empirical study as to society's actual expectations and indicting at 372 that "the results indicate that courts often misjudge what 'society' is prepared to embrace as a reasonable expectation of privacy."

And thus some have strongly urged that the "privacy" focus of Fourth Amendment theory should be either replaced or supplemented by the rec-

ognition of some other interest. See, e.g., Castiglione, Human Dignity Under the Fourth Amendment, 2008 Wis.L.Rev. 655 (proposing "that human dignity * * * should stand alongside privacy as a primary animating principle"); Rubenfeld, The End of Privacy, 61 Stan.L.Rev. 101, 104 (2008) ("The Fourth Amendment does not guarantee a right to privacy. It guarantees-if its actual words mean anything-a right to security").

[129]Smith v. Maryland, 442 U.S. 735, 99 S.Ct. 2577, 61 L.Ed.2d 220 (1979) (Marshall, J., dissenting).

[130]Florida v. Riley, 488 U.S. 445, 109 S.Ct. 693, 102 L.Ed.2d 835 (1989).

[131]Brennan, J., dissenting in *Riley*.

[132]Kyllo v. United States, 533 U.S. 27, 121 S.Ct. 2038, 150 L.Ed.2d 94 (2001).

[133]Ferguson v. City of Charleston,

cally refused to say that vulnerability to exposure is the equivalent of privacy forfeiture and left open the possibility that more robust doctrines of * * * partial exposure are in the offing."[134] This appears to be a rejection of the all-or-nothing approach of the earlier cases, under which it would seem that "*Katz* itself would have to be overruled."[135]

§ 2.1(e) Trespass as an alternate theory

While the Supreme Court's decision in *Katz v. United States*[136] seemed to sound the death knell for the pre-*Katz* "trespass" approach to determining the scope of the Fourth Amendment's coverage, over fifty years later, in *United States v. Jones*,[137] the trespass doctrine re-emerged as an alternate theory to the *Katz* expectation-of-privacy approach. *Jones* involved the government's actions in installing a GPS tracking device on the undercarriage of a vehicle then used by defendant and the subsequent tracking of the vehicle's movements with that device for the next 28 days. Remarkably, all nine of the Justices agreed that the government's activities amounted to a Fourth Amendment "search." Four of the Justices, concurring, reached this conclusion via *Katz,* but the majority concluded it was unnecessary to go that route, as "Jones's Fourth Amendment rights do not rise or fall with the *Katz* formulation," as "the *Katz* reasonable-expectation-of-privacy test has been *added to*, not *substituted for*, the common-law trespassory test." Hence it was enough in *Jones* that the "Government physically occupied private property for the purpose of obtaining information," as "such a physical intrusion would have been considered a 'search' within the meaning of the Fourth Amendment when it was adopted."

The four concurring Justices in *Jones* argued that the majority's approach had been put to rest in *Katz*–where, after all, it had been emphatically asserted that the reach of the Fourth Amendment "cannot turn upon the presence or absence of a physical

---

532 U.S. 67, 121 S.Ct. 1281, 149 L.Ed.2d 205 (2001).

[134]Colb, What is a Search? Two Conceptual Flaws in Fourth Amendment Doctrine and Some Hints of a Remedy, 55 Stan.L.Rev. 119, 187 (2002).

[135]Serr, Great Expectations of Privacy: A New Model for Fourth Amendment Protection, 73 Minn.L. Rev. 583, 626 (1989).

[Section 2.1(e)]

[136]Katz v. United States, 389 U.S. 347, 88 S.Ct. 507, 19 L.Ed.2d 576 (1967).

[137]United States v. Jones, __ U.S. __, 132 S.Ct. 945, 181 L.Ed.2d 911 (2012), discussed in Goldberg, How United States v. Jones Can Restore Our Faith in the Fourth Amendment, 110 Mich.L.Rev. First Impressions 62 (2011); Morrison, The Drug Dealer, The Narc, and the Very Tiny Constable: Reflections on United States v. Jones, 3 Cal.L.Rev.Circuit 113 (2012); Priester, Five Answers and Three Questions After United States v. Jones (2012), the Fourth Amendment "GPS case," http://papers.ssrn.com/sol3/papers.cfm?abstract_id=2030390 (2012); Spencer, GPS Monitoring Device Leads the Supreme Court to a Crossroads in Privacy Law, http://papers.ssrn.com/sol3/papers.cfm?abstract_id=2014233 (2012).

intrusion"–and had not been resurrected since.[138] Moreover, they found the trespass approach an unhelpful way to go about resolving the instant case. Application of the trespass doctrine in *Jones*, the concurring Justices argued, attached "great significance" to the "relatively minor" act of affixing a small object to the underside of a vehicle, an act "generally regarded as so trivial that it does not provide a basis for recovery under modern tort law." Also, the concurring Justices observed, "reliance on the law of trespass will present particularly vexing problems" in subsequent cases, such as whether "only electronic, as opposed to physical, contact with the item to be tracked" will suffice.[139] (To this, the majority responded that it was actually avoiding the "particularly vexing problems" presented by "the concurrence's insistence on the exclusivity of the *Katz* test," such as the need to distinguish between "short term" non-search monitoring vs. "longer term" monitoring that the concurring Justices concluded was a search under *Katz*.)

But there is another aspect of the disagreement between the majority Justices and concurring Justices in *Jones* that has drawn the most attention, which is whether the majority is correct in asserting that the *Jones* result is simply an instance of the Court "preserv[ing] that degree of privacy against government that existed when the Fourth Amendment was adopted." The concurring Justices object:

> But it is almost impossible to think of late-18th century situations that are analogous to what took place in this case. (Is it possible to imagine a case in which a constable secreted himself somewhere in a coach and remained there for a period of time in order to monitor the movements of the coach's owner?)

Appended to that query was this (by now, oft-quoted) footnote: "The Court suggests that something like this might have occurred in 1791, but this would have required either a gigantic coach, a very tiny constable, or both-not to mention a constable with incredible fortitude and patience." The *Jones* majority, also responding via footnote, thanked the concurrence for actually supplying an analogy "that is not far afield,"[140] but then, significantly, added:

---

[138]The majority opinion had argued otherwise, relying upon Soldal v. Cook County, 506 U.S. 56, 113 S.Ct. 538, 121 L.Ed.2d 450 (1992); and Alderman v. United States, 394 U.S. 165, 89 S.Ct. 961, 22 L.Ed.2d 176 (1969). But, as the concurring Justices aptly noted, *Soldal* merely concluded that a seizure can occur independent of any search, while *Alderman* only established that homeowners had a legitimate expectation of privacy as to all conversations taking place under their roof.

[139]One supporter of *Jones* has argued that the rationale of that case could readily be "updated to consider electronic penetration a form of trespass," which "would permit the labeling of more intrusions as searches, whether they look like traditional trespasses or modern-day, electronic trespasses." Goldberg, 110 Mich.L. Rev. First Impressions 62, 68 (2011).

[140]However, it has been aptly noted, even the constable-in-coach hy-

In any case, it is quite irrelevant whether there was an 18th-century analog. Whatever new methods of investigation may be devised, our task, *at a minimum*, is to decide whether the action in question would have constituted a "search" within the original meaning of the Fourth Amendment.

As one perceptive commentator has noted, the *Jones* majority thereby "acknowledged that the Court's holding was not simply an exercise in translating original expected applications," and instead offered something that "sounds like semantic original-ism,"[141] an approach that "seems to offer little help in a case like *Jones*" because "the original semantic meaning of the Fourth Amendment's prohibition on unreasonable search and seizures was so expansive."[142] Hence this verdict:

> The holding in *Jones* is likely defensible if one thinks that technological advance may not erode legal protections against any form of official scrutiny, but this is a nonoriginalist claim-it is not an original expected application, nor is it premised on any histori-cal evidence about the original semantic meaning of the prohibition on "unreasonable search and seizure" divorced from original expected applications.[143]

Precisely what impact the *Jones* trespass rule will have upon the totality of Fourth Amendment jurisprudence remains to be seen. One view is that "the practical impact of the *Jones* addition is likely to minimal," given "that a great deal of the most helpful investigatory techniques in the digital age can be accomplished without ever making contact, physical or electronic, with the person or property under investigation."[144] Another, perhaps con-sistent with the verdict on *Jones* quoted above, is that "over time * * * *Jones* may cover most of the territory currently protected by *Katz* and could ultimately replace *Katz* as a clearer, cleaner

---

pothetical does not provide the perfect analogy to what happened in *Jones*, for, on the one hand, "by using all his senses, the constable would have learned more than the limited infor-mation transmitted by a GPS device," but, on the other, "could not have simultaneously informed his col-leagues of his location in the manner that a GPS device instantaneously transmits data." Rosenthal, Original-ism in Practice, 87 Ind. L.J. 1183, 1209 (2012). Or, as it was put in Morrison, The Drug Dealer, the Narc, and the Very Tiny Constable, Reflections on United States v. Jones, 3 Cal.L.Rev. Circuit 113, 115 n. 17 (2012), "the tiny constable would only have approxi-mated the usefulness of a tracking de-vice if he also had been able to signal his location in real time, perhaps by using a trail of breadcrumbs."

[141] As the author elsewhere ex-plains, "a semantic form of originalism is the predominant approach, in which constitutional interpretation is not based on the intentions of the framers or the original expected applications of constitutional text, but rather on the original meaning of the text stated at the level of generality found in the text." Rosenthal, 87 Ind.L.J. 1183, 1210 (2012).

[142] Rosenthal, 87 Ind.L.J. 1183, 1209–10 (2012)

[143] Rosenthal, 87 Ind.L.J. 1183, 1211 (2012).

[144] Priester, Five Answers and Three Questions After United States v. Jones (2012), the Fourth Amend-ment "GPS case," http://papers.ssrn.co m/sol3/papers.cfm?abstract_id= 2030390 (2012).

metric of when the Fourth Amendment is implicated."[145]

§ 2.2 Plain view, smell, hearing, and touch; aiding the senses

§ 2.2(a)   Plain view, smell, hearing or touch
§ 2.2(b)   Use of flashlight or other means of illumination
§ 2.2(c)   Use of binoculars or telescope; photo enlargement
§ 2.2(d)   Use of magnetometer, x-ray, weapons detector, etc., to "see" what the naked eye cannot see
§ 2.2(e)   Use of thermal imager to detect and measure heat
§ 2.2(f)   Use of electronic surveillance to discover and decrypt communications
§ 2.2(g)   Use of canine to detect drugs, etc.
§ 2.2(h)   Use of "electronic canine" to detect explosives, alcohol, etc.

Research References

West's Key Number Digest
Automobiles ☞349.5(8); Controlled Substances ☞106; Searches and Seizures ☞13.1 to 22, 26, 47.1 to 51, 57, 63; Telecommunications ☞494

Legal Encyclopedias
C.J.S., Motor Vehicles § 1333; Searches and Seizures §§ 8, 13, 18, 20 to 24, 27 to 28, 30 to 35, 37 to 38, 41, 66 to 76, 78, 102 to 103; Telecommunications §§ 235 to 237, 245 to 252, 254, 261, 263 to 268, 307

Introduction

As a general proposition, it is fair to say that when a law enforcement officer is able to detect something by utilization of one or more of his senses while lawfully present[1] at the vantage point where those senses are used, that detection does not constitute a "search" within the meaning of the Fourth Amendment. Illustrations of this general rule are described and discussed in later sections of this Chapter. The concern herein is with the outer boundaries of the rule—in particular, the extent to which it is applicable to those cases where the detection has been possible only by aiding or enhancing the natural senses in some way,

---

[145]Goldberg, How United States v. Jones Can Restore Our Faith in the Fourth Amendment, 110 Mich.L.Rev. First Impressions 62, 68–69 (2011).

[Section 2.2]

[1]It must be cautioned that this phrase "lawfully present" is used throughout this Chapter as a shorthand way of describing a no-search-so-far situation, and thus should not be read literally. The important point is that it is *possible* for an officer to be lawfully present at a certain location, but yet his discovery by using natural senses might still constitute a search. In Florida v. Riley, 488 U.S. 445, 109 S.Ct. 693, 102 L.Ed.2d 835 (1989), as Blackmun, J., dissenting, correctly observed, a "majority of this Court agrees" that observation from a "helicopter * * * flying at a lawful altitude under FAA regulations" would constitute a search if there was not sufficient "frequency of nonpolice helicopter flights at [that] altitude."

often by reliance upon modern technology.[2]

§ 2.2(a) Plain view, smell, hearing or touch

The Supreme Court decision most frequently cited in support of the so-called plain view doctrine is *Coolidge v. New Hampshire*.[3] There, the plurality opinion of Justice Stewart stated:

> It is well established that under certain circumstances the police may seize evidence in plain view without a warrant. But it is important to keep in mind that, in the vast majority of cases, *any* evidence seized by the police will be in plain view, at least at the moment of seizure. The problem with the "plain view" doctrine has been to identify the circumstances in which plain view has legal significance rather than being simply the normal concomitant of any search, legal or illegal.

An example of the applicability of the "plain view" doctrine is the situation in which the police have a warrant to search a given area

---

[2]On technology and the Fourth Amendment generally, consult Bandes, Power, Privacy and Thermal Imaging, 86 Minn.L.Rev. 1379 (2002); Clancy, What is a "Search" Within the Meaning of the Fourth Amendment?, 70 Alb.L. Rev. 1 (2006); Clancy, Coping With Technological Change: Kyllo and the Proper Analytical Structure to Measure the Scope of Fourth Amendment Rights, 72 Miss.L.J. 525 (2002); Colb, The World Without Privacy: Why Property Does Not Define the Limits of the Right Against Unreasonable Searches and Seizures, 102 Mich.L. Rev. 889 (2004); Kerr, An Equilibrium-Adjustment Theory of the Fourth Amendment, 125 Harv.L.Rev. 476 (2011); Kerr, The Fourth Amendment and New Technologies: Constitutional Myths and the Case for Caution, 102 Mich.L.Rev. 801 (2004); Kerr, Technology, Privacy, and the Courts: A Reply to Colb and Swire, 102 Mich.L.Rev. 933 (2004); Kuh, The Founders' Privacy: The Fourth Amendment and the Power of Technological Surveillance, 86 Minn.L.Rev. 1325 (2002); Milligan, Analogy Breakers: A Reality Check on Emerging Technologies, 80 Miss.L.J. 1319 (2011); Ohm, The Fourth Amendment in a World Without Privacy, 81 Miss.L.J. 1309 (2012); Penney, Reasonable Expectations of Privacy and Novel Search Technologies: An Economic Approach, 97 J.Crim.L. & Criminology 477 (2007); Simmons, Why 2007 is Not Like 1984: A Broader Perspective on Technology's Effect on Privacy and Fourth Amend-ment Jurisprudence, 97 J.Crim.L. & Criminology 531 (2007); Simmons, From Katz to Kyllo: A Blueprint for Adapting the Fourth Amendment to Twenty-First Century Technologies, 53 Hastings L.J. 1303 (2002); Steinberg, Sense-Enhanced Searches and the Irrelevance of the Fourth Amendment, 16 Wm. & Mary Bill Rts.J. 465 (2007); Strandburg, Home, Home on the Web and Other Fourth Amendment Implications of Technosocial Change, 70 Md.L.Rev. 614 (2011); Swire, Katz is Dead, Long Live Katz, 102 Mich.L.Rev. 904 (2004); Taslitz, The Fourth Amendment in the Twenty-First Century: Technology, Privacy, and Human Emotions, 65 Law & Contemp.Probs. 125 (2002); Terrell & Jacobs, Privacy, Technology, and Terrorism: Bartnicki, Kyllo, and the Normative Struggle Behind Competing Claims to Solitude and Security, 51 Emory L.J. 1469 (2002); Tomkovicz, Technology and the Threshold of the Fourth Amendment: A Tale of Two Futures, 72 Miss.L.J. 317 (2002); Urbonya, A Fourth Amendment "Search" for the Age of Technology: Postmodern Perspectives, 72 Miss.L.J. 447 (2002); Weaver, The Fourth Amendment, Privacy and Advancing Technology, 80 Miss.L.J. 1131 (2011); Note, 44 Ariz.L.Rev. 967 (2002).

[Section 2.2(a)]

[3]Coolidge v. New Hampshire, 403 U.S. 443, 91 S.Ct. 2022, 29 L.Ed.2d 564 (1971).

for specified objects, and in the course of the search come across some other article of incriminating character. * * * Where the initial intrusion that brings the police within plain view of such an article is supported, not by a warrant, but by one of the recognized exceptions to the warrant requirement, the seizure is also legitimate. Thus the police may inadvertently come across evidence while in "hot pursuit" of a fleeing suspect. * * * And an object that comes into view during a search incident to arrest that is appropriately limited in scope under existing law may be seized without a warrant. * * * Finally, the "plain view" doctrine has been applied where a police officer is not searching for evidence against the accused, but nonetheless inadvertently comes across an incriminating object. * * *

What the "plain view" cases have in common is that the police officer in each of them had a prior justification for an intrusion in the course of which he came inadvertently across a piece of evidence incriminating the accused. The doctrine serves to supplement the prior justification—whether it be a warrant for another object, hot pursuit, search incident to lawful arrest, or some other legitimate reason for being present unconnected with a search directed against the accused—and permits the warrantless seizure. Of course, the extension of the original justification is legitimate only where it is immediately apparent to the police that they have evidence before them; the "plain view" doctrine may not be used to extend a general exploratory search from one object to another until something incriminating at last emerges.

As close examination of this language makes apparent, the plain view doctrine discussed in *Coolidge* is intended to provide a basis for making a *seizure* without a warrant.[4] The fact that there is a plain view in the *Coolidge* sense does not mean that there has been no search; indeed, the situations described by Justice Stewart are in the main search situations—search pursuant to a warrant naming other objects, search during hot pursuit, search incident to arrest, and a search for purposes other than finding evidence. Rather, the effort in *Coolidge* is to describe when items so found may be seized even though they were not the items that were legitimate objectives of that search. The *Coolidge* plurality[5] identifies three requirements: (1) there must be a prior valid

---

[4]What *Coolidge* and its progeny make clear is "that there is no additional requirement of exigency for the seizure of property that is in plain view, provided that the police officer's presence on the property is lawful and the incriminating character of the evidence is immediately apparent." G & G Jewelry, Inc. v. City of Oakland, 989 F.2d 1093 (9th Cir.1993). See also Sanders v. City of San Diego, 93 F.3d 1423 (9th Cir.1996).

[5]In Texas v. Brown, 460 U.S. 730, 103 S.Ct. 1535, 75 L.Ed.2d 502 (1983), four members of the Court stated that because "the *Coolidge* plurality's discussion of 'plain view' * * * has never been expressly adopted by a majority of this Court," it was "not a binding precedent" but "should obviously be the point of reference for further discussion of the issue." Two other members of the Court saw "no reason at this late date to imply criticism of [*Coolidge*'s] articulation of this exception" because it "has been accepted generally for over a decade." The remaining three Justices, without addressing this point, cited

intrusion; (2) the discovery of the seized items must be inadvertent;[6] and (3) it must be immediately apparent to the police that they have evidence before them.[7] The significance of these requirements in terms of justifying a warrantless seizure of evidence is discussed at several points in this Treatise.[8]

By comparison, the concern here is with plain view in a quite different sense, namely, as descriptive of a situation in which there has been no Fourth Amendment search at all. This situation, which perhaps is deserving of a different label so as to avoid confusion of it with that discussed in *Coolidge*,[9] encompasses those circumstances in which an observation is made by a police officer without a prior physical intrusion into a constitutionally protected area. This includes the case in which an officer discov-

---

Coolidge as a precedent on the plain view doctrine. The plurality opinion in *Brown* also asserted that "the phrase 'immediately apparent' [in *Coolidge*] was very likely an unhappy choice of words, since it can be taken to imply that an unduly high degree of certainty as to the incriminatory character of evidence is necessary for an application of the 'plain view' doctrine," and then concluded it was intended to be merely a "statement of the rule * * * requiring probable cause for seizure in the ordinary case."

[6]This dictum in *Coolidge* was later rejected in Horton v. California, 496 U.S. 128, 110 S.Ct. 2301, 110 L.Ed.2d 112 (1990).

[7]For a useful discussion of these requirements, see Moylan, The Plain View Doctrine: Unexpected Child of the Great "Search Incident" Geography Battle, 26 Mercer L.Rev. 1047, 1073–78, 1081–88 (1975).

[8]See § 4.11 (re plain view in execution of search warrants), § 5.2(j) (re plain view upon search of the person), § 6.7 (re plain view and warrantless entry of premises), § 7.5 (re plain view and warrantless search of vehicles), and § 8.1(c) (re plain view and search by consent).

[9]As noted in Scales v. State, 13 Md.App. 474, 284 A.2d 45 (1971): "In this context, we studiously avoid the phraseology 'in plain view' to avoid any implication that the so-called 'plain view doctrine' is being invoked. That doctrine is not here applicable.

Needless confusion is frequently engendered by the employment in many opinions of the same phrase—'in plain view'—to describe two visually similar but legally distinct situations. The 'plain view doctrine,' as described in *Coolidge* * * *, refers exclusively to the legal justification—the reasonableness—for the seizure of evidence which has not been particularly described in a warrant and which is inadvertently spotted in the course of a constitutional search already in progress or in the course of an otherwise justifiable intrusion into a constitutionally protected area. It has no applicability when the vantage point from which the 'plain view' is made is not within a constitutionally protected area. It is, therefore, literally discreet to use for such latter situations some alternative phraseology such as 'clearly visible,' 'readily observable,' 'open to public gaze,' etc., rather than to employ the words 'in plain view' in their purely descriptive capacity lest the unwary reader read them in their other and talismanic capacity as an invocation of the doctrine of the same name in non-intrusive situations where it is not applicable."

See also State v. Kaaheena, 59 Haw. 23, 575 P.2d 462 (1978); State v. Taylor, 61 Ohio App.2d 209, 401 N.E.2d 459, 15 O.O.3d 323 (1978) (then-extant *Coolidge* inadvertence limitation not applicable to police officer at lawful location looking through apartment window and seeing marijuana transaction).

ers an object which has been left in an "open field"[10] or similar nonprotected area,[11] and also those cases in which an officer—again, without making a prior physical intrusion—sees an object on the person of an individual,[12] within premises,[13] or within a vehicle,[14] or other container.[15] In each of these instances there has been no search at all because of the plain view character of the situation, and this means that the observation is lawful without the necessity of establishing either pre-existing probable cause or the existence of a search warrant or one of the traditional exceptions to the warrant requirement.[16]

---

[10]Hester v. United States, 265 U.S. 57, 44 S.Ct. 445, 68 L.Ed. 898 (1924). For more on open fields, see § 2.4(a).

[11]State v. Coleman, 122 Ariz. 130, 593 P.2d 684 (App.1978), approved in part 122 Ariz. 99, 593 P.2d 653 (shoes leaning against outside wall of apartment building).

[12]E.g., United States v. Jones, 187 F.3d 210 (1st Cir.1999) (counterfeit bills in defendant's hand); State v. Calhoun, 502 So.2d 808 (Ala.1986) (observation of marijuana cigarette in defendant's open pocket); Commonwealth v. Meehan, 377 Mass. 552, 387 N.E.2d 527 (1979) (blood on suspect's shoes); Ford v. State, 122 Nev. 796, 138 P.3d 500 (2006) (bloody cap and sweatshirt on murder suspect).

Compare United States v. Askew, 529 F.3d 1119 (D.C.Cir.2008) (unzipping defendant's sweatshirt *is* a search, as it "renders visible whatever lies underneath").

[13]E.g., Sumdum v. State, 612 P.2d 1018 (Alaska 1980) (where "police officers who are lawfully positioned" were able to look into defendant's door, the inadvertence requirement did not have to be met because it applies only "after there has been an initial search or intrusion"); State v. Dickerson, 313 N.W.2d 526 (Iowa 1981) (same); State v. Johnson, 171 N.J. 192, 793 A.2d 619 (2002) (where police officers came onto porch of building "for a legitimate investigative purpose," they "had a right to be where they could make observations" of package of drugs in hole beside porch post).

[14]E.g., United States v. Campbell, 549 F.3d 364 (6th Cir.2008) (no search to shine flashlight into car, revealing gun); United States v. Martin, 806 F.2d 204 (8th Cir.1986) (district court erred in applying *Coolidge* requirements to looking into window of parked car); Commonwealth v. Sergienko, 399 Mass. 291, 503 N.E.2d 1282 (1987) (trial judge erred in requiring *Coolidge* "prior justification" for looking into window of parked car); Johnson v. State, 999 So.2d 360 (Miss. 2008) (no search to look in lawfully stopped car and set fruits of robbery); State v. Powell, 99 N.M. 381, 658 P.2d 456 (App.1983) (no search to look into lawfully stopped car and thus *Coolidge* limits on plain view not applicable); State v. Planz, 304 N.W.2d 74 (N.D.1981) (where officer looked through car window, he "made his observation without the aid of a *Coolidge*-type intrusion and the requirements of the 'plain view' doctrine therefore do not apply"); State v. Byerley, 635 S.W.2d 511 (Tenn.1982) (*Coolidge* plain view limits not applicable where, for example, officer looks into car and "the discovery he makes is not preceded by an otherwise valid Fourth Amendment search"); Delong v. Commonwealth, 234 Va. 357, 362 S.E.2d 669 (1987) (seeing gun by looking through car window need not be inadvertent, which it wasn't here in that car stopped because occupants involved in shooting).

[15]E.g., State v. Youngblood, 117 Idaho 160, 786 P.2d 551 (1990) (no search where officer looked down into top of open paper bag defendant left on parking lot pavement).

[16]And where there is no search, it is permissible for the officer to "rec-

It is extremely important to understand that the kind of plain view described in the preceding paragraph, because it involves no intrusion covered by the Fourth Amendment, need not meet the three requirements set out in the *Coolidge* plurality opinion.[17] By definition, there is no prior valid intrusion. Whether it is immediately apparent that what has been observed is evidence of crime may have a bearing upon what the police may do as a result of this nonsearch observation, but it is clearly irrelevant to the threshold issue of whether the observation was a search. And even before the repudiation of the *Coolidge* "inadvertent discovery" requirement,[18] it was clear that the observation need not have been inadvertent. As Judge Moylan has pointed out, in such a case

> the condition of inadvertence is certainly not operational. In surveying sidewalks, streets and gutters and in roaming the "open fields" (even as technical trespassers), the police would seem to be free to go on fishing expeditions or to go on planned reconnaissances * * * in such nonprotected places, whether the viewing be inadvertent or

ord" his observation by camera or videotape. See, e.g., United States v. McMillon, 350 F.Supp. 593 (D.D.C. 1972) (pictures and videotape of marijuana growing in defendant's back yard, taken without a warrant, admissible because plants were in plain view); People v. Edelbacher, 47 Cal.3d 983, 254 Cal.Rptr. 586, 766 P.2d 1 (1989) (no search to photograph shoe tracks seen by officer when on normal route visitors would use at private premises); People v. Green, 298 Ill.App.3d 1054, 233 Ill.Dec. 389, 700 N.E.2d 1097 (1998) (photography of lawfully stopped suspect no search where officer "took the photographs of the defendant in a public place where it was lawful for him to be"); State v. Cain, 400 N.W.2d 582 (Iowa 1987) (no search to press camera lens against car window and photograph interior); State v. Marini, 638 A.2d 507 (R.I.1994) (videotaping of defendant's confession to police). See Annot., 27 A.L.R.4th 532 (1984); Note, 35 Wash. & Lee L.Rev. 1043 (1978).

And, where defendant's conduct occurs where he has no reasonable expectation of privacy, it is not a search for the defendant's activity to be captured by a camera triggered by motion in the area and without the immediate presence of a police officer making the same observation directly. United States v. McIver, 186 F.3d

1119 (9th Cir.1999) (use of unmanned still and video cameras in a national forest no search; court rejects "the notion that the visual observation of the site became unconstitutional merely because law enforcement chose to use a more cost-effective 'mechanical eye' to continue the surveillance"). See also Hudspeth v. State, 349 Ark. 315, 78 S.W.3d 99 (2002) (no search for police to set up video camera near "a crude hut" on "an undeveloped ten-acre tract" and later return and check it, discovering defendant and others engaged in drug manufacturing, as surveillance was "used to record activity in an area where the suspect has no reasonable expectation of privacy").

[17]See, generally, Wallin, The Uncertain Scope of the Plain View Doctrine, 16 U.Balt.L.Rev. 266 (1987).

[18]Horton v. California, 496 U.S. 128, 110 S.Ct. 2301, 110 L.Ed.2d 112 (1990). "Some state courts have followed *Horton* and completely abolished the inadvertency requirement," a few "have declined to follow *Horton* and continue to require inadvertency," and a few others "have recognized the exception for objects that are 'contraband,' 'stolen,' or 'dangerous in themselves.'" State v. Nieves, 160 N.H. 245, 999 A.2d 389 (2010) (citing cases in each category).

not.[19]

It is equally important to understand that while the characterization of an observation as a nonsearch plain view situation settles the lawfulness of the observation itself, it does not determine whether a seizure of the observed object would likewise be lawful. Though the Supreme Court in another context has rather loosely asserted that "objects falling in the plain view of an officer who has a right to be in the position to have the view are subject to seizure,"[20] this is quite clearly not so as to the type of plain view under discussion here. Again Judge Moylan:

> Seeing something in open view does not, of course, dispose, ipso facto, of the problem of crossing constitutionally protected thresholds. Those who thoughtlessly over-apply the plain view doctrine to every situation where there is a visual open view have not yet learned the simple lesson long since mastered by old hands at the burlesque houses, "You can't touch everything you can see."
>
> Light waves cross thresholds with a constitutional impunity not permitted arms and legs. Wherever the eye may go, the body of the policeman may not necessarily follow.[21]

The point was made by the Supreme Court in *Illinois v. Andreas*,[22] where it was cautioned that the plain view doctrine "authorizes seizure of illegal or evidentiary items visible to a police officer" only if the officer's "access to the object" itself has a "Fourth Amendment justification."[23]

Assume, for example, one of the plain view situations listed earlier: an officer while standing on the public way is able to look through the window of a private residence and see contraband present therein. The fact that the presence of the contraband in the residence was discovered by resort to plain view instead of, say, information supplied by a reliable informant, has no bearing upon the question of whether an intrusion into those premises may now be made for the purpose of seizing that contraband. As the Court stated in *Coolidge,*

> plain view *alone* is never enough to justify the warrantless seizure of evidence. This is simply a corollary of the familiar principle * * * that no amount of probable cause can justify a warrantless search

---

[19]Moylan, 26 Mercer L.Rev. 1047, 1097–98 (1975).

[20]Harris v. United States, 390 U.S. 234, 88 S.Ct. 992, 19 L.Ed.2d 1067 (1968).

[21]Moylan, 26 Mercer L.Rev. 1047, 1096 (1975).

[22]Illinois v. Andreas, 463 U.S. 765, 103 S.Ct. 3319, 77 L.Ed.2d 1003 (1983).

[23]See also Horton v. California, 496 U.S. 128, 110 S.Ct. 2301, 110 L.Ed.2d 112 (1990) (for plain view doctrine to operate, "not only must the officer be lawfully located in a place from which the object can be plainly seen, but he or she must also have a lawful right of access to the object itself"); Texas v. Brown, 460 U.S. 730, 103 S.Ct. 1535, 75 L.Ed.2d 502 (1983) (plurality states that " 'plain view' provides grounds for seizure of an item when an officer's access to an object has some prior justification under the Fourth Amendment").

or seizure absent "exigent circumstances." Incontrovertible testimony of the senses that an incriminating object is on premises belonging to a criminal suspect may establish the fullest possible measure of probable cause. But even where the object is contraband, this Court has repeatedly stated and enforced the basic rule that the police may not enter and make a warrantless seizure.[24]

By the same token, if the plain view is of an object on the person of some individual, it is still necessary that the seizure of that object from the person occur pursuant to a warrant, incident to arrest, or without a warrant but under exigent circumstances.[25] And even when the plainly viewed object could be seized without

---

[24]Compare Taylor v. United States, 286 U.S. 1, 52 S.Ct. 466, 76 L.Ed. 951 (1932) (though police, standing where they had a right to be, saw contraband in open view in a garage by looking through a small opening, their warrantless entry to seize the contraband was unconstitutional); with Steele v. United States, 267 U.S. 498, 45 S.Ct. 414, 69 L.Ed. 757 (1925) (police, standing where they had a right to be, looked into garage and saw contraband in open view through doorway; this furnished probable cause for obtaining warrant by which they lawfully entered and seized the contraband).

See also State v. David, 269 Ga. 533, 501 S.E.2d 494 (1998) ("officer's observation of the contraband from outside the apartment and his recognition of it as contraband, standing alone, did not authorize the officer to make a warrantless entry into the apartment to arrest the occupants and seize the material"); State v. Rickard, 420 So.2d 303 (Fla.1982) (fact marijuana plants could be seen in defendant's back yard from neighbor's property did not permit warrantless entry onto defendant's land); People v. Pakula, 89 Ill.App.3d 789, 44 Ill.Dec. 919, 411 N.E.2d 1385 (1980) (fact marijuana plants seen in defendant's back yard did not alone justify entry of yard and seizure of plants, as "the warrantless intrusion into the defendant's privacy is not justifiable merely by a pre-intrusion plain view observation"); State v. Fisher, 283 Kan. 272, 154 P.3d 455 (2007) ("absent a justifiable intrusion onto Fisher's curtilage, the mere observation of the bag from the highway does not itself allow the

bag's seizure"); Strange v. State, 530 So.2d 1336 (Miss.1988) ("plain smell" of marijuana within premises does not, absent exigent circumstances, justify warrantless entry to seize the marijuana).

Compare Wien v. State, 882 A.2d 183 (Del.2005) (where defendant owned waterfront property, part of which was designated as wetlands, and from road outside defendant's property environmental officer observed circumstances constituting a violation of state wetlands law, officer's entry of land lawful because "officer may enter onto property to conduct a warrantless search where he sees evidence of a crime in plain view"); Corry v. State, 710 So.2d 853 (Miss.1998) (where from adjoining property officer observed hunting violations then occurring on defendant's land, he "had the authority to enter Cupit's land and make a warrantless arrest" in order "to thwart the commission of a crime in progress").

[25]See, e.g., Cupp v. Murphy, 412 U.S. 291, 93 S.Ct. 2000, 36 L.Ed.2d 900 (1973), finding exigent circumstances to be present. Consider also Moore v. State, 997 A.2d 656 (Del.2010) (where defendant stopped on reasonable suspicion he committing crime of carrying concealed weapon, and when he sat down gun fell from his pocket, after such "plain view" officer "was entitled to seize the gun").

Compare Commonwealth v. Meehan, 377 Mass. 552, 387 N.E.2d 527 (1979), where officers investigating a homicide asked defendant to come to the station for an interview, which he did, and then saw red stains on his shoes, which they took from him

interfering with a person or entering upon protected premises, it cannot be said that the right of seizure flows automatically from the plain view. Except when the object has been abandoned,[26] the seizure itself constitutes an interference with "effects" protected by the Fourth Amendment, and this means that in the absence of a search warrant some recognized ground for warrantless seizure, equally applicable outside plain view cases, must be present.[27] This last point was highlighted in *Soldal v. Cook County*,[28] where the Supreme Court rejected language in the court of appeals opinion which, as the Court put it, "seemingly construes the Amendment to protect only against seizures that are the outcome of a search." The Court put a plain view situation in which no search had occurred, as where police see an object while inside private premises entered with consent, and noted that in such circumstances any seizure of the observed object would be "scrupulously subjected to Fourth Amendment inquiry," under which the seizure would ordinarily pass muster only if "the probable cause standard" was met.[29]

As for the contents of a container, the mere fact that the container itself is in plain view provides no basis for a warrantless seizure and search of it, even assuming probable cause as to

---

and subjected to chemical analysis. The court held that defendant had come to the station and handed over the shoes by consent, but then in the alternative upheld the police action because the shoes were in plain view and "the whole going situation was one where a requirement of procuring a warrant for the sneakers would seem extravagant." The court was not as careful as it might have been in its analysis, especially as to whether there was probable cause for the seizure. If there was probable cause for the seizure, then on the facts of this case there was probable cause for arrest as well, and thus the court may have been influenced (if that was the assumption) by the fact that defendant could have been arrested, in which case the seizure of his shoes clearly would have been lawful. See § 5.2(j) concerning seizure incident to arrest, and compare the situations where seizure occurs before or without arrest, discussed in § 5.4(b) and (c).

[26]See Hester v. United States, 265 U.S. 57, 44 S.Ct. 445, 68 L.Ed. 898 (1924). For more on abandoned property, see § 2.6(b).

[27]See §§ 4.11, 5.2(j), 6.7(a), 7.5(b).

Thus, in State v. Sweatt, 427 A.2d 940 (Me.1981), where defendants had left gems at a store on consignment for sale and an officer lawfully entered the store and examined the gems and then seized them, the court in holding the seizure unlawful noted that the defendants by their conduct had lost any expectation of privacy in terms of viewing of the gems but that they retained an "expectation that their gems would not be taken except after purchase by customers."

[28]Soldal v. Cook County, 506 U.S. 56, 113 S.Ct. 538, 121 L.Ed.2d 450 (1992).

[29]Such a probable cause showing would be required, the Court noted, "in the absence of consent or a warrant permitting the seizure of the items in question." See, e.g., Waltman v. Payne, 535 F.3d 342 (5th Cir.2008) (where sheriff had plaintiff's 500 kenaf plants removed from open field, part of his 1500-acre hunting lease, such action lawful only because, considering the plants had the physical appearance of marijuana and were planted in a manner common to illegal marijuana crops, sheriff had probable cause the plants were contraband).

the contents.[30] But if the contents themselves are in plain view within an accessible container,[31] then there exists no reasonable expectation of privacy as to those contents and thus no need for a warrant to open the container.[32]

Just as what an officer sees where he is lawfully present is a nonsearch plain view, what he learns by reliance upon his other senses while so located is likewise no search and thus per se lawful. In effect, the plain view doctrine "has been expanded to cover that evidence that can be perceived by the sense of smell or what the officer may hear."[33] As for what might be called the "plain hearing" situation, a useful illustration is provided by *United States v. Fisch.*[34] There, investigators obtained a motel room adjoining the room being used by persons suspected of being involved in a narcotics conspiracy. From that room, often by

---

[30]United States v. Chadwick, 433 U.S. 1, 97 S.Ct. 2476, 53 L.Ed.2d 538 (1977). See, e.g., Matter of Welfare of G.M., 560 N.W.2d 687 (Minn.1997) (court of appeals erred in concluding "that because the *pouch* was in plain view, and because the police officer had probable cause to believe the pouch *contained* contraband, that this case fit under" the plain view doctrine). Cases contrary to *G.M.* are to be found, e.g., Casey v. United States, 788 A.2d 155 (D.C.App.2002), reflecting that the continued vitality of *Chadwick*, is in some doubt. See § 5.5(c).

Of course, "plain view" only of the container, reasonably believed to contain seizable items, will sometimes allow search of the container without first obtaining a warrant. See, e.g., State v. Roper, 305 Mont. 212, 26 P.3d 741 (2001) (warrantless search justified because of probation condition).

[31]That is, one not within a protected place, or one within a place (e.g., an automobile) that in the circumstances may be searched on probable cause without a warrant.

[32]Indeed, some other circumstances making it virtually certain what the contents are will also justify a warrantless opening of the container. See the discussion in § 5.5(f).

[33]United States v. Pagan, 395 F.Supp. 1052 (D.P.R.1975).

[34]United States v. Fisch, 474 F.2d 1071 (9th Cir.1973). See also United States v. Hessling, 845 F.2d 617 (6th

Cir.1988); United States v. Mankani, 738 F.2d 538 (2d Cir.1984); United States v. Jackson, 588 F.2d 1046 (5th Cir.1979); State v. Moses, 367 So.2d 800 (La.1979); State v. Day, 50 Ohio App.2d 315, 362 N.E.2d 1253 (1976), all reaching the same result on similar facts.

Likewise, it is no search to overhear with the naked ear a telephone conversation at an unenclosed telephone in a public place. United States v. Muckenthaler, 584 F.2d 240 (8th Cir.1978). See also United States v. Ceballos, 385 F.3d 1120 (7th Cir.2004) (because "the defendants did not have a reasonable expectation of privacy in their voices during their booking interviews, their voices fall within the exception of the plain hearing exception," and thus no search to compare defendant's voices with those captured on surveillance tapes); United States v. Gann, 732 F.2d 714 (9th Cir.1984) (no search where officers executing search warrant heard what defendant said on phone in their presence); Holt v. State, 481 N.E.2d 1324 (Ind.1985) (no search where officer with naked ear heard prisoner talk on phone 12 ft. away); State v. Christianson, 361 N.W.2d 30 (Minn.1985) (no search where arrested defendant, in police station interview room while officers present, was overheard when he talked on phone); Pierre v. State, 607 So.2d 43 (Miss.1992) (no search where defendant's telephone call from police detectives' office overheard by detective 5 feet away).

lying prone at the connecting door, the agents overheard incriminating remarks by the conspirators. In holding that this conduct did not constitute a search, the court reasoned:

> The officers were exercising their investigative duties in a place where they had a right to be and they were relying upon their naked ears. So using their natural senses, they heard discussion of criminal acts. What was heard, however, was expressed by speakers who insist that they were justifiably relying upon their right of privacy, who sought to keep their conversation private, who "did not expect that law enforcement officers would be located just a few inches away from the crack below the door connecting the two adjoining rooms," and who thus conclude that "If one justifiably relies on his privacy any eavesdropping constitutes a search and seizure within the meaning of the Fourth Amendment." * * *
>
> But it is clear from *Katz* that for suppression of overheard speech the speaker must have "justifiably relied" on his privacy. * * * There must, first of all, have been a reliance on, an actual and reasonable expectation of, privacy. But beyond the individual's expectations, the needs of society are involved. The individual's subjective, self-centered expectation of privacy is not enough. We live in an organized society and the individual's expectation of privacy must be justifiable, "one that society is prepared to recognize as 'reasonable.'"
>
> The statements before us fail of suppression on both aspects. * * * Here the conversations complained of were audible by the naked ear in the next room. True the listening ear was at the keyhole, so to speak, but another listening ear was also, at one time, on the bed in the middle of the room, where was heard the pilot's story. Appellants would have us divide the listening room into privileged or burdened areas, and the conversation into degrees of audibility to, we presume, the normal ear, thus a remark heard on the bed arguably admissible, but not those heard at the door, a loud remark admissible, arguably one uttered in "normal" tones, but definitely not one whispered. We find no precedent for a categorization involving such hair-splitting distinctions and we are not disposed to create one.

Essentially the same reasoning supports what might be called the "plain smell" rule; there is no "reasonable expectation of privacy" from lawfully positioned agents "with inquisitive nostrils."[35] This means, for example, that no search in a Fourth Amendment sense has occurred when a law enforcement officer, lawfully present at a certain place, detects odors emanating from private premises,[36] from a vehicle,[37] or from some personal ef-

---

[35]United States v. Johnston, 497 F.2d 397 (9th Cir.1974).

[36]United States v. Ventresca, 380 U.S. 102, 85 S.Ct. 741, 13 L.Ed.2d 684 (1965) (search warrant properly based in part on allegation investigators "smelled the odor of fermenting mash in the vicinity of the suspected dwell-

ing"); Taylor v. United States, 286 U.S. 1, 52 S.Ct. 466, 76 L.Ed. 951 (1932) (agents determined by sight and smell that contraband liquor was in garage; that established probable cause, but agents improperly entered without first obtaining a search warrant).

[37]United States v. Pierre, 958

fects[38] nearby. But if the officer has to force air out of the effects in order to detect the odor, that conduct may be found to constitute a search. Such was the result in *Hernandez v. United States*,[39] where an officer detected the odor of marijuana coming from some suitcases after pressing their sides together and forcing air from the interior. The court reasoned:

> The manipulation of appellant's bags by Sergeant Butler prior to appellant's arrest constituted a "search" within the meaning of the Fourth Amendment. The contents of the bags were not exposed to Sergeant Butler's sight or smell before the bags were squeezed. He detected the odor of marihuana as the result of an "exploratory investigation," an "invasion or quest," a "prying into hidden places for that which was concealed"—conduct which has been repeatedly said to characterize a "search." * * * Technical trespass is not required. * * * But even if it were, it occurred here. "A trespass to a chattel may be committed by intentionally * * * using or intermeddling with a chattel in the possession of another."

The *Hernandez* result, however, is not beyond dispute. Assuming that Sergeant Butler was lawfully present in the storage area where the bags were located, it might be contended that his squeezing of the bags did not intrude upon the appellant's justified expectation of privacy in that Hernandez could not have reasonably expected that suitcases placed with an airline for load-

---

F.2d 1304 (5th Cir.1992); United States v. Rivera, 595 F.2d 1095 (5th Cir. 1979); United States v. Martinez-Miramontes, 494 F.2d 808 (9th Cir.1974) (relying on the analysis in *Fisch* and concluding that just as the court there "refused to make 'hair-splitting' constitutional distinctions," it could "likewise find no distinction in the use of the olfactory organs whether the revealing odor is detected in a stroll around the car or by a sniff over the trunk compartment").

Compare United States v. Ryles, 988 F.2d 13 (5th Cir.1993) (if officer "pierced the airspace inside the van before he smelled the burnt marijuana," this a search, albeit a reasonable one because, once driver who smelled of alcohol admitted he had no driver's license, officer was so acting to determine if any passenger had a license and was not similarly impaired).

[38]United States v. Gault, 92 F.3d 990 (10th Cir.1996) (where defendant train passenger "left his bag unattended" on floor in front of his seat so that it "protruded nearly a foot into the aisle," agent's smelling of bag no search); United States v. Johnston, 497 F.2d 397 (9th Cir.1974) (agent smelled odor coming from suitcase in vestibule of railroad car; court says it "not prepared to hold that, under the circumstances here, suitcase sniffing (whether the sniffer is erect or bending over) is a search within the meaning of the Fourth Amendment"); State v. Browne, 291 Conn. 720, 970 A.2d 81 (2009) (where defendant's freezer opened in search warrant execution and two large bricks wrapped in plastic found within, the "very definite odor of marijuana" made this a "plain smell" discovery of drugs); Sims v. State, 425 So.2d 563 (Fla.App.1982) (odor of marijuana from packages); State v. Coleman, 412 So.2d 532 (La.1982) (where police in baggage area with consent of airline, smelling odor of marijuana coming from checked bags no search).

As for whether a warrant is nonetheless needed to open the containers, see § 5.5(f).

[39]Hernandez v. United States, 353 F.2d 624 (9th Cir.1965).

ing, shipment and unloading would be handled more delicately.[40] But such reasoning hardly explains the highly questionable conclusion reached by another court, namely, that these checked-luggage-squeezing cases somehow support the holding that police about to have a drug dog sniff a vehicle stopped for a traffic violation may order the driver to roll up her windows and turn on the vehicle's ventilation system blowers on high in order "to force air inside the vehicle out through the seams."[41]

What this suggests, of course, is that there is also a "plain touch" doctrine[42] which likewise identifies yet another variety of nonsearch police activity. Thus, assuming a case somewhat like *Hernandez* in which it is conceded that the defendant had "no reasonable expectation that his luggage would not be moved or handled,"[43] if Sgt. Butler had squeezed a piece of soft-sided luggage and felt the unmistakable outline of a gun, that discovery would not constitute a search.[44] On the other hand, if the defendant had *not* dealt with the container in such a way as to surrender any justified privacy expectation vis-a-vis tactile examination, then of course the touching *would* be a search. Illustrative is *United States v. Most*,[45] where the defendant, pursuant to grocery store policy, checked his bag with a clerk prior to shop-

---

[40]United States v. Lovell, 849 F.2d 910 (5th Cir.1988), holding that "where agents detect an odor of marijuana emanating from luggage by using their own sense of smell" this is not a search. The defendant relied upon Arizona v. Hicks, 480 U.S. 321, 107 S.Ct. 1149, 94 L.Ed.2d 347 (1987), holding the mere movement of a stereo set to expose its serial number was a search, in arguing the agent made a search when he removed the suitcase from the airline's convey belt and squeezed it. The Court responded that *Hicks* was concerned with police activity inside defendant's apartment, where he clearly had a legitimate expectation of privacy, and distinguished the instant case because here the agent's actions occurred in a semi-public area after defendant had entrusted the handling of his bags to a common carrier and thus at that point had "no reasonable expectation that his luggage would not be moved or handled." Accord: United States v. Viera, 644 F.2d 509 (5th Cir.1981); State v. Peters, 189 Ariz. 216, 941 P.2d 228 (1997).

[41]People v. Bartelt, 241 Ill.2d 217, 349 Ill.Dec. 949, 948 N.E.2d 52 (2011).

Bartelt is a 4-3 decision; the dissenters rely upon the analysis in United States v. Ladeaux, 454 F.3d 1107 (10th Cir.2006), where, however, because of the procedural posture of the case, the court did not reach the merits of defendant's claim.

[42]See Holtz, The "Plain Touch" Corollary: A Natural and Foreseeable Consequence of the Plain View Doctrine, 95 Dick.L.Rev. 521 (1991).

[43]See United States v. Lovell, 849 F.2d 910 (5th Cir.1988), discussed in note 40 supra.

[44]Cf. United States v. Russell, 670 F.2d 323 (D.C.Cir.1982) (gun in paper bag "fell securely within the well-established 'plain view' exception" where officer felt outline of gun as he grasped the bag; plain view "encompasses 'plain touch'").

[45]United States v. Most, 876 F.2d 191 (D.C.Cir.1989). See also United States v. Jenkins, 396 F.3d 751 (6th Cir.2005) (where police officer present within hotel room with consent saw several luggage bags in the room and "proceeded to pick up all of the bags and feel them, noting that they were full (of 'bricks') and very heavy," that

ping there. A detective squeezed the bag and, based on its feel and the prior suspicion, concluded it contained packages of the cocaine derivative crack. In holding that the trial court had erred in upholding this police conduct on a "plain touch" theory, the court stated:

> We may assume, *arguendo,* that the "plain touch" doctrine would permit the opening of Most's bag *if* Sgt. Simms was authorized to feel the bag's exterior. "Plain touch" analysis is appropriate, however, only after the initial contact has been determined to be lawful. The doctrine applies to a narrow range of situations, such as *Terry* stops,[46] in which police are authorized to perform a limited inspection but not to conduct a full-scale search. It does not, however, allow police officers to eviscerate the fourth amendment by performing warrantless searches one layer at a time.

Somewhere between the *Hernandez* and *Most* fact situations, it would seem, are those cases (increasing in number as drug interdiction efforts are being directed at bus travelers) dealing with police feeling of the carry-on luggage of bus passengers, a matter about which courts were in general disagreement[47] until the Supreme Court decided *Bond v. United States.*[48] *Bond* involved a situation in which, during a lawful stop of a Greyhound bus, federal agents walked through the bus and squeezed the soft luggage passengers had placed in the overhead storage spaces. An agent noticed that one bag contained a brick-like object, and when passenger Downs admitted the bag was his and allowed the agent to open it, a brick of methamphetamine was discovered. Before the Supreme Court, the government argued that matters open to public observation are not protected by the Fourth Amendment, relying upon the overflight cases, *California v. Ciraolo*[49] and *Florida v. Riley.*[50] To this, the Court quite correctly responded that "*Ciraolo* and *Riley* are different from this case

---

a search).

[46]The reference is to Terry v. Ohio, 392 U.S. 1, 88 S.Ct. 1868, 20 L.Ed.2d 889 (1968), where the Court held such a patdown was a search, though a limited one permissible on less than the traditional, full quantum of probable cause. See § 9.6(a).

[47]E.g., compare United States v. Nicholson, 144 F.3d 632 (10th Cir.1998) ("placing a bag in an overhead rack of a commercial bus exposes it to certain intrusions," i.e., that "other passengers may push and move the bag" in order to make room for their own articles, but not manipulations that "reveal the contents of a bag, for example clothes, shoes, or toiletries, in which the owner has a legitimate expectation of privacy"); with United States v.

McDonald, 100 F.3d 1320 (7th Cir.1996) (where defendant "placed her bags in an overhead rack on a common carrier that was accessible to other passengers," the "feeling and pressing of [defendant's] bags that the officers undertook" was no search).

[48]Bond v. United States, 529 U.S. 334, 120 S.Ct. 1462, 146 L.Ed.2d 365 (2000), discussed in Derry, Lost Luggage: Searching for a Rule Regarding Privacy Expectations in Bond v. U.S., 69 U.Cin.L.Rev. 535 (2001); Comment, 29 Sw.U.L.Rev. 109 (1999); Notes, 27 Am.J.Crim.L. 411 (2000); 53 Baylor L.Rev. 713 (2001); 31 Cumb.L. Rev. 813 (2001); 37 Tul.L.Rev. 425 (2001); 33 U.Tol.L.Rev. 457 (2002); 27 Wm. Mitchell L.Rev. 2003 (2001).

[49]California v. Ciraolo, 476 U.S.

because they involved only visual, as opposed to tactile, observation. Physically invasive inspection is simply more intrusive than purely visual inspection."[51] The Court then turned to the real issue presented by *Bond*, whether "by using an opaque bag and placing that bag directly above his seat" the defendant had a justified expectation of privacy against the kind of tactile intrusion that occurred, and concluded:

> When a bus passenger places a bag in an overhead bin, he expects that other passengers or bus employees may move it for one reason or another. Thus, a bus passenger clearly expects that his bag may be handled. He does not expect that other passengers or bus employees will, as a matter of course, feel the bag in an exploratory manner.[52] But this is exactly what the agent did here.[53] We therefore hold that the agent's physical manipulation of petitioner's bag violated the Fourth Amendment.

The two *Bond* dissenters, who apparently would reserve the Fourth Amendment's protections for those passengers with the foresight to use hard-sided luggage,[54] objected that the *Bond* case "will lead to a constitutional jurisprudence of 'squeezes,' thereby complicating further already complex Fourth Amendment law." This seems somewhat of an overstatement, but in any event it would seem that an honest application of the *Katz* test in this context, as in many others, necessitates some consideration, on a case-by-case basis, of what degree of intrusion was undertaken by the police and what degree of protection from such an intrusion could fairly be expected from persons in the defendant's position. In the passenger luggage case, then, there is no escaping the task of evaluating the extent of control the passenger maintained over the luggage, the extent of protection afforded by the nature of the luggage itself, and the extent and character of the police efforts to ascertain what was inside that luggage.

207, 106 S.Ct. 1809, 90 L.Ed.2d 210 (1986), discussed in § 2.3(g).

[50]Florida v. Riley, 488 U.S. 445, 109 S.Ct. 693, 102 L.Ed.2d 835 (1989), discussed in § 2.3(e).

[51]The two dissenters in *Bond* disagreed with this latter conclusion, reasoning that "[w]hether tactile manipulation (say, of the exterior of luggage) is more intrusive or less intrusive than visual observation (say, through a lighted window) necessarily depends on the particular circumstances."

[52]This should not be read as a reference to the officer's purpose. Elsewhere the *Bond* majority noted the parties' agreement "that the subjective intent of the law enforcement officer is irrelevant," and then added that this "principle applies to the agent's acts in this case as well; the issue is not his state of mind, but the objective effect of his actions."

[53]The two dissenters, on the other hand, perceived no difference between what the officer had done and what could reasonably be expected from fellow passengers, stating that the "squeezing" by the officer did not "differ from the treatment that overhead luggage is likely to receive from strangers in a world of travel that is somewhat less gentle than it used to be."

[54]They stated that "the traveler who wants to place a bag in a shared overhead bin and yet safeguard its contents from public touch should plan to pack those contents in a suitcase with hard sides."

This being so, it would seem that, in the case of carry-on luggage, it makes some difference exactly where the passenger places the bag,[55] and also some difference how the officer manipulates the bag (e.g., feeling it for shapes within, as opposed to lifting it to determine overall weight).[56] In the case of airline passengers, it may well be that carry-on luggage will be deemed to carry a justified expectation of privacy of a lesser degree because the luggage must pass inspection to be taken aboard; the x-raying and the squeezing may be seen as near equivalents in the sense that both can reveal the shape of specific contents. As for the checked luggage of passengers on public conveyances, it would seem from the language already quoted from *Bond*, plus the Court's added observation that "travelers are particularly concerned about their carry-on luggage" because "they generally use it to transport personal items that, for whatever reason, they prefer to keep close at hand," that *Bond* cannot be viewed as covering checked luggage as well. But in the case of bus passengers, where it is common practice for the passengers to set their larger luggage beside the bus so that the driver can place it into the underneath compartment, it is to be doubted that the circumstances are that much different from those that actually obtained in *Bond* so as to call for a different result. At the other extreme, where an airline passenger checks his luggage at the terminal and that luggage is thereafter handled several times as it makes its way to and into the plane the passenger will be traveling upon, the opportunities for manipulation of the bag by baggage handlers is more substantial. This certainly increases the chances a police officer's manipulation of that luggage will not be deemed a search, though surely the magnitude of the officer's manipulation must still be taken into account, all of which perhaps accounts for the pre-*Bond* difference of opinion regarding that situation.[57]

Even in the *Terry* situation alluded to in *Most*, the so-called "plain touch" does not ordinarily serve to distinguish a search from a nonsearch, but rather to distinguish a legal search from an illegal one: the fundamental question is whether the touching relied upon to establish the probable cause for a further intrusion was part of a legitimate frisk of the suspect or his effects under

---

[55]See, e.g., United States v. Gault, 92 F.3d 990 (10th Cir.1996) (holding that officer's kicking and lifting of a gym bag located on the floor in front of a train seat, and protruding into the aisle, did not constitute a search, reasoning that the information the officer "obtained from the kick and lift of the bag, its weight and the solidity of its contents, was the same information

that a passenger would have obtained by kicking the bag accidentally or by lifting it to clear the aisle").

[56]See, e.g., United States v. Gault, 92 F.3d 990 (10th Cir.1996).

[57]Compare Arizona v. Hicks, 480 U.S. 321, 107 S.Ct. 1149, 94 L.Ed.2d 347 (1987), and United Sttes v. Lovell, 849 F.2d 910 (5th Cir.1988), both discussed in note 40 supra.

Terry.[58] This was the essential point in *Minnesota v. Dickerson*,[59] where the officer commenced a lawful frisk for a weapon but felt only a lump no bigger than a marble. The state court had concluded that because there was at that moment *no* "possibility that the object in the defendant's pocket was a weapon," the officer's subsequent "squeezing, sliding and otherwise manipulating the contents of the defendant's pocket" (necessary to reveal that the lump was crack cocaine in a plastic bag) was illegal.[60] The Supreme Court agreed, noting that "the officer's continued exploration of respondent's pocket after having concluded that it contained no weapon was unrelated to '[t]he sole justification of

---

[58]See United States v. Proctor, 148 F.3d 39 (1st Cir.1998) (during lawful pat-down officer "made an immediate determination that the bulge was in fact a glassine bag containing marijuana"); State v. Clark, 255 Conn. 268, 764 A.2d 1251 (2001) (*Dickerson* distinguished, as here during lawful "open, flat-handed patdown," when officer touched bulge in defendant's sock "he immediately recognized it as crack cocaine based on the fact of the 'plasticky packaging material' and the 'rock or-chunk-like' substance"); Dickerson v. United States, 677 A.2d 509 (D.C.App.1996) (during "authorized patdown for weapons, the officer came upon a package that he said immediately felt like the kind of drug package he had touched on numerous occasions in the same unusual location on the body, namely the crotch area," and thus probable cause to search the package); People v. Mitchell, 165 Ill.2d 211, 209 Ill.Dec. 41, 650 N.E.2d 1014 (1995) (in pat-down for weapons, officer felt in defendant's shirt pocket an object "like a piece of rock inside a small baggie"; that information plus earlier observation of drug paraphernalia in defendant's car constituted probable cause to arrest); State v. James, 795 So.2d 1146 (La.2000) ("the officer exceeded the scope of a valid *Terry* stop when he removed the [film] canister from relator's pocket and began manipulating it to determine its contents"); People v. Custer, 465 Mich. 319, 630 N.W.2d 870 (2001) (during lawful pat-down "the officer felt a two-by-three inch object in defendant's pocket that he believed was a card of blotter acid," "based on his knowledge that blotter acid was often contained on sheets of cardboard," "that cards of blotter acid were capable of fitting into a pants pocket," etc., and thus "officer had probable cause to believe the object he felt in defendant's pocket was contraband" and "was justified in removing [what turned out to be] photographs from the defendant's pocket pursuant to the plain feel exception to the warrant requirement"); State v. Rushing, 935 S.W.2d 30 (Mo.1996), discussed in Note, 63 Mo.L.Rev. 243 (1998) (in *Terry* frisk officer immediately felt tubular item of kind commonly used to carry crack; that and other circumstances constituted probable cause to search further); State v. Winn, 974 S.W.2d 700 (Tenn.Crim. App.1998) (feeling "bulge" during frisk no basis to search for contraband, as "the officer provided no objective facts upon which to base his determination that the bundle in the defendant's rear pocket was contraband").

[59]Minnesota v. Dickerson, 508 U.S. 366, 113 S.Ct. 2130, 124 L.Ed.2d 334 (1993). See Atneosen & Wolfe, The "Plain Feel" Exception: Is the Standard Sufficiently Plain?, 29 Wm.Mitchell L.Rev. 81 (1994); Poulin, The Plain Feel Doctrine and the Evolution of the Fourth Amendment, 42 Vill.L.Rev. 741 (1997); Comment, 58 Alb.L.Rev. 871 (1995); Notes, 36 B.C.L.Rev. 125 (1994); 44 DePaul L.Rev. 167 (1994); 39 Loyola L.Rev. 685 (1993); 14 N.Ill. L.Rev. 585 (1994); 21 Ohio N.U.L.Rev. 343 (1994); 47 Okla.L.Rev. 711 (1994); 39 St. Louis U.L.Rev. 1053 (1995); 1994 Wis.L.Rev. 1303.

[60]State v. Dickerson, 481 N.W.2d 840 (Minn.1992).

the search [under *Terry:*] . . . the protection of the police officer and others nearby.'"

Significantly, however, the Supreme Court in *Dickerson* did not stop there but went on to disagree with the state court on another point as to which the lower courts had been divided:[61] whether there exists a "plain feel" equivalent to the plain view doctrine. The state court had rejected the analogy on two grounds: (i) because "the sense of touch is inherently less immediate and less reliable than the sense of sight," and (ii) because "the sense of touch is far more intrusive into the personal privacy that is at the core of the fourth amendment." But the Supreme Court disagreed on both counts. As to the first, the Court responded that often touch is very reliable, as in a *Terry* frisk detecting the presence of a weapon. Moreover, any lack of reliability generally merely means "that officers will less often be able to justify seizures of unseen contraband," as in any event the Fourth Amendment requires probable cause as a prerequisite to seizure. As to the second, the Supreme Court concluded it was "inapposite" because the feared intrusion "has already been authorized by the lawful search for weapons" and the subsequent seizure of the identified item "occasions no further invasion of privacy."

That focus on the concept of "plain touch" in *Dickerson* is somewhat confusing. Again, the real question presented by the facts of that case was whether the search which uncovered the crack cocaine had some independent justification. In concluding it did not, the Court apparently found it useful to draw an analogy between the instant so-called "plain touch" situation and the well-established plain view doctrine; the squeeze in *Dickerson,* the Court said, was just as lacking in justification as was the moving of the stereo in the plain view case of *Arizona v. Hicks*.[62] But much of the Court's discussion, especially that disagreeing with the state court, goes to a quite different point: that a "plain touch" is like a plain view in that it can (i) not only establish probable cause, but (ii) obviate whatever search warrant requirement would otherwise exist. This is the sense of the *Dickerson* Court's assertion that a "plain touch" justifies a "warrantless seizure" because the touching makes so certain what the object is that going the search warrant route "would do little to promote the objectives of the Fourth Amendment." But *Dickerson* really does not present a seizure-based-on-touch issue! The touching there resulted not in a seizure but in further searching, which revealed a plastic bag of crack cocaine; then came the seizure of what was apparently at that point in plain view (not merely plain touch).

[61]The pre-*Dickerson* cases on both sides are collected in the Supreme Court's opinion. After *Dickerson,* however, as noted in State v. Wonders, 263 Kan. 582, 952 P.2d 1351 (1998), "almost all other states which have been asked to extend this exception to the Fourth Amendment search warrant requirement" have done so.

[62]Arizona v. Hicks, 480 U.S. 321, 107 S.Ct. 1149, 94 L.Ed.2d 347 (1987).

Moreover, even if the search in *Dickerson* had been upon probable cause, so that it then would have been appropriate to move on to the question of justifying a warrantless seizure, surely such a seizure could quite readily be upheld without any reliance upon the concept of "plain touch."[63]

If, as the Supreme Court concluded in *Dickerson,* the state court was wrong in saying that "the sense of touch is * * * less reliable than the sense of sight," that conclusion is most likely to prove important in the future in still another context, where the question is whether a container that otherwise could be searched only pursuant to a search warrant may be opened without such a warrant because the container itself sufficiently reveals its contents.[64] But the resolution of that question depends *not* on whether the "plain touch" amounts to probable cause, deemed a critical point in the *Dickerson* discussion, but rather on whether it manifests the contents of the container to such a "virtual certainty" that the warrant process would serve no meaningful function. Some plain touches doubtless meet that more demanding test as well,[65] but it should not be assumed that the discussion in *Dickerson* sheds any light on just when that is so.

§ 2.2(b) Use of flashlight or other means of illumination

Over eighty years ago the Supreme Court had occasion to consider whether observation by means of artificial illumination constituted a search under the Fourth Amendment. In *United*

---

[63]Such probable cause the defendant presently possessed contraband would be a basis for his arrest, which would support an incidental search of the person even if the search came before the arrest, Rawlings v. Kentucky, 448 U.S. 98, 100 S.Ct. 2556, 65 L.Ed.2d 633 (1980), and that search could extend to the opening of small containers on the person and could be followed by a warrantless seizure of discovered contraband, United States v. Robinson, 414 U.S. 218, 94 S.Ct. 467, 38 L.Ed.2d 427 (1973).

Compare Commonwealth v. Stevenson, 560 Pa. 345, 744 A.2d 1261 (2000) (full search proper "where the officer conducting the frisk feels an object whose mass or contour makes its criminal character immediately apparent," which not the case "when an officer conducting a *Terry* frisk merely feels and recognizes by touch an object that could be used to hold either legal or illegal substances, even when the

officer has previously seen others use that object to carry or ingest drugs," as with pill bottles, cigars and fold paper in instant case).

[64]See § 5.5(f).

[65]As where the "plain touch" clearly reveals the shape of a gun. See United States v. Williams, 822 F.2d 1174 (D.C.Cir.1987); United States v. Portillo, 633 F.2d 1313 (9th Cir.1980).

Compare People v. Diaz, 81 N.Y.2d 106, 595 N.Y.S.2d 940, 612 N.E.2d 298 (1993) (in pre-*Dickerson* decision, court appears to conclude that a "plain touch" can *never* excuse a warrant requirement for a search because, unlike a plain view situation, "the identity and nature of the concealed item cannot be confirmed until seen," necessitating "a further *search*"instead of merely a warrantless seizure, which is what the plain view doctrine permits).

States v. Lee,[66] a Coast Guard patrol boat following a motorboat lost sight of the boat after sundown, but the boat was later discovered alongside a schooner. The boatswain testified that upon locating the motorboat he shined a searchlight on it and saw a number of cans of alcohol on board. The court of appeals ruled that this constituted an illegal search, but the Supreme Court disagreed:

> But no search on the high seas is shown. The testimony of the boatswain shows that he used a searchlight. It is not shown that there was any exploration below decks or under hatches. For aught that appears, the cases of liquor were on deck and, like the defendants, were discovered before the motorboat was boarded. Such use of a searchlight is comparable to the use of a marine glass or a field glass. It is not prohibited by the Constitution.

In *Katz v. United States*,[67] of course, the Court later took a drastically different approach to the fundamental question of what constitutes a search, and in particular held that a search could occur without physical penetration of a constitutionally protected area. Although at first blush this might appear to cast some doubt upon the continued vitality of *Lee,* it is noteworthy that the *Katz* Court cited *Lee* in support of the proposition that "[w]hat a person knowingly exposes to the public, even in his own home or office, is not a subject of Fourth Amendment protection." That reference has not gone unnoticed; indeed, it has been relied upon in more recent cases holding that use of artificial illumination by a lawfully positioned officer does not constitute a search.[68]

Particularly in light of the Supreme Court's declaration that a diminished expectation of privacy surrounds the automobile because "[i]t travels public thoroughfares where both its occupants and its contents are in plain view,"[69] it is not surprising that the use of a flashlight or similar artificial illumination has been most readily upheld when it has permitted an officer to see objects inside a vehicle. When the vehicle was parked or was lawfully stopped on the public way, the courts have consistently held that the officer's conduct in illuminating the interior of the automobile does not constitute a search.[70] "The fact that the contents of the vehicle may not have been visible without the use

---

[Section 2.2(b)]

[66]United States v. Lee, 274 U.S. 559, 47 S.Ct. 746, 71 L.Ed. 1202 (1927). See also United States v. Hernandez, 715 F.2d 548 (11th Cir.1983) (no search on similar facts, as defendants "had no expectation of privacy in the marijuana they carried aboard its deck" even though they "travelling in darkness").

[67]Katz v. United States, 389 U.S. 347, 88 S.Ct. 507, 19 L.Ed.2d 576 (1967).

[68]E.g., United States v. Wright, 449 F.2d 1355 (D.C.Cir.1971).

[69]United States v. Chadwick, 433 U.S. 1, 97 S.Ct. 2476, 53 L.Ed.2d 538 (1977), quoting from the plurality opinion in Cardwell v. Lewis, 417 U.S. 583, 94 S.Ct. 2464, 41 L.Ed.2d 325 (1974).

[70]United States v. Allen, 573 F.3d 42 (1st Cir.2009); United States v. Desir, 257 F.3d 1233 (11th Cir.2001);

of artificial illumination does not preclude such observation from application of the 'plain view' doctrine."[71]

To the extent that courts have felt compelled to offer some reason for this conclusion, the reason typically given is that the owner or operator of an automobile parked or being operated upon a public thoroughfare does not have a justified expectation that such a common device as a flashlight would not be used during the nighttime to see what would be visible without such illumination during daylight hours. It is said that property lying within the vehicle has been "knowingly exposed to public view" even when "artificial illumination, specifically directed, might be required to render the property visible."[72] As noted in *Marshall v.*

United States v. Beatty, 170 F.3d 811 (8th Cir.1999); United States v. Weatherspoon, 82 F.3d 697 (6th Cir.1996); United States v. Landry, 903 F.2d 334 (5th Cir.1990); United States v. Hood, 493 F.2d 677 (9th Cir.1974); State v. Brierly, 109 Ariz. 310, 509 P.2d 203 (1973); People v. Dickinson, 928 P.2d 1309 (Colo.1996); State v. Graham, 200 Conn. 9, 509 A.2d 493 (1986); Robertson v. State, 704 A.2d 267 (Del. 1997); Beachum v. United States, 19 A.3d 311 (D.C.App.2011); Redd v. State, 242 Ga. 876, 252 S.E.2d 383 (1979); State v. Naeole, 80 Haw. 419, 910 P.2d 732 (1996); State v. Post, 98 Idaho 834, 573 P.2d 153 (1978); People v. Bombacino, 51 Ill.2d 17, 280 N.E.2d 697 (1972); Avant v. State, 528 N.E.2d 74 (Ind.1988); State v. Lamp, 322 N.W.2d 48 (Iowa 1982); State v. Doile, 244 Kan. 493, 769 P.2d 666 (1989); State v. Hunt, 25 So. 3d 746 (La.2009); State v. Chattley, 390 A.2d 472 (Me. 1978); Commonwealth v. Doulette, 414 Mass. 653, 609 N.E.2d 473 (1993); People v. Whalen, 390 Mich. 672, 213 N.W.2d 116 (1973); State v. Alesso, 328 N.W.2d 685 (Minn.1982); Smith v. State, 729 So.2d 1191 (Miss.1998); State v. Renfrew, 122 N.H. 308, 444 A.2d 527 (1982); State v. Parizek, 678 N.W.2d 154 (N.D.2004); Dick v. State, 596 P.2d 1265 (Okl.Crim.App.1979); State v. Miller, 45 Or.App. 407, 608 P.2d 595 (1980); Commonwealth v. Milyak, 508 Pa. 2, 493 A.2d 1346 (1985); State v. Trudeau, 165 Vt. 355, 683 A.2d 725 (1996).

See also United States v. Rascon-Ortiz, 994 F.2d 749 (10th Cir.1993) (no search for officer to kneel down and look at undercarriage, even though flashlight and mirror used); Commonwealth v. A Juvenile (No. 2), 411 Mass. 157, 580 N.E.2d 1014 (1991) (no search for officer to use spotlight to see from road exterior damage to car parked in driveway of residence).

To the same effect are United States v. Coplen, 541 F.2d 211 (9th Cir.1976), concerning use of a flashlight to look into an airplane parked on the ramp at an airport; and Albo v. State, 379 So.2d 648 (Fla.1980), concerning use of a flashlight to look inside a parked motor home.

[71]United States v. Johnson, 506 F.2d 674 (8th Cir.1974). As the Court put it in Texas v. Brown, 460 U.S. 730, 103 S.Ct. 1535, 75 L.Ed.2d 502 (1983), it is "beyond dispute that [officer] Maples' action in shining his flashlight to illuminate the interior of [driver] Brown's car trenched upon no right secured to the latter by the Fourth Amendment."

And, such use of "plain view" analysis as to discovery of a weapon by shining a flashlight does not mean the defendant cannot be convicted of carrying a concealed weapon when concealment is defined as hidden from ordinary observation. Robertson v. State, 704 A.2d 267 (Del.1997).

[72]State v. Stone, 294 A.2d 683 (Me.1972). The result is otherwise, of course, if the vehicle is parked on private property as to which the defendant has a justified expectation of privacy. See People v. Apodaca, 194 Colo. 324, 571 P.2d 1109 (1977). But,

United States:[73]

> When the circumstances of a particular case are such that the police officer's observation would not have constituted a search had it occurred in daylight, then the fact that the officer used a flashlight to pierce the nighttime darkness does not transform his observation into a search. Regardless of the time of day or night, the plain view rule must be upheld where the viewer is rightfully positioned * * *. The plain view rule does not go into hibernation at sunset.[74]

This suggests that there may be certain instances in which using a flashlight to look inside a vehicle *is* a search because the circumstances indicate an intrusion upon a justified expectation of privacy occurred. Illustrative is *Berryhill v. State*,[75] where a flashlight was used to enable a viewing of the contents of a truck through an opening in the van door about the width of a penny; the court quite correctly concluded a search had occurred.[76]

It must be emphasized once again that the officer's position vis-a-vis the vehicle, whereby he is able to shine a light into the car and see what is thereby illuminated, must have been lawfully acquired. No problem is presented when the vehicle is parked in an area accessible to the public. If the vehicle is parked on private property, the officer must have a legitimate reason for being on the property at the place where the flashlight viewing occurs.[77] When the police have stopped the car, it is of course essential

---

entry onto the private property on reasonable suspicion has been allowed, so that while thus lawfully positioned a light may be shined into the vehicle. Garrett v. State, 466 N.E.2d 8 (Ind. 1984).

[73]Marshall v. United States, 422 F.2d 185 (5th Cir.1970).

[74]See also United States v. Booker, 461 F.2d 990 (6th Cir.1972) ("Since it would not constitute a search for the officer to observe objects in plain view in the automobile in daylight, it ought not to constitute a search for him to flash a light in the car as he was walking past it in the night season"); State v. Cobb, 115 Ariz. 484, 566 P.2d 285 (1977) ("To say that what would have been clearly visible to the police * * * within a few short hours when daylight arrived, was not properly seized because it was nighttime and a policeman used his flashlight, stretches the legal imagination too far"); People v. Whalen, 390 Mich. 672, 213 N.W.2d 116 (1973) ("the plain view rule does not slink away at sunset to emerge again at the break of day"); State v. O'Neill, 148 Wash.2d 564, 62 P.3d 489

(2003) ("The use of a flashlight to illuminate at night what is plainly visible during the day is not an unconstitutional intrusion into a citizen's privacy interests").

[75]Berryhill v. State, 372 So.2d 355 (Ala.Civ.App.1979). See also Raettig v. State, 406 So.2d 1273 (Fla.App.1981) (observation in kneeling position made by flashlight through crack between bed of truck and base of camper 6'8" long and 1/2" wide was a search, as when a person "has taken affirmative measures to safeguard his property within an area from public view, a minute crack on the surface of such area can hardly be regarded as an implied invitation to any curious passerby to take a look").

[76]The analysis here is similar to that of the dissent in United States v. Wright, 449 F.2d 1385 (D.C.Cir.1971), discussed in the text at note 88 infra.

[77]United States v. Carter, 360 F.3d 1235 (10th Cir.2004) (officers' actions in "walking up the driveway, and shining their flashlight into a car in the driveway * * * do not implicate the Fourth Amendment"); State v. Lee,

that the stopping have been lawful.[78] And in any event, if either the illumination or observation is accomplished by opening or entering the car, it is likewise essential that this conduct have a lawful basis. Illustrative is *Tyler v. United States*,[79] where an officer came upon a person in the early morning hours sitting in a parked car in an alley. The policeman opened the car door on the passenger side and shined his flashlight into the car, discovering thereby the handle of a pistol protruding from under the front seat. In holding the weapon inadmissible, the court correctly reasoned:

> In the case at bar, the opening of the car door was an intrusion that has not been justified by appellee as coming within any of the exceptions to the need for a warrant to search. The Government has not shown that the officer who opened the door and upon using a flashlight saw the gun in plain view had "a right to be in the position to have that view." The officer had opened the car door in order to see what was inside. He could not have been searching for the fruits, implements or evidence of a crime since there would be none for the offense of parking in an alley for which the only possible police action was a citation to the driver.

Occurring much less frequently, but governed by essentially the same considerations, is the use of artificial illumination to detect what an individual has on his person. *State v. Bainch*[80] is such a case. There a policeman on patrol during the early morning hours saw a man either sleeping or passed out on a bench. The officer approached and shined his flashlight around the bench, after which he directed the light into the sleeping man's pocket and saw marijuana cigarettes. The court held that the officer had found the cigarettes in plain view and that "the fact that he observed them with the aid of the flashlight did not make this a 'search.' " *Bainch,* of course, is an unusual case in that it was not necessary for the officer to stop the suspect prior to the viewing of the incriminating evidence. If a suspect is lawfully stopped for investigation, then here again the use of a flashlight to see what is on the person of the suspect is constitutionally permissible.[81] But if, on the other hand, the initial detention of the suspect was illegal, then the viewing of the suspect's posses-

---

633 P.2d 48 (Utah 1981) (no search, as officer taking appropriate path to front door).

[78] See § 9.5.

[79] Tyler v. United States, 302 A.2d 748 (D.C.App.1973).

[80] State v. Bainch, 24 Ariz.App. 140, 536 P.2d 709 (1975).

[81] In People v. Woods, 6 Cal.App.3d 832, 86 Cal.Rptr. 264 (1970), the officer lawfully stopped the suspect and then, "without spreading the pocket or pulling it open, shined his flashlight into the pocket and discovered therein a clear plastic bag containing a green, leafy substance that looked like marijuana." In holding this was not a search, the court reasoned: "Officer Convey was on a public street where he was entitled to be. He illuminated the interior of defendant's pocket with his flashlight without in any way otherwise improving his view. * * * We do not regard this conduct on the officer's part as being equivalent to his

sions by flashlight is tainted by that illegality.[82]

Finally, there is the infrequent but troublesome practice of using artificial illumination to detect what is inside premises. In at least some circumstances it is fair to conclude that such observations are likewise not searches in the Fourth Amendment sense, although it is less than clear just how far this notion can be pushed. A comparatively easy situation is that presented in *People v. Wheeler*,[83] where an eyewitness to a burglary told police he saw the burglars take a stereo cabinet into a nearby garage. From a lawful position near that unlighted garage, one of the officers shined his flashlight through the open garage door and immediately saw the cabinet. In upholding this action, the court asserted:

> It is well established law that the observation of that which is in the plain sight of an officer standing in a place where he has a lawful right to be does not constitute a search and such observation is lawful regardless of whether the illumination permitting the observation is natural light, artificial light, or light from a flashlight held by the officer viewing the object in question.

reaching into the pocket and forcibly withdrawing therefrom the clear plastic bag of marijuana."

Compare Commonwealth v. Graham, 554 Pa. 472, 721 A.2d 1075 (1998) (shining flashlight into detainee's pocket, revealing cocaine in container for Lifesavers Holes, was a search, as reasoning "that a flashlight may properly illuminate items that would be in plain view during daylight hours, does not apply here, as the Lifesavers Holes container was not an exposed object"; court fails to note what might have been a more convincing rationale, that the looking was no search but was a fruit of an illegal detention because the only basis for the officer dealing with defendant at all was for self-protection, given that he a companion of a person to be arrested on an outstanding warrant, but a patdown had already revealed that defendant not armed); People v. Snider, 76 Cal.App.3d 560, 142 Cal.Rptr. 900 (1978) (after a vehicle stopped for defective tail light, officer shined flashlight on driver's face to check it against picture on tendered driver's license; noting defendant's "pinned eyes," officer then subjected him to flashlight test for addiction and thereby determined that there was no pupillary reaction to the change from light to darkness; first use of the flashlight was no search, the second was a limited form of search requiring a degree of suspicion somewhat short of the usual quantum of probable cause present here).

[82]In State v. Evans, 16 Or.App. 189, 517 P.2d 1225 (1974), the officer again shined a light into the suspect's pocket and saw a bag of marijuana, but here the result was different than in *Woods*. The court concluded: "The defendant, by refusing to disclose the contents of his other pocket and by turning to avoid observation was guilty only of an unsophisticated attempt to assert his right to privacy and would clearly, had he felt free, have walked away. At the moment Officer Straughan bent over and shined his flashlight upward, he was able to observe marijuana in the visible quarter to half inch of the plastic bag showing in the corner of defendant's pocket only because defendant was present for such examination by virtue of a minor detention which was not justified under the Fourth Amendment. Therefore the fruits of that observation are not admissible into evidence and the motion to suppress was properly granted."

[83]People v. Wheeler, 28 Cal.App.3d 1065, 105 Cal.Rptr. 56 (1972).

Given the facts in *Wheeler,* especially the open garage door, this result is not objectionable.[84] Thus on somewhat similar facts the Supreme Court readily concluded that "the officers' use of the beam of a flashlight, directed through the essentially open front of respondent's barn, did not transform their observations into an unreasonable search within the meaning of the Fourth Amendment."[85] That decision also supports the conclusion that it is not a search to use a flashlight to look through a window into residential premises from a lawful vantage point,[86] just as it is no search to use such illumination to see objects outside the premises while within the curtilage on legitimate business.[87]

It is less apparent that the like result reached in *United States v. Wright*[88] is correct. In that case, police located the remains of a stolen car under circumstances indicating that it had been stripped in that general vicinity, and then found tell-tale sweepings of nuts and bolts in front of a three-car garage facing onto an alley. The sliding doors of the garage were not completely closed because of their construction and age, so an officer employed his flashlight to look through the gap into the "relatively dark" interior and saw parts that had been removed from the stolen car. The majority, even on the assumption that "what Officer Huffstutler saw when he beamed his flashlight through the crack in the doors could only have been otherwise observed if the light in the garage had been turned on," concluded there had been no search. Taking note of the decision in *Katz,* they reasoned that

> even under this basic principle, the appellant cannot prevail. For it cannot be said that his actions in storing the stolen transmission—

---

[84]See also United States v. Garner, 907 F.2d 60 (8th Cir.1990) (no search when officer investigating burglary complaint shined headlights into garden adjacent to residence and saw marijuana plants); People v. Glick, 250 P.3d 578 (Colo.2011) (where police lawfully at front door and person who answered door left it open when he went to find another occupant, no search for police to shine flashlight into home from that position and "make plain view observations that during daylight would not constitute a search"); Commonwealth v. Johnson, 777 S.W.2d 876 (Ky.1989) (no search to look inside motel room by shining flashlight through ajar door and uncurtained window; court stresses flashlight "a widely available device" and that motel lodgers must do more to preserve privacy because rooms are "in close proximity to places of public passage"); State v. Winkler, 552 N.W.2d

347 (N.D.1996) (no search where officers drove onto driveway and shined headlights of patrol car through open garage door).

[85]United States v. Dunn, 480 U.S. 294, 107 S.Ct. 1134, 94 L.Ed.2d 326 (1987).

[86]Commonwealth v. Pietrass, 392 Mass. 892, 467 N.E.2d 1368 (1984) (use of flashlight to look through window from enclosed porch no search if officer lawfully on the porch); State v. Rose, 128 Wash.2d 388, 909 P.2d 280 (1996) (use of flashlight, "an exceedingly common device," to look through picture window from porch no search, as officer lawfully on porch).

[87]State v. Johnson, 171 N.J. 192, 793 A.2d 619 (2002).

[88]United States v. Wright, 449 F.2d 1355 (D.C.Cir.1971).

which, no doubt, he would like to have kept hidden—in a garage having a nine-inch gap between the doors were calculated to keep his possession of it "strictly private and free from perception by others" any more than the petitioner in *Lee, supra,*[89] could have expected the presence at night of the contraband liquor on the deck of his boat to be so.

Judge Wright, in his dissent, after noting that what the majority preferred to call a "nine-inch gap" was in fact "an eight-inch slit one half inch wide," asked:

> But isn't it at least troubling that here * * * the garage door was *locked* and the police * * * had to use special equipment such as a flashlight to see inside? Certainly a flashlight is not standard equipment for "any curious passerby,"[90] particularly in the daytime. Isn't there also a serious danger that the "plain view" holding of the majority in this case is inconsistent with the Supreme Court decision in *Katz,* which held that what a person "seeks to preserve as private, even in an area accessible to the public may be constitutionally protected"? * * * Is it not important to our American way of life that when a citizen does as much as ordinary care requires to shield his sanctuary from strangers his constitutional right to maintain his privacy should not be made to depend upon the resources of skillful peepers and eavesdroppers who can always find ways to intrude?

These are tough questions, to be sure, and it would be foolhardy to claim that *Katz* provides ready answers to them. It may be suggested, however, that these provocative inquiries cast a fair degree of doubt upon the generalization that all such flashlight observations into private premises are deserving of the nonsearch plain view characterization. It is not enough, of course, that the defendants in *Wright* subjectively believed they had a secure hiding place for the fruits of their criminal activity. But surely there comes a point where it can be said that a person has "justifiably relied"[91] upon the privacy of his premises even though he has not taken the extraordinary step of sealing off every minute aperture in that structure. Precisely when that point is reached is a matter upon which reasonable minds might differ. But in making that judgment in a particular case, it certainly is not irrelevant that the officer was able to pierce the privacy-by-darkness inside the premises only by directing an artificial light into the building. It is one thing to say that "[t]he plain view rule

---

[89] The reference is to United States v. Lee, 274 U.S. 559, 47 S.Ct. 746, 71 L.Ed. 1202 (1927), discussed in text at note 66 supra.

[90] This is a reference to the majority's quotation of James v. United States, 418 F.2d 1150 (D.C.Cir.1969), where it is said: "That the policeman may have to crane his neck, or bend over, or squat, does not render the doctrine inapplicable, so long as what he saw would have been visible to any curious passerby."

[91] This, of course, is the critical language in *Katz.*

does not go into hibernation at sunset,"[92] so that a person cannot claim a justified expectation of privacy based upon nothing more than the fact that what could be seen during the day can be seen during the nighttime only by artificial light.[93] It is quite another, however, to conclude that when a person, in effect, "creates" darkness within premises by the manner in which he closes and secures the building, there can never be a constitutionally-protected expectation that this privacy will not be breached by artificial illumination manipulated from outside. Preferable to *Wright,* therefore, is the reasoning in *State v. Tarantino*[94] that it *is* a search for an officer to observe items within a locked store building by shining a light through a minute crack in the wall, for to hold otherwise "would require owners of non-residential buildings who want to enjoy their Fourth Amendment rights to maintain their structures almost as air tight containers."[95] Such a search-by-flashlight conclusion "is even more compelling than in *Tarantino*"when the building thereby looked into is a dwelling, considering "the enormous expectation of privacy with regard to the interior of a personal residence."[96]

In cases of the *Wright* genre, it is in a sense understandable that courts find themselves inextricably pushed in the direction of holding that the flashlight observation is not a search. In the *Wright* case itself, for example, one is inclined to view sympathetically the action taken by the police; once the sweepings were found immediately in front of the garage, the officers understandably concluded that the most logical next step was to respond to this "challenging situation"[97] by peering through the crack in the door directly before them. A court that deems this a reasonable

---

[92]Marshall v. United States, 422 F.2d 185 (5th Cir.1970).

[93]State v. Curtin, 175 W.Va. 318, 332 S.E.2d 619 (1985) (where police lawfully on defendant's premises to execute search warrant for house, shining flashlight into garden no search, as a "flashlight merely provides at night what the sun does during the day").

[94]State v. Tarantino, 322 N.C. 386, 368 S.E.2d 588 (1988).

[95]The court added the instant case was distinguishable from the Supreme Court's decision in United States v. Dunn, 480 U.S. 294, 107 S.Ct. 1134, 94 L.Ed.2d 326 (1987), text at note 85 supra, because here the officer "had to bend and peer with a flashlight through quarter-inch cracks near the floor. Nothing indicates, as in *Dunn,* that had [the officer] conducted

his investigation during the day he could have viewed the building's interior without making the same searching inquiry."

[96]State v. Rose, 75 Wash.App. 28, 876 P.2d 925 (1994) (a search to look inside mobile home through curtained windows by using flashlight at night, as this "not simply a case wherein the flashlight illuminated what could normally have been seen during the day").

[97]In *Wright,* the majority set forth an alternative ground of decision to the plain view approach, namely, that under the circumstances it was reasonable for the officer to take a "closer look at a challenging situation." In support, the court relied upon Dorsey v. United States, 372 F.2d 928 (D.C. Cir.1967), where an officer shined a light into a parked car. In *Dorsey,* without either characterizing the officer's action as a search or attempting

response by the police is tempted to validate that response by declaring it was not a search, especially if it appears an assertion the police action *was* a search compels the conclusion Judge Wright reached in his dissent, namely, that the police should have sought out a magistrate and tried to persuade him to issue a search warrant. As Professor Amsterdam has cogently pointed out, "[i]t would obviously be easier and more likely for a court to say that a patrolman's shining of a flashlight into the interior * * * was a 'search' if that conclusion did not encumber the flashlight with a warrant requirement but simply required, for example, that the patrolman 'be able to point to specific and articulable facts' supporting a reasonable inference that something [inside] required his attention."[98]

That comment tends to explain a case such as *State v. Crea*,[99] which otherwise might appear to be in irresolvable conflict with *Wright*. In *Crea* the police, who were investigating the theft of two snowmobiles and a snowmobile trailer, were advised that the car earlier observed towing the stolen articles had been seen leaving certain premises. The police then went to those premises for the purpose of questioning whoever might be there and, while on the property for this lawful purpose, shined a flashlight through a window of the basement door and saw the stolen snowmobiles in the basement. The court did not go the *Wright* route of declaring that no search had occurred, but yet upheld the police action:

> The difficult question, in our view, is whether the police violated the Fourth Amendment in looking into the walk-in basement window without a warrant. We hold that under the circumstances they were justified in doing so. The test is not whether it would have been reasonable for the police to obtain a warrant but whether the police acted reasonably in proceeding without one. * * * We believe they acted reasonably in looking in the window. First, they had very strong probable cause to believe that if they shined the flashlight into the window, they would see the stolen snowmobiles for which they were looking. Second, their intrusion, being visual and involving a basement window only, was minimal. Third, they might have had difficulty obtaining a search warrant at that hour. For these reasons we hold that the police acted reasonably in looking into the basement window.

The questions that courts have had to answer concerning the

---

to justify it as a search, the court held: "If policemen are to serve any purpose of detecting and preventing crime by being out on the streets at all, they must be able to take a closer look at challenging situations as they encounter them. All we hold here is that this was one of those situations, and that the police response to it was a justifiable one which did not project their

law enforcement responsibilities beyond permissible constitutional limits."

[98] Amsterdam, Perspectives on the Fourth Amendment, 58 Minn.L.Rev. 349, 393 (1974).

[99] State v. Crea, 305 Minn. 342, 233 N.W.2d 736 (1975).

use of flashlights and like implements can also arise as to the employment of other, more sophisticated means for piercing the veil of darkness. Such other devices, most notably infra-red equipment, are currently being utilized by law enforcement authorities,[100] and thus it is not surprising that Fourth Amendment issues concerning their use have occasionally surfaced in the law reports. Illustrative is *State v. Denton*,[101] where from adjoining property 100 feet away police using a night scope observed activity on a private dock "which was located on a public navigable waterway," meaning the defendants "actions could have been viewed by anyone passing on the waterway." The court in those circumstances could "see no significant difference between binoculars that magnify and a 'night scope' that clarifies the observations made by the naked eye." A concurring judge helpfully commented:

> However, I do not agree with the comments of the majority opinion which approve of the reliance on observations through a night scope to establish probable cause. As I understand this device, it not only magnifies what the viewer could see with the naked eye, but also makes possible the observation of activities which the viewer could not see because of darkness. There is no difference, therefore, between a nightscope and electronic bugging devices or telephone wiretapping instruments. By electronic means, the investigator is able to gather evidence which could not be obtained without the use of ingenious scientific devices.

> The constitution does not authorize the invasion by electronics of the reasonable expectations of privacy enjoyed by our citizens. In the present case, the evidence is that the investigating officers could see and did see sufficiently with the naked eye to give them probable cause for arresting defendants.

Whether the result reached in *Denton* is sound as to out-of-doors activity, as some other courts have concluded,[102] is itself

---

[100]In United States v. Coplen, 541 F.2d 211 (9th Cir.1976), agents investigating a narcotics smuggling operation conducted a surveillance of the movement of certain vehicles at night by using an aircraft with infra-red equipment. The court did not have occasion to pass upon this aspect of the investigation.

[101]State v. Denton, 387 So.2d 578 (La.1980).

[102]United States v. Ward, 546 F.Supp. 300 (W.D.Ark.1982), aff'd in part, rev'd in part, 703 F.2d 1058 (8th Cir.1983) (court, declining to say that use of such a device would never be a search, concluded it was not a search to use it to identify defendant as he

was moving around in the darkness outside his barn, where it was not also used to look inside darkened premises); Newberry v. State, 421 So.2d 546 (Fla.App.1982) (drawing same distinction, court says there "is no license to engage in criminal activity with impunity after sunset in an open area that would not be so protected after sunrise"); State v. Wacker, 317 Or. 419, 856 P.2d 1029 (1993) (use of "starlight scope" from second-story window to see what occurring within parked car no search, as activity in car would have been readily observable by passersby, as car "in the parking lot of a tavern that was open for business" and defendant in car "chose to carry out his activities in a car with its console

open to dispute. Even if, as concluded herein,[103] it is no search for police to use binoculars to see outdoor activity, employment of this more sophisticated equipment seems, as the *Denton* concurrence concludes, more analogous to the use of electronic eavesdropping equipment. Utilization of the latter equipment, even for the purpose of overhearing conversations occurring outdoors, constitutes a search.[104] But in any event, the use of a night scope or similar device to view activity occurring within private premises and not otherwise open to observation must be deemed a search. Were there any doubts on this score, surely they are put to rest by *Commonwealth v. Williams*,[105] where police from an observation post 30 to 40 feet away watched activity within an apartment for 9 days using binoculars and, when it was night and no lights were on within, a startron. The court declared:

> It is not necessary at this time and in this case to hold that every time a startron or other device that "sees" through darkness is used by authorities to obtain evidence without a search warrant the evidence must be suppressed. However, when such a device is used for nine days to observe a private apartment frequented by other than those sought by the police, including two acts of sexual intercourse not involving the person, the subject for detection, for whom the surveillance was established, then the warrantless observation of a third floor apartment in darkness has truly impermissibly invaded privacy to which all citizens, including petitioner, are guaranteed by the Fourth Amendment.

§ 2.2(c) Use of binoculars or telescope; photo enlargement

On occasion, the United States Supreme Court has indicated that the use of binoculars or similar device to magnify a distant object does not constitute a search. In *United States v. Lee*,[106] holding that no search had occurred where the boatswain on a Coast Guard patrol boat shined a searchlight on the deck of a motorboat discovered alongside a schooner, the Court commented that "[s]uch use of a searchlight is comparable to the use of a marine glass or a field glass." And in *On Lee v. United States*,[107] in the course of holding that evidence gathered by a "false friend" wired for sound by the police could be introduced, the Court gratuitously observed that "[t]he use of bifocals, field glasses or the telescope to magnify the object of a witness' vision is not a forbidden search or seizure, even if they focus without his knowl-

---

or overhead light on"); State v. Cannon, 634 S.W.2d 648 (Tenn.Crim.App.1982) (emphasizing that the device was used to facilitate surveillance of outside activity and that there was no indication it was used to look inside premises).

[103] See § 2.2(c).

[104] See § 2.2(f).

[105] Commonwealth v. Williams, 494 Pa. 496, 431 A.2d 964 (1981).

[Section 2.2(c)]

[106] United States v. Lee, 274 U.S. 559, 47 S.Ct. 746, 71 L.Ed. 1202 (1927).

[107] On Lee v. United States, 343 U.S. 747, 72 S.Ct. 967, 96 L.Ed. 1270 (1952).

edge or consent upon what one supposes to be private indiscretions."

Although these statements by the Supreme Court were dicta, it is fair to say that they were in all respects consistent with the interpretation of the Fourth Amendment that then obtained. In *Goldman v. United States*,[108] the Court had held that the use of an electronic listening device did not constitute a search if the surveillance was not accompanied by a physical intrusion or trespass. It is by no means remarkable, therefore, that a lower court, relying upon the *Goldman* analysis, would conclude that no search had occurred where police observed criminal activity in the defendant's house by watching with binoculars from another house about 150 away.[109] Moreover, the Supreme Court had held that certain technical trespasses did not intrude into a constitutionally protected area; in *Hester v. United States*,[110] it was held that observations made by officers trespassing on defendant's land without a warrant were not within the Fourth Amendment protection of "persons, houses, papers, and effects" because the police were in the "open fields" at the time of their observations. It is equally unsurprising, therefore, that lower courts readily concluded that binocular observation while in an "open field" or other unprotected area did not constitute a search within the meaning of the Fourth Amendment.[111] The prevailing rule, in short, was that if the user of the binoculars had not violated the Fourth Amendment in taking the position from which he used them, the observations made by their use amounted to a nonsearch plain view.[112]

But in *Katz v. United States*,[113] holding that overhearing a telephone conversation by the use of eavesdropping equipment placed on the outside of the telephone booth was a search, the Court expressly disapproved of the *Goldman* trespass rule and declared that the central inquiry in determining whether a Fourth Amendment search has occurred is whether the police conduct "violated the privacy upon which [the defendant] justifiably relied." This dramatic shift in *Katz* made it quite clear that the earlier decisions upholding the use of telescopic devices by reliance upon *Goldman* and *Hester* could no longer be safely relied upon. As Justice Harlan noted in his concurring opinion, *Katz* did not render totally obsolete the notion of constitutionally protected

---

[108]Goldman v. United States, 316 U.S. 129, 62 S.Ct. 993, 86 L.Ed. 1322 (1942).

[109]Johnson v. State, 2 Md.App. 300, 234 A.2d 464 (1967).

[110]Hester v. United States, 265 U.S. 57, 44 S.Ct. 445, 68 L.Ed. 898 (1924).

[111]Fullbright v. United States, 392 F.2d 432 (10th Cir.1968); Hodges v. United States, 243 F.2d 281 (5th Cir. 1957).

[112]For further discussion of the pre-*Katz* cases, see Annot., 48 A.L.R.3d 1178 (1973).

[113]Katz v. United States, 389 U.S. 347, 88 S.Ct. 507, 19 L.Ed.2d 576 (1967).

areas, and thus it is true after *Katz* (just as it was before) that a binocular observation from within such an area constitutes a search.[114] But the reverse of this proposition is no longer true; it cannot be said that such an observation is not a search merely because it was made from a vantage point where the officer was authorized to be. No such easy generalization is now available to resolve these cases.[115] Although "[t]he use of binoculars does not, per se, constitute an unreasonable search,"[116] it is no longer so "that anything observed with the use of binoculars can automatically be categorized as 'within the plain-view doctrine.'"[117]

Under the *Katz* expectation of privacy test, particular attention must be given to the nature of the place at which the observed objects or activities are located, for this will bear directly upon whether there was a justified expectation of privacy as to those objects or activities.[118] Perhaps the easiest situation with which to deal is that in which the incriminating evidence or conduct is seen out in the open, whether in a public place or on private property. It may sometimes be true that in this situation the defendant can honestly say that he had an actual expectation of privacy, at least in the sense that he was confident there was no one in such immediate proximity as to be able to detect the incriminating character of those objects or activities with the naked eye. But under *Katz* the expectation must be justified; it must be one, as Justice Harlan helpfully put it, "that society is prepared to recognize as 'reasonable.'"

Under this particular balancing of privacy and law enforcement interests, it is submitted, Fourth Amendment restrictions should not be imposed when the police have done no more than: (1) use binoculars to observe more clearly or carefully that which was in the open and thus subject to some scrutiny by the naked eye from the same location; or (2) use binoculars to view at a distance that which they could have lawfully observed from closer proximity but for their desire not to reveal the ongoing

---

[114]People v. Fly, 34 Cal.App.3d 665, 110 Cal.Rptr. 158 (1973).

[115]See Power, Technology and the Fourth Amendment: A Proposed Formulation for Visual Searches, 80 J.Crim.L. & Criminology 1 (1989) (noting that post-*Katz* lower courts "have moved in a variety of different directions, each supposedly mandated by *Katz*," id. at 5, and proposing a model of analysis for enhanced visual observations).

[116]People v. Ciochon, 23 Ill.App.3d 363, 319 N.E.2d 332 (1974).

[117]People v. Ciochon, 23 Ill.App.3d 363, 319 N.E.2d 332 (1974).

[118]A striking example is provided by State v. Abislaiman, 437 So.2d 181 (Fla.App.1983), where hospital security personnel activated a zoom lens on a surveillance camera in the emergency room parking lot to see inside a car that had been parked there about 5 minutes during early morning without anyone entering or exiting, and thereby discovered defendant was carrying a gun. The court held the defendant "had no reasonable expectation of privacy even from such an intrusion as occurred here," given the fact there was traffic in that lot at all hours and the hospital could be expected to employ security measures there.

surveillance. When this is the nature of the police conduct vis-a-vis evidence or conduct located in the open, the assistance provided by the binoculars should not be characterized as a search.[119] Fully consistent with *Katz,* therefore, are those holdings that it is not a search to make a binocular observation of the gathering of marijuana in an open field,[120] bookmaking activity on the street,[121] drug sales on the street[122] or in a car,[123] the loading[124] or unloading[125] of contraband from a vehicle in the open, the markings on a truck parked at the rear of defendant's premises abutting a public golf course,[126] or the characteristics of a marijuana plant on a sun deck and visible from a neighbor's yard.[127] This is not to suggest, however, that use of binoculars to look into a curtilage is never a search.[128]

Much more difficult to deal with, because they are not all of a kind, are those cases in which law enforcement agents have used

---

[119]United States v. Lace, 669 F.2d 46 (2d Cir.1982).

[120]Patterson v. State, 133 Ga.App. 742, 212 S.E.2d 858 (1975). See also Murphy v. State, 413 So.2d 1268 (Fla.App.1982) (no search to see marijuana growing with binoculars from helicopter flying at usual height); State v. Holbron, 65 Haw. 152, 648 P.2d 194 (1982) (no search to see marijuana growing in defendant's back yard by using binoculars from adjacent public tennis courts); State v. Bennett, 205 Mont. 117, 666 P.2d 747 (1983) (no search to see marijuana growing in open field using 60-power scope from road).

[121]United States v. Loundmannz, 472 F.2d 1376 (D.C.Cir.1972).

[122]Commonwealth v. Ortiz, 376 Mass. 349, 380 N.E.2d 669 (1978). See also State v. Barr, 98 Nev. 428, 651 P.2d 649 (1982) (no search to see what defendant had in his hand in public alleyway by using binoculars); State v. Jones, 33 Wash.App. 275, 653 P.2d 1369 (1982) (no search to see defendant's conduct in parked car in parking lot).

[123]State v. Wong, 68 Haw. 221, 708 P.2d 825 (1985) (no search for officer from 40 yds. away to see exchange of marijuana in car where vehicle's interior illuminated by interior light and parking lot lights).

[124]United States v. Grimes, 426 F.2d 706 (5th Cir.1970).

[125]United States v. Minton, 488 F.2d 37 (4th Cir.1973).

[126]People v. Spinelli, 35 N.Y.2d 77, 358 N.Y.S.2d 743, 315 N.E.2d 792 (1974).

[127]People v. Vermouth, 42 Cal.App.3d 353, 116 Cal.Rptr. 675 (1974).

[128]See State v. Kender, 60 Haw. 301, 588 P.2d 447 (1978) (where officer on neighboring property climbed three-quarters of way up fence and braced himself on fellow officer's shoulder and then, using a 60-power telescope, was able to see marijuana plants in defendant's back yard, this a search; notion that it no search for an officer to see something from a vantage point where he lawfully present is correct only if the situation "involved observations by police officers which were facilitated by the defendant's failure to take sufficient steps to protect his privacy," not true here given the fence around and heavy foliage on defendant's property). Broader than *Kender* is State v. Barnes, 390 So.2d 1243 (Fla.App.1980), holding it was a search for an officer on adjoining property to identify plants on defendant's land as marijuana by using a high-powered telescope, reasoning that under *Katz* "the public to whom something is knowingly exposed must be 'the ordinary run of people, not those who happen to possess powerful and sophisticated devices and the curiosity to use them to spy on their fellows.'"

binoculars or similar equipment to look inside of premises. There are instances, of course, in which the fact that the observation was into premises is of relatively little significance because it is readily apparent that there could have been no reasonable expectation of privacy with respect to the object or conduct seen.[129] If, for example, a person places a marijuana plant directly on his window sill so that it is observable from the street, his expectation of privacy concerning the plant is not significantly different from that in the case described above where the plant was on the sun deck, and thus it is no search to scrutinize that plant with binoculars.[130] Similarly, if a person operates an illegal still inside a shed with the doors wide open and the lights on, so that the activity could be seen by the naked eye by anyone in the immediate vicinity, it is not objectionable that agents made distant observation of that conduct by use of binoculars.[131] And if a person injects narcotics at a lighted window, a justified expectation of privacy cannot be claimed merely because the surveilling officer was no longer in the street, where the defendant had earlier seen him, but instead was watching with binoculars from a more distant location.[132]

But these are rather unusual situations, and in no sense undermine the general notion that under *Katz* "an individual might be justified in expecting freedom from telescopic intrusion in the confines of a private place such as his own home."[133] In assessing in a particular case whether the expectation was in fact justified, there would appear to be two primary considerations: (1) the level of sophistication of the equipment utilized by the po-

---

[129]State v. Littleton, 407 So.2d 1208 (La.1981) (no search to use binoculars to look into hangar with a 30'40" wide opening); State v. Louis, 296 Or. 57, 672 P.2d 708 (1983) (no expectation of privacy re photographing defendant with telephoto lens while he repeatedly exposed himself at his living room window so as to be observable to passersby and neighbors).

[130]Cf. State v. Manly, 85 Wash.2d 120, 530 P.2d 306 (1975) ("The fact that the evidence does not disclose the proximity of the plants to the window is relatively unimportant as applying simple principles of geometry at the various points of observation indicates that the plants were near or in the window and not secreted within the room or hidden from public view").

[131]Fullbright v. United States, 392 F.2d 432 (10th Cir.1968). See also United States v. Van Damme, 48 F.3d 461 (9th Cir.1995) (no search where officer in helicopter looked through 600 mm. telephoto lens to see marijuana through open doors of greenhouses outside curtilage).

[132]Cf. People v. Ciochon, 23 Ill.App.3d 363, 319 N.E.2d 332 (1974) (remanding for a determination as to whether these were actually the facts). See also United States v. Whaley, 779 F.2d 585 (11th Cir.1986) (no search to observe with binoculars operation of drug lab in basement with large, uncurtained windows while lights on within, especially because activity visible by naked eye on neighboring property).

[133]Note, 43 N.Y.U.L.Rev. 968, 985 (1968). See also Annot., 59 A.L.R.5th 615 (1998).

lice[134]; and (2) the extent to which the incriminating objects or actions were out of the line of normal sight from contiguous areas where passersby or others might be.

An illustration of less than adequate analysis of these factors is provided by *Commonwealth v. Hernley*.[135] There, an FBI agent began a surveillance of defendant's printshop because he suspected that football gambling forms were being produced there. He could tell that the presses inside the shop were operating, but could not see inside because of the location and size of the windows, which were at a level to preclude observation of activities within the shop by anyone standing on the ground outside the building. To remedy this problem, the agent mounted a four-foot ladder that he placed on the railroad tracks abutting defendant's property, and from a distance of 30 to 35 feet looked through a side window. By using binoculars, the agent was actually able to ascertain from this distance the content of the printed material being run off the press, which he identified as "Las Vegas" football parlay sheets. On the basis of this information, a warrant to search the shop was obtained, which the trial court ruled was based upon an unreasonable search. The appellate court, after noting the pre-*Katz* decisions holding that use of binoculars without trespass is no search, concluded "that *Katz* does not require a different result"[136]:

In *Katz*, the suspect entered a phone booth, closed the door and

---

[134]Concern about this has been expressed in the decisions. In addition to the *Kim* case quoted in the text following, consider People v. Spinelli, 35 N.Y.2d 77, 358 N.Y.S.2d 743, 315 N.E.2d 792 (1974): "We are aware that with the increasingly sophisticated modern equipment available to law enforcement agencies, it is becoming increasingly possible to view objects that would not be observed by a person not in possession of such sophisticated equipment. In this case we need not reach the question of when such a technologically aided viewing of an object in and of itself rises to the level of a constitutionally cognizable search."

[135]Commonwealth v. Hernley, 216 Pa.Super. 177, 263 A.2d 904 (1970).

See also People v. Ferguson, 47 Ill.App.3d 654, 7 Ill.Dec. 792, 365 N.E.2d 77 (1977) (officer in vacant lot 60 feet away used binoculars to look through windows of second floor apartment and saw two women at table reading "policy results slips"; held, this proper, as the "defendant made no ef-

fort to block an outsider's view"); People v. Hicks, 49 Ill.App.3d 421, 7 Ill.Dec. 279, 364 N.E.2d 440 (1977) (officer using "night binoculars" looked through window of first floor hotel room and saw many people within engaged in gambling; held, the reasoning of *Hernley* is applicable here, as "since the defendants were aware of a need to pull the curtains on two occasions, they cannot claim that they expected privacy on the other occasions"); State v. Thompson, 196 Neb. 55, 241 N.W.2d 511 (1976) (officers in alley used binoculars to look through rear window and into living room, by which they saw man smoking a marijuana cigarette; held, no search occurred, as the "officers had a right to be in the alley and there was nothing unlawful in their use of binoculars").

[136]In addition to the reason given in the quotation following in the text, the court also stated *Katz* was in any event inapplicable to the instant case because the Supreme Court had given it "wholly prospective application."

paid the toll, thereby seeking to effectively exclude the listening ear. The Court held that his expectation in this regard was justifiable. Our case presents the situation in which it was incumbent on the suspect to preserve his privacy from visual observation. To do that the appellees had only to curtain the windows. Absent such obvious action we cannot find that their expectation of privacy was justifiable or reasonable. The law will not shield criminal activity from visual observation when the actor shows such little regard for his privacy.

This is a perversion of the reasoning underlying *Katz*. As Professor Amsterdam has aptly put it,

this approach raises the question of how tightly the fourth amendment permits people to be driven back into the recesses of their lives by the risk of surveillance. Mr. Katz could, of course, have protected himself against surveillance by forbearing to use the phone; and—so far as I am presently advised of the state of the mechanical arts—anyone can protect himself against surveillance by retiring to the cellar, cloaking all the windows with thick caulking, turning off the lights and remaining absolutely quiet. This much withdrawal is not required in order to claim the benefit of the amendment because, if it were, the amendment's benefit would be too stingy to preserve the kind of open society to which we are committed and in which the amendment is supposed to function. What kind of society is that? Is it one in which a homeowner is put to the choice of shuttering up his windows or of having a policeman look in?[137]

Given the configuration of the building in which Hernley carried on his printing business, he certainly had a justified expectation of privacy. "[T]o hold otherwise," the dissenting opinion in *Hernley* notes, "would be to unreasonably restrict the right of our citizens to feel safe in leaving their windows uncurtained to the skies, free from intrusion by all but the occasional passing airplane or helicopter." The situation is aggravated by the officer's use of binoculars; the defendant, who with good reason expected that he could carry on his printing business in private, now learns that the very contents of the matter he was printing were subject to unrestrained scrutiny by the authorities.

Much more in keeping with the spirit of *Katz* is the carefully reasoned opinion in *United States v. Kim*.[138] In that case, FBI agents used an 800 millimeter telescope with a 60 millimeter opening to observe activities in Kim's apartment. The building from which the surveillance was conducted was approximately a quarter of a mile away; there were no buildings in the line of sight located significantly closer to Kim's building. Despite the distance, the sophisticated equipment enabled the agents to observe closely the activities in the apartment—even to the extent

---

[137]Amsterdam, Perspectives on the Fourth Amendment, 58 Minn.L.Rev. 349, 402 (1974).

[138]United States v. Kim, 415 F.Supp. 1252 (D.Haw.1976), discussed in Comment, 63 Iowa L.Rev. 708 (1978).

of learning what Kim was reading. The information acquired by this surveillance was used to obtain a wiretap order, which the defendant later challenged on the ground that it was based upon the fruits of an illegal search. In rejecting the government's contention that the surveillance had been nothing more than a nonsearch plain view, the court stated:

It is of the utmost significance, however, and this court so finds, that the sophisticated visual aids available to the government can intrude on individual privacy as severely as the electronic surveillance in *Katz* * * * . It is inconceivable that the government can intrude so far into an individual's home that it can detect the material he is reading and still not be considered to have engaged in a search. * * * If government agents have probable cause to suspect criminal activity and feel the need for telescopic surveillance, they may apply for a warrant; otherwise, they have no right to peer into people's windows with special equipment not generally in use.

The quest for evidence directed at Kim's apartment is not exempted from Fourth Amendment regulation by the plain view doctrine. * * * A "plain" view of Kim's apartment was impossible; only an aided view could penetrate. In view of the powerful technology used by the law enforcement agents in this case, the "plain" in plain view must be interpreted as permitting only an unaided plain view.[139] * * *

It is urged that Kim had no subjective expectation of privacy since he did not draw his curtains * * * . Such an interpretation is totally at war with Fourth Amendment values. * * *

[W]hether and when Kim's curtains were open or shut has no relevance in this case. By opening his curtains, an individual does not thereby open his person, house, papers and effects to telescopic scrutiny by the government. * * * [A]s the technological capability of law enforcement agencies increases, the Fourth Amendment must likewise grow in response. To permit governmental intrusions of the sort at issue in this case to remain uncontrolled would violate the basic foundations of privacy, security and decency which distinguish free societies from controlled societies.

More recently, a number of other courts have wisely adopted the *Kim* approach.[140]

Finally, there are those cases in which the police surveillance

---

[139]This statement should not be read literally. At this point the court dropped a footnote which, consistent with the analysis recommended herein, cautioned: "This case does not present a situation where private parties have a plain (unaided) view of the defendant's premises but government agents are forced to use visual aids because they were not able to get as close to the defendant's premises as the private parties."

Consider also Comment, 24 Cal.W.L.Rev. 83, 94 (1987), defining a search as "the use of technology to augment the senses in order to obtain information that could not have otherwise been obtained from a lawful vantage point without such an augmentation."

[140]United States v. Taborda, 635 F.2d 131 (2d Cir.1980) ("Absent exposure to such unenhanced viewing, however, we do not believe the inference of intended privacy at home is rebutted by a failure to obstruct telescopic viewing by closing the curtains," as the vice of such viewing is that "it

involves the use of photography in such a fashion as to not only memorialize what was seen with the naked eye,[141] but also to enhance that perception by photographs improving in some way upon what was observable with the naked eye. One type of case, illustrated by *United States v. Allen*,[142] is that in which a camera with a telescopic lens is utilized to improve the ultimate picture over what the photographer was able to see with the naked eye. In such cases, the required analysis is essentially identical to that discussed above. Thus, the court in *Allen* held that photographing from a helicopter was no search, although a camera with a 70–230 mm. zoom lens was used, because such equipment is widely available commercially and not any more sophisticated than equipment generally available to the public.[143]

Another type of case is that in which the enhancement results from enlarging the pictures taken with standard photographic

---

risks observation * * * of intimate details of a person's private life"); State v. Knight, 63 Haw. 90, 621 P.2d 370 (1980) (use of 7 × 50 highpowered binoculars from adjoining land to identify marijuana plants in greenhouse a search where "the contents * * * were not visible to the naked eye"); State v. Ward, 62 Haw. 509, 617 P.2d 568 (1980) (use of 10 × 30 binoculars to see crap game in 7th-story apartment from another building in eighth of a mile away, closest vantage point, was a search, as "the constitution does not require that in all cases a person, in order to protect his privacy, must shut himself off from fresh air, sunlight and scenery"); State v. Kender, 60 Haw. 301, 588 P.2d 447 (1978) (discussed in note 128 supra); State v. Blacker, 52 Or.App. 1077, 630 P.2d 413 (1981) (a search to use spotting scope that magnified 16–36 times to see marijuana plant through second story window; "where, as here, only an enhanced eye could penetrate, we do not think defendant's failure to draw the curtain should be interpreted as a renunciation of his expectation of privacy"); Wheeler v. State, 659 S.W.2d 381 (Tex.Crim.App.1982) (when police used 600 mm. lens to get glimpse through fan louvres of marijuana plants in opaque greenhouse 100 yards from nearest vantage point and surrounded by brush and two fences, this a search).

Sometimes *Kim* has been distin-

guished, as where there really was no justified expectation of privacy as to what was occurring in the premises. See, e.g., United States v. Bifield, 498 F.Supp. 497 (D.Conn.1980), aff'd 659 F.2d 1063 (2d Cir.1981) (correctly holding that it is no search to use binoculars to see display of weapons in lighted office of gas station located on major thoroughfare in commercial district, as the activities would have been plainly visible to passersby without artificial aids).

For additional discussion of the cases, see Note, 67 Cornell L.Rev. 379 (1982).

[141] This is clearly no search if the observation itself was not. See note 16 supra. This is not to suggest that use of an unmanned cameras, so that there is no contemporary naked-eye observation, necessarily means the photography is a search. See United States v. McIver, 186 F.3d 1119 (9th Cir.1999), note 16 supra.

[142] United States v. Allen, 675 F.2d 1373 (9th Cir.1980).

[143] See also L. R. Willson & Sons v. OSHRC, 134 F.3d 1235 (4th Cir.1998) (no search to inspect company's construction worksite, revealing that employees working on structural steel more than 80 feet above ground not wearing fall protective devices, by videotaping such activity through a 16-power camera lens from the roof of a nearby hotel).

equipment. Illustrative is *State v. Dickerson*,[144] where police lawfully made certain observations through the window of the front door of a residence, photographed what they had just seen, and then made enlargements of the photos. The court held, quite correctly it would seem, that the photography-plus-enlargement did not constitute a Fourth Amendment search, for it "merely enabled the officers to see the exposed items in more detail."

It is by no means inconsistent with *Allen* and *Dickerson* to suggest that there certainly comes a point, because of the sophistication of the photographic equipment and what it is able to accomplish over naked-eye observation, that photo enhancement becomes a search. The Supreme Court agrees that this is so, though—as is evident from *Dow Chemical Company v. United States*[145]—a majority of the Court has taken a rather extreme view as to just what is necessary for photo surveillance to fall into the search category. In *Dow,* the EPA employed a commercial aerial photographer to photograph the company's 2,000-acre chemical manufacturing factory from altitudes of 12,000, 3,000 and 1,200 feet, all within navigable airspace. Dow conceded that a flyover with naked-eye observation would be no search, but claimed that use of an aerial mapping camera in such circumstances was a search. A majority of the Court disagreed:

> Here, the EPA was not employing some unique sensory device that, for example, could penetrate the walls of buildings and record conversations in Dow's plants, offices or laboratories, but rather a conventional, albeit precise, commercial camera commonly used in map-making. The Government asserts it has not yet enlarged the photographs to any significant degree, but Dow points out that simple magnification permits identification of objects such as wires as small as one-half inch diameter.
>
> It may well be, as the Government concedes, that surveillance of private property by using highly sophisticated surveillance equipment not generally available to the public, such as satellite technology, might be constitutionally proscribed absent a warrant.[146] But the photographs here are not so revealing of intimate details as to raise constitutional concerns. Although they undoubtedly give EPA more detailed information than naked-eye views, they remain limited to an outline of the facility's buildings and equipment. The mere fact that human vision is enhanced somewhat, at least to the degree here, does not give rise to constitutional problems.

The four dissenters in *Dow* characterized the equipment rather differently. They noted that the camera "cost in excess of $22,000.00 and is described by the company as the 'finest preci-

---

[144]State v. Dickerson, 313 N.W.2d 526 (Iowa 1981).

[145]Dow Chemical Co. v. United States, 476 U.S. 227, 106 S.Ct. 1819, 90 L.Ed.2d 226 (1986).

[146]See Note, 13 J.Marshall J. Computer & Info.L. 729, 761–62 (1995) ("law enforcement agencies will eventually use the satellite in surveillance," and when they do it necessary to "require a warrant").

sion aerial camera available,'" that it "was capable of taking several photographs in precise and rapid succession," and that such a "technique facilitates stereoscopic examination, a type of examination that permits depth perception." Also, they observed that the district court had found that "some of the photographs taken from directly above the plant at 1,200 feet are capable of enlargement to a scale of 1 inch equals 20 feet *or greater,* without significant loss of detail or resolution. When enlarged in this manner, and viewed under magnification, it is possible to discern equipment, pipes, and power lines as small as ½ inch in diameter."

In view of these facts, the majority's no-search conclusion is certainly suspect, to say the least. As previously discussed, it is hardly sensible to read *Katz* as meaning that we assume the risk of whatever technology the government can bring to bear upon its investigative efforts. Nor is it particularly consoling to be told—as the dissenters aptly describe the majority's approach— "that the photography was not a Fourth Amendment 'search' because it was not accompanied by a physical trespass and because the equipment used was not the most highly sophisticated form of technology available to the Government." But the essential point is that the *Dow* majority's distinction between the equipment used in that case and "satellite technology" "not generally available to the public" is hardly a compelling one. As the dissenters explained,

> the camera used in this case was highly sophisticated in terms of its capability to reveal minute details of Dow's confidential technology and equipment. * * * Satellite photography hardly could have been more informative about Dow's technology. Nor are "members of the public" likely to purchase $22,000.00 cameras.

It would be a mistake, however, to read *Dow* as having pronounced that "anything goes"—at least short of the majority's satellite—in the realm of photographic surveillance. That is not the case, as is apparent from the context in which the camera was assessed in *Dow* and from certain words of qualification and caution expressed by the majority in that case. The context, surveillance of a vast industrial complex, is significant precisely because the majority treats the place at which the camera was directed as a most important consideration in determining whether Fourth Amendment activity occurred.[147] The Court emphasized that the "narrow issue" being considered "concerns aerial observation of a 2,000-acre outdoor manufacturing facility," and footnoted that circumscription with this: "We find it important that this is *not* an area immediately adjacent to a private home, where privacy expectations are most heightened." That is, critical to the Court's holding in *Dow* is the conclusion "that the open areas of an industrial plant complex with numerous plant structures spread over an area of 2,000 acres are not

---

[147]Whether this is sound is an-   other matter. See § 2.4(b).

analogous to the 'curtilage' of a dwelling for purposes of aerial surveillance." This certainly suggests (which, hopefully, would be the case) that use of the same equipment in the companion case of *California v. Ciraolo*,[148] involving overflight of and viewing into the curtilage, would have produced a different result.[149]

Moreover, especially in a curtilage situation but by no means limited to it, it would be incorrect to interpret *Dow* as declaring that any use of equipment making it possible to view from great distance objects as small as 1/2-inch in diameter falls outside the Fourth Amendment. Although power lines that small were apparently observable under magnification in *Dow,* the majority explained that this was so

> only because of their stark contrast with the snow-white background. No objects as small as 1/2-inch diameter such as a class ring, for example, are recognizable, nor are there any identifiable human faces or secret documents captured in such a fashion as to implicate more serious privacy concerns.

That is an important qualification; *Dow* is thus not inconsistent with and does not put into doubt the previously discussed holding in the *Kim* case.[150]

§ 2.2(d) Use of magnetometer, x-ray, weapons detector, etc., to "see" what the naked eye cannot see

The devices discussed in the preceding subsections, such as flashlights and binoculars, are an aid to the sense of sight in that they permit one to see that which would otherwise go undetected because of darkness or distance. There are a variety of other devices in current use by law enforcement agents which also permit them to "see" (perhaps not in a literal sense) that which otherwise

---

[148]California v. Ciraolo, 476 U.S. 207, 106 S.Ct. 1809, 90 L.Ed.2d 210 (1986).

[149]Critical to the holding in *Ciraolo* was the fact that "any member of the public flying in this airspace who glanced down could have seen everything that these officers observed." Also, the *Ciraolo* majority (after referring to *Dow*) deemed it necessary to recite the state's acknowledgment in the instant case that "[a]erial observation of curtilage may become invasive, either due to physical intrusiveness or through modern technology which discloses to the senses those intimate associations, objects or activities otherwise imperceptible to police or fellow citizens."

But, the distinction was missed in State v. Vogel, 428 N.W.2d 272 (S. D.1988), where an officer conducted aerial surveillance of defendant's residence and took pictures of the *interior* of that residence, a geodesic dome, with a camera equipped with a zoom lens. The court distinguished *Kim* by saying that here the defendant "has made no showing that the cameras and lenses used * * * were 'sophisticated visual aids' or 'special equipment not generally in use,'" and added that given the fact the Supreme Court upheld use of a $22,000 camera in *Dow,* "the objection to the photography here is futile." By comparison, in State v. Lange, 158 Wis.2d 609, 463 N.W.2d 390 (App.1990), the court, noting the distinction in *Dow* between industrial property and a home, limited its holdings re surveillance of the latter "to approval of the use of standard binoculars and cameras equipped with generally available standard and zoom lenses."

[150]See text at note 138 supra.

would go unseen. The concern here is with whether the utilization of this equipment constitutes a search within the meaning of the Fourth Amendment.

One type of device is that which makes it possible to determine a certain characteristic (e.g., size, shape, density, or ingredients) of some object that is covered and thus not subject to direct viewing. The magnetometer, to which all air travelers have been subjected in recent years, is this kind of instrument.

> Its operation is based upon the physical fact that the earth is surrounded by a relatively constant magnetic field composed of lines of flux. Steel and other ferromagnetic metals are much better conductors than the air. As a result, when any such metal moves through an area, nearby magnetic lines of flux are distorted to some degree as they tend to converge and pass through the metal while seeking the path of least resistance. Such distortions occurring near a "flux-gate magnetometer" create a signal which can be amplified and calibrated to detect magnetic disturbances.[151]

When used as a part of an airport hijacker detection system,[152] the magnetometer is set so that it will give a warning signal whenever a person or luggage passing through the device contains the amount of metal that would be in a pistol.

As might be expected, courts have consistently held that use of a magnetometer to detect metal on a person or in an object constitutes a search.[153] In *United States v. Epperson*,[154] for example, the court stated:

> We agree that the use of the magnetometer in these circumstances was a "search" within the meaning of the Fourth Amendment. By this device a government officer, without permission, discerned metal on Epperson's person. That he did so electronically rather than by patting down his outer clothing or "frisking" may make the search more tolerable and less offensive—but it is still a search. Indeed, that is the very purpose and function of a magnetometer: to search for metal and disclose its presence in areas where there is a normal expectation of privacy.

This conclusion is fully consistent with the expectation of privacy approach of *Katz v. United States*,[155] and is equally applicable to other devices that also reveal the characteristics of concealed objects. Thus, it is a search to use an X-ray machine or radiographic scanner to project electronic emanations through an

---

[Section 2.2(d)]

[151]United States v. Lopez, 328 F.Supp. 1077 (E.D.N.Y.1971).

[152]See § 10.6, discussing that system and the fact that use of the magnetometer in that context is a reasonable search.

[153]Bourgeois v. Peters, 387 F.3d 1303 (11th Cir.2004); United States v. Albarado, 495 F.2d 799 (2d Cir.1974);

United States v. Bell, 464 F.2d 667 (2d Cir.1972); State v. David, 130 Ga.App. 872, 204 S.E.2d 773 (1974); People v. Kuhn, 33 N.Y.2d 203, 351 N.Y.S.2d 649, 306 N.E.2d 777 (1973).

[154]United States v. Epperson, 454 F.2d 769 (4th Cir.1972).

[155]Katz v. United States, 389 U.S. 347, 88 S.Ct. 507, 19 L.Ed.2d 576 (1967).

object and reveal, in picture form, by virtue of the density of the resistance encountered, the shape of objects within the container examined.[156] Surely the same is true of the more recently developed Body Scan Imaging Technology, where a narrow beam of low-level x-ray energy scans a person, as a consequence of which (unlike medical x-rays) "the emissions reflect off of an image instead of fully penetrating it, revealing features near the body's surface" on a total image displayed essentially as a naked body.[157] *Katz* likewise supports the conclusion that use of a scintillator, an instrument sensitive to radiation, to determine the presence of certain concealed objects is also a search.[158] From this it follows that discovery of explosives by use of an Explosive Detection System (EDS), deployed to commercial airports by the Transportation Security Administration in the post-9/11 era to meet its responsibility for screening all checked luggage,[159] also constitutes a search. EDS "is a sophisticated million-dollar machine that uses computerized tomography technology similar to that used for CAT scans in hospitals. By taking the equivalent

---

[156]United States v. Young, 350 F.3d 1302 (11th Cir.2003) (x-ray); United States v. Haynie, 637 F.2d 227 (4th Cir.1980) (x-ray scanner); United States v. Henry, 615 F.2d 1223 (9th Cir.1980) (noting airport x-ray scanner is certainly a more intrusive device than a magnetometer); United States v. Albarado, 495 F.2d 799 (2d Cir.1974); People v. Fritschler, 81 Misc.2d 106, 364 N.Y.S.2d 801 (1975).

Compare United States v. Allman, 336 F.3d 555 (7th Cir.2003) ("we have trouble seeing how, in this age of routine, soon to be universal, x-raying of containers shipped by air, the defendant could have had a reasonable expectation that his package would not be x-rayed at any point during transit"); State v. Gallant, 308 A.2d 274 (Me.1973) (where customs agent, suspicious of certain pieces of mail entering country, took several thick envelopes to private lab and had them subjected to radiograph scanning, which penetrated fabric of the envelopes sufficiently to reveal that each envelope contained stapled packets of powdery substance, because scrutiny had been conducted "without opening the sealed envelope or disclosing the private thoughts communicated therein," it "stopped short of being the kind of invasion which must properly be considered a 'search'").

[157]Comment, 8 Tex.Wesleyan L.Rev. 417, 420 (2002); Note, 44 Creighton L.Rev. 1357 (2011), discussing use of these devices as an alternative to frisking during customs inspections. See § 10.5(e). On use of these machines by the TSA, see Comment, 49 Santa Clara L.Rev. 213 (2009); Note, 41 Loy.L.A.L.Rev. 385 (2007).

[158]In the pre-*Katz* case of Corngold v. United States, 367 F.2d 1 (9th Cir. 1966), agents employed a scintillator in the public hallway outside defendant's apartment to detect the presence of a large quantity of radium-dial watches therein. Relying upon the no trespass-no search rule of Goldman v. United States, 316 U.S. 129, 62 S.Ct. 993, 86 L.Ed. 1322 (1942), the court held that "appellant's Fourth Amendment rights were not violated." *Katz* would compel a contrary result.

[159]Such screening is mandated by 49 U.S.C.A. § 44901. The TSA has decided to utilize both the very large EDS units and also the smaller Explosive Trace Detection (ETD) devices in complying with this requirement. Bester, The Birth of the Transportation Security Administration: A View From the Chief Counsel, 17 Air & Space Law 1, 22 (Summer 2002). The ETD devices are considered herein at § 2.2(h).

of hundreds of x-ray pictures of a suitcase from different angles, this device can create a 3-D view of what is inside, including some indication of the relative density of the objects."[160] In contradistinction to all this equipment it may well be that a merchant's use of a sensormatic detection system, which will alert *only* to tags on the store's merchandise when they are being removed from the store, is not a search because there is no *justified* expectation in successful shoplifting.[161]

As a result of Department of Justice funding, three organizations have undertaken to develop concealed weapons detection technology. "The idea," as one commentator has explained, "is to produce a commercially and technologically viable device that could do an 'electronic frisk' of a suspect from a distance of ten or twenty feet."[162] Two of the detectors under development use magnetic fields, albeit in quite different ways. Raytheon's device would illuminate the subject with a low intensity electromagnetic pulse and then measure the time decay of the radiated energy from metal objects carried by the person. The device detects only metal objects, but produces no images. Rather, by measurement of the intensity and the time decay of the secondary radiation, there are produced "signatures" that can be identified as indicating whether the detected metal object is or is not a gun. By

---

[160]Goodman, Airline Security 10 (2002), at <www.angelfire.com/ga4/clgoodma/paper.phf>.

[161]In Lucas v. United States, 411 A.2d 360 (D.C.App.1980), discussed in Annot., 10 A.L.R.4th 376 (1981), the court found it unnecessary to resolve this issue. In concluding that *if* this was a search it was reasonable, the court stressed "that the intrusion of this sensormatic device is minimal for * * * it meets the test of being as limited as possible. It is quite different from, and far less intrusive, than the magnetometer used at airports which can be triggered not only by weapons, but by a wide variety of other metal objects not infrequently carried by law-abiding citizens. * * *

"Unlike any technique heretofore passed upon by this court, this device does not search or scan generally for items in which the subject has a proprietary interest. It reveals nothing about the subject or his belongings other than whether he is carrying store merchandise with live tags beyond the point where he should have paid for the merchandise and had the tags removed.

"It is the preciseness of the sensormatic equipment, not in terms of detecting what it searches for but, more importantly, in terms of not detecting anything it is not searching for that makes its use reasonable."

The *Lucas* analysis finds considerable support in two more recent Supreme Court decisions, namely, United States v. Jacobsen, 466 U.S. 109, 104 S.Ct. 1652, 80 L.Ed.2d 85 (1984) (where police in lawful possession of package of white powder and lawfully opened it to extent previously opened by private party, chemical test of trace of powder no search, as test would only reveal if the powder was cocaine and thus would not "compromise any legitimate interest in privacy"); United States v. Place, 462 U.S. 696, 103 S.Ct. 2637, 77 L.Ed.2d 110 (1983) (where federal agents had lawful custody of luggage, dog sniff of luggage no search, as "the sniff discloses only the presence or absence of narcotics, a contraband item").

[162]Harris, Superman's X-Ray Vision and the Fourth Amendment: The New Gun Detection Technology, 69 Temple L.Rev. 1 (1996).

comparison, the INEL system uses magnetic gradiometers to measure fluctuations produced when anything made of ferromagnetic material moves through the earth's magnetic field. No electronic energy is directed at the subject, as these instruments merely measure what certain objects do to the earth's magnetic field. The readings would be compared with known "signatures" of weapons of similar mass, shape and density to determine the likelihood that the device has focused upon a weapon. The third device, under development by Millitech, uses passive millimeter wave imaging technology:

> Millitech's system begins with the principle that the human body—and everything else—emits radiation. The amplitude of radiation at which the waves are emitted is a product of the emitting object's temperature and its material and surface properties other than temperature. A living person is a "good emitter"; metal objects are "poor emitters." Plastics and ceramics are somewhere in between. These waves pass through clothing and even many building materials, making them "virtually transparent." Millitech's gun detector scans the waves emitted by both a human body and any objects concealed on them and produces a small image on the back of the device in which the outlines of concealed objects, usually dark, are clearly visible against the much brighter image of the body. The subject of the scan is not exposed to any artificial radiation from the device itself. Millitech's device directs no energy of any kind *at* subjects; rather, it utilizes invisible high frequency waves *coming from* the subject.[163]

Given the present state of this technology, there is every reason to believe that police departments will soon have available devices that can detect concealed weapons in one of the ways just described. That being the case, it is well to consider the status of these devices under the Fourth Amendment—in particular, whether the detection of a concealed weapon by utilization of such technology constitutes a "search" within the meaning of the Fourth Amendment. Because, as we have seen earlier,[164] it is generally the case that police use of such devices as flashlights and binoculars are not a search, it might be argued that it follows that gun detectors can be similarly characterized. But this is not the case, for

> gun detectors do not do what lights, telescopes, binoculars, and like devices do—put police officers artificially closer or provide illumination enabling them to observe what would be visible anyway but for distance or darkness. Rather, gun detectors allow police to see what

---

[163]Harris, 69 Temple L.Rev. 1, 7 n.38 (1996). For a most useful and more detailed description of these devices, including their common characteristics and their differences, see Harris, at 7–14; Iraola, New Detection Technologies and the Fourth Amendment, 47 S.D.L.Rev. 8 (2002). For more on the Millitech device, see Dery, Remote Frisking Down to the Skin: Government Searching Technology Powerful Enough to Locate Holes in Fourth Amendment Fundamentals, 30 Creighton L.Rev. 353 (1997); Comment, 9 Alb.L.J.Sci. & Tech. 135 (1998).

[164]See § 2.2(b),(c).

they *never could*, regardless of how close they stood or how bright the sunshine. The contents of one's pockets and the areas under one's clothing remain hidden even to those with the sharpest vision. * * * Gun detectors do not so much *enhance* police senses as they do *replace* them with something superhuman, an ability to perceive that people simply do not have. Concealed weapons are not merely *hard* to see under clothes; they are *impossible* to see. Thus, only by semantic slight of hand could a court call gun detectors sense enhancing; the label seems ill fitting and disingenuous.[165]

If an analogy is to be sought, then, it should be from those devices that do not "see" in a literal sense. One approach of this kind is to link concealed weapons detection devices (at least those that are "passive" in nature) with the thermal imager, which in pre-*Kyllo* days produced the contention that because use of the imager is not a search (as then was the prevailing view) the use of a gun detector is not either.[166] *Kyllo*, of course, holds that use of a thermal imager on a home *is* a search, but given the Court's analysis as discussed herein,[167] it is apparent that *Kyllo* sheds no light on the practice of using weapons detector devices on persons then out in public. Thus it is doubtless still true "that an older technology—magnetometers that detect weapons in airports—represents a much better analogy to gun detectors."[168] Because it is well-settled that the use of a magnetometer (or an x-ray machine, another likely analogy) constitutes a "search" within the meaning of the Fourth Amendment,[169] it might seem apparent that the same conclusion is compelled as to the more sophisticated gun detectors made possible by modern technology.

That is certainly the correct result *unless* it can be said that the more sophisticated gun detectors are significantly different, in a Fourth Amendment sense, from the x-ray and magnetometer because of what is revealed. X-rays reveal a variety of shapes, some of which may or may not be shapes unique to a gun. Magnetometers reveal the presence of a certain quantity of metal, but again that quantity might be a gun or an innocuous object. But at least some of the gun detectors are intended to detect

---

[165]Harris, 69 Temple L.Rev. 1, 24 (1996). See also Slobogin, Physical Surveillance: The American Bar Association's Tentative Draft Standards, 10 Harv.J.L. & Tech. 383, 447–52 (1997) (reaching same conclusion and discussing proposed limitations on use of such devices); Comment, 45 UCLA L.Rev. 281 (1997) (concluding "police use of the concealed weapon detectors would constitute a search" and discussing limited circumstances in which such would be permissible); Notes, 48 Fla.L.Rev. 299 (1996) (reaching the same conclusion and discuss-ing what limits consequently must be followed in using such devices in making individual *Terry* stops or in operating checkpoints); 25 Rutgers Computer Tech.L.J. 135 (1999) (is a search and thus limited to certain "special needs" situations).

[166]Note, 46 Duke L.J. 575, 596–604 (1996).

[167]See § 2.2(f).

[168]Harris, 69 Temple L.Rev. 1, 3 (1996).

[169]See text at notes 153–156 supra.

guns and nothing else,[170] so that we may have arrived at that situation that was only a matter of speculation when, some years ago, it was asserted that "if a device could be invented that accurately detected weapons and did not disrupt the normal movement of people, there could be no fourth amendment objection to its use."[171] That assertion, the Supreme Court's cases seem to indicate, might well be correct—at least in some circumstances. In *United States v. Jacobsen*,[172] where a federal drug agent, after gaining lawful access to white powder in a package, subjected the powder to a field test revealing it was cocaine, seven Justices took the position that this testing was no search because a "chemical test that merely discloses whether or not a particular substance is cocaine does not compromise any legitimate interest in privacy." This conclusion, the *Jacobsen* Court added, was dictated by the holding a year earlier in *United States v. Place*[173] that a canine sniff is no search. That holding in *Place* was grounded in the facts that a canine sniff "does not require opening the luggage, * * * does not expose noncontraband items that otherwise would remain hidden from public view," and "discloses only the presence or absence of narcotics, a contraband item."

Does the *Jacobsen-Place* doctrine support the conclusion that use of a gun detector is no search, so that (as some proponents of this hardware apparently contemplate[174]) these detectors may be directed at persons without any prior individualized suspicion whatsoever? Well, that depends. For one thing, it is important to appreciate that the *Jacobsen-Place* doctrine presupposes not merely an item-specific detection device, but rather one that is *contraband*-specific. This means that a gun detector might qualify as a no-search investigative technique if and only if the concealed possession of a gun is criminal under the circumstances. Use of the detector thus would not be a search when used in certain special settings where there is a general prohibition on carrying a weapon (e.g., when attempting to board a commercial aircraft[175]), but would be a search if used more generally *unless* it is

---

[170]Raytheon's device "produces no image" and "simply detects metal objects that fit the 'signature' of a gun," Harris, 69 Temple L.Rev. 1, 7 n.38 (1996); the INEL device uses "target recognition software" to identify those fluctuations matching "known 'signatures' of weapons," id. at 8 n.38; while the Millitech device has at least the potential reveal the "size, shape, and form" of other objects, id. at 13, though perhaps it could somehow be programmed to respond only to known weapons shapes.

[171]Loewy, The Fourth Amendment as a Device for Protecting the Innocent, 81 Mich.L.Rev. 1229, 1248 (1983).

[172]United States v. Jacobsen, 466 U.S. 109, 104 S.Ct. 1652, 80 L.Ed.2d 85 (1984), discussed in § 1.8(b).

[173]United States v. Place, 462 U.S. 696, 103 S.Ct. 2637, 77 L.Ed.2d 110 (1983), discussed in § 2.2(g).

[174]Wilson, Just Take Away Their Guns, N.Y. Times, Mar. 20, 1994, § 6 (Magazine), at 47.

[175]See § 10.8 on the hijacker detection system.

true, subject perhaps to very limited exceptions,[176] that carrying a
concealed weapon is otherwise a criminal offense. But in a great
many jurisdictions it is *not* true; it may be the ultimate irony
that at precisely the time when these weapons detection devices
are being perfected, more and more states have adopted laws
under which large numbers of citizens can lawfully carry concealed weapons.[177] At best, then, the no-search characterization
will be possible as to gun detection devices in only about half of
the states. (Which half of the states will have the most desirable
environment is, of course, debatable. Those jurisdictions proscribing the carrying of concealed weapons generally will be able to
use weapons detectors freely—at least free of Fourth Amendment
restraints—and presumably will reduce somewhat the amount of
criminality involving use of weapons. Those jurisdictions not
proscribing the carrying of concealed weapons will have to follow
Fourth Amendment limitations[178] in the use of weapons detection
devices, which presumably would reduce—but not entirely eliminate—the chance of questionable practices, such as an arbitrary
selection of those who are to be the object of such scrutiny.[179])

Assume now a jurisdiction in which the carrying of a concealed
weapon *is* a criminal offense. May it be concluded beyond question that in such a locale the *Jacobsen-Place* doctrine will operate
to make the use of the contraband-specific weapons detector an

---

[176]Something a bit short of 100%
prohibition should suffice to bring the
Place-Jacobsen doctrine into play, as
where carrying a concealed weapon is
generally criminal but a few persons
(e.g., police) are privileged to do so
because of the nature of their employment. Cf. United States v. DeBerry,
76 F.3d 884 (7th Cir.1996) (tip that a
person was carrying a firearm constitutes reasonable suspicion of the crime
of carrying a concealed weapon despite
the fact the statute had "the usual
exceptions for police officers and the
like"). This conclusion is especially
compelling where the exception covers
only government employees and others, such as private detectives, amenable to a degree of state regulation beyond that applicable to the general
public.

[177]Harris, 69 Temple L.Rev. 1, 57
(1996), observes: "As of this writing,
at least twenty-five states have enacted some variety of these new concealed weapon permit statutes. In
some of the jurisdictions that have
adopted these laws, hundred of thousands of people have obtained permits
and may now legally carry concealed

firearms."

[178]One question, of course, is
whether the nature of the device bears
on just when this variety of search
activity is permissible. See discussion
of this point in § 9.6 at note 153.

[179]Indeed, Wilson, Just Take Away
Their Guns, N.Y. Times, Mar. 20,
1994, § 6 (Magazine), at 47, an apparent advocate of the widespread use of
gun detection devices, has conceded
that under his proposed regime "innocent people will be stopped. Young
black and Hispanic men will probably
be stopped more often than older white
Anglo males or women of any race."
For more on this prospect, see
Schwartz, "Just Take Away Their
Guns": The Hidden Racism of Terry v.
Ohio, 23 Fordham Urb.L.J. 317 (1996).

The problem is very similar to
that which already exists as to making traffic stops, likely possible as to
any driver who is scrutinized briefly,
on racial or other arbitrary grounds.
See the discussion of Whren v. United
States, 517 U.S. 806, 116 S.Ct. 1769,
135 L.Ed.2d 89 (1996), in § 1.4(f).

activity uncontrolled by the Fourth Amendment? It is impossible to say for sure, for there are questions about the breadth of the *Jacobsen-Place* rule that have not yet been fully resolved. In *Place*, the dog sniff was of a piece of luggage then in the lawful possession of the police outside the defendant's presence, and thus it cannot be said for sure that the Court would have felt the same way about the sniffing of a person.[180] (*Jacobsen* does not address that issue either, for there the testing was of the contents of a package lawfully opened by the authorities, again out of the presence of the owner.[181]) Given the emphasis in *Place* on the fact that the detection procedures at issue there ensured "that the owner of the property is not subjected to the embarrassment and inconvenience entailed in less discriminate and more intrusive investigative methods," it might be argued, for example, that directing a weapons detection device at a particular individual is a search if that activity is known to the object of the police scrutiny and to bystanders.

Still another problem, which cannot be resolved without knowing more about both the boundaries of *Jacobsen-Place* and the reliability of the new gun detection devices, has to do with the relevance of accuracy to a determination that a certain detection device is sufficiently contraband-specific. It remains to be seen just how reliable the various gun detection devices will turn out to be, though it has been speculated that "eliminating error altogether may prove difficult, if not impossible."[182] It would be remarkable if the *Jacobsen* and *Place* decisions were grounded in an unstated assumption of total infallibility of either the field test kit or the canine nose, so it is probably the case that the chance of error need not be totally eliminated. But, despite the Supreme Court's failure to address this point,[183] it would seem that the tolerable margin of error must be slight—certainly much less than the margin of error that is allowable in the context of determining that the purported nonsearch activity has now supplied probable cause for a real search,[184] for the underlying principle of *Jacobsen* and *Place* is that the privacy of innocent

[180]See § 2.2(g).

[181]For more on this general point, see Harris, 69 Temple L.Rev. 1, 33–34 (1996).

[182]Harris, 69 Temple L.Rev. 1, 35 (1996).

[183]In *Place*, for example, the Court made the flat-out assertion that the trained canine nose "discloses only the presence or absence of narcotics, a contraband item." But the fact of the matter is that mistakes made by the dog or (perhaps more likely) the dog's handler can—and more than rarely do—result in a false positive identification of drugs. See Bird, An Examination of the Training and Reliability of the Narcotics Detection Dog, 85 Ky.L.J. 405 (1997).

[184]Certainly the was-there-a-search issue and the is-there-now-probable-cause issue are separate and distinct and require different analysis. Given the low level of probability required to establish probable cause, see § 3.2(e), it is possible to establish grounds to search in a particular instance despite a rather significant likelihood that the search will turn out

activities is not significantly jeopardized. Moreover, as one perceptive commentator has noted, this latter consideration is especially telling in the present context:

> To the extent that gun detectors make some mistakes, such as identifying as carriers of concealed weapons people who are, in fact, carrying keys, tools, or some other innocent object, they create a whole new problem. Those people for whom the device generates a false positive will likely be searched in some more thorough, presumably physical manner.[185]

Yet another emerging technology deserving mention here is the "Enclosed Space Detection System" (ESDS), a search tool developed by the Department of Energy that enables officials to detect the presence of a person within, for example, a vehicle by detecting the beating of the occupant's heart.[186] Because a physical search of a vehicle to find a person is unquestionably a search,[187] it would seem, based upon the same analysis used above regarding the gun detector, that employment of ESDS to acquire the same information would constitute a search. But, while this conclusion, as a general matter, would "seem to be beyond question,"[188] here again it must be asked whether the *Jacobsen-Place* doctrine comes into play. One commentator has answered that question in the affirmative, reasoning that "the heartbeat detector is as limited as a canine sniff both in manner of obtaining facts and in the content of the information it reveals."[189] But, as discussed earlier, the Supreme Court in *Place* put great emphasis upon the fact that the drug dog's sniff reveals "only the presence or absence of narcotics, a contraband item," which would indicate that *Place* may not be a useful analogy here. This commentator has suggested otherwise, reasoning, in effect, that the *Place* rationale would extend to those situations in which "ESDS discloses only the presence or absence of a hidden person, who would be present only for an illegal purpose whether at a nuclear facility, prison, border checkpoint, or airport."[190] Although it is less than apparent that this is so, this is not to suggest that employment of ESDS in the particular circumstances mentioned would constitute an illegal search. Perhaps it would be a search, but under

---

to be fruitless. But it makes no sense whatsoever to assert that a certain variety of detection activity, merely because it is more often accurate than in error, deserves to be characterized as no search.

[185]Harris, 69 Temple L.Rev. 1, 35 (1996).

[186]For further description of this technology, see Dery, The Loss of Privacy is Just a Heartbeat Away: An Exploration of Government Heartbeat Detection Technology and Its Impact on Fourth Amendment Protections, 7

Wm. & Mary Bill Rts.J. 401, 403–08 (1999); Iraola, New Detection Technologies and the Fourth Amendment, 47 S.D.L.Rev. 8 (2002).

[187]United States v. Ortiz, 422 U.S. 891, 95 S.Ct. 2585, 45 L.Ed.2d 623 (1975).

[188]Dery, 7 Wm. & Mary Bill Rts.J. 401, 423 (1999).

[189]Dery, 7 Wm. & Mary Bill Rts.J. 401, 424 (1999).

[190]Dery, 7 Wm. & Mary Bill Rts.J. 401, 424 (1999).

the Supreme Court's "special needs" approach it might well past muster as a limited intrusion serving compelling interests "beyond normal law enforcement."[191]

Those devices must be distinguished from equipment used to disclose the presence of something that is not concealed in the sense of being covered or enclosed but yet cannot be perceived by the naked eye. Sometimes the extensiveness of the examination by this equipment makes it apparent that the disclosure was achieved by a search; it has thus rightly been deemed "obvious" that using a gas chromatograph to identify organic compounds in a person's clothing constitutes a search.[192] But what then of an ultraviolet lamp, which is used to establish that a suspect has recently been in contact with a certain incriminating object? The technique involves treating the object (often[193] but not always[194] drugs found in an inspection of incoming international mail[195]) by dusting it with fluorescent powder[196] or coating it with fluorescent grease.[197] At some later time, after it is thought that a particular person has been in physical contact with the treated object, an ultraviolet light is shined upon the hands of the suspect. If the suspect has in fact had contact with the object so treated, the light will make the hands glow where traces of the powder or grease are present.

Courts have experienced considerable difficulty with the question of whether such use of an ultraviolet lamp itself constitutes a search,[198] which is none too surprising, for the *Katz* formula does not provide a ready answer. Of the few decisions in point,

[191]Skinner v. Railway Labor Executives' Ass'n, 489 U.S. 602, 109 S.Ct. 1402, 103 L.Ed.2d 639 (1989). For discussion of why these situations fit within the "special needs" category, see Dery, 7 Wm. & Mary Bill Rts.J. 401, 429–37 (1999).

[192]State v. Joyce, 229 Conn. 10, 639 A.2d 1007 (1994). The Court distinguished United States v. Jacobsen, 466 U.S. 109, 104 S.Ct. 1652, 80 L.Ed.2d 85 (1984) (field test of powder no search because limited to determining presence or absence of illegal cocaine), and United States v. Place, 462 U.S. 696, 103 S.Ct. 2637, 77 L.Ed.2d 110 (1983) (dog sniff no search because it detects only presence or absence of contraband), because "the gas chromatograph test is not designed to detect the presence of contraband, and in fact detects the presence and identity of many organic substances."

Use of a gas chromatograph, especially in its more recent variation as

a portable device testing for explosives or drugs, is discussed further in § 2.2(h).

[193]E.g., United States v. Millen, 338 F.Supp. 747 (E.D.Wis.1972).

[194]E.g., United States v. Richardson, 388 F.2d 842 (6th Cir.1968) (witness saw bank burglary and placing of loot in hiding place; police put fluorescent powder in hidden bags).

[195]On the validity of such an inspection, see § 10.5(k).

[196]E.g., United States v. Millen, 338 F.Supp. 747 (E.D.Wis.1972).

[197]E.g., Commonwealth v. DeWitt, 226 Pa.Super. 372, 314 A.2d 27 (1973).

[198]This, of course, is a distinct issue from that of whether a detention of the suspect in order to use the lamp was an illegal seizure. If an illegal seizure was made, then the evidence obtained thereby would be inadmissible without regard to whether what

the numerical majority have reached the conclusion that this conduct is not a search in the Fourth Amendment sense. Illustrative is *Commonwealth v. DeWitt*,[199] where customs agents, after finding hashish in a table with a false top being shipped from abroad, treated it with fluorescent grease, repackaged it and sent it on its way. After the package was delivered, agents entered the premises of delivery to execute a warrant for the contraband. While there the agents passed an ultraviolet light over the hands of the defendants and learned that they had handled the treated hashish. In response to the defendants' claim that this was an illegal search not authorized by the warrant, the court stated:

> In any event, defendants had no reasonable expectation of privacy as to the presence of foreign matter on their hands independent of the expectation of the privacy of their premises, which had been legitimately invaded by the police. The grease may be compared to a physical characteristic, such as a fingerprint or one's voice, which is "constantly exposed to the public." * * * The Fourth Amendment provides no protection for what "a person knowingly exposes to the public." * * * It is true that the grease could not be detected with the naked eye, but then, neither may a fingerprint be examined until there has been an application of ink. Furthermore, the examination was both limited and controlled, affording no opportunity to learn any information other than that specifically sought: Have the person's hands been in contact with the treated contraband? In this respect, the examination was more circumscribed than any eavesdropping, electronic surveillance, long-distance viewing with binoculars, or even the use of a flashlight. Also, it involves no personal indignities or physical discomfort, and was neither annoying, frightening, or humiliating. * * *
>
> In these circumstances the use of the ultraviolet light to examine defendants' hands did not amount to a search. It may well be that in other circumstances an examination by ultraviolet light would amount to a search. Each case turns upon its own facts.[200]

---

followed was itself a search. Davis v. Mississippi, 394 U.S. 721, 89 S.Ct. 1394, 22 L.Ed.2d 676 (1969).

For another assessment of these cases, see Comment, 22 J. Marshall L.Rev. 877 (1989).

[199] Commonwealth v. DeWitt, 226 Pa.Super. 372, 314 A.2d 27 (1973).

[200] The court noted that two other cases were in accord but that neither court "offered reasons for its conclusion." The two cases are United States v. Richardson, 388 F.2d 842 (6th Cir.1968) (witness saw bags taken in bank burglary being hidden behind the bank; bags were dusted with powder; man fitting general description of defendant seen approaching and then running from that area; agents went to restaurant where defendant worked and asked him to step over to socket where they plugged in the lamp; the light indicated fluorescent powder in the creases of his hands; court declared it did "not regard the examination of appellant's hands under the ultraviolet light as a search within the meaning of the Fourth Amendment," but in alternative stated that if it was a search defendant had consented to it); United States v. Millen, 338 F.Supp. 747 (E.D.Wis.1972) (lamp used on defendant after his arrest; court says that "an examination by law enforcement agents of a person's hands under a fluorescent light while he is in custody does not constitute a search subject to Fourth Amendment constraints"; court cites to Schmerber v.

The contrary position is represented by *United States v. Kenaan*,[201] involving facts like those in *DeWitt* in all material respects. The *Kenaan* court concluded:

> Appellant contends that the results of the inspection of his hands should have been suppressed at trial, since the inspection was, in effect, a personal search unauthorized by the warrant to search the premises. There can be little doubt that an inspection of one's hands, under an ultraviolet lamp, is the kind of governmental intrusion into one's private domain that is protected by the Fourth Amendment. * * * If the reach of the Fourth Amendment extends to fingerprinting, * * * and a search of one's clothing or personal effects, * * * it should certainly encompass a detailed inspection, by special instrument, of one's skin.
>
> It is no answer for the government to argue that the ultraviolet inspection actually protected appellant's privacy by obviating the necessity of a physical search of his person, since the search warrant gave the government agents no authority to conduct a personal search. * * * The protection afforded an individual by the Fourth Amendment would be eviscerated if, under authority of a warrant to search premises, government agents could scan an individual's body with sensitive instruments capable of picking up the most minute or intimate object lodged thereon.[202]

Because "the *Katz* decision was written to resist captivation in any formula,"[203] there is no easy litmus-paper test whereby either *DeWitt* or *Kenaan* can be declared to be the "correct" application of *Katz*. However, some tentative comments on this exceedingly difficult issue may be offered. For one thing, it may be questioned whether the *DeWitt* court is correct in asserting that the fluorescent substance was knowingly exposed to the public. Certainly it was not exposed in the sense of the characteristics the Court discussed in *United States v. Dionisio*,[204] where it was said:

> Like a man's facial characteristics, or handwriting, his voice is

---

California, 384 U.S. 757, 86 S.Ct. 1826, 16 L.Ed.2d 908 (1966), and thus may have simply meant that it was a valid search incident to arrest).

See also United States v. Ukomadu, 236 F.3d 333 (6th Cir.2001) (use of black light to detect phosphorescent powder on defendant's hands and clothing no search); State v. Holzapfel, 230 Mont. 105, 748 P.2d 953 (1988) (exposing arrestee's hands to ultraviolet light no search; analogy to fingerprinting).

[201] United States v. Kenaan, 496 F.2d 181 (1st Cir.1974).

[202] Similarly, in State v. Howell, 524 S.W.2d 11 (Mo.1975), defendant was arrested and then had his hands swabbed with a solution allowing the police to determine that he had recently fired a gun. The court concluded that this evidence was not admissible because the defendant had been illegally arrested, and then went on to state unnecessarily: "Additionally, there is no question but what the performance of the test on defendant's hands and the taking of sample residue therefrom was a search and seizure."

[203] Amsterdam, Perspectives on the Fourth Amendment, 58 Minn.L.Rev. 349, 385 (1974).

[204] United States v. Dionisio, 410 U.S. 1, 93 S.Ct. 764, 35 L.Ed.2d 67 (1973).

repeatedly produced for others to hear. No person can have a reasonable expectation that others will not know the sound of his voice, any more than he can reasonably expect that his face will be a mystery to the world.

It certainly cannot be said in the same fashion that the defendants in *DeWitt* and *Kenaan* were knowingly exposing to others the fact that they had recently handled contraband.

But this does not advance matters very far, for while *Katz* says it is no search to discover what one "knowingly exposes," it does not declare the exact reverse of this proposition. That is, the Court did not say that discovery of what was not knowingly exposed is inevitably a search. Rather, the Court cautiously stated that what one "seeks to preserve as private * * * *may* be constitutionally protected."[205] This means, for example (as we have seen in the earlier discussion in this section), that if one seeks to preserve something as private by reliance upon darkness or distance, the discovery of it by flashlight or binoculars is not necessarily a search.

It is also interesting to note that both *Kenaan* and *DeWitt* analogize the use of the lamp to fingerprinting. This, however, leads the two courts in opposite directions, for *Kenaan* asserts that fingerprinting is a search while *DeWitt* declares that it is not.[206] *Dionisio* also addresses this point, albeit in uncertain terms. The Court there likened the taking of a voice exemplar to

the fingerprinting in *Davis,* where, though the initial dragnet detentions were constitutionally impermissible, we noted that the fingerprinting itself "involves none of the probing into an individual's private life and thoughts that marks an interrogation or search."

But this characterization in *Davis v. Mississippi*[207] was made for a quite different purpose,[208] and thus it is to be doubted that the question of whether fingerprinting is a search can be taken as settled.

Moreover, even if it may be assumed that the act of fingerprinting by itself is not a Fourth Amendment search, this does not really resolve the issue at hand. That is, the analogy between fingerprinting and use of an ultraviolet lamp is not as close as was assumed in both *DeWitt* and *Kenaan*. *Dionisio* says that because one's voice has "previously been exposed to the public"[209] it is no search to require one to speak again on a particular

---

[205]Emphasis added.

[206]Other courts have likewise disagreed on this point. Compare Paulson v. Florida, 360 F.Supp. 156 (S.D.Fla. 1973); with State v. Inman, 301 A.2d 348 (Me.1973).

[207]Davis v. Mississippi, 394 U.S. 721, 89 S.Ct. 1394, 22 L.Ed.2d 676 (1969).

[208]Namely, to suggest that the fingerprinting was a lesser intrusion that would justify a brief detention for that purpose upon less than the traditional quantum of probable cause. See § 9.8(b).

[209]Quoting from United States v. Doe (Schwartz), 457 F.2d 895 (2d Cir. 1972).

occasion. Similarly, the companion case of *United States v. Mara*[210] teaches that because handwriting "is repeatedly shown to the public," it is not a search to compel the giving of an exemplar on an occasion when the defendant would doubtless prefer not to do so. By a parity of reasoning, it might be contended that the act of taking fingerprints is no search because, "[e]xcept for the rare recluse who chooses to live his life in complete solitude,"[211] we constantly leave our fingerprints in public places. But it cannot be said that by our frequent appearances in public we reveal whether we have handled contraband in the privacy of our own homes.

This suggests that a no less apt analogy could be drawn between the use of an ultraviolet lamp and the conduct in *Cupp v. Murphy*.[212] There, Murphy appeared at the station in connection with the police investigation of the strangling of his wife; the police saw dried blood on his finger and then took scrapings from his fingernails, which turned out to contain traces of skin, blood cells, and fabric from his wife's nightgown. The Court without hesitation concluded that a search had occurred:

> Unlike the fingerprinting in *Davis,* the voice exemplar obtained in * * * *Dionisio,* * * * or the handwriting exemplar obtained in * * * *Mara,* * * * the search of the respondent's fingernails went beyond mere "physical characteristics . . . constantly exposed to the public" * * * .

Cupp tells us, then, that when one voluntarily walks into a police station with evidence connecting him with a homicide on his hands, that person nonetheless has a protected expectation of privacy with respect to that evidence when its incriminating character is not evident to the naked eye and it must be taken and analyzed to be of evidentiary value. If this is so, then it is not far-fetched to suggest that the defendants in *DeWitt* and *Kenaan* also had a protected expectation of privacy with respect to the substance on their hands[213] which, like the scrapings in *Cupp,* were not incriminating to the naked eye.[214]

None of this, of course, supplies a definitive answer to the ques-

---

[210]United States v. Mara, 410 U.S. 19, 93 S.Ct. 774, 35 L.Ed.2d 99 (1973).

[211]United States v. Doe (Schwartz), 457 F.2d 895 (2d Cir.1972), quoted in *Dionisio*.

[212]Cupp v. Murphy, 412 U.S. 291, 93 S.Ct. 2000, 36 L.Ed.2d 900 (1973).

[213]The substance, it should be emphasized, is a powder or grease having evidentiary significance in terms of showing the suspect recently handled the treated contraband. The discovery is not of the contraband itself, and thus the Supreme Court decisions discussed in note 161 supra are of doubtful applicability here, even assuming they could otherwise be extended to limited intrusions upon a *person* revealing only contraband.

[214]In *Cupp,* of course, there is the added fact that a physical thing, the scrapings, were actually seized, but this standing alone seems a weak basis for distinguishing *Cupp.* The defendant's possessory interest in the dirt under his nails, as compared to his privacy interest in his person, is rather insignificant.

tion we started with: whether using an ultraviolet light to detect a fluorescent substance on one's hands constitutes a search. It only confirms the earlier assertion that there is no readily apparent "correct" answer. In the final analysis, *Katz* requires that a value judgment be made; though it "begs the question,"[215] "the basis of the *Katz* decision seems to be that the fourth amendment protects those interests that may justifiably claim fourth amendment protection."[216] To say that a particular type of police practice is not a search is to conclude, in effect, that such activities "may be as unreasonable as the police please to make them,"[217] and thus the push must be in the direction of applying the "search" appellation to those varieties of police conduct we are not prepared to leave totally uncontrolled. One such practice, it is submitted, is the scanning of "an individual's body with sensitive instruments capable of picking up the most minute or intimate object lodged thereon."[218]

This conclusion takes on greater force when it is considered that imposing some Fourth Amendment limits upon this practice would not be particularly burdensome to law enforcement. It is quite unlike, say, requiring the police to provide justification every time they turn on a flashlight. There is no reason to utilize an ultraviolet light on a general or random basis; rather, as the *DeWitt* and *Kenaan* cases themselves illustrate, the occasion for using this investigative technique arises when suspicion has focused upon one person or a small group of individuals. When there are grounds to arrest a particular suspect, he may be arrested and then the lamp may be used as a legitimate search incident to arrest.[219] Use of the lamp, as previously noted, is not unlike the search made in *Cupp v. Murphy*,[220] and thus there will be instances in which the lamp could be used without either a warrant or arrest to make "the very limited search necessary to preserve highly evanescent evidence." Moreover, because the search is very limited, it could be lawfully directed at a small group of suspects[221] even absent full probable cause with respect to any particular member of the group.[222]

---

[215]Amsterdam, 58 Minn.L.Rev. 349, 385 (1974).

[216]Amsterdam, 58 Minn.L.Rev. 349, 385 (1974).

[217]Amsterdam, 58 Minn.L.Rev. 349, 388 (1974).

[218]United States v. Kenaan, 496 F.2d 181 (1st Cir.1974).

[219]In United States v. Kenaan, 496 F.2d 181 (1st Cir.1974), the court, in remanding the case, noted that "the district court will have further opportunity to decide whether there was

probable cause for arrest before inspection of appellant's hands."

[220]Cupp v. Murphy, 412 U.S. 291, 93 S.Ct. 2000, 36 L.Ed.2d 900 (1973).

[221]The greatest value of this particular kind of search, it would seem, would be in identifying the guilty party from a small group, as where there is a controlled delivery of a package containing narcotics to a certain address and the police do not know which occupant opened the package.

[222]See § 9.8(b).

§ 2.2(e) Use of thermal imager to detect and measure heat

Yet another type of equipment utilized by law enforcement is a thermal-imaging device.[223] As described in *Kyllo v. United States*:[224] "Thermal imagers detect infrared radiation, which virtually all objects emit but is not visible to the naked eye. The imager converts radiation into images based on relative warmth—black is cool, white is hot, shades of gray connote relative differences; in that respect, it operates somewhat like a video camera showing heat images." When directed at a particular structure, the imager does not intrude into the interior, but rather it passively measures heat emitted from the exterior surfaces of that structure. The most common use of the imager is as in *Kyllo*: when directed at a building the police suspect is being used to grow marijuana, the device can confirm those suspicions by detecting an abnormal heating pattern suggestive of a marijuana growing operation. That and other information is then collectively presented to a magistrate in order to obtain a warrant to search that building for marijuana.

The question of whether use of a thermal imager constitutes a

---

[Section 2.2(e)]

[223]For other discussions of such equipment, see Kash, Prewarrant Thermal Imaging as a Fourth Amendment Violation: A Supreme Court Question in the Making, 60 Alb.L.Rev. 1295 (1997); Comments, 49 Cath.U.L. Rev. 575 (2000); 36 Duq.L.Rev. 415 (1998); 29 Ga.L.Rev. 819 (1995); 59 La.L.Rev. 1243 (1999); 90 Nw.U.L.Rev. 267 (1995); 53 SMU L.Rev. 1645 (2000); 12 T.M. Cooley L.Rev. 597 (1995); 46 Vill.L.Rev. 241 (2001); Notes, 37 Am.Crim.L.Rev. 127 (2000); 27 Ariz.St.L.J. 295 (1995); 46 Drake L.Rev. 173 (1997); 29 Ind.L.Rev. 231 (1995); 13 J.Marshall J. Computer & Info.L. 453 (1995); 83 Ky.L.J. 891 (1995); 25 Ohio N.U.L.Rev. 593 (1999); 16 QLR 419 (1997); 3 Tex.Wesleyan L.Rev. 393 (1997); 49 Wash.U.J.Urb. & Contemp.L. 247 (1996).

[224]Kyllo v. United States, 533 U.S. 27, 121 S.Ct. 2038, 150 L.Ed.2d 94 (2001), discussed in Cloud, Rube Goldberg Meets the Constitution: Virtual Fourth Amendment Protection in the Twenty-First Century, 72 Miss.L.J. 51 (2002); Fisher, Cracking Down on Soccer Moms and Other Urban Legends on the Frontier of the Fourth Amendment, 38 Willamette L.Rev. 137 (2002); Seamon, Kyllo v. United States and the Partial Ascendance of Justice Scalia's Fourth Amendment, 79 Wash.U.L.Q. 1013 (2001); Sklansky, Back to the Future: Kyllo, Katz, and the Common Law, 72 Miss.L.J. 143 (2002); Slobogin, Peeping Techno-Toms and the Fourth Amendment: Seeing Through Kyllo's Rules Governing Technological Surveillance, 86 Minn.L.Rev. 1393 (2002); Comments, 80 Denv.U.L.Rev. 463 (2002); 107 Dick.L.Rev. 179 (2002); 36 J.Marshall L.Rev. 507 (2003); 46 N.Y.L. Sch.L.Rev. 319 (2003); 81 N.C.L.Rev. 728 (2003); 78 N.D.L.Rev. 99 (2002); 34 U.Tol.L.Rev. 351 (2003); Notes, 56 Ark.L.Rev. 431 (2003); 41 Brandeis L.J. 939 (2003); 24 Campbell L.Rev. 53 (2001); 32 Cumb.L.Rev. 675 (2002); 52 DePaul L.Rev. 201 (2002); 2002 Geo.J.L. & Pub.Pol'y 155; 90 Geo.L.J. 2175 (2002); 45 How.L.J. 177 (2001); 62 La.L.Rev. 929 (2002); 64 Mont.L. Rev. 519 (2003); 78 NYU L.Rev. 1789 (2003); 56 Okla.L.Rev. 153 (2003); 12 Seton Hall Const.L.J. 769 (2002); 43 S.Tex.L.Rev. 837 (2002); 19 T.M.Cooley L.Rev. 247 (2002); 24 U.Haw.L.Rev. 383 (2002); 51 U.Kan.L.Rev. 181 (2002); Recent Decision, 71 Miss.L.J. 325 (2001); 2 Wyo.L.Rev. 169 (2002).

search began hitting the appellate courts in the early 1990's. One view, as concluded in *State v. Young*,[225] was that an affirmative answer was called for by *United States v. Karo*,[226] holding that use of a beeper to "reveal a critical fact about the interior of the premises" was a search. But the overwhelming majority of appellate decisions were to the contrary.[227] The two most common reasons given for reaching that result were less than satisfying: (i) that the device only reveals "heat waste," which is like the garbage set out for collection held not to merit Fourth Amendment protection in *California v. Greenwood*,[228] and (ii) that infrared surveillance was comparable to the use of drug-sniffing dogs, held in *United States v. Place*[229] not to constitute a search when it revealed contraband within luggage lawfully held by the police. Then came the *Kyllo* case, where the Supreme Court, albeit in a 5-4 opinion,[230] turned everything around. The question before the Court in *Kyllo* was "whether the use of a thermal-imaging device aimed at a private home from a public street to detect relative amounts of heat within the home constitutes a 'search' within the meaning of the Fourth Amendment,"[231] and Justice Scalia, for the majority, answered with a resounding "yes."

Beginning with the much-maligned *Katz* "expectation of privacy" test, the Court proceeded to apply it to a situation as to

[225]State v. Young, 123 Wash.2d 173, 867 P.2d 593 (1994), discussed in Note, 30 Gonz.L.Rev. 135 (1994). Accord: People v. Deutsch, 44 Cal.App. 4th 1224, 52 Cal.Rptr.2d 366 (1996); State v. Siegal, 281 Mont. 250, 934 P.2d 176 (1997).

[226]United States v. Karo, 468 U.S. 705, 104 S.Ct. 3296, 82 L.Ed.2d 530 (1984), discussed in § 2.7(g).

[227]United States v. Real Property Located at 15324 Cty. Hwy. E, 219 F.3d 602 (7th Cir.2000); United States v. Depew, 210 F.3d 1061 (9th Cir. 2000); Kyllo v. U.S., 190 F.3d 1041 (9th Cir.1999); United States v. Robinson, 62 F.3d 1325 (11th Cir. 1995); United States v. Ishmael, 48 F.3d 850 (5th Cir.1995); United States v. Myers, 46 F.3d 668 (7th Cir.1995); United States v. Ford, 34 F.3d 992 (11th Cir.1994); United States v. Pinson, 24 F.3d 1056 (8th Cir.1994); State v. Cramer, 174 Ariz. 522, 851 P.2d 147 (App.1992); LaFollette v. Commonwealth, 915 S.W.2d 747 (Ky. 1996); State v. McKee, 181 Wis.2d 354, 510 N.W.2d 807 (App.1993).

In the *Depew* case, following a middle position of sorts—that the use of a thermal imager is no search *only*

if "the scan did not reveal any details of the inside of Depew's home"—the court also recognized that in any event warrantless use of a thermal imager may be objectionable because of its location within the curtilage, and remanded for further inquiry into that matter.

[228]California v. Greenwood, 486 U.S. 35, 108 S.Ct. 1625, 100 L.Ed.2d 30 (1988), discussed in § 2.6(c).

[229]United States v. Place, 462 U.S. 696, 103 S.Ct. 2637, 77 L.Ed.2d 110 (1983), discussed in § 2.2(g).

[230]With some unusual alignments. Scalia, who wrote the majority opinion, was joined by Souter, Thomas, Ginsburg, and Breyer; and Stevens filed a dissent joined by Rehnquist, O'Connor and Kennedy.

[231]*Kyllo* thus does *not* mean courts "are required to weigh the evidence of probable cause against the privacy interests of the individual whose property was subject to search," as the case concerns only "the threshold determination of whether a search occurred." United States v. Lopez, 380 F.3d 538 (1st Cir.2004).

which the Court had "previously reserved judgment,"[232] that is, regarding "how much technological enhancement of ordinary perception" was permissible as to surveillance of a home from a public vantage point before that perception would constitute a Fourth Amendment search. Although admitting that some technological advances do indeed "shrink the realm of guaranteed privacy," as with "the technology enabling human flight" that the Court had held in *California v. Ciraolo*[233] did not make looking down into an otherwise private curtilage a search, the Court deemed it necessary to draw a clear line regarding surveillance of the home: "We think that obtaining by sense-enhancing technology any information regarding the interior of the home that could not otherwise have been obtained without physical 'intrusion into a constitutionally protected area' * * * constitutes a search—at least where (as here) the technology in question is not in general public use." Application of that test, which, as Justice Scalia explained, "assures preservation of that degree of privacy against government that existed when the Fourth Amendment was adopted," meant that the surveillance in the instant case had amounted to a search, for a thermal imager "reveals the relative heat of various rooms in the home," which is most certainly "information regarding the interior of the home."[234]

There are many things to like about the majority opinion in *Kyllo*, perhaps the most important being that the opinion is true to the teaching of *Katz* that what is most important is whether there has been an intrusion upon a justified expectation of privacy, and not (as in the pre-*Katz* era) whether there had been a physical intrusion into some protected area. The significance of this distinction dramatically appears when the *Kyllo* rationale is compared with that of the four dissenters in that case. The dis-

---

[232]In Dow Chemical Co. v. United States, 476 U.S. 227, 106 S.Ct. 1819, 90 L.Ed.2d 226 (1986), discussed in § 2.4(b).

[233]California v. Ciraolo, 476 U.S. 207, 106 S.Ct. 1809, 90 L.Ed.2d 210 (1986), discussed in § 2.3(g).

[234]The Court added that consequently such surveillance "is presumptively unreasonable without a warrant," which would seem to mean that a showing of probable cause would be required. But in United States v. Kattaria, 503 F.3d 703 (8th Cir.2007), opinion vacated 519 F.3d 930 (8th Cir. 2007), discussed in Note, 73 Mo.L.Rev. 881 (2008), the court concluded "that the same Fourth Amendment reasonable suspicion standard that applies to *Terry* investigative stops should apply to the issuance of a purely investigative warrant to conduct a limited thermal imaging search from well outside the home." The court's reasoning in support seems rather circular (since the thermal imaging was to get information supporting a full search of the house, that preliminary search must therefore have a lower threshold, as "[i]f the same probable cause is required to obtain both kinds of warrants, law enforcement will have little incentive to incur the expense of a minimally intrusive thermal imaging search before conducting a highly intrusive physical search"), and, while otherwise it might seem sensible (see comparable argument re dog sniffs in § 2.2(g)), it cannot be squared with the current position of the Supreme Court. See text at notes 442–445 infra.

senters, in an approach decidedly reminiscent of the pre-*Katz* approach, draw a distinction between "through-the-wall surveillance" and "off-the-wall" surveillance, and conclude that it is decisive that "the equipment in this case did not penetrate the walls of petitioner's home" but instead did no more than "passively measure heat emitted from the exterior surfaces of petitioner's home." But such an approach, which most likely would have produced a different result in *Katz* itself,[235] is most certainly inconsistent with the teaching of *Katz*, as the *Kyllo* majority explained:

> But just as a thermal imager captures only heat emanating from a house, so also a powerful directional microphone picks up only sound emanating from a house—and a satellite capable of scanning from many miles away would pick up only visible light emanating from a house. We rejected such a mechanical interpretation of the Fourth Amendment in *Katz*, where the eavesdropping device picked up only sound waves that reached the exterior of the phone booth.

The basic point, as it was put in one of the few pre-*Kyllo* cases finding use of a thermal imager to constitute a search, is that "*Katz* looked not to the tools employed by the government nor to the phenomena measured by those tools but to the object of the government's efforts."[236]

A second praiseworthy characteristic of the *Kyllo* majority opinion is the Court's forthright recognition of the need to take a stand *now* against the increasing intrusiveness of modern technology, instead of waiting, as would the dissenters, until the equipment is even more sophisticated and the intrusions even more severe. It is the dissenters' position in *Kyllo* that there is no need to take a stand in the instant case because it involves only "a fairly primitive thermal imager" that "merely discloses that the exterior of one house or one area of the house, is much warmer than another." But the majority rightly opted for "the

---

[235]As stated in the excellent opinion in United States v. Cusumano, 67 F.3d 1497 (10th Cir.1995), vacated on rehearing en banc, 83 F.3d 1247 (10th Cir.1996), but only on the ground that this issue need not be reached because evidence other than the thermal imager scan provided probable cause for the challenged search warrant: "It must be remembered that the bug at issue in *Katz* was fixed to the outside of a public phone booth. Reduced to its operational fundamentals, that bug did not monitor the interior of the phone booth at all; rather, it measured the molecular vibrations of the glass that encompassed that interior. Alternatively, it might fairly be said that the bug passively recorded the propagation of waste vibrational energy into the public sphere. Drawing upon the logic embraced by our fellow circuits, one could reason that the translation of the vibrational record into an account of that which transpired within the phone booth was simply a useful interpretation of abandoned energy—an analysis which would condone the search condemned in *Katz*."

[236]United States v. Cusumano, 67 F.3d 1497 (10th Cir.1995), vacated on rehearing en banc, 83 F.3d 1247 (10th Cir.1996), but only on the ground that this issue need not be reached because evidence other than the thermal imager scan provided probable cause for the challenged search warrant.

long view," fearing that the dissenters'

approach would leave the homeowner at the mercy of advancing technology—including imaging technology that could discern all human activity in the home. While the technology used in the present case was relatively crude, the rule we adopt must take account of more sophisticated systems that are already in use or in development.

In this respect, the majority opinion is true to the wisdom imparted long ago in *Boyd v. United States*,[237] where, much as in *Kyllo*, the government's position was that the conduct in issue should not trouble the Court because it lacked "many of the aggravating incidents of actual search and seizure." This prompted Justice Bradley's oft-quoted response that "unconstitutional practices get their first footing * * * by silent approaches and slight deviations from legal modes of procedure," so that it "is the duty of courts to be watchful for the constitutional rights of the citizen, and against any stealthy encroachments thereon. Their motto should be *obsta principiis*." Unlike some of the Court's earlier decisions,[238] *Kyllo* is true to that motto, for it indeed does "resist the opening wedge"[239] of intrusion into the home via technology.

Third and finally, the *Kyllo* majority opinion also deserves praise for foregoing the various privacy-belittling techniques that have become rather common in efforts to narrow the protections of the *Katz* doctrine. One of these techniques is to claim that the defendant's privacy really does not deserve protection because he failed to do all that he might have done to prevent the information in question from being accessible in some fashion by the authorities. A perfect illustration of that technique is the assertion by the *Kyllo* dissenters that if the defendant did not want his in-premises activities discovered in this way, it was his burden to "make sure that the surrounding area is well insulated." This is much like the cases criticized elsewhere herein[240] on the ground that they left apartment dwellers with the burden of papering over the transom and stuffing the keyhole in order to achieve protected privacy.

A second technique for diminishing privacy is through elaborate hypotheses about how law enforcement authorities might have lawfully acquired the same information. Here again the *Kyllo* dissenters provide an example, claiming in essence that the use of technology here should be of no concern because "any member of the public might notice that one part of a house is warmer than another part or a nearby building if, for example,

---

[237] Boyd v. United States, 116 U.S. 616, 6 S.Ct. 524, 29 L.Ed. 746 (1886).

[238] As discussed in LaFave, The Forgotten Motto of Obsta Principiis in Fourth Amendment Jurisprudence, 28 Ariz.L.Rev. 291 (1986).

[239] The nonliteral translation. See Guindagh, Dictionary of Foreign Phrases and Abbreviations 179 (1965).

[240] See § 2.3(c).

rainwater evaporates or snow melts at different rates across its surfaces." To this, the majority aptly responds that such a comparison

> is quite irrelevant. The fact that equivalent information could sometimes be obtained by other means does not make lawful the use of means that violate the Fourth Amendment. The police might, for example, learn how many people are in a particular house by setting up year-round surveillance; but that does not make breaking and entering to find out the same information lawful. In any event, on the night of January 16, 1992, no outside observer could have discerned the relative heat of Kyllo's home without thermal imaging.

The example put by the *Kyllo* majority is especially telling, for one of the major threats of law enforcement use of modern technology is that the technology can replace means of surveillance that would have been so expensive and time-consuming as to be unlikely undertakings absent rather strong evidence at the outset that fruitful evidence would be forthcoming.

A third technique by which privacy is belittled is by insisting that the intrusion must be rather substantial and must reveal specifically certain intimate details, as reflected in both the dissenting opinion and the argument of the government. As the *Kyllo* majority responded:

> The Fourth Amendment's protection of the home has never been tied to measurement of the quality or quantity of information obtained. * * * In the home, our cases show, *all* details are intimate details, because the entire area is held safe from prying government eyes.[241] [They] were intimate details because they were details of the home, just as was the detail of how warm—or even how relatively warm—Kyllo was heating his residence.

While there are thus many reasons to look with favor upon the majority opinion in *Kyllo*—especially in light of the nearly uniform pre-*Kyllo* view in the lower courts that use of a thermal imager is no search—there is some reason for concern about certain aspects of that opinion. First and foremost is the fact that the Court gave warning of a possible limitation upon its holding by adding at the end: "at least where (as here) the technology in question is not in general public use." That prompted the objection from the dissenters that "this criterion is somewhat perverse because it seems likely that the threat to privacy will grow, rather than recede, as the use of intrusive equipment becomes more readily available." The majority's response to that criticism is brief; there is no denial of its validity, but only the protest that the dissent's "quarrel * * * is not with us but with this Court's

---

[241]Noting that in United States v. Karo, 468 U.S. 705, 104 S.Ct. 3296, 82 L.Ed.2d 530 (1984), "the only thing detected was a can of ether in the home," while in Arizona v. Hicks, 480 U.S. 321, 107 S.Ct. 1149, 94 L.Ed.2d 347 (1987), "the only thing detected * * * was the registration number of a phonograph turntable."

precedent," given the statement of the majority in *Ciraolo* that defendant's fenced curtilage was not constitutionally protected from naked-eye viewing from 1,000 feet because "private and commercial flight in the public airways is routine."

Perhaps one should not make too much of the tentative qualification attached to the holding in *Kyllo*. After all, the Court does *not* assert that there *is* a "general public use" exception, but only that its search conclusion applies "at least" when the technology is not in public use. That cautious language, therefore, might be taken merely as an indication that the Court has left the "general public use" situation for another day, which certainly square's with the majority's later explanation that the instant case was not the occasion "to reexamine that factor," considering that it was obvious that thermal imaging could not by any stretch of the imagination be characterized as "routine." But none of that totally dissipates the concern stated earlier, for even the most tentatively stated exceptions to a rule have a tendency to harden into immutable limitations with the passage of time. It thus may be well to bring into question, hard on the heels of the *Kyllo* decision, whether the "general public use" limitation the Court finds in *Ciraolo* in fact merits application in cases where, as in *Kyllo*, the issue is whether police use of sophisticated surveillance equipment to enhance the human senses constitutes a search.

In exploring that question, it is well to begin with the same structural approach to the *Katz* doctrine used elsewhere herein,[242] which is to say that it may generally be said under *Katz* that courts should not bestow the nonsearch appellation upon police surveillance (1) that does not occur at a "public vantage point"; or (2) that is offensive in its intrusiveness in the sense that it uncovers that which the resident may fairly be said to have protected from scrutiny by the "curious passerby." The *Ciraolo* case is definitely a pure category (1) case, and thus establishes no more than that in figuring out what locations may fairly be characterized as a public vantage point, it is quite proper to take into account the fact that public presence at the location in question is "routine." That is, the Court in that case relied upon the fact the observation, which occurred at an altitude of 1,000 feet in public navigable airspace, was "where private and commercial flight in the public airways is routine," for only one conclusion, namely, that the officer's actions were no search because his observations were "from a public vantage point where he has a right to be and which renders the activities clearly visible."[243] What perhaps is even more important is that the *Ciraolo* Court took pains to em-

---

[242]E.g., § 2.3(c).

[243]Similarly, in Florida v. Riley, 488 U.S. 445, 109 S.Ct. 693, 102 L.Ed.2d 835 (1989), likewise involving naked-eye observation and thus also involving only category (1), the plurality opinion based its no-search conclusion on the fact the observations were from a public vantage point, as "[a]ny member of the public could legally

phasize that its comments about what was "routine" for the public had no application in a category (2) case, that is, one where the concern was with a different kind of technological advancement—not one merely adding to the list of public vantage points, but one allowing the police to perceive from some public vantage point information they could not acquire by their natural senses. Hence the *Ciraolo* majority, following some discussion of Justice Harlan's oft-quoted concurrence in *Katz, immediately precedes* the sentence about "routine" public flight with the important comment that one "can reasonably doubt that in 1967 Justice Harlan considered an aircraft within the category of future 'electronic' developments that could stealthily intrude upon an individual's privacy." In short, the Court in *Ciraolo* cautiously applied what is now called a possible "general public use" exception only to category (1) and carefully distinguished the category (2) situation. That there should be such a distinction is by no means shocking, as a "public vantage point" inquiry quite naturally entails inquiry into what places are "routinely" used by members of the public, but it hardly follows from the fact that a particular piece of equipment is available for "general public use" that such use by police is not unduly intrusive, in the sense that the burden of countering such an intrusion by thicker walls (or whatever else it would take to thwart the technology) is fairly imposed upon those occupying the premises surveilled.[244]

Having said that, it must be admitted that on one occasion the Court did consider the "general public use" concept in a category (2) context. The case is *Dow Chemical Co. v. United States*,[245] another overflight case, but this time one with a category (2) component because the evidence in question was photographs taken at 12,000, 3,000 and 1,200 feet using a "precision aerial mapping camera." The *Dow* majority appeared to be making a "general public use" type of argument when it declared that the photos at issue "are essentially like those commonly used in mapmaking," that "[a]ny person with an airplane and an aerial camera could readily duplicate them," that the camera in question was a "commercial camera commonly used in mapmaking,"

---

have been flying over Riley's property in a helicopter at the altitude of 400 feet and could have observed Riley's greenhouse," and "there is nothing in the record or before us to suggest that helicopters flying at 400 feet are sufficiently rare in this country to lend substance to respondent's claim that he reasonably anticipated that his greenhouse would not be subject to observation from that altitude."

[244]For more on this point, see Slobogin, Peeping Techno-Toms and the Fourth Amendment: Seeing Through Kyllo's Rules Governing Technological Surveillance, 86 Minn.L. Rev. 1393 (2002), where he argues at 1396 "that the extent to which a particular technological device is used by the general public, and the related inquiries into whether it is 'generally available' or 'highly sophisticated,' should be irrelevant to Fourth Amendment analysis."

[245]Dow Chemical Co. v. United States, 476 U.S. 227, 106 S.Ct. 1819, 90 L.Ed.2d 226 (1986).

and that consequently the case was quite different from one in which the government engages in "surveillance of private property by using highly sophisticated surveillance equipment not generally available to the public, such as satellite technology." That distinction is an unfortunate one, for, as the dissenters aptly pointed out, it "simply cannot be supported in fact or by the reasoning of any prior Fourth Amendment decision of this Court." But *Dow* does not in any event lend support to the argument that *Kyllo* would come out differently were the thermal imager deemed to be in "general public use," for *Dow* expressly disclaims any relevance of its holding to the surveillance of dwellings, as the bottom line in *Dow* was that the place surveilled, "the open areas of an industrial plant complex," was deemed "not analogous to the 'curtilage' of a dwelling for purposes of aerial surveillance [because] such an industrial complex is more comparable to an open field."

Perhaps it is also worth noting in this connection that even if it were assumed that there does exist a "general public use" exception to a category (2) issue even with respect to surveillance of a private home, the *Kyllo* majority at least takes a more demanding stance as to what it takes to establish such use than is found in either *Dow* or in the *Kyllo* dissent. The dissenters find "somewhat doubtful" the majority's assumption the thermal imager does not fall within that exception, given that the record

> describes a device that numbers close to a thousand manufactured units; that has a predecessor numbering in the neighborhood of 4,000 to 5,000 units; that competes with a similar product numbering from 5,000 to 6,000 units; and that is "readily available to the public" for commercial, personal, or law enforcement purposes, and is just an 800-number away from being rented from "half a dozen national companies" by anyone who wants one.

Perhaps that is correct if *Dow* is used as a guide, considering that there the Court was prepared to say that "any person" might be taking aerial photographs with a $22,000 aerial camera. But surely *Dow* is wrong, just as are the *Kyllo* dissenters. Certainly under the *Katz* interpretation of the Fourth Amendment, it should take much more than the mere theoretical possibility of a member of the public engaging in surveillance of equivalent intensity to undo one's justified expectation of privacy. In the case of the thermal imager, for example, it seems fanciful to suggest that "any person" might have decided to check out the heat emissions at Kyllo's house, and this is so even though there are admittedly many thermal imagers out there being used for a variety of uses other than law enforcement, including firefighting, medical diagnosis regarding both humans and animals, maritime navigation, predictive maintenance of electrical apparatus, product development and industrial production quality assurance.[246]

Yet another complaint by the *Kyllo* dissenters worthy of note is their objection that because the majority's

> new rule applies to information regarding the "interior" of the home, it is too narrow * * * . Clearly, a rule that is designed to protect individuals from the overly intrusive use of sense-enhancing equipment should not be limited to a home. If such equipment did provide its user with the functional equivalent of access to a private place—such as, for example, the telephone booth involved in *Katz*, or an office building—then the rule should apply to such an area as well as to a home.

Considering the state of Fourth Amendment jurisprudence *before* the *Kyllo* decision, that complaint is hardly justified. After all, the Court had previously concluded that the right of a person to be free from governmental intrusion in his own home lies at "the very core" of the Fourth Amendment,[247] and that a private home and its environs are where "privacy expectations are most heightened."[248] That being the case, it certainly makes little sense to criticize a case dealing *only* with the acquisition of "information regarding the interior of the home" for its failure to give assurances that precisely the same degree of protection would obtain at all other locations. Indeed, any sort of one-size-fits-all restructuring of Fourth Amendment doctrine would not likely be an improvement in any event, even putting aside the inappropriateness of deciding hypothetical cases, because the chances are that the consequence would be a watering-down of the protections afforded the home rather than an upgrading of privacy as to everything else. But the central point is that *Kyllo* decided only the issue then before the Court, leaving for another day questions about whether the *Kyllo* rule or some lesser variety thereof is appropriate as to places having a somewhat lesser privacy expectation[249] or, in the case of the thermal imaging lie detector, as to a person.[250] The case should not be read as settling anything beyond that, and certainly ought not be used to support a claim

---

[246]On these and other uses, see, e.g., <www.flir.com>.

[247]Silverman v. United States, 365 U.S. 505, 81 S.Ct. 679, 5 L.Ed.2d 734 (1961).

[248]Dow Chemical Co. v. United States, 476 U.S. 227, 106 S.Ct. 1819, 90 L.Ed.2d 226 (1986).

[249]In State v. Mordowanec, 259 Conn. 94, 788 A.2d 48 (2002), the court found it did not have to address one issue left open in *Kyllo*: "whether a search warrant would be required to conduct a thermal imaging scan of premises other than a home, such as commercial property." So too in United States v. Elkins, 300 F.3d 638 (6th Cir.2002) (noting "little federal precedent * * * and none since *Kyllo*" on the issue, but that in pre-*Kyllo* case of United States v. Ishmael, 843 F.Supp. 205 (E.D.Tex.1994), it held that warrantless thermal imaging of commercial building was a search). See also United States v. Lopez, 380 F.3d 538 (1st Cir.2004) (*Kyllo* not relevant in this case "because the search involved a home rather than a car").

[250]Dery, Lying Eyes: Constitutional Implications of New Thermal Imaging Lie Detector Technology, 31 Am.J.Crim.L. 217, 219, 244 (2004), discussing such a detector that "mea-

that technologically-enhanced surveillance is, no matter what, outside Fourth Amendment constraints when directed at activity occurring outside the home (even though the Court on prior occasions may have gone too far in that direction.)[251]

Finally, there is the objection by the *Kyllo* dissenters that the majority's rule "is far too broad" because it would "embrace potential mechanical substitutes for dogs trained to react when they sniff narcotics," even though it follows from the Court's earlier decision in *United States v. Place*[252] "that sense-enhancing equipment that identifies nothing but illegal activity is not a search either." But that is a particularly odorous red herring, for the open question of whether *Place* applies to dog sniffs of residences just as it does to containers in the lawful possession of the police existed well before *Kyllo* was decided, and *Kyllo* does nothing more than highlight the pre-existing issue. A claim that *Kyllo*, involving a home but not dogs, is defective for not resolving that issue, is on a par with a contention that *Place*, involving dogs but not a home, is faulty for not spelling out all applications of the drug-dog exception.

§ 2.2(f) Use of electronic surveillance to discover and decrypt communications

An awesome array of equipment has been developed making it possible to hear that which cannot be detected with the naked ear. Law enforcement authorities have long had the capacity for wiretapping, and there now exists a wide range of sophisticated gadgetry by which eavesdropping may be carried out.

> Tiny microphones can be secreted behind a picture or built into a coat button. Highly directive microphones known as "parabolic microphones" are capable of eavesdropping on a conversation taking place in an office on the opposite side of a busy street or on a park bench or outdoor restaurant terrace hundreds of feet away. Laser beams can pick sound waves off closed windows. A small, continuously operating transmitter can be placed beneath the fender of an automobile and its signal picked up by a receiver in another car or in a fixed plant.[253] A special gun developed for American military authorities can shoot a small dart containing a wireless radio microphone into a tree, window pane, awning or any other object near the subject of investigation.[254]

It is no exaggeration, therefore, to say that electronic eavesdrop-

---

sures warming that occurs around a liar's eyes," and concluding that in light of *Kyllo* "the person who leaves the home therefore may not be able to rely on Fourth Amendment search precedent against government use of a thermal imager to detect lies."

[251]See, e.g., the discussion of United States v. Knotts, 460 U.S. 276, 103 S.Ct. 1081, 75 L.Ed.2d 55 (1983), in

§ 2.7(f).

[252]United States v. Place, 462 U.S. 696, 103 S.Ct. 2637, 77 L.Ed.2d 110 (1983).

[Section 2.2(f)]

[253]This particular practice is discussed in § 2.7(f).

[254]Y. Kamisar, W. LaFave, J. Israel & N. King, Modern Criminal Proce-

ping looms as "the ultimate invasion of privacy."[255] And though it was once otherwise, today it is clear that resort to such equipment to hear that which cannot be heard except by artificial means constitutes a search within the meaning of the Fourth Amendment.

In *Olmstead v. United States*,[256] today best remembered for the ringing dissent of Justice Brandeis,[257] the Supreme Court held, 5-4, that messages passing over telephone wires are not within the protection of the Fourth Amendment. "The Amendment itself," declared Chief Justice Taft for the majority, "shows that the search is to be of material things—the person, the house, his papers or his effects. The description of the warrant necessary to make the proceeding lawful, is that it must specify the place to be searched and the person or *things* to be seized." The Chief Justice went on to say that not only did the police fail to violate the Amendment by tapping, as such, but neither did they do so at any point along the way in gaining access to the wiretap evidence: "The evidence was secured by the use of the sense of hearing and that only. There was no entry of the houses or offices of the defendants. * * * The intervening wires are not part of his house or office."

The Chief Justice noted in his *Olmstead* opinion that "Congress may of course protect the secrecy of telephone messages by making them when intercepted, inadmissible in evidence in federal criminal trials, by direct legislation, and thus depart from the common law of evidence." Such a development occurred with the enactment of the Federal Communications Act of 1934, which read in part: "[N]o person not being authorized by the sender shall intercept any communication and divulge or publish the existence, contents, substance, purport, effect, or meaning of such intercepted communication to any person." This wording was held to cover wiretapping by state or federal officers as well as by private persons,[258] and to apply to intrastate as well as interstate communications.[259] Although the Act was interpreted as barring wiretap evidence in a federal prosecution even if gathered by state officers,[260] by analogy to *Wolf v. Colorado*[261] the Court held that state-gathered wiretap evidence need not be excluded in

---

dure 466–67 (11th ed.2005).

[255]Williams, The Wiretapping-Eavesdropping Problem: A Defense Counsel's View, 44 Minn.L.Rev. 855, 866 (1960).

[256]Olmstead v. United States, 277 U.S. 438, 48 S.Ct. 564, 72 L.Ed. 944 (1928).

[257]See Steiker, Brandeis in Olmstead: "Our Government is the Potent, the Omnipresent Teacher," 79

Miss.L.J. 149 (2009).

[258]Benanti v. United States, 355 U.S. 96, 78 S.Ct. 155, 2 L.Ed.2d 126 (1957); Nardone v. United States, 302 U.S. 379, 58 S.Ct. 275, 82 L.Ed. 314 (1937), 308 U.S. 338, 60 S.Ct. 266, 84 L.Ed. 307 (1939).

[259]Weiss v. United States, 308 U.S. 321, 60 S.Ct. 269, 84 L.Ed. 298 (1939).

[260]Benanti v. United States, 355 U.S. 96, 78 S.Ct. 155, 2 L.Ed.2d 126

state prosecutions.[262] With the demise of *Wolf,* this latter holding was brought into question, and finally, two days before the electronic surveillance provisions of the Crime Control Act of 1968 were signed into law, the Court held that the fruits of a violation of the 1934 Act were inadmissible in state courts.[263]

Title III of the 1968 Act prohibits wiretapping except under the very limited circumstances provided for therein. The fruits of any other wiretapping are inadmissible "in any trial, hearing, or other proceeding in or before any court, grand jury, department, officer, agency, regulatory body, legislative committee, or other authority of the United States, a State, or a political subdivision thereof."[264] Moreover, state officials may engage in wiretapping only if authorized by a state statute meeting the standards specified in Title III.[265] Consequently, contemporary litigation concerning wiretapping tends to focus almost exclusively upon the meaning and application of Title III, a matter which is beyond the scope of this Treatise.[266] Suffice it to note here that it is now clear beyond question that wiretapping *is* a search within the meaning of the Fourth Amendment. This follows from the declaration in *Katz v. United States*[267] that *Olmstead* had "been so eroded by our subsequent decisions that the 'trespass' doctrine there enunciated can no longer be regarded as controlling," and the holding in *Katz* that even nontrespassory electronic eavesdropping which picks up only one end of a telephone conversation is a search. By contrast, interception of the radio portion of conversations over a cordless phone has often been held not to be a Fourth Amendment search,[268] though it could be a search under special circum-

---

(1957).

[261]Wolf v. Colorado, 338 U.S. 25, 69 S.Ct. 1359, 93 L.Ed. 1782 (1949).

[262]Schwartz v. Texas, 344 U.S. 199, 73 S.Ct. 232, 97 L.Ed. 231 (1952).

[263]Lee v. Florida, 392 U.S. 378, 88 S.Ct. 2096, 20 L.Ed.2d 1166 (1968).

[264]18 U.S.C.A. § 2515.

[265]18 U.S.C.A. § 2516(2).

[266]See J. Carr & P. Bellia, The Law of Electronic Surveillance (2010); C. Fishman & A. McKenna, Wiretapping and Eavesdropping (3d ed.2007).

[267]Katz v. United States, 389 U.S. 347, 88 S.Ct. 507, 19 L.Ed.2d 576 (1967).

[268]Price v. Turner, 260 F.3d 1144 (9th Cir.2001) (no search, as "at the time of Price's cordless phone conversations, they were readily susceptible to interception," unlike situation to-

day); In re Askin, 47 F.3d 100 (4th Cir.1995) (at time of this interception, not covered by Title III, though "Congress has since extended Title III's coverage to include the radio portion of cordless communications"; person using regular phone had no Fourth Amendment expectation of privacy where other party to conversation used cordless phone; latter conclusion follows from *White,* discussed in text following herein, as "common characteristic of the government informant and the cordless phone user is that they are both unreliable recipients of the communicated information: one because he repeats the conversation to law enforcement officers and the other because he broadcasts the conversation over radio waves to all within range who wish to overhear"); United States v. Smith, 978 F.2d 171 (5th Cir.1992) (not then covered by Title III, as not a "wire" or "oral" com-

stances[269] (and could now more generally be deemed a search "as technological advances make cordless communications more private"[270]). Moreover, when a telephone caller "voluntarily speaks to someone whose identity he has made no attempt to ascertain" and, as it turns out, made incriminating statements to a police officer who answered the phone of the person being called, this does not constitute a search.[271] And, the caller has no justified expectation of privacy against the recipient allowing the police to listen in via an extension phone[272] or a cell phone on speaker mode.[273]

The history with respect to non-telephonic electronic eavesdropping is rather similar. The first "bugging" case reached the Supreme Court in 1942 in *Goldman v. United States*.[274] There the Court found that the use of a detectaphone placed against an of-

---

munication and "electronic" communication defined to exclude such communication, 18 U.S.C.A. § 2510(12); generally such interception also no search because "there could have been no reasonable expectation of privacy in the cordless phone transmissions due to the ease with which they could be monitored"); Tyler v. Berodt, 877 F.2d 705 (8th Cir.1989); State v. Howard, 235 Kan. 236, 679 P.2d 197 (1984); State v. Neisler, 655 So.2d 252 (La.1995), in that part unanimously adopted in superceding opinion, 666 So.2d 1064 (La.1996) ("any expectation of privacy in conversations carried out over this medium is not objectively reasonable"); State v. Delaurier, 488 A.2d 688 (R.I.1985); State v. Smith, 149 Wis.2d 89, 438 N.W.2d 571 (1989) ("the Federal Communications Commission has ordered that a cordless telephone base unit must bear the legend, 'Privacy of communications may not be ensured while using this phone,' " and thus "the expectation of privacy cannot be a reasonable one").

[269]United States v. Smith, 978 F.2d 171 (5th Cir.1992) (thus, "trial court must be prepared to consider the reasonableness of the privacy expectation in light of all the particular circumstances and the particular phone at issue,"; defendant here does not prevail because he merely argued he "did not know that his conversations would not be private," insufficient under *Katz,* and he "introduced absolutely no evidence—such as the phone's frequency or range—that

would tend to show that his subjective expectation of privacy was reasonable").

[270]United States v. Smith, 978 F.2d 171 (5th Cir.1992) (noting that newer cordless phones "are limited to a range of about sixty feet, barely beyond the average house or yard," that they monitor all frequencies and select an unused one, which "greatly reduces the chance that a cordless phone will pick up conversations from other cordless phones," and that they "actually scramble the radio signal so that even radio scanners cannot intercept the conversation"); State v. Neisler, 655 So.2d 252 (La.1995), in that part unanimously adopted in superceding opinion, 666 So.2d 1064 (La.1996) (warning "that technology in this area is undergoing constant evolution," so that "as broadcasts emanating from such devices become harder to intercept, the reasonableness of privacy expectations in communications conducted over such media will increase proportionately"). See also Note, 56 Syrac.L.Rev. 459 (2006).

[271]State v. Gonzalez, 278 Conn. 341, 898 A.2d 149 (2006). Accord: United States v. Lee, 359 F.3d 194 (3d Cir.2004); United States v. Congote, 656 F.2d 971 (5th Cir.1981).

[272]Commonwealth v. Eason, 427 Mass. 595, 694 N.E.2d 1264 (1998).

[273]State v. Wetter, __ Vt. __, 35 A.3d 962 (2011).

[274]Goldman v. United States, 316 U.S. 129, 62 S.Ct. 993, 86 L.Ed. 1322

fice wall in order to hear private conversations in the office next door did not violate the Fourth Amendment because there was no physical trespass in connection with the relevant interception. That the Constitution does furnish some protection against the electronic seizure of conversations was made plain by *Silverman v. United States*,[275] where a unanimous Court held that listening to conversations within a house by inserting a "spike mike" into a party wall and making contact with a heating duct serving the house, "thus converting their entire heating system into a conductor of sound," amounted to an illegal search and seizure. *Silverman* made it clear, as the Court later noted in *Wong Sun v. United States*,[276] "that the Fourth Amendment may protect against the overhearing of verbal statements as well as against the more traditional seizure of 'papers and effects.'" It was much less clear, however, whether *Silverman* made any inroads upon the trespass doctrine of *Goldman*. True, the Court asserted it "need not pause to consider whether or not there was a technical trespass under the local property law relating to party walls," but the Court also stated "that the eavesdropping was accomplished by means of an unauthorized physical penetration into the premises occupied by the petitioners." But when the Court thereafter, in the per curiam opinion in *Clinton v. Virginia*,[277] barred the use of evidence obtained by means of a mechanical listening device stuck into the wall of an apartment adjoining petitioner's, though the state court had found that "the penetration was very slight such as one made by a thumb tack," it appeared that no physical intrusion was necessary for the electronic eavesdropping to constitute a search.

Any doubts were removed by *Katz v. United States*,[278] for there FBI agents had attached an electronic listening and recording device to the *outside* of a public telephone booth and thereby overheard Katz transmitting wagering information over that phone. Declaring that after *Silverman* "it becomes clear that the reach of [the Fourth] Amendment cannot turn upon the presence or absence of a physical intrusion into any given enclosure," the Court declined to decide *Katz* upon whether or not it could be said that the booth was a "constitutionally protected area." Rather, the Court held that the "Government's activities in electronically listening to and recording the petitioner's words violated the privacy upon which he justifiably relied while using

---

(1942).

[275]Silverman v. United States, 365 U.S. 505, 81 S.Ct. 679, 5 L.Ed.2d 734 (1961).

[276]Wong Sun v. United States, 371 U.S. 471, 83 S.Ct. 407, 9 L.Ed.2d 441 (1963).

[277]Clinton v. Virginia, 377 U.S. 158, 84 S.Ct. 1186, 12 L.Ed.2d 213

(1964).

[278]Katz v. United States, 389 U.S. 347, 88 S.Ct. 507, 19 L.Ed.2d 576 (1967). Regarding the effect of *Katz* on the entire field of electronic surveillance, see Casey, Electronic Surveillance and the Right to be Secure, 41 U.C.Davis L.Rev. 977 (2008).

the telephone booth and thus constituted a 'search and seizure' within the meaning of the Fourth Amendment." As for the government's argument "that the telephone booth from which the petitioner made his calls was constructed partly of glass, so that he was as visible after he entered it as he would have been if he had remained outside," the Court responded:

> But what he sought to exclude when he entered the booth was not the intruding eye—it was the uninvited ear. He did not shed his right to do so simply because he made his calls from a place where he might be seen. No less than an individual in a business office, in a friend's apartment, or in a taxicab, a person in a telephone booth may rely upon the protection of the Fourth Amendment. One who occupies it, shuts the door behind him, and pays the toll that permits him to place a call, is surely entitled to assume that the words he utters into the mouthpiece will not be broadcast to the world. To read the Constitution more narrowly is to ignore the vital role that the public telephone has come to play in private communication.

Although the majority in *Katz* asserted that the issue was *not* whether a public telephone booth is a constitutionally protected area, the passage quoted above does seem to focus upon the fact that Katz was inside a protected place, i.e., a phone booth,[279] and thus gives rise to the question whether it is also a search to use eavesdropping equipment to overhear conversations in public places. As Professor Kitch has asked:

> Suppose that instead of speaking in a public telephone booth, Katz had gone with a friend for a walk in a deserted section of a public park to discuss his illegal activities, but that that area of the park had been extensively covered by sensitive microphones so that police officers could listen to the conversation. Would this be a search within the meaning of the amendment? Would Katz have "justifiably" relied on the privacy afforded by the park's seclusion? Mr. Justice Harlan, in his specially concurring opinion, took the position that "conversations in the open" are not protected because "the expectation of privacy under the circumstances would be unreasonable." But what is either unjustifiable or unreasonable about such an expectation? One ground for making a distinction is suggested by the Court's opinion when it mentions the vital role the public telephone has come to play in private communication. It can be argued that discussions in parks are infrequent and unimportant in our harried age. But surely that is not so. The telephone is important for transacting business, legal and illegal, while long walks in parks are far more likely actually to involve significant communication of private thoughts and feelings.

A different problem might be presented if, instead of going to a

---

[279]Similarly, Harlan, J., concurring, stated: "The critical fact in this case is that '[o]ne who occupies [a telephone booth] shuts the door behind him, and pays the toll that permits him to place a call is surely entitled to assume' that his conversation is not being intercepted. * * * The point is not that the booth is 'accessible to the public' at other times, * * * but that it is a temporarily private place whose momentary occupants' expectations of freedom from intrusion are recognized as reasonable."

park, Katz had gone with his associate to his favorite restaurant and asked for his favorite table, located in a secluded alcove. Unbeknown to him, police might have bugged the table to hear the conversation. Would Katz be justified in relying on the privacy of the table? Is Katz entitled to assume that words he utters in a restaurant will not be broadcast to the world? The only basis for distinguishing this case from that considered in the opinion is that there is no "door" for Katz to close. But is that really an important difference? Would the case have been different if the pay phone had not been surrounded by a booth?[280]

In the cases put by Professor Kitch, it is submitted, the use of artificial means to overhear a conversation law enforcement agents are not in a position to discover by use of the naked ear should be deemed a Fourth Amendment search. This is because

an expectation of privacy will be reasonable if in a given context it is one normally shared by people in that setting and at the same time falls within some tolerance level which represents the limit of what society can accept given its interest in law enforcement.

As applied to the typical eavesdropping case, however, the first half of this test would appear always to be satisfied. Electronic eavesdropping by its very nature is meant to be secret and undetectable. Indeed, it depends for its efficacy on the very fact that it violates the normal expectation that one can rely on his senses to warn him when someone is in hearing range. Whether the conversation takes place in a home, in a private office, or in a more public place such as a phone booth or a restaurant, as long as the conversants appear to be secluded they will not expect to be overheard.[281] Hence if this were the test of whether a justifiable expectation of privacy has been invaded, the conclusion would seem to follow that all secret electronic eavesdropping constitutes a fourth amendment intrusion.[282]

It is not inconsistent with that analysis to conclude that in certain exceptional circumstances no justified expectation of privacy against electronic eavesdropping exists, as where persons converse inside a squad car but outside the natural hearing of

---

[280]Kitch, Katz v. United States: The Limits of the Fourth Amendment, 1968 Sup.Ct.Rev. 133, 139–40.

[281]Compare Kee v. City of Rowlett, 247 F.3d 206 (5th Cir.2001), where police placed an electronic surveillance tap in a funereal urn in close proximity to a grave site situated in an outdoor and publicly accessible cemetery for 14 hours, including the time of burial services there for two murdered children. In upholding a grant of summary judgment against family members who sued for violation of their Fourth Amendment rights, the court held that while "the open fields approach cannot automatically be ad-

opted for use in the oral communication context," the plaintiffs could not prevail because they did "not specify which conversations were conducted in a manner inaudible to others and provide no information about who was present and to whom their conversations were directed," especially since the defendants "submitted evidence to demonstrate that the grave site services were attended by representatives of the media and that third parties were in close proximity to the grave site."

[282]The Supreme Court, 1967 Term, 82 Harv.L.Rev. 93, 192 (1968).

any officer.[283]

In an earlier discussion,[284] it was concluded that where the police use binoculars to view from a distance public conduct they could have viewed with the naked eye from closer proximity but for their desire not to reveal their surveillance, the use of the binoculars should not be deemed a search. Consistency, it might be argued, thus compels the conclusion that when conversations occur in a public place it is no search to hear with an eavesdropping device that which could have been heard with the naked ear but for the difficulty of getting close enough to the suspect without disclosing the surveillance. But *Katz* does not demand this kind of consistency; it does not protect every expectation of privacy, but only those (as Justice Harlan helpfully put it) "that society is prepared to recognize as 'reasonable.'" That is, *Katz* requires that a value judgment be made, and the suggestion here is that privacy of conversations—at the bottom of the Fourth Amendment totem pole in the era of *Olmstead* and *Goldman*—is more deserving of constitutional protection, even when the conversations occur in a public place, than is privacy as to conduct occurring in a public or semi-public place. Put another way, the notion here is that in assigning values to various privacy interests in our society, there is more reason to protect the expectation that one can converse in private when no one else is in hearing range than there is to protect the expectation that public conduct will

---

[283]United States v. Dunbar, 553 F.3d 48 (1st Cir.2009); United States v. Turner, 209 F.3d 1198 (10th Cir.2000) (rejecting defendant's argument "that his expectation of privacy is reasonable because of the circumstances: he was not in custody or being threatened with arrest, and the officer deliberately represented the car as a safe haven" for defendant and the passenger in defendant's vehicle); United States v. McKinnon, 985 F.2d 525 (11th Cir.1993); Farina v. State, 679 So.2d 1151 (Fla.1996); Campos v. State, 885 N.E.2d 590 (Ind.2008); People v. Marland, 135 Mich.App. 297, 355 N.W.2d 378 (1984); State v. Turner, 371 S.C. 595, 641 S.E.2d 436 (2007) (collecting cases in accord); State v. Ramirez, 535 N.W.2d 847 (S.D.1995).

Consider also Napper v. United States, 22 A.3d 758 (D.C.App.2011) ("individuals do not typically have a reasonable expectation of privacy in police interview rooms," and thus defendant had no such expectation re his cell phone call while officers out of the room).

The aforementioned cases hold there is no privacy expectation regardless of the status of the person engaging in the conversation, and they are to be distinguished from those decisions holding only that a prisoner, even when in a police car, has no right of privacy, e.g., State v. McAdams, 559 So.2d 601 (Fla.App.1990).

Compare *Turner* with State v. Munn, 56 S.W.3d 486 (Tenn.2001) (electronic eavesdropping upon private conversations between defendant, voluntarily present for questioning, and his mother while they alone in interview room in police station *was* a search, as the "police officers' collective actions in turning off the audio tape recorder at the defendant's request; asking if he wanted to talk alone with his mother; excusing themselves from the room; and closing the door both deceived and assured the defendant and his mother that they would be free to talk in private without anyone hearing their conversation").

[284]See §2.2(c).

be unobserved when no one is within range to see it with the naked eye. This distinction, it must be emphasized, is based upon the nature of the thing to be protected rather than the nature of the instrument that makes the intrusion. Thus, if the police were to station a lipreader with binoculars some distance from persons conversing in public and in that way were able to determine the contents of that conversation, this should not be dismissed as just another nonsearch use of binoculars. That conduct intrudes upon a justified expectation of privacy in conversations just as much as the use of eavesdropping equipment, and thus should be treated in the same way for Fourth Amendment purposes.

Courts have not had occasion to struggle with the question of whether the use of eavesdropping equipment in other circumstances is a search under *Katz*. Here again, this is because of the impact of Title III of the Crime Control Act of 1968. That Act prohibits, with the force of an exclusionary sanction applicable in federal and state proceedings, the interception of any oral communication by the use of any electronic, mechanical or other device except in specified limited circumstances and in accordance with procedures proscribed therein.[285] An "oral communication" is "any oral communication uttered by a person exhibiting an expectation that such communication is not subject to interception under circumstances justifying such expectation."[286] The word "intercept" means "the aural acquisition of the contents of any wire, electric or oral communication through the use of any electronic, mechanical, or other device."[287] And "electronic, mechanical, or other device" means, with very limited exceptions, "any device or apparatus which can be used to intercept a wire, oral or electronic communication."[288] The general assumption is that the Act, at least as to the matter here under discussion, proscribes at least as much as is forbidden by the Fourth Amendment, and thus in recent litigation the focus has been upon the meaning and application of the aforementioned parts of the 1968 Act.[289]

There remains to be mentioned one particular way in which eavesdropping equipment may be utilized without violating either Title III[290] or the Fourth Amendment: in conjunction with a secret agent, where the equipment makes a record of or permits

[285]18 U.S.C.A. § 2515.

[286]18 U.S.C.A. § 2510(2), which goes on to say that "such term does not include any electronic communication."

[287]18 U.S.C.A. § 2510(4).

[288]18 U.S.C.A. § 2510(5).

[289]The Act is beyond the scope of this Treatise. See J. Carr & P. Bellia, The Law of Electronic Surveillance

(2011); C. Fishman & A. McKenna, Wiretapping and Eavesdropping (3d ed.2007).

[290]18 U.S.C.A. § 2511(2) (c) states: "It shall not be unlawful under this chapter for a person acting under color of law to intercept a wire, oral or electronic communication, where such person is a party to the communication or one of the parties to the communication has given prior consent to

others to hear that which the suspect has said in his conversation with the agent. In *On Lee v. United States*,[291] an undercover agent "wired for sound" entered the defendant's laundry and engaged him in an incriminating conversation, which an agent outside the laundry was able to hear on a receiving set. In a 5-4 decision, the Court rejected the claim that the undercover agent had committed a trespass because consent to his entry was obtained by fraud,[292] and dismissed as "verging on the frivolous" the further contention that the agent outside "was a trespasser because by these aids he overheard what went on inside." Justice Jackson, for the majority, likened the use of the transmitter and receiver to the use of a telescope, and declared that the utilization of this equipment had "the same effect on his privacy as if [the agent outside] had been eavesdropping outside an open window."[293] Similarly, in *Lopez v. United States*,[294] where the secret agent had a recording device concealed on his person, the majority, relying upon *On Lee*, concluded that

> this case involves no "eavesdropping" whatever in any proper sense of that term. The Government did not use an electronic device to listen in on conversations it could not otherwise have heard. Instead, the device was used only to obtain the most reliable evidence possible of a conversation in which the Government's own agent was a participant and which that agent was fully entitled to disclose. And the device was not planted by means of an unlawful physical invasion of petitioner's premises under circumstances which would violate the Fourth Amendment. It was carried in and out by an agent who was there with petitioner's assent, and it neither saw nor heard more than the agent himself.[295]

The effect of *Katz* upon *On Lee* and *Lopez* remained a matter of considerable speculation until the Supreme Court decided the

---

such interception."

[291]On Lee v. United States, 343 U.S. 747, 72 S.Ct. 967, 96 L.Ed. 1270 (1952).

[292]On consent by deception, see § 8.2(m), (n).

[293]There were four separate dissenting opinions. Burton, J., joined by Frankfurter, J., maintained that by means of the concealed radio transmitter, the narcotics agents "without warrant or consent" picked up "words * * * *within* the constitutionally inviolate 'house' of a person entitled to protection against unreasonable searches and seizures." In a separate dissent Frankfurter, J., adhered to the views expressed in *Goldman* that *Olmstead* should be overruled. Douglas, J., announced that he was wrong to have joined the majority opinion in *Gold-*

man. Black, J., would have excluded the evidence in the exercise of the Court's supervisory authority over federal criminal justice.

[294]Lopez v. United States, 373 U.S. 427, 83 S.Ct. 1381, 10 L.Ed.2d 462 (1963).

[295]Brennan, J., joined by Douglas and Goldberg, JJ., dissented, finding *On Lee* indistinguishable from the instant case and maintaining that the evidence should have been excluded in both cases. Chief Justice Warren, concurring, agreed that *On Lee* was wrongly decided, but found the instant case "quite dissimilar constitutionally" because in *On Lee* the use of the transmitter was not to corroborate the testimony of the secret agent but rather "to obviate the need to put him on the stand."

case of *United States v. White*,[296] where a government informer engaged defendant in conversations in a restaurant, defendant's home, and the informer's car while the informer was carrying a concealed radio transmitter.[297] The court of appeals held that this electronic eavesdropping constituted a search, but the Supreme Court did not agree. Justice White, writing the opinion of the Court,[298] first concluded that *Katz* "left undisturbed" the notion "that however strongly a defendant may trust an apparent colleague, his expectations in this respect are not protected by the Fourth Amendment when it turns out that the colleague is a government agent regularly communicating with the authorities,"[299] and then continued:

> If the law gives no protection to the wrongdoer whose trusted accomplice is or becomes a police agent, neither should it protect him when that same agent has recorded or transmitted the conversations which are later offered in evidence to prove the State's case.[300]

Inescapably, one contemplating illegal activities must realize and risk that his companions may be reporting to the police. If he sufficiently doubts their trustworthiness, the association will very probably end or never materialize. But if he has no doubts, or al-

---

[296]United States v. White, 401 U.S. 745, 91 S.Ct. 1122, 28 L.Ed.2d 453 (1971).

[297]The claim that therefore *White* applies only when such a device is on the informant's person was rejected in United States v. Yonn, 702 F.2d 1341 (11th Cir.1983), where the device was installed in a room the informant rented for defendant but was activated only when the informant was also in the room. The court concluded that the "location of the electrical equipment does not alter the irrefutable fact that Yonn had no justified expectation of privacy in his conversation with" the informant.

[298]The Chief Justice and Stewart and Blackmun, JJ., joined in that opinion. Brennan, J., concurred in the result on the ground that *Katz* was not retroactive, but opined that both *On Lee* and *Lopez* were "no longer sound law." Black, J., concurred with the result for the reasons stated in his *Katz* dissent.

Because of this division of the Court, some doubt remained as to the vitality of *White* in a genuine post-*Katz* context. However, in United States v. Caceres, 440 U.S. 741, 99 S.Ct. 1465, 59 L.Ed.2d 733 (1979), the Court held without discussion (with

Marshall and Brennan, JJ., dissenting on other grounds) that a violation of an IRS regulation concerning warrantless monitoring by transmitter of conversations between IRS agents and taxpayers does "not raise any constitutional questions."

[299]Even a promise of confidentiality or anonymity by a known government official may not suffice to create a justified expectation of privacy. See People v. Maury, 30 Cal.4th 342, 133 Cal.Rptr.2d 561, 68 P.3d 1 (2003) (notwithstanding promise of anonymity to callers telephoning in tips to receive possible rewards, breach of that promise by recording defendant's calls not deemed an intrusion on a reasonable expectation of privacy, especially where "the information the caller divulges reasonably gives law enforcement probable cause to believe that the caller may be the perpetrator of a serious crime to which the information relates").

[300]Though the matter was put this way, there seems to be no doubt but that *White* also covers situations in which an undercover law enforcement agent has assumed a fictitious identity. United States v. Sileven, 985 F.2d 962 (8th Cir.1993).

lays them, or risks what doubt he has, the risk is his. In terms of what his course will be, what he will or will not do or say, we are unpersuaded that he would distinguish between probable informers on the one hand and probable informers with transmitters on the other. Given the possibility or probability that one of his colleagues is cooperating with the police, it is only speculation to assert that the defendant's utterances would be substantially different or his sense of security any less if he also thought it possible that the suspected colleague is wired for sound. At least there is no persuasive evidence that the difference in this respect between the electronically equipped and the unequipped agent is substantial enough to require discrete constitutional recognition, particularly under the Fourth Amendment which is ruled by fluid concepts of "reasonableness."

Nor should we be too ready to erect constitutional barriers to relevant and probative evidence which is also accurate and reliable. An electronic recording will many times produce a more reliable rendition of what a defendant has said than will the unaided memory of a police agent. It may also be that with the recording in existence it is less likely that the informant will change his mind, less chance that threat or injury will suppress unfavorable evidence and less chance that cross-examination will confound the testimony. Considerations like these obviously do not favor the defendant, but we are not prepared to hold that a defendant who has no constitutional right to exclude the informer's unaided testimony nevertheless has a Fourth Amendment privilege against a more accurate version of the events in question.

The difficulty with this analysis is that undue emphasis has been placed upon subjective expectations, and not enough attention has been given to the critical value judgments which must be made under the *Katz* formula. As Justice Harlan stated in his dissent in *White:*

Since it is the task of the law to form and project, as well as mirror and reflect, we should not, as judges, merely recite the expectations and risks without examining the desirability of saddling them upon society. The critical question, therefore, is whether under our system of government, as reflected in the Constitution, we should impose on our citizens the risks of the electronic listener or observer without at least the protection of a warrant requirement.

This question must, in my view, be answered by assessing the nature of a particular practice and the likely extent of its impact on the individual's sense of security balanced against the utility of the conduct as a technique of law enforcement.

That, it is submitted, is the proper approach. And while it does not indisputably lead to a particular conclusion, there is much to be said in favor of Justice Harlan's assessment. He continued:

The argument of the plurality opinion, to the effect that it is irrelevant whether secrets are revealed by the mere tattletale or the transistor, ignores the differences occasioned by third-party monitoring and recording which insures full and accurate disclosure of all that is said, free of the possibility of error and oversight that inheres in human reporting.

Authority is hardly required to support the proposition that words would be measured a good deal more carefully and communication inhibited if one suspected his conversations were being transmitted and transcribed. Were third-party bugging a prevalent practice, it might well smother that spontaneity—reflected in frivolous, impetuous, sacrilegious, and defiant discourse—that liberates daily life. Much offhand exchange is easily forgotten and one may count on the obscurity of his remarks, protected by the very fact of a limited audience, and the likelihood that the listener will either overlook or forget what is said, as well as the listener's inability to reformulate a conversation without having to contend with a documented record. All these values are sacrificed by a rule of law that permits official monitoring of private discourse limited only by the need to locate a willing assistant.

* * * The interest *On Lee* fails to protect is the expectation of the ordinary citizen, who has never engaged in illegal conduct in his life, that he may carry on his private discourse freely, openly, and spontaneously without measuring his every word against the connotations it might carry when instantaneously heard by others unknown to him and unfamiliar with his situation or analyzed in a cold, formal record played days, months, or years after the conversation. Interposition of a warrant requirement is designed not to shield "wrongdoers," but to secure a measure of privacy and a sense of personal security throughout our society.

The Fourth Amendment does, of course, leave room for the employment of modern technology in criminal law enforcement, but in the stream of current developments in Fourth Amendment law I think it must be held that third-party electronic monitoring, subject only to the self-restraint of law enforcement officials, has no place in our society.[301]

In *On Lee*, *Lopez* and *White*, the equipment that was recording

---

[301]For other critical assessments of *White*, see Note, 52 B.U.L.Rev. 831 (1972); The Supreme Court, 1970 Term, 85 Harv.L.Rev. 38, 250–58 (1971).

While most states follow *White*, e.g., Smithey v. State, 269 Ark. 538, 602 S.W.2d 676 (1980); State v. Grullon, 212 Conn. 195, 562 A.2d 481 (1989); United States v. Sell, 487 A.2d 225 (D.C.App.1985); Morningstar v. State, 428 So.2d 220 (Fla.1982); Green v. State, 250 Ga. 610, 299 S.E.2d 544 (1983); State v. Lester, 64 Haw. 659, 649 P.2d 346 (1982); State v. Jennings, 101 Idaho 265, 611 P.2d 1050 (1980); People v. Kezerian, 77 Ill.2d 121, 32 Ill.Dec. 321, 395 N.E.2d 551 (1979); Lawhorn v. State, 452 N.E.2d 915 (Ind. 1983); State v. Olkon, 299 N.W.2d 89 (Minn.1980); People v. Collins, 438 Mich. 8, 475 N.W.2d 684 (1991); Lee v. State, 489 So.2d 1382 (Miss.1986); State v. Engleman, 653 S.W.2d 198 (Mo.1983); State v. Levan, 326 N.C. 155, 388 S.E.2d 429 (1990); State v. Loh, 780 N.W.2d 719 (N.D.2010); Commonwealth v. Blystone, 519 Pa. 450, 549 A.2d 81 (1988); State v. Iverson, 364 N.W.2d 518 (S.D.1985); Rovinsky v. State, 605 S.W.2d 578 (Tex.Crim.App.1980); State v. Boone, 581 P.2d 571 (Utah 1978); Cogdill v. Commonwealth, 219 Va. 272, 247 S.E.2d 392 (1978); State v. Corliss, 123 Wash.2d 656, 870 P.2d 317 (1994); Blackburn v. State, 170 W.Va. 96, 290 S.E.2d 22 (1982), some, often employing reasoning similar to that of Harlan, take a stricter view as a matter of state law. See, e.g., Coffey v. State, 585 P.2d 514 (Alaska 1978); Commonwealth v. Blood, 400 Mass. 61, 507 N.E.2d 1029 (1987); State v. Allen, 357 Mont. 495, 241 P.3d 1045 (2010); State v. Blow, 157 Vt. 513, 602 A.2d 552 (1991) (limited by State v. Brooks, 157 Vt. 490, 601 A.2d 963 (1991), to participant monitoring in defendant's home as compared to in a public parking lot but extended to secret recording by a known police of-

and/or transmitting the defendant's conversations was on the person of the informer or undercover agent who was a party to those conversations. What then if that equipment is instead installed at a certain place without a warrant or a showing of probable cause and exigent circumstances? In one such case, *United States v. Padilla*,[302] it was held that the defendant's Fourth Amendment rights were violated when agents placed an audio recording device in the defendant's hotel room and recorded conversations between the defendant and another person who consented to the recordings. That court "expressed concern that if law enforcement officers were permitted to leave a monitoring or recording device in a hotel for a lengthy period of time the officers would be tempted to monitor or record conversations that occurred when no consenting participant was present."[303]

The prevailing view, however, is to the contrary.[304] The leading case is *United States v. Lee*,[305] which accurately noted that

> *Padilla* appears to be based, not on the conclusion that the recordings in that case had been obtained in violation of the Fourth Amendment, but on a prophylactic rule designed to stamp out a law enforcement technique that the Court viewed as creating an unacceptable risk of abuse.

The *Lee* court concluded that there was not "much risk of such abuse" and thus no need for such a prophylactic remedy, but then went on to caution that there were three circumstances where the distinction between the recording device being placed in the room rather than on the cooperating individual's person

> would matter for Fourth Amendment purposes. First, if the defendant had an expectation of privacy in the premises at the time when the device was installed, the entry to install the device would constitute a search. Second, the cases involving consensual monitoring do not apply if recordings are made when the cooperating individual is not present. Third, the logic of those cases is likewise inapplicable if the placement of the recording device permits it to pick up evidence that the cooperating individual could not have heard or seen while in the room. Unless one of these circumstances is present, however, it does not matter for Fourth Amendment purposes whether the device is placed in the room or carried on the person of the cooperating individual. In either event, the recording will not gather any evidence other than that about which the cooperating witness could have testified.[306]

What has been said herein with respect to the use of

---

ficer in State v. Geraw, 173 Vt. 350, 795 A.2d 1219 (2002)).

[302] United States v. Padilla, 520 F.2d 526 (1st Cir.1975).

[303] As *Padilla* was summarized in United States v. Lee, 359 F.3d 194 (3d Cir.2004).

[304] United States v. Lee, 359 F.3d 194 (3d Cir.2004); United States v.

Yonn, 702 F.2d 1341 (11th Cir.1983); United States v. Myers, 692 F.2d 823 (2d Cir.1982).

[305] United States v. Lee, 359 F.3d 194 (3d Cir.2004).

[306] The court then concluded that there was no violation of the Fourth Amendment in the instant case because the "monitoring devices were

eavesdropping-wiretapping equipment is generally true as well as to electronic visual surveillance.[307] It is no search to videotape what a police officer is observing in a plain view situation,[308] nor is any justified expectation of privacy violated by the videotaping of activity occurring in full public view.[309] By analogy to the *White*

---

installed in the suite's living room at a time when Lee had no expectation of privacy in the premises," there "is no evidence that conversations were monitored when [government informer] Beavers was absent from the room, and Beavers was plainly there at the time of the incriminating meetings shown on the tapes that were introduced at Lee's trial." Also, the court concluded it could not "draw a constitutional distinction between consensual audio and video surveillance," both of which were involved in the instant case.

See also United States v. Diaz-Diaz, 433 F.3d 128 (1st Cir.2005) (no *Padilla* problem here, as monitoring equipment was installed on premises of a business controlled by government's cooperating witness, and defendant's use of those premises "was limited to his connection with the underlying conspiracy, thus tailoring the use of electronic monitoring to meetings relevant thereto," and that "connection was narrowed further by the fact that control of the device was given to" that witness, who activated it only during his meeting with defendant or other conspirators).

[307] See Guirguis, Electronic Visual Surveillance and the Reasonable Expectation of Privacy, 9 J.Tech.L. & Pol'y 143 (2004); Comments, 21 Ariz.St. L.J. 445 (1989); 58 U.Chi.L.Rev. 1045 (1991); Note, 35 Wash. & Lee L.Rev. 1043 (1978). As for the video surveillance of the future via a wearable computing device, see Note, 32 Suffolk U.L.Rev. 729 (1999).

[308] See note 16 supra, which also includes cases holding it is likewise no search when the police leave a camera in an area where there is no expectation of privacy, even though the officer does not remain at the scene to view first-hand the recorded conduct.

[309] United States v. Gonzalez, 328

F.3d 543 (9th Cir.2003) (video surveillance no search here; "given the public nature of the mailroom in a community hospital where individuals—even DEA agents—strolled nearby without impediment during the transaction, * * * the defendant had no objectively reasonable expectation of privacy"); McCray v. State, 84 Md.App. 513, 581 A.2d 45 (1990) ("videotaping of activity occurring in full public view" no search); Sponick v. City of Detroit Police Dept., 49 Mich.App. 162, 211 N.W.2d 674 (1973) (police officer videotaped in bar talking with known criminals did not have a "reasonable expectation of privacy" because observations occurred in public place).

This is not to suggest that the videotaping must be at a location entirely "public" for Fourth Amendment restraints to be inapplicable. See, e.g., Vega-Rodriguez v. Puerto Rico Telephone Co., 110 F.3d 174 (1st Cir.1997) (lawsuit by employees of quasi-public telephone company challenging videotaping of their workplace properly dismissed, as employees had no justified expectation of privacy "while toiling in the Center's open and undifferentiated work area"); Cowles v. State, 23 P.3d 1168 (Alaska 2001) (distinguishing *Taketa* and *Bonnell*, infra, court holds that where defendant suspected of theft from ticket sales, covert video surveillance during business hours of her desk from camera hidden in ceiling vent no search, as "Cowles's desk could be seen by members of the public through the ticket window and the open door, and by her fellow employees who were walking around the office almost continuously during the videotaping," and the "fact that the video camera may have been in an especially good position from which to view Cowles's acts of transferring money from the University money pouch to her desk and thence to her purse is not sufficient to

case, it has also been held that Fourth Amendment protections
do not extend to the videotaping of "private" activities between
the defendant and another when the other party has consented
to the taping,[310] though this is the case *only* when the consenting
party is also present.[311] But the surreptitious placement of a

---

create a reasonable expectation of
privacy in an open and public setting
where no such expectation could reasonably exist"); State v. McLellan, 144
N.H. 602, 744 A.2d 611 (1999) (videotaping of activity within classroom of
elementary school during evening
hours established janitor stealing
money; janitor had no expectation of
privacy there, as this "not an area over
which the defendant enjoyed exclusive
use and control," as "the classroom
was not his personal space," and it
makes no difference that "he was the
only person who had access to the
classroom during the time the video
camera was set to record"). Compare
United States v. Taketa, 923 F.2d 665
(9th Cir.1991); State v. Bonnell, 75
Haw. 124, 856 P.2d 1265 (1993), § 2.4
note 84.

For a useful discussion of police
use of closed circuit television, See
Note, 13 U.Mich.J.L.Ref. 571 (1980).
As noted therein at 582: "One walking
along a public sidewalk or standing in
a public park cannot reasonably expect
that his activity will be immune from
the public eye or from observation by
police. Where police use CCTV to
observe such public areas there is no
basis for a defendant to claim a reasonable expectation of privacy." Even
if video surveillance is sufficiently public as to not constitute a Fourth Amendment search, surely controls on governmental use of this technique are
needed. See Slobogin, Physical Surveillance: The American Bar Association's
Tentative Draft Standards, 10
Harv.L.J. & Tech. 383, 440–44 (1997)
(tentative standards on video surveillance, private and public); Note, 31
Val.U.L.Rev. 1979 (1997) (proposed
statute limiting street video surveillance systems).

[310]United States v. Shryock, 342
F.3d 948 (9th Cir.2003) (video surveillance within hotel room rented by accomplice who consented to recording);

United States v. Corona-Chavez, 328
F.3d 974 (8th Cir.2003) (video surveillance of defendant while in hotel room
meeting with co-conspirator now cooperating with government); United
States v. Davis, 326 F.3d 361 (2d
Cir.2003) (video surveillance with
camera hidden in informant's jacket
during controlled drug buy); United
States v. Laetividal-Gonzalez, 939
F.2d 1455 (11th Cir.1991) (video surveillance within office rented by undercover agent); Avery v. State, 15
Md.App. 520, 292 A.2d 728 (1972)
(observation of defendant sexually
molesting woman in her premises
through use of closed-circuit TV secreted there with her consent not
within protection of Fourth Amendment).

[311]United States v. Nerber, 222
F.3d 597 (9th Cir.2000), concluding
that while, "when the informants were
in the room the video surveillance was
conducted with their consent, and
defendants bore the risk that their
activities with the informants were being surveilled," "once the informants
left the room, defendants' expectation
to be free from hidden video surveillance was objectively reasonable.
When defendants were left alone, their
expectation of privacy increased to the
point that the intrusion of a hidden
video camera became unacceptable.
People feel comfortable saying and doing things alone that they would not
say or do in the presence of others.
This is clearly true when people are
alone in their own home or hotel room,
but it is also true to a significant
extent when they are in someone else's
home or hotel room. * * *

"The fact that society is prepared to accept as reasonable defendants' expectation to be free from
video surveillance while alone in the
hotel room is confirmed by the way the
law treats audio surveillance in identical circumstances. The government

video camera in a place where a defendant does have a justified expectation of privacy and the subsequent use of that camera quite clearly *is* activity governed by the Fourth Amendment,[312] which means that a search warrant with adequate safeguards[313]

---

conceded that audio surveillance conducted after the informants departed was inadmissible, because the federal wiretap statute permits warrantless audio surveillance only if one of the participants in the monitored conversation consents."

See also United States v. Brathwaite, 458 F.3d 376 (5th Cir.2006) (stressing "videotape evidence here only depicted what was viewable by the CI, to whose presence Brathwaite consented"). Compare United States v. Yang, 281 F.3d 534 (6th Cir.2002) (where because of error by taping technicians, contrary to instructions tapes included brief periods when consenting party was not in the room, but prosecutor had unauthorized periods redacted, no basis for exclusion of redacted tape).

[312]Brannum v. Overton County School Board, 516 F.3d 489 (6th Cir.2008) ("the locker room videotaping was a search"); State v. Howard, 728 A.2d 1178 (Del.Super.1998) (videotaping of husband and wife following their arrest, after police left them together in a locked interview room; court distinguishes cases holding no reasonable expectation of privacy in police interview rooms, as "the fact that the subjects of the videotaped conversations * * * were married to each other significantly changes the analysis of this issue"); People v. Dezek, 107 Mich.App. 78, 308 N.W.2d 652 (1981) (video surveillance of activity within stalls of public restroom); People v. Teicher, 52 N.Y.2d 638, 439 N.Y.S.2d 846, 422 N.E.2d 506 (1981) (upholding with warrant videotaping of dentist molesting female patient in his office).

Compare United States v. Vankesteren, 553 F.3d 286 (4th Cir.2009) (no search to videotape activity in defendant's fields "a mile or more from his home," an area "classified as open fields and not curtilage," where defendant "has no reasonable expectation of privacy"); United States

v. Jackson, 213 F.3d 1269 (10th Cir.2000) (video surveillance from cameras installed on telephone poles outside defendant's premises no search, as "use of video equipment and cameras to record activity visible to the naked eye does not ordinarily violate the Fourth Amendment," and here the cameras "were incapable of viewing inside the houses, and were capable of observing only what any passerby would easily have been able to observe").

[313]As observed in Note, 35 Wash. & Lee L.Rev. 1043 (1978), what is needed here is not an ordinary search warrant, but rather one requiring minimization and other safeguards of the kind required when a warrant authorizes eavesdropping or wiretapping. See United States v. Apperson, 441 F.3d 1162 (10th Cir.2006) (necessity requirement met by showing "other 'real-time' surveillance techniques * * * could not be used" at that site); United States v. Jackson, 213 F.3d 1269 (10th Cir.2000) (while Title I—formerly Title III—does not regulate silent video surveillance, it "provides guidelines for establishing video surveillance under the Fourth Amendment"); United States v. Williams, 124 F.3d 411 (3d Cir.1997) (assuming correctness of view taken by "every court of appeals that has addressed video surveillance," i.e., "that video surveillance conforming to the standards set out in Title III is constitutional"); United States v. Falls, 34 F.3d 674 (8th Cir.1994) (search warrant adhering to four basic requirements of Title I (formerly Title III) is sufficient); United States v. Koyomejian, 970 F.2d 536 (9th Cir.1992) (four basic requirements of Title I (formerly Title III) adopted); United States v. Cuevas-Sanchez, 821 F.2d 248 (5th Cir.1987) (court decides "to use Title III as a guide for the constitutional standard"); United States v. Torres, 751 F.2d 875 (7th Cir.1984) (rejecting notion secret televising inherently unreasonable but

would ordinarily be required. (By analogy to electronic visual surveillance, it may well be that certain other investigative techniques, such as the use of the Keystroke Logger System, which monitors and records keystrokes entered into a computer in order to decipher encrypted data,[314] also require warrants with special safeguards.[315])

Yet another form of electronic surveillance, "essentially an online version of a wiretap,"[316] involves an Internet surveillance software originally known as Carnivore and now denominated DCS1000.[317]

The software is housed in a computer and connected to an Internet service provider (ISP) such as AOL, Earthlink, or Prodigy. The ISP

cautioning it may not "be used as generally as less intrusive techniques," court concludes that such surveillance "is identical in its indiscriminate character to a wiretapping and bugging," so that "a warrant for television surveillance that did not satisfy the four provisions of Title III that implement the Fourth Amendment's requirement of particularity would violate the Fourth Amendment"); Ricks v. State, 312 Md. 11, 537 A.2d 612 (1988) (for video surveillance, it must be shown that normal investigative techniques have failed or are not likely to succeed or are too dangerous; must be particularized description of targeted communications; definite duration must be set; minimization required); People v. Dezek, 107 Mich.App. 78, 308 N.W.2d 652 (1981) (search warrant authorizing video surveillance of restroom defective, for it did not limit search to "precise and discriminate circumstances" as Supreme Court has required for eavesdropping warrants); People v. Teicher, 52 N.Y.2d 638, 439 N.Y.S.2d 846, 422 N.E.2d 506 (1981) (court rejects defendant's contention that video surveillance is so intrusive that it is always unreasonable, but holds that warrant here must and does meet the special requirements the Supreme Court has imposed upon warrants for electronic eavesdropping).

[314]Further discussed in text at note 331 infra.

[315]See Note, 2002 U.Ill.J.L.Tech. & Pol'y 193, arguing that while use of KLS is not directly covered by Title III, because both KLS and nonaudio video surveillance involve "an invasion

of privacy more intrusive than that imposed through execution of a traditional search warrant," it follows that the "added protections" required in the cases in note 313 also apply to KLS use.

[316]Comment, 80 N.C.L.Rev. 315, 317 (2001).

[317]For other discussions of Carnivore/DCS1000, see Heflin, Who's Afraid of the Big Bad Wolf: Why the Fear of Carnivore is an Irrational Product of the Digital Age, 107 Dick.L. Rev. 343 (2002); Lewis, Carnivore— The FBI's Internet Surveillance System, 23 Whittier L.Rev. 317 (2001); McCarthy, Don't Fear Carnivore: It Won't Devour Individual Privacy, 66 Mo.L.Rev. 827 (2001); Comments, 9 Comm.Law.Conspectus 111 (2001); 80 N.C.L.Rev. 315 (2001); 52 S.C.L.Rev. 875 (2001); 19 Temp. Envt'l L. & Tech.J. 155 (2001); 32 Tex.Tech.L.Rev. 1053 (2001); 18 T.M.Cooley L.Rev. 183 (2001); 74 UMKC L.Rev. 945 (2006); Notes, 27 Brook.J.Int'l L. 245 (2001); 20 Cardozo Arts & Ent. L.J. 231 (2002); 34 Conn.L.Rev. 261 (2001); 29 Fordham Urb.L.J. 2233 (2002); 35 Ind.L.Rev. 303 (2001); 21 Loy.L.A.Ent. L.Rev. 481 (2001); 8 Mich. Telecomm. & Tech.L.Rev. 219 (2001); 18 N.Y.U.L. Sch.J.Hum.Rts. 305 (2002); 76 Notre Dame L.Rev. 1215 (2001); 62 Ohio St.L.J. 1831 (2001); 28 Okla.City U.L.Rev. 291 (2003); 1 Okla.J.L. & Tech. 2 (2003); 7 Roger Williams U.L.Rev. 247 (2001); 28 Rutgers Computer & Tech.L.J. 155 (2002); 75 S.Cal.L.Rev. 231 (2001); 11 Wash.U. J.L & Pol'y 351 (2003); 10 Wm. & Mary Bill of Rts.J. 827 (2002).

then provides the FBI with an access point containing all traffic from the suspect. Using a one-way tapping device, all data at the access point is copied. Carnivore then filters this copied data, sniffing out and retrieving "packets" of information that are subject to court orders while theoretically rejecting all extraneous data. FBI administrators have the ability to calibrate Carnivore to capture packets based on Internet Protocol (IP) address or e-mail username. "Packets can be recorded in their entirety (full mode) or recording can be limited to addressing information (pen mode), i.e., IP addresses and usernames."[318]

Federal statutes on electronic surveillance have set the procedures for use of Carnivore/DCS1000 in both modes. Probable cause is not required when the software is in pen mode on the assumption that such activity does not constitute a search, a conclusion not entirely free of doubt.[319] In most instances, however, those using e-mail have a justified expectation of privacy as to the contents of such messages,[320] and when that is the case it is apparent that obtaining those contents is a search for which the Fourth Amendment requires probable cause and (usually) a search warrant.

It has been said that as "a general proposition, the use of Carnivore by government agents likely will meet the Fourth Amendment's requirements."[321] That is very likely the case, although there is understandably concern about the frequency and the extent to which Carnivore/DCS1000 surveillance might turn out in practice to be excessive. These fears stem from "the fact that Carnivore is easily abused, either intentionally or unintentionally," given that the "system must be specifically configured by an agent to exclude certain communications," and that "the system lacks fundamental audit and accountability safeguards to protect against this type of mistake."[322]

Especially because of the development of this technology for Internet surveillance, more sophisticated criminals have undertaken to safeguard their data and communications by encryption, which

> gives Internet users a heightened degree of privacy in Internet communications and a data storage capacity unequaled in the physical world. One of the most common encryption methods used is Pretty Good Privacy (PGP). PGP uses a two key system with a passphrase to encrypt plain text into ciphertext, and to decrypt the ciphertext back to plain text. PGP is such a strong cryptography that it has been said, " . . . even a billion computers doing a billion checks a second . . . [could] not decipher the result . . . before the end of the universe."
> * * * Plain text can only be encrypted with the public key; it can-

---

[318]Comment, 52 S.C.L.Rev. 875, 876 (2001).

[319]See § 2.7(b).

[320]See § 2.6(f).

[321]Comment, 80 N.C.L.Rev. 315, 347 (2001).

[322]Note, 34 Conn.L.Rev. 261, 287 (2001).

not be decrypted. To decrypt the ciphertext the corresponding private key is needed. Although they are related, the private key cannot feasibly be mathematically deduced from the public key. Data, which can be encrypted by anyone, can only be decrypted by the possessor of the private key, thus ensuring the ability of one recipient to maintain secure communications with multiple senders. This allows secure data to be transmitted over the Internet or any other data channel in which the secure data is encrypted by the sender so that only the recipient can decrypt it. This eliminates the need for sharing passwords and decreases possible security breaches associated with conventional cryptography. Public and private keys are kept on the computer in encrypted form (keyrings). Because the private key can be long and complicated, it is encrypted on the recipient's machine using a passphrase or secret key. The passphrase can be any one of a number of combinations of uppercase and lowercase letters, numbers, and punctuation marks. A passphrase is generally longer than a password so it is less susceptible to dictionary attacks and other standard code-breaking attempts. The advent of two-key encryption has enabled criminals to encrypt and transfer files without divulging their passwords or passphrases to others who might eventually share that information with law enforcement personnel.[323]

In response, the federal government some time ago began proposing legislation that would require every developer of encryption software to provide a key to the code, which would be retained by "trusted third parties" and be available to law enforcement personnel upon issuance of an appropriate subpoena or search warrant. These proposals are said to involve "key escrow" because of the fact that the key that unlocks encrypted messages would be stored and made readily available to law enforcement. Debate about such proposals became particularly intense in the mid-1990s when the Clinton administration proposed a form of this back-door technology called the "Clipper Chip." While the Clinton administration eventually abandoned the Clipper Chip initiative, of interest here is that part of the aforementioned debate directed to the question of whether, assuming legal grounds to obtain the encrypted message, permitting decryption via "key escrow" would itself constitute a Fourth Amendment search. The "yes" and "no" positions on this question have been usefully summarized as follows:

[The yes position is] that encrypting an electronic communication creates a "reasonable expectation of privacy" in the communication's contents, triggering Fourth Amendment protection. The near impossibility of decrypting a strongly encrypted Internet communication makes it "reasonable" to expect that the communication will remain private. Therefore, any regulatory scheme that allows the government to obtain a user's key and decrypt the communication without a warrant would violate her "reasonable expectation of privacy" and violate the Fourth Amendment. Some commentators have analogized encryption to a lock and key: just as locking a box with a key

---

[323]Note, 2002 U.Ill.J.L.Tech. &   Pol'y 193, 195–97.

creates a reasonable expectation of privacy in its contents, locking a communication by encrypting it with an encryption key does the same.

[The no position is] that encryption cannot create Fourth Amendment protection because the Fourth Amendment regulates government access to communications, not the cognitive understanding of communications already obtained. Once ciphertext is in plain view, the communication itself is in plain view for Fourth Amendment purposes. Although the government must unscramble the communication to understand it, the Fourth Amendment cannot regulate the cognitive process by which the government attempts to extract meaning from an encrypted communication in its possession. As counterintuitive as it seems, any expectation that the government will be unable to decrypt ciphertext cannot be constitutionally "reasonable"—no matter how statistically justified it is—because it is not based on an extraconstitutional right to enjoin the invasion of privacy. Whenever the government obtains ciphertext consistently with Fourth Amendment standards, decrypting the communication into plaintext without a warrant cannot violate the Fourth Amendment.[324]

Because a "key escrow" system never came into being, there are, of course, no court decisions directly on point. Useful analogies, at least in the eyes of the "no" camp, are such cases as *United States v. Scott*,[325] *United States v. Longoria*,[326] and *Commonwealth v. Copenhefer*.[327] *Scott* held that no warrant was needed to reconstruct documents from their shredded state, the many 5/32 inch-wide strips of paper lawfully recovered from defendant's garbage, for defendant lacked a justified expectation of privacy notwithstanding his "use of more sophisticated 'higher' technology" to maintain secrecy, just as would be the case regarding one who sought privacy by putting the communication "in a secret code" or "in some obscure foreign language." *Longoria* is a foreign language case in which the court concluded that drug conspirators had no justified expectation of privacy regarding their oral communications in Spanish while in the presence of English-speaking outsiders, one of whom recorded the conversations so that law enforcement authorities could translate them into English. As for *Copenhefer*, where in a search of defendant's computer the police used special technology to retrieve files defendant assumed he had erased by executing the "delete" command, the court concluded that defendant's hope for secrecy "did

---

[324]Kerr, The Fourth Amendment in Cyberspace: Can Encryption Create a "Reasonable Expectation of Privacy"?, 33 Conn.L.Rev. 503, 504–05 (2001). Kerr himself takes the "no" position; the several commentators taking the "yes" position are cited id. at 504 nn. 6, 7 and 8. Also disagreeing with *Kerr* are Henderson, Nothing New Under the Sun? A Technologically Rational Doctrine of Fourth Amendment Search, 56 Mercer L.Rev. 507, 529–35 (2005); Comment, 30 Pepp.L.Rev. 339 (2003).

[325]United States v. Scott, 975 F.2d 927 (1st Cir.1992).

[326]United States v. Longoria, 177 F.3d 1179 (10th Cir.1999).

[327]Commonwealth v. Copenhefer, 526 Pa. 555, 587 A.2d 1353 (1991).

not prohibit the state from subjecting validly seized physical evidence from any scientific analysis possible within current technology," and thus a second warrant was not required to perform the "undeletion"—just as would be the case as to police efforts to decipher a seized document found to be written in code.

At least some of those in the "yes" camp question the relevance of these cases to the "key escrow" issue. It is asserted, for example, that *Longoria* and *Scott*, respectively, have to do with speaking in the presence of others and with abandonment of property, affirmative actions by which the defendants in those cases lost any justified privacy expectation, while there is no comparable act by a person whose encrypted document could be decrypted under a "key escrow" system.[328] However, if the issue is the status of decryption of a file or message otherwise lawfully acquired by law enforcement, then that distinction seems beside the point. But the central objection from the "yes" camp is that these three cases merely involved a "hope" that speaking in Spanish would not ultimately come to the attention of one of the many who understand that language, that shredding papers placed in the garbage would discourage painstaking efforts to properly connect the shreds, and that pressing "delete" would dispose of files in the computer's memory, while encryption "encodes a digital document and leaves the user with the only key" so that "no one but the user can read its contents."[329] Of course, if a "key escrow" system were extant, this latter assertion would be less than correct, which suggests that a judgment about legislation creating such a system involves not so much a traditional Fourth Amendment what-is-a-search inquiry[330] as it does broader questions about whether having, in effect, an unbreakable code that makes totally unavailable certain evidence of crime is tolerable, and whether any possible "key escrow" scheme can be structured so as to sufficiently ensure against government abuse of the technology.

At least for now, "key escrow" is off the table, and thus those exceedingly difficult questions need not be answered. Meanwhile, without any "key escrow" system in place, law enforcement has

---

[328]Comment, 30 Pepp.L.Rev. 339, 355–59 (2003).

[329]Comment, 30 Pepp.L.Rev. 339, 356, 361 (2003).

[330]On this point, I find certain language in Froomkin, The Metaphor is the Key: Cryptography, the Clipper, and the Constitution, 143 U.Pa.L.Rev. 709 (1995)—which, however, takes the view that mandatory escrow of a key *is* a Fourth Amendment "search or seizure," id. at 827—quite helpful. He correctly notes that there is nothing in the Fourth Amendment itself that empowers the government "to require that people help to create the conditions that would make such searches effective," and says that the question is whether "the government might make preemptive rules designed * * * to preserve the government's ability to carry out a valid search by taking action in advance of any warrant." Id. at 826, 829. For more on this question, see Tien, Doors, Envelopes, and Encryption: The Uncertain Role of Precautions in Fourth Amendment Law, 54 DePaul L.Rev. 873 (2005).

had to look to other technology in order to access encrypted materials, namely, a "keystroke logging" system or a variation thereof known as "Magic Lantern."[331] A "keystroke logging" system (KLS) has been characterized as "the best way for law enforcement to crack strong encryption used by criminals and terrorists to hide information," for it "allows for immediate access to encrypted information because it 'watches' the [computer] user type his passphrase and relays the passphrase to the party that installed the logger."[332]

> Although the precise technical specifications are unavailable, the KLS records keystrokes entered into a computer keyboard when the computer's modem or other communication devices are not in use. The KLS consists of a combination of firmware, software and/or hardware, and is embedded into the host computer to conceal its existence. The KLS program examines each keystroke individually, and if no communications device is being used simultaneously, the keystroke is recorded. This eliminates the possibility of recording information that is being transmitted through or in route to a modem or other communication device. This system has allowed the government to utilize traditional search warrants,[333] thereby

---

[331]For other discussion of keystroke logging and Magic Lantern, see Etzioni, Implications of Selective New Technologies for Individual Rights and Public Safety, 15 Harv.J.L. & Tech. 257 (2002); Kuh, The Founders' Privacy: The Fourth Amendment and the Power of Technological Surveillance, 86 Minn.L.Rev. 1325 (2002); Voors, Encryption Regulation in the Wake of September 11, 2001: Must We Protect National Security at the Expense of the Economy, 55 Fed.Comm.L.J. 331 (2003); Woo & So, The Case for Magic Lantern: September 11 Highlights the Need for Increased Surveillance, 15 Harv.J.L. & Tech. 521 (2002); Comment, 20 J.Marshall J.Comp. & Inf.L. 287 (2002); Notes, 40 Am.Crim.L.Rev. 1271 (2003); 2002 U.Ill.J.L.Tech. & Pol'y 193; 70 U.M.K.C.L.Rev. 751 (2002).

[332]Woo & So, 15 Harv.J.L. & Tech. 521, 525 (2002).

[333]In United States v. Scarfo, 180 F.Supp.2d 572 (D.N.J.2001), pursuant to a traditional search warrant police entered a business operated by a New Jersey mob boss and installed KLS on his computer, as a result of which the password to encrypted files was obtained after monitoring the key strok-

ing on the machine for almost two months. The warrant authorized surreptitious entry and reentry as necessary to recover data and perform maintenance on the KLS. The officers entered four times and recovered 27 pages of text, the final item of which was the password. The principal argument upon Scarfo's motion to suppress the evidence ultimately acquired was that the keystrokes constituted "electronic communications" for which a more demanding Title III warrant was required. In response, the government successfully argued that because the data recorded by the KLS was not being transmitted contemporaneously through a modem or other communications device, the data was not intercepted under Title III, and consequently a traditional warrant sufficed. That conclusion has been questioned on a somewhat different basis, namely, that just as courts have ruled that a warrant essentially in the style of a Title III warrant is required as a Fourth Amendment matter for non-audio video surveillance, see note 313 supra, the same should be true of KLS installation and use, for both "video surveillance and the KLS record ongoing activities over a period of time, and are not limited to what is available at the time the warrant is executed." Note,

avoiding more stringent wiretapping statute requirements.[334]
Such use of KLS as originally developed requires, as in *United
States v. Scarfo*,[335] that law enforcement agents surreptitiously
physically enter the premises where the computer in question is
located and physically install the KLS device on that computer.
As seemingly was accepted without question in *Scarfo*,[336] that
kind of activity obviously constitutes a search under the Fourth
Amendment, meaning it is unnecessary to ponder the more difficult question of whether retrieving key strokes is itself a search
in light of the fact that equipment for doing precisely this is
available to the public and is used to check on employees' and
family members' use of computers.[337] This is because activity that
in and of itself is not a search (e.g., a drug dog sniff) constitutes
part of an illegal search if done while not "lawfully present" in a
Fourth Amendment sense when that activity occurs.[338]

More recently, the FBI has developed a software version of the
KLS known as "Magic Lantern." It

> utilizes a computer virus for remote installation on a suspect's
> machine to obtain the suspect's password or passphrase. This
> program could be e-mailed to the suspect by relatives or friends or
> installed through network vulnerabilities in the computer system,
> thereby eliminating the need for a physical break-in and the
> dangers associated therewith. Like the KLS, Magic Lantern records
> keystrokes typed on the computer, but it is also capable of e-mailing
> an output data file back to law enforcement personnel.[339]

It remains to be seen whether this Magic Lantern version of the
KLS will prove to be effective or, on the other hand, will be ineffective because "vulnerable to detection by the latest anti-virus
software."[340] Assuming it is employed and proves effective, there
will doubtless arise the question of whether utilization of the

---

2002 U.Ill.J.L.Tech. & Pol'y 193, 212.

[334]Note, 2002 U.Ill.J.L.Tech. &
Pol'y 193, 198.

[335]United States v. Scarfo, 180
F.Supp.2d 572 (D.N.J.2001), discussed
in Note, 40 Am.Crim.L.Rev. 1271
(2003).

[336]It was assumed by all that a
search had occurred, for the court
entertained and ruled upon defendant's objections that the warrant issued was a general warrant and also
violated the particularity requirement
of the Fourth Amendment.

[337]"Hundred of these products are
available, and the most frequent civilian consumers are companies who
monitor employees' computer habits
while on the job, parents interested in
knowing what their children do online,

and suspicious spouses who try to
short-circuit the dreaded on-line love
affair." Note, 70 U.M.K.C.L.Rev. 751,
768 (2002).

[338]See, e.g., United States v.
Meindl, 83 F.Supp.2d 1207 (D.Kan.
1999) ("As long as the canine unit is
lawfully present when the sniff occurs,
the 'canine sniff is not a search within
the meaning of the Fourth Amendment' ").

[339]Note, 2002 U.Ill.J.L.Tech. &
Pol'y 193, 198–99.

[340]Note, 70 U.M.K.C.L.Rev. 751,
770 (2002), further noting at 770–71:
"When the 'Magic Lantern' story first
broke, the Associated Press reported
that McAfee Corporation contacted the
FBI to make sure that its well-known
McAfee anti-virus product would not
alert targeted suspects of the surveil-

Magic Lantern technology itself constitutes a Fourth Amendment search.

One commentator has suggested that the answer to this question is "no," reasoning that such programs are merely "the cyber-equivalent of the dog sniff in *Place*."[341] But surely this is not the case, for, even putting to one side the status after *United States v. Kyllo*[342] of a dog sniff that uncovered narcotics located inside premises, the decision in *United States v. Place*[343] extends only to the discovery of contraband,[344] which the key strokes are not. Another basis given for the no-search characterization, related to the fact that such "software versions of a keystroke logging system are commercially available on the Internet,"[345] is that "to the extent that some members of the public (i.e., hackers) may access the same information through the Internet, a court may conclude that the information is not private because individuals assume the risk that others, including the government, may access this information once a computer is connected to the Internet."[346] This raises, of course, the troublesome qualification in *Kyllo*, namely, that acquiring by "sense-enhancing technology" information otherwise unavailable without physical entry of a home is a search "at least where (as here) the technology in question is not in general public use," which harks back to the Court's earlier holding in *Dow Chemical Co. v. United States*[347] that it was no search to employ a precision aerial mapping camera, as distinguished from surveillance "by using highly sophisticated surveillance equipment not generally available to the public." The error of such distinctions has been discussed elsewhere herein,[348] and thus suffice it to note here that this "generally available" qualification is especially pernicious in this context, for

---

lance. If that report was initially correct, McAfee soon reversed field and, along with the rest of the anti-virus industry, spoke out to reassure customers that they would create no 'back door' for the FBI in any of their products.

"With that in mind, privacy advocates can probably rest easier because the practical hurdles for the FBI's crime fighting virus are legion. First, absent a global conspiracy between the FBI and every anti-virus software company, 'Magic Lantern' will fail in its silent purpose; if just one program detects it the proverbial cat would be out of the bag. The detecting company's products would instantly become the leader in the market to the exclusion of any of those that agreed to collude with the FBI, and it is unlikely that any sensible business would take such a risk in relation to its competitors."

[341]Kuh, 86 Minn.L.Rev. 1325, 1352 (2002).

[342]Kyllo v. United States, 533 U.S. 27, 121 S.Ct. 2038, 150 L.Ed.2d 94 (2001).

[343]United States v. Place, 462 U.S. 696, 103 S.Ct. 2637, 77 L.Ed.2d 110 (1983).

[344]See § 2.2(d).

[345]Note, 2002 U.Ill.J.L.Tech. & Pol'y 193, 199.

[346]Kuh, 86 Minn.L.Rev. 1325, 1352 (2002).

[347]Dow Chemical Co. v. United States, 476 U.S. 227, 106 S.Ct. 1819, 90 L.Ed.2d 226 (1986).

[348]See § 2.2(c), (d).

it in essence would mean that the government is free to engage in those intrusions open to the most unprincipled of hackers.

It is also important, however, to note that the distinction suggested in *Kyllo* had to do with "sense-enhancing technology," and of course that was precisely what was at issue in *Dow* as well, while Magic Lantern involves something well beyond that: it does not merely allow the police to see or hear more distant or more clearly. Rather, Magic Lantern actually sends something to the computer located within the suspect's premises that will be able to report back to law enforcement agents certain facts—what keys are being stricken by the computer user—that (in the language of *Kyllo*) "could not otherwise have been obtained without 'physical intrusion into a constitutionally protected area,'"[349] as indicated by the procedures found necessary in *Scarfo*. The essential point is that *Kyllo* indicates acceptance by the Court of the proposition (as put in a thoughtful lower-court thermal imager case) that "*Katz* looked not to the tools employed by the government nor the phenomena measured by those tools but to the object of the government's efforts."[350] The object of those efforts via Magic Lantern is to make a record of the key strokes on a computer, which "would certainly be a search under the Fourth Amendment,"[351] as "computers have become an integral and personal part of people's lives,"[352] and the key strokes made on those computers "are used to compose e-mails, type 'real-time' messages over an 'instant messenger,' and—at the heart of the matter—type passwords, which, by their nature

---

[349]And consider the possible relevance here of United States v. Jones, __ U.S. __, 132 S.Ct. 945, 181 L.Ed.2d 911 (2012), holding that a trespass "for the purpose of obtaining information" is a search, if the holding were "updated to consider electronic penetration a form of trespass," Goldberg, How United States v. Jones Can Restore Our Faith in the Fourth Amendment, 110 Mich.L.Rev. First Impressions 62, 68 (2011).

[350]United States v. Cusumano, 67 F.3d 1497 (10th Cir.1995), vacated on rehearing en banc, 83 F.3d 1247 (10th Cir.1996), but only on the ground that this issue need not be reached because evidence other than the thermal imager scan provided probable cause for the challenged search warrant.

[351]Note, 70 U.M.K.C.L.Rev. 751, 772 (2002). In light of *Kyllo*, this would most assuredly be the case as to a computer used in the home, but this is not to suggest that if Magic Lantern had been used in the previously discussed *Scarfo* case, where defendant used the computer at his place of business, that the result would be otherwise. It must be remembered that the *Kyllo* holding specified the home because a home was there involved, leaving open what the result would be as to other structures, and also that the fact a home was involved in *Kyllo* made it possible for the majority to assert that in such a locale "*all* details are intimate details" safe from government surveillance. While the same may not be true of all details in a place of business, surely it would be true as to the keys an individual strikes on a computer while beyond direct observation of a bystander.

[352]Woo & So, 15 Harv.J.L. & Tech. 521, 530 (2002).

necessitate secrecy."[353]

The proper conclusion, then, as one commentator has aptly put it, is

> that the computer user whose hard drive is invaded by a law enforcement Trojan Horse program is in a situation functionally analogous to the one Katz found himself in. Both utilize methods of "online" communication that rely on technology; both assume their "content" is private-the computer user because she is on her computer in her home or office, and Katz because he was in a phone booth the door of which was securely closed. In neither scenario can law enforcement access the content in question without utilizing dedicated technology that lets the officers invade a private enclave (hard drive, phone booth) in a fashion a reasonable person would not expect. In neither scenario do we have the target of that invasion engaging in conduct that abrogates a Fourth Amendment expectation of privacy in the area that is invaded, i.e., neither Katz nor our hypothetical computer user knowingly engaged in conduct that exposed their respective content to the public, and thereby to law enforcement.[354]

§ 2.2(g) Use of canine to detect drugs, etc.[355]

In recent years police have made extensive use of specially

---

[353]Comment, 20 J.Marshall J.Comp. & Inf.L. 287, 296 (2002).

[354]Brenner, Fourth Amendment Future: Remote Computer Searches and the Use of Virtual Force, 81 Miss.L.J. 1229, 1243–44 (2012). Regarding the last point, the author also observes, id. at 1242–43, that while a "number of courts have found that one who installs and enables 'peer-to-peer' file sharing on his computer thereby giving anyone with internet access the ability to gain entrance to his computer,' has 'no reasonable expectation of privacy,'" those courts "have, at least implicitly, found that the user of file-sharing software defeats a Fourth Amendment expectation of privacy only as to the files the person has made available for sharing."

[Section 2.2(g)]

[355]See also Bird, An Examination of the Training and Reliability of the Narcotics Detection Dog, 85 Ky.L.J. 405 (1997); Gardner, Sniffing for Drugs in the Classroom—Perspectives on Fourth Amendment Scope, 74 Nw.U.L. Rev. 803 (1980); Hunt, Calling in the Dogs: Suspicionless Sniff Searches and Reasonable Expectations of Privacy, 56 Case W.Res.L.Rev. 285 (2005); Kingham, Marijuana Detection Dogs as an Instrument of Search: The Real Question, The Army Lawyer 10 (May 1973); Lederer & Lederer, Marijuana Dog Searches After United States v. Unrue, The Army Lawyer 6 (Dec. 1973); Lederer & Lederer, Admissibility of Evidence Found by Marijuana Detection Dogs, The Army Lawyer 12 (April 1973); Lichtenstein, Drug Detector Dogs and the Fourth Amendment: A Model Plan, 11 Am.J.Crim.L. 67 (1983); Peebles, The Uninvited Canine Nose and the Right to Privacy: Some Thoughts on Katz and Dogs, 11 Ga.L.Rev. 75 (1976); Smith, Going to the Dogs: Evaluating the Proper Standard for Narcotics Detector Dog Searches of Private Residences, 46 Houst.L.Rev. 103 (2009); Annots., 117 A.L.R.5th 407 (2004),150 A.L.R.Fed. 399 (1998); Comments, 17 Akron L.Rev. 739 (1984); 85 Dick.L.Rev. 143 (1980); 71 Geo.L.J. 1232 (1983); 68 Marq.L. Rev. 57 (1984); 46 Me.L.Rev. 161 (1994); 48 Mont.L.Rev. 101 (1987); 13 San Diego L.Rev. 410 (1976); Notes, 72 Brook.L.Rev. 279 (2006); 44 Fordham L.Rev. 973 (1976); Notes, 71 J.Crim.L. & Crim. 39 (1980); 31 Okla.L. Rev. 709 (1978); 2 U.Dayton L.Rev. 149 (1977); 1977 U.Ill.L.F. 1167, 1197–1201; Annot., 31 A.L.R.Fed. 931

trained dogs to detect the presence of explosives[356] or, more commonly, narcotics.[357] These dogs are utilized in checking persons and effects crossing the border into the United States,[358] luggage accompanying persons traveling by airline,[359] train,[360] or bus,[361] freight shipped by airline,[362] and the contents of vehicles[363] and storage facilities.[364] In light of the careful training these dogs receive,[365] an "alert"[366] by a dog is deemed to constitute probable

---

(1977).

[356]State v. Quatsling, 24 Ariz.App. 105, 536 P.2d 226 (1975).

[357]E.g., United States v. Eura, 440 F.3d 625 (4th Cir.2006); United States v. Solis, 536 F.2d 880 (9th Cir.1976); People v. Campbell, 67 Ill.2d 308, 10 Ill.Dec. 340, 367 N.E.2d 949 (1977).

[358]The Customs Service has estimated that for the fiscal year 1974 their trained dogs "screened 90,500 vehicles, 4 million mail packages, and 6,052,049 units of cargo in just a fraction of the time it would have taken customs inspectors. The dog teams accounted for the seizure of 22,722 pounds of marijuana, 2,166 pounds of hashish, 25 pounds of cocaine, 13 pounds of heroin and 2 million units of the dangerous drugs (detected because of similar chemical properties)." Comment, 13 San Diego L.Rev. 410, 416 n. 31 (1976).

[359]United States v. Bronstein, 521 F.2d 459 (2d Cir.1975); People v. Williams, 51 Cal.App.3d 346, 124 Cal.Rptr. 253 (1975); People v. Furman, 30 Cal.App.3d 454, 106 Cal.Rptr. 366 (1973); People v. Campbell, 67 Ill.2d 308, 10 Ill.Dec. 340, 367 N.E.2d 949 (1977); State v. Scheetz, 286 Mont. 41, 950 P.2d 722 (1997).

[360]United States v. Garcia, 42 F.3d 604 (10th Cir.1994) (luggage in baggage car); United States v. Trayer, 898 F.2d 805 (D.C.Cir.1990); United States v. Colyer, 878 F.2d 469 (D.C.Cir.1989); United States v. Whitehead, 849 F.2d 849 (4th Cir.1988).

[361]United States v. Gant, 112 F.3d 239 (6th Cir.1997); United States v. Harvey, 961 F.2d 1361 (8th Cir.1992); United States v. Fulero, 498 F.2d 748 (D.C.Cir.1974); Scott v. State, 927 P.2d 1066 (Okl.Cr.1996).

[362]United States v. Daniel, 982 F.2d 146 (5th Cir.1993) (dog-sniffing of package shipped with airline lawful, as reasonable suspicion justified 45-minute "temporary seizure" to facilitate sniff); State v. Elkins, 47 Ohio App.2d 307, 354 N.E.2d 716 (1976).

[363]United States v. Dyson, 639 F.3d 230 (6th Cir.2011); United States v. Eura, 440 F.3d 625 (4th Cir.2006); United States v. Duffaut, 314 F.3d 203 (5th Cir.2002); United States v. Glinton, 154 F.3d 1245 (11th Cir. 1998); United States v. Brown, 24 F.3d 1223 (10th Cir.1994); United States v. Rodriguez-Morales, 929 F.2d 780 (1st Cir.1991); United States v. Solis, 536 F.2d 880 (9th Cir.1976); State v. Martinez, 26 Ariz.App. 210, 547 P.2d 62 (1976); Dowty v. State, 363 Ark. 1, 210 S.W.3d 850 (2005); State v. Bergmann, 633 N.W.2d 328 (Iowa 2001); State v. Barker, 252 Kan. 949, 850 P.2d 885 (1993); State v. Cleave, 131 N.M. 82, 33 P.3d 633 (2001).

[364]United States v. Venema, 563 F.2d 1003 (10th Cir.1977); State v. Quatsling, 24 Ariz.App. 105, 536 P.2d 226 (1975); People v. Evans, 65 Cal.App.3d 924, 134 Cal.Rptr. 436 (1977).

[365]"The entrance requirements are rigid, and the dogs are screened throughout the training program. During the training period, a dog will work with the same handler so that the handler can learn which movement or action by the dog is an indication of a drug find. For the dogs, training is a hide-and-seek game. In the initial training, the trainer tosses a packet of marijuana to the dog. This develops into a large-scale exercise in which narcotics are hidden in open fields, buildings, cars, and other locations dogs encounter when they graduate from the training course.

"A dog can alert to the drug in a

cause for an arrest or search[367] if a sufficient showing is made as to the reliability of the particular dog used in detecting the presence of a particular type of contraband.[368] The more difficult question, which is of primary concern here, is whether such use of

variety of ways; the dog can snarl, bark, whine, or paw at a container. Each dog may respond differently." Comment, 13 San Diego L.Rev. 410, 415 (1976).

[366]If the dog does not alert but merely shows "interest" in the object, this alone is not probable cause but can be part of the totality of circumstances establishing probable cause. United States v. Guzman, 75 F.3d 1090 (6th Cir.1996).

[367]E.g., United States v. Morales-Zamora, 914 F.2d 200 (10th Cir.1990); United States v. Race, 529 F.2d 12 (1st Cir.1976); Doe v. Renfrow, 475 F.Supp. 1012 (N.D.Ind.1979), aff'd in part, 631 F.2d 91 (7th Cir.) (dog's alert to student in classroom established probable cause student had drugs, though it turned out student did not and dog apparently alerted because student recently handled dog in heat).

It has been estimated that most of the cash in circulation (the estimates range from 70% to 97% of all bills) contains sufficient quantities of cocaine to alert a trained dog. See United States v. Six Hundred Thirty-Nine Thousand Five Hundred and Fifty-Eight Dollars ($639,558) in U.S. Currency, 955 F.2d 712 (D.C.Cir.1992). Thus it sometimes happens in practice that a drug dog alert will lead to nothing but currency. See, e.g., United States v. Trayer, 898 F.2d 805 (D.C. Cir.1990); Taslitz, Does the Cold Nose Know? The Unscientific Myth of the Dog Scent Lineup, 42 Hastings L.J. 15, 29 & n. 71 (1990). It has thus been suggested that "a court considering whether a dog sniff provides probable cause * * * may have to take into account the possibility that the dog signalled only the presence of money, not drugs." United States v. Six Hundred Thirty-Nine Thousand Five Hundred and Fifty-Eight Dollars ($639,558) in U.S. Currency, 955 F.2d 712 (D.C.Cir.1992).

[368]"Various methods of providing an index of the dog's reliability and credibility narrow down to some basic elements. The magistrate should be advised of the following: the exact training the detector dog has received; the standards or criteria employed in selecting dogs for marijuana detection training; the standards the dog was required to meet to successfully complete his training program; the 'track record' of the dog up until the search (emphasis must be placed on the amount of false alerts or mistakes the dog has furnished). Only after this information has been furnished, is a magistrate justified in issuing a warrant." Comment, 13 San Diego L.Rev. 410, 416–17 (1976). Consider also Myers, Detector Dogs and Probable Cause, 14 Geo.Mason L.Rev. 16 (2006) ("argues that an alert, even by a well-trained dog with an excellent track record in the field, cannot by itself constitute probable cause to search. By using Bayesian analysis of the value of dog alerts, this article demonstrates that a finding of probable cause requires additional evidence"); and see related discussion in § 9.3, text following note 355.

See, e.g., State v. Barker, 252 Kan. 949, 850 P.2d 885 (1993) (probable cause requires testimony "from the handler of the dog as to the training, background, characteristics, capabilities, and behavior of the dog," so remand for such testimony necessary); cases collected in § 3.3(d) note 265. Compare United States v. Daniel, 982 F.2d 146 (5th Cir.1993) (probable cause where prior reasonable suspicion plus dog alert; it sufficient that affidavit "specifically explained that the dog was trained to detect the presence of controlled substances," and defendant in error in claiming "that an affidavit must show how reliable a drug-detecting dog has been in the past"). See also § 3.3(d) note 257.

Checking on the reliability of the dog may not be sufficient. It has been noted that "handler error ac-

"canine cannabis connoisseurs"[369] or similarly trained dogs itself constitutes a search so as to be subject to the limitations of the Fourth Amendment.

Before the Supreme Court addressed this issue, a few courts held that reliance upon the trained canine nose to detect that which the officer could not discover by his own sense of smell constitutes a search.[370] Most courts, however, either held or assumed otherwise.[371] One reason given for the latter conclusion was that the practice is essentially no different from the officer using his own sense of smell. In *United States v. Bronstein*,[372] for example, the court asserted:

> If the police officers here had detected the aroma of the drug through their own olfactory senses, there could be no serious contention that their sniffing in the area of the bags would be tantamount to an unlawful search. * * * We fail to understand how the detection of the odoriferous drug by the use of the sensitive and schooled canine senses here employed alters the situation and renders the police procedure constitutionally suspect.[373]

But this simply is not so. As one commentator has rightly noted, "application of a 'plain smell' doctrine to dog searches * * * stretches the imagination," for the fact of the matter is that in *Bronstein* and all the other cases "none of the officers involved

---

counts for almost all false detections" and that consequently "examination of a handler's qualifications should receive particular judicial scrutiny." Bird, An Examination of the Training and Reliability of the Narcotics Detection Dog, 85 Ky.L.J. 405, 432 (1997).

[369] People v. Evans, 65 Cal.App.3d 924, 134 Cal.Rptr. 436 (1977).

[370] Jones v. Latexo Independent School Dist., 499 F.Supp. 223 (E.D. Tex.1980), noted in 9 Am.J.Crim.L. 127 (1981); (use of dog to detect which public school students had drugs was a search because the dog "was able to detect odors completely outside the range of the human sense of smell," and "this replaced, rather than enhanced, the perceptive abilities of school officials," and thus was more like use of electronic bugging or x-rays than flashlight); Doe v. Renfrow, 475 F.Supp. 1012 (N.D.Ind.1979), aff'd in part 631 F.2d 91 (7th Cir.); People v. Evans, 65 Cal.App.3d 924, 134 Cal.Rptr. 436 (1977); State v. Elkins, 47 Ohio App.2d 307, 354 N.E.2d 716 (1976). Virtually all of the commentators (see sources cited in note 355 supra) reached this conclusion.

See also State v. Pellici, 133 N.H. 523, 580 A.2d 710 (1990) (so holding as a matter of state constitutional law and rejecting *Place*); People v. Devone, 15 N.Y.3d 106, 905 N.Y.S.2d 101, 931 N.E.2d 70 (2010), discussed in Begeal, People v. Devone: New York Offers, Drivers More Protection from Warrantless Canine-Sniff Searches or Does It?, 4 Alb.Gov't L.Rev. 827 (2011) (canine sniff of exterior of car is a search under state constitution, but given reduced expectation of privacy only a "founded suspicion" necessary to justify such a search). The other pre-*Place* decisions taking the *Pellici* approach are collected in Morgan v. State, 95 P.3d 802 (Wyo.2004).

[371] E.g., United States v. McCranie, 703 F.2d 1213 (10th Cir.1983); United States v. Waltzer, 682 F.2d 370 (2d Cir.1982); State v. Morrow, 128 Ariz. 309, 625 P.2d 898 (1981); People v. Mayberry, 31 Cal.3d 335, 182 Cal.Rptr. 617, 644 P.2d 810 (1982); People v. Price, 54 N.Y.2d 557, 446 N.Y.S.2d 906, 431 N.E.2d 267 (1981).

[372] United States v. Bronstein, 521 F.2d 459 (2d Cir.1975).

[373] To the same effect is People v. Campbell, 67 Ill.2d 308, 10 Ill.Dec. 340, 367 N.E.2d 949 (1977).

was able to detect the odor of narcotics; the drugs were not in the plain smell of the officers. The officers needed trained dogs to sniff out the contraband."[374]

Bronstein also asserts that the use of the trained dogs is no search because this is simply another instance of the police utilizing "certain 'sense-enhancing' instruments to aid in the detection of contraband." Because, so the argument goes, the cases have generally held that the use of a flashlight[375] or binoculars[376] to aid the natural senses does not constitute a Fourth Amendment search, it follows that it is not a search to resort to "canine assistance in pursuit of the criminal." This analogy is equally unsound. As Judge Mansfield noted in his concurring opinion in *Bronstein,*

> the police have been permitted to enhance or magnify the human senses with the aid of instruments such as binoculars or flashlights * * *. But that is not the case here where the "nose" being put into others' business was clearly an intrusion. The police agents here did not smell or see any contraband, nor were their senses enhanced. Their only indication that marijuana was present was the action of the dog. Their own senses were replaced by the more sensitive nose of the dog in the same manner that a police officer's ears are replaced by a hidden microphone in areas where he could not otherwise hear because of the inaudibility of the sounds. The illegality of the latter practice in the absence of a search warrant or special circumstances has long been established.[377]

A seemingly closer analogy is to the utilization of magnetometers and similar devices,[378] which have consistently been held to amount to a search within the meaning of the Fourth Amendment.[379]

This issue was resolved by the Supreme Court in *United States v. Place,*[380] where a suspected drug courier's luggage was seized for a period of 90 minutes so that it could be transported to another airport and exposed to a drug detection dog there. The majority held that on the facts presented a dispossession of this length could not be justified under the *Terry* balancing test,[381] but then went on to say that a shorter dispossession for this purpose would be lawful because it could not be said that "this investiga-

---

[374]Comment, 13 San Diego L.Rev. 410, 423 (1976).

[375]See § 2.2(b).

[376]See § 2.2(c).

[377]See also Note, 2 U.Dayton L.Rev. 149, 155 (1977); Jones v. Latexo Independent School Dist., 499 F.Supp. 223 (E.D.Tex.1980); State v. Elkins, 47 Ohio App.2d 307, 354 N.E.2d 716 (1976).

[378]The commentators have frequently drawn this analogy. See Kingham, Marijuana Detection Dogs as an Instrument of Search: The Real

Question, The Army Lawyer 10, 11–12 (May 1973); Lederer & Lederer, Marijuana Dog Searches After United States v. Unrue, The Army Lawyer 6, 7 (Dec. 1973); Comment, 13 San Diego L.Rev. 410, 423 (1976); Note, 1977 U.Ill.L.F. 1167, 1199.

[379]See § 2.2(d).

[380]United States v. Place, 462 U.S. 696, 103 S.Ct. 2637, 77 L.Ed.2d 110 (1983).

[381]On this branch of the *Place* case, see § 9.8(e).

tive procedure is itself a search requiring probable cause." In reaching this conclusion, the Court did not rely upon the theories often used by the lower courts and criticized above. That is, the Court did *not* say that use of the dog was equivalent to the officer using his own sense of smell or that it simply augmented the officer's sense of smell.[382] Rather, the Court placed primary emphasis upon the unique nature of the investigative technique, which disclosed only criminality and nothing else:

> We have affirmed that a person possesses a privacy interest in the contents of personal luggage that is protected by the Fourth Amendment. * * * A "canine sniff" by a well-trained narcotics detection dog, however, does not require opening the luggage. It does not expose noncontraband items that otherwise would remain hidden from public view, as does, for example, an officer's rummaging through the contents of the luggage. Thus, the manner in which information is obtained through this investigative technique is much less intrusive than a typical search. Moreover, the sniff discloses only the presence or absence of narcotics, a contraband item. Thus, despite the fact that the sniff tells the authorities something about the contents of the luggage, the information obtained is limited. This limited disclosure also ensures that the owner of the property is not subjected to the embarrassment and inconvenience entailed in less discriminate and more intrusive investigative methods.
>
> In these respects, the canine sniff is *sui generis*.[383] We are aware of no other investigative procedure that is so limited both in the manner in which the information is obtained and in the content of the information revealed by the procedure. Therefore, we conclude that the particular course of investigation that the agents intended to pursue here—exposure of respondent's luggage, which was located in a public place, to a trained canine—did not constitute a "search" within the meaning of the Fourth Amendment.[384]

The three concurring members of the Court quite properly chided the majority for getting into this issue at all. As they correctly noted, resolution of the dog sniff issue was not necessary to the decision.[385] Moreover, the Court's decision on this point can hardly be characterized as an informed one; as Justice Brennan

---

[382]Brennan, J., joined by Marshall, J., concurring in the result, quite correctly noted that "a dog does more than merely allow the police to do more efficiently what they could do using only their own senses. A dog adds a new and previously unobtainable dimension to human perception."

[383]However, some other devices have been developed that are at least arguably of the same character. See § 2.2(h).

[384]As noted in State v. Scheetz, 286 Mont. 41, 950 P.2d 722 (1997), regarding the outcome under state constitutional provisions, "most states that have addressed the use of drug-detecting canines have followed *Place* and have held that the use of drug-detecting canines does not constitute a search." But see post-*Place* cases in note 370 supra.

[385]This is because once it was decided that the dispossession of the luggage was too long in any event, there was no need for the Court to address the question of the permissibility of the dog sniffing had the seizure been for a shorter duration. Such was the manner in which the court of appeals resolved the case. United States v. Place, 660 F.2d 44 (2d Cir.1981).

Yet, the Supreme Court has

observed, the matter was not at issue in the district court, was not reached or discussed by the court of appeals, and "was not briefed or argued in this Court." Reaching out in such circumstances is especially unwise when there is more than one solution with sufficient merit to deserve careful consideration. As Justice Blackmun put it: "While the Court has adopted one plausible analysis of the issue, there are others. For example, a dog sniff may be a search, but a minimally intrusive one that could be justified in this situation under *Terry* upon mere reasonable suspicion."

Whether the *Place* majority's explanation or that suggested by Justice Blackmun (discussed further herein[386]) should prevail is, to be sure, a close question. The choice between the two turns on whether the authorities need to be constitutionally restrained in the use of this investigative device so that it is permitted only in particular instances where there exists a reasonable suspicion (which, incidentally, there was in *Place*), or whether instead the police should be unrestrained and thus free to utilize this procedure in a wholesale fashion, at random, or on nothing more than a whim or hunch.[387] The argument in support of the *Place* approach is that use of this very limited procedure even in these

---

since dealt with its resolution of this issue as a holding, see United States v. Jacobsen, 466 U.S. 109, 104 S.Ct. 1652, 80 L.Ed.2d 85 (1984), note 387 infra, and thus, as one court put it, "[w]hether or not the statement in *Place* was a holding or dictum, the Supreme Court has clearly directed the lower courts to follow its pronouncement." United States v. Beale, 736 F.2d 1289 (9th Cir.1984).

[386]See text at note 437 and following.

[387]Some pre-*Place* decisions held such uses of dogs to constitute a search-.Jones v. Latexo Independent School Dist., 499 F.Supp. 223 (E.D.Tex.1980) (is a search to use dog on all public school students to see who carrying drugs); People v. Evans, 65 Cal.App.3d 924, 134 Cal.Rptr. 436 (1977) (surveillance of mini-warehouse compartment; illegal search, as "the record is totally devoid of facts relative to whether the customs agents, the narcotics agent or the detectives had any information prior to going to the mini-warehouse area that marijuana could be found in compartments 20 and 21," and "the dogs were used to sniff around all of the compartments"); People v.

Williams, 51 Cal.App.3d 346, 124 Cal.Rptr. 253 (1975) (illegal search where dog and handler entered baggage area to "engage in a fishing expedition, or more accurately in this instance in a sniffing expedition, of a general, routine, exploratory nature").

In United States v. Jacobsen, 466 U.S. 109, 104 S.Ct. 1652, 80 L.Ed.2d 85 (1984), the majority utilized the *Place* rule to hold it was by the same reasoning no search to conduct a field test "that merely discloses whether or not a particular substance is cocaine." Brennan and Marshall, JJ., dissenting, objected:

It is certainly true that a surveillance technique that identifies only the presence or absence of contraband is less intrusive than a technique that reveals the precise nature of an item regardless of whether it is contraband. But by seizing upon this distinction alone to conclude that the first type of technique, as a general matter, is not a search, the Court has foreclosed any consideration of the circumstances under which the technique is used, and may very well have paved the way for technology to override the limits of law in the area of criminal investigation.

For example, under the Court's analysis in these cases, law enforcement of-

latter circumstances is unobjectionable because no intrusion upon an innocent person's privacy interests occurs. On this theory, it is unobjectionable (to take the facts revealed in a few recent cases) that the police work these dogs at random on vehicles parked in a motel parking lot,[388] or school[389] parking lot, baggage passing through a certain airport,[390] luggage in the luggage racks of a bus stopped for cleaning and refueling,[391] luggage stored in the baggage car of a train,[392] or packages awaiting delivery by a certain freight service.[393] No one has his possessory interest interfered

---

ficers could release a trained cocaine-sensitive dog * * * to roam the streets at random, alerting the officers to people carrying cocaine. * * * Or, if a device were developed that, when aimed at a person, would detect instantaneously whether the person is carrying cocaine, there would be no Fourth Amendment bar, under the Court's approach, to the police setting up such a device on a street corner and scanning all passersby. In fact, the Court's analysis is so unbounded that if a device were developed that could detect, from the outside of a building, the presence of cocaine inside, there would be no constitutional obstacle to the police cruising through a residential neighborhood and using the device to identify all homes in which the drug is present. In short, under the interpretation of the Fourth Amendment first suggested in *Place* and first applied in this case, these surveillance techniques would not constitute searches and therefore could be freely pursued whenever and wherever law enforcement officers desire. Hence, at some point in the future, if the Court stands by the theory it has adopted today, search warrants, probable cause, and even 'reasonable suspicion' may very well become notions of the past.

[388]United States v. Ludwig, 10 F.3d 1523 (10th Cir.1993) ("random dog sniffing of vehicles and other objects without prior lawful detention or reasonable suspicion * * * are not searches").

[389]Hearn v. Board of Public Education, 191 F.3d 1329 (11th Cir.1999); Myers v. State, 839 N.E.2d 1154 (Ind. 2005).

[390]State v. Morrow, 128 Ariz. 309, 625 P.2d 898 (1981) (dog handler for customs service worked dog on random domestic baggage, as he did 3 times a week, to keep his dog in practice; court

dismissed defendant's observation that in all prior cases approving use of dogs there was reason to suspect the presence of contraband, reasoning that "if a dog's sniff is not a search, then it is immaterial whether there was pre-sniff knowledge"); People v. Mayberry, 31 Cal.3d 335, 182 Cal.Rptr. 617, 644 P.2d 810 (1982); (though dogs were used on all luggage coming into San Diego on flights from Florida, court held it no search to detect "the escaping smell of contraband"); State v. Scheetz, 286 Mont. 41, 950 P.2d 722 (1997) (no search for canine to sniff bags of certain arriving flight).

[391]United States v. Gant, 112 F.3d 239 (6th Cir.1997); United States v. Harvey, 961 F.2d 1361 (8th Cir.1992) (stressing "the canine sniff did not require any contact with the owners of the unattended luggage" and "did not cause the appellants to be detained or inconvenienced" or cause them "any annoyance or embarrassment").

See also Scott v. State, 927 P.2d 1066 (Okl.Cr.1996) (random checking at regular bus stop of luggage checked with bus company and stored in bus undercarriage no search).

[392]United States v. Garcia, 42 F.3d 604 (10th Cir.1994).

[393]In State v. Snitkin, 67 Haw. 168, 681 P.2d 980 (1984), where dogs were used to sniff all packages in a cargo holding room of a private mail carrier, known to drug enforcement officials as a high volume drug conduit, the court by reliance on *Place* concluded it was no search, but then seemed to hedge by talking about the need to determine "the reasonableness of the dog's use in the particular circumstances" by a balancing test and by finding the government interest

with, and only the traveler or shipper who is transporting drugs has his privacy interest interfered with. Any thought that *Place* was limited to its own facts and therefore would not apply to such random uses of drug-sniffing dogs was ultimately dispelled in *City of Indianapolis v. Edmond*.[394] The majority, holding a drug checkpoint involving use of such dogs on all vehicles stopped at the checkpoint in violation of the Fourth Amendment because "the primary purpose" of the checkpoint was "to uncover evidence of ordinary criminal wrongdoing," first concluded that the checkpoints amounted to a seizure, but that the "fact that officers walk a narcotics-detection dog around the exterior of each car * * * does not transform the seizure into a search."[395] And just a few years later, in *Illinois v. Caballes*,[396] the Court concluded there was no search where a "dog sniff was performed on the exterior of respondent's car while he was lawfully seized for a traffic violation." That reaffirmation of *Place* in *Edmond* and *Caballes* lends additional support to the conclusion that *Kyllo v. United States*,[397] involving use of a thermal imager to gain information from inside a house that would not otherwise be apparent, "does not disturb the nearly twenty years of precedent regarding dog sniffs and vehicles,"[398] and that "a drug sniffing dog is not 'technology' of the type addressed in *Kyllo*."[399]

One commentator has suggested that "the fourth amendment

---

here particularly strong because of the statistical information that drugs often come to Hawaii via Federal Express. In State v. Wolohan, 23 Wash.App. 813, 598 P.2d 421 (1979), the court held no search had occurred though a police officer and his drug-sniffing dog regularly patrolled the Greyhound package express area as part of a regular assignment and without the necessity of any suspicion concerning any of the packages examined. The court reached this outrageous result notwithstanding the dissenting judge's objection that "the cases are virtually unanimous in requiring or finding that the police officer entertained a reasonable suspicion regarding the presence of contraband in the particular area to be searched prior to employing the canine's drug-sensitive senses."

[394]City of Indianapolis v. Edmond, 531 U.S. 32, 121 S.Ct. 447, 148 L.Ed.2d 333 (2000).

[395]As the Court elaborated: "Just as in *Place*, an exterior sniff of an automobile does not require entry into the car and is not designed to disclose any information other than the presence or absence of narcotics. * * * Like the dog sniff in *Place*, a sniff by a dog that simply walks around a car is 'much less intrusive than a typical search.'"

However, the three dissenters in *Edmond*, unwilling to accept the majority's purpose distinction, criticized the majority by stating that the "State's use of a drug-sniffing dog, according to the Court's holding, annuls what is otherwise plainly constitutional."

[396]Illinois v. Caballes, 543 U.S. 405, 125 S.Ct. 834, 160 L.Ed.2d 842 (2005), discussed in § 9.3(b).

[397]Kyllo v. United States, 533 U.S. 27, 121 S.Ct. 2038, 150 L.Ed.2d 94 (2001).

[398]State v. Bergmann, 633 N.W.2d 328 (Iowa 2001). Accord: Morgan v. State, 95 P.3d 802 (Wyo.2004).

[399]State v. Bergmann, 633 N.W.2d 328 (Iowa 2001). In distinguishing *Kyllo* in *Caballes*, the Court stated: "The legitimate expectation that information about perfectly lawful activity will remain private is categorically dis-

exists to protect the innocent and may normally be invoked by the guilty only when necessary to protect the innocent," so that "if a device could be invented that accurately detected weapons and did not disrupt the normal movement of people, there could be no fourth amendment objection to its use."[400] But this reasoning, he goes on to note, does not support the "carte blanche use of marijuana-sniffing dogs"[401] such as is permissible under the *Place* decision. This is because these dogs are not fool-proof and thus their use sometimes leads to serious intrusions upon the privacy of innocent people.[402] The classic example is *Doe v. Renfrow*,[403] where such a dog "alerted" to a 13-year-old girl during a school-wide "sniff" of all students. This dog continued to "alert" even after she emptied her pockets, so she was then subjected to a nude search by two women; no drugs were found, but it was later discovered that she had been playing that morning with her dog, who was in heat. This was not an isolated instance of error. The dogs used in this undertaking alerted to some fifty students, only 17 of whom were found to be in possession of drugs.[404] The benefit of the approach suggested by Justice Blackmun, whereby the sniff would be deemed a minor search permissible only on reasonable suspicion, is that it would reduce considerably the likelihood of such unfortunate consequences as occurred in *Doe*. That is, if the dogs could not be used wholesale fashion but only against persons and effects for which there already existed an independent reasonable suspicion of drug possession, then the opportunity for such erroneous alerts would be substantially reduced.[405]

It may be argued, of course, that this objection is irrelevant to the matter here under discussion. If these dogs are not as ac-

---

tinguishable from respondent's hopes or expectations concerning the nondetection of contraband in the trunk of his car."

[400]Loewy, The Fourth Amendment as a Device for Protecting the Innocent, 81 Mich.L.Rev. 1229, 1246, 1248 (1983).

[401]Loewy, 81 Mich.L.Rev. 1229, 1246 (1983).

[402]This point is developed further in § 9.3(f).

[403]Doe v. Renfrow, 475 F.Supp. 1012 (N.D.Ind.1979), aff'd in part 631 F.2d 91 (7th Cir.1980).

[404]Consider, in this regard, State v. Nguyen, 726 N.W.2d 871 (S.D.2007), where records on the use of the drug dog relied upon in that case showed that the dog's handler had conducted 183 searches based on that dog's alerts

but had found controlled substances in only 84 instances. The dog's handler explained these results by noting that when the dog alerts "he is responding to the *odor* of a controlled substance, not its conclusive presence," and that many of the purported "failures" were "later explained by the fact that the person in the car searched was an admitted user or that the person was in the presence of someone who had used drugs."

[405]As stated in Bird, An Examination of the Training and Reliability of the Narcotics Detection Dog, 85 Ky.L.J. 405, 433–34 (1997): "The judiciary should be most skeptical of sniffs conducted in a random, unfocused manner. All but the most carefully planned random sniffs using highly-trained dog teams will likely result in many false detections."

curate as the Court assumed in *Place* then, it might be reasoned, this bears not so much on the question of whether the dog's sniffing is itself a search as it does on the question of whether the dog's "alert" standing alone constitutes probable cause supporting a *real* search of the effects or person to which the dog reacted. By thus focusing upon the probable cause issue, one of two conclusions would be reached: (1) that the "well-trained narcotics detection dog" referred to in *Place* may sometimes be mistaken (as in *Doe*), but nonetheless is sufficiently accurate to provide the degree of probability of contraband[406] needed under the Fourth Amendment probable cause test; or (2) that because of the possible unreliability some independent corroboration is needed, meaning not that the wholesale use of dogs described earlier would be impermissible, but rather that once the dog alerted to a particular container additional investigation disclosing other suspicious circumstances would be necessary before a warrant could issue. While the lower courts[407] and a plurality of the Supreme Court[408] appear to accept the first of these conclusions, it is well to remember that with rare exception[409] the cases have involved situations in which the alert occurred after a pre-existing reasonable suspicion.[410] In any event, acceptance of the latter conclusion would make the *Place* reasoning more convincing, for whether this problem of reliability is seen as one of probable cause or Fourth Amendment intrusion, unquestionably the extent to which there exists a risk of error weakens the Court's claim that "only the presence or absence of narcotics" will be disclosed.

Dissenting in *Illinois v. Caballes*,[411] Justice Souter convincingly argued that because the "infallible dog * * * was a creature of legal fiction," the dog sniff deserves to be characterized as a search in the Fourth Amendment lexicon. As the matter was put in his rather compelling reasoning:

> Once the dog's fallibility is recognized, however, that ends the justification claimed in *Place* for treating the sniff as sui generis under the Fourth Amendment: the sniff alert does not necessarily

---

[406]Courts typically require a higher probability on the question of whether any crime has occurred; see § 3.2(e).

[407]See text following note 364 supra.

[408]In Florida v. Royer, 460 U.S. 491, 103 S.Ct. 1319, 75 L.Ed.2d 229 (1983), the plurality stated: "If [a drug detection dog] had been used, Royer and his luggage could have been momentarily detained while this investigative procedure was carried out. Indeed, it may be that no detention at all would have been necessary. A negative result would have freed Royer in

short order; a positive result would have resulted in his justifiable arrest on probable cause."

[409]See cases in notes 388 through 392 supra.

[410]It is interesting that in one case where this was not so, the court held that a "canine alert, however, does not constitute probable cause in a completely random setting, such as an airport, because of its questionable accuracy." United States v. Galloway, 316 F.3d 624 (6th Cir.2003).

[411]Illinois v. Caballes, 543 U.S. 405, 125 S.Ct. 834, 160 L.Ed.2d 842 (2005), discussed in 9.3(6).

signal hidden contraband, and opening the container or enclosed space whose emanations the dog has sensed will not necessarily reveal contraband or any other evidence of crime. This is not, of course, to deny that a dog's reaction may provide reasonable suspicion, or probable cause, to search the container or enclosure; the Fourth Amendment does not demand certainty of success to justify a search for evidence or contraband. The point is simply that the sniff and alert cannot claim the certainty that *Place* assumed, both in treating the deliberate use of sniffing dogs as sui generis and then taking that characterization as a reason to say they are not searches subject to Fourth Amendment scrutiny. And when that aura of uniqueness disappears, there is no basis in *Place*'s reasoning, and no good reason otherwise, to ignore the actual function that dog sniffs perform. They are conducted to obtain information about the contents of private spaces beyond anything that human senses could perceive, even when conventionally enhanced. The information is not provided by independent third parties beyond the reach of constitutional limitations, but gathered by the government's own officers in order to justify searches of the traditional sort, which may or may not reveal evidence of crime but will disclose anything meant to be kept private in the area searched. Thus in practice the government's use of a trained narcotics dog functions as a limited search to reveal undisclosed facts about private enclosures, to be used to justify a further and complete search of the enclosed area. And given the fallibility of the dog, the sniff is the first step in a process that may disclose "intimate details" without revealing contraband, just as a thermal-imaging device might do, as described in *Kyllo*.[412]

It is extremely important to recognize that the *Place* holding does not validate the use of drug detection dogs in all circumstances. The Court said only "that the particular course of investigation that the agents intended to pursue here—exposure of respondent's luggage, which was located in a public place, to a trained canine—did not constitute a 'search' within the meaning of the Fourth Amendment." For one thing, this means that if an encounter between the dog and a person or object is achieved by

---

[412]See also Blair, Illinois v. Caballes: Love Affair With a Drug-Sniffing Dog. 41 Tulsa L.Rev. 179 (2005); Dery, Who Let the Dogs Out? The Supreme Court Did in Illinois v. Caballes by Placing Absolute Faith in Canine Sniffs,. 58 Rutgers L. Rev. 3778 (2006); Hunt, Calling in the Dogs: Suspicionless Sniff Searches and Reasonable Expectations of Privacy, 56 Case W.Res.L.Rev. 285 (2005); Johnston, Drugs, Dogs, and the Fourth Amendment: An Analysis of Justice Stevens' Opinion in Illinois v. Caballes, 24 QLR 659 (2006); Katz & Golembiewski, Curbing the Dog: Extending the Protection of the Fourth Amend-ment to Police Drug Dogs, 85 Neb.L. Rev. 735, 737–38 (2007) ("The *Place* doctrine is based on three specific principles attributed to a dog sniff that render it 'sui generis': a dog sniff is a minimal intrusion; a dog only sniffs for the presence of contraband; and, by implication, a dog is highly accurate. In fact, a dog sniff fails on all three accounts, rendering the theoretical basis offered by Justice O'Connor meaningless"); Myers, In the Wake of Caballes, Should We Let Sniffing Dogs Lie?, 20 Crim.Just. 4 (Winter, 2006); Myers, Detector Dogs and Probable Cause, 14 Geo.Mason L.Rev. 16 (2006); Note, 39 Loy.L.A.L.Rev. 1471 (2006).

bringing the dog into an area entitled to Fourth Amendment protection, that entry is itself a search subject to constitutional restrictions.[413] For another, it means that if the place is public

---

[413]United States v. Winningham, 140 F.3d 1328 (10th Cir.1998) (where drug dog used on lawfully stopped vehicle jumped through open door and alerted to rear vent therein, this a search; *Stone*, deemed "inapposite" because here, unlike there, "the officers themselves opened the door," making apparent a "desire to *facilitate* a dog sniff of the van's interior"); United States v. Whitehead, 849 F.2d 849 (4th Cir.1988) (bringing dogs into train roomette to smell interior is a search; "*Place* obviously did not sanction the indiscriminate, blanket use of trained dogs in all contexts," and there was Fourth Amendment activity here because "occupants of train roomettes may properly expect some degree of privacy, [albeit] less than the reasonable expectations that individuals rightfully possess in their homes or their hotel rooms"); United States v. DiCesare, 765 F.2d 890 (9th Cir.1985) (concurring opinion reasons that bringing a canine into an apartment to smell at particular occupant's door is a search); People v. Williams, 51 Cal.App.3d 346, 124 Cal.Rptr. 253 (1975) (trainer and dog made unauthorized entry into baggage staging area of American Airlines, not open to the public).

But see United States v. Lyons, 486 F.3d 367 (8th Cir.2007) (where on canine sniff of vehicle dog, on second lap, stuck his head through open window and then alerted, no Fourth Amendment violation, as passenger opened window earlier and no police order to keep window open, and officer "did not direct the dog to stick his head through the window"); United States v. Stone, 866 F.2d 359 (10th Cir.1989) (though "the dog created a troubling issue under the Fourth Amendment when it entered the hatchback," given finding below that dog keyed on the drugs only after he inside the car, "the dog's instinctive actions did not violate the Fourth Amendment. There is no evidence, nor does Stone contend, that

the police asked Stone to open the hatchback so the dog could jump in. Nor is there any evidence the police handler encouraged the dog to jump into the car"). In light of *Stone*, other courts have similarly concluded that the instinctive acts of trained canines, such as trying to open a container containing narcotics, do not violate the Fourth Amendment. United States v. Pierce, 622 F.3d 209 (3d Cir.2010) (after driver left car door open, dog jumped inside and alerted to front seat and glove box, "and in so doing acted instinctively and without facilitation by his handler"); United States v. Vazquez, 555 F.3d 923 (10th Cir.2009) (dog instinctively jumped into vehicle through point of entry police did not ask driver to open); United States v. Olivera-Mendez, 484 F.3d 505 (8th Cir.2007) (fact dog "placed his front paws on the body of the car in several places during a walk-around" not objectionable, as it a "minimal and incidental contact with the exterior of the car" and "not a tactile inspection"); United States v. Reed, 141 F.3d 644 (6th Cir.1998).

Compare United States v. Diaz, 25 F.3d 392 (6th Cir.1994) (use of dog as to vehicle in motel parking lot proper, as defendant motel guest had no expectation of privacy as to the lot); United States v. Gonzalez-Basulto, 898 F.2d 1011 (5th Cir.1990) (though dog and handler hoisted up into trailer of tractor-trailer rig, that search activity fell within consent of driver to inspection of trailer, as driver knew such dogs on scene and being used); Commonwealth v. Welch, 420 Mass. 646, 651 N.E.2d 392 (1995) (bringing dog into fire department's "common room, shared by the various officers on duty," where dog alerted to defendant's locker, no search; court stresses defendant had limited expectation of privacy because "he shared the room in common with others who were as free to come and go and use the room as he was").

but the encounter can be accomplished only by a temporary seizure of the person or object,[414] then the encounter will again be constitutionally impermissible, unless there are *Terry-Place* grounds for such a seizure[415] or it is otherwise permissible under a *Delaware v. Prouse*[416] standardized procedure approach[417] or

---

[414]Compare B.C. v. Plumas Unified School District, 192 F.3d 1260 (9th Cir.1999) (requiring high school students to leave classroom for 10 minutes while their effects therein sniffed by drug dog no seizure, as "a student is required to be on school premises, subject to the direction of school authorities, during the course of the schoolday").

[415]United States v. Eura, 440 F.3d 625 (4th Cir.2006) (court assumes, unnecessarily it would seem, that a temporary seizure was involved in having dog sniff vehicle parked on street in front of residence where search warrant executed, and thus upholds sniff only after concluding reasonable suspicion existed); United States v. Duffaut, 314 F.3d 203 (5th Cir.2002) (where vehicle lawfully stopped for traffic violation, "walking around it with a drug-sniffing dog" no search); United States v. $404,905.00 in U.S. Currency, 182 F.3d 643 (8th Cir.1999) (where stop was for traffic violation, the 2-minute canine sniff of truck and U-Haul trailer "was a *de minimis* intrusion" not amounting to a search); United States v. Glinton, 154 F.3d 1245 (11th Cir.1998) (dog sniff of vehicle after it stopped on reasonable suspicion no search); United States v. Stone, 866 F.2d 359 (10th Cir.1989) ("police may employ a narcotic dog to sniff an automobile which they have stopped upon reasonable suspicion to believe it contains narcotics"); People v. Esparza, 272 P.3d 367 (Colo.2012) (no search where drug dog alerted to defendant's vehicle after his lawful arrest for driving under suspension); State v. Bergmann, 633 N.W.2d 328 (Iowa 2001) (re traffic stop, "all that we have required in Iowa is that the dog sniff be conducted within a reasonable amount of time from the initial, lawful stop and that the stop is not unduly prolonged"; such the case here, as "the dog sniff occurred no more than a few

minutes after Bergmann was pulled over," and there were "facts which support the reasonableness of expanding the scope of the stop to wait for a drug dog to arrive"); State v. Aguilar, 809 N.W.2d 285 (N.D.2011) (dog sniff of vehicle no search, as driver lawfully arrested for traffic offense); State v. England, 19 S.W.3d 762 (Tenn.2000) (*Place* applies "in the context of canine sweeps around the perimeter of a legally detained vehicle");Crockett v. State, 803 S.W.2d 308 (Tex.Crim.App. 1991) (canine sniff of defendant's carried luggage tainted by stop of defendant without reasonable suspicion).

Compare State v. Wiegand, 645 N.W.2d 125 (Minn.2002) (notwithstanding agreement that "a dog sniff around the exterior of a motor vehicle located in a public place is not a search requiring probable cause," court construes reasonableness requirement of Fourth Amendment and state constitutional equivalent "to limit the scope of a *Terry* investigation to that which occasioned the stop," so that, even where as in the instant case the stop was *not* "extended in duration beyond that which would have been necessary to issue the warning ticket," a dog sniff, which constitutes at least "some intrusion into privacy interests," is permissible following a traffic stop *only* upon "a reasonable, articulable suspicion of drug-related criminal activity"). Cf. People v. Haley, 41 P.3d 666 (Colo. 2001) (under *state* constitution, "a dog sniff of a person's automobile in connection with a traffic stop that is prolonged beyond its purpose to conduct a drug investigation intrudes upon a reasonable expectation of privacy and constitutes a search").

[416]Delaware v. Prouse, 440 U.S. 648, 99 S.Ct. 1391, 59 L.Ed.2d 660 (1979).

[417]United States v. Hernandez, 976 F.2d 929 (5th Cir.1992) (use of dog at border patrol checkpoint "does not

some other theory.[418] In that connection, it is well to note that the use of a drug sniffing dog against a person or effects in possession of a person may itself be an important consideration in determining that an illegal seizure had occurred and that the dog sniff is a fruit thereof.[419]

Moreover, even if there has been no search into a protected area and no seizure of a person or container, there *still* may be instances in which utilization of the dogs is properly subject to

---

constitute a search"); United States v. Dovali-Avila, 895 F.2d 206 (5th Cir.1990) (same).

Compare United States v. Morales-Zamora, 914 F.2d 200 (10th Cir.1990) (use of dogs at driver's license and vehicle registration check roadblock no search, *but* case remanded for consideration of defendant's argument that their detention "at the roadblock was an unlawful seizure because the roadblock's stated purpose was a pretext for searching the stopped vehicles for drugs").

Even a broader objection was stated in United States v. Beale, 674 F.2d 1327 (9th Cir.1982), asserting that "it goes without saying that the alternative to random checkpoint stops cited in *Delaware v. Prouse*, i.e., '[q]uestioning . . . all incoming traffic at roadblock-type stops,' * * * is totally unpalatable in the canine sniffing context. Nothing would invoke the specter of a totalitarian police state as much as the indiscriminate, blanket use of trained dogs at roadblocks, airports, and train stations. * * * Similarly, the use of dogs to sniff people, rather than objects, is highly intrusive and is normally inconsistent with the concepts embodied in our Constitution. We would not preclude, however, the use of a trained canine who sniffs from a distance as an alternative where a more intrusive strip search or search of the body cavities is justified." This dictum was not specifically addressed on rehearing, 736 F.2d 1289 (9th Cir.1984).

[418]United States v. Engles, 481 F.3d 1243 (10th Cir.2007) (reasonable suspicion not needed for dog sniff of vehicle, as vehicle had been parked in restaurant parking lot by defendant at time of traffic stop resulting his arrest

for driving while under suspension, as "an officer who later came upon the scene could have employed a dog to sniff the exterior of the vehicle"); United States v. Rodriguez-Morales, 929 F.2d 780 (1st Cir.1991) (no search to use dog on vehicle seized as a result of reasonable discretionary police action under "community caretaking function"); State v. Cleave, 131 N.M. 82, 33 P.3d 633 (2001) (after lawful stopping of vehicle at Border Patrol interior checkpoint, defendant consented to allow agent to "look in" or "inspect" trunk, but after defendant opened trunk an agent approached with a narcotics dog, who alerted to the trunk; lower court's holding this an illegal search because it outside the scope of the consent rejected; "the scope of consent is not an issue in this case because the use of the dog was not a Fourth Amendment search").

Compare State v. Carlson, 302 Mont. 508, 15 P.3d 893 (2000) (use of dog on van parked on another's property fruit of illegal seizure, as occupants of van, who had offered to drive van off the property of complainant, were detained for half an hour awaiting arrival of drug dog).

[419]United States v. Buchanon, 72 F.3d 1217 (6th Cir.1995) (where police brought out drug dog to sniff vehicles already parked by side of road, that turned encounter with defendants into a seizure for which grounds here lacking; "the drug sniff is more coercive than police questioning of a citizen in a place where he or she may easily leave the police presence because a person who wants to end the canine sniff has to either 1) remove their personal property from the presence of the dog, or 2) has to convince the police to stop their actions").

Fourth Amendment restraints even after *Place*. In that case, it is well to recall, the court addressed only the situation of exposure of luggage to the dog in the suspect's absence. What then if the agents, anticipating Place's arrival, had simply been standing by with a drug detection dog and, when Place paused momentarily in the corridor, had confronted him with the dog who reacted positively? Or what if, as in *Doe,* the tactic is exposure of the dog to people only, rather than only containers (as in *Place*) or people carrying containers (as in the hypothetical just put)? Such practices are not covered by the *Place* holding[420] nor by the many lower court cases allowing use of these dogs for "the sniffing of inanimate and unattended objects rather than persons,"[421] and might well require a different result.[422] Certainly "the very act of being subjected to a body sniff by a German Shepherd may be of-

---

[420]Shortly after *Place* was decided, the Court refused to hear an appeal by a Texas school district from the ruling in Horton v. Goose Creek Independent School District, 690 F.2d 470 (5th Cir.1982), that use of specially trained dogs to sniff students in class was a search. 463 U.S. 1207, 103 S.Ct. 3536, 77 L.Ed.2d 1387 (1983). Also noteworthy is the fact that when the Supreme Court concluded in City of Indianapolis v. Edmond, 531 U.S. 32, 121 S.Ct. 447, 148 L.Ed.2d 333 (2000), that *Place* was applicable to the use of dogs at a drug checkpoint, explaining that "a sniff by a dog that simply walks around a car" is "much less intrusive than a typical search," the Court followed that statement with a "cf." citation to United States v. Turpin, 920 F.2d 1377 (8th Cir.1990), a case noting the various judicial views regarding whether use of a dog directly against a person is a search.

Some of the post-*Place* lower court decisions have emphasized that the use of dogs in the case at hand did not involve the sniffing of persons or luggage carried by persons. United States v. Beale, 736 F.2d 1289 (9th Cir.1984); State v. Snitkin, 67 Haw. 168, 681 P.2d 980 (1984). But see United States v. Dovali-Avila, 895 F.2d 206 (5th Cir.1990) (use of dog on vehicle lawfully stopped at checkpoint deemed no search, though defendant seated in vehicle at the time).

[421]Brennan, J., dissenting from denial of certiorari, Doe v. Renfrow, 451 U.S. 1022, 101 S.Ct. 3015, 69 L.Ed.2d 395 (1981).

Consider in this regard a case holding otherwise under the *state* constitution, State v. Tackitt, 315 Mont. 59, 67 P.3d 295 (2003) (reaffirming earlier state court decision it no search to use drug dog on checked luggage, but now concluding the result otherwise as to defendant's parked but unoccupied car, as he "had a reasonable expectation of privacy in the enclosed and concealed space of his vehicle [which] is in no way dependent on where his vehicle was parked"). See also State v. Hart, 320 Mont. 154, 85 P.3d 1275 (2004) (applying *Tackitt* to dog sniff of vehicle incident to stopping of vehicle to serve arrest warrant on motorist).

[422]United States v. Kelly, 302 F.3d 291 (5th Cir.2002) (where defendant was "subjected to a canine sniff of his person, including a brief touching of his groin area," that "was a Fourth Amendment search," albeit a lawful border search, as defendant was at the time crossing an international bridge from Mexico to U.S.); B.C. v. Plumas Unified School District, 192 F.3d 1260 (9th Cir.1999) (court holds that it was a search for a drug-sniffing dog to sniff high school students as they were directed to exit and then reenter their classroom, relying on Horton v. Goose Creek Independent School District, 690 F.2d 470 (5th Cir.1982)).

Compare United States v. Reyes, 349 F.3d 219 (5th Cir.2003) (noting that "*Horton* and *Plumas* emphasize the 'close proximity' of the sniff, an el-

fensive at best or harrowing at worst" even "to the innocent sniffee,"[423] and a sniff directed at objects being carried by the person is no less objectionable, especially when done in an airport corridor in circumstances amounting to a public accusation of crime.[424] (The Supreme Court's decision in *Illinois v. Caballes*,[425] concluding there was no search in that case, where a "dog sniff was performed on the exterior of respondent's car while he was lawfully seized for a traffic violation," hardly settles the matter, for at the time of the dog sniff Caballes was neither seated in his car nor standing adjacent thereto, but instead was seated in the patrol car with the officer who had stopped him.)

Perhaps these investigative activities do not involve an intrusion into privacy or possession or freedom of movement, the interests traditionally protected by the Fourth Amendment. But such cases as *Place* and *Terry* suggest that there are other interests also deserving such protection. In *Place,* allowing use of the dogs on luggage not then in the suspect's possession, it was emphasized that the practice lacked the "embarrassment * * * entailed in less discriminate and more intrusive investigative methods." And in *Terry* the Court stressed that the Fourth Amendment imposes upon courts the "responsibility to guard against police conduct which is overbearing or harassing." The kind of confrontation under discussion here—which, again, was not present in *Place*—is embarrassing, overbearing and harassing, and thus should be subject to Fourth Amendment restraints.

Yet another possible use of these specially trained canines is to discover the presence of contraband inside private premises. Such was the case in *United States v. Thomas*,[426] concerning a search warrant obtained on the basis of a canine sniff outside a certain apartment indicating the presence of narcotics inside. The court held the warrant was based upon information acquired in an illegal search.[427] After noting that in the analogous area of use of beepers the Supreme Court had distinguished between their use to ascertain the presence of objects inside premises from their use to track vehicles on the road,[428] the court reasoned:

Thus, a practice that is not intrusive in a public airport may be

---

ement not present in this case," in that defendant was "approximately four to five feet away from the dog" when he and all other passengers exited the bus, so "the sniff does not constitute a search" in this case).

[423]Loewy, 81 Mich.L.Rev. 1229, 1246–47 (1983).

[424]But in Merrett v. Moore, 58 F.3d 1547 (11th Cir.1995), involving dog sniffing of occupied vehicles lawfully stopped at a roadblock, the plaintiff's argument "that the Court's hold-

ing in *Place* should be limited to sniffs of unattended property" was rejected.

[425]Illinois v. Caballes, 543 U.S. 405, 125 S.Ct. 834, 160 L.Ed.2d 842 (2005), discussed in § 9.3(b).

[426]United States v. Thomas, 757 F.2d 1359 (2d Cir.1985).

[427]However, the evidence was deemed admissible nonetheless under the *Leon* "good faith" rule, discussed in § 1.3.

[428]See § 2.7(f).

intrusive when employed at a person's home. Although using a dog sniff for narcotics may be discriminating and unoffensive relative to other detection methods, and will disclose only the presence or absence of narcotics, * * * it remains a way of detecting the contents of a private, enclosed space. With a trained dog police may obtain information about what is inside a dwelling that they could not derive from the use of their own senses. Consequently, the officers' use of a dog is not a mere improvement of their sense of smell, as ordinary eye glasses improve vision, but is a significant enhancement accomplished by a different, and far superior, sensory instrument. Here the defendant had a legitimate expectation that the contents of his closed apartment would remain private, that they could not be "sensed" from outside his door. Use of the trained dog impermissibly intruded upon that legitimate expectation. The Supreme Court in *Place* found only "that the particular course of investigation that the agents intended to pursue here—exposure of respondent's luggage, which was located in a public place, to a trained canine—did not constitute a 'search' within the meaning of the Fourth Amendment." * * * Because of defendant Wheelings' heightened expectation of privacy inside his dwelling, the canine sniff at his door constituted a search.[429]

---

[429]See also People v. Wieser, 796 P.2d 982 (Colo.1990) (court divided 4-3 in favor of view that dog sniff from public walkway outside rented locker in storage facility intruded upon defendant's justified expectation of privacy, but majority concludes either no search or search on reasonable suspicion); Jardines v. State, 73 So.3d 34 (Fla.2011) ("a 'sniff test' by a drug detection dog conducted at a private residence does not *only* reveal the presence of contraband, * * * but it also constitutes an intrusive procedure that may expose the resident to public opprobrium, humiliation and embarrassment, and it raises the specter of arbitrary and discriminatory application," and thus "is a substantial government intrusion into the sanctity of the home and constitutes a 'search' within the meaning of the Fourth Amendment"); State v. Davis, 732 N.W.2d 173 (Minn.2007) (under *state* constitution dog sniff outside defendant's apartment door but in common hallway is a search); State v. Ortiz, 257 Neb. 784, 600 N.W.2d 805 (1999) ("an individual's Fourth Amendment privacy interests may extend in a limited manner beyond the four walls of the home, depending on the facts, including the expectation of privacy to be free from police canine sniffs for il-

legal drugs in the hallway outside an apartment or at the threshold of a residence, and [thus] a canine sniff under these circumstances must be based on no less than reasonable, articulable suspicion"); People v. Dunn, 77 N.Y.2d 19, 563 N.Y.S.2d 388, 564 N.E.2d 1054 (1990) (use of dogs to sniff drugs within apartment a search under *state* law, as to hold otherwise "would raise the specter of the police roaming indiscriminately through the corridors of public housing projects with trained dogs in search of drugs"); Commonwealth v. Johnston, 515 Pa. 454, 530 A.2d 74 (1987) (requiring, as a matter of *state* constitutional law, that there be reasonable suspicion for a dog sniffing at the door of a rented space in a warehouse entered with the landlord's consent); Lunney, Has the Fourth Amendment Gone to the Dogs? Unreasonable Expansion of Canine Sniff Doctrine to Include Sniffs of the Home, 88 Or.L.Rev. 829 (2009) (arguing such use of dogs a seizure); MacDonnell, Orwellian Ramifications: The Contraband Exception to the Fourth Amendment, 41 U.Mem.L.Rev. 299 (2010); Comment, 11 Loy.J.Publ.Int.L. 131, 132 (2009) (concluding "a dog sniff at the threshold of our home constitutes a search within the meaning of the Fourth Amendment"). Contra: Brown v. United States, 627 A.2d 499

Thomas was questioned and distinguished in *United States v. Colyer*,[430] where a drug dog in the public corridor of a train "alerted" to a particular sleeper compartment and thus indicated the presence of drugs therein. The court first concluded the mere fact the dog revealed contraband was within the compartment did not make the sniff a search, as "*Place* and *Jacobsen*[431] stand for the proposition that a possessor of contraband can maintain no legitimate expectation that its presence will not be revealed." Thus the court turned to the other reasoning in *Place*, which stressed the unobtrusive manner in which the information was obtained without embarrassment or inconvenience to the owner of the luggage. This was equally true here, the court reasoned, as though the defendant was within the roomette at the time of the sniff the dog's actions were not then even known to him, and thus there did not exist the threatening circumstances that arguably would distinguish from *Place* a direct sniffing of a person. As for *Thomas*, it was distinguished on the ground that it involved the "heightened privacy interest" one has in his dwelling. A roomette in a train, the *Colyer* court reasoned, is more analogous to an automobile[432] than to a home.[433] Finally, *Colyer* questioned the correctness of *Thomas* on two grounds: (i) the *Thomas* court's as-

---

(D.C.App.1993); State v. Taylor, 763 S.W.2d 756 (Tenn.Crim.App.1988).

Compare United States v. Hayes, 551 F.3d 138 (2d Cir.2008) (*Thomas* distinguished where contents of bag smelled by dog was in scrub brush located 65 ft. from defendant's back door and bordering an adjacent property, and dog first alerted while in front yard); United States v. Brock, 417 F.3d 692 (7th Cir.2005) (dog sniff outside locked door of bedroom rented by defendant not a search where police had obtained consent of suspect's housemate to enter common areas); United States v. Esquilin, 208 F.3d 315 (1st Cir.2000) (where occupant of motel room consented to entry by officer and dog so that officer could question him, but person then said they could look around to ensure he had no drugs there, dog's opening of bag in response to command to "find the dope" no search); Commonwealth v. Welch, 420 Mass. 646, 651 N.E.2d 392 (1995) (discussed in note 413 supra); State v. Slowikowski, 307 Or. 19, 761 P.2d 1315 (1988) (police were "testing" dogs at storage facility with permission of owner by placing drugs in unused locker, but dog alerted to a rented locker; held, no search because

the dog's discovery was not "the result of a purposive intrusion into the defendant's privacy" because it was unexpected).

Other cases are collected in State v. Guillen, 223 Ariz. 314, 223 P.3d 658 (2010).

[430]United States v. Colyer, 878 F.2d 469 (D.C.Cir.1989).

[431]The reference is to United States v. Jacobsen, 466 U.S. 109, 104 S.Ct. 1652, 80 L.Ed.2d 85 (1984), discussed in § 1.8(b).

[432]See City of Indianapolis v. Edmond, 531 U.S. 32, 121 S.Ct. 447, 148 L.Ed.2d 333 (2000); United States v. Massie, 65 F.3d 843 (10th Cir.1995) (dog sniff of vehicle at border patrol fixed checkpoint no search); Merrett v. Moore, 58 F.3d 1547 (11th Cir.1995) (dog sniff of vehicle lawfully stopped at roadblock no search); United States v. Friend, 50 F.3d 548 (8th Cir.1995) (just as "a dog sniff of a car parked on a public street or alley" is no search, same true where car parked on defendant's property but not within curtilage); United States v. Ludwig, 10 F.3d 1523 (10th Cir.1993) (dog sniff of vehicle parked in motel parking lot no search, as only contraband revealed).

sertion the defendant there had a legitimate expectation the contents of his apartment would remain private was said to be contrary to the *Place-Jacobsen* indication that a possessor of contraband has no legitimate expectation that its presence will not be revealed; and (ii) the *Thomas* court's reliance on the beeper cases was said to be incorrect, for the beepers were used to reveal the location (not contents) of containers known to contain a noncontraband substance.[434] The issue is highlighted by *Kyllo v.*

---

[433]Accord: United States v. Trayer, 898 F.2d 805 (D.C.Cir.1990); United States v. Tartaglia, 864 F.2d 837 (D.C. Cir.1989); United States v. Whitehead, 849 F.2d 849 (4th Cir.1988).

Consider also United States v. Garcia, 42 F.3d 604 (10th Cir.1994) (relying on *Colyer*, court holds dog sniff of luggage in train's baggage car no search; court collects other cases which "have determined that a dog sniff in a baggage area does not constitute a search for Fourth Amendment purposes").

Similarly, in State v. Phaneuf, 597 A.2d 55 (Me.1991), involving use of a dog to sniff first-class mail, the court rejected defendant's "contention that the fourth amendment creates a *heightened* expectation of privacy in the mail akin to that in one's domicile."

[434]See also United States v. Scott, 610 F.3d 1009 (8th Cir.2010) (dog's "sniff of the apartment door frame from a common hallway did not constitute a search"); United States v. Reed, 141 F.3d 644 (6th Cir.1998) (*Thomas* rejected; court holds that where police dog entered apartment to search for intruder but instead alerted to drugs, such was no search in light of fact that "the canine team was lawfully present" therein); United States v. Roby, 122 F.3d 1120 (8th Cir.1997) (*Thomas* position rejected; court holds "a trained dog's detection of odor in a common corridor [of a motel] does not contravene the Fourth Amendment"); United States v. Lingenfelter, 997 F.2d 632 (9th Cir.1993) (no search where drug dog in public alleyway smelled marijuana in nearby warehouse; "because *Thomas* rests on an incorrect statement of the law, we expressly reject its reasoning"); People v. Guenther, 225 Ill.App.3d 574, 167 Ill.Dec. 705, 588 N.E.2d 346 (1992) (officer lawfully in premises to arrest could threaten to bring in drug dog to determine presence of marijuana there, as such "a canine sniff does not constitute a search"; court relies on *Dunn* analysis); Fitzgerald v. State, 384 Md. 484, 864 A.2d 1006 (2004) (where dog and handler "lawfully were present, as the apartment building's common area and hallways were accessible to the public through an entrance of unlocked glass doors," dog sniff of drugs in apartment no search); State v. Carter, 697 N.W.2d 199 (Minn.2005), discussed in Bond & Gaitas, State v. Carter: The Minnesota Constitution Protects Against Random and Suspicionless Dog Sniffs of Storage Units, 32 Wm.Mitchell L.Rev. 1287 (2006), and Note, Ga.L.Rev. 1209 (2006) (collecting cases in accord, court holds "that a dog sniff outside a storage unit is not a search under the Fourth Amendment," but emphasizing "that the expectation of privacy under the Fourth Amendment is less for a storage unit than for a home"); People v. Dunn, 77 N.Y.2d 19, 563 N.Y.S.2d 388, 564 N.E.2d 1054 (1990) (use of dogs in apartment hallway a state search but not a federal search; *Thomas* "unpersuasive," as the "distinction it relies upon, namely, the heightened expectation of privacy that a person has in his residence, is irrelevant under the *Place* rationale"); State v. Smith, 327 Or. 366, 963 P.2d 642 (1998) (*Thomas* is "questionable law" and in any event "irrelevant to the present facts," which "more closely resembled the circumstances in *Lingenfelter*, i.e., a sniff of the exterior of a warehouse").

United States,[435] holding use of a thermal imager to acquire "any information regarding the interior of the home" was a search, where the dissenters unfairly criticized the majority for not resolving just where that rule stops and *Place* starts.[436]

Assuming now that *some* uses of these dogs constitutes a search, it does not inevitably follow that they should be encumbered by the restrictions ordinarily applicable to other types of searches clearly more intrusive in character. While it has sometimes been asserted that if the use of trained dogs is a search then such surveillance is unconstitutional if "conducted in absence of a warrant supported by probable cause,"[437] it may be argued that the Fourth Amendment does not demand such a result. In *Terry v. Ohio*,[438] the Court upheld a limited warrantless search made upon less than full probable cause "by balancing the need to search [or seize] against the invasion which the search [or seizure] entails," and thus a similar approach might be taken as to the kind of search here under discussion.[439] Although there are sound reasons for not employing too generously "a graduated model of the fourth amendment,"[440] the notion that searches by use of dogs trained to detect narcotics or explosives is a lesser

---

[435]Kyllo v. United States, 533 U.S. 27, 121 S.Ct. 2038, 150 L.Ed.2d 94 (2001).

[436]See § 2.2(d) at note 252.

Compare United States v. Scott, 610 F.3d 1009 (8th Cir.2010) ("[u]nlike the thermal imaging technology at issue in *Kyllo*, narcotics dog sniffs are not 'capable of detecting lawful activity,'" so dog sniff at apartment door no search); State v. Bergmann, 633 N.W.2d 328 (Iowa 2001) (concerning use of a drug dog to discover drugs in a vehicle rather than a home, where the court concluded that *Kyllo* "does not disturb the nearly twenty years of precedent regarding dog sniffs and vehicles," but also that "a drug sniffing dog is not 'technology' of the type addressed in *Kyllo*"); Fitzgerald v. State, 384 Md. 484, 864 A.2d 1006 (2004) (*Kyllo* "does not apply to dog sniffs," as "a dog is not technology," is not "advancing technology," and "dog sniffs are unique in their narrow yes/no determination of the presence of a narcotic"); with State v. Wiegand, 645 N.W.2d 125 (Minn.2002) (in case involving dog sniff of vehicle, court observes: "While *Kyllo* involved both the home and a piece of technical equipment much different from a dog, its reasoning suggests that a dog sniff

of a home might lead a court to conclude that a search requiring probable cause took place"). See also Note, 26 Seattle U.L.Rev. 337 (2002), on "rethinking canine sniffs" in light of *Kyllo*.

[437]United States v. Solis, 393 F.Supp. 325 (C.D.Cal.1975), rev'd, 536 F.2d 880 (9th Cir.1976).

[438]Terry v. Ohio, 392 U.S. 1, 88 S.Ct. 1868, 20 L.Ed.2d 889 (1968).

[439]See Note, 1977 U.Ill.L.F. 1167, 1201. This theory is helpfully set out in detail in Peebles, The Uninvited Canine Nose and the Right to Privacy: Some Thoughts on Katz and Dogs, 11 Ga.L.Rev. 75, 98–104 (1976). See also State v. Wiegand, 645 N.W.2d 125 (Minn.2002) (relying on "*Terry* principles" to require reasonable suspicion of drug-related criminality re vehicle stopped for traffic violation, and noting the parties have not "pointed to any state or federal court that has required probable cause for the use of a drug-sniffing dog on a vehicle, whether based on the U.S. or a state constitution").

[440]I.e., that it would convert "the fourth amendment into one immense Rorschach blot." Amsterdam, Perspectives on the Fourth Amendment, 58 Minn.L.Rev. 349, 393 (1974). See also id. at 374–77.

intrusion subject to lesser Fourth Amendment restrictions is an appealing one. This is because this particular investigative technique is a distinct police practice which quite obviously is much less intrusive than other searches.[441] It seems rather unlikely, however, that the Supreme Court would now reach such a conclusion.[442] The Court has declared that the Fourth Amendment knows no search but a "full-blown search,"[443] asserted that *Terry* provides no support for "any search whatever for anything but weapons,"[444] and cautioned that the balancing process is appropriate only when warranted by "special needs beyond the normal need for law enforcement."[445]

Some lower courts, however, have held[446] that a search conducted by using a canine nose to detect contraband is permissible provided the police had a "founded suspicion"[447] or "reasonable suspicion,"[448] based upon articulable facts, that contraband

---

[441]See State v. Pellicci, 133 N.H. 523, 580 A.2d 710 (1990) (adopting this position as a matter of state constitutional law).

[442]See United States v. Colyer, 878 F.2d 469 (D.C.Cir.1989), for a helpful discussion of this point. See also Jardines v. State, 73 So.3d 34 (Fla.2011) (agreeing with analysis in text following and noting that "the parties in the present case have failed to point to a single case in which the United States Supreme Court has indicated that a search for evidence for use in a criminal prosecution, absent special needs beyond the normal needs of law enforcement, may be based on anything other than probable cause").

[443]Arizona v. Hicks, 480 U.S. 321, 107 S.Ct. 1149, 94 L.Ed.2d 347 (1987).

[444]Ybarra v. Illinois, 444 U.S. 85, 100 S.Ct. 338, 62 L.Ed.2d 238 (1979).

[445]Skinner v. Railway Labor Executives' Ass'n, 489 U.S. 602, 109 S.Ct. 1402, 103 L.Ed.2d 639 (1989).

In a "special needs" case, of course, whether the balancing will permit the dog sniffs upon less than an individualized suspicion depends upon the weight of the competing interests. See, e.g., B.C. v. Plumas Unified School District, 192 F.3d 1260 (9th Cir.1999) (sniffing of persons of high school students was unlawful, as it was "highly intrusive" because "the body and its odors are highly per-

sonal," and there was no "drug problem or crisis" at that high school necessitating suspicionless sniffing).

[446]These cases, in the main, predate *Place* and thus sometimes involve the kinds of uses of these dogs not constituting a search under that decision.

[447]United States v. Solis, 536 F.2d 880 (9th Cir.1976); Mata v. State, 380 So.2d 1157 (Fla.App.1980).

[448]United States v. Klein, 626 F.2d 22 (7th Cir.1980) (noting this "not a case in which we need confront this thorny problem of an indiscriminate dragnet-type sniffing expedition," as here the "authorities already had a reasonable suspicion to believe that the luggage contained contraband"); People v. Boylan, 854 P.2d 807 (Colo. 1993) (under state constitution, "a dog-sniff search need be justified * * * by reasonable suspicion"); State v. Waz, 240 Conn. 365, 692 A.2d 1217 (1997), noted at 19 QLR 625 (2000) (assuming canine sniff a search under state constitution, this "requires no more than a showing that the investigating officers had a reasonable and articulable suspicion that the parcel contained contraband"); Fitzgerald v. State, 384 Md. 484, 864 A.2d 1006 (2004) (assuming without deciding that dog sniffing of drugs in apartment a search under state constitution, it lawful because the "police had reasonable suspicion"); State v. Davis, 732 N.W.2d 173 (Minn.

was present within the object to which the animal was directed.[449] Several other cases, although appearing to uphold the practice upon some broader basis, are consistent upon their facts, for they indicate that the approved surveillance was actually undertaken upon a reasonable suspicion.[450] And a few other cases, though not

---

2007) (reasonable suspicion basis even for dog sniff outside defendant's apartment door but in common hallway; *Kyllo* distinguished because device there used "capable of detecting lawful as well as unlawful activity"); State v. Carter, 697 N.W.2d 199 (Minn.2005) (reasonable suspicion required under *state* constitution to sniff rented self-storage unit); State v. Meza, 333 Mont. 305, 143 P.3d 422 (2006) (canine sniff a search under state constitution, but permissible here because of particularized suspicion); to public a search under state constitution, but permissible on reasonable suspicion); State v. Ortiz, 257 Neb. 784, 600 N.W.2d 805 (1999) (under Fourth Amendment, "before a drug-detecting canine can be deployed to test the threshold of a home, the officers must possess at a minimum reasonable, articulable suspicion"); Latham v. State, 97 Nev. 279, 629 P.2d 780 (1981) (use of dog pursuant to warrant lawful when affidavit showed this not "an indiscriminate canine exploratory search" but rather a case in which "the dog was used as corroboration of the suspicions or preknowledge of the police"); People v. Dunn, 77 N.Y.2d 19, 563 N.Y.S.2d 388, 564 N.E.2d 1054 (1990) (per *state* constitution, it necessary "police have a reasonable suspicion that a residence contains illicit contraband"); State v. Elkins, 47 Ohio App.2d 307, 354 N.E.2d 716 (1976); Commonwealth v. Rogers, 578 Pa. 127, 849 A.2d 1185 (2004) (sniffing exterior of car stopped for traffic violation requires reasonable suspicion).

See also Doe v. Renfrow, 475 F.Supp. 1012 (N.D.Ind.1979), aff'd in part 631 F.2d 91 (7th Cir.1980), stressing the diminished expectation of privacy of high school students in upholding use of such dogs to detect drugs on students while the students were in their classes. The court said that while the officials had no infor-

mation about specific students, there was sufficient suspicion regarding the student body generally because of the extensive list of previous drug use within the school.

Compare Commonwealth v. Martin, 534 Pa. 136, 626 A.2d 556 (1993) (but where canine search of a person, full probable cause required).

[449] Actually, in some instances the dog may be directed to a group of objects, e.g., all the luggage unloaded from a particular flight, because there is a reasonable suspicion as to some of the luggage. See, e.g., United States v. Bronstein, 521 F.2d 459 (2d Cir.1975) (dog walked by conveyor belt containing about 50 pieces of luggage, alerted to two suitcases).

[450] United States v. Bronstein, 521 F.2d 459 (2d Cir.1975) (stressing that the dog "was not employed in a dragnet operation directed against all flight passengers but rather on the basis of reliable information that reasonably triggered the surveillance employed here"); United States v. Fulero, 498 F.2d 748 (D.C.Cir.1974) (dog used only after bus depot employee reported suspicious circumstances and officer detected smell of moth balls, frequently used to conceal odor of marijuana, emanating from footlockers); State v. Martinez, 26 Ariz.App. 210, 547 P.2d 62 (1976) (dog alerted to car stopped on reasonable suspicion it involved in narcotics traffic); People v. Furman, 30 Cal.App.3d 454, 106 Cal.Rptr. 366 (1973) (dog used to check airline passenger's luggage after narcotics agent received information from reliable informant that defendant might be in possession of narcotics); State v. Goodley, 381 So.2d 1180 (Fla.App.1980) (no search, but alternative holding is that defendant's furtive actions at airport made it a lawful search on reasonable suspicion); People v. Campbell, 67 Ill.2d 308, 10 Ill.Dec. 340, 367 N.E.2d 949 (1977)

treating the use of trained dogs as a search or requiring a reasonable suspicion, indicate that such activity will not be upheld if engaged in indiscriminately.[451]

Although these cases also take the position that the police are under no obligation to obtain a search warrant before utilizing trained dogs to make a search,[452] it is less than apparent that this is correct. The no-warrant conclusion is not an inevitable consequence of the fact that a lesser quantum of evidence will suffice, for surely this lesser standard could be made the basis upon which warrants for this purpose would issue.[453] Indeed, it could be argued with some force that the risk of police error is greater when something other than the usual probable cause standard is applied, so that there is even more reason to have the neutral and detached judgment of a magistrate in this context.[454] Nor can the no-warrant conclusion be explained on the ground that trained dogs are almost always used in exigent circumstances, for the facts of the cases show that this is not true.[455] Also unavailable is the contention that the warrant clause does not extend to searches of personal effects outside the home, for this claim was rejected by the Supreme Court in *United States v. Chadwick*.[456]

Chadwick notwithstanding, an argument might be made that the warrant process should not be extended to such minimal

---

(suspicious circumstances telephoned to police by other law enforcement agents; court says that the "use of trained dogs as a follow-up investigative technique to partially corroborate information received is, in our judgment, a useful, entirely reasonable and permissible procedure"); People v. Price, 54 N.Y.2d 557, 446 N.Y.S.2d 906, 431 N.E.2d 267 (1981) (used on luggage of suspected drug courier); State v. Rogers, 43 N.C.App. 475, 259 S.E.2d 572 (1979) (dog alerted to safety deposit box of person suspected of being involved in narcotics traffic).

[451]United States v. McCranie, 703 F.2d 1213 (10th Cir.1983) ("authorities must have some suspicion luggage contains contraband before it can be sniffed"); State v. Groves, 65 Haw. 104, 649 P.2d 366 (1982) (court says it "will not condone the use of these dogs on general exploratory searches or for indiscriminate dragnet-type searches").

[452]But see Commonwealth v. Martin, 534 Pa. 136, 626 A.2d 556 (1993) (where canine search is of a person, a search warrant is required, but suspect may be detained a reason-

able time while warrant sought).

[453]Cf. Camara v. Municipal Court, 387 U.S. 523, 87 S.Ct. 1727, 18 L.Ed.2d 930 (1967) (search warrant ordinarily required for safety inspection of premises notwithstanding fact usual probable cause standard not applicable).

[454]Cf. Davis v. Mississippi, 394 U.S. 721, 89 S.Ct. 1394, 22 L.Ed.2d 676 (1969) (dictum that suspect could be detained for fingerprinting on less than full probable cause, but that a warrant would be needed in such a case notwithstanding fact no warrant generally needed to make custodial arrest on full probable cause).

[455]E.g., United States v. Venema, 563 F.2d 1003 (10th Cir.1977) (dogs used at storage locker day following observation of suspect there); People v. Campbell, 67 Ill.2d 308, 10 Ill.Dec. 340, 367 N.E.2d 949 (1977) (information received by telephone 2½ hours before scheduled time of flight on which defendant due to arrive).

[456]United States v. Chadwick, 433 U.S. 1, 97 S.Ct. 2476, 53 L.Ed.2d 538 (1977).

privacy invasions as the use of trained dogs to sniff out drugs or explosives. Use of the warrant process to deal with police practices presenting only a "minor peril to Fourth Amendment protections,"[457] it could well be argued, would tend to downgrade that process and thus might tempt magistrates to be less cautious in exercising their warrant-issuing authority. That is, it may well be that, as a practical matter, the warrant process can best serve as a meaningful device for the protection of Fourth Amendment rights if it is used somewhat selectively to prevent those police practices that would be most destructive of Fourth Amendment values.[458] However, this position has not as yet received attention from the courts.

§ 2.2(h) Use of "electronic canine" to detect explosives, alcohol, etc.[459]

Gas chromatography (GC) is an increasingly important technology for providing reliable information in a variety of circumstances. It has been usefully summarized as follows:[460]

The gas chromatograph, which is essentially an extremely sensitive filtering machine, is instrumental in breaking down a gas sample or a liquid mixture into its molecular subcomponents. If, for example, an individual wanted to ascertain the molecular compounds in a particular liquid, the sample would be mixed with a liquid solvent. The mixture is then heated until it forms a gas. The gas is then forced through a column, which is a glass tube filled with special filtration material. Each molecular compound in the sample will elute through a given column and temperature at a specific rate. A detector is attached at the outgoing end of the column which records the quantity and concentration of each particular molecular compound contained in the sample.

During this process, a mass spectrometer may be used in conjunction with the gas chromatograph. A mass spectrometer bombards the sample with high-energy electrons to generate extensive fragmentation ions. Because the sample is broken up to such a degree, the equipment can accurately determine which compounds are present. Using GC and MS (GC/MS) simultaneously yields information about the sample with a high specificity level.

---

[457]This characterization was used by the plurality in Coolidge v. New Hampshire, 403 U.S. 443, 91 S.Ct. 2022, 29 L.Ed.2d 564 (1971), to explain why the police may seize without a warrant evidence found in the course of a lawful search for other objects.

[458]See LaFave, Warrantless Searches and the Supreme Court: Further Ventures Into the "Quagmire," 8 Crim.L.Bull. 9, 27–29 (1972).

[Section 2.2(h)]

[459]See also Costantino, Electronic Sniffers' Place: The Use of Electronic Sniffers Under the Search and Seizure

Clause of the Fourth Amendment, 2 Charlotte L.Rev. 333 (2010), assessing use of such devices directed at the home, the individual, personal effects, and automobiles.

[460]This summary is from Bober, The "Chemical Signature" of the Fourth Amendment: Gas Chromatography/ Mass Spectometry and the War on Drugs, 8 Seton Hall Const.L.J. 75, 79–80 (1997), which at 78 n.20 cites several book-length technical treatments of the subject. See also Iraola, New Detection Technologies and the Fourth Amendment, 47 S.D.L.Rev. 8 (2002).

The gas chromatograph is an instrument used within the confines of the scientific laboratory. Courts have recognized gas chromatography as an extremely accurate technique in detecting the chemical/molecular makeup of perfume samples, the cause of a fire suspected of being arson,[461] the presence of illicit drugs in urine samples,[462] and the "fingerprinting" of different oil samples.[463]

In recent years, product development has turned GC from simply "a scientific laboratory technique" to one that is also used "on the streets,"[464] and it is precisely this development, creating a variety of opportunities for such technology to reveal information about what people are carrying on their persons or what is being transported in containers, which highlights the question of concern here: whether use of such technology constitutes a Fourth Amendment search. Law enforcement officers are now utilizing two varieties of this "electronic canine"[465] developed by Thermedics, Inc.: Egis, which has to do with the discovery of explosives, and Sentor, which has to do with the discovery of drugs.

Egis is a 300-pound explosives-detection system made of two components. One, the hand-held sampling unit, weighs only 8 pounds, and it works like a vacuum and sucks in vapors and particles from the vicinity of a suspected container or individual. The other, the analytical unit, takes this sample and produces a chemical sketch of it, which is then compared to the make-up of known explosives. In this fashion, the portable unit can automatically trace the chemical signature of plastic explosives, TNT and nitroglycerin, which is used in dynamite. Egis was originally used mainly at foreign airports, but is increasingly being utilized for domestic explosives detection. An Egis-type of system, generically referred to as an Explosive Trace Detector (ETD),[466] has been deployed to commercial airports by the Transportation Security Administration in the post-9/11 era to meet its responsibility for screening all checked luggage.[467] (A more recent version of the device is built in the shape of an archway and blows mildly

---

[461]See Lane, Preparing a Fire Related Case, 22 Vt.B.J. & L.Dig. 41 (Aug.1996); Note, 18 W.N.Engl.L.Rev. 305 (1996).

[462]Manfield, Imposing Liability on Drug Testing Laboratories for "False Positives": Getting Around Privity, 64 U.Chi.L.Rev. 287, 289–90 (1997).

[463]On the use of the technology in pollution forensics generally, see Bowman, Dirt Detectives, 17 Cal.Law. 26 (Feb.1997); Note, 7 Fordham Envtl. L.J. 483 (1996).

[464]Bober, 8 Seton Hall Const.L.J. 75, 119 (1997).

[465]Bober, 8 Seton Hall Const.L.J. 75, 104 (1997).

[466]"ETDs work by collecting samples and detecting vapors and residues of explosives. Operators collect samples by using swabs to rub different areas of the bags. Swabs are then cropped into chemical analyzers that separate and identify any threat explosives are present in less than 10 seconds. ETDs are smaller in weight and size than EDS machines [see note 159 supra] and are relatively low cost, about $40,000 each." <http://www.boeing.com/ids/airport_security/faq.html>.

[467]Such screening is mandated by 49 U.S.C.A. § 44901. The TSA has decided to utilize both the smaller ETD devices and also the very large

warm air over persons passing through it to detect explosive vapors or particles on their clothes and belongings.[468])

As for Sentor, it is a machine that is essentially identical to Egis in terms of hardware, but which picks up the chemical signatures of drugs rather than high explosives. It also involves use of a hand-held object about the size of a large flashlight that vacuums in a large volume of air around a suspect person or package. The device filters a volume of air and screens out smoke, auto exhausts and a multitude of other compounds and then in about 30 seconds identifies the amount of cocaine, heroin, or methamphetamine that is present. Sentor is currently being used by the Customs Service, the Drug Enforcement Administration, and the FBI.[469]

Given the characterization of Sentor and Egis as two varieties of "electronic canine,"[470] it is rather easy to move to the conclusion that under *United States v. Place*,[471] discussed earlier,[472] the use of either of these devices does not constitute a search within the meaning of the Fourth Amendment. That might well be the conclusion the Supreme Court would reach if confronted with the issue, but before this result is accepted out of hand, it may be well to consider the issue further, beginning with a consideration of the extent to which these devices (especially Sentor, which, given its function, appears to have a potential for use in a much broader variety of circumstances) differs from that of a *real* trained canine nose. One commentator has asserted that there are two significant differences: (1) That while "drug sniffing canines are usually trained to detect usable or larger quantities of drugs, Sentor uses high-speed gas chromatography to search for narcotic particles on a much smaller scale"; it is, in short, a highly-sophisticated and not-generally-available piece of equipment (price tag: $150,000.00) which "can detect trace amounts of narcotics that no canine could," down to "amounts of narcotics that may only be molecular in size."[473] (2) That while a "drug sniffing canine is able to * * * both * * * detect the presence of narcotics via its olfactory senses [and] detect the location of the

---

Explosive Detection System (EDS) units in complying with this requirement. Bester, The Birth of the Transportation Security Administration: A View From the Chief Counsel, 17 Air & Space Law 1, 22 (Summer 2002). The EDS unit is considered herein at § 2.2(d).

[468]Bober, 8 Seton Hall Const.L.J. 75, 81–82 (1997); Fahy, Bomb Squad, Mass. High Tech, <http://www.boston.com/mht/issue/w82696/lead1.html>;

Note, 41 Loy.L.A.L.Rev. 385 (2007).

[469]Bober, 8 Seton Hall Const.L.J. 75, 76–77, 81–82 (1997).

[470]Bober, 8 Seton Hall Const.L.J. 75, 104 (1997).

[471]United States v. Place, 462 U.S. 696, 103 S.Ct. 2637, 77 L.Ed.2d 110 (1983).

[472]See § 2.2(g).

[473]Bober, 8 Seton Hall Const.L.J. 75, 111, 119 (1997).

contraband," Sentor "can only tell you that drugs are in the air."[474]

One thing clearly suggested by the first of these particulars is that use of the Sentor might well qualify as a search under the analysis used by the Supreme Court in *Dow Chemical Co. v. United States*.[475] As one commentator has explained:

In *Dow*, the Court made a distinction between sophisticated technology used by the state that is or is not "generally available to the public." The $20,000 aerial camera used in that case was commonly used in map-making, and was in the final analysis, simply a camera, albeit more powerful than a conventional one. But, it does appear that there is a threshold at work in *Dow*: the level of technology employed by the government to conduct surveillance does matter, and that it may have limits. * * *

In relation to the Sentor's use of gas chromatography, it could be argued that the "in general use" principle in *Dow* should become a standard for the Supreme Court to follow. For example, the Sentor device costs $150,000.00. Even though the majority in *Dow* did not wish to heed the dissent's observation that "members of the public are unlikely to purchase $22,000 cameras," perhaps there may be an amount that is too much. Maybe Sentor's $150,000 price tag is or surpasses that threshold amount.[476]

It may well be, of course, "that the Court's decision in *Dow* places too much emphasis on the level of technology being employed,"[477] when in actuality the focus should be upon the nature of the intrusion brought about by the surveillance technique at issue. But, there is more than one way of characterizing that intrusion. Considering the second of the distinctions between the real and electronic canine listed above, it might be contended that there is an even *greater* reason for treating the latter as no search, for it merely reveals what is "in the air," as to which even one who causes himself or his effects to be in the proximity of that air can hardly have a justified expectation of privacy. Of course, such an approach might necessitate a more particularized inquiry into the relevant physics, especially as to whether the vacuuming done as the first step of utilizing either the Egis or Sentor is merely taking nearby air or is drawing air from the suspect container or from the interstices of a suspect's clothing. But good physics (and, for that matter, good metaphysics) may make bad law, as is best illustrated by many of the pre-*Kyllo* cases dealing with use of thermal imagers, discussed earlier.[478] Some of those cases have held such use *not* to be a search on the ground that the device employed does not penetrate the protected place but merely collects a telltale characteristic (there, heat) which has escaped from that place. If that is correct, it might be

[474]Bober, 8 Seton Hall Const.L.J. 75, 108–09 (1997).

[475]Dow Chemical Co. v. United States, 476 U.S. 227, 106 S.Ct. 1819, 90 L.Ed.2d 226 (1986).

[476]Bober, 8 Seton Hall Const.L.J. 75, 118–19 (1997).

[477]Bober, 8 Seton Hall Const.L.J. 75, 118 (1997).

[478]See § 2.2(d).

contended that the Sentor likewise is essentially passive in nature and only collects minute particles escaping into the air. But that kind of analysis was rejected in *Kyllo* and would have produced a different result even in *Katz v. United States*,[479] where it might be said the escaping characteristic was the vibrations on the glass of the phone booth that conveyed defendant's conversations to the police bug. And thus it is apparent that "*Katz* looked not to the tools employed by the government nor to the phenomena measured by those tools but to the object of the government's efforts."[480]

If the latter approach is taken here, then it is at least clear that the more traditional in-the-laboratory use of gas chromatography *is* a search, as held in *State v. Joyce*.[481] That case involved an in-the-lab testing of an arson suspect's clothing which involved heating the garments to vaporize any organic material present and then running the vapors through a column designed to separate the mixture of chemical compounds inside the vapor, which produced a printout of a pattern representing the compounds present in the vapor, which when compared with a library of known signature patterns of organic substance, by which it was determined that there were traces of gasoline on the suspect's clothing. The court in *Joyce* quite correctly concluded that such "government conduct invaded the defendant's reasonable expectation of privacy through the use of a machine designed to detect the presence and identity of many organic compounds by heating clothing items and analyzing the resultant vapor," meaning "that this chemical test, capable of determining a multitude of private facts about an individual,[482] constituted a search." (Consistent with *Joyce*, it may be concluded that resort to gas chromatography is *not* a search if the nature of the object tested is such that there could be no privacy expectation in the information revealed by the test.[483])

But the court in *Joyce* also found it necessary to say that the

---

[479]Katz v. United States, 389 U.S. 347, 88 S.Ct. 507, 19 L.Ed.2d 576 (1967).

[480]United States v. Cusumano, 67 F.3d 1497 (10th Cir.1995), vacated en banc on rehearing, 83 F.3d 1247 (10th Cir.1996), but only on the ground that this issue need not be reached because evidence other than the thermal imager scan provided probable cause for the challenged search warrant.

[481]State v. Joyce, 229 Conn. 10, 639 A.2d 1007 (1994).

[482]At this point, the court in *Joyce* dropped this footnote: "That the gas chromatograph utilized by Hubball was capable of exposing rather private facts about an individual is evidenced by Hubball's testimony before the jury that his machine detected the presence of an organic material in the defendant's underwear that was not an accelerant."

[483]*Joyce* was distinguished in State v. Bernier, 246 Conn. 63, 717 A.2d 652 (1998), where, after charred wood flooring samples were lawfully seized from defendant's home pursuant to a fire investigation, authorities performed gas chromatography analysis on these samples: "The defendant adduced no evidence as to the type of private information the test conducted on the flooring could or did reveal about him. We are unpersuaded by the

state's reliance on *Place* and its offspring, *United States v. Jacobsen*,[484] was misplaced because those cases said that a device which merely determines the presence or absence of contraband is no search, while by comparison "the gas chromatograph test is not designed to detect the presence of contraband, and in fact detects the presence and identity of many organic substances." This certainly suggests that if the Sentor *really* detects only illegal drugs and deals with all noncontraband organic substances in a fashion that ensures the operator of the equipment is unable to identify them, then the *Place/Jacobsen* rule would come into play,[485] meaning that use of the device would itself not constitute a search and thus would be constitutionally permissible provided, of course, that its use did not first necessitate an illegal seizure of the person or thing to be examined. And if this were so, then this would mean that there would be no constitutional prohibition on the police operating a Sentor nonseizure checkpoint by, for example, setting up the device in some area known for drug activity and then directing it at some or all passersby.

This is a troubling thought, at least if some of the claims made about Sentor are correct. For one thing, it is claimed that the device is sensitive to a fault, so that it will respond positively to "possession of molecular amounts of cocaine,"[486] which could be and often is innocent[487] and thus cannot alone serve as a basis for a criminal conviction.[488] For another, as noted earlier, it is contended that a Sentor positive reaction is less focused than a drug dog's alert because the device "can only tell you that drugs are in the air" but not "*exactly* where they are," for the reason that "air is fluid and moves whether individuals pass through it

---

defendant's contention that our conclusion in *Joyce* that the defendant in that case had a reasonable expectation of privacy in the information the gas chromatography might reveal from his clothing necessarily means that the same type of private facts might be revealed by the use of this test on the defendant's flooring. We decline to impute to the defendant's burnt flooring the degree and nature of personal information contained in one's clothing. The flooring samples, as compared to the clothes in *Joyce*, are such an unlikely repository of personal information as to render the defendant's expectation of privacy unreasonable."

[484]United States v. Jacobsen, 466 U.S. 109, 104 S.Ct. 1652, 80 L.Ed.2d 85 (1984).

[485]So too as to Egis, if it identifies only explosive materials and no innocent substance and does so in a context in which possession of such material is criminal.

[486]Bober, 8 Seton Hall Const.L.J. 75, 112 (1997).

[487]Bober, 8 Seton Hall Const.L.J. 75, 117 (1997), reporting on an experiment in which eleven highly respected citizens in south Florida were asked to provide $20 bills from their wallets; all of these bills contained traces of cocaine except the one provided by a sheriff who apparently was aware of the purpose of the experiment and deliberately washed his bill beforehand!

[488]Lord v. State, 616 So.2d 1065 (Fla.App.1993).

or not."[489] Even assuming these two claims are true, of course, it could be contended that such doubts go only to the legitimate legal consequences of a positive report from Sentor—e.g., whether such a report alone supplies probable cause for arrest, or whether it alone furnishes reasonable suspicion for a brief detention—and have nothing to do with the question of whether acquiring such information in the first instance is a search. But because it is difficult to believe that courts will not accept a Sentor alert as providing a basis for some sort of intrusive activity thereafter, the two questions cannot be separated that neatly. After all, a central point in *Place* was that a person who was the object of the nonsearch activity there would not be "subjected to the embarrassment and inconvenience entailed in less discriminate and more intrusive investigative methods." Nor will it do to contend that the Fourth Amendment is intended to protect only the innocent, for one advocate of that perspective even disapproved of the "carte blanche use of marijuana-sniffing dogs"[490] because of the margin for error.

Yet another variety of "electronic canine," one which is used much more commonly in contemporary law enforcement, is known as the Passive Alcohol Sensor. As described by one commentator:

> The latest invention in fighting crime is the P.A.S. III. Developed under the direction of various insurance and highway safety organizations and touted as non-intrusive, this innocuous looking flashlight with a built-in breathalyzer is being used to analyze a driver's breath without their participation or consent. The sensor that is attached to the flashlight is an electrochemical fuel cell that detects the presence of alcohol in the air of the car.

> In order to analyze a driver's breath, the tool needs to be held within ten inches from the driver as the driver is exhaling. In order to obtain a sample of exhaled air, the Sniffer's manufacturer, PAS Systems International, suggests that the officer request the driver to give their name, address, and date of birth. A pump within the sensor draws in a sample of the exhaled breath as well as the air in the car and the fuel cell analyzes the amount of alcohol in the sample. A bar display on the flashlight indicates the possible blood alcohol content detected. The display ranges from green to red, which corresponds to an approximate blood alcohol content range of.01 to.12. For daytime use, an innocuous looking clipboard with an attached breathalyzer serves the same function.[491]

In considering whether utilization of the Passive Alcohol Sensor (hereinafter, the P.A.S.) constitutes a search under the Fourth Amendment, it is appropriate to begin with the understanding that use of the more traditional breathalyzer most definitely *is* a search. As the Supreme Court put it in *Skinner v. Railway Labor*

---

[489]Bober, 8 Seton Hall Const.L.J. 75, 109 (1997).

[490]Loewy, The Fourth Amendment as a Device for Protecting the Innocent, 81 Mich.L.Rev. 1229, 1246 (1983).

[491]Note, 9 J.L. & Pol'y 835, 857–58 (2001).

Executives' Ass'n:[492] "Subjecting a person to a breathalyzer test, which generally requires the production of alveolar or 'deep lung' breath for chemical analysis, * * * implicates similar concerns about bodily integrity and, like the blood-alcohol test we considered in *Schmerber*,[493] should also be deemed a search." Read literally, that declaration can hardly be said to encompass what occurs when the P.A.S. is used, as there is no "production" by the suspect, and it is the breath otherwise necessarily exhaled by the suspect that is being measured.[494]

That is the beginning, but hardly the end, of the inquiry into this issue, which as yet appears not to have been resolved by any reported appellate court decision. The question has been discussed by the commentators, however, who have (until recently[495]) consistently taken the view that employment of a P.A.S. is *not* a search.[496] (They do not dispute, however, that information so acquired could be the fruit of a prior illegal seizure of the person; in the discussion following it is assumed that there has been no such illegal seizure because the P.A.S. has been employed in connection with a lawful *Terry* stop, a lawful DWI checkpoint, or a lawful accident investigation.[497])

Here as well, there has been reliance upon the dog-sniff case,

---

[492]Skinner v. Railway Labor Executives' Ass'n, 489 U.S. 602, 109 S.Ct. 1402, 103 L.Ed.2d 639 (1989). See also State v. Jones, 279 Kan. 71, 106 P.3d 1 (2005) (given stipulation that preliminary breath test "requires a sample of deep lung air which can only be extracted from a person if the person forcibly blows air into the PBT device for a period of 3 to 5 seconds and that deep lung air is 'not normally held out to the public,'" subjecting defendant to the test a search).

[493]The reference is to Schmerber v. California, 384 U.S. 757, 86 S.Ct. 1826, 16 L.Ed.2d 908 (1966), discussed with *Skinner* in this context in § 2.6(a).

[494]As stated in an advertisement for the P.A.S. III: "The passive sensor does not require the co-operation of the subject nor does it require the individual to produce a deep lung sample of air by blowing into the mouthpiece. Rather it samples from the general environment air which is in front of the face of the individual." See http://a lcoholism.about.com/library/weekly/aa 000823a.htm.

[495]Comments, 39 San Diego L.Rev. 563 (2002); 34 Tex.Tech.L.Rev. 129 (2001), both present arguments in support of the conclusion that use of the P.A.S. *is* a search.

[496]Fields & Hricko, Passive Alcohol Sensors—Constitutional Implications, 20 The Prosecutor 45 (Summer 1986); Grey, Passive Alcohol Sensors and the Fourth Amendment, at http://www.nd aa.org/apri/programs/traffic/passive_ alcohol_sensors_fourth_amendmen t_2.html; Manak, Constitutional Aspects of the Use of Passive Alcohol Screening Devices as Law Enforcement Tools for DWI Enforcement, 19 The Prosecutor 29 (Winter 1986); Note, 9 J.L. & Pol'y 835 (2001) (arguing at 859 that "the device unnecessarily intrudes upon the privacy of an individual," but then agreeing at 862 that it "is likely to pass any Fourth Amendment challenge on its use").

[497]For more on the use of P.A.S. in connection with these procedures, see Manak, 19 The Prosecutor 29, 33–34 (Winter 1986).

United States v. Place,[498] to justify the no-search conclusion.[499] In one respect, the *Place* decision does lend some support; the Court there, discussing discovery of the contents of luggage, emphasized the "manner" in which the information there was obtained, deemed "less intrusive than a typical search" because there was no opening of the container and no rummaging through the contents. Similarly, the P.A.S. is also much less intrusive than the search of which the Court spoke in *Skinner;* indeed, it can even be said that in some respects use of the P.A.S. is less intrusive than dog sniffs generally.[500] But it must be remembered that there was a second ingredient in *Place,* namely, that "the sniff discloses only the presence or absence of narcotics, a contraband item," which took on even greater significance when the Court later relied on the same reasoning in holding the field test "that merely discloses whether or not a particular substance is cocaine."[501] With the arguable exception of the case in which the P.A.S. discovers a range of blood alcohol content on a person too young to consume alcohol legally, it does not uncover contraband but rather evidence tending to show[502] that the object of the P.A.S. scrutiny has been engaged in criminal conduct, such as driving under the influence or driving recklessly.

Another argument made in favor of the conclusion that use of the P.A.S. is no search in that it simply acquires an aspect of a person's appearance/demeanor as to which there exists no reasonable expectation of privacy.[503] In *United States v. Dionisio,*[504] for example, the Supreme Court held that the "physical characteristics of a person's voice, its tone and manner, as opposed to the specific content of the conversation, are constantly exposed to the public," as "[l]ike a man's facial characteristics, or handwriting, his voice is repeatedly produced for others to hear," meaning that "[n]o person can have a reasonable expectation that others will not know the sound of his voice, any more than he can reasonably expect that his face will be a mystery to the world." On similar analysis, the Court has held one does not have a justified

---

[498]United States v. Place, 462 U.S. 696, 103 S.Ct. 2637, 77 L.Ed.2d 110 (1983).

[499]Fields & Hricko, 20 The Prosecutor 45, 48–49 (Summer 1986); Manak, 19 The Prosecutor 29, 32 (Winter 1986).

[500]"A factor that militates strongly in the passive alcohol sensor's favor, particularly on the issue that it is a person that it 'sniffs,' is that it is unobtrusive. The image of a dog sniffing around a person can be frightening and police use of dogs has negative connotations. The passive alcohol sensor is not threatening." Fields & Hricko,

20 The Prosecutor 45, 49 (Summer 1986).

[501]United States v. Jacobsen, 466 U.S. 109, 104 S.Ct. 1652, 80 L.Ed.2d 85 (1984).

[502]Indeed, the breath test may be just one of several facts needed even to show probable cause. See, e.g., People v. Hanna, 223 Mich.App. 466, 567 N.W.2d 12 (1997).

[503]See § 2.6(a).

[504]United States v. Dionisio, 410 U.S. 1, 93 S.Ct. 764, 35 L.Ed.2d 67 (1973).

expectation of privacy in his handwriting[505] or fingerprints.[506] And thus, so the argument goes, there is likewise no reasonable privacy expectation as to one's breath, which is likewise "constantly before the public"[507] and "repeatedly exposed to the public."[508] Here again, however, the analogy is far from perfect. All of the characteristics referred to in the Supreme Court's cases, sound of voice, style of handwriting, facial characteristics and fingerprints, refer to aspects of a person's character/demeanor that remain more or less unchanged over time. By contrast, when the police resort to a P.A.S. test, the purpose is not to determine whether the subject of the test suffers from halitosis, but rather is to acquire a fair estimation of his blood alcohol level on a particular occasion (a condition that conceivably will never or rarely be duplicated again). That seems quite different from the *Dionisio* line of cases, and instead much like the situation in *Cupp v. Murphy*,[509] where the Court held that scraping the fingernails of a voluntarily present murder suspect *was* a search notwithstanding the police observation of dried blood on the suspect's finger.

Much more promising is a plain view (or, more precisely, plain smell) analysis of a P.A.S. test. Given the fact that it is well established[510] that a lawfully-positioned officer may, using his own nostrils, acquire smells emanating from a vehicle without having conducted a search, it can be argued that the same is true when those smells are captured and analyzed by a P.A.S.[511]—at least so long as the device is not intruded inside the vehicle in the course of doing so.[512] Of course, the P.A.S. test is different in that a device is being employed to acquire information the officer could not obtain by his own unenhanced senses, but this only suggests that the proper analogy is to the many, many cases upholding the shining of a flashlight into a vehicle.[513] True, the P.A.S. device is a more sophisticated instrument than a flashlight, but it is a far cry from the $150,000 Sentor discussed earlier, and

[505]United States v. Mara, 410 U.S. 19, 93 S.Ct. 774, 35 L.Ed.2d 99 (1973).

[506]Cupp v. Murphy, 412 U.S. 291, 93 S.Ct. 2000, 36 L.Ed.2d 900 (1973).

[507]Fields & Hricko, 20 The Prosecutor 45, 47 (Summer 1986).

[508]Grey, Passive Alcohol Sensors and the Fourth Amendment, at http://www.ndaa.org/apri/programs/traffic/passive_alcohol_sensors_fourth_amendment_2.html at 6.

[509]Cupp v. Murphy, 412 U.S. 291, 93 S.Ct. 2000, 36 L.Ed.2d 900 (1973).

[510]See § 2.5(c).

[511]Fields & Hricko, 20 The Prosecutor 45, 46–49 (Summer 1986); Grey, Passive Alcohol Sensors and the Fourth Amendment, at http://www.ndaa.org/apri/programs/traffic/passive_alcohol_sensors_fourth_amendment_2.html, at 2–4; Manak, 19 The Prosecutor 29, 33 (Winter 1986).

[512]Fields & Hricko, 20 The Prosecutor 45, 49 (Summer 1986), putting this questionable assertion: "The flashlight cases do not indicate if the light was shone through the window or inserted in the car's open window. This vagueness suggests that the distinction is irrelevant. In fact, the flashlight cases provide direct authority for use of the sensor inside a vehicle because the light generated by the flashlight passes through the vehicle's window whether it is open or closed."

[513]See § 2.5(c).

thus it arguably escapes the Court's caution in *Dow Chemical Co. v. United States*[514] that resort to highly sophisticated technology might be viewed differently. That is, the P.A.S. device might be analogized not only to a flashlight, but also to the beeper device deemed no search in *United States v. Knotts*,[515] where the Court declared that "nothing in the Fourth Amendment prohibited the police from augmenting the sensory faculties bestowed upon them at birth with such enhancement as science and technology afforded them in this case."

The unresolved question, which makes the result as to P.A.S. use problematical, is just how far that quoted proposition can be pushed. In *Knotts*, for example, the Court deemed it necessary to point out that the device used there revealed only the whereabouts of a vehicle as it traveled on the highway, a fact that was at least theoretically obtainable from bystanders to the defendant's peregrinations. A comparable statement cannot be made as the information acquired by a P.A.S., although it can at least be said that the chances are that the officer standing aside the suspect's vehicle would likely acquire *some* smell of alcohol, so that the P.A.S. simply provided a more precise measurement of something that the officer ordinarily would otherwise obtain. That brings us to *Kyllo v. United States*,[516] where the Court held that "the use of a thermal-imaging device aimed at a private home from a public street to detect relative amounts of heat within the home constitutes a 'search' within the meaning of the Fourth Amendment." There is one sense, of course, in which *Kyllo* can be immediately distinguished from the issue here under discussion: the *Kyllo* holding had to do with obtaining "information regarding the interior of the home," a place where "privacy expectations are most heightened," while P.A.S. use is ordinarily directed at those traveling by vehicle on the public way, where the Court had indicated a lesser degree of privacy obtains.[517] But *Kyllo* is also important because it reminds us of something about the overarching expectation of privacy test of *Katz*:

> But just as a thermal imager captures only heat emanating from a house, so also a powerful directional microphone picks up only sound emanating from a house—and a satellite capable of scanning from many miles away would pick up only visible light emanating from a house. We rejected such a mechanical interpretation of the Fourth Amendment in *Katz*, where the eavesdropping device picked up only sound waves that reached the exterior of the phone booth.

The basic point, as another court put it, is that "*Katz* looked not to the tools employed by the government nor to the phenomena

---

[514]Dow Chemical Co. v. United States, 476 U.S. 227, 106 S.Ct. 1819, 90 L.Ed.2d 226 (1986).

[515]United States v. Knotts, 460 U.S. 276, 103 S.Ct. 1081, 75 L.Ed.2d 55 (1983).

[516]Kyllo v. United States, 533 U.S. 27, 121 S.Ct. 2038, 150 L.Ed.2d 94 (2001).

[517]See § 7.2(b).

measured by those tools but to the object of the government's efforts."[518] This suggests that in assessing whether or not P.A.S. use is a search, it is important to keep in mind that while the P.A.S. can in one sense be said to be merely "sampling the air around the person," this is for the purpose of detecting "the presence of ethyl alcohol in the breath," which in turn makes possible an estimation of the quantity "of alcohol in a person's blood."[519]

All of this suggests the significant possibility that P.A.S. use could be deemed a Fourth Amendment search, a prospect acknowledged in a sense by most of those commentators arguing that the result would be otherwise, for they present the alternative argument that P.A.S. might be characterized as a minimally-intrusive type of search permissible without a warrant and upon reasonable suspicion.[520] This latter possibility would mean that a P.A.S. could be employed upon stopping a driver reasonably suspected of DWI or reckless driving, or in further screening a driver who, at a DWI checkpoint, acted in a manner providing reasonable suspicion, so that its "chief utility" would be as "a screening device producing information which, when taken with other facts known to the police officer, will give probable cause to arrest."[521] The trouble with this minimally-intrusive/reasonable suspicion thesis, however, is that it conflicts with much of the Supreme Court's Fourth Amendment jurisprudence: the Court has asserted that the Fourth Amendment knows no search but a "full-blown search,"[522] that *Terry* provides no support for "any search whatever for anything but weapons,"[523] and that a balancing process is appropriate only when warranted by "special needs beyond the normal need for law enforcement."[524] Whether all that has fallen by the wayside as a result of the Court's more recent holding in *United States v. Knights*,[525] upholding a warrantless probation search of reasonable suspicion *not* on a "special needs" theory but purportedly by a balancing of governmental and individual interests "under our general Fourth Amendment approach," remains to be seen.

---

[518]United States v. Cusumano, 67 F.3d 1497 (10th Cir.1995), vacated on rehearing en banc, 83 F.3d 1247 (10th Cir.1996), but only on the ground that this issue need not be reached because evidence other than the challenged thermal imager scan provided probable cause for the warrant at issue.

[519]Manak, 19 The Prosecutor 29, 30 (Winter 1986).

[520]Manak, 19 The Prosecutor 29, 35 (Winter 1986); Note, 9 J.L. & Pol'y 835, 874 (2001).

[521]Manak, 19 The Prosecutor 29, 30 (Winter 1986).

[522]Arizona v. Hicks, 480 U.S. 321, 107 S.Ct. 1149, 94 L.Ed.2d 347 (1987).

[523]Ybarra v. Illinois, 444 U.S. 85, 100 S.Ct. 338, 62 L.Ed.2d 238 (1979).

[524]Skinner v. Railway Labor Executives' Ass'n, 489 U.S. 602, 109 S.Ct. 1402, 103 L.Ed.2d 639 (1989).

[525]United States v. Knights, 534 U.S. 112, 122 S.Ct. 587, 151 L.Ed.2d 497 (2001).

§ 2.3 Residential premises

Research References

West's Key Number Digest

Arrest ☞68(6); Controlled Substances ☞134; Searches and Seizures ☞16 to 21, 25.1 to 28, 47.1

Legal Encyclopedias

C.J.S., Arrest §§ 3 to 4, 3 to 54, 38, 43 to 49; Searches and Seizures §§ 8, 13, 18, 20 to 24, 27 to 38, 41, 66 to 67, 70 to 73, 78, 102

Introduction

Prior to the decision in *Katz v. United States*,[1] the Supreme Court often used the concept of "a constitutionally protected area"[2] to define the reach of the Fourth Amendment's protections. One such area, specifically enumerated in the Amendment, is a person's house. Indeed, one's dwelling has generally been viewed as the area most resolutely protected by the Fourth Amendment.[3] "At the very core," the Court cautioned in *Silverman v. United States*,[4] "stands the right of a man to retreat into his own home and there be free from unreasonable governmental intrusion." This constitutional protection of houses has been extended to other residential premises as well, including apartments,[5] hotel and motel rooms,[6] and rooms in rooming houses[7] or hospitals.[8]

Katz teaches that the Amendment "protects people, not places,"

[Section 2.3]

[1]Katz v. United States, 389 U.S. 347, 88 S.Ct. 507, 19 L.Ed.2d 576 (1967).

[2]E.g., Silverman v. United States, 365 U.S. 505, 81 S.Ct. 679, 5 L.Ed.2d 734 (1961).

[3]See Hafetz, "A Man's Home Is His Castle?": Reflections on the Home, the Family, and Privacy During the Late Nineteenth and Early Twentieth Centuries, 8 Wm. & Mary J.Women & L. 173 (2002).

[4]Silverman v. United States, 365 U.S. 505, 81 S.Ct. 679, 5 L.Ed.2d 734 (1961).

[5]E.g., Clinton v. Virginia, 377 U.S. 158, 84 S.Ct. 1186, 12 L.Ed.2d 213 (1964).

[6]E.g., Stoner v. California, 376 U.S. 483, 84 S.Ct. 889, 11 L.Ed.2d 856 (1964); Commonwealth v. Lopez, 458 Mass. 383, 937 N.E.2d 949 (2010). "Private sleeper cars on passenger trains are comparable to hotel rooms in that the occupant enjoys a heightened expectation of privacy." United States v. Dimick, 990 F.2d 1164 (10th Cir.1993).

[7]E.g., McDonald v. United States, 335 U.S. 451, 69 S.Ct. 191, 93 L.Ed. 153 (1948). Commonwealth v. Porter P., 456 Mass. 254, 923 N.E.2d 36 (2010) (defendant had reasonable expectation of privacy in room he shared with

and that the "constitutionally protected area" concept cannot "serve as a talismanic solution to every Fourth Amendment problem." But even under the *Katz* justified-expectation-of-privacy approach, it is still useful to view residential premises as a place especially protected against unreasonable police intrusion. As Justice Harlan noted in his concurring opinion in *Katz*, "reference to a 'place' " is ordinarily necessary in deciding what protection the Fourth Amendment affords to people. And it is still true, he added, that "a man's home is, for most purposes, a place where he expects privacy."[9] The concern herein is with what police investigative practices, when directed at residential premises, do not intrude upon a protected privacy expectation as to those premises.

§ 2.3(a) Abandoned premises

It has often been held that if a defendant has in fact abandoned the place where he formerly resided, then he may not have suppressed from evidence what the police find on those premises after the time of abandonment. Sometimes such a holding is premised on the conclusion that by abandonment the defendant lost standing to object,[10] sometimes on the notion that the landlord was in a position to give effective consent after the

---

mother at homeless shelter, even though his use of room was limited and shelter staff had master key and could enter "for professional business purposes").

[8]Jones v. State, 648 So.2d 669 (Fla.1994); People v. Brown, 88 Cal.App.3d 283, 151 Cal.Rptr. 749 (1979); State v. Stott, 171 N.J. 343, 794 A.2d 120 (2002) (where defendant shared room at state-run psychiatric hospital under circumstances where his "stay would be of some duration," and "defendant's room had many of the attributes of a private living area and * * * had served as such a place throughout defendant's occupancy," "defendant had a reasonable expectation of privacy in the area searched by the police," who looked within hem of curtain, though "case might be different if the police had searched [deceased roommate's] personal wardrobe"); Morris v. Commonwealth, 208 Va. 331, 157 S.E.2d 191 (1967).

[9]One commentator objects that the "Fourth Amendment has disproportionately protected residential privacy rights on the basis of property

law concepts and the rhetoric of the inviolate physical home," and "advocate[s] replacing housing exceptionalism and formalistic property approaches with a strong and consistent doctrinal focus on harm to substantive privacy and intimate association." Stern, The Inviolate Home: Housing Exceptionalism in the Fourth Amendment, 95 Cornell L.Rev. 905, 955–56 (2010).

[Section 2.3(a)]

[10]See § 11.3(a).

When the question is one of standing, the perspective of the inquiry regarding the "abandonment" changes. "The object of measurement shifts from reasonable appearances to historic reality. What finally matters shifts from what the policeman reasonably believed out on the street to what the suppression hearing judge ultimately knows in the courtroom." Faulkner v. State, 317 Md. 441, 564 A.2d 785 (1989). See also Oken v. State, 327 Md. 628, 612 A.2d 258 (1992) (thus *all* facts presented to court at time of hearing relevant).

abandonment occurred,[11] and sometimes upon the general proposition that the abandonment terminated any justified expectation of privacy the defendant previously had with respect to those premises.[12] The concern here is with what constitutes such an abandonment that it may be fairly said the one-time occupant no longer has a protected expectation of privacy in the residence.[13]

One question that arises with some frequency is what it takes to terminate a tenant's justified expectation of privacy as to a house or apartment he had been renting. May it be said, for example, that this expectation ends merely by virtue of nonpayment of rent by the tenant, or must the landlord pursue established legal procedures for eviction? Instructive on this question is *United States v. Botelho*,[14] where the oral lease of a cottage was from period to period with payments of rent to be prepaid every two weeks. After the tenants were delinquent in the rental payments and also failed to pay electricity and telephone bills, the landlady informed them they would be evicted on July 15 unless all bills were paid by July 14. No money was received, so she entered on the 15th, observed a sawed-off shotgun, and then summoned the police, who searched the cottage. The landlady later instituted summary eviction proceedings, but before they could be carried to their completion the tenants vacated the premises about the end of July. No rental payments were ever received for the period following June 30. In holding that the tenants had a justified expectation of privacy in the cottage at the time of the search, the court reasoned:

> Rephrased in the terms of Justice Harlan's test, it is the government's argument that the notice to vacate terminated defendant's tenancy and therefore any expectation of privacy he may have had was unreasonable. It seems to me that this argument would be sound except for the fact that the notice given by Mrs. MacIsaac on July 10th was clearly inadequate under Hawaii law. * * * The requirement of written notice is not a paper formality because statutes providing for possessory or summary remedies of a landlord against a tenant must be strictly construed. * * * Accordingly, the tenancy of the premises was not terminated by Mrs. MacIsaac's verbal notice of eviction.
>
> Nor do I believe that the non-payment of rent would, without more, make the defendant's expectation of privacy unreasonable. * * * Moreover, in view of the mandatory and exclusive nature of [the aforementioned statute], the fact that the landlady reserved a right to re-enter on the failure to pay rent is immaterial. It is the better and more modern rule that a landlord entitled to possession by right of re-entry or otherwise must, on the refusal of the tenant to surrender the leased premises, resort to the remedy given by law to secure it. Any other rule is prejudicial to the public peace and

---

[11]See § 8.5(a).

[12]E.g., United States v. Wilson, 472 F.2d 901 (9th Cir.1972).

[13]As for purported abandonment merely by disclaimer of ownership, see § 11.3(a).

[14]United States v. Botelho, 360 F.Supp. 620 (D. Haw. 1973).

order. * * *

The government argues alternatively that property law should not be controlling in determining the scope of Fourth Amendment protections. It reasons that despite the invalidity of the notice of eviction the defendant could not have had a reasonable expectation of privacy in any part of the cottage when the rent, electricity and telephone bills were unpaid, and the landlady had informed him to be out of the premises by July 15. While persuasive in some respects, I cannot agree with the government's contention. Although the Supreme Court has stated that it is "unnecessary and ill-advised" to import property law concepts into the law surrounding Fourth Amendment rights, * * * it is obvious that this was intended to broaden the protection afforded against unreasonable searches and seizures, not narrow it. Furthermore, I am not prepared to hold that a defendant with a perfectly legal right to possession or occupancy of leased premises can be found to have an "unreasonable" expectation of privacy.[15]

The reasoning in *Botelho* is generally sound. Although, as the court concedes, property law concepts are not necessarily controlling on Fourth Amendment issues, the justified expectation of privacy one has in his place of residence certainly includes the expectation that the processes of the law rather than self-help will be utilized to terminate a tenant's occupancy[16] (or, for that

---

[15]Compare United States v. Bolden, 545 F.3d 609 (8th Cir.2008) (where police, on basis of Jan. 2003 information from defendant's accomplice, retrieved gun from bag under gutter on outside of residence defendant had rented, defendant without expectation of privacy, as landlord had commenced eviction proceedings in Nov. 2002 and retook possession in Dec. 2002; court rejects defendant's claim "that the landlord's history of forgiving his rent deficiencies and the fact that eviction notices were returned undelivered gave him a reasonable expectation of privacy," as defendant "knew he was facing eviction * * *, yet made no attempt to prevent eviction and asserted no continuing possessory interest in the residence"); Marshall v. State, 232 P.3d 467 (Okla. Crim.App.2010) (where defendant "evicted from the house * * * approximately one month before" and "[e]verything had been moved out except for a twin bed, some clothing and trash" and "the front door was ajar," defendant "did not have an expectation of privacy in the house").

[16]In People v. Stadtmore, 52 A.D.2d 853, 382 N.Y.S.2d 807 (1976), the landlord instituted a summary proceeding culminating in the issuance of a warrant to evict the defendant for nonpayment of rent. As the defendant was finishing packing and moving his effects into the hallway, two officers entered and searched the apartment. Though the state contended that "the landlord-tenant relationship terminates upon the issuance of a warrant to evict," the court held: "Until the moment of his actual eviction defendant, regardless of his technical status under property law, was lawfully occupying the apartment in question. In our view, respondent seeks to convert civil process into a warrant for a general search. In short, the single fact of non-payment of rent should not result in the forfeiture of one's Fourth Amendment rights.

"Turning to the District Attorney's remaining contentions, we note that a defendant's reasonable expectation of privacy has been considered a factor in determining the reasonableness of a warrantless search * * *. In terms of reasonable expectations, we do not believe that a tenant who is about to be evicted should anticipate

matter, an owner's occupancy).[17]

But the language in *Botelho* should not be taken to mean that no abandonment by the tenant is possible before the rental term expires, for this is not the case.

> The question of abandonment for Fourth Amendment purposes does not turn on strict property concepts but on whether the accused has relinquished his interest in the property to the extent that he no longer has a reasonable expectation of privacy in the premises at the time of the search. * * * This principle has been applied to find abandonment where a tenant has left residential premises even though he may retain the lawful right to possession.[18]

---

that police officers will be present to conduct a general search for contraband on the pretense of insuring the total removal of his belongings * * *."

See also United States v. Curlin, 638 F.3d 562 (7th Cir.2011) (where landlord obtained eviction order for defendant's nonpayment of rent, and after defendant flouted order police executed the eviction order and made a "safety sweep" incident thereto, finding drugs and guns in plain view, defendant without expectation of privacy given his "wrongful" presence); United States v. Sanford, 493 F.Supp. 78 (D.D.C.1980) (where marshal executed writ of restitution for nonpayment of rent, tenant "was entitled to an expectation that his personal effects and property would be not subject to a full-scale exploratory search even though they would be displaced and removed to the public street"); Boone v. State, 39 Md.App. 20, 383 A.2d 412 (1978) (where landlord pursues statutory procedure for repossession, this terminates tenant's expectation of privacy in apartment, but diminished his expectation of privacy as to his effects only to extent necessary for removal of them); State v. McNichols, 106 Nev. 651, 799 P.2d 550 (1990) (where defendant "lost his legal interest in the property when it was foreclosed" and "lost his possessory interest in the property when he was evicted," and "new owner changed the locks, and the constable's office placed court seals on the entry," defendant's "trespassory re-entry did not create an objective expectation of privacy").

Compare United States v. Buchanan, 633 F.2d 423 (5th Cir.1980)

(no expectation of privacy where search was one month after tenant failed to pay rent, lease said it expired 5 days after nonpayment, and 10 days before search landlord changed the locks).

[17]Although the law may recognize that certain legal processes may be combined with some degree of self-help, in which case those processes plus the self-help will likely be deemed sufficient to work an abandonment. See Laney v. State, 379 Md. 522, 842 A.2d 773 (2004) (where defendant purchased improved real property and, to finance purchase acquired loan secured by mortgage on purchased property, after which defendant failed to make payments according to loan agreement, following which necessary legal steps to terminate the mortgagor's interest in and right to possession of the property—notice, foreclosure, sale, and judicial ratification—were taken, so that the law then recognizes that the purchaser may *either* obtain a court order to remove holdover mortgagor or take possession of the property peacefully without court's assistance and purchaser did latter, that made defendant a trespasser without any reasonable expectation of privacy in the premises, considering (i) that he "no longer had any right to occupy the premises," (ii) that defendant "had been notified that the foreclosure sale would take place," and (iii) that state law did not require new owner "to pursue some additional judicial remedy to evict").

[18]Bloodworth v. State, 233 Ga. 589, 212 S.E.2d 774 (1975). See also United States v. Stevenson, 396 F.3d

This means that if by all appearances the tenant has vacated the premises by the time the lease has ended, then *Botelho* is inapplicable, for there would be no occasion for the landlord to seek eviction in such circumstances.[19] Thus, in *United States v. Wilson*,[20] where the tenant was over two weeks overdue with his rent, the landlord learned from neighbors that the tenant had

---

538 (4th Cir.2005) (where defendant rented his apartment on week-to-week basis and was behind in rent but landlord did not attempt to evict him and indicated he could pay rent later, defendant deemed to have abandoned the apartment after his arrest, as he manifested intention not to return by letter to his girlfriend, giving her ownership of the personal property in his apartment and referring to himself as the "former renter"); United States v. Levasseur, 816 F.2d 37 (2d Cir.1987) (defendants had abandoned the premises notwithstanding their failure to take their weapons, clothing and personal belongings; "subsequently discovered events may support an inference that appellants had already chosen, and manifested their decision, not to return," and such the case here, as all circumstances indicated that when they learned of arrest of confederates elsewhere they fled to another city to avoid arrest and thus "forfeited their reasonable expectation of privacy"); United States v. De Parias, 805 F.2d 1447 (11th Cir.1986) (defendant had abandoned his apartment when he left for another city and told his girl friend, with whom he shared apartment, that he was not returning; though he "fled Miami to avoid capture, a lawful police investigation does not constitute such coercion that the abandonment should be considered involuntary"); People v. Morrison, 196 Colo. 319, 583 P.2d 924 (1978) (though defendant had moved into apartment 1 week ago and paid half of first month's rent and security deposit, premises were abandoned where all clothing, bedding and personal effects had been removed, the only items found were in trash pile, and defendant never returned to apartment or paid balance of first month's rent but instead left the state); State v. Grissom, 251 Kan. 851, 840 P.2d 1142 (1992) (where defendant, who used storage locker with Thibido in painting business, told Thibido that he going to California and was giving Thibido "complete custody and control of the painting business," and Thibido later found the lock securing the locker was gone, and defendant with Thibido's help loaded most of his personal effects from his apartment into his car and, before departing, told Thibido he "could have the remaining contents of the apartment," defendant had abandoned the locker and apartment even if rental periods had not expired).

Compare People v. Brewer, 690 P.2d 860 (Colo.1984) (where rent on month-to-month tenancy overdue but defendant's effects known to still be there and defendant had arranged to move them out the coming weekend without objection from landlord, this showed a continued expectation of privacy and no abandonment).

[19] State v. Christian, 95 Wash.2d 655, 628 P.2d 806 (1981).

[20] United States v. Wilson, 472 F.2d 901 (9th Cir.1972).

Compare Wilson v. Health & Hospital Corporation of Marion Co., 620 F.2d 1201 (7th Cir.1980) (with respect to *owner* of the property, one is not required to "keep his doors closed and locked * * * to maintain in full effectiveness an expectation of privacy," and thus corporation not entitled to summary judgment upon the "fact that the basement and apartment doors were open"); People v. Pitman, 211 Ill.2d 502, 286 Ill.Dec. 36, 813 N.E.2d 93 (2004) (where, though defendant did not own the farm, he had possessory interest in entire farm and had ability to exclude others, and owner had conferred on defendant legal authority to take care of the farm, barn outside the curtilage not abandoned just because doors were unlocked and wide open).

moved out, and the landlord went to the apartment in question and found the door standing open and the apartment in disarray, the court quite properly held that the tenant had abandoned the apartment. "The proper test for abandonment," the court noted, "is not whether all formal property rights have been relinquished, but whether the complaining party retains a reasonable expectation of privacy in the articles alleged to be abandoned."[21]

[21]See also United States v. Hoey, 983 F.2d 890 (8th Cir.1993) (abandonment where defendant "personally told her landlord that she was leaving," she "was six weeks behind on her rent," "held a moving sale, and her neighbor saw her leaving the apartment"); United States v. Binder, 794 F.2d 1195 (7th Cir.1986) (business office abandoned where defendant, substantially arrears in rent, had moved out and taken many business records); United States v. Sellers, 667 F.2d 1123 (4th Cir.1981) (defendant had no expectation of privacy where he had departed the community, was 5 months delinquent in rental payments, and left a note for his landlady saying he was sorry he could not pay and that he was leaving his effects behind and that she could have them); United States v. Sledge, 650 F.2d 1075 (9th Cir.1981) (defendant gave landlord notice of intent to vacate by March 31, rent paid through March, landlord left note for tenant to call on March 15 but no call received, on March 29 landlord saw apartment door wide open and premises empty, landlord entered on March 30 when circumstances unchanged; held, premises abandoned); State v. Tucker, 268 Ark. 427, 597 S.W.2d 584 (1980) (defendant had no expectation of privacy where he had not been at apartment he shared with deceased for a month, he left the state by bus without advising anyone of an intention to return, and he established residence and obtained employment in another state); Caraballo v. State, 39 So.3d 1234 (Fla.2010) (despite "lack of a final order of eviction" defendant had abandoned apartment where he served with a 3-day eviction notice for nonpayment of rent and thereafter "the apartment maintenance supervisor conducted a walk-through of the apartment and determined that it had been abandoned," following which a vendor's lock placed on door to allow access for cleaners and painters); Thomas v. State, 274 Ga. 156, 549 S.E.2d 359 (2001) (where defendant not tenant of landlord and landlord had never given permission to sublet the townhouse and two weeks earlier ordered defendant to vacate the premises, and "townhouse was abandoned by the time of the search," defendant "had no expectation of privacy at [that] time of the searches"); Criss v. State, 512 N.E.2d 858 (Ind.1987) (apartment was abandoned where left empty except for trash, and rent past due); State v. Hunt, 682 A.2d 690 (Me.1996) (where defendant testified "that he had removed from the apartment everything that he wanted, leaving behind only 'trash,' and that he left the apartment on October 5 intending never to return," he "voluntarily abandoned his apartment and the items left therein"); Commonwealth v. Lanigan, 12 Mass.App.Ct. 913, 423 N.E.2d 800 (1981) (where "the defendant immediately on learning that the police were investigating him, fled from the Commonwealth with the intention of not returning to the apartment during the short period, if any, which remained of his rental period," he had abandoned the premises; it irrelevant that police unaware of this, as a "relinquishment of rights by abandonment does not depend on knowledge by the police that the abandonment has occurred"); State v. Madera, 206 Mont. 140, 670 P.2d 552 (1983) (apartment abandoned where defendant two days overdue on rent, his car gone and curtains drawn, and landlord found key inside and personal effects gone and garbage strewn about); State v. Hodge, 225 Neb. 94, 402 N.W.2d 867 (1987) (where defendants relinquished control of house and vacated premises when lease ended, they had abandoned the

It is a fair generalization that abandonment is more readily found as to rooms occupied on a transient basis. Thus, in *Botelho* the court cautioned: "Because of the transitory nature of most motel and hotel rental arrangements, non-payment of rent in that context might well require a different rule." Illustrative is *United States v. Parizo*,[22] where defendant rented a motel room for a single night, paid only for one night, and never informed the desk that he wished to stay on beyond that time. After check-out time the following day, the manager entered the room, saw a weapon, and summoned the police. In upholding the police entry of that room, the court reasoned:

> [W]hen the term of a guest's occupancy of a room expires, the guest loses his exclusive right to privacy in the room. The manager of a motel then has the right to enter the room and may consent to a search of the room and the seizure of the items there found.[23] * * *

premises and thus had no expectation of privacy as to padlocked attic); Swearingen v. State, 101 S.W.3d 89 (Tex.Crim.App.2003) (where defendant and wife decided to move from trailer to his parent's home and landlord so advised on Dec. 24 and both keys returned to landlord by Jan. 1, and landlord cleaned trailer on Jan. 6, defendant had abandoned pair of pantyhose with leg missing that landlord had taken away with other trash); State v. Christian, 26 Wash.App. 542, 613 P.2d 1199 (1980), judgment aff'd, 95 Wash.2d 655, 628 P.2d 806 (1981) (defendant had no justified expectation of privacy in apartment on June 1 where he told landlord he would not continue tenancy after May 31, defendant put personal effects in truck and drove off on May 31, and landlord had advised him of plans to enter and clean on June 1, notwithstanding fact defendant unknownst to landlord returned and stayed another night; fact possession not terminated per landlord-tenant statute not relevant where, as here, tenant was vacating voluntarily and was not being evicted).

[22] United States v. Parizo, 514 F.2d 52 (2d Cir.1975).

[23] See also United States v. Lanier, 636 F.3d 228 (6th Cir.2011) ("general rule" is that occupant's expectation of privacy ends when the rental period has expired or been lawfully terminated); United States v. Kitchens, 114 F.3d 29 (4th Cir.1997) ("absent a pattern or practice to the contrary, a person's legitimate expectation of privacy in a motel room terminates at check-out time"); United States v. Huffhines, 967 F.2d 314 (9th Cir.1992) ("guest in a motel has no reasonable expectation of privacy in a room after the rental period has expired"); United States v. Rahme, 813 F.2d 31 (2d Cir.1987) ("when a hotel guest's rental period has expired or been lawfully terminated, the guest does not have a legitimate expectation of privacy in the hotel room or in any articles therein of which the hotel lawfully takes possession"); United States v. Larson, 760 F.2d 852 (8th Cir.1985) (defendant's expectation of privacy in motel room had lapsed where he stayed 7 hrs. past checkout time and 5 hrs. past time he allowed to stay over without paying next day's rent in advance); United States v. Diggs, 649 F.2d 731 (9th Cir.1981) (*Botelho*, note 14 supra, not applicable in motel context; abandonment existed without formal notice of eviction where defendant left owing $1,000 and was not seen or heard from thereafter and motel terminated the tenancy upon receiving room key in the mail); Sumdum v. State, 612 P.2d 1018 (Alaska 1980) ("after the rental period has terminated, a guest's reasonable expectations of privacy are greatly diminished," and thus after checkout hour motel personnel, who had been unable to reach guest by phone or by knocking, could enter); State v.

Appellant argues that, notwithstanding the expiration of the rental period, his intent to retain possession of the room remains the decisive factor and that we ordered the trial court to turn its decision upon findings bearing upon whether he had such an intent. However, intentional abandonment is relevant in different factual situations from the situation here. Had the search occurred during the rental period, appellant would have standing to object to an unauthorized search of the premises, unless prior to the search he had abandoned the premises, thereby forfeiting his right to occupancy and privacy. * * * Preliminary to the inquiry into intentional abandonment by the defendant, it must be shown that the defendant had sufficient control over the premises to establish a right to privacy therein.

Thus, if the search in *Parizo* had been conducted before check-out time, then it would be necessary to establish that the defendant had abandoned the premises "in the sense of having no apparent intention to return and make further use of them,"[24] unless the defendant's prior conduct had been such to constitute a waiver of

---

Ahumada, 125 Ariz. 316, 609 P.2d 586 (App.1980) (abandonment where defendant failed to check out of motel at room checkout time or to pay for another day in advance, as required by motel policy); State v. Kirksey, 647 S.W.2d 799 (Mo.1983) (where defendant's companion paid part of hotel bill and said they had no more money and party was leaving hotel and defendant, when questioned by police, "gave a name different from that of the room registration and told the officers that he was not a registered guest of the hotel," premises were abandoned-);Brimage v. State, 918 S.W.2d 466 (Tex.Crim.App.1994) ("logic [of this point in *Parizo*] is sound and should be applied to the present case").

[24]Paty v. State, 276 So.2d 195 (Fla.App.1973). In *Paty*, when the motel owner smelled marijuana in defendant's room and told defendant the police would be summoned, defendant fled to a building across the street carrying a footlocker. When the police arrived, they saw defendant's other personal effects in the room, but proceeded to search there and found marijuana. Defendant returned shortly thereafter and was arrested. The trial court upheld the search on the ground that the police were justified in assuming defendant had abandoned the premises, but this ruling was overturned on appeal: "While it is true that appellant fled from the room carrying

a footlocker, he left in the room his jacket and motorcycle helmet, and he left parked outside of the room the motorbike. It was then well before the checkout time for the day, and appellant had already advised the manager that he wished to have the room for another day. Within a matter of a few minutes after fleeing the scene, appellant was back sans footlocker. He confirmed that the room was his and there is no evidence to indicate that had he not been arrested he would not have remained in the room for some additional period of time. It would not seem reasonable, especially at that point in time, for the police officer to assume that appellant had vacated the premises in the sense of having no apparent intention to return and make further use of them. It is significant that there is no evidence indicating that the officer himself had assumed or believed that appellant had abandoned or vacated the room."

See alsoFarmer v. State, 759 P.2d 1031 (Okla.Crim.App.1988) (though defendant "had told the clerk to tell anyone who called that he had checked out," motel room not abandoned where "motel receipts showed that he had paid for another night, he had retained his key, and he had left his belongings").

Compare United States v. James, 534 F.3d 868 (8th Cir.2008) (motel room deemed abandoned by defendant, as while motel management

his privacy expectation.[25] And doubtless there are cases in which

only said defendant "scheduled to leave that day," assault victim "reported that James fled with all his belongings after the assault," and room "contained no personal belongings"); United States v. Hunter, 647 F.2d 566 (5th Cir.1981) (motel room abandoned before checkout time where defendant paid bill in full and left motel room with room key locked inside the room); United States v. Akin, 562 F.2d 459 (7th Cir.1977) (hotel room abandoned where tenant left door wide open and no luggage or suits were in the room); State v. Jackson, 304 Conn. 383, 40 A.3d 290 (2012) (hotel room abandoned, as "defendant manifested an intent never to return * * * when he jumped out of the hotel window in an attempt to kill himself," and "there is no reason to believe that, when he fortuitously survived the fall, his intent to return to the room was somehow revived"); Buttrum v. State, 249 Ga. 652, 293 S.E.2d 334 (1982) (motel room abandoned, even though rent paid in advance for 2 more days, where key left on counter in office and all personal belongings had been removed from room); State v. Oken, 569 A.2d 1218 (Me.1990) (though defendant had taken key with him and had left a few effects—jersey, vodka, orange juice, and pair of socks—in room, room abandoned by 8:30 a.m., before 11 a.m. checkout; court stresses no luggage there, bed never turned down, defendant paid in advance for one night by credit card, and defendant on prior day drove to another motel an hour away and checked in there and next day paid for extra day there); Commonwealth v. Paszko, 391 Mass. 164, 461 N.E.2d 222 (1984) (motel room abandoned though one-week rental period had another day to run, as defendant had already checked into another motel and had moved all his personal effects there except a few items he apparently overlooked).

[25] United States v. Molsbarger, 551 F.3d 809 (8th Cir.2009) (defendant had no reasonable expectation of privacy in hotel room after manager ordered him and other occupants

evicted for continued raucous behavior after prior warnings); Young v. Harrison, 284 F.3d 863 (8th Cir.2002) (hotel eviction of unruly guests effective, so that subsequent police entry of their room lawful, even though hotel "did not follow the procedures set out in South Dakota's Forcible Entry and Detainer statute," as presumably "South Dakota would join many other jurisdictions in concluding that a hotel guest is not a tenant and is subject to self-help eviction"); Johnson v. State, 285 Ga. 571, 679 S.E.2d 340 (2009) (when police advised hotel manager defendant selling drugs from his room, and manager decided to evict defendant and followed established protocol of calling room, then going to room and knocking when no answer to phone, and then opening door when no answer to knock, defendant "lost his expectation of privacy in the hotel room when he was properly evicted" in that manner); Commonwealth v. Molina, 459 Mass. 819, 948 N.E.2d 402 (2011) (where hotel guest on notice manager had authority to evict guest for violation of law, and smell of marijuana detected outside room and hotel employees found marijuana within, and manager then "took affirmative steps to effectuate the eviction by physically preventing the defendant's entry into the room by double-locking the door," defendant's "occupancy rights" and "his privacy interest in the room" were "properly terminated" before police entry); State v. Perkins, 588 N.W.2d 491 (Minn.1999) (where registration card defendant signed gave notice guest would be "removed" if other guests were disturbed by a guest or his associates, and defendant aware of two earlier complaints and warnings prior to the time manager asked him to leave, and of fact "the 'party' remained excessively loud," defendant no longer had a reasonable expectation of privacy in the room).

Compare United States v. Bautista, 362 F.3d 584 (9th Cir.2004) (where motel manager had taken "no affirmative steps to repossess the room once she learned that it had been reserved with a stolen credit card," but

no abandonment will be deemed to have occurred even after the initially indicated term of rental, as where the tenant had arranged for credit card payment of all charges and both the motel and tenant treated the tenant's nondeparture as extending the term.[26] Indeed, an abandonment conclusion may sometimes be inappropriate because of "the hotel's generally lax practices in enforcing its checkout time."[27]

Another difference between houses and apartments, on the one hand, and transient quarters, on the other, is discernible in those cases where the defendant has been arrested prior to the time of the search. When a person is regularly residing at certain premises, "[a]bsence due to arrest and incarceration while awaiting trial is not of itself a sufficient basis upon which to conclude that the accused has abandoned any reasonable expectation of privacy in his home."[28] By comparison, where a person occupying a hotel or motel room is arrested under circumstances indicating that his incarceration will be more than temporary, the arrest may be viewed as terminating the occupancy of the room.[29] This

---

merely "asked the police to investigate the matter * * * and would have evicted Bautista only if he later failed to provide either a satisfactory explanation or another form of payment," and "manager did not ask the police to evict Bautista," defendant "was still a lawful occupant who retained a legitimate expectation of privacy in the room"). The court distinguished People v. Satz, 61 Cal.App.4th 322, 71 Cal.Rptr.2d 433 (1998), where defendant used a stolen credit card to register and admitted she had no money to pay for the room, and the manager specifically asked the police to assist her in evicting the defendant.

[26]United States v. Mulder, 808 F.2d 1346 (9th Cir.1987) (defendant secured payment of bill with American Express card and indicated one-day stay, defendant returned seeking his bag 48 hours later and hotel had billed his card for another day; no abandonment).

[27]United States v. Dorais, 241 F.3d 1124 (9th Cir.2001) (where hotel did not strictly enforce noon checkout and defendant indicated he would stay until 12:30, abandonment occurred only after latter time). Consider also United States v. Lanier, 636 F.3d 228 (6th Cir.2011) (citing cases in support,

court notes exceptions to general rule where defendant "ask[ed] the hotel to extend his stay" and thus "receive[d] permission from the hotel for a later check-out time," or where "the hotel had [a] history of acquiescing in delayed departures by" defendant, not present in this case; also, while hotel, upon discovery of drugs in defendant's room allowed police to search the room before one-hour "traditional grace period" had expired, since defendant "knew nothing about the one-hour grace period" hotel free to retract it in specific cases, as where drugs seen).

[28]Commonwealth v. Strickland, 457 Pa. 631, 326 A.2d 379 (1974).

But, additional facts may show abandonment in such circumstances. See, e.g., Commonwealth v. Jackson, 384 Mass. 572, 428 N.E.2d 289 (1981) (defendant, arrested Dec. 26, had paid rent through Jan. 1, but after arrest he told cotenants to move out and remove his belongings; this "protection of one's belongings is not inconsistent with an intent to abandon the premises," and thus police entry of empty apartment in mid-January proper).

[29]State v. Rhodes, 337 So.2d 207 (La.1976) (where armed robber was arrested in his motel room and at time of arrest locker with his personal ef-

is particularly likely if, as in *Abel v. United States*,[30] the arresting officers see to it that the defendant checks out of the hotel after his arrest. In *Abel* the Supreme Court upheld a search of the room defendant had occupied at the time of his arrest, reasoning that because he "had vacated the room" the hotel "had the exclusive right to its possession" at the time of the search.

At least one commentator has called *Abel* into question, stating:

> It may be argued that the petitioner had not voluntarily relinquished control of the premises, and therefore the theory of abandonment is most tenuous. Additionally, subsequent movement of Fourth Amendment conceptualization toward an increased emphasis on constitutionally protected privacy renders the viability of *Abel* increasingly dubious.[31]

But, while it may be true that an intent to abandon cannot be presumed merely from the fact of arrest and incarceration, it does not follow that a person lawfully arrested cannot be said to have abandoned the room by electing to check out after the arrest. The problem here, as a practical matter, is that the arrested transient may find himself in a "Catch-22" situation; he may be confronted with the choice of abandoning the room and certain personal effects there (thus subjecting them to police scrutiny because of the abandonment) or of taking the effects with him (thus subjecting them to inventory at the station). Perhaps limits upon the inventory authority would alleviate this situation somewhat.[32]

Another variation of the problem arises when the defendant has not checked out but, by virtue of being in police custody, is not in a position to extend his occupancy. Such was the situation in *United States v. Croft*,[33] where the court asserted:

> Defendant argues that the expiration of the rental period should

---

fects was taken to station, it was not "unreasonable on the succeeding day to search the motel room, the occupancy of which had been terminated by the prior day's arrest and incarceration of defendant on a fugitive warrant"); Commonwealth v. Netto, 438 Mass. 686, 783 N.E.2d 439 (2003) (day after motel room occupants arrested on murder warrants, manager asked police to take items remaining in the room; "even if the motel manager let the police into the room slightly prior to the customary checkout time," effects were abandoned due to "the guests' abandonment of the room * * * due to their arrest on murder charges," and fact that the following day "they had not returned to retrieve their belongings, made any arrangements to have someone else retrieve their

belongings, or taken any steps to extend the rental period").

[30] Abel v. United States, 362 U.S. 217, 80 S.Ct. 683, 4 L.Ed.2d 668 (1960).

[31] J. Cook, Constitutional Rights of the Accused—Pretrial Rights 314 (1972).

[32] See § 5.5(b).

[33] United States v. Croft, 429 F.2d 884 (10th Cir.1970). See also United States v. Huffhines, 967 F.2d 314 (9th Cir.1992) (defendant's argument he had continuing expectation of privacy in motel room "because his arrest prevented him from returning to the motel to renew the rental agreement" rejected, as he "cannot rely on his own misconduct to extend the period of his expectation of privacy"); United States

not control in this case because his arrest prior to check-out time prevented him from returning to the motel and perhaps extending the rental period. We are not persuaded by this argument for it was defendant's own conduct that prevented his return to the motel.

It may be questioned, however, whether expiration of the rental period—especially under these circumstances—can be said to terminate fully the guest's justified expectation of privacy as to personal property he had secured in the privacy of his room. Certainly the innkeeper must be able to remove those effects from the room so that it can be rented to another, and if in that process he finds evidence of crime it may well be that the former guest cannot complain if, as in *Parizo*, that incriminating evidence is made available to the police. But the innkeeper is not without responsibility as to personalty left behind,[34] and thus it might be doubted whether he can give the police carte blanche to rummage through those effects.[35] However, if the hotel places the guest's effects in storage and then, upon learning of the guest's

v. Rahme, 813 F.2d 31 (2d Cir.1987) ("when a defendant has been arrested, it was presumably his 'own conduct that prevented his return to the [h]otel'"); United States v. Ramirez, 810 F.2d 1338 (5th Cir.1987) (makes no difference abandonment involuntary because of defendant's arrest); United States v. Lee, 700 F.2d 424 (10th Cir.1983) (following *Croft* on similar facts); Gardner v. State, 296 Ark. 41, 754 S.W.2d 518 (1988) (after defendant's arrest motel employees took possession of his effects per standard procedures and later turned purse over to police on their request; held, notwithstanding fact defendant's "inability to return to his room was not of his own choosing," no "expectation of privacy in the purse after employees of the Inn had removed it from Gardner's former room and had taken it into their possession"); Myers v. State, 454 N.E.2d 861 (Ind.1983) (after defendant's arrest his two-day rental of motel room expired, at which point "he no longer had an expectation of privacy" in it); Blades v. Commonwealth, 339 S.W.3d 450 (Ky.2011) (following *Croft*, court declines "to require police to obtain a search warrant every time an arrest potentially inhibits a guest from returning and extending his or her rental period"); Obermeyer v. State, 97 Nev. 158, 625 P.2d 95 (1981) (defendant arrested, hotel keys found on

his person, so 2 days later officer went to hotel and searched room with hotel personnel; proper, as defendant's rent past due, notwithstanding fact defendant's effects still in the room).

[34] R. Anderson, The Hotelman's Basic Law § 16:9 (1965).

[35] The leading case in point is Commonwealth v. Brundidge, 533 Pa. 167, 620 A.2d 1115 (1993), where the court concluded that while after the rental period on a motel room has run no justified expectation of privacy "exists in the room or in any item in plain view to anyone readying the room after checkout time for the next occupant," "a motel guest has a reasonable expectation of privacy to the contents of discrete and concealed personal effects in a motel room after checkout time.

"While the motel personnel must have access to and use of the motel room after the rental period expires, this does not extend to items of personal luggage or other containers which do not reveal the nature of their contents. In this case, the motel management had no economic or other justification to examine the contents of the closed personal possessions of its guests, especially where only a relatively short period of time had elapsed since checkout time, appellee's car remained parked at the motel, the room remained locked, and petitioner returned shortly thereafter to register

arrest, turns them over to the police, this provides a basis for police inventory of those effects.[36]

Yet another situation in which courts have had to decide whether the premises have been abandoned to the extent that the occupant's justified expectation of privacy therein has ceased is where those premises have been seriously damaged by fire. Certainly there will be instances in which it may fairly be concluded that the tenant in those premises has left without any intention to return,[37] but the notion that the owner of the burned premises has abandoned them merely because they are not inhabitable[38] is a highly questionable one. No such abandonment should be found when the owner has boarded up the premises[39] or when it appears that there are salvageable items of personal property

---

for a second night. Therefore, the search of the jacket [found in the closet with a protective bag over it] should have been accomplished pursuant to a judicial warrant issued upon probable cause."

See also United States v. Ramos, 12 F.3d 1019 (11th Cir.1994) (at end of 5-month lease of condo unit, when defendant to check out by 10 a.m. and another renter due later that day, cleaners entered that afternoon and summoned police, who looked inside locked briefcase; in holding lower court erred in ruling briefcase abandoned, court stresses testimony that general practice when cleaner finds effects was "to pack the personal belongings and *hold* them until the owner of the items-the departing lessee-could be located"); United States v. Huffhines, 967 F.2d 314 (9th Cir.1992) ("Although the assistant manager lacked the authority to consent to a search of Huffhines belongings left in the room, it was not clearly erroneous for the court to find that the assistant manager's consent to a search of the room included the area under the mattress where the gun was found"); Johnson v. State, 285 Ga. 571, 679 S.E.2d 340 (2009) (eviction from hotel room, resulting in "loss of the expectation of privacy in the room does not mean that [defendant] had lost his expectation of privacy with regard to personal items in the room," but police check on bulge in jacket justified by safety concerns).

[36]United States v. Rahme, 813 F.2d 31 (2d Cir.1987).

[37]E.g., State v. Felger, 19 Or.App. 39, 526 P.2d 611 (1974); State v. Disbrow, 266 N.W.2d 246 (S.D.1978) (abandonment re May 1 inspection where all personal effects in defendant's apartment destroyed in April 25 fire, defendant never paid rent for April or May, and after living with friend for short time defendant moved to another state).

Even if the tenant is deemed to have abandoned the burned premises, it does not inevitably follow that this would cause his "privacy interest to shift automatically to [the owner] like some reversionary property interest." State v. Smith, 656 S.W.2d 882 (Tenn. Crim.App.1983) (no expectation of privacy in landlord, as he also made no efforts to secure the premises).

[38]E.g., People v. Bailey, 42 Mich.App. 359, 202 N.W.2d 557 (1972).

The condition of the premises may have some bearing, however, upon the question of whether an arson investigation into the premises would be a reasonable search. See § 10.4.

[39]Swan v. Superior Court, 8 Cal.App.3d 392, 87 Cal.Rptr. 280 (1970). See also State v. Zindros, 189 Conn. 228, 456 A.2d 288 (1983) (no abandonment where tenant came to premises after fire several times and on leaving each time secured the premises).

in the premises that the owner could be expected to retrieve.[40] However, even absent a fire, it sometimes happens that premises are in such an extreme state of disrepair and apparently unoccupied as to support the conclusion that those premises apparently have been abandoned.[41]

It is also necessary to distinguish abandoned premises from those that are merely unoccupied, for justified privacy expectations are not totally lacking as to the latter. The point is illustrated by *State v. Finnell*,[42] where the owner of vacant residential structures challenged city code provisions regarding warrantless inspection of the interior of vacant buildings. The city argued "that no reasonable expectation of privacy exists in a location without the occurrence of intimate and personal activities traditionally associated with the home," but the court responded that "this is not the appropriate test." Emphasizing that the defendant "is the owner and maintains both possession and control of the building" and "regulates access to the building," the court concluded that he had "a subjective expectation of privacy" in those premises "that is reasonable-albeit an expectation that is protected to a lesser extent than such expectations

---

[40]People v. Dorney, 17 Ill.App.3d 785, 308 N.E.2d 646 (1974): "On the record before this court we cannot say that the trial court's finding of non-abandonment was clearly erroneous. Although the trailer was rendered uninhabitable by the fire, defendant returned on at least one occasion to pick up salvageable items of personal property. When the defendant returned a second time for similar reasons, the trailer had been removed by the authorities without his permission and without notice to defendant of its new location. These facts certainly do not warrant the inference that defendant intended to abandon his trailer."

See also State v. Hansen, 286 N.W.2d 163 (Iowa 1979) (rejecting the "habitability" standard as inconsistent with *Katz* and finding a search had occurred of house not damaged extensively where defendant, temporarily housed with relatives, still had much personal property therein).

[41]McKenney v. Harrison, 635 F.3d 354 (8th Cir.2011) (reasonable for police to conclude house abandoned where they "found the house in disrepair, with an unkept yard and a fence that was incomplete and falling apart," there "no vehicles parked in the drive-

way," no one "responded when the officers knocked on the front door," "back door was open" and officers "could see into kitchen, where the cabinets were open and empty, the refrigerator was open and empty," and "there was no furniture or personal effects" and "no lights on, sounds from appliances, or other indications that the house had electrical power").

Compare State v. Carter, 54 So.3d 1093 (La.2011) (no showing officers "reasonably believed that the house was abandoned, as detective merely stated conclusion that residence was "abandoned" and "did *not* testify that the house appeared abandoned," and "officers on the scene evidently did not report that they viewed a dilapidated structure boarded up and surrounded by overgrown weeds, or that the officer came by a belief the home had been abandoned from any other reliable basis").

[42]State v. Finnell, 115 Ohio App.3d 583, 685 N.E.2d 1267 (1996). Compare State v. Perry, 124 N.J. 128, 590 A.2d 624 (1991) (no search for officers to enter house "that appeared vacant and whose front door was not only unlocked but open").

where the owner is active and the site was in productive use."[43]

§ 2.3(b) Entry of residence

The home "is accorded the full range of Fourth Amendment protections,"[44] for it is quite clearly a place as to which there exists a justified expectation of privacy against unreasonable intrusion. It is beyond question, therefore, that an unconsented police entry[45] (sometimes involving no more than the opening of a screen door)[46] into a residential unit, be it a house or an apartment or a hotel or motel room,[47] constitutes a search within the

---

[43]Thus, the court added, defendant's "privacy interest in his vacant buildings is less than that of home owners in their homes, or business owners in their business premises." And if, which was unknown, defendant "uses the buildings for storage," the court added, "the city admits that his interest would be greater than if the buildings were completely empty."

[Section 2.3(b)]

[44]Lewis v. United States, 385 U.S. 206, 87 S.Ct. 424, 17 L.Ed.2d 312 (1966).

[45]Even if "very limited." McNairy v. State, 835 S.W.2d 101 (Tex.Crim. App.1991). See also Martin v. United States, 952 A.2d 181 (D.C.App.2008) (where unconsented police entry of house, after which defendant retrieved weapon from closet, trial court's "no search" ruling in error, as "the Fourth Amendment was implicated as soon as the police entered").

[46]As explained in United States v. Arellano-Ochoa, 461 F.3d 1142 (9th Cir.2006), whether "opening a screen door breaches a reasonable expectation of privacy depends on the circumstances. During winter in a cold climate, people ordinarily keep the solid door shut. About the only way for mail and package delivery people, solicitors, missionaries, children funding school trips, and neighbors to knock on the door is to open the screen door and knock on the solid door. People understand that visitors will need to open the screen door, and have no expectation to the contrary. The reason why people do not feel that their privacy is breached by opening the screen door to knock is that it isn't; the solid door

protects their privacy.

"In the summer, when people leave their solid doors open for ventilation, the screen door is all that separates the inside from the outside. People can get a resident's attention by knocking on the screen door without opening it. Where the solid door is wide open, the screen door is what protects the privacy of the people inside—not just their visual privacy, which it protects only partially, but also their privacy from undesired intrusion. Where the solid door is open so that the screen door is all that protects the privacy of the residents, opening the screen door infringes upon a reasonable and legitimate expectation of privacy."

[47]Or, indeed, even a tent, for though "a tent may not provide the sturdy protection against the winds, the rains, the heat, and the cold which a customary house provides, the tent-dweller is no less protected from unreasonable government intrusions merely because his dwelling has walls of canvas rather than walls of stone." Kelley v. State, 146 Ga.App. 179, 245 S.E.2d 872 (1978). See also United States v. Sandoval, 200 F.3d 659 (9th Cir.2000) (defendant had expectation of privacy as to tent, closed on all 4 sides and in area "heavily covered by vegetation and virtually impenetrable," on Bureau of Land Management land, without regard to whether he had permission, as "camping on public land, even without permission, is far different from squatting in a private residence," and defendant "was never instructed to vacate or risk eviction"); People v. Schafer, 946 P.2d 938 (Colo. 1997) (defendant had reasonable ex-

meaning of *Katz v. United States*.[48] Moreover, this Fourth Amendment protection (and thus this search characterization of an entry) extends even to "occupants of flimsily constructed dwellings with unobstructed windows or other openings directly on public lands, streets, or sidewalks, who failed to lock their doors to bar entrance."[49]

Sometimes the police or a person acting on their behalf will resort to a subterfuge in order to gain entry into a home. Illustrative is *Lewis v. United States*,[50] where an undercover narcotics agent falsely identified himself as "Jimmy the Pollack" and claimed that a mutual friend had told him defendant might be able to supply marijuana, at which the defendant received the agent into his house and sold him marijuana there. The Court was not sympathetic to the defendant's contention that his justified expectation of privacy in his home had been breached:

> [W]hen, as here, the home is converted into a commercial center to which outsiders are invited for purposes of transacting unlawful business, that business is entitled to no greater sanctity than if it were carried on in a store, a garage, a car, or on the street. A government agent, in the same manner as a private person, may accept an invitation to do business and may enter upon the premises for the very purposes contemplated by the occupant.

The breadth of the *Lewis* exception, especially as to the kinds of deception that are permissible, is considered elsewhere in this Treatise.[51]

It is not improper for a police officer to call at a particular house and seek admission for the purpose of investigating a com-

---

pectation of privacy as to interior of his tent where he "camping on unimproved publicly accessible land which was neither fenced nor posted"); State v. Pruss, 145 Idaho 623, 181 P.3d 1231 (2008) (defendant had reasonable expectation of privacy in his "hooch," a camouflaged frame structure in the woods with a backpacking tent erected inside wooden frame); Alward v. State, 112 Nev. 141, 912 P.2d 243 (1996) (defendants "had an objectively reasonable expectation of privacy in the tent," which was "their temporary residence," notwithstanding fact they "camped on land managed by the Bureau of Land Management"). For more on the expectation of privacy in tents and other camping shelters, see Note, 26 U.Mem.L.Rev. 293 (1995). For more on the expectation of privacy of those trespassing on federal lands, as in *Sandoval*, see Annot., 66 A.L.R.5th 373 (1999); Comment, 50 Emory L.J. 1357 (2001).

Or, indeed, even a fish house, "erected and equipped to protect its occupants from the elements and often providing eating, sleeping, and other facilities." State v. Larsen, 650 N.W.2d 144 (Minn.2002).

Compare United States v. Ruckman, 806 F.2d 1471 (10th Cir.1986) (cave in which defendant residing on land owned by U.S. and controlled by Bureau of Land Management not within Fourth Amendment's protection).

[48]Katz v. United States, 389 U.S. 347, 88 S.Ct. 507, 19 L.Ed.2d 576 (1967).

[49]United States v. Moss, 963 F.2d 673 (4th Cir.1992).

[50]Lewis v. United States, 385 U.S. 206, 87 S.Ct. 424, 17 L.Ed.2d 312 (1966).

[51]See § 8.2(m).

plaint or conducting other official business. If admission is voluntarily granted by a person who is in a position to give such effective consent,[52] then the policeman may enter and make observations while therein consistent with the scope of the permission he was given.[53] But the mere fact that the door of the house is opened in response to the officer's knock or ring does not mean that the officer is entitled to walk past the person so responding into the interior of the residence.[54] Nor may the officer enter the home when there is no response at all,[55] even if the door is open.[56] As stated in *State v. Crider*:[57]

> It is not unreasonable for police officers, in the pursuit of criminal investigations, to seek interviews with suspects or witnesses at their homes, but their right to call upon them at their homes for such purposes does not include the right to walk in uninvited merely because there is no response to a knock or a ring.

The court in *Crider* pointed out that the "mere presence of a hallway in the interior of a single family dwelling, without more, is not in itself an invitation to the public to enter," so that police entry only into the hallway "must be viewed as an intrusion into an area in which the defendant was entitled to a reasonable expectation of privacy."[58]

The *Crider* rule is applicable to a building containing only one

---

[52]On who may consent, see §§ 8.4, 8.5. As noted there, some persons who could not give a valid consent to a full search of the residence (e.g., children residing there) might nonetheless be able to consent to entry of a policeman to that area where visitors are normally received.

[53]See § 8.1(c).

[54]United States v. Curran, 498 F.2d 30 (9th Cir.1974); People v. O'Hearn, 931 P.2d 1168 (Colo.1997).

So too, a police officer is not free to enter an open garage door. United States v. Oaxaca, 233 F.3d 1154 (9th Cir.2000).

[55]Compare United States v. Walker, 474 F.3d 1249 (10th Cir.2007) (where officer knocked several times on the storm door but got no response, and then opened the storm door and knocked on the inner wooden door, which was about ten inches ajar, that "not a Fourth Amendment intrusion," as "most visitors would have done the same").

[56]State v. Kochel, 744 N.W.2d 771 (N.D.2008) ("While an open door may 'invite the gaze of curious passers-by

and lessen the reasonable anticipation of privacy in the home,' it does not alone justify an officer's entry").

[57]State v. Crider, 341 A.2d 1 (Me. 1975).

[58]Similarly, where a residence has a front door and a patio door and also a door leading through the garage to a kitchen door, an officer wanting to serve civil process may not opt for walking through the garage, which "is an intimate part of a person's residence." State v. Blumler, 458 N.W.2d 300 (N.D.1990). See also State v. Kochel, 744 N.W.2d 771 (N.D.2008) (distinguishing *Kitchen*, infra, improper for police to enter addition to mobile home, as "the structure is fully enclosed by wooden walls complete with a door and a window").

Compare State v. Breuer, 577 N.W.2d 41 (Iowa 1998) (where house divided into 2 apartments had porch with 2 doors, and officer desiring to question defendant rang his doorbell but received no response and then opened door and walked up stairs to second floor apartment and knocked on door at top of stairs and, when defendant opened door, smelled burning

residential unit, and does not carry over in its entirety to such multiple-occupancy structures as apartment buildings, hotels and motels. As *Crider* elaborates:

> Police officers in the performance of their duties may, without violating the constitution, peaceably enter upon the common hallway of a multiple dwelling without a warrant or express permission to do so. * * * There is no invasion of privacy when a policeman without force enters the common hallway of a multiple-family house in the furtherance of an investigation.[59]

This is somewhat of an overstatement. It is correct when the circumstances indicate that the hallway is readily accessible to the general public,[60] but not otherwise. For example, in *United*

---

marijuana, court holds defendant had legitimate expectation of privacy as to the stairway and landing because it "was not an area used by other people," but that because police "may go onto a person's private property, approach the residence, and knock on a door to speak with a person regarding a police investigation," climbing stairs was a legitimate "minimal intrusion" equivalent to trying a back door when no response at front door); State v. Kitchen, 572 N.W.2d 106 (N.D.1997) (though area entered by police characterized as an "enclosed entryway," defendant's reliance on *Crider* unavailing, as court concludes area is "a porch-type entrance," as inner door flush with original exterior wall of house and "vestibule-like addition" had an unlocked screen door, so space "was impliedly open to at least some access by the public").

[59]Assuming circumstances in which this is so, it is another matter whether the officer, while there, may make use of that vantage point to look into or listen at a particular residential unit. This matter is explored in the immediately following subsection.

As for what other investigative techniques are permissible, consider Harvin v. United States, 228 Ct.Cl. 605, 661 F.2d 885 (Ct.Cl.1981) (where investigator put match sticks between door and door jam of plaintiff's motel room to keep track of his comings and goings, this no search; "plaintiff had no reasonable expectation of privacy which was invaded when the match sticks fell after someone opened the door"); Commonwealth v. Montanez, 410 Mass. 290, 571 N.E.2d 1372 (1991) (no search for officer to move tile in dropped ceiling directly outside door to defendant's apartment and thereby discover defendant's narcotics stash).

[60]United States v. Rheault, 561 F.3d 55 (1st Cir.2009) (tenant of apartment on second floor without expectation of privacy in washing machine on third floor landing, to which third floor tenants and their guests had relatively unfettered access); United States v. Dillard, 438 F.3d 675 (6th Cir.2006) ("Dillard did not have a reasonable expectation of privacy in the common hallway and stairway of his duplex that were unlocked and open to the public"; court also stresses door was ajar and that "there was no visible way for the police or anyone else to alert the duplex tenant of their presence"); United States v. Mendoza, 281 F.3d 712 (8th Cir.2002) (duplex, where outer door to vestibule not secured, there were two mailboxes outside, and "there was no signal to the officers that knocking on the outer door would have been necessary"); United States v. Cephas, 254 F.3d 488 (4th Cir.2001) (police officer's movement from door of house containing apartments to door of defendant's apartment was with consent of another resident, but in any event was "through an area common to the several separate apartments in the house, an area where any pollster or salesman could have presented himself"); United States v. Brown, 169 F.3d 89 (1st Cir.1999); United States v. Clark, 67 F.3d 1154 (5th Cir.1995) (apartment building upper level walk-

States v. Carriger[61] the entrances to the apartment building were locked and could only be opened by a key or by someone within activating a buzzer system. A federal agent slipped into the building by holding the door when several workmen exited the premises; he then went to the third floor via a stairway, where he observed an exchange of drugs in the hallway. Relying upon Justice Jackson's concurring opinion in *McDonald v. United States*,[62] the court in *Carriger* held that the "officer's entry into this locked apartment building without permission[63] and without a warrant of any kind was an illegal entry and violated appellant's Fourth Amendment rights." The court reasoned:

> We cannot agree with the district court that *McDonald* may be distinguished upon the basis that it proscribed a forcible entry into an apartment building while the entry here was peaceable. Whether the officer entered forcibly through a landlady's window or by guile through a normally locked entrance door, there can be no difference in the tenant's subjective expectation of privacy, and no difference in the degree of privacy that the Fourth Amendment protects. A tenant expects other tenants and invited guests to enter in the common areas of the building, but he does not expect trespassers.

Other courts have reached the same conclusion upon similar

---

way "neither enclosed nor locked"); United States v. Acosta, 965 F.2d 1248 (3d Cir.1992); United States v. Sewell, 942 F.2d 1209 (7th Cir.1991); United States v. Penco, 612 F.2d 19 (2d Cir. 1979); Brown v. United States, 627 A.2d 499 (D.C.App.1993); Cox v. State, 160 Ga.App. 199, 286 S.E.2d 482 (1981); People v. Smith, 152 Ill.2d 229, 178 Ill.Dec. 335, 604 N.E.2d 858 (1992) (unlocked "common area shared by other tenants, the landlord, their social guests and other invitees"); Commonwealth v. Acosta, 416 Mass. 279, 627 N.E.2d 466 (1993); State v. Macke, 594 S.W.2d 300 (Mo.App.1980); Commonwealth v. Miley, 314 Pa.Super. 88, 460 A.2d 778 (1983); State v. Eddy, 519 A.2d 1137 (R.I.1987).

[61]United States v. Carriger, 541 F.2d 545 (6th Cir.1976).

[62]McDonald v. United States, 335 U.S. 451, 69 S.Ct. 191, 93 L.Ed. 153 (1948), where an officer climbed through a window into the landlady's room and then proceeded to the second floor and, by standing on a chair, looked through the transom into defendant's room and saw gambling paraphernalia. Justice Jackson asserted "that each tenant of a building, while

he has no right to exclude from the common hallways those who enter lawfully, does have a personal and constitutionally protected interest in the integrity and security of the entire building against unlawful breaking and entry."

[63]By contrast, entry with permission, even if obtained by a ruse, does not violate the Fourth Amendment. See, e.g., State v. Anderson, 517 N.W.2d 208 (Iowa 1994) (officers "gained entry to the apartment building by randomly pushing apartment buzzers until someone let them in the locked building"; despite such "ruse" officers' presence "was not unlawful until such time as someone with authority requested them to leave," and thus overhearing conversation in hallway no search).

As for consent without a ruse, see United States v. Taylor, 248 F.3d 506 (6th Cir.2001) (officers communicated via intercom with residents "until they found a resident who was willing to let them in, provided that she not be identified as the one giving them access," and thus entry of locked common areas lawful under *Carriger*).

facts,[64] but there are also quite a few cases to the contrary,[65]

[64]United States v. Werra, 638 F.3d 326 (1st Cir.2011) (defendant had a justified expectation of privacy in foyer area of house within which he lived with about a half dozen others, unrelated, as operation of premises was "in some respects a collective undertaking, with both the financial arrangements and the informal relationship among the residents suggestive of a single household"); United States v. Heath, 259 F.3d 522 (6th Cir.2001) ("the holding of *Carriger* is applicable here," as the officers "entered a locked building without utilizing the proper procedure"; fact they used key lawfully seized from defendant makes no difference, as "the mere possession of a key will not transform an illegal entry into a valid one," for it "is the *authority* to enter, not the manner of entry, that provides the legality for the officers' conduct"); Reardon v. Wroan, 811 F.2d 1025 (7th Cir.1987) (expectation of privacy in hallway of fraternity house; "fraternity members could best be characterized as 'roommates in the same house,' not simply co-tenants sharing certain common areas. Moreover, a fraternity, by definition, is intended to be something of an exclusive living arrangement with the goal of maximizing the privacy of its affairs"); United States v. Booth, 455 A.2d 1351 (D.C.App.1983) (police not entitled to enter hallway of rooming house where nothing about the premises suggested strangers free to enter); People v. Trull, 64 Ill.App.3d 385, 20 Ill.Dec. 960, 380 N.E.2d 1169 (1978) (holding "that the common entries and hallways of a locked apartment building are protected by the fourth amendment"); State v. Di Bartolo, 276 So.2d 291 (La.1973) ("apparently the building was kept locked and only tenants who had keys and guests whom they admitted could gain entrance to the building"); Garrison v. State, 28 Md.App. 257, 345 A.2d 86 (1975) ("the entrance door was kept locked and only tenants and management personnel had keys to the door," and the "only way one visiting a tenant could gain entrance was by telephoning a tenant who 'would come down' and unlock the door"); People v. Beachman, 98 Mich.App. 544, 296 N.W.2d 305 (1980) (Fourth Amendment protections extend to lobby of locked residential hotel). See also Note, 101 Mich.L. Rev. 273, 310 (2002) (concluding upon well-reasoned analysis that "Supreme Court precedent, the history of the Fourth Amendment, the intent of the Framers, and considerations of sound public policy all necessitate the recognition of a constitutionally protected privacy interest within the locked common-areas of an apartment building").

[65]United States v. Nohara, 3 F.3d 1239 (9th Cir.1993) (police entry of "high security" apartment building when defendant "buzzed" in one Nobrega who contacted defendant via intercom and who then cooperating with police in investigation of Nobrega's drug supplier; "an apartment dweller has no reasonable expectation of privacy in the common areas of the building whether the officer trespasses or not"); United States v. Barrios-Moriera, 872 F.2d 12 (2d Cir.1989) ("common hallway" in apartment building is "an area where there is no legitimate expectation of privacy * * * even though the area is guarded by a locked door"); United States v. Luschen, 614 F.2d 1164 (8th Cir.1980) (no expectation of privacy in apartment building hallway even though it within "a security building" officer only able to enter by getting "security key" from manager); State v. Talley, 307 S.W.3d 723 (Tenn.2010) (collecting federal and state cases in accord with view that there is no "reasonable expectation of privacy in the common areas of a locked apartment building," court holds that police entry of locked condominium building by virtue of assistance from unknown person who opened the door for the officers was lawful, especially in light of fact "that the condominium residents had collectively provided not only the police department but also several others with the entry code for use in the ordinary course of their duties").

which now represent "the majority position."[66] One court distinguished *Carriger* in answering in the negative the question "whether tenants in a large, high-rise apartment building, the front door of which has an undependable lock that was inoperable on the day in question, have a reasonable expectation of privacy in the common areas of their building."[67]

We have seen that the absence of a lock on the premises is typically viewed as manifesting that hallways and other common areas are open to the public when the place is an apartment building, hotel or motel, but not when the place is a one-unit residence. What then if the place is a rooming house? The better view is represented by *State v. Titus*,[68] holding that except in the case in which it is very obvious from other circumstances that the rooming house is open to the general public,[69] a rooming house is to be treated in this respect as if it were a single-unit dwelling, so that an unlocked or even open outer door cannot be treated by the police as alone manifesting an invitation to enter.[70] As explained in *Titus*:

> This holding does not extend to common hallways in unlocked apartment buildings, which generally serve only to connect separate, self-contained living units typically complete with all of the traditional living areas (i.e., bathrooms, dining rooms, living rooms, kitchens, etc.). Interior hallways in rooming houses are protected only by virtue of linking such traditional rooms within the house— they provide rooming house residents with the only means of access to those rooms, and are an inseparable feature of their "home." In other words, it is not any inherent nature of a hallway that controls, but rather what the hallway links (i.e., individual self-contained living units versus shared traditional living areas).

Like analysis is called for when the police have entered other areas of a multiple-occupancy structure, such as a laundry room,[71] an attic,[72] a basement[73] or parking facility.[74] Observations therein do not constitute a Fourth Amendment search if that area is

[66]State v. Talley, 307 S.W.3d 723 (Tenn.2010).

[67]United States v. Miravalles, 280 F.3d 1328 (11th Cir.2002).

[68]State v. Titus, 707 So.2d 706 (Fla.1998).

[69]And thus the *Titus* court distinguished City of Evanston v. Hopkins, 330 Ill.App. 337, 71 N.E.2d 209 (1947), upholding police entry of a rooming house where there was a "Public Telephone" sign at the entrance and the door was open.

[70]Accord: People v. Douglas, 2 Cal.App.3d 592, 82 Cal.Rptr. 718 (1969); Bryant v. United States, 599 A.2d 1107 (D.C.App.1991); United States v. Booth, 455 A.2d 1351 (D.C. App.1983); State v. Berlow, 284 N.J.Super. 356, 665 A.2d 404 (Ct.Law Div.1995).

Contra: United States v. Anderson, 533 F.2d 1210 (D.C.Cir. 1976); United States v. Perkins, 286 F.Supp. 259 (D.D.C.1968), aff'd 432 F.2d 612 (D.C.Cir.); State v. Kechrid, 822 S.W.2d 552 (Mo.App.1992).

[71]United States v. Marrero, 651 F.3d 453 (6th Cir.2011) ("it was a common area of the apartment complex").

[72]Griffin v. West RS, Inc., 143 Wash.2d 81, 18 P.3d 558 (2001) (in this civil case, it a proper instruction that tenant of apartment building had reasonable expectation of privacy in

readily accessible to the public, but do if the area in question has been sufficiently secured so as to give the tenants a justified expectation of privacy in that place. In making that determination, it must be kept in mind that not all multiple-occupancy buildings should be treated in like fashion; there is, for example, a difference between "a two-family dwelling such as a duplex" and a large apartment building.[75] In all such cases, however, it must be remembered that the fact the area is not open to the

---

attic area accessible only through living space of that tenant).

[73]State v. Reddick, 207 Conn. 323, 541 A.2d 1209 (1988) (it a search for police to enter basement of 2-apartment house; "the basement was secured from the outside and readily accessible only from the two apartments within the dwelling" and thus "is an area where a tenant might expect other tenants and invited guests but would not expect deliverymen, salesmen, mailmen, policemen or trespassers"); Bryant v. United States, 599 A.2d 1107 (D.C.App.1991) (was a search for police to enter basement of rooming house where, as trial judge concluded, there no indication it "open to the general public"); Garrison v. State, 28 Md.App. 257, 345 A.2d 86 (1975) (police made a search when they entered "a basement area closed to the public and to be used only by tenants of the building").

But see United States v. Brooks, 645 F.3d 971 (8th Cir.2011) (tenant had no reasonable expectation of privacy as to staircase that "leads to the basement of the multifamily dwelling, in which there is a common area shared by all tenants," as "there exists no 'generalized expectation of privacy in the common areas of an apartment building'"); United States v. Hawkins, 139 F.3d 29 (1st Cir.1998) (where entry of building lawful to execute search warrant for defendant's apartment, defendant "had no reasonable expectation of privacy in the basement common area," and thus police entry there no search); United States v. McGrane, 746 F.2d 632 (8th Cir.1984) (visual inspection of defendant's storage locker in basement no search, as this a common area accessible to all tenants and the landlord, though the office gained entry to the basement by

trespass); Penny v. United States, 694 A.2d 872 (D.C.App.1997) (where, as here, front door of apartment building unlocked and immediately inside stairway led down to unlocked basement, police entry of basement no search, as "the tenant of an apartment in a multitenant building has no reasonable expectation of privacy in the common areas of that building, such as * * * basements"); Commonwealth v. Williams, 453 Mass. 203, 900 N.E.2d 871 (2009) (defendant without reasonable expectation of privacy in basement, unlocked and used by various tenants in the building).

[74]United States v. Penco, 612 F.2d 19 (2d Cir.1979) (garage of apartment building open to all); United States v. Cruz Pagan, 537 F.2d 554 (1st Cir.1976) (police entered underground parking garage of condominium; held, "a person cannot have a reasonable expectation of privacy * * * in such a well travelled common area of an apartment house or condominium").

[75]United States v. King, 227 F.3d 732 (6th Cir.2000) ("the nature of the living arrangements of a duplex, as opposed to a multi-unit apartment building, affords the tenant of the duplex a greater expectation of privacy in areas the tenant of the multi-unit apartment building would not enjoy, because in the case of a duplex, access to such areas is limited to the duplex's tenants and landlord"); United States v. Fluker, 543 F.2d 709 (9th Cir.1976) (given "particular circumstances" of the case, defendant who occupied one unit in duplex had a legitimate expectation of privacy in a common hallway of duplex normally locked to outsiders).

Compare United States v. Villegas, 495 F.3d 761 (7th Cir.2007) (defendant had no reasonable expectation

general public merely means that the police cannot constitutionally enter that area without express permission. Certain persons, such as the landlord or his representative,[76] may consent to police entry into a common area even when the character of that area is such that it cannot be said there was an implied invitation to the general public to enter.

Finally, it should be noted that a search-by-entry can occur without the necessity of the officer fully intruding his person inside the residence. *Dinkens v. State*[77] is such a case. There, an officer who had been advised that defendant had a pistol under his dwelling went there and, after finding no one home, walked to the rear of the house, reached into a small vent underneath the house and found the pistol. Characterizing this as "an intrusion into the home itself,"[78] the court held the officer had conducted a search by making that intrusion into the householder's privacy. Authority in accord with *Dinkens* is to be found,[79] although one pre-*Katz* case held that such an area is "not within the protection of the Fourth Amendment."[80] The better view is that such action *is* a search which, because it is not highly intrusive, would be reasonable in somewhat broader circumstances than would permit a complete physical entry into a residential unit.[81]

---

of privacy in duplex common hallway, where outer door open and screen door unlocked, and hallway used not only by residents, but also by customers of other unit, which advertised business on sign outside building; court distinguished *King* because there occupants of two units all related, so that situation there "more closely resembled a single family house," and distinguished *Fluker* because there residents of both units were co-conspirators in drug distribution operations and thus "would maintain the privacy of all occupants of the duplex to advance their common purpose").

[76]See § 8.5(a). Thus, for example, where the hallway could be entered only through a locked door opened by key or a buzzer activated by someone in an apartment, but the building's manager had authorized the police to enter and had given them a key, the entry was lawful. People v. Howard, 63 Cal.App.3d 249, 133 Cal.Rptr. 689 (1976).

[77]Dinkens v. State, 291 So.2d 122 (Fla.App.1974).

[78]Compare the investigative techniques discussed in note 64 supra.

[79]E.g., United States v. Pacheco-Ruiz, 549 F.2d 1204 (9th Cir.1976); People v. Hurst, 325 F.2d 891 (9th Cir. 1963).

[80]Marullo v. United States, 328 F.2d 361 (5th Cir.1964).

See also United States v. Romano, 388 F.Supp. 101 (E.D.Pa. 1975) (officer found cocaine in newspapers concealed in drainpipe attached to rear wall of townhouse on college campus occupied by defendant and four other students; held, no search, as common areas of multiple dwellings are "not within the curtilage of the individual tenant," and defendant had no justified expectation of privacy because the area was not in his "exclusive control").

[81]As explained in Amsterdam, Perspectives on the Fourth Amendment, 58 Minn.L.Rev. 349, 389–90 (1974), this thinking may underlie *Marullo*. The court first declared that this was a reasonable warrantless search, but when the defendant in his petition for rehearing pointed to authority that a warrantless search of a dwelling is per se unreasonable, the court then asserted that no search had

What then of the situation in *United States v. Concepcion*,[82] where the police arrested the defendant, found keys on his person, used one of them to unlock an apartment in a nearby apartment house, and then used the information that defendant had access to this apartment to induce him to consent to a search of it? In response to the defendant's claim that the consent was the fruit of an illegal search, the court first noted that a "keyhole contains *information*—information about who has access to the space beyond" and that "the tumbler of a lock is not accessible to strangers," and then concluded: "Because the agents obtain information from the inside of the lock,[83] which is both used frequently by the owner and not open to public view, it seems irresistible that inserting and turning the key is a 'search.' "[84] The court went on to conclude, quite reasonably, that the intrusion upon "privacy interests is so small" that neither a search warrant nor full probable cause was necessary as a prerequisite to such a search.[85] However, the prevailing view today is that such activity does *not* constitute a search.[86]

---

occurred. As Amsterdam says, id. at 390: "Confronted with the necessity of enforcing the warrant requirement all the way to the boundary line of the fourth amendment, the court moved the boundary line over a couple of feet."

[82]United States v. Concepcion, 942 F.2d 1170 (7th Cir.1991).

[83]In Reeves v. Churchich, 484 F.3d 1244 (10th Cir.2007), where a police officer pointed a rifle at an occupant of a duplex from a noncurtilage space, see note 239 infra, but the end of the rifle intruded into the home's interior, the court distinguished *Concepcion* and held the insertion of the rifle "was not a search because the rifle was incapable of obtaining information and did not obtain any information," and was at most "a common law trespass."

[84]The court found "a close parallel" in Arizona v. Hicks, 480 U.S. 321, 107 S.Ct. 1149, 94 L.Ed.2d 347 (1987), holding it is a search to turn over a phonograph to read its serial number.
Accord: United States v. DeBardeleben, 740 F.2d 440 (6th Cir. 1984); United States v. Portillo-Reyes, 529 F.2d 844 (9th Cir.1975), questioned in United States v. Grandstaff, 813 F.2d 1353 (9th Cir.1987); Cole v.

State, 858 S.W.2d 915 (Tenn.Crim. App.1993) (but "the intrusion requires neither a search warrant nor probable cause, only a founded suspicion").

[85]The court noted that Arizona v. Hicks, 480 U.S. 321, 107 S.Ct. 1149, 94 L.Ed.2d 347 (1987), said a warrant is unnecessary and that *Hicks*, requiring probable cause, was distinguishable because there the privacy interest was more substantial because the officers obtained information "they could not have come by in any other way." See also United States v. $109,179 in U.S. Currency, 228 F.3d 1080 (9th Cir.2000) (insertion of car key into a nearby parked car "for the sole purpose of aiding the police in identification of an individual" detained on reasonable suspicion deemed not an unreasonable search, as it was "a 'minimally intrusive' action" serving "the strong governmental interests in investigating drug crimes"); Commonwealth v. Alvarez, 422 Mass. 198, 661 N.E.2d 1293 (1996) (assuming putting key in lock of apartment a search, it legal, as "for such an unobtrusive search the police needed only a founded or reasonable suspicion to insert the key").

[86]United States v. Moses, 540 F.3d 263 (4th Cir.2008) ("the discrete act of inserting the key into the lock

§ 2.3(c) Looking in or listening at the residence

Although it is generally true that a person has a justified expectation of privacy with respect to the interior of his place of residence, it does not follow that it is inevitably a search for a law enforcement officer to see or hear what is occurring therein. At least when the officer only employs his natural senses,[87] the prevailing rule is that such uses of the senses "made from a place where a police officer has a right to be do not amount to a search in the constitutional sense."[88] In assessing just what circumstances fall within this rule, it is useful to give separate consideration to single-unit dwellings and then to such multiple-occupancy premises as apartment houses, hotels and motels.

As for a dwelling house, it certainly is not a search for an officer to see or hear what is occurring inside a dwelling while he is in an area adjacent to that dwelling's curtilage that is open to the public. Illustrative is *People v. Wright*,[89] where the surveilling officer so employed his senses of sight and hearing while standing on the nearby railroad right of way. In response to the defendant's argument that *Katz* had rejected the "trespass" doctrine and that therefore this was a search despite the absence of a trespass, the court reasoned:

> We do not, however, read *Katz* as indicating any constitutional infirmity in the instant search, for we believe the seemingly restrictive ruling in *Katz* is applicable only to those instances where electronic eavesdropping devices or other artificial means are employed in addition to the natural senses. We read the reaffirmation of the lawful position aspect of the plain-view doctrine in *Har-*

---

and discovering whether or not it fit did not offend the Fourth Amendment"); United States v. Salgado, 250 F.3d 438 (6th Cir.2001) (trying key in lock of defendant's apartment, "accessible by means of an unlocked, common hallway," no search, as "the mere insertion of a key into a lock, by an officer who lawfully possesses the key and is in a location where he has a right to be, to determine whether this key operates the lock, is not a search"); United States v. Hawkins, 139 F.3d 29 (1st Cir.1998) (trying key found in defendant's apartment during execution of search warrant there in storage locker found in common area of basement no search); People v. Trull, 64 Ill.App.3d 385, 20 Ill.Dec. 960, 380 N.E.2d 1169 (1978) (determining key fit lock no search); Commonwealth v. DeJesus, 439 Mass. 616, 790 N.E.2d 231 (2003) ("Inserting a key into a lock and turning it to see whether it fits cannot be construed as a warrantless search of a lock tumbler"); State v. Robinson, 158 N.H. 792, 973 A.2d 277 (2009) (no Fourth Amendment violation, as "the mere information of ownership obtained from inserting a key into a door is not the type of information in which a defendant has a reasonable expectation of privacy"); State v. Jackson, 268 N.J.Super. 194, 632 A.2d 1285 (1993) ("the 'testing' of Jackson's validly seized keys" in two doors "did not constitute a search").

[Section 2.3(c)]

[87] On the use of various aids to the senses, see § 2.2.

[88] Lorenzana v. Superior Court, 9 Cal.3d 626, 108 Cal.Rptr. 585, 511 P.2d 33 (1973).

[89] People v. Wright, 41 Ill.2d 170, 242 N.E.2d 180 (1968). Though this case involved an apartment house, the reasoning is equally applicable to a single-family dwelling.

ris[90] as retaining the viability of the trespass doctrine in those cases where law enforcement officers gain information concerning crimes by use of their natural senses. Therefore, while the absence of a trespass is no longer to be an adequate ground to justify the admission of evidence secured through the use of the natural senses assisted by artificial means, the lack of a trespass is still a highly relevant consideration in sustaining the admission of evidence which has fallen into the plain view of an officer, i.e., gathered solely by the use of his natural senses.

This result is fully consistent with the *Katz* rationale, for the defendant in *Wright* cannot be said to have justifiably relied upon the privacy of his residence when his activities could be both seen and heard from a nearby public area.

By like reasoning, it may be concluded that no justified reliance is present when a person's in-premises activities may be readily observed or heard by neighbors, so that it is not a search for an officer to see or hear those activities from a neighbor's property.[91] In *Commonwealth v. Busfield*,[92] for example, the surveilling officer obtained a neighbor's permission to look from his residence into the window of the suspect premises across the way. From that vantage point, he could see through the sheer curtain in the suspect premises to the narcotics activity then occurring. The court correctly concluded that because that activity was in plain sight of the defendant's neighbor, he had "exposed his transaction to the public."

This is not to suggest, however, that in every conceivable instance in which surveillance by the natural senses is conducted without entering the curtilage, it may be concluded that no Fourth Amendment search has occurred. *Wright* merely says that the lack of trespass is a "highly relevant consideration," not that it is controlling, and certainly there are circumstances in which it must be concluded that the occupant's justified expectation of privacy was breached notwithstanding the absence of a trespass. For example, what if policemen were to climb up a telephone pole and peer beneath a second-story window shade, thereby observing what could not be seen either from ground level or from nearby buildings? In such a case, "[a]lthough they use no

---

[90]The reference is to the post-*Katz* decision in Harris v. United States, 390 U.S. 234, 88 S.Ct. 992, 19 L.Ed.2d 1067 (1968), concerning "the plain view of an officer who has a right to be in the position to have that view."

[91]United States v. Whaley, 779 F.2d 585 (11th Cir.1986) (no search to surveil from neighbor's property and on nearby canal open only to area landowners; court rejects defendant's argument it is a search because officer's vantage point not open to general public); State v. Texeira, 62 Haw. 44, 609 P.2d 131 (1980) (gambling seen and heard from adjoining property); Turner v. State, 499 S.W.2d 182 (Tex.Crim.App.1973); State v. Vogel, 428 N.W.2d 272 (S.D.1988) (no search to look into defendant's house from hilltop outside curtilage; "Anyone on the neighbor's property could have walked, unobstructed, to the hilltop, and seen the plants").

[92]Commonwealth v. Busfield, 242 Pa.Super. 194, 363 A.2d 1227 (1976).

electronic gadgetry, the interests on which their activities intrude appear to be indistinguishable from the interest protected in *Katz*."[93] It will not do in such a case to say that the occupant of the premises could have closed off that window more completely.[94] It is one thing to assert that an occupant cannot claim a justified expectation of privacy as to activities within his dwelling when that conduct is carried out in such a manner as to be readily seen or heard by neighbors or by the passing public. It is quite another to declare that citizens cannot "feel safe in leaving their windows uncurtained to the skies"[95] or in otherwise failing to seal off each and every aperture in their dwellings. And thus when police surveillance takes place at a position that cannot be called a "public vantage point,"[96] i.e., when the police-though not trespassing upon the defendant's curtilage-resort to the extraordinary step of positioning themselves where neither neighbors nor the general public would ordinarily be expected to be, the observation or overhearing of what is occurring within a dwelling constitutes a Fourth Amendment search. This is really what *Katz* is all about.

The *Wright* rule also should not be taken to mean that any viewing or hearing of what is occurring in premises *is* a search if the police were within the curtilage[97] at the time. "A sidewalk, pathway, common entrance or similar passageway offers an

---

[93]Amsterdam, Perspectives on the Fourth Amendment, 58 Minn.L.Rev. 349, 402 (1974).

[94]As in Commonwealth v. Hernley, 216 Pa.Super. 177, 263 A.2d 904 (1970), holding the defendant had no justified expectation of privacy re the interior of his print shop because he failed "to curtain the windows," though the windows were well above eye level and the officer had looked in by standing on a four-foot ladder and using binoculars.

In Commonwealth v. Williams, 494 Pa. 496, 431 A.2d 964 (1981), involving a 9-day surveillance of a third story apartment from another apartment 30–40 feet away, including use of binoculars and a startron permitting the police to see into the apartment even in darkness, the court timidly distinguished *Hernley* because in the instant case the police observed "two acts of sexual intercourse not involving the person * * * for whom the surveillance was established."

[95]Montgomery, J., dissenting in Commonwealth v. Hernley, 216 Pa.Super. 177, 263 A.2d 904 (1970).

[96]Pate v. Municipal Court, 11 Cal.App.3d 721, 89 Cal.Rptr. 893 (1970).

[97]As the Court stated in Oliver v. United States, 466 U.S. 170, 104 S.Ct. 1735, 80 L.Ed.2d 214 (1984), "the curtilage is the area to which extends the intimate activity associated with the 'sanctity of a man's home and the privacies of life,' * * * and therefore has been considered part of home itself for Fourth Amendment purposes. Thus, courts have extended Fourth Amendment protection to the curtilage; and they have defined the curtilage, as did the common law, by reference to the factors that determine whether an individual reasonably may expect that an area immediately adjacent to the home will remain private." The Court added that "for most homes, the boundaries of the curtilage will be clearly marked; and the conception defining the curtilage—as the area around the home to which the activity of home life extends—is a familiar one easily understood from our daily experience."

implied permission to the public to enter which necessarily negates any reasonable expectancy of privacy in regard to observations made there."[98]

> Absent express orders from the person in possession against any possible trespass, there is no rule of private or public conduct which makes it illegal per se, or a condemned invasion of the person's right of privacy, for anyone openly and peaceably, at high noon, to walk up the steps and knock on the front door of any man's "castle" with the honest intent of asking questions of the occupant thereof— whether the questioner be a pollster, a salesman, or an officer of the law.[99]

Thus, courts have held "that police with legitimate business may enter the areas of the curtilage which are impliedly open to use by the public," and that in so doing they "are free to keep their eyes open and use their other senses."[100] This means, therefore, that if police utilize "normal means of access to and egress from the house"[101] for some legitimate purpose,[102] such as to make in-

---

[98]Lorenzana v. Superior Court, 9 Cal.3d 626, 108 Cal.Rptr. 585, 511 P.2d 33 (1973).

[99]United States v. Hersh, 464 F.2d 228 (9th Cir.1972), quoting from Davis v. United States, 327 F.2d 301 (9th Cir.1964).

See also United States v. Cephas, 254 F.3d 488 (4th Cir.2001) ("A voluntary response to an officer's knock at the front door of a dwelling does not generally implicate the Fourth Amendment, and thus an officer generally does not need probable cause or reasonable suspicion to justify knocking on the door and then making verbal inquiry"); United States v. Cormier, 220 F.3d 1103 (9th Cir.2000) (officer acted properly, as he "knocked on the door for only a short period spanning seconds," "there was no police demand to open the door," and officer "was not unreasonably persistent in her attempt to obtain access to Cormier's motel room"); United States v. Tobin, 923 F.2d 1506 (11th Cir.1991); United States v. Peters, 912 F.2d 208 (8th Cir.1990) ("After Peters opened the door to the hotel room in which he was staying, in response to the simple knock on the door by the police officers, a search did not occur when the detectives looked into Peters' room through the open doorway"); People v. Rivera, 41 Cal.4th 304, 59 Cal.Rptr.3d 473, 159 P.3d 60 (2007) (police officer may

approach and knock on door of residence, and such actions "require no articulable suspicion of criminal activity"); People v. Holmes, 981 P.2d 168 (Colo.1999) (where police officer called because of loud party knocked hard on door in effort to get attention of occupant over the noise, and door swung open because not properly latched, allowing officer to observe bong within, no search; "Knocking on the door of a residence for the purpose of investigating a crime is reasonable police conduct and does not infringe upon the occupant's right of privacy"); State v. Sanders, 374 So.2d 1186 (La.1979) ("It is an almost implicit understanding and custom in this country that, in the absence of signs or warning, a residence may be approached and the occupants summoned to the door by knocking"); Commonwealth v. Acosta, 416 Mass. 279, 627 N.E.2d 466 (1993) (no search where officer viewed defendant when he opened door in response to a knock; officer "did not announce himself as a police officer" and "did no more than any citizen could do by entering a common area and knocking on the door").

[100]State v. Crea, 305 Minn. 342, 233 N.W.2d 736 (1975).

[101]Lorenzana v. Superior Court, 9 Cal.3d 626, 108 Cal.Rptr. 585, 511 P.2d 33 (1973). Sometimes a departure from the most direct route will be

quiries of the occupant,[103] to serve a subpoena,[104] or to introduce

permissible. See United States v. Garcia, 997 F.2d 1273 (9th Cir.1993) (looking in back door no search where, as here, both front and back door "are readily accessible from a public place like the driveway and parking area here," so that police went to back door "reasonably believing it is used as a principal entrance to the building"); United States v. Daoust, 916 F.2d 757 (1st Cir.1990) (where front door "is inaccessible there is nothing unlawful or unreasonable about going to the back of the house to look for another door"); United States v. Anderson, 552 F.2d 1296 (8th Cir.1977) (when officer who wished to question defendant received no answer to knock on front door, but lights were on and dog heard barking in back, it reasonable for officer to walk to the rear of the premises to see if defendant with dog); Miller v. State, 342 Ark. 213, 27 S.W.3d 427 (2000) (where police entered curtilage during legitimate police investigation and knocked at front door but received no response, and then followed path around unfenced property to back porch and knocked on rear door, and smelled marijuana from that vantage point, no search); State v. Glines, 134 Or.App. 21, 894 P.2d 516 (1995) (officer properly went to side door to knock on door where, as here, "side entry is about eight feet from the front wall of defendant's house" and "adjacent to a common driveway that defendant shares with his neighbor, is visible from the public sidewalk and is equipped with a doorbell").

Also, what are "normal means" may depend somewhat on the circumstances. See United States v. Jackson, 585 F.2d 653 (4th Cir.1978) (no search for officer to stand on chair under window and look in open window of house with "for rent" sign in front, as it would be expected that prospective tenants "would inspect the house, look in the windows and view the surrounding premises in order to determine what interest they might have in renting").

Compare People v. Camacho, 23 Cal.4th 824, 98 Cal.Rptr.2d 232, 3 P.3d 878 (2000), where police, responding to a complaint of a loud party at defendant's home, arrived there at 11 p.m. and heard no excessive noise. The officers walked into a side yard open area covered with grass without any path or walkway and with no entrance to the home on that side, and looked in a large side window, visible from the public street or sidewalk though the interior was not, and saw defendant with drugs. In holding this was a search, the court emphasized that the officers had "proceeded directly into [defendant's] darkened side yard" "without bothering to knock on defendant's front door," though they arrived there "late in the evening and heard no such noise." The court added that "had the officers on their arrival at defendant's house heard a raucous party, confirming the anonymous complaint that brought them there in the first place, and had they then banged on the front door to no avail, their entry into the side yard in an attempt to seek the source of the noise would likely have been justified."

[102]"To come within the implied invitation, a police officer must be on some police business. That does not necessarily mean that the officer has to have probable cause or even an objectively reasonable suspicion that criminal activity is afoot. The police business may be administrative as well as investigative, and it may be action based on a suspicion that turns out to be without substantial basis, provided the suspicion is held in good faith rather than as a pretext for an arbitrary search. Officer Sabin's burglary suspicion, based on recent reports of burglaries in the community and the fact that Cloutier's basement was the only illuminated room in the house, although tenuous, was held in good faith and was not pretextual." State v. Cloutier, 544 A.2d 1277 (Me. 1988).

[103]United States v. Hersh, 464 F.2d 228 (9th Cir.1972); State v. Deary, 753 So.2d 200 (La.2000) (officer was "conducting a legitimate police investigation" when he came onto porch and

an undercover agent into the activities occurring there,[105] it is not a Fourth Amendment search for the police to see[106] or hear[107] or

---

knocked on side of house and looked through open door, as purpose was "to question the occupants about the individual the officer had observed leave the premises in the company of another person known to [the officer] from prior narcotics arrests"); Jones v. State, 407 Md. 33, 962 A.2d 393 (2008); State v. Crea, 305 Minn. 342, 233 N.W.2d 736 (1975); State v. Perez, 85 S.W.3d 817 (Tex.Crim.App.2002) (knocking on door of apartment to which theft suspect fled, at which defendant opened door, was only an encounter and thus no reasonable suspicion required).

[104]State v. Poling, 207 W.Va. 299, 531 S.E.2d 678 (2000).

[105]Hall v. State, 15 Md.App. 363, 290 A.2d 803 (1972); State v. White, 18 Or.App. 352, 525 P.2d 188 (1974).

[106]Taylor v. Michigan Dept. of Natural Resources, 502 F.3d 452 (6th Cir.2007) (under "conditions consistent with a winter-time break in of a potentially-seasonal home" that "warranted a brief protective check," it not objectionable that officer, in "broad daylight, * * * spent approximately five minutes looking in open windows"); United States v. Khabeer, 410 F.3d 477 (8th Cir.2005) (no search for officer to see TV set through front window of home while standing in driveway); United States v. Hammett, 236 F.3d 1054 (9th Cir.2001) (no search for officer to look through gap in siding on house while completing circling of house looking for another door after no one answered front door); United States v. Taylor, 90 F.3d 903 (4th Cir.1996) (where defendant's "front entrance was as open to the law enforcement officers as to any delivery person, guest, or other member of the public," it no search for officer on front porch to look through picture window); United States v. Evans, 27 F.3d 1219 (7th Cir.1994) (looking into house from driveway no search, as "no evidence that the public had limited access to Glenn's driveway"); United States v. Daoust, 916 F.2d 757 (1st Cir.1990)

(officer, properly at rear of premises seeking "an accessible main floor entrance" then "looked up through the window simply to see if someone was at home"); People v. Glick, 250 P.3d 578 (Colo.2011) (where police lawfully at front door and person who answered door left it open when he went to find another occupant, no search for police to shine flashlight into home from that position and "make plain view observations that during daylight would not constitute a search"); State v. David, 269 Ga. 533, 501 S.E.2d 494 (1998) (where official accompanied landlord checking on possible unauthorized occupancy, and when landlord knocked on door it was opened and officer then saw through the open door a marijuana pipe, this no search); Hardister v. State, 849 N.E.2d 563 (Ind.2006) (where officers lawfully went to back yard in reasonable anticipation that suspects within would flee out back door, but they did not, once officers "lawfully present in the backyard, their looking into the kitchen through the side and rear windows, was also reasonable as an effort to locate the fleeing suspects"); State v. Dickerson, 313 N.W.2d 526 (Iowa 1981) (no search to look through window of front door and then photograph what seen); Commonwealth v. Hatcher, 199 S.W.3d 124 (Ky.2006) (since officer "authorized to knock on Hatcher's door to respond to the report of an allegedly abandoned minor," no Fourth Amendment violation when he "looked into her house through the open door"); State v. Brisban, 809 So.2d 923 (La.2002) (officer was "on the porch for a legitimate purpose when he looked through the screen door and saw what appeared to be contraband"); State v. Cloutier, 544 A.2d 1277 (Me.1988) (no search where officer on path from side door looked in basement window); State v. Gott, 456 S.W.2d 38 (Mo.1970) (while standing at front door, officer looked in window and saw defendant rolling a marijuana cigarette); State v. Rose, 128 Wash.2d 388, 909 P.2d 280 (1996) (looking through picture win-

---

smell[108] from that vantage point what is happening inside the dwelling. This is so even if such discovery occurs only by virtue of an occupant opening the door in response to the officer's conduct.[109]

dow from porch no search, as officer "entitled to walk up onto the porch," for it "was accessible from a large parking area" nearby and thus "was impliedly open to the public"); State v. Poling, 207 W.Va. 299, 531 S.E.2d 678 (2000) (no search where officer on front porch on lawful business saw marijuana plants through uncovered window).

    Considering Lorenzana v. Superior Court, 9 Cal.3d 626, 108 Cal.Rptr. 585, 511 P.2d 33 (1973), text at note 111 infra, it may sometimes be argued that the observation was not a search because the defendant had not made reasonable efforts to maintain privacy. Generally, it would appear that somewhat greater efforts might be required as to windows at or by an entrance to the premises as compared to the kind of windows involved in *Lorenzana.* But see State v. Jordan, 29 Wash.App. 924, 631 P.2d 989 (1981) (where police on porch responding to complaint of noisy party, looking into 6" space between drape and window casing a search, as "by drawing the curtains the individuals inside the duplex had clearly demonstrated a reasonable expectation of privacy"; dissent objects this a valid plain view because it cannot be said "the officers had to strain and contort so that they might see through a tiny opening").

[107]People v. Smith, 152 Ill.2d 229, 178 Ill.Dec. 335, 604 N.E.2d 858 (1992) (defendant's confession to murder overheard by officers in unlocked apartment building common-area hallway); Hall v. State, 15 Md.App. 363, 290 A.2d 803 (1972) (officer overheard words while on front porch).

[108]Miller v. State, 342 Ark. 213, 27 S.W.3d 427 (2000) (smelling marijuana within while lawfully at back door no search); People v. Baker, 813 P.2d 331 (Colo.1991) (officer smelled odor of marijuana from outside open front door); State v. Garcia, 374 So.2d 601 (Fla.App.1979) (officer smelled odor of marijuana from front porch); State v.

Prevette, 43 N.C.App. 450, 259 S.E.2d 595 (1979) (same); State v. Glines, 134 Or.App. 21, 894 P.2d 516 (1995) (while at side door, officer smelled odor of marijuana coming from basement, interior access to which was located by that door); State v. Perez, 85 S.W.3d 817 (Tex.Crim.App.2002) (smelling of marijuana inside apartment after defendant answered lawful knock on door).

    Sometimes a court will, in the alternative, deem the approach and smelling a search, albeit one justified by exigent circumstances. See, e.g., Holder v. State, 847 N.E.2d 930 (Ind.2006) (where officers detected odor of ether from as far away as 100 yards from defendant's home, which "led them to walk across the private property of several residents in the neighborhood and ultimately to crouch near the defendant's basement window to take a sniff," the "significant degree of the fumes from a known explosive and flammable chemical in a residential area compelled the officers to find its source for the sake of the safety and health of the nearby residents").

[109]In summoning the occupant to the door, it is not objectionable that the police resorted to a ruse. United States v. Leung, 929 F.2d 1204 (7th Cir.1991). But the result is otherwise if the door is opened in response to a police command. United States v. Mowatt, 513 F.3d 395 (4th Cir.2008) (seeing inside through open door a search where, as here, occupant opened door in response to police command); United States v. Poe, 462 F.3d 997 (8th Cir.2006) (opening door not consensual when after "over ten minutes of persistent knocks" by one officer and another "had commanded Poe to open the door"). United States v. Conner, 127 F.3d 663 (8th Cir.1997) ("an unconstitutional search occurs when officers gain visual * * * access to a motel room after an occupant opens the door not voluntarily, but in response to a demand under color of authority"). Likewise if the door is

On the other hand, if the police stray from that path to other

kept open in response to a police threat or command. United States v. Washington, 387 F.3d 1060 (9th Cir. 2004). As for the distinction between an order and a request, see Bailey v. Newland, 263 F.3d 1022 (9th Cir.2001) (when officers approached motel room, Cowans stepped outside, after which Bailey slammed the door; police put Cowans in police car and then one officer "began knocking on the door and * * * identified himself as a police officer"; "he knocked for about one-minute-and-a-half to two minutes while continuing to identify himself as a police officer but issued no commands or orders"; Bailey then opened the door and stepped out, permitting police to see gun and drug paraphernalia within; court concludes it has "no basis to conclude that Bailey voluntarily answered the door"); United States v. Tobin, 923 F.2d 1506 (11th Cir.1991) (where officer knocked 3–4 minutes and called out, "I'm a police officer, I would like to talk to you, I need for you to come here," this not an order, as the officer "did not use the imperative" and "he phrased his words in the form of a request"); Commonwealth v. Hamilton, 24 Mass.App.Ct. 290, 508 N.E.2d 870 (1987). In such a case, the fact that "the officers gained visual access to the interior of a dwelling without physically entering it is irrelevant to the question whether a search was effected." United States v. Winsor, 846 F.2d 1569 (9th Cir.1988).

Also, note that in some circumstances an insistent effort to get the occupant to come to the door can amount to a *seizure* of those within. See United States v. Jerez, 108 F.3d 684 (7th Cir.1997) (where deputies knocked on motel room door at 11:00 p.m. for 3 minutes, made commands and requests to open the door, knocked for 1½ to 2 minutes on outside of window, and shone flashlight through small opening in window's drapes into face of one defendant as he lay in bed, collectively manifesting "the law enforcement officers refusal to take 'no' for an answer," this constituted a seizure).

But, while it is doubtless true that "as a matter of public policy * * * [l]ate-night intrusions into people's homes are, and should be, discouraged and should not be permitted unless necessary," "courts have declined to find a seizure based on a night-time 'knock and talk' in the absence of other coercive circumstances." Scott v. State, 366 Md. 121, 782 A.2d 862 (2001) (random knocking on motel room doors at 11:30 p.m. in hopes occupants would allow police to enter and ultimately consent to search). See also United States v. Cormier, 220 F.3d 1103 (9th Cir.2000) (after 8:00 p.m.); United States v. Taylor, 90 F.3d 903 (4th Cir.1996) (at 9:15 p.m.); State v. Warren, 949 So.2d 1215 (La.2007) (at 2:30 a.m., police "detected a strong odor of marijuana smoke coming from the room"); but compare United States v. Wells, 648 F.3d 671 (8th Cir.2011), discussed in note 234 infra. And the "knock and talk" procedure is unquestionably proper when utilized during daylight hours. See, e.g., United States v. Adeyeye, 359 F.3d 457 (7th Cir. 2004); State v. Johnston, 150 N.H. 448, 839 A.2d 830 (2004), especially where the tactic does not result in police entry of the residence. Jones v. State, 407 Md. 33, 962 A.2d 393 (2008).

For further discussion of the "knock and talk" procedure, see Annot., 15 A.L.R.6th 515 (2006); Notes, 32 B.C.J.L. & Soc.Just. 119 (2012); 41 Suffolk U.L.Rev. 561 (2008); Consider also Bradley, "Knock and Talk" and the Fourth Amendment, 84 Ind.L.J. 1099 (2009), proposing "possible solutions to the intrusiveness that the 'knock and talk' technique imposes on the home," the most severe of which would be "to ban 'knock and talk' entirely when a particular home or suspect is the focus of police investigation." This, Bradley contents, would constitute a "return to the principles" of Johnson v. United States, 333 U.S. 10, 68 S.Ct. 367, 92 L.Ed. 436 (1948), claimed to stand for the proposition that "police cannot get people to open their doors without a warrant and then use evidence obtained as a result

parts of the curtilage in order to conduct the surveillance, then the use of natural sight or hearing or smell to detect what is inside is a search within the meaning of the Fourth Amendment.[110] Illustrative is *Lorenzana v. Superior Court*,[111]

of that opening as the basis for a valid search or arrest." Bradley, supra, at 1103. However, in *Johnson*, where the government attempted to justify search of a hotel room as incident to the valid arrest of an occupant, the Court never questioned the police conduct that caused the "opening" of the door in response to their knock, as compared to the subsequent unlawful police "entry * * * under color of their police authority": the Court held that defendant's arrest was unlawful precisely because based "on the knowledge that she was alone in the room, gained only after, and wholly by reason of, their entry."

[110]Lundstrom v. Romero, 616 F.3d 1108 (10th Cir.2010) (a search where officer "either scaled a fence or opened a gate to gain access to Lundstrom's backyard, taking up a position that allowed him to observe Lundstrom in the rear of the house"); United States v. Blount, 98 F.3d 1489 (5th Cir.1996) (where no walkway to back yard and no indication back door a principal means of access to that residence, "when a police officer walks into the partially fenced back yard of a residential dwelling, using a passage not open to the general public, and places his face within inches of a small opening in an almost completely covered rear window to look into the house and at the inhabitants, that officer has performed a 'search' "); People v. Camacho, 23 Cal.4th 824, 98 Cal.Rptr.2d 232, 3 P.3d 878 (2000) (illegal search where police, responding to a complaint of a loud party at defendant's home, arrived there at 11 p.m. and heard no excessive noise. The officers walked into a side yard open area covered with grass without any path or walkway and with no entrance to the home on that side, and looked in a large side window, visible from the public street or sidewalk though the interior was not, and saw defendant with drugs); Olivera v. State, 315 So.2d 487 (Fla.App.1975) (officer overheard incriminating discussions at rear bedroom window; "the implications of sanctioning police surveillance by standing in a yard at one's window in the middle of the night are too obvious to require elaboration"); State v. Kaaheena, 59 Haw. 23, 575 P.2d 462 (1978) (officer searched by standing on crates to gain access to 1-inch opening between drapes and blinds); Quintana v. Commonwealth, 276 S.W.3d 753 (Ky.2008) (when no one answered front door, officer walked to back yard to window where air conditioner was located and smelled marijuana from air coming out; this a search, as "back yard is not normally an area that the general public would perceive as public access"); State v. Ragsdale, 381 So.2d 492 (La.1980) (officer went to rear patio, completely enclosed by tall and solid wooden fence, and looked through narrow gap in closed curtains; this is a search); State v. Foster, 347 Or. 1, 217 P.3d 168 (2009) (no "lawful vantage point" here, as officer "had walked past the front door to look in the window," but this justified by legitimate safety concerns of police present to serve restraining order at residence where they had encountered many difficulties in the past); State v. Artic, 327 Wis.2d 392, 786 N.W.2d 430 (2010) (where police officer walked around house and entered fenced-in back yard and approached rear door, such "presence within the curtilage was not lawful," and thus what seen and heard within by officer may not be considered in determining lawfulness of entry of house).

Compare McDougall v. State, 316 So.2d 624 (Fla.App.1975), distinguishing such cases "on the basis that there the law enforcement officers had no right to be on the premises in the first instance," and holding there was no search where a police officer looked in the rear window of a duplex after receiving a call to investigate a possible burglary at that duplex. The

where an officer, unable to see into the suspect house from the street or adjacent driveway, crossed a ten foot strip of land on a side of the house where there were no doors or defined pathways and took a position beneath a window. Although the window was closed and the shade was drawn down to two inches of the bottom sill, this officer was able to overhear a telephone conversation about a pending narcotics pickup and to see heroin. The court quite understandably concluded "that the questioned police procedure too closely resembles the process of the police state, too dangerously intrudes upon the individual's reasonable expectancy of privacy, and thus too clearly transgresses constitutional principle." As for the contention that the defendant had no justified expectation of privacy because he had not succeeded in totally concealing his criminal activity from such surveillance by the natural senses, the *Lorenzana* court responded:

> The fact that apertures existed in the window, so that an unlawfully intruding individual so motivated could spy into the residence, does not dispel the reasonableness of the occupants' expectation of privacy. * * * To the contrary, the facts of this case demonstrate that by drawing the window shade petitioner Lorenzana exhibited a reasonable expectation to be free from surveillance conducted from a vantage point in the surrounding property not open to public or common use.[112] Surely our state and federal Constitutions and the cases interpreting them foreclose a regression into an Orwellian society in which a citizen, in order to preserve a modicum of privacy, would be compelled to encase himself in a light-tight, air-proof box.[113]

Turning now to multiple-occupancy dwellings, such as apart-

---

court could just as well have said that it *was* a search but a reasonable one under the circumstances. Consider also Nordskog v. Wainwright, 546 F.2d 69 (5th Cir.1977), holding that when police have probable cause to arrest and receive no answer to their knock on the front door, they may look in a side window and rear door to see if defendant is there.

[111]Lorenzana v. Superior Court, 9 Cal.3d 626, 108 Cal.Rptr. 585, 511 P.2d 33 (1973).

[112]This is not to suggest that drawing a shade or closing blinds is inevitably necessary. In People v. Camacho, 23 Cal.4th 824, 98 Cal.Rptr.2d 232, 3 P.3d 878 (2000), where the state attempted to distinguish *Lorenzana* on the ground that in the instant case "defendant's rather large (four-by-eight-foot) window was completely uncovered," the court nonetheless held the 11 p.m. side-yard windowpeeping

was nonetheless a search. That result is correct, given that the "window is visible from the public street or sidewalk, but the inside of the room is not" (perhaps because "a red bulb dimly lit the room").

[113]Compare United States v. Hammett, 236 F.3d 1054 (9th Cir. 2001), where police, receiving no answer to their knock at the front door, circled the house looking for another entrance. When they had almost completed the trip, they saw drugs within by looking through a 1/2 inch to 1 inch wide crack in overlapping pieces of corrugated steel siding forming the walls of the residence. In holding there was no search, the court emphasized that "the officers were able to view the marijuana plants through the crack from a distance of approximately five to six feet without making any contortions."

ment houses, rooming houses, hotels, and motels, it may be noted
at the outset that certain situations are not unlike those previously discussed. If, for example, an officer is able to see or hear
what is occurring within a particular unit without intruding into
the building or surrounding curtilage and while stationed at what
may be fairly characterized a public vantage point, then here
again there has been no search.[114] But what is different about the
multiple-occupancy dwelling cases generally is that an occupant
can claim an exclusive privacy interest in only a portion of the
premises, and areas immediately adjacent to that portion will be
open to public or common usage, so that courts are inclined to
view those occupying such dwellings as having a reduced privacy
expectation.[115]

Rather typical of this view is *Moody v. State*,[116] holding it was
no search for a detective to look through the partially opened
blinds into a motel room:

> Our courts have accorded a high degree of judicial sanctity to
> people in their homes, however, this security against unreasonable
> searches of homes should be distinguished from the scope of protec-
> tion afforded a motel resident. * * *

> "A private home is quite different from a place of business or
> from a motel cabin. A home owner or tenant has the exclusive enjoy-
> ment of his home, his garage, his barn or other buildings, and also
> the area under his home. But a transient occupant of a motel must
> share corridors, sidewalks, yards, and trees with the other
> occupants. Granted that a tenant has standing to protect the room
> he occupies, there is nevertheless an element of public or shared
> property in motel surroundings that is entirely lacking in the enjoy-
> ment of one's home."[117]

> In the present case, the detectives observed appellant while they
> were standing outside the motel in an area used by guests or
> persons having business there. As an occupant of the motel, appel-
> lant only shared in the property surrounding the motel whereas if
> he were a homeowner, he would have exclusive enjoyment of his
> property.

> The occupants of the motel room had no right to expect any
> privacy with relation to what they did inside the window as it was

---

[114]Williamson v. State, 707 A.2d
350 (Del.1998); People v. Wright, 41
Ill.2d 170, 242 N.E.2d 180 (1968).

[115]E.g., State v. Benton, 206 Conn.
90, 536 A.2d 572 (1988) (rejecting
defendant's contention "that a different rule should apply to multiple family dwellings in general and duplex
apartments in particular").

Similarly, when the defendant
was a long-time squatter on government property, he may have had a justified expectation of privacy as to the
interior of the dwelling, but had no
expectation of privacy in the immediately adjacent property, which any
member of the public might well enter.
State v. Dias, 62 Haw. 52, 609 P.2d
637 (1980). And if the defendants
choose to engage in their activity in a
vacant house without any curtains,
there is again a reduced expectation of
privacy, so that police may enter the
back yard. State v. Johnson, 580
S.W.2d 254 (Mo.1979).

[116]Moody v. State, 52 Ala.App.
552, 295 So.2d 272 (1974).

[117]Quoting from Marullo v. United
States, 328 F.2d 361 (5th Cir.1964).

within easy view of those utilizing the motel surroundings. It is not unreasonable to hold motel residents to the expectation that persons using the motel area might peer into open windows.

Other courts have likewise held that it is not a search for the police to look into a motel room from the parking lot or a similar area used by the public,[118] or for the police to listen with the naked ear from such a vantage point[119] or from an adjoining room.[120]

---

[118]Ponce v. Craven, 409 F.2d 621 (9th Cir.1969); People v. Gomez, 632 P.2d 586 (Colo.1981) (no search to look into motel room from sidewalk); State v. Holtz, 300 N.W.2d 888 (Iowa 1981) (no search to look into motel room window from common walkway); Commonwealth v. Johnson, 777 S.W.2d 876 (Ky.1989) ("what would be sufficient vigilance to preserve one's privacy in a home, apartment or office may be insufficient in a motel room" and thus it no search to look through partially open motel room door and window); State v. Brown, 9 Wash.App. 937, 515 P.2d 1008 (1973).

   Cf. State v. Cardenas, 146 Wash.2d 400, 47 P.3d 127 (2002) (as for looking into motel room window, court says, citing illustrative cases, that "failure to completely close the curtains is not necessarily determinative" on the lack of a reasonable expectation of privacy, and says instant case, where "the curtains were partially closed, leaving a three-inch gap," and "the officers were required to peer through the opening on bended knees, presents a close question" the court need not answer because justification existed for looking in even if it a search).

[119]United States v. Burns, 624 F.2d 95 (10th Cir.1980) (no search to listen from motel hallway, as if guests "converse in a fashion insensitive to the public, or semipublic, nature of walkways adjoining such rooms, reasonable expectations of privacy are correspondingly less"); Ponce v. Craven, 409 F.2d 621 (9th Cir.1969); Satterfield v. State, 127 Ga.App. 528, 194 S.E.2d 295 (1972).

[120]United States v. Hearn, 563 F.3d 95 (5th Cir.2009); United States v. Hessling, 845 F.2d 617 (6th Cir. 1988); United States v. Mankani, 738

F.2d 538 (2d Cir.1984) ("the presence of a visible door, crack or opening in the wall adjacent to another hotel room, as was the case here, should suggest to the average person that his or her privacy may be limited"); United States v. Sin Nagh Fong, 490 F.2d 527 (9th Cir.1974); United States v. Lopez, 475 F.2d 537 (7th Cir.1973); State v. Moses, 367 So.2d 800 (La.1979); State v. Gerry, 23 Wash.App. 166, 595 P.2d 49 (1979).

   In United States v. Agapito, 620 F.2d 324 (2d Cir.1980), the court rejected defendant's argument that it *is* a search to hear with the naked ear that which can be heard only by pressing the ear to the separating door, relying "upon three critical factors.

   "First, appellants' conversations were heard by the *naked human ear*. Regardless of whether the tones may be described as loud or normal, the fact remains that appellants were talking *loud enough* to be heard by others in an adjoining room. The agents were unaided by any artificial, mechanical or electronic device.

   "Second, the agents had a legal right to be in the adjoining room. We decline to restrict their movements in their own room in order to prevent the overhearing of conversations in an adjoining room. It strikes us as impractical to permit an agent in an adjoining room to listen while standing immediately next to a wall or connecting door without touching it but to prohibit him from listening by moving his ear several inches and pressing it against the wall or connecting door. * * *

   "Third, appellants were in a hotel room. True, the occupants of a hotel room are entitled to the protection of the Fourth Amendment. * * * But the reasonable privacy expectations in a hotel room differ from those

By like reasoning, similar conduct in a public area or adjoining room of a hotel[121] or rooming house[122] is deemed not to be a search. Apartment dwellers fare no better. It is not a search for an officer to look into an apartment while in a common passageway[123] or other common area[124] of the apartment complex, or to listen from

in a residence. * * *

"In view of the transient nature of hotel guests, moreover, one cannot be sure who his neighbors are in a hotel room. A person in a residence generally knows who his neighbors are. A person in a hotel room therefore takes a greater risk than one in a residence that, instead of neighbors, an adjoining room may contain strangers or, as in this case, even persons with interests adverse to his own."

Fisch involved the added fact that the agents, with the aid of the motel operator, had the suspects moved to a different room so that a vacant adjoining room could be made available to the agents, but the court concluded that the "accomplishment of the move of the defendants' room to one more accessible for surveillance violated no constitutional right of the appellants. They could, had they wished, refused the transfer. The officers were in a room open to anyone who might care to rent."

[121]United States v. Leung, 929 F.2d 1204 (7th Cir.1991) (no search where officer looked through motel room door when occupant opened it, and this so even though police resorted to ruse by having housekeeper knock and ask to clean the room); Borum v. United States, 318 A.2d 590 (D.C.App. 1974) (officer in hallway looked through crack in door and saw use of drugs; no search, as the hallway "is open to the general public" and the "crack was readily apparent and accessible to anyone walking along that hall"); Hatcher v. State, 141 Ga.App. 756, 234 S.E.2d 388 (1977) (no search where officers in hallway knocked on door and saw stolen goods in room when defendant opened door); People v. Miller, 30 Ill.App.3d 643, 332 N.E.2d 440 (1975) (observation from hallway through open door no search, as "this area was open to the public").

[122]Ray v. United States, 288 A.2d 239 (D.C.App.1972) (listening from adjoining room).

[123]United States v. Acevedo, 627 F.2d 68 (7th Cir.1980) (no search to look into apartment window from gangway used by general public to reach adjoining tavern); Gross v. State, 8 Ark.App. 241, 650 S.W.2d 603 (1983) (conversation overheard from "residential walkway" of apartment house); People v. Berutko, 71 Cal.2d 84, 77 Cal.Rptr. 217, 453 P.2d 721 (1969) (observation from common passageway bordering defendant's apartment); State v. Macke, 594 S.W.2d 300 (Mo.App.1980) (observation through open door from common area); Commonwealth v. Johnson, 247 Pa.Super. 208, 372 A.2d 11 (1977) (observation from patio steps used by anyone entering apartment building from the rear).

[124]United States v. Fields, 113 F.3d 313 (2d Cir.1997) (no search where police entered fenced side-yard of apartment house and looked through 6-inch opening into defendant's illuminated bedroom, as defendants' activity was in plain view of "a common area accessible to the other tenants in the multi-family apartment building-in which they had no legitimate expectation of privacy"); United States v. Lloyd, 36 F.3d 761 (8th Cir.1994) (no search to look through open door of apartment from unlocked hallway); People v. Becker, 188 Colo. 160, 533 P.2d 494 (1975) (observation was "from a common area in front of the apartment * * * through the uncurtained part of a large picture window adjacent to the front door"); Latham v. Sullivan, 295 N.W.2d 472 (Iowa App.1980) (no search to look in apartment window from ordinary outside route used to reach apartment door); People v. Funches, 89 N.Y.2d 1005, 657 N.Y.S.2d 396, 679 N.E.2d

an adjoining apartment.[125] Moreover, at least when the hallways of the apartment building have not been made inaccessible to the general public,[126] listening with the naked ear from the hallway outside a particular apartment is not deemed to intrude upon any justified expectation of privacy of the apartment's occupants.[127] In *United States v. Llanes*,[128] for example, where a narcotics agent overheard incriminating comments by standing in the hallway near the imperfectly hung apartment door, the court declared "that conversations carried on in a tone of voice quite audible to a person standing outside the home are conversations knowingly exposed to the public."

Decisions such as *Llanes* are particularly worrisome, for they leave the unfortunate resident of a multiple-occupancy dwelling with very little privacy. For the reasons stated so well by Professor Amsterdam, it would appear that this line of authority has diminished the privacy of such persons "to a compass inconsis-

---

635 (1997) (no search when officer came down fire escape to landing outside defendant's second-story apartment and looked in, given "defendant's lack of exclusive control over the use of the fire escape"); State v. Taylor, 61 Ohio App.2d 209, 401 N.E.2d 459, 15 O.O.3d 323 (1978) (no search to look into apartment from "the semi-public walkway" leading to building); Rodriguez v. State, 653 S.W.2d 305 (Tex.Crim.App.1983) (no search where police in hallway looked through open door).

[125] State v. Benton, 206 Conn. 90, 536 A.2d 572 (1988) (listening with naked ear while "not closer than twelve to eighteen inches to the common wall" of the duplex).

[126] In Commonwealth v. Hall, 366 Mass. 790, 323 N.E.2d 319 (1975), the apartment building in question had double doors; after passing through the first one into the vestibule, a visitor confronted another door and three doorbells, one for each apartment. This door could be opened by key or by a buzzer mechanism activated from one of the apartments. The police gained entry twice—once when the door happened to be unlocked, once by immediately following a person who had rung a doorbell and had been admitted by buzzer. The court held the hallway was not a public area because "the arrangement made—the lock on the downstairs door and the buzzer

system—was designed to exclude members of the public and to admit none but the defendant's own guests and invitees. * * * A justified expectation of privacy therefore arose. That the lock on the vestibule door could be and was bypassed on the two occasions when the eavesdropping took place cannot alter the picture, for police do not have carte blanche to pass through doors that are unlocked or even ajar if the area beyond has a private character."

See also People v. Killebrew, 76 Mich.App. 215, 256 N.W.2d 581 (1977); State v. Ortiz, 257 Neb. 784, 600 N.W.2d 805 (1999) ("under the case law, the degree of privacy society is willing to accord an apartment hallway may depend on the facts, such as whether there is an outer door locked to the street which limits access * * *; the number of residents using the hallway * * *; the number of units in the apartment complex * * *; and the presence or absence of no trespassing signage").

[127] United States v. Moore, 463 F.Supp. 1266 (S.D.N.Y.1979); People v. Foster, 19 Cal.App.3d 649, 97 Cal.Rptr. 94 (1971); Commonwealth v. Dinnall, 366 Mass. 165, 314 N.E.2d 903 (1974); State v. Kuznitz, 105 N.J.Super. 33, 250 A.2d 802 (1969).

[128] United States v. Llanes, 398 F.2d 880 (2d Cir.1968).

tent with the aims of a free and open society."[129] After accurately predicting that *Katz* would undergo a "rapid transmutation into a rule to the effect that if an officer conducts his observations from a vantage point accessible to the general public and uses no artificial aids to vision, he is clear of the amendment,"[130] Amsterdam asks:

> Is this a satisfactory result? It does not seem so to me. The problem began, I think, when the simplification of *Katz* began, in terms of categorical concepts such as "privacy." People who live in single houses or well-insulated apartments tend to take a rather parochial view of privacy. Because we are accustomed to having something approaching absolute privacy when we lock our outer doors, we tend to conceive of privacy as an absolute phenomenon and to denigrate the importance of degrees of privacy. To us it seems intuitively evident that anything a person does within sight or hearing of his neighbors or the general public is not private—and that, as to such things, it makes no difference whether they are observed by a neighbor or a policeman—because *we* retire to our homes when we want *real* privacy. But if you live in a cheap hotel or in a ghetto flat, your neighbors can hear you breathing quietly even in temperate weather when it is possible to keep the windows and the doors closed. For the tenement dweller, the difference between observation by neighbors and visitors who ordinarily use the common hallways and observation by policemen who come into the hallways to "check up" or "look around" is the difference between all the privacy that his condition allows and none. Is that small difference too unimportant to claim fourth amendment protection?[131]

The argument is a compelling one, and justifies the conclusion that conduct such as that in *Llanes* should not go entirely unregulated. And while it may be true that "no court is going to say that policemen may not enter apartment hallways without a search warrant, it would be quite possible for a court to say that police entries into apartment hallways are 'searches' subject to some lesser form of regulation."[132]

Even if courts do not go this far (and there is unfortunately no evidence to date that they are inclined to embrace the Amsterdam approach), the *Katz* justified-expectation-of-privacy approach should nonetheless be interpreted to give the resident of a multiple-occupancy structure greater protection than he had under the pre-*Katz* trespass rule. In particular, as perhaps the

---

[129] Amsterdam, 58 Minn.L.Rev. 349, 403 (1974).

[130] Amsterdam, 58 Minn.L.Rev. 349, 404 (1974).

[131] Amsterdam, 58 Minn.L.Rev. 349, 404 (1974).

[132] Amsterdam, 58 Minn.L.Rev. 349, 405 (1974). Some courts have indicated that surveillance into prem- ises, even when a search, is not of the same order as a search involving a physical entry of the premises and scrutiny of possessions therein, so that somewhat different Fourth Amendment standards are applicable in the surveillance cases. See, e.g., Texas v. Gonzales, 388 F.2d 145 (5th Cir.1968); Borum v. United States, 318 A.2d 590 (D.C.App.1974).

Supreme Court is coming to realize,[133] courts should not bestow the nonsearch appellation upon police surveillance (1) that does not occur at a "public vantage point";[134] or (2) that is offensive in its intrusiveness in the sense that it uncovers that which the resident may fairly be said to have protected from scrutiny by the "curious passerby."[135]

With respect to the first point, it is useful to consider the facts of *Cohen v. Superior Court*.[136] After receiving an anonymous tip that prostitution was occurring in a particular fourth-floor apartment at a certain address, officers went to those premises to investigate. Noting that a metal fire escape was attached to the side of the building, one of the officers went out onto the fire escape from the fourth-floor hallway and then took a position on that part of the fire escape landing which extended to the balcony under the window of the suspect apartment. From that vantage point the officer saw a woman inside the apartment handling what was recognized as marijuana. On the question of whether this constituted a search, the trial court thought that "the issue resolves itself by whether or not the officer did commit a trespass in going out on the balcony," and then answered in the negative because the fire escape was not intended for the exclusive use of the occupants of the surveilled apartment. Under the pre-*Katz* trespass doctrine, this would by no means be a remarkable result, but it is disheartening to find essentially the same analysis sometimes accepted as consistent with the rule of the *Katz* case,[137] for, as the appellate court in *Cohen* concluded:

> The test to be applied in determining whether observation into a residence violates the Fourth Amendment is whether there has been an unreasonable invasion of the privacy of the occupants, not the extent of the trespass which was necessary to reach the observa-

---

[133]See Florida v. Riley, 488 U.S. 445, 109 S.Ct. 693, 102 L.Ed.2d 835 (1989), involving helicopter surveillance. Though a majority of the Court held on the facts presented that the defendant had not established a search had occurred, Blackmun, J., dissenting, observed that a majority of the Court accepted the notion that it *is* a search to so view within defendant's curtilage if "private helicopters rarely fly over curtilages" at that altitude, though such flight was "at a lawful altitude under FAA regulations." That is, in essence, the "public vantage point" concept. Also, no less than four Justices in *Riley* discuss the second point of whether the resident has done all that can be expected of him by way of protecting his property from outside scrutiny.

[134]Pate v. Municipal Court, 11 Cal.App.3d 721, 89 Cal.Rptr. 893 (1970).

[135]United States v. Wright, 449 F.2d 1355 (D.C.Cir.1971). Consider, in this regard, the bringing of a drug-sniffing dog into the hallway, discussed in § 2.2(g).

[136]Cohen v. Superior Court, 5 Cal.App.3d 429, 85 Cal.Rptr. 354 (1970).

[137]In State v. Clarke, 242 So.2d 791 (Fla.App.1970), the court held that because "the fire escape of the apartment complex was a common escape route for use by any persons," "the occupants of the apartment in question had no reasonable right to expect any privacy with relation to what they did inside the window within easy view of any person on that fire escape."

tion point. Whether a particular search involves an unconstitutional intrusion into the privacy of an individual is dependent upon the total facts and circumstances of the case. * * *

In the instant matter the police made their observations from an outside fire escape which was available to tenants, guests, and other persons lawfully on the fourth floor in case of fire. It is a tenable argument that tenants whose apartments had windows on the outside wall four stories above the street could reasonably expect privacy from any observations from the fire escape except during an emergency evacuation. In such a crisis, it is unlikely that anyone would pause to look into windows.

The *Cohen* court thus remanded the case for a determination of the critical facts, such as "the customary use or nonuse of the fire escape platform for purposes other than emergency escape from a fire, and on the extent of view into the apartment by a person using the escape ladders and not walking away from the escape route." Consistent with *Cohen*, some other decisions also recognize that the resident of a multiple-occupancy dwelling has a justified expectation of privacy against being heard or seen from vantage points about the building not ordinarily utilized by the public or other residents.[138]

As for the second point, the 1948 Supreme Court case of *McDonald v. United States*[139] provides a relevant fact situation. There the police suspected a tenant in a rooming house, McDonald, of being involved in a numbers operation. One of them climbed through a window leading into the room of Mrs. Terry, the landlady, and then proceeded to the second floor to McDonald's room. The door to the room was closed, so the officer stood on a chair and looked through the transom, by which he was able to see two men handling gambling paraphernalia. This, the

---

[138]Pate v. Municipal Court, 11 Cal.App.3d 721, 89 Cal.Rptr. 893 (1970) (where occupants of motel room had drawn curtains so that observations could not be made from adjacent ground area, it a search for officers to climb onto a second-story trellis and there look into window); Borum v. United States, 318 A.2d 590 (D.C.App. 1974) (surveillance from roof atop the lobby into second floor hotel room is a search); Commonwealth v. Panetti, 406 Mass. 230, 547 N.E.2d 46 (1989) (it a search for police to overhear defendant's conversations from crawl space under his first floor apartment, given defendant's justified expectation "that no one would be in the crawl space to which neither the public nor tenants had access"); State v. Carter, 569 N.W.2d 169 (Minn.1997) (police conducted search by looking in apartment window, as even if "the area just

outside the apartment window was a common area, the fact that [the officer] left the sidewalk, walked across the grass, climbed over the bushes, placed his face within 12 to 18 inches of the window * * * makes it clear that he took extraordinary measures to enable himself to view the inside of a private building"); State v. Alexander, 170 N.J.Super. 298, 406 A.2d 313 (1979), order aff'd, 173 N.J.Super. 260, 414 A.2d 36 (1980) (police looked in defendant's second-story apartment by leaning over fire escape railing to see in window 8 feet from fire escape; this a search as the window was "well out of the view of anyone engaged in normal use of the fire escape").

[139]McDonald v. United States, 335 U.S. 451, 69 S.Ct. 191, 93 L.Ed. 153 (1948).

government argued, amounted to no search vis-a-vis McDonald:

> Although it was an invasion of privacy for the officers to enter Mrs.
> Terry's room, that was a trespass which violated her rights under
> the Fourth Amendment, not McDonald's. Therefore so far as he was
> concerned, the officers were lawfully within the hallway, as much
> so as if Mrs. Terry had admitted them. Looking over the transom
> was not a search, for the eye cannot commit the trespass condemned
> by the Fourth Amendment.

Justice Douglas, writing the opinion of the Court, did not "stop to
examine that syllogism for flaws," but merely announced: "we
reject the result."[140] Justice Jackson, concurring, thought it desirable to identify the flaw; he concluded that tenant McDonald had
"a personal and constitutionally protected interest in the integrity and security of the entire building against unlawful breaking
and entry." He thus proceeded to make it clear that had the officers made a lawful entry into the common area of the premises,
they would then have had virtual carte blanche to conduct a
surveillance there:

> Like any other stranger, they could then spy or eavesdrop on others
> without being trespassers. If they peeped through the keyhole or
> climbed on a chair or on one another's shoulders to look through
> the transom, I should see no grounds on which the defendant could
> complain.

In the context of the pre-*Katz* trespass rule which then obtained,
there is certainly nothing remarkable about this assertion by
Justice Jackson. But the great virtue of the *Katz* decision is that
it liberates courts from the trespass straightjacket and permits a
reasoned value judgment to be made concerning what types of
police surveillance are not to go unregulated by constitutional
restraints. And in making that judgment, it is submitted, there is
no necessity to conclude that apartment and hotel dwellers must
be deemed to have no justified expectation of privacy against
such highly intrusive snooping merely because they live under
conditions requiring that others must be allowed to pass their
door. Even if we are prepared to say that these residents must
pay the price, in terms of loss of privacy against police scrutiny,
for having the misfortune to reside where the doors are cracked[141]
or imperfectly hung,[142] surely at some point the limit is reached.
And certainly that limit *is* reached when the conduct in question

---

[140]As Amsterdam, 58 Minn.L.Rev.
349, 389 (1974), notes: "Examination
of the syllogism would, I think, have
stirred some of the fourth amendment's deeper difficulties. But the
rejection of its result was as foreor-
dained as Zarathustra's rejection of
the gods, and for much the same reason. If this totally unreasonable conduct were not a search and seizure,
how could the Supreme Court condemn it as an unreasonable search
and seizure? *Therefore*, it was a search
and seizure."

[141]Borum v. United States, 318
A.2d 590 (D.C.App.1974).

[142]United States v. Llanes, 398
F.2d 880 (2d Cir.1968).

is keyhole-peeping,[143] transom-peeping,[144] or looking though minute openings in covered windows.[145] To assert that the tenant in a hotel or apartment building has an expectation of privacy in his place of residence is to say very little if that tenant is put to the choice of papering over his transom and stuffing his keyhole or else having a policeman look in.

§ 2.3(d) Entry of related structures

Under the traditional pre-*Katz* interpretation of the Fourth Amendment, the "right of the people to be secure in their * * * houses" extended not merely to a person's dwelling, but also to other structures located within the curtilage.

> Generally speaking, curtilage has been held to include all buildings in close proximity to a dwelling, which are continually used for carrying on domestic employment; or such place as is necessary and convenient to a dwelling, and is habitually used for family purposes.[146]

Applying the curtilage test to the facts of particular cases, courts

---

[143]State v. Person, 34 Ohio Misc. 97, 298 N.E.2d 922 (1973) (concluding that even though the landlord's son could admit the police to the hallway of the rooming house, the police officer's actions in "surreptitiously peering through a keyhole" constituted a Fourth Amendment search). Cf. State v. Morrow, 95 Wis.2d 595, 291 N.W.2d 298 (App.1980) (where officer assumed prone position on floor of hotel hallway and looked under door into room, this a search, but one made on probable cause and in exigent circumstances on facts of this case).

[144]Cf. State v. Adams, 378 So.2d 72 (Fla.App.1979) (where police looked in defendant's room in a rooming house by going onto the porch and then standing on a chair to peer through a window above eye level, this was a search because defendant had a reasonable expectation of privacy against such surveillance).

[145]State v. Carter, 569 N.W.2d 169 (Minn.1997), described in note 138 supra (also emphasizing officer "peered through a small gap between the blinds").

Compare United States v. Fields, 113 F.3d 313 (2d Cir.1997) (distinguishing case in which court held it a search to look through a very small opening in a sheet of plywood covering a broken window, court concludes looking from common area of apart-ment complex into bedroom no search, given "the five-to six-inch opening beneath the blinds in this case" that was "sufficiently large to be clearly visible from the interior of the room to anyone who cared enough about his privacy to close the blinds").

[Section 2.3(d)]

[146]United States v. Potts, 297 F.2d 68 (6th Cir.1961). The Supreme Court stated in Oliver v. United States, 466 U.S. 170, 104 S.Ct. 1735, 80 L.Ed.2d 214 (1984), that "the curtilage is the area to which extends the intimate activity associated with the 'sanctity of a man's home and the privacies of life,' * * * and therefore has been considered part of home itself for Fourth Amendment purposes. Thus, courts have extended Fourth Amendment protection to the curtilage; and they have defined the curtilage, as did the common law, by reference to the factors that determine whether an individual reasonably may expect that an area immediately adjacent to the home will remain private." The Court added that "for most homes, the boundaries of the curtilage will be clearly marked; and the conception defining the curtilage—as the area around the home to which the activity of home life extends—is a familiar one easily understood from our daily experience."

The extent of the curtilage de-

held that it was a search within the meaning of the Fourth Amendment for police to enter a garage,[147] a barn,[148] a smokehouse,[149] a bathhouse,[150] or a hen house.[151] But this by no means meant that these and like structures were inevitably within the protection of the Amendment. Other decisions, sometimes involving different facts and sometimes reflecting a different judicial attitude concerning the scope of the curtilage (especially as to just how close a "close proximity" is), found the following structures to be outside the curtilage and thus subject to unrestrained entry at the whim of the police: garages,[152] barns,[153] hen houses,[154] stables,[155] lean-tos,[156] and outbuildings.[157]

As perhaps is apparent from these lists, it is bizarre that the curious concept of curtilage, originally taken to refer to the land

---

pends upon the nature of the premises. As stated in Commonwealth v. Thomas, 358 Mass. 771, 267 N.E.2d 489 (1971): "In a modern urban multifamily apartment house, the area within the 'curtilage' is necessarily much more limited than in the case of a rural dwelling subject to one owner's control. * * * In such an apartment house, a tenant's 'dwelling' cannot reasonably be said to extend beyond his own apartment and perhaps any separate areas subject to his exclusive control."

[147]Taylor v. United States, 286 U.S. 1, 52 S.Ct. 466, 76 L.Ed. 951 (1932); Martin v. United States, 183 F.2d 436 (4th Cir.1950); State v. Jenkins, 143 Idaho 918, 155 P.3d 1157 (2007); State v. Brochu, 237 A.2d 418 (Me.1967); State v. Winkler, 552 N.W.2d 347 (N.D.1996).

Distinguishable from those decisions is City of Whitefish v. Large, 318 Mont. 310, 80 P.3d 427 (2003) (where defendant's carport was attached to but beneath her condominium unit, police could enter the carport because "it would be comparable to the front porch" in other cases, as "casual visitors might easily walk through her carport to reach the stairs to her front door"). Consider also Coffin v. Brandau, 642 F.3d 999 (11th Cir.2011) (where door to attached garage open when police arrived, court says it "need not decide * * * whether entering an open garage to gain access to a visible door to the home is a violation of the Fourth Amendment," as here facts show defendant's wife "attempted to close the

garage door" prior to police entry).

[148]Rosencranz v. United States, 356 F.2d 310 (1st Cir.1966); Walker v. United States, 225 F.2d 447 (5th Cir. 1955).

[149]Roberson v. United States, 165 F.2d 752 (6th Cir.1948).

[150]Wakkuri v. United States, 67 F.2d 844 (6th Cir.1933).

[151]People v. Lind, 370 Ill. 131, 18 N.E.2d 189 (1938); Cantu v. State, 557 S.W.2d 107 (Tex.Crim.App.1977).

[152]Carney v. United States, 163 F.2d 784 (9th Cir.1947); Guaresimo v. United States, 13 F.2d 848 (6th Cir. 1926); People v. Lees, 257 Cal.App.2d 363, 64 Cal.Rptr. 888 (1967); People v. Swanberg, 22 A.D.2d 902, 255 N.Y.S.2d 267 (1964).

[153]Schnorenberg v. United States, 23 F.2d 38 (7th Cir.1927); Guaresimo v. United States, 13 F.2d 848 (6th Cir. 1926).

[154]Hodges v. United States, 243 F.2d 281 (5th Cir.1957); Schnorenberg v. United States, 23 F.2d 38 (7th Cir. 1927).

[155]United States v. McBride, 287 F. 214 (S.D.Ala.1922).

[156]United States v. Mitchell, 12 F.2d 88 (S.D.Tex.1926).

[157]Brock v. United States, 256 F.2d 55 (5th Cir.1958) (was 150 to 180 feet from residence). For further discussion of a reasonable expectation of privacy in "outbuildings" in a broader sense, see Annot., 67 A.L.R.6th 531 (2011).

and buildings within the baron's stone walls, should ever have been deemed to be of controlling significance as to the constitutional limits upon the powers of the police. The Fourth Amendment also protects a person's "papers, and effects," and it was never satisfactorily explained why these papers and effects were with or without protection from unreasonable search and seizure depending upon whether they were kept in a building close to or distant from the dwelling. As one federal judge observed some years ago,

> the "curtilage" test * * * would imply * * * that buildings outside the curtilage are *not* within the protection of the Fourth Amendment, and, while I am aware of cases so holding, I can see no reason why a farmer should be afforded less protection in the barn where he actually does business, whether located within the curtilage or not, than is accorded a city dweller in his office.[158]

The same could be said of structures not having a business use. It is difficult to understand, for example, why police should be required to conform to the restraints of the Fourth Amendment when they enter an urban dweller's garage attached to or immediately adjacent to his dwelling, but should be permitted to enter at will a garage some distance from or having no connection with the dwelling. The absurdity of that distinction led at least one court to conclude that "a garage * * * is protected against unreasonable searches without regard to whether or not it is within the curtilage of a private dwelling."[159]

One of the virtues of *Katz v. United States*[160] is that it makes it apparent that the curtilage concept should not be employed to limit arbitrarily the reach of the Fourth Amendment's protections. Under *Katz*, it is a search to violate "the privacy upon which [one] justifiably relied," and unquestionably a person can have such an expectation of privacy as to garages and barns and the like even when they are not in "close proximity" to his dwelling.

Some of the post-*Katz* cases still rely upon the curtilage concept in the process of holding that it is a search to enter a structure located within the curtilage.[161] This is not particularly objectionable, for there is no reason to view *Katz* as having somehow reduced the protection of in-curtilage structures; surely a justi-

---

[158]Rives, J., dissenting in Walker v. United States, 225 F.2d 447 (5th Cir.1955).

[159]United States v. Hayden, 140 F.Supp. 429 (D.Md.1956).

[160]Katz v. United States, 389 U.S. 347, 88 S.Ct. 507, 19 L.Ed.2d 576 (1967).

[161]E.g., Los Angeles Police Protective League v. Gates, 907 F.2d 879 (9th Cir.1990) (garage connected to home); Kishel v. State, 287 So.2d 414 (Fla.App.1974) (building located 30 feet from residence); McGee v. State, 133 Ga.App. 184, 210 S.E.2d 355 (1974) (shed within 45 to 69 feet of the house on a country farm); State v. Legg, 633 N.W.2d 763 (Iowa 2001) (garage attached to house); State v. Trusiani, 854 A.2d 860 (Me.2004) (attached garage used for storage and used as entry by family but not by visitors); State v. Winkler, 552 N.W.2d 347 (N.D.1996) (garage near house).

fied expectation of privacy exists as to them. But it will no longer do to declare routinely that any entry of a structure beyond the curtilage is not a Fourth Amendment search. Rather, *Katz* dictates the approach taken in *People v. Weisenberger*,[162] where, in the course of holding that the discovery of three 2-pound bags of marijuana in a chicken house was a search, the court reasoned:

> In our view the court's reliance on the curtilage doctrine was misplaced. Even though the area of the search might have been outside the curtilage, nevertheless, if it was a place where the owner had a reasonable expectation of privacy, then it was a constitutionally protected area where warrantless intrusions are forbidden under the federal and state constitutions. * * *
>
> The record reflects that the chicken house was in proximity to the Weisenberger home and was being put to an active domestic use. It housed ten to fifteen laying hens and contained necessary feed and water for their maintenance. There was no public exposure of illicit activity being conducted in or about the chicken house. * * *
>
> In light of these circumstances, we think it clear that appellant had a reasonable expectation of privacy in this outbuilding.

In the more recent case of *Oliver v. United States*,[163] the Supreme Court utilized the curtilage concept for purposes of distinction in reaffirming the "open fields" rule of *Hester v. United States*.[164] But, despite the *Oliver* Court's unwillingness to recognize that an expectation of privacy could be grounded in one's use of fences and no trespassing signs around his property,[165] that decision casts no doubt upon the soundness of the *Weisenberger* reasoning. The Court in *Oliver* only held "that an individual may not legitimately demand privacy for activities conducted out of doors in fields," and acknowledged that the Fourth Amendment's protections extend to structures other than homes. Similarly, in applying *Oliver* in *United States v. Dunn*,[166] the Court ruled that merely looking into a barn outside the curtilage was no search,[167] but did not challenge the defendant's assertion "that he possessed an expectation of privacy, independent from his home's curtilage, in the barn and its contents, because the barn is an essential part of his business," meaning "his barn enjoyed Fourth

---

[162]People v. Weisenberger, 183 Colo. 353, 516 P.2d 1128 (1973). See also State v. Showalter, 427 N.W.2d 166 (Iowa 1988) (entry of barn outside curtilage a search, as defendant has expectation of privacy as to it independent from house and curtilage); State v. Vicars, 207 Neb. 325, 299 N.W.2d 421 (1980) (was a search to enter calf shed 100 feet from residence and on opposite side of chain link fence surrounding yard, as "shed was clearly used by the defendant's family in their farming operation in such a manner

that there was certainly a reasonable expectation of privacy in the shed").

[163]Oliver v. United States, 466 U.S. 170, 104 S.Ct. 1735, 80 L.Ed.2d 214 (1984).

[164]Hester v. United States, 265 U.S. 57, 44 S.Ct. 445, 68 L.Ed. 898 (1924).

[165]See § 2.4(a).

[166]United States v. Dunn, 480 U.S. 294, 107 S.Ct. 1134, 94 L.Ed.2d 326 (1987).

[167]See § 2.3(e).

Amendment protection and could not be entered and its contents seized without a warrant."[168]

§ 2.3(e) Looking into or listening at related structures

Even if a certain related structure is protected by the Fourth Amendment in the sense that a physical intrusion into that place would constitute a search, it does not necessarily follow that it is also a search for the police simply to look inside that structure. In determining whether the looking was a search, the fundamental question under *Katz* is whether the looking intruded upon the justified expectation of privacy of the occupant. This, in turn, ordinarily requires consideration of two factors: (1) the location of the officer at the time of the viewing; and (2) the precise manner in which the view was achieved.

As for the location of the officer, the easiest case is that in which the policeman is able to look inside without entering upon the land of the owner or occupant of the garage or similar structure. It is not objectionable, for example, that the officer made his observations from a public sidewalk[169] or alley.[170] As is equally true of multiple-occupancy residences,[171] a somewhat lesser expectation of privacy is likely to exist where the structure in question is divided up into separate units. Thus, where the defendant's garage was one of a row of garages rented to separate individuals, no intrusion into his privacy occurred where an officer was able to look into his garage from "the common area shared by all the users of the rented garages."[172] Similarly, where one garage is partitioned off and separate sections are rented to different individuals, it is no search for an officer to enter one section with the permission of the person renting that stall and from there to look through an opening into defendant's portion of the garage.[173]

When the view is achieved by entering upon the defendant's

---

[168]Thus in State v. Showalter, 427 N.W.2d 166 (Iowa 1988), the court viewed *Dunn* as no bar to concluding the defendant had an expectation of privacy as to his barn outside the curtilage. Accord: Siebert v. Severino, 256 F.3d 648 (7th Cir.2001); People v. Pitman, 211 Ill.2d 502, 286 Ill.Dec. 36, 813 N.E.2d 93 (2004).

Compare State v. Martin, 553 A.2d 1264 (Me.1989) (no search to enter "a shanty for animals to get in out of the weather" located 50 ft. from defendant's dwelling, as it not within curtilage; because freezer in shed apparently not connected to electrical supply, the shed not an area that "harbors the intimate activities associated with the sanctity of a home and the privacies of life").

See other cases in note 50, § 2.4(a).

[Section 2.3(e)]

[169]United States v. Hanahan, 442 F.2d 649 (7th Cir.1971).

[170]United States v. Wright, 449 F.2d 1355 (D.C.Cir.1971); Bruce v. State, 268 Ind. 180, 375 N.E.2d 1042 (1978).

[171]See § 2.3(c).

[172]State v. Mack, 21 Or.App. 522, 535 P.2d 766 (1975).

[173]United States v. Hufford, 539 F.2d 32 (9th Cir.1976). See also State v. Bobic, 140 Wash.2d 250, 996 P.2d 610 (2000) (relying on *Hufford*, court

property, a closer examination of the facts of the particular case is essential. Especially in rural or other rather open areas, the so-called open fields doctrine[174] may prove significant, in that a viewing accomplished while in an open field area is not likely to be considered an intrusion upon the defendant's justified expectation of privacy.[175] Instructive in this regard is *Fullbright v. United States*,[176] where federal investigators came upon the farm of one Marzett and while there looked through the open door of a shed and saw three persons operating a still therein. In concluding that this was not a search, the court in *Fullbright* commented:

> When the investigators made their initial observation, the door to the shed was open and its light was sufficient to reveal what was going on. The extent of the investigators' action at the time was to look. And the use of binoculars did not change the character or admissibility of the evidence or information gained.[177] It has been consistently held that open fields are not protected by the Fourth Amendment. The investigator here did not make a "search" of any papers, houses, persons, or effects in the usual sense but rather made distant observations of a house and shed the direct search of which we shall assume would have been constitutionally prohibited without a warrant as being within the "curtilage". If the investigators had physically breached the curtilage there would be little doubt that any observations made therein would have been proscribed. But observations from outside the curtilage of activities within are not generally interdicted by the Constitution. Indeed, to so hold might require passing officers to close their eyes to the commission of felonies on front doorsteps. * * * By this we do not mean to say that surveillance from outside a curtilage under no circumstances could constitute an illegal search in view of the teachings of *Katz v. United States* * * *. It is our opinion, however, that on the record before us in light of *Hester*[178] the observations in question may not be deemed an unreasonable search if they were made from outside the curtilage of the Marzett farm.

Although the open fields-curtilage distinction will often be helpful in this context, *Fullbright* correctly cautions that this distinction as to the character of the property on which the officer was positioned will not inevitably be controlling. The ultimate judgment to be made under *Katz* is whether, by taking that position, the officer intruded upon a privacy expectation deserving of

---

holds there no search where officer looked into defendant's rented storage unit from unrented adjoining unit by looking through small hole in the wall without aid of flashlight; no search, considering that "the detective's observations were made without extraordinary or invasive means and could be seen by anyone renting the unit").

[174] See § 2.4(a).

[175] United States v. Mooring, 137 F.3d 595 (8th Cir.1998); United States v. Brady, 993 F.2d 177 (9th Cir.1993); Whistenant v. State, 50 Ala.App. 182, 278 So.2d 183 (1973).

[176] Fullbright v. United States, 392 F.2d 432 (10th Cir.1968).

[177] For more on the use of binoculars, see § 2.2(b).

[178] The reference is to the "open fields" case of Hester v. United States, 265 U.S. 57, 44 S.Ct. 445, 68 L.Ed. 898 (1924).

Fourth Amendment protection.[179] In *United States v. Minton*,[180] for example, officers stationed themselves at the top of a 12–14 foot embankment about 80–90 feet away and from there, with the aid of binoculars, saw illicit liquor plainly visible in a truck and through the open doorway of a building. Although it was unclear whether the embankment belonged to Minton, the court declared that

> even if it did, such a location at such a distance is probably not within the curtilage. * * * More important than the rubric of realty * * * there was here, we think, no reasonable expectation of privacy—considering the time of day and all the surrounding circumstances.

If the officer was in closer proximity to the structure, as commonly is the case when the events occur in an urban setting, it must be considered just how private the particular vantage point actually was. It is not objectionable for an officer to come upon that part of the property which "has been opened to public common use."[181] The route any visitor to a residence would use is not private in the Fourth Amendment sense, and thus if police take

---

[179]Another way in which the curtilage concept is occasionally used inconsistently with the *Katz* test, though fully consistent with the traditional curtilage definition, see text at note 146 supra, is by assuming that a protected privacy expectation in a structure such as a barn can exist only if the adjacent residence is occupied. See, e.g., Norman v. State, 362 So.2d 444 (Fla.App.1978) (because house on farm not occupied, the barn "did not have the same protected status" it would otherwise have, and thus police could climb fence and walk 250 yards to barn and look through windows with flashlight, though they knew a man living elsewhere was working the farm). As was recognized in overturning that decision, Norman v. State, 379 So.2d 643 (Fla.1980), it makes no sense to say that a farmer has a justified expectation of privacy as to his "business premises" (e.g., a barn) only if he lives immediately adjacent thereto.

[180]United States v. Minton, 488 F.2d 37 (4th Cir.1973).

[181]People v. Superior Court, 33 Cal.App.3d 475, 109 Cal.Rptr. 106 (1973). See also United States v. French, 291 F.3d 945 (7th Cir.2002) (no search where officer looked into shed from gravel walkway, as it a

"route which any visitor * * * would use"); Pistro v. State, 590 P.2d 884 (Alaska 1979) (officer could see through garage window from driveway, "a normal means of ingress and egress impliedly open to public use by one desiring to speak to occupants of the garage, or to park off the street while visiting occupants of the house"); People v. Houze, 425 Mich. 82, 387 N.W.2d 807 (1986) (no search where police "looked into an unattached garage which abutted a public alley from a common access route"); State v. Winkler, 552 N.W.2d 347 (N.D.1996) (where officers "entered Winkler's property on the driveway, which extends over 200 feet from the public road to Winker's home, and followed the driveway's right-hand turn behind the home" to where they could see into the open garage, this no search, as "any member of the public would have entered upon Winkler's property in the manner the officers did").

Compare State v. Christensen, 131 Idaho 143, 953 P.2d 583 (1998) (under state constitution, where officer approached residence and in doing so saw marijuana in hot hut, this an illegal search, as while property not fenced, officer passed over or by gate clearly posted with "No Trespassing" sign, as a "reasonable respectful citizen when confronted with a closed

that route "for the purpose of making a general inquiry"[182] or for some other legitimate reason,[183] they are "free to keep their eyes open,"[184] and thus it is permissible for them to look into a garage or similar structure from that location.[185] On the other hand, if the police depart from that route and go to other, more private parts of the curtilage in order to look into a structure there,[186] this constitutes a search,[187] even if the police might have been

---

gate and a no trespassing sign does not proceed further"; sign does not create "an absolute barrier to warrantless entry into the curtilage by police," who could nonetheless approach the house in a more serious matter than here, where police came upon premises "only to make general inquiries about nearby residents").

[182]United States v. Knight, 451 F.2d 275 (5th Cir.1971).

[183]United States v. French, 291 F.3d 945 (7th Cir.2002) (stressing "that Kelly came to French's property not to conduct a search, but for the *express purpose* of locating an errant probationer" he believed was on that property). Compare State v. Ross, 141 Wash.2d 304, 4 P.3d 130 (2000) (officers here were not "on legitimate police business," as "the officers' purpose was not to investigate criminal activity but to obtain information to prepare the affidavit in order to obtain a search warrant," for they "entered the property at 12:10 a.m., an hour when no reasonably respectful citizen would be welcome absent actual invitation or an emergency," and they "had no intention of contacting the defendant," but rather walked up the driveway to the garage, where they smelled marijuana therein, in an attempt to determine whether that was the smell noticed on an earlier visit).

[184]State v. Crea, 305 Minn. 342, 233 N.W.2d 736 (1975).

[185]United States v. Knight, 451 F.2d 275 (5th Cir.1971); Bower v. State, 769 S.W.2d 887 (Tex.Crim.App. 1989) (officer looked in garage while approaching "front door by the only means of access—the driveway"); Bies v. State, 76 Wis.2d 457, 251 N.W.2d 461 (1977).

[186]However, an officer may have

some other legitimate reason for departing from that route, in which case observations made within structures will still come within the plain view doctrine. See Doe v. State, 131 Idaho 851, 965 P.2d 816 (1998) (where police, seeking to question defendant, implicated in a burglary, went to dairy farm where he resided with parents and, when no one answered door of residence, walked to area of a shop 40–50 ft. away and there saw a vehicle and shotgun through open shop doors, this no search, for "[a]fter finding no one in the home, it was reasonable for the officer to look for Doe in the shop, especially when the area was well lit," and it "reasonable to conclude that the occupants could be found working somewhere on the property"); State v. DeWitt, 324 Mont. 39, 101 P.3d 277 (2004) (where defendant did not answer residence door when police knocked, but his truck was parking in driveway with warm engine and light was on inside garage, police properly knocked on side entry door to garage, so when door swung open because of the knock police made no search in seeing smoke and smelling exhaust); State v. Krout, 100 N.M. 661, 674 P.2d 1121 (1984) (seeking out a person to be arrested).

[187]Daughenbaugh v. City of Tiffin, 150 F.3d 594 (6th Cir.1998) (looking into plaintiff's open garage from plaintiff's back yard, where police not lawfully present, a search); United States v. Morehead, 959 F.2d 1489 (10th Cir.1992) (looking in window of shop building near residence a search, but was lawful because police there with a warrant to arrest defendant and had reason to believe defendant inside shop building because light on there and no one answered at residence); Ex parte Maddox, 502 So.2d 786 (Ala.1986) (looking into greenhouse from within

able to (but didn't) make the same observation from outside the curtilage.[188]

Despite the importance of making these kinds of assessments concerning the position of the officer at the time he makes his observations, it cannot be asserted dogmatically that the viewing is never a search whenever the police conduct in taking that position did not itself intrude upon the defendant's justified privacy expectation. Attention must also be given to the manner of viewing, for the "ultimate question" put by *Katz* "is whether, if the particular form of surveillance practiced by the police is permitted to go unregulated by constitutional restraints, the amount of privacy and freedom remaining to citizens would be diminished to a compass inconsistent with the aims of a free and open society."[189] Certainly that privacy would be so diminished if persons were put to the choice of sealing up their premises air tight or else assuming the risk that a policeman will look in. And even if a garage is not entitled to "the special Fourth Amendment protections afforded a dwelling,"[190] it is still true that "when a citizen does as much as ordinary care requires to shield his sanctuary from strangers his constitutional right to maintain his privacy should not be made to depend upon the resources of skillful peepers and eavesdroppers who can always find ways to intrude."[191]

When the conduct of the officer in gaining access to the vantage point is itself unobjectionable, privacy interests are not threatened by allowing the officer so positioned to use his naked eye[192]

---

curtilage is a search; vantage point not on regular route of visitors to farm); Norman v. State, 379 So.2d 643 (Fla.1980) (it a search for officer to climb fence to which gate locked and then look into barn; privacy expectation justified because defendant "took overt steps to designate his farm and barn not open to the public"; the "barn, an integral part of petitioner's farming business, enjoyed the same Fourth Amendment protection as do other business premises"); Huffer v. State, 344 So.2d 1332 (Fla.App.1977) (officers walked through side yard to back yard and shined light through small tear in plastic cover of hothouse and saw marijuana plants inside; held, "[u]nder either the traditional curtilage approach or the more contemporary reasonable expectation of privacy approach, the appellant's hothouse was deserving of constitutional protection"); Gonzalez v. State, 588 S.W.2d 355 (Tex.Crim.App.1979) (it a search when officer deviated from normal

route of visitor on property to peek into outdoor toilet near dwelling); State v. Daugherty, 94 Wash.2d 263, 616 P.2d 649 (1980) (it a search to look into garage where defendant had backed up 2 trucks to open garage door to block view and officer went between the trucks, beyond that part of the driveway which was a pathway to the house, to gain view).

[188]State v. Christensen, 131 Idaho 143, 953 P.2d 583 (1998).

[189]Amsterdam, Perspectives on the Fourth Amendment, 58 Minn.L.Rev. 349, 403 (1974).

[190]United States v. Wright, 449 F.2d 1355 (D.C.Cir.1971).

[191]Wright, J., dissenting in United States v. Wright, 449 F.2d 1355 (D.C. Cir.1971).

[192]As to whether it should be otherwise when aids to the natural senses are employed, see § 2.2.

to look into a garage, barn or shed through an open door[193] or an uncovered window.[194] In such a case, it cannot be said that the occupant of those premises has done "as much as ordinary care requires." But when the premises are more carefully secured and the officer consequently has to resort to other techniques, there comes a point at which the surveillance deserves to be characterized as a search and thus brought within the restraints of the Fourth Amendment.[195] And this can be so even as to structures not technically within the curtilage, as is illustrated by *United States v. Dunn.*[196] To look into a barn fifty yards from the curtilage boundary, agents crossed four fences and then used a flashlight to look through a fishnet covering to determine what was inside. In holding that notwithstanding the Supreme Court's generous "open fields" rule of *Oliver v. United States*[197] this was a search, the court noted it had "found no case * * * applying the term [open fields] to a building of any consequence."[198] The court in *Dunn* quite correctly emphasized that a

> barn is as much a part of a rancher's place of business as a warehouse or outbuilding is part of an urban merchant's place of business. It is and ought to be constitutionally protected from warrantless searches if the owner or occupier takes reasonable steps to effect privacy.

The court of appeals in *Dunn* later declined to rely on that reasoning and instead claimed the barn was within the curtilage,[199] a holding the Supreme Court reversed in *United States v. Dunn.*[200] Examining several "factors" deemed to bear upon the "open fields"-curtilage distinction, the Court first concluded that the barn in fact was outside the curtilage.[201] The importance of that conclusion, in the majority's judgment, was that consequently the

---

[193]United States v. Minton, 488 F.2d 37 (4th Cir.1973); Fullbright v. United States, 392 F.2d 432 (10th Cir. 1968); Bies v. State, 76 Wis.2d 457, 251 N.W.2d 461 (1977).

[194]United States v. Hanahan, 442 F.2d 649 (7th Cir.1971); State v. Mack, 21 Or.App. 522, 535 P.2d 766 (1975).

[195]This is not to say that all of the restrictions applicable to entry of such a structure should necessarily be imposed as to such a lesser intrusion. See Amsterdam, 58 Minn.L.Rev. 349, 388–95 (1974).

[196]United States v. Dunn, 766 F.2d 880 (5th Cir.1985).

[197]Oliver v. United States, 466 U.S. 170, 104 S.Ct. 1735, 80 L.Ed.2d 214 (1984).

[198]But, the term might be applied to a lesser structure. See, e.g., Rainey v. Hartness, 339 Ark. 293, 5 S.W.3d 410 (1999) (entry of wooded area no search because it within open field doctrine, and it likewise no search to look into deer stand there, as it "little more than a metal box, with sides three to four feet high and a roof elevated on poles," as persons within "were exposed to the public's view," and there no evidence plaintiff "used the stand to engage in private activity, other than eating meals, or that he attempted to shield his activities from the public").

[199]United States v. Dunn, 782 F.2d 1226 (5th Cir.1986).

[200]United States v. Dunn, 480 U.S. 294, 107 S.Ct. 1134, 94 L.Ed.2d 326 (1987), discussed in Note, 18 Golden Gate U.L.Rev. 397 (1988).

[201]This aspect of the case is discussed in § 2.4(a).

officers at the time of their viewing were themselves outside the curtilage and thus *could not* have been engaging in Fourth Amendment activity. Why? Because "under *Oliver* and *Hester*, there is no constitutional difference between police observations conducted while in a public place and while standing in the open fields."[202] *Dunn* thus was governed by the previous Term's decision in *California v. Ciraolo*,[203] involving aerial surveillance into a curtilage yard.[204]

The two dissenters in *Dunn* concluded that the barn was in the curtilage and that, even if it were not, the police activity intruded upon the defendant's reasonable expectation of privacy. They wisely concluded:

> The Fourth Amendment prohibits police activity which, if left unrestricted, would jeopardize individuals' sense of security or would too heavily burden those who wished to guard their privacy. In this case, in order to look inside respondent's barn, the DEA agents traveled a half-mile off a public road over respondent's fenced-in property, crossed over three additional wooden and barbed wire fences, stepped under the eaves of the barn, and then used a flashlight to peer through otherwise opaque fishnetting. For the police habitually to engage in such surveillance—without a warrant-is constitutionally intolerable.

Although courts have given less than adequate attention to that point,[205] it is useful here to take note of the carefully reasoned opinion in *United States v. Vilhotti*.[206] In that case, an officer standing in a service alley abutting a garage was able, with the aid of a flashlight, to peer through a small space between the boards covering a rear window and see stolen goods stored therein. Finding that these facts presented "a close question under the Fourth Amendment," the court reasoned that

> to ascertain what constitutes an unreasonable search the court must evaluate a person's efforts to insure the privacy of an area or activity in view of both contemporary norms of social conduct and the imperatives of a viable democratic society. * * *
>
> The two most important variables in deciding whether a visual search contravenes the Fourth Amendment are accessibility to view and the nature of the premises. Thus, for example, "objects falling within the plain view of an officer who has a right to be in the posi-

---

[202]See also United States v. Gerard, 362 F.3d 484 (8th Cir.2004) (where garage outside curtilage of farmhouse, officer did not conduct illegal warrantless search of 2-story garage when he climbed ladder to peer through vent into lighted and locked garage in attempt to locate or ascertain safety of owner).

[203]California v. Ciraolo, 476 U.S. 207, 106 S.Ct. 1809, 90 L.Ed.2d 210 (1986).

[204]See § 2.3(g).

[205]See, e.g., United States v. Wright, 449 F.2d 1355 (D.C.Cir.1971) (use of flashlight to look through small crack between garage doors); People v. Superior Court, 33 Cal.App.3d 475, 109 Cal.Rptr. 106 (1973) (looking through cracks in garage door, aided however by fact lights were on inside the garage).

[206]United States v. Vilhotti, 323 F.Supp. 425 (S.D.N.Y.1971).

tion to have that view" are not constitutionally protected. * * * While Kelly's vantage point was a well-travelled public right of way, it would be distorting the "plain view" doctrine to hold that it encompasses peering through cracks in a boarded window. * * *

The photographs submitted in evidence by the government show, however, that the gaps between the boards covering the windows were readily apparent to any passerby. The fact that private citizens have peered through these gaps does not necessarily permit a government agent to do the same. * * * But under *Katz*, an agent is permitted the same license to intrude as a reasonably respectful citizen would take. Therefore, the nature of the premises inspected—e.g., whether residential, commercial, inhabited or abandoned—is decisive; it determines the extent of social inhibition on natural curiosity and, inversely, the degree of care required to ensure privacy. Here, given that an unattached garage was the object of search, neither social nor physical barriers were sufficient to protect its interior from intrusion by a casual observer. Kelly's flashlight search, therefore, did not encroach upon defendants' reasonable expectations of privacy. Indeed, it is not unlikely that police officers would routinely make such inspections as part of their peacekeeping functions.[207]

Without suggesting that the result ultimately reached in *Vilhotti* is beyond dispute,[208] the fundamental approach taken deserves to be emulated by other courts. The court in *Vilhotti* asks the right kinds of questions-questions that must be answered in order to keep faith with *Katz*.

---

[207]See also State v. Bowling, 867 S.W.2d 338 (Tenn.Crim.App.1993) (police viewing of defendant's truck, parked in his garage, was a search, as "truck was behind a solid, completely closed garage door," and while "the only other garage door was open, it had been raised a mere one and a half feet to allegedly enable the dog to come and go," so officer's "actions of getting on his hands and knees with his head very near to the ground and looking into the garage are not those actions which society would permit of a reasonably respectful citizen").

Compare United States v. Pace, 955 F.2d 270 (5th Cir.1992) (declining, on basis of Supreme Court's *Dunn* case, supra, to reach same result where a barn outside the curtilage involved; while "officers could not see inside the barn from any distance, but had to press their faces close to the opening to see inside," court concluded controlling fact was that police were still outside curtilage at time of observation; decision subject to question in that one of the four factors in *Dunn* was that the defendants there had done little to prevent someone stand-

ing in the open fields from viewing the interior of the barn); State v. Buzzard, 112 Ohio St.3d 451, 860 N.E.2d 1006 (2007) (where tracks from burglarized business led to driveway ending at nearby windowless building, but locked double door was "warped and loose fitting" so that quarter-inch gap allowed police to see stolen goods within, that no search, as "the viewing took place in front of the garage, where there is a diminished expectation of privacy").

[208]See the dissent by Wright, J., in the rather similar case of United States v. Wright, 449 F.2d 1355 (D.C.Cir. 1971). It may be, however, that *Wright* is a better case than *Vilhotti* for finding that a search had occurred. In *Vilhotti* the gaps were "readily apparent to any passerby"; In *Wright*, the majority said there was "a nine-inch gap" between the doors," but the dissent points out that the "records shows that the 'nine-inch gap' was actually an eight-inch slit one half inch wide * * * and the police may have pulled on the doors so they could see inside."

Yet another type of situation addressed by the Supreme Court is that in which the looking into a related structure occurs from the vantage point of an aircraft. In *Florida v. Riley*,[209] an officer in a helicopter hovering 400 feet above defendant's residence looked into a partially covered greenhouse in the backyard and saw marijuana plants. Relying on *California v. Ciraolo*,[210] the Court held no search had occurred. In *Ciraolo*, involving a viewing into defendant's fenced back yard from a fixed-wing aircraft flying at 1,000 feet, the Court reached the highly questionable[211] conclusion that defendant had no reasonable expectation of privacy because "any member of the public flying in this airspace who glanced down could have seen everything that these officers observed." A four-Justice plurality in *Riley* reached the conclusion, surely no less vulnerable than that in *Ciraolo*, that "any member of the public could legally have been flying over Riley's property in a helicopter at the altitude of 400 feet and could have observed Riley's greenhouse."

Is there *any* form of aerial surveillance without sense-enhancing devices[212] that *does* constitute a "search" so as to be subject to Fourth Amendment limitations? The *Riley* plurality appears to assume the answer is yes,[213] but is not very helpful as to what additional facts will push a case across the Fourth Amendment line. Somewhat curiously, they note that there was no "intimation here that the helicopter interfered with respondent's normal use of the greenhouse or of other parts of the curtilage. As far as this record reveals, no intimate details connected with the use of the home or curtilage were observed, and there was no undue noise, no wind, dust, or threat of injury."[214] Also, *all* members of the Court seem to agree that flights at some

---

[209]Florida v. Riley, 488 U.S. 445, 109 S.Ct. 693, 102 L.Ed.2d 835 (1989), discussed in Foster, Warrantless Aerial Surveillance and the Right to Privacy: The Flight of the Fourth Amendment, 56 J. Air & Com. 719 (1991); 28 Duq.L. Rev. 327 (1990); 17 Fla.St.U.L.Rev. 157 (1989); 17 Hastings Const.L.Q. 725 (1990); 19 Stetson L.Rev. 273 (1989); 23 Suffolk U.L.Rev. 866 (1989); 62 U.Colo.L.Rev. 407 (1991); 67 U.Detr. L.Rev. 143 (1989); 38 U.Kan.L.Rev. 107 (1990); 1990 Utah L.Rev. 407; 43 Vand.L.Rev. 275 (1990).

[210]California v. Ciraolo, 476 U.S. 207, 106 S.Ct. 1809, 90 L.Ed.2d 210 (1986).

[211]See the discussion of *Ciraolo* in § 2.3(g).

[212]On use of such devices, see § 2.2(b), (c) and (d).

[213]They assert: "This is not to say that an inspection of the curtilage of a house from an aircraft will always pass muster under the Fourth Amendment simply because the plane is within the navigable airspace specified by law."

[214]See also Henderson v. People, 879 P.2d 383 (Colo.1994) (no search where helicopter overflight, by which marijuana plants in shed spotted, was between 500 and 700 ft. and notwithstanding five passes there was "little evidence of the noise, wind, dust, threat of injury, or interference with the use of the curtilage" required by *Riley*).

Compare Commonwealth v. Oglialoro, 525 Pa. 250, 579 A.2d 1288 (1990) (where police in helicopter "reduced their altitude to 50 feet, where they hovered over the property

particular altitude could be sufficiently "rare" to make a house-holder's expectation of privacy reasonable, but there is no agreement on just what degree of rarity is required[215] or on who has to prove what on the degree-of-rarity issue.[216]

§ 2.3(f) Entry of adjoining lands

Certain lands adjacent to a dwelling[217] called the "curtilage" have always been viewed as falling within the coverage of the Fourth Amendment.[218] This is still the case under the approach

---

for 15 seconds and then made 3 passes over the property over a five minute period," so the defendant's wife "experienced sensations caused by the helicopter's proximity, including loud noise and vibration of the house and windows," "such evidence is sufficient to establish that the helicopter's presence at 50 feet above the barn represented a hazard to persons and property on the ground and that the conduct of the police in flying at this level was unreasonable").

[215]The plurality ambiguously refers to where flights are "sufficiently rare"; O'Connor, J., concurring, asks whether "members of the public travel with sufficient regularity" at that altitude; Brennan, J. (joined by two other Justices), dissenting, inquiries whether "public observation" of Riley's curtilage was "commonplace"; and Blackmun, J., dissenting, asks whether "private helicopters rarely fly over curtilages at an altitude of 400 feet."

[216]The 4-Justice plurality assumed nonrarity from the collective facts that there are over 10,000 helicopters in the U.S. and that it is lawful to operate them at 400 feet. By reference to "the record not suggesting otherwise," they seemed to assume the defendant had the burden (unmet here) of showing otherwise. O'Connor, J., concurring, more specifically relied on the fact "the defendant must bear the burden of proving that his expectation of privacy was a reasonable one," which included proof of the rarity of helicopters at 400 feet. Blackmun, J., dissenting, "would impose upon the prosecution the burden of proving contrary facts necessary to show Riley lacked a reasonable expectation of

privacy," and would remand to permit such a showing (i.e., nonrarity of helicopter flights at 400 feet) "because our prior cases gave the parties little guidance on the burden of proof issue." The other three dissenters would simply "take judicial notice that * * * such flights are a rarity," but added that in burden-of-proof terms the burden should be on the prosecution because it "has greater access to information concerning customary flight patterns and because the coercive power of the State ought not be brought to bear in cases in which it is unclear whether the prosecution is a product of an unconstitutional, warrantless search."

[Section 2.3(f)]

[217]Compare United States v. Basher, 629 F.3d 1161 (9th Cir.2011) ("classifying the area outside of a tent in a National Park or National Forest land campsite as curtilage would be very problematic," as such sites "are open to the public and exposed"); United States v. Barajas-Avalos, 359 F.3d 1204 (9th Cir.2004), as amended, 377 F.3d 1040 (9th Cir.2004) (where 12-foot travel trailer was parked in "natural clearing" on defendant's farm land, while interior of such "a 'non-traditional' house" protected by Fourth Amendment against entry, police did not violate defendant's rights "by viewing the interior of the travel trailer through a window," as the clearing was not a "curtilage" because "there is no evidence that the travel trailer was used as a permanent or temporary home since 1993"); Olson v. State, 166 Ga.App. 104, 303 S.E.2d 309 (1983) (uninhabited house is not a dwelling and thus lacks a protected curtilage).

[218]Care v. United States, 231 F.2d 22 (10th Cir.1956).

to Fourth Amendment issues adopted by the Supreme Court in *Katz v. United States*[219] As for the extent of the home's curtilage, the Supreme Court in *United States v. Dunn*[220] decided

> that curtilage questions should be resolved with particular reference to four factors: the proximity of the area claimed to be curtilage to the home, whether the area is included within an enclosure surrounding the home, the nature of the uses to which the area is put, and the steps taken by the resident to protect the area from observation by people passing by.[221]

But under the *Katz* approach, certain observations (albeit not into the residence or some other structure) made while the police are within the curtilage are covered by the Fourth Amendment,[222] while some others are not, depending upon whether there was an intrusion upon a justified expectation of privacy. In making that judgment, perhaps the most important consideration is precisely where on the adjacent lands the police were positioned. This is because a portion of the curtilage, being the normal route of access for anyone visiting the premises, is "only a semi-private area."[223] As elaborated in *State v. Corbett*:[224]

> People commonly have different expectations, whether considered or not, for the access areas of their premises than they do for more secluded areas. Thus, we do not place things of a private nature on our front porches that we may very well entrust to the seclusion of

---

[219]Katz v. United States, 389 U.S. 347, 88 S.Ct. 507, 19 L.Ed.2d 576 (1967).

Compare Wattenburg v. United States, 388 F.2d 853 (9th Cir.1968) (asserting that after *Katz* "a more appropriate test in determining if a search and seizure adjacent to a house is constitutionally forbidden is whether it constitutes an intrusion upon what the resident seeks to preserve as private even in an area which, although adjacent to his home, is accessible to the public").

[220]United States v. Dunn, 480 U.S. 294, 107 S.Ct. 1134, 94 L.Ed.2d 326 (1987).

[221]On the interpretation of these factors by the lower courts, see § 2.4(a).

[222]This is not to say, however, that for such a search to be lawful all of the restrictions upon a search into premises must necessarily be complied with. See, e.g., People v. Doerbecker, 39 N.Y.2d 448, 384 N.Y.S.2d 400, 348 N.E.2d 875 (1976), where an officer without a warrant came upon land adjoining a residence and found a package containing guns and pills

under some leaves. This surveillance was at the headquarters of one of two motorcycle gangs between which a feud was under way, and members of one of the gangs had already been apprehended with dynamite. After concluding that the officer had made a Fourth Amendment search because he had intruded upon a justified expectation of privacy, the court continued: "That expectation, however, was only one of the elements to be considered in determining the reasonableness of the search. Also relevant was the relatively limited extent of the intrusion on the privacy when measured against the justification which existed for it. * * * Here, the intrusion was lesser rather than greater, not extending into the primary building of the landowner or indeed into any building at all * * *; at the same time the justification—the preservation of the public safety—was more than adequate."

[223]United States v. Magana, 512 F.2d 1169 (9th Cir.1975).

[224]State v. Corbett, 15 Or.App. 470, 516 P.2d 487 (1973).

a backyard, patio or deck. In the course of urban life, we have come
to expect various members of the public to enter upon such a
driveway, e.g., brush salesmen, newspaper boys, postmen, Girl
Scout cookie sellers, distressed motorists, neighbors, friends. Any
one of them may be reasonably expected to report observations of
criminal activity to the police * * *. If one has a reasonable expectation that various members of society may enter the property in
their personal or business pursuits, he should find it equally likely
that police will do so.

Thus, when the police come on to private property to conduct an
investigation[225] or for some other legitimate purpose[226] and re-

[225]In *Corbett*, the court stated:
"Criminal investigation is as legitimate a societal purpose as is census
taking or mail delivery." See also
Nikolas v. City of Omaha, 605 F.3d
539 (8th Cir.2010) (officer "could enter
the property through its open gate and
proceed up the driveway to the front
door of the main residence to ask for
consent to search"); United States v.
Lakoskey, 462 F.3d 965 (8th Cir.2006)
(postal inspector was "lawfully allowed
to approach * * * front door and contact [defendant] for investigative purposes" re suspicious package); United
States v. Taylor, 458 F.3d 1201 (11th
Cir.2006) (police came on property on
"legitimate police business" after "911
hangup call" followed by more hangups
in response to two call-backs); Estate
of Smith v. Marasco, 430 F.3d 140 (3d
Cir.2005) (upon responding to neighbor's complaint of bright light on suspect's property, when officers did not
receive response at front door but
believed suspect was at home and
knew he sometimes sat on back porch,
entry into backyard lawful, but same
not true of subsequent entry after it
learned suspect not there); United
States v. Hammett, 236 F.3d 1054 (9th
Cir.2001) ("officer may encroach upon
the curtilage of a home for the purpose
of asking questions of the occupants");
Alvarez v. Montgomery County, 147
F.3d 354 (4th Cir.1998) (police lawfully entered curtilage to investigate
911 call re underage drinking party);
United States v. Daoust, 916 F.2d 757
(1st Cir.1990) ("policeman may lawfully go to a person's home to interview
him"); Scott v. State, 347 Ark. 767, 67
S.W.3d 567 (2002) (officers who came
onto defendant's front porch and

knocked on his door "were justified in
approaching Mr. Scott's residence to
question him about potential criminal
activity"); People v. Rivera, 41 Cal.4th
304, 59 Cal.Rptr.3d 473, 159 P.3d 60
(2007) (police officer may approach and
knock on door of residence, and such
actions "require no articulable suspicion of criminal activity"); People v.
Shorty, 731 P.2d 679 (Colo.1987) ("In
conducting a criminal investigation, a
police officer may enter those residential areas that are expressly or impliedly held open to casual visitors");
Trimble v. State, 842 N.E.2d 798
(Ind.2006) ("police entry onto private
property and their observations do not
violate the Fourth Amendment when
the police have a legitimate investigatory purpose for being on the property
and limit their entry to places visitors
would be expected to go"); Quintana v.
Commonwealth, 276 S.W.3d 753
(Ky.2008) ("the officer who approaches
the main entrance of a house has a
right to be there, just as any member
of the public might be"); State v.
Townsend, 571 A.2d 1206 (Me.1990)
(proper for officer to come into defendant's driveway "pursuing his investigation of the defendant, * * * even
though he chose to disguise his real
purpose by engaging the defendant in
conversation about another matter");
State v. Rand, 430 A.2d 808 (Me.1981)
("not unreasonable for the police officers, in the pursuit of criminal investigations, to seek interviews with
suspects or witnesses at their homes");
Doering v. State, 313 Md. 384, 545
A.2d 1281 (1988) (police properly entered curtilage "in the course of a legitimate investigation of a serious
crime"); Commonwealth v. A Juvenile
(No. 2), 411 Mass. 157, 580 N.E.2d

1014 (1991) (to investigate possible hit-and-run vehicle in driveway); State v. Alayon, 459 N.W.2d 325 (Minn. 1990) (officer "did not need a warrant or probable cause to walk up to defendant's home, knock on the door and say the things he said"); Waldrop v. State, 544 So.2d 834 (Miss.1989) (where owner of house trailer consented to search of it, police properly crossed defendant's land to accomplish their "right of ingress and egress" to the trailer); State v. Johnson, 171 N.J. 192, 793 A.2d 619 (2002) (officers came onto porch "for a legitimate investigative purpose," i.e., "to investigate a report of drug activity"); People v. Kozlowski, 69 N.Y.2d 761, 513 N.Y.S.2d 101, 505 N.E.2d 611 (1987) ("Nor were defendant's constitutional rights violated when the officer investigating the reported traffic incident entered upon defendant's property, knocked on the front door, and asked questions which defendant chose to answer"); State v. Beane, 770 N.W.2d 283 (N.D.2009) (police on "legitimate business" may enter curtilage, as here, where they seeking parole violator known to associate with resident); State v. Wright, 391 S.C. 436, 706 S.E.2d 324 (2011) ("A police officer without a warrant is privileged to enter private property to investigate a complaint or a report of an ongoing crime"); State v. Lodermeier, 481 N.W.2d 614 (S.D.1992) (officers there to question defendant "about a ladder he had reported stolen"); State v. Ryea, 153 Vt. 451, 571 A.2d 674 (1990) (officer properly approached defendant after he pulled into his driveway to make *Terry* stop on suspicion defendant had been driving on suspended license); State v. Byrne, 149 Vt. 224, 542 A.2d 276 (1988) (game warden properly entered curtilage "to conduct an investigation"); Gompf v. State, 120 P.3d 980 (Wyo.2005) ("absent a clear expression by the owner to the contrary, police officers are permitted to approach a dwelling and seek permission to question an occupant in the course of their official business," and such the case here though officers ar-

rived at 2 a.m., as the "lights were on in the house and the officers, therefore, assumed people were awake inside").

Compare Jacob v. Township of West Bloomfield, 531 F.3d 385 (6th Cir.2008) (code enforcement officer's repeated entry of defendant's curtilage and thereby discovering "castoff material" violating land use ordinance was a search); Knott v. Sullivan, 418 F.3d 561 (6th Cir.2005) (inspecting pile of ashes within curtilage was a search); Estate of Smith v. Marasco, 318 F.3d 497 (3d Cir.2003) (rejecting "sweeping proposition" that "officers may proceed to the back of a home when they do not receive an answer at the front door any time they have a legitimate purpose for approaching the house in the first place," court holds officers may so proceed only if it "the only practical way of attempting to contact the resident," as "where the front door was inaccessible," or if the "officers reasonably may believe * * * that the person they seek to interview may be located elsewhere on property within the curtilage," or because of "the presence of an exigency justifying entry into the curtilage"); Rogers v. Pendleton, 249 F.3d 279 (4th Cir.2001) (right of police is "to knock on a residence's door or otherwise approach the residence seeking to speak to the inhabitants, not the right to make a general investigation in the curtilage based on reasonable suspicion," and right of police to "approach a home to speak to the inhabitants * * * clearly fails to encompass a continued search of the curtilage for people or things *after* officers have spoken to the owner of a home and been asked to leave").

[226]In *Corbett*, the purpose of the visit was to obtain some descriptive information to be used in applying for a search warrant. See also United States v. Frencher, 503 F.3d 701 (8th Cir.2007) (officers properly came onto property "to serve an eviction notice," and properly continued knocking on door when they detected movements within); Widgren v. Maple Grove Township, 429 F.3d 575 (6th Cir.2005) (zoning administrator's intrusion onto

strict their movements to places visitors could be expected to go[227]
(e.g., walkways,[228] driveways,[229] porches),[230] observations made

owner's property to post civil infraction notice on front door of house not a search); United States v. Morehead, 959 F.2d 1489 (10th Cir.1992) (entry to serve arrest warrant on defendant); Causey v. State, 374 So.2d 406 (Ala.Crim.App.1979) (proper for officer to go to door of defendant, "to whom it would seem he owed the courtesy of at least reporting to him that one of the stolen tires had been found in his driveway"); Johnson v. State, 291 Ark. 260, 724 S.W.2d 160 (1987) (entry to arrest defendant for observed offense, observation of marijuana thereafter a plain view situation); Gilreath v. State, 247 Ga. 814, 279 S.E.2d 650 (1981) (proper for officer to call at house after woman's father expressed concern for her safety); State v. Orde, 161 N.H. 260, 13 A.3d 338 (2010) ("police officer has a right to enter a person's curtilage or legitimate business," here "to serve a dog complaint").

    Compare State v. Shepherd, 303 Ark. 447, 798 S.W.2d 45 (1990) (from driveway police looked through partially open garage door; this not a lawful plain view, as police "were there on the pretext of serving an illegal subpoena"; dissent objects invalidity of subpoena irrelevant where, as here, "an officer has come upon the land in the same way that any member of the public could be expected to do").

[227]In some instances, visitors may be barred from approaching the house. See, e.g., State v. Ryder, 301 Conn. 810, 23 A.3d 694 (2011) (in instant case, where "police could not drive up to the immediate front of the house because a stone wall, approximately five or six feet high, extended across the front of the property, and an electronic security gate [three feet high], made out of white fencing posts and located between the road and the interior driveway, was closed," "the defendant had a reasonable expectation of privacy in the area between his front door and the gate").

[228]United States v. Cousins, 455 F.3d 1116 (10th Cir.2006) (entry of

sideyard area lawful, as it was expected path one would take on paved walkway); United States v. Raines, 243 F.3d 419 (8th Cir.2001) (where no one answered front door, but several cars parked on driveway and it a summer evening, it proper for officer to walk through 10-foot opening in fence to backyard); United States v. Hammett, 236 F.3d 1054 (9th Cir.2001) (where no one answered front door, officer properly "circled the house with the intent of locating another door"); United States v. Thomas, 120 F.3d 564 (5th Cir.1997) (police could take walkway to front door notwithstanding privacy fence 3 feet from front door, as gate was open and there no door bell or knocker at the gate, so it "reasonable for the officers to believe the front door was readily accessible to the general public"); United States v. James, 40 F.3d 850 (7th Cir.1994) (no search, as officer "used a paved walkway along the side of the duplex leading to the rear side door," "passage to the rear side door was not impeded by a gate or fence," and both "the paved walkway and the rear side door were accessible to the general public"); United States v. Daoust, 916 F.2d 757 (1st Cir.1990) (where front door "is inaccessible there is nothing unlawful or unreasonable about going to the back of the house to look for another door"); People v. Bradley, 1 Cal.3d 80, 81 Cal.Rptr. 457, 460 P.2d 129 (1969) (discovery of marijuana plants no search, as "they were located a scant 20 feet from defendant's door to which presumably delivery men and others came"); People v. Terrazas-Urquidi, 172 P.3d 453 (Colo.2007) (police approach of backyard shed lawful where defendant "using the shed as living quarters, and the front door contained a peephole and a dead bolt, suggesting that he expected casual visitors"); State v. Duda, 437 So.2d 794 (Fla.App.1983) (marijuana seen when officer went to rear door, which proper for him to do, as he sent to investigate domestic disturbance and noise was heard at rear of house); State v. Lyons, 167 Ga.App.

from such vantage points are not covered by the Fourth

747, 307 S.E.2d 285 (1983) (proper for officer investigating animal complaint to go to back door, from which he saw marijuana plants, as he "unable to elicit a response at the front door of a residence reasonably believed to be occupied"); Hardister v. State, 849 N.E.2d 563 (Ind.2006) (defendant living at 407 "had no cognizable expectation of privacy because the backyard and sidewalk were shared with the residents of 405 and were not enclosed by a fence"); State v. Nine, 315 So.2d 667 (La.1975) (officer on a sideyard "used as a passageway"); Clausell v. State, 326 Mont. 63, 106 P.3d 1175 (2005) ("officers were well within their authority to proceed on the open walkway to the front door, where they saw evidence in plain view"); State v. Ramaekers, 257 Neb. 391, 597 N.W.2d 608 (1999) (officer "was lawfully on the front walk when he observed the ongoing party" in the yard, and thus observation no intrusion on justified expectation of privacy); State v. Byrne, 149 Vt. 224, 542 A.2d 276 (1988) (officer took walkway to steps, where hair and blood observed); State v. Seagull, 26 Wash.App. 58, 613 P.2d 528 (1980), aff'd, 95 Wash.2d 898, 632 P.2d 44 (1981) (no search for officer to take sideyard path from south porch to north porch upon recalling being told occupants could not hear knocking on south porch; though officer "strayed slightly from the most absolutely direct route between the two doors," it "would be unreasonable to require, in every case, that police officers walk a tight rope while on private property engaging in legitimate police business").

[229]United States v. Brown, 653 F.3d 656 (8th Cir.2011) (shining flashlight into car no search, as officer lawfully on driveway where it parked "to investigate a call for police assistance"); United States v. Galaviz, 645 F.3d 347 (6th Cir.2011) (police entry of part of driveway "directly abutting the public sidewalk" lawful and thus seeing gun within car parked there a lawful plain view); United States v. Brown, 510 F.3d 57 (1st Cir.2007) (ar-

rest made where officer properly positioned, in driveway next to garage, especially considering that defendant ran a motor repair business from the garage and allowed customers to enter the driveway and garage); United States v. Taylor, 458 F.3d 1201 (11th Cir.2006) (proper that officer "proceeded down the driveway that provided access to the house" and "went to the front door"); United States v. Carter, 360 F.3d 1235 (10th Cir.2004) (officers' actions in "walking up the driveway, and shining their flashlight into a car in the driveway * * * do not implicate the Fourth Amendment"); United States v. Reyes, 283 F.3d 446 (2d Cir.2002) ("we have found no Fourth Amendment violation based on a law enforcement officer's presence on an individual's driveway where," as here, "that officer was in pursuit of legitimate law enforcement business"); United States v. Roberts, 747 F.2d 537 (9th Cir.1984) (police drove up shared unobstructed but private road and then onto lawn of residence where cars parked, where no driveway as such); Tryon v. State, 371 Ark. 25, 263 S.W.3d 475 (2007) (no search as to what police viewed on defendant's premises from his driveway); People v. Edelbacher, 47 Cal.3d 983, 254 Cal.Rptr. 586, 766 P.2d 1 (1989) (driveway a "normal route used by visitors approaching the front doors"); Trimble v. State, 842 N.E.2d 798 (Ind.2006) (police properly on driveway where it "wraps around the back of [defendant's] house" to the "back door, the main entryway for visitors"); State v. Lewis, 675 N.W.2d 516 (Iowa 2004) ("the Fourth Amendment did not prohibit the police from entering Lewis's driveway" and thus observation of backyard activities from there lawful); State v. Townsend, 571 A.2d 1206 (Me.1990) (in entering driveway "the police officer did not exceed the 'implied invitation' to use it when he entered on legitimate police business"); Commonwealth v. A Juvenile (No. 2), 411 Mass. 157, 580 N.E.2d 1014 (1991) (examination of car in driveway no search where "the driveway was the normal route by which to approach the front door"); Mitchell v. State, 792 So.2d 192 (Miss.2001) (officer "was in an area of common use, near the driveway"); State v. Hubbel, 286 Mont. 200, 951 P.2d 971 (1997) ("police were thus well within their authority when they drove into the driveway and parked in the general parking area where they observed evidence in plain view"); State v. Merrill, 252 Neb. 510, 563 N.W.2d 340 (1997) (given "the accessibility and visibility of the driveway from the public roadway," "any member of the public could have entered upon Merrill's property in the same manner the officers did," and thus officers viewing of marihuana plants from driveway no search); State v. Johnston, 150 N.H. 448, 839 A.2d 830 (2004) (police conduct proper, as "the defendant's driveway was semi-private in nature, and the officers entered the property for a legitimate purpose"); State v. Wright, 391 S.C. 436, 706 S.E.2d 324 (2011) (lawful observation where police "could properly drive up the dirt driveway to get to the front door"); State v. Lodermeier, 481 N.W.2d 614 (S.D.1992) (officer examined exterior of garden tractor parked in driveway lawful, as "officer with legitimate business may enter a driveway and, while there, may inspect objects in open view"); State v. Pike, 143 Vt. 283, 465 A.2d 1348 (1983) (driveway "the normal route of access for anyone visiting the premises"); Robinson v. Commonwealth, 273 Va. 26, 639 S.E.2d 217 (2007) (officer could properly drive up driveway, at least to point where it intersected with path to front door); State v. Maxfield, 125 Wash.2d 378, 886 P.2d 123 (1994) (no search, as officer "stayed on the pathway, the driveway or the immediate access routes to the house and garage"). See also Annot., 60 A.L.R.5th 1 (1998).

[230]United States v. Cooke, 674 F.3d 491 (5th Cir.2012) (given "the peculiarities of the residence," with barn-like outer shell within which there a dirt floor and paved sidewalk leading to another door, to the living quarters, going to and knocking at in-ner door proper, as "any member of the public would reasonably think that they would have to enter and knock on the interior doors when visiting"; district court described area as "akin to a covered porch"); United States v. Titemore, 437 F.3d 251 (2d Cir.2006) (while porch was on side of building, it "was in fact a primary entrance visible to and used by the public," as manifested by fact "steps led up to the porch" and there a doorbell "suggest-[ing] to visitors that they could visit the home from the porch"); United States v. Thomas, 430 F.3d 274 (6th Cir.2005) (encounter with defendant at back deck of residence proper, for "the rear deck was adjacent to the driveway and served as the primary entrance to Hopper's home"); People v. Edelbacher, 47 Cal.3d 983, 254 Cal.Rptr. 586, 766 P.2d 1 (1989) (no search to observe and photograph shoe tracks on front porch); State v. Detlefson, 335 So.2d 371 (Fla.App.1976) ("It cannot be said the defendant had a reasonable expectation of privacy in the front porch of his home where, presumably, delivery men and others were free to observe"); State v. Tye, 276 Ga. 559, 580 S.E.2d 528 (2003) (where police came onto defendant's porch to question him in connection with murder investigation, they "were in an authorized location" when they saw defendant's bloodstained clothing); Gilreath v. State, 247 Ga. 814, 279 S.E.2d 650 (1981) (where no answer at front door, proper to go to side door and enter screened porch there); State v. Johnson, 171 N.J. 192, 793 A.2d 619 (2002) (officer "did not go beyond the porch, thus restricting his movements to the places that any other visitor could be expected to go"); State v. Kitchen, 572 N.W.2d 106 (N.D.1997) (though police entered what court at one point refers to as an "enclosed entryway," court concludes it a "porch-type entrance," as officer knocked on inside door flush with original exterior wall of the house after entering a "vestibule-like addition" with an unlocked screen door, and police entry no search because that space "was impliedly open to at least some

Amendment.[231] But other portions of the lands adjoining the residence are protected, and thus if the police go upon these other portions and make observations there, this amounts to a Fourth Amendment search,[232] and this is so even if these other portions

access by the public"); State v. Rose, 128 Wash.2d 388, 909 P.2d 280 (1996).

Cf. State v. Wilbourn, 364 So.2d 995 (La.1978) (proper for police to view evidence of hit-run accident on exterior of car parked in carport, where carport must be entered by anyone "knocking at the sidedoor to find out if someone was home or to deliver or sell something").

Compare State v. Reinier, 628 N.W.2d 460 (Iowa 2001) ("The porch of Reinier's house was just like any other portion of her house. It had glass-encased windows covered with blinds. The entrance to the porch had a solid wood door with a deadbolt lock and a screen door. Reinier stored personal belongings in the porch and kept the wood door locked at night. These circumstances reveal Reinier maintained an expectation of privacy which society clearly recognizes as reasonable. Thus, entry into the area by police constituted a search").

[231]But consider Brown v. State, 392 So.2d 280 (Fla.App.1980), where defendant was seen on his back porch by police who had driven past the gate and all the way up the driveway, and the court concluded this was a search because the events occurred at 1:45 a.m., a time when visitors would not ordinarily call, and thus defendant was entitled to expect privacy within his enclosed yard at that time.

[232]United States v. Wells, 648 F.3d 671 (8th Cir.2011) (expectation of privacy in "backyard that is accessible only by walking around the side of a home" on unpaved driveway); United States v. Struckman, 603 F.3d 731 (9th Cir.2010) (defendant's "backyard—a small, enclosed yard adjacent to a home in a residential neighborhood—is unquestionably" part of curtilage, and thus police entry without exigent circumstances unreasonable); United States v. Van Dyke, 643 F.2d 992 (4th Cir.1981) (it a search for officers to climb fence and watch from honeysuckle patch 150 feet from house in rural area; curtilage not limited to nearer mowed area; assuming "that sheer distance could in some instances lead us to conclude that a particular area was outside the curtilage even though inside a fence surrounding a residence, this case does not present such a situation"); Griffin v. State, 347 Ark. 788, 67 S.W.3d 582 (2002) (though police obtained consent to enter after knocking on door, that consent invalid because police had already made stealthy entry of the property after 10 p.m. and had first "checked out a shed and walked around the premises"); State v. Lewis, 675 N.W.2d 516 (Iowa 2004) (where "backyard was located adjacent to the home" and a "fence with a gate completely enclosed the backyard" and "enclosed rear porch was located in the fenced backyard" and "screens and or windows with a door fully enclosed the rear porch," entry of yard and porch a search); State v. Fisher, 283 Kan. 272, 154 P.3d 455 (2007) (search here, as "once [police officer's] knock and talk was complete, instead of driving away from the house to the highway, he simply drove deeper into the property on the driveway—according to the photographs, perhaps as much as 50 yards—directly to the previously observed bag"); State v. Silva, 509 A.2d 659 (Me.1986) (entry of backyard area within curtilage a search); State v. Orde, 161 N.H. 260, 13 A.3d 338 (2010) (where police officer walked up onto deck at side of house and saw marijuana plants there, that illegal search, considering that items on deck not visible from the road, the driveway, or the side door reached by path from driveway, and given officer's "departure from the obvious paths on the property"); People v. Doerbecker, 39 N.Y.2d 448, 384 N.Y.S.2d 400, 348 N.E.2d 875 (1976) (see note 222 supra for facts); State v. Johnson, 301 N.W.2d

are themselves clearly visible from outside the curtilage.[233] (However, legitimate police business may occasionally take officers to parts of the premises not ordinarily used by visitors,[234] as

---

625 (N.D.1981) (it a search to look behind entry structure to area not observable from road or nearby driveway to mobile home);Dale v. State, 38 P.3d 910 (Okla.Crim.App.2002) (agent's entry of defendant's property "by climbing over the locked driveway gate, which was part of a secure perimeter fence, and proceeding between the two residential structures in order to confront [him] was an unlawful entry onto the curtilage of the home"); State v. Prier, 725 S.W.2d 667 (Tenn.1987) (entry of garden area within curtilage a search); Gonzalez v. State, 588 S.W.2d 355 (Tex.Crim.App.1979) (it a search where officer deviated from normal route to explore weeded area in back yard); State v. Harris, 671 P.2d 175 (Utah 1983) (a search where officer went to defendant's garden, at rear of his property behind farm building and well screened). On the reasonable expectation of privacy in backyards, see Annot., 62 A.L.R.6th 413 (2011).

[233]Hoffman v. People, 780 P.2d 471 (Colo.1989).

[234]The cases upholding such police activity do not necessarily make it clear whether such action is deemed to be no search or a reasonable search. See, e.g., United States v. Taylor, 458 F.3d 1201 (11th Cir.2006) ("to the extent that the officers moved away from the front door and toward Taylor" when he walked out from behind the barn, "this small departure from the front door also does not trigger the protections of the Fourth Amendment"); Alvarez v. Montgomery County, 147 F.3d 354 (4th Cir.1998) (where police responding to 911 call re underage drinking party approached front door to notify residents of complaint but, seeing sign reading "Party In Back," walked around house to back yard where party going on and asked to see host, such entry "did not exceed their legitimate purpose for being there" and thus "satisfied the Fourth Amendment's reasonableness requirement");

Tryon v. State, 371 Ark. 25, 263 S.W.3d 475 (2007) (officer "did not violate Tryon's constitutional rights by merely walking into the backyard after he saw Tryon take off running"); Vidos v. State, 367 Ark. 296, 239 S.W.3d 467 (2006) (where officer "knocked at the residence and discovered that no one was home," his "merely walking from the house to the barn" in search of person he sought lawful); State v. Hider, 649 A.2d 14 (Me.1994) (officer tracking thief from airport with tracking dog lawfully entered rear of defendant's curtilage); State v. Dunn, 340 Mont. 31, 172 P.3d 110 (2007) (defendant "did not have a reasonable expectation of privacy in his backyard area" vis-a-vis police entry to investigate neighbors' complaint of loud party there, where "noise was coming from the backyard"); State v. Domicz, 188 N.J. 285, 907 A.2d 395 (2006) (not objectionable that police "passed through the rear gate and entered the curtilage for the purpose of knocking on defendant's door and speaking with him," as "position of the parked cars in defendant's driveway led the officers to believe that the back door was used by residents and visitors"); State v. Beane, 770 N.W.2d 283 (N.D.2009) ("The officers' 'small departure' from the front door of the residence to meet Beane coming from the unattached garage also did not trigger the protections of the Fourth Amendment");State v. Curtin, 175 W.Va. 318, 332 S.E.2d 619 (1985) (police properly in yard at rear of house to secure premises while others executed search warrant within).

Compare United States v. Wells, 648 F.3d 671 (8th Cir.2011) (distinguishing *Anderson*, note 101 supra, and *Raines*, note 228 supra, court holds that where police made no effort to contact defendant at his front door but instead, at 4 a.m., walked to back yard and knocked on door of outbuilding there, such action unreasonable, as there no "reason for them to think that Wells generally would receive

---

"where knocking at the front door is unsuccessful in spite of indications that someone is in or around the house.")[235]

Account must also be taken of the nature of the premises. Whether considered from the perspective of the curtilage concept[236] or the more modern justified-expectation-of-privacy approach,[237] it is a fair generalization that the lands adjoining a multiple-occupancy residence are less likely to receive Fourth Amendment protection than the yard of a single-family residence. Under the *Katz* test, the privacy expectation as to such an area is often diminished because it is not subject to the exclusive control of one tenant and is utilized by tenants generally and the numerous visitors attracted to a multiple-occupancy building. Thus, it has been held that tenants in an apartment building have no justified expectation of privacy as to "a portion of the home which all residents and visitors must use to enter,"[238] "the common yard

---

'visitors' there").

[235]Hardesty v. Hamburg Township, 461 F.3d 646 (6th Cir.2006). Accord: Estate of Smith v. Marasco, 318 F.3d 497 (3d Cir.2003); United States v. Hammett, 236 F.3d 1054 (9th Cir. 2001); United States v. Anderson, 552 F.2d 1296 (8th Cir. 1977); United States v. Bradshaw, 490 F.2d 1097 (4th Cir.1974).

[236]As stated in Commonwealth v. Thomas, 358 Mass. 771, 267 N.E.2d 489 (1971): "In a modern urban multi-family apartment house, the area within the 'curtilage' is necessarily much more limited than in the case of a rural dwelling subject to one owner's control. * * * In such an apartment house, a tenant's 'dwelling' cannot reasonably be said to extend beyond his own apartment and perhaps any separate areas subject to his exclusive control."

Compare United States v. Maestas, 639 F.3d 1032 (10th Cir.2011) (guest of one tenant in triplex had no reasonable expectation of privacy in adjacent enclosed garbage storage area, even assuming it within curtilage, as this was "a common area shared by all three tenants (and presumably their guests) and the landlord (and presumably his or her agents)"); United States v. Williams, 581 F.2d 451 (5th Cir.1978) (concluding, as to farm, that where the outbuildings "are not encompassed by a fence that also

includes the house, or perhaps a privacy or exclusionary one around them, the outer limits of the curtilage are defined by the walls of the remote outbuildings," so that it was no search to smell illegal liquor while positioned near a shed but more distant from the main house than the shed); Sanders v. State, 264 Ark. 433, 572 S.W.2d 397 (1978) (garden some 100–200 yards behind house trailer, though separated by fence from trailer, was within curtilage, as police knew given fact they first tried to justify search of garden as incident to execution of warrant for premises later held invalid).

[237]United States v. Acosta, 965 F.2d 1248 (3d Cir.1992) (where "landlord gave the defendants permission to use the backyard" but "the right to grant permission to others remained with the landlord" and "the landlord used the backyard freely, as did his employees," "the fact that defendants had permission to use the yard did not create any legal expectation of privacy in it").

[238]State v. Johnson, 171 N.J. 192, 793 A.2d 619 (2002) (questioning proposition that the "curtilage concept has limited applicability with respect to multi-occupancy premises because none of the occupants can have a reasonable expectation of privacy in areas that are also used by other occupants").

open to the public"[239] or the parking lot open to all users of the apartment building.[240]

This is not to say, however, that tenants in multiple-occupancy buildings may *never* have a protected privacy expectation as to adjoining lands merely because no one tenant has exclusive control. Just as the tenants in such a building may have a collective expectation of privacy vis-a-vis the general public in their corridors and hallways because of the manner in which the building is secured,[241] they will sometimes have a protected collective expectation as to certain areas outside. A case in point is *Fixel v. Wainwright*,[242] where an officer entered a fenced backyard behind a four-unit apartment building and discovered a bag of heroin there. To the government's argument that "the multi-unit character of this residence results in a relinquishment of any right of privacy relating to the backyard," the court responded:

> The backyard of Fixel's home was not a common passageway normally used by the building's tenants for gaining access to the apartments. * * * Nor is the backyard an area open as a corridor to salesmen or other businessmen who might approach the tenants in the course of their trade. * * * This apartment was Fixel's home, he lived there and the backyard of the building was completely removed from the street and surrounded by a chain link fence. * * * While the enjoyment of his backyard is not as exclusive as the backyard of a purely private residence, this area is not as public or shared as the corridors, yards or other common areas of a large apartment complex or motel. Contemporary concepts of living such as multi-unit dwellings must not dilute Fixel's right to privacy any more than is absolutely required. We believe that the backyard area of Fixel's home is sufficiently removed and private in character that he could reasonably expect privacy.[243]

Yet another relevant consideration is the precise manner the

---

[239]State v. Hines, 323 So.2d 449 (La.1975). See also Reeves v. Churchich, 484 F.3d 1244 (10th Cir.2007) (front yard of duplex not part of building's curtilage, where yard not enclosed and residents could not exclude others from the yard, which they shared with other residents); People v. Holt, 91 Ill.2d 480, 64 Ill.Dec. 550, 440 N.E.2d 102 (1982) (area under porch of apartment building). The same is true of a motel, State v. Berry, 223 Kan. 102, 573 P.2d 584 (1977), a duplex, State v. Hook, 60 Haw. 197, 587 P.2d 1224 (1978), or when two buildings have a common curtilage, Walley v. State, 353 Ark. 586, 112 S.W.3d 349 (2003) ("a person does not have an objectively reasonable expectation of privacy in the area around a rental residence, especially where, as here, a second building on the prop-

erty is rented to another person who shares the curtilage with the accused").

[240]United States v. Soliz, 129 F.3d 499 (9th Cir.1997) (no search for officer to enter parking area used by residents and guests, located between buildings in 2-building apartment complex; court doubts whether "a shared common area in a multi-unit dwelling compound is sufficiently privacy oriented to constitute curtilage"); State v. Coburne, 10 Wash.App. 298, 518 P.2d 747 (1973). The same is true of a motel parking lot. United States v. Diaz, 25 F.3d 392 (6th Cir.1994).

[241]See § 2.3(b).

[242]Fixel v. Wainwright, 492 F.2d 480 (5th Cir.1974).

[243]See also Espinoza v. State, 265 Ga. 171, 454 S.E.2d 765 (1995) (where

police observation occurs, especially the degree of scrutiny involved. In those cases saying, in effect, that no justified expectation of privacy was intruded upon because the police entered as would a tradesman or any other visitor, it is ordinarily the case that the police merely saw from their vantage point what would have been readily apparent to anyone coming upon the premises. Illustrative is *State v. Detlefson*,[244] where police came on the front porch and saw marijuana plants there; the court understandably said that defendant had no "reasonable expectation of privacy in the front porch of his home where, presumably, delivery men and others were free to observe the plants there." Delivery men, unlike the police, might not have recognized the plants as marijuana, but that is not significant, as the critical fact is that the police did not do anything on the porch that any other visitor would be unlikely to do. When that is not the case, the expectation-of-privacy issue deserves another look.

An excellent example is provided by *Wattenburg v. United States*,[245] where the defendant, who resided at and operated a certain motel, claimed that federal officers conducted an illegal search when they examined a stockpile of cut trees near the motel and determined that the trees had been removed from government lands without authority. The stockpile was twenty to thirty-five feet from the motel, but was only five feet from a parking area used by personnel and patrons of the lodge. The court first

---

defendant lived in left side of duplex and his apartment reached by left half of a private driveway shaped like a stethoscope, search that uncovered garbage bag among bushes 7–8' to left of his driveway and outside the stethoscope, "a place where visitors to the duplex would not be expected to go," intruded on defendant's justified expectation of privacy).

Compare United States v. Arboleda, 633 F.2d 985 (2d Cir.1980) (where defendant threw package out window of third-floor apartment and it landed on ledge, officer could examine package, as there was no evidence defendant "exercised any exclusive control over the ledge," and "it is doubtful that the curtilage concept has much applicability to multi-family dwellings"); Bunn v. State, 153 Ga.App. 270, 265 S.E.2d 88 (1980) (where common grassy area had 6-foot privacy fence, but there was an opening between the fence and building permitting persons to pass through the area and area was used by all tenants and their invitees, it no search to enter that area; but this did not justify of-

ficer going onto adjoining concrete patio of particular apartment, as that area qualifies as the curtilage of that apartment).

[244]State v. Detlefson, 335 So.2d 371 (Fla.App.1976). See also United States v. Miller, 589 F.2d 1117 (1st Cir.1978) (court concluded defendant had no justified expectation of privacy as to 40 lb. bale of marijuana on his residential land, though the bale was covered by a tarpaulin, where nearby marijuana debris would have been apparent to any passerby).

[245]Wattenburg v. United States, 388 F.2d 853 (9th Cir.1968). Also illustrative is State v. Goude, 49 Or.App. 721, 620 P.2d 957 (1980), where police examined a car up on blocks in defendant's driveway. Noting that this was not a casual inspection, but included looking inside and under the car, the court concluded this was a search because the defendant "could reasonably expect that people would not be crawling around his car, opening the hood and possibly getting inside to inspect the interior."

reached the dubious conclusion[246] "that the stockpile of Christmas trees here in question was within the curtilage of Wattenburg's abode at the Hideaway Lodge, and therefore, at least as to him, protected by the Fourth Amendment," and then proceeded to assess the facts under the "more appropriate" *Katz* test. The court concluded that the conduct of the agents was also a search under that test, which would seem equally dubious if a mere observation of the *Detlefson* type had occurred, for it would not seem that motel grounds so close to the much-used parking area could themselves be characterized as private. But more than a casual observation was involved, and this made the difference:

> Measured by the test we suggest, Wattenburg was, without doubt, protected by the Fourth Amendment from a warrantless search and seizure of the kind described above. In the daytime and in the dark, from 2:35 p.m. to 9:00 p.m. on November 8, 1965, several law enforcement officials meticulously went through the stockpile of trees * * *. It must have been necessary to move most of the trees from one place to another in order to make the kind of examination which the officers carried on. Lights must have been required as the men moved about after dark and there was undoubtedly a certain amount of noise. There can be no doubt that Wattenburg, in placing the stockpile this close to his place of residence, sought to protect it from this kind of governmental intrusion.

Whether the foregoing analysis can in all respects be squared with the Supreme Court's more recent decision in *Oliver v. United States*[247] is not entirely clear. In the course of reaffirming the "open fields" doctrine,[248] the Court there seemed to attach greater significance to the common law "curtilage" concept than had, for example, the lower court in *Wattenburg*. The Supreme Court in *Oliver* asserted that the curtilage, as distinguished from open fields, is "part of the home itself for Fourth Amendment purposes," and that "Fourth Amendment protection" extends to the curtilage as "defined [by] the common law." But the Court stressed also that this definition necessitates "reference to the factors that determine whether an individual reasonably may expect that an area immediately adjacent to the home will remain private." This suggests that it is still quite proper to take into account the nature of the premises in the manner previously described, but it is less apparent that the precise manner of the police observation remains as a separate consideration.

§ 2.3(g) Looking into or listening at adjoining lands

If, as concluded above, there are certain parts of the grounds surrounding a residence which are private in the *Katz* sense, so that a physical intrusion upon them is covered by the Fourth Amendment, it remains to be determined whether it is also a

---

[246]See note 237 supra.

[247]Oliver v. United States, 466 U.S. 170, 104 S.Ct. 1735, 80 L.Ed.2d

214 (1984).

[248]See § 2.4(a).

search to view objects or activities on those grounds or to overhear conversations occurring on those grounds while at some other location. In many instances the answer is no,[249] but this is not inevitably so; depending upon the circumstances of the individual case, it may appear that the occupant of the premises in question had a justified expectation of privacy against such intrusions.

Certainly no justified expectation is present when the physical facts are such that the incriminating objects or activities were readily visible to persons on the public way[250] or neighboring lands.[251] Illustrative is *State v. Pontier*,[252] where police, after

---

[Section 2.3(g)]

[249]Of course, this conclusion merely establishes the lawfulness of the viewing or overhearing, and it does not follow that a warrantless entry onto the premises to seize evidence would also be lawful. United States v. Whaley, 781 F.2d 417 (5th Cir.1986).

[250]United States v. Bucci, 582 F.3d 108 (1st Cir.2009) (no search to view defendant's driveway and garage interior for 8 months from video camera on utility pole across the street, where those areas "plainly visible" from the street); United States v. Poole, 407 F.3d 767 (6th Cir.2005) (where "officers here merely looked into Appellant's backyard from their position in the public alley," no search); Causey v. State, 374 So.2d 406 (Ala.Crim.App. 1979) (no search for officer to look into defendant's property from public road); Tryon v. State, 371 Ark. 25, 263 S.W.3d 475 (2007) (no search where officer saw defendant's truck with air compressor in bed, parked on defendant's property, "from the road," "a lawful vantage point"); Hoffman v. People, 780 P.2d 471 (Colo.1989) (no search to look into curtilage through wire mesh fence from service alley); State v. Holbron, 65 Haw. 152, 648 P.2d 194 (1982) (no search to look into defendant's yard from adjacent public tennis courts); State v. Wright, 391 S.C. 436, 706 S.E.2d 324 (2011) (activities outside adjacent to defendant's residence "were knowingly exposed to the public" when observed by deputies "driving by the residence on a public road").

[251]Widgren v. Maple Grove Township, 429 F.3d 575 (6th Cir.2005)

(no search to observe exterior of owner's house for tax assessment purposes from neighbor's property); United States v. Campbell, 395 F.2d 848 (4th Cir.1968) ("the viewing by Alcohol and Tobacco Tax Division agents from an adjacent cornfield of a transaction in illicit whiskey which took place in the back yard of Campbell's home" was not a search); Miller v. State, 342 Ark. 213, 27 S.W.3d 427 (2000) (no search to view marijuana plants from neighbor's property); People v. Superior Court, 37 Cal.App.3d 836, 112 Cal.Rptr. 764 (1974) (no search, as the "observations made by the officers looking over the five-foot fence from the neighbor's yard disclosed no more than what was in plain view of the neighboring householders and anyone else who might be on their premises with or without an invitation"); People v. Ortega, 175 Colo. 136, 485 P.2d 894 (1971) (no search for police to watch defendant's actions in back yard of apartment house from adjoining property); State v. Rickard, 420 So.2d 303 (Fla.1982) (no search to observe marijuana plants in defendant's yard from nearby citrus grove); State v. Dupuis, 378 So.2d 934 (La.1979) (no search to look in from neighbor's field, as "any stranger could have * * * been in the field and observed the defendant's loading activities"); State v. Pease, 520 A.2d 698 (Me.1987) (no search to look into curtilage from nearby wooded area); State v. Nason, 498 A.2d 252 (Me.1985) (proper for police to observe comings and goings at defendant's house from vantage point at which they had a right to be); State v. Peakes, 440 A.2d 350 (Me.1982) (marijuana plants observable from neighbor's

receiving an anonymous tip that marijuana was growing in the back yard of a certain residence, entered a neighbor's back yard with permission and from there looked over a short picket fence and through some overhanging foliage and saw marijuana plants. Noting that in *Katz* the Court had stated that "[w]hat a person knowingly exposes to the public, even in his own home or office, is not a subject of Fourth Amendment protection," the *Pontier* court concluded:

> The back yard of appellant's home was enclosed by a waist high picket fence and foliage growing at various locations along the fence. Planting marijuana plants in a back yard enclosed only by a picket fence and intermittent vegetation is not an action reasonably calculated to keep the plants from observation since it is certainly foreseeable that a reasonably curious neighbor, while working in his yard, might look over the picket fence into appellant's yard and see the plants, whether or not he knew what they were.

More difficult are those cases in which the yard is much better secured from outside viewing and the police consequently have to engage in conduct arguably exceeding that which could be expected of "a reasonably curious neighbor." Consider, for example, the facts of *United States v. McMillon*,[253] where the back yard was enclosed by a six-foot high stake fence overgrown with vines and bushes. The officers managed to pierce this visual barrier by standing on a neighbor's back porch, which was separated from defendant's porch by a partition and was slightly recessed from defendant's porch. One officer was able to photograph the plants in the yard by standing on his toes or a box, but the other officer testified that he was able to videotape the plants by aiming the camera over the fence while holding it at eye level. The court concluded that no search had occurred:

> There is no doubt that the officers had the right to stand on the porch, having been invited to do so by occupants of the premises.[254] Nor are the indications that some of the observations were made by the officers while standing on their toes, or leaning around the side of the partition, or perhaps standing on a box on the porch sufficient to constitute their actions a search within the proscriptions of the Fourth Amendment. As stated by Judge Leventhal in *James v. United States*[255] * * *: "That the policeman may have to crane his neck, or bend over, or squat, does not render the doctrine inapplicable, so long as what he saw would have been visible to any

---

yard).

[252]State v. Pontier, 95 Idaho 707, 518 P.2d 969 (1974).

[253]United States v. McMillon, 350 F.Supp. 593 (D.D.C.1972).

[254]This is not to suggest that such an invitation is essential. See, e.g., Sarantopoulos v. State, 629 So.2d 121 (Fla.1993) (where police looked over fence from neighbor's back yard, which he entered without obtaining permission, this no search; court relies on United States v. Dunn, 480 U.S. 294, 107 S.Ct. 1134, 94 L.Ed.2d 326 (1987), holding a trespass even on defendant's own property not sufficient to establish that a search occurred).

[255]James v. United States, 418 F.2d 1150 (D.C.Cir.1969).

curious passerby."

If it is true that one of the officers was able to make the observations from eye level, then the result reached in *McMillon* may be correct. The case comes very close, however, to the limit of non-search surveillance. Although admittedly yards are not as private as houses, "the amount of privacy and freedom remaining to citizens would be diminished to a compass inconsistent with the aims of a free society"[256] if all such nontrespassory observations were unregulated by constitutional restraints. Surely there comes a point at which it can be said that the householder has done all that can be reasonably expected of him to keep his yard private, even though the police by some extraordinary measure have been able to breach that privacy without physical entry. Thus, if a person has surrounded his property with a solid wooden fence eight feet high,[257] it is fair to say that he has a justified expectation of privacy there even if the police are able to locate some small crack or knothole by which to peer inside.[258] Similarly, if the police can view the incriminating object in defendant's back yard only by squeezing into a narrow area between the neighbor's garage and defendant's fence, almost blocked off by heavy foliage and weeds, and from that vantage point using a telescope,[259] such viewing deserves to be characterized as a search under the *Katz* test.[260]

Sometimes the incriminating object or activity is not observ-

---

[256]Amsterdam, Perspectives on the Fourth Amendment, 58 Minn.L.Rev. 349, 403 (1974).

[257]Compare Sarantopoulos v. State, 629 So.2d 121 (Fla.1993) (defendant's "extraordinary efforts" objection rejected where 6'2" officer on neighbor's property was able by standing on his tiptoes to see over 6 ft. high solid board fence; court said defendant without reasonable expectation of privacy because fence "protected from view only as to those who remained on the ground and who were unable to see over the six-foot fence unaided").

[258]These were the facts in George v. State, 509 S.W.2d 347 (Tex.Crim. App.1974). The court did not say that no search had occurred; rather, the court held "that the limited investigation by the officer which resulted in the observation of the marijuana was not unreasonable under the circumstances." The surveillance was undertaken on the basis of information from an informant to the effect that marijuana was growing in that yard, which

the court acknowledged "did not constitute probable cause for an arrest or search within the house or within the fence." *George* illustrates the important point that to say looking into the curtilage is a search is not to conclude that a search of that limited nature may be undertaken only upon facts that would justify a much more intrusive search.

[259]On other uses of telescopes and binoculars, see § 2.2(c).

Mere use of binoculars from a more readily accessible vantage point, such as the woods just outside defendant's curtilage, is no search. Ex parte Maddox, 502 So.2d 786 (Ala.1986).

[260]People v. Fly, 34 Cal.App.3d 665, 110 Cal.Rptr. 158 (1973). See also United States v. Cuevas-Sanchez, 821 F.2d 248 (5th Cir.1987) (distinguishing *Ciraolo*, text at note 273 infra, court holds it is a search to look into defendant's back yard, surrounded by 10 ft. high solid fence, by installing video camera on top of power pole); State v. Kender, 60 Haw. 301, 588

able from a neighbor's land, but can be (and is) seen from some other portion of the defendant's land. This is no search if the observations were made while the officer was located at a place where "visitors could be expected to go."[261] In other circumstances, the "open fields" doctrine[262] comes into play, so that such viewing by the police is unobjectionable-even if what is seen is itself within the protected area called the "curtilage"-if the police vantage point was itself in the "open fields." Illustrative is *State v. Rogers*,[263] where police came onto defendant's tract of wooded property and viewed marijuana plants growing in the garden near his house. Though the garden itself was deemed to be within the curtilage, the court concluded no search had occurred because, in cases of this genre, "the place of observation is normally more important than the place observed."[264] In reaching that holding, the court emphasized "the absence of two factors that could have changed our conclusion: affirmative action by defendants to block observation of the garden from the surrounding woods and use of technology by the trooper to aid his observation."

Sometimes the police obtain a view of residential lands from the air by using a helicopter or an airplane.[265] Two California

---

P.2d 447 (1978) (where officer had to climb three-quarters of way up fence and support himself on fellow officer's shoulder and then use 60-power telescope to see marijuana plants in defendant's back yard, this a search; court says notion it no search for officer to see from vantage point where he lawfully present applies only when the situation "involved observations by police officers which were facilitated by the defendant's failure to take sufficient steps to protect his privacy," which not so here given fence around and heavy foliage on defendant's yard).

[261]State v. Beauchemin, 161 N.H. 654, 20 A.3d 936 (2011) (no search for conservation officer to photograph possible deer baiting site while on defendant's front porch at main entrance to house).

[262]See § 2.4(a).

[263]State v. Rogers, 161 Vt. 236, 638 A.2d 569 (1993).

[264]In support, the court quite properly relied upon United States v. Dunn, 480 U.S. 294, 107 S.Ct. 1134, 94 L.Ed.2d 326 (1987), holding that looking into a barn from outside the curtilage was no search. *Dunn* says that

"there is no constitutional difference between police observations conducted while in a public place and while standing in the open fields. Similarly, the fact that the objects observed by the officers lay within an area that we have assumed * * * was protected by the Fourth Amendment does not affect our conclusion."

See also Widgren v. Maple Grove Township, 429 F.3d 575 (6th Cir.2005) (observation for tax purposes of exterior of owner's house from owner's open fields no search); United States v. Hatfield, 333 F.3d 1189 (10th Cir.2003) ("police observation of a defendant's curtilage from a vantage point in the defendant's open field is not a search").

[265]See Granberg, Is Warrantless Aerial Surveillance Constitutional?, 55 Cal.St.B.J. 451 (1980); Kaye, Aerial Surveillance: Private Versus Public Expectations, 56 Cal.St.B.J. 258 (1981); Comments, 15 Ariz.L.Rev. 145 (1973); 18 Gonzaga L.Rev. 307 (1983); 17 J. Marshall L.Rev. 455 (1984); Notes, 50 Fordham L.Rev. 271 (1981); 60 N.Y.U.L.Rev. 725 (1985); 17 Val.U. L.Rev. 309 (1983); 35 Vand.L.Rev. 409 (1982).

cases illustrate the possibilities. In *People v. Sneed*[266] officers saw marijuana plants growing in defendant's back yard from a helicopter hovering as low as 20 to 25 feet above the property; in *People v. Superior Court*[267] an officer using binoculars saw stolen auto parts in defendant's back yard from a plane that flew over the area at an altitude of about 500 feet. The viewing from the helicopter was held to be a search, while the observation from the plane was held not to be a search.

When considered from the perspective of the *Katz* test, the two decisions are not inconsistent. In *Sneed*, the court reasoned that

> [w]hile appellant certainly had no reasonable expectation of privacy from * * * airplanes and helicopters flying at legal and reasonable heights, we have concluded that he did have a reasonable expectation of privacy to be free from noisy police observation by helicopter from the air at 20 to 25 feet and that such an invasion was an unreasonable governmental intrusion into the serenity and privacy of his back yard.

In the other case, by comparison, the court noted:

> Patrol by police helicopter has been a part of the protection afforded the citizens of the Los Angeles metropolitan area for some time. The observations made from the air in this case must be regarded as routine. An article as conspicuous and readily identifiable as an automobile hood in a residential yard hardly can be regarded as hidden from such a view.

But these two cases do not suggest that whether the aerial surveillance is or is not a search should be determined merely by the altitude of the aircraft. The fundamental question is whether this surveillance permitted the police to see that which the occupant justifiably believed was private. In *Superior Court*, therefore, it would seem highly relevant that the officers in the airplane saw a large object readily observable by the defendant's neighbors.[268] By contrast, in *Sneed* it was not conclusively established that the marijuana plants could have otherwise been

---

[266]People v. Sneed, 32 Cal.App.3d 535, 108 Cal.Rptr. 146 (1973).

[267]People v. Superior Court, 37 Cal.App.3d 836, 112 Cal.Rptr. 764 (1974). See also People v. Lashmett, 71 Ill.App.3d 429, 27 Ill.Dec. 657, 389 N.E.2d 888 (1979) (no search to see tractor and similar farm machinery from plane at 2400 feet).

[268]Indeed, the police later looked at the auto parts again from the neighbor's yard, which was separated from defendant's property by a five-foot fence. See also United States v. Allen, 633 F.2d 1282 (9th Cir.1980) (helicopter surveillance not a search where "the objects observed were large scale modifications of the Allen Ranch landscape and barn"); Reece v. State, 152 Ga.App. 760, 264 S.E.2d 258 (1979) (no search to discover from airplane stolen vehicles in open field); People v. Lashmett, 71 Ill.App.3d 429, 27 Ill.Dec. 657, 389 N.E.2d 888 (1979) (no search to see large farm machinery from plane at 2400 feet); State v. Ryder, 315 N.W.2d 786 (Iowa 1982) (no search to view farm machinery from airplane); State v. Bridges, 513 A.2d 1365 (Me.1986) (post-*Ciraolo* case cautiously notes defendant's conduct observed from plane also readily observable from passersby on road, so it "immaterial that their activities happened to be observed from the air").

observed without intruding onto protected property.[269] But some later lower court cases seemed to proceed as if it was simply a matter of whether the surveilling aircraft was at a lawful height.[270]

More and more cases of this genre reached the courts, with the ultimate result of "doctrinal incoherence and conflict among the court decisions"[271] on just how *Katz* applied to aerial surveillance of the curtilage. As for whether society is prepared to recognize the dweller's actual expectation of privacy as reasonable,

> courts have taken two sharply conflicting approaches. The first, best described as the "reasonable passerby" approach, holds that if a dweller has exhibited an expectation of privacy, the reasonableness of the dweller's expectation must then be determined by comparing the nature and conduct of the aerial surveillance with the range of normal aerial behavior of the public in the vicinity. The second approach, best described as the "reasonable per se" approach, holds that if a dweller has exhibited an expectation of privacy, it is per se one that society will find may not reasonably be violated from the air.[272]

Then came *California v. Ciraolo*,[273] where police, proceeding on an anonymous tip that defendant was growing marijuana in his backyard, surrounded by a 6-foot outer fence and 10-foot inner fence, flew over the property at an altitude of 1,000 feet and saw marijuana plants 8 to 10 feet in height, which they photographed with a standard 35 mm. camera. The observation, on which a search warrant was thereafter grounded, was held by the court of

---

[269]The court in *Sneed* was not as careful with respect to this point as it might have been. The court did say that there was no evidence "that anyone had viewed the plants from the neighbor's corn field," but did not declare unequivocally that such a viewing could not readily have been made. It is significant, however, that in discussing the question of whether there is a reasonable expectation of privacy in a back yard, the court stated that this depended upon the facts of the individual case and then recited factors which would be relevant in terms of viewing from adjacent property rather than from the air: "the location of the premises, that is, whether in an urban or isolated area, the existence or nonexistence and height of natural or artificial structures adjacent to the premises, the height and sight-proof character of the fencing, the location of public or common private walkways adjacent to the premises."

[270]Williams v. State, 157 Ga.App. 476, 277 S.E.2d 923 (1981) (no search, as aircraft at lawful height); State v. Layne, 623 S.W.2d 629 (Tenn.Crim. App.1981) (no search, as plane in navigable air space).

[271]Note, 60 N.Y.U.L.Rev. 725, 749 (1985).

[272]Note, 60 N.Y.U.L.Rev. 725, 746 (1985).

[273]California v. Ciraolo, 476 U.S. 207, 106 S.Ct. 1809, 90 L.Ed.2d 210 (1986), discussed in Junker, The Structure of the Fourth Amendment: The Scope of the Protection, 79 J.Crim.L. & C. 1105, 1152–55 (1989); Comments, 30 Ariz.L.Rev. 361 (1988); 75 Cal.L.Rev. 1767 (1987); 36 Cath.U. L.Rev. 667 (1987); 22 Gonzaga L.Rev. 393 (1987); Notes, 73 Cornell L.Rev. 97 (1987); 53 J.Air.L. & C. 291 (1987); 47 La.L.Rev. 1365 (1987); 18 Loyola U.L.J. 285 (1986); 52 Mo.L.Rev. 507 (1987); 40 Sw.L.Rev. 1133 (1986); 23 Tulsa L.J. 259 (1987); 66 Wash.U.L.Q. 111 (1988).

appeals to be an illegal search, but the Supreme Court, in a 5-4 decision, disagreed. Stating the question as "whether naked-eye observation of the curtilage by police from an aircraft lawfully operating at an altitude of 1,000 feet violates an expectation of privacy[274] that is reasonable," the majority responded:

> The observations by Officers Shutz and Rodriguez in this case took place within public navigable airspace, see 49 U.S.C.App. § 1304, in a physically nonintrusive manner; from this point they were able to observe plants readily discernable to the naked eye as marijuana. That the observation from aircraft was directed at identifying the plants and the officers were trained to recognize marijuana is irrelevant. Such observation is precisely what a judicial officer needs to provide a basis for a warrant. Any member of the public flying in this airspace who glanced down could have seen everything that these officers observed. On this record, we readily conclude that respondent's expectation that his garden was not protected from such observation is unreasonable and is not an expectation that society is prepared to honor.[275]

As discussed earlier,[276] the most sensible way to apply the *Katz* justified-expectation-of-privacy test is to characterize police surveillance as a search unless it occurs from a "public vantage point" and uncovers what the person has not protected from scrutiny by the "curious passerby." Under that approach, the *Ciraolo* case should have come out the other way. The fact that the aircraft was in "public navigable airspace" does show that the surveillance occurred from a "public vantage point," but that is all. As the four *Ciraolo* dissenters correctly observed,

> the actual risk to privacy from commercial or pleasure aircraft is virtually nonexistent. Travelers on commercial flights, as well as private planes used for business or personal reasons, normally obtain at most a fleeting, anonymous, and nondiscriminating glimpse of the landscape and buildings over which they pass. The risk that a passenger on such a plane might observe private activities, and might connect those activities with particular people, is

---

[274]The Court "assumed" the defendant had an actual expectation of privacy, but nonetheless made some troublesome observations in that connection. See § 2.1(c).

[275]*Ciraolo* was followed in Florida v. Riley, 488 U.S. 445, 109 S.Ct. 693, 102 L.Ed.2d 835 (1989), upholding police surveillance from a helicopter at an altitude of 400 feet. The surveillance was of the interior of a greenhouse, and thus the case is further discussed at note 209 supra.

See also United States v. Warford, 439 F.3d 836 (8th Cir.2006) (though helicopter sometimes "dropped to an altitude of 200 or 300" feet, that legally permissible and not shown to

be so rare as to violate reasonable expectation of privacy); United States v. Boyster, 436 F.3d 986 (8th Cir.2006) (even if lands viewed within curtilage and helicopter was "at an altitude of around one hundred feet," there no search, as defendant did not claim flight at that level illegal or "so rare as to make aerial surveillance at that level unreasonable"); State v. Ainsworth, 310 Or. 613, 801 P.2d 749 (1990) (relying on *Ciraolo*, court holds no search where naked eye police observation from helicopter and "they lawfully were in the air above defendants' land").

[276]E.g., text at note 132 supra.

simply too trivial to protect against. * * *

* * * The only possible basis for this holding is a judgment that
the risk to privacy posed by the remote possibility that a private
airplane passenger will notice outdoor activities is equivalent to the
risk of official aerial surveillance. But the Court fails to acknowledge the qualitative difference between police surveillance and
other uses made of the air space. Members of the public use the air
space for travel, business, or pleasure, not for the purpose of observing activities taking place within residential yards.[277]

It is important to note, however, that *Ciraolo* only holds it is no
search to make a naked-eye observation into the curtilage from
navigable air space. That result, therefore, is not inconsistent
with the decision in *Sneed* (though, at the same time, it must be
recognized that *Ciraolo* does not settle that any surveillance from
a flight in violation of FAA regulations is by that fact alone a
search).[278] The Supreme Court's more recent decision in *Florida
v. Riley*[279] supports this conclusion. In the course of concluding
that surveillance by helicopter at 400 feet was no search, the

[277]On this dissent, see Hancock,
Justice Powell's Garden: The Ciraolo
Dissent and Fourth Amendment
Protection for Curtilage-Home Privacy,
44 San Diego L.Rev. 551 (2007). On
such analysis, the court in People v.
Mayoff, 42 Cal.3d 1302, 233 Cal.Rptr.
2, 729 P.2d 166 (1986), decided to
reject *Ciraolo* "and thus adhere to the
contrary state view."

[278]In State v. Davis, 51 Or.App.
827, 627 P.2d 492 (1981), the court
rejected the trial court's position that
the viewing by aircraft was a search
solely because the flight at 600–700
feet was lower than permitted by the
FAA for fixed–wing aircraft:

The trial court's application of the
FAA regulation is not an appropriate
method of analysis in a search and
seizure area for several reasons. It
provides a mechanical approach to
search and seizure issues—one merely
determines whether an aircraft was
above or below the prescribed minimum altitude, and Fourth Amendment
protection is or is not afforded based
on this demarcation. * * *

We also find little attraction in the
idea of using FAA regulations because
they were not formulated for the purpose of defining the reasonableness of
citizens' expectation of privacy. They
were designed to promote air safety.
* * *

Lastly, we wish to point out that the
FAA regulations distinguish between

the types of aircraft involved. The
regulation in this case was applied to a
fixed-wing aircraft. The regulation allows helicopters to be flown at lower
altitudes. To use the regulation would
make "a crazy quilt" out of the Fourth
Amendment, with the "pattern of protection" being dictated by the type of
aircraft used for surveillance.

Comment, 24 Cal.W.L.Rev. 379,
380 (1988), concludes "that aerial
surveillance by a helicopter at an
altitude of 300 to 500 feet does not offend the fourth amendment and is not
unreasonable if the aircraft is (1) being lawfully operated, and (2) not
unreasonably intrusive."

[279]Florida v. Riley, 488 U.S. 445,
109 S.Ct. 693, 102 L.Ed.2d 835 (1989).
See also United States v. Breza, 308
F.3d 430 (4th Cir.2002) (spotting marijuana plants in defendant's noncurtilage garden from helicopter no search
here, where "the helicopter fully complied with applicable regulations regarding proper altitude" and "such
flights were a regular occurrence in
the area"); United States v. Fernan-
dez, 58 F.3d 593 (11th Cir.1995) (under *Riley*, observation of marijuana
plants from helicopter at 500 feet no
search); Commonwealth v. One 1985
Ford Thunderbird Automobile, 416
Mass. 603, 624 N.E.2d 547 (1993) (no
Fourth Amendment violation when
helicopter flew over defendant's home
at altitude of 1,500, 800 and 700 ft., so

four-Justice plurality cautioned that there was no "intimation here that the helicopter interfered with respondent's normal use of the greenhouse or of other parts of the curtilage. As far as this record reveals, no intimate details connected with the use of the home or curtilage were observed, and there was no undue noise, no wind, dust, or threat of injury."[280]

If it is still correct to say that the conduct in *Sneed* was a search, then it is certainly arguable that it would still be a search if the same discovery had been made from a high-altitude aircraft employing sophisticated observation equipment. As noted in *Dean v. Superior Court*:[281]

> At a recent but relatively primitive time, an X-2 plane could spy on ground activity from a height of 50,000 feet. Today's sophisticated technology permits overflights by vehicles orbiting at an altitude of several hundred miles. Tomorrow's sophisticated technology will supply optic and photographic devices for minute observations from extended heights. Judicial implementations of the Fourth Amendment need constant accommodation to the ever–intensifying technology of surveillance. In analyzing claims of immunity from aerial surveillance by agents of government, the observer's altitude is a minor factor. Horizontal extensions of the occupant's terrestrial activity form a more realistic and reliable measure of privacy than the vertical dimension of altitude.

In this regard, it is important to take note of the companion case to *Dow Chemical Company v. United States*,[282] where the aerial surveillance did involve the use of rather sophisticated equipment-as the dissenters described it, "the finest precision aerial camera available" which "cost in excess of $22,000.00" and "was capable of taking several photographs in precise and rapid succession," thus facilitating "stereoscopic examination, a type of examination that permits depth perception," and which produced photographs "capable of enlargement to a scale of 1 inch equals 20 feet *or greater*, without significant loss of detail or resolution," by which "it is possible to discern equipment, pipes, and power lines as small as 1/2 inch in diameter." The *Dow* majority strongly

---

that visible to naked eye view were hundreds of marijuana plants in empty swimming pool).

[280]Such analysis was challenged by 3 of the 4 dissenters: "If indeed the purpose of the restraints imposed by the Fourth Amendment is to 'safeguard the privacy and security of individuals,' then it is puzzling why it should be the helicopter's noise, wind, and dust that provides the measure of whether this constitutional safeguard has been infringed."

Consider also Commonwealth v. One 1985 Ford Thunderbird Automobile, 416 Mass. 603, 624 N.E.2d

547 (1993) (cautiously concluding that under the *state* constitution such overflight is lawful "when the police have a reasonable suspicion that illegal activity is occurring in a backyard"); State v. Bryant, 183 Vt. 355, 950 A.2d 467 (2008) (helicopter surveillance by circling over defendant's yard at 100 feet for 15–30 minutes, contrary to law, violated *state* constitution).

[281]Dean v. Superior Court, 35 Cal.App.3d 112, 110 Cal.Rptr. 585 (1973).

[282]Dow Chemical Co. v. United States, 476 U.S. 227, 106 S.Ct. 1819, 90 L.Ed.2d 226 (1986).

implied that the use of such equipment was no search *only* because it was directed at "a 2,000-acre outdoor manufacturing facility," and further cautioned: "We find it important that this is *not* an area immediately adjacent to a private home, where privacy expectations are most heightened." In addition, the Court asserted "that surveillance of private property by using highly sophisticated surveillance equipment not generally available to the public, such as satellite technology, might be constitutionally proscribed absent a warrant."[283] Reading *Ciraolo* with *Dow*, then, by no stretch of the imagination can it be asserted that the Court has manifested its approval of aerial surveillance of the curtilage that involves use of sophisticated sense-enhancing equipment.

In the not too distant future, the question may be whether police surveillance from an unmanned aircraft system constitutes a Fourth Amendment search. Such systems, as compared with manned airplanes and helicopters, "bear unique risks to society's expectation of privacy," as they are "practically invisible at altitudes where a manned aircraft could be seen from the ground," "operate almost silently, making them significantly harder to detect," and, especially, have "the ability to hover or circle in the sky for hours" and thus "present a potential for intrusion far more pervasive than the merely flyover of a plane or helicopter."[284] Given these characteristics, it has understandably been contended that "UAS surveillance of the curtilage of the home is an unconstitutional search within the meaning of the Fourth Amendment."[285] But it is less than certain that such cases

---

[283]Governments are beginning to use satellite imagery for a variety of enforcement purposes, such as to detect the growing of crops without an irrigation permit, unreported property improvements, and unreported timber cutting. This practice will doubtless increase, for, as compared with taking photographs from airplanes, "satellite imagery can be much more cost-effective" and "is faster as well. * * * And as sharper-resolution photos become available, * * * the program could be used to look for objects as small as backyard porches, to check if homeowners have their construction permits in order." Kerber, When Is a Satellite Photo an Unreasonable Search?, Wall St.J., Jan. 27, 1998, p. B.1, col. 3–4; p. B4, col. 4–5. For an updated description and assessment of satellite surveillance, see Note, 65 Ohio St.L.J. 1627 (2004).

[284]Comment, 51 S.Tex.L.Rev. 173, 201 (2009). By virtue of a change in FAA regulations, police departments "across the country can now fly drones weighing up to 25 pounds, as long as the aircraft stay within sight of the operator and fly no higher than 400 feet (so as not to get in the way of commercial aircraft). More rules easing restrictions on commercial drones are expected by 2015. By the end of the decade, the FAA expects 30,000 unmanned aerial vehicles—some as small as birds—to be peering down on American soil." The Drone Over Your Backyard, http://theweek.com/article/index/228830/ the drone over your backyard a guide.

[285]Comment, 74 J.Air L. & Com. 627, 661 (2009), reasoning: "This conclusion follows from a variety of factors, such as the rarity of UAS use within the public sector, the ability of technology to perceive details that would otherwise be imperceptible without physically entering the curti-

as *Ciraolo*, *Riley* and *Dow* mandate such a conclusion,[286] and thus it remains "speculative at best."[287]

Instances of aural surveillance resulting in the police overhearing conversations occurring outside but near residential premises must be analyzed in essentially the same fashion. Certainly "one who lives in a built-up city or suburban neighborhood must expect that his conversations in his home or in his yard may be audible to his neighbors or to passersby."[288] Thus, if police in such circumstances are able to hear such conversations with the naked ear while in a neighbor's yard, this would not constitute a search under *Katz*. In a rural setting, if the eavesdropping officers were positioned in an "open field" and did not physically intrude into the curtilage, then it would appear that what they hear with the unaided ear is no search.[289] But the use of electronic eavesdropping equipment brings the police conduct within *Katz* even when the conversations are in the open rather than, as in *Katz*, an enclosed space.[290]

§ 2.4 Other premises and places

§ 2.4(a)   "Open fields"

§ 2.4(b)   Business and commercial premises

§ 2.4(c)   Private areas in public places: rest rooms and fitting
          rooms

§ 2.4(d)   Detention facilities

---

lage of the home, and the invasive nature of UAS surveillance conducted through stealth."

[286]See, generally, Comments, 74 J.Air L. & Com. 627 (2009); 49 Jurimetrics J. 491 (2009); 51 S.Tex.L.Rev. 173 (2009).

[287]Comment, 74 J.Air L. & Com. 627, 661 (2009).

[288]United States ex rel. Gedko v. Heer, 406 F.Supp. 609 (W.D.Wis. 1975).

[289]To the contrary is United States ex rel. Gedko v. Heer, 406 F.Supp. 609 (W.D.Wis.1975), where officers gained entrance to petitioner's farm through an adjoining field. The officers climbed a fence at the boundary of petitioner's farm premises and proceeded thereupon through open fields and timber to a point about 300 to 400 feet from petitioner's farm buildings. After a surveillance plane criss-crossed over the property several times, the officers heard the petitioner and his wife shouting to one another about the need to dispose of the marijuana. Petitioner's farm was fenced; the farm yard was six-tenths of a mile from the public road; and a no trespassing sign was posted at the gate. In holding that the officers had intruded upon petitioner's justified expectation of privacy, the court stated: "In this case * * * there was nothing to indicate that petitioner and his wife should have had any reason to expect their conversations, even their shouted conversations, to be overheard by anyone. They had taken deliberate measures to ensure that their activities and conversations would be protected from other persons, official or non-official." However, such analysis cannot be squared with the Supreme Court's more recent *Oliver* decision, discussed in § 2.4(a).

[290]See § 2.2(e).

Research References

West's Key Number Digest
Controlled Substances ⊕134 to 136; Prisons ⊕4(7); Searches and Seizures
⊕15 to 17, 25.1 to 27, 47.1, 76, 79

Legal Encyclopedias
C.J.S., Prisons and Rights of Prisoners §§ 7, 58, 60, 74 to 75, 122; Searches and
Seizures §§ 8, 13, 18, 20 to 24, 26 to 38, 41, 66 to 67, 70 to 72, 99 to 102, 189

Introduction

The concern herein is with the application of the justified
expectation of privacy test of *Katz v. United States*[1] to various
places other than residential premises. Long before *Katz* it was
settled that so-called "open fields" are not protected by the Fourth
Amendment, but it is necessary to inquire to what extent this is
still true in light of the *Katz* reasoning. It is also useful to give
separate attention to business premises, for generally speaking
such places are less private than residential premises. There are
certain places, such as public rest rooms, which are open to the
public but yet are used by particular members of the public under
circumstances suggesting they expect privacy, and thus the application of *Katz* to those locations also presents a discrete
problem for analysis. Finally, consideration is also given here to
the question of whether there is a protected privacy interest in
jails and other detention facilities.

§ 2.4(a) "Open fields"[2]

What has come to be referred to as the "open fields" doctrine
was first stated by the United States Supreme Court in 1924 in
the case of *Hester v. United States*.[3] There, a revenue agent staked
out the home of Hester's father and, from a distance of 50 to 100
yards, saw Hester hand a bottle to a person who was thought to
be a customer for bootleg whiskey. Hester took alarm, went to his
car and removed a jug from it, and then ran through the fields.
Both the bottle carried by the customer and the jug carried by
Hester were thrown into an open field. Both broke, but each
contained enough liquid so that it could be determined they had
contained bootleg whiskey. The broken containers were examined
by revenue agents where they had been dropped.

[Section 2.4]

[1]Katz v. United States, 389 U.S.
347, 88 S.Ct. 507, 19 L.Ed.2d 576
(1967).

[Section 2.4(a)]

[2]The concern herein is with
whether police conduct taking place in
an "open field" and resulting in the
discovery of incriminating evidence or
conduct there is a Fourth Amendment
search. This is to be distinguished

from the question of whether the police, while in an open field, have engaged in a search if from that vantage
point they are able to hear or see into
a residence, into related buildings, or
into lands immediately adjacent to
those structures. This latter question
is discussed in § 2.3.

[3]Hester v. United States, 265
U.S. 57, 44 S.Ct. 445, 68 L.Ed. 898
(1924).

In a unanimous and very brief opinion by Justice Holmes, the Court in *Hester* held that the evidence was not obtained by an illegal search even though there had been a technical trespass. The Court, although pointing out that the whiskey was "abandoned," rested its holding upon the nature of the place where the revenue agent located the containers:

> The only shadow of a ground for bringing up the case is drawn from the hypothesis that the examination of the vessels took place upon Hester's father's land. As to that, it is enough to say that * * * the special protection accorded by the Fourth Amendment to the people in their "persons, houses, papers and effects," is not extended to the open fields. The distinction between the latter and the house is as old as the common law.

In applying the *Hester* doctrine over the years, lower courts have applied the open fields characterization to virtually any lands not falling within the curtilage. In *Care v. United States*,[4] for example, the "open fields" doctrine was applied to permit the introduction of evidence relating to the discovery of a still concealed in a cave about 125 yards from the house. The cave was deemed to be in the open fields because it was not located in the curtilage:

> Whether the place searched is within the curtilage is to be determined from the facts, including its proximity or annexation to the dwelling, its inclusion within the general enclosure surrounding the dwelling, and its use and enjoyment as an adjunct to the domestic economy of the family.[5]

Courts never took the word "open" in the *Hester* rule too seriously; the rule was applied even when the land was fenced,[6] even when it was posted with no trespassing signs,[7] and even when the evidence discovered was not itself in plain view.[8] Similarly, the word "fields" was never restricted to a literal or technical definition of a place suitable for pasture or tillage. *Hester*-type analysis has been applied to police intrusions into wooded areas,[9]

---

[4]Care v. United States, 231 F.2d 22 (10th Cir.1956).

[5]See, e.g., Olson v. State, 166 Ga.App. 104, 303 S.E.2d 309 (1983) (uninhabited house is not a dwelling and thus lacked a protected curtilage).

[6]United States v. Rapanos, 115 F.3d 367 (6th Cir.1997); Janney v. United States, 206 F.2d 601 (4th Cir. 1953); Stark v. United States, 44 F.2d 946 (8th Cir.1930).

[7]McDowell v. United States, 383 F.2d 599 (8th Cir.1967).

[8]Care v. United States, 231 F.2d 22 (10th Cir.1956). See also United States v. Pinter, 984 F.2d 376 (10th Cir.1993) (fact "the laboratory location was not visible from a public place likewise is of no significance").

[9]United States v. McIver, 186 F.3d 1119 (9th Cir.1999) (national forest); United States v. Eastland, 989 F.2d 760 (5th Cir.1993); United States v. Pinter, 984 F.2d 376 (10th Cir. 1993); Rainey v. Hartness, 339 Ark. 293, 5 S.W.3d 410 (1999); Pruitt v. State, 258 Ga. 583, 373 S.E.2d 192 (1988); Cornman v. State, 156 Ind.App. 112, 294 N.E.2d 812 (1973); State v. Pelletier, 673 A.2d 1327 (Me.1996); State v. Sorensen, 243 Mont. 321, 792 P.2d 363 (1990); State v. Pinder, 128 N.H. 66, 514 A.2d 1241 (1986); State

desert,[10] vacant lots in urban areas,[11] open beaches,[12] reservoirs,[13] and open waters.[14] ("There is no case, however, where the open field doctrine has been applied to allow a search . . . of a commercial structure in a field."[15]) And thus in reaffirming the *Hester* "open fields" rule, the Supreme Court stated:

> It is clear, however, that the term "open fields" may include any unoccupied or undeveloped area outside of the curtilage. An open field need be neither "open" nor a "field" as those terms are used in common speech. For example, * * * a thickly wooded area nonetheless may be an open field as that term is used in construing the Fourth Amendment.[16]

In *Katz v. United States*,[17] the Court rejected the notion that the "constitutionally protected areas" concept "can serve as a talismanic solution to every Fourth Amendment problem," and held that it should instead be asked, in deciding whether a Fourth Amendment search had occurred, whether the police conduct "violated the privacy upon which [the defendant] justifiably relied." As might be expected, defendants thereafter urged that *Katz* "sounded the death knell of the 'open fields' doctrine, and overruled, *sub silentio, Hester*."[18] Some courts expressly or impliedly accepted this contention,[19] but a substantial number held otherwise or at least assumed that a straightforward ap-

v. Hall, 168 Vt. 327, 719 A.2d 435 (1998); State v. Jeffries, 105 Wash.2d 398, 717 P.2d 722 (1986).

[10]United States v. Fahey, 769 F.2d 829 (1st Cir.1985) (no search to take soil samples at mine site in desert); State v. Caldwell, 20 Ariz.App. 331, 512 P.2d 863 (1973).

[11]State v. Stavricos, 506 S.W.2d 51 (Mo.App.1974); State v. Aragon, 89 N.M. 91, 547 P.2d 574 (1976).

[12]Anderson v. State, 133 Ga.App. 45, 209 S.E.2d 665 (1974). See also State v. Glenner, 513 A.2d 1361 (Me.1986) (shoreline is open field).

[13]State v. Borchard, 24 Ohio App.2d 95, 264 N.E.2d 646 (1970).

[14]Nathanson v. State, 554 P.2d 456 (Alaska 1976).

[15]Allinder v. State of Ohio, 808 F.2d 1180 (6th Cir.1987) (Fourth Amendment thus applicable to search of apiaries). But, the mere fact the *land* has been put to commercial use does not take it out of the "open fields" category. United States v. Rapanos, 115 F.3d 367 (6th Cir.1997) (175-acre tract without buildings was open field notwithstanding fact it "had under-

gone extensive alteration and development" and "was clearly 'commercial property' "); Department of Environmental Protection v. Emerson, 616 A.2d 1268 (Me.1992) (large disposal area for tires and demolition debris).

[16]Oliver v. United States, 466 U.S. 170, 104 S.Ct. 1735, 80 L.Ed.2d 214 (1984).

As stated in United States v. Van Damme, 48 F.3d 461 (9th Cir. 1995): "The unfortunate use of the term 'open fields' in this body of law causes misunderstanding and confusion, and should be replaced by a term which means what it says, such as 'unprotected area.' "

[17]Katz v. United States, 389 U.S. 347, 88 S.Ct. 507, 19 L.Ed.2d 576 (1967).

[18]Conrad v. State, 63 Wis.2d 616, 218 N.W.2d 252 (1974).

[19]E.g., State v. Byers, 359 So.2d 84 (La.1978); State v. Chort, 91 N.M. 584, 577 P.2d 892 (1978); State v. Walle, 52 Or.App. 963, 630 P.2d 377 (1981); State v. Doelman, 620 S.W.2d 96 (Tenn.Crim.App.1981); State v. Weigand, 169 W.Va. 739, 289 S.E.2d

plication of *Hester* was still proper.[20] Then came *Oliver v. United States*,[21] where the Supreme Court held, 6-3, that the *Hester* "open fields" doctrine fully survived the *Katz* reformulation of Fourth Amendment interests. *Oliver* made it relatively easy for lower courts to conclude that exploration of open areas outside the curtilage[22] does not constitute Fourth Amendment activity,[23]

---

508 (1982).

[20]E.g., United States v. Baldwin, 691 F.2d 718 (5th Cir.1982); Skipper v. State, 387 So.2d 261 (Ala.Crim.App. 1980); State v. Simpson, 639 S.W.2d 230 (Mo.App.1982); State v. Bennett, 205 Mont. 117, 666 P.2d 747 (1983); State v. Bernath, 3 Ohio App.3d 229, 444 N.E.2d 439 (1981); Teague v. State, 674 P.2d 560 (Okl.Crim.App. 1984).

[21]Oliver v. United States, 466 U.S. 170, 104 S.Ct. 1735, 80 L.Ed.2d 214 (1984), discussed in Junker, The Structure of the Fourth Amendment: The Scope of the Protection, 79 J.Crim.L. & C. 1105, 1147–51 (1989); Saltzburg, Another Victim of Illegal Narcotics: The Fourth Amendment (As Illustrated by the Open Field Doctrine), 48 U.Pitt.L.Rev. 1 (1986); Annot., 80 L.Ed.2d 860 (1986); Comment, 12 Fla.St.U.L.Rev. 637 (1984).

[22]The mere fact "the officers have to cross curtilage in order to get to the open field" does not mean there is a Fourth Amendment violation, at least when what was involved was "traveling down a road which ran through the curtilage area," as such action does "not violate any expectation of privacy." Cosgrove v. State, 806 P.2d 75 (Okl.Crim.App.1991). For more on permissible entries of the curtilage, see § 2.3(f).

[23]Nikolas v. City of Omaha, 605 F.3d 539 (8th Cir.2010) (no search for officer "to inspect portions of the property that fall within the open fields doctrine, such as the ravine" and garage "not part of the curtilage of the residence some thirty to forty-five fee away"); Waltman v. Payne, 535 F.3d 342 (5th Cir.2008) (sheriff's entry onto portion of plaintiff's 1500-acre hunting lease, posted as under control of a certain hunt club, but where many plants growing, was lawful under

open-fields doctrine); United States v. Hutchings, 127 F.3d 1255 (10th Cir.1997) (open field on government-owned property some distance from trailer of defendants, employees charged with maintaining the property); United States v. Rigsby, 943 F.2d 631 (6th Cir.1991) (picnic site in publicly accessible wooded area); United States v. Burton, 894 F.2d 188 (6th Cir.1990) (no search though officer had to climb 2 fences to get to where marijuana growing on defendant's farm); United States v. Eng, 753 F.2d 683 (8th Cir.1985) (area of farm 400 yards from residence outside curtilage and thus within *Oliver* open fields rule); United States v. Roberts, 747 F.2d 537 (9th Cir.1984) (based on *Oliver,* shared private road with many "no trespassing" and "private property keep out" signs deemed outside curtilage and thus open field); United States v. Hoskins, 735 F.2d 1006 (6th Cir.1984) (area 100 yards away from house outside curtilage and thus open field under *Oliver*); United States v. Marbury, 732 F.2d 390 (5th Cir.1984) (*Oliver* allows flyover surveillance of "plainly noncurtilage portions of this large tract, such as the sand dunes and roadway"); People v. Mayoff, 42 Cal.3d 1302, 233 Cal.Rptr. 2, 729 P.2d 166 (1986) (aerial surveillance of planted fields no search); State v. Flynn, 360 N.W.2d 762 (Iowa 1985) (peat moss pile at open area of country club comes within *Oliver* open fields rule); Foley v. Commonwealth, 953 S.W.2d 924 (Ky.1997) ("rural, open property" 50–100 yards from cabin); State v. Smith, 983 So.2d 65 (La.2008) ("defendant surrendered any reasonable expectation of privacy in the contents of the closed and locked bag * * * by concealing the bag * * * in the woods on land belonging to someone else"); State v. Wing, 559 A.2d 783 (Me.1989) (3 marijuana patches, one separated from residence by wooded

meaning such areas may be entered by police even when probable cause is lacking,[24] and, indeed, even where there does not exist a reasonable suspicion.[25]

The majority in *Oliver* gave three reasons in support of this conclusion.[26] The first was grounded in "the explicit language of the Fourth Amendment": the Amendment affords protection only to "persons, houses, papers, and effects," and an open field is none of these, so consequently such a field is itself[27] totally lacking any constitutional protection against government intrusion.

---

area, one nearby it 139 feet from residence, and third 60 feet from residence and separated by gully and wooded area, outside the curtilage); State v. Sorenson, 441 N.W.2d 455 (Minn. 1989) (*Oliver* allows entry of field though gate blocked the road and "No Trespassing" signs posted at entrance); State v. Nolan, 356 N.W.2d 670 (Minn. 1984) (flyover of cornfields comes within *Oliver* rule); State v. Pinder, 128 N.H. 66, 514 A.2d 1241 (1986) (wooded area within *Oliver*, and state constitution does not protect either); State v. Mittleider, 809 N.W.2d 303 (N.D.2011) (" 'no trespassing' signs in open fields do not create an increased expectation of privacy"); Horner v. State, 836 P.2d 679 (Okl.Crim.App. 1992) (no search where officers entered "open fields" area where defendant had an oil production lease, though "officers gained access to the property by climbing over a gate"); Wellford v. Commonwealth, 227 Va. 297, 315 S.E.2d 235 (1984) (corn field quarter of mile from dwelling within *Oliver* rule); State v. Cord, 103 Wash.2d 361, 693 P.2d 81 (1985) (flyover of ranch within *Oliver* rule).

Compare State v. Barnett, 68 Haw. 32, 703 P.2d 680 (1985) (it a search to discover marijuana plants 400, 250 and 150 ft. from dwelling, as discovery occurred when police came onto property after specifically being denied permission to enter; "these facts make any analogy to the *Oliver* case inapt"); People v. Scott, 79 N.Y.2d 474, 583 N.Y.S.2d 920, 593 N.E.2d 1328 (1992) (*Oliver* rejected as a matter of state constitutional law, deemed to protect even outside the curtilage "where landowners fence or post 'No Trespassing' signs on their property, or, by some other means, indicate

unmistakably that entry is not permitted"). Other decisions rejecting the open fields doctrine as a matter of state constitutional law, as well as a larger number of decisions declining to go that route, are collected in Commonwealth v. Russo, 594 Pa. 119, 934 A.2d 1199 (2007).

[24]State v. Sorenson, 441 N.W.2d 455 (Minn.1989): "Appellant first argues that *Oliver v. United States* does not apply in this case because, in the cases discussed in *Oliver*, the police had probable cause to believe that illegal activity was taking place on the land before making their warrantless entry. * * *

"Appellant's reliance on the existence of probable cause is incorrect. If police or other law enforcement officers enter land which is found to be an open field, then the existence of probable cause is irrelevant and unnecessary."

[25]United States v. Pinter, 984 F.2d 376 (10th Cir.1993).

[26]White, J., concurring, argued the *Katz* expectation of privacy test did not have to be discussed at all because the case could be fully disposed of on the ground that open fields did not come within the list of things protected by the Fourth Amendment.

[27]The Court noted that "the Fourth Amendment provides ample protection to activities in the open fields that might implicate an individual's privacy. An individual who enters a place defined to be 'public' for Fourth Amendment analysis does not lose all claims to privacy or personal security. * * * For example, the Fourth Amendment's protections against unreasonable arrest or unreasonable seizure of effects upon the person remain fully appli-

However, as the dissenters[28] pointed out, such reasoning not only "is inconsistent with the results of many of our previous decisions,"[29] none which the Court purports to overrule,"[30] but more fundamentally ignores the fact that "when interpreting these seminal constitutional provisions" the Court should strive "to lend them meanings that ensure that the liberties the Framers sought to protect are not undermined by the changing activities of government officials."

The second ground put forward by the majority in *Oliver* is that any interest a landowner might have in the privacy of his land[31] outside the curtilage is not one that "society is prepared to recognize as reasonable." In thus applying the *Katz* doctrine, the Court reasoned that

> open fields do not provide the setting for those intimate activities that the Amendment is intended to shelter from government interference or surveillance. There is no societal interest in protecting the privacy of those activities, such as the cultivation of crops, that occur in open fields. Moreover, as a practical matter these lands usually are accessible to the public and the police in ways that a home, an office or commercial structure would not be. It is not generally true that fences or no trespassing signs effectively bar the public from viewing open fields in rural areas.

But more in keeping with the *Katz* rationale is the contrary conclusion of the *Oliver* dissenters. In support of the conclusion that a landowner *does* have a legitimate expectation of privacy in his fields in some circumstances, they emphasized (i) that the defendants here, as owners of the land intruded upon, had a right of exclusive use of those lands protected by both civil and criminal law; (ii) that the "privately-owned woods and fields that are not exposed to public view regularly are employed in a variety of ways that society acknowledges deserve privacy," and (iii) that the defendants had taken normal precautions to maintain

---

cable."

[28] Marshall, J., joined by Brennan and Stevens, JJ.

[29] E.g., Marshall v. Barlow's, Inc., 436 U.S. 307, 98 S.Ct. 1816, 56 L.Ed.2d 305 (1978), applying the Fourth Amendment to commercial structures.

[30] And, it seems unlikely that the literal approach taken in *Oliver* will result in those decisions being overruled. As the dissenters note: "Sensitive to the weakness of its argument that the 'persons and things' mentioned in the Fourth Amendment exhaust the coverage of the provision, the Court goes on to analyze at length the privacy interests that might legitimately be asserted in 'open fields.' [This] strongly suggest[s] that the plain-language theory sketched in Part II of the Court's opinion will have little or no effect on our future decisions in this area."

[31] A much easier case, of course, is where the open field adjoins defendant's property but is not a part of defendant's property. See, e.g., United States v. Hamilton, 931 F.2d 1046 (5th Cir.1991) (defendant's home set apart by fence from woods apparently belonging to defendant's grandmother; defendant had no justified expectation of privacy re marijuana in washing machine defendant buried there, as he "failed to show that he had any power to exclude others from the wooded area").

privacy by erecting "no trespassing" signs on their property.[32]

Lastly, the *Oliver* majority rejected a case-by-case approach by which a more careful examination of the legitimate privacy expectations attaching to a particular field would be made in light of all the attendant circumstances. Such an approach, the Court concluded, would not

> provide a workable accommodation between the needs of law enforcement and the interests protected by the Fourth Amendment. Under this approach, police officers would have to guess before every search whether landowners had erected fences sufficiently high, posted a sufficient number of warning signs, or located contraband in an area sufficiently secluded to establish a right of privacy. * * * The *ad hoc* approach not only makes it difficult for the policeman to discern the scope of his authority * * *; it also creates a danger that constitutional rights will be arbitrarily and inequitably enforced.[33]

Though the concern is a legitimate one, the difficulties that would be presented by a case-by-case approach (as in *Katz* itself[34]) appear to be exaggerated.[35] The dissenters argued with some force that it would not be an unfair imposition upon the police to expect

---

[32]See also Saltzburg, Another Victim of Illegal Narcotics: The Fourth Amendment (As Illustrated by the Open Field Doctrine), 48 U.Pitt.L.Rev. 1 (1986), defending this position. Consider also Annot., 45 A.L.R.6th 643 (2009).

[33]This means that after *Oliver* the use of fencing, locked gates and numerous "No Trespassing" signs will not suffice to show a reasonable expectation of privacy in a so-called "open fields" area. See, e.g., United States v. Lewis, 240 F.3d 866 (10th Cir.2001).

Relying upon this language in *Oliver*, the court in United States v. Rapanos, 115 F.3d 367 (6th Cir.1997), concluded it was foreclosed from adopting the defendant's suggestion which perhaps "as a matter of public policy * * * makes good sense," that the open fields doctrine should be inapplicable when the landowner is present because in such circumstances "there is a great risk of violence if an angry property owner uses force or threats of force to deny access to his property."

[34]As noted in Cloud, Pragmatism, Positivism, and Principles of Fourth Amendment Theory, 41 UCLA L.Rev. 199, 255 (1993): "This per se rule also conflicts with the Court's treatment of

the facts in *Katz*. If a public telephone booth supports a reasonable expectation of conversational privacy, it is not immediately obvious why a secluded woods, surrounded by acres of private land enclosed by fences and 'No Trespassing' signs, supports no privacy expectations for any kind of activities, including the intimate activities often associated with the home."

[35]See State v. Dixson, 307 Or. 195, 766 P.2d 1015 (1988), adopting a case-by-case approach as a matter of state constitutional law: "A person who wishes to preserve a constitutionally protected privacy interest in land outside the curtilage must manifest an intention to exclude the public by erecting barriers to entry, such as fences, or by posting signs. This rule will not unduly hamper law enforcement officers in their attempts to curtail the manufacture of and trafficking in illegal drugs, because it does not require investigating officers to draw any deduction other than that required of the general public." See also State v. Romain, 295 Mont. 152, 983 P.2d 322 (1999) (following *Bullock,* infra; reasonable expectation of privacy where fence and gate marked with flourescent orange paint, means recognized by statute for indicating no trespassing allowed); State v. Bullock,

them to make precisely the same kinds of judgments that the rest of us must make to avoid violating the criminal trespass laws: "A clear, easily administrable rule emerges * * *: Private land marked in a fashion sufficient to render entry thereon a criminal trespass under the law of the state in which the land lies is protected by the Fourth Amendment's proscription of unreasonable searches and seizures."[36]

Because *Oliver* takes the position that to fall within the "open fields" classification the area in question must be outside the curtilage, the meaning of that concept has become increasingly important. It is understandable, therefore, that more recently the Court in *United States v. Dunn*[37] undertook to provide further guidance on this point:

> Drawing upon the Court's own cases and the cumulative experience of the lower courts that have grappled with the task of defining the extent of a home's curtilage, we believe that curtilage questions should be resolved with particular reference to four factors: the proximity of the area claimed to be curtilage to the home,[38] whether the area is included within an enclosure surrounding the

272 Mont. 361, 901 P.2d 61 (1995) (following *Dixson* approach and concluding that under state constitution "a person may have an expectation of privacy in an area of land that is beyond the curtilage which the society of this State is willing to recognize as reasonable," as "where that expectation is evidenced by fencing, 'No Trespassing,' or similar signs, or 'by some other means [which] indicate[s] unmistakably that entry is not permitted'"); State v. Kirchoff, 156 Vt. 1, 587 A.2d 988 (1991) (rejecting per se rule of *Oliver* under state constitution, and concluding that "where the indicia, such as fences, barriers or 'no trespassing' signs reasonably indicate that strangers are not welcome on the land, the owner or occupant may reasonably expect privacy").

[36] The majority responded that "the common law of trespass furthers a range of interests that have nothing to do with privacy and that would not be served by applying the strictures of trespass law to public officers."

[37] United States v. Dunn, 480 U.S. 294, 107 S.Ct. 1134, 94 L.Ed.2d 326 (1987), discussed in Fishman, Police Trespass and the Fourth Amendment: A Wall in Need of Mending, 22 J. Marshall L.Rev. 795 (1989); Notes, 18 Golden Gate U.L.Rev. 397 (1988); 23

Land & Water L.Rev. 257 (1988); 14 So.U.L.Rev. 283 (1987); 56 Stan.L.Rev. 943 (2004).

[38] See, e.g., United States v. Noriega, 676 F.3d 1252 (11th Cir.2012) (where officer smelled odor of marijuana coming from outbuilding, he outside curtilage, as "the outbuilding was located 50 to 75 yards away from the house"); Rieck v. Jensen, 651 F.3d 1188 (10th Cir.2011) (driveway just within gate not within curtilage, as it several hundred feet from house); United States v. Hayes, 551 F.3d 138 (2d Cir.2008) (65-ft. distance from back door to scrub brush area "weighs against the proximity factor"); United States v. Davis, 530 F.3d 1069 (9th Cir.2008) (where areas police entered were 180 and 200 ft. from house, "the proximity factor weights against finding the area * * * lay within the curtilage"); United States v. Boyster, 436 F.3d 986 (8th Cir.2006) ("field was located over 100 yards from the residence"); United States v. Breza, 308 F.3d 430 (4th Cir.2002) (fact entrance to defendant's garden only 50 ft. from house "would permit" but "does not compel" conclusion garden within curtilage; distance "must be considered in light of the other *Dunn* factors"); United States v. Jenkins, 124 F.3d 768 (6th Cir.1997) (defendant's backyard within curtilage, as it "is not large and is im-

home,[39] the nature of the uses to which the area is put,[40] and the

mediately accessible from a sliding glass door located in the back of the house"); State v. Webb, 130 Idaho 462, 943 P.2d 52 (1997) (marijuana plot outside curtilage; was 230 feet from defendant's trailer and 150 feet from his shop); People v. Pitman, 211 Ill.2d 502, 286 Ill.Dec. 36, 813 N.E.2d 93 (2004) (barn outside curtilage; 40–60 yards from farmhouse); Dunn v. Commonwealth, 360 S.W.3d 751 (Ky.2012) (place "more than 300 to 400 feet" outside curtilage); State v. Pelletier, 673 A.2d 1327 (Me.1996) (wooded area 250–300 yards behind defendant's residence not within curtilage); State v. Cody, 248 Neb. 683, 539 N.W.2d 18 (1995) (large marijuana patch 75–100 yards beyond shed that served as garage and stable not within curtilage); State v. Smith, 163 N.H. 169, 37 A.3d 409 (2012) (where wooded area was 5–70 ft. from defendant's home, such proximity alone "alone is not dispositive"); State v. Rogers, 161 Vt. 236, 638 A.2d 569 (1993) (garden within curtilage though 150 ft. from house); State v. Martwick, 231 Wis.2d 801, 604 N.W.2d 552 (2000) (marijuana plants growing 50–75 feet from house deemed in open field, "a close case" except that "it is helpful to examine the distance in relation to the total size of the property").

[39]See, e.g., United States v. Noriega, 676 F.3d 1252 (11th Cir.2012) (where officer smelled odor of marijuana coming from outbuilding, he outside curtilage, as fence "separated the outbuilding from the back yard"); Rieck v. Jensen, 651 F.3d 1188 (10th Cir.2011) (while officer was just inside fence that completely surrounds the property, "this fence around 17 acres is not the sort of 'enclosure surrounding the home' contemplated by *Dunn*"); United States v. Davis, 530 F.3d 1069 (9th Cir.2008) (area "not within any enclosure that also encompassed the house," and also outside fence around workshop "set apart from the house"); United States v. Boyster, 436 F.3d 986 (8th Cir.2006) (field "was not enclosed by a fence"); Bleavins v. Bartels, 422 F.3d 445 (7th Cir.2005) (trailers seized

without warrant for back taxes not within curtilage, as field where they found enclosed with interior fence separating field from home, deck and garage); United States v. Gerard, 362 F.3d 484 (8th Cir.2004) (garage outside curtilage, as it not within fence that surrounded farmhouse); United States v. Breza, 308 F.3d 430 (4th Cir.2002) (vegetable garden outside curtilage, as it separated from remainder of yard by "an interior fence and a line of landscaping that included an ornamental garden and several trees"); United States v. Diehl, 276 F.3d 32 (1st Cir.2002) (magistrate "placed too much emphasis on the need for artificial enclosures in a fairly small clearing, already enclosed by forest, where the home-related uses did not require such enclosures"); United States v. Jenkins, 124 F.3d 768 (6th Cir.1997) (backyard within curtilage, as it "enclosed on three sides by a wire fence," and "yard and the house lie within the same fenced-off area"); United States v. Reilly, 76 F.3d 1271 (2d Cir.1996) (stressing enclosures at outer edges of property and no "internal fencing" that "courts may well view * * * as a boundary that sets curtilage apart from the open fields"); People v. Pitman, 211 Ill.2d 502, 286 Ill.Dec. 36, 813 N.E.2d 93 (2004) (barn outside curtilage; not within enclosure surrounding farmhouse); State v. Fisher, 283 Kan. 272, 154 P.3d 455 (2007) (area within curtilage because within enclosure of barbed wire fencing around house); Dunn v. Commonwealth, 360 S.W.3d 751 (Ky.2012) (within fence, but still outside curtilage, as fence "marked portions of the edge of Appellant's large property rather than enclosing a relatively small area around the house"); State v. Smith, 163 N.H. 169, 37 A.3d 409 (2012) (woods not within curtilage, as "no general enclosure * * * surrounding both"); State v. Hall, 168 Vt. 327, 719 A.2d 435 (1998) (woods behind defendant's home not within curtilage, as "only fencing behind defendant's house was ornamental" and wooded area "was located beyond the ornamental fence"); State v. Rogers, 161 Vt. 236, 638 A.2d 569

steps taken by the resident to protect the area from observation by people passing by.[41] * * * We do not suggest that combining these factors produces a finely tuned formula that when mechanically ap-

---

(1993) (garden within curtilage, as "house and garden are surrounded by a thickly wooded band of property that serves as a natural enclosure"); State v. Martwick, 231 Wis.2d 801, 604 N.W.2d 552 (2000) (marijuana plants outside curtilage, as beyond point where "curtilage is clearly marked by the low-cut weeds and brush," after which "tree line then suddenly appears").

But see United States v. Perdue, 8 F.3d 1455 (10th Cir.1993) (fact there a low picket fence between house and area in question not determinative where, as here, the area otherwise identifiable as associated with house).

[40]See, e.g., Rieck v. Jensen, 651 F.3d 1188 (10th Cir.2011) (stressing area within fence several hundred feet from house "not a suitable setting for intimate activities associated with a home"); United States v. Hayes, 551 F.3d 138 (2d Cir.2008) (area not used "for other intimate purposes" than hiding place for drugs); United States v. Davis, 530 F.3d 1069 (9th Cir.2008) (as to area outside workshop set apart from house, there "no signs of domestic activity" but rather of marijuana growing activity, "not an 'intimate activity of the home'"); United States v. Boyster, 436 F.3d 986 (8th Cir.2006) (nothing "indicates that the land was used for any legitimate purpose associated with a residence"); Bleavins v. Bartels, 422 F.3d 445 (7th Cir.2005) (trailers seized without warrant for back taxes not within curtilage, as field where they found not intimately associated with the house, as used only to store boat and trailers); United States v. Breza, 308 F.3d 430 (4th Cir.2002) (stressing trial court's finding that in light of the size of the garden, it was "not just a domestic activity"); United States v. Diehl, 276 F.3d 32 (1st Cir.2002) ("we are not willing to * * * require that, to invoke curtilage protection, there must be objective evidence of intimate uses possessed by officers," as such "would totally eviscerate the protection, mak-

ing it depend on the exigencies of night or day, rain or shine, and winter or summer"); United States v. Jenkins, 124 F.3d 768 (6th Cir.1997) (backyard within curtilage, as it used "as an area to garden" and for "hanging their wet laundry on a clothesline to dry"); United States v. Brady, 993 F.2d 177 (9th Cir.1993) (outbuilding used primarily for growing marijuana not within curtilage); United States v. Swepston, 987 F.2d 1510 (10th Cir.1993) (shed within curtilage; court emphasizes there a path from shed to house and that shed regularly used by occupant of house); United States v. Hatch, 931 F.2d 1478 (11th Cir.1991) (stock pens, tac room, etc., near where marijuana growing shows use of area not "connected with the intimate activities of the home"); People v. Pitman, 211 Ill.2d 502, 286 Ill.Dec. 36, 813 N.E.2d 93 (2004) (barn outside curtilage; none of the tenants used it for "intimate activities of the home"); State v. Fisher, 283 Kan. 272, 154 P.3d 455 (2007) (fact area used for gardening indicative of curtilage); State v. Smith, 163 N.H. 169, 37 A.3d 409 (2012) (no evidence defendant "used the 'unmaintained' forest for domestic purposes"); State v. Rogers, 161 Vt. 236, 638 A.2d 569 (1993) (garden within curtilage, as "gardening is an act often associated with the curtilage of a home"); State v. Lange, 158 Wis.2d 609, 463 N.W.2d 390 (App.1990) (garden where marijuana grown within curtilage, as it also contained "a variety of garden vegetables," and it also "significant that laundry was hanging on a line even farther from the house").

[41]See, e.g., Rieck v. Jensen, 651 F.3d 1188 (10th Cir.2011) (stressing area within fence several hundred feet from house was "clearly visible from a public highway"); United States v. Davis, 530 F.3d 1069 (9th Cir.2008) (stressing chain-link fence around workshop "not designed to prevent observation"); United States v. Boyster, 436 F.3d 986 (8th Cir.2006) (does not appear defendant "took any ordinary precautions to keep the marijuana

plied, yields a "correct" answer to all extent-of-curtilage questions.[42] Rather, these factors are useful analytical tools only to the degree that, in any given case, they bear upon the centrally relevant consideration–whether the area in question is so intimately tied to the home itself that it should be placed under the home's "umbrella" of Fourth Amendment protection.[43]

Applying those considerations, the Court next ruled that the lower court had erred in concluding that defendant's barn was within the curtilage and that consequently looking into it was a search.[44] Specifically: (1) the barn was 50 yards outside the fence surrounding the house and 60 yards from the house itself; (2) the barn was not within the area surrounding the house that was enclosed by a fence; (3) "the law enforcement officials possessed objective data indicating that the barn was not being used for intimate activities of the home";[45] and (4) the defendant had done little to protect the barn area from observation from adjacent

---

from being visible to onlookers"); Bleavins v. Bartels, 422 F.3d 445 (7th Cir.2005) (trailers seized without warrant for back taxes not within curtilage, as field where they found visible to passersby from public vantage point); United States v. Breza, 308 F.3d 430 (4th Cir.2002) (in concluding garden not within curtilage, court notes that though home in "remote location," defendant apparently made no "additional effort to conceal the vegetable garden from public view"); United States v. Diehl, 276 F.3d 32 (1st Cir.2002) ("the location of the property, the bend in the long driveway, the surrounding woodland, and the efforts of the inhabitants to discourage mail delivery and visits from neighbors and officials all seem to have created a locus as free from observation by passersby as one could conceive"); United States v. Jenkins, 124 F.3d 768 (6th Cir.1997) (backyard within curtilage, as it "well shielded" from those on public road by house and from others by woods); United States v. Reilly, 76 F.3d 1271 (2d Cir.1996) (cottage and wooded area within curtilage, as both were "several hundred feet away from the road" and defendant had "planted trees along the perimeter of the property to block visibility"); People v. Pitman, 211 Ill.2d 502, 286 Ill.Dec. 36, 813 N.E.2d 93 (2004) (barn outside curtilage; "nothing prohibited observation of the barn area from those standing in the open field"); State v. Boying-

ton, 714 A.2d 141 (Me.1998) (pond "plainly visible from the public road" not within curtilage); State v. Lange, 158 Wis.2d 609, 463 N.W.2d 390 (App.1990) (heavy tree line around area relevant whether defendant "planted the trees himself, or merely chose to live on the property because the trees afforded privacy").

[42]See, e.g., United States v. Hatch, 931 F.2d 1478 (11th Cir.1991) (fact marijuana plants "not visible to passersby" did not outweigh 3 factors favoring outside-the-curtilage conclusion).

[43]It has been noted that these four factors are most likely to be determinative when the area at issue "is rural and remote from public view and is therefore similar to the area at issue in *Dunn*." United States v. Swepston, 987 F.2d 1510 (10th Cir. 1993). Compare United States v. Acosta, 965 F.2d 1248 (3d Cir.1992) (*Dunn* factors less analytically useful in solving curtilage question because area in question was apartment dwelling in urban area).

[44]This is not to suggest that if the barn *was* in the curtilage that merely looking into it would necessarily be a search. See § 2.3(e).

[45]This is not quite the way the matter should have been put. As Scalia, J., noted in his concurrence: "What is significant is that the barn was not being so used, whether or not the law enforcement officials knew it. The of-

open fields.[46]

Despite the emphasis in *Oliver* upon the concept of "curtilage" in defining the scope of the Fourth Amendment's protections, it should not be assumed that under this revitalized "open fields" doctrine anything goes provided it occurs outside the curtilage.[47] *Oliver* only holds "that an individual may not legitimately demand privacy for activities conducted out of doors in fields"; the Court recognized that the Fourth Amendment protects structures other than houses. Fully consistent with *Oliver*, therefore, is *United States v. Dunn*,[48] holding police had conducted a search when they used a flashlight to look inside a barn which, though fifty yards beyond the curtilage, they had reached only by scaling several fences. Noting it had "found no case * * * applying the term [open fields] to a building of any consequence," the court in *Dunn* properly concluded:

> A barn is as much a part of a rancher's place of business as a warehouse or outbuilding is part of an urban merchant's place of business. It is and ought to be constitutionally protected from warrantless searches if the owner or occupier takes reasonable steps to effect privacy.

As discussed above, the Supreme Court reversed in *Dunn* (albeit following the court of appeals' shift in a later opinion to a curtilage theory[49]). This reversal should not be taken to signal a rejection of the basic point made above, for that is not the case. Taking note of defendant's alternative theory that he "possessed an expectation of privacy in his barn and its contents because the barn was an essential part of his business," the Court merely

---

ficers' perceptions might be relevant to whether the intrusion upon curtilage was nevertheless reasonable, but they are no more relevant to whether the barn was curtilage than to whether the house was a house."

[46] The two dissenters objected that the majority's conclusion the barn was not within the curtilage "overlooks the role a barn plays in rural life and ignores extensive authority holding that a barn, when clustered with other outbuildings near the residence, is part of the curtilage." They went on to conclude that in any event the defendant had a reasonable expectation of privacy in his barn, which had been intruded upon by looking into the building from a vantage point inaccessible to the public.

In United States v. Pace, 955 F.2d 270 (5th Cir.1992), where the first three factual considerations in *Dunn* were clearly present, but "officers could not see inside the barn from any distance, but had to press their faces close to the opening to see inside," the court reached the questionable conclusion that *Dunn* still governed because this up-close observation still was outside the curtilage.

[47] State v. Sorenson, 441 N.W.2d 455 (Minn.1989) ("fact that the open-fields doctrine permitted Officer Buria's warrantless entry onto appellant's land does not suspend all privacy and personal security projections of the fourth amendment," and thus defendant could challenge the officer's stopping of him while in the field).

[48] United States v. Dunn, 766 F.2d 880 (5th Cir.1985).

[49] United States v. Dunn, 782 F.2d 1226 (5th Cir.1986).

responded that assuming this was so,[50] this merely meant the barn "could not be entered and its contents seized without a warrant" and did not bar looking into the barn while standing at an open fields vantage point.[51]

§ 2.4(b) Business and commercial premises

Although the Fourth Amendment guarantees the right of the people to be secure in their "houses," this protection is by no means limited to residential buildings. The Supreme Court has consistently held that offices and stores and other business and commercial premises are likewise entitled to protection against

---

[50]See, e.g., United States v. Santa Maria, 15 F.3d 879 (9th Cir.1994) (trailer outside curtilage protected); United States v. Broadhurst, 805 F.2d 849 (9th Cir.1986) ("a structure need not be within the curtilage in order to have Fourth Amendment protection"); United States v. Trickey, 711 F.2d 56 (6th Cir.1983) (outbuilding outside curtilage located on residential property protected);Allinder v. State of Ohio, 808 F.2d 1180 (6th Cir.1987) (involving search of apiaries and similar premises; court holds open fields doctrine not applicable to "a commercial structure in a field"); Fite v. State, 873 P.2d 293 (Okl.Cr.App.1993) (entry of well house and storage building illegal, as "the open fields doctrine does not permit the officers to enter *the building* in the field without a warrant"); State v. Townsend, 186 W.Va. 283, 412 S.E.2d 477 (1991) (defendant "had a reasonable expectation of privacy in the interior of his hog house * * * outside the curtilage * * * where the defendant used the building as an adjunct to his farming business").

Compare United States v. Pennington, 287 F.3d 739 (8th Cir.2002) (though *Dunn* and *Oliver* made it clear that "the open fields doctrine only allows a search of what is in plain view in the open field," and "does not justify a warrantless search of a man-made enclosure found in an open field," "given the location of the underground bunker in an open field, its readily visible entryway with an unprotected ladder facilitating access to the tunnel, and no lock or door imped-

ing access," police entry of bunker permissible); State v. Martin, 553 A.2d 1264 (Me.1989) (no search to enter "a shanty for animals to get in out of the weather" located 50 ft. from defendant's dwelling, as it not within curtilage; because freezer in shed apparently not connected to electrical supply, the shed not an area that "harbors the intimate activities associated with the sanctity of a home and the privacies of life"); State v. Forshey, 182 W.Va. 87, 386 S.E.2d 15 (1989) (entry into unspecified "outbuilding" not within curtilage upheld as no search under open fields doctrine; strong dissent).

See other cases in § 2.3(d), note 168.

[51]See also United States v. Van Damme, 48 F.3d 461 (9th Cir.1995) (no search where police looked through open doors of greenhouses located outside the curtilage from vantage point of helicopter flying overhead above FAA limits and from open fields area where inside of greenhouses could be seen notwithstanding presence of high board fence); State v. Pruss, 145 Idaho 623, 181 P.3d 1231 (2008) ("Although the State is correct that Pruss did not have a reasonable expectation of privacy in the forest land surrounding his campsite, the interior of Pruss's hooch was not an open field. * * * Although the police could certainly have walked up to Pruss's hooch and while doing so could have lawfully observed anything in plain view, the open fields doctrine would not justify their entry into the hooch").

unreasonable searches and seizures.[52] As the Court stated in *See v. City of Seattle*,[53] "[t]he businessman, like the occupant of a residence, has a constitutional right to go about his business free from unreasonable official entries upon his private commercial property."

It is a fair generalization, however, that business and commercial premises are not as private as residential premises, and that consequently there are various police investigative procedures which may be directed at such premises without the police conduct constituting a Fourth Amendment search.[54] *Katz v. United States*[55] teaches that "[w]hat a person knowingly exposes to the public, even in his own home or office, is not a subject of Fourth Amendment protection." This means "that as an ordinary matter law enforcement officials may accept a general public invitation to enter commercial premises for purposes not related to the trade conducted thereupon."[56] On this basis, courts have consistently held that police, albeit motivated by an investigative purpose, conducted no search by merely entering such premises as a bus terminal,[57] auto repair shop,[58] salvage yard,[59] used car

[Section 2.4(b)]

[52]O'Connor v. Ortega, 480 U.S. 709, 107 S.Ct. 1492, 94 L.Ed.2d 714 (1987); New York v. Burger, 482 U.S. 691, 107 S.Ct. 2636, 96 L.Ed.2d 601 (1987); Mancusi v. DeForte, 392 U.S. 364, 88 S.Ct. 2120, 20 L.Ed.2d 1154 (1968); Go-Bart Importing Co. v. United States, 282 U.S. 344, 51 S.Ct. 153, 75 L.Ed. 374 (1931); Gouled v. United States, 255 U.S. 298, 41 S.Ct. 261, 65 L.Ed. 647 (1921); Silverthorne Lumber Co. v. United States, 251 U.S. 385, 40 S.Ct. 182, 64 L.Ed. 319 (1920).

[53]See v. City of Seattle, 387 U.S. 541, 87 S.Ct. 1737, 18 L.Ed.2d 943 (1967).

[54]That proposition must be distinguished from the notion that "an expectation of privacy in commercial premises, however, is different from, and indeed less than, a similar expectation in an individual's home." New York v. Burger, 482 U.S. 691, 107 S.Ct. 2636, 96 L.Ed.2d 601 (1987). This latter principle has to do not with the search-no search distinction but rather with when searches may be conducted of business premises pursuant to restrictions less onerous than usually obtain as a Fourth Amendment matter. See § 10.2.

[55]Katz v. United States, 389 U.S. 347, 88 S.Ct. 507, 19 L.Ed.2d 576 (1967).

[56]United States v. Berrett, 513 F.2d 154 (1st Cir.1975). See also Andree v. Ashland County, 818 F.2d 1306 (7th Cir.1987) (ordinance requiring police presence at rock concert valid; no expectation of privacy, as general public invited); United States v. Edmonds, 611 F.2d 1386 (5th Cir.1980) (officers came onto a dock by using entrance road posted with "no trespassing" sign; was implied invitation notwithstanding sign, as reputation in community was that public welcome to use dock area and public did use it; it was place where boats docked and were unloaded and where business activity conducted).

[57]Commonwealth v. Adams, 234 Pa.Super. 475, 341 A.2d 206 (1975).

[58]United States v. Ealy, 363 F.3d 292 (4th Cir.2004); United States v. Morton, 17 F.3d 911 (6th Cir.1994); Koster v. State, 374 Ark. 74, 286 S.W.3d 152 (2008); Shaw v. State, 253 Ga. 382, 320 S.E.2d 371 (1984); Murphy v. State, 426 So.2d 786 (Miss.1983); State v. De Marco, 157 N.J.Super. 341, 384 A.2d 1113 (1978).

But see United States v. Pantoja-

lot,[60] parking lot,[61] dock,[62] real estate office,[63] construction company office,[64] courier company office,[65] motel,[66] hospital,[67] pool hall,[68] bar,[69] restaurant,[70] furniture store,[71] bookstore,[72] or variety

---

Soto, 739 F.2d 1520 (11th Cir.1984) (Fourth Amendment applicable to service bay of gas station, but officer lawfully present pursuing person to be arrested).

[59]State v. Dahms, 310 N.W.2d 479 (Minn.1981); Delay v. State, 563 S.W.2d 905 (Tenn.Crim.App.1977).

[60]United States v. Brandon, 599 F.2d 112 (6th Cir.1979); Commonwealth v. Baldwin, 11 Mass.App.Ct. 386, 416 N.E.2d 544 (1981).

[61]United States v. Gooch, 499 F.3d 596 (6th Cir.2007) (police lawfully positioned when they saw gun in defendant's car, notwithstanding car owner's claim of reasonable expectation in that area because it VIP parking area for nearby club, as the "area was within a large parking lot that was shared by several commercial establishments" and "there was no barrier * * * that prevented pedestrians from walking through the VIP area of the parking lot during the hours the valet service was in operation"); United States v. Reed, 733 F.2d 492 (8th Cir.1984) (defendants without expectation of privacy in construction company parking lot located in commercial area, bounded on 3 sides by public streets, with fenced gate left open).

[62]United States v. Edmonds, 611 F.2d 1386 (5th Cir.1980); Cuevas v. State, 151 Ga.App. 605, 260 S.E.2d 737 (1979).

[63]Northside Realty Associates, Inc. v. United States, 605 F.2d 1348 (5th Cir.1979).

[64]State v. Albaugh, 732 N.W.2d 712 (N.D.2007) ("no individual would reasonably expect a great amount of privacy in a commercial business location, where the public was apparently welcome").

[65]Cantizano v. United States, 614 A.2d 870 (D.C.App.1992) ("the office was open to those who walked in, as

the officer did here").

[66]In Donovan v. Lone Steer, Inc., 464 U.S. 408, 104 S.Ct. 769, 78 L.Ed.2d 567 (1984), the Court concluded: "An entry into the public lobby of a motel and restaurant for the purpose of serving an administrative subpoena is scarcely the sort of governmental act which is forbidden by the Fourth Amendment."

[67]State v. Herbest, 551 A.2d 442 (Me.1988) (defendant "had no reasonable expectation of privacy in a reception area of a hospital emergency room"); State v. Rheaume, 179 Vt. 39, 889 A.2d 711 (2005) (defendant without reasonable expectation of privacy in emergency ward treatment room, as "medical personnel, hospital staff, patients and their families, and emergency workers—including police officers—are, as a matter of course, frequently, and not unexpectedly, moving through the area"; collecting cases in accord). See also Annot., 28 A.L.R.6th 245 (2007).

[68]Washington v. State, 42 Ark.App. 188, 856 S.W.2d 631 (1993); People v. Johnson, 21 Ill.App.3d 769, 315 N.E.2d 579 (1974).

[69]State v. Lund, 409 So.2d 569 (La.1982) (club); Birkenshaw v. City of Detroit, 110 Mich.App. 500, 313 N.W.2d 334 (1981); Commonwealth v. Monteririo, 4 Mass.App.Ct. 349, 348 N.E.2d 449 (1976); Gordon v. State, 640 S.W.2d 743 (Tex.App.1982).

[70]Sullivan v. District Ct. of Hampshire, 384 Mass. 736, 429 N.E.2d 335 (1981) (canteen at hospital); Jones v. City of Ridgeland, 48 So.3d 530 (Miss. 2010) (restaurant parking lot); State v. Russo, 470 S.W.2d 164 (Mo.App. 1971).

[71]Wilson v. Commonwealth, 475 S.W.2d 895 (Ky.1971).

[72]Abilene Retail No. 30, Inc. v. Board of Com'rs of Dickinson County, Kan., 492 F.3d 1164 (10th Cir.2007); State, ex rel. Rear Door Bookstore v.

store.[73] The "implied invitation for customers to come in," of course, extends only to those times when the premises are in fact "open to the public"[74]; the mere fact that certain premises are open to the public at certain times does not justify entry by the police on other occasions.[75]

If a police officer has entered as would any member of the public,[76] it is not a search for the officer to conduct himself therein as might be expected of any other person who would enter. Quite clearly, the officer is "entitled to take note of objects in plain view."[77] He may also examine merchandise in the fashion that a

Tenth District Court of Appeals, 63 Ohio St.3d 354, 588 N.E.2d 116 (1992).

[73]State v. Doukales, 111 R.I. 443, 303 A.2d 769 (1973).

[74]Wilson v. Commonwealth, 475 S.W.2d 895 (Ky.1971). See also United States v. Sandoval–Vasquez, 435 F.3d 739 (7th Cir.2006) (police entry of iron works no search, as "at the time of entry, the door through which customers entered was open, the garage door was open, and the establishment was still open for business").

[75]O'Rourke v. Hayes, 378 F.3d 1201 (11th Cir.2004) (was a search for officers to enter medical office "while the office was not yet open to patients"); United States v. Swart, 679 F.2d 698 (7th Cir.1982) ("Commercial establishments do not extend an explicit invitation to enter during non-business hours or when there are no employees on the premises"); People v. Ramsey, 272 Cal.App.2d 302, 77 Cal.Rptr. 249 (1969); State v. Foreman, 662 N.E.2d 929 (Ind.1996) (was a search for officers to enter room adjoining bingo center when room not open to public, notwithstanding fact "the room was open to the general public during business hours").

[76]Compare Club Retro, L.L.C. v. Hilton, 568 F.3d 181 (5th Cir.2009) (raid on club not justified by fact it an establishment then open to the public, as the members of the raiding party "did not enter Club Retro as would a typical patron; instead they chose to project official authority by entering with guns drawn in a S.W.A.T. team raid," and thus the police "entry and search was not a reasonable acceptance of Club Retro's invitation to the

public").

[77]United States v. Berrett, 513 F.2d 154 (1st Cir.1975). See also O'Neill v. Louisville/Jefferson County Metro Government, 662 F.3d 723 (6th Cir.2011) (plaintiffs "opened a portion of their home to the public when they invited those who responded to their newspaper ad to come and look at the puppies," and undercover officers did not intrude "any more than permitted or any more than any other person who responded to the ad"); Zimmerman v. City of Oakland, 255 F.3d 734 (9th Cir.2001) (where police came onto property zoned for light industrial use and tagged derelict bus stored there, and "area where the bus was parked was open to people who wished to transact business with tenants of the lot," and § 1983 plaintiff "did nothing to prevent people from seeing the bus," police entry of lot and viewing of bus no search, as when "a police officer entered a commercial area in the same manner as any member of the public, and examines the area in the same way as might be expected of any other person, the officer has not conducted a 'search' within the meaning of the Fourth Amendment"); Northside Realty Associates, Inc. v. United States, 605 F.2d 1348 (5th Cir.1979) (government agents "behaved exactly as a prospective home buyer visiting a real estate office would be expected to behave"); Koster v. State, 374 Ark. 74, 286 S.W.3d 152 (2008) (officers observed items "in plain view in Koster's shop, a commercial business establishment open to the public"); State v. Merchandise Seized, 225 N.W.2d 921 (Iowa 1975); State v. Russo, 470 S.W.2d 164 (Mo.App.1971); State v. Marshall,

prospective customer could be expected to do. In *People v. Superior Court*,[78] for example, where a policeman entered a pawn shop, picked up a typewriter, and looked at the serial number on the machine, the court concluded:

> Under the facts of this case there was no search. The typewriter was not intentionally put out of the way or concealed in a private or hidden place. The cover was not on the typewriter when it was first viewed by the officers. Had the serial number been on the surface on top of the typewriter, the officer would have been able to examine it without touching it. The fortuitous circumstance that the serial number was placed in such a manner as to require that the typewriter be moved in order to be read cannot be construed to turn reasonable conduct into misconduct of constitutional dimensions.[79]

As the Supreme Court explained in *Maryland v. Macon*,[80] holding an "officer's action in entering the bookstore and examining the wares that were intentionally exposed to all who frequent the place of business did not infringe a legitimate expectation of privacy and hence did not constitute a search": "The mere expectation that the possibly illegal nature of a product will not come to the attention of the authorities, whether because a customer will not complain or because undercover officers will not transact business with the store,[81] is not one that society is prepared to recognize as reasonable." Similarly, an officer may examine other objects to which the public has ready access. This means, for example, that when a policeman followed a suspect into a lounge and saw her place a bar towel on the shelf beneath

---

123 N.J. 1, 586 A.2d 85 (1991) (no search for officer to read words "To be opened in the event of my death" on envelope defendant dropped in open, uncovered box on motel office counter for outgoing mail); State, ex rel. Rear Door Bookstore v. Tenth District Court of Appeals, 63 Ohio St.3d 354, 588 N.E.2d 116 (1992) (no search for officer to discover items "within the plain view of anyone who entered the arcade area of the bookstore"); Commonwealth v. Adams, 234 Pa.Super. 475, 341 A.2d 206 (1975); State v. Doukales, 111 R.I. 443, 303 A.2d 769 (1973).

[78]People v. Superior Court, 2 Cal.App.3d 131, 82 Cal.Rptr. 507 (1969). See also United States v. Ealy, 363 F.3d 292 (4th Cir.2004) (police entering garage where commercial auto work done could take note of license number of vehicle); State v. Cockrum, 592 S.W.2d 300 (Mo.App. 1979) (no search for officer to examine serial numbers on refrigerator and other major appliances displayed for

sale in store).

[79]Compare Winters v. Board of County Commissioners, 4 F.3d 848 (10th Cir.1993) ("facts of this case do not support the conclusion that the warrantless seizure was justified under the plain view doctrine," as though "the ring may have been visible in a display case, [the officer] did not have a lawful right of access to it," and he "never saw the ring until it was provided to him by" the pawnshop clerk, after the officer asked the clerk to produce the ring described in a particular pawn shop record).

[80]Maryland v. Macon, 472 U.S. 463, 105 S.Ct. 2778, 86 L.Ed.2d 370 (1985), discussed in Note, 36 Am.U.L. Rev. 773 (1987).

[81]Also, the act of the undercover officer in purchasing a magazine for sale was no search, for the seller had "voluntarily transferred any possessory interest he may have had in the magazine."

a public wall phone next to the directory normally stored there, he could remove and unroll the towel; because "the shelf under the public telephone where the defendant put the towel was open to public use, she had no reasonable expectation of privacy with respect to it."[82]

Those situations must be contrasted with that in *Lo-Ji Sales, Inc. v. New York*,[83] where police accompanied by a Town Justice made a search of an adult bookstore during the hours it was open for business. The Justice examined the contents of magazines from which the police first removed the cellophane wrappers, and he also looked at films on coin-operated projectors after the clerk on duty was made to adjust the machines so that coins were not needed. After concluding that those searches could not be upheld under the search warrant the search party had, the Court turned to the state's suggestion

> that by virtue of its display of the items at issue to the general public in areas of its store open to them, petitioner had no legitimate expectation of privacy against governmental intrusion * * *, and that accordingly no warrant was needed. But there is no basis for the notion that because a retail store invites the public to enter, it consents to wholesale searches and seizures that do not conform to Fourth Amendment guarantees. * * * The Town Justice viewed the films, not as a customer, but without the payment a member of the public would be required to make. Similarly, in examining the books and in the manner of viewing the containers in which the films were packaged for sale, he was not seeing them as a customer would ordinarily see them.

For his actions not to constitute a Fourth Amendment search, the officer must remain in that portion of the premises open to the public.[84] In *State v. Baker*,[85] for example, where the policeman walked into the back room, the court declared:

---

[82]Commonwealth v. Monteririo, 4 Mass.App.Ct. 349, 348 N.E.2d 449 (1976). See also United States v. Lyons, 898 F.2d 210 (1st Cir.1990) (where incident to defendant's arrest police found keys and rental agreement for a storage compartment, and police knew friend of defendant had rented another compartment at same place, determining that one of defendant's keys fit lock to latter compartment "is so minimally intrusive that it does not implicate a reasonable expectation of privacy" and is no search because defendant only had "an expectation that the *contents* would be free from public view"); People v. Loveless, 80 Ill.App.3d 1052, 36 Ill.Dec. 120, 400 N.E.2d 540 (1980) (no search for officer in busy tavern to merely pick up a jacket lying on table,

as an "individual who places a coat on a table in a busy tavern must reasonably expect that the coat will be touched or handled by an employee or by any member of the public who desires to use or sit at that table").

[83]Lo-Ji Sales, Inc. v. New York, 442 U.S. 319, 99 S.Ct. 2319, 60 L.Ed.2d 920 (1979).

[84]Unless, of course, he obtains consent from one in a position to give effective consent. See, e.g., PPS, Inc. v. Faulkner County, 630 F.3d 1098 (8th Cir.2011) (during business hours, police entered pawn shop and asked if paint sprayer was on premises and manager then consented to police entry of back room behind closed door to view it; such lawful presence justified plain-view seizure). On consent by

821

The search is not sustainable on the theory of the right of police officers to enter a public store. The implied invitation does not extend beyond the area to which the public is admitted, i.e., the store premises proper. * * * Observations made in that area by police are not a "search." * * * Here the rear room was not visible from the combination barber shop, shoeshine, and poolroom store, and the incursion to the rear room in the course of a thorough search of the whole first floor of the building beyond the store was plainly not justified on the theory of store premises open to the public.[86]

---

an employee, see § 8.6(c); on consent by an employer with respect to parts of the business premises used by a particular employee, see § 8.6(d).

[85]State v. Baker, 112 N.J.Super. 351, 271 A.2d 435 (1970).

[86]See also United States v. Ziegler, 474 F.3d 1184 (9th Cir.2007) (examination of items in defendant's office a search, as "office was not shared by coworkers, and kept locked," and it makes no difference that "there was a master key"); United States v. Taketa, 923 F.2d 665 (9th Cir.1991) (use of covert video surveillance by camera placed in ceiling of defendant's private office was a search, as the office was not open to the public and the only three other people with regular access to it were defendant's co-conspirators in the conduct charged); People v. Williams, 51 Cal.App.3d 346, 124 Cal.Rptr. 253 (1975) (officer illegally entered airline baggage room, as it not open to general public); Harper v. State, 283 Ga. 102, 657 S.E.2d 213 (2008) (rejecting argument no search of employee's desk "because it was unlocked and was in a workspace shared by numerous coworkers"); State v. Bonnell, 75 Haw. 124, 856 P.2d 1265 (1993) (was a search for police to secretly videotape activities in post office's employee break room, which "was neither a public place nor subject to public view or hearing," in that postal employees on break "could see anyone approaching and could avoid being surprised by an untrusted intruder"); State v. Foreman, 662 N.E.2d 929 (Ind.1996) (though no search for officers to enter bingo center then open, it was a search for them to enter adjoining room, not then open to public, by removing door from hinges);

Commonwealth v. Gabrielle, 269 Pa.Super. 338, 409 A.2d 1173 (1979) (officer illegally looked into employee's locker at plant); State v. Weaver, 349 S.W.3d 521 (Tex.Crim.App.2011) (officers entered a welding shop, consisting of a front office and a workshop in the rear, while it was open, seeking a wanted person but, not finding him, led a drug dog around a van backed up to the workshop bay door, and then searched the van on the basis of the dog's alert; held, dog sniff illegal, as "this area was not part of the 'public' area of his welding shop"); Crosby v. State, 750 S.W.2d 768 (Tex.Crim.App. 1987) (officer in night club open to public engaged in search when he entered private dressing room of entertainer).

Compare United States v. Boden, 854 F.2d 983 (7th Cir.1988) (no search when officer entered storage facility where individual units rented out, as officer remained in common area and did not intrude into individual units); Northside Realty Associates, Inc. v. United States, 605 F.2d 1348 (5th Cir.1979) (stressing government agents entering real estate office made no search because they "did not enter into any restricted areas of the office, such as an employee's lounge"); Cowles v. State, 23 P.3d 1168 (Alaska 2001) (distinguishing *Taketa* and *Bonnell*, supra, court holds that where defendant suspected of theft from ticket sales, covert video surveillance during business hours of her desk from camera hidden in ceiling vent no search, as "Cowles's desk could be seen by members of the public through the ticket window and the open door, and by her fellow employees who were walking around the office almost continuously during the videotaping," and the "fact that the video camera may

Not all business or commercial premises are open to the public at large. A factory, for example, may be readily accessible to the employees of the company, but it does not follow from this that police may enter those premises at will.[87] And an office "is seldom a private enclave free from entry by supervisors, other employees and business and personal invitees,"[88] yet an expectation of privacy protected by the Fourth Amendment exists as to such work areas as offices and the desks and files therein.[89] Similarly, a club or other business that is operated for a select clientele may not be public. "Charging admission to a closely restricted group would not necessarily convert the premises into a public place, even though it may be a place of business."[90] This means, for example, that if a club is operated only for members of a particular organization, the "implied invitation" to enter extends only to such persons.[91] But the actual practice as to admitting persons

---

have been in an especially good position from which to view Cowles's acts of transferring money from the University money pouch to her desk and thence to her purse is not sufficient to create a reasonable expectation of privacy in an open and public setting where no such expectation could reasonably exist"); Nelson v. Salem State College, 446 Mass. 525, 845 N.E.2d 338 (2006) (state college employee videotaped by hidden camera as she changed clothes and applied sunburn medication while "she thought she was alone"; no Fourth Amendment violation, as her office "was open to the public throughout the day" and window "provided passersby a full view of the interior of the office," and space behind partitions where she changed "was no more private," as it "lacked a door" and "was located near the stairs").

[87]Gateway 2000, Inc. v. Limoges, 1996 SD 81, 552 N.W.2d 591 (1996) (where, as to its factory producing computers, "Gateway maintains an internal security department and prohibits access beyond the visitor center to members of the public for security and safety reasons," it "is clear that Gateway has a justified expectation of privacy in its employees' work areas which are not open to the public," and thus sheriff's entry of those areas to serve civil process is an illegal search).

See § 10.2 re administrative inspection of factories and other commercial premises.

[88]O'Connor v. Ortega, 480 U.S. 709, 107 S.Ct. 1492, 94 L.Ed.2d 714 (1987).

[89]In Ortega, the plurality opinion stated that "the question of whether an employee has a reasonable expectation of privacy must be addressed on a case-by-case basis." Scalia, J. concurring, chided the plurality for not accepting the broader proposition "that the offices of government employees, and a fortiori the drawers and files within those offices, are covered by Fourth Amendment protections as a general matter," except in "such unusual situations" as where "the office is subject to unrestricted public access." The four dissenters (and thus a majority of the Court) expressed approval of this broader view.

[90]Asher v. City of Little Rock, 248 Ark. 96, 449 S.W.2d 933 (1970).

[91]State v. Oregon City Elks Lodge No. 1189, 17 Or.App. 124, 520 P.2d 900 (1974) (Elks club open to members of other Elks lodges, and thus it no search for district attorney to employ such member as undercover agent and have him gain entry to observe gambling). Cf. Iowa Beta Chapter of Phi Delta Theta Fraternity v. University of Iowa, 763 N.W.2d 250 (Iowa 2009) (fraternity had a reasonable expectation of privacy as to conversations in basement meeting room of fraternity house, where it stationed wardens at the door of the room to exclude non-members).

into such facilities must be considered in making the determination of whether there was in fact a justified expectation of privacy therein. In *Ouimette v. Howard*,[92] for example, where an officer entered a social club to request that a person move an illegally parked car and while there saw evidence of crime, the court quite correctly concluded that under *Katz* the question was not "whether the officers, while on the Club's premises, were trespassers or licensees," but rather whether the entry "defeated Ouimette's reasonable expectation of privacy." The court held that it did not; the door was not locked, there was no door man to keep out nonmembers, and nonmembers frequently did enter the club.

Especially when the business or commercial premises are not open to the public or are not open at that particular time, the surveillance may take a different form. For example, the police may approach the building and, without an actual physical entry, see or hear what is occurring therein. Application of the *Katz* justified-expectation-of-privacy test in such cases requires consideration of where the police were at the time of the surveillance and how the surveillance was conducted. If police using the naked eye or ear[93] are able to see or hear while located on adjoining property or even on property of the business readily accessible to the general public, this is not a search.[94] The same is true if the police were in a corridor of a building used by the public to

---

As for the use of subterfuge concerning identity to gain entry to such premises, see § 8.2(m).

[92]Ouimette v. Howard, 468 F.2d 1363 (1st Cir.1972). See also United States v. Perry, 548 F.3d 688 (8th Cir.2008) (defendant had no reasonable expectation of privacy within gathering club for veterans, given that club was commercial establishment in an area open to the general public, and there no evidence as to what policy of club was re admission of nonmembers); Commonwealth v. Cadoret, 388 Mass. 148, 445 N.E.2d 1050 (1983) ("fact that premises are maintained as a club with a membership policy is not conclusive in favor of the club. Failure to enforce limitations on admittance would warrant the conclusion that the persons operating the club had no reasonable expectation of privacy"); State v. Posey, 40 Ohio St.3d 420, 534 N.E.2d 61 (1988) (police officer's entry of Eagles' Club with club member no search, as he "entered the post as the guest of a member as could any member of the general public");

Commonwealth v. Weimer, 262 Pa.Super. 69, 396 A.2d 649 (1978) (though private club had 1-way mirror and buzzer system, but practice was to release door whenever buzzer pressed, there was no expectation of privacy, as for "all the owner and bartender knew, or apparently cared, the door might have been opening for a thief, a nonmember, a uniformed officer, or, as in this case, a plainclothes trooper").

[93]As to the significance of using aids to enhance the senses, see § 2.2.

[94]Christensen v. County of Boone, Illinois, 483 F.3d 454 (7th Cir.2007) (no search for police officer to watch plaintiff as "she went about her duties as an employee of a local gas station," as at such times "she appeared in plain view of the public"); United States v. Elkins, 300 F.3d 638 (6th Cir.2002) ("areas that adjoin a commercial building but are accessible to the public do not receive curtilage-like protection," and thus it no search for police to come onto a "path apparently used to gain access to an apartment

reach the commercial establishments there, but not if the hallway is only used by a limited group such as the proprietors of the various shops in the building.[95]

On the other hand, if the police engage in a much more intense form of surveillance, especially from places not ordinarily used by the public, this is a search under *Katz*. Illustrative is *Commonwealth v. Soychak*,[96] where an officer, suspecting that gambling was occurring in a certain club, climbed onto the roof of the building and looked through the louvers of an exhaust fan. The court quite properly concluded that this action constituted a Fourth Amendment search, for it intruded upon the occupants' justified expectation of privacy even though they "failed to completely block the view of police investigators." *Soychak* thus illustrates a very important point: *Katz* covers that surveillance which, "if not restricted by the fourth amendment, would curtail the liberties of citizens to a compass inconsistent with a free society,"[97] and thus the occupants of business and commercial premises should not be put to the choice of taking extraordinary methods of sealing off those premises or else submitting to

---

building behind the [commercial] property"; it also no search for officer at that vantage point to look through open gap about an inch wide around exposed PVC pipe 2–3 ft. off the ground, where in darkness bright light from within was shining through the gap); United States v. Conner, 478 F.2d 1320 (7th Cir.1973) (observation from apron outside door of garage where auto repair business conducted); Howard v. State, 583 P.2d 827 (Alaska 1978) (no search if officer was on driveway to which general public had access to make lumber purchases); State v. Denton, 387 So.2d 578 (La.1980) (no search for officer to watch activity on wharf from adjoining land where, though "it was a private dock, it was located on a public navigable waterway * * * and their actions could have been viewed by anyone passing on the waterway"); Delay v. State, 563 S.W.2d 905 (Tenn.Crim.App.1977) (open lot adjacent to building at salvage yard); Hamilton v. State, 590 S.W.2d 503 (Tex.Crim.App.1979) (no search for officer on public sidewalk to look in restaurant window).

[95]United States v. Case, 435 F.2d 766 (7th Cir.1970) (hallway outside store not public, as it "was kept locked" and "was used by a very confined group, and, most of the time, limited

to the proprietors of the stores in the building," and thus eavesdropping by officer from hallway was a search).

[96]Commonwealth v. Soychak, 221 Pa.Super. 458, 289 A.2d 119 (1972). See also State v. Lamartiniere, 362 So.2d 526 (La.1978) (officer looked into defendant's rented 10 ft. × 30 ft. storage unit by looking through ventilation space between units at roof; this a search, as "the defendant would not be unreasonable in believing that no one would scale the twelve foot wall in order to see the contents of the unit"); State v. Tarantino, 322 N.C. 386, 368 S.E.2d 588 (1988) (is a search to shine flashlight into store through small cracks in wall).

Compare United States v. Hendrickson, 940 F.2d 320 (8th Cir.1991) (no search for police to look through chicken-wire ceiling of commercial storage unit from adjoining unit, as "given the open ceiling of unit #56, a reasonable person would assume that its contents could be viewed from above by the owner or manager of the units and by other persons renting or using the units for any number of reasons").

[97]Amsterdam, Perspectives on the Fourth Amendment, 58 Minn.L.Rev. 349, 404 (1974).

unrestrained police surveillance.[98]

Unfortunately, the decided cases do not always reflect adherence to this significant principle. In *Commonwealth v. Hernley*,[99] for example, an FBI agent suspected that football parlay cards were being printed at a certain print shop. He could hear the presses running in the shop, but could not see inside because the height of the windows was such that no one standing on the ground could see in. The agent therefore mounted a four-foot ladder he placed on the railroad tracks abutting the property; though he was about 35 feet from the window, by the use of binoculars he was able to determine the contents of the material then being run off the presses. The court held that the defendant had no justified expectation of privacy because he had failed "to curtain the windows." But this is not so. As the *Hernley* dissent notes, our privacy is unduly circumscribed if citizens cannot "feel safe in leaving their windows uncurtained to the skies." "This much withdrawal is not required in order to claim the benefit of the amendment because, if it were, the amendment's benefit would be too stingy to preserve the kind of open society to which we are committed and in which the amendment is supposed to function."[100]

As we have seen,[101] the traditional means for determining whether surveillance of land near residential premises constitutes a search is to distinguish between the curtilage and open fields. If this approach were used as to land adjoining business premises, such land would be open to unrestrained police scrutiny, for it is clear that "the concept of curtilage does not apply to buildings other than dwellings."[102] However, "mechanical application of the curtilage concept"[103] so as to deprive business lands of any Fourth Amendment protection is inappropriate after

---

[98]As stated in State v. Tarantino, 322 N.C. 386, 368 S.E.2d 588 (1988): "The presence of tiny cracks near the floor of the interior wall of a second-floor porch is not the kind of exposure which serves to eliminate a reasonable expectation of privacy. To hold otherwise would result in an unfairly exacting standard. It would require owners of non-residential buildings who want to enjoy their Fourth Amendment rights to maintain their structures almost as air tight containers."

But see United States v. Pace, 955 F.2d 270 (5th Cir.1992), described in note 46 supra, reaching a different conclusion as to a barn.

[99]Commonwealth v. Hernley, 216 Pa.Super. 177, 263 A.2d 904 (1970).

[100]Amsterdam, 58 Minn.L.Rev. 349, 402 (1974).

[101]See §§ 2.3(g), 2.4(a).

[102]United States v. Wolfe, 375 F.Supp. 949 (E.D.Pa.1974). See also People v. Janis, 139 Ill.2d 300, 152 Ill.Dec. 100, 565 N.E.2d 633 (1990) (rejecting defendant's "business curtilage" claim, as the "area immediately adjacent to a commercial establishment, unlike the curtilage of a home, does not provide the setting for those intimate activities that the amendment is intended to shelter").

Compare United States v. Swart, 679 F.2d 698 (7th Cir.1982) (asserting "the cars may have been within the curtilage of the business buildings").

[103]People v. Ramsey, 272 Cal.App.2d 302, 77 Cal.Rptr. 249 (1969).

Katz.[104] The question now is whether the police intruded upon a justified expectation of privacy, and this requires a more careful assessment of how private the particular lands were and how intense the police scrutiny was. Thus, in *United States v. FMC Corp.*,[105] where agents entered upon the land of an industrial plant, the court concluded this was a search because the area was surrounded by an 8-foot high fence topped with barbed wire and the gates were closed and locked except when plant personnel were in the area. The court distinguished *Air Pollution Variance Board v. Western Alfalfa Corp.*,[106] where the Supreme Court held no search had occurred. In that case, an inspector made a warrantless and unconsented entry onto the corporation's land and from that vantage point made an opacity reading of smoke being emitted from the corporation's chimneys. A unanimous Court, per Douglas, J., concluded that the "invasion of privacy * * * is abstract and theoretical," as the inspector was not "on premises from which the public was excluded," and he "sighted what anyone in the city who was near the plant could see in the sky–plumes of smoke."[107]

Cases falling somewhere between *FMC* and *Western Alfalfa* can be more difficult to resolve, as the Supreme Court discovered

---

[104]See Note, 23 Del.J.Corp.L. 513, 516 (1998) (noting "the development of the 'business curtilage' concept and the ongoing debate in federal and state courts about whether the Fourth Amendment requires recognition of the concept," and arguing for "Fourth Amendment protection to secure commercial areas in which a business owner has affirmatively precluded public entry and view").

[105]United States v. FMC Corp., 428 F.Supp. 615 (W.D.N.Y.1977).

[106]Air Pollution Variance Bd. v. Western Alfalfa Corp., 416 U.S. 861, 94 S.Ct. 2114, 40 L.Ed.2d 607 (1974). See also United States v. Tolar, 268 F.3d 530 (7th Cir.2001) (no search for agent to enter through open gate fenced lot of business during business hours "to find the owner and ask his permission to do more"); United States v. Hall, 47 F.3d 1091 (11th Cir.1995) (no expectation of privacy as to dumpster located in parking lot the business shares with other businesses and no steps taken to limit public's access; court opines that if Supreme Court were "to embrace the so-called 'business curtilage' concept, it would, at a minimum, require that the commercial proprietor take affirmative steps to exclude the public"); United States v. Ludwig, 10 F.3d 1523 (10th Cir.1993) (no expectation of privacy in motel parking lot that "was open and visible from the public roads bordering it"); United States v. Reed, 733 F.2d 492 (8th Cir.1984) (no expectation of privacy in fenced but open parking lot of construction company); State v. Baker, 65 N.C.App. 430, 310 S.E.2d 101 (1983) (no expectation of privacy on parking lot of antique store even when store closed); State v. Bell, 832 S.W.2d 583 (Tenn.Crim.App.1991) (no expectation of privacy as to open dumpster located on parking lot used by customers).

[107]Unfortunately, Justice Douglas relied upon the "open fields" doctrine of Hester v. United States, 265 U.S. 57, 44 S.Ct. 445, 68 L.Ed. 898 (1924), and never even cited *Katz,* thus creating the mistaken impression that the "open fields" doctrine continues to have independent significance after *Katz.* Quite clearly, however, the inspector did not engage in a search within the meaning of *Katz.*

in *Dow Chemical Company v. United States*,[108] holding, 5-4, "that EPA's aerial photography of petitioner's 2,000-acre plant complex without a warrant was not a search under the Fourth Amendment." The equipment utilized was sufficiently sophisticated and beyond that one might anticipate being used by a member of the general public to justify characterizing its use as Fourth Amendment activity, and the *Dow* majority rather strongly indicated it would so conclude had it been used to surveil "an area immediately adjacent to a private home, where privacy expectations are most heightened."[109] In other words, the Court in *Dow* took into account the nature of the place being photographed–the exterior of business premises–in concluding that a search had not occurred. That place, the Court reasoned, "can perhaps be seen as falling somewhere between 'open fields' and curtilage, but lacking some of the critical characteristics of both." But, "for purposes of aerial surveillance," the *Dow* majority concluded, "the open areas of an industrial plant complex * * * are not analogous to the 'curtilage' of a dwelling"; instead,

> such an industrial complex is more comparable to an open field and as such it is open to the view and observation of persons in aircraft lawfully in the public airspace immediately above or sufficiently near the area for the reach of cameras.

As the four dissenting Justices in *Dow* complained, the majority never satisfactorily explained precisely why this is so, "nor does it explain how its result squares with *Katz* and its progeny." The Court does comment that the "intimate activities associated with family privacy and the home and its curtilage simply do not reach the outdoor area or spaces between structures and buildings of a manufacturing plant," but it is not apparent why that observation should alone carry the day. As the dissenters pointed out, certainly Dow "has a legitimate interest in preserving the privacy of the relevant portions of its open-air plants," as manifested by the company's considerable efforts in that regard. Indeed, the majority seems to concede as much with respect to physical intrusion into such areas. That leaves unexplained why the absence of physical trespass is not just as irrelevant here as it was in *Katz,* unless the explanation lies in the majority's reliance upon *Donovan v. Dewey*[110] and *Marshall v. Barlow's, Inc.*,[111] having to do with the proposition that business premises are subject to inspection pursuant to different and less strict Fourth

---

[108]Dow Chemical Co. v. United States, 476 U.S. 227, 106 S.Ct. 1819, 90 L.Ed.2d 226 (1986), discussed in Comments, 30 Ariz.L.Rev. 361 (1988); 75 Cal.L.Rev. 1767 (1987); 36 Cath.U. L.Rev. 667 (1987); 63 N.Y.U.L.Rev. 191 (1988); Notes, 18 Loyola U.L.J. 285 (1986); 40 Okla.L.Rev. 248 (1987); 56 U.Cin.L.Rev. 361 (1987); 66 Wash.U.

L.Q. 111 (1988).

[109]For further discussion of this point, see § 2.2(c).

[110]Donovan v. Dewey, 452 U.S. 594, 101 S.Ct. 2534, 69 L.Ed.2d 262 (1981).

[111]Marshall v. Barlow's, Inc., 436 U.S. 307, 98 S.Ct. 1816, 56 L.Ed.2d 305 (1978).

Amendment limitations.[112] But those cases concern *when* a search is constitutionally permissible, not with the *Dow* issue of *whether* any search has occurred. Moreover, as the *Dow* dissenters properly remind us, that line of cases "is not founded solely on the differences between the premises occupied by such business and homes, or on a conclusion that administrative inspections do not intrude on protected privacy interests and therefore do not implicate Fourth Amendment concerns," but rather "on a determination that the reasonable expectation of privacy that the owner of a business does enjoy may be adequately protected by the regulatory scheme itself." That this is so is highlighted by the fact that lesser Fourth Amendment standards also apply to safety inspections of residential premises.[113]

In any event, *Dow* does not cast doubt upon the other decisions discussed earlier. Certainly it does not conflict with *Soychak*, involving looking into a business building from a nonpublic vantage point; indeed, the majority in *Dow* emphasizes that "Dow plainly has a reasonable, legitimate, and objective expectation of privacy within the interior of its covered buildings, and it is equally clear that expectation is one society is prepared to observe."[114] Nor does the Court's decision conflict with *FMC*, involving a physical entry of a plant complex, for the "narrow issue raised" in *Dow* concerns observation "*without* physical entry," and the Court cautioned that "any actual physical entry by EPA into any enclosed area would raise significantly different questions."[115] Finally, it is well to note that *Dow* does not settle that any and all forms of photographic surveillance of the out-

---

[112]See § 10.2.

[113]See § 10.1.

[114]But see United States v. Pace, 955 F.2d 270 (5th Cir.1992), holding it no search to look into a windowless barn made of corrugated steel panels by looking through a small crack in the wall, where the court concluded *Dow Chemical* was trumped by the Court's later decision in United States v. Dunn, 480 U.S. 294, 107 S.Ct. 1134, 94 L.Ed.2d 326 (1987), text at note 37 supra: "Whatever *Dow Chemical* may have left open concerning the concept of a curtilage surrounding a business or commercial establishment, *Dunn* indicates that there is no business curtilage surrounding a barn lying within an open field."

[115]As stated in the post-*Dow* case of People v. Janis, 139 Ill.2d 300, 152 Ill.Dec. 100, 565 N.E.2d 633 (1990): "Outdoor commercial premises, like the interior of commercial buildings,

are protected from unreasonable searches under the fourth amendment. This is particularly true in cases where the business, by its nature, must be conducted outside."

See New York v. Burger, 482 U.S. 691, 107 S.Ct. 2636, 96 L.Ed.2d 601 (1987) (automobile junkyard); Donovan v. Dewey, 452 U.S. 594, 101 S.Ct. 2534, 69 L.Ed.2d 262 (1981) (stone quarries); People v. Janis, supra (it a search for police to enter rear yard behind plumbing business when business was closed, as area "is not open to the public for parking or any other use, and is not visible from any point of public access," and "is not accessible from any public ingress or egress" and no one permitted to use area "other than employees and other persons associated with the plumbing business during business hours"); Commonwealth v. Lutz, 512 Pa. 192, 516 A.2d 339 (1986) (relying on this qualification in *Dow*, court rules Fourth

door portions of business premises will fall outside the Fourth Amendment. For one thing, the majority acknowledges "that surveillance of private property by using highly sophisticated surveillance equipment not generally available to the public, such as satellite technology, might be constitutionally proscribed absent a warrant."[116] For another, and perhaps more significant, the Court in *Dow* intimates that whether the use of sophisticated equipment short of a satellite is a search, even in this context, depends to some extent on just what is discovered. Though the photograph in *Dow* apparently made it possible to see "power lines as small as 1/2-inch in diameter," the Court cautioned: "No objects as small as 1/2-inch in diameter such as a class ring, for example, are recognizable, nor are there any identifiable human faces or secret documents captured in such a fashion as to implicate more serious privacy concerns."[117]

Finally, mention must be made of the fact that a justified expectation of privacy in business premises terminates upon abandonment of those premises, just as is true of residential premises.[118] Illustrative is *Mullins v. United States*,[119] where the court concluded

> that the evidence clearly, unequivocally, and decisively established that no records were seized until *after* defendant had abandoned the property, including his records, in the office previously rented from Mrs. McCracken. Defendant does not contest the fact that no rent was paid for the office beginning November 1, 1971, and that he and his wife did not visit the office after November 1, 1971. Further, no business associate or employee was in the office after the last week of October, 1971. Mrs. McCracken testified that the United States District Attorney padlocked the office during Febru-

---

Amendment protections extend to business inspection involving entry of business premises even "where the business must, by its nature, be conducted outside").

[116]Governments are beginning to use satellite imagery for a variety of enforcement purposes, such as to detect the growing of crops without an irrigation permit, unreported property improvements, and unreported timber cutting. This practice will doubtless increase, for, as compared with taking photographs from airplanes, "satellite imagery can be much more cost-effective" and "is faster as well. * * * And as sharper-resolution photos become available, * * * the program could be used to look for objects as small as backyard porches, to check if homeowners have their construction permits in order." Kerber, When Is a Satellite Photo an Unreasonable Search?, Wall St.J., Jan. 27, 1998, p.

B.1, col. 3–4; p. B4, col. 4–5. See also Note, 13 J.Marshall J. Computer & Info.L. 729, 761–62 (1995) ("law enforcement agencies will eventually use the satellite in surveillance," and when they do it necessary to "require a warrant").

[117]See also L. R. Willson & Sons v. OSHRC, 134 F.3d 1235 (4th Cir.1998) (no search to inspect company's construction worksite, revealing that employees working on structural steel more than 80 feet above ground not wearing fall protective devices, by videotaping such activity through a 16-power camera lense from the roof of a nearby hotel; here, as in *Dow*, photography was limited to outside area).

[118]See § 2.3(a).

[119]Mullins v. United States, 487 F.2d 581 (8th Cir.1973).

ary, 1972, and both Mrs. McCracken and Ludtke testified that the business records of defendant were seized on June 12, 1972. * * * Defendant only asserts without any other evidentiary support that he did not intend to abandon the office and the records kept there. His subjective statement of intent is entitled to little weight and is patently at odds with the physical facts.

Different from all the foregoing situations are those in which the police intrusion into business premises is to obtain information regarding effects left by a customer for business purposes.[120] Illustrative is *Wabun-Inini v. Sessions*,[121] where, shortly after appellant left two rolls of film at a photo store for processing, an FBI agent entered and convinced the clerk to prepare and sell to him an extra set of prints from appellant's negatives. Appellant claimed this action intruded upon his Fourth Amendment rights, which it would seem was the case, for surely (except perhaps when the photographs depict criminal activity[122]) there should generally be recognized a justified expectation that when one takes film in for processing, the resulting photographs will be examined only by persons necessarily involved in that processing. But in light of such Supreme Court decisions as *Smith v. Maryland*[123] and *United States v. Miller*,[124] holding there is no expectation of privacy vis-a-vis the police when information is conveyed to a business entity for limited business purposes, it would not be surprising if the customer did not prevail on such an expectation-of-privacy analysis. In *Wabun-Inini* the court found it unnecessary to pass on the FBI's position—"that Wabun-Inini, by voluntarily conveying the film to a third party, lost all reasonable expectation of privacy in it"[125]—but ruled against the appellant upon a line of reasoning almost as troubling. Wabun-Inini lacked a privacy expectation (in the language of Justice Harlan in *Katz*)"that society is prepared to recognize as 'reasonable,'" because the "photographs were exposed to public view during the development process." Although there was no showing that the photographs were actually seen by any member of the public as

---

[120]Often cases of this kind are discussed in terms of standing. See § 11.3(d).

[121]Wabun-Inini v. Sessions, 900 F.2d 1234 (8th Cir.1990).

[122]United States v. Taylor, 515 F.Supp. 1321 (D.Me.1981) (photos of marijuana smuggling); People v. Hebel, 174 Ill.App.3d 1, 123 Ill.Dec. 592, 527 N.E.2d 1367 (1988) (lewd photos); Deemer v. Commonwealth, 920 S.W.2d 48 (Ky.1996).

[123]Smith v. Maryland, 442 U.S. 735, 99 S.Ct. 2577, 61 L.Ed.2d 220 (1979), discussed in § 2.7(c).

[124]United States v. Miller, 425 U.S. 435, 96 S.Ct. 1619, 48 L.Ed.2d 71 (1976), discussed in § 2.7(c).

[125]But see State v. Simmons, 955 S.W.2d 752 (Mo.1997) (after lawful inventory revealed pawn tickets and claim checks for photographs being developed, police went to the named premises and recovered the pawned jewelry and the photographs; defendant "relinquished any right of privacy he had in the phonographs or negatives themselves by giving them to the developer," and lacked "any expectation of privacy * * * in stolen jewelry located in a public pawn shop").

that process was carried out, the court explained it was enough to defeat the appellant's privacy claim that there was a "theoretical possibility" of such exposure. Specifically, when appellant's photos emerged from the printing machine they would be visible for 10–15 seconds to any member of the public who from a counter two and a half feet away managed to look past a pillar and freestanding sign. This conclusion makes a mockery of the *Katz* test, though perhaps no more so than the Supreme Court cases the court relied upon: *California v. Ciraolo*[126] and *California v. Greenwood*.[127]

However, a ruling against the customer will often be unobjectionable, as illustrated by *United States v. Ruiz*.[128] The defendant, after landing his aircraft at a small airport, paid to have it stored overnight in a certain hangar commonly used to store transient aircraft. Customers and employees had access to the premises during the daytime, but the facility was closed to customers at night, when owner Lyddon admitted police with a drug dog, who alerted to the presence of narcotics in defendant's plane, resulting in issuance and execution of a search warrant for that aircraft. While Ruiz claimed "he had a reasonable expectation of privacy in the hangar comparable to a tenant's expectation of privacy in his rented house or a motel occupant's expectation of privacy in his motel room," the court quite correctly concluded otherwise, noting that "this case is quite different because Mr. Ruiz stored the airplane in a hangar entirely controlled by Mr. Lyddon. And unlike the occupant of a rented home or motel room, Mr. Ruiz shared the hangar space with other Lyddon Aero Center customers."[129]

§ 2.4(c) Private areas in public places: rest rooms and fitting rooms

Police sometimes engage in clandestine surveillance of public rest rooms in an attempt to detect criminal conduct—typically use of drugs or homosexual activity—occurring therein.[130] Often this is accomplished by an officer taking a position on the roof or in a compartment above an enclosed stall and looking therein

---

[126]California v. Ciraolo, 476 U.S. 207, 106 S.Ct. 1809, 90 L.Ed.2d 210 (1986), discussed in § 2.3(g).

[127]California v. Greenwood, 486 U.S. 35, 108 S.Ct. 1625, 100 L.Ed.2d 30 (1988), discussed in § 2.6(c).

[128]United States v. Ruiz, 664 F.3d 833 (10th Cir.2012).

[129]The court added that the instant case was "more analogous to Minnesota v. Olson, 495 U.S. 91, 110 S.Ct. 1684, 109 L.Ed.2d 85 (1990), where the Supreme Court held that 'an overnight guest has a legitimate expecta-

tion of privacy in his host's home,' but '[t]he host may admit or exclude from the house as he prefers.' Thus, even if we assume that Mr. Ruiz had an expectation of privacy in the hangar akin to that of a houseguest, Mr. Lyddon as the owner could nevertheless admit law enforcement officials into the hangar."

[Section 2.4(c)]

[130]See J. Wambaugh, The New Centurions 198 (1970); Comment, 25 Willamette L.Rev. 855 (1989).

through a hole or vent. At least since the *Katz* decision,[131] it is clear beyond question that such surveillance into a closed rest room stall constitutes a Fourth Amendment search.[132]

Illustrative is *State v. Bryant*.[133] Suspecting that stalls in the St. Paul Montgomery Ward department store were being illegally used by homosexuals, the manager enlisted the aid of the police. An officer stationed himself over a ventilator in the ceiling above the rest room, which enabled him to view the toilet stalls below. The stalls were all enclosed by metal partitions and had doors that could be closed and secured from the inside; when the door was closed it was impossible to see into a stall from the public area of the rest room, other than to see the feet of the occupant. From his vantage point, the officer observed the defendant and another engaged in sodomy. Noting Justice Harlan's observation in *Katz* that a phone booth, though " 'accessible to the public' at other times, * * * is a temporarily private place whose momentary occupants' expectations of freedom from intrusion are recognized as reasonable," the *Bryant* court rightly concluded that "this language applies here, where the facilities provided assure the user of privacy as much as a telephone booth does."[134]

The court in *Bryant* noted at one point that the store "could have removed the doors if it saw fit, so that anyone using the facilities would have no expectation of privacy," thus suggesting that if there had been no doors on the stalls the case would have

---

[131]In the pre-*Katz* case of Smayda v. United States, 352 F.2d 251 (9th Cir.1965), such surveillance was upheld on the ground that no trespass had occurred. The case was severely criticized, see Notes, 17 Hastings L.J. 835 (1966); 19 Vand.L.Rev. 945 (1966); Comment, 23 Wash. & Lee L.Rev. 423 (1966), and has rightly been considered as undeserving of reliance since *Katz*. Kroehler v. Scott, 391 F.Supp. 1114 (E.D.Pa.1975).

Indeed, it has been suggested that "[a]nxieties about peepholes and undercover decoys in public lavatories, and about related investigative tactics targeted at homosexuality elsewhere, helped shape what the Court thought about the police and about the kinds of threats they posed." Sklansky, "One Train May Hide Another": Katz, Stonewall, and the Secret Subtext of Criminal Procedure, 41 U.C.Davis L.Rev. 875 (2008).

[132]This is not to suggest that a search warrant would always be required to conduct such a surveillance. In Kroehler v. Scott, 391 F.Supp. 1114

(E.D.Pa.1975), the court stated that it recognized "circumstances in which such surveillance practices might well satisfy Constitutional requirements. For example, should a law enforcement officer observe an individual enter the stall with drug-related paraphernalia or what appears to be such, his immediate surveillance of the stall in the manner here followed appears warranted. Similarly, when two individuals enter the stall, neither of whom appears to be an invalid or handicapped as to require assistance, the immediate surveillance of the stall, without the delay incident to a warrant appears to pass Constitutional muster."

[133]State v. Bryant, 287 Minn. 205, 177 N.W.2d 800 (1970).

[134]See also Britt v. Superior Court, 58 Cal.2d 469, 24 Cal.Rptr. 849, 374 P.2d 817 (1962); Bielicki v. Superior Court, 57 Cal.2d 602, 21 Cal.Rptr. 552, 371 P.2d 288 (1962); People v. Dezek, 107 Mich.App. 78, 308 N.W.2d 652 (1981) (use of video tape recorder as to conduct within stalls).

come out differently. Some courts have viewed the presence or absence of doors on the individual stalls in a public rest room as controlling.[135] The most striking illustration of this is *Buchanan v. State*,[136] a consolidated appeal of two cases both involving police surveillance from a concealed position above a men's room:

> The occupants are entitled to the modicum of privacy its design affords. * * * Where, however, the design is such that there is no right to expect privacy there can be no invasion of privacy. The men's restroom at the Sears store had commode stalls with doors which locked from the inside. A person inside such a stall with the door locked could be said to have some reasonable expectation of privacy. * * * The commode stalls in Reverchon Park had no doors and were visible to all in the general restroom area. In such a design there is no reasonable expectation of privacy from viewers. * * * Hence, while the method of the alleged clandestine surveillance was identical in each instance, the appellant's expectation of privacy under the circumstances was not reasonable where no doors were provided for the stalls.

To the contrary is *People v. Triggs*,[137] where an officer looked through an overhead vent into a doorless stall within a restroom in a public park and observed defendant and another engaged in sodomy:

> The People here urge us to hold that clandestine observation of doorless stalls in public rest rooms is not a "search," and hence is not subject to the Fourth Amendment's prohibition of unreasonable searches. This would permit the police to make it a routine practice to observe from hidden vantage points the rest room conduct of the public whenever such activities do not occur within fully enclosed toilet stalls and would permit spying on the "innocent and guilty alike." Most persons using public rest rooms have no reason to suspect that a hidden agent of the state will observe them. The expectation of privacy a person has when he enters a rest room is reasonable and is not diminished or destroyed because the toilet stall being used lacks a door. * * *
>
> The clandestine observations of rest rooms does not fall from the

---

[135]See the many cases cited and disapproved in People v. Triggs, 8 Cal.3d 884, 106 Cal.Rptr. 408, 506 P.2d 232 (1973). See also Young v. State, 109 Nev. 205, 849 P.2d 336 (1993) (though stalls doorless, they positioned so one does not look into the stalls from entrance or basin/urinal area of men's room at park; video surveillance through small hole in wall between rest room and adjoining maintenance room no search, as defendants "had no reasonable expectation of privacy in the doorless toilet stalls," especially in light of fact their homosexual activities "could be observed over or under the partitions and through holes in the partitions"). Cf. Liebman v. State, 652 S.W.2d 942 (Tex.Crim.App.1983) (defendant within booth of coin-operated movie arcade of adult theatre had justified expectation of privacy, as booths had 7 foot high walls and doors and locks). *Liebman* was distinguished in State v. Cooper, 29 Kan.App.2d 177, 23 P.3d 163 (2001) (defendant within video booth of adult entertainment establishment had no reasonable expectation of privacy, as door could not be locked and had gap at the top and the bottom).

[136]Buchanan v. State, 471 S.W.2d 401 (Tex.Crim.App.1971).

[137]People v. Triggs, 8 Cal.3d 884, 106 Cal.Rptr. 408, 506 P.2d 232 (1973).

purview of the Fourth Amendment merely through the removal of toilet stall doors. * * *

In seeking to honor reasonable expectations of privacy through our application of search and seizure law, we must consider the expectations of the innocent as well as the guilty. When innocent people are subjected to illegal searches—including when, as here, they do not even know their private parts and bodily functions are being exposed to the gaze of the law—their rights are violated even though such searches turn up no evidence of guilt.[138]

Katz, properly viewed, extends the limitations of the Fourth Amendment to those forms of police surveillance that cannot be "permitted to go unregulated by constitutional restraints."[139] Clandestine peeping into rest rooms is surely one type of surveillance that cannot be left to the whim of the police, whether there are doors on the stalls or not, and thus *Triggs* rather than *Buchanan* represents the better view. As one commentator has noted:

> *People v. Triggs* reflects the true spirit of the *Katz* case * * *. In *Katz,* the Supreme Court held that where the petitioner had sealed himself in a glass phone booth there was an expectation of privacy regarding his auditory transmissions, although there was no such expectation as to his visually observable conduct. The Court held, in effect, that one can have an expectation of privacy which is reasonable in one form while unreasonable in another. Specifically, the defendant in *Katz* had privacy from one *means* of surveillance, auditory, but not from another, visual. *Triggs* carries this concept of the expectation of privacy one step further and reflects its potential extrapolation by the court's emphasis on the *method* by which the observation was carried out.[140]

It does not follow, of course, that every instance of police observation in a public rest room constitutes a Fourth Amendment search. There is no justified expectation of privacy as to incriminating conduct occurring in the public area of a rest room rather than inside one of the stalls.[141] Moreover, if the police merely enter a rest room and see conduct occurring within a stall

---

[138]See also Kroehler v. Scott, 391 F.Supp. 1114 (E.D.Pa.1975) ("Since we find that the expectation of privacy is generated by the nature of the activity involved, rather than by the precise physical characteristics of the stall, whether or not the stalls had doors is not a crucially material inquiry"); State v. Holt, 291 Or. 343, 630 P.2d 854 (1981) (mere fact stall without door does not mean that observation by any means no search, but observation from adjoining stall through hole in partition no search; defendant had no reasonable expectation of privacy as to such observation because he had earlier peeked through the same hole).

[139]Amsterdam, Perspectives on the Fourth Amendment, 58 Minn.L.Rev. 349, 403 (1974).

[140]Note, 25 Hastings L.J. 575, 596 (1974). See also Comment, 55 Minn.L. Rev. 1255 (1971); Note, 22 Hastings Const.L.Q. 867 (1995).

[141]People v. Lynch, 179 Mich.App. 63, 445 N.W.2d 803 (1989) (no expectation of privacy as to conduct in public area of restroom at highway rest area, and this so though persons entering from outside have to pass through two separate doors); State v. Holt, 291 Or. 343, 630 P.2d 854 (1981) (defendant "had no reasonable expectation of privacy while in the common area of a

that is "readily visible and accessible"[142] to any member of the public who so enters, there is again no intrusion into a justified expectation of privacy.[143] This includes the situation in which the

---

public restroom").

    In State v. Jarrell, 24 N.C.App. 610, 211 S.E.2d 837 (1975), the act of oral copulation observed and photographed by the police from the attic of the rest room occurred near a window in the public area of the rest room. The court stated: "By using such a public place for their activities, defendants had no such expectation of privacy as society, or at least as this Court, is prepared to recognize as 'reasonable.' On the contrary, they risked observation, and we find here no constitutional right in defendants to demand that such observation be made only by some person of whose presence they were aware. In our opinion defendants here did not acquire the right to insulate their activities with Fourth Amendment protection merely by attempting to maintain a lookout for persons who might enter the restroom." The court rejected defendant's reliance upon Triggs.

    Jarrell is a hard case, for here again it could be contended that it is the nature of the surveillance that should be determinative, not how public the conduct was otherwise. It does seem, however, that the police conduct in Jarrell is not as offensive as that in Triggs.

    On covert electronic surveillance of common areas of public restrooms, see Comment, 6 Cooley L.Rev. 495 (1989).

[142]Bielicki v. Superior Court, 57 Cal.2d 602, 21 Cal.Rptr. 552, 371 P.2d 288 (1962).

[143]As the court stated in Triggs: "The Attorney General claims that criminal acts are often committed inside rest rooms within plain view of any member of the public who should happen to enter. Under such circumstances, the police need not resort to clandestine observation to apprehend individuals involved in such activities. When law enforcement officers suspect that crimes are being perpetrated, they are as free to enter rest rooms as

is any member of the public. Should they discover from a location open to the public, the commission of criminal acts, their observation of what is in plain view involves no search, and is not subject to the strictures of the Fourth Amendment."

    Consider in this regard Brown v. State, 3 Md.App. 90, 238 A.2d 147 (1968). An officer went into the men's room of a bar "to make a routine check," and saw defendant, whom he knew to be a drug addict, inside the booth. The officer was 6 feet tall, and the door of the booth was about 5 feet 5 inches, so the officer looked over the door (he testified: "I just stuck my head over. I didn't have to tip toe, or get up on my toes") and saw narcotics paraphernalia. The court held this was a search because of the "head physically intruding into the area," reasoning that Katz was not to be read "as overruling the rule that evidence is inadmissible because obtained by a physical trespass or actual intrusion into a constitutionally protected area." Consider also Wylie v. State, 164 Ga.App. 174, 296 S.E.2d 743 (1982) (looking into closed stall through crack in door was a limited search, justified on reasonable suspicion upon seeing two pairs of feet facing each other therein); People v. Mercado, 68 N.Y.2d 874, 508 N.Y.S.2d 419, 501 N.E.2d 27 (1986) (looking over wall from adjoining stall by standing on commode is a search, justified by reasonable suspicion in that one pair of feet but two voices heard in stall).

    Compare United States v. Billings, 858 F.2d 617 (10th Cir.1988) (no search for officer standing in public area to see leg within stall with package of white substance taped to ankle); Moore v. State, 355 So.2d 1219 (Fla.App.1978) (no search where officer walked into bus station rest room and then looked through 1/2" crack into stall and saw defendant taking cocaine); Swann v. State, 637 P.2d 888 (Okl.Crim.App.1981) (no search for officer to look under door to stall in

officer looks "through a gap between the bathroom stall door and the bathroom stall wall," at least where the officer "did not position herself in any way that would be unexpected by someone using the restroom."[144] Under certain circumstances, even an entry into a locked rest room will not amount to a search. *Kirsch v. State*[145] is such a case. There an officer was called to a gas station and told by the attendant that "there were three males in the restroom, and they had been in there for approximately thirty minutes, and didn't know whether anything was wrong with them or not." The officer opened the door with the key provided by the attendant and saw the men with narcotics paraphernalia. The court concluded that "no reasonable person would be justified in expecting absolute privacy in, or exclusive use of, the whole of such a facility, particularly where the length of such occupancy and use far exceeded, as here, normally permissible limits."[146]

Sometimes surveillance of fitting rooms in clothing stores is undertaken in an effort to detect shoplifting.[147] Such conduct should be assessed in the same fashion as rest room surveillance. Illustrative is *State v. McDaniel*,[148] where surveillance was conducted from a concealed position above the fitting room. The court there stated:

> A customer entering a fitting room of a department store for the purpose of partially disrobing and trying on clothing and closing the door or curtain of the fitting room behind her obviously is at-

bookstore where he heard sounds of defendant masturbating; "where the appellant's conduct is audible to the public we hold that there is no justified expectation of privacy"); State v. Holt, 291 Or. 343, 630 P.2d 854 (1981) (no search to look into open restroom stall); Green v. State, 566 S.W.2d 578 (Tex.Crim.App.1978) (no search where officer entered bookstore and, upon seeing two men enter booth for showing sex films, approached booth and through 3′5″ gap between curtain and edge of booth saw deviate sexual conduct).

[144]United States v. White, 890 F.2d 1012 (8th Cir.1989).

[145]Kirsch v. State, 10 Md.App. 565, 271 A.2d 770 (1970). See also United States v. Delaney, 52 F.3d 182 (8th Cir.1995) (where after defendant's lawful seizure for investigation defendant allowed to go to bathroom and defendant disobeyed officer's instructions by locking stall door, officer's looking into and entry of stall no search, as "there was no clandestine or surreptitious police surveillance"); People v.

Hunt, 77 Mich.App. 590, 259 N.W.2d 147 (1977) (gas station rest room not locked, but lack of reasonable expectation of privacy again based on conduct of defendant remaining there with another person over 30 minutes).

[146]See also United States v. Hill, 393 F.3d 839 (8th Cir.2005) (where "the restroom was designed for use by one person, it was located in a convenience store, and available for use by customers ane guests of the store," and defendant and female companion entered together and "remained there after being asked to leave," their reasonable expectation of privacy in the room "had expired").

[147]Another issue that often arises as to this practice, see, e.g., State v. Jensen, 83 Or.App. 231, 730 P.2d 1282 (1986), is whether the store detective engaging in the practice, perhaps with a grant of some law enforcement authority, is subject to the Fourth Amendment. See § 1.8.

[148]State v. McDaniel, 44 Ohio App.2d 163, 337 N.E.2d 173 (1975).

tempting to preserve as private her conduct in the fitting room area, even though to some degree it may be accessible to the public. Even though the customer may be aware, and may be deemed to have consented, to the possible intrusion into her privacy by the inadvertence of another customer or by a salesclerk who intends to assist the customer, the customer using the fitting room has a reasonable expectation that her privacy will not be invaded by an intruding eye from a concealed vantage point.[149]

§ 2.4(d) Detention facilities

In the pre-*Katz* case of *Lanza v. New York,*[150] the defendant objected to the electronic interception of a conversation he had with his brother, then confined in a New York jail, in a room at the jail set aside for such visits. Although the conviction was affirmed upon an independent state ground without resolving the constitutional claim, Justice Stewart observed for the majority:

> [W]ithout attempting either to define or to predict the ultimate scope of Fourth Amendment protection, it is obvious that a jail shares none of the attributes of privacy of a home, an automobile, an office, or a hotel room. In prison, official surveillance has traditionally been the order of the day. Though it may be assumed that even in a jail, or perhaps especially there, the relationships which the law has endowed with particularized confidentiality must continue to receive unceasing protection, there is no claimed violation of any such special relationship here.

After *Katz,* some courts relied upon this language in the course of holding that a prisoner has no justified expectation of privacy in his cell. Illustrative is *United States v. Hitchcock,*[151] refusing to suppress papers found in defendant's penitentiary cell because it is not "reasonable for a prisoner to consider his cell private." Some courts, however, took the view that while "entry into a controlled environment entails a dramatic loss of privacy" (so that "the justifiable reasons for invading an inmate's privacy are both obvious and easily established"), "the surrender of privacy is not total and * * * some residuum meriting the protection of the

---

[149]Consistent with *McDaniel* is In re Deborah C., 30 Cal.3d 125, 177 Cal.Rptr. 852, 635 P.2d 446 (1981) (no search where officer merely looked from corridor to see conduct visible through 2 ft. gap between door and floor).

Compare Gillett v. State, 588 S.W.2d 361 (Tex.Crim.App.1979) (over strong dissent objection that subjective expectations are not controlling and that therefore a justified expectation of privacy within a fitting room cannot be destroyed by a sign declaring there is no such privacy, court holds it no search for security officer to peek under door of fitting room, as

the "room was for use by the public on conditions established by the business").

[Section 2.4(d)]

[150]Lanza v. New York, 370 U.S. 139, 82 S.Ct. 1218, 8 L.Ed.2d 384 (1962).

[151]United States v. Hitchcock, 467 F.2d 1107 (9th Cir.1972). See also Donaldson v. Superior Court, 35 Cal.3d 24, 196 Cal.Rptr. 704, 672 P.2d 110 (1983) ("no federal case has repudiated the *Lanza* dictum or excluded a jail or police station conversation from evidence").

Fourth Amendment survives the transfer into custody."[152] But, at least as to the privacy interest in his cell and the possessory interest in his effects there of a convicted person incarcerated in prison, the Supreme Court held in *Hudson v. Palmer*[153] "that the Fourth Amendment has no applicability." This case is discussed elsewhere herein.[154]

On occasion an arrestee will be held in custody for some time at a place other than a jail, as where such a person is hospitalized because of illness or injury. When that is the case, the arrestee will not have the same expectation of privacy as would a nonarrested person in the same locale. Illustrative is *United States v. George*,[155] where police came into the arrestee's hospital room and searched the excrement in his bedpan for drugs, which were seized. In rejecting the defendant's claim this infringed upon his reasonable expectation of privacy, the court noted that the cases relied upon by the defendant regarding hospital room privacy involved persons not then under arrest.

§ 2.5 Vehicles

§ 2.5(a) Abandoned vehicles
§ 2.5(b) Examination of exterior of vehicle
§ 2.5(c) Determination of contents of vehicle without physical intrusion
§ 2.5(d) Examination of vehicle identification numbers

Research References

West's Key Number Digest
Automobiles ⬥349.5; Controlled Substances ⬥115; Searches and Seizures ⬥18, 28, 59 to 63, 165

Legal Encyclopedias
C.J.S., Motor Vehicles §§ 1333 to 1334; Searches and Seizures §§ 8, 13, 18, 20 to 24, 31 to 32, 37 to 38, 51, 70, 72, 78, 102

Introduction

Although automobiles and other means of transportation are not specifically mentioned in the Fourth Amendment, it is clear beyond question that vehicles are protected by the Amendment.[1]

---

[152]Bonner v. Coughlin, 517 F.2d 1311 (7th Cir.1975).

[153]Hudson v. Palmer, 468 U.S. 517, 104 S.Ct. 3194, 82 L.Ed.2d 393 (1984).

[154]See § 10.9. Suffice it to note here that the courts are not in agreement as to whether *Hudson* applies to pretrial detainees. See People v. Davis,

36 Cal.4th 510, 31 Cal.Rptr.3d 96, 115 P.3d 417 (2005) (collecting cases in both categories).

[155]United States v. George, 987 F.2d 1428 (9th Cir.1993).

[Section 2.5]

[1]See, e.g., Preston v. United States, 376 U.S. 364, 84 S.Ct. 881, 11 L.Ed.2d 777 (1964); Rios v. United

As the court put it in *United States v. Chadwick*,[2] "automobiles
are 'effects' under the Fourth Amendment, and searches and
seizures of automobiles are therefore subject to the constitutional
standard of reasonableness." It is true, of course, that "there is a
constitutional difference between houses and cars,"[3] in the sense
that vehicles are subject to lawful search in broader circumstances than would permit search of a house. The significance of
that difference is explored elsewhere in this Treatise.[4] The
concern here, by contrast, is with those situations in which it
may be said that a police investigative practice directed at a vehicle is no search at all, and thus not subject to the restraints of
the Fourth Amendment.

§ 2.5(a) Abandoned vehicles

Courts have frequently admitted into evidence objects found by
the police during the examination of an abandoned vehicle.
Sometimes this is done on the ground that the defendant, by
abandoning the vehicle, had no standing to object,[5] and sometimes
on the more general ground that such an examination is not a
search under the justified-expectation-of-privacy test of *Katz v.
United States*.[6] It is the latter ground that is of primary concern
here.

It is sometimes said that when the state relies upon an
abandonment theory to justify the discovery by police of evidence
in a vehicle there is presented "a question of intent."[7] Presumably
this means that it must be determined whether the "owner has
relinquished all right, title, claim, and possession, with intention
of not reclaiming it or resuming its ownership, possession or
enjoyment,"[8] for this is the classic approach of property law on
this issue. Assuming the owner has dealt with the vehicle in this
fashion, it would seem clear that police entry of the vehicle is not
objectionable on Fourth Amendment grounds.[9] However, many of
the decided cases cannot be explained on the basis of this property law definition of abandonment, and thus it appears that a
somewhat broader principle, derived from the *Katz* test, is ap-

---

States, 364 U.S. 253, 80 S.Ct. 1431, 4
L.Ed.2d 1688 (1960); Henry v. United
States, 361 U.S. 98, 80 S.Ct. 168, 4
L.Ed.2d 134 (1959); Brinegar v. United
States, 338 U.S. 160, 69 S.Ct. 1302, 93
L.Ed. 1879 (1949); Carroll v. United
States, 267 U.S. 132, 45 S.Ct. 280, 69
L.Ed. 543 (1925).

[2]United States v. Chadwick, 433
U.S. 1, 97 S.Ct. 2476, 53 L.Ed.2d 538
(1977).

[3]Chambers v. Maroney, 399 U.S.
42, 90 S.Ct. 1975, 26 L.Ed.2d 419
(1970).

[4]See ch. 7.

[Section 2.5(a)]

[5]E.g., State v. Achter, 512 S.W.2d
894 (Mo.App.1974). For more on the
standing issue, see § 11.3(e).

[6]Katz v. United States, 389 U.S.
347, 88 S.Ct. 507, 19 L.Ed.2d 576
(1967).

[7]United States v. D'Avanzo, 443
F.2d 1224 (2d Cir.1971).

[8]Black's Law Dictionary 13 (rev.
4th ed. 1968).

[9]State v. Lingar, 726 S.W.2d 728
(Mo.1987) (defendant pawned vehicle
at salvage yard, but then left town and
circumstances indicate "that he did

plicable here. As stated in *State v. Achter*,[10] the question is not whether someone "had a proprietary or possessory interest in the automobile at the time of the police activity in question," taking into account the "subtle distinctions of common law property concepts," but rather whether "defendant was entitled to and did have a reasonable expectation that the automobile would be free from governmental intrusion."

In determining whether the vehicle was dealt with in such a fashion as to dissipate any justified expectation of privacy therein, it is necessary to assess all the surrounding circumstances. In *United States v. Gulledge*,[11] for example, two men left a U-Haul trailer at a service station because their car was running hot; they were granted permission to leave the trailer for two or three days. After ten days passed without the trailer being removed, the attendant became suspicious and called the police, who looked inside and found stolen liquor. The court correctly held "that the trailer had been abandoned," for the men who left the trailer could hardly expect their privacy in it to continue after this passage of time in light of the condition upon which it was left at the station.[12]

---

not intend to return for it," thus vehicle abandoned); McDuff v. State, 939 S.W.2d 607 (Tex.Crim.App.1997) (where defendant had left his unattended car on motel parking lot for 6 days, and in interim had moved to Kansas City and was found there living under an alias, this shows defendant "intended to abandon the car").

[10]State v. Achter, 512 S.W.2d 894 (Mo.App.1974). See also United States v. Barlow, 17 F.3d 85 (5th Cir.1994); Duncan v. State, 281 Md. 247, 378 A.2d 1108 (1977); State v. Anderson, 548 N.W.2d 40 (S.D. 1996).

[11]United States v. Gulledge, 469 F.2d 713 (5th Cir.1972).

[12]See also United States v. Ramirez, 145 F.3d 345 (5th Cir.1998) (where defendant left his car in parking lot of restaurant and fled the area, and his family later told police he had fled to Mexico, car was abandoned); United States v. Taylor, 683 F.2d 18 (1st Cir.1982) (abandonment for Fourth Amendment purposes where yacht left ashore without a line made fast and without any writing indicating name of owner or intent to return); United States v. Hunter, 647 F.2d 566 (5th Cir.1981) (where defendant left disabled aircraft unattended and unlocked and in position where it a hazard to other planes using runway and did not notify an official at airport of his intention to move the plane to a safer location, plane was abandoned); United States v. Ramapuram, 632 F.2d 1149 (4th Cir.1980) (though defendant still owned a "junker" car kept immobilized and unlocked in an open field on a farm owned by defendant's family but rented to others, where defendant did not live, his "possessory interest in the farm and 'junker' was sufficiently lessened to compel the judgment that he could not legitimately expect [it] would remain secure from prying eyes"); State v. Sivri, 231 Conn. 115, 646 A.2d 169 (1994) (*Gulledge* deemed controlling, as defendant, upon learning of police desire to search his car in connection with murder, left it on street several miles from his home, removed the license plates, and then fled to Canada, and thus "cannot claim a reasonable expectation of privacy in its contents"); Hyde v. State, 275 Ga. 693, 572 S.E.2d 562 (2002) (irrelevant whether probable cause for search warrant for murder victim's car found in parking lot, as affidavit described car "as abandoned"

Gulledge should be compared with *Muegel v. State*,[13] where an officer saw a car parked along side a highway, looked in the glove compartment to find evidence of ownership, and found drugs. The defendant then arrived with a wrecker and was arrested. The court declared that the officer's action "was not a 'search' within the constitutional proscription" because this was an "abandoned car." But, while the result reached may have been correct because the officer was pursuing a legitimate "community caretaking" function with respect to the car,[14] it does not seem correct to say that one who leaves a car by the side of the road only temporarily has either abandoned the car or has lost any justified expectation of privacy as to the contents.[15]

---

by defendant, who "had regularly driven this car" before the murder and "was seen driving it in the days after the stabbing" two months earlier); State v. Tungland, 281 N.W.2d 646 (Minn.1979) (though defendant "continued to own the car," it was temporarily abandoned where "he parked the car on [a service station] lot without permission (express or implied), left intoxicating liquor in the car in open view, left the keys in the ignition, and failed to lock the doors"); State v. Sweet, 796 S.W.2d 607 (Mo.1990) (no expectation of privacy in junked vehicle left with trunk lid ajar and windows broken in rural area, near but not within curtilage of friend's residence); State v. Lemacks, 275 S.C. 181, 268 S.E.2d 285 (1980) (where defendant left car unattended, with keys in ignition and parked so as to constitute a hazard to vehicular traffic, this "constituted an abandonment for constitutional purposes").

[13]Muegel v. State, 257 Ind. 146, 272 N.E.2d 617 (1971). See also State v. Lawson, 394 So.2d 1139 (Fla.App. 1981), taking the remarkable position that if defendant was illegally stopped and questioned and then departed on foot, leaving his car parked in a parking lot, he had thereby abandoned the car.

[14]See § 7.4(b).

[15]See also United States v. Scrivner, 680 F.2d 1099 (5th Cir.1982) (no abandonment by leaving loaded trucks unlocked and with keys in them near own premises; "Such an act is doubtless careless and imprudent, but it scarcely suffices to support a conclusion that he has cast the vehicles aside, relinquishing his interest in them"); Agnew v. State, 376 So.2d 13 (Fla.App.1979) (airplane in flyable condition parked in an area where repairs were often made was not abandoned merely because no one was on board); State v. Baldwin, 396 N.W.2d 192 (Iowa 1986) (though occupants had quickly entered truck stop building on approach of police, "there was no police chase" or even a showing suspects aware of police presence; thus defendant "did not relinquish his reasonable expectation of privacy in the van and its contents by leaving the van unattended for 20–30 minutes at this interstate highway truck stop"); Duncan v. State, 281 Md. 247, 378 A.2d 1108 (1977) (court declared that when there has been no flight— compare cases in notes 18 and 19 infra—it is necessary to consider "such factors as the condition of the vehicle, its location, and the length of time it has remained there" in determining if the car has been abandoned, and then concluded that these factors did not show abandonment of a car parked for a brief period on a lawn, as there were no curbs and the area was by a shopping mall; court then concluded the car was abandoned because of defendant's "unequivocal disclaimer" of any interest in it; on this theory, see § 2.6(b)); Shum v. State, 97 Nev. 15, 621 P.2d 1114 (1981) (facts similar to *Muegel;* car not abandoned, and officer had no right to enter to seek identification where car had not been involved in accident, was not parked illegally,

Another type of case is that in which an automobile is deemed to be abandoned because it was left behind at the scene of a crime, apparently because of a hurried departure on foot by the perpetrator of the crime. In *Kurtz v. People*,[16] for example, evidence was found in a car parked at the back door of burglarized premises, and all indications were that the burglars had brought the car to the scene and had intended to use it to effect their escape. In holding that the car had been abandoned, the court adopted the following reasoning from *Thom v. State*:[17]

> Sometimes an automobile takes on the characteristics of a man's castle. Other times an automobile takes on the characteristics of an overcoat—that is, it is movable and can be discarded by the possessor at will. If appellant in his endeavors to avoid the clutches of the law had discarded his overcoat to make his flight more speedy, no one would think that an officer was unreasonably invading his privacy or security in picking up the overcoat and searching it thoroughly. In that situation most people would agree that the fleeing suspect had abandoned his coat as a matter of expediency as well as any rights relative to its search and seizure. What difference can there be when a fleeing burglar abandons his automobile to escape the clutches of the law? We can see no distinction and consequently hold that when property is abandoned officers in making a search thereof do not violate any rights or security of a citizen guaranteed under the Fourth Amendment.

Certainly there are circumstances where, from the manner in which a car was left at a crime scene, it may fairly be concluded

---

and was creating no hazard); State v. Guebara, 119 N.M. 662, 894 P.2d 1018 (App.1995) ("parking of a locked vehicle on private property for several weeks, with the consent of the property owners, did not signify that the vehicle was abandoned").

Compare State v. Amaya, 227 Mont. 390, 739 P.2d 955 (1987) (stolen car left impaled on guard rail of highway was abandoned).

Muegel does not really say that the defendant lost his expectation of privacy in all respects, for the court stressed that the officer's actions were "strictly limited to those areas of a vehicle where it would reasonably be expected that such a certification of registration might be found." Thus, the notion may be that by leaving the vehicle unattended and unlocked in these circumstances, the defendant had no justified expectation of privacy as to a certain part of the interior. Consider also United States v. Barlow, 17 F.3d 85 (5th Cir.1994) (court reaches questionable conclusion that car abandoned where defendant "left his car parked at night at the end of a public street, away from public parking, behind a shopping center and near its back alley where only deliveries occur, unlocked, and with key in the ignition," but then adds that this justifies only a limited intrusion, including in the glove compartment, "to identify its owner"); United States v. D'Avanzo, 443 F.2d 1224 (2d Cir.1971) (FBI agent followed certain truck, and when driver parked truck and ran off into nearby swamp, officer climbed onto truck and looked down into open top without disturbing tarpaulin; court held district court's finding of abandonment not clearly erroneous, but then cautiously stated "defendants relinquished any interest they may otherwise have had in protecting the privacy of the exposed portion of the dump truck").

[16]Kurtz v. People, 177 Colo. 306, 494 P.2d 97 (1972).

[17]Thom v. State, 248 Ark. 180, 450 S.W.2d 550 (1970).

that no justified expectation of privacy as to that vehicle exists.[18] However, the *Thom* reasoning overshoots the mark somewhat, and thus should not be taken to mean that a vehicle is abandoned, in the sense in which that word is here being used, whenever it is left parked in the vicinity of the place where a crime was committed. The fact of the matter is that a car and an overcoat are different; one can hardly expect privacy in an overcoat left on the street, but cars are regularly parked on the street for brief periods of time without an expectation that they will thereby be subject to entry.

Courts have also found cars to be abandoned when it appeared that the operator of the vehicle left the car behind in an effort to avoid apprehension by the police. Sometimes the car had actually been pursued by the police for some distance, after which the driver jumped from the car and fled on foot.[19] On other occasions the vehicle was parked when the occupant, upon seeing the police

[18]E.g., United States v. Washington, 12 F.3d 1128 (D.C.Cir. 1994) (in response to attempted *Terry* stop by police, car sped away and overturned; "the vehicle was abandoned once the defendants left it overturned in the alley and fled the scene"); United States v. Tate, 821 F.2d 1328 (8th Cir.1987) (defendant shot officer and then fled, leaving van on highway with windows down and door unlocked); Rodriquez v. State, 299 Ark. 421, 773 S.W.2d 821 (1989) (after high-speed chase, defendant fled car and left motor running and door open); People v. Hampton, 198 Colo. 566, 603 P.2d 133 (1979) (police stakeout interrupted attempted robbery, the 3 robbers fled on foot and left behind in parking lot with keys in ignition the car in which they arrived); People v. Washington, 90 Ill.App.3d 631, 45 Ill.Dec. 837, 413 N.E.2d 170 (1980) (defendant, bailee of car, abandoned it when, as reported by witnesses to robbery, he fled scene and left the car on the street unlocked and with keys in ignition); Henderson v. State, 695 P.2d 879 (Okl.Crim.App.1985) (high speed chase by police, defendant then stopped car and escaped on foot).

[19]United States v. Vasquez, 635 F.3d 889 (7th Cir.2011) (vehicle abandoned where defendant "ditched it and bolted off on the run"); United States v. Edwards, 441 F.2d 749 (5th Cir. 1971); State v. Asbury, 124 Ariz. 170,

602 P.2d 838 (App.1979); People v. Turner, 8 Cal.4th 137, 32 Cal.Rptr.2d 762, 878 P.2d 521 (1994) (car "abandoned" where driver and passenger left car parked, running, unlocked and with lights on); State v. Branam, 334 Mont. 457, 148 P.3d 635 (2006) (defendant's "act of fleeing from law enforcement and leaving the Escalade and its contents on the street constitutes abandonment," justifying impoundment and inventory); State v. Green, 44 Or.App. 253, 605 P.2d 746 (1980). Cf. United States v. Williams, 569 F.2d 823 (5th Cir.1978) (abandonment where defendant, upon noting he was being followed, unhooked trailer and left it in roadside rest area).

Compare United States v. Moody, 485 F.2d 531 (3d Cir.1973) (defendant fled from car he left in street during high speed chase by police, but government did not meet its burden to show abandonment, as it unclear whether defendant knew persons chasing him were police; if he did know, then he "was seeking both to avoid arrest and abandon the incriminating evidence in the trunk of his car," if he did not know, then "he only left his car temporarily in order to escape this danger"); State v. Dean, 206 Ariz. 158, 76 P.3d 429 (2003) (where defendant ignored police signal to stop and continued on until he parked in own driveway and ran into his residence, car "was not abandoned").

approach, exited the vehicle and took flight.[20] On still others, the automobile was left by the driver at the scene of an accident.[21]

Yet another type of abandonment case is that in which the owner turns permanent control of the vehicle over to another person, as in *Commonwealth v. Sero*.[22] After someone shot and killed defendant's wife while she was seated in his car, defendant gave the car to one of his employees, saying he never wanted to be in that car again in light of what had happened. That employee later allowed police to make certain tests on the car, a procedure that was upheld because of defendant's abandonment of the vehicle. Stressing that the "test for abandonment is whether the complaining party could retain a reasonable expectation of privacy in the property allegedly abandoned," the court correctly concluded that the fact "legal title had not been transferred is not determinative," and that defendant had no reasonable expectation because he had "expressed a desire not to maintain control over the car in any way."[23]

Some courts also find abandonment based upon the defendant's disclaimer to the police of any interest in the vehicle. Illustrative is *United States v. Hastamorir*,[24] where Lopez and another were observed placing brick-like packages into a station wagon. When

---

[20]United States v. Smith, 648 F.3d 654 (8th Cir.2011) (defendant "abandoned the Cadillac in the Taco Bell drive-through lane when he fled on foot" on approach of police); United States v. D'Avanzo, 443 F.2d 1224 (2d Cir.1971) (suspect truck was parked by driver, after which FBI agent approached, upon which the driver fled into swamp; held, truck abandoned, at least to the extent that would permit climbing onto truck and looking down into open portion); State v. Grissom, 251 Kan. 851, 840 P.2d 1142 (1992) (abandonment where defendant "was parked on private property without authorization" and "fled the apartment complex because of the arrival of the police"); Hunt v. Commonwealth, 488 S.W.2d 692 (Ky.App.1972) (officer entered roadside park, at which three men near car fled into the woods; two of them, who claimed to have been hitchhiking, were apprehended, but car was watched for four hours without driver returning; held, car had been abandoned). Consider also Hudson v. State, 642 S.W.2d 562 (Tex.App.1982) (car abandoned when driver of it, upon questioning by the police, ran away).

Compare Rambo v. State, 481 S.W.2d 378 (Tenn.1972) (no abandon-ment where driver fled after arrest, as "[b]efore the defendant made his escape the officers already had assumed custody of the car and had summoned a wrecker").

[21]State v. Anderson, 548 N.W.2d 40 (S.D. 1996) (abandonment where defendant, when his car collided with another vehicle, departed on foot and left car with keys in it at accident scene).

[22]Commonwealth v. Sero, 478 Pa. 440, 387 A.2d 63 (1978). See also People v. Sutherland, 223 Ill.2d 187, 307 Ill.Dec. 524, 860 N.E.2d 178 (2006) ("where, as here, an individual has left his vehicle unattended in a public place, transferred title to another person, expressed in writing his intention not to return for the vehicle, and later confirmed that he had no further use for the vehicle, that vehicle has been abandoned").

[23]Absent such a complete and permanent surrender of control, the issue would be whether the bailee could give consent effective against the bailor. See § 8.6(a).

[24]United States v. Hastamorir, 881 F.2d 1551 (11th Cir.1989).

he was questioned promptly thereafter, Lopez "denied any knowledge of the station wagon or its cargo," by which, the court concluded, he "effectively abandoned any fourth amendment rights he possessed in the station wagon and its contents." As discussed later,[25] a different result is called for when the disclaimer is of ownership but not possession or when the disclaimer is itself a consequence of improper police action.

§ 2.5(b) Examination of exterior of vehicle

"What a person knowingly exposes to the public," the Supreme Court declared in *Katz v. United States*,[26] "is not a subject of Fourth Amendment protection." This being so, it is apparent that when a vehicle is parked on the street or in a lot or at some other location where it is readily subject to observation by members of the public, it is no search for the police to look at the exterior of the vehicle.[27] In like circumstances, it is also not a search for the

---

[25]See § 2.6(b).

[Section 2.5(b)]

[26]Katz v. United States, 389 U.S. 347, 88 S.Ct. 507, 19 L.Ed.2d 576 (1967).

[27]United States v. Diaz-Castaneda, 494 F.3d 1146 (9th Cir.2007) ("license plate checks do not count as searches under the Fourth Amendment"); United States v. Ellison, 462 F.3d 557 (6th Cir.2006) ("a motorist has no reasonable expectation of privacy in the information contained on his license plate under the Fourth Amendment"); United States v. $109,179 in U.S. Currency, 228 F.3d 1080 (9th Cir.2000) ("insertion of the key into a car door [to] determine whether the key fit the lock" no search); Olabisiomotosho v. City of Houston, 185 F.3d 521 (5th Cir.1999) ("motorist has no privacy interest in her license plate number," and thus computer check may be run on observed number without reasonable suspicion); United States v. Rascon-Ortiz, 994 F.2d 749 (10th Cir.1993) (no search for officer to kneel down and look at undercarriage, even though flashlight and mirror used); United States v. Hensel, 699 F.2d 18 (1st Cir.1983) (no search to view license on car parked in driveway); Dorris v. State, 656 P.2d 578 (Alaska App.1982) (examination of tires no search); State v. Harding, 137 Ariz. 278, 670 P.2d

383 (1983) (noting license plate number on car being driven and calling in for license check no search); People v. Petersen, 110 Ill.App.3d 647, 66 Ill.Dec. 380, 442 N.E.2d 941 (1982) (no search to check damage to body of car parked on owner's property but parallel to railroad tracks). State v. Wilbourn, 364 So.2d 995 (La.1978) (police lawfully present in carport serving as entryway to defendant's house saw blood and hairs on front of car); Commonwealth v. A Juvenile (No. 2), 411 Mass. 157, 580 N.E.2d 1014 (1991) (no search to view exterior damage to car parked in driveway either from the road or from the driveway itself where it "the normal route by which to approach the front door of the residence"); State v. Weaver, 912 S.W.2d 499 (Mo.1995) ("Simply trying a key in an exterior lock of an automobile does not constitute a search"); State v. Neil, 350 Mont. 268, 207 P.3d 296 (2009) ("license plates contain public information," and defendant had "no expectation of privacy in a license plate which is knowingly exposed to the public"); State v. Robinson, 158 N.H. 792, 973 A.2d 277 (2009) (insertion of key in lock of car door no search, as "the mere information of ownership obtained from inserting a key into a door is not the type of information in which a defendant has a reasonable expectation of privacy"); State v. Richter, 145 N.H. 640, 765 A.2d 687 (2000), followed in State v.

police to take photographs of the vehicle,[28] and this includes the situation in which an officer utilizes ALPR (Automatic License Plate Recognition) technology[29] to determine that the vehicle is connected to past criminality.[30]

Reno, 150 N.H. 466, 840 A.2d 786 (2004) (visual inspection of license plate mounted on moving car in public view, as well as random computer check of such license, no search); Commonwealth v. Mangini, 478 Pa. 147, 386 A.2d 482 (1978) (examination of tread and groove patterns on tires of car parked on public high school parking lot).

Compare United States v. DeBardeleben, 740 F.2d 440 (6th Cir.1984) (placing key in door as means of identifying car is a search, but a minimal intrusion permissible on reasonable suspicion); State v. Goude, 49 Or.App. 721, 620 P.2d 957 (1980) (where car up on blocks in defendant's driveway, inspection to extent of crawling around on hands and knees near the rear of the car to view the rear end, brake line and suspension was a search, a defendant "could reasonably expect that people would not be crawling around his car"). For further discussion of use of keys as a minimally intrusive search, see § 2.3 at note 82.

Consider also United States v. Cowan, 674 F.3d 947 (8th Cir.2012) (where police lawfully acquired suspect's set of keys and key fob, and then pressed the alarm button on the fob to determine the suspect had a car parked nearby, this no search, as defendant "did not have a reasonable expectation of privacy in the identity of his car," as the "officers could have obtained the identification information by conducting a background check on the car's license plates or vehicle identification number").

[28]Dumbsky v. State, 508 N.E.2d 1274 (Ind.1987) (truck parked in defendant's driveway and police properly on premises to execute arrest warrant); Fisher v. State, 259 Ind. 633, 291 N.E.2d 76 (1973) (pictures taken "of a vehicle sitting in open view in a vacant lot"); Hudson v. State, 588 S.W.2d 348 (Tex.Crim.App.1979) (pic-

tures taken of car parked on street). State v. Wettstein, 28 Utah 2d 295, 501 P.2d 1084 (1972) (photographs taken from alley of vehicle parked at apartment building parking lot).

Also, assuming a lawful seizure of a car by the police, it is no search to then photograph the exterior of the seized car. State v. Serna, 290 N.W.2d 446 (Minn.1980).

[29]"Cameras mounted on top of patrol cars automatically photograph license plates at the rate of hundreds per minute. The images are converted into letters and numbers and sent to a computer located in the trunk of the police vehicle. The computer compares the information to a database containing a list of license plates corresponding to cars that have been reported stolen, where registration or insurance coverage has lapsed, or other similar violations of law. These lists are known in law enforcement as 'hot lists'. If a license plate read by the camera matches one in the database, an alarm sounds on the laptop computer mounted between the driver and passenger seats, alerting the officer to the nature of the crime or violation associated with the plate." People v. Davila, 27 Misc.3d 921, 901 N.Y.S.2d 787 (2010). For further descriptions, see Hubbard, Automatic License Plate Recognition: An Exciting New Law Enforcement Tool with Potentially Scary Consequences, 18 Syrac.Sci. & Tech.L.Rep. 3 (2008); Rushin, The Judicial Response to Mass Police Surveillance, 2001 U.Ill.J.L.Tech. & Pol'y 281.

[30]See Hubbard, Automatic License Plate Recognition: An Exciting New Law Enforcement Tool with Potentially Scary Consequences, 18 Syrac.Sci. & Tech.L.Rep. 3 (2008) (as "no expectation of privacy in the information contained on the plates," though defendant might claim "an expectation of anonymity, while driving on a crowded freeway where a human could

Worthy of note in this connection is the Supreme Court case of *Cardwell v. Lewis*,[31] where the defendant, in response to a request that he appear for questioning in connection with a homicide investigation, parked his car in a commercial parking lot nearby before appearing as requested. After some questioning, the police placed him under formal arrest and then had his car towed from the parking lot to the police impoundment lot. The next day a technician matched the cast of a tire impression made at the crime scene with the tread of the right rear tire on the car, and also took a small paint sample from the car and determined it matched paint on the fender of the victim's car. One issue presented by these facts was whether the warrantless seizure of the car, that is, the towing in of the car, was constitutionally permissible.[32] On this question, the Court was divided.[33] Of interest here, however, is the later examination of the car. As to this, the plurality opinion[34] appears to have concluded[35] that this was not a search:

---

not possibly process all the license plates that passed at a high rate of speed"); Rushin, The Judicial Response to Mass Police Surveillance, 2001 U.Ill.J.L.Tech. & Pol'y 281, 310, 312 (as "every time a person enters a public highway, their actions are visible to police officers, traffic cameras, tollbooth surveillance, and all other persons on the thoroughfare," and "ALPR does not give law enforcement any extrasensory ability"). More troublesome is the data collection aspect of ALPR; see § 2.7, text at note 325.

[31]Cardwell v. Lewis, 417 U.S. 583, 94 S.Ct. 2464, 41 L.Ed.2d 325 (1974).

[32]On this aspect of the case, see § 7.2.

[33]The plurality opinion answered in the affirmative; the four dissenters answered in the negative; Powell, J., concurring, did not reach the issue.

[34]The dissenters found it unnecessary to confront this question. They stated: "In casting about for some way to avoid the impact of our previous decisions, the plurality opinion first suggests * * * that no 'search' really took place in this case, since all that the police did was to scrape paint from the respondent's car and make observations of its tires. Whatever merit this argument might possess in the abstract, it is irrelevant in the circumstances disclosed by this record. The argument is irrelevant for the simple

reason that the police before taking the paint scrapings and looking at the tires, first took possession of the car itself. The Fourth and Fourteenth Amendments protect against 'unreasonable searches and *seizures*,' and there most assuredly was a seizure here."

This type of problem is reflected in some lower court cases. See, e.g., United States v. George, 971 F.2d 1113 (4th Cir.1992) (defendant's truck was impounded and tires *seized* therefrom; though warrant to search truck for the tires invalid as lacking probable cause, admission into evidence of the tires upheld on ground defendant "does not have an objectively reasonable expectation of privacy in tires on a truck that he drives and parks in public places").

[35]Actually, the case can just as easily be read as saying that there was a reasonable search. Immediately following the excerpt set out in the text here the plurality opinion states: "Under circumstances such as these, where probable cause exists, a warrantless examination of the exterior of a car is not unreasonable under the Fourth and Fourteenth Amendments." This more cautious approach may have been taken so as to avoid the necessity of expressly concluding that the taking of a paint sample is within the "plain view" concept.

In the present case, nothing from the interior of the car and no personal effects, which the Fourth Amendment traditionally has been deemed to protect, were searched or seized and introduced in evidence. With the "search" limited to the examination of the tire on the wheel and the taking of paint scrapings from the exterior of the vehicle left in the public parking lot, we fail to comprehend what expectation of privacy was infringed. Stated simply, the invasion of privacy, "if it can be said to exist, is abstract and theoretical."[36]

More recently, a five-member majority of the Supreme Court, in the *Class* case described below, expressly endorsed the *Cardwell* plurality's conclusion that examination of the exterior of an automobile "does not constitute a 'search' " because the vehicle "is thrust into the public eye."[37]

---

[36]See also United States v. Muniz-Melchor, 894 F.2d 1430 (5th Cir.1990) (where truck lawfully stopped at Border Patrol checkpoint 70 miles from border, it no search for agent to tap side of propane tank, which by absence of a ringing sound indicated the tank's exterior had been penetrated in some manner; "tapping did not expose its contents," the "tank was a part of the exposed exterior of the truck," and this defendant "must have reasonably expected that someone, such as a gasoline station attendant, might lean against the tank or touch it in some manner"); Watkins v. State, 296 Ark. 345, 756 S.W.2d 907 (1988) (relying on *Cardwell*, court approves police conduct, when they observed one license plate on top of another, of removing top plate—already determined not to be registered to any vehicle—to see underneath plate, as the "very purpose of a license plate is to identify the owner of a car should the need arise"); Deshazier v. State, 155 Ga.App. 526, 271 S.E.2d 664 (1980) (relying on *Cardwell*, court holds photographing and taking paint scrapings from car not an intrusion into any reasonable expectation of privacy); Dumbsky v. State, 508 N.E.2d 1274 (Ind.1987) (police lawfully on property tried gas cap left at crime scene on truck and found it fit; this no search, as "the experiment with the gas cap was even less intrusive than the removal of paint allowed in *Cardwell*"); State v. Skelton, 247 Kan. 34, 795 P.2d 349 (1990) ("no Fourth Amendment violation occurred

in the seizure of the vegetation and soil from the exterior of the car under *Cardwell* because an individual has no reasonable expectation of privacy in the exterior of a car parked in a public lot"); State v. Pratt, 16 So. 3d 1163 (La.2009) (officer's "discovery of the magnetic key boxes attached to the underside frame of the car [parked at gas station] did not constitute a search"); Department of Transportation v. Armacost, 299 Md. 392, 474 A.2d 191 (1984) (vehicle emission inspection by inserting test probe 10″ into exhaust pipe; applying *Cardwell,* court concludes "it unlikely that vehicle owners have a reasonable expectation of privacy in the exhaust gases located 10 inches from the end of their exhaust systems"); State v. Timms, 505 A.2d 1132 (R.I.1986) (removal of wire from front grill of seized car "is analogous to [situation] where police, having already lawfully seized a car, scraped mud from the tire to use it as evidence"); Pellatz v. State, 711 P.2d 1138 (Wyo.1986) (no search to examine backhoe on open semi-truck trailer parked on public parking lot).

[37]"There is thus little question in the aftermath of *Cardwell* and *Class* that one does not have a reasonable expectation of privacy in the visible exterior parts of an automobile that travels the public roads and highways." United States v. George, 971 F.2d 1113 (4th Cir.1992).

In United States v. Jones, __ U.S. __, 132 S.Ct. 945, 181 L.Ed.2d 911 (2012), the Court held that attach-

§ 2.5(c) Determination of contents of vehicle without physical intrusion

It is a fair generalization that if a law enforcement officer is able, by the use of his natural senses,[38] to discover what is inside a vehicle while "standing in a place where he had a right to be,"[39] this discovery does not constitute a Fourth Amendment search. This is true even if the vehicle had been in motion and was stopped by the officer in advance of the viewing, provided of course that the stopping was lawful, for otherwise the viewing would be a fruit of the illegal seizure of the vehicle.[40] And thus

---

ing a GPS device to the undercarriage of a vehicle "for the purpose of obtaining information" was a search, and distinguished *Cardwell* by asserting it was unclear whether the plurality there was saying that "no search occurred" or that "the search was reasonable."

[Section 2.5(c)]

[38]On the significance of using aids to the senses, see § 2.2. Where the windows are coated with a substance which darkens them, so that the interior of the van can be seen only by placing one's face against the glass and cupping one's hands around one's eyes, such actions "did not convert his view into a search," as they are "less intrusive than the use of artificial means to illuminate the interior." United States v. Head, 783 F.2d 1422 (9th Cir.1986). Also, the police may photograph that which is observable from outside the vehicle. State v. Cain, 400 N.W.2d 582 (Iowa 1987).

[39]United States v. Fuentes, 379 F.Supp. 1145 (S.D.Tex.1974).

[40]United States v. Rumley, 588 F.3d 202 (4th Cir.2009) (gun seen in car after traffic stop and passenger asked to step out of vehicle); United States v. Desir, 257 F.3d 1233 (11th Cir.2001) (vehicle stopped for traffic violation); United States v. Beatty, 170 F.3d 811 (8th Cir.1999); United States v. Lloyd, 13 F.3d 1450 (10th Cir.1994) (vehicle stopped for erratic driving); United States v. Lara, 517 F.2d 209 (5th Cir.1975) (vehicle lawfully stopped on reasonable suspicion of criminal activity); People v. Lomax, 49 Cal.4th 530, 112 Cal.Rptr.3d 96, 234 P.3d 377 (2010) (gun seen within vehi-

cle after lawful traffic stop); People v. Naranjo, 686 P.2d 1343 (Colo.1984) (car stopped for speeding); State v. Aillon, 202 Conn. 385, 521 A.2d 555 (1987) (vehicle lawfully stopped on reasonable suspicion of criminal activity); State v. Wyatt, 67 Haw. 293, 687 P.2d 544 (1984) (car stopped for driving without lights); State v. Munoz, 149 Idaho 121, 233 P.3d 52 (2010) (marijuana seen within car after stop on reasonable suspicion passenger was person wanted for felony probation violation); Avant v. State, 528 N.E.2d 74 (Ind.1988) (car stopped on reasonable suspicion of criminal activity); State v. Lamp, 322 N.W.2d 48 (Iowa 1982) (vehicle lawfully stopped); State v. Graham, 273 Kan. 844, 46 P.3d 1177 (2002) (vehicle stopped to arrest passenger, wanted on outstanding probation violation warrant); Chavies v. Commonwealth, 354 S.W.3d 103 (Ky.2011) (vehicle stopped for reckless driving); State v. Hunt, 25 So. 3d 746 (La.2009) (vehicle stopped for traffic violation); Commonwealth v. Alvarado, 420 Mass. 542, 651 N.E.2d 824 (1995) (valid traffic stop of vehicle); Walter v. State, 28 S.W.3d 538 (Tex.Crim.App. 2000) (valid stop; it makes no difference that looking inside was preparatory for anticipated search that would have been illegal); Carson v. Commonwealth, 244 Va. 293, 421 S.E.2d 415 (1992) (vehicle lawfully stopped at toll booth; approach of uniformed officer not itself a seizure illegally extending the lawful stop); Delong v. Commonwealth, 234 Va. 357, 362 S.E.2d 669 (1987) (car lawfully stopped because occupants involved in shooting).

Compare Hicks v. United States, 705 A.2d 636 (D.C.App.1997) (though

the Supreme Court in *New York v. Class*[41] concluded, as to a car lawfully stopped for traffic violations, that a "mere viewing" of the interior would not constitute a search.

The most common case is that in which the officer uses the sense of sight to detect what is inside the vehicle.[42] "It is not unlawful, but entirely lawful, for a police officer who is on a public street or sidewalk to look, either deliberately or inadvertently, into an automobile parked on the street and to observe what is exposed therein to open view."[43] Likewise, there is "no rule which

car parked when police approached, police blocked vehicle with their car to ensure against defendant's departure before looking through window and seeing drugs within, and thus observation a fruit of that illegality); State v. Hoven, 269 N.W.2d 849 (Minn.1978) (viewing of bag of marijuana in truck not lawful plain view where police control of truck due to pretext arrest); State v. Meadows, 170 W.Va. 191, 292 S.E.2d 50 (1982), overruled on other grounds by, State v. Dunbar, 229 W. Va. 293, 728 S.E.2d 539 (2012) (viewing of marijuana in car not lawful where prior stopping illegal).

Consider also the unduly strict view taken in State v. Banks, 363 So.2d 491 (La.1978), holding that where a car was stopped for reckless driving and the driver arrested, the later act of the police in looking through the car window while it was parked on the shoulder of the highway was illegal because the state "failed to show that the police officers had prior justification for approaching defendant's car after his full custodial arrest." Just why there must be some special justification even to approach a car parked by the highway is not explained. The *Banks* limitation was rejected in Commonwealth v. Lehman, 265 Pa.Super. 480, 402 A.2d 539 (1979) (rejecting trial judge's suppression on theory that officer lawfully stopped car but had no reason to stand by car once driver exited). See also State v. Powell, 99 N.M. 381, 658 P.2d 456 (App.1983) (no search to look into window of vehicle lawfully stopped even though investigation justifying the stop had been completed); State v. Jackson, 296 Or. 430, 677 P.2d 21 (1984) (looking into stopped car proper though car

stopped for traffic violation and officer had already returned license to driver, and though officer walked around the car rather than directly back to squad car).

[41]New York v. Class, 475 U.S. 106, 106 S.Ct. 960, 89 L.Ed.2d 81 (1986). See Maclin, New York v. Class: A Little-Noticed Case with Disturbing Implications, 78 J.Crim.L. & C. 1 (1987).

[42]E.g., Colorado v. Bannister, 449 U.S. 1, 101 S.Ct. 42, 66 L.Ed.2d 1 (1980); United States v. Rumley, 588 F.3d 202 (4th Cir.2009); Boone v. Spurgess, 385 F.3d 923 (6th Cir.2004); Redd v. State, 240 Ga. 753, 243 S.E.2d 16 (1978); State v. Graham, 273 Kan. 844, 46 P.3d 1177 (2002); Chavies v. Commonwealth, 354 S.W.3d 103 (Ky. 2011); State v. Hunt, 25 So. 3d 746 (La.2009); State v. Renfrew, 122 N.H. 308, 444 A.2d 527 (1982); Commonwealth v. Petroll, 558 Pa. 565, 738 A.2d 993 (1999); Delong v. Commonwealth, 234 Va. 357, 362 S.E.2d 669 (1987).

[43]Beachum v. United States, 19 A.3d 311 (D.C.App.2011) (no search to shine flashlight into parked car, revealing handgun); Cook v. Commonwealth, 216 Va. 71, 216 S.E.2d 48 (1975). See also United States v. Allen, 573 F.3d 42 (1st Cir.2009) (police saw gun in car "by simply leaning over the hood and shining his flashlight into the window"); United States v. Thornton, 197 F.3d 241 (7th Cir.1999) (package seen through open door when passenger got out of car parked on street, prior to any police illegality); United States v. Martin, 806 F.2d 204 (8th Cir.1986); State v. Munoz, 149 Idaho 121, 233 P.3d 52 (2010) (police saw marijuana in car af-

precludes the introduction into evidence of objects seen through the window of an automobile by a law officer who in the performance of his duties is making a blanket surveillance of automobiles in a public parking lot by looking through the windows."[44]

---

ter looking in door driver left open upon exiting); State v. Cullor, 315 N.W.2d 808 (Iowa 1982); Hodge v. State, 761 P.2d 492 (Okl.Crim.App. 1988) (police looked in window of parked pickup truck and saw couple engaged in intercourse); State v. Campbell, 103 Wash.2d 1, 691 P.2d 929 (1984).

[44]State v. Flores, 305 So.2d 292 (Fla.App.1974) (parking lot on school campus). See also United States v. Gooch, 499 F.3d 596 (6th Cir.2007) (police lawfully positioned when they saw gun in defendant's car, notwithstanding car owner's claim of reasonable expectation in that area because it VIP parking area for nearby club, as the "area was within a large parking lot that was shared by several commercial establishments" and "there was no barrier * * * that prevented pedestrians from walking through the VIP area of the parking lot during the hours the valet service was in operation"); United States v. Reed, 733 F.2d 492 (8th Cir.1984) (defendants without expectation of privacy in construction company parking lot located in commercial area, bounded on 3 sides by public streets, with fenced gate left open) United States v. Sparks, 291 F.3d 683 (10th Cir.2002) (no search to look through open door of parked truck where defendant had left door open upon alighting to examine package by side of road); United States v. Hatten, 68 F.3d 257 (8th Cir.1995) (no search to look into vehicle parked on lot of night club); United States v. Ware, 914 F.2d 997 (7th Cir.1990) (vehicle parked on parking lot of hospital); United States v. Head, 783 F.2d 1422 (9th Cir.1986) (van on store parking lot; no search even though van had darkened glass and officer could see inside only by pressing face to glass and cupping hands around eyes); United States v. Bellina, 665 F.2d 1335 (4th Cir.1981) (no search to look in window of airplane, as a "plane parked at a public

airport without any coverings over all of its windows and with the curtains open on some of the windows is not an object in which it can be said a party has a legitimate expectation of privacy"); United States v. Finch, 679 F.2d 1083 (4th Cir.1982) (no search to look into camper on motel parking lot); State v. Kuskowski, 200 Conn. 82, 510 A.2d 172 (1986) (vehicle parked in public boat launch area); State v. Graham, 200 Conn. 9, 509 A.2d 493 (1986) (vehicle parked in lot accessible to public); Albo v. State, 379 So.2d 648 (Fla.1980) (no search to look into motor home parked on restaurant parking lot); Catchings v. State, 256 Ga. 241, 347 S.E.2d 572 (1986) (vehicle parked in lot of apartment complex); State v. Wong, 68 Haw. 221, 708 P.2d 825 (1985) (no search to watch marijuana transfer in car parked on shopping center parking lot); State v. Rusher, 468 A.2d 1008 (Me.1983) (no search to look in open door of motor home on parking lot); State v. Harriman, 467 A.2d 745 (Me.1983) (no search to look in windows of van on shopping mall parking lot); Commonwealth v. Sergienko, 399 Mass. 291, 503 N.E.2d 1282 (1987) (vehicle in public parking lot); State v. Vohnoutka, 292 N.W.2d 756 (Minn. 1980) (vehicle parked in parking lot of closed gas station at 5 a.m.); State v. Mann, 203 N.J. 328, 2 A.3d 379 (2010) (no search to look through open window into vehicle parked in restaurant parking lot); State v. Garrett, 584 N.W.2d 502 (N.D.1998) (vehicle parked in public parking area of recreational area); Roney v. State, 819 P.2d 286 (Okl.Crim.App.1991) (car parked in parking lot of store, officer approached because license plate could not be read); Commonwealth v. Milyak, 508 Pa. 2, 493 A.2d 1346 (1985) (no search to shine light into van parked on restaurant parking lot); State v. Trudeau, 165 Vt. 355, 683 A.2d 725 (1996) (vehicle parked in parking lot of closed commercial establishment);

The same is true of a vehicle parked in an open "public place" such as a gas station[45] or inside a structure, such as a repair shop, that is open to the public.[46] If a vehicle is located on private property, but the police have made a lawful entry upon that property for some legitimate reason, what they see in plain view in the car while present at a place on that property consistent with the reason for their presence is also admissible.[47]

Sometimes the police detect the contents of a vehicle by the sense of smell, in which case same result obtains. "This olfactory impression * * * comes under the plain view doctrine which applies to all sensory impressions gained by an officer who is legally present in the position from which he gains them."[48] In *United States v. Martinez-Miramontes*,[49] where a customs agent approached a parked car and, by sniffing around a crevice where the trunk closed, detected the odor of marijuana, the court concluded that this degree of scrutiny was not objectionable: "We find no distinction of substance between leaning down and turning the head to look inside a motor vehicle to see articles which then come within the 'plain view' doctrine * * * and leaning down and sniffing to detect the odor of marijuana."[50] But if the officer leans into an open window to detect the odor, then there *has*

State v. Hanshaw, 170 W.Va. 354, 294 S.E.2d 157 (1982) (no search to look at what visible in back of truck parked on public lot).

[45]United States v. Thornton, 463 F.3d 693 (7th Cir.2006).

[46]United States v. Mercado, 307 F.3d 1226 (10th Cir.2002) ("officer was at liberty to look in the windows of the van" after defendant "left it at a [repair] shop open to the public twenty-four hours a day").

[47]United States v. Brown, 653 F.3d 656 (8th Cir.2011) (shining flashlight into car no search, as officer lawfully on driveway where it parked "to investigate a call for police assistance"); United States v. Galaviz, 645 F.3d 347 (6th Cir.2011) (police entry of part of driveway "directly abutting the public sidewalk" lawful and thus seeing gun within car parked there a lawful plain view); United States v. Good, 780 F.2d 773 (9th Cir.1986); Scott v. State, 599 So.2d 1222 (Ala.Crim. App.1992) (officers "legitimately on the premises of the apartment complex in which the appellant resided because they were attempting to execute two warrants to arrest the appellant");

State v. Garcia, 374 So.2d 601 (Fla. App.1979); State v. Doile, 244 Kan. 493, 769 P.2d 666 (1989) (car parked on parking lot of private club, where officers were "on official business—to quell a fight reported in the club"); State v. Daigle, 344 So.2d 1380 (La.1977); State v. Godsey, 202 Mont. 100, 656 P.2d 811 (1982); State v. Byerley, 635 S.W.2d 511 (Tenn.1982); State v. Lee, 633 P.2d 48 (Utah 1981); McDermott v. State, 870 P.2d 339 (Wyo.1994) (officers "had a right to be where they were" when they saw evidence in defendant's car, parking in driveway, as police on way to house to question occupants).

[48]United States v. Fuentes, 379 F.Supp. 1145 (S.D.Tex.1974).

[49]United States v. Martinez-Miramontes, 494 F.2d 808 (9th Cir. 1974).

[50]See also State v. Villa-Perez, 835 S.W.2d 897 (Mo.1992) ("act of standing near and inhaling or sniffing at the truck's rear door was not a search").

As for use of a drug dog to smell drugs within a vehicle, see § 2.2(g).

been a search.[51]

There may be circumstances, however, in which the nature of the scrutiny—albeit not involving a trespass inside the vehicle—will be such as to warrant the search appellation under the test of *Katz v. United States*.[52] *Katz* rejects the no-trespass-ergo-no-search notion in favor of a value judgment as to what privacy expectations are deserving of constitutional protection, and it is fully consistent with that approach to suggest that people should be entitled to expect privacy within their vehicles without resorting to extraordinary measures to conceal all their contents. That is, while it has been said one "has a lesser expectation of privacy in a motor vehicle" because it "travels public thoroughfares where both its occupants and its contents are in plain view,"[53] the fact remains that in some instances the contents are not readily viewable because the owner of the vehicle has taken reasonable steps to keep them private. When that is the case, that privacy is deserving of protection even though some nontrespassory means of breaching the privacy are in fact available to the police.

Instructive in this regard is the case of *United States v. Bradshaw*.[54] Agents came onto defendant's property for the legitimate purpose of questioning him, and while there detected a suspicious odor coming from defendant's truck. One agent then looked through a crack between the rear doors of the truck and observed incriminating evidence. The court concluded that what was detected by the sense of smell was no search, but that on these facts the visual observation was a search:

> It was not possible for Agent Williams to make this confirmatory observation without exceeding the original purpose of his intrusion, which had justified his presence on defendant's property up to that point, and making a further intrusion into an area of protected privacy. Objects lying on the bed of the truck could not be seen except by someone who took special pains to look through the crack. The truck was parked on defendant's property very near to his residence. Under such circumstances, the defendant had a reasonable expectation that the contents of his truck would remain unknown to the general public. Thus, we believe that when Agent Williams looked through the crack between the closed rear doors of

---

[51]United States v. Ryles, 988 F.2d 13 (5th Cir.1993) (officer's action in "placing his head inside the interior of the van through an open window" is a search, albeit a reasonable one because, once driver who smelled of alcohol admitted he had no driver's license, officer was so acting to determine if any passenger had a license and was not similarly impaired); United States v. Pierre, 932 F.2d 377 (5th Cir.1991) (such "reaching into the automobile" a search even though, unlike in Supreme Court's *Class* case, of-

ficer had not "made physical contact with objects inside the car").

[52]Katz v. United States, 389 U.S. 347, 88 S.Ct. 507, 19 L.Ed.2d 576 (1967).

[53]Cardwell v. Lewis, 417 U.S. 583, 94 S.Ct. 2464, 41 L.Ed.2d 325 (1974) (plurality opinion), quoted with approval in United States v. Chadwick, 433 U.S. 1, 97 S.Ct. 2476, 53 L.Ed.2d 538 (1977).

[54]United States v. Bradshaw, 490 F.2d 1097 (4th Cir.1974).

the truck, he "searched" the truck within the meaning of the fourth amendment.[55]

Bradshaw is obviously quite different from *Texas v. Brown*,[56] where an officer outside the lawfully stopped vehicle, upon seeing a suspicious object therein, bent over to get a better view of the interior. As the plurality opinion put it, that event was

> irrelevant to Fourth Amendment analysis. The general public could peer into the interior of Brown's automobile from any number of angles; there is no reason Maples should be precluded from observing as an officer what would be entirely visible to him as a private citizen. There is no legitimate expectation of privacy * * * shielding that portion of the interior of an automobile which may be viewed from outside the vehicle by either inquisitive passersby or diligent police officers.

Brown is in turn distinguishable from *State v. Epperson*,[57] where the officer could obtain the view only by leaning *into* the car; the court quite correctly concluded this was a search,[58] just as where the view is obtained by opening a car door.[59] As the Supreme Court later explained in *New York v. Class*,[60] "a car's interior [is] subject to Fourth Amendment protection," and thus even a minor "intrusion into that space constituted a 'search.' "[61]

---

[55]See also Berryhill v. State, 372 So.2d 355 (Ala.Civ.App.1979) ("the disclosure of contraband in a closed and locked van by shining a flashlight through an aperture the width of a penny cannot be classified as 'plain view' "); Commonwealth v. Podgurski, 386 Mass. 385, 436 N.E.2d 150 (1982) (concludes "the defendants' expectation of privacy in the interior of a windowless van, parked with its sliding door ajar in broad daylight and in a lot to which the public has access, is one which society could recognize as reasonable," so that officer's conduct in opening the door farther and looking in was a search; it would be otherwise had he merely looked into the partially open door).

[56]Texas v. Brown, 460 U.S. 730, 103 S.Ct. 1535, 75 L.Ed.2d 502 (1983).

[57]State v. Epperson, 237 Kan. 707, 703 P.2d 761 (1985).

[58]Compare Commonwealth v. Santana, 420 Mass. 205, 649 N.E.2d 717 (1995) (though ordinarily "the leaning into an automobile is a search," here, where passenger of lawfully stopped vehicle inexplicably handed officer a bag containing a half gallon container of milk, the officer's "leaning into the automobile to return the bag containing the milk was not a search").

[59]People v. Superior Court, 3 Cal.3d 807, 91 Cal.Rptr. 729, 478 P.2d 449 (1970); State v. Schlosser, 774 P.2d 1132 (Utah 1989). See also United States v. Frisbie, 550 F.2d 335 (5th Cir.1977) (lowering of vehicle's tailgate a search).

[60]New York v. Class, 475 U.S. 106, 106 S.Ct. 960, 89 L.Ed.2d 81 (1986).

[61]Compare State v. Aubin, 622 A.2d 444 (R.I.1993) (no mention of *Class,* but court concludes that leaning into a lawfully stopped vehicle, like the order to the driver to step out upheld in Pennsylvania v. Mimms, 434 U.S. 106, 98 S.Ct. 330, 54 L.Ed.2d 331 (1977), "was a de minimis intrusion and did not violate the Fourth Amendment"; result seems correct on particular facts—"suspiciously parked vehicle, with defendant's companion fleeing the scene, was approached at 3:15 a.m."—which show grounds for officer taking such action "in order to have plain view of defendant's hands" as de-

§ 2.5(d) Examination of vehicle identification numbers

The police not infrequently examine identification numbers on vehicles in order to determine if those vehicles have been stolen. As a consequence, the question has sometimes been raised as to whether that practice constitutes a Fourth Amendment search.

In recent years, car manufacturers have been placing what is called the "public vehicle identification number" (or PVIN) inside the automobile in such a location that it may be read through the windshield without in any way opening or entering the vehicle. Cases in which the police have merely looked through the windshield at that number present no problem. If the officer is lawfully present at that location and the vehicle, if stopped by the police, was lawfully detained,[62] then quite clearly no intrusion upon Fourth Amendment rights has occurred.[63] And if in like circumstances the police merely read an identification number on the outside of a motorcycle,[64] camper,[65] tractor,[66] or backhoe,[67] it again may be said that no search has occurred. Such cases are really no different than those previously discussed concerning other looking at or into vehicles.

More difficult are those cases in which the officer has had to open the vehicle in some way in order to read the number. Sometimes, for example, the officer will open a car door to facilitate observation of the identification plate on the door post; sometimes the officer will open the hood of the vehicle to find a number; and sometimes other types of entries will be necessary

---

fendant reached into glove compartment).

[Section 2.5(d)]

[62] See State v. Colon, 6 Conn.Cir. 722, 316 A.2d 797 (1973) (car stopped on reasonable suspicion); Conner v. State, 34 Md.App. 124, 366 A.2d 385 (1976) (motorcycle stopped for traffic violation); State v. Miller, 45 Or.App. 407, 608 P.2d 595 (1980) (vehicle stopped for traffic violations).

Compare United States v. Swart, 679 F.2d 698 (7th Cir.1982) (government's claim there never an expectation of privacy in VIN is too broad, as it "would allow police to enter a closed garage or closed premises to get a car's vehicle identification number"; police entry of premises here for that purpose illegal).

[63] Ramer v. State, 530 So.2d 915 (Fla.1988) (no search to view VIN by crawling under vehicle); State v. Cote, 518 A.2d 454 (Me.1986); Commonwealth v. Hason, 387 Mass. 169, 439 N.E.2d 251 (1982); People v. Brooks, 405 Mich. 225, 274 N.W.2d 430 (1979) (viewing VIN stamped on frame by merely crawling under car); Dick v. State, 596 P.2d 1265 (Okl. Crim.App.1979); Commonwealth v. Grabowski, 306 Pa.Super. 483, 452 A.2d 827 (1982) (no search to look at VIN on under side of car).

See also United States v. Gunn, 428 F.2d 1057 (5th Cir.1970) (observation of serial numbers on tires on vehicle).

Compare United States v. $277,000.00 U.S. Currency, 941 F.2d 898 (9th Cir.1991) (removal of opaque cover from parked car is a search even though purpose is to look for PVIN).

[64] Conner v. State, 34 Md.App. 124, 366 A.2d 385 (1976).

[65] Tate v. State, 544 P.2d 531 (Okl. Crim.App.1975).

[66] State v. Lodermeier, 481 N.W.2d 614 (S.D.1992).

[67] Pellatz v. State, 711 P.2d 1138 (Wyo.1986).

to get at numbers now stamped on vehicles in secret locations generally known only to law enforcement personnel. One view that has been taken with respect to such conduct by the police is that it does not constitute a Fourth Amendment search. This position became well established in the Fifth Circuit Court of Appeals,[68] and was accepted by some other courts as well.[69]

Cases taking this position are, in the main, short on analysis. An exception is *United States v. Polk*,[70] where the court held

that such a limited inspection[71] of a vehicle identification number is not a search within the meaning of the fourth amendment. The rationale for this holding is that an automobile owner can have no reasonable expectation of privacy with respect to the car's VIN. * * *

Vehicle identification numbers are put on automobiles by the manufacturers to aid in identifying the vehicles. There are so many similar cars that individual vehicles can be identified only through the use of such individual numbering. State laws contain many requirements for disclosing and recording such VIN's, showing a generally accepted mode of disclosure and the lack of any reasonable expectation of privacy with respect to the numbers.

Most states require that automobiles be registered with a state agency to establish a record of car ownership. The registration, which must be carried in the car, identifies the car by its VIN.

---

[68]United States v. Forrest, 620 F.2d 446 (5th Cir.1980); United States v. Wood, 500 F.2d 681 (5th Cir.1974); United States v. Polk, 433 F.2d 644 (5th Cir.1970); United States v. Johnson, 413 F.2d 1396 (5th Cir.1969), aff'd, 431 F.2d 441 (5th Cir.1970).

[69]United States v. Ware, 457 F.2d 828 (7th Cir.1972); United States v. Graham, 391 F.2d 439 (6th Cir.1968); People v. Valoppi, 61 Mich.App. 470, 233 N.W.2d 41 (1975); People v. Hart, 75 Misc.2d 908, 349 N.Y.S.2d 289 (1973); Wood v. State, 632 S.W.2d 734 (Tex.Crim.App.1982). Fox v. Commonwealth, 213 Va. 97, 189 S.E.2d 367 (1972).

Contra: State v. Moore, 66 Haw. 202, 659 P.2d 70 (1983).

[70]United States v. Polk, 433 F.2d 644 (5th Cir.1970).

[71]The court earlier stated: "It is important to point out what is not involved in this case: (1) the car door was not locked; (2) there was no damage to the car in making the inspection; (3) there was no search of private areas of the automobile, for instance the glove compartment, for identification; (4) there was no seizure of the car; (5) there was no infringement of other property rights of the defendant, since the car was located in a repair garage, the owner of which gave the officer permission to check the car; (6) there was no stopping of the car in transit that might infringe the rights of persons to free movement."

In United States v. Baker, 452 F.2d 21 (5th Cir.1971), the car was locked and the officer opened it by prying open the vent window with a pen knife. The government argued that this still was not a search, but the court found it unnecessary to resolve this issue. In State v. Simpson, 95 Wash.2d 170, 622 P.2d 1199 (1980), the court, after noting that "no court has ever resolved the precise question which is presented in this case: the degree of expectation of privacy in a VIN which is located in the interior of a closed, locked door of a lawfully parked, immobile vehicle," concluded that "although respondent did not have a legitimate expectation of privacy in the VIN itself, he had a legitimate expectation that other people would not break open the locked door of the truck in order to view the VIN."

These requirements proceed from a purpose to keep track of the ownership of potential instruments of personal and property injury, so that drivers in automobile accidents can be traced and so that compulsory insurance requirements can be enforced. * * *

It is routine practice for policemen stopping cars in traffic control operations to ask for the automobile registration papers in addition to the driver's license. Viewing registration papers is part of the accepted regulatory scheme.

VIN's are typically disclosed to private parties also. Automobile purchase and sale documents usually identify the car by its VIN. Automobile insurance policies also identify cars by their VIN's. There can therefore be no reasonable expectation of privacy with respect to the identity of the VIN. Opening the car door, looking under the hood, or crawling under the car to inspect the rear axle does not independently bring an inspection of the VIN within the scope of the Fourth Amendment. * * *

Thus the VIN on the rear axle or on the car frame are outside any reasonable expectations of privacy. Those that may be seen only by opening the car door or hood are no more private: doors and hoods are continually opened to the eyes of observers. Although opening the door of a car may involve a technical trespass, such action does not invade any expectations of privacy.

The current status of *Polk* and like decisions is somewhat uncertain in light of the Supreme Court's curiously disjointed opinion in *New York v. Class*,[72] holding (5-4) that the action of a police officer, who stopped the defendant for two traffic violations, in reaching into the interior of defendant's automobile to move papers on the dashboard obscuring the VIN was reasonable, thereby justifying seizure of a weapon observed in the car during that intrusion. The majority opinion in *Class,* in a manner not unlike *Polk,* begins by concluding that "because of the important role played by the VIN in the pervasive governmental regulation of the automobile and the efforts by the Federal Government to ensure that the VIN is placed in plain view, * * * there was no reasonable expectation of privacy in the VIN." Moreover, the Court added, "the placement of the obscuring papers was insufficient to create a privacy interest in the VIN" that did not otherwise exist; the "mere viewing of the formerly obscured VIN was not, therefore, a violation of the Fourth Amendment." But the Court in *Class* then explained that the analysis could not end there, for the "evidence that respondent sought to have suppressed was not the VIN, however, but a gun, the handle of which the officer saw from the interior of the car," and proceeded to express agreement with the state court's conclusion "that the intrusion into that space [i.e., "a car's interior"] constituted a 'search.'"

---

[72]New York v. Class, 475 U.S. 106, 106 S.Ct. 960, 89 L.Ed.2d 81 (1986), discussed in Maclin, New York v. Class: A Little-Noticed Case With Disturbing Implications, 78 J.Crim.L. & C. 1 (1987); Notes, 37 Case W.Res. L.Rev. 339 (1986); 26 Washburn L.J. 195 (1986).

Though the Court went on to hold that this search was reasonable under the circumstances (about which more in a moment), it is first necessary to focus upon just what the *Class* case tells us about when taking steps to uncover a VIN constitutes Fourth Amendment activity. Given the sequence of analysis just described, some lower courts will doubtless be tempted to read *Class* as meaning that entry of a vehicle to uncover a VIN is no search at all (and thus needs no justification whatsoever) whenever it is the VIN itself rather than some other item that is the object of the defendant's suppression motion. But this is not what the Court said, and such a conclusion would hardly be a sensible one. The Court in *Class* quite correctly characterized the officer's decision to enter the car as a "decision to conduct [a] search," which it most certainly was. Even if it is true in some sense that the defendant's placement of the papers on the dashboard did not create a privacy interest in the VIN, the Court can hardly have meant by that observation that actions taken to uncover the VIN do not *ever* constitute a search. If the officer was not making a search when he reached into the automobile, there would be no basis for saying it became a search ab initio merely because while so positioned he saw (and then seized) a gun the defendant later sought to suppress.

Another what-is-a-search question prompted by *Class* is whether police action undertaken to discover a VIN is *never* a search unless that action consists of a physical intrusion into the interior of the car. That is, may *Class* fairly be read as meaning that if an officer merely opens a car door to examine a VIN on the door jamb that this is not a search and thus needs no justification whatsoever? Such an interpretation might appear to be suggested by the following language:

> The VIN, which was the clear initial objective of the officer, is by law present in one of two locations—either inside the door jamb, or atop the dashboard and thus ordinarily in plain view of someone outside the automobile. *Neither of those locations is subject to a reasonable expectation of privacy.* The officer here checked both those locations, and only those two locations. The officer did not root about the interior of the respondent's automobile before proceeding to examine the VIN. He did not reach into any compartments or open any containers. He did not even intrude into the interior at all until after he had checked the door jamb for the VIN. When he did intrude, the officer simply reached directly for the unprotected space where the VIN was located to move the offending papers. We hold that *this search* was sufficiently unintrusive to be constitutionally permissible * * *.[73]

But an assumption that the phrase "this search" refers only to the physical intrusion into the interior is hardly a compelling one. Nor is the matter settled by the Court's statement that there is no privacy expectation as to the VIN on the door jamb, for that

---

[73]Emphasis added.

is also true of the dashboard VIN but yet did not stop the Court from concluding that very limited steps to reveal that VIN still had to be characterized as a search. Given the Supreme Court's earlier conclusion in *Katz* that a physical entry into a "constitutionally protected area" is not essential in order for there to have occurred a Fourth Amendment search, it would seem that opening a vehicle door to see an otherwise hidden VIN is likewise a search,[74] albeit of a limited nature and thus permissible in the circumstances recognized in *Class*.

Turning now to just what those circumstances are, it is necessary first to recite the facts of *Class* in a bit more detail. As soon as Class was stopped for speeding and driving with a cracked windshield, he emerged from his car and approached one of the officers; he tendered a registration certificate and proof of insurance but stated he had no driver's license. Meanwhile, the other officer undertook the previously described search for the VIN. In holding that this was a reasonable search, the majority in *Class* emphasized these considerations: (i) "a demand to inspect the VIN, like a demand to see licenses and registration papers, is within the scope of police authority pursuant to a traffic violation stop"; (ii) "If respondent had stayed in his vehicle and acceded to such a request from the officer, the officer would not have needed to intrude into the passenger compartment"; (iii) *Pennsylvania v. Mimms*,[75] which "allows an officer to guard against [the possibility a traffic violator is armed] by requiring the driver to exit the car briefly," "also allowed the officers here to detain respondent briefly outside the car that he voluntarily exited while they complete their investigation"; and (iv) the police could reasonably search for the VIN rather than have the defendant uncover it, for "[t]o have returned respondent immediately to the automobile would have placed the officers in the same situation that the

---

[74]State v. Larocco, 794 P.2d 460 (Utah 1990) (under state constitution, opening door to see VIN on inside edge of door a search; court says it would also so hold as to Fourth Amendment). See also United States v. $277,000.00 U.S. Currency, 941 F.2d 898 (9th Cir.1991) (removal of opaque car cover from vehicle to see PVIN is a search).

Some pre-*Class* authority both ways is to be found. Compare United States v. Forrest, 620 F.2d 446 (5th Cir.1980) ("An inspection by police officers is not a search merely because the police must open the door of the vehicle in order to examine the VIN plate"); with People v. Piper, 101 Ill.App.3d 296, 56 Ill.Dec. 815, 427 N.E.2d 1361 (1981) ("Where, as here, the VIN can be seen by the policeman only when he himself has opened the door to the vehicle, a search has begun").

Compare the post-*Class* decision in United States v. Chavira, 467 F.3d 1286 (10th Cir.2006) (court notes that district court held, and government does not dispute, that opening door to see VIN on doorjamb was a search, but then in extensive footnote court seems to say no impropriety "if the officer remains physically outside the car when he examines the VIN on the dashboard, the doorjamb, or both").

[75]Pennsylvania v. Mimms, 434 U.S. 106, 98 S.Ct. 330, 54 L.Ed.2d 331 (1977).

holding in *Mimms* allows officers to avoid—permitting an individual being detained to have possible access to a dangerous weapon and the benefit of the partial concealment provided by the car's exterior." In response to the objection that this, in effect, permitted the making of a search without probable cause, the *Class* majority reasoned that such cases as *Mimms* and *Michigan v. Summers*[76] showed that certain police action undertaken in the interest of self-protection could be "piggy-backed" onto some other police action (a traffic stop in *Mimms,* execution of a search warrant in *Summers*) grounded in probable cause (albeit not probable cause the person was armed). (The *Class* dissenters, on the other hand, rather persuasively argued that "none of the factors the Court relies upon—the lack of reasonable expectation of privacy in the VIN, the officers' observing respondent commit minor traffic violations, the government's interest both in promoting highway safety and in shielding officers from danger, and the allegedly limited nature of the search that took place—gave the police *any reason* to search for the VIN.")

Although the *Class* majority cautioned that "our holding today does not authorize police officers to enter a vehicle to obtain a dashboard-mounted VIN when the VIN is visible from outside the automobile," the holding certainly has the potential to expand in other directions. Given the Court's earlier recognition in *Mimms* that police may order the traffic violator out of his vehicle for their protection, the fact that the defendant in *Class* exited the car on his own volition may well turn out to be insignificant. That is, the concerns for police protection expressed in *Mimms* and *Class* would make it easy for a lower court to conclude that it is unobjectionable that the police first ordered the driver out of the vehicle and then searched for the concealed VIN.[77] Whether there must always be an observed traffic violation on which to "piggy-back" the VIN search is unclear,[78] though the Court's statements about the importance of the VIN and the consequent lack of an expectation of privacy as to the VIN would lend support to the conclusion, suggested also by lower courts in some pre-*Class*

---

[76]Michigan v. Summers, 452 U.S. 692, 101 S.Ct. 2587, 69 L.Ed.2d 340 (1981).

[77]United States v. Villa-Chaparro, 115 F.3d 797 (10th Cir.1997) (where officer unable to find VIN on dashboard, he "properly asked Defendant to step outside the vehicle so he could check for the VIN on the doorjamb"); United States v. Miller, 84 F.3d 1244 (10th Cir.1996) (though officer ordered driver of car stopped for speeding to step out of car, the *Class* notion that if "the VIN on the dashboard is covered and the driver is not in the vehicle,

the officer may open the door to read the VIN on the doorjamb" is nonetheless applicable).

[78]But see United States v. Villa-Chaparro, 115 F.3d 797 (10th Cir.1997) (court emphasizes vehicle stopped for seat belt violation and thereafter suspicion vehicle stolen developed); United States v. Miller, 84 F.3d 1244 (10th Cir.1996) ("A driver who has committed a traffic violation does not have a reasonable expectation of privacy in his vehicle's VIN, even if it is not in plain view").

cases,[79] that checking in a vehicle for a VIN is a lesser intrusion than the usual search and thus may be undertaken upon a lesser quantum of evidence. As stated in *United States v. Powers*:[80]

> Since identification numbers are, at the least, quasi-public information, a search of that part of the car displaying the number is but a minimal invasion of a person's privacy. A police officer, therefore, should be freer to inspect the numbers without a warrant than he is to search a car for purely private property. Because of the car's mobility, he may have little opportunity to do so if he must first secure a warrant or have probable cause for a search or arrest. Nevertheless, the legality of the search cannot be predicated on the "inarticulate hunches" or subjective "good faith" of the officer. * * * Instead it should be tested by the objective standard stated in *Terry* * * *.

However, there is authority that "the careful balancing revealed in the *Class* opinion is not to be extended so as to permit a search of any parked vehicle without probable cause just because the VIN is obscured in some way."[81]

The language from *Class* quoted at the outset of the preceding paragraph naturally raises the question of whether the visibility of the dashboard VIN likewise means the police may not take steps to examine another, hidden VIN in that vehicle. Such was the issue in *United States v. Caro*,[82] where, after a traffic stop, the officer suspected the vehicle might be stolen but then, upon looking through the windshield at the dashboard VIN, saw that it matched the VIN on the vehicle registration the defendant had supplied. The defendant claimed this dispelled the suspicion, meaning the detention should have been terminated at that point, and that therefore the officer acted improperly in checking for a VIN on the side panel of a door (which led to the serendipitous

---

[79]United States v. Forrest, 620 F.2d 446 (5th Cir.1980) (explaining some prior 5th Cir. cases on the ground that "the officers had legitimate reasons to suspect criminal activity was afoot"); People v. Piper, 101 Ill.App.3d 296, 56 Ill.Dec. 815, 427 N.E.2d 1361 (1981) (no basis to inspect car VIN merely because it one of two cars involved in accident, given "absence of any articulable facts upon which the police might reasonably suspect the car was stolen").

[80]United States v. Powers, 439 F.2d 373 (4th Cir.1971).

[81]United States v. $277,000.00 U.S. Currency, 941 F.2d 898 (9th Cir. 1991), holding illegal the removal of opaque car covers from two parked vehicles in an effort to see the VIN. The court stated:

> In the case at hand, the vehicles

were not being driven on the roads; they were parked in a backyard. The occasion for the inspection was not brought about by traffic violations; it was merely the discovery of two vehicles with Mexican license plates parked in a backyard. The factors carefully balanced in the *Class* opinion, such as the necessity of vehicle regulation on the public highways, officer safety and the minimal intrusion involved by removing a paper from the dashboard of a vehicle already stopped for traffic violations, are simply inapplicable here.

See also State v. Guebara, 119 N.M. 662, 894 P.2d 1018 (App.1995) (following *$277,000 U.S. Currency*, which is "factually similar to the present case").

[82]United States v. Caro, 248 F.3d 1240 (10th Cir.2001).

discovery of air fresheners, creating reasonable suspicion of the presence of drugs). In response the government argued "that the presence of an unobscured and apparently accurate VIN on Mr. Caro's dashboard should not have barred Trooper Avery from checking other locations for an additional VIN, because here, unlike *Class*, there were facts that suggested Mr. Caro's car might have been stolen." The court concluded:

> But the fact that dashboard VIN plates can be altered tells us nothing. Door VIN plates can be altered. All VIN plates can be altered. * * * The government's mere conjectures as to the likelihood of any particular VIN having been modified are therefore insufficient to overcome *Class*['s] specific bar to the course of conduct pursued here by Trooper Avery.

> The government's reading of *Class* would transform the valid dashboard VIN, which would at least suggest that Mr. Caro's car was not stolen, into a legal reason to penetrate further into the vehicle. We decline to extend *Class* in this manner. Instead, * * * we affirm that where the dashboard VIN plate is readable from outside the passenger compartment, that VIN matches the VIN listed on the registration, and there are no signs the plate has been tampered with, there is insufficient cause for an officer to extend the scope of a detention by entering a vehicle's passenger compartment for the purpose of further examining any VIN.

§ 2.6 Persons and effects

Research References

West's Key Number Digest
Controlled Substances ☞138; Criminal Law ☞393; Searches and Seizures ☞13.1 to 16, 25.1 to 28, 74 to 78

Legal Encyclopedias
C.J.S., Criminal Law §§ 645 to 654; Internal Revenue § 807; Searches and Seizures §§ 8, 13, 18, 20 to 38, 41, 66 to 67, 70 to 72, 92 to 94, 102 to 106

Introduction

The Fourth Amendment protects the "right of the people to be secure in their persons * * * and effects, against unreasonable searches and seizures." There are, of course, many circumstances in which a seizure or search of either a person or certain effects may be lawfully undertaken. Persons and effects may be searched pursuant to a valid search warrant.[1] A person may be seized upon a valid arrest warrant[2] or upon probable cause without a warrant,[3] and under certain circumstances may be detained briefly upon a lesser quantum of evidence.[4] It is lawful to search a person incident to a valid arrest[5] and under certain other limited circumstances.[6] Also, there are certain circumstances in which effects may be seized and searched without a warrant.[7] However, the concern here is not with these matters, but rather with the question of what police investigative techniques directed at persons and effects do not constitute a search and thus are not subject to the restraints of the Fourth Amendment. Under *Katz v. United States*,[8] the fundamental inquiry is what techniques do not violate a justified expectation of privacy.

§ 2.6(a) Personal characteristics

In the overwhelming majority of cases in which an objection is raised concerning the obtaining of incriminating evidence from a person, the central issue is whether the antecedent "seizure" of the person was in compliance with the Fourth Amendment. This is because it is not ordinarily possible to obtain such evidence without first making a seizure, and because the determination of the seizure issue is likely to govern without regard to whether what happened thereafter was or was not a search. It is clear that "the legal arrest of a person * * * does—for at least a reasonable time and to a reasonable extent—take his own privacy out of the realm of protection from police interest in weapons, means of escape and evidence,"[9] and thus if a person has been lawfully arrested it really is not significant whether certain types of in-custody investigation (e.g., fingerprinting) constitute a Fourth Amendment search; the investigation is lawful in any event because a valid arrest was made.[10] By the same token, if an investigation of a person is accomplished by making an illegal

---

[Section 2.6]

[1] See ch. 4.

[2] See § 5.1(h).

[3] See § 5.1(b).

[4] See § 9.5.

[5] See § 5.2.

[6] See § 5.4.

[7] See § 5.5.

[8] Katz v. United States, 389 U.S. 347, 88 S.Ct. 507, 19 L.Ed.2d 576 (1967).

[Section 2.6(a)]

[9] United States v. Edwards, 415 U.S. 800, 94 S.Ct. 1234, 39 L.Ed.2d 771 (1974), quoting from United States v. DeLeo, 422 F.2d 487 (1st Cir.1970).

Thus, where a defendant in custody for another crime was put in a lineup merely to fill it up but was identified as the perpetrator of that crime as well, this is not a violation of his Fourth Amendment rights. His initial seizure was lawful, placing him in the lineup was "at best a minimal, and in our view constitutionally inconsequential, additional restraint," and one has no expectation of privacy as to physical characteristics constantly exposed to the public. People v. Whitaker, 64 N.Y.2d 347, 486 N.Y.S.2d 895, 476 N.E.2d 294 (1985).

[10] On the other hand, as discussed in § 9.2(f), if there is merely a lawful brief detention and no grounds for arrest, a problem may arise as to how

seizure of that individual, the evidence obtained is inadmissible as a fruit of the illegal seizure whether or not the post-seizure police action itself qualifies as a search. In *Davis v. Mississippi*,[11] for example, Justice Brennan quite correctly stated: "The only issue before us is whether fingerprints obtained from petitioner should have been excluded from evidence as the product of a detention which was illegal under the Fourth and Fourteenth Amendments." As for what *is* a search in this context, generally "courts have implicitly assumed that an individual has a reasonable expectation of privacy with respect to those portions of his or her person that are hidden from public view, including hidden recesses in both one's clothing and body."[12]

This means that the question here under consideration—whether obtaining evidence of an individual's personal characteristics in certain ways constitutes a Fourth Amendment search—will be of central importance only in rather unusual circumstances. One such circumstance is that present in *United States v. Dionisio*,[13] namely, where the person is subpoenaed to appear before a grand jury and there provide evidence of certain physical characteristics (in *Dionisio*, voice exemplars). In order to hold, as it did, that this procedure was not subject to the reasonableness requirement of the Fourth Amendment, the Court had to conclude that neither the appearance under compulsion of the subpoena nor the subsequent obtaining of the exemplar was covered by the Amendment. After concluding "that a subpoena to appear before a grand jury is not a 'seizure' in the Fourth Amendment sense,"[14] the Court confronted defendant's claim "that the grand jury's subsequent directive to make the voice recording was itself an infringement of his rights under the Fourth Amendment." The Court, per Stewart, J., responded:

> In *Katz v. United States,* * * * we said that the Fourth Amendment provides no protection for what "a person knowingly exposes to the public, even in his own home or office . . . ." * * * The physical characteristics of a person's voice, its tone and manner, as opposed to the content of a specific conversation, are constantly exposed to the public. Like a man's facial characteristics, or handwriting, his voice is repeatedly produced for others to hear. No person can have a reasonable expectation that others will not know the sound of his voice, any more than he can reasonably expect that his face will be a mystery to the world. As the Court of Appeals for

---

closely the suspect may be scrutinized. See, e.g., State v. Selvidge, 30 Wash.App. 406, 635 P.2d 736 (1981) (proper to require suspects to display soles of shoes, as they did not have "a subjective expectation of privacy in their shoe patterns, patterns shown to the world with every step").

[11]Davis v. Mississippi, 394 U.S. 721, 89 S.Ct. 1394, 22 L.Ed.2d 676 (1969).

[12]State v. Smith, 279 Neb. 918, 782 N.W.2d 913 (2010).

[13]United States v. Dionisio, 410 U.S. 1, 93 S.Ct. 764, 35 L.Ed.2d 67 (1973).

[14]For discussion of this aspect of the case, see § 9.7(a).

the Second Circuit stated:

> Except for the rare recluse who chooses to live his life in complete solitude, in our daily lives we constantly speak and write, and while the content of a communication is entitled to Fourth Amendment protection, . . . the underlying identifying characteristics—the constant factor throughout both public and private communications—are open for all to see or hear. There is no basis for constructing a wall of privacy against the grand jury which does not exist in casual contacts with strangers. Hence no intrusion into an individual's privacy results from compelled execution of handwriting or voice exemplars; nothing is being exposed to the grand jury that has not previously been exposed to the public at large.[15] * * *

The required disclosure of a person's voice is thus immeasurably further removed from the Fourth Amendment protection than was the intrusion into the body effected by the blood extraction in *Schmerber*.[16] "The interests in human dignity and privacy which the Fourth Amendment protects forbid any such intrusions on the mere chance that desired evidence might be obtained." * * * Similarly, a seizure of voice exemplars does not involve the "severe, though brief, intrusion upon cherished personal security," effected by the "pat down" in *Terry*[17]—"surely . . . an annoying, frightening, and perhaps humiliating experience." * * * Rather, this is like the fingerprinting in *Davis,* where, though the initial dragnet detentions were constitutionally impermissible, we noted that the fingerprinting itself, "involves none of the probing into an individual's private life and thoughts that marks an interrogation or search."[18]

In the companion case of *United States v. Mara,*[19] the Court reached the same result where the grand jury witness was required to furnish handwriting exemplars, stating: "Handwriting, like speech, is repeatedly shown to the public, and there is no more expectation of privacy in the physical characteristics of a person's script than there is in the tone of his voice."[20]

The Court in *Dionisio* likened the sound of a person's voice to a

---

[15]Quoting from United States v. Doe (Schwartz), 457 F.2d 895 (2d Cir. 1972).

[16]The reference is to Schmerber v. California, 384 U.S. 757, 86 S.Ct. 1826, 16 L.Ed.2d 908 (1966).

[17]The reference is to Terry v. Ohio, 392 U.S. 1, 88 S.Ct. 1868, 20 L.Ed.2d 889 (1968).

[18]See also United States v. Ceballos, 385 F.3d 1120 (7th Cir.2004) (evaluation of defendants' voices heard during booking after lawful arrest and comparison of them with those captured on surveillance tapes within *Dionisio*).

[19]United States v. Mara, 410 U.S. 19, 93 S.Ct. 774, 35 L.Ed.2d 99 (1973). See also United States v. Euge, 444 U.S. 707, 100 S.Ct. 874, 63 L.Ed.2d 141 (1980) (citing *Mara* for proposition that "compulsion of handwriting exemplars is neither a search of seizure subject to Fourth Amendment protections," and holding IRS can compel handwriting exemplars under its summons authority conferred by 26 U.S.C.A. § 7602).

[20]See also Burns v. State, 813 So.2d 668 (Miss.2001) (because there "no privacy interest in handwriting," no Fourth Amendment violation where handwriting exemplars were "obtained through trickery" of jailed defendant).

person's "facial characteristics," which are also "constantly exposed to the public." It does not seem open to question, therefore, that mere observation of those characteristics or other physical characteristics[21] does not constitute a Fourth Amendment

---

[21]In People v. Carlson, 677 P.2d 310 (Colo.1984), the court, after concluding that the driver of a lawfully stopped vehicle could be ordered out of and away from the car, held it was no search to observe his gait, as it "is no different than the viewing of his general physical characteristics, such as height, weight or build, all of which would be 'in the plain view of an officer who has a right to be in a position to have that view.' * * * In short, a driver of a motor vehicle has no legitimate expectation of privacy in his physical traits and demeanor that are in the plain sight of an officer during a valid traffic stop." But, the court continued, the same is not true of a roadside sobriety test: "Since these are maneuvers which the ordinary person seeks to preserve as private, there is a constitutionally protected privacy interest in the coordinative characteristics sought by the testing process." In accord with the latter holding in Carlson are Hulse v. State, Dept. of Justice, 289 Mont. 1, 961 P.2d 75 (1998) ("field sobriety tests are not 'merely observations' of a person's physical behavior, but, rather, constitute a search under the Fourth Amendment," for "an individual has a legitimate privacy interest in both the process of conducting the field sobriety tests and in the information revealed by the tests"); State v. Nagel, 320 Or. 24, 880 P.2d 451 (1994) ("field sobriety tests administered in this case are counter to a reasonable expectation of privacy," as they "require defendant to perform certain maneuvers that are not regularly performed in public"). As also noted in Hulse, the prevailing but not unanimous view is that such tests do not require probable cause but only reasonable suspicion, for the reason "that public safety is equally threatened by a person driving under the influence of alcohol as by a person illegally concealing a gun." To the same

effect as Hulse is Commonwealth v. Blais, 428 Mass. 294, 701 N.E.2d 314 (1998).

Consider also State v. Aldridge, 172 W.Va. 218, 304 S.E.2d 671 (1983) (where lawfully detained suspect had previously exposed injury to hand to others, no search to require him to remove gloves).

Compare United States v. Askew, 529 F.3d 1119 (D.C.Cir.2008) (rejecting government's reliance on Dionisio in claiming unzipping defendant's sweatshirt no search; "there is nothing about a sweatshirt that * * * must necessarily be revealed to the public in the course of daily life," and government erroneously "assumes that the unzipping of appellant's jacket would reveal only appellant's already partially visible sweatshirt"); People v. Harper, 237 Ill.App.3d 202, 177 Ill.Dec. 334, 603 N.E.2d 115 (1992) (search occurred when officers ordered suspect to open his mouth, shined flashlights into mouth, and ordered him to spit out observed packet); State v. Hardy, 577 N.W.2d 212 (Minn.1998) (officer's "request that Hardy open his mouth," "made while physically blocking the stairs from which Hardy attempted to exit the porch, constituted a show of authority designed to obtain compliance," and thus "constituted a sufficient intrusion upon Hardy's privacy interests to qualify as a search protected by the Fourth Amendment"); Hawkins v. State, 853 S.W.2d 598 (Tex.App.1993) (officer's actions constituted search when he placed his cupped hand out in front of driver detained in Terry stop). But, to the extent that these cases indicate that an order, even without compliance, is a search, consider California v. Hodari D., 499 U.S. 621, 111 S.Ct. 1547, 113 L.Ed.2d 690 (1991) (holding no seizure absent "either physical force" or "submission to the assertion of authority").

search.[22] Moreover, it is no search to "record" those characteristics, in effect, by taking a picture of the individual.[23]

It is noteworthy that the *Dionisio* Court also drew an analogy between taking voice exemplars and taking fingerprints, thus suggesting that fingerprinting is no search. (Although it is well established that the taking of fingerprints is permissible incident to a lawful arrest,[24] courts have rarely addressed the question of whether the act of fingerprinting is itself a search.[25]) This dictum in *Dionisio* might be considered suspect, however, for the Court's reliance upon *Davis* for support is not as sound as might first appear. The language quoted from *Davis* was not included therein for the purpose of showing that fingerprinting is not a search but rather for the purpose of showing that detention for such a limited intrusion might "comply with the Fourth Amendment even though there is no probable cause in the traditional sense." Yet, the Court has more recently referred to fingerprinting as nothing more than obtaining "physical characteristics . . . constantly exposed to the public,"[26] and lower courts have upheld the fingerprinting of grand jury witnesses without a showing of probable cause.[27]

The obtaining of some physical characteristics quite clearly is a search. The *Dionisio* Court cited with approval its earlier decision in *Schmerber v. California*,[28] holding that the taking of a blood sample is a Fourth Amendment search. By analogy to *Schmerber,* it has been held that subjecting a person to a

---

[22]Cf. United States v. Holland, 378 F.Supp. 144 (E.D.Pa.1974) (lawful for court to order defendant to submit to dental exam to determine if he was missing a tooth, as victim of crime said was the case as to the perpetrator, for "the defendant could not harbor a reasonable expectation of privacy with respect to his missing tooth").

[23]United States v. Holland, 438 F.2d 887 (6th Cir.1971) (photographing of person who voluntarily came to police station); Application of Rodgers, 359 F.Supp. 576 (E.D.N.Y.1973) (photographing of grand jury witness); State v. McDowell, 301 N.C. 279, 271 S.E.2d 286 (1980) (photographing of person who reported as required to his parole officer).

Cf. Commonwealth v. Mahoney, 400 Mass. 524, 510 N.E.2d 759 (1987) (no search to videotape booking of defendant arrested for driving under influence where booking "took place in an open area of the police station where any officers or passersby could observe the defendant").

[24]Napolitano v. United States, 340 F.2d 313 (1st Cir.1965); Smith v. United States, 324 F.2d 879 (D.C.Cir. 1963); United States v. Iacullo, 226 F.2d 788 (7th Cir.1955); United States v. Laub Baking Co., 283 F.Supp. 217 (N.D.Ohio 1968); State v. Inman, 301 A.2d 348 (Me.1973); McGovern v. Van Riper, 137 N.J.Eq. 548, 45 A.2d 842 (1946).

[25]Compare Paulson v. Florida, 360 F.Supp. 156 (S.D.Fla.1973) (asserting fingerprinting is a search); with Commonwealth v. DeWitt, 226 Pa.Super. 372, 314 A.2d 27 (1973) (asserting fingerprinting is not a search).

[26]Cupp v. Murphy, 412 U.S. 291, 93 S.Ct. 2000, 36 L.Ed.2d 900 (1973).

[27]E.g., In re Grand Jury Proceedings (Schofield), 507 F.2d 963 (3d Cir. 1975).

[28]Schmerber v. California, 384 U.S. 757, 86 S.Ct. 1826, 16 L.Ed.2d 908 (1966).

breathalizer test is likewise a search, for in that instance as well "the material seized comes from within the suspect's body."[29] So too as for requiring a person to submit a saliva sample.[30] It is not surprising, therefore, that the Supreme Court ruled in *Skinner v. Railway Labor Executives' Ass'n*[31] that drug and alcohol testing of railroad employees by taking blood or breath samples constitutes a Fourth Amendment search. The Court in *Skinner* went on to hold that the third technique at issue, collecting and testing urine samples, is also a search, though it does not entail intrusion into the body, as

> chemical analysis of urine, like that of blood, can reveal a host of private medical facts about an employee, including whether she is epileptic, pregnant, or diabetic. Nor can it be disputed that the process of collecting the sample to be tested, which may in some cases involve visual or aural monitoring of the act of urination, itself implicates privacy interests.[32]

The line between *Schmerber* and *Dionisio* is not always easy to draw. Assume, for example, that a person is subpoenaed to appear before a grand jury and to supply samples of the hair on his head and arms, so that the samples may be compared with hairs found at a crime scene. Does the person subpoenaed have a legitimate claim that the taking of hair samples is governed by the Fourth Amendment so that, unlike *Dionisio*, the reasonableness requirement of the Amendment applies? It may be said, of course, that "[h]air, like fingerprints or a man's facial characteristics or the body itself, is an identifying physical characteristic and is constantly exposed to public view."[33] In that respect, the situation is like that in *Dionisio*, but in other respects it is not. For one thing, nothing was seized from Dionisio, but "[u]nquestionably

---

[29]Commonwealth v. Quarles, 229 Pa.Super. 363, 324 A.2d 452 (1974). See also Blank v. State, 3 P.3d 359 (Alaska App.2000); City of Fargo v. Wonder, 651 N.W.2d 665 (N.D.2002); Blair v. Commonwealth, 115 Pa.Cmwlth. 293, 539 A.2d 958 (1988); State v. Locke, 418 A.2d 843 (R.I. 1980); State v. McGuigan, 184 Vt. 441, 965 A.2d 511 (2008).

As for use of a Passive Alcohol Sensor instead of the more traditional breathalyzer, see § 2.2(h).

[30]Kohler v. Englade, 470 F.3d 1104 (5th Cir.2006); Padgett v. Donald, 401 F.3d 1273 (11th Cir.2005); State v. Martinez, 276 Kan. 527, 78 P.3d 769 (2003); Commonwealth v. Draheim, 447 Mass. 113, 849 N.E.2d 823 (2006).

[31]Skinner v. Railway Labor Executives' Ass'n, 489 U.S. 602, 109 S.Ct. 1402, 103 L.Ed.2d 639 (1989).

[32]Accord: Ferguson v. City of Charleston, 532 U.S. 67, 121 S.Ct. 1281, 149 L.Ed.2d 205 (2001); Chandler v. Miller, 520 U.S. 305, 117 S.Ct. 1295, 137 L.Ed.2d 513 (1997); Vernonia School Dist. 47J v. Acton, 515 U.S. 646, 115 S.Ct. 2386, 132 L.Ed.2d 564 (1995); National Treasury Employees Union v. Von Raab, 489 U.S. 656, 109 S.Ct. 1384, 103 L.Ed.2d 685 (1989).

[33]State v. Sharpe, 284 N.C. 157, 200 S.E.2d 44 (1973). See also In re Grand Jury Proceedings, 686 F.2d 135 (3d Cir.1982) ("there is no greater expectation of privacy with respect to hair which is on public display than with respect to voice, handwriting or fingerprints").

the plucking of * * * hairs * * * constitute[s] a 'seizure.' "[34] For another, while the hair is "constantly exposed" in the sense that the person knowingly exposes the color and style of his hair, it cannot really be said that the hair is exposed in the sense of revealing those characteristics that can be determined only by microscopic examination. This is a distinction that has proved significant in another Supreme Court case. In *Cupp v. Murphy*,[35] the Court did not hesitate in concluding that the police made a search when they took scrapings from Murphy's fingernails after observing dried blood on his finger while Murphy was voluntarily present at the station. *Cupp* indicates, therefore, that even though one walks into a police station with evidence connecting him with a homicide on his hands in plain view, that person nonetheless has a protected expectation of privacy with respect to that evidence when its incriminating character is not evident to the naked eye and it must be seized and then subjected to microscopic analysis to be of evidentiary value.[36]

On the ground that "the collection and analysis of biological samples from an individual constitutes a search for purposes of the Fourth Amendment," the taking of such samples for purposes of DNA analysis constitutes a search, "regardless of whether the samples were obtained by drawing blood[37] or by [obtaining saliva[38] via] cheek swabs."[39] However, given "the technological advancement of DNA collection science," whereby a DNA sample can be obtained "simply by applying a 'sticky patch' to the skin," it has

---

[34]State v. Sharpe, 284 N.C. 157, 200 S.E.2d 44 (1973).

[35]Cupp v. Murphy, 412 U.S. 291, 93 S.Ct. 2000, 36 L.Ed.2d 900 (1973).

[36]The future will doubtless bring into play other techniques for obtaining quite different personal characteristics. "Advances in modern scientific technique, including a proprietary process called Brain Fingerprinting have, by some accounts, made it possible to determine whether an individual possesses specific and detailed information—Brain Fingerprinting can tell the operator what an individual does or does not know without any voluntary action, response or consent of the subject." Halliburton, Letting Katz Out of the Bag: Cognitive Freedom and Fourth Amendment Fidelity, 59 Hastings L.J. 309, 309–10 (2007).

[37]Nicholas v. Goord, 430 F.3d 652 (2d Cir.2005); United States v. Sczubelek, 402 F.3d 175 (3d Cir.2005); United States v. Kincade, 379 F.3d 813 (9th Cir.2004); Schlicher v. (NFN) Peters, I & I, 103 F.3d 940 (10th Cir.

1996); Landry v. Attorney General, 429 Mass. 336, 709 N.E.2d 1085 (1999); Doles v. State, 994 P.2d 315 (Wyo.1999).

[38]Friedman v. Boucher, 580 F.3d 847 (9th Cir.2009); Padgett v. Donald, 401 F.3d 1273 (11th Cir.2005); Schlicher v. (NFN) Peters, I & I, 103 F.3d 940 (10th Cir.1996): Boling v. Romer, 101 F.3d 1336 (10th Cir.1996); In re Shabazz, 200 F.Supp.2d 578 (D.S.C. 2002); State v. Lee, 976 So.2d 109 (La. 2008); Doles v. State, 994 P.2d 315 (Wyo.1999).

But consider Garcia-Torres v. State, 949 N.E.2d 1229 (Ind.2011) (opining cheek swabs procedure "has more in common with fingerprints than it does with blood alcohol content" and thus may be no search, but then proceeding on parties' agreement it a search).

[39]State v. Surge, 122 Wash.App. 448, 94 P.3d 345 (2004). Accord: State v. Martin, 184 Vt. 23, 955 A.2d 1144 (2008).

been opined that "a considerable amount of doubt is cast on whether DNA collection continues to constitute a search within the scope of Fourth Amendment protection at all."[40] On the other hand, it has been rather persuasively argued that "all the forms of DNA sampling * * * should be denominated searches for the purpose of the Fourth Amendment" because DNA sampling "is closer to urinalysis in that subsequent biochemical testing can reveal 'private medical facts.' "[41]

§ 2.6(b) Abandoned effects generally

As one commentator has noted:

> The significance of abandoned property in the law of search and seizure lies in the maxim that the protection of the fourth amendment does not extend to it. Thus, where one abandons property, he is said to bring his right of privacy therein to an end, and may not later complain about its subsequent seizure and use in evidence against him. In short, the theory of abandonment is that no issue of search is presented in such a situation, and the property so abandoned may be seized without probable cause.[42]

Sometimes the fact of abandonment is relied upon in order to find that a particular defendant was without standing,[43] but more often courts take the position that if certain property is abandoned

---

[40]Note, 33 Hofstra L.Rev. 1017, 1030–31 (2005).

[41]Kaye, The Constitutionality of DNA Sampling on Arrest, 10 Cornell J.L. & Pub. Pol'y 455, 480–82 (2001). (The quoted term is from Skinner v. Railway Labor Executives' Ass'n, 489 U.S. 602, 109 S.Ct. 1402, 103 L.Ed.2d 639 (1989), where the Court, in concluding that urine sampling followed by urinalysis is a search, emphasized "the chemical analysis of urine, like that of blood, can reveal a host of private medical facts about an employee, including whether he or she is epileptic, pregnant, or diabetic.")

See also Kaye, Who Needs Special Needs? On the Constitutionality of Collecting DNA and Other Biometric Data From Arrestees, 34 J.L.Med. & Ethics 188, 191 (2006) ("Under a line of cases involving blood sampling, breathalysers, urine specimens, and nail scrapings, the Court could rely on the dignitary interests related to physical invasions to find that buccal swabbing or saliva sampling for DNA analysis is a bona fide Fourth Amendment event"); Kaye & Smith, DNA Identification Databases: Legality, Legitimacy, and the Case for Population-Wide Coverage, 2003

Wis.L.Rev. 413, 444 ("The sensitive nature of some of the information locked in the helices of the DNA molecule leads us to believe that DNA sampling is a Fourth Amendment search, even if the sample is obtained noninvasively"); Lowenberg, Applying the Fourth Amendment When DNA Collected for One Purpose is Tested for Another, 79 U.Cin.L.Rev. 1289, 1291–92 (2011) (considering "the many additional tests that might be conducted on DNA," "the Fourth Amendment would require a warrant or an applicable warrant exception before a DNA sample can be retested for additional genetic information").

[Section 2.6(b)]

[42]Mascolo, The Role of Abandonment in the Law of Search and Seizure: An Application of Misdirected Emphasis, 20 Buff.L.Rev. 399, 400–01 (1971).

[43]See § 11.3(f). Also illustrative are Buza v. State, 529 N.E.2d 334 (Ind.1988) (where defendant gave earrings to girl friend and manifested no intent to retrieve them, these items abandoned and thus defendant without standing as to their seizure from her residence); Commonwealth v. Richardson, 476 Pa. 571, 383 A.2d 510

it is beyond the protections of the Fourth Amendment. It is this broader notion that is of primary concern here.

The Supreme Court has on more than one occasion relied upon an abandonment theory. In *Hester v. United States*,[44] agents were observing an illegal liquor sale from a distance when an alarm was given. The two participants ran and were pursued into a field by the officers, where the agents found a jug and bottle which had been dropped or thrown by the two men. The Court declared: "The defendant's own acts, and those of his associates, disclosed the jug, the jar and the bottle—and there was no seizure in the sense of the law when the officers examined the contents of each after it had been abandoned." Similarly, in *Abel v. United States*,[45] where defendant, arrested in his hotel room, packed his effects and checked out of the hotel but left certain items behind in the waste basket, the Court concluded that it was not

> unlawful to seize the entire contents of the wastepaper basket, even though some of its contents had no connection with crime. So far as the record shows, petitioner had abandoned these articles. He had thrown them away. So far as he was concerned, they were *bona vacantia*. There can be nothing unlawful in the Government's appropriation of such abandoned property.

It appears that the Court in *Abel* is referring to abandonment in the property law sense; the reference to "bona vacantia," for example, is to those "things in which nobody claims a property, and which belonged, under the common law, to the finder."[46] But, while it is true that such abandonment will at least sometimes suffice in this context, it should not be assumed that the property law concept of abandonment is controlling as to the reach of the Fourth Amendment. "The test for abandonment in the search and seizure context is distinct from the property law notion of abandonment: it is possible for a person to retain a property interest in an item, but nonetheless to relinquish his or her reasonable expectation of privacy in the object."[47] Instructive on this point is *City of St. Paul v. Vaughn*,[48] where police followed a suspect into a drycleaning establishment, saw him tuck something underneath the counter, retrieved the item (an eyeglass case) and found narcotics paraphernalia inside. Though the de-

---

(1978) (where defendant gave earring to one person with instructions to flush it down toilet and sold rings to another person, these items were abandoned and defendant lacked standing as to their seizure).

[44] Hester v. United States, 265 U.S. 57, 44 S.Ct. 445, 68 L.Ed. 898 (1924).

[45] Abel v. United States, 362 U.S. 217, 80 S.Ct. 683, 4 L.Ed.2d 668 (1960). The Court in *Abel* also stressed

that defendant had vacated the hotel room. For a discussion of other cases in which abandonment of the premises permits examination of effects left there, see § 2.3(a).

[46] Black's Law Dictionary 223 (rev. 4th ed. 1968).

[47] United States v. Thomas, 864 F.2d 843 (D.C.Cir.1989).

[48] City of St. Paul v. Vaughn, 306 Minn. 337, 237 N.W.2d 365 (1975).

fendant had "discarded the eyeglass case in a location to which any member of the public had equal access," he contended it could not be said that he had abandoned it because "his intention was merely to hide the case, not to relinquish his right of ownership." The court did not agree:

> The distinction between abandonment in the property—law sense and abandonment in the constitutional sense is critical to a proper analysis of the issue. In the law of property, the question, as defendant correctly states, is whether the owner has voluntarily, intentionally, and unconditionally relinquished his interest in the property so that another, having acquired possession, may successfully assert his superior interest. * * * In the law of search and seizure, however, the question is whether the defendant has, in discarding the property, relinquished his reasonable expectation of privacy so that its seizure and search is reasonable within the limits of the Fourth Amendment. * * * In essence, what is abandoned is not necessarily the defendant's property, but his reasonable expectation of privacy therein.

> Where the presence of the police is lawful and the discard occurs in a public place where the defendant cannot reasonably have any continued expectancy of privacy in the discarded property, the property will be deemed abandoned for purposes of search and seizure.[49]

---

[49]See also United States v. Hayes, 551 F.3d 138 (2d Cir.2008) (defendant without expectation of privacy as to contents of black bag that he concealed in "the non-curtilage area where the black bag was discovered," an area as to which there no expectation of privacy); United States v. Richardson, 537 F.3d 951 (8th Cir.2008) (where police saw defendant abruptly stop his vehicle and walk beyond dumpster, and officer then found handgun at base of tree there, the gun had been abandoned); United States v. Simpson, 439 F.3d 490 (8th Cir.2006) (where defendant "threw the rifle and magazines on the ground while being chased by police," and thereby "physically relinquished" the property in order "to disclaim ownership of this evidence," defendant had abandoned the property); United States v. Basinski, 226 F.3d 829 (7th Cir.2000) (abandonment involves "an objective test," and thus "it does not matter whether the defendant harbors a desire to later reclaim an item"); United States v. Tugwell, 125 F.3d 600 (8th Cir.1997) (defendant, upon seeing drug dog alert to his checked suitcase at bus station, departed the terminal; after several announcements for owner to pick up bag, it then opened; bag was abandoned notwithstanding fact defendant returned 2 hours later to claim it, as "issue 'is not abandonment in the strict property right sense, but rather, whether the defendant in leaving the property has relinquished her reasonable expectation of privacy'"); United States v. Rem, 984 F.2d 806 (7th Cir.1993) (where defendant jumped off train before reaching his destination and left his suitcases on the train in area open to public, abandonment can be found notwithstanding defendant's subjective intent to regain possession of suitcase later); United States v. Ramos, 960 F.2d 1065 (D.C.Cir.1992) (despite defendant's claim he merely "stowed" plastic bag of drugs in crevice between seats on bus before taking seat in next row, implying intent to recover same once investigating officer left bus, bag was abandoned because hiding place not private, as passengers "may move freely about the vehicle while on board"); United States v. Oswald, 783 F.2d 663 (6th Cir.1986) (where defendant after several hours made no effort to retrieve metal case from burned-out car he had been driving, car was abandoned because of lack of expectation of privacy, and it makes no difference that defendant may have

This analysis is fully consistent with *Katz v. United States*,[50]

entertained hope of regaining possession at some future time); State v. Jackson, 304 Conn. 383, 40 A.3d 290 (2012) (where defendant "jumped out of his hotel window in an attempt to kill himself," his socks, later found on a nearby rooftop, "a public place, open to the view of anyone who happened to look out a window of the hotel," deemed "abandoned"); Spriggs v. United States, 618 A.2d 701 (D.C.App. 1992) (where defendant placed a key case on a small curb next to a fence post and then walked away, after which case was immediately retrieved by an officer, case had been abandoned because "any passerby could have picked it up in that period of time"); Teal v. State, 282 Ga. 319, 647 S.E.2d 15 (2007) (abandonment "does not turn on strict property concepts but on whether the accused has relinquished his interest in the property to the extent that he no longer has a reasonable expectation of privacy"); State v. Britton, 633 So.2d 1208 (La.1994) (where defendant walked into gas station, "removed a packet containing several rocks of cocaine from his pants pocket, and placed it in a gum rack," and "then moved over to a large walk-in cooler as if he were making a selection," at which point officer retrieved packet, this no search as defendant had abandoned the packet); Commonwealth v. Bly, 448 Mass. 473, 862 N.E.2d 341 (2007) (defendant had no reasonable expectation of privacy in cigarette butts and water bottle he left behind in interview room at institution where he incarcerated, where items used to obtain DNA sample); State v. Crandall, 340 Or. 645, 136 P.3d 30 (2006) (where, upon being summoned by police officer, defendant in apartment parking lot "ducked down and put the baggie underneath one of the parked cars, defendant left the baggie where any person using the parking lot could have seen it" and thus "had no right to privacy in the baggie," without regard to whether it actually abandoned); State v. Jimenez, 729 A.2d 693 (R.I.1999) (where defendant, a police officer, gave department

his uniform with bullet holes for display at news conference, had not planned to wear it again, would eventually have thrown it away, and stated it of no use to him, uniform was abandoned); State v. Rynhart, 125 P.3d 938 (Utah 2005) (stressing "distinction between the concept of abandonment in property law and in the context of the Fourth Amendment," court concludes a "property owner need not intend to permanently relinquish ownership or possession to forfeit a reasonable expectation of privacy; she need only leave an item unsecured in a public place," and thus when defendant ran her car off road and left her purse in the unlocked vehicle and did not notify police or owner of the property, purse was abandoned).

Compare State v. Westover, 140 N.H. 375, 666 A.2d 1344 (1995) (under state constitution only intent to abandon will suffice, and thus defendant did not abandon clothing that he "gently" threw to ground before entering store); People v. Howard, 50 N.Y.2d 583, 430 N.Y.S.2d 578, 408 N.E.2d 908 (1980) (where officer with grounds to stop defendant for investigation pursued him into basement of building and found on top of pile of junk vanity case defendant had been seen carrying, in 5-4 decision majority, utilizing only "intent to abandon" test, found there no abandonment, while dissenters, apparently using expectation of privacy approach, concluded there was abandonment); Joh, Reclaiming "Abandoned" DNA: The Fourth Amendment and Genetic Privacy, 100 Nw.U.L. Rev. 857 (2006); and Giannelli, ABA Standards on DNA Evidence: Nontestimonial Identification Orders, 24 Crim.Just. 24, 31–32 (Spring 2009) (both questioning cases like *Bly*, supra, where an abandonment theory is utilized to acquire a person's DNA). And, it is argued that, in any event, these cases should not apply with respect to naturally shed DNA. Comment, 41 U.Balt.L.Rev. 165 (2011).

[50]Katz v. United States, 389 U.S. 347, 88 S.Ct. 507, 19 L.Ed.2d 576 (1967).

which the court in *Vaughn* cited in support. (Moreover, it justifies the conclusion that even an inadvertent leaving of effects in a public place,[51] whether or not an abandonment in the true sense of that word, can amount to a loss of any justified expectation of privacy.[52])

The great majority of the court decisions having to do with the abandonment of effects in a search and seizure context are similar to *Vaughn* in that it appears[53] the defendant tried to dispose of certain incriminating objects upon the lawful approach of or pursuit by the police. Thus, effects have been held to be abandoned when they were thrown from a car[54] or motorcycle,[55] when they were dropped to the ground by a pedestrian,[56] when they

---

[51]Compare State v. Dunn, 653 N.W.2d 688 (N.D.2002) (where instead police properly "upon the private residence property to investigate the report of a loud party" found a jacket lying on the side of the driveway, looking in pockets of jacket was a search where done "prior to any inquiry or ascertainment by the officer whether the jacket was lost or abandoned and unclaimed").

[52]State v. Barrett, 401 N.W.2d 184 (Iowa 1987) (143-page personal journal left at fast food restaurant). Cf. Holt v. United States, 675 A.2d 474 (D.C.App.1996) ("public exposure of Holt's clothing was not inadvertent, he elected to wear it into the hospital's emergency room obviously anticipating relinquishment of control over it to hospital staff during his treatment," and there "is no indication that Holt ever asked to secure his clothes in a secured locker or in some other manner consistent with a desire to remove them from public view," and thus situation analogous to where effects are left in a public place).

Compare State v. Hamilton, 314 Mont. 507, 67 P.3d 871 (2003) (under *state* constitution, distinction drawn "between a person who abandoned property and a person who loses property but retains the right and desire to regain possession of that property"); Morris v. State, 908 P.2d 931 (Wyo.1995) (where defendant apparently inadvertently left his wallet in police car, he "did not abandon his expectation of privacy; rather the wal-

let was mislaid or lost").

[53]It should be noted, however, that officers have been known to claim the defendant abandoned the property in question even though in fact the property was found in a search of defendant's person. See Younger, The Perjury Routine, The Nation 596 (May 8, 1967); Comment, 60 Geo.L.J. 507 (1971).

[54]United States v. Hollman, 541 F.2d 196 (8th Cir.1976); United States v. McLaughlin, 525 F.2d 517 (9th Cir. 1975); State v. Spears, 395 So.2d 762 (La.1981); Jackson v. State, 654 P.2d 1057 (Okl.Crim.App.1982).

[55]State v. Monk, 315 So.2d 727 (La.1975).

[56]United States v. Richardson, 427 F.3d 1128 (8th Cir.2005) (defendant abandoned gun and wallet containing cocaine dropped upon approach by police); United States v. Martin, 399 F.3d 750 (6th Cir.2005) (defendant abandoned pistol while being chased by police); United States v. Cofield, 272 F.3d 1303 (11th Cir.2001) (distinguishing Smith v. Ohio, 494 U.S. 541, 110 S.Ct. 1288, 108 L.Ed.2d 464 (1990), text at note 69 infra, court notes that here defendant, "rather than attempting to protect the contents of the bag[s], placed them on the ground and walked away"); United States v. Wilson, 36 F.3d 205 (1st Cir.1994) (defendant "had no reasonable expectation of privacy in the packet dropped and left behind in a public street"); United States v. Trimble, 986 F.2d 394 (10th Cir.1993)

were left behind in a taxi[57] or place accessible to the general public,[58] and when they were thrown out of the window of a

(defendant removed amber vial from pants and attempted to throw it to the ground; vial was "voluntarily abandoned"); People v. McClain, 149 P.3d 787 (Colo.2007) (property was abandoned, as defendant "dropped the clear plastic baggy *before* the officers called him over and seized him"); Jackson v. State, 990 A.2d 1281 (Del.2009) ("the bag Jackson threw away and the bicycle he left behind as he fled" were "abandoned property," as he had not yet been seized); Teal v. State, 282 Ga. 319, 647 S.E.2d 15 (2007) (defendant left duffel bag on ground when he fled from police); People v. Hoskins, 101 Ill.2d 209, 78 Ill.Dec. 107, 461 N.E.2d 941 (1984); Gipson v. State, 459 N.E.2d 366 (Ind.1984); State v. McGee, 381 N.W.2d 630 (Iowa 1986) (defendant dropped small package of drugs to ground); State v. Hamilton, 36 So.3d 209 (La.2010) ("defendant was approaching the officers voluntarily with his hands in his pockets, and discarded the cocaine before the police showed an intent to seize him"); People v. Mamon, 435 Mich. 1, 457 N.W.2d 623 (1990) (defendant threw bag to ground); State v. Lisenbee, 116 Nev. 1124, 13 P.3d 947 (2000) (defendant dropped baggie of drugs while running away from police); Cooper v. State, 806 P.2d 1136 (Okl.Crim.App.1991) (suspect dropped cigarette package to floor under table when officer entered bar); Atterberry v. State, 726 P.2d 898 (Okl.Crim.App.1986) (suspect lawfully stopped for investigation dropped small package to ground); State v. Dupree, 319 S.C. 454, 462 S.E.2d 279 (1995) (where defendant threw plastic bag to floor at officer's feet, bag was abandoned).

But see State v. May, 608 A.2d 772 (Me.1992) (after arrestee's release, police discovered his wallet in back of police cruiser; because "defendant did not intentionally discard his wallet but merely lost it, he did not at that time relinquish his expectation of privacy in it and thereby abandon it"); People v. Anderson, 24 N.Y.2d 12, 298 N.Y.S.2d 698, 246 N.E.2d 508 (1969)

(abandonment not established, as "the police officer's testimony reveals that he picked up the box so soon after it had been dropped that it is impossible to determine whether or not the defendant, if given the opportunity, would have picked up the box himself"); State v. Pidcock, 306 Or. 335, 759 P.2d 1092 (1988) (briefcase found by side of road not abandoned, as defendant was then actively engaged in trying to locate it; officer's examination of contents a search, albeit a reasonable one undertaken in an effort to identify the owner).

[57]Shackleford v. Commonwealth, 262 Va. 196, 547 S.E.2d 899 (2001) (defendant, questioned at train station by police re contents of his bag, which he refused to open, was followed by them when he traveled via taxi to a motel; he had no expectation of privacy as to gun and drugs he concealed in the taxi and left behind when he exited).

[58]United States v. Kelly, 329 F.3d 624 (8th Cir.2003) (after defendant's lawful arrest, his wallet found on floor at police station; "when Kelly discarded the wallet to avoid its discovery he also discarded any privacy interest he may have had in the wallet or its contents"); United States v. Liu, 180 F.3d 957 (8th Cir.1999) (where defendant, passenger on train, when questioned about his luggage during scheduled stop of the train, abruptly left the train, quickened his pace and then ran until seized, this constituted abandonment of luggage in the train, as "such behavior is not indicative of an intent to return"); United States v. Lewis, 40 F.3d 1325 (1st Cir.1994) (gun and drugs were abandoned when upon approach of police they placed under car parked in store's parking lot); United States v. Rem, 984 F.2d 806 (7th Cir.1993) (defendant abandoned his suitcase when "he chose to place the suitcase, which had no identification on it, in a public luggage rack on the train, and then abruptly left the train without it before reaching his destination"); United States v. Wider, 951

residence.[59] (On occasion, however, the abandonment concept is utilized in quite different circumstances; it has been held, for example, that one abandons the hair he has cut off by a barber[60], the saliva he expectorates onto a public sidewalk[61] leaves on a discarded paper cup,[62] or uses in licking an envelope he then

---

F.2d 1283 (D.C.Cir.1991) (paper sack left on steps of courtyard adjacent to street); United States v. Nordling, 804 F.2d 1466 (9th Cir.1986) (defendant, removed from airplane about to leave, left luggage on plane and disclaimed having any; court stresses "in circumstances it was virtually certain that the bag would be opened, inspected and turned over to law enforcement authorities"); United States v. McFillin, 713 F.2d 57 (4th Cir.1981) (explosives abandoned in public area); United States v. Smith, 293 A.2d 856 (D.C. App.1972); Maxwell v. State, 443 So.2d 967 (Fla.1983) (where 2 passengers on bus arrested and told to claim their bags but they left one behind, it abandoned); State v. Dobard, 824 So.2d 1127 (La.2002) (defendant, up seeing police approaching booth in which he seated in bar, dropped objects to floor and got up from booth and began walking away; four pieces of crack cocaine found on floor had been abandoned); People v. Ramirez-Portoreal, 88 N.Y.2d 99, 643 N.Y.S.2d 502, 666 N.E.2d 207 (1996) (where paper bags placed, respectively, in tail pipe of parked van and in trash pile on city street, by defendants who then remained in the vicinity, no objectively reasonable expectation of privacy in such places); State v. Freeman, 64 Ohio St.2d 291, 414 N.E.2d 1044 (1980) (defendant lawfully arrested at bus station dropped his luggage and fled; luggage abandoned); State v. Belcher, 306 Or. 343, 759 P.2d 1096 (1988) (defendant had abandoned his backpack in tavern when he fled just before police arrived to deal with fight defendant involved in).

Compare United States v. Garzon, 119 F.3d 1446 (10th Cir.1997) (bus passenger did not abandon his backpacks during layover when "he left them in a secure overhead internal luggage rack just as he was told he could by the bus driver"); State v.

Parker, 399 So.2d 24 (Fla.App.1981) (no abandonment when gun left under ladder next to basement stairwell in defendant's fenced back yard; for abandonment "the property must be discarded in a place where the person has no reasonable expectation of privacy, such as an open field, or public street").

[59]United States v. Soto-Beniquez, 356 F.3d 1 (1st Cir.2003); United States v. Pirolli, 673 F.2d 1200 (11th Cir.1982); United States v. Lewis, 227 F.Supp. 433 (S.D.N.Y.1964); Commonwealth v. Harper, 485 Pa. 572, 403 A.2d 536 (1979).

Compare Hobson v. United States, 226 F.2d 890 (8th Cir.1955) (bag of heroin thrown out window landed in curtilage of defendant's house and thus was still protected by Fourth Amendment); Commonwealth v. Straw, 422 Mass. 756, 665 N.E.2d 80 (1996) (where "the defendant intended to protect his property from any public scrutiny because he placed the property in a closed and locked briefcase and disposed of the briefcase by throwing it into the fenced-in curtilage of his family's home," where "only he and members of his family normally would have a right of access," property was not abandoned).

[60]United States v. Cox, 428 F.2d 683 (7th Cir.1970) ("Defendant's intent in discarding his severed hair is no less clear because it involved no affirmative act on his part").

[61]Commonwealth v. Cabral, 69 Mass.App. 68, 866 N.E.2d 429 (2007) (defendant had no reasonable expectation of privacy in his abandoned spittle, which investigator retrieved and had tested for DNA).

[62]Williamson v. State, 413 Md. 521, 993 A.2d 626 (2010) (after defendant arrested he served a meal from McDonald's in his cell, and defendant discarded wrappers and paper cup on floor, and police retrieved cup and had

places in the mail,[63] and the excreta he deposits in a hospital bedpan.[64] But in *Ferguson v. City of Charleston*,[65] where the dissent claimed that a hospital patient's urine tested for drugs could be regarded "as one of the 'effects' * * * of the person who has passed and abandoned it," the majority responded that the "reasonable expectation of privacy enjoyed by the typical patient undergoing diagnostic tests in a hospital is that the results of those tests will not be shared with nonmedical personnel without her consent.") But effects not otherwise abandoned cannot be deemed abandoned merely because the defendant failed to comply with an illegal police order regarding the placement of those effects.[66]

It should not be assumed, however, that in every instance in which a defendant relinquishes possession or control, albeit briefly, an abandonment for Fourth Amendment purposes has occurred. The fundamental question is whether the relinquishment occurred under circumstances indicating he retained no justified expectation of privacy in the object. Thus, as the Supreme Court concluded in *Rios v. United States*,[67] a "passenger who lets a package drop to the floor of the taxicab in which he is riding can hardly be said to have 'abandoned' it."[68] Even when the place where the object is put is somewhat more public than the interior of an occupied taxicab, there still may be a justified expectation

---

it tested for DNA; defendant "could not reasonably expect that the police would not collect, and potentially investigate, the trash he discarded in his cell," and since defendant "did not retain a reasonable expectation of privacy" re the "lawfully acquired DNA," testing same not objectionable).

[63]State v. Athan, 160 Wash.2d 354, 158 P.3d 27 (2007) (letter sent to police officer in response to undercover officer's letter to murder suspect on another matter, sent for specific purpose of obtaining material from which to determine suspect's DNA; court concludes there "is no subjective expectation of privacy in discarded genetic material just as there is no subjective expectation of privacy in fingerprints or footprints left in a public place").

[64]Venner v. State, 279 Md. 47, 367 A.2d 949 (1977) ("Venner could not have had an 'expectation . . . that society [would be] prepared to recognize as "reasonable"' a property right in human excreta for the simple reason that human experience is to abandon it immediately").

A hospitalized patient lacks an expectation of privacy as to various

other things coming from his body as well, including a bullet removed from his arm by surgery. Commonwealth v. Johnson, 556 Pa. 216, 727 A.2d 1089 (1999).

[65]Ferguson v. City of Charleston, 532 U.S. 67, 121 S.Ct. 1281, 149 L.Ed.2d 205 (2001).

[66]United States v. Garzon, 119 F.3d 1446 (10th Cir.1997) (where during layover bus passenger left backpack "in a secure overhead internal luggage rack just as he was told he could by the bus driver," this cannot be deemed abandonment because of defendant's failure to obey an officer's "unlawful order to move his personal belongings from the bus and to parade them past a drug-sniffing dog").

[67]Rios v. United States, 364 U.S. 253, 80 S.Ct. 1431, 4 L.Ed.2d 1688 (1960).

[68]Nor is the container abandoned merely because the passenger gets out of the vehicle at the request or command of the police. People v. James, 163 Ill.2d 302, 206 Ill.Dec. 190, 645 N.E.2d 195 (1994).

of privacy. Thus in *Smith v. Ohio,*[69] where the defendant tossed the grocery bag he was carrying onto the hood of his car in response to a police officer's inquiry and then attempted to protect the bag from the officer's inspection, the Court unhesitantly concluded that he "clearly has not abandoned that property." Also illustrative is *United States v. Boswell,*[70] where the defendant carried an object covered with a blanket into the hallway of a building and set it down in the hallway while he made a telephone call at a phone some 20 to 30 feet away. The court quite correctly concluded that this did not constitute an abandonment.[71] *Boswell* is clearly distinguishable from *Anderson*

---

[69]Smith v. Ohio, 494 U.S. 541, 110 S.Ct. 1288, 108 L.Ed.2d 464 (1990).

[70]United States v. Boswell, 347 A.2d 270 (D.C.App.1975).

[71]While the court erroneously based this conclusion on the assumption that an actual "intent to abandon" was necessary, which drew a sharp dissent, the result is correct if viewed in justified-expectation-of-privacy terms. A more cautious and correct statement re the significance of intent in this context appears in State v. May, 608 A.2d 772 (Me.1992): "While it may not be necessary for defendant actually to 'intend' to abandon the property, whether he intentionally discarded the item or merely lost or mislaid it is plainly relevant to ascertaining whether he had a 'substantive expectation of privacy' in the item."

See also United States v. Jackson, 544 F.2d 407 (9th Cir.1976) (putting suitcase down and taking a few steps away from it not abandonment); State v. Joyce, 229 Conn. 10, 639 A.2d 1007 (1994) (fact defendant, who thereafter suffered serious burns to self and clothing, had spilled gasoline on his clothing does not manifest absence of intent to preserve privacy interest in the clothing, even after the clothing damaged by fire); State v. Mooney, 218 Conn. 85, 588 A.2d 145 (1991) (defendant, a homeless person, had reasonable expectation of privacy in and had not abandoned his duffel bag and cardboard box, seized by police from a highway bridge abutment, as (1) "society has traditionally afforded a high degree of deference to

expectations of privacy in closed containers because such an area is normally intended as a repository of personal effects"; (2) the containers were at a place the police knew "defendant regarded as his home"; (3) defendant had not abandoned them, but could not be there to assert his Fourth Amendment rights because he had been arrested; and (4) the purpose of the search was to gather evidence of crime); State v. Philbrick, 436 A.2d 844 (Me.1981) (where defendant, injured in fight, left his knapsack by side of road and hitched ride to police station and reported same, knapsack had not been abandoned; court erroneously says abandonment "is primarily a question of intent," but adds the more relevant observation that the police were aware "the defendant merely left his property behind him, more or less of necessity, making no attempt, however, to discard it or disassociate it from himself"); Stanberry v. State, 343 Md. 720, 684 A.2d 823 (1996) (defendant bus passenger, by placing his bag on overhead rack and leaving it there while he used the facilities at a scheduled rest stop, did not lose his reasonable expectation of privacy in bag's contents); State v. Cook, 332 Or. 601, 34 P.3d 156 (2001) (defendant did not abandon clothing, as "leaving the items on the ground in compliance with the officer's request to 'step out' [of the area near the dumpster] is not conduct demonstrating an intent permanently to relinquish possession of the items").

For more on the Fourth Amendment rights of the homeless, see Morrison, The Fourth Amendment's

v. State,[72] where the defendant put a margarine carton under a rock on a public beach. There, though the defendant was still on the beach in the general vicinity, the court properly held that the carton had been abandoned for Fourth Amendment purposes. The nature of the object and the place where it was put indicate that there was no justified expectation of privacy as to the carton, for any curious passerby might have examined it.[73] Similarly, in

---

Applicability to Residents of Homeless Shelters, 32 Hamline L.Rev. 319 (2009); Stec, Search and Seizure Laws Strip Personhood from the Homeless, 53 Fed.Law. 53 (May 2006); Townsend, Cardboard Castles: The Fourth Amendment's Protection of the Homeless's Makeshift Shelters in Public Areas, 35 Cal.W.L.Rev. 223 (1999); Note, 101 Yale L.J. 1305, 1330 (1992) (proposing "a standard focusing on private activities," which "would not invalidate all searches of the areas shelterless people inhabit" but "would simply prevent searches of these areas from being automatically excluded from the Fourth Amendment's protection of houses"); and other student commentary at 72 B.U.L.Rev. 425 & 443 (1992); 41 Duke L.J. 1508 (1992); 60 Fordham L.Rev. 1003 (1992); 36 How.L.J. 75 (1993); 18 N.Engl.L.Rev. 305 (1996); 53 Ohio St.L.J. 869 (1992); 13 Pace L.Rev. 229 (1993); 26 Suffolk U.L.Rev. 279 (1992); 39 Wayne L.Rev. 155 (1992).

[72]Anderson v. State, 133 Ga.App. 45, 209 S.E.2d 665 (1974).

[73]The dissent in *Anderson* objects: "If I put my shirt, shoes, or wallet on a public beach and walk into the water, or walk 75 feet down the beach, I do not give the world leave to search my pockets or my purse." This is true, and it is also true (and more relevant) that one would not expect a casual passerby to conduct such a search, and thus if such objects had been left by the defendant in *Anderson* a different result would have been called for. A curious passerby, however, might well look in a margarine carton under a rock.

Anderson is thus distinguishable from United States v. Sylvester, 848 F.2d 520 (5th Cir.1988) (hunters in a field had not abandoned an un-

locked "hunter's box" merely by being briefly out of sight of the box); Morton v. State, 284 Md. 526, 397 A.2d 1385 (1979) ("Persons who avail themselves of the facilities at a public recreation center and place their belongings on the sidelines of a basketball court do not, without more, forfeit the legitimate expectation that those belongings will remain undisturbed, free from unreasonable governmental intrusion").

Morton should in turn be distinguished from United States v. Morgan, 936 F.2d 1561 (10th Cir.1991) (defendant, being pursued by police, threw down gym bag "in the backyard of someone he knew or was acquainted with," still no expectation of privacy, as that yard "abutted an open field," "the bag would have been plainly visible to those passing by," and defendant had not "requested the assistance of anyone to help recover or protect the bag, and the record discloses no one else was present who could have provided such assistance"); Buchanan v. State, 432 So.2d 147 (Fla.App.1983) (defendant had no expectation of privacy as to drugs he put under mattress of hospital emergency room "where medical personnel were constantly walking in and out and where he could have expected to remain only a few hours at most"); People v. Loveless, 80 Ill.App.3d 1052, 36 Ill.Dec. 120, 400 N.E.2d 540 (1980) (no search for police officer merely to pick up jacket lying on table in crowded bar, as one "who places a coat on a table in a busy tavern must reasonably expect that that coat will be touched or handled by an employee or by any member of the public who desires to use or sit at that table").

Anderson is also distinguishable from situations in which circumstances have dictated that defendant

---

United States v. Oswald,[74] where defendant left his burning car by the roadside and after the passage of several hours had made no effort to retrieve from it a metal case or to notify the authorities of the event, the case had been abandoned. As the court explained:

> Not only will privacy expectations vary with the type of property involved, * * * but they will vary with the location of the property. When one leaves a suitcase in an airport baggage claim area, he leaves it in a place where there is normally some measure of security. It is reasonable to expect that checked luggage will be locked up, if not claimed within a reasonable time, and will be kept safe until the person holding the claim check comes to retrieve it. One who chooses to leave luggage in an unlocked burned-out automobile at the side of a highway in the country can fairly be thought to have a much lower expectation of privacy—and Oswald's expectation, as we know, was very low indeed. Flaming cars do tend to attract a certain amount of attention. Flames may keep people at a respectful distance for a time, but fires eventually die out; and a fire-ravaged automobile, left unprotected in the open countryside invites just the kind of examination Oswald feared his would receive.[75]

There are circumstances, of course, in which a person may surrender immediate control of an object for a much longer period of time without surrendering his justified expectation of privacy with respect to that object. *People v. Laursen*[76] is such a case. There the owner of a home permitted the police to carry off boxes

---

surrender control but it would be expected the police would aid him in keeping his effects secure. See, e.g., United States v. Markland, 489 F.Supp. 932 (D.Conn.1980), order reversed on other grounds, 635 F.2d 174 (2d Cir.1980) (defendant taken to hospital after vehicle he driving involved in accident, causing personal effects in the car to be scattered about the area; held, "neither the involuntary expulsion of the bag from the car during the accident or Markland's failure to collect his possessions before leaving the scene of the accident can be interpreted to indicate an intent to abandon"). In such a case, the next issue is whether the police may inventory the effects while holding them for defendant; see § 5.5(b).

[74] United States v. Oswald, 783 F.2d 663 (6th Cir.1986).

[75] See also United States v. Gillis, 358 F.3d 386 (6th Cir.2004) (defendant did not have reasonable expectation of privacy in contents of abandoned vehicle nearby his residence, as vehicle was unlocked, windshield and other windows were missing, allowing anyone to reach inside).

[76] People v. Laursen, 22 Cal.App.3d 1033, 99 Cal.Rptr. 841 (1972), aff'd, 8 Cal.3d 192, 104 Cal.Rptr. 425, 501 P.2d 1145 (1972). See also United States v. James, 353 F.3d 606 (8th Cir.2003) ("a person does not abandon his property merely because he gives it to someone else to store"); United States v. Neely, 345 F.3d 366 (5th Cir.2003) (hospital patient's clothing, kept in storeroom at hospital, had not been abandoned by patient; "an emergency room patient does not forfeit his possessory rights to clothing simply by walking (or in many cases being carried) through the hospital door"); United States v. Basinski, 226 F.3d 829 (7th Cir.2000) (no abandonment where defendant "entrusted the *locked* briefcase to a lifelong friend so that Friedman might hide it on private property owned by Friedman, in a locked barn, surrounded by a locked gate, in a remote part of Wisconsin" and "specifically ask[ed] Friedman to

of clothing the defendant had left there in his custody. The court

keep the case hidden in a private place, until the time he asked him to destroy it"); United States v. Most, 876 F.2d 191 (D.C.Cir.1989) (where defendant checked his bag with store clerk before shopping there, as was store policy, and then left bag with clerk when he left the store briefly, as was not uncommon, no abandonment, as defendant "did not place his bag within the reach of the world generally" but instead "entrusted his belongings to the professional supervision of the cashiers with the clear understanding that they would protect the property from intrusion by the public"); Hackett v. State, 386 So.2d 35 (Fla.App.1980) (defendant checked out of motel owing $600 and left luggage behind, then and later informed owner that money was being wired to him and bill would be paid, but after 1 day police summoned and they searched the luggage; held, no abandonment, as defendant "had at all times exhibited an intention to return for his luggage as soon as he had obtained the funds to pay his outstanding bill; he had in effect left his luggage as collateral, which he intended to redeem"); State v. Boone, 284 Md. 1, 393 A.2d 1361 (1978) (notwithstanding defendant's failure to pay rent on his apartment or to be present at time of eviction, he did not thereby "relinquish his right to [his personal effects in the apartment] or to a reasonable expectation of privacy therein," but only gave up "a right to have the goods remain in the apartment"); State v. Taylor, 114 Nev. 1071, 968 P.2d 315 (1998) (fact defendant's suitcase had been checked by his niece and traveling companion did not mean defendant had abandoned it, as one "does not abandon property upon a merely failure to openly exercise control over it prior to its search or where access and control over property is shared with a third party").

Hackett and *Boone* must be distinguished from those cases in which the tenant's personal effects are subject to a lien for nonpayment of rent. See United States v. Poulsen, 41 F.3d 1330 (9th Cir.1994) ("a lien on the contents of a rental unit is sufficient to extinguish the renter's legitimate expectation of privacy," and thus after "expiration of the rental period [defendant] no longer had a legitimate expectation of privacy in the contents of his storage unit," notwithstanding his claim "that he did not intend to abandon his property"); United States v. Rahme, 813 F.2d 31 (2d Cir.1987) (once hotel "properly takes possession of the luggage, the guest no longer has the right to control access to it and can have no legitimate expectation of privacy in it").

Compare United States v. Hershenow, 680 F.2d 847 (1st Cir.1982) (where defendant left sealed box with maintenance man at nursing home, box deemed abandoned 4 months later, as defendant "did not know the location of the box," had not "inquired about the box * * * or done anything to assert control over it"); United States v. Davis, 624 F.3d 508 (2d Cir.2010) (defendant had abandoned safe left in home of estranged wife, as he had returned to retrieve some of his belongings but failed to respond to her calls to retrieve the remainder, and wife never prevented defendant from retrieving property); United States v. Thomas, 451 F.3d 543 (8th Cir.2006) (defendant abandoned mail in rented mailbox in private postal service store where no one had picked up mail or paid for mail box for over a year and defendant's contract with store authorized store to dispose of mail unclaimed after 30 days); United States v. Robinson, 390 F.3d 853 (6th Cir.2004) (where defendant's rental agreement at Mailboxes, Etc. store had lapsed at time package delivered there, and standard service agreement said packages sent to expired mailbox "may be discarded or destroyed" after 30 days if no arrangement for forwarding made, package seized by police more than 30 days after deliver "could properly be characterized as abandoned"); United States v. Chandler, 197 F.3d 1198 (8th Cir.1999) (where defendant left his duty bag at police station when he suspended without

held that the defendant "had a reasonable expectation of privacy with respect to the boxes and clothing he left in the custody of Graham with the advice that he would be in touch with him later with regard to their disposition. He had not abandoned them."[77] Indeed, sometimes the justified expectation of privacy will remain even though the defendant's surrender of control has been permanent, as is illustrated by *State v. Comeaux*.[78] The defendant, hospitalized after an automobile accident, gave a blood sample to the hospital for treatment purposes, after which an officer by a false claim of authority obtained from a nurse a portion of that sample, which was then tested for alcohol content. In rejecting the state's claim there had been no intrusion upon the patient's Fourth Amendment rights, the court cogently stated:

pay for suspected drug trafficking, and left it in supervisory officer's office rather than his own locker and over the following 7 months "failed to reclaim or even inquire about the bag," it abandoned); United States v. McCarthy, 77 F.3d 522 (1st Cir.1996) (defendant had no expectation of privacy re suitcase where "he left the open suitcase in Henderson's trailer after Henderson told McCarthy that he and Hunter had to leave"); United States v. Austin, 66 F.3d 1115 (10th Cir.1995) (where defendant left his bag with perfect stranger at airport, bag had been abandoned; defendant's reliance on *Most* rejected because here "defendant voluntarily relinquished his bag without any conditions or agreements"); Wilson v. State, 297 Ark. 568, 765 S.W.2d 1 (1989) (defendants stayed one night with friend and then departed, leaving his jacket with pistol in it behind, and host first took jacket and gun to nearby vacant lot and covered with leaves and then took the police there; because "no evidence that the appellant made any attempt to recover or retrieve these items," he "had renounced or abandoned his right to privacy"); People v. Ayala, 24 Cal.4th 243, 99 Cal.Rptr.2d 532, 6 P.3d 193 (2000) (where invitee or social guest at automobile body shop left behind two orange juice containers, one full and one nearly empty, the containers were abandoned); State v. Shelton, 345 Mont. 330, 191 P.3d 420 (2008) (defendant, while a temporary guest for a few hours in apartment of one Wood, left bag of rubbish in garbage can

inside apartment; since there "no evidence to suggest that he had entrusted the bag of trash to Wood for safekeeping," the bag was abandoned property); State v. Buckman, 259 Neb. 924, 613 N.W.2d 463 (2000) (where defendant, lawfully arrested, smoked two cigarettes at police station and discarded butts, they were abandoned property); State v. Howe, 159 N.H. 366, 986 A.2d 631 (2009) (where defendant, who rented bedroom, was asked by landlady to leave for nonpayment of rent and was told to remove his belongings within 7 days and did so but left behind a few items, including manila folder and CDs containing child porn, and gave no indication he would return for them and had not returned 12 days after deadline, when landlady found the items while cleaning the room, "defendant's actions demonstrate a clear intent to abandon" the property); State v. Gould, 131 Ohio St.3d 179, 963 N.E.2d 136 (2012) (where defendant left hard drive in his apartment with other belongings when he stole brother's truck and left Toledo in Aug. 2006, and until his arrest in June 2007 "never inquired about the hard drive or attempted to assert control over it," and instead "concealed his whereabouts," defendant had abandoned the hard drive).

[77] In this type of case, the central issue usually is whether the bailee can give effective consent to the search. See § 8.6(a).

[78] State v. Comeaux, 818 S.W.2d 46 (Tex.Crim.App.1991).

The record reflects that appellee gave a sample of his blood in order to receive medical help only; he had no intention of allowing that sample to be used for any other purpose. Common sense dictates, in this age of blood testing for everything from HIV infection to drug use, that a person does not assume that, by giving a sample of blood for private testing, that blood sample could then be submitted to the State, or to any other person or entity, for a purpose other than that for which it was given.

By similar reasoning, it has been held that where a person has left an object with another person for safekeeping, as in *Laursen*, but then directed that person to destroy the property, such a request has not "necessarily entailed an abandonment."[79]

A number of courts have held that an abandonment may arise out of a disclaimer of ownership[80] made in response to police questioning.[81] The leading case is *United States v. Colbert*,[82] where officers approached two men carrying briefcases to question them

---

[79]United States v. Basinski, 226 F.3d 829 (7th Cir.2000) ("By ordering Friedman to destroy the briefcase, Basinski did not invite all the world to rummage through the briefcase at will, as a defendant in abandonment situations essentially does. Rather, his command manifested a desire that nobody possess or examine the contents of the briefcase"). Accord: United States v. Johnston, 353 F.3d 617 (8th Cir.2003).

[80]To be distinguished from mere silence in response to police questioning about ownership, which is not to be characterized in the same way. "To equate a passive failure to claim potentially incriminating evidence with an affirmative abandonment of property would be to twist both logic and experience in a most uncomfortable knot." State v. Joyner, 66 Haw. 543, 669 P.2d 152 (1983). See also State v. May, 608 A.2d 772 (Me.1992) (where arrestee shrugged his shoulders when asked what had become of his wallet, which in fact he had mislaid in police car, his answer not proof of abandonment, as "abandonment cannot be * * * inferred from mere silence in response to police questioning"); Stanberry v. State, 343 Md. 720, 684 A.2d 823 (1996) (where police boarded bus during rest stop and held up item of luggage from overhead rack and asked all passengers if anyone owned it and no one answered, police did not reasonably believe bag abandoned, as "police may

not infer abandonment from the owner's passive failure to claim property"; court emphasizes such result necessary for such drug interdiction activity to meet constitutional requirements under Florida v. Bostick, 501 U.S. 429, 111 S.Ct. 2382, 115 L.Ed.2d 389 (1991), which says nonseizure if passenger free to remain silent in response to police questioning). United States v. Adams, 583 F.3d 457 (6th Cir.2009) (police, in hotel room by consent, asked to whom jacket on floor belonged, and no one, including defendant, claimed ownership; defendant had thus abandoned any privacy interest in the jacket).

[81]United States v. Alexander, 573 F.3d 465 (7th Cir.2009) (defendant had abandoned vehicle where, upon police inquiry, he "repeatedly said that it wasn't his car"); United States v. Ojeda-Ramos, 455 F.3d 1178 (10th Cir.2006) (where officer asked defendant bus passenger "whether the blue suitcase was his, he expressly disclaimed any interest in it" and thereby "abandoned the blue suitcase"); United States v. Fulani, 368 F.3d 351 (3d Cir.2004) (where defendant bus passenger denied that any luggage on overhead rack was his and also remained silent when police officer asked all passengers who owned bag, defendant "abandoned ownership in his bag, effectively waiving his right to bar its search," notwithstanding presence of his nametag on the luggage); United States v. Sanders, 196 F.3d 910 (8th

Cir.1999) (where passenger Sanders in pickup truck denied bag in bed of pickup was his, property deemed abandoned even if officers "knew that Sanders was lying"); United States v. Welbeck, 145 F.3d 493 (2d Cir.1998) (where defendant, passenger on train, denied owning bag under seat in front of his, he "cannot be heard to complain that the officers violated his privacy interest in a bag he denied was his," as it thereby became "abandoned property"); United States v. McDonald, 100 F.3d 1320 (7th Cir.1996) (where bus passenger repeatedly denied owning bags in overhead rack, this constituted abandonment); United States v. Hernandez, 7 F.3d 944 (10th Cir.1993) (when bus stopped at immigration checkpoint, officer asked all passengers who owned backpack on rack above empty seat, and no one answered, and when passenger said it belonged to defendant, defendant denied ownership; defendant "had abandoned his backpack"); United States v. Alvarez, 6 F.3d 287 (5th Cir.1993) (abandonment where defendant, upon his arrest in motel room, asserted none of effects there were his); United States v. De Los Santos Ferrer, 999 F.2d 7 (1st Cir.1993) (airline passenger's disclaimer that checked suitcase was hers, even if disclaimer was "immediately suspect" and thus disbelieved by police, treated as equivalent of abandonment); United States v. Gonzales, 979 F.2d 711 (9th Cir.1992) (bus passenger's denial that bags next to him were his constitutes abandonment though his "location with respect to the bags suggested that they were his"); United States v. Frazier, 936 F.2d 262 (6th Cir.1991) (abandonment where "defendant's companion placed the bag on the floor" and "defendant stated that it was not his"); United States v. Lewis, 921 F.2d 1294 (D.C.Cir. 1990) (bus passenger's denial tote bag on rack above her owned by her constituted abandonment; it "irrelevant" she "might have repossessed the bag if the detective had not taken it"); United States v. Clark, 891 F.2d 501 (4th Cir.1989) (defendant lacked reasonable expectation of privacy as to suit-

case in baggage claim area, as to which police knew defendant had claim stub, given defendant's "denial of ownership, or even knowledge of, the suitcase"); United States v. McBean, 861 F.2d 1570 (11th Cir.1988) (even if defendant's consent to search of car was exceeded by searching luggage in trunk, defendant cannot object, as he had abandoned the luggage by asserting it was not his and that he did not know what it contained); State v. Mahone, 67 Haw. 644, 701 P.2d 171 (1985) (woman consented to search of apartment, defendant cannot complain about search extending to canvas-type bag there, though he a known overnight guest, as he denied ownership of bag and made no protest when it searched); State v. Carvajal, 202 N.J. 214, 996 A.2d 1029 (2010) (where defendant bus passenger "denied having any luggage on the bus" and other passengers all claimed their luggage, leaving "one unclaimed duffel bag with no apparent or known owner," defendant had abandoned the bag); State v. Brown, 348 Or. 293, 232 P.3d 962 (2010) (where defendant "disclaimed ownership of the bags and voluntarily left them behind" in hotel room rented by another, "she no longer retained a reasonable expectation of privacy in the bags," and thus consent of renter sufficient for search of bags); Commonwealth v. Smith, 575 Pa. 203, 836 A.2d 5 (2003) (where during drug interdiction of bus police searched bag after defendant's "repeated and affirmative denial of ownership of the bag" and "the failure of any of the other passengers to claim the bag, police [properly] concluded that it was abandoned"); Faulkner v. State, 317 Md. 441, 564 A.2d 785 (1989) (employee who identified one locker as his and denied that second locker was his had no expectation of privacy in second locker); Commonwealth v. Dowds, 563 Pa. 377, 761 A.2d 1125 (2000) (where airline passenger denied that bag with tags bearing her name and located in baggage claim area was hers, that "an act from which an intention to abandon may be inferred"); State v. Velasquez, 994 S.W.2d 676 (Tex.Crim.

because one of the men fit the description of a wanted felon. As the officers approached, the two men set their briefcases on the sidewalk. They identified themselves as book salesmen, but when the officers asked to see their wares they replied that they did not have to show the officers anything and denied that they owned the briefcases or had any knowledge about them. The officers then asked the two men for their draft cards, and when neither produced one they were both arrested for failure to carry a Selective Service registration certification. After being placed in the patrol car, they again denied knowing anything about the briefcases; one of the officers returned to the briefcases, opened them, and found sawed-off shotguns inside. The court held:

> The facts of this case show conclusively that Colbert and Reese abandoned their briefcases before the searches took place. In response to police questions they both disclaimed any interest in the briefcases and began to walk away from them. The police officers in no way compelled these actions. Under these circumstances appellants could entertain no reasonable expectation of privacy in them.[83]

Judge Goldberg wrote a ringing dissent which casts serious doubt upon the holding in *Colbert*. He observed that "the patently unbelievable disclaimer of possession was accompanied by statements" that the defendants did not have to show the police anything, and that the "first inkling of any 'abandonment' came only after the appellants were apprehended by the state officers, arrested on wholly unrelated and somewhat dubious grounds, and given the Hobson's choice of making either an incriminating admission or the obviously false disclaimer."[84] As Judge Goldberg saw it, the defendants had not surrendered their expectation of

---

App.1999) (abandonment where bus passenger "at least twice denied ownership of the bag" and "there is no evidence of police misconduct"); State v. Milashoski, 163 Wis.2d 72, 471 N.W.2d 42 (1991) (firemen removed containers from basement of home where fire occurred, resident lacked expectation of privacy as to their contents when he said "he had no idea what was in the containers in the basement" and "speculated that they could have been left there by the previous owner"); Andrews v. State, 40 P.3d 708 (Wyo.2002) (defendant "repeatedly renounced ownership of the third duffel bag").

Compare State v. Taylor, 114 Nev. 1071, 968 P.2d 315 (1998) (defendant did not abandon his suitcase upon denying to police that he knew his niece and traveling companion, who had checked it with airline, as "a disclaimer of ownership of the subject property must be express)."

This is not to suggest that such a disclaimer is essential for abandonment, for that is not the case. State v. Farinich, 179 N.J.Super. 1, 430 A.2d 233 (1981), judgment aff'd, 89 N.J. 378, 446 A.2d 120.

[82]United States v. Colbert, 474 F.2d 174 (5th Cir.1973).

[83]Actually, as the dissent points out, in this en banc case six members of the court subscribed to that view, and six others upheld the admission of the evidence on other grounds.

[84]Consider, in this regard, Walter v. United States, 447 U.S. 649, 100 S.Ct. 2395, 65 L.Ed.2d 410 (1980), where packages of obscene films, shipped by defendants, were misdelivered and then turned over to the FBI. In the course of concluding that the FBI could not screen the films without a warrant, in that this action would

privacy in the briefcases, but rather had been tricked out of it. He observed:

> A coerced lie cannot effect an abandonment. No one, but no one, could have believed that defendants were not in possession of the briefcases. To say that defendants knew they were waiving a constitutional right when they uttered these meaningless lies under the threat of imminent discovery is a fiction, pure and simple. This was not a case of physical abandonment * * * where it is fair to say that the defendant knowingly relinquished any expectation of privacy he might have had in the item. Here, the "abandonment" consisted of an unknowing response to custodial interrogation. Are we to say that defendants should have known that despite all that had preceded the disclaimer, they still had a right to privacy in respect to the briefcases that the police would respect if the correct answer was given to the police query? * * * Neither the police officers, the defendants, nor anyone on the streets of Birmingham that day could possibly have believed that anything was "abandoned," voluntarily or otherwise, as a result of defendants' lie.[85]

In order to further assess *Colbert,* it is useful to note at the outset that it is clearly established that, although abandoned property may normally be obtained and used for evidentiary purposes by the police, this is not so if the abandonment was coerced by[86] or otherwise the fruit of[87] unlawful police action. "Property is not considered abandoned when a person throws

---

exceed that earlier undertaken by private persons examining the packages, the opinion of Stevens, J., announcing the judgment of the Court but joined only by Stewart, J., states:

> Nor can petitioner's failure to make a more prompt claim to the Government for return of the films be fairly regarded as an abandonment of their interest in preserving the privacy of the shipment. As subsequent events have demonstrated, such a request could reasonably be expected to precipitate criminal proceedings. We cannot equate an unwillingness to invite a criminal prosecution with a voluntary abandonment of any interest in the contents of the cartons.

[85]Even more incredible in this regard is United States v. Miller, 589 F.2d 1117 (1st Cir.1978). After a federal agent removed four suitcases from defendant's car, defendant disclaimed any ownership or knowledge of them but yet admitted knowing the combination to one of them. Notwithstanding this scenario, the court upheld the agent's actions in looking inside the suitcase on the ground "that one who disclaims any interest in luggage thereby disclaims any concern about whether or not the contents of the luggage remain private."

Compare United States v. Burnette, 698 F.2d 1038 (9th Cir.1983) (notwithstanding defendant's initial disclaimer of ownership of purse, this not abandonment where her subsequent conduct indicated her desire to maintain physical possession of it and the privacy of its contents); State v. Morton, 326 Or. 466, 953 P.2d 374 (1998) (though defendant "denied vehemently any ownership interest in or knowledge of the contents of the container" dropped while being illegally arrested, such disclaimer cannot be treated as abandonment where defendant "had, in fact, been in personal possession of the container in question only moments before").

[86]United States v. Gwinn, 191 F.3d 874 (8th Cir.1999) (in response to government's claim defendant, passenger on train, abandoned his bag when he twice denied to police that he owned it, court says that because defendant "denied that he owned the black bag only after he had been seized and handcuffed by the officers," defendant's "actions can hardly be charac-

away incriminating articles due to the unlawful activities of police officers."[88] Thus, where a person has disposed of property in response to an illegal seizure or search by the police,[89] courts

---

terized as a voluntary act"); Commonwealth v. Pollard, 450 Pa. 138, 299 A.2d 233 (1973).

[87]United States v. King, 990 F.2d 1552 (10th Cir.1993) (taking into account the Brown v. Illinois, 422 U.S. 590, 95 S.Ct. 2254, 45 L.Ed.2d 416 (1975), factors of "temporal proximity," "intervening circumstances," and "purpose and flagrancy of the official misconduct").

[88]State v. Reed, 284 So.2d 574 (La.1973).

[89]There must be a cause and effect relationship, and thus in United States v. Pirolli, 673 F.2d 1200 (11th Cir.1982), where after an illegal search of defendant's residence the evidence was found in the yard, the court stated: "Appellant contends that the abandonment by Pirolli was caused by the illegal conduct of the agents, when they made the illegal search of the house. This does not, however, fit within the facts since at the time Pirolli was heard slamming the back door to the house the agents had not yet knocked on the door to seek admission. Nothing they had done thus far was illegal. The fact that Pirolli abandoned the articles in an effort to evade his being caught with them does not amount to his abandonment being the product of police misconduct." See also United States v. Roman, 849 F.2d 920 (5th Cir.1988) (illegal x-raying of suitcase checked with airline not relevant as to defendant's abandonment by disclaimer he had checked any luggage, as defendant unaware of the x-raying; the "connection between Roman's abandonment and the prior, improper, police conduct, therefore, was far too tenuous to provide the requisite causal nexus"); State v. Oquendo, 223 Conn. 635, 613 A.2d 1300 (1992) (where flight after illegal seizure, defendant did not abandon duffle bag he threw away during the unlawful pursuit, but abandonment theory applied to defendant's wallet found in woods to which defendant

fled, as "the record does not disclose that the wallet was discarded in response to Birney's pursuit"); State v. Reynolds, 144 Wash.2d 282, 27 P.3d 200 (2001) ("whether the deputy's directive constituted an unlawful seizure of Reynolds constituted an unlawful seizure is immaterial" because defendant failed to establish he "discarded the item *after* the allegedly unlawful police conduct occurred").

In State v. Oliver, 368 So.2d 1331 (Fla.App.1979), where the alleged "abandonment" occurred after the police, without grounds for making a stop, directed two bike riders to stop. The court ruled that "a person's otherwise voluntary abandonment of property cannot be tainted or made involuntary by a prior illegal police stop of such person. * * * Only when the police begin to conduct an illegal search can a subsequent abandonment of property be held involuntary as being tainted by the prior illegal search * * *, and even that result may vary depending on the facts of the case. * * *

"Fundamental Fourth Amendment interests as well as sound logic support the prevailing case law in this subject. Until an actual police search has begun, it cannot be assumed that the police will search a person whom they have temporarily stopped on the street or that they will search such a person's car or other personal belongings. Not every temporary detention necessitates such action. * * * As a consequence, a person's abandonment of property subsequent to an illegal police stop can hardly be considered the product of a stop."

The *Oliver* reasoning is not convincing. The question is not whether, but for the throwing away of the objects, the police would have found them in an illegal search. Rather, the question is whether the prior illegality has promoted the disposal, which it most assuredly did. *Oliver* is an invitation to police to engage in illegal stops. The better view, therefore, is reflected

have not hesitated to hold that property inadmissible.[90] This

in Monahan v. State, 390 So.2d 756 (Fla.App.1980) (abandonment argument rejected, as abandonment came after illegal stop of defendant).

　Just as troublesome as *Oliver* are United States v. Liu, 180 F.3d 957 (8th Cir.1999) (where defendant, train passenger, claimed officer's manipulation of his bag a search, court rules defendant's subsequent departure from train and flight was abandonment, and since such was a "voluntary act" the abandonment would not constitute a fruit of the prior police activity even if it was a search); People v. Boodle, 47 N.Y.2d 398, 418 N.Y.S.2d 352, 391 N.E.2d 1329 (1979) (where police illegally seized defendant by having him get in police car and then driving off, after which defendant threw gun out window, court remarkably concluded this "abandonment" not the fruit of the illegal seizure because defendant, "in seeking to rid himself of the weapon, did not respond directly to the illegal police action" because it was not "a spontaneous reaction" but instead "an independent act involving a calculated risk"). *Boodle,* like *Oliver,* is an invitation to police to engage in illegal stops.

　[90]United States v. Stephens, 206 F.3d 914 (9th Cir.2000) (while bus passenger's repeated denials of ownership of bag constituted abandonment of the bag, such was "a result of an unlawful seizure," for the agents had confronted the bus passengers with "a Hobson's choice," either "stay on the bus and consent to the search, or get off the bus"); United States v. Acosta-Colon, 157 F.3d 9 (1st Cir.1998) (baggage claim tickets defendant tried to swallow in response to illegal detention presumed to be a suppressible fruit); United States v. Nicholson, 144 F.3d 632 (10th Cir.1998) (because earlier police contact in manipulating bus passenger's luggage was an illegal search, defendant's subsequent failure to claim ownership did not justify opening of the luggage, as "any abandonment was a direct consequence of the detective's Fourth Amendment

violation"); United States v. Wood, 981 F.2d 536 (D.C.Cir.1992) (after defendant illegally stopped, he dropped gun to ground; noting the "arguably dubious reasoning" of the *Boodle* case, note 89 supra, court concludes defendant's response was not "some sort of independent effort to get rid of the gun," and was tainted by the illegality, as defendant "did not attempt to hide the gun" and "no time elapsed and no intervening events occurred between the commencement of the seizure and the dropping of the gun"); United States v. Wilson, 953 F.2d 116 (4th Cir.1991) (defendant threw coat away while fleeing from illegal *Terry* stop); United States v. Beck, 602 F.2d 726 (5th Cir.1979) (objects thrown out of car window after illegal stop); Jones v. State, 28 A.3d 1046 (Del.2011) (where defendant illegal stopped without reasonable suspicion, after which defendant "dropped the bag of cocaine," "the abandonment was a direct consequence of the illegal seizure"); State v. James, 795 So.2d 1146 (La.2000) ("Relator's flight in response to the officer's unjustified conduct [in removing a film canister from his pocket and manipulating it] did not constitute an abandonment of his privacy interests in the closed container"); State v. Tucker, 136 N.J. 158, 642 A.2d 401 (1994) (object thrown to ground after illegal seizure); State v. Garcia, 147 N.M. 134, 217 P.3d 1032 (2009) (where defendant seized without reasonable suspicion by being pepper-sprayed and defendant after "several strides" dropped cocaine, that a fruit of illegal seizure and not admissible on abandonment theory); State v. Harbison, 141 N.M. 392, 156 P.3d 30 (2007) ("at the time Defendant threw the evidence under the car he had already stopped in response to the show of authority and was under police seizure"); State v. Morton, 326 Or. 466, 953 P.2d 374 (1998) (where "defendant dropped the container only after the police had begun the process of taking defendant into custody," because arrest illegal dropping cannot be treated as abandonment); Commonwealth v. Jackson, 548 Pa.

means that the court in *Colbert* may be faulted for not having given sufficient attention to the question of whether either the initial detention or the subsequent arrest was in violation of the Fourth Amendment, for if there was such a violation the so-called abandonment clearly was a fruit of that illegally.[91]

The more interesting and difficult question posed by *Colbert,* however, is whether certain police conduct short of an illegal seizure or search should also be deemed to nullify the abandonment for Fourth Amendment purposes. That is, assuming now that both the initial detention and later arrest were lawful, may it still be said that the police improperly maneuvered the suspects into the abandonment in a way inconsistent with the protections of the Fourth Amendment? One commentator answers in the affirmative:

> If the officer does nothing, or if he simply places the individual under surveillance, in the belief that he may possibly witness some criminal activity, then there will be no issue of unreasonableness. If, however, the officer, without benefit of probable cause, and acting strictly on a "hunch," or because of suspicion based upon

---

484, 698 A.2d 571 (1997) (defendant dropped package of drugs while being illegally searched); Hawkins v. State, 758 S.W.2d 255 (Tex.Crim.App.1988) (defendant threw bag in ditch after illegal pedestrian stop); State v. Reichenbach, 153 Wash.2d 126, 101 P.3d 80 (2004) (where vehicle passenger dropped baggie on floor when police unlawfully "ordered him to raise his hands at gunpoint," "the baggie was abandoned in response to the unlawful seizure"). But the point is sometimes missed; see, e.g., United States v. Washington, 146 F.3d 536 (8th Cir.1998) (in case much like *Nicholson*, defendant deemed to have "voluntarily abandoned" his luggage by disclaiming it, and such voluntary act viewed as breaking causal chain); Rodriguez v. State, 689 S.W.2d 227 (Tex.Crim. App.1985) (court declined to determine if stop lawful, after which defendant threw package of heroin out of car, as "the heroin was not obtained as a result of a search").

On the other hand, as noted in United States v. Maryland, 479 F.2d 566 (5th Cir.1973), citing the Supreme Court's decision in *Abel* in support, "a lawful arrest does not in itself amount to such compulsion as will render an otherwise voluntary abandonment involuntary." In this case, the defendant left certain items in the police car in which he had been transported to jail.

Compare Commonwealth v. Laureano, 411 Mass. 708, 584 N.E.2d 1132 (1992) (where defendant, upon seeing plainclothes police enter bar, walked hastily into men's room, police following of defendant there no seizure, so drugs thrown into urinal by defendant not tainted).

[91]United States v. Morin, 665 F.2d 765 (5th Cir.1982) ("there is a clear nexus between the illegal arrest of Morin and the subsequent verbal disclaimer of his luggage," as he "perceived no other option * * * than a denial of possession"); United States v. Jackson, 544 F.2d 407 (9th Cir.1976) (defendant's disclaimer of ownership of suitcase could not be considered in determining if suitcase was abandoned, as disclaimer was made immediately after—and was a fruit of—an illegal arrest); State v. Cooke, 54 N.C.App. 33, 282 S.E.2d 800 (1981), decision aff'd, 306 N.C. 132, 291 S.E.2d 618 (disclaimer following illegal stop no abandonment; "[d]efendants who disclaim ownership of property or reflexively discard property in their possession when alarmed by, or suspicious of, illegal police activity do so without necessarily abandoning all expectations of privacy in the property").

personal knowledge or hearsay, decides to follow the individual, and proceeds to hound him in a harassing manner, hoping that the individual will panic in the belief that he had better "ditch the stuff" before there is a shakedown, then an issue of major constitutional proportions will arise. Since the individual cannot possibly know in advance how far the officer will go, he has no way of gauging a prudent course. If the officer continues to close in, the individual has to anticipate a search. To do nothing means certain discovery. To attempt a discard is to invite a retrieve, thereby giving the officer probable cause to arrest. * * *

There is no meaningful distinction of constitutional significance between unreasonable search and seizure activity, and harassing official conduct outside the legitimate investigative sphere which prompts an individual to reveal what would otherwise be impermissible for the police to seek by means of a search of his person. In short, the police may not do indirectly what is denied to them directly. In either event, they will be engaging in conduct equally unreasonable under the fourth amendment, which, apparently, has been recognized by both the Supreme Court and several lower courts.[92] If a question, an observation, or an act of hearing, can each be considered part of the search process, there seems little reason why the same reasoning may not equally apply to harassing police conduct that seeks to prompt the victim into revealing what would otherwise be the product of an unreasonable search and seizure if conducted by the officer. Therefore, if overbearing conduct outside the realm of legitimate investigation falls beyond the pale of the fourth amendment, any attempt to exploit it by retrieving its fruits for subsequent use in a criminal prosecution should be condemned and suppressed under the same authority.[93]

This argument has considerable appeal. The difficulty, however, lies in identifying precisely what it is that constitutes "harassing

---

[92]This commentator's footnote at this point refers to Terry v. Ohio, 392 U.S. 1, 88 S.Ct. 1868, 20 L.Ed.2d 889 (1968) (stating "courts still retain their traditional responsibility to guard against police conduct which is overbearing or harassing"); and People v. Bridges, 123 Ill.App.2d 58, 259 N.E.2d 626 (1970) (stressing that there had been "no provocation by the officers which could be said to have forced defendant to drop it"). See also Commonwealth v. Wooden, 13 Mass.App.Ct. 417, 433 N.E.2d 1234 (1982) (before defendants threw envelope away, plainclothes officer had done no more than pull abreast of them in unmarked car, and thus abandonment effective); People v. Williams, 109 Mich.App. 768, 312 N.W.2d 155 (1981) (abandonment, as officer merely walked toward defendant).

Compare with *Bridges* the prov-

ocation in State v. Chopin, 372 So.2d 1222 (La.1979), where officers, without grounds for a stop, swung their car around into defendant's path, switched on bright lights, and braked not more than 3–4 feet in front of him. Because that "approach clearly indicated that some form of official detention was imminent," the abandonment was provoked by the police. *Chopin* was distinguished in State v. Wheeler, 416 So.2d 78 (La.1982), finding of abandonment where the officer merely walked toward the defendant and "did not approach the defendant in a manner or under circumstances which made it seem that some form of detention was imminent."

[93]Mascolo, The Role of Abandonment in the Law of Search and Seizure: An Application of Misdirected Emphasis, 20 Buff.L.Rev. 399, 416–17, 419 (1971).

official conduct." Assume this scenario: officer *A* parks his car, steps out, and walks down the street in the direction of *B,* who, upon seeing the officer approaching him, proceeds to "ditch the stuff" because he fears that the officer will search him. Surely the Fourth Amendment does not protect people from decisions that, in retrospect, appear unwise, and thus the mere fact that *B* (correctly or incorrectly) thought he was going to be searched and consequently attempted to get rid of the incriminating evidence is not enough to negate his abandonment.[94] Nor is it particularly helpful to look to the state of mind of officer *A* rather than suspect *B*. Even assuming that it can be established that it was *A* 's intention to make what would have been an illegal seizure of search of *B,* this is likewise not enough to warrant holding the abandonment ineffective; the unexecuted intention of the officer should not govern in light of the fact that the incriminating evidence was come by without the necessity of a seizure or search.[95] Yet, this case cannot be disposed of upon the generalization that the mere act of approaching a person can never amount to "provocation by the officers which could be said to have forced defendant to drop"[96] the object. If officer *A* had on several previous occasions, upon seeing *B* on the street, stopped, approached him, and then subjected him to a search, then certainly the mere act of approaching on this occasion deserves to be characterized as "harassing official conduct."[97]

However, as discussed more fully elsewhere herein,[98] this issue appears to have been abrogated by the Supreme Court's decision in *California v. Hodari D.,*[99] holding that even a clearly manifested intent to seize on the present occasion is not a basis for suppression of evidence "abandoned" in response. Such conduct does not constitute a Fourth Amendment "seizure," the Court reasoned, for that term encompasses "a laying on of hands or application of physical force to restrain movement, even when it is

---

[94]As noted in State v. Washington, 364 So.2d 949 (La.1978): "Defendant's erroneous belief that the officers, a significant distance away, intended to confront him is not chargeable to the police."

[95]See § 1.4(b).

[96]People v. Bridges, 123 Ill.App.2d 58, 259 N.E.2d 626 (1970).

[97]Consider State v. Belton, 441 So.2d 1195 (La.1983), where police saw defendant in front of a bar where drug dealers congregated, stopped their car and got out and approached defendant, at which he ran inside the bar and dropped a paper bag on the floor, which the officers recovered and

opened and found contained narcotics. The court ruled that though perhaps there were not grounds to detain defendant, his abandonment was effective because no "actual or imminent unlawful detention" had occurred. The court failed to assess the police conduct in light of defendant's testimony that these same officers had confronted him at the same location the previous week and told him they would arrest him the next time they found him there, which was emphasized in the dissent.

[98]See text in § 9.4(d).

[99]California v. Hodari D., 499 U.S. 621, 111 S.Ct. 1547, 113 L.Ed.2d 690 (1991).

ultimately unsuccessful,"[100] and also *"submission* to the assertion of authority," but not a "show of authority" as to which "the subject does not yield." (The *Hodari D.* dissenters cogently argued that "the character of the citizen's response should not govern the constitutionality of the officer's conduct," and noted that the majority's holding could well "encourage unlawful displays of force that will frighten countless innocent citizens into surrendering whatever privacy rights they may still have."[101]) In line with *Hodari D.,* it has been held that if an officer makes a lawful seizure of a person and then threatens to make what would be an illegal search of that person, evidence abandoned in response to that threat is admissible because there was no "search."[102]

Even if there is no such conduct, it should not be assumed from *Colbert* that a disclaimer of ownership always constitutes an abandonment for Fourth Amendment purposes. This is not the case, as is illustrated by *People v. Cameron.*[103] An officer, after seeing a black satchel in a car, asked the two occupants of the vehicle for permission to look in the satchel. The two men responded that they did not own the satchel, and the officer then proceeded to search it. In rejecting the state's claim that this was a lawful

---

[100]See, e.g., United States v. Flynn, 309 F.3d 736 (10th Cir.2002) (where police placed sign on interstate highway warning of drug checkpoint ahead and then detained and checked vehicles taking little-used exit just after sign, and defendant pulled off at that exit and dropped sack from car before reaching point where police were concealed, the abandonment was voluntary, as "posting of signs to create a ruse does not constitute illegal police activity," and defendant was stopped by police only later upon reasonable suspicion based on examination of contents of sack); State v. Lisenbee, 116 Nev. 1124, 13 P.3d 947 (2000) (reaching such a result on such facts by relying on that language).

But, the majority went on to say that if it was unsuccessful the seizure would terminate, for it is incorrect "to say that for Fourth Amendment purposes there is a *continuing* arrest during the period of fugitivity." This means, the Court added, that if the officer had grabbed Hodari "but Hodari had broken away and had *then* cast away the cocaine, it would hardly be realistic to say that the disclosure had been made during the course of an arrest."

[101]See also State v. Tucker, 136 N.J. 158, 642 A.2d 401 (1994), rejecting the *Hodari D.* analysis as a matter of state law.

[102]State v. Rawlings, 121 Idaho 930, 829 P.2d 520 (1992) (even if officer's threat to search defendant for identification asserted authority beyond what *Terry* allows, that itself was not a "search," as officer "did not touch defendant or take any action other than the questioned statement before the defendant abandoned the property").

Compare State v. Garcia, 147 N.M. 134, 217 P.3d 1032 (2009) (because words used in *Hodari D.* "connote a complete, even extended, separation between the suspect and the officer" before the purported abandonment, court finds "serious uncertainty" as to whether Supreme Court would suppress the evidence in instant case, where officer without reasonable suspicion stopped defendant by pepper-spraying him, and then defendant, after taking "only several strides" and while he "continued to be under the effects of the pepper spray," dropped cocaine; court then proceeds to reject *Hodari D.* as a matter of state law).

[103]People v. Cameron, 73 Misc.2d 790, 342 N.Y.S.2d 773 (1973).

examination of abandoned property, not subject to Fourth Amendment restraints, the court stated:

> Defendants, as already stated, only denied ownership, not possession. There is a great deal of difference between denial of ownership of property on a public street where no possession is claimed or indicated and denial of ownership of property in a car where possession is conceded, although ownership denied. * * * I therefore find no abandonment in this case.[104]

---

[104]See also United States v. Burbage, 365 F.3d 1174 (10th Cir.2004) (train passenger, who said backpack in overhead rack belonged to another passenger who allowed him to put a portfolio in it, thereby "lost any objectively reasonable expectation of privacy in the backpack as a whole"); United States v. Scott, 987 A.2d 1180 (D.C.App.2010) (where defendant denied having car in vicinity but then "retracted" the disclaimer and said nearby car he used belonged to his cousin, "the police were not entitled to conclude that he had abandoned" the car); Robles v. State, 510 N.E.2d 660 (Ind.1987) (defendant's statement that bag he checked with airline not owned by him not abandonment; he had reasonable expectation of privacy as person who admittedly was transporting the bag); State v. Casey, 59 N.C.App. 99, 296 S.E.2d 473 (1982) (defendant's denial that bags he carrying in airport were his not abandonment, as he "had the right to exclude all others from the bags by virtue of his right of possession and control"); State v. Huether, 453 N.W.2d 778 (N.D.1990) (where bag containing controlled substance found in defendant's car, he did not abandon bag by denying both ownership of bag and knowledge of contents; this "especially true where, as here, the paper bag is contained and controlled within an area where there is a legitimate expectation of privacy," defendant "did not discard or place the bag in a public place," and disclaimer came "only after the search"); State v. Cook, 332 Or. 601, 34 P.3d 156 (2001) (where defendant seen by dumpster sorting clothing, "fact that defendant told the officers that he did not own the bag and clothes did not, however, permit the officers to conclude that defendant intended to relinquish all his

constitutionally protected interest in those items," especially since defendant then "relinquished his immediate physical possession of the bag and clothing by leaving them on the ground" after officer "instructed him to 'step out' of the area"); State v. Evans, 159 Wash.2d 402, 150 P.3d 105 (2007) ("disclaiming ownership is not sufficient, by itself, to constitute abandonment" where, as here, defendant "had a privacy interest in the area searched [his vehicle], the item that was seized-the briefcase-was locked, and he objected to its seizure").

And quite clearly a claim of surrender of possession known to be false is not an abandonment either. See Morton v. State, 284 Md. 526, 397 A.2d 1385 (1979) (defendant illegally arrested in recreation center told police he had given his jacket and bag to his cousin who had left the center; police knew no one had left and found effects in the center; held, no abandonment).

Compare with Cameron United States v. Denny, 441 F.3d 1220 (10th Cir.2006) (even if defendant intended to hide plastic bag and cracker box it contained under his seat on train, once he "explicitly disavowed any ownership interest in them," he without reasonable expectation of privacy as to them, so police could seize and inspect them); United States v. Fulani, 368 F.3d 351 (3d Cir.2004) (in holding bus passenger abandoned luggage in overhead rack by denying luggage was his, court rejects defendant's argument "that he could not have abandoned his luggage without physically removing himself from it"); United States v. Sanders, 130 F.3d 1316 (8th Cir.1997) (where passengers exiting bus at completion of journey left 3 bags unclaimed and upon police inquiry all of

Of course, a denial of ownership in some other circumstances, as where there is doubt as to which person is in possession, would be a different matter.[105]

§ 2.6(c) Garbage in particular[106]

There is one particular type of abandoned property situation that has proved to be especially troublesome: where law enforcement authorities[107] look through refuse a person has set out for disposal. Consequently, that situation is given separate attention at this point.

The traditional approach to a case of this type, as it developed prior to *Katz v. United States*,[108] was to apply property concepts in order to determine whether the police examination of the defendant's garbage constituted a Fourth Amendment search. In particular, courts deemed it necessary to resolve two property law issues: (1) whether the defendant had intended to abandon the object the police discovered; and (2) whether the discovery was accomplished by an intrusion upon the curtilage. This may be illustrated by comparing the two leading pre-*Katz* cases in point: *Work v. United States*;[109] and *United States v. Minker*.[110] In *Work,* officers went to defendant's home after receiving informa-

---

them, including defendant, disclaimed ownership of them, defendant thereby "surrendered any legitimate expectation of privacy he had in the bag" police opened); United States v. Ruiz, 935 F.2d 982 (8th Cir.1991) (disclaimer of ownership constituted abandonment where, in addition, defendant had already placed suitcase into car other than that defendant himself entered, manifesting he had "abandoned any privacy interest he may have had"); United States v. Canady, 615 F.2d 694 (5th Cir.1980) (where suitcase defendant carrying did not pass the airport X-ray scan, and defendant repeatedly said suitcase not his and that his purpose in carrying it was to turn it over to airline, such disclaimer meant defendant was without any expectation of privacy as to the contents); State v. Morrow, 128 Ariz. 309, 625 P.2d 898 (1981) (upholding a search of the attache case defendant was carrying at an airport and from which he withdrew some of his effects, on the ground that defendant's declaration it was not his constituted abandonment); People v. Grainger, 117 Mich.App. 740, 324 N.W.2d 762 (1982) (defendant had abandoned briefcase he carrying at airport by say-

ing he did not own it but that it belonged to friend).

[105]State v. Mahone, 67 Haw. 644, 701 P.2d 171 (1985) (where police knew defendant an overnight guest in woman's apartment and woman consented to search of apartment, defendant cannot now complain about search of his canvas-type bag in the apartment where he disclaimed ownership of it and watched the search-by-consent extend to it without protest); State v. Zaitseva, 135 Idaho 11, 13 P.3d 338 (2000) (where absent owner of car gave consent to search of it, defendant, who had been a passenger in that car, could not later object to search of bag in car, as both defendant and driver, owner's sister, had denied ownership of bag).

[Section 2.6(c)]

[106]See also Annot., 62 A.L.R.5th 1 (1998); Notes, 23 Ariz.L.Rev. 283 (1981); 1987 Wis.L.Rev. 191.

[107]Sometimes with the assistance of public or private refuse haulers.

[108]Katz v. United States, 389 U.S. 347, 88 S.Ct. 507, 19 L.Ed.2d 576 (1967).

[109]Work v. United States, 243 F.2d

tion that a young girl was using narcotics there; they knocked on the door and, when no one answered, took a few steps into the first floor hallway. The defendant then walked past the officers out the front door and down the steps to an area under the porch, where she was seen placing something in a trash can. The officers then lifted the top of the trash can and retrieved a phial of pills. In holding that this was an illegal search, the court stressed: (i) the pills had not been abandoned by the defendant, for the circumstances indicated she was trying to hide the pills in the can rather than permanently dispose of them; and (ii) the "trash receptacle in which the phial was found was in close proximity to the house," and thus was within the curtilage—an area protected by the Fourth Amendment. In *Minker,* on the other hand, IRS agents arranged for a trash collector to segregate the trash he collected from a four-unit apartment building where defendant resided and to turn that trash over to them. The court concluded that this action did not intrude upon the defendant's Fourth Amendment rights, as: (i) the defendant had intended to abandon the adding machine tapes and other slips of paper the agents found in the trash; and (ii) the trash receptacle located outside the building was not within the curtilage of the defendant's second-floor apartment.

In *Katz,* the Supreme Court rejected the notion that "a talismanic solution to every Fourth Amendment problem" could be found by reliance upon property law concepts, and thus held that the overriding issue is whether the police conduct "violated the privacy upon which [the defendant] justifiably relied." Despite *Katz,* some courts continued to resolve the garbage cases in essentially the same way as in *Work* and *Minker,* so that if the police had not trespassed onto an area that can be called the "curtilage" and if they took only what the defendant intended to abandon, there was deemed to have been no Fourth Amendment search.[111] It appears, however, that *Katz* requires a somewhat different type of analysis of such cases in terms of whether the police conduct intruded upon a justified expectation of privacy.

Illustrative of a *Katz*-type approach is *People v. Edwards.*[112] Defendant's neighbor told police that he had seen a plastic bag containing a green vegetable substance on defendant's back porch. The officers then entered the open back yard area of that

660 (D.C.Cir.1957).

[110]United States v. Minker, 312 F.2d 632 (3d Cir.1962).

[111]United States v. Kramer, 711 F.2d 789 (7th Cir.1983); United States v. Terry, 702 F.2d 299 (2d Cir.1983); United States v. Vahalik, 606 F.2d 99 (5th Cir.1979); Magda v. Benson, 536 F.2d 111 (6th Cir.1976); United States v. Mustone, 469 F.2d 970 (1st Cir. 1972); United States v. Jackson, 448 F.2d 963 (9th Cir.1971); State v. Fassler, 108 Ariz. 586, 503 P.2d 807 (1972); Campbell v. State, 278 So.2d 420 (Miss.1973); Commonwealth v. Minton, 288 Pa.Super. 381, 432 A.2d 212 (1981).

[112]People v. Edwards, 71 Cal.2d 1096, 80 Cal.Rptr. 633, 458 P.2d 713 (1969).

residence and looked in three trash cans located two or three feet from the back porch door; in one can they found a bag containing a small amount of marijuana. The court held that

> the search of the trash can was unlawful. As we have seen, the trash can was within a few feet of the back door of defendant's home and required trespass for its inspection. It was an adjunct to the domestic economy. * * * Placing the marijuana in the trash can, so situated and used, was not an abandonment unless as to persons authorized to remove the receptacle's contents, such as trashmen. * * * The marijuana itself was not visible without "rummaging" in the receptacle. So far as appears defendants alone resided at the house. In the light of the combined facts and circumstances it appears that defendants exhibited an expectation of privacy, and we believe that expectation was reasonable under the circumstances of the case. We can readily ascribe many reasons why residents would not want their castaway clothing, letters, medicine bottles or other telltale refuse and trash to be examined by neighbors or others, at least not until the trash has lost its identity and meaning by becoming part of a large conglomeration of trash elsewhere. Half truths leading to rumor and gossip may readily flow from an attempt to "read" the contents of another's trash.

Though the court in *Edwards* implied that defendant had not really abandoned the items in the trash cans, the more significant part of the holding is that which recognizes there can be a justified expectation of privacy in garbage. It does seem clear that Edwards had abandoned the objects he placed in his trash cans; unlike the defendant in *Work,* he demonstrated an unequivocal intention to part with them forever. But this is not determinative. A justified expectation of privacy may exist as to items which have been abandoned in the property law sense, just as it is true that no such expectation may exist on some occasions even though the property has not been abandoned.[113] This is because under *Katz* "the question is not whether there has been abandonment in the property law sense, * * * but rather whether there has been abandonment of a reasonable expectation of privacy as to the area searched or the property seized."[114]

Certainly, for the reasons articulated in *Edwards,* people intend that their refuse, though placed outside their dwelling for collection, remain private. As one court commented, "almost every human activity ultimately manifests itself in waste products and * * * any individual may understandably wish to maintain the confidentiality of his refuse."[115] This is unquestionably so,[116] for one's trash may expose "intimate areas of an individual's personal

---

[113]As noted in the preceding subdivision, sometimes a person may put an object in a public place without intending to abandon it, but yet may be said to have lost his justified expectation of privacy as to that object by this action.

[114]United States v. Kahan, 350 F.Supp. 784 (S.D.N.Y.1972), rev'd on other grounds, 415 U.S. 239, 94 S.Ct. 1179, 39 L.Ed.2d 297 (1974).

[115]Smith v. State, 510 P.2d 793 (Alaska 1973).

affairs" and "can reveal much about a person's activities, associations, and beliefs."[117]

Under *Katz,* for the expectation of privacy to receive Fourth Amendment protection, it must be one "that society is prepared to recognize as 'reasonable.' "[118] This means that the ultimate question put by *Katz* is "whether, if the particular form of surveillance practiced by the police is permitted to go unregulated by constitutional restraints, the amount of privacy and freedom remaining to citizens would be diminished to a compass inconsistent with the aims of a free and open society."[119] Surely the type of police surveillance employed in *Edwards* should not go unregulated, for a society in which all "our citizens' trash cans could be made the subject of police inspection"[120] for evidence of the more intimate aspects of their personal life upon nothing more than a whim is not "free and open."

Nor will it do to suggest that the citizen who desires privacy as to his trash should arrange to dispose of it in a way other than did the defendant in *Edwards.*[121] It would be a perversion of *Katz* to interpret it as extending protection only to those who resort to

---

[116]But see (later Chief Justice) Burger's dissent in Work v. United States, 243 F.2d 660 (D.C.Cir.1957), for the incredible assertion that "[h]onest citizens neither need nor, I think, want protection for their privacy extended to these artificial limits."

[117]This language, used by Powell, J., concurring in California Bankers Ass'n v. Shultz, 416 U.S. 21, 94 S.Ct. 1494, 39 L.Ed.2d 812 (1974), to describe bank records of financial transactions, is equally apropos here, as was concluded in State v. Tanaka, 67 Haw. 658, 701 P.2d 1274 (1985), holding on *state* constitutional grounds that police inspection of trash is a search: "People reasonably believe that police will not indiscriminately rummage through their trash bags to discover their personal effects. Business records, bills, correspondence, magazines, tax records, and other telltale refuse can reveal much about a person's activities, associations and beliefs. If we were to hold otherwise, police could search everyone's trash bags and on their property without any reason and thereby learn of their activities, associations and beliefs."

[118]Harlan, J., concurring.

[119]Amsterdam, Perspectives on the Fourth Amendment, 58 Minn.L.Rev.

349, 403 (1974).

[120]People v. Krivda, 5 Cal.3d 357, 96 Cal.Rptr. 62, 486 P.2d 1262 (1971).

[121]But see United States v. Kramer, 711 F.2d 789 (7th Cir.1983), asserting: "Of course people sometimes do not want others to see things—e.g., magazines, financial records, correspondence, doctor bills—that they sometimes throw away. But people can easily prevent this by destroying what they want to keep secret before they discard it, or by not discarding it. Defendant could have burned or shredded his drug records before he discarded them or kept them hidden somewhere inside his house. * * * There is nothing unfair about requiring that people not discard things they want to keep secret, or destroy them before they do."

Consider, in this regard, that courts tend not to be more protective of other errors at disposal. In United States v. Alden, 576 F.2d 772 (8th Cir. 1978), defendant tried to dispose of his garbage by burning it in a trash pile in his yard, but the court concluded this did not give him a greater expectation of privacy, as "no one could reasonably expect that partially burned trash dumped in an open area of yard and exposed to the wind would remain secure."

extraordinary means to keep information regarding their personal lives out of the hands of the police. "Mr. Katz could, of course, have protected himself against surveillance by forbearing to use the phone,"[122] but the fact that he did not do so did not deprive him of a justified expectation of privacy in the public phone booth. Similarly, the mere fact that a citizen elects to dispose of his garbage in the customary way by making it available for pickup by a municipal or privately-retained hauler is no basis for concluding that his expectation of privacy as to that garbage is unjustified. True, disposal of garbage in the customary way is attended with some risks to privacy, but this "hardly means that government is constitutionally unconstrained in adding to those risks."[123] To assert otherwise, Justice Rabinowitz has pointed out,

> fails to recognize that citizens might expect a few, infrequent invasions of their privacy by third persons, but might simultaneously expect their privacy to remain immune from governmental intrusion. I disagree. A telephone caller, for example, who conducts a conversation on a "party line" might reasonably expect brief interruptions from others who were attempting to ascertain if the line were in use. It does not necessarily follow, however, that the same caller would also expect that government agents might be conducting a full-scale warrantless "search" or tap of his conversations. Similarly, one who deposits refuse into a dumpster might expect some minor, inadvertent examination by garbagemen[124] or other third persons, but such expectations would not necessarily include a detailed, systematized inspection of the garbage by law enforcement personnel.[125]

The facts of *Edwards* make it a strong case for recognition of a justified expectation of privacy; as the court stressed, Edwards resided in a single-family dwelling, he kept his trash in a relatively private area by the back door, and the police obtained the evidence by intercepting the garbage by going onto his property before it was picked up. The question now is how significant these facts alone are, for in *California v. Greenwood*[126] the Supreme Court rejected the kind of analysis utilized by Justice

---

[122]Amsterdam, 58 Minn.L.Rev. 349, 402 (1974).

[123]Amsterdam, 58 Minn.L.Rev. 349, 406 (1974).

[124]If the person who collects the trash rummages through it on his own initiative, finds incriminating evidence, and takes it to the police, no Fourth Amendment issue is presented. People v. Gray, 63 Cal.App.3d 282, 133 Cal.Rptr. 698 (1976).

[125]Smith v. State, 510 P.2d 793 (Alaska 1973) (dissenting opinion).

[126]California v. Greenwood, 486 U.S. 35, 108 S.Ct. 1625, 100 L.Ed.2d 30 (1988), also discussed in Watson, The Homeowner's Right to Privacy in Garbage Left for Collection, 25 Crim.L. Bull. 257 (1989); Notes, 38 Am.U.L. Rev. 993 (1989); 38 Buff.L.Rev. 647 (1990); 41 Case W.Res.L.Rev. 581 (1991); 39 Case W.Res.L.Rev. 955 (1989); 38 Cath.U.L.Rev. 543 (1989); 39 Drake L.Rev. 775 (1990); 79 J.Crim.L. & Criminology 623 (1988); 33 Loyola L.Rev. 549 (1989); 24 N.Engl. L.Rev. 1169 (1990); 67 N.Car.L.Rev. 1191 (1989); 20 Pace L.Rev. 541 (2000); 24 Tulsa L.J. 401 (1989); 58 U.Cin.L. Rev. 361 (1989); 91 W.Va.L.Rev. 597

Rabinowitz. *Greenwood* involved bags of trash placed at the curb for pickup, which the police arranged for the trash collector[127] to segregate and turn over to them for inspection of the contents. In holding such activity did not intrude upon a reasonable expectation of privacy, the Court emphasized (i) that "bags left on or at the side of a public street are readily accessible to * * * members of the public";[128] and (ii) that defendant had put out his garbage

---

(1989); Annot., 62 A.L.R.5th 1 (1998).

Compare Beltz v. State, 221 P.3d 328 (Alaska 2009) (under state constitution, "person who sets out garbage for routine collection on or adjacent to a public street * * * has some objectively reasonable expectation of privacy in that garbage," and thus warrantless search of it permissible only upon reasonable suspicion); State v. Tanaka, 67 Haw. 658, 701 P.2d 1274 (1985) (pre-*Greenwood* broader protection under state constitution); Litchfield v. State, 824 N.E.2d 356 (Ind. 2005), not retroactive, Membres v. State, 889 N.E.2d 265 (Ind.2008) (garbage covered by state constitutional provision, but search reasonable if no "arbitrary selection of the subject" and garbage is "retrieved in substantially the same manner as the trash collector would take it"); State v. 1993 Chevrolet Pickup, 328 Mont. 10, 116 P.3d 800 (2005) (adopting *Litchfield* rule as a matter of state constitutional law); State v. Gross, 150 N.H. 46, 834 A.2d 316 (2003) (*Greenwood* rejected because state constitution construed "to provide greater protection"); State v. Hempele, 120 N.J. 182, 576 A.2d 793 (1990) (rejecting *Greenwood* as a matter of state constitutional law, so that "the State must secure a warrant based on probable cause in order to search garbage bags left on the curb for collection"); State v. Granville, 140 N.M. 345, 142 P.3d 933 (App.2006) (following *Hempele* as a matter of state constitutional law); State v. Morris, 165 Vt. 111, 680 A.2d 90 (1996) (as a matter of state constitutional law, "we decline to follow the *Greenwood* majority's decision allowing warrantless trash searches"); State v. Boland, 115 Wash.2d 571, 800 P.2d 1112 (1990) (rejecting *Greenwood* under state constitution, where "the focus is whether the 'private affairs' of

an individual have been unreasonably violated"). However, "a majority of state courts have generally found that there is no reasonable expectation of privacy in garbage when placed for collection, under both state and federal constitutional guarantees." People v. Hillman, 834 P.2d 1271 (Colo.1992) (collecting cases). See also Rikard v. State, 354 Ark. 345, 123 S.W.3d 114 (2003); State v. Ranken, 25 A.3d 845 (Del.2010); State v. Schwartz, 689 N.W.2d 430 (S.D.2004).

[127]While the collector in *Greenwood* was a public collector, that fact has not been deemed critical. As stated in United States v. Hall, 47 F.3d 1091 (11th Cir.1995): "We fail to see how contracting with a private garbage collection service diminishes the probative value of the fact that the garbage was conveyed to a third party. Presumably, both private and public garbage collectors are equally able to sort through the garbage they collect."

[128]Courts have been disinclined to conclude that there *is* a reasonable expectation of privacy even under the state constitution merely because of local ordinances regulating waste management. See Rikard v. State, 354 Ark. 345, 123 S.W.3d 114 (2003) (given emphasis in ordinance "on cleanliness and preventing any scattering of that garbage," it does not create expectation of privacy in garbage); Commonwealth v. Pratt, 407 Mass. 647, 555 N.E.2d 559 (1990) ("fact * * * ordinance allowed only licensed trash collectors to transport garbage does not make the defendant's subjective expectation of privacy any more reasonable"); Commonwealth v. Minton, 288 Pa.Super. 381, 432 A.2d 212 (1981) (purpose of township code proscription of removing covers from refuse receptacles was "presumably sanitation and cleanliness not privacy"); State v.

"for the express purpose of conveying it to a third party, the trash collector, who might himself have sorted through respondents' trash or permitted others, such as the police, to do so."[129] The first of these reasons is inapplicable in an *Edwards*-type situation, and the *Greenwood* majority seems to view this first reason as rather critical,[130] for the Court repeatedly refers to the issue and holding in the case in terms of garbage "outside the curtilage,"[131] "on or at the side of a public street," "at the curb," "in an area accessible to the public," and "in public areas."[132] As

---

Stevens, 734 N.W.2d 344 (S.D.2007) ("While city ordinances may, in some cases, be reflective of societal expectations of privacy, they do not manifest such an expectation simply because they dictate how persons are to place their trash for collection or how the trash is to be collected").

[129]Compare State v. Fisher, 283 Kan. 272, 154 P.3d 455 (2007) (*Greenwood* distinguished, as here police, by entry of curtilage, seized garbage that "was not left out for commercial trash collection" but rather "for eventual disposition" by property owner).

[130]See, e.g., State v. Fisher, 283 Kan. 272, 154 P.3d 455 (2007) (*Greenwood* not applicable here, as trash in question had been "placed approximately 100 yards from the highway and behind a rural home").

[131]Despite the use of this phrase in *Greenwood*, it would seem that cases of this genre are not to be worked out by exclusive attention to the question of whether the garbage was within or outside the curtilage, as the Court also talked about the garbage being "accessible to the public," which is also true of much garbage placed just inside the curtilage or even farther inside when on the most obvious route for visitors. However, this point can produce sharp disagreements. See, e.g., the several opinions in United States v. Redmon, 138 F.3d 1109 (7th Cir.1998), noted at 9 Widener J.Pub.L. 61 (1999).

[132]This would include, for example, the situation where defendant left his bags of trash at the curb for pick-up, United States v. Williams, 669 F.3d 903 (8th Cir.2012); where defendant placed his garbage 3–6 feet from the curb, United States v. Segura-Baltazar, 448 F.3d 1281 (11th Cir.2006); where defendant's garbage cans were just outside his garage but on a driveway defendant used in common with his next door neighbors and also serving as the walkway to defendant's front door, United States v. Redmon, 138 F.3d 1109 (7th Cir.1998); where defendant placed four sealed trash bags on the curb, United States v. Bowman, 215 F.3d 951 (9th Cir.2000); where defendant placed garbage bags for garbage collection on a trailer 3 ft. from the alley, United States v. Long, 176 F.3d 1304 (10th Cir.1999); where the defendant placed his garbage cans "for collection on his own lawn next to the curb," United States v. Wilkinson, 926 F.2d 22 (1st Cir.1991); where defendant "placed his garbage on public property at the end of his driveway," Beltz v. State, 221 P.3d 328 (Alaska 2009); where defendant "placed the garbage bags directly adjacent to the sidewalk in front of his residence," People v. Hillman, 834 P.2d 1271 (Colo.1992); where defendant placed his garbage can "on the public sidewalk," State v. Ranken, 25 A.3d 845 (Del.2010); where defendant placed his garbage bags 35–40 ft. from house, 5–8 ft. from street, with no barrier other than drainage ditch, within area of city easement and where trash placed "regularly for collection by sanitation crews," State v. Kimberlin, 267 Kan. 659, 984 P.2d 141 (1999); where defendant "placed his garbage at the alley's edge for collection," State v. 1993 Chevrolet Pickup, 328 Mont. 10, 116 P.3d 800 (2005); where defendant's trash was placed "next to the street in trash bags," State v. Sorenson, 770 N.W.2d 701 (N.D.2009); where defendant's trash was "set out by the curb,"

noted earlier,[133] police have only limited authority to come onto the curtilage, for they must conduct themselves as would an ordinary social visitor to the premises. That hardly includes rummaging through the garbage cans of one's host.[134] As for the second reason given in *Greenwood*, it might support the conclusion the police can enlist the aid of the garbage hauler even as to garbage within the curtilage,[135] but it hardly means that the police may themselves intrude. There is no principle in Fourth Amendment jurisprudence to the effect that the police are free to do what *some* individual has been authorized to do. Moreover, this second reason should not be read as an endorsement of the broad and unsound concept that one's garbage is abandoned property and thus is always without Fourth Amendment protection.[136] As the dissenters noted, the author of *Greenwood* had declared

State v. Stevens, 734 N.W.2d 344 (S. D.2007). And, in the case of a commercial establishment, as to which the "curtilage" concept may have little meaning, this would include placing the garbage on adjoining land used by customers and others. United States v. Hall, 47 F.3d 1091 (11th Cir.1995) (dumpster in parking lot business shared with another business); State v. Bell, 832 S.W.2d 583 (Tenn.Crim. App.1991) (dumpster in parking lot for customers).

But lower courts in the post-*Greenwood* era are not always as careful as they should be with regard to this factor. See United States v. Simms, 626 F.3d 966 (7th Cir.2010) (police passed through open door to seize garbage from garbage cart inside 6-foot high fence; upheld solely on notion that open gate manifested consent to such entry by the garbage collector, a procedure contemplated by a "winter rules" ordinance); United States v. Segura-Baltazar, supra (court appears to rely almost exclusively upon the second *Greenwood* factor as to a second set of garbage cans "at the left side of the residence near the garage," upholding lower court's conclusion "that the trash was sufficiently exposed to the public to defeat a reasonable expectation of privacy because it was left in a location where the sanitation workers regularly would, on Wednesdays, remove it along with trash left by the street"); State v. Trahan, 229 Neb. 683, 428 N.W.2d 619 (1988) (police searched defendant's garbage contain-

ers, placed for pickup 4 feet from the back door of his trailer house, where defendant had use of an area extending 12 feet behind the trailer; notwithstanding that the district court "made no finding as to whether the garbage in question was within the curtilage of defendant's property," the appellate court satisfied that "the placement of the garbage was in a location accessible to the public and placed for collection").

[133] See § 2.3(f).

[134] But see State v. Hempele, 120 N.J. 182, 576 A.2d 793 (1990), concluding that under *Greenwood* the central question is whether the garbage was left at a location "accessible to the public," meaning the "privacy expectation is the same whether the garbage is left outside or just inside the property line."

[135] See text at note 154 infra.

[136] As stated in United States v. Hedrick, 922 F.2d 396 (7th Cir.1991), the notion "that the intent eventually to convey the garbage to the garbage collector is itself sufficient to eliminate any expectation of privacy in garbage" is "not consistent with Supreme Court protection of the curtilage and with its opinion in *Greenwood*."

There are, understandably, differences of opinion as to whether abandonment analysis continues to have any place in the garbage cases. See, e.g., the various opinions in United States v. Redmon, 138 F.3d 1109 (7th Cir.1998) (some judges claim abandon-

just months earlier that a defendant's "property interest [in trash] does not settle the matter for Fourth Amendment purposes."[137]

Some authority is to be found to the effect that a resident of a multiple-occupancy dwelling does not have the same justified expectation of privacy as to a trash container made available for the use of all persons occupying the several individual residential units in that structure.[138] Illustrative is *Smith v. State*,[139] where police, suspecting that narcotics activity was occurring in a certain apartment, undertook a 24-hour-per-day "stakeout" of the area for a period of 12 days. Whenever an occupant of the suspect apartment placed a container of garbage into the dumpster by the apartment building, an officer would retrieve it. On the basis of the evidence found in these packages, a warrant to search the apartment was obtained. Though opining that "trash located close to a single-family dwelling * * * would be a strong case for holding the expectation of privacy to be reasonable," the court concluded that no comparable expectation existed in the instant case:

> No attempt was made to empty the bags or boxes or to commingle their contents with the collective mess of garbage. Any person later emptying refuse in the dumpster could easily segregate the items placed therein by the Smiths. * * * [T]his dumpster accommodated several apartments. Therefore many people living in the building— and certainly the superintendent—would conceivably have occasion to look into it and scavenge about in the collective heap.

Smith is, to be sure, a more difficult case than *Edwards*. However, it is submitted that the court reached the wrong result. It may well be that "an apartment house tenant, using trash barrels in common with other tenants, has less reason to believe what he deposits in the trash will remain private than does the home dweller who provides and uses his own individual trash cans."[140] But this should not be determinative. As one court put it:

> Users of the communal receptacle undoubtedly do recognize the possibility that another tenant will discover the contents of their garbage after it is placed in the container. But they have no more reason than the householder [in a single family dwelling] to expect

---

ment not relevant because Court in *Greenwood* "certainly did not embrace the abandonment theory"; others rely on abandonment because *Greenwood* "never expressly, nor implicitly for that matter, rejected the abandonment theory").

[137] California v. Rooney, 483 U.S. 307, 107 S.Ct. 2852, 97 L.Ed.2d 258 (1987) (White, J., dissenting).

[138] United States v. Harruff, 352 F.Supp. 224 (E.D.Mich.1972); Smith v. State, 510 P.2d 793 (Alaska 1973); People v. Whotte, 113 Mich.App. 12, 317 N.W.2d 266 (1982); State v. Ronngren, 361 N.W.2d 224 (N.D.1985); Willis v. State, 518 S.W.2d 247 (Tex. Crim.App.1975).

[139] Smith v. State, 510 P.2d 793 (Alaska 1973).

[140] People v. Stewart, 34 Cal.App.3d 695, 110 Cal.Rptr. 227 (1973).

their trash to be examined by police officers.[141]

It seems likely, however, in light of *California v. Greenwood,*[142] that the Supreme Court would agree with the result in *Smith.* In *Greenwood*, where police arranged with a trash collector to keep separate bags of garbage picked up at Greenwood's curb, the Court ruled this intruded upon no justified expectation of privacy. In reaching this conclusion, the Court recognized *both* (i) that "bags left on or at the side of a public street are readily accessible to * * * members of the public"; and (ii) that defendant had put out his garbage "for the express purpose of conveying it to a third party, the trash collector, who might himself have sorted through respondents' trash or permitted others, such as the police, to do so." The first point is true to a significant degree as to areas of multiple-occupancy dwellings readily accessible to all tenants and visitors,[143] and the Court is no more likely to be sympathetic to the special plight of the apartment dweller,[144] in terms of his difficulty in trying to make a private disposal of effects, than it was with the plight of Greenwood, who by county ordinance was required to place his trash at the curb. The second *Greenwood* point is also applicable here; it reflects that one's expectation—whatever the nature of his residence—that his garbage will promptly be commingled with other trash is not to receive Fourth

---

[141] People v. Smith, 52 Cal.App.3d 514, 125 Cal.Rptr. 192 (1975) reversed on other grounds, 17 Cal.3d 845, 132 Cal.Rptr. 397, 553 P.2d 557 (1976).

[142] California v. Greenwood, 486 U.S. 35, 108 S.Ct. 1625, 100 L.Ed.2d 30 (1988).

[143] And even more true as to multi-occupancy business premises. See United States v. Hall, 47 F.3d 1091 (11th Cir.1995) (a "commercial proprietor incurs a similarly diminished expectation of privacy when garbage is placed in a dumpster which is located in a parking lot that the business shares with other businesses, and no steps are taken to limit the public's access to the dumpster"); United States v. Dunkel, 900 F.2d 105 (7th Cir.1990) judgment vac'd on other grounds, 498 U.S. 1043, 111 S.Ct. 747, 112 L.Ed.2d 768 (1991) (under *Greenwood,* dentist had no expectation of privacy re dumpster, used by all 8 business or professional tenants of building, where dumpster located off parking lot used by employees and customers of all ten-

ants).

From such cases as *Hall* and *Dunkel,* it has been concluded that while "activities or objects in the home * * * need only be removed if in plain view to be protected, one seeking to protect his or her privacy in a commercial location must take affirmative steps to bar the public from the area they wish to keep private." Commonwealth v. Krisco Corp., 421 Mass. 37, 653 N.E.2d 579 (1995) (such steps taken here, as defendant "installed gates at either end of the fenced alley" within which dumpster located "and kept them closed until the waste hauler arrived").

[144] Or, for that matter, to that of a mere guest at a single-family residence, who may be deemed to have abandoned his property by placing it in a trash receptacle on his host's property. See State v. Strickland, 683 So.2d 218 (La.1996) (guest's property deemed "clearly abandoned property" once put in trash bin "located near" house trailer of host).

Amendment protection.[145]

A number of the cases that have reached the courts are different from *Edwards* because the garbage had been placed at curbside or at some other location making it more accessible to the public than Edwards' back yard. In the pre-*Greenwood* cases, the police examination of such garbage was usually upheld either by reliance upon pre-*Katz* criteria (such as that the garbage was not protected by the Fourth Amendment simply because it was abandoned[146] or because it was not located within the curtilage[147]), or by justified-expectation-of-privacy analysis.[148]

---

[145]State v. Briggs, 756 A.2d 731 (R.I.2000) (where defendant, "absentee landlord of the multidwelling property," had his garbage placed in "communal dumpster" in parking lot there, "the fact that so many people," i.e., "the tenants in the property, as well as the tenants' guests, solicitors, strangers, postal people, animals," and "the private company that collected the trash," "had access to the dumpster" means "the defendant had no objective reasonable expectation of privacy" in his trash placed there).

[146]United States v. Dela Espriella, 781 F.2d 1432 (9th Cir.1986) (trash container placed for curbside collection); United States v. Terry, 702 F.2d 299 (2d Cir.1983); Magda v. Benson, 536 F.2d 111 (6th Cir.1976) (garbage bag placed on tree lawn for pickup); United States v. Mustone, 469 F.2d 970 (1st Cir.1972) (bags tied and left on sidewalk next to garbage can by store); Cooks v. State, 699 P.2d 653 (Okl.Crim.App.1985) (trashcan at front curb).

[147]United States v. Wolfe, 375 F.Supp. 949 (E.D.Pa.1974).

[148]United States v. O'Bryant, 775 F.2d 1528 (11th Cir.1985) (fact defendant himself did not place briefcase, which had been in car when it stolen, in trash makes no difference); United States v. Kramer, 711 F.2d 789 (7th Cir.1983) (no expectation of privacy where defendant placed garbage container at roadside, even though police had to trespass a few feet inside defendant's knee-high chain-link fence to get at container); United States v. Reicherter, 647 F.2d 397 (3d Cir.1981) ("Having placed the trash in an area particularly suited for public inspection and, in a manner of speaking, public consumption, for the express purpose of having strangers take it, is inconceivable that the defendant intended to retain a privacy interest in the discarded objects"); Smith v. State, 510 P.2d 793 (Alaska 1973); State v. Slatko, 432 So.2d 635 (Fla.App.1983) ("A person has no expectation of privacy in trash which he has bagged and placed on his property adjacent to an alley so that it may be picked up by the local trash collectors"); People v. Collins, 106 Ill.2d 237, 87 Ill.Dec. 910, 478 N.E.2d 267 (1985) (no expectation of privacy where defendant placed bag of garbage in apartment house hallway; police examination of contents "was no more intrusive than what the defendant might have expected from passing tenants, vagrants, neighborhood children, or animals"); Commonwealth v. Chappee, 397 Mass. 508, 492 N.E.2d 719 (1986) ("Although the fact that the trash bags were placed on public property may not be controlling, it is a significant factor to be considered in determining whether the defendant had a reasonable expectation of privacy"; no such expectation here, plastic bags placed by street on town property); State v. Oquist, 327 N.W.2d 587 (Minn.1982) (though "a householder may ordinarily have some expectation of privacy in the items he places in his garbage can," this defendant "had no reasonable expectation of privacy with respect to the contents of the plastic bags placed in or near his open garbage can" where the examination "was procured without trespassing on the defendant's premises").

Contra: People v. Krivda, 5

Then came *Greenwood,* where police twice obtained from the regular trash collector garbage bags left on the curb in front of Greenwood's house. In each instance the trash collector at police request cleaned his truck bin of other refuse, picked up the bags from Greenwood's curb, and then turned the bags over to the police. The majority in *Greenwood,* per White, J., concluded

> that respondents exposed their garbage to the public sufficiently to defeat their claim to Fourth Amendment protection. It is common knowledge that plastic garbage bags left on or at the side of a public street are readily accessible to animals, children, scavengers, snoops, and other members of the public.[149] * * * Moreover, respondents placed their refuse at the curb for the express purpose of conveying it to a third party, the trash collector, who might himself have sorted through respondents' trash or permitted others, such as the police, to do so. Accordingly, having deposited their garbage "in an area particularly suited for public inspection and, in a manner of speaking, public consumption, for the express purpose of having strangers take it," * * * respondents could have had no reasonable expectation of privacy in the inculpatory items that they discarded.

(This reasoning supports the conclusion that the result would be the same if the police themselves had intruded into garbage bags so located.[150])

Cal.3d 357, 96 Cal.Rptr. 62, 486 P.2d 1262 (1971), vacated and remanded for a determination of whether the holding had a state or federal basis, 409 U.S. 33, 93 S.Ct. 32, 34 L.Ed.2d 45 (1972), affirmed on basis of both state and federal constitutions, 8 Cal.3d 623, 105 Cal.Rptr. 521, 504 P.2d 457 (1973).

[149]This does not mean that *Greenwood* is limited to instances in which bags instead of cans are used. As stated in United States v. Trice, 864 F.2d 1421 (8th Cir.1988): "While the garbage in *Greenwood* was merely placed in a bag and the trash at Kepka's property was kept in a garbage can, this difference does not give Kepka an *objectively* reasonable expectation of privacy. While a trash can is less accessible to animals than a garbage bag, a trash can placed at the curb is still readily accessible to children, scavengers, snoops and other members of the public. * * * A person must do more than place trash for collection in a trash can, that the public has access to, to create an objectively reasonable expectation of privacy. Kepka did not take that extra step." The court gave no hint of what a suf-

ficient "extra step" would be. Accord: United States v. Segura-Baltazar, 448 F.3d 1281 (11th Cir.2006); United States v. Wilkinson, 926 F.2d 22 (1st Cir.1991).

[150]United States v. Spotted Elk, 548 F.3d 641 (8th Cir.2008) (no search where FBI agent examined contents of "two trash containers that were 'set out' in the alley outside the fence"); United States v. Bowman, 215 F.3d 951 (9th Cir.2000) (*Greenwood* applies where police looked through trash bags located "on the curb"); United States v. Shanks, 97 F.3d 977 (7th Cir.1996) (*Greenwood* applies to police search of defendant's garbage containers "located adjacent to the alley"); United States v. Wilkinson, 926 F.2d 22 (1st Cir.1991) (*Greenwood* applicable to police search of garbage cans defendant left "for collection on his own lawn next to the curb"); United States v. Carmona, 858 F.2d 66 (2d Cir.1988) (*Greenwood* applied to uphold police search of "trashcans placed on the street curb, outside the private grounds of the house"); State v. Donato, 135 Idaho 469, 20 P.3d 5 (2001) (police seized garbage "which had been set at

Once again the Court construed *Katz* in an extraordinarily narrow fashion, requiring that a defendant's expectation of privacy be virtually absolute to receive Fourth Amendment protection. As the two *Greenwood* dissenters cogently argued, because the Court's precedents make it clear that such containers are entitled to Fourth Amendment protection when used to transport personal effects, the same should be true when they are used to discard personal effects in the manner Greenwood did:

The mere *possibility* that unwelcome meddlers *might* open and rummage through the containers does not negate the expectation of privacy in its contents any more than the possibility of a burglary negates an expectation of privacy in the home; or the possibility of a private intrusion negates an expectation of privacy in an unopened package; or the possibility that an operator will listen in on a telephone conversation negates an expectation of privacy in the words spoken on the telephone. "What a person . . . seeks to preserve as private, *even in an area accessible to the public,* may be constitutionally protected." *Katz* * * *.[151]

Nor is it dispositive that "respondents placed their refuse at the curb for the express purpose of conveying it to a third party, . . . who might himself have sorted through respondents' trash or permitted others, such as police, to do so." * * * In the first place, Greenwood can hardly be faulted for leaving trash on his curb when a county ordinance commanded him to do so * * *. More importantly, even the voluntary relinquishment of possession or control over an effect does not necessarily amount to a relinquishment of a privacy expectation in it. Were it otherwise, a letter or package would lose all Fourth Amendment protection when placed in a mail box or other depository with the "express purpose" of entrusting it to the postal officer or a private carrier; those bailees are just as likely as trash collectors (and certainly have greater incentive) to "sor[t] through" the personal effects entrusted to them, "or permi[t] others, such as police, to do so." Yet, it has been clear for at least 110 years that the possibility of such an intrusion does not justify a warrantless search by police in the first instance.

[I]n the instant case the contraband was concealed in paper sacks

---

the edge of Donato's property for collection" just as garbage man preparing to dump it in truck); Moran v. State, 644 N.E.2d 536 (Ind.1994) (*Greenwood* governs where police searched "garbage cans * * * sitting about a foot from the street"); State v. Sampson, 362 Md. 438, 765 A.2d 629 (2001) (*Greenwood* applicable where bags could be reached from sidewalk, and "it matters not whether that area is technically within or without the boundary of the curtilage"); State v. Hempele, 120 N.J. 182, 576 A.2d 793 (1990) (in instant case "the police themselves removed the garbage from the curb," but this "distinction has no fourth amendment significance"); State

v. Carriere, 545 N.W.2d 773 (N.D.1996) (*Greenwood* applies to police search of garbage defendant "placed at the end of his driveway near the street, but on his property"); Barekman v. State, 200 P.3d 802 (Wyo.2009) (*Greenwood* applies here, where police retrieved trash from barrels "on the curb" and about 25–30 ft. from defendant's residence).

[151] For useful elaboration of this essential point, see Kamin, The Private is Public: The Relevance of Private Actors in Defining the Fourth Amendment, 46 B.C.L.Rev. 83 (2004); Serr, Great Expectations of Privacy: A New Model for Fourth Amendment Protection, 73 Minn.L.Rev. 583 (1989).

within the barrels, and was not visible without emptying or searching through the barrels' contents. * * * Under such circumstances, we hold that defendants had a reasonable expectation that their trash would not be rummaged through and picked over by police officers acting without a search warrant.

It remains to be asked whether the police may achieve by indirection that which they may not do directly. This was the issue presented in *Croker v. State*.[152] Garbage collectors for the city at regular intervals would enter the defendant's back yard through the gate and empty the contents of his garbage cans into a large green plastic barrel used for that purpose, which they would in turn deposit in a truck in the alley to be transported to the city dump. Police asked the garbage collectors not to dump the contents of their barrel into the truck when picking up defendant's garbage, but instead to turn that material over to the police. This was done on four separate occasions, which resulted in the police discovery of plant stems and seeds of marijuana in the garbage, and this in turn was used to obtain a warrant to search defendant's premises. The court concluded:

> Under those circumstances, and as we analyze the evidence, the trial court was not in error when it impliedly found by its order denying defendant's motion to suppress that no invasion of defendant's right of privacy occurred. Even assuming under the rationale of *Katz* * * * that defendant did have a reasonable expectation of privacy to the contents of his garbage cans as long as the contents were on his premises it would be most unrealistic to hold that such reasonable expectation of privacy would reach beyond the confines of defendant's premises. It is our view that when defendant put his garbage in his garbage cans for purposes of removal he impliedly consented to entry upon his premises by the garbage collectors in the regular performance of their duties and to the removal of the garbage by them to the alley, which was open to the public. At that time the officers or anyone else, if the garbage collectors did not object, were free to examine the contents of the collectors' barrel.[153]

If there is a protected expectation of privacy in trash, so that

---

[152]Croker v. State, 477 P.2d 122 (Wyo.1970). See also United States v. Crowell, 586 F.2d 1020 (4th Cir.1978); United States v. Shelby, 573 F.2d 971 (7th Cir.1978), both involving similar facts and analysis.

[153]The court relied upon State v. Purvis, 249 Or. 404, 438 P.2d 1002 (1968). After police were informed by employees of a hotel that a certain guest was suspected of using narcotics, a detective asked the maids to keep the trash from his room separate from the other trash they collected, and they did so. The court reasoned: "The evidence in this case would support a finding that the maids were authorized by defendant to clean the room when they did and to remove the trash, including the cigarette butt found on the floor of the room. Defendant's claim to privacy terminated with respect to items discarded by him and which he impliedly authorized to be hauled away. Certainly, once the discarded items were outside of the room they were in the public domain and open to inspection by anyone. And so, in the present case if the police had given no instructions to the maids and simply waited until the trash from room 705 was brought out into the hallway and then intercepted it, de-

the police must comply with the Fourth Amendment when they directly search a person's garbage can, then it is rather difficult to swallow *Croker*. An expectation of privacy that can so easily be thwarted is not worth much. Yet, *Croker* cannot be dismissed summarily, for it is clear that in other contexts the police may rely upon the aid of others to obtain that which they are in no position to acquire on their own. In *Hoffa v. United States*[154] the Court held "that no interest legitimately protected by the Fourth Amendment is involved" when by misplaced trust a person takes into his confidence a government informer, and in *United States v. White*[155] the *Hoffa* rule was deemed to have survived even after

---

fendant would have had no legitimate claim to privacy in the items examined. The same result would obtain if the assistance of the maids was enlisted only to the extent of requiring them to deliver the trash to the police so that it could be examined by them.

"In the present case the maids were recruited by the police to carry on a form of search within the room, but only for items which had been discarded by defendant and which eventually would be available to the police for inspection even if no instructions had been given. Although the cooperation of the maids in keeping the objects from room 705 separate from objects taken from the other rooms was helpful to the police and, in fact, could be regarded as a part of the process of search, we do not think that the recruitment of the maids by the police for this purpose constituted an invasion of defendant's constitutional right of privacy."

See also United States v. Bruce, 396 F.3d 697 (6th Cir.2005) (defendant, tenant of hotel room, "had no reasonable expectation of privacy in this trash, as he and his travel companions had placed items in the trash bins where they would be picked up during the routine daily cleaning of the rooms, and neither Defendant nor his companions had taken any measures to prevent this typical daily task"); Riverdale Mills Corp. v. Pimpare, 392 F.3d 55 (1st Cir.2004) (EPA sampling of wastewater at manhole # 1, on road on corporation's property, no search, as such water "is *irretrievably* flowing into the public sewer, which is only 300 feet away," for such

water "is similar to trash left out on the curb for pick-up by the trash collector, which enjoyed no reasonable expectation of privacy"); United States v. Biondich, 652 F.2d 743 (8th Cir.1981) ("When a person makes arrangements with a sanitation service to have the items picked up, however, and when the items are placed in the designated place for collection and the regular collector makes the pickup in the usual manner on the scheduled collection day, the person loses his or her legitimate expectation of privacy in the items at the time they are taken off his or her premises"); Danai v. Canal Square Associates, 862 A.2d 395 (D.C.App.2004) (where trash is collected from various commercial suites and accumulated in building's trash room, and management exercises control and authority over the building's trash room, the contents of which are ultimately disposed of offsite, office tenant had no expectation of privacy in discarded letter that landlord obtained from trash room); State v. Howard, 342 Or. 635, 157 P.3d 1189 (2007) (defendants did not retain protected privacy interest in their garbage after sanitation company picked it up in the regular course of business and then turned it over to police for inspection). For more on testing of waste water, as in *Riverdale*, see Note, 51 Ariz.L. Rev. 741 (2009).

[154]Hoffa v. United States, 385 U.S. 293, 87 S.Ct. 408, 17 L.Ed.2d 374 (1966).

[155]United States v. White, 401 U.S. 745, 91 S.Ct. 1122, 28 L.Ed.2d 453 (1971).

Katz. But *Hoffa* is quite different from *Croker*, as Justice Rabinowitz has pointed out:

> *Hoffa* and the instant case, however, are distinguishable. There, the defendants knowingly and voluntarily communicated certain incriminating information to a third person who turned out to be a paid informer; a communication to another was intentionally initiated and undertaken. Having intentionally conducted such communication, the defendants were obliged to assume the risk that the recipient of the communication might turn out to be a government agent. Their expectation of privacy, under such circumstances, was necessarily diminished. Here, the facts suggest that no such knowing or voluntary disclosure of the contents of the closed garbage bag to the collectors or any other person was initiated or attempted by appellant. If anything, the facts would seem to suggest that appellant and her husband expected the refuse collectors to "commingle" or destroy the garbage. If appellant had deposited personal letters rather than contraband into the dumpster, it could not be seriously maintained that she voluntarily and knowingly meant to communicate the contents of such letters to the collectors or police. It is more reasonable to infer that she expected the contents of her garbage to be intermingled with other refuse in the well of the truck, and ultimately dumped into a central collection place where the forces of nature would destroy them. In short, without some attempt at knowingly communicating to a third person or knowingly disclosing to the public, appellant did not have to assume the risk that such third persons might be paid informers or agents of the police. Her reasonable expectation of privacy against governmental intrusion remains intact.[156]

Though the foregoing analysis by Justice Rabinowitz is eminently sensible, the likelihood the Supreme Court would come out that way is certainly less than substantial. In *California v. Greenwood*,[157] having to do with similar use of a trash collector as to bags of refuse placed at the curb, the Court, in concluding the defendant lacked a reasonable expectation of privacy in the contents of those bags, emphasized both (i) that "bags left on or at the side of a public street are readily accessible to * * * members of the public"; and (ii) that defendant had put out his garbage "for the express purpose of conveying it to a third party, the trash collector, who might himself have sorted through respondents' trash or permitted others, such as the police, to do so." The first of these reasons is inapplicable in a *Croker*-type situation, but the second does apply and may well alone suffice to defeat the householder's claim. Even if the police may not themselves enter the curtilage to take the garbage,[158] *Greenwood* does not suggest that their dealings with the trash collector will taint his actions. In coming onto the curtilage and taking the trash, the collector is doing exactly what the householder

---

[156]Smith v. State, 510 P.2d 793 (Alaska 1973) (dissenting opinion).

[157]California v. Greenwood, 486 U.S. 35, 108 S.Ct. 1625, 100 L.Ed.2d 30 (1988).

[158]See text at note 126 supra.

contemplated. What the householder obviously did not contemplate is that the collector would fail to "commingle" that garbage as he ordinarily does, but the *Greenwood* majority appears to reject the notion that anticipation of commingling is a reasonable expectation under *Katz.*[159]

In any case where the examination of the garbage is otherwise permissible under *Greenwood,* does it make any difference that the defendant has resorted to rather extraordinary means to ensure that its incriminating character would not be perceived by others? Consider, for example, *United States v. Scott,*[160] where IRS agents painstakingly reassembled documents defendant shredded into 5/32-inch strips before putting them in the garbage later placed outside his curtilage. In answering the above question in the negative, the court reasoned:

> What we have here is a failed attempt at secrecy by reason of underestimation of police resourcefulness, not invasion of constitutionally protected privacy. There is no constitutional protection from police scrutiny as to information received from a failed attempt at secrecy. * * *
>
> Appellee here thought that reducing the documents to 5/32-inch pieces made them undecipherable. It turned out he was wrong. He is in no better position than the citizen who merely tears up a document by hand and discards the pieces onto the sidewalk. * * *[161]
>
> In our view, shredding garbage and placing it in the public domain subjects it to the same risks regarding privacy, as engaging

---

[159]The majority did take specific note of the respondents' claim of a privacy expectation because the bags were ones "which the garbage collector was expected to pick up, mingle with the trash of others, and deposit at the garbage dump." See State v. Hauser, 342 N.C. 382, 464 S.E.2d 443 (1995) (where at police request defendant's "garbage was picked up by the regular garbage collector [from defendant's back yard], in the usual manner and on the scheduled collection day," and "no one other than those authorized by defendant entered defendant's property, and no unusual procedures were followed other than to keep defendant's garbage separate," this no search under *Greenwood,* as "the clear intention to convey the garbage to a third party, so as to allow the trash collector to make such use and disposed of it as he desires, is a factor which merits substantial weight").

But see State v. Hauser, 115 N.C.App. 431, 445 S.E.2d 73 (1994) (where at police request city sanitation worker picked up defendant's

garbage from behind his house and then turned it over to police instead of commingling it with other refuse in his truck, this an illegal search, as *Greenwood* read as based exclusively on "the accessibility of the garbage, not the defendant's intent to convey it to a third party").

[160]United States v. Scott, 975 F.2d 927 (1st Cir.1992), discussed in Note, 79 Cornell L.Rev. 452 (1994).

[161]The court elaborated: "A person who prepares incriminatory documents in a secret code (or for that matter in some obscure foreign language), and thereafter blithely discards them as trash, relying on the premise or hope that they will not be deciphered [or translated] by the authorities could well be in for an unpleasant surprise if his code is 'broken' by the police [or a translator is found for the abstruse language], but he cannot make a valid claim that his subjective expectation in keeping the contents private by use of the secret code [or language] was reasonable in a constitutional sense."

in a private conversation in public where it is subject to the possibility that it may be overheard by other persons. Both are failed attempts at maintaining privacy whose failure can only be attributed to the conscious acceptance by the actor of obvious risk factors. In the case of the conversation, the risk is that conversation in a public area may be overheard by a third person. In the disposal of trash, the risk is that it may be rummaged through and deciphered once it leaves the control of the trasher. In both situations the expectation of privacy has been practically eliminated by the citizen's own action. Law enforcement officials are entitled to apply human ingenuity and scientific advances to collect freely available evidence from the public domain.[162]

Though this result may well be consistent with the analysis in *Greenwood,* it is troubling precisely because it illustrates just how difficult it can be to dispose of personal effects without surrendering one's privacy interest in them.[163]

§ 2.6(d) Effects that are "mere evidence"

Historically, the right to search for and seize property depended upon the assertion by the Government of a valid claim of superior interest; it was not enough that the purpose of the search and seizure was to obtain evidence for the apprehension or conviction of a criminal. This notion, which came to be known as the "mere evidence" rule, had its origin in the celebrated English case of *Entick v. Carrington.*[164] This case recognized publisher Entick's right to recover damages in trespass against three agents of the Crown who, empowered with a warrant, had entered his home and seized countless books and records. In response to the defendants' argument that the warrant was valid because it served as "a means of detecting offenders by discovering evidence," Lord Camden replied:

> I wish some cases had been shewn, where the law forceth evidence out of the owner's custody by process. * * * In the criminal law such a proceeding was never heard of; and yet there are some crimes * * * that are more atrocious than libelling. But our law has provided no paper-search in these cases to help forward the conviction. * * * It is very certain, that the law obligeth no man to accuse himself; because the necessary means of compelling self-accusation, falling upon the innocent as well as the guilty, would be both cruel and unjust; and it would seem, that search for evidence is disallowed upon the same principle. Then, too, the innocent would be confounded with the guilty.

---

[162]Compare United States v. Upham, 168 F.3d 532 (1st Cir.1999) (court summarily rejects government's suggestion, relying on *Greenwood* and *Scott,* that one abandons material supposedly deleted by pushing computer's "delete" button but which can be recovered by a specialized utility program until the deleted information is actually overwritten by new information; "to compare deletion to putting one's trash on the street where it can be searched by every passerby * * * is to reason by false analogy").

[163]See text at note 111 supra.

[Section 2.6(d)]

[164]Entick v. Carrington, 19 How.St. Tri. 1029 (1765).

Though "the rationale of the passage is not crystal-clear," it appears "that Lord Camden was simply observing * * * that neither statute nor common law authorized the use of search warrants to obtain evidence of crime," in which "respect he was quite right."[165]

Over a century later, in the famous case of *Boyd v. United States*,[166] "the first Supreme Court decision in which the fourth amendment looms large,"[167] this passage from *Entick* was quoted with ringing approval by Justice Bradley. *Entick* was described as "one of the landmarks of English liberty" and its propositions as "sufficiently explanatory of what was meant by unreasonable searches and seizures." The Court in *Boyd* thus deemed it appropriate to draw a distinction between cases where a warrant was issued for articles to which the government or the owner was entitled to possession (as in, respectively, revenue cases and stolen goods cases), and the instant case, where the books and records were subject to no such possessory claim and were the legitimate property of the party from whom they were sought. The "modern cornerstone of the 'mere evidence' rule,"[168] however, is *Gouled v. United States*,[169] which involved the admissibility into evidence of certain contracts seized from defendant and used against him at his trial for conspiracy to defraud the government. The Court in *Gouled* concluded it was clear that search warrants

> may not be used as a means of gaining access to a man's house or office and papers solely for the purpose of making search to secure evidence to be used against him in a criminal or penal proceeding, but that they may be resorted to only when a primary right to such search and seizure may be found in the interest which the public or the complainant may have in the property to be seized, or in the right to the possession of it, or when a valid exercise of the police power renders possession of the property by the accused unlawful and provides that it may be taken. * * *
>
> There is no special sanctity in papers, as distinguished from other forms of property, to render them immune from search and seizure, if only they fall within the scope of the principles of the cases in which other property may be seized, and if they be adequately described in the affidavit and warrant. Stolen or forged papers have been so seized, * * * and lottery tickets, under a statute prohibiting their possession with intent to sell them, * * * and we cannot doubt that contracts may be so used as instruments or agencies for perpetrating frauds upon the government as to give the public an interest in them which would justify the search for and seizure of them, under a properly issued search warrant, for the purpose of

---

[165]T. Taylor, Two Studies in Constitutional Interpretation 53 (1969).

[166]Boyd v. United States, 116 U.S. 616, 6 S.Ct. 524, 29 L.Ed. 746 (1886).

[167]T. Taylor, Two Studies in Constitutional Interpretation 53 (1969).

[168]T. Taylor, Two Studies in Constitutional Interpretation 55 (1969).

[169]Gouled v. United States, 255 U.S. 298, 41 S.Ct. 261, 65 L.Ed. 647 (1921).

preventing further frauds.

As to each of the contracts involved in *Gouled*, the Court concluded that "[t]he government could desire its possession only to use it as evidence against the defendant and to search for and seize it for such purpose was unlawful."

It must be emphasized that the Court in *Gouled* distinguished between mere evidence and other effects, not between papers and other effects. The Court specifically upheld on later occasions the seizure of documents that were the instrumentalities of crime.[170] On the other hand, the *Gouled* rule was unhesitantly applied to bar seizure of mere evidence not documentary in nature.[171] The "mere evidence" rule was later extended to warrantless searches of premises incident to arrest, on the theory that such searches could not be "greater than that conferred by a search warrant."[172] Curiously, however, the Court never extended the rule to searches of the person incident to arrest.[173]

Over the years, the "mere evidence" rule fell upon hard times. The distinction the Court had drawn between seizure of items of evidential value only and seizure of instrumentalities, fruits or contraband was rather consistently and severely criticized by the commentators.[174] Even after *Mapp v. Ohio*,[175] the rule of the *Gouled* case was rejected in several well-reasoned state court decisions.[176] And federal courts were inclined to go to great lengths to avoid what was perceived as an artificial distinction. In *United States v. Guido*,[177] for example, the court, in upholding the seizure of defendant's shoes for matching with a heel print

---

[170]Zap v. United States, 328 U.S. 624, 66 S.Ct. 1277, 90 L.Ed. 1477 (1946); Marron v. United States, 275 U.S. 192, 48 S.Ct. 74, 72 L.Ed. 231 (1927).

[171]E.g., Morrison v. United States, 262 F.2d 449 (D.C.Cir.1958) (excluding a stained handkerchief that was evidence of a perverted act).

[172]United States v. Lefkowitz, 285 U.S. 452, 52 S.Ct. 420, 76 L.Ed. 877 (1932).

[173]As early as 1914 the Supreme Court, by way of dictum, referred to the recognized right "to search the person of the accused when legally arrested to discover and seize the fruits or evidences of crime." Weeks v. United States, 232 U.S. 383, 34 S.Ct. 341, 58 L.Ed. 652 (1914). In Schmerber v. California, 384 U.S. 757, 86 S.Ct. 1826, 16 L.Ed.2d 908 (1966), the Court upheld the taking of a blood sample from a person though the search obvi-ously was for evidentiary purposes only.

[174]E.g., Chafee, The Progress of the Law 1919–1922, 35 Harv.L.Rev. 673 (1922); Kamisar, The Wiretapping-Eavesdropping Problem: A Professor's View, 44 Minn.L.Rev. 891, 914–18 (1960); Kaplan, Search and Seizure: A No-Man's Land in the Criminal Law, 49 Cal.L.Rev. 474, 478 (1961); Traynor, Mapp v. Ohio at Large in the Fifth States, 1962 Duke L.J. 319, 332; Comments, 45 N.C.L.Rev. 512 (1967) 66 Colum.L.Rev. 355 (1966); 20 U.Chi. L.Rev. 319 (1953); 31 Yale L.J. 518 (1922).

[175]Mapp v. Ohio, 367 U.S. 643, 81 S.Ct. 1684, 6 L.Ed.2d 1081 (1961).

[176]E.g., People v. Thayer, 63 Cal.2d 635, 47 Cal.Rptr. 780, 408 P.2d 108 (1965); State v. Bisaccia, 45 N.J. 504, 213 A.2d 185 (1965).

[177]United States v. Guido, 251 F.2d 1 (7th Cir.1958).

left at the scene of a bank robbery, asserted that the shoes were instrumentalities of the crime because they "would facilitate a robber's get-away and would not attract as much public attention as a robber fleeing barefooted from the scene of the holdup." Finally, in *Warden v. Hayden*,[178] the Supreme Court sounded the death knell for the "mere evidence" rule.

In *Hayden,* the police entered a house in hot pursuit of a man who had just committed an armed robbery and, during the course of a search therein for the perpetrator, found and seized several items of clothing. The court of appeals held that this search was lawful but that the clothing was nonetheless inadmissible because they were of "evidential value only" and thus not lawfully subject to seizure.[179] The Supreme Court reversed. Stressing that "the principal object of the Fourth Amendment is the protection of privacy rather than property," the Court, per Justice Brennan, concluded that this protection was not advanced by the "mere evidence" rule:

> Nothing in the language of the Fourth Amendment supports the distinction between "mere evidence" and instrumentalities, fruits of crime, or contraband. On its face, the provision assures the "right of the people to be secure in their persons, houses, papers, and effects * * *," without regard to the use to which any of these things are applied. This "right of the people" is certainly unrelated to the "mere evidence" limitation. Privacy is disturbed no more by a search directed to a purely evidentiary object than it is by a search directed to an instrumentality, fruit, or contraband. A magistrate can intervene in both situations, and the requirements of probable cause and specificity can be preserved intact. Moreover, nothing in the nature of property seized as evidence renders it more private than property seized, for example, as an instrumentality; quite the opposite may be true. Indeed, the distinction is wholly irrational, since, depending on the circumstances, the same "papers and effects" may be "mere evidence" in one case and "instrumentality" in another. * * *
>
> The premise in *Gouled* that government may not seize evidence simply for the purpose of proving crime has likewise been discredited. The requirement that the Government assert in addition some property interest in material it seizes has long been a fiction, obscuring the reality that government has an interest in solving crime. * * *
>
> The rationale most frequently suggested for the rule preventing the seizure of evidence is that "limitations upon the fruit to be gathered tend to limit the quest itself." * * * But privacy "would be just as well served by a restriction on search to the even-numbered days of the month. * * * And it would have the extra advantage of avoiding hair-splitting questions. * * *" * * * The "mere evidence" limitation has spawned exceptions so numerous and confusion so great, in fact, that it is questionable whether it affords meaningful

---

[178]Warden v. Hayden, 387 U.S. 294, 87 S.Ct. 1642, 18 L.Ed.2d 782 (1967).

[179]363 F.2d 647 (4th Cir.1966).

protection. But if its rejection does enlarge the area of permissible searches, the intrusions are nevertheless made after fulfilling the probable cause and particularity requirements of the Fourth Amendment and after the intervention of "a neutral and detached magistrate * * *." The Fourth Amendment allows intrusions upon privacy under these circumstances, and there is no viable reason to distinguish intrusions to secure "mere evidence" from intrusions to secure fruits, instrumentalities, or contraband.[180]

§ 2.6(e) Private papers

The Court's repudiation of the "mere evidence" rule in *Warden v. Hayden*[181] was unquestionably justified. As the excerpts from Justice Brennan's opinion set out above amply illustrate, that rule "is both historically and analytically unsound"[182] and relied upon property-based distinctions having little to do with "the protection of privacy," which is "the principal object of the Fourth Amendment." This is not to say, of course, that Justice Douglas was wrong when he asserted in his *Hayden* dissent that the Constitution "creates a zone of privacy that may not be invaded by the police through raids, by the legislator through laws, or by magistrates through the issuance of warrants." One might consistently reject the arbitrary distinctions of the "mere evidence" rule and still hold to the view that certain matters are so private that they should be absolutely immune from search and seizure. Indeed, some of the harshest critics of the rule felt that it "should not be simply scrapped, without replacement."[183]

But, how should the replacement be formulated, and what would be its constitutional underpinnings? One possibility was suggested in the Court's opinion in *Hayden,* where Justice Brennan cautioned:

> The items of clothing involved in this case are not "testimonial" or "communicative" in nature, and their introduction therefore did not compel respondent to become a witness against himself in violation of the Fifth Amendment. * * * This case thus does not require that we consider whether there are items of evidential value whose very nature precludes them from being the object of a reasonable search and seizure.

It is quite understandable that the Court on this occasion intimated that the Fifth Amendment prohibition against compulsory self-incrimination barred the seizure of private papers even

---

[180]Fortas, J., joined by the Chief Justice, concurring, declined to "join in the majority's broad—and in my judgment, totally unnecessary—repudiation of the so-called 'mere evidence' rule." Douglas, J., dissenting, concluded that "[t]he personal effects and possessions of the individual (all contraband and the like excepted) are sacrosanct from prying eyes, from the long arm of the law, from any rummaging by police."

[Section 2.6(e)]

[181]Warden v. Hayden, 387 U.S. 294, 87 S.Ct. 1642, 18 L.Ed.2d 782 (1967).

[182]T. Taylor, Two Studies in Constitutional Interpretation 63 (1969).

[183]T. Taylor, Two Studies in Constitutional Interpretation 69 (1969).

under an otherwise valid search warrant, for this had been asserted or implied in dicta on several prior occasions. In *Boyd v. United States,*[184] the Court said: "[W]e have been unable to perceive that the seizure of a man's private books and papers to be used in evidence against him is substantially different from compelling him to be a witness against himself." Similarly, in *Hale v. Henkel*[185] it was observed that "the substance of the offense is the compulsory production of private papers, whether under a search warrant or a subpoena duces tecum, against which the person * * * is entitled to protection."

The Fifth Amendment issue was to plague the lower courts in the years following *Hayden.* In *Hill v. Philpott,*[186] where internal revenue agents seized a doctor's records pursuant to a warrant, the court concluded that the doctor's Fifth Amendment objection was well taken. Looking to the *Hayden* caveat, the court asserted: "In overruling *Gouled* as to its Fourth Amendment teachings, we do not believe that the Court intended to in any way diminish the Fifth Amendment characteristics which might attach to certain items of property such as personal books and records." In *United States v. Bennett,*[187] on the other hand, the court rejected a Fifth Amendment challenge to a seizure of a letter. The court viewed any relationship existing between the Fourth and Fifth Amendments as "largely repudiated by *Hayden*" and concluded that "the Fourth Amendment does not protect broadly against the seizure of things whose compulsory production would be forbidden by the Fifth." Most lower courts took the *Bennett* position,[188] as did the Supreme Court when it finally confronted the issue in *Andresen v. Maryland.*[189]

In *Andresen,* state authorities obtained search warrants to search defendant's law office and also corporate offices for specified documents pertaining to a fraudulent sale of land. The papers found in the execution of the warrants were admitted against him at his trial, and he was convicted. Noting that the "historic function" of the privilege against self-incrimination has been to protect a "natural individual from compulsory incrimination

[184]Boyd v. United States, 116 U.S. 616, 6 S.Ct. 524, 29 L.Ed. 746 (1886).

[185]Hale v. Henkel, 201 U.S. 43, 26 S.Ct. 370, 50 L.Ed. 652 (1906).

[186]Hill v. Philpott, 445 F.2d 144 (7th Cir.1971).

[187]United States v. Bennett, 409 F.2d 888 (2d Cir.1969).

[188]Shaffer v. Wilson, 523 F.2d 175 (10th Cir.1975); United States v. Murray, 492 F.2d 178 (9th Cir.1973); Taylor v. Minnesota, 466 F.2d 1119 (8th Cir.1972); United States v. Blank, 459 F.2d 383 (6th Cir.1972); United States v. Scharfman, 448 F.2d 1352 (2d Cir.1971). The majority position accords with the view taken in 8 J. Wigmore, Evidence § 2264 (McNaughton rev. 1961).

[189]Andresen v. Maryland, 427 U.S. 463, 96 S.Ct. 2737, 49 L.Ed.2d 627 (1976).

through his own testimony or personal records,"[190] the Court, per Justice Blackmun, concluded that there had been no Fifth Amendment violation in this case because there was no compulsion.

[I]n this case, petitioner was not asked to say or to do anything. The records seized contained statements that petitioner had voluntarily committed to writing. The search for and seizure of these records were conducted by law enforcement personnel. Finally, when these records were introduced at trial, they were authenticated by a handwriting expert, not by petitioner. Any compulsion of petitioner to speak, other than the inherent psychological pressure to respond at trial to unfavorable evidence, was not present.

This case thus falls within the principle stated by Mr. Justice Holmes: "A party is privileged from producing the evidence but not from its production." * * * This principle recognizes that the protection afforded by the self-incrimination clause of the Fifth Amendment "adheres basically to the person, not to information that may incriminate him." * * * Thus, although the Fifth Amendment may protect an individual from complying with a subpoena for the production of his personal records in his possession because the very act of production may constitute a compulsory authentication of incriminating information, * * * a seizure of the same materials by law enforcement officers differs in a crucial respect—the individual against whom the search is directed is not required to aid in the discovery, production, or authentication of incriminating evidence. * * *

Finally, we do not believe that permitting the introduction into evidence of a person's business records seized during an otherwise lawful search would offend or undermine any of the policies undergirding the privilege. * * *

In this case, petitioner, at the time he recorded his communication, at the time of the search, and at the time the records were admitted at trial, was not subjected to "the cruel trilemma of self-accusation, perjury or contempt." * * * Indeed, he was never required to say or to do anything under penalty of sanction. Similarly, permitting the admission of the records in question does not convert our accusatorial system of justice into an inquisitorial system. * * * Further, the search for and seizure of business records pose no danger greater than that inherent in every search that evidence will be "elicited by inhumane treatment and abuses." * * * In this case, the statements seized were voluntarily committed to paper before the police arrived to search for them, and petitioner was not treated discourteously during the search. Also, the "good cause" to "disturb" * * * petitioner was independently determined by the judge who issued the warrants; and the State bore the burden of executing them. Finally, there is no chance in this case, of petitioner's statements being self-deprecatory and untrustworthy because they were extracted from him—they were already in existence and had been made voluntarily.

The papers seized in *Andresen* were, as the Court repeatedly

---

[190]Bellis v. United States, 417 U.S. 85, 94 S.Ct. 2179, 40 L.Ed.2d 678 (1974), quoting from United States v. White, 322 U.S. 694, 64 S.Ct. 1248, 88 L.Ed. 1542 (1944).

took pains to point out, "business records." "We are not so outraged by the intrusion on privacy which accompanies the seizure of these records as we are by the seizure of a diary,"[191] and thus it might be thought that the Court has not slammed the Fifth Amendment door shut entirely and that notwithstanding *Andresen* the Court might on some later occasion hold that the Fifth Amendment does protect certain private papers more private than Andresen's documents concerning the land sales. This, however, seems unlikely. Given the kind of analysis employed in *Andresen,* "[n]o distinction can be drawn between business records and diaries * * *—in all such cases the fact that evidence is obtained without requiring the accused to act or speak means 'testimonial compulsion' is lacking."[192] While some have ascribed to the Fifth Amendment the broad purpose of protecting privacy,[193] this is not the case. This is apparent when it is considered that the privilege is inapplicable when the possibility of incrimination is absent[194] or has been removed by a grant of immunity.[195] As Judge Friendly has aptly observed: "It seems a strange concept of a right to privacy that, although this does not protect the most sensitive communications against disclosure in court so long as they are innocent, it demands absolute immunity for incriminating testimony alone."[196] Thus, while there is a sense in which the claiming of the privilege can result in the protection of some aspects of one's privacy, "there is no coherent notion of privacy that explains the privilege."[197] Given this fact and the added fact that *Andresen* makes the manner in which the documents were obtained determinative, there is no reason to believe that the Fifth Amendment will hereafter be utilized to bar search warrants directed at the most private of

---

[191]Marshall, J., dissenting in Couch v. United States, 409 U.S. 322, 93 S.Ct. 611, 34 L.Ed.2d 548 (1973).

[192]Note, 90 Harv.L.Rev. 945, 978 (1977). See also Bacigal, The Fourth Amendment in Flux: The Rise and Fall of Probable Cause, 1979 U.Ill.L.F. 763, 791 (concluding that after *Andresen* there is no kind of evidence which is always beyond reach); Note, 76 Mich.L. Rev. 184, 211 (1977) ("No zone of privacy now exists that the government cannot enter to take an individual's property for the purpose of obtaining incriminating information").

[193]See Couch v. United States, 409 U.S. 322, 93 S.Ct. 611, 34 L.Ed.2d 548 (1973) (Douglas, J., dissenting); California v. Byers, 402 U.S. 424, 91 S.Ct. 1535, 29 L.Ed.2d 9 (1971) (Harlan, J., concurring); McKay, Self-Incrimination and the New

Privacy, 1967 Sup.Ct.Rev. 193.

[194]Thus, there is no Fifth Amendment privilege to refuse to testify or surrender papers on the ground that one would thereby incriminate another or betray a trust. Burdeau v. McDowell, 256 U.S. 465, 41 S.Ct. 574, 65 L.Ed. 1048 (1921); Hale v. Henkel, 201 U.S. 43, 26 S.Ct. 370, 50 L.Ed. 652 (1906).

[195]Kastigar v. United States, 406 U.S. 441, 92 S.Ct. 1653, 32 L.Ed.2d 212 (1972).

[196]In re Horowitz, 482 F.2d 72 (2d Cir.1973). See also Friendly, The Fifth Amendment Tomorrow: The Case for Constitutional Change, 37 U.Cin.L. Rev. 671, 688 (1968).

[197]Meltzer, Privileges Against Self-Incrimination and the Hit-and-Run Opinions, 1971 Sup.Ct.Rev. 1, 21.

papers.[198]

This is not to say, however, that there are *no* circumstances in which a Fifth Amendment-type objection could be properly raised with respect to a search warrant, as is illustrated by the interesting case of *United States v. Howell*.[199] Six black books prepared by and in the possession of the defendant were sought by grand jury subpoena, and were produced for in camera inspection by a judge for determination of defendant's Fifth Amendment objection. After the subpoena was quashed as to some of the books but before that order could be implemented, the prosecutor sought search warrants for the same books. The court refused to issue the warrants, finding it "obvious" that "documents submitted by a defendant to a judge for in camera inspection cannot thereupon be seized from the judge's chambers by the United States Attorney pursuant to a search warrant." As for the government's claim it was doing no more than it could do once the books were returned to defendant, the court responded:

> The problem in this case is with the documents that Judge Burns held *were* covered by the Fifth Amendment. Because of the *in camera* inspection, the United States Attorney has now verified the existence of the documents, their relevance, and their location. My concern is that the government is attempting to accomplish indirectly what it may not have been able to do directly.
>
> * * * Neither *Andresen* nor any of the other cases that I have reviewed involve the "one-two" punch that the government is attempting to use here: A subpoena duces tecum quashed on Fifth Amendment grounds followed by a search warrant for the same documents. This unusual procedural background infuses the element of coercion that is not normally found in search and seizure cases. The defendant has in fact been required to aid in the discovery, production, and authentication of the documents submitted for *in camera* inspection. It would be a cruel hoax on the defendant to grant the motion to quash the subpoena and then turn around and make the documents available by a search warrant. Such a procedure could raise the "trilemma of self-accusation, perjury or contempt." * * *
>
> Granting the application for the search warrant in this situation

---

[198]Cf. State v. Barrett, 401 N.W.2d 184 (Iowa 1987) (involving state use of a personal journal left by defendant at a fast food restaurant and, when found by an employee there to contain death threats, turned over to police; referring to above analysis, court "find[s] no fifth amendment protection against the State's evidentiary use of defendant's personal journals"); State v. Andrei, 574 A.2d 295 (Me.1990) (where defendant's diary turned over to police by her husband, no Fifth Amendment violation, as "diary was voluntarily created and was delivered to the po-

lice in the absence of any form of compulsion").

Nor will the First Amendment. See United States v. Moody, 977 F.2d 1425 (11th Cir.1992) (upholding warrant for various writings of the defendant, including "a journal or notebook about the bombings" he had engaged in, against defendant's claim the warrant "violated his free speech and free press rights under the First Amendment").

[199]United States v. Howell, 466 F.Supp. 835 (D.Or.1979).

could open up the possibility of abuse by the government. The requirements for issuance of a subpoena duces tecum are much less stringent than for a search warrant. Furthermore, no judicial determination is made prior to the subpoena's issuance. The government could use the defendant's Fifth Amendment claim to specific documents under the subpoena to establish probable cause that the documents actually exist. The government could then use that probable cause to justify a search warrant. The effect of this would be to negate any Fifth Amendment defense to a subpoena duces tecum. I cannot believe that the Supreme Court in *Andresen* intended its holding to be that broad.

I realize that the effect of my ruling in this case is to force the government to an election between using a subpoena duces tecum or a search warrant when it wishes to reach documents in the hands of a defendant or potential defendant. If the government has probable cause and can meet the other Fourth Amendment requirements, it can proceed with a search warrant. If not, it can use a subpoena duces tecum to obtain any documents that are not protected by the Fifth Amendment. The government cannot, however, "piggyback" the subpoena and search warrant powers to circumvent the protections of the Fourth and Fifth Amendments.

But what of the Fourth Amendment? It *is* concerned with privacy; as the Court stressed in *Warden v. Hayden,*[200] "the principal object of the Fourth Amendment is the protection of privacy." "Diaries and personal letters that record only their author's personal thoughts lie at the heart of our sense of privacy,"[201] and thus it is not fanciful to suggest that perhaps private papers of that particular type are absolutely protected by the Fourth Amendment from seizure. The fundamental and difficult policy question is whether certain aspects of our privacy are so precious that the privacy interest can be said *never* to be outweighed by a law enforcement interest, so that there is

---

[200]Warden v. Hayden, 387 U.S. 294, 87 S.Ct. 1642, 18 L.Ed.2d 782 (1967).

[201]Marshall, J., dissenting in Couch v. United States, 409 U.S. 322, 93 S.Ct. 611, 34 L.Ed.2d 548 (1973). See also Hayden v. Warden, 363 F.2d 647 (4th Cir.1966) (seizure of "a diary containing incriminating entries" would be "prohibited by the Fourth and Fourteenth Amendments"); United States v. Boyette, 299 F.2d 92 (4th Cir.1962) ("a diary in which its author has recited his criminal conduct, seized in an otherwise lawful search, should not be used against him"); T. Taylor, Two Studies in Constitutional Interpretation 70 (1969) ("There is no good reason why a diary or personal letter * * * should be subject to seizure"); Comments, 69 Nw.U.L.Rev. 626, 649 (1974) ("If the papers are *intrapersonal* in nature (such as diaries) * * * use of the materials against the author should be prohibited"); 45 Texas L.Rev. 526, 559 (1967) (if "the book contained mere after-the-fact recording of criminal activity," then "these thoughts should be excluded from evidence"); Notes, 90 Harv.L.Rev. 945, 989 (1977) ("a presumption of privacy attaches to one's diary and conversations or letters passed between personal friends and acquaintances"); 33 McGeorge L.Rev. 129, 140 (2001) ("a diary deserves a higher degree of protection than other pieces of physical evidence"); 19 Rutgers L.J. 389, 417 (1988) ("the fourth amendment requires that a seizure of a personal diary be met with the strictest of scrutiny").

absolute immunity from seizure of certain highly personal documents, or whether all aspects of our privacy must be balanced against the needs of law enforcement pursuant to the traditional probable cause and particularity requirements of the Fourth Amendment. This question was neither raised nor resolved in *Andresen*.[202]

The case for absolute privacy in certain personal papers has been forcefully made by one commentator, and deserves to be quoted here:

> Belief in the uniqueness of each individual is one of the fundamental moral tenets of Western society. Such uniqueness inheres in being human and is not an entitlement to be granted or withheld by the state. In fact, one of the primary purposes of law is to ensure respect for this belief by preserving each person's right to a private life free from unwanted intrusion and disclosure.[203] Justice Brandeis saw this as the purpose underlying the fourth amendment:
>
> > The makers of our Constitution undertook to secure conditions favorable to the pursuit of happiness. They recognized the significance of man's spiritual nature, of his feelings and of his intellect . . . . They sought to protect Americans in their beliefs, their thoughts, their emotions and their sensations. They conferred, as against the Government, the right to be let alone . . . .[204]
>
> A record of one's private beliefs and emotions tells a good deal about the person. Similarly, when one intimately and privately shares such thoughts and feelings with others he reveals much of the inner person he is. Such experiences may include the exchange of letters, tapes, or phone conversations as well as actual gathering and conversation. Just as recognition of the relationship between private reflection, socialization, and personality has led the Court to block legislative attempts to control intimate private conduct,[205] interference with the private life by search or subpoena should be proscribed under the fourth and fifth amendments rather than tolerated as a necessary incident of criminal law enforcement. The

---

[202]As observed in Note, 67 J.Crim.L. & C. 389, 396 (1976): "*Andresen* leaves open the perplexing question of whether there is any kind of evidence which, because of its intimate nature, would be immune from search and seizure, regardless of its location. It is likely that further attempts to put some limits on the permissible target of a search warrant will center around what the Court has deemed the right of privacy. *Andresen*, having involved an office rather than a home, and business papers rather than some more intimate possession, does leave some room for the Court to maneuver."

[203]Murphy v. Waterfront Comm'n, 378 U.S. 52, 84 S.Ct. 1594, 12 L.Ed.2d 678 (1964), identified among the "fundamental values" underlying the priv-

ilege against self-incrimination "our respect for the inviolability of the human personality and of the right of each individual 'to a private enclave where he may lead a private life.'"

[204]Olmstead v. United States, 277 U.S. 438, 48 S.Ct. 564, 72 L.Ed. 944 (1928) (Brandeis, J., dissenting).

[205]Roe v. Wade, 410 U.S. 113, 93 S.Ct. 705, 35 L.Ed.2d 147 (1973) (abortion); Eisenstadt v. Baird, 405 U.S. 438, 92 S.Ct. 1029, 31 L.Ed.2d 349 (1972) (contraceptives for unmarried persons); Stanley v. Georgia, 394 U.S. 557, 89 S.Ct. 1243, 22 L.Ed.2d 542 (1969) (private possession of obscene material); Griswold v. Connecticut, 381 U.S. 479, 85 S.Ct. 1678, 14 L.Ed.2d 510 (1965) (right of marital privacy).

privacy value should not suffer abridgement simply because there is reason to believe a person is involved in criminal activity.[206] While it seems unlikely that the Fourth Amendment, which after all "cannot be translated into a general constitutional 'right to privacy,' "[207] could be extended this far,[208] a statutory prohibition upon the seizure of certain highly private documents might well be deserving of adoption.[209] The formulation appearing in the Model Code of Pre-Arraignment Procedure has much to commend it.[210]

Even if it is thought that the case for granting absolute protection to certain private papers is not a compelling one, there nonetheless remains a legitimate concern unique to the search of private papers. The point has been developed very well by Professor Taylor:

> The question in hand transcends the procedural safeguards of particularity and probability in the second clause [of the Fourth Amendment]. To be sure, a general warrant to seize all papers of a specified category may be even more oppressive than a warrant to seize particularly designated papers, especially if the latter be found early in the search, since the former requires a search of all the papers to isolate those which are to be seized. But, where personal papers are concerned, specificity of category is no real safeguard against the most grievous intrusions on privacy, as was pointed out over two hundred years ago during the House of Commons debates on general warrants:
>
> > . . . Even a particular warrant to seize seditious papers alone, without mentioning the titles of them, may prove highly detrimental, since in that case, all a man's papers must be indiscriminately examined, and such examination may bring things to light which it may not concern the public to know, and which yet it may prove highly detrimental to the owner to have made public

---

[206]Note, 90 Harv.L.Rev. 945, 985–86 (1977).

[207]Katz v. United States, 389 U.S. 347, 88 S.Ct. 507, 19 L.Ed.2d 576 (1967).

[208]See State v. Andrei, 574 A.2d 295 (Me.1990), rejecting defendant's "argument, for which she has failed to cite any controlling authority, that her privacy interests in her own diary are so precious that the Fourth and Fifth Amendments, operating together, protect her journal absolutely from any seizure by law enforcement agents without regard to the circumstances of the seizure." See also State v. Lewis, 123 Idaho 336, 848 P.2d 394 (1993) (upholding, without discussion of this point, search warrant for pedophile's premises for various objects, including "a diary listing names of victims and activities engaged in").

[209]T. Taylor, Two Studies in Constitutional Interpretation 71 (1969).

[210]Model Code of Pre-Arraignment Procedure § SS 210.3(2) (1975) provides: "With the exception of handwriting samples, and other writings or recordings of evidentiary value for reasons other than their testimonial content, things subject to seizure * * * shall not include personal diaries, letters, or other writings or recordings, made solely for private use or communication to an individual occupying a family, personal or other confidential relation, other than a relation in criminal enterprise, unless such things have served or are serving a substantial purpose in furtherance of a criminal enterprise."

. . . .[211]

Of course, a search for a tiny object, such as a stolen or smuggled diamond, which can be concealed among papers or in some other small recess, may involve much the same kind of ransacking search. But at least in such a case it is unnecessary to read papers and anyhow, exceptional cases apart, it is clear that documentary searches involve deeper inroads on personal security than searches for the traditional fruits and instrumentalities of crime.[212] In short, "the vice lies in the unlimited search"[213] that may well be necessary even when the warrant complies with the Fourth Amendment particularity requirement.

This problem was briefly noted by the Court in *Andresen*. It was observed that similar dangers "are present in executing a warrant for the seizure of telephone conversations," and that in both kinds of searches "responsible officials, including judicial officials, must take care to assure that they are conducted in a manner that minimizes unwarranted intrusions upon privacy." Efforts at realistic minimization have been none too successful in the wiretapping area,[214] and are unlikely to succeed as to private papers either unless some unique procedures are developed. One approach deserving serious consideration is that provided for in the Model Code of Pre-Arraignment Procedure:

If the documents to be seized cannot be searched for or identified without examining the contents of other documents, or if they con-

---

[211] 16 The Parliamentary History of England 10–11 (1813), proceedings on Jan. 29, 1765.

[212] T. Taylor, Two Studies in Constitutional Interpretation 67–68 (1969). See also McKenna, The Constitutional Protection of Private Papers: The Role of a Hierarchical Fourth Amendment, 53 Ind.L.J. 55, 91 (1977), arguing that "a hierarchical conception of fourth amendment protection should be recognized," with "private papers at or near the summit of such a hierarchy."

Consider also Schnapper, Unreasonable Searches and Seizures of Papers, 71 Va.L.Rev. 869 (1985), concluding: "Read in light of its historical background, the fourth amendment's search and seizure clause condemns the inspection of innocent private papers by government officials in search of a document that by itself may be unprotected," so as a consequence the government should normally be limited to the subpoena power, but if "the government has reason to believe that documents are in

danger of destruction it may seek a warrant directing that the documents be seized unread, placed under seal, and brought to a judge for a prompt in camera examination." Id. at 921–22.

[213] United States v. Bennett, 409 F.2d 888 (2d Cir.1969). Judge Friendly continues: "The reason why we shrink from allowing a personal diary to be the object of a search is that the entire diary must be read to discover whether there are incriminating entries; most of us would feel rather differently with respect to a 'diary' whose cover page bore the title 'Robberies I Have Performed.' Similarly the abhorrence generally felt with respect to 'rummaging' through the contents of a desk to find an incriminating letter would not exist in the same measure if the letter were lying in plain view."

[214] See opinions of Brennan and Marshall, JJ., dissenting from the denial of certiorari in Bynum v. United States, 423 U.S. 952, 96 S.Ct. 357, 46 L.Ed.2d 277 (1975); and Scott v. United States, 425 U.S. 917, 96 S.Ct. 1519, 47 L.Ed.2d 768 (1976).

stitute items or entries in account books, diaries, or other documents containing matter not specified in the warrant, the executing officer shall not examine the documents but shall either impound them under appropriate protection where found, or seal and remove them for safekeeping pending * * * a hearing * * * at which the person from whose possession or control the documents were taken, and any other person asserting any right or interest in the documents, may appear, in person or by counsel, and move (a) for the return of the documents * * *, in whole or in part, or (b) for specification of such conditions and limitations on the further search for the documents to be seized as may be appropriate to prevent unnecessary or unreasonable invasion of privacy.[215]

§ 2.6(f) Computer data

Even if neither the Fourth Amendment nor the Fifth Amendment confers a mantle of absolute privacy upon private papers, it is apparent that in most instances any police effort to examine such papers will constitute a search, so that at least the usual Fourth Amendment constraints will apply. This is because such records are usually kept in one's home or business office, where a justified expectation of privacy obtains. But one cannot as confidently say that computerized records accessed at such places are equally private, for these records

have several unique characteristics that a court might find to affect the scope of their fourth amendment protection.

First, computer records are stored in a technologically innovative form, raising the question whether they are sufficiently like other records to engender the "reasonable expectation of privacy" required for fourth amendment protection.[216] Second, people frequently store computer records on computers owned by third parties. The storage of records on another party's computer could be seen as a disclosure of the records to that party, lessening the individual's expectation of privacy, or as a grant of authority to consent to a search of the records.[217] Finally, many computer records can be obtained—both legitimately and illegitimately—by telephone. Telephone access to computerized records, especially when there is a strong possibility of unauthorized access, might be seen as precluding the reasonableness of the individual's expectation of privacy in the records, thereby eliminating fourth amendment protection.[218]

Whether and when the protections of the Fourth Amendment extend to computer data is emerging as a most significant issue, for "[c]omputer services are becoming increasingly important to

---

[215]Model Code of Pre-Arraignment Procedure § SS 220.5(2) & (3) (1975).

[Section 2.6(f)]

[216]This is also so as to, e.g., data stored on an electronic pager device. "As a general rule, there is a reasonable expectation of privacy in the contents of one's pager." State v. DeLuca, 168 N.J. 626, 775 A.2d 1284 (2001). Accord: United States v. Lynch, 908 F.Supp. 284 (D.V.I.1995); People v. Bullock, 226 Cal.App.3d 380, 277 Cal.Rptr. 63 (1990).

[217]As for the third party consent issues that can arise in this context, see § 8.6(f).

[218]Note, 67 B.U.L.Rev. 179, 180 (1987).

large segments of society."[219] However, it is an issue that as yet has rarely been addressed by the courts, and thus some degree of speculation is necessary here. In part the uncertainty is attributable to the Supreme Court's overall approach to questions regarding the Fourth Amendment's scope, involving a balancing of privacy claims against crime control interests, which for various reasons means that the "choice of values and the legal reasoning that will be used in future cases are difficult to predict."[220] But application of the *Katz* formula is especially problematical in the present context, involving "new technologies," for "societal expectations linked to a technology evolve with time."[221]

Of the three "unique characteristics" listed above, the first may be disposed of with relative ease. Certainly the fact that "records are stored in computerized form should not, by itself, render them unprotected by the fourth amendment," for by "holding that the fourth amendment protects privacy interests, and by rejecting the claim that the amendment protects only tangible property," the Court in *Katz* "demonstrated the irrelevance of physical form to the issue of fourth amendment protection."[222] This means that police activity in accessing records in a one-user single computer system is comparable to looking at records stored in a one-user filing cabinet;[223] ordinarily it is a search, just as merely making a copy of the information instead may well constitute a seizure.[224]

As for the second characteristic, storage of records on another party's computer, this typically occurs through a process of "timesharing" in which multiple users share concurrently the resources of a single computer system. Illustrative is the commercial sale of computer time, provision of computer resources to faculty and students by a university, and provision of such resources to employees by a business organization. Through the use of passwords and other devices, the data stored on the system by one user is made unavailable to the other users.[225] But another threat to the privacy of these files exists:

---

[219]Note, 60 U.M.K.C.L.Rev. 139, 140 (1991).

[220]Note, 81 Va.L.Rev. 1181, 1193 (1995) (elaborating those reasons at 1193–95).

[221]Note, 67 B.U.L.Rev. 179, 197 (1987).

[222]Note, 67 B.U.L.Rev. 179, 196 (1987).

[223]Sometimes, when the police obtain supposedly deleted computer files, the attempted analogy may be to the garbage can rather than the filing cabinet. See note 162 supra.

[224]For a discussion of that question, see text at note 293 infra.

[225]Occasionally such safeguards are absent, in which case a reasonable expectation of privacy as to that data clearly does not exist. See, e.g., United States v. King, 509 F.3d 1338 (11th Cir.2007) (when defendant's personal laptop computer was connected to military base's network, defendant's "files were 'shared' over the entire base network, and * * * everyone on the network had access to all of his files," and thus "the contents of his computer's hard drive were akin to items stored in the unsecured common areas of a multi-unit apartment building"); Commonwealth v. Kaupp, 453 Mass.

As a practical matter, computer operators will always be able to obtain records stored on their computers, regardless of password requirements or other file access protection schemes. Because computer operators possess the physical media upon which records are stored, they are able to circumvent file protection schemes by reading the files using different equipment. Furthermore, many operating systems are not intended to restrict the computer operator's access to files. In fact, the computer operator must have access to certain type of individual records in order to perform necessary functions. For example, to bill the user for storage space, or to make "backup" copies of the user's files to safeguard against data loss, the operator must have access to the "directory" specifying the names, locations, and lengths of the user's files.[226]

Because of this disclosure, it might be argued that there is no justified expectation of privacy in the computer files in light of such Supreme Court decisions as *United States v. Miller*[227] and *Smith v. Maryland*.[228] In *Miller*, where police served two banks with defective subpoenas requiring production of defendant's account records, the Court held the defendant had no legitimate expectation of privacy in the bank's records of his accounts, as (i) the records were the property of the bank, and (ii) the information in them had been "voluntarily conveyed to the banks" by the defendant. In *Smith*, involving police use of a pen register, the Court held that a person who disclosed to the telephone company numbers he dialed could not have a reasonable expectation of privacy in those numbers because the telephone company was capable of recording them and in fact did use the numbers for legitimate business purposes.[229]

However, the critical fact in both *Miller* and *Smith* was that "the information was given to a third party for that party's use"; in both cases, "this information had to be disclosed for the telephone company or bank to provide the requested service."[230] This means that "[r]ecords that the computer operator must routinely use, such as 'file directories,' probably have been 'disclosed' within the meaning of *Miller* and *Smith*," for they

---

102, 899 N.E.2d 809 (2009) (defendant "did not have any reasonable expectation of privacy in the files in [his computer's] open share, which were accessible to all network users").

[226]Note, 67 B.U.L.Rev. 179, 193–94 (1987).

[227]United States v. Miller, 425 U.S. 435, 96 S.Ct. 1619, 48 L.Ed.2d 71 (1976), discussed in § 2.7(c).

[228]Smith v. Maryland, 442 U.S. 735, 99 S.Ct. 2577, 61 L.Ed.2d 220 (1979), discussed in § 2.7(b).

[229]In *Smith*, discussed further in § 2.7(b), the Court deemed a justified expectation of privacy to be lacking as to information conveyed to the telephone company's "switching equipment." In Tokson, Automation and the Fourth Amendment, 96 Iowa L.Rev. 581, 586–87 (2011), it is concluded that this "automation rationale arose from the unique context of telephone routing" and thus "can easily be limited to the facts of *Smith*," meaning "that users whose information is exposed to automated Internet systems incur no loss of privacy" sufficient to defeat a justified expectation of privacy in that information.

[230]Note, 81 Va.L.Rev. 1181, 1200 (1995).

"relate to business between the timesharer and the computer operator, analogous to the bank records in *Miller* and the numbers dialed in *Smith*,"[231] although this is not inevitably the case.[232] But "computer operators have no legitimate purpose in reading records unrelated to the operator's function, just as the telephone company has no legitimate purpose in listening to the contents of conversations,"[233] and thus the user *does* have a legit-

---

[231]Note, 67 B.U.L.Rev. 179, 204 (1987).

Even more clearly, under *Miller* and *Smith* there is no protected Fourth Amendment privacy interest in subscriber information given to an Internet service provider. Doe v. Shurtleff, 628 F.3d 1217 (10th Cir.2010) (thus requirement that registered sex offender report "his online identifiers" to state does not violate Fourth Amendment); United States v. Christie, 624 F.3d 558 (3d Cir.2010); United States v. Bynum, 604 F.3d 161 (4th Cir.2010); United States v. Perrine, 518 F.3d 1196 (10th Cir.2008); Guest v. Leis, 255 F.3d 325 (6th Cir.2001); State v. Evers, 175 N.J. 355, 815 A.2d 432 (2003). This is so notwithstanding the fact that the federal Electronic Communications Act of 1986 requires that a government entity seeking to procure subscriber information from an Internet service provider do so by warrant, court order, subpoena, or consent of the subscriber. 18 U.S.C.A. § 2703(c)(1).

But see State v. Reid, 194 N.J. 386, 945 A.2d 26 (2008), reaching a different conclusion as to subscriber information as a matter of *state* constitutional law.

[232]In Leventhal v. Knapek, 266 F.3d 64 (2d Cir.2001), in the course of a state DOT investigation into whether certain employees had nonstandard software on their office computers and thus might be spending their time at work on personal matters, DOT investigators entered plaintiff's office, turned on his computer (which had no power-on password) and printed out lists of file names, including some on bypassed password-protected menus, and opened a few files. The court held that *all* this activity was a search, considering that plaintiff "occupied a private office" and "did not share use of his computer with other employees." The court emphasized that this public employee's privacy expectation had not been "reduced by virtue of actual office practices and procedures, or by legitimate regulation," as (1) there was no "general practice of routinely conducting searches of office computers"; (2) plaintiff "had not been placed * * * on notice that he should have no expectation of privacy in the contents of his office computer," distinguishing United States v. Simons, 206 F.3d 392 (4th Cir.2000), text at note 238 infra; (3) existing policies "did not prohibit the mere storage of personal materials in his office computer"; and (4) the "infrequent and selective search for maintenance purposes or to retrieve a needed document" did not destroy the employees' expectation of privacy.

[233]Note, 67 B.U.L.Rev. 179, 204 (1987). This argument is ably developed in Bellia, Surveillance Law Through Cyberlaw's Lens, 72 Geo.Wash.L.Rev. 1375, 1402–12 (2004); and Mulligan, Reasonable Expectations in Electronic Communications: A Critical Perspective on the Electronic Communications Privacy Act, 72 Geo.Wash.L.Rev. 1557, 1576–96 (2004). "The fact that her system administrator has the ability to monitor a computer user's electronic communication should not constitute a disclosure of that communication to the administrator (thereby vitiating a reasonable expectation of privacy in that communication): that a telephone operator has the ability to monitor phone calls and may listen to parts of them for administrative purposes does not render unreasonable an expectation of privacy in those conversations." Note, 110 Harv.L.Rev. 1591, 1602 (1997).

imate expectation of privacy as to "the contents of electronic mail messages[234] or personal files."[235] This is so even when the system manager makes backup copies of such records,[236] and even when the users are all employees of the system operator.[237]

---

[234]For more on Fourth Amendment protection of e-mail, see text at notes 273–285 infra; Bellia, Surveillance Law Through Cyberlaw's Lens, 72 Geo.Wash.L.Rev. 1375, esp. 1385–88, 1396–1413 (2004); Henderson, Nothing New Under the Sun? A Technologically Rational Doctrine of Fourth Amendment Search, 56 Mercer L.Rev. 507, 521–28 (2005); Katopis, "Searching" Cyberspace: The Fourth Amendment and Electronic Mail, 14 Temp.Envtl.L. & Tech. 175 (1995); Mulligan, Reasonable Expectations in Electronic Communications: A Critical Perspective on the Electronic Communications Privacy Act, 72 Geo.Wash.L.Rev. 1557, esp. 1576–82 (2004); Pikowsky, The Need for Revisions to the Law of Wiretapping and Interception of E-Mail, 10 Mich.Telecomm. & Tech.L.Rev. 1 (2003); Ray, The Warrantless Interception of E-Mail: Fourth Amendment Search or Free Rein for the Police?, 36 Rutgers Computer & Tech.L.J. 178 (2010); Sundstrom, You've Got Mail! (And the Government Knows It): Applying the Fourth Amendment to Workplace E-Mail Monitoring, 73 N.Y.U.L.Rev. 2064 (1998); Comments, 14 Alb.L.J.Sci. & Tech. 245 (2003); 4 J.Bus. & Tech.L. 411 (2009); 22 J.Marshall J.Computer & Info.L. 493 (2004); Notes, 110 Harv.L.Rev. 1591 (1997); 43 Val.U.L.Rev. 671 (2009).

Statutory limits on the surveillance of electronic mail were imposed by the Electronic Communications Act of 1986, Pub.L. 99-508, 100 Stat. 1859. For a summary of those limits, see Bellia, supra; Mulligan, supra; Winick, Searches and Seizures of Computers and Computer Data, 8 Harv.J.L. & Tech. 75, 90–98 (1994); Notes, 78 Fordham L.Rev. 349 (2009); 60 U.M.K. C.L.Rev. 139, 149–52 (1991). However, the Title III exclusionary rule was not extended correspondingly to apply to violations of law relating to electronic communications. 18 U.S.C.A.

§ 2518(10)(c). One court has observed: "While it is clear to this court that Congress intended to create a statutory expectation of privacy in e-mail files, it is less clear that an analogous expectation of privacy derives from the Constitution." United States v. Bach, 310 F.3d 1063 (8th Cir.2002).

As for resort to something comparable to a mail cover regarding e-mail, see § 2.7(a).

[235]Note, 81 Va.L.Rev. 1181, 1201 (1995). See, e.g., United States v. Slanina, 283 F.3d 670 (5th Cir.2002) (re search of files in defendant's office computer at fire station, court concludes defendant "did not forfeit his expectation of privacy in the files by providing the BIOS password to Smith, as he gave Smith the password for the limited purpose of installing the network, not perusing his files"; as for claim "that the city's need to develop network systems and upgrade equipment required complete computer access," court responds that "even though network administrators had some access to his computer, there is no evidence that such access was routine").

[236]"In making a backup copy, the system manager copies all data on the system to a different set of media, over which he has complete and exclusive control. The purpose of making a backup copy, however, is limited to protecting the data in case of a computer failure. The system manager need not know the contents of the copied data files, and the user's knowledge that the system manager will create backup copies does not mean that the user expects the system manager to examine the contents of that data." Note, 81 Va.L.Rev. 1181, 1203 (1995).

[237]"Users also should be found to have reasonable expectations of privacy on group systems, such as those owned by employers. When data is stored on an employer's computer,

The situation as to multiple users of a single computer system may be different because of previously announced policies regarding such use, as is illustrated by *United States v. Simons*.[238] The defendant was employed by a division of the CIA, and in that connection was provided with a private office and a computer with Internet access. Thereafter, the division instituted a policy to the effect that employees could use the Internet for official government business only, and it was explained that the division would conduct electronic audits to ensure compliance, which would include a determination of Web sites visited and of inbound and outbound file transfers. During an audit in which the keyword "sex" was entered into the firewall database, a large number of Internet "hits" originating from defendant's computer were found. From another workstation, it was determined that defendant had downloaded over 1,000 picture files from the Internet, so the files on defendant's hard drive were copied, again from another workstation. When some of the images were determined to be child pornography, criminal charges were filed against defendant. The court concluded that while government employees may have a legitimate expectation of privacy in their offices, "office practices, procedures, or regulations may reduce legitimate privacy expectation," which was the case here given the division's Internet policy. Specifically, the court held "that the remote searches of Simons' computer did not violate his Fourth Amendment rights because, in light of the Internet policy, Simons lacked a legitimate expectation of privacy in the files downloaded from the Internet."[239] *Simons* has been distinguished, and an opposite result reached, where no such policy had been

---

there are situations where the employer will need to have access to the contents of user files. Unlike the case involving disclosure, however, the employer has no general need to examine every private user file. This situation is no different from an employer's need to access an employee's private office, desk or filing cabinet. The employee has a reasonable expectation of privacy in those areas, and should also have a reasonable expectation of privacy in her 'data area.' " Note, 81 Va.L.Rev. 1181, 1202 (1995).

[238]United States v. Simons, 206 F.3d 392 (4th Cir.2000).

[239]There were later physical entries into defendant's office to seize his hard drive, which the court noted "presented a distinct question." That branch of the case is considered in § 10.3(d).

In accord with *Simons*: United States v. Thorn, 375 F.3d 679 (8th Cir.2004) (where defendant employed in government office with established policy providing "that employees have no personal right of privacy with respect to their use of the agency's computers" and "expressly provides * * * the right to access all of the agency's computers in order to audit their use," defendant without legitimate expectation of privacy as to contents of his office computer, and thus it no search for computer technician to make reasonable examination of contents of hard drive); United States v. Angevine, 281 F.3d 1130 (10th Cir.2002) (university professor had no justified expectation of privacy as to erased files on his office computer, obtained by use of special technology to retrieve data remaining latent in the computer's memory; because university "policy explicitly cautions users that information flowing through the University

Persons and Effects § 2.6(f)

disseminated.[240]

This leaves the third unique characteristic of many computerized records: telephonic access, as with the computer bulletin board system "in which a single computer acts as a repository for information exchanged among a number of different users."[241] When a bulletin board system is truly open to the public, then surely there is no expectation of privacy as to information disseminated in that fashion.[242] But many of these systems "restrict

---

network is not confidential either in transit or in storage on a University computer," "University computer users should have been aware network administrators and others were free to view data downloaded from the Internet"; "the University computer policy warned system administrators kept file logs recording when and by whom files were deleted," and "given his transmission of the pornographic data through a monitored University network, deleting the files alone was not sufficient to establish a reasonable expectation of privacy"); State v. Robinson, 293 Kan. 1002, 270 P.3d 1183 (2012) (where Reisig allowed defendant, a nonemployee, to use a networked computer at Reisig's place of business, and defendant knew his Internet activity was monitored by a network filter and that Reisig could monitor that activity, and defendant's Internet search activity was not password protected, defendant lacked a reasonable expectation of privacy re his Internet searches on that computer).

[240]United States v. Heckenkamp, 482 F.3d 1142 (9th Cir.2007) (defendant's "objectively reasonable expectation of privacy in his computer" was *not* "eliminated when he attached it to the university network," as "the mere act of accessing a network does not itself extinguish privacy expectation" where 'there was no announced monitoring policy on the network"); United States v. Slanina, 283 F.3d 670 (5th Cir.2002) (city employee had reasonable expectation of privacy as to files on city-owned computer in his office, as "city did not disseminate any policy that prevented the storage of personal information on city computers and also did not inform its employees that com-

puter usage and internet access would be monitored").

[241]Note, 67 B.U.L.Rev. 179, 195 (1987).

[242]"Because police have the right to 'go' on the Internet anywhere that members of the public may go, an open list-serve, newsgroup, chat room, telnet-able file, or Web page with no restrictions on its use is in plain view and cannot be considered private for Fourth Amendment purposes." Note, 110 Harv.L.Rev. 1591, 1603 (1997).

See, e.g., United States v. Borowy, 595 F.3d 1045 (9th Cir.2010) (despite defendant's "ineffectual effort to prevent LimeWire from showing his files," his "files were still entirely exposed to public view," in that "anyone with access to LimeWire could download and view his files," and thus case not distinguishable from *Ganoe*, infra); United States v. Stults, 575 F.3d 834 (8th Cir.2009) ("Stults had no reasonable expectation of privacy in files that the FBI retrieved from his personal computer where Stults admittedly installed and used LimeWire to make his files accessible to others for file sharing"); United States v. Ganoe, 538 F.3d 1117 (9th Cir.2008) (where defendant "installed and used file-sharing software on his computer" and "knew or should have known that the folder into which he downloaded files was accessible to others on the peer-to-peer network," that is, "anyone else with the same freely available program," he "lacked an objectively reasonable expectation of privacy in those files," as he thereby "opened up his download folder to the world," and argument that defendant "lacked the technical savvy or good sense to configure Lime-Wire to prevent access to his pornography files is like saying that

access through the use of passwords or user identification," and when this has occurred there is much to be said for the position that "the system's owner has manifested an expectation of privacy that should not be considered unreasonable merely because telephone access is available."[243] There is no reason why the teaching of *Katz*, that individuals may hold reasonable expectations of privacy in communications, should be limited to instances in which there is an effort to communicate with but a single person.

The technology for limiting telephone access to computer files is not foolproof, and thus "hackers" sometimes manage to penetrate through the safeguards and reach supposedly private information. However, that risk alone is hardly sufficient to deprive these records of a justified expectation of privacy under *Katz*. "Reliance on protections such an individual computer accounts, password protection, and perhaps encryption of data[244] should be no less reasonable than reliance upon locks, bolts, and

---

he did not know enough to close his drapes").

Ganoe does not apply where the police conduct did not involve "use of peer-to-peer software to remotely access" defendant's shared files, but rather add a situation where an officer "manually accessed and searched [defendant's] computer," as he "has a reasonable expectation of privacy in his computer and its contents when it is not being accessed through the peer-to-peer network." State v. Bailey, 989 A.2d 716 (Me.2010).

[243]Note, 67 B.U.L.Rev. 179, 208 (1987). "The password functions like a closed container or a seal on a letter; it hides from view the contents of the message until the password is given. By placing information within 'a closed, opaque container,' an individual manifests an objectively reasonable expectation of privacy in that information. If the password can be bypassed, the communication can be observed without providing the password, or the illegal nature of the communication is obvious from the outward aspect of the communication, then the password will not establish a reasonable expectation of privacy." Note, 110 Harv.L.Rev. 1591, 1603–04 (1997). "While a chat room or electronic bulletin board user might intend to broadcast his or her messages to the world at large, this is increasingly not true of social networking users. Privacy settings remain an advanced feature of social networking websites." Comment, 93 Marq.L.Rev. 1495, 1526 (2010).

It has also been suggested that the Privacy Protection Act of 1980, affording special protection to "any work product materials possessed by a person reasonably believed to have a purpose to disseminate to the public a newspaper, book, broadcast or other similar form of public communication," 42 U.S.C.A. § 2000aa(a), covers bulletin board systems. See Winick, Searches and Seizures of Computers and Computer Data, 8 Harv.J.L. & Tech. 75, 99–101 (1994). It is important to note, however, that violation of those statutory limitations is not a basis for evidence suppression. 42 U.S.C.A. § 2000aa-6(e). On the "suspect exception" to the Act, see, e.g., Sennett v. United States, 667 F.3d 531 (6th Cir.2012).

[244]Compare Note, 110 Harv.L.Rev. 1591, 1604 (1997), arguing that "encrypting one's communication is insufficient to establish a reasonable expectation of privacy. The encryption may obscure the meaning of a message but the encrypted message itself remains in plain view; thus, an officer's observation of that encrypted message is not a search and does not implicate the Fourth Amendment. Furthermore,

burglar alarms, even though each form of protection is penetrable."[245] "For this reason, whether to treat a particular social media platform as an extension of the home or office should depend primarily on whether the platform generally is set up for the kinds of social interactions typical of a home * * * and whether the individual 'residing' at the site has granted access to the public at large or maintained control over who can enter."[246]

Although the above analysis supports the conclusion that a justified expectation of privacy attaches to most computer data, there remains to be considered a few special techniques for acquiring this information that present other problems regarding the scope of the Fourth Amendment's coverage. One such technique is use of what is known as a "CRT microspy" device.[247]

> Due to the electromagnetic nature of computer equipment it is possible to monitor activity from a location as remote as five hundred feet with specialized electronic surveillance equipment. Computers, monitors, keyboards, and printers leak electronic signals in all directions in the form of radio frequency energy. A receiver specifically designed for the task can pick up these radio waves and display the captured images on a monitor screen. * * *

> Computers can be shielded from remote surveillance, but such protection is quite expense [and thus] it seems unlikely that ordinary computer users would take this precaution * * *.[248]

As one commentator has noted, an argument can be made that the remote scanning of private computer activity using a CRT microspy device is no search and thus is not subject to the restraints of the Fourth Amendment:

---

the encoded message, once observed, may be decoded without implicating the Fourth Amendment, just as law enforcement agents may 'decode' communications that they overhear in other languages."

　　Similarly, Kerr, The Fourth Amendment in Cyberspace: Can Encryption Create a "Reasonable Expectation of Privacy"?, 33 Conn.L. Rev. 503, 532 (2001), concludes: "Although the Internet is a recent development with great promise for revolutionary change, the Fourth Amendment questions raised by encrypting Internet communications are decades (if not centuries) old. Applying the rights-based conception of the Fourth Amendment to encrypted communications reveals that decrypting an Internet communication cannot itself violate a 'reasonable expectation of privacy' and therefore cannot violate the Fourth Amendment. As a result, proposals that would permit the gov-

ernment to access encryption keys and have the power to decrypt communications do not suffer the constitutional defects that their opponents have claimed."

　　For more on encryption, see § 2.2(e).

[245]Note, 81 Va.L.Rev. 1181, 1200 (1995). "Individuals retain reasonable expectations of privacy in their homes even though roughly one of every fifteen households is burglarized each year." Note, 67 B.U.L.Rev. 179, 205–06 (1987).

[246]Strandburg, Home, Home on the Web and Other Fourth Amendment Implications of Technosocial Change, 70 Md.L.Rev. 614, 663 (2011).

[247]CRT is short for "cathode ray tube," in this instance a computer monitor.

[248]Note, 60 U.M.K.C.L.Rev. 139, 143 (1991).

Courts have considered two factors important in denying Fourth Amendment protections to the users of cordless telephones. The first is that the telephones broadcast radio signals from the receiver in all directions, thus making conversations open to the public. One court imaginatively described the emanations from cordless telephones as "analogous to a stone dropped into a pool of water, which results in the transmission of equal waves of energy in all directions, which will lap against any obstacle in the path of the emanating and ever enlarging concentric circles until the wave energy transmitted is totally diminished." The second fact of significance is that the FCC has ordered that cordless telephone base units bear the legend "privacy of communications may not be ensured when using this phone," so the court reasoned no one using the phone can reasonably expect privacy.

Both of these facts are equally true of computers. Computers and their peripherals broadcast radio signals in all directions, just like waves emanating from a stone dropped in water. Also, computer monitors bear an FCC warning alerting users to the fact that they are unintentional radiators. The following statement can be found on the back of most computer monitors: "Certified to comply with the limits for a Class B computing device pursuant to subpart J of Part 15 of FCC Rules." This notice informs users that a computer monitor is a Class B device which means it "generates, uses, and can radiate radio frequency energy." If the rationale applied to cordless phones is used for monitors, then computer users should have no reasonable expectation of privacy and remote scans could be conducted without a warrant.[249]

But, while it is true that interception of the radio portion of conversations over a cordless phone has been deemed to be no search,[250] it is *not* correct to say that this rule supports a like conclusion as to use of a CRT microspy. To take the most obvious distinction first, it is apparent that the rather cryptic message on the back of the computer monitor is quite unlike the warning on the cordless telephone base units, for it provides not the slightest clue to the average computer owner or user that use of the monitor might in any way disseminate the images on the screen to others in the area. Even more important, however, is the fact that the cordless phone cases are *not* grounded in the notion that one's privacy expectations can be defeated by the mere fact that some kind of device has been invented (and might be in use by law enforcement) which can retrieve otherwise private information. Rather, the point of those cases is that there is no reasonable expectation of privacy vis-a-vis cordless phones because anyone who uses that device "broadcasts the conversation over radio waves to all within range who wish to overhear."[251] The critical word "all" is appropriate in that context because the

---

[249]Note, 60 U.M.K.C.L.Rev. 139, 163–64 (1991).

[250]See cases collected in § 2.2(f)

note 268.

[251]In re Askin, 47 F.3d 100 (4th Cir.1995).

original cordless phones[252] were "subject to ready interception by standard radio scanners, radio receivers, or other cordless telephones."[253]

In other words, the reason such cordless phones are not private is because of "the ease with which they could be monitored"[254] by neighbors and passersby using devices common employed for lawful nonsurveillance purposes. But it can hardly be contended that a computer user likewise "broadcasts * * * to all within range" the images on his monitor merely because research has now developed "an effective, low-cost 'CRT microspy' device"[255] with that capability. Indeed, to conclude that use of that device is no search merely because of its capacity to retrieve in understandable form the electronic signals emanating from the computer user's premises would, in effect, constitute a rejection of *Katz v. United States,*[256] where meaningful retrieval of another sort of emanation was deemed a search.[257]

The other special technique for acquiring otherwise—private computer data to be considered here is unique because it discovers only "digital contraband" (that is, "any computer file that, outside of very specific authorized exceptions, cannot be legally possessed," such as "digital videos of child pornography" or "a 'cracked' copy of a commercial program—one that has been illegally modified to remove licensing protection").[258] Apparently a computer program can be designed to search through any hard drive connected to the Internet for a file matching one already in possession of the person making such a search. Indeed, it even may be possible to run such a search program on a large number

---

[252] The situation has changed considerably, so that conversations on modern cordless phones are not readily intercepted. These phones "monitor all available frequencies and automatically select one that is unused," "broadcast on radio frequencies not utilized by commercial radio," and "actually scramble the radio signal." United States v. Smith, 978 F.2d 171 (5th Cir. 1992). The court in *Smith*, after taking note of these changes, concluded that because of the wide variety of cordless phones in use there exists no "general rule that it either is or is not reasonable to expect privacy for cordless telephone conversations." That reasoning certainly squares with the argument here that the so-called cordless phone rule cannot be relied upon to conclude that use of a CRT microspy is no search. Regarding the point in *Smith,* see also Note, 56 Syrac.L.Rev. 459 (2006).

[253] State v. Smith, 149 Wis.2d 89, 438 N.W.2d 571 (1989).

[254] United States v. Smith, 978 F.2d 171 (5th Cir.1992).

[255] Note, 60 U.M.K.C.L.Rev. 139, 143 (1991).

[256] Katz v. United States, 389 U.S. 347, 88 S.Ct. 507, 19 L.Ed.2d 576 (1967).

[257] "It must be remembered that the bug at issue in *Katz* was fixed to the outside of a public phone booth. Reduced to its operational fundamentals, that bug did not monitor the interior of the phone booth at all; rather, it measured the molecular vibrations of the glass that encompassed that interior." United States v. Cusumano, 67 F.3d 1497 (10th Cir.1995), vacated on rehearing en banc, 83 F.3d 1247 (10th Cir.1996), on other grounds.

[258] Note, 105 Yale L.J. 1093, 1097 (1996).

of networked hard drives simultaneously. And thus a law enforcement officer who had come into possession of one specific piece of digital contraband might then run a Net-wide search for that very contraband. In doing so, he might "identify dozens, hundreds, or even thousands of individuals who did have a copy on their computer and for whom he would then have probable cause to request a search warrant."[259] Such a search, to be sure,

> presents a novel set of characteristics: As part of a dragnet search, individuals' hard drives are searched without their permission and without any particularized cause to believe them guilty, and the search scans through a vast amount of very personal information located within people's offices and homes. At the same time, however, the search has a minimal impact on property, produces no false positives, need not be noticeable, and reveals nothing to officials beyond the identity of some individuals who possess this particular piece of digital contraband.[260]

That description naturally brings to mind two Supreme Court decisions, *United States v. Place*[261] and *United States v. Jacobsen*.[262] In *Place*, which concerned a dog sniffing of a suspect's luggage for narcotics, the Court reasoned that since such a sniff "does not require opening the luggage [and] does not expose noncontraband items that would otherwise remain hidden from public view," it was an investigative procedure "that is so limited both in the manner in which the information is obtained and in the content of the information revealed by the procedure" that it did not constitute a Fourth Amendment search. In *Jacobsen*, the Court reiterated that the decisive fact in *Place* was "that the government conduct could reveal nothing about noncontraband items," and then concluded that because the same was true in the instant case there again had been no search. The activity at issue in *Jacobsen* was the testing of a small quantity of white powder, accidentally found by Federal Express employees in a shipment, which determined that the substance was cocaine. As the Court put it, the testing "could, at most, have only a de minimis impact on any protected property interest," and "compromise[d] no legitimate privacy interest" because it revealed only contraband "and no other arguably 'private' fact." The same can be said of the discovery of computer contraband in the manner described above, and thus it might well be concluded that "the officers who ran the Net-wide program would not be conducting a Fourth Amendment search."[263]

Whether this is either a desirable result or one which the Supreme Court would reach on the hypothetical facts set out

---

[259]Note, 105 Yale L.J. 1093, 1099 (1996).

[260]Note, 105 Yale L.J. 1093, 1100 (1996).

[261]United States v. Place, 462 U.S. 696, 103 S.Ct. 2637, 77 L.Ed.2d 110

(1983), discussed in § 2.2(g).

[262]United States v. Jacobsen, 466 U.S. 109, 104 S.Ct. 1652, 80 L.Ed.2d 85 (1984), discussed in § 1.8(b).

[263]Note, 105 Yale L.J. 1093, 1108 (1996).

above is difficult to say. There is a sense in which the discovery of digital contraband located within a person's computer system itself located in the privacy of a person's home or office is qualitatively different from the seemingly less intrusive actions in *Place* and *Jacobsen*. In *Place*, after all, the dog was merely used on luggage already in the lawful temporary custody of the police, while in *Jacobsen* the testing was of material the defendant had put in the hands of a shipper and which was already within the lawful plain-view scrutiny of a police officer.[264] And thus it might be contended that the discovery of the computer contraband *is* a search, for the same reason that *United States v. Thomas*[265] held that using a canine sniff to discover narcotics within a particular apartment was a search: there was an intrusion upon a person's "heightened expectation of privacy inside his dwelling." But the *Thomas* reasoning has itself been challenged on the ground that any assertion of heightened expectations runs contrary to the teaching of *Place* and *Jacobsen* that a possessor of contraband has no legitimate expectation that its presence will not be revealed.[266]

The ultimate question here thus seems to be whether there is any limitation or qualification to the notion—as it was originally put by Professor Loewy—that "if a device could be invented that accurately detected [contraband] and did not disrupt the normal [activities] of people, there could be no fourth amendment objection to its use.,"[267] There is no obvious or apparent answer to this question, and thus the best that can be done here is to identify what other consideration might most logically support the speculation that "the Court may not extend [the *Place-Jacobsen*] approach to its logical end."[268] Simply put, it is the need for autonomy and refuge, explained by one thoughtful commentator in these terms:

> It is true that the Net-wide search finds only "relevant" information, but it is society at large and not the individual who defines what is illegal and thus what is relevant. Outside of the limited number of enumerated substantive restrictions, virtually any socially disfavored act can be criminalized at the discretion of the

---

[264]*Place* and *Jacobsen* would be more analogous to the conduct at issue in United States v. Borowy, 595 F.3d 1045 (9th Cir.2010), where defendant's files were "entirely exposed to public view" in that "anyone with access to LimeWire could download and view them," and the officer searched through his files "using a software program that verifies the 'hash marks' of files and displays a red flag next to known images of child pornography." The court ruled that "the hash-mark analysis functioned simply as a sorting mechanism to prevent the govern-

ment from having to sift, one by one, through Borowy's already publically exposed files."

[265]United States v. Thomas, 757 F.2d 1359 (2d Cir.1985), discussed in § 2.2(g).

[266]United States v. Colyer, 878 F.2d 469 (D.C.Cir.1989).

[267]Loewy, the Fourth Amendment as a Device for Protecting the Innocent, 81 Mich.L.Rev. 1229, 1246 (1983).

[268]Note, 81 Va.L.Rev. 1181, 1205 (1995).

majority; the individual would then retain no control over whether or not information relevant to such an act would be revealed. In this light, one critical problem with the Net-wide search or any other form of an "evidence-detecting divining rod" is that it denies to the individual any space in which she can be sure of controlling information about herself. In short, no refuge remains in which the individual would not have to worry about the risk of exposure, for as control over the boundary between the area of security and the area of public life disappears, so too does the area of security itself.[269] The point is *not* that there is a zone of absolute privacy around the home and office (a proposition rejected by the Supreme Court in *Bowers v. Hardwick*),[270] but only that there should be "a space in which the government's enforcement power is handicapped,"[271] at least to the extent that ordinarily[272] even surveillance which can discover only contraband is not permissible when done at random and without individualized suspicion.

While all of the foregoing discussion has concerned records kept on a computer, it is now necessary to turn to the use of a computer to communicate with others, as by e-mail, and to ask whether there is a justified expectation of privacy in such communications. (Whether government interception of such communications is a search, mandating compliance with the usual Fourth Amendment safeguards, is a matter of some significance in light of the fact that the FBI has developed software, originally called Carnivore and now denominated DCS1000, that has the capability of making such interceptions.[273]) As a general matter, the answer should be yes. As one commentator rightly concluded:

---

[269]Note, 105 Yale L.J. 1093, 1111–12 (1996).

[270]Bowers v. Hardwick, 478 U.S. 186, 106 S.Ct. 2841, 92 L.Ed.2d 140 (1986). That rejection was not questioned when *Bowers* was itself overruled in Lawrence v. Texas, 539 U.S. 558, 123 S.Ct. 2472, 156 L.Ed.2d 508 (2003).

[271]Note, 105 Yale L.J. 1093, 1118 (1996).

[272]There may be exceptions. It has been argued that "while the Fourth Amendment ought to prevent routine uses of the Net-wide search for nonviolent criminals such as software pirates or possessors of child pornography, it would not have prevented a Net-wide search on the day the Unabomber delivered his manifesto to the New York Times and the Washington Post. On the extraordinary occasion when a search might yield reliable evidence tying its possessor directly to violent

crime, the interests protected by the Fourth Amendment clearly yield." Note, 105 Yale L.J. 1093, 1119 (1996).

[273]For further discussion of Carnivore/DCS1000, see Lewis, Carnivore—The FBI's Internet Surveillance System, 23 Whittier L.Rev. 317 (2001); McCarthy, Don't Fear Carnivore: It Won't Devour Individual Privacy, 66 Mo.L.Rev. 827 (2001); Comments, 9 Comm.Law.Conspectus 111 (2001); 89 N.C.L.Rev. 315 (2001); 52 S.C.L.Rev. 875 (2001); 19 Temp. Envt'l L. & Tech.J. 155 (2001); 32 Tex.Tech.L.Rev. 1053 (2001); 18 T.M.Cooley L.Rev. 183 (2001); Notes, 27 Brook.J.Int'l L. 245 (2001); 20 Cardozo Arts & Ent. L.J. 231 (2002); 34 Conn.L.Rev. 261 (2001); 35 Ind.L. Rev. 303 (2001); 21 Loy.L.A.Ent.L.Rev. 481 (2001); 8 Mich. Telecomm. & Tech.L.Rev. 219 (2001); 18 N.Y.U.L. Sch.J.Hum.Rts. 305 (2002); 76 Notre Dame L.Rev. 1215 (2001); 62 Ohio St.L.J. 1831 (2001); 7 Roger Williams

"Because e-mail offers security equal to or greater than U.S. and commercial mail, faxes, and land-line telephone conversations, an e-mail user's expectation of privacy should be equal to or greater than those forms of communications."[274] And thus the seminal case on this issue, *United States v. Maxwell*,[275] drew upon those parallels and then concluded without hesitation "that the transmitter of an e-mail message enjoys a reasonable expectation that police officials will not intercept the transmission without probable cause and a search warrant." And in *United States v. Warshak*,[276] the court held "that a subscriber enjoys a reasonable expectation of privacy in the contents of emails 'that are stored with, or sent or received through, a commercial ISP,'" meaning the "government may not compel a commercial ISP to turn over the contents of a subscriber's emails without first obtaining a warrant based on probable cause."[277] This justified privacy expectation exists notwithstanding the fact that e-mailing (just as with telephoning) is not risk free, and thus *Maxwell* goes on to declare: "The fact that an unauthorized 'hacker' might intercept an e-mail message does not diminish the legitimate expectation of privacy in any way."[278] So too, as the *Warshak* decision emphasizes, e-mail is distinguishable from the bank re-

---

U.L.Rev. 247 (2001); 28 Rutgers Computer & Tech.L.J. 155 (2002); 75 S.Cal.L.Rev. 231 (2001).

[274] Comment, 80 N.C.L.Rev. 315, 342 (2001). Consider also Kerr, Applying the Fourth Amendment to the Internet: A General Approach, 62 Stan.L.Rev. 1005, 1029–30 (2010), relying upon the postal letters and telephone precedents to conclude, as does the "sparse" case authority, that in applying "the Fourth Amendment to the Internet and computer communications networks in a technology-neutral way, courts should adopt the content/non-content distinction," so that only contents would receive Fourth Amendment protection. "In the case of e-mail, for example, the subject line, the body of the message, and any attachments count as the contents of the communication. They are the actual message to be sent. Everything else in the e-mail, including the to/from address and the size of the e-mail, counts as non-content information."

For other articles on Fourth Amendment protection of e-mail, see note 234 supra.

[275] United States v. Maxwell, 45 M.J. 406 (A.F.Ct.Crim.App.1996).

[276] United States v. Warshak, 631 F.3d 266 (6th Cir.2010), discussed in Recent Development, 12 N.C.J.L. & Tech. 345 (2011).

[277] Meaning, the court added, that to the extent that the Stored Communications Act, 18 U.S.C.A. §§ 2701 et seq., "purports to permit the government to obtain such emails warrantlessly, the SCA is unconstitutional."

Kerr, 62 Stan.L.Rev. 1005, 1039 (2010), concludes "that the Fourth Amendment ordinarily requires a warrant for the collection of the contents of Internet communications," but that "the Fourth Amendment should require a narrow exception permitting the warrantless copying of data pending a warrant," which "would mirror similar authority to temporarily detain a package pending a warrant to open it, and would allow for a warrant requirement for access to contents of communications," thus meaning that 18 U.S.C.A. § 2703(b), permitting "the government to compel access to stored files without a warrant," "is unconstitutional in many of its applications." For further discussion, see § 5.5, text at note 126.

[278] As for encrypted messages and

cords in *United States v. Miller*,[279] as the latter records are intended for use by the bank "in the ordinary course of business," while the ISP is only "an *intermediary*, not the intended recipient of the emails."

This is not to suggest, however, that this expectation of privacy in the communication exists in all circumstances or against all risks. And thus, just as a letter writer's "expectation of privacy ordinarily terminates upon delivery" of the letter,[280] *Maxwell* cautions that once e-mail "transmissions are received by another person, the transmitter no longer controls its destiny." This means, for example, that the person sending the e-mail has no valid Fourth Amendment complaint should the recipient turn the message over to the police[281] or forward it on to others,[282] or should the recipient turn out to be an undercover police officer.[283] Moreover, as *Maxwell* also warns, "the more open the method of transmission, such as the 'chat room,' the less privacy one can reasonably expect."[284] Finally, the relationship between the person sending the e-mail and the business or governmental entity operating the system used to send it may sometimes be such that there is not a strong privacy expectation vis-a-vis that entity.[285]

By virtue of a "shift in Internet usage from consumption to

---

the steps possible by law enforcement to decrypt them, see § 2.2(f).

[279] United States v. Miller, 425 U.S. 435, 96 S.Ct. 1619, 48 L.Ed.2d 71 (1976).

[280] United States v. King, 55 F.3d 1193 (6th Cir.1995).

[281] As in Commonwealth v. Proetto, 2001 Pa.Super. 95, 771 A.2d 823 (2001).

[282] United States v. Maxwell, 45 M.J. 406 (A.F.Ct.Crim.App.1996), states: "One always bears the risk that a recipient of an e-mail message will redistribute the e-mail."

[283] United States v. Charbonneau, 979 F.Supp. 1177 (S.D.Ohio 1997); State v. Evers, 175 N.J. 355, 815 A.2d 432 (2003) (defendant "transmitted the forbidden e-mail at peril that one of the recipients would disclose his wrongdoing").

[284] "Appellant could not have a reasonable expectation of privacy in his chat-room communications. When appellant engaged in chat-room conversations, he did not know to whom he was speaking. Oftentimes individuals engaging in chat-room conversations pretend to be someone other than who

they are. Appellant could not have a reasonable expectation of privacy in engaging in chat-room conversations." Commonwealth v. Proetto, 2001 Pa.Super. 95, 771 A.2d 823 (2001).

As noted in Kerr, 62 Stan.L. Rev. 1005, 1030–31 (2010): "Because many people use the Internet to communicate with large groups, the presumption [of Fourth Amendment protection] will be overcome in many cases online. For example, if an Internet user posts information on a public web page that is available to the public, the information will be unprotected. If a person shares files with others on a network, the sharing ordinarily will waive the individual's reasonable expectation of privacy in the shared data. Similarly, if a person posts a message to a large group, but a member of that group is a confidential informant, the informant can read the message and relay it to the police without violating the Fourth Amendment." See also Comment, 93 Marq.L. Rev. 1495 (2010).

[285] In United States v. Monroe, 52 M.J. 326 (A.F.Ct.Crim.App.2000), the court distinguished *Maxwell* because there the e-mail service was provided by AOL, which "stored e-mail mes-

participation,"[286] there is now much data other than e-mails that is stored at locations other than the hard drive of a computer. By virtue of what is termed "cloud computing," Internet "users now interact with applications and store data remotely rather than on their own computers. A central aspect of this shift is the ability to 'outsource storage' to service providers like Google rather than saving things such as e-mails, photos, calendars, or other documents on a personal hard drive."[287] Because such "remotely stored data are not intended for public access, they are generally protected by unlimited links, password protection, or encryption."[288] Consistent with the previous discussion, one thoughtful commentator has reached these conclusions regarding the Fourth Amendment protection of data so stored: (1) that "users expect their information to be treated the same on this virtual cloud as it would be if it were stored on their own computer";[289] (2) that such an expectation of privacy is reasonable provided "reasonable concealment efforts"[290] are undertaken via such "virtual concealment efforts" as "encryption, password protection, and the practical obscurity of unlisted links";[291] and (3) that because the service provider "is merely providing a platform for using and storing the content via the cloud," then despite any "minimal right the service provider reserves to access the contents of those files or containers, the service provider is not a party to the contents any more than a landlord is a party what goes on behind his tenants' closed doors due to his limited right of entry."[292]

To be contrasted from the instances of *search* of computer data,

---

sages for retrieval on AOL's centralized and privately-owned computers rather than on the Internet itself, and [had] contractually agreed not to read or disclose subscribers' e-mail to anyone other than authorized users," while in the instant case "the system was owned by the Government and instead of a contractual agreement not to read or disclose the messages, there was a specific notice that 'users logging on to this system consent to monitoring by the Hostadm,'" meaning defendant "had no reasonable expectation of privacy in his e-mail messages or e-mail box at least from the personnel charged with maintaining the EMH system." Consider also United States v. Warshak, 631 F.3d 266 (6th Cir.2010) ("we are unwilling to hold that a subscriber agreement will *never* be broad enough to snuff out a reasonable expectation of privacy," as "if the ISP expresses an intention to 'audit, inspect and monitor' its

subscribers' emails, that might be enough to render an expectation of privacy unreasonable").

[286]Note, 93 Minn.L.Rev. 2205 (2009).

[287]Note, 93 Minn.L.Rev. 2205, 2215 (2009).

[288]Note, 93 Minn.L.Rev. 2205, 2217 (2009).

[289]Note, 93 Minn.L.Rev. 2205, 2205–06 (2009).

[290]Note, 93 Minn.L.Rev. 2205, 2233 (2009).

[291]Note, 93 Minn.L.Rev. 2205, 2236 (2009).

[292]Note, 93 Minn.L.Rev. 2205, 2237 (2009). See also Bagley, Don't be Evil: The Fourth Amendment in the Age of Google, National Security, and Digital Papers and Effects, 21 Alb.L.J.Sci. & Tech. 153, 190 (201) ("Citizens should enjoy a reasonable expectation of privacy from unwanted government in-

the subject of the preceding discussion, is the case in which investigators instead make a copy of that data for possible examination on some future occasion. This scenario is by no means uncommon.

> Computer search and seizure inverts the usual pattern of criminal investigations. When searching for traditional physical evidence, the police first search for property and then seize it. Computer technologies often require investigators to obtain a copy first and then search it later. Nearly every case begins with copying data that will later be searched, and government investigators often will prefer to copy more rather than less if the Fourth Amendment allows it.[293]

Is the copying a "seizure" within the meaning of the Fourth Amendment, so that it is subject to the Amendment's limitations as to when a seizure may be made, or is it no seizure, in which case the Fourth Amendment will come into play only if and when on some subsequent occasion (perhaps now with more compelling grounds) the authorities conduct a search of the copied data?

This is currently a matter of some uncertainty. One the one hand, the leading case on the question of whether copying is a search, *Arizona v. Hicks*,[294] holding that police conduct in copying down the serial number on a stereo "did not constitute a seizure," suggests the answer to the above question is: no seizure. *Hicks* has been relied upon by lower courts in a variety of circumstances,[295] including the copying of computer files.[296] On the other

---

trusion in their password-protected digital documents and effect repositories in the cloud"); Kerr, Applying the Fourth Amendment to the Internet: A General Approach, 62 Stan.L.Rev. 1005, 1029 (2010) ("The Fourth Amendment should generally protect the contents of communications stored in 'the cloud' of the Internet, including remotely stored files maintained on a server that is hosted for individual users"); Strandburg, Home, Home on the Web and Other Fourth Amendment Implications of Technosocial Change, 70 Md.L.Rev. 614, 661 (2011) ("Storage in the cloud is a fairly straightforward extension of Fourth Amendment protection if one acknowledges its social equivalence to storage at home or in the office * * *. Cloud computing * * * may raise somewhat more difficult issues[, but] at the very least * * * a mere relocation of calculations from an account book to a private computer and then to the cloud [should] not undermine Fourth Amendment

protections").

For other discussions of this subject, see Comment, 12 U.Pa.J. Const.L. 223 (2009); Notes, 25 Berkeley Tech.L.J. 621 (2010); 89 Or.L.Rev. 351 (2010). A broad coalition of technology companies and advocacy groups known as the Digital Due Process coalition is seeking federal legislation "to ensure that as millions of people move private documents from their filing cabinets and personal computers to the Web, those documents remain protected from easy access by law enforcement and other government authorities." Helft, A Wide Call to Improve Web Privacy, N.Y.Times, Mar. 31, 2010, p. B1.

[293]Kerr, Fourth Amendment Seizures of Computer Data, 119 Yale L.J. 700, 702 (2010).

[294]Arizona v. Hicks, 480 U.S. 321, 107 S.Ct. 1149, 94 L.Ed.2d 347 (1987).

[295]E.g., Bills v. Aseltine, 958 F.2d 697 (6th Cir.1992) (thus recording by

hand, the Supreme Court in *Berger v. New York*[297] and *Katz v. United States*,[298] dealing with wiretapping and eavesdropping, respectively, characterized the conduct at issue in those cases as a "search and seizure," which certainly "suggests that recording the surveillance was understood as a seizure."[299] That approach is reflected by lower court characterization of copied computer files as "seized data."[300]

One thoughtful commentator has suggested a solution to this "seizure puzzle," arguing that

> electronic copying by the government ordinarily constitutes a Fourth Amendment seizure. The reason is that the Fourth Amendment power to seize is the power to freeze. That is, the seizure power is the power to hold the crime scene and control evidence. Generating an electronic copy of data freezes that data for future use just like taking physical property freezes it: it adds to the amount of evidence under the government's control. From the standpoint of regulating the government's power to collect and use evidence, generating an electronic copy is not substantially different from controlling access to a house or making an arrest. Each of these seizures ensures that the government has control over the person, place, or thing that it suspects has evidentiary value. As a result, copying Fourth Amendment protected data should ordinarily be considered a Fourth Amendment seizure.[301]

Under this approach, the seizure rule has "two key limitations":[302] (1) Only copying of data that has not been exposed to human observation by a government agent amounts to a seizure, because only that copying involves freezing the scene and adding to the information in the government's possession."[303] (2) "A seizure of moving or movable property occurs only when government action

---

photography does not amount to a seizure); Schirber v. State, 142 P.3d 1169 (Wyo.206) (copying down serial number of radios no search).

[296] In re U.S., 665 F.Supp.2d 1210 (D.Or.2009); United States v. Gorshkov, 2001 WL 1024026 ((W.D.Wash. 2001).

[297] Berger v. New York, 388 U.S. 41, 87 S.Ct. 1873, 18 L.Ed.2d 1040 (1967).

[298] Katz v. United States, 389 U.S. 347, 88 S.Ct. 507, 19 L.Ed.2d 576 (1967).

[299] Kerr, 119 Yale L.J. 700, 708 (2010).

[300] United States v. Comprehensive Drug Testing, Inc., 621 F.3d 1162 (9th Cir.2010).

[301] Kerr, 119 Yale L.J. 700, 709 (2010).

[302] Kerr, 119 Yale L.J. 700, 704 (2010).

[303] Kerr, 119 Yale L.J. 700, 714–15 (2010). This serves to distinguish the conduct in *Hicks*, which "merely preserves the human observation in a fixed form." Id. at 714.

In any event, a copying that *is* deemed a seizure might be deemed permissible without a warrant in certain exigent circumstances. As concluded in Kerr, Applying the Fourth Amendment to the Internet: A General Approach, 62 Stan.L.Rev. 1005, 1041–42 (2010): "At most, the exigency should permit the government either to make a copy of the data and store it until a warrant is obtained or else to order a third party like an ISP to do so and hold the data pending a warrant. The Supreme Court has interpreted the Fourth Amendment to allow an analogous power to temporarily detain a package sent through the mail while a warrant is obtained al-

alters the path or timing of its intended possession or transmission. Copying data as part of its usual course of transmission or storage does not seize anything, because its intended path or timing has not been interrupted."[304] (Others have attempted to distinguish *Hicks* in a somewhat different fashion, which would produce a "seizure" category with somewhat different dimensions.)[305]

§ 2.7 Surveillance of relationships and movements

Research References

West's Key Number Digest
Criminal Law ☞394.3; Postal Service ☞47; Records ☞31; Searches and Seizures ☞13.1, 26, 76, 78; Telecommunications ☞494.1, 521, 540, 541

lowing its opening. So long as the police move quickly to obtain a warrant, the temporary seizure of the package is constitutionally reasonable without a warrant. The same rule should apply to Internet communications. So long as investigators move quickly to obtain a warrant, they should be allowed to run off a copy of the data without a warrant but then not actually observe the data until a warrant is obtained."

[304]Kerr, 119 Yale L.J. 700, 721 (2010).

[305]See Note, 78 Geo.Wash.L.Rev. 476, 496 (2010) (proposing "the Supreme Court should broaden its definition of possessory interest beyond mere physical possession to include an individual's right to exclude the government from her written or digital information," so that "any duplication process, such as photography or photocopying, that yields a perfect copy of a document in the owner's possession would be a seizure," as "creating the copy would strip the owner of her ability to control the use and disposition of that information"; disagreeing with Kerr re exclusion when information before it was copied, as "[e]ven if that viewing destroys her privacy interest, that should be irrelevant to the seizure analysis"); Note, 81 Va.L.Rev. 1181, 1186 (1995) ("One could reconcile *Katz* and *Hicks* by arguing the possessory interest in a document or conversation consists of controlling the dissemination and use of the information contained therein, whereas the possessory interest in a tangible item, such as a stereo, lies almost entirely in its use. Copying the information from a document or conversation interferes with control and thus interferes with the possessory interest. Photographing a scene or copying a serial number, on the other hand, does not meaningfully interfere with possession. Because the value of a computer file lies in the information therein, it is much more analogous to a written document or oral conversation. Although *Hicks* could logically extend to all intangible information, copying a computer file should constitute a seizure under the Fourth Amendment").

Introduction

Most of the investigative techniques heretofore discussed in this Chapter, such as peering in a window, examining the exterior of a vehicle, taking a handwriting sample, or picking up an abandoned object, are ordinarily utilized to detect an incriminating object or action on a particular occasion. That is, even though some of them (e.g., window peeking) might be employed against a suspect on a continuing basis, typically this is not the case, and the claim of the defendant usually is that the investigative technique in question unjustly intruded into his private affairs at a particular point in time. By contrast, there are certain investigative techniques which, either because they are ongoing or because of the kind of information they uncover, might be deemed objectionable primarily because they reveal private affairs over a broader span of time. The use of mail covers or pen registers, for example, often results in the discovery of one's continuing associations with other persons. Similarly, the use of an electronic tracking device allows the authorities to keep track of a person's movements over a significant period of time. It is the cumulative effect of these techniques which provides the strongest basis for the claim that they constitute an intrusion into a justified expectation of privacy under *Katz v. United States*.[1] That is, it is the breadth of the intrusion rather than its depth at any particular instant in time which is most threatening to privacy. The concern herein is with these techniques.

§ 2.7(a) Mail covers

One investigative technique employed to determine the relationships and associations of a person[2] and to obtain leads into other details of his life[3] is the mail cover.

Mail covers have been a technique of investigation widely used by various governmental agencies.[4] In a mail cover, information appearing on the outside of envelopes intended for a specified ad-

---

[Section 2.7]

[1] Katz v. United States, 389 U.S. 347, 88 S.Ct. 507, 19 L.Ed.2d 576 (1967).

[Section 2.7(a)]

[2] See, e.g., United States v. Schwartz, 283 F.2d 107 (3d Cir.1960) (used to obtain names of persons who might be victims of individual suspected of mail fraud).

[3] See, e.g., United States v. Costello, 255 F.2d 876 (2d Cir.1958) (used to track down evidence of defendant's expenditures, which was important evidence in presentation of a net worth tax evasion case).

[4] The practice was investigated by the Senate Subcommittee on Administrative Practice and Procedure in 1965. Note, 4 Colum.J.L. & Soc.Probs. 165, 170–71 (1968)

dressee is recorded by postal employees before the letters are delivered. This information, which includes the postmark and the return address, is given by the post office to the agency which requested that the cover be imposed. Usually mail covers are placed on the mail of persons under suspicion of having committed crimes or those associated with them. Information obtained from such a cover may be used to discover the identity of conspirators or evidence which will incriminate the suspect. Mail covers are also used to ascertain the whereabouts of persons sought by police. The postmarks on letters sent by a fugitive to his family or girl friend, for instance, provide police with a convenient list of cities where the fugitive has been and may lead to his capture.[5]

In the days before the *Katz* decision, it was commonly assumed that the use of a mail cover presented no Fourth Amendment issue. In *Lustiger v. United States*,[6] decided a month before *Katz*, the court casually asserted that "the Fourth Amendment does not preclude postal inspectors from copying information contained on the outside of sealed envelopes in the mail, where no substantial delay in the delivery of the mail is involved." Earlier decisions upheld the use of mail covers without even a mention of the Fourth Amendment; they deemed it sufficient that the practice did not violate statutes on obstruction of mail or the postal regulations then in force.[7]

Cases such as *Lustiger* could readily be explained under pre-*Katz* Fourth Amendment doctrine by the simple observation that a mail cover did not intrude into the letter and determine the contents of the communication, but instead only obtained that which was in plain view on the surface of the envelope. But in *Katz* the Court abandoned property-based Fourth Amendment analysis and adopted the concept that "the Fourth Amendment protects people, not places." It thus became apparent that the mere fact the return address appears on the outside of the envelope is not dispositive, for under *Katz* physical location in and of itself is no longer the controlling parameter.

In the post-*Katz* case of *United States v. Choate*,[8] an FBI agent sent a letter to the postal inspector in charge in Los Angeles and requested a 30-day mail cover be placed on Choate, explaining that he was "currently under investigation by this office for the

---

observes: "The Subcommittee learned that at the time, there were approximately 1000 covers instituted per month, running for an average of two weeks each. The principal uses of covers were reported to be in the apprehension of fugitives from justice; investigation of sabotage, espionage, narcotics, pornography, firearms, mail fraud, income tax violations, gambling, racketeering. The number of covers in force on June 26, 1964 was 730 * * *."

[5]Note, 4 Colum.J.L. & Soc.Probs. 165 (1968).

[6]Lustiger v. United States, 386 F.2d 132 (9th Cir.1967).

[7]Cohen v. United States, 378 F.2d 751 (9th Cir.1967); Canaday v. United States, 354 F.2d 849 (8th Cir. 1966); United States v. Schwartz, 283 F.2d 107 (3d Cir.1960); United States v. Costello, 255 F.2d 876 (2d Cir.1958).

[8]United States v. Choate, 422 F.Supp. 261 (C.D.Cal.1976).

suspected smuggling of large quantities of narcotics into the United States." The request was honored, and the mail cover disclosed, among other things, the name of a bank in which Choate had an account. This became a crucial piece of evidence with respect to the charge of attempted tax evasion brought against Choate. The district court in *Choate* first concluded that "the mail cover procedure * * * failed to comply with relevant postal regulations,"[9] and then went on to find that the cover constituted a Fourth Amendment search:

> It cannot be denied that a reasonable person's expectation of privacy with regard to return addresses on mail is a somewhat limited one. He understands that this information is necessary to postal operations and will be examined and utilized in order to route items when the name and address of the addressee is incorrect, absent, or illegible. But the disclosure mandated by these circumstances is not broad or for all purposes: a reasonable person still expects (1) that the information contained in the return address will only be used for postal purposes, and (2) that it will be utilized in only a mechanical fashion without any records being kept. The recording and disclosure to non-postal authorities for non-postal purposes that results from a mail cover extends far beyond these narrow bounds.

> No extraordinary governmental interest is raised to justify the resulting incursion into the realm of privacy delimited by such reasonable expectations. No claim is made that mail covers further the business of the Postal Service. The sole interest of the Postal Service in undertaking this form of surveillance with regard to the defendant was to assist governmental agencies in snooping. The only stated basis for the warrantless intrusion was a "feeling," in the acknowledged absence of probable cause, that a crime was being committed. * * *

> Nor can the invasion of privacy which resulted in this case be excused as minimal. Although the flow of Choate's mail may not have been materially disrupted, the Supreme Court "has never sustained a search upon the sole ground that officers reasonably

---

[9]The relevant regulation provided that a postal inspector in charge could order a mail cover: "Where written request is received from any law enforcement agency of the Federal, State, or local governments, wherein the requesting authority stipulates and specifies the reasonable grounds that exist which demonstrate the mail cover would aid in the location of a fugitive, or that it would assist in obtaining information concerning the commission or attempted commission of a crime." 39 C.F.R. § 233.2(e)(1)(ii) (1975). Noting that the "reasonable grounds" language and other restrictions had been added to the regulations in 1965 in response to congres-

sional pressure, the court concluded that "[t]o allow any law enforcement agency to obtain a mail cover without specification of any tangible justification would clearly run counter to the intent of the revision or at least the congressional action which led to its promulgation." Because the letter from the FBI agent did not specify any "reasonable grounds," the cover was in violation of postal regulations.

As discussed in § 1.5(b), violation of the postal regulations is not itself a basis for application of an exclusionary rule. See, e.g., United States v. Hinton, 222 F.3d 664 (9th Cir.2000).

expected to find evidence of a particular crime and voluntarily confined their activities to the least intrusive means consistent with that end."[10] * * *

Finally, the fact that the Postal Service is a government-sanctioned monopoly cannot be ignored. While one desiring to protect his privacy may be put to a choice as to whether or not to install a telephone,[11] there are few alternatives to the mail. Surely, in a free society, citizens should be left at least one unfettered means of communication which cannot be invaded without the showing of probable cause necessary for a search warrant. To allow the government to give an absolute monopoly and then to use it to invade the privacy of the citizenry without the protection of judicial scrutiny is to license the blatant circumvention of constitutional rights.

This reasoning is faithful to the rationale underlying *Katz,* which in the last analysis requires the making of an important value judgment: "whether, if the particular form of surveillance practiced by the police is permitted to go unregulated by constitutional restraints, the amount of privacy and freedom remaining to citizens would be diminished to a compass inconsistent with the aims of a free and open society."[12] That judgment was properly made by the district court in *Choate,* for we do not have an open society if a citizen is put to the choice of foregoing use of the postal service or of having investigators record the names and addresses of his correspondents. The mere fact that certain information is not absolutely private and is made available on a limited basis for a limited purpose should not mean there is no justified expectation of privacy against "snooping" by government agents.

Unfortunately, *Choate* was reversed on appeal.[13] The court of appeals followed an all-or-nothing approach to privacy, and thus

---

[10]This quotation, significantly, is from *Katz.*

[11]This concession, which may have been unnecessary (see immediately following subsection), was made in order to distinguish Ninth Circuit cases holding there is no reasonable expectation of privacy as to the fact that telephone calls were placed on particular dates to particular phone numbers from a residential telephone.

[12]Amsterdam, Perspectives on the Fourth Amendment, 58 Minn.L.Rev. 349, 403 (1974).

Just what the restraints should be is another matter. See, e.g., Uviller, Evidence from the Mind of the Criminal Suspect: A Reconsideration of the Current Rules of Access and Restraint, 87 Colum.L.Rev. 1137 (1987), charac-

terizing mail covers as one variety of "surveillance of semisecure behavior," id. at 1197, for which it should suffice that the police get a court order "predicated upon a belief less certain than probable cause," id. at 1210.

[13]United States v. Choate, 576 F.2d 165 (9th Cir.1978). See also United States v. Quoc Viet Hoang, 486 F.3d 1156 (9th Cir.2007) ("the Fourth Amendment is not implicated when only the external features of a package, like the address label are examined"); United States v. Burnette, 375 F.3d 10 (1st Cir.2004) (defendant "has no reasonable expectation of privacy in the outside of mail that is sorted or stored in the open, common office area" of a commercial mail receiving agency; defendant's claim "her mail was stored in her private mailbox in a private

concluded there was no Fourth Amendment protection from use of mail covers given the fact that "the information would foreseeably be available to postal employees."[14] In light of the similar analysis by the Supreme Court in its holding that use of a pen register is not a search,[15] the court of appeals decision here may well reflect how the Supreme Court would come out on the mail cover issue.

Something comparable to a mail cover might be undertaken with respect to electronic mail, that is, the transmission of letters and messages among computers via telephone lines. Statutory limits on surveillance of electronic mail were imposed by the Electronic Communications Act of 1986.[16] However, the statute does not bar interception limited to learning of the existence of such a communication or the parties to it,[17] and, in any event, the Title III statutory exclusionary rule was not extended correspondingly to apply to violations of law relating to electronic

---

mailroom that was guarded by an attendant at all times * * * presents a more colorable claim," but record does not support claim); United States v. Hinton, 222 F.3d 664 (9th Cir.2000) ("There is no expectation of privacy in the address on a package, regardless of its class," and there "also is no reasonable expectation of privacy in a parcel locker" in a postal annex, given the continuing access of postal employees to that space, and thus no search for federal agents to look at and remove package from locker so that defendant would have to go to counter to pick it up); United States v. Osunegbu, 822 F.2d 472 (5th Cir.1987) (where defendant rented a private postal box open at the back and to which manager of facility had continued access to retrieve misdelivered mail, no search for manager at postal inspector's request to let inspector examine outside of mail earlier placed in defendant's box); United States v. Huie, 593 F.2d 14 (5th Cir.1979) (reaching same result as *Choate*.) For another discussion of the cases, see Annot., 57 A.L.R. Fed. 742 (1982). Consider also United States v. Gering, 716 F.2d 615 (9th Cir.1983) (claim mail cover violated First Amendment right of association rejected).

[14]Hufstedler, J., in her excellent dissent, pointed out: "In order to execute the mail cover request, a postal employee was required to search through and segregate all mail being sent to find that posted to the subject addressee. He then carefully scrutinized the covers of first- and fourth-class mail in order to record the requested categories of information. This was patently a 'search' of Choate's mail and a 'seizure' of the information on its cover. Like the utilization of a pen register which has been held to constitute a search of a telephone and a seizure of evidence thereby produced * * *, a mail cover intrudes into a channel of communication and seizes evidence of who is being communicated with.

"The fact that the information is on the cover of the envelope may affect the reasonableness of the invasion but it renders the activity no less a search. But for the mail cover, the information would have been noticed only momentarily and certainly unrecorded. Further, of critical import is the fact that the information was doubtless 'seized' in that the Government made a permanent record of what was written on the surface of the mail."

[15]Smith v. Maryland, 442 U.S. 735, 99 S.Ct. 2577, 61 L.Ed.2d 220 (1979), discussed in more detail in § 2.7(b).

[16]Pub.L. 99-508, 100 Stat. 1859.

[17]18 U.S.C.A. § 2510(8).

communications.[18] As for a Fourth Amendment challenge to an electronic mail cover, it would likely be unavailing in light of the prior decisions on pen registers (discussed below) and covers on traditional forms of mail.[19]

§ 2.7(b) Pen registers

Another device employed by law enforcement authorities in order to determine what persons are in communication with a suspected individual is the pen register.

> The pen register is a device attached to a given telephone line usually at a central telephone office. A pulsation of the dial on the line to which the pen register is attached records on a paper tape dashes equal in number to the number dialed. The paper tape then becomes a permanent and complete record of outgoing numbers called on the particular line. With reference to incoming calls, the pen register records only a dash for each ring of the telephone but does not identify the number from which the incoming call originated. The pen register cuts off after the number is dialed on outgoing calls and after the ringing is concluded on incoming calls without determining whether the call is completed or the receiver is answered. There is neither recording nor monitoring of the conversation.[20]

Title III of the Omnibus Crime Control and Safe Streets Act of 1968 prohibits the interception of "any wire, oral or electronic communication" except in accordance with the strict procedures set out therein.[21] Courts have consistently held that those provisions are not applicable to pen registers,[22] and in *United States v. New York Telephone Company*[23] the Supreme Court reached the same conclusion:

> Pen registers do not "intercept" because they do not acquire the "contents" of communications, as that term is defined by 18 U.S.C.A. § 2511(8). Indeed, a law enforcement official could not even determine from the use of a pen register whether a communication existed. These devices do not hear sound. They disclose only the telephone numbers that have been dialed—a means of establishing communication. Neither the purport of any communication between the caller and the recipient of the call, their identities, nor whether the call was even completed are disclosed by pen registers. Furthermore, pen registers do not accomplish the "aural acquisi-

---

[18]18 U.S.C.A. § 2518(10)(c).

[19]Note, 14 Hastings Const.L.Q. 421, 438–44 (1987).

[Section 2.7(b)]

[20]United States v. Caplan, 255 F.Supp. 805 (E.D.Mich.1966).

[21]18 U.S.C.A. §§ 2510 to 2520.

[22]Hodge v. Mountain States Telephone and Telegraph Co., 555 F.2d 254 (9th Cir.1977); United States v. Southwestern Bell Telephone Co., 546 F.2d 243 (8th Cir.1976); United

States v. Illinois Bell Telephone Co., 531 F.2d 809 (7th Cir.1976); United States v. Clegg, 509 F.2d 605 (5th Cir. 1975); United States v. Falcone, 505 F.2d 478 (3d Cir.1974).

Compare Ellis v. State, 256 Ga. 751, 353 S.E.2d 19 (1987) (*state* wiretap statute interpreted as encompassing use of pen register).

[23]United States v. New York Telephone Co., 434 U.S. 159, 98 S.Ct. 364, 54 L.Ed.2d 376 (1977).

tion" of anything. They decode outgoing telephone numbers by responding to changes in electrical voltage caused by the turning of the telephone dial (or the pressing of buttons on push button telephones) and present the information in a form to be interpreted by sight rather than by hearing.

The legislative history confirms that there was no congressional intent to subject pen registers to the requirements of Title III. The Senate Report explained that the definition of "intercept" was designed to exclude pen registers:

"Paragraph 4 [of § 2510] defines 'intercept' to include the aural acquisition of the contents of any wire or oral communication by any electronic, mechanical, or other device. Other forms of surveillance are not within the proposed legislation. . . . The proposed legislation is not designed to prevent the tracing of phone calls. The use of a 'pen register,' for example would be permissible. * * * The proposed legislation is intended to protect the privacy of the communication itself and not the means of communication."[24] * * *

It is clear that Congress did not view pen registers as posing a threat to privacy of the same dimension as the interception of oral communications and did not intend to impose Title III restrictions upon their use.

The Court in *New York Telephone* went on to hold that the district court had power under Fed.R.Crim.P. 41 to authorize the installation of pen registers, for the reason that this rule was sufficiently flexible to include within its scope electronic intrusions authorized upon a finding of probable cause, and that the court's order compelling the telephone company to provide assistance was clearly authorized by the All Writs Act.[25]

The holding in *New York Telephone* that pen registers are not governed by Title III made even more significant the issue of concern here: whether the utilization of such a device constitutes a "search" under the test of *Katz v. United States*[26] so as to be subject to the limitations of the Fourth Amendment. Some lower courts assumed that a pen register order involves a search and seizure under the Fourth Amendment,[27] but in *Smith v. Maryland*[28] the Supreme Court ruled to the contrary. Justice Black-

---

[24]Quoting from S.Rep. No. 1097, 90th Cong., 2d Sess. 90 (1968).

[25]Stevens, J., joined by Brennan and Marshall, JJ., dissented as to both of these points. Stewart, J., concurring in part and dissenting in part, also believed the district court was without power to order the telephone company to assist the government.

[26]Katz v. United States, 389 U.S. 347, 88 S.Ct. 507, 19 L.Ed.2d 576 (1967).

[27]Application of the United States

of America in the Matter of an Order Authorizing the Use of a Pen Register, 538 F.2d 956 (2d Cir.1976), rev'd on other grounds in *New York Telephone*. See also Application of the United States for an Order Authorizing Installation and Use of a Pen Register, 546 F.2d 243 (8th Cir.1976); State v. Ramirez, 351 A.2d 566 (Del.Super. 1976).

[28]Smith v. Maryland, 442 U.S. 735, 99 S.Ct. 2577, 61 L.Ed.2d 220 (1979); discussed in Burkoff, When is a Search Not a "Search"? Fourth

mun, for the majority, while recognizing that "our lodestar is *Katz*," rejected petitioner's claim that he had a "legitimate expectation of privacy" regarding the numbers he dialed on his phone:

First, we doubt that people in general entertain any actual expectation of privacy in the numbers they dial. All telephone users realize that they must "convey" phone numbers to the telephone company, since it is through telephone company switching equipment that their calls are completed. All subscribers realize, moreover, that the phone company has facilities for making permanent records of the numbers they dial, for they see a list of their long-distance (toll) calls on their monthly bills. In fact, pen registers and similar devices are routinely used by telephone companies "for the purposes of checking billing operations, detecting fraud, and preventing violations of law." * * * Telephone users, in sum, typically know that they must convey numerical information to the phone company; that the phone company has facilities for recording this information; and that the phone company does in fact record this information for a variety of legitimate business purposes. Although subjective expectations cannot be scientifically gauged, it is too much to believe that telephone subscribers, under these circumstances, harbor any general expectation that the numbers they dial will remain secret. * * *

Second, even if petitioner did harbor some subjective expectation that the phone numbers he dialed would remain private, this expectation is not "one that society is prepared to recognize as 'reasonable.'" This Court consistently has held that a person has no legitimate expectation of privacy in information he voluntarily turns over to third parties. * * * In *Miller*,[29] for example, the Court held that a bank depositor has no "legitimate 'expectation of privacy'" in financial information "voluntarily conveyed to . . . banks and exposed to their employees in the ordinary course of business." * * *

This analysis dictates that petitioner can claim no legitimate expectation of privacy here. When he used his phone, petitioner voluntarily conveyed numerical information to the telephone company and "exposed" that information to its equipment in the ordinary course of business. In so doing, petitioner assumed the risk that the company would reveal to police the numbers he dialed.[30] The switch-

---

Amendment Doublespeak, 15 U.Tol.L. Rev. 515, 537–41 (1984); Fishman, Pen Registers and Privacy: Risks, Expectations, and the Nullification of Congressional Intent, 29 Cath.U.L.Rev. 557 (1980); Guzik, The Assumption of Risk Doctrine: Erosion of Fourth Amendment Protection Through Fictitious Consent to Search and Seizure, 22 Santa Clara L.Rev. 1051, 1073–78 (1982); Comment, 15 Harv.Civ.Rts.-Civ.Lib.L.Rev. 753 (1980); Note, 38 Md.L.Rev. 767 (1979); 33 Sw.L.J. 1283 (1980).

[29] The reference is to United States v. Miller, 425 U.S. 435, 96 S.Ct. 1619, 48 L.Ed.2d 71 (1976), criticized herein in § 2.7(c).

[30] In State v. Boyd, 295 Conn. 707, 992 A.2d 1071 (2010), police seized defendant's cell phone from his car at the time of his arrest and later found the cell phone's subscriber number on the phone. The state, relying on *Smith*, argued defendant had no reasonable expectation of privacy in the number because he had revealed it to third parties. The court responded that *Smith* and related cases "stand for the proposition that the government can

ing equipment that processed those numbers is merely the modern counterpart of the operator who, in an earlier day, personally completed calls for the subscriber. Petitioner concedes that if he had placed his calls through an operator, he could claim no legitimate expectation of privacy.

Having thus announced, in effect, the ominous proposition that modern technology cannot add to one's justified expectation of privacy, but can only detract from it, the Court turned to petitioner's contention that he had a legitimate expectation of privacy as to the particular incriminating call because it was a local one, which "telephone companies, in view of their present billing practices, usually do not record":

> This argument does not withstand scrutiny. The fortuity of whether or not the phone company in fact elects to make a quasi-permanent record of a particular number dialed does not, in our view, make any constitutional difference. Regardless of the phone company's election, petitioner voluntarily conveyed to it information that it had facilities for recording and that it was free to record. In these circumstances, petitioner assumed the risk that the information would be divulged to police. * * * We are not inclined to make a crazy quilt of the Fourth Amendment, especially in circumstances where (as here) the pattern of protection would be dictated by billing practices of a private corporation.[31]

---

obtain information that the defendant has provided to a third party *from that third party* without implicating the defendant's fourth amendment rights. * * * [H]owever, nothing in [those cases] supports a conclusion that, if a defendant has a reasonable expectation of privacy in an area or item, the government may search that area or item for any information that the defendant had provided to third parties without triggering fourth amendment protections."

[31]See also Rehberg v. Paulk, 611 F.3d 828 (11th Cir.2010), aff'd on other grounds., -- U.S. --, 132 S.Ct. 1497, 182 L.Ed.2d 593 (2012) (defendant "lacked a legitimate expectation of privacy in the phone and fax numbers he dialed," obtained by prosecutor via subpoena to phone companies); United States v. German, 486 F.3d 849 (5th Cir.2007) ("non-content surveillance of a pen register is an insufficient invasion of privacy to implicate the Fourth Amendment"); People of State of California v. F.C.C., 75 F.3d 1350 (9th Cir.1996) (because "phone number is not among the select privacy interests protected by a federal constitutional right to privacy," FCC rule re caller identification telephone service does not infringe upon Fourth Amendment rights); United States v. Meriwether, 917 F.2d 955 (6th Cir.1990) (relying on *Smith,* court holds that "when one transmits a message to a pager, he runs the risk that the message will be received by whomever is in possession of the pager," as "unlike the phone conversation where a caller can hear a voice and decide whether to converse, one who sends a message to a pager has no external indicia that the message actually is received by the intended recipient"); United States v. Whitten, 706 F.2d 1000 (9th Cir.1983) (no reasonable expectation of privacy in audible message left on telephone answering machine); State v. Miller, 449 A.2d 1065 (Del.Super.1982) (relying on *Smith,* court holds that use of a DNR, that is, a dialed number recorder, which records both incoming and outgoing telephone numbers as well as the duration of the calls, is not a search); Ohio Domestic Violence Network v. Public Utilities Comm'n, 70 Ohio St.3d 311, 638 N.E.2d 1012 (1994) (relying on *Smith,* court holds caller identification telephone service

Such a crabbed interpretation of the *Katz* test makes a mockery of the Fourth Amendment.[32] Under *Smith,* the police may without any cause whatsoever and for whatever purpose they choose uncover private relationships[33] with impunity merely because the telephone company might under *some* circumstances for *certain limited purposes* make a record of such relationships for the company's *own* use. Indeed, it is enough for the majority in *Smith* that the telephone company has the capacity to make a record of such relationships, even though the company has had the good sense not to offend its subscribers by making or keeping those records for no reason.

But the basic point, as noted by Justice Marshall in his dissent,[34] is that even if it may be said that subscribers know

> that a phone company monitors calls for internal reasons, * * * it does not follow that they expect this information to be made available to the public in general or the government in particular. Privacy is not a discrete commodity, possessed absolutely or not at all. Those who disclose certain facts to a bank or phone company for a limited business purpose need not assume that this information will be released to other persons for other purposes.

This is especially true in this particular context. As Justice Marshall went on to note, it is one thing to say that a person assumes the risk of disclosure when he elects to make incriminat-

---

does not infringe upon the Fourth Amendment privacy rights of the caller); Southern Bell Tel. & Tel. Co. v. Hamm, 306 S.C. 70, 409 S.E.2d 775 (1991) (relying on *Smith,* court holds caller identification telephone service does not violate Fourth Amendment).

[32] See also Fishman, 29 Cath.U.L. Rev. 557, 568–74 (1980), for similar criticism. And see People v. Sporleder, 666 P.2d 135 (Colo.1983) (pen register governed by state constitution); Shaktman v. State, 553 So.2d 148 (Fla.1989) (pen register governed by state constitution); State v. Thompson, 114 Idaho 746, 760 P.2d 1162 (1988) (pen register governed by state constitution); Commonwealth v. Melilli, 521 Pa. 405, 555 A.2d 1254 (1989) (pen register covered by state constitution); Richardson v. State, 865 S.W.2d 944 (Tex.Crim.App.1993) ("use of a pen register may well constitute a 'search'" under state constitution); State v. Gunwall, 106 Wash.2d 54, 720 P.2d 808 (1986) (pen register covered by state constitution).

Compare State v. Valenzuela, 130 N.H. 175, 536 A.2d 1252 (1987)

(declining to follow those other states which have adopted a stricter view); State v. Schultz, 252 Kan. 819, 850 P.2d 818 (1993) (summarizing authorities and arguments for rejecting *Smith*, but declining to do so).

[33] Underlying the majority opinion in *Smith* appears to be the assumption that the relationships here at issue are not worth protecting. But surely this is not the case. As Justice Stewart correctly notes in his dissent, "I doubt there are any who would be happy to have broadcast to the world a list of the local or long distance numbers they have called. This is not because such a list might in some sense be incriminating, but because it easily could reveal the identities of the persons and the places called, and thus reveal the most intimate details of a person's life."

[34] The Marshall dissent is joined by Brennan, J., who also joined the separate dissent by Stewart, J. Powell, J., took no part in the consideration or decision of this case.

ing remarks to or in the presence of another person,[35] but "here, unless a person is prepared to forego use of what for many has become a personal or professional necessity, he cannot help but accept the risk of surveillance."[36]

It was clear even before *Katz* that the protections of the Fourth Amendment extend to certain matters that are not absolutely, 100% private. Thus, even though a tenant may not have absolute privacy in his home because the landlord may enter "to view waste," the Supreme Court did not hesitate to hold that the residence is protected by the Fourth Amendment from police intrusion even with the landlord's permission.[37] Similarly, a person who rents a hotel room cannot be said to have absolute privacy in that room, for "he gives 'implied or express permission' to 'such persons as maids, janitors or repairmen' to enter his room 'in the performance of their duties,'" but this certainly does not mean that a hotel room is not protected by the Fourth Amendment against unreasonable police entry.[38] *Katz* did not overrule those decisions, but rather extended them to situations in which no physical trespass is necessary for the police to obtain that which an individual has sought to preserve as private. This being so, it makes no sense to say that the telephone subscriber (any more than the tenant or hotel occupant) is fair game for unrestrained police scrutiny merely because he has surrendered some degree of his privacy for a limited purpose to those with whom he is doing business. As Professor Amsterdam put it, "[t]he fact that our ordinary social intercourse, uncontrolled by government, imposes certain risks upon us hardly means that government is constitutionally unconstrained in adding to those risks."[39]

New York Telephone and *Smith* do not govern, however, if the pen register is used in such a way as to intercept conversations, as in *United States v. Lucht*.[40] A pen register had already been installed and the police expected to have court approval for a wiretap soon, so they "conducted 'audio tests' with the pen register," that is, "converted the pen register into a listening device in order to check sound quality and test the recording equipment." The court ruled that the conversations thereby intercepted had to

---

[35]The reference, of course, is to the line of cases represented by Hoffa v. United States, 385 U.S. 293, 87 S.Ct. 408, 17 L.Ed.2d 374 (1966).

[36]*Smith* "erroneously assumes Smith had a choice. In fact, since [he] had no way to shield the numbers he dialed from the telephone company, the only choice Smith had to minimize his risk of being observed was to leave home and use a pay phone." Brenner, The Fourth Amendment in an Era of Ubiquitous Technology, 75 Miss.L.J.

1, 68 (2005).

[37]Chapman v. United States, 365 U.S. 610, 81 S.Ct. 776, 5 L.Ed.2d 828 (1961).

[38]Stoner v. California, 376 U.S. 483, 84 S.Ct. 889, 11 L.Ed.2d 856 (1964).

[39]Amsterdam, Perspectives on the Fourth Amendment, 58 Minn.L.Rev. 349, 406 (1974).

[40]United States v. Lucht, 18 F.3d 541 (8th Cir.1994).

be suppressed, as those actions "violated the Fourth Amendment and state and federal wiretapping statutes."

In response to *Smith,* Congress enacted legislation providing procedures to govern the installation and use of a pen register. An attorney for the government may obtain a court order authorizing such installation and use by making an application identifying the applicant and the law enforcement agency conducting the investigation and certifying under oath or affirmation that "the information likely to be obtained is relevant to an ongoing criminal investigation."[41] This legislation, which provides only for fines and possible imprisonment for knowing violation,[42] has been interpreted as not also carrying an exclusionary-rule type remedy.[43]

The Communications Assistance for Law Enforcement Act of 1994[44] was enacted in order "to further define the industry duty to cooperate [with law enforcement agencies] and to establish procedures based on public accountability and industry standards-setting."[45] FCC rulemaking under the Act resulted in the promulgation of final rules on August 26, 1999, which, among other things, requires telecommunication carriers to provide law enforcement agencies with "dialed digit extraction."[46] In contrast to the traditional pen register, which "can only intercept the first set of numbers dialed from a telephone,"[47] this new DDE capability "would allow law enforcement agencies to record any digits dialed after the call has been cut through," that is, "the additional numbers provided to a long distance source provider, an automated system, a bank, voicemail, a paging device, or any other numbers dialed after the connection."[48] Assuming such DDE authorization is contemplated by CALEA,[49] there remains the important question of the status of DDE under the Fourth Amendment, as to which one thoughtful commentator has offered

---

[41]18 U.S.C.A. § 3122(b)(2).

[42]18 U.S.C.A. § 3121(c).

[43]United States v. Thompson, 936 F.2d 1249 (11th Cir.1991) ("Absent a specific reference to an exclusionary rule, it is not appropriate for the courts to read such a provision into the act").

[44]Codified as amended at 47 U.S.C.A. §§ 1001 to 1010 and in scattered sections of 18 U.S.C.A., See BeVier, The Communications Assistance for Law Enforcement Act of 1994: A Surprising Sequel to the Breakup of AT & T, 51 Stan.L.Rev. 1049 (1999); Comment, 21 Whittier L.Rev. 767 (2000).

[45]H.R.Rep. No. 103-827, at 14 (1994).

[46]47 C.F.R. § 1.20007(b)(6).

[47]Note, 84 Minn.L.Rev. 1051 (2000).

[48]Note, 84 Minn.L.Rev. 1051, 1064 (2000).

[49]That matter is open to question. "Dialed digit extraction violates three specific provisions of CALEA. Post-cut-through numbers are not call-identifying information nor are they reasonably available to the initial carrier. Additionally, including dialed digit extraction breached the framework established for technical standards in 47 U.S.C.A. § 1006(b). Requiring telecommunication carriers to provide law enforcement agencies with dialed digit extraction overreaches the authority that Congress gave to the FCC in CALEA." Note, 84 Minn.L.Rev.

this cogent analysis:

> While the Supreme Court has held that the unauthorized use of a Title III wiretap violates the Fourth Amendment, there is no Fourth Amendment violation for unauthorized use of a pen register. However, the expansion of a pen register to include dialed digit extraction alters this analysis because it expands the type and amount of information that a pen register obtains. Pen registers with dialed digit extraction capabilities should receive the same treatment as Title III wiretaps do under the Fourth Amendment.

> The Court has previously held that the Fourth Amendment applies when there is a "legitimate expectation of privacy." Determining if there is a "legitimate expectation of privacy" involves a two prong test: the first prong looks at the subjective expectation of the individual targeted for electronic surveillance. The second prong looks at whether or not society recognizes that individual's subjective expectation of privacy. Obtaining post-cut-through numbers with a pen register violates both prongs of the test. While individuals may not have a subjective expectation of privacy in the numbers that they dial, they most likely do have such an expectation when it comes to content transmitted over the telephone line in the form of post-cut-through digits. There is no functional difference, in terms of expectations, between an individual who calls a bank and speaks to an actual banker to get his balance or an individual who calls a bank and uses an automated system to get his balance. Either way, the individuals are transmitting information over the telephone wire that they do not wish to expose to the public. The type of information typically transmitted over the telephone by use of post-cut-through numbers is incredibly far-reaching: bank account numbers and codes, prescription identification numbers, paging messages, social security numbers, driver license numbers, airline flight information, credit card numbers, voicemail passwords, general account passwords, and responses to automated systems. In *Smith v. Maryland*,[50] the Court noted that individuals know or should know that the numbers dialed to connect a call are made into a permanent record. Accordingly, an individual has no expectation of privacy in the numbers dialed. However, post-cut-through numbers present a different issue. These numbers do not appear on the monthly bill, nor are they documented on a permanent record. Thus, while individuals may knowingly expose the telephone numbers they dial to make a telephone call, they may still wish to keep information communicated via post-cut-through numbers private, a subjective expectation of privacy that warrants Fourth Amendment protection.

> Furthermore, the subjective expectation of privacy is one that society recognizes as reasonable. In the past, information carried in post-cut-through numbers was transmitted via voice communications over telephone systems. For instance, the information now dialed into a telephone to transfer money from one bank account to another used to be done by talking to a banker instead of using an automated system. The different method of communication does not change the type of information that is transmitted, nor should it change the type of protection that it receives. This information has

---

1051, 1081 (2000).

[50] Smith v. Maryland, 442 U.S. 735, 99 S.Ct. 2577, 61 L.Ed.2d 220 (1979).

generally been viewed as protected by the Fourth Amendment and should continue to be so protected.[51]

Because the "most common type of such communication today is a text message, a message typed out on a cell phone that converts numbers into letters and sends the communication much like an old-fashioned Western Union telegram,"[52] it is not surprising that the first significant holding on government acquisition of post cut-through digits had to do with investigators obtaining text messages from a company providing wireless text-messaging services. In *Quon v. Arch Wireless Operating Co., Inc.*,[53] the court, after noting that *Smith* had distinguished *Katz* by noting that "pen registers do not acquire the *contents* of communications," and that this distinction had also been drawn in prior cases dealing with letters and e-mails, concluded:

> We see no meaningful difference between the e-mails at issue in *Forrester*[54] and the text messages at issue here. Both are sent from user to user via a service provider that stores the messages on its servers. Similarly, * * * we also see no meaningful distinction between text messages and letters. As with letters and e-mails, it is not reasonable to expect privacy in the information used to "address" a text message, such as the dialing of a phone number to send a message. However, users do have a reasonable expectation of privacy in the content of their text messages vis-a-vis the service provider. * * * The [service provider] may have been able to access the contents of the messages for its own purposes is irrelevant. * * * Appellants did not expect that [the service provider] would monitor their text messages, much less turn over the messages to third parties without Appellants' consent.

The *Quon* case had to do with a city police department reviewing text messages sent and received by Quon, a sergeant in that department, by obtaining those messages from the company that had contracted to provide wireless text-messaging services for the city. At issue in this § 1983 action was whether that activity had violated the Fourth Amendment rights of Quon and those with whom he exchanged text messages. Significantly, the court qualified the conclusion quoted above by cautioning that it did

---

[51]Note, 84 Minn.L.Rev. 1051, 1077–78 (2000). See also Notes, 41 Am.Crim.L.Rev. 1321 (2004); 74 Brook. L.Rev. 1109 (2009); In re U.S. for Orders (1) Authorizing Use of Pen Registers and Trap and Trace Devices, 515 F.Supp.2d 325 (E.D.N.Y.2007) (telephone callers had a reasonable expectation of privacy in their post-cut-through dialed digits, and government in error in reading Pen/Trap statute as authorizing access to all dialed digits of telephone calls, including post-cut-through dialed digits).

[52]2 W. LaFave, J. Israel, N. King & O. Kerr, Criminal Procedure § 4.3(c) (3d ed.2007).

[53]Quon v. Arch Wireless Operating Co., Inc., 529 F.3d 892 (9th Cir. 2008), discussed in Case Summary, 39 Golden Gate U.L.Rev. 351 (2009); Comment, 5 Seton Hall Cir.Rev. 461(2009); Note, 17 Geo.Mason L.Rev. 295 (2009).

[54]The reference is to United States v. Forrester, 512 F.3d 500 (9th Cir. 2008), discussed in text at note 76 infra.

"not endorse a monolithic view of text message users' reasonable expectation of privacy, as this is necessarily a context-specific inquiry." Thus, if Quon had "voluntarily permitted the Department to review his text messages," the other plaintiffs "would have no claims." As for Quon's own reasonable expectation of privacy, this, the court explained, "turns on the Department's policies regarding privacy in his text messages." The court then went on to conclude "that the Department's informal policy that text messages would not be audited if he paid the overages[55] rendered Quon's expectation of privacy in those messages reasonable."

On review by the Supreme Court in *City of Ontario v. Quon*,[56] that Court declined to pass judgment upon the assertions appearing in the paragraph quoted above, purportedly because of the risk of "error by elaborating too fully on the Fourth Amendment implications of emerging technology before its role in society has become clear." The Court thus simply proceeded to "assume several propositions *arguendo*": (1) that "Quon had a reasonable expectation of privacy in the text messages sent on the pager provided to him by the City"; (2) that the City's "review of the transcript constituted a search within the meaning of the Fourth Amendment"; and (3) that the existing "principles applicable to a government employer's search of a physical office" also apply in the instant context. As discussed elsewhere herein,[57] the Court then concluded the City's search of Quon's text messages was reasonable, which also thwarted the claim of those who had texted Quon, for they made "no corollary argument that the search, if reasonable as to Quon, could nonetheless be unreasonable as to" them.

Because of an FCC regulation requiring cellular telephone companies to have the capability of determining the location from which a cellular phone call originates to within 125 meters,[58] yet another type of information will be available from such phone companies: the location of each cellular phone every few minutes during the period it is turned on. As to such practice, it has been

---

[55]Under the city's contract, each pager was allotted 25,000 characters, after which the city was required to pay overage charges, and the practice was that such overages would be paid by the employee using that pager. Quon went over the monthly limit several times, but each time paid the overage charges, but nonetheless his superiors decided to examine transcripts of the text messages to determine if they were exclusively work-related.

[56]City of Ontario v. Quon, __ U.S.

__, 130 S.Ct. 2619, 177 L.Ed.2d 216 (2010), discussed in Dery, Legal Limbo: The Supreme Court's Discomfort with Technology in City of Ontario v. Quon Cause it to Confuse the Definition of a Fourth Amendment Search, 22 Geo.Mason U.Civ.Rts.L.J. 61 (2007); Notes, 26 Berkeley Tech.L.J. 859 (2011); 90 Neb.L.Rev. 559 (2011).

[57]See § 10.3, text at note 186.

[58]See § 2.7(f), describing the mandated technology in further detail and assessing it from the "tracking device" perspective.

argued "that cellular call location information is sufficiently different from information about the phone numbers dialed from a telephone—that location information reveals so much more about an individual's private life—that the analysis applied by the Supreme Court in *Smith* is inapplicable."[59] Though there is much to be said for this contention, because of "the sweeping language of the Supreme Court's opinion in *Smith v. Maryland*, it seems likely that courts will use the case as a basis for denying Fourth Amendment protection to cellular call location information."[60]

Information about e-mail messages similar to that obtained by the traditional pen register can now be acquired for use in criminal investigations by utilizing the FBI's electronic surveillance software originally known as Carnivore and now designated as DCS1000.

> The software is housed in a computer and connected to an Internet service provider (ISP) such as AOL, Earthlink, or Prodigy. The ISP then provides the FBI with an access point containing all traffic from the suspect. Using a one-way tapping device, all data at the access point is copied. Carnivore then filters this copied data, sniffing out and retrieving "packets" of information that are subject to court orders while theoretically rejecting all extraneous data. FBI administrators have the ability to calibrate Carnivore to capture packets based on Internet Protocol (IP) address or e-mail username. "Packets can be recorded in their entirety (full mode) or recording can be limited to addressing information (pen mode), i.e., IP addresses and usernames."[61]

Because a court order for an e-mail pen register may also be acquired without a showing of probable cause,[62] it becomes important to determine whether acquiring information via

---

[59]Note, 10 Stan.L. & Pol'y Rev. 103, 108 (1998).

[60]Note, 10 Stan.L. & Pol'y Rev. 103, 107 (1998).

[61]Comment, 52 S.C.L.Rev. 875, 876 (2001). For other discussions of Carnivore/DCS1000, see Lewis, Carnivore—The FBI's Internet Surveillance System, 23 Whittier L.Rev. 317 (2001); McCarthy, Don't Fear Carnivore: It Won't Devour Individual Privacy, 66 Mo.L.Rev. 827 (2001); Comments, 9 Comm.Law.Conspectus 111 (2001); 89 N.C.L.Rev. 315 (2001); 19 Temp. Envt'l L. & Tech.J. 155 (2001); 32 Tex.Tech.L.Rev. 1053 (2001); 18 T.M.Cooley L.Rev. 183 (2001); Notes, 27 Brook.J.Int'l L. 245 (2001); 20 Cardozo Arts & Ent.L.J. 231 (2002); 34 Conn.L.Rev. 261 (2001); 35 Ind.L.Rev. 303 (2001); 21 Loy.L.A.Ent. L.Rev. 481 (2001); 8 Mich. Telecomm. & Tech.L.Rev. 219 (2001); 18 N.Y.U.L.

Sch.J.Hum.Rts. 305 (2002); 76 Notre Dame L.Rev. 1215 (2001); 62 Ohio St.L.J. 1831 (2001); 7 Roger Williams U.L.Rev. 247 (2001); 28 Rutgers Computer & Tech.L.J. 155 (2002); 75 S.Cal.L.Rev. 231 (2001).

[62]18 U.S.C.A. § 3123(a).

By virtue of a 2001 amendment to § 3121 adding the terms "routing" and "addressing" to the phrase "dialing and signaling information," it is made perfectly clear that the pen register and trap and trace authority applies to Internet traffic. Another amendment makes it clear that the information retrieved "shall not include the contents of any communication," defined in 18 U.S.C.A. § 2510(8) as including "any information concerning the substance, purport, or meaning of [the] communication." It remains to be seen exactly what information, if any, may be obtained under the new language beyond the "to" and "from"

Carnivore/DCS1000 when in "pen mode" constitutes a search under the Fourth Amendment.

In pursuing that inquiry, it is necessary, of course, to again examine *Smith v. Maryland*,[63] having to do with the more traditional type of pen register, one revealing the numbers dialed from a particular phone. In holding resort to that procedure was no Fourth Amendment search, the Court stressed that telephone numbers called are conveyed to the telephone company in order to complete the call and are recorded by the company for billing purposes. "Telephone users, in sum, typically know that they must convey numerical information to the phone company; that the phone company has facilities for recording this information; and that the phone company does in fact record this information for a variety of legitimate business purposes," says *Smith*, and thus it "is too much to believe that telephone subscribers, under these circumstances, harbor any general expectation that the numbers they dial will remain secret." That language, as one perceptive commentator has put it,

> provides the strongest support for denying that Internet users hold a subjective expectation of privacy in e-mail addressing information. On the one hand, the billing structure of ISPs, typically consisting of a flat monthly fee or a fee based on time spent online, never considers the distance over which messages are sent. Consequently, the recipient addresses of such messages play no part in determining billing, and no itemized list of "numbers dialed" is received by users to destroy an expectation of privacy. But when users send e-mail messages, they certainly know that addressing information is being "conveyed" to their ISP, if for no other reason than to route their messages to the proper destination. Moreover, because e-mail is typically stored on an ISP's server computer before it is read by a recipient, and often remains there after reading, users know ISPs possess "facilities for recording" e-mail addressing information. The recordability of e-mail addresses is further supported by the knowledge that e-mail, like all Internet traffic, is composed of digital data that may easily be recorded by any computer receiving it. And for many of the reasons articulated by the *Smith* Court—particularly detecting fraud and identifying the source of harassing or obscene messages—users likely expect their ISPs to occasionally or regularly record the addressing information of certain messages for "legitimate business purposes." Considering these auxiliary functions of e-mail addressing, it is "too much to believe" that Internet users expect their addressing information to remain private.[64]

Moreover, the *Smith* Court added, when a telephone user "voluntarily conveyed numerical information to the telephone company and 'exposed' that information to its equipment in the ordinary course of business," he has "assumed the risk that the

---

header information received under the pre-amendment version of the law.

[63]Smith v. Maryland, 442 U.S. 735, 99 S.Ct. 2577, 61 L.Ed.2d 220 (1979).

[64]Note, 8 Mich. Telecomm. & Tech.L.Rev. 219, 227–28 (2001).

company would reveal to police the numbers he dialed. The switching equipment that processed those numbers is merely the modern counterpart of the operator who, in an earlier day, personally completed calls to the subscriber." Put into an e-mail context, that language makes it clear

> that e-mail addressing information revealed to no one other than an ISP's equipment nevertheless falls squarely within the * * * assumption of risk doctrine * * *. Telephone numbers dialed and e-mail addressing information serve the same legitimate business purpose—both tell network switching equipment where to send the call or message of the initiating party. The fact that no human being may ever view the header information is of no consequence. When an Internet user sends a message over an ISP's network, she has revealed the addressing information to the ISP's equipment in the ordinary course of business, and she assumes the risk that the ISP will reveal her addressing information to the government. A Carnivore installation on the ISP network simply facilitates this "revelation" by the ISP.[65]

There is, however, another aspect of the *Smith* decision that must be taken into account at this point, for it involves a factor that casts at least *some* doubt upon the conclusion that use of Carnivore/DCS1000 in "pen mode" does not constitute a Fourth Amendment search. As the Court put it, in the case of a telephone pen register, "a law enforcement official could not even determine from the use of a pen register whether a communication existed. * * * Neither the purport of any communication between the caller and the recipient of the call, their identities, nor whether the call was even completed is disclosed by pen registers." Carnivore/DCS1000 is different in two respects: (i) it collects *more* than simple addressing information; and (ii) it collects addressing information which arguably is itself more revealing than the sequence of dialed numbers in *Smith*.

As for the first of these, Carnivore/DCS1000 in pen mode "captures the entire e-mail message and all of its fields (including the 'SUBJECT' line and contents of the message), but replaces each character in fields other than 'To:' and 'From:' with an X."[66] Because each X represents a unit of data ("an e-mail sent containing seventeen bytes of data is represented by eighteen Xs, while an e-mail containing twenty-nine bytes is represented by thirty Xs"[67]), the result is that it "it is easy to determine the length of each field in the header and the length of the entire message."[68] While one commentator has asserted that "it is unlikely that 'society is prepared to recognize as "reasonable"' an expectation of

---

[65]Note, 8 Mich. Telecomm. & Tech.L.Rev. 219, 229 (2001).

[66]Note, 8 Mich. Telecomm. & Tech.L.Rev. 219, 230 (2001).

[67]Comment, 52 S.C.L.Rev. 875, 886 (2001).

[68]Note, 34 Conn.L.Rev. 261, 288 (2001).

privacy in the length of e-mail messages,"[69] it is to be doubted that the matter can be dismissed so cavalierly, considering that this added information "would often allow an agent to perform traffic analysis,"[70] and, when the suspected criminality involves the communication of images, would provide information that images have indeed been sent.[71]

As for the second difference between telephone and e-mail pen registers, the basic point is that "the e-mail addressing information is more personal, and thus more revealing, than a phone number. An e-mail address may specifically identify an individual (for example, JohnDoe aol.com) or at least refer to him in a personal, idiosyncratic manner (for example, BigJohn aol.com.). A phone number, on the other hand, provides no personal information other than the location from which the phone call was placed."[72] One response, that "e-mail addressing information is not necessary personal," and "is only as personal as the user chooses it to be,"[73] is hardly adequate in many instances, for in institutional settings (e.g., university, business) "usernames are often assigned by a central authority and typically contain some part of the user's proper name."[74] A more comprehensive and convincing response is that it is to be doubted

> whether an e-mail address more accurately reveals the actual sender or recipient of an e-mail than does a telephone number. For someone other than the owner named in the records of the telephone company or ISP to use either type of account, access must be gained. For an e-mail account, this means the user must be privy to the owner's password. However, e-mail accounts can typically be accessed from almost any geographic location. For a telephone call, the user must gain access to the owner's actual home, where the telephone line terminates. In either case, such access is most likely to be had by other members of the owner's household. Indeed, access to both telephones and e-mail accounts by multiple members of the same household is quite common. Thus, it is unclear whether e-mail addresses really reveal that much more about the identity of

---

[69]McCarthy, Don't Fear Carnivore: It Won't Devour Individual Privacy, 66 Mo.L.Rev. 827 (2001).

[70]Note, 34 Conn.L.Rev. 261, 288 (2001), adding: "One example * * * is 'in the case of a user visiting a web site, [where] knowing the length of the objects returned can often be used to identify which web page he was visiting.'"

[71]"This data may seem insignificant, but consider the following hypothetical: A judge authorizes FBI agents to use Carnivore to capture e-mail addresses sent to and from a person suspected of violating child pornography laws. While the agents are viewing this information, they no-

tice most messages are small but some are extraordinarily large, perhaps indicating that illegal pictures are being transmitted. Therefore, in some cases the FBI has the ability to ascertain, or at least accurately guess, the nature of an e-mail without first obtaining Title III authorization." Comment, 52 S.C.L.Rev. 875, 886–87 (2001).

[72]Comment, 52 S.C.L.Rev. 875, 887 (2001).

[73]McCarthy, Don't Fear Carnivore: It Won't Devour Individual Privacy, 66 Mo.L.Rev. 827, 845 (2001).

[74]Note, 8 Mich. Telecomm. & Tech.L.Rev. 219, 230 (2001).

message senders and recipients.[75]

In *United States v. Forrester*,[76] the very first federal circuit court opinion that "has spoken to the constitutionality of computer surveillance techniques that reveal the to/from addresses of e-mail messages," the court not surprisingly concluded that such "surveillance techniques * * * are constitutionally indistinguishable from the use of a pen register that the Court approved in *Smith*." In reaching this conclusion, the *Forrester* court emphasized three points: (i) "e-mail * * * users, like the telephone users in *Smith*, rely on third-party equipment in order to engage in communication"; (ii) "e-mail to/from addresses * * * constitute addressing information and do not necessarily reveal any more about the underlying contents of communications than do phone numbers"; and (iii) since "the pen register in *Smith* was able to disclose not only the phone numbers dialed but also the number of calls made," there "is no difference of constitutional magnitude between this aspect of the pen register and the government's monitoring here of the total volume of data transmitted to or from Alba's account. Devices that obtain addressing information also inevitably reveal the amount of information coming and going, and do not thereby breach the line between mere addressing to more content-rich information."

But, while "the analogy between telephone numbers and the source or destination of an electronic communication works well for information necessary to route an e-mail, the analogy is imperfect when address information may reveal or direct law enforcement officials to content."[77] Such is the case when the acquired information is that a particular computer has made contact with a particular website on the Internet. For one thing, "information that ostensibly identifies the location of the relevant file on a web server may embed certain clues as to content";[78] for another, "even when a URL reveals nothing at all about content,

---

[75]Note, 8 Mich. Telecomm. & Tech.L.Rev. 219, 231 (2001). And, consider the analogy to postal mail: "The postal mail precedents have obvious force in the case of e-mail and other person-to-person Internet messages. The body of an e-mail message, the subject line, and the contents of any attachments are analogous to the contents inside a postal envelope or package. They constitute the message that the sender wants to share with the intended recipient. The e-mail header (minus the subject line) containing the to/from address, size of the e-mail, and mail servers that routed the message are analogous to the to/from address dimensions, and post-

mark of a postal letter." Kerr, Applying the Fourth Amendment to the Internet: A General Approach, 62 Stan.L.Rev. 1005, 1023 (2010).

[76]United States v. Forrester, 512 F.3d 500 (9th Cir.2008), discussed in Comment, 41 Loy.L.A.L.Rev. 1121 (2008); Note, 22 BYU J.Pub.L. 499 (2008).

[77]Bellia, Surveillance Law Through Cyberlaw's Lens, 72 Geo.Wash.L.Rev. 1375, 1429 (2004).

[78]Bellia, 72 Geo.Wash.L.Rev. 1375, 1429 (2004). "Consider, for example, a user searching the Barnes & Noble web site for a book on breast cancer. The address—known as the universal resource locator, or URL—of

when a publicly available web site is involved, the address information is all that law enforcement officials need to determine what information a user has viewed."[79] While this lends support to the conclusion that acquiring such information is a search, there are other factors at play here which, when taken into account, may well make it "likely that a court would deem a user's expectation of privacy in URLs of the pages the user views to be unreasonable."[80] Of particular significance is the fact that "in various contexts URLs are passed to web servers other than the server providing the particular page the user views."[81]

In the previously-discussed case of *United States v. Forrester*,[82] which was also the first federal circuit opinion to pass on "the constitutionality of computer surveillance techniques that reveal * * * the IP addresses of websites visited," the court held such surveillance to be constitutional by the same analysis, discussed above, it used regarding e-mail to/from addresses. As for the concerns stated in the preceding paragraph, the court reasoned that "[w]hen the government obtains * * * the IP address of websites visited, it does not find out * * * the particular pages on the websites the person viewed," so that, "[a]t best, the government may make educated guesses about what* * * was viewed on the websites based on its knowledge of the * * * IP addresses," which is "no different from speculation about the contents of a phone conversation on the basis of the identity of the person or entity that was dialed." But, the court importantly added: "Surveillance techniques that enable the government to determine not only the IP addresses that a person accesses but also the uniform resource locators ("URL") of the pages visited might be more constitutionally problematic."[83]

---

the page displaying the search results will likely contain the search terms, as in the example http://search.barnes andnoble.com/booksearch/results.asp? WRD=breast+cancer&userid=2TJNSO YMEW." Id.

[79]Bellia, 72 Geo.Wash.L.Rev. 1375, 1429 (2004).

[80]Bellia, 72 Geo.Wash.L.Rev. 1375, 1430 (2004).

[81]Bellia, 72 Geo.Wash.L.Rev. 1375, 1430 (2004). "For example, a web site may have an arrangement with a third-party advertiser for the advertiser to serve banner ads to the site; the user's browser will transmit the URL of the page the user is viewing to the advertiser's server. Similarly, when a user transmits a request

to view a particular web page, the server hosting that page typically can log the URL of the preceding page the user viewed." Id.

[82]United States v. Forrester, 512 F.3d 500 (9th Cir.2008).

[83]The court elaborated: "A URL, unlike an IP address, identifies the particular document within a website that a person views and thus reveals much more information about the person's Internet activity. For instance, a surveillance technique that captures IP addresses would show only that a person visited the New York Times' website at http://www.nyt imes.com, whereas a technique that captures URLs would also divulge the particular articles the person viewed."

§ 2.7(c) Examination of financial and other business records

Yet another way in which law enforcement agents can obtain information concerning a person's associations and activities over a considerable span of time is by examination of the detailed records kept by those agencies with whom that person has had occasion to do business. The opportunities for such surveillance are greater today than ever before, and are bound to increase substantially in the years ahead.

> In a highly industrialized society, second and third party institutions—banks, telephone companies, hospitals, doctors' offices, credit bureaus—collect and maintain an enormous quantity of personal information. Data which were once either nonexistent or confined solely to the individual's personal records are now reposited in files, computer discs, and microfilm beyond the individual's physical control.[84]

Despite the fact that the volume and personal nature of this information is such that access by government agents unrestrained by constitutional limitations would seem to constitute a devastating intrusion into privacy, courts have not been receptive to the assertion that the subjects of this information are at all protected by the Fourth Amendment against this kind of surveillance. In light of the unfortunate decision of the Supreme Court in *United States v. Miller*,[85] they are even less likely to accept such a contention.[86]

In *Miller,* local authorities discovered distilling equipment in

---

[Section 2.7(c)]

[84]Note, 83 Yale L.J. 1439 (1974). See also National Academy of Sciences, Databanks in a Free Society (1972); V. Packard, The Naked Society (1964); J. Rule, Private Lives and Public Surveillance (1973); M. Warner & M. Stone, The Data Bank Society (1970); Karst, "The Files": Legal Controls Over the Accuracy and Accessibility of Stored Personal Data, 31 Law & Contemp. Prob. 342 (1966). Consider also Doran, Privacy and Smart Grid: When Progress and Privacy Collide, 41 Tol.L. Rev. 909, 910 (2010) (re privacy problems relating to forthcoming "smart grid," involving "highly detailed electricity usage data communicated by and between the utility, the consumer, and, in many instances, third-party vendors").

The concern here is with what expectation of privacy a customer or similarly-situated person has with regard to examination of such records. By contrast, the question of what privacy expectation a *user* of a computer system has, either within or without a business context, with respect to that person's files in a multiple-user computer system is discussed in § 2.6(f).

[85]United States v. Miller, 425 U.S. 435, 96 S.Ct. 1619, 48 L.Ed.2d 71 (1976).

[86]See, e.g., United States v. McIntyre, 646 F.3d 1107 (8th Cir.2011) (no expectation of privacy re power-usage information re defendant's home, obtained from utility company); United States v. Christie, 624 F.3d 558 (3d Cir.2010) (rejecting defendant's claim "that he possessed a reasonable expectation of privacy in his IP address," obtained by police with assistance of website administrator); United States v. Bynum, 604 F.3d 161 (4th Cir.2010) (defendant lacked "a subjective expectation of privacy in his internet and phone 'subscriber information'"); United States v. Perrine, 518 F.3d 1196 (10th Cir.2008) ("subscriber

information provided to an internet provider is not protected by the Fourth Amendment's privacy expectation"); Nelson v. National Aeronautics and Space Administration, 512 F.3d 1134 (9th Cir.2008) (background investigations of employees of Jet Propulsion Lab, whereby adverse information sought from "the applicants references, employers, and landlords," no search in light of *Miller*); Guest v. Leis, 255 F.3d 325 (6th Cir.2001) ("computer users do not have a legitimate expectation of privacy in their subscriber information because they have conveyed it to another person— the system operator"); United States v. Bradford, 246 F.3d 1107 (8th Cir.2001) (defendants, who used Western Union to wire money to California for drug buys, had no "Fourth Amendment right to privacy in the records of the Western Union transfers"); United States v. Phibbs, 999 F.2d 1053 (6th Cir.1993) (no reasonable expectation of privacy in records re defendant kept by various businesses, "including his credit card statements and telephone records"); United States v. Sturman, 951 F.2d 1466 (6th Cir.1991) (no Fourth Amendment reasonable expectation of privacy in Swiss banking records covered by strict banking secrecy laws of that country; court emphasizes that privacy right and remedy for violation limited by treaty); In re Grand Jury Proceedings: Subpoena Duces Tecum, 827 F.2d 301 (8th Cir.1987) ("Western Union customers have no privacy interest in Western Union records, as they are not the customers' property"); State v. Hamzy, 288 Ark. 561, 709 S.W.2d 397 (1986) (no expectation of privacy in phone company records); Gibbs v. State, 479 A.2d 266 (Del.1984) (no expectation of privacy in toll call records); Kesler v. State, 249 Ga. 462, 291 S.E.2d 497 (1982) (no expectation of privacy in telephone toll and billing records); In re Order for Indiana Bell Telephone to Disclose Records, 274 Ind. 131, 409 N.E.2d 1089 (1980) (no expectation of privacy in long distance call records of phone company); State v. Bank of America, 272 Kan. 182, 31 P.3d 952 (2001) (bank's customers had

no reasonable expectation of privacy in their bank records, and thus State Securities Commissioner could prohibit bank from notifying its customers of subpoena for bank records); Commonwealth v. Cote, 407 Mass. 827, 556 N.E.2d 45 (1990) (no expectation of privacy in messages taken down by contracted answering service, as use of such service "necessarily involved a voluntary conveyance of information to that third party"); State v. Mello, 162 N.H. 115, 27 A.3d 771 (2011) ("a defendant has no reasonable expectation of privacy in subscriber information voluntarily provided to an Internet service provider"); State v. Gubitosi, 152 N.H. 673, 886 A.2d 1029 (2005) (no reasonable expectation of privacy re billing records regarding defendant's cellular telephone calls); State v. Domicz, 188 N.J. 285, 907 A.2d 395 (2006) (though Kyllo v. United States, 533 U.S. 27, 121 S.Ct. 2038, 150 L.Ed.2d 94 (2001), held use of thermal imager on house a search, it does not follow that obtaining and inspecting utility records to obtain much the same information is a Fourth Amendment search, but latter subject to *McAllister*, infra); State v. Hammer, 787 N.W.2d 716 (N.D.2010) ("There is no legitimate expectation of privacy in the information kept in bank records"); State v. Evers, 175 N.J. 355, 815 A.2d 432 (2003) (no expectation of privacy "in subscriber information given to an Internet service provider"); People v. Di Raffaele, 55 N.Y.2d 234, 448 N.Y.S.2d 448, 433 N.E.2d 513 (1982) (no expectation of privacy in telephone toll billing records); State v. Lind, 322 N.W.2d 826 (N.D.1982) (no expectation of privacy in telephone company records); State v. Makuch, 340 Or. 658, 136 P.3d 35 (2006) (defendants without privacy interest in records at their lawyer's home showing they his clients or that their names written on lawyer's personal organizer, as lawyer's "representation of defendants was a matter of public record"); State v. Johnson, 340 Or. 319, 131 P.3d 173 (2006) (no expectation of privacy re records kept by defendant's "cellular telephone provider, respecting his cel-

defendant's warehouse as a result of a fire there. Two weeks later federal agents presented grand jury subpoenas to the presidents of two banks in which defendant had accounts; these subpoenas ordered production of "all records of accounts, i.e., savings, check-

---

lular telephone usage," where provider "generated and maintained these records from the provider's own equipment and for the provider's own, separate, and legitimate business purposes (such as billing)"); State v. McGoff, 517 A.2d 232 (R.I.1986) (no expectation of privacy in phone company records); State v. Fears, 659 S.W.2d 370 (Tenn. Crim.App.1983) (no expectation of privacy in medical records); State v. Simmons, 190 Vt. 141, 27 A.3d 1065 (2011) (defendant had no reasonable expectation of privacy as to his internet protocol (IP) address, obtained from internet service provider); State v. Maxfield, 125 Wash.2d 378, 886 P.2d 123 (1994) (no reasonable expectation of privacy in power consumption records); Saldana v. State, 846 P.2d 604 (Wyo.1993) ("procurement of Saldana's telephone records, including those linking his name to his unlisted telephone number, does not constitute a 'search' invading a 'legitimate expectation of privacy'"); Lafond v. State, 89 P.3d 324 (Wyo.2004) (no expectation of privacy in bank records).

However, a few jurisdictions *have* accepted the contention as a matter of state constitutional law. See, e.g., People v. Chapman, 36 Cal.3d 98, 201 Cal.Rptr. 628, 679 P.2d 62 (1984); People v. Lopez, 776 P.2d 390 (Colo. 1989) (but, no reasonable expectation under state constitution if defendant wrote bad checks); Winfield v. Division of Pari-Mutuel Wagering, 477 So.2d 544 (Fla.1985); State v. Reid, 194 N.J. 386, 945 A.2d 26 (2008) (privacy interest in subscriber information given to Internet service provider); State v. McAllister, 184 N.J. 17, 875 A.2d 866 (2005) (person has "reasonable expectation of privacy in his or her bank records, even when those records are in the possession of the bank"); Commonwealth v. DeJohn, 486 Pa. 32, 403 A.2d 1283 (1979); State v. Thompson, 810 P.2d 415 (Utah 1991); Matter of Maxfield, 133 Wash.2d 332, 945 P.2d 196 (1997) ("there is a privacy

interest in electrical consumption records preventing their disclosure by a public utility district employee without authority of law"); State v. Welch, 160 Vt. 70, 624 A.2d 1105 (1992) ("defendant does have a privacy interest that derives from her expectation that [her prescriptions on file at pharmacies] cannot be arbitrarily disclosed"); State v. Miles, 160 Wash.2d 236, 156 P.3d 864 (2007) (banking records protected by state constitution). For more on state law contrary to *Miller*, see Henderson, The Timely Demise of the Fourth Amendment Third Party Doctrine, 96 Iowa L.Rev.Bull. 39 (2011); Henderson, Beyond the (Current) Fourth Amendment: Protecting Third-Party Information, Third Parties, and the Rest of Us Too, 34 Pepp.L.Rev. 975 (2007); Henderson, Learning from All Fifty States: How to Apply the Fourth Amendment and Its State Analogs to Protect Third Party Information from Unreasonable Search, 55 Cath.U.L.Rev. 373 (2006).

Compare United States v. Knoll, 16 F.3d 1313 (2d Cir.1994) (generally, one has standing as to "those papers that a person leaves with his or her lawyer," as "the client has a subjective expectation that such papers will be kept private and such expectation is one society recognizes as reasonable," but no such expectation here because documents in question were letters which defendant had sent "to an individual with whom he had no relationship of confidentiality").

Also covered by *Miller* is the government's actions in conducting a background investigation of prospective government employees by written inquiries to the applicants' acquaintances. Nelson v. National Aeronautics and Space Administration, 530 F.3d 865 (9th Cir.2008) (such inquiries "fit squarely under *Miller*'s brightline rule," though they "may disclose highly personal information about the applicant").

ing, loan or otherwise, in the name of" defendant or his company. The banks provided microfilm records of the relevant accounts and copies of checks, deposit slips, financial statements and monthly statements. After defendant was charged with various federal offenses relating to his illegal distilling operation, he unsuccessfully sought the suppression of these records on the ground that the subpoenas were defective. The court of appeals reversed,[87] but the Supreme Court found "that there was no intrusion into any area of which respondent had a protected Fourth Amendment interest."

The court of appeals had assumed that Miller had the necessary Fourth Amendment interest, pointing to the language in *Boyd v. United States*[88] that describes that Amendment's protection against the "compulsory production of a man's private papers." But a majority of the Supreme Court[89] disagreed:

> We think that the Court of Appeals erred in finding the subpoenaed documents to fall within a protected zone of privacy.
>
> On their face, the documents subpoenaed here are not respondent's "private papers." Unlike the claimant in *Boyd,* respondent can assert neither ownership nor possession. Instead, these are the business records of the banks. * * *
>
> Respondent urges that he has a Fourth Amendment interest in the records kept by the banks because they are merely copies of personal records that were made available to the banks for a limited purpose and in which he has a reasonable expectation of privacy. He relies on this Court's statement in *Katz v. United States*[90] * * * that "we have . . . departed from the narrow view" that "property interests control the right of the Government to search and seize," and that a "search and seizure" become unreasonable when the Government's activities violate "the privacy upon which [a person] justifiably relie[s]." But in *Katz* the Court also stressed that "[w]hat a person knowingly exposes to the public . . . is not a subject of Fourth Amendment protection." * * * We must examine the nature of the particular documents sought to be protected in order to determine whether there is a legitimate "expectation of privacy" concerning their contents. * * *
>
> Even if we direct our attention to the original checks and deposit slips, rather than to the microfilm copies actually viewed and obtained by means of the subpoena, we perceive no legitimate "expectation of privacy" in their contents. The checks are not confidential communications but negotiable instruments to be used in commercial transactions. All of the documents obtained, including financial statements and deposit slips, contain only information voluntarily conveyed to the banks and exposed to their employees in the ordinary course of business. The lack of any legitimate expectation of privacy concerning the information kept in bank re-

----

[87]United States v. Miller, 500 F.2d 751 (5th Cir.1974).

[88]Boyd v. United States, 116 U.S. 616, 6 S.Ct. 524, 29 L.Ed. 746 (1886).

[89]Brennan and Marshall, JJ., wrote separate dissents.

[90]Katz v. United States, 389 U.S. 347, 88 S.Ct. 507, 19 L.Ed.2d 576 (1967).

cords was assumed by Congress in enacting the Bank Secrecy Act, the expressed purpose of which is to require records to be maintained because they "have a high degree of usefulness in criminal tax, and regulatory investigations and proceedings." * * *

The depositor takes the risk, in revealing his affairs to another, that the information will be conveyed by that person to the government. * * * This Court has held repeatedly that the Fourth Amendment does not prohibit the obtaining of information revealed to a third party and conveyed by him to Government authorities, even if the information is revealed on the assumption that it will be used only for a limited purpose and the confidence placed in the third party will not be betrayed.

In support, the Court cited the "false friend" cases of *United States v. White*,[91] *Hoffa v. United States*,[92] and *Lopez v. United States*.[93]

The result reached in *Miller* is dead wrong,[94] and the Court's woefully inadequate reasoning does great violence to the theory of Fourth Amendment protection the Court had developed in *Katz*. A bank depositor's informational control over his financial transactions "deserves Fourth Amendment protection surely as much as occupancy of telephone booths."[95] Especially "[i]n light of the massive recordkeeping of personal financial transactions, un-

---

[91]United States v. White, 401 U.S. 745, 91 S.Ct. 1122, 28 L.Ed.2d 453 (1971).

[92]Hoffa v. United States, 385 U.S. 293, 87 S.Ct. 408, 17 L.Ed.2d 374 (1966), discussed in Taslitz, Privacy as Struggle, 44 San Diego L.Rev. 501 (2007).

[93]Lopez v. United States, 373 U.S. 427, 83 S.Ct. 1381, 10 L.Ed.2d 462 (1963).

[94]For other telling criticism, see Alschuler, Interpersonal Privacy and the Fourth Amendment, 4 N.Ill.U.L. Rev. 1, 21–28 (1983); Crocker, From Privacy to Liberty: The Fourth Amendment After Lawrence, 57 UCLA L.Rev. 1 (2009); Guzik, The Assumption of Risk Doctrine: Erosion of Fourth Amendment Protection Through Fictitious Consent to Search and Seizure, 22 Santa Clara L.Rev. 1051, 1068–72 (1982); Comment, 72 J.Crim.L. & Criminology 243 (1981).

But a strong defense of the third-party doctrine is mounted in Kerr, The Case for the Third-Party Doctrine, 107 Mich.L.Rev. 561, 564–65 (2009), acknowledging that the "Supreme Court has never offered a clear argument in its favor," but contending

the doctrine "serves two roles that critics have missed": (1) maintaining "the technological neutrality of Fourth Amendment rules," in that without the doctrine "savvy wrongdoers could use third-party services in a tactical way to enshroud the entirety of their crimes in zones of Fourth Amendment protection," thus allowing "technology to upset the Fourth Amendment's traditional balance between privacy and security"; and (2) providing "ex ante clarity," in that without the doctrine "courts would face the difficult challenge of creating a clear regime of Fourth Amendment protection for third-party information." These contentions have not gone unchallenged. See Epstein, Privacy and the Third Hand: Lessons from the Common Law of Reasonable Expectations, 24 Berkeley Tech.L.J. 1199 (2009); Murphy, The Case Against the Case for Third-Party Doctrine: A Response to Epstein and Kerr, 24 Berkeley Tech.L.J. 1239 (2009); both responded to in Kerr, Defending the Third-Party Doctrine: A Response to Epstein and Murphy, 24 Berkeley Tech.L.J. 1229 (2009).

[95]Note, 83 Yale L.J. 1439, 1465 (1974).

restricted government access to bank records poses a severe threat to civil liberties and privacy,"[96] and this is true in spades as to the post–9/11 high-volume government acquisition of financial records.[97] But *Miller* holds that this access is not at all restricted by the Fourth Amendment,[98] and thus it is unquestionably true that this case has "a substantial adverse impact upon values the Fourth Amendment seeks to preserve."[99]

The Court's assertion in *Miller* that there can be no protected Fourth Amendment interest where there is "neither ownership nor possession" is contrary to the purposes underlying the Fourth Amendment, the teachings of *Katz,* and the realities of modern-day life.[100] Ownership and possession are property concepts which, the Court wisely concluded in *Katz,* cannot "serve as a talismanic solution to every Fourth Amendment problem," and which surely do not lead to the proper solution in this context.

---

[96]Note, 83 Yale L.J. 1439, 1442 (1974).

[97]Lichtblau & Bisen, Bank Data Sifted in Secret by U.S. to Block Terror, N.Y. Times, June 23, 2006, p. A1 (nat'l ed.), report that "counterterrorism officials have gained access to financial records from a vast international database and examined banking transactions involving thousands of Americans and others in the United States," "by reviewing records from the nerve center of the global banking industry, a Belgian cooperative that routes about $6 trillion daily between banks, brokerages, stock exchanges and other institutions," which "mostly involve wire transfers and other methods of moving money overseas and into and out of the United States." "The program, however, is a significant departure from typical practice in how the government acquires Americans' financial records," as "officials did not seek individual court-approved warrants or subpoenas to examine specific transactions, instead relying on broad administrative subpoenas for millions of records." This report added that "[s]everal people familiar with [this] program said they believed that they were exploiting a 'gray area' in the law and that a case could be made for restricting the government's access to the records on Fourth Amendment and statutory grounds."

[98]Though in *Miller* the authorities proceeded by subpoena, the thrust of the opinion is that the bank customer has no expectation of privacy and thus no Fourth Amendment protection no matter how egregious the police conduct resulting in government acquisition of the information in the bank records. Thus, in United States v. Payner, 447 U.S. 727, 100 S.Ct. 2439, 65 L.Ed.2d 468 (1980), where IRS agents arranged to have the bank records obtained by *burglary,* the Court without hesitation concluded that under *Miller* "a depositor has no expectation of privacy and thus no 'protectable Fourth Amendment interest' in copies of checks and deposits slips retained by his bank."

[99]Note, 83 Yale L.J. 1439, 1465 (1974).

[100]As stated by Justice Sotomayor in her concurring opinion in United States v. Jones, __ U.S. __, 132 S.Ct. 945, 181 L.Ed.2d 911 (2012), the GPS monitoring case, "it may be necessary to reconsider the premise that an individual has no reasonable expectation of privacy in information voluntarily disclosed to third parties. This approach is ill suited to the digital age, in which people reveal a great deal of information about themselves to third parties in the course of carrying out mundane tasks. * * * I would not assume that all information voluntarily disclosed to some member of the public for a limited purpose is, for that reason alone, disentitled to Fourth Amendment protection."

Unquestionably, the "Fourth Amendment's drafters were * * * concerned with privacy in the sense of control over information."[101] In simpler times, that type of privacy could be and was expressed in terms of property relationships, as information about one's personal affairs was ordinarily kept only within that individual's control and most likely within his own house. But this is no longer the case:

> Dramatic increases in urbanization and technology have caused property and privacy interests to diverge. Economic specialization has largely supplanted the individual's house or papers as repositories for personal information; computers are more efficient. There is today dependence upon hospitals and doctors' offices rather than upon bedside physicians, telephonic communications rather than direct conversation, and bank-intermediated transactions in place of direct payments, all of which generate second or third party records. Rather than suppress personal information or confine it to his home, which would be—if not impossible—grossly inefficient and severely restrictive of social and financial intercourse, the individual chooses third party intermediaries whom he believes will protect his privacy. Custom, statutory restrictions, and private remedies serve to enforce these expectations of privacy. Yet, under a "proprietary interests" interpretation of the Fourth Amendment, these nonproperty modes of informational control go unrecognized: Privacy is protected only if embodied in a proprietary relationship.[102]

Miller, by resorting to a "proprietary interest" interpretation that seemingly had been abandoned in Katz, fails to give protection to information which surely deserves to be characterized as private.[103]

Admittedly it cannot be said that all information about a person is private in the Fourth Amendment sense. Katz instructs that "[w]hat a person knowingly exposes to the public * * * is not a subject of Fourth Amendment protection," and certainly some of the information institutions collect in the course of business transactions fits that description. For example, if law enforce-

---

[101]Note, 83 Yale L.J. 1439, 1457 (1974). As noted there: "In particular the framers sought to incorporate the decision of Entick v. Carrington [19 How.St.Tr. 1029 (C.P.1765)] into the Constitution. That case involved a civil suit against agents of the Crown for their seizure of the books and papers of John Entick, an author who, Lord Halifax believed, had published several seditious pamphlets. In outlawing the use of general warrants, Entick v. Carrington was concerned with more than physical intrusion: another aspect of privacy—the individual's loss of control of information—was at stake. Lord Camden's famous opinion expressed abhorrence that the individual's 'house is rifled, his most valu-

able secrets are taken out of his possession . . . .' A fear that 'the secret cabinets and bureaus of every subject in this kingdom will be thrown open to the search and inspection of a messenger' prompted the court's holding."

[102]Note, 83 Yale L.J. 1439, 1458–59 (1974).

[103]"In other words, the privacy interest has in fact followed the information, while the law has followed the material records as tangible objects of possession. It is this discordance between fact and law which undermines the reasoning used in cases such as United States v. Miller." Comment, 14 San Diego L.Rev. 414, 424 (1977).

ment agents were allowed to consult business records that merely revealed a person's name or address or telephone number, this does not offend any interests protected by the Fourth Amendment.[104] (So too, there is no legitimate expectation of privacy as to certain other information acquired by police examination of the government's own files.[105]) But bank records are an-

---

[104]In People v. Elder, 63 Cal.App.3d 731, 134 Cal.Rptr. 212 (1976), the court concluded that the action of the gas company and telephone company in revealing names, addresses and telephone numbers from their records did not intrude upon constitutionally protected privacy:

Name and address relate to identification rather than disclosure of private, personal affairs. It is virtually impossible to live in our current society without repeated disclosure of name and address, both privately and to the government. While a myriad of reasons motivate some to reduce the degree of their identity before the public eye which includes, for example, subscribing to an unlisted telephone number, this quest for anonymity does not compel the conclusion that a reasonable expectation of privacy existed on the facts before us.

See also United States v. Cormier, 220 F.3d 1103 (9th Cir.2000) (defendant lacked reasonable expectation as to motel guest registration records of motel where he had stayed; "Miller rationale is even more compelling in the context of guest registration records because no highly personal information is disclosed to the police"); United States v. Willis, 759 F.2d 1486 (11th Cir.1985) (examination of motel records to determine when defendant registered there no search); State v. Smith, 367 N.W.2d 497 (Minn.1985) (examination of county bureau of social services records to ascertain defendant's address no search, as "any constitutional right that a person has to informational privacy clearly does not extend to his address"); Commonwealth v. Duncan, 572 Pa. 438, 817 A.2d 455 (2003) (where police merely "asked the bank only for the name and address that corresponded to the suspected rapist's ATM card number," no intrusion upon defendant's privacy merely because his

"mere name and address happened to have been obtained from a bank, as opposed to some other source"); Saldana v. State, 846 P.2d 604 (Wyo.1993) (state's acquisition of defendant's unlisted telephone number from telephone records no search); Kerr, 62 Stan.L.Rev. 1005, 1026–27 (2010) (name and address of subscriber to specific Internet account or holder of specific Internet protocol address not protected by Fourth Amendment, a conclusion reached by courts that "did not require any intellectual heavy lifting, however: it has been long established that the Fourth Amendment doesn't apply to basic subscriber information for telephone accounts, Western Union accounts, and other similar third-party accounts, and it is difficult to articulate a reason why the name and address of an Internet account should receive a different rule").

Compare People v. Chapman, 36 Cal.3d 98, 201 Cal.Rptr. 628, 679 P.2d 62 (1984) (under state constitution, defendant had reasonable expectation of privacy in her unlisted name, address and telephone number; Elder, disapproved); State v. Butterworth, 48 Wash.App. 152, 737 P.2d 1297 (1987) (state constitution protected defendant's unpublished telephone listing).

[105]United States v. Ellison, 462 F.3d 557 (6th Cir.2006) (using license plate number to run computer check of Law Enforcement Information Network ("LEIN") files no search, as such "technology * * * does not allow officers to access any previously-unobtainable information"); United States v. Bowley, 435 F.3d 426 (3d Cir.2006) ("an alien has no reasonable expectation of privacy in a file that is maintained solely by a government agency for official purposes and kept in the custody of that agency"); Willan v. Columbia County, 280 F.3d 1160 (7th Cir.2002) ("Records of conviction

other matter, for unquestionably they "can reveal much about a

are public rather than private documents, however; the information in them is not the property of the convicted persons, and therefore the National Crime Information Center had every right, at least so far as the Constitution is concerned, to record and disseminate Willan's conviction"); People v. Bailey, 232 Ill.2d 285, 328 Ill.Dec. 22, 903 N.E.2d 409 (2009) ("a warrant check is not a search"); Smith v. State, 744 N.E.2d 437 (Ind.2001) (collecting cases in accord, court rules that where defendant's body and blood samples used to develop DNA profile, that profile may be maintained as a government record and later used to compare with other DNA evidence); State v. Bowman, 337 S.W.3d 679 (Mo.2011) (re transfer of DNA sample to another state 6 years after acquired, "the subsequent use of the DNA sample obtained from the valid search and seizure does not constitute a Fourth Amendment violation"); State v. Sloane, 193 N.J. 423, 939 A.2d 796 (2008) ("an NCIC check is not a search," as "the NCIC database is comprised of matters of public record"); State v. Boyd, 654 N.W.2d 392 (N.D.2002) ("an officer's check of a license plate does not implicate an individual's Fourth Amendment rights," and thus officer "did not need a reasonable suspicion of criminal activity to initially check Boyd's license plate" before stop); State v. Bjerke, 697 A.2d 1069 (R.I.1997) (computer check re defendant's license plate no search, as such information "within the control and custody of the state through the Registry of Motor Vehicles," and it "well known to all that the state is the very body that issues, controls, and regulates motor vehicle registration license plates"); State v. McKinney, 148 Wash.2d 20, 60 P.3d 46 (2002) (checking vehicle registration and records of associated drivers' license records without probable cause or reasonable suspicion no violation of *state* right to privacy, considering "the historical treatment of driver's license records, the fact that these records reveal little about a person's associa-

tions, financial dealings, or movements, and the purpose for which the state complies and maintains these records").

But see Commonwealth v. Buccella, 434 Mass. 473, 751 N.E.2d 373 (2001) (court proceeds to "assume" without deciding that defendant, a high school student, "had a reasonable expectation of privacy with respect to his school papers, notwithstanding the fact that he had turned them over to his teachers"; court opines it "would appear reasonable to expect that a government agency, to which a citizen is required to submit certain materials, will use those materials solely for the purposes intended and not disclose them to others in ways that are unconnected with those intended purposes"); State v. Donis, 157 N.J. 44, 723 A.2d 35 (1998) (under *state* constitution, court holds random license plate checks using mobile data units in police cars to check state and federal records lawful provided terminals reprogrammed so that initial random license plate look-up would display information regarding only registration status of vehicle, license plate statute of registered owner, and whether vehicle has been reported stolen; if original inquiry disclosed basis for further police action, then police officer would proceed to second step, which would allow access to personal information of registered owner, including name, address, social security number, and if available, criminal record). For more on the use of these mobile data terminals and proposed suggestions for limitations on their use, see Amirante, People v. Barnes-George Orwell's 1994 Revisited: Unbridled and Impermissible Police Use of Computer Power in the Modern Age, 28 Loy.U.Chi.L.J. 667 (1997); Cedres, Mobile Data Terminals and Random License Plate Checks: The Need for Uniform Guidelines and a Reasonable Suspicion Requirement, 23 Rutgers Computer & Tech. L.J. 391 (1997); Note, 17 J.Marshall J. Computer & Info.L. 1235 (1999).

person's activities, associations, and beliefs."[106]

The records of checks—now available to investigators—are highly useful. In a sense a person is defined by the checks he writes. By examining them the agents get to know his doctors, lawyers, creditors, political allies, social connections, religious affiliation, education interests, the papers and magazines he reads and so on *ad infinitum.* These are all tied to one's social security number; and now that we have the data banks, these other items will enrich that storehouse and make it possible for a bureaucrat—by pushing one button—to get in an instant the names of the 190 million Americans who are subversives or potential and likely candidates.[107]

Had the Court in *Miller* been true to *Katz,* it would have focused on two critical questions: (i) whether it may fairly be said that a bank depositor has "exhibited an actual (subjective) expectation of privacy" in the bank records of his financial transactions; and (ii) if so, whether that expectation is "one that society is prepared to recognize as 'reasonable.' "[108] Both of these inquiries deserve an affirmative answer. "It cannot be gainsaid that the customer of a bank expects that the documents, such as checks, which he transmits to the bank in the course of his business operations will remain private."[109]

Commercial banks have rigorously maintained the confidentiality of checking account transactions. Generally information is released to private parties only upon consent of the depositor and is confined to credit information. Raw transactional data usually desired by government agencies are never released to private parties, and breaches of this customary secrecy are rare. This confidential rela-

---

[106]Powell, J., concurring in California Bankers Ass'n v. Shultz, 416 U.S. 21, 94 S.Ct. 1494, 39 L.Ed.2d 812 (1974).

As can telephone toll records, as is apparent from the fact that "law enforcement agencies and grand juries currently issue subpoenas and summonses for toll-call records relevant to felony investigations at the rate of approximately 2,000–3,000 each month." Reporters Committee for Freedom of the Press v. American Telephone & Telegraph Co., 192 U.S.App.D.C. 376, 593 F.2d 1030 (1978). The same may be said of records of one's purchases kept by a credit card company, held to be deserving of protection as a matter of state law in People v. Blair, 25 Cal.3d 640, 159 Cal.Rptr. 818, 602 P.2d 738 (1979), relying upon *Burrows,* note 109 infra.

As can even library records disclosing who is reading what. See Comment, 30 Am.U.L.Rev. 275 (1980). It is concluded therein at 321 that

limited disclosure should be allowed when relevant to a criminal case: "Disclosure, however, should take place only under judicial supervision, with close attention paid to the degree to which the state's interest in the information is content-neutral, as indicated by the relevance of the individual's reading practices to the criminal act under investigation." For criticism of the broader availability of patrons' library records under the PATRIOT Act, see Note, 29 J.Legis. 283 (2003).

[107]Douglas, J., dissenting in California Bankers Ass'n v. Shultz, 416 U.S. 21, 94 S.Ct. 1494, 39 L.Ed.2d 812 (1974).

[108]This is the formulation in Justice Harlan's concurring opinion, which lower courts have typically utilized in applying *Katz.*

[109]Burrows v. Superior Court, 13 Cal.3d 238, 118 Cal.Rptr. 166, 529 P.2d 590 (1974).

tionship is supported by more than custom: Banks are under a legal obligation to maintain the secrecy of their depositors' transactions. Although the duty of secrecy is not unqualified, the courts have made it clear that the banker functions as an agent in handling account information: He can release data only if consistent with that role. Thus even without property rights, the depositor has customary and legal rights to control the revelation of checking account information.[110]

The *Miller* Court purports to rebut all of this with the observation that there can be no expectation of privacy in bank records because Congress enacted the Bank Secrecy Act for the express purpose of requiring the keeping of records that would be useful to criminal investigators. But surely the *Katz* expectation of privacy cannot be defeated in this fashion. "If it could, the government could diminish each person's subjective expectation of privacy merely by announcing half-hourly on television that * * * we were all forthwith being placed under comprehensive electronic surveillance."[111]

The second *Katz* inquiry in essence calls for a value judgment, namely, whether if the police practice in question were not regulated by the constitution our privacy "would be diminished to a compass inconsistent with the aims of a free and open society."[112] Although in many contexts this question cannot be resolutely answered, there is no need for uncertainty upon the facts of *Miller*. Given the enormous quantity of information about people which can be gleaned from business records, and the highly personal character of much of this information (especially when it is all sorted and related to particular individuals), unrestrained police access to such data would constitute a devastating imposition upon privacy. As was stated in *Burrows v. Superior Court*:[113]

> To permit a police officer access to these records merely upon his request, without any judicial control as to relevancy or other traditional requirements of legal process, and to allow the evidence to be used in any subsequent criminal prosecution against a defendant, opens the door to a vast and unlimited range of very real abuses of police power.

There remains for consideration the *Miller* Court's reliance upon the "false friend" cases: *White, Hoffa,* and *Lopez.* As noted in *White*, "*Hoffa*, * * * which was left undisturbed by *Katz*, held that however strongly a defendant may trust an apparent colleague, his expectations in this respect are not protected by the Fourth Amendment when it turns out that the colleague is a government agent regularly communicating with the authorities." If it could be said in *Hoffa* that "no interest legitimately protected

---

[110]Note, 83 Yale L.J. 1439, 1463–64 (1974).

[111]Amsterdam, Perspectives on the Fourth Amendment, 58 Minn.L.Rev. 349, 384 (1974).

[112]Amsterdam, 58 Minn.L.Rev. 349, 403 (1974).

[113]Burrows v. Superior Court, 13 Cal.3d 238, 118 Cal.Rptr. 166, 529 P.2d 590 (1974).

by the Fourth Amendment is involved" when what is said in confidence to an old friend is by prearrangement related by that friend to the authorities, then, the Court in effect says in *Miller,* surely no such interest is involved when what was revealed in confidence to the bank is revealed to the police. But this will not wash, for *Miller* is different from *White, Hoffa* and *Lopez* in two significant respects.

For one thing, *Hoffa* stresses that the Fourth Amendment will not come to the rescue of one who "voluntarily confides his wrongdoing" to another. Hoffa could have been more circumspect in his choice of associates, and having taken Partin into his confidence, he cannot now complain. Miller's disclosures to his two banks, however, are certainly not voluntary in the same sense. As noted in *Burrows,* "[f]or all practical purposes, the disclosure by individuals or business firms of their financial affairs to a bank is not entirely volitional, since it is impossible to participate in the economic life of contemporary society without maintaining a bank account." Because "banks are inescapable intermediaries in modern commercial transactions,"[114] an individual's decision to utilize the facilities of a bank cannot be fairly said to constitute a surrender of his privacy. Even if it may be said that the risk Hoffa took "is the kind of risk we necessarily assume whenever we speak,"[115] it by no means follows that the Fourth Amendment likewise leaves the potential bank customer with "the unsavory dilemma of either not using the banking system or using it and waiving his protectible privacy interest."[116]

Secondly, in *Hoffa* there is no question but that the authorities obtained nothing more than facts Hoffa willingly revealed to his false friend Partin. Hoffa made incriminating statements in the immediate presence of Partin, and quite clearly he knew that Partin perceived the significance of those comments. But this was not the case in *Miller.* There, what the government learned as a result of examining several checks was that Miller had made certain purchases of various items from certain specified individuals. That is, the government was interested in and learned of the underlying transactional information, but this is not the information Miller would expect the bank to be interested in. One discloses his private papers to a bank "for a limited

---

[114]Comment, 14 San Diego L.Rev. 414, 431 (1977).

[115]As the Court put it in the *Hoffa* case.

[116]Comment, 14 San Diego L.Rev. 414, 431 (1977). Indeed, "most third party record-holders possess information about us because we cannot otherwise realistically function in the modern world. Thus, contrary to the Supreme Court's assertion in *Miller,* the surrender of personal information to these third parties is hardly 'voluntary.' Nor does it, or should it, lead us to 'assume' that the third party will function as an institutional undercover agent, a conduit for any information the government wants." Slobogin, Transaction Surveillance by the Government, 75 Miss.L.J. 139, 171 (2005).

977

purpose," and thus he "has a reasonable expectation that his check will be examined for bank purposes only—to credit, debit or balance his account."[117] This expectation accords with reality, as "the banker has virtually no occasion to gain access to or make use of the underlying transactional information."[118]

> With the exception of a cursory inspection of the original item to insure that the check is not postdated and that signatures and endorsements are genuine, bankers rarely have any legitimate business use for the underlying transactional data. Once a check is paid and returned, these data—names of payees, dates on checks, endorsements, and other memoranda—are recorded only in microfilms of checks. A considerable effort may thereafter be required to obtain the information * * *. The cursory nature of the bank's inspection of checks cannot be overemphasized. The banking system currently processes some 30 billion checks per year.

> The increasing mechanization of the banking industry continues to reduce the chances that any human agent would come into any direct, significant contact with the underlying transactional information.[119]

Thus, it cannot be said, as claimed in *Miller,* that when a law enforcement agent is allowed to give detailed scrutiny to an individual's banking records, he is only discovering that which the bank customer expected bank employees to be aware of. Bank employees see a particular customer's checks only briefly and not all at one time, and thus they are not in a position "to construct accurate conclusions about the customer's lifestyle."[120] But when the police are permitted to give all of that customer's banking records a thorough and exhaustive examination, they will have learned a great deal more about the customer; "the totality of bank records provides a virtual current biography."[121] It is the acquiring of such detailed personal information the Court declined to subject to Fourth Amendment restraints, and this is why the *Miller* decision is so pernicious.[122]

Miller 's application to search of computerized information

---

[117]Marshall, J., dissenting in California Bankers Ass'n v. Shultz, 416 U.S. 21, 94 S.Ct. 1494, 39 L.Ed.2d 812 (1974).

[118]Note, 83 Yale L.J. 1439, 1463 (1974).

[119]Note, 83 Yale. L.J. 1439, 1463 n. 114 (1974).

[120]Comment, 14 San Diego L.Rev. 414, 425 n. 81 (1977).

[121]Burrows v. Superior Court, 13 Cal.3d 238, 118 Cal.Rptr. 166, 529 P.2d 590 (1974).

[122]Although *statutory* protections of such records are beyond the scope of this Treatise, note should be made here of the "Right to Financial Privacy Act of 1978," 12 U.S.C.A. §§ 3401 et seq., which requires that a copy of any federal subpoena or summons for financial records be served on the customer with full notice of his right to challenge the subpoena or summons in court prior to its execution 10 days hence, unless a "protective order" is obtained upon a showing that such notice would seriously jeopardize the investigation. For discussion of the Act, see Comments, 8 Fordham Urb.L.J. 597 (1980); 13 U.S.F.L.Rev. 485 (1979). The Act does not itself require suppression of evidence obtained in violation of the Act, and courts have declined to suppress in

when, as is increasingly common, one person's records are stored on another party's computer under a timesharing system, remains to be determined.[123] Though it doubtless will be claimed that the *Miller* assumption of risk analysis readily applies here as well, one commentator has plausibly argued the correct result is otherwise. This is because "computer operators have no legitimate purpose in reading records unrelated to the operator's function, just as the telephone company has no legitimate purpose in listening to the contents of conversations."[124] But even if this is so, the situation is different as to file directories, for they "relate to business between the timesharer and the computer operator, analogous to the bank records in *Miller* and the numbers dialed in *Smith*."[125] (This result is wrong for the very same reasons that *Miller* and *Smith* are wrong; the timesharer should not lose his expectation of privacy vis-a-vis the government merely because he has made certain information accessible to one other person.)

Also deserving mention here is the increasingly popular law enforcement practice of obtaining information from a company operating an internet search engine (e.g., Google) regarding the kinds of searches conducted from a particular computer. Such information, which can sometimes be highly incriminating,[126] is available because the companies operating search engines maintain records, at least for some period of time, of "every search query ever sent from a specific IP address" as well as "which links users click after inputting search queries."[127] As yet, "[n]o case has decided whether there is a constitutional right to privacy

---

such circumstances in the exercise of their supervisory power. United States v. Kington, 801 F.2d 733 (5th Cir. 1986); United States v. Frazin, 780 F.2d 1461 (9th Cir.1986). The limit on use of subpoenaed financial records in § 3420(a) "does not prohibit the Government from using the subpoenaed bank records to obtain a search warrant." United States v. Jackson, 11 F.3d 953 (10th Cir.1993).

About one-third of the states have enacted similar legislation. See citations collected in State v. Schultz, 252 Kan. 819, 850 P.2d 818 (1993). For more on search of bank records as a violation of state law, see Annot., 33 A.L.R.5th 453 (1995).

[123]This subject is discussed in more detail in § 2.6(f).

[124]Note, 67 B.U.L.Rev. 179, 204 (1987).

[125]Note, 67 B.U.L.Rev. 179, 204 (1987).

[126]Lawless, The Third Party Doctrine Redux: Internet Search Records and the Case for a "Crazy Quilt" of Fourth Amendment Protection, 2007 UCLA J.L. & Tech. 1, ¶ 2 (describing homicide case in which it established that what appeared to be a robbery in which defendant was wounded in the chest and his wife was killed was actually an instance of the defendant killing his wife and wounding himself to divert suspicion; useful evidence was defendant's earlier Google search for "trauma cases gunshot right chest" to learn how to survive such injury); Soghkoian, The Problem of Anonymous Vanity Searches, 3 I/S 299, 301 (2007) ("In one case, a murder suspect's search records were produced in court to prove that he had searched for the words 'neck,' 'snap,' and 'break' before killing his wife").

[127]Foley, Are Google Searches Private? An Originalist Interpretation of the Fourth Amendment in Online Communication Cases, 22 Berkeley

in queries entered into a search engine,"[128] but clearly "the broad 'assumption-of-risk' language in *Miller* and *Smith* provides the basis for arguments that search engine users lack an expectation of privacy in communications held by search engines."[129] Nor, so the argument goes, is the "exception to the third party doctrine * * * known as the 'content/envelope' distinction"[130] relevant here, as "individuals disclose information to search engines in order to locate information on the Web. Consequently, there would be no Fourth Amendment protection for Internet search records under the third party doctrine because any disclosure of that information to the government would be done by a recipient of the communication, not a messenger."[131] Perhaps, then, this is simply yet another instance in which *Miller* and *Smith* produce the wrong result, considering the fact that "it is increasingly more difficult for Americans to function without the Internet."[132] But there is something to be said for the proposition that, even in the face of *Miller* and *Smith*, a different result ought to be reached in the situation here under discussion. As one commentator put it,

> there is a qualitative difference between search query entries and other kinds of transactional data routinely provided to third parties in the course of business. A phone number is "content neutral" and does not give law enforcement any means to reconstruct the conversation itself. By contrast, search terms contain precise language that reveals topics researched. This allows government access to types of information it never had when *Katz*, *Miller*, and *Smith* were decided. * * *
>
> [I]nternet searches are more akin to the "private papers" traditionally protected by the Fourth Amendment than "business records" at issue in *Miller* and *Smith*. In *Miller* and *Smith*, the Court noted that the content intercepted was not "personal," but "business records." When the government obtains bank records, as in *Miller*, it learns what transactions were made and by whom, but not the underlying subjects and circumstances of the transactions. By contrast, a Google search query * * * allows the government to research responsive URLs, and may prompt subpoenas to obtain a user's IP address and identity. * * * The "content" of these queries

---

Tech.L.J. 447, 449–50 (2007).

[128]Foley, 22 Berkeley Tech.L.J. 447, 467 (2007).

[129]Foley, 22 Berkeley Tech.L.J. 447, 457 (2007).

[130]Lawless, 2007 UCLA J.L. & Tech. 1, ¶ 16, citing Kerr, Internet Surveillance Law After the USA Patriot Act: The Big Brother That Isn't, 97 Nw.U.L.Rev. 607, 611(2003). In *Katz*, the Court referred to the overheard phone conversation as "content," while in *Smith* the telephone numbers obtained by the pen register device were "envelope" information. See also

Tokson, The Content/Envelope Distinction in Internet Law, 50 Wm. & Mary L.Rev. 2105 (2009).

[131]Lawless, 2007 UCLA J.L. & Tech. 1, ¶ 34.

[132]Scribner, Subpoena to Google Inc. in ACLU v. Gonzales: "Big Brother" is Watching Your Internet Searches Through Government Subpoenas, 75 U.Cin.L.Rev. 1273, 1292 (2007). See also Bagley, Don't be Evil: The Fourth Amendment in the Age of Google, National Security, and Digital Papers and Effects, 21 Alb.L.J.Sci. & Tech. 153 (2011).

is more closely aligned with the phone conversation in *Katz* than to digits dialed on a phone or bank records one knows a human teller might read, at issue in *Smith* and *Miller*.[133]

Given the many unfortunate consequences that have followed the lamentable *Miller* decision, it may well be, as one thoughtful commentator has proposed, that there is a need

> for privity analysis to replace privacy analysis in cases involving information held outside the custody of its originator. In such cases, privity provides a more precise way of describing the potential harms that result from the government's seizure of personal data. Unlike privacy, privity is a highly intersubjective concept that would require judges to ask not only "whether the information has been exposed," but also "to whom" and "to what end." Put simply, privity describes a particular type of privacy interest that is affected when the government compels individuals to turn over others' confidential information or communications.[134]

Miller notwithstanding, one court has held that the client of an attorney has a legitimate expectation of privacy in his file. Deeming it irrelevant that the client had no general expectation of privacy as to the attorney's offices and had no possessory or ownership interest even in his own file, the court in *DeMassa v. Nunez*[135] reasoned:

> It is axiomatic that the attorney-client privilege confers upon the *client* an expectation of privacy in his or her confidential communications with the attorney. * * *
>
> Constitutional guarantees also support the legitimacy of the client's expectation of privacy in this case. To the extent that the right to effective assistance of counsel in a separate criminal case is at stake, the Sixth Amendment provides an additional "source" and "understanding" of this expectation of privacy. * * * Because the Fifth Amendment's protection against testimonial self-incrimination may be threatened by the act of disclosure of legal files, that constitutional guarantee also supports the clients' legitimate expectation of privacy. * * *
>
> The expectation of privacy in an attorney-client file thus has roots in federal and state statutory and common law and in the United States Constitution, among other sources. Indeed, there is no body of law or recognized source of professional ethics in which this "source" or "understanding" is lacking.

But this expectation of privacy does not extend to incriminating physical objects where "the attorney had an ethical obligation * * * to deliver the physical items to the police * * * in advance

---

[133]Foley, 22 Berkeley Tech.L.J. 447, 467, 469–70 (2007).

[134]Note, 115 Yale L.J. 1086, 1090 (2006). Similarly, Brenner, The Fourth Amendment in a Era of Ubiquitous Technology, 75 Miss.L.J. 1, 76 (2005), suggests we should "incorporate another, broader conception of shared privacy into the Fourth Amendment in order to protect the privacy of information I share with certain third parties."

[135]DeMassa v. Nunez, 770 F.2d 1505 (9th Cir.1985).

of trial."[136]

While *DeMassa* merely relied upon the attorney-client privilege, it has been forcefully argued that the Fourth Amendment itself "is violated whenever law enforcement officials have reason to believe that a search or seizure is likely to expose them to privileged attorney-client communications and fail to take reasonable steps to minimize their exposure.[137] As explained,

> there are cases in which a search and seizure is unreasonable even if supported by probable cause and authorized by a judicial official. For example, in *Winston v Lee*,[138] the Supreme Court held that performing a court-ordered surgery on a suspect in order to remove a bullet from his chest would violate the suspect's Fourth Amendment rights. The Court reasoned that "(a) compelled surgical intrusion into an individual's body for evidence ( ) implicates expectations of privacy and security of such magnitude that the intrusion may be 'unreasonable' even if likely to produce evidence of a crime." [T]he attorney-client privilege embodies a privacy interest of such magnitude that searches and seizures of privileged attorney-client communications are unreasonable even if likely to produce evidence of a crime.[139]

As concluded in the carefully reasoned decision in *People v. Gutierrez*,[140] yet another situation in which *Miller* "is inapplicable" is with regard to an individual's tax return information stored in the files of a professional tax preparer. For one thing, the laws of the several states as well as federal law protect the privacy of tax return information even when it is in the custody of the IRS, a state department of revenue, or a tax preparer.

> [T]his reflects a broad societal understanding that, when an individual prepares and files a tax return, he does so for the IRS and no one else. And he retains an expectation of privacy in such information against intrusion by criminal law enforcement agencies, even when disclosed to others for the purpose of facilitating compliance with state and federal tax laws.

Moreover, "the facts giving rise to an individual's privacy interest in his or her tax return contrast starkly from the facts presented in *Miller*." This is because *Miller* concerned records maintained under the Bank Secrecy Act that would "have a high degree of usefulness in criminal tax, and regulatory investigations and proceedings,"[141] while the applicable federal statute regarding tax materials[142] "makes it more difficult for law enforcement agencies to obtain tax returns for non-tax criminal investigations and prosecutions." This being the case, the *Gutierrez* court concluded,

[136]Rubin v. State, 325 Md. 552, 602 A.2d 677 (1992).

[137]Comment, 72 U.Chi.L.Rev. 729, 730 (2005).

[138]Winston v. Lee, 470 U.S. 753, 105 S.Ct. 1611, 84 L.Ed.2d 662 (1985), discussed in § 4.1(e).

[139]Comment, 72 U.Chi.L.Rev. 729, 732 (2005).

[140]People v. Gutierrez, 222 P.3d 925 (Colo.2009).

[141]12 U.S.C.A. § 1829b(b)(1).

[142]26 U.S.C.A. § 6103.

"a taxpayer who entrusts his tax return to the care of a tax preparer for purposes of complying with federal and state tax law does *not* assume the risk that the tax preparer will voluntarily divulge the information to law enforcement."[143]

§ 2.7(d) Examination of medical records

The previously discussed *Miller* decision of the Supreme Court has also been relied upon in cases where the issue is whether one has a protected expectation of privacy in one's medical records. A leading case is *People v. Perlos,*[144] involving several defendants who were involved in automobile accidents as drivers and who, after they were hospitalized, were subjected to blood tests to measure the alcohol content in their blood. These tests were made for purposes of medical treatment and consequently did not themselves violate the Fourth Amendment.[145] The results of those tests, which showed each of the defendants had been intoxicated, were later turned over to the prosecutor pursuant to a state statute declaring such test results "admissible in a criminal prosecution" and further requiring that the "medical facility or person performing the chemical analysis shall disclose the results of the analysis to a prosecuting attorney who requests the results for use in a criminal prosecution."

Although some of the court's discussion in *Perlos* might be construed as saying the statute involved Fourth Amendment activity which was reasonable in light of "the need for effective laws to curtail drunken driving," the central issue as perceived by the court was: "did defendants have privacy interests in their blood alcohol test results?" The court answered in the negative, declaring it agreed

> with the rationale underlying *United States v. Miller* suggesting that there is no objectively reasonable expectation of privacy in the test results. Clearly, defendants cannot claim ownership or possession of the results. Also, as stated in *Miller,* information revealed to a third party, even for a limited purpose, can properly be conveyed to the government even if the information was revealed in confidence. In these cases, blood was taken for a limited purpose, medical treatment. As in *Miller,* * * * the information conveyed was not privileged. Under the *Miller* analysis, once the hospitals obtained the results for medical purposes, it would have been unreasonable for defendants to assume that the results would necessarily remain private. At the very least, various hospital employees become aware of the test results in the normal course of their work. Society places a risk on persons in their dealings with third parties that information conveyed to third parties will not remain private.

---

[143]The court went on to hold that "unless the custodian or business itself is pervaded by fraud, probable cause must be analyzed in relation to each individual's constitutionally protected interests," that is, in the instant case there needed to be "probable cause to search Gutierrez's individual file," which was lacking.

[Section 2.7(d)]

[144]People v. Perlos, 436 Mich. 305, 462 N.W.2d 310 (1990).

[145]See § 1.8(d) at note 187.

Moreover, while in *Miller* the government was allowed access to all of the respondent's bank records, in the instant case, the state could only obtain an extremely limited and well-defined portion of defendants' overall medical records.

Other cases supporting the *Perlos* decision are to be found,[146] but there is also authority reaching the contrary conclusion.[147]

---

[146]Young v. Murphy, 90 F.3d 1225 (7th Cir.1996) ("nursing home records reporting his condition and treatment"); Pollard v. State, 439 N.E.2d 177 (Ind.App.1982); State v. Davis, 161 N.H. 292, 12 A.3d 1271 (2010) ("society does not recognize a reasonable expectation of privacy in blood alcohol test results obtained and recorded by a hospital as part of its consensual treatment of a patient, where these results are requested by law enforcement and for law enforcement purposes in connection with an incident giving rise to an investigation for driving while under the influence"); State v. Dyal, 97 N.J. 229, 478 A.2d 390 (1984); State v. Guido, 698 A.2d 729 (R.I.1997) ("defendant had no legitimate expectation of privacy in Rhode Island Hospital's medical records relating to his emergency treatment," as "those records were produced by medical personnel for their use in providing medical treatment"); State v. Hardy, 963 S.W.2d 516 (Tex.Crim. App.1997); State v. Jenkins, 80 Wis.2d 426, 259 N.W.2d 109 (1977).

As for the penumbral right to privacy recognized in Griswold v. Connecticut, 381 U.S. 479, 85 S.Ct. 1678, 14 L.Ed.2d 510 (1965), though its "boundaries * * * have not been delineated clearly," the prevailing view is that "this constitutionally protected right to confidentiality extends to medical information or records," and therefore "a person reasonably may expect that his or her prescription records or information contained therein will not be disseminated publicly," but this right is subject to a balancing test whereby it has been "reduced drastically," and there is "no case * * * in which a court has held that a law enforcement officer's access to prescription records violates the patient's right of privacy." State v. Russo, 259 Conn. 436, 790

A.2d 1132 (2002).

[147]Doe v. Broderick, 225 F.3d 440 (4th Cir.2000) (in holding patient at methadone clinic had a legitimate expectation of privacy in his records on file there, court stated: "The reason for this is apparent: medical treatment records contain intimate and private details that people do not wish to have disclosed, expect will remain private, and, as a result, believe are entitled to some measure of protection from unfettered access by government officials"); King v. State, 276 Ga. 126, 577 S.E.2d 764 (2003) (*state* constitutional right to privacy in personal medical records means that if records to be obtained by subpoena, then person affected to be given advance notice and opportunity to object, but such procedure not necessary if records obtained pursuant to search warrant); State v. Skinner, 10 So. 3d 1212 (La.2009) (collecting cases concluding "the constitutional right to privacy extends to medical and/or prescription records," court thus holds "the Fourth Amendment * * * require[s] a search warrant before a search of prescription and medical records for criminal investigative purposes is permitted"); State v. Copeland, 680 S.W.2d 327 (Mo.App.1984); State v. Bilant, 307 Mont. 113, 36 P.3d 883 (2001) (medical record information possessed by defendant's health care provider protected by guarantee of "informational privacy" in *state* constitution); State v. Nelson, 283 Mont. 231, 941 P.2d 441 (1997) (under state constitution, defendant had a protected privacy expectation in his medical records); In re Search Warrant for Medical Records of C.T., 160 N.H. 214, 999 A.2d 210 (2010) (in light of physician-patient privilege statute, court per supervisory powers requires that when warrant executed for medical records they be produced under seal for in camera

The criticism of *Miller* set out earlier[148] is perhaps even more applicable to the reasoning in *Perlos,* as the *Perlos* dissent effectively elaborated:

> A person's medical records are an intensely personal matter. Few persons would willingly share their medical records with the state. In today's society, a person has little choice but to undergo medical treatment at a medical facility, generally licensed by and authorized to operate by the state. Few persons have the ability to obtain medical treatment in their homes, and even such persons would, of necessity, employ physicians and other medically trained persons who would be subject to the statutory edict.

> * * *

> Under the circumstances that a person who becomes involved in an automobile accident, in need of medical treatment, ordinarily has no choice but to permit himself to be transported to a medical facility and to allow blood to be withdrawn for the purpose of emergent medical treatment, and having in mind the intensely personal nature of medical records, the permission granted by the driver for such purpose—to the medical facility and not to the state—differs from lodging, in nonemergent circumstances, tax records with an accountant, or financial records with a bank.

By like reasoning it has been held that a hospital patient has a legitimate expectation of privacy in the blood taken for medical treatment itself, so that it is an illegal search for the police to induce hospital personnel to provide some of the blood that is then tested by a police agency to determine blood alcohol content.[149]

Although the Supreme Court declared in *Ferguson v. City of*

---

review by court with notice to patient and medical provider of opportunity to object to disclosure, in which case state must establish "essential need" for the information); Commonwealth v. Riedel, 539 Pa. 172, 651 A.2d 135 (1994) ("appellant does have a reasonable expectation of privacy in his medical records," but search here lawful, as on probable cause and by officer who could have earlier obtained warrantless testing because of exigent circumstances). See also Comment, 34 Seton Hall L.Rev. 943 (2004) (on need for privacy in medical records).

Cf. State v. Mubita, 145 Idaho 925, 188 P.3d 867 (2008) (when defendant tested HIV positive, he requested HIV-related services from local health department, which required that he execute and give department documents certifying his HIV status; department later gave those documents to prosecutor in response to request;

in holding this case governed by *Miller,* the court stressed that the "documents are the Health Department's own forms, which Mubita executed in order to receive the desired services. These are not medical records, containing information he revealed to his own physician in order to obtain medical treatment, but rather business records maintained by the Health Department to administer its HIV services").

Consider also Bowling v. State, 289 Ga. 881, 717 S.E.2d 190 (2011) (even assuming defendant had a reasonable expectation of privacy in his medical records, such privacy "not absolute," and thus records could be obtained via search warrant, as here).

[148]See § 2.7(c).

[149]State v. Comeaux, 818 S.W.2d 46 (Tex.Crim.App.1991), discussed in § 2.6(b).

Charleston[150] that the "reasonable expectation of privacy enjoyed by the typical patient undergoing diagnostic tests in a hospital is that the results of those tests will not be shared with nonmedical personnel without her consent," this should not be taken as an expression of disapproval of the result in cases such as *Perlos*.[151] This is because the very taking of the urine sample in *Ferguson* was pursuant to a program developed with the participation of law enforcement for the testing of pregnant women for drugs at a state hospital with the understanding that the results would be turned over to law enforcement agents, and the purported "special need" justifying such action was found wanting precisely because this program was thus shown to be insufficiently "divorced from the State's general interest in law enforcement."[152] *Ferguson,* then, as the majority put it at one point, was a case where the "hospital staff * * * intentionally set out to obtain incriminating evidence from their patients for law enforcement purposes."[153]

§ 2.7(e) Data aggregation and mining

In recent years, an immense amount of personal information has been collected and stored by governments and also in the private sector, a process greatly facilitated by the advent of sophisticated computers. "As computer processing speeds accelerated, and as computer memory ballooned, computers provided a vastly increased ability to collect, search, analyze, copy, and transfer records."[154] With respect to the federal government, "agencies and departments maintain almost 2000 databases, including records pertaining to immigration, bankruptcy, Social Security, military personnel, as well as countless other matters. * * * States maintain public records of arrest, births, criminal proceedings, marriages, divorces, property ownership, voter registration, workers compensation, and scores of other types of

---

[150]Ferguson v. City of Charleston, 532 U.S. 67, 121 S.Ct. 1281, 149 L.Ed.2d 205 (2001).

[151]See, e.g., Kerns v. Bader, 663 F.3d 1173 (10th Cir.2011), relying upon analysis in text following.

[152]Even the dissenters in *Charleston* agreed that if the taking of the urine sample was a search, then "the subsequent testing and reporting of the results to the police are obviously part of (or infected by) the same search."

[153]The Court put it this way to emphasize that the holding in *Ferguson* did not extend to a case "in which state hospital employees, like other citizens, may have a duty to provide law enforcement officials with evidence of criminal conduct acquired in the

course of routine treatment."

In Reedy v. Evanson, 615 F.3d 197 (3d Cir.2010), plaintiff provided a blood sample as part of a rape kit examination following her sexual assault. Later, a police officer who suspected her of drug use asked hospital personnel to do additional testing of plaintiff's blood sample. Relying upon the above-quoted language in *Ferguson*, the court held that such testing, beyond the bounds of the consent she had initially given, "violated the Fourth Amendment."

[Section 2.7(e)]

[154]Solove, Privacy and Power: Computer Databases and Metaphors for Information Privacy, 53 Stan.L. Rev. 1393, 1402 (2001).

records," including licensing records "on numerous professionals such as doctors, lawyers, engineers, insurance agents, nurses, police, accountants, and teachers."[155] In the private sector, the demand for information useful in developing marketing and advertising strategies has increased to the point where today "corporations are desperate for whatever consumer information they can glean," and they now seek "information about the consumer herself, often including lifestyle details and even a full-scale psychological profile."[156] This has given rise to "the creation of a new industry: the database industry," where "personal data collections are bartered and sold";[157] along "with companies whose databases were an outgrowth of their business, a new breed of firms devotes their primary business to the collection of personal information."[158] The public and private data collections are by no means separate and distinct; the public sector has "obtained * * * demographic information from the federal government,"[159] while in turn federal law enforcement agencies have acquired data that was collected in the private sector.[160]

In the post-9/11 era, many responsible analysts have called for "the increased use of data aggregation (information sharing) and automated analysis (in particular data mining) technologies."[161] Data mining, which clearly has value as an antiterrorism enter-

---

[155] Solove, 53 Stan.L.Rev. 1393, 1403 (2001).

[156] Solove, 53 Stan.L.Rev. 1393, 1404 (2001). Yet another source of information is the pictures and data displayed on the Internet in social networking sites. See Comment, 31 S.Ill.U.L.J. 95 (2006); Recent Development, 10 N.C.J.L. & Tech. 171 (2008).

[157] Solove, 53 Stan.L.Rev. 1393, 1407 (2001). For example: "Experian maintains a database of credit information on about 215 million people and demographic information on about 215 million consumers in 110 million U.S. households"; "ChoicePoint has 14 billion records on individuals and businesses that can be used for tasks like pre-employment screening of job candidates; "MIBInc., has profiles of medical information on about 15 million individuals collected from its association of 600 insurance companies"; and "Catalina Marketing, Inc. began to collect shopping data" and by 1998 "had reportedly amassed a 2-terabyte database with 18 billion rows of data." Tien, Privacy, Technology and Data Mining, 30 Ohio N.U.L.Rev. 389 (2004).

[158] Solove, 53 Stan.L.Rev. 1393,

1408 (2001). For more on these "commercial data brokers," see Solove & Hoofnagle, A Model Regime of Privacy Protection, 2006 U.Ill.L.Rev. 357.

[159] Solove, 53 Stan.L.Rev. 1393, 1406 (2001).

[160] "The FBI buys files of information about individuals from Choice-Point, Inc., a major data aggregation company that 'cull[s], sort[s] and packag[es] data on individuals from scores of sources, including credit bureaus, marketers and regulatory agencies,' and 'FBI agents can also go to a dedicated Web intranet site for help in conducting their own searches.' * * * In the counter-terrorism context, the FBI is particularly interested in private-sector data from: the travel industry (airlines, rail, car rental); the telecommunications industry (cellular, land line, Internet); the financial industry (banks, credit card, money transmitters, casinos, brokerage firms); and the service industry (insurance, pharmaceuticals, weapons, chemicals, precursors)." Tien, 30 Ohio N.U.L.Rev. 389, 390 n. 10 (2004).

[161] Taipale, Technology, Security and Privacy: The Fear of Frankenstein,

prise,[162]

is the process of looking for new knowledge in existing data. The basic problem addressed by data mining is turning low-level data, usually too voluminous to understand, into higher forms (information or knowledge) that might be more compact (for example, a summary), more abstract (for example, a descriptive model), or more useful (for example, a predictive model). At the core of the data mining process is the application of data analysis and discovery algorithms to enumerate and extract patterns from data in a database. A formal definition of data mining is "the non-trivial extraction of implicit, previously unknown, and potentially useful information from data." Each aspect of this definition has important implications for our purposes in trying to understand what data mining is and in distinguishing it from previously familiar data-processing and database query technologies.

Extracting implicit information means that the results of data mining are not existing data items in the database. Traditional information retrieval from a database returns arrays consisting of data from individual fields of records (or entire records) from the database in response to a defined or specified database query. The results of the traditional database query are explicit in the database, that is, the answer returned to a query is itself a data item (or an array of many items) in the database. Data mining techniques, however, extract knowledge from the database that is implicit—knowledge that "typically [does] not exist a priori" is revealed. Data mining generally identifies patterns or relationships among data items or records that were not previously identified (and are not themselves data items) but that are revealed in the data itself.

Thus, data mining extracts information that was previously unknown. That is, data mining employs complex techniques that can provide answers to questions that have not been asked (or elicit questions for problems that have not been identified). [I]t is this aspect—the creation of new knowledge without previously particularized suspicion—that creates the most unease among privacy advocates in the context of law enforcement use of these techniques.[163]

That such data collection and mining, if totally unrestrained,

---

the Mythology of Privacy and the Lessons of King Ludd, 7 Yale J.L. & Tech. 123 (2005).

[162]"As Mary DeRosa points out in her report on data mining for the Center for Strategic and International Studies, basic data mining using government watch list information, airline reservations records, and aggregated publicly available data would have linked together and identified all nineteen of the September 11, 2001 hijackers." Berkower, Sliding Down a Slippery Slope? The Future Use of Administrative Subpoenas in Criminal Investigations, 73 Fordham L.Rev.

2251 (2005).

But see Solove, Data Mining and the Security-Liberty Debate, 75 U.Chi.L.Rev. 343, 345, 362 (2008), concluding (i) that it "is not clear * * * that data mining is an effective security measure," and (ii) that, in any event, "the privacy concerns are significantly greater than currently acknowledged."

[163]Taipale, Data Mining and Domestic Security: Connecting the Dots to Make Sense of Data, 5 Colum. Sci. & Tech.L.Rev. 2 (2003). For other descriptions of "data mining," see Cate, Government Data Mining: The Need

impinges upon "American values concerning privacy," so that there is needed a "framework of legal, technological, training, and oversight mechanisms necessary to guarantee the privacy of U.S. persons in the context of national security and law enforcement activities," seems apparent.[164] But, especially in light of the Supreme Court's caution in *Katz v. United States*[165] that "the protection of a person's *general* right to privacy" for the most part falls outside the Fourth Amendment, it hardly follows that either data collection or data mining or the two in combination necessarily are subject to the Amendment's limitations. Indeed, it is far from apparent that the aggregation or mining of data involves any Fourth Amendment activity—more particularly, that such collection or manipulation of data available to the government can be said to constitute a "search" within the meaning of the Amendment. This would seem to follow from the Supreme Court decisions previously discussed, especially *Smith v. Maryland*[166] and *United States v. Miller*,[167] which collectively support the proposition that when "information maintained by third parties is exposed to others, it is not private, and therefore not protected by the Fourth Amendment."[168]

That this line of cases apparently leaves data aggregation and

---

for a Legal Framework, 43 Harv.C.R.-C.L.L.Rev. 435 (2008); Rubinstein, Data Mining and Internet Profiling: Emerging Regulatory and Technological Approaches,75 U.Chi.L.Rev. 261, 262–73 (2008); Slobogin, Government Data Mining and the Fourth Amendment, 75 U.Chi.L.Rev. 317, 322–27 (2008); Solberg, Data Mining on Facebook: A Free Space for Researchers or an IRB Nightmare?, 2010 U.Ill. J.L.Tech. & Pol'y 311; Steinbock, Data Matching, Data Mining, and Due Process, 40 Ga.L.Rev. 1, 13–16 (2005); Zarsky, Government Data Mining and Its Alternatives, 116 Penn.St.L.Rev. 285, 291–94 (2011).

[164]Tech. And Privacy Advisory Comm., U.S. Dep't of Defense, Safeguarding Privacy in the Fight Against Terrorism (Mar.2004), available at htt p:www.cdt.org/security/usapatriot/ 20040300tapac.pdf. For legislative proposals, see Solove & Hoofnagle, 2006 U.Ill.L.Rev. 357. Consider also the proposals in Slobogin, Transaction Surveillance by the Government, 75 Miss.L.J. 139 (2005); Zarsky, Government Data Mining and Its Alternatives, 116 Penn.St.L.Rev. 285 (2011).

[165]Katz v. United States, 389 U.S. 347, 88 S.Ct. 507, 19 L.Ed.2d 576 (1967).

[166]Smith v. Maryland, 442 U.S. 735, 99 S.Ct. 2577, 61 L.Ed.2d 220 (1979), discussed in § 2.7(b).

[167]United States v. Miller, 425 U.S. 435, 96 S.Ct. 1619, 48 L.Ed.2d 71 (1976), discussed in § 2.7(c).

[168]Solove, Digital Dossiers and the Dissipation of Fourth Amendment Privacy, 75 S. Cal. L. Rev. 1083, 1087 (2002). See also Thai, Is Data Mining Ever a Search Under Justice Stevens' Fourth Amendment?, 74 Fordham L.Rev. 1731 (2006).

But consider Slobogin, 75 U.Chi. L.Rev. 317, 322, 330–31 (2008), concluding there may be "a few" and "very small" "chinks in *Miller*'s armor," as illustrated by Ferguson v. City of Charleston, 532 U.S. 67, 121 S.Ct. 1281, 149 L.Ed.2d 205 (2001), discussed in § 10.3(a), and Georgia v. Randolph, 547 U.S. 103, 126 S.Ct. 1515, 164 L.Ed.2d 208 (2006), discussed in § 8.3(d), which "signal that the Court is willing to consider at least minor exceptions to *Miller*'s dictate that the government does not effect a constitutionally regulated search when it accrues information the subject

data mining unrestrained by the Fourth Amendment, some say, shows that these decisions have lost whatever luster they once had. "*Smith* and *Miller*," one commentator asserts, "are the new *Olmstead* and *Goldman*,"[169] in that they are no more protective against the data gathering/mining process than the latter cases were against wiretapping. Another says: "The current definition of what constitutes a Fourth Amendment search was crafted in light of one developing technology, the telephone networks. Now is the time to craft a definition that accommodates the amazing but intrusive technologies of the twenty-first century."[170] Underlying such expressions, it would seem, is the judgment that it can be said of modern information technology what I concluded some

---

shares with a third party." Slobogin then goes on to describe "how that doctrine might be interpreted to require limitations on government data mining. The proposed framework requires attention to the type of records obtained via data mining, the extent to which they can be connected to particular individuals, and the government's goal in obtaining them. Based on proportionality reasoning * * *, the highest degree of justification for data mining should be required when the data is private in nature and sought in connection with investigation of a particular target. In contrast, data mining that relies on impersonal or anonymized records, or that is sought in an effort to identify a perpetrator of a past or future vent, need not be as strictly regulated."

Also noteworthy is Justice Sotomayor's concurring opinion in United States v. Jones, __ U.S. __, 132 S.Ct. 945, 181 L.Ed.2d 911 (2012), the GPS monitoring case, asserting that "it may be necessary to reconsider the premise that an individual has no reasonable expectation of privacy in information voluntarily disclosed to third parties. This approach is ill suited to the digital age, in which people reveal a great deal of information about themselves to third parties in the course of carrying out mundane tasks. * * * I would not assume that all information voluntarily disclosed to some member of the public for a limited purpose is, for that reason alone, disentitled to Fourth Amendment protection."

[169]Solove, 75 S. Cal. L. Rev. 1083, 1137 (2002). On the shortcomings of *Olmstead* and *Goldman*, see § 2.2(f).

[170]Henderson, Nothing New Under the Sun? A Technologically Rational Doctrine of Fourth Amendment Search, 56 Mercer L.Rev. 507, 510 (2005). So too, Palfrey, The Public and Private at the United States Border with Cyberspace, 78 Miss.L.J. 241, 294 (2008) ("it is time to rethink whether the scope of the Fourth Amendment is sufficient to protect individual privacy from intrusion by the state, especially with respect to data initially collected by private parties," and "also time to consider whether the public-private distinction, as it has developed over the past century and a half, makes sense in a digital age"); Slobogin, 75 U.Chi.L.Rev. 317, 341 (2008), ("that the Supreme Court's current hands-off approach to record searches cannot justifiably be applied to data mining if societal views about privacy expectations are taken seriously").

Thus, Brenner & Clark, Fourth Amendment Protection for Shared Privacy Rights in Stored Transactional Data, 14 J.L. & Pol'y 211, 280 (2006), "have proposed a principle of 'relation-based shared privacy' which distinguishes Data that should be protected because it is in society's interests to facilitate trust-based relationships and efficient sharing of information. By focusing on specific attributes of those relationships while protecting Government's ability to investigate crimes efficiently, our principle assures that Consumers who take advantage of pervasive technologies will not thereby sacrifice their right to privacy under the Fourth Amendment." And consider Slobogin's assessment, note 168 supra.

years ago was the vice of other forms of technology then being made available to law enforcement:

> The inevitable consequence of such technology * * * is that it will skew the cost-benefit principle significantly. That is, it simply makes it too easy, without the loss of a lot of shoe leather and the other costs police traditionally have had to take into account in determining the realistic limits upon their enforcement activities, to engage in random and wholesale snooping. Posnerian cost-benefit balancing is thus no longer a sufficient deterrent to such enlarged investigative strategies, and this is *precisely* why this activity needs to be brought within the purview of the fourth amendment.[171]

Whether this will happen with respect to the aggregation and mining of data via modern computer technology is hard to say; indeed, whether it *should* happen is a proposition hardly beyond dispute. Perhaps the best that can be done in this brief treatment of the subject is to identify more clearly what legitimate privacy concerns attend the investigative processes here under discussion. This can best be accomplished, one very thoughtful commentator has explained, by separately considering "those that arise from the aggregation (or integration) of data," which "might be called the 'database' problem," and "those that arise from the automated analysis of data that may not be based on any individualized suspicion," that is, "the 'mining' problem."[172]

With respect to the first category, the so-called database problem, it is clearly of the kind mentioned above. That problem has aptly been summarized as follows:

> The efficiencies inherent in data aggregation itself cannot be denied; indeed, it is these efficiencies that provide the impetus for developing and employing data aggregation technologies in the first place. Nor can the impact of this efficiency on privacy be denied. New technologies that provide easy access to distributed data and efficiency in processing are obviously challenging to a system that is at least partially based on protecting certain rights by insisting on inefficiencies. On the one hand there is a need to "connect the dots" and on the other hand the notion of a free society is at least partially built on keeping the power to "connect the dots" out of the control any one actor, particularly the central government. Making access to data easier and more efficient (in a sense, lowering the transaction cost of data use) magnifies and enhances government power.[173]

The problem, then, is the loss of "practical obscurity," to use a term of central importance in a Supreme Court case not involving the Fourth Amendment. In *Department of Justice v. Reporters Committee for Freedom of the Press*,[174] denying a reporter's FOIA request for a rap sheet that was officially part of the public

---

[171]LaFave, The Forgotten Motto of Obsta Principiis in Fourth Amendment Jurisprudence, 28 Ariz.L.Rev. 291, 309 (1986).

[172]Taipale, 5 Colum.Sci. & Tech.L. Rev. 2 (2003).

[173]Taipale, 5 Colum.Sci. & Tech.L. Rev. 2 (2003). For more on the problems of data aggregation, see Solove, A Taxonomy of Privacy, 154 U.Pa.L. Rev. 477, 506–11 (2006).

[174]Department of Justice v. Report-

record, the Court was concerned with the aggregation of public records in such a fashion as to negate the "practical obscurity" that otherwise protected those records: "[T]here is a vast difference between the public records that might be found after a diligent search of courthouse files, county archives and local police stations throughout the country and a computerized summary located in a single clearinghouse of information." The question that remains to be answered "is whether that same analysis, when applied to government aggregation or integration of previously discrete, distributed sources of information—each which it may have the perfect legal right to access individually—is itself problematic under the Fourth Amendment's right to be free from 'unreasonable' search."[175]

Turning now to the mining problem, it is useful to begin by noting the full dimensions of such activity:

> In the technical literature, data mining is more narrowly defined as the "nontrivial process of identifying valid, novel, potentially useful and ultimately understandable patterns in data." Similarly, the General Accounting Office defines data mining as "the application of database technology and techniques—such as statistical analysis and modeling—to uncover hidden patterns and subtle relationships in data and to infer rules that allow for the prediction of future results." Both of these definitions seek to distinguish mere information retrieval using traditional query and report tools, which describe what is in a database, from "true" data mining, which uses automated processes to discover patterns. Because such patterns are themselves knowledge, the field is often referred to as "knowledge discovery."[176]

As another writer succinctly put it, "Data mining is the intelligent search for new knowledge in existing masses of data."[177] For some, it is this "new knowledge" fruit of data-mining which provides a basis for characterizing it as Fourth Amendment activity, notwithstanding the continued vitality of such cases as *Miller* and *Smith*. Thus, one commentator argues

> that data mining is a search, even when the government has lawfully acquired the individual facts in the database being mined, because the patterns or inferences discovered via data mining often deserve to be private and go beyond the information that can fairly be said to be "knowingly exposed" to others. * * * As noted earlier, the data-mining literature distinguishes between traditional "query and report tools," which describe what is in a database, and "true" data mining, which identifies "valid, novel, potentially useful and ultimately understandable patterns in data." Because "such patterns are themselves knowledge," it is completely reasonable to say that finding such patterns or relationships exposes information that

---

ers Committee for Freedom of the Press, 489 U.S. 749, 109 S.Ct. 1468, 103 L.Ed.2d 774 (1989).

[175]Taipale, 5 Colum.Sci. & Tech.L. Rev. 2 (2003).

[176]Tien, 30 Ohio N.U.L.Rev. 389, 393–94 (2004).

[177]Fulda, Data Mining and Privacy, 11 Alb. L.J. Sci. & Tech. 105, 106 (2000).

is not "in" the database. * * * In short, the proper response to the obstacle posed by the "knowing exposure" doctrine is that the underlying patterns or associations are not the same as the surface facts in the database, and that these patterns may themselves be "private."[178]

Whether or not this analysis is correct in all respects, it does seem to focus particular attention upon a central issue posed by data mining: "Is it possible for data that does not in itself deserve legal protection to contain implicit knowledge that does deserve legal protection?"[179] It is worth noting, however, that the above analysis does appear to ignore one important characteristic of those varieties of data mining being discussed, which include "pattern-analysis (or data mining in the narrow sense), that is, automated analysis to develop a descriptive or predictive model based on discovered patterns; and pattern matching, that is, automated analysis using a descriptive or predictive model * * * against additional datasets to identify other related (or 'like') data subjects (people, places, things, relationships, etc.)."[180] The so-called "new knowledge" thus obtained, whether it is new patterns or new people fitting the pattern, is grounded not in data which a single person has released to third parties, but rather in a much larger array of data surrendered by a very large number of people. That being the case, it is not immediately apparent that it is relevant that no particular person has made a "knowing exposure" of this new knowledge, any more than a person could circumvent *Miller* or *Smith* by saying he did not knowingly expose the knowledge the police obtained by considering his bank or phone records not in isolation, but with a vast quantity of other information acquired from other sources.

Much of the concern about data mining has focused upon what is described above as pattern matching. Hence, it is said that pattern analysis "raises the most serious privacy and civil liberties concerns because it involves examination of the lawful daily activities of millions of people" and hence "poses concerns under both the constitutional presumption of innocence and the Fourth Amendment principle that the government must have individualized suspicion before it can conduct a search."[181] Such "mass dataveillance," it is said, "possesses some of the same dangers that the framers of the Fourth Amendment intended to prohibit," i.e., "the general warrant, which allowed the king to break into

---

[178]Tien, 30 Ohio N.U.L.Rev. 389, 408–09 (2004).

[179]Fulda, 11 Alb.L.J. Sci. & Tech. 105, 109 (2000).

[180]Taipale, 7 Yale J.L. & Tech. 123 (2005).

[181]Dempsey & Flint, Commercial Data and National Security, 72 Geo.Wash.L.Rev. 1459, 1466–67

(2004). Similarly, others object that pattern matching puts "the government in the business of maintaining constant surveillance on millions of people," and "investigate[s] everyone, and most people who are investigated are innocent." See Taipale, 5 Colum. Sci. & Tech.L.Rev. 2 (2003) (quoting such critics).

the homes of any number of citizens in search of suspicious information without particularized suspicion."[182] But, while from a
broad privacy perspective it may fairly be said that "much of the
concern behind these criticisms is legitimate,"[183] it can hardly be
said that data mining is a search without individualized suspicion
unless it is in fact a "search" in the Fourth Amendment sense,
which, as noted above, is problematical at best. The Fourth
Amendment presents no barrier to law enforcement agencies
engaging in a variety of nonsearch, nonseizure surveillance activities directed at apparently innocent conduct, which may ultimately culminate in reasonable suspicion or even probable
cause.[184]

Of course, a part of the concern is that information acquired by
data mining may ultimately be relied upon to justify some Fourth
Amendment activity, be it a seizure or a search.[185] Thus, the
"general warrant" objection quoted above is preceded with the
suggestion that as a consequence of data mining "if a traveler
bought fertilizer and a one-way ticket and took flight lessons in
Florida, he or she might be tagged for special searches," because
the "possibility that this traveler might be a retired business
person who was a gardening aficionado would not be evidently
detectable by the system."[186] Two points deserve to be made in
this regard: (1) It does not follow that pattern-matching is "inherently unreasonable,"[187] for the question is "what confidence
interval for the technology and methodology are required to meet
the 'reasonableness' test, and what procedural protections are
imposed between their application and any consequence to the
individual."[188] If the consequences are a seizure or a search, it
still must be asked whether fertilizer + one-way ticket + flight
lessons adds up to probable cause or reasonable suspicion, or
whatever test applies in the circumstances. (Most troublesome, of
course, is the possibility that a dubious pattern matching might
prompt a search or seizure in a "special needs" context where not
even an individualized suspicion barrier exists, as might well be
true of the airport search in the above example.) (2) It is not nec-

---

[182]Rosen, The Naked Crowd:
Balancing Privacy and Security in an
Age of Terror, 46 Ariz.L.Rev. 607, 611
(2004).

[183]Taipale, 5 Colum.Sci. & Tech.L.
Rev. 2 (2003).

[184]See the discussion in United
States v. Sokolow, 490 U.S. 1, 109
S.Ct. 1581, 104 L.Ed.2d 1 (1989).

[185]See Steinbock, 40 Ga.L.Rev. 1,
28–36 (2005).

But if instead the information
is used to support some other official
action, and even if acquiring the infor-

mation did not intrude upon justified
privacy expectations so as to make it a
Fourth Amendment search, it may be
argued that the process nonetheless
violates due process. See generally
Steinbock, 40 Ga.L.Rev. 1 (2005).

[186]Rosen, 46 Ariz.L.Rev. 607, 611
(2004).

[187]See Taipale, 7 Yale J.L. & Tech.
123 (2005), explaining why such a
conclusion is "analytically unsound."

[188]Taipale, 5 Colum.Sci. & Tech.L.
Rev. 2 (2003).

essary for the data aggregation or data mining itself to be deemed a Fourth Amendment search in order to call into question a seizure or search made in reliance upon the purported knowledge derived therefrom. That is, it can in any event be questioned whether fertilizer + one-way ticket + flight lessons adds up to the amount of individualized suspicion required. Moreover, "the Constitution constrains governmental dependence on incriminating leads generated by computer if the underlying data is of dubious accuracy," for *Arizona v. Evans*[189] "provides a constitutional basis for the principle that the government should not rely on databases to arrest or detain individuals unless those databases and the method of searching them are accurate."[190] However, making a judgment about the accuracy of a database, and about whether the cause of any inaccuracy is of a kind justifying application of the exclusionary rule,[191] can be exceedingly difficult tasks: there often will be no way to establish that a particular database is faulty[192] or to pinpoint the source of any particular mistake discovered.[193]

In the final analysis, whether data aggregation and mining is subject to Fourth Amendment restraints depends upon whether what is now referred to as the "mosaic theory" (i.e., "that the ag-

---

[189]Arizona v. Evans, 514 U.S. 1, 115 S.Ct. 1185, 131 L.Ed.2d 34 (1995), discussed in § 1.8(e). See also Herring v. United States, 555 U.S. 135, 129 S.Ct. 695, 172 L.Ed.2d 496 (2009) (stressing that here police were not "reckless" in maintaining the computer records system, and that there no showing that errors in the system "are routine or widespread").

[190]Dempsey & Flint, 72 Geo.Wash. L.Rev. 1459, 1486–87 (2004).

[191]See Herring v. United States, 555 U.S. 135, 129 S.Ct. 695, 172 L.Ed.2d 496 (2009), discussed in § 1.6(i).

[192]As noted in Murphy, Databases, Doctrine and Constitutional Criminal Procedure, 37 Fordham Urb.L.J. 803, 823 (2010), "the faulty products of a database can go entirely unnoticed under current doctrine even when they are common and recurring. Consider the debate in *Herring* itself: the majority demanded evidence that the database routinely produced bad information, refusing to consider the absence of quality control mechanisms itself a sufficient 'harm.' Yet a database that generates bad information— say, that falsely reports arrest war-

rants—may produce many arrests, but little record of those arrests. Unless the arrested person sues civilly, or is found in violation of contraband (as in the case of *Herring*), no formal record of the error may be made. And even if formal suits are filed, it may be difficult to link them to one another as the product of a faulty database. The only proof of the reliability of the database in *Herring* itself were the statements of its keepers—hardly disinterested parties—and yet, even those were contested factually."

[193]As noted in Murphy, 37 Fordham Urb.L.J. 803, 827 (2010): "Databases are rarely the product of one individual's action, and rarely contain easily separable individual information. Instead, they tend to be the product of numerous actors and inputs and collate numerous tiers of information. Think about *Herring*: an anonymous person put in the erroneous information, or else failed to remove it; then the information was accessed by one clerk and transmitted to another who failed to undertake any steps to verify it. It is difficult, and maybe impossible, to identify the moment the error occurred or the individual who perpetrated it."

gregation of information might be covered by a reasonable expectation of privacy even though each particular discrete bit of data on its own would not"[194]) becomes a part of accepted Fourth Amendment analysis. As discussed later herein,[195] it is quite noteworthy in this regard that in *United States v. Jones*,[196] the GPS monitoring case, concurring opinions representing the position of five Justices "expressly gave their imprimatur to at least some version of the mosaic theory,"[197] which certainly amounts "to an invitation for lower courts to consider embracing the mosaic logic."[198]

§ 2.7(f) Electronic tracking devices[199]

Another surveillance technique that has become increasingly common involves the use of an electronic tracking device to monitor the changing location of some object, typically an automobile. The Supreme Court has had occasion to address this practice first in two cases decided in the early 1980s, and then again in another case that reached the Court nearly thirty years later, during which time there occurred a rather significant change in the sophistication of the equipment being employed in such surveillance. The two earlier cases involved what is commonly referred to as a "beeper." "Comparatively simplistic technology in today's hindsight, such a beeper device emitted a radio-signal pulse at regular intervals, and could only be followed manually by a police officer with a signal detector who stayed within signal range to avoid losing track of the device."[200] In *United States v. Knotts*,[201] where use of a beeper facilitated keeping track of a vehicle during a trip from Minneapolis to a cabin 100 miles away,

---

[194]Priester, Five Answers and Three Questions After United States v. Jones (2012), the Fourth Amendment "GPS case," http://papers.ssrn.com/sol3/papers.cfm?abstract_id=2030390 (2012).

[195]See § 2.7(f).

[196]United States v. Jones, __ U.S. __, 132 S.Ct. 945, 181 L.Ed.2d 911 (2012).

[197]Preister, http://papers.ssrn.com/sol3/papers.cfm?abstract_id=2030390 (2012).

[198]Kerr, 110 Mich.L.Rev. __, __ (2012).

[Section 2.7(f)]

[199]See Dowling, "Bumper Beepers" and the Fourth Amendment, 13 Crim.L.Bull. 266 (1977); Junker, The Structure of the Fourth Amendment: The Scope of the Protection, 79 J.Crim.L. & C. 1105, 1127–36 (1989);

Marks & Batey, Electronic Tracking Devices: Fourth Amendment Problems and Solutions, 67 Ky.L.J. 987 (1979); Slobogin, Physical Surveillance: The American Bar Association's Tentative Draft Standards, 10 Harv.L.J. & Tech. 383, 444–46 (1997); Comments, 46 Cin.L.Rev. 243 (1977); 16 Ga.L.Rev. 197 (1981); 13 U.S.F.L.Rev. 203 (1978); Notes, 1977 U.Ill.L.F. 1167, 1183–89; 22 Vill.L.Rev. 1067 (1977); 86 Yale L.J. 1461 (1977).

[200]Priester, Five Answers and Three Questions After United States v. Jones (2012), the Fourth Amendment "GPS case," http://papers.ssrn.com/sol3/papers.cfm?abstract_id=2030390 (2012). For further description, see Note, 86 Yale L.J. 1461, 1463–64 (1977).

[201]United States v. Knotts, United States v. Knotts, 460 U.S. 276, 103 S.Ct. 1081, 75 L.Ed.2d 55 (1983), discussed in Notes, 58 Tul.L.Rev. 849

the Court concluded there had been no Fourth Amendment activity under the *Katz* test, for a "person travelling in an automobile on public thoroughfares has no reasonable expectation of privacy in his movements from one place to another." By contrast, the Court in *United States v. Karo*[202] held that "the monitoring of a beeper in a private residence, a location not open to visual surveillance," constituted a search intruding upon those having a privacy interest in the premises.

By the time the Supreme Court revisited the subject in 2012, "far more sophisticated technology enabled much more detailed and extensive tracking of public movements."[203] In that case, *United States v. Jones*,[204]

> the police attached a small GPS device to the undercarriage of a Jeep; using access to satellites and cellphone networks, the device transmitted its location to a police computer at frequent intervals, producing over 2,000 pages of location-information data in four weeks. Rather than requiring constant real-time monitoring by an officer, the police could simply view the ongoing log of the device's location transmissions at any time.[205]

Remarkably, all nine Justices in *Jones* agreed that the police activity constituted a search under the Fourth Amendment, although they were divided as to the proper rationale. The five-Justice majority, relying upon pre-*Katz* trespass theory,[206] deemed it enough that the "Government physically occupied private property for the purpose of obtaining information," as "such a physical intrusion would have been considered a 'search' within the meaning of the Fourth Amendment when it was adopted." The four concurring Justices, on the other hand, applied *Katz* and concluded that the defendant's "reasonable expectations of privacy were violated by the long-term monitoring of the movements of the vehicle he drove."[207]

While *Jones,* in a sense, renders irrelevant the Court's earlier

---

(1984); 45 U.Pitt.L.Rev. 741 (1984); 30 Wayne L.Rev. 1151 (1984).

[202]United States v. Karo, 468 U.S. 705, 104 S.Ct. 3296, 82 L.Ed.2d 530 (1984).

[203]Priester, http://papers.ssrn.com/sol3/papers.cfm?abstract_id=2030390 (2012).

[204]United States v. Jones, __ U.S. __, 132 S.Ct. 945, 181 L.Ed.2d 911 (2012), discussed in Goldberg, How United States v. Jones Can Restore Our Faith in the Fourth Amendment, 110 Mich.L.Rev. First Impressions 62 (2011); Morrison, The Drug Dealer, The Narc, and the Very Tiny Constable: Reflections on United States v. Jones, 3 Cal.L.Rev. Circuit 113 (2012); Priester, Five Answers and Three Questions After United States v. Jones (2012), the Fourth Amendment "GPS case," http://papers.ssrn.com/sol3/papers.cfm?abstract_id=2030390 (2012); Spencer, GPS Monitoring Device Leads the Supreme Court to a Crossroads in Privacy Law, http://papers.ssrn.com/sol3/papers.cfm?abstract_id=2014233 (2012).

[205]Priester, http://papers.ssrn.com/sol3/papers.cfm?abstract_id=2030390 (2012).

[206]Regarding this aspect of *Jones*, see § 2.1, text at note 136.

[207]In addition, one member of the majority, Justice Sotomayor, indicated in a separate concurrence that she agreed with the other four concurring Justices "that, at the very least, 'lon-

treatment of the tracking issue, some background and perspective (especially why the *Katz* approach did not earlier provide a basis for treating such surveillance as a search) can be gained by first taking a closer look at *Knotts*. A beeper was placed inside a five-gallon container of chloroform then sold by a Minneapolis chemical company to Armstrong, who delivered it in that city to Petschen, who in turn delivered it to Knotts' cabin nearly 100 miles away in rural Wisconsin. For a time police kept track of the container by both visual surveillance and monitoring of the beeper's signals, but during the latter part of the journey the visual surveillance was ended because of Petschen's evasive maneuvers and the signal from the beeper was lost at about the same time. An hour later the now stationary signal was picked up at the cabin, for which a search warrant was obtained after three days of intermittent visual surveillance. The Court concluded that the monitoring was "neither a 'search' nor a 'seizure' within the contemplation of the Fourth Amendment" because it did not "invade any legitimate expectation of privacy":

> A person travelling in an automobile on public thoroughfares has no reasonable expectation of privacy in his movements from one place to another. When Petschen travelled over the public streets he voluntarily conveyed to anyone who wanted to look the fact that he was travelling over particular roads in a particular direction, the fact of whatever stops he made, and the fact of his final destination when he exited from public roads onto private property.
>
> * * * Admittedly, because of the failure of the visual surveillance, the beeper enabled the law enforcement officials in this case to ascertain the ultimate resting place of the chloroform when they would not have been able to do so had they relied solely on their naked eyes. But scientific enhancement of this sort raises no constitutional issues which visual surveillance would not also raise. A police car following Petschen at a distance throughout his journey could have observed him leaving the public highway and arriving at the cabin owned by respondent, with the drum of chloroform still in the car.[208]

Knotts, it is submitted, marked yet another occasion on which

---

ger term GPS monitoring in investigations of most offenses impinges on expectations of privacy.'"

Consequently, in the post-*Jones* decision in State v. Zahn, 812 N.W.2d 490 (S.D.2012), the court relied upon the various opinions in *Jones* to support the conclusion that the long-term GPS monitoring in that case constituted a search under *both* the "physical trespass" test and the "reasonable expectation of privacy" test.

[208]There was, somewhat surprisingly, no dissent in *Knotts*. Brennan, J., joined by Marshall, J., concurring in the judgment, added that "this would have been a much more difficult case if respondent had challenged, not merely certain aspects of the monitoring of the beeper installed in the chloroform container purchased by respondent's compatriot, but also its original installation," which he apparently did not question because he was not the purchaser and thus assumed he was without standing, in that "when the government does engage in physical intrusion of a constitutionally protected area in order to obtain information, that intrusion may constitute a violation of the Fourth Amendment even if the same information could have been obtained by other means."

the *Katz* expectation-of-privacy test was distorted and narrowed. In *Knotts,* it is extremely doubtful that visual surveillance alone would have revealed the delivery point of the container—even with monitoring of the beeper, the police lost track of Petschen for an hour when he began evasive maneuvers after apparently discovering he was being followed. But this makes no difference, the Court concluded, because Petschen "voluntarily conveyed to anyone who wanted to look the fact that he was travelling over particular roads in a particular direction * * * and the fact of his final destination when he exited from public roads onto private property." But "anyone who wanted to look" would not have known what the beeper revealed: that the container purchased at the Minneapolis chemical company was now at a certain cabin in a secluded area of rural northern Wisconsin. Only an army of bystanders, conveniently strung out on Petschen's route and who not only "wanted to look" but also wanted to pass on what they observed to the next in line, would—to use the language in *Knotts*—"have sufficed to reveal all of these facts to the police." Just why the disclosure of these fragments to an imaginary line of bystanders must be treated as a total surrender of one's expectation of privacy concerning his travels is never explained in *Knotts.*

In light of *Jones,* another facet of *Knotts* is worth noting. The Court there observed that the defendant did not really "quarrel with" its no-expectation-of-privacy analysis, except to say that if the defendant did not prevail in the instant case then the result down the road would be unchecked surveillance of a much more severe nature. As the defendant put it, the result of the Court ruling against the defendant would be that "twenty-four hour surveillance of any citizen of this country will be possible, without judicial knowledge or supervision." To this, the Court responded that "if such dragnet-type law enforcement practices as respondent envisions should eventually occur, there will be time enough then to determine whether different constitutional principles may be applicable." Given the unanimous ruling in the defendant's favor in *Jones,* involving 28-day surveillance, it is clear that the time had arrived, albeit without a consensus of just what "different" principles should be thrown into the breach. It has been suggested that this split, together with "a concurring opinion that seemingly agreed with both of the two camps while

---

Blackmun, J., joined by Brennan, Marshall and Stevens, JJ., concurring in the judgment, objected to the "unnecessary" reliance upon the open fields doctrine. Stevens, J., joined by Brennan and Marshall, JJ., concurring in the judgment, objected to the broad implication that the Fourth Amendment does not ever inhibit the police "from augmenting the sensory facilities bestowed upon them at birth with such enhancement as science and technology afforded them."

simultaneously staking out a position broader than either,"[209] "showed a Court seemingly intent on avoiding the complex and difficult issues of Fourth Amendment rights in a digital, internet-interconnected age and putting off the tough judgment calls for another case another day."[210]

The four-Justice concurrence in *Jones* clearly expresses a distaste for getting into this subject at all, noting:

> In circumstances involving dramatic technological change, the best solution to privacy concerns may be legislative. A legislative body is well situated to gauge changing public attitudes, to draw detailed lines, and to balance privacy and public safety in a comprehensive way.

In the absence of such legislation, they then conclude, the "best that we can do in this case is to apply existing Fourth Amendment doctrine and to ask whether the use of GPS tracking in a particular case involved a degree of intrusion that a reasonable person would not have anticipated." But the concurrence has little to say about precisely how a court should go about that task, other than that "relatively short-term monitoring" would pass muster while "longer term GPS monitoring" would not, and that the line between the two "was surely crossed before the 4-week mark." This, as the majority opinion notes, leaves a lot of "vexing problems" to be sorted out in the future.[211] Absent the Court drawing a *Shatzer*-style arbitrary time limit,[212] it is to expected that it would take a considerable amount of litigation before the how-long-is-too-long question was answered. Indeed, that task may well be even more complicated if it turns out that

---

[209]The reference is to the concurring opinion by Justice Sotomayor. She joined the majority's trespass approach because "that principle suffices to decide this case," but then seemingly went well beyond the four concurring Justices position by adding that even in cases of "short-term monitoring, some unique attributes of GPS surveillance relevant to the *Katz* analysis will required particular attention." Those attributes, she noted, are (1) that GPS monitoring generates a record about a person's public movements "that reflects a wealth of detail about her familial, political, professional, religious, and sexual associations"; (2) that the government "can store such records and efficiently mine them for information years into the future"; and (3) that because such monitoring "is cheap in comparison to conventional surveillance techniques and, by design, proceeds surreptitiously, it evades the ordinary checks that constrain abusive law enforcement practices: 'limited police resources and community hostility.'"

[210]Priestly, http://papers.ssrn.com/sol3/papers.cfm?abstract_id=2030390 (2012).

[211]The majority admits that it may be necessary at some future point "to grapple with these 'vexing problems * * * where a classic trespassory search is not involved and resort must be had to *Katz* analysis," but insisted "there is no reason for rushing forward to resolve them here."

[212]The reference is to Maryland v. Shatzer, __ U.S. __, 130 S.Ct. 1213, 175 L.Ed.2d 1045 (2010), adopting a break-in-custody rule regarding *Miranda* for when "a suspect has been released from his pretrial custody and has returned to his normal life for some time," but then, deeming it unadvisable to leave the "some time" qualifier open to subsequent litigation, opted for a period of 14 days.

the "degree of intrusion" inquiry involves not merely the passage of a specified period of time, but other characteristics of the particular surveillance at issue (as the Sotomayor concurrence suggests[213]). Yet another added complication is suggested by the four-Justice concurrence, namely that the degree of intrusion not within the anticipation of a reasonable person may depend upon the nature and seriousness of the offense under investigation.[214]

Whatever else might be said about the *Jones* majority's resurrection of the pre-*Katz* trespass doctrine,[215] that approach might be viewed with favor by some merely because it saves lower courts—at least for the time being[216]—from the difficult task of sorting out GPS surveillances on the basis of the "degree of intrusion" involved in the individual case. As compared to the approach of the four-Justice concurrence in *Jones*, the majority's thesis is relatively straightforward:

> The Fourth Amendment provides in relevant part that "[t]he right of the people to be secure in their persons, houses, papers, and effects, against unreasonable searches and seizures, shall not be violated." It is beyond dispute that a vehicle is an "effect" as that term is used in the Amendment. * * * We hold that the Government's installation of a GPS device on a target's vehicle, and its use of that device to monitor the vehicle's movements, constitutes a "search."

Thus, as the majority continued, because in the instant case the "Government physically occupied private property for the purpose of obtaining information," that alone is sufficient, for "such a physical intrusion would have been considered a "search' within the meaning of the Fourth Amendment when it was adopted." (While the concurrence questioned that approach because "it is almost impossible to think of late-18th century situations that are analogous to what took place in this case," the majority responded that "it is quite irrelevant whether there was an 18th-century analog," as "[w]hatever new methods of investigation may be devised, our task, *at a minimum*, is to decide whether the action in question would have constituted a 'search' within the original meaning of the Fourth Amendment.") Thus, in contrast to the position of the concurrence, the majority's approach in *Jones* means that even a surveillance as brief as that in *Knotts* would be tainted had it been preceded by the requisite physical[217]

---

[213] See note 209 supra.

[214] They state: "We also need not consider whether prolonged GPS monitoring in the context of investigations involving extraordinary offenses would similarly intrude on a constitutionally protected sphere of privacy."

[215] See § 2.1(e).

[216] See note 2113 supra.

[217] One supporter of *Jones* has argued that the rationale of that case could readily be "updated to consider electronic penetration a form of trespass," which "would permit the labeling of more intrusions as searches, whether they look like traditional trespasses or modern-day, electronic trespasses." Goldberg, 110 Mich.L. Rev. First Impressions 62, 68 (2011).

trespass.[218]

One major objection to this approach, sounded by the *Jones* concurrence, is that

> the Court's reasoning largely disregards what is really important (the *use* of a GPS for the purpose of long-term tracking) and instead attaches great significance to something that most would view as relatively minor (attaching to the bottom of a car a small, light object that does not interfere in any way with the car's operation). Attaching such an object is generally regarded as so trivial that it does not provide a basis for recovery under modern tort law.

Hence, as one commentator aptly put it, "what is so dissatisfying about the majority opinion in *Jones* is that, despite its doctrinal boldness, it is devoid of normative judgment."[219] Of course, if focusing on the "trivial," the minor trespass, always served as an indirect means of subjecting what is "really important," the subsequent surveillance, to Fourth Amendment control, then that objection might lose some of its force. But that is sometimes not the case, as can be see by separate consideration of two situations: (i) where the device is attached to an automobile not then controlled by the person later monitored; and (ii) where the device is attached to some other object subsequently transferred to the person later monitored.

The first of these two situations was not far from the surface in *Jones*. The majority's holding was expressly limited to instances in which the requisite "trespass" is to "a target's vehicle," at which point a footnote was dropped revealing a potential problem in the instant case. The vehicle in question, it was there noted, "was registered to Jones's wife," although the government had acknowledged Jones was "the exclusive driver" so that, the Court asserted, "he had at least the property rights of a bailee." But the Court declined to "consider the Fourth Amendment significance of Jones's status," especially since the court of appeals had concluded Jones had the ability to make a Fourth Amendment objection. Of course, the court of appeals had employed a theory more in keeping with the four-Justice concurrence in *Jones*, in which case it would seem that any calculation of "standing" would relate to the user of the vehicle on during the period of surveillance. But under the approach of the *Jones* majority it is the fact that the "Government physically occupied private property" that counts, meaning that existing standing-re-automobile

---

[218]Regarding *Knotts*, the *Jones* majority says: "*Knotts* would be relevant, perhaps, if the Government were making the argument that what would otherwise be an unconstitutional search is not such were it produces only public information. The Government does not make that argument, and we know of no case that would support it."

[219]Morrison, 3 Cal.L.Rev. Circuit 113, 124 (2012).

doctrine[220] would be applied only to the date of the requisite trespass. This means, as the four-Justice concurrence observes, that "if the GPS device had been installed before respondent's wife gave him the keys, respondent would have no claim for trespass–and, presumably, no Fourth Amendment claim either." But if the 28 days of surveillance would not "count" in such circumstances, this suggests there is something seriously wrong with *Jones* majority's approach.

As for the second situation, involving transfer of an object containing a surveillance device, it was addressed in *United States v. Karo*,[221] where, upon learning that defendants had ordered 50 gallons of ether from a government informant, agents installed a beeper in that shipment with the informant's consent, and the shipment was thereafter transferred to the defendants. While the lower court ruling in Karo's favor rested largely upon the acts of installation and transfer, the Supreme Court disagreed. The installation was unobjectionable because done with consent of the person then in possession of the items to be shipped. As for the transfer, it was deemed no search because it "conveyed no information at all," and no seizure because no one's "possessory interest was interfered with in a meaningful way."[222] As for the fact the shipment "contained an unknown and unwanted foreign object," the Court characterized this as a "technical trespass" but then added that under *Katz* " an actual trespass is neither necessary nor sufficient to establish a constitutional violation." Given the reliance in *Jones* upon an information-seeking trespass, it might be thought that this branch of *Karo* has now been rejected, but this is not the case. Instead, the *Jones* majority opinion embraced that conclusion in *Karo* as "perfectly consistent with the one we reach here."

The reaffirmation of this part of *Karo* is another reason to question the majority's approach in *Jones*. At least when there has been a lawful sale of goods, the fact the seller consented to putting the beeper in the goods should not itself legitimate the later monitoring of the beeper. The privacy rights of the buyer cannot be surrendered by the seller of the goods, "any more than the telephone company could have sanctioned the installation of the recording device in *Katz*."[223] Whatever the legal situation at the moment the beeper was installed, the significant fact is that the

---

[220]See § 11.3(e).

[221]United States v. Karo, 468 U.S. 705, 104 S.Ct. 3296, 82 L.Ed.2d 530 (1984).

[222]*Karo* was distinguished in State v. Kelly, 68 Haw. 213, 708 P.2d 820 (1985), where, after a package shipped from Peru was found to have cocaine in it, the package was held for ten days until a beeper could be hidden in the cover of a photo album therein, after which a controlled delivery was made. The court concluded that the addressee of the mailed package "had a possessory interest in the photo album during the time the album was in mail transit."

[223]United States v. Bobisink, 415

government intended for the device to be operative after the goods were sold and in the possession of someone else.[224] Nor does it make any sense to say that a participant in a transaction not itself unlawful (though it may have an unlawful objective) must be said to have assumed the risk that the seller has arranged to have the subsequent movement of the goods monitored. "A citizen is entitled to assume that property he buys does not contain an electronic spy."[225] (There is some authority that a citizen is not entitled to make such an assumption when he has engaged in an illegal transaction,[226] but it could just as logically be argued that Katz had no justified expectation of privacy in his telephone conversation because that conversation was itself the criminal act of transmitting wagering information in violation of federal law.)

Because the majority opinion in *Jones* makes it perfectly clear that the Court is adding to, and not subtracting from, existing authority on the subject of electronic tracking, it is thus apparent that in some circumstances a defendant can prevail even without showing the trespass critical to the result in *Jones*. Relevant here is another branch of the *Karo* case in which the Court answered in the affirmative a question reserved in *Knotts*: "whether monitoring of a beeper falls within the ambit of the Fourth Amendment when it reveals information that could not have been obtained through visual surveillance." Noting first that unquestionably it would be an unreasonable search to surreptitiously enter a residence without a warrant to verify that the container was there, the Court reasoned:

> For purposes of the Amendment, the result is the same where, without a warrant, the Government surreptitiously employs an electronic device to obtain information that it could not have obtained by observation from outside the curtilage of the home. The beeper tells the agent that a particular article is actually located at a particular time in the private residence and is in the possession of the person or persons whose residence is being surveilled. Even if visual surveillance has revealed that the article to which the beeper is attached has entered the house, the later monitoring not only

F.Supp. 1334 (D.Mass.1976).

[224]United States v. Bailey, 628 F.2d 938 (6th Cir.1980); United States v. Moore, 562 F.2d 106 (1st Cir.1977).

[225]United States v. Bobisink, 415 F.Supp. 1334 (D.Mass.1976).

[226]United States v. Emery, 541 F.2d 887 (1st Cir.1976), followed on similar facts in United States v. Pringle, 576 F.2d 1114 (5th Cir.1978); United States v. Perez, 526 F.2d 859 (5th Cir.1976).

Compare United States v. Bailey, 628 F.2d 938 (6th Cir.1980) (*Emery-Perez* not applicable where "non-contraband items will be used for criminal purposes," as "the Government's argument would authorize warrantless beeper surveillance of laboratory equipment, hand guns, or any other legitimately owned item the Government suspected would be used to commit a crime"); United States v. Moore, 562 F.2d 106 (1st Cir.1977) (declining to apply the *Emery-Perez* rule as to "legally-possessed substances * * * which * * * are destined later to be used in the commission of a crime").

verifies the officers' observations but also establishes that the article remains on the premises.[227]
Karo was deemed to be such a case, as the affidavit for the challenged search warrant indicated that police surveillance established the arrival at a certain residence of a vehicle containing a can of ether, but that the agents did not maintain tight surveillance for fear of detection and thus learned only by use of a beeper earlier placed in the can that the can remained there when several vehicles left the premises.

Although the majority in *Karo* at one point characterized the question presented in terms of "whether the monitoring of a beeper in a private residence, a location not open to visual surveillance," is a search, the opinion begins with a somewhat broader statement of one of the issues: "whether monitoring of a beeper falls within the ambit of the Fourth Amendment when it reveals information that could not have been obtained through visual surveillance." These two characterizations are different in some respects, and thus they together create some uncertainty as to the dimensions of the *Karo* decision. It may be suggested, however, that the underlying principle is by no means limited to "the monitoring of a beeper in a private residence." As three Justices[228] noted, the Court also recognized more generally "that concealment of personal property from public view gives rise to Fourth Amendment protection." This would appear to mean, for one thing, that using a beeper to discover a container in a vehicle can constitute a search.[229] For another, it means that structures not qualifying as "a private residence" also come within the *Karo* rule. (The majority acknowledged as much when it asserted that use of a beeper to determine that a container was in a particular locker in a public warehouse would be a search.) For still an-

---

[227]O'Connor, J., joined by Rehnquist, J., proposed "a different and generally narrower test than the one proposed by the Court for determining when an activated beeper in a closed container violates the privacy of a homeowner into whose home the container is moved. I would use as the touchstone the defendant's interest in the container in which the beeper is placed. When a closed container is moved by permission into a home, the homeowner and others with an expectation of privacy in the home itself surrender any expectation of privacy they might otherwise retain in the movements of the container—unless it is *their* container or under *their* dominion and control."

[228]Stevens, J., joined by Brennan and Marshall, JJ.

[229]As those three Justices in *Karo* put it: "When a person drives down a public thoroughfare in a car with a can of ether concealed in the trunk, he is not exposing to public view the fact that he is in possession of a can of ether; the can is still 'withdrawn from public view' and hence its location is entitled to constitutional protection." *Knotts* is not inconsistent with that conclusion, as there the agents had by visual surveillance seen the codefendant take possession of the container, and thus the monitoring of the beeper never revealed a previously unknown fact as to the vehicle the container was in, but only revealed the location of the vehicle the container was known to be in.

other, it means that it is not inevitably necessary that at the time of the critical monitoring the beeper be within the protected place. As those three Justices correctly point out with respect to an earlier use of the beeper in connection with the container's delivery to another home,

> even if it is assumed that a beeper infringes privacy interests only with respect to the location of items concealed within a home, the "search" that the Court concludes began when the can containing the beeper went into Karo's home did not end when it left the home. When the agents monitored the beeper at a later point and learned that the can was no longer in the home, the invasion of the privacy of Karo's home continued; by learning that the can was no longer in the home the monitoring told the agents something they otherwise would not have known about what was in Karo's home. If monitoring a beeper constitutes a search because it "establishes that the article remains on the premises," * * * it is no less a search when it establishes that the article has left the premises.[230]

Another question concerns how significant it is that the *Karo* majority initially characterized the issue in terms of a beeper monitoring that "reveals information that could not have been obtained through visual surveillance." Does that mean *absolutely* could not have been obtained by that other means, or only *practically* could not have been obtained? The latter alternative, it might be said, can hardly be what was intended, for this would amount to a sub silentio overruling of *Knotts;* as noted earlier, use of the beeper was essential in that case because it was not feasible, given the terrain, the length of the journey, and the possibility of discovery were closer tailing attempted, for the police to keep track of the suspect's peregrinations with only visual surveillance. Yet a look at the facts in *Karo* strongly suggests that what the Court there characterized as a search uncovered a fact—that the can was presently within the home—which could have otherwise been discovered (at least in the sense of the unrealistic approach followed in *Knotts*). Agents saw the vehicle known to be carrying the container come to the house for which they later obtained a warrant, and the agents also saw that vehicle depart later. What they did not see, however, was whether the can with the beeper was still in the rear bed of the pickup truck, apparently because (as the Court noted) "the agents did not maintain tight surveillance for fear of detection."

Thus, *Karo* appears to accept that use of a beeper can be a search even in an instance where the ascertained fact *might* have been discoverable by closer and more intense visual surveillance. But if, as appears to be the case, the Court is not prepared to overrule *Knotts,* the seeming inconsistency in results is to be preferred over an interpretation of *Karo* whereunder the Court's

---

[230]The majority in *Karo* did not respond directly to this contention, but simply concluded that "no prior monitoring of the beeper contributed to * * * discovery" of the container later in a warehouse.

"could not have been obtained through visual surveillance" language is taken literally. That is, it makes great sense to interpret *Karo* as holding it is a search to engage in "monitoring of property that has been withdrawn from public view," as the Court put it at still another point. Were it otherwise, *Karo* would impose upon lower courts the herculean task of ascertaining in each case whether the police, if they had conducted themselves differently than they did, could have made the same discovery by visual surveillance.[231]

If, as the majority concludes in *Karo,* "indiscriminate monitoring of property that has been withdrawn from public view" must be subject to "Fourth Amendment oversight," then it would seem that one particular conclusion reached by the Court in that case is in error. In the course of holding that the warrant issued for search of the premises was untainted because based upon sufficient facts other than the previous warrantless monitoring of the beeper there, the Court first had to conclude that other critical facts in the warrant affidavit were lawfully obtained. Some of these facts were acquired by earlier surveillance of the removal of the container from a public warehouse, where it had been located by picking up the beeper's signal. The agents' equipment was not sensitive enough to reveal which of the rental lockers in the warehouse held the container, which prompted the majority to conclude: "Monitoring the beeper revealed nothing about the contents of the locker that Horton and Harley had rented and hence was not a search of that locker." But this simply is not so. As three of the Justices, dissenting in part, correctly noted: "The property was concealed from public view; its location was a secret and hence by revealing its location the beeper infringed an expectation of privacy. Without the beeper, the agents would have never found the warehouse, and hence would have never set up visual surveillance of the locker containing the can of ether."

While *Karo,* whatever it means, continues to exist as an exception to the *Jones* requirement of a trespass at the time of installation of the tracking device, it remains to be seen whether other exceptions will emerge in the future. However, such a develop-

---

[231]Consider in this regard United States v. Gbemisola, 225 F.3d 753 (D. C.Cir.2000), holding that no warrant was needed while tracking the container holding the device, as it was carried by defendant during his travels by taxi, considering that the location of the box was simultaneously determined by "the agents' visual surveillance." But defendant objected that because "the device also reported when the box was opened—an event the officers did not see," a warrant *was* required. The court responded: "At any time, the surveillance vehicle could have pulled alongside of the taxi and the officers could have watched Gbemisola through its window. Indeed, the taxi driver himself could have seen the event simply by looking in his rearview mirror or turning around. As one cannot have a reasonable expectation of privacy concerning an act performed within the visual range of a complete stranger, the Fourth Amendment's warrant requirement was not implicated."

ment hardly seems unlikely. The majority in *Jones* acknowledged: "It may be that achieving the same result through electronic means, without an accompanying trespass, is an unconstitutional invasion of privacy, but the present case does not require us to answer that question." Even more significant is the fact that *Jones* is not merely a case in which five Justices were willing to embrace the trespass theory, but is also a case in which five Justices quite clearly manifested that they were prepared to go further. The four Justices joining in the concurrence, of course, were prepared to apply their "long-term tracking" rule whether or not there had been a trespass. In addition there is the separate concurrence by Justice Sotomayor; she joined the majority opinion because it "supplies a narrower basis for decision," but also not only agreed with the other concurring Justices regarding "long term GPS monitoring," but appeared to go further in also expressing concern with "even short-term monitoring."[232]

Also significant here is that from these concurring opinions in *Jones* it is apparent that "at least five justices on the Court expressly gave their imprimatur to at least some version of the mosaic theory,"[233] i.e., "that the aggregation of information might be covered by a reasonable expectation of privacy even though each particular discrete bit of data on its own would not."[234] Justice Sotomayor's concurrence "clearly echoes the mosaic theory,"[235] as reflected in her comment that she would "ask whether people reasonably expect that their movements will be recorded and aggregated in a manner that enables the Government to ascertain, more or less at will, their political and religious beliefs, sexual habits, and so on." While the four-Justice concurrence instead "focused on whether the investigation exceeded society's expectations for how the police would investigate a particular crime," it is nonetheless clear that "both opinions clearly look to the collective sum of government action, rather than individual steps, to determine what is a Fourth Amendment search."[236] Whether an express embrace by the Supreme Court of the mosaic theory would be a good idea or a bad idea is a matter on which there is a difference of opinion. Certainly "there are good arguments on both sides"[237] of this issue, but there is no denying that adoption of the mosaic theory will confront courts with many difficult issues. As Prof. Kerr has noted,

> implementing the mosaic theory requires courts to ask and answer
> a remarkable set of novel questions. The mosaic theory is so differ-

---

[232] See note 209 supra.

[233] Priester, http://papers.ssrn.com/sol3/papers.cfm?abstract_id=2030390 (2012).

[234] Priester, http://papers.ssrn.com/sol3/papers.cfm?abstract_id=2030390 (2012).

[235] Kerr, the Mosaic Theory of the Fourth Amendment, 110 Mich.L.Rev. —, — (2012).

[236] Kerr, 110 Mich.L.Rev. —, — (2012)l

[237] Priester, http://papers.ssrn.com/sol3/papers.cfm?abstract_id=2030390 (2012).

ent from what has come before that implementing it requires the creation of what amounts to a parallel set of Fourth Amendment rules. For every settled question of law under the discrete steps approach, courts will need to reanalyze the framework for the mosaic approach. And, for the most part, the challenge is exponentially more complicated. Under the discrete steps approach, searches are simple points. Replacing those points with complex aggregates over space and time is akin to introducing *Flatland*s square to a three dimensional world.[238]

Assuming now a case in which the use of a tracking device *does* constitute a Fourth Amendment search, the next question is whether such a search, absent true exigent circumstances, must be undertaken pursuant to a warrant. As to the in-premises monitoring at issue in *Karo*, the Court answered in the affirmative, rejecting in the process the government's claim that the protections of the search warrant procedure are unnecessary because "the beeper constitutes only a minuscule intrusion on protected privacy interests." In mandating a warrant except in "truly exigent circumstances," the Court emphasized that "requiring a warrant will have the salutary effect of ensuring that use of beepers is not abused." Moreover, the Court in *Karo* indicated that claims of exigent circumstances would not be legitimate when based upon the assertion that at the time of the installation of the beeper it was not known whether it would ultimately be used to engage in the type of monitoring which constitutes a search or, if it were to be so used, what particular place would be so surveilled. The Court was not persuaded by the government's objection that "for all practical purposes they will be forced to obtain warrants in every case in which they seek to use a beeper, because they have no way of knowing in advance whether the beeper will be transmitting its signals from inside private premises." And as for the government's claim the warrant requirement is impractical because at the commencement of the beeper monitoring it is usually unknown to what premises the container holding it will be taken, so that the Fourth Amendment's particularity requirement could not then be met, the Court answered that it would "still be possible to describe the object into which the beeper is to be placed, the circumstances that led agents to wish to install the beeper, and the length of time for which beeper surveillance is requested. In our view, this information will suffice to permit issuance of a warrant authorizing

[238]Kerr, 110 Mich.L.Rev.—,— (2012). The Kerr article contains a most useful discussion of four major questions: (1) the standard question, i.e., what test determines when a mosaic has been created? (2) the grouping question, i.e., which non-searches should be grouped to assess whether the group crossed the mosaic line? (3) the reasonableness question, i.e., how is the reasonableness of each mosaic to be determined, considering that a mosaic may aggregate across many different kinds of surveillance? (4) the remedies question, including when the exclusionary rule applies and who has standing.

beeper installation and surveillance."[239]

Less clear is the situation involving the trespass on a vehicle to install a tracking device and the subsequent tracking of that vehicle on the highway, as in *Jones*. (The government there "argue[d] in the alternative that even if the [warrantless][240] attachment and use of the device was a search, it was reasonable— and thus lawful—under the Fourth Amendment because 'officers had reasonable suspicion,[241] and indeed probable cause, to believe that [Jones] was a dealer in a large-scale cocaine distribution conspiracy,' " but since that argument had not been raised before, the Court deemed "the argument forfeited.") Given that searches of vehicles without a warrant have otherwise been upheld, even absent any showing of exigent circumstances, because of the "lesser expectation of privacy in a motor vehicle,"[242] it might be contended that the same must be true with respect to a vehicle search under *Jones*. The objection to that, of course, is that 28 days of nonstop surveillance is a far cry from the typical search, so that the added protections of a warrant requirement make special sense in that context. But here again the particular theory embraced by the majority in *Jones* may have an adverse ef-

---

[239]While *Karo* thus appears to mean that search inside premises for the beeper-laden object is permissible without any identification of the premises in the search warrant, the Court later declined to take a similar step with respect to so-called "anticipatory" search warrants, discussed in § 3.7(c). In United States v. Grubbs, 547 U.S. 90, 126 S.Ct. 1494, 164 L.Ed.2d 195 (2006), the Court declared that probable cause for such a search warrant has two prongs: (i) probable cause that seizable items will be in a particular place if a certain "triggering condition" first occurs, and (ii) "probable cause to believe the triggering condition will occur" with respect to a "single location." This appears to mean that, contrary to some pre-*Grubbs* case law, an anticipatory search warrant cannot be obtained based upon the "triggering condition" that a specified package known to contain specified seizable effect is observed being taken into previously unknown premises.

[240]Actually, in *Jones* the agents did obtain a warrant but did not comply with two of the warrant's restrictions: (i) that the installation occur within 10 days; and (ii) that the installation occur within the District of Columbia. As to this, the four-

Justice concurrence in *Jones* noted: "In the courts below the Government did not argue, and has not argued here, that the Fourth Amendment does not impose those precise restrictions and that the violation of those restrictions does not demand the suppression of evidence obtained using the tracking device."

[241]Some authority is to be found to the effect that reasonable suspicion suffices. United States v. Michael, 645 F.2d 252 (5th Cir.1981). However, *Michael* dealt with a form of surveillance not deemed a search under the Supreme Court's later decisions, and was distinguished in United States v. Butts, 710 F.2d 1139 (5th Cir.19830, on reh., 729 F.2d 1514 (5th Cir.,), where full probable cause was deemed necessary for physical entry of an aircraft to install the beeper. And in any event, the Supreme Court later, in another context, rejected the notion that a less-intrusive search for evidence would only require reasonable suspicion instead of probable cause. Arizona v. Hicks, 480 U.S. 321, 107 S.Ct. 1149, 94 L.Ed.2d 347 (1987).

[242]United States v. Chadwick, 433 U.S. 1, 97 S.Ct. 2476, 53 L.Ed.2d 538 (1977). See § 7.2.

fect, for its focus is not upon the resulting surveillance but rather upon the act of installing the tracking device, that is, the point at which the "Government physically occupied private property for the purpose of obtaining information."[243]

Other forms of technology are also used for the purpose of tracking persons or things or determining their present or past location. One such possibility has been created by an FCC rule requiring cellular telephone companies to have the capability of determining the location from which a cellular phone call originates to within 125 meters.

> The cellular telephone call location technology now mandated by the FCC will turn each of the more than fifty million cell phones in the United States into a tracking device. It will enable police not just to pinpoint the location of cell phone calls to 911 operators, but to track the location of all cellular phone users, no matter who they are calling, both as they are actually making calls and after the fact through phone company computer records. Moreover, because cellular telephones send out signals to the cellular system every few minutes to keep the system informed of their location, police will be able to remotely track any individual with a cellular telephone that is turned on, whether or not they are actually placing a call. Cellular telephone location technology thus will provide law enforcement with an extraordinarily powerful new tool for monitoring the movement of individuals.[244]

As one commentator has noted, because of "the broad language employed by the Court, the opinion in *Knotts* is clearly applicable to at least some uses of cellular call location technology,"[245] as police are most likely "to use the technology to track cellular

---

[243]In the post-*Jones* decision in State v. Zahn, 812 N.W.2d 490 (S.D. 2012), the court held "that the attachment and use of a GPS device to monitor an individual's activities over an extended period of time requires a search warrant." However, *Zahn* cannot be read as concluding that such a warrant requirement exists under the *Jones* majority's trespass doctrine, as the *Zahn* case also adopts, in the alternative, the position seemingly accepted by another group of Justices in *Jones* that long-term monitoring, without regard to trespass, constitutes a search.

[244]Note, 10 Stan.L. & Pol'y Rev. 103, 104 (1998).

[245]See, e.g., In re Application of the United States for an Order Directing a Provider of Electronic Communication Service to Disclose Records to Government, 620 F.3d 304 (3d Cir. 2010), discussed in Freiwald, Cell Phone Location Data and the Fourth

Amendment: A Question of Law, Not Fact, 70 Md.L.Rev. 681 (2011) (relying on *Knotts* in rejecting ruling below that a search warrant is always required to obtain from a cell phone provider a customer's historical cellular tower data, also known as cell site location information); United States v. Forest, 355 F.3d 942 (6th Cir.2004) (where DEA agents, in order to reestablish visual contact with defendant, dialed his cellular phone, without allowing it to ring, and used Sprint's computer data to determine which cellular transmission towers being "hit" by defendant's phone, all in order "to track his movements only on public highways," *Knotts* governs notwithstanding defendant's claim "he had a legitimate expectation of privacy in the cell-site data itself," as "the distinction between the cell-site data and Garner's location is not legally significant under the particular facts of this case");Devega v. State, 286 Ga. 448, 689 S.E.2d 293 (2010) (police had

telephone users as they travel on public streets and highways," which under *Knotts* "does not violate any reasonable expectation of privacy."[246] There are, however, as this same analyst notes, two arguments that could be made in an effort to distinguish *Knotts*: (1) because "tracking with cellular call location technology, [which] can be done virtually automatically by computer,[247] will allow the police to monitor the movements of many more people for longer periods of time,"[248] the greater potential for what the Court in *Knotts* called "dragnet type law enforcement" mandates, as the Court there suggested, "different constitutional principles"; and (2) because "cellular call location technology makes it possible for police to monitor the movement of individuals after the fact,"[249] this is more than what the Court in *Knotts* called "augmenting the sensory faculties." This same commentator

---

defendant's cell phone provider "ping" his phone, thus sending signal to phone to locate it by its GPS, and by following signal police located defendant as he traveled along highway; no search, as "the warrantless monitoring of his cell phone location revealed the same information as visual surveillance").

[246]Note, 10 Stan.L. & Pol'y Rev. 103, 108 (1998). See also Comment, 43 Ariz.St.L.J. 591, 592 (2011) (concluding such monitoring "is not a search within the meaning of the Fourth Amendment so long as the shifting position of the thing being tracked could be determined by visual observation from a spot where one is legally permitted to be."

[247]In a very revealing description of current police practices, it was noted that often the police will seek the assistance of a wireless carrier to conduct the real-time surveillance of movements, but that "even small police departments found cell surveillance so valuable that they acquired their own tracking equipment to avoid the time and expense of having the phone companies carry out the operation for them." Lichtblau, Police Are Using Phone Tracking as Routine Tool, New York Times, April 1, 2012, p. A.1, col. 6.

[248]Note, 10 Stan.L. & Pol'y Rev. 103, 109 (1998).

[249]Note, 10 Stan.L. & Pol'y Rev. 103, 109 (1998). See also Clark, Cell Phones as Tracking Devices, 41 Val.U.

L.Rev. 1413 (2007) (noting at 1416–17 that "most of the courts concluded that an order based upon probable cause * * * is required to compel cell phone providers to divulge real-time/prospective cell site location information"); McLaughlin, The Fourth Amendment and Cell Phone Location Tracking: Where Are We?, 29 Hastings Comm. & Ent.L.J. 421 (2007) (presenting other arguments); Comment, 16 CommLaw Conspectus 283 (2007) (concluding at 319 that "proof of probable cause is required to obtain access to tracking data derived from cell phones"); Notes, 73 Brook.L.Rev. 421 (383 (2007) (concluding at 384 "that a warrant issued upon probable cause is the appropriate form of authorization for law enforcement to conduct certain types of surveillance made possible by cell location data"); 29 Hastings Comm. & Ent.L.J. 421 (2007) (concluding at 425 "that because cell phones location tracking implicates a number of core Fourth Amendment doctrines, it should constitute an unreasonable search"); 39 Pepp.L.Rev. 701 (2012) (concluding obtaining historical cell site location information is no search, and thus probable cause not required); 13 Rich.J.L. & Tech. 16 (2007) (concluding at 98 that "a cellular phone user retains a reasonable expectation of privacy in his cell site data"); 64 U.Miami L.Rev. 1061 (2010) (concluding at 1086 that "government acquisition of cellular phone site location information constitutes a search").

As noted in In re Application of the United States for an Order Direct-

deems it less than apparent that the Supreme Court would buy either of these arguments,[250] and certainly the cell phone monitoring practices in question here do not fall within the *Jones* trespass rule, just as it is unlikely that the limitations imposed by *Karo* will have any significant impact here.[251] But the fact that five Justices in *Jones* expressed a readiness to go further, at least with respect to long-term surveillance, suggests that Fourth Amendment controls on cell phone surveillance are not out of the

---

ing a Provider of Electronic Communication Service to Disclose Records to Government, 620 F.3d 304 (3d Cir.2010), discussed in Freiwald, Cell Phone Location Data and the Fourth Amendment: A Question of Law, Not Fact, 70 Md.L.Rev. 681 (2011), "there is no dispute" that historical cell site location information is a "record or other information pertaining to a subscriber * * * or customer" and thus falls within § 2703(c)(1) of the Stored Communications Act. The court went on to construe this provision as meaning the government could seek a court order for such information upon a showing (as the statute says) "that there are reasonable grounds to believe that * * * the records or other information sought, are relevant and material to an ongoing criminal investigation," and that such an order could thus be issued upon a standard that "is a lesser one than probable cause," but that a court in its discretion could instead require in a particular case that the government instead pursue the other procedure included in the statute, obtaining a search warrant upon a showing of probable cause, though the latter "is an option to be used sparingly."

[250] As this commentator notes, the first argument is unlikely to prevail "without strong evidence of widespread police abuse of the technology," while the second might well be rejected on the ground that this after-the-fact capability is simply "augmenting" the existing police power to interview bystanders about their recollections. Note, 10 Stan.L. & Pol'y Rev. 103, 109 (1998). Moreover, examination of phone company records to determine the past activity might be viewed as analogous to consulting such records

to determine numbers called. See § 2.7(b). But that analogy was rejected in In re Application of the United States for an Order Directing a Provider of Electronic Communication Service to Disclose Records to Government, 620 F.3d 304 (3d Cir.2010): "A cell phone customer has not 'voluntarily' shared his location information with a cellular provider in any meaningful way. [I]t is unlikely that cell phone customers are aware that their cell phone providers *collect* and store historical location information. Therefore, '[w]hen a cell phone user makes a call, the only information that is voluntarily and knowingly conveyed to the phone company is the number that is dialed and there is no indication to the user that making that call will also located the caller; when a cell phone user receives a call, he hasn't voluntarily exposed anything at all.'"

[251] Because "the main reason people buy cell phones is to be able to make telephone calls when they are away from the wireline phones in their home or office, law enforcement is likely to have relatively few opportunities to apply cellular call location technology to people inside private residences regardless of the holding in *Karo*." Note, 10 Stan.L. & Pol'y Rev. 103, 109 (1998). As noted in Application of the United States for an Order Directing a Provider of Electronic Communication Service to Disclose Records to Government, 620 F.3d 304 (3d Cir.2010): "The *Knotts/Karo* opinions make clear that the privacy interests at issue are confined to the interior of the home. There is no evidence in this record that historical [cell site location information], even when focused on cell phones that are equipped with GPS, extends to that realm."

question.

There are a variety of other tracking mechanisms currently in use by government, although apparently only for purposes other than law enforcement, that hold potential benefits for police investigators. There is, for example, the federally-funded Intelligent Transportation Systems (ITS) project, whose surveillance technologies initially "collected aggregate information about traffic flows, such as the rate of use of a segment of highway," though "ITS applications can track the locations a traveler visits and maintain itineraries of an individual's past travel," and "are sometimes even used to predict the individual's future movements and activities."[252] Another illustration concerns the use of toll tag transponders, intended for use in automatically paying tolls, but by which "it is possible to follow the successive locations of transponders, and the vehicles to which these devices are attached, as they move past toll tag readers located at places along roads and highways."[253] Should these tracking mechanisms be put to use by law enforcement, their use as well will doubtless be assessed under *Knotts*, *Karo* and *Jones*.

Also deserving mention here is the "increased use of Vessel Monitoring systems (VMS)," which are "electronic transmitting devices placed on vessels to intermittently transmit information via satellite link to a land-based receiver," including a "vessel's location, speed, and direction of movement."[254] Current regulations require an approved VMS system be on board many commercial fishing vessels and that the units remain "turned on and transmitting 24 hours per day, regardless of the vessel's location and irrespective of whether the vessel is engaging in commercial fishing activities."[255] Given the 24-hour surveillance and the statutory mandate for sharing VMS data among relevant state and

---

[252]Glancy, Privacy on the Open Road, 30 Ohio N.U.L.Rev. 295, 303 (2004).

Consider also Joh, Discretionless Policing: Technology and the Fourth Amendment, 95 Cal.L.Rev. 199 (2007), suggesting ITS technology could permit "remote and automatic enforcement of the traffic laws, thereby reducing or eliminating traffic stops by police").

Similarly, by use of radio frequency identification tags it may be possible in the future to keep track of the movements and actions of individuals. See Note, 40 Loy.L.A.L.Rev. 853 (2007); Recent Developments, 8 N.C.J.L. & Tech. 249 (2007), discussing the technology and its Fourth

Amendment implications.

[253]Glancy, 30 Ohio N.U.L.Rev. 295, 307 (2004).

[254]Crance & Mastry, Fourth Amendment Privacy Rights at Sea and Governmental Use of Visual Monitoring Systems: There's Something Fishy About This, 22 J.Envtl.L. & Litig. 231, 233 (2007).

[255]Crance & Mastry, 22 J.Envtl.L. & Litig. 231, 233 (2007), adding that there are two limited power-down exceptions: (i) when the vessel is continuously out of the water over 72 hours; and (ii) when the vessel had both a commercial and valid for-hire reef fish permit.

federal agencies,[256] it has been argued that, "in the absence of a warrant, continuous 24-hour surveillance of commercial fishing vessels should be struck down as unconstitutional."[257]

§ 2.7(g) Ongoing surveillance of public movements and relationships

In certain types of investigations, police have occasion to engage in ongoing surveillance of movements and relationships occurring in public.[258] A fixed surveillance may be established with respect to certain premises and conducted there for some period of time in an effort to uncover evidence of criminal activity occurring at or being directed from those premises.[259] Yet another kind of fixed surveillance involves installing closed circuit television cameras in certain high-crime areas and monitoring the TV screens at the stationhouse.[260] A moving surveillance may be conducted, either briefly or as long as several months, in order to determine if a particular individual is engaged in criminal activity or—more likely—to identify all of the participants in an ongoing criminal conspiracy.[261] In addition, law enforcement agents may, either as a matter of routine or in connection with a partic-

---

[256] 16 U.S.C.A. § 1861(b)(1)(A).

[257] Crance & Mastry, 22 J.Envtl.L. & Litig. 231, 243–44 (2007).

[Section 2.7(g)]

[258] R. Ferguson, Vice Control 40–48 (1974); A. Sutor, Police Operations 160–77 (1976).

[259] Illustrative is this incident, set out in Law Enforcement in the Metropolis 24 (D. McIntyre ed. 1967): "Two officers rented a room in a flophouse and let it be known that they had just been discharged from service, had lots of money, and were going to have a good time for themselves. They selected a room which overlooked the rear of a hotel on the opposite side of the street in which the bawdy house was operated. Using a motion picture camera, and occasionally a telescopic lens, they photographed the activity taking place at this house. Each morning, they photographed the girls as they reported for work. The customers were photographed as they approached the house and were directed to the door by one of the girls or the madam, who would appear on a rear porch. On completion of their assignment, the officers had photographed approximately 150 men entering and leaving this establishment. On one occasion, so

many men were being entertained that it was necessary for them to wait on the back porch, which was in plain view."

[260] Under this technique, "police officers monitor the CCTV screens and can dispatch assistance immediately when anything unusual appears on the screen. The officer on monitoring duty can adjust the camera for a better viewing angle and focus on suspected criminal activity. The most sophisticated aspect of the system, however, is a technological breakthrough known as light amplification ability. This feature permits the system to be used at night, thus giving constant twenty-four hour surveillance." Note, 13 U.Mich.J.L.Ref. 571, 573 (1980). On the current extent and effects of CCTV use, see Slobogin, Public Privacy: Camera Surveillance of Public Places and the Right to Anonymity, 72 Miss.L.J. 213, 219–33 (2002).

[261] Illustrative is the following incident, set out in Law Enforcement in the Metropolis 28 (D. McIntyre ed. 1967): "To build conspiracy cases against gambling rackets, surveillance must be maintained for protracted periods of time. Depending upon the size of the 'numbers' operation, the

ular ongoing investigation, attend certain kinds of public gatherings and take note of what occurs on those occasions.

"When 'surveillance' involves the observation of the public activities of an individual and the collection and maintenance of publicly available information about an individual, it is hard to pin down any fourth amendment rights that have been violated."[262] Indeed, it is a fair generalization that none of the activities described above constitutes a search and that conse-

---

conspiracy squad of the Detroit Vice Bureau may spend as long as 14 months observing the process of how bets are placed and routed through syndicate headquarters. Daily observations are made of the movements of all syndicate members, ranging in importance from those working on house-to-house collections to those suspected of being the 'big boss.' As the investigation progresses, the officers may conceal themselves in a truck parked close to the premises in order to better identify the individuals entering and leaving such an establishment. In all surveillance work, a daily journal of the officer's observations is maintained so that an organizational chart of the syndicate operation can be pieced together. In addition to serving as a means of obtaining warrants for the seizure of evidence and for arrest purposes, these observations serve to tie together the various individuals to prove a conspiracy charge in court."

[262] Christie, Government Surveillance and Individual Freedom: A Proposed Statutory Response to Laird v. Tatum and the Broader Problem of Government Surveillance of the Individual, 47 N.Y.U.L.Rev. 871, 885 n. 68 (1972). Note, 13 U.Mich.L.Ref. 571, 582 (1980), observes: "One walking along a public sidewalk or standing in a public park cannot reasonably expect that his activity will be immune from the public eye or from observation by police. Where police use CCTV to observe such public areas there is no basis for a defendant to claim a reasonable expectation of privacy." Thus, it has been held that visual surveillance, even if aided by binoculars and extending over a substantial period of time, is not governed by the Fourth Amendment when the person or vehi-

cle being watched is moving about on the public streets and highways. United States v. Gonzalez-Rodriguez, 513 F.2d 928 (9th Cir.1975); United States v. McCall, 243 F.2d 858 (10th Cir.1957). Compare Aronov, Privacy in a Public Setting: The Constitutionality of Street Surveillance, 22 QLR 769 (2004), asserting at 809 that "Dragnet scanning of individuals' daily activities for signs of illegality amounts to an unreasonable search"; Blitz, Video Surveillance and the Constitution of Public Space: Fitting the Fourth Amendment to a World that Tracks Image and Identity, 82 Tex.L.Rev. 1349 (2004), concluding at 1480 that "the invasiveness and inescapability of emerging public camera systems make it hard to understand how courts can invoke the Fourth Amendment to block government officials from rummaging through purses, containers, or suitcases, but ignore the more substantial threat to privacy presented by ubiquitous video surveillance"; Granholm, Video Surveillance of Public Streets: The Constitutionality of Invisible Citizen Searches, 64 U.Det.L.Rev. 687 (1987), arguing the public has a justified expectation of privacy of a limited nature, so that reasonable suspicion should be required; and Slobogin, Public Privacy: Camera Surveillance of Public Places and the Right to Anonymity, 72 Miss.L.J. 213, 286 (2002), proposing that "constitutional regulation of government efforts to pierce public anonymity through CCTV consist of four components. First, law enforcement should have to justify both the establishment of a particular camera system and its use to scrutinize particular individuals. Second, it should have to develop policies regarding the procedure for conducting camera surveillance. Third, it should have to develop policies regard-

quently these investigative practices are not at all limited by the Fourth Amendment. In *Katz v. United States*[263] the Court declared that "[w]hat a person knowingly exposes to the public * * * is not a subject of Fourth Amendment protection."

For one thing, this means that covert "visual surveillance"[264] of a person while he moves about in public is not subject to Fourth Amendment restraints. This surveillance does not intrude upon anyone's justified expectation of privacy, for members of the public have "no reason to believe that their movements on the public highway would remain private.":[265] As the Supreme Court noted in *Cardwell v. Lewis*[266]: "A car has little capacity for escaping public scrutiny. It travels public thoroughfares where both its occupants and its contents are in plain view." One commentator has taken the view that one "knowingly exposes to the public" only what a reasonably curious person might observe, and thus has suggested that because such a person would not engage in "continuous tailing * * * for a long distance or time, * * * longterm visual surveillance may result in a search subject to Fourth Amendment warrant requirements."[267] However, no court decision has been found adopting this position or even intimating that it might be adopted. On the contrary, arrests and searches have been upheld when based upon the fruits of an extended surveillance of the suspect's activities and movements in public.[268]

This question was more directly confronted by the Supreme

---

ing storage and dissemination of recorded materials to other entities. Finally, and most importantly, it should be accountable to entities outside law enforcement when it fails to follow these three requirements."

[263]Katz v. United States, 389 U.S. 347, 88 S.Ct. 507, 19 L.Ed.2d 576 (1967).

[264]United States v. Holmes, 521 F.2d 859 (5th Cir.1975), aff'd en banc by equally divided court, 537 F.2d 227 (5th Cir.1976), concluding such surveillance is not governed by the Fourth Amendment. See also State v. Abislaiman, 437 So.2d 181 (Fla.App. 1983) (no search to operate and monitor camera with zoom lens as security measure in hospital parking lot); State v. Pelletier, 541 A.2d 1296 (Me.1988) (no search to follow defendant's car several miles, thus observing erratic driving); State v. Littlefield, 408 A.2d 695 (Me.1979) (no search to follow pedestrian several blocks).

[265]United States v. Moore, 562 F.2d 106 (1st Cir.1977).

[266]Cardwell v. Lewis, 417 U.S. 583, 94 S.Ct. 2464, 41 L.Ed.2d 325 (1974).

[267]Note, 86 Yale L.J. 1461, 1494 (1977).

[268]E.g., Christensen v. County of Boone, Illinois, 483 F.3d 454 (7th Cir.2007) (deputy's actions in repeatedly following plaintiffs as they drove on country roads and in repeatedly sitting outside businesses that plaintiffs patronized not a search); United States v. Gonzalez-Rodriguez, 513 F.2d 928 (9th Cir.1975) (over a month of continued surveillance).

Consider also Vega-Rodriguez v. Puerto Rico Telephone Co., 110 F.3d 174 (1st Cir.1997) (lawsuit by employees of quasi-public telephone company challenging videotaping of their workplace properly dismissed, as no reasonable expectation of privacy in the open and undifferentiated work area; as for employees' argument that this is different from direct observation by supervisors because the "surveillance is electronic and, therefore, unremitting," court responds that "this sort of

Court in *United States v. Knotts,*[269] where by a combination of visual surveillance and monitoring of an electronic tracking device installed in a container the suspect was transporting he was tracked about 100 miles to where he delivered the container. The Court held that the monitoring was no search because it revealed only facts that could have been ascertained by visual surveillance, which likewise does not constitute Fourth Amendment activity:

> A person travelling in an automobile on public thoroughfares has no reasonable expectation of privacy in his movements from one place to another. When Petschen travelled over the public streets he voluntarily conveyed to anyone who wanted to look the fact that he was travelling over particular roads in a particular direction, the fact of whatever stops he made, and the fact of his final destination when he exited from public roads onto private property.

That conclusion is not at all affected by the majority's holding in *United States v. Jones*[270] that such surveillance *is* a search if accomplished by a trespass onto defendant's vehicle to install the surveillance device, and even the five concurring Justices in *Jones* do not appear to be proposing any change in this regard.[271]

This kind of surveillance, in which the objective is to keep the subject under observation without his becoming aware that he is being followed, must be distinguished from a so-called "rough" surveillance. In the latter type of surveillance

> no attempt is made to conceal the surveillant's actions. The object is to stay with the subject at all times whether he likes it or not. It is used to harass, and restrict his movements and generally upset the operation. (Used on known racketeers, narcotics dealers, etc.,

---

argument has failed consistently under the plain view doctrine, and it musters no greater persuasiveness in the present context").

[269] United States v. Knotts, 460 U.S. 276, 103 S.Ct. 1081, 75 L.Ed.2d 55 (1983).

[270] United States v. Jones, __ U.S. __, 132 S.Ct. 945, 181 L.Ed.2d 911 (2012).

[271] In the four-Justice concurrence, it is asserted at one point that the trespass theory "leads to incongruous results," in that brief surveillance following such attachment is deemed a search, while "if the police follow the same car for a much longer period using unmarked cars and aerial assistance, this tracking is not subject to any Fourth Amendment constraints." If this is really "incongruous," one might think this means these four Jus-

tices believe the latter situation also involves a search. But those Justices later seem to say that the problem re GPS monitoring is that it makes "long-term monitoring relatively easy and cheap," while by comparison long-term monitoring without such technological assistance is sufficiently restrained by the fact it would require a significant "expenditure of law enforcement resources." Likewise, Justice Sotomayor, in her separate concurrence, seems concerned generally by surveillance that is so intense that it "reflects a wealth of detail about [a person's] familial, political, professional, religious, and sexual associations," but then adds to that the concern that "GPS monitoring is cheap in comparison to conventional surveillance techniques" and thus "evades the ordinary checks that constrain abusive law enforcement practices."

when it is very difficult to obtain evidence against them.)[272] As the Supreme Court noted in *Terry v. Ohio*,[273] the Fourth Amendment imposes upon courts the "responsibility to guard against police conduct which is overbearing or harassing." This suggests that such harassment-by-surveillance, at least when there is "harassment bordering on arrest,"[274] should be viewed as a violation of the Fourth Amendment.[275]

As for the collection of data concerning what occurs at public gatherings, it has been held that "such activity by law enforcement authorities, without more, is legally unobjectionable."[276] Illustrative is *United States v. Cogwell*,[277] where the defendants were convicted of defrauding the government of monies which were supposed to be used for job training. At trial several policemen testified that in the course of several hundred visits to the job training centers they observed only limited trainee attendance and practically no instruction, which was at variance with reports filed by the defendants. As to the defendants' claim that these visits violated their Fourth Amendment rights, the court responded:

> Defendants were voluntary participants in an educational program subject to continual monitoring by United States government of-

---

[272]A. Sutor, Police Operations 165 (1976).

[273]Terry v. Ohio, 392 U.S. 1, 88 S.Ct. 1868, 20 L.Ed.2d 889 (1968).

[274]In Giancana v. Johnson, No. 63 C 1145 (N.D.Ill.1963), where plaintiff Sam Giancana established that for over a month FBI agents had kept from two to five vehicles outside his residence on a 24-hour basis, had observed him and his home, and had followed him as he went to places of public accommodation such as restaurants, stores and golf courses, Judge Austin concluded that such activity "is an arbitrary intrusion into plaintiff's right of privacy, his right to be left alone, and is harassment bordering on arrest." He issued a preliminary injunction restraining the FBI agents from (a) maintaining more than one car within one block of plaintiff's residence, (b) following plaintiff with more than one car, or (c) playing in the foursome immediately behind plaintiff on the golf course. The injunction was stayed four days later, Giancana v. Hoover, 322 F.2d 789 (7th Cir.1963), and was later reversed on the ground that the district court had lacked jurisdiction because of plaintiff's failure to allege $10,000 damages, Giancana v. Johnson, 335 F.2d 366 (7th Cir. 1964). Consider also Scherer v. Brennan, 266 F.Supp. 758 (N.D.Ill. 1966), aff'd 379 F.2d 609 (7th Cir. 1967), holding Secret Service agents immune from tort suit for their actions in keeping plaintiff (a dealer in firearms who kept in his home rifles, pistols, a machine gun, and a 25 m.m. cannon) under "constant direct surveillance" on the day the President was visiting "within easy rifle shot" of plaintiff's residence.

[275]Similarly, surveillance of business premises may be open and harassing in nature to the extent that customers are kept away from the business. See Donnelly, Judicial Control of Informants, Spies, Stool Pigeons, and Agent Provocateurs, 60 Yale L.J. 1091, 1096 (1951). In Bee See Books, Inc. v. Leary, 291 F.Supp. 622 (S.D.N.Y.1968), such conduct directed at a book store was held to unconstitutionally chill First Amendment rights.

[276]Philadelphia Yearly Meeting of the Religious Society of Friends v. Tate, 519 F.2d 1335 (3d Cir.1975).

[277]United States v. Cogwell, 486 F.2d 823 (7th Cir.1973).

ficials * * *. They cannot, therefore, reasonably claim the same expectancy of privacy which might shroud their purely personal activity. Further, the locations do not suggest an expectation of privacy. The training centers were generally accessible to anyone having an interest in the program, including some nonparticipants. * * * The nature of the activity belies an expectation of privacy. Educational classes are inherently group activities open to the full view of fellow participants, instructors, and administrative and supervisory personnel.

Similarly, it has been held that it is not a Fourth Amendment search for the police to photograph[278] or videotape[279] or tape record[280] what occurs at a public meeting (or, for that matter, at an organization's meeting, where such is deemed to be within the scope of the invitation given by the organization or its representatives to the investigating undercover officer.[281]) Such activities have also been challenged on the ground that they unduly chill the First Amendment freedoms of speech and association, generally without success.[282]

If, as concluded earlier, it is generally true that using surveillance cameras in public areas is not a search, it must then be asked whether the result is different when the camera in question is employed together with some other technology that facilitates identification. One such technology, one of many modern forms of biometric identification,[283] is called "facial recognition," which has been described as follows:

FaceIt is a facial recognition software engine helping a network of cameras and computers to quickly detect and recognize faces. When a head-like object moves within the camera's field of vision—both eyes have to be visible and the face cannot be turned more than 45 degrees from the camera—the computer guesses whether it is a face. If the answer is yes, FaceIt crops the face from the background and "normalizes" the image by compensating for size

[278]Philadelphia Yearly Meeting of the Religious Society of Friends v. Tate, 519 F.2d 1335 (3d Cir.1975).

[279]Sponick v. City of Detroit Police Dept., 49 Mich.App. 162, 211 N.W.2d 674 (1973) (police officer videotaped in bar talking with known criminals did not have a "reasonable expectation of privacy" because observation occurred in public place).

But see State v. Solis, 214 Mont. 310, 693 P.2d 518 (1984) (warrantless videotaping of transactions in pawn shop operated undercover by police illegal under *state* constitution, as "there is a reasonable expectation that hidden monitoring is not taking place").

[280]United States v. Tijerina, 412

F.2d 661 (10th Cir.1969).

[281]United States v. Mayer, 503 F.3d 740 (9th Cir.2007) (where undercover agent joined organization opposed to sexual age-of-consent laws, he did not exceed scope of consent in recording his conversations with other members at organization conference).

[282]See Laird v. Tatum, 408 U.S. 1, 92 S.Ct. 2318, 33 L.Ed.2d 154 (1972); United States v. Mayer, 503 F.3d 740 (9th Cir.2007); Anderson v. Sills, 56 N.J. 210, 265 A.2d 678 (1970).

[283]Others include voice recognition, signature recognition, fingerprint imaging, hand measurement scans, hand vein mapping, iris recognition, and retinal scans. See Note, 9 S.Cal. Interdisc.L.J. 295, 307–09 (1995).

and lighting. The image is then subjected to a Local Feature Analysis that essentially generates a faceprint—a digital code encapsulating the measurements of the landmarks of a face and how they correlate. * * * Accessories such as wigs, moustaches, glasses, even basic plastic surgery, will not affect identification.[284]

There "are two main uses for facial recognition technology: first, for identification purposes, and second, for access control or authorization purposes."[285] The second of these, also called "authentication," that is, "the ability to verify a person's identity through a comparison with their previously recorded biometric measurements,"[286] is used by private industry to prevent fraud, but can also be used by government agencies as a check on identity when the government is entitled to require a person to identify themselves. Illustrative would be a state Department of Motor Vehicles using the technology "to scan databases to insure that individuals attempting to get a driver's license are who they say they are."[287] This is certainly the least objectionable use of this technology, and it would appear that its use in this manner by the government presents no serious Fourth Amendment issue.

However, the "most important and prominent use" of this technology "is use for identification, or one-to-many searching. In this mode, cameras sweep their field of vision for every face present and then FaceIt compares each face it scans in a crowd to those in a database of facial images, returning a list of matches with associated confidence levels. The system can match over a million faces per second."[288] Government use of the technology in this way, which "carries with it the largest privacy implications,"[289] has occurred on occasion, mainly at major sporting events and on streets where large numbers of people congregate.[290] In light of studies questioning the reliability and effectiveness of using the technology for identification purposes,[291] it may be doubted how common police use of the technology in this way will become, although renewed post-9/11 government interest in using face recognition as part of the "war on terrorism" may bring

---

[284]Nguyen, Here's Looking at You, Kid: Has Face-Recognition Technology Completely Outflanked the Fourth Amendment?, 7 Va.J.L. & Tech. (Summer 2002), article 2, par. 7, appearing at <http://www.vjolt.net/vol7/issue1/index.html>.

[285]Note, 9 S.Cal.Interdisc.L.J. 295, 305 (1995).

[286]Note, 9 S.Cal.Interdisc.L.J. 295, 306 (1995).

[287]Note, 9 S.Cal.Interdisc.L.J. 295, 306 (1995).

[288]Nguyen, 7 Va.J.L. & Tech. (Summer 2002), art. 2, par. 8.

[289]Nguyen, 7 Va.J.L. & Tech. (Summer 2002), art. 2, par. 8.

[290]Comment, 20 J.Marshall J.Computer & Info.L. 321, 326–29 (2002), noting such use at the January 2001 Super Bowl and the 2002 Winter Olympics in Salt Lake City, and in the Tampa entertainment district.

[291]See Rotenberg, Privacy and Secrecy After September 11, 80 Minn.L. Rev. 1115, 1121 (2002); Slobogin, Public Privacy: Camera Surveillance of Public Places and the Right to Anonymity, 72 Miss.L.J. 213, 315 n.67 (2002).

about improvements in and greater use of the technology.[292]

Does the use of facial recognition technology for identification purposes constitute a "search" within the meaning of the Fourth Amendment? The commentators have usually answered this question in the negative,[293] which is hardly surprising. As one of them succinctly put it, "facial recognition technology is no different from an officer comparing a photograph of a known criminal to the faces of people the officer passes in the street. Both methods involve comparing a face while in a public place with pictures of known criminals: one method is merely more efficient than the other. Since the content of information received by the officer is identical in the two cases, the Fourth Amendment analysis under *Katz* should also be identical."[294] That judgment, of course, is quiet similar to that made by the Supreme Court in *Knotts* regarding the tracker surveillance in that case,[295] where the Court in effect stated that such surveillance was no search because unaided visual surveillance of the defendant's movements in public places would have yielded the same information.

Of course, for the reasons stated earlier,[296] there is reason to be troubled about this assumed equivalence between "visual surveillance" and "scientific enhancement" in *Knotts*. Somewhat the same concern might be voiced regarding the use of facial recognition technology. As one commentator aptly put it: "On the one hand, FaceIt is no different from a police officer standing at the corner with a set of mugshots and scanning for faces in the crowd. On the other hand, however, FaceIt is * * * like having thousands of police officers standing in the square and monitoring citizens as they walk past to buy their groceries or enter restaurants."[297] But so long as *Knotts* stands, that distinction is unlikely to carry the day, for in that case the "scientific enhancement" was deemed to have no Fourth Amendment significance because an army of bystanders along the defendant's 100-mile journey would have acquired the same information.

---

[292]Comment, 20 J. Marshall J. Computer & Info.L. 321, 327–28n (2002).

[293]Benjamin, ShotSpotter and FaceIt: The Tools of Mass Monitoring, 2002 UCLA J.L. & Tech. 2, available at <www.lawtechjournal.com/articles/2002/02__020421__benjamin.pdf>; Fretty, Face-Recognition Surveillance: A Moment of Truth for Fourth Amendment Rights in Public Places, 16 Va.J.L. & Tech. 430, 441–44 (2011); Nguyen, 7 Va.J.L. & Tech. (Summer 2002), pars. 9–24; Simmons, From Katz to Kyllo: A Blueprint for Adapting the Fourth Amendment to Twenty-First Century Technologies, 53 Hastings L.J. 1303, 1358 n.99 (2002); Comment, 20 Temp.Envtl.L. & Tech.J. 251, 257–61 (2002); Note, 9 So.Cal. Interdisc.L.J. 295, 331 (1999).

But see Brogan, Facing the Music: The Dubious Constitutionality of Facial Recognition Technology, 25 Hastings Comm. & Ent.L.J. 65 (2003); Comment, 20 J.Marshall J. Computer & Info. L. 321, 339–41 (2002).

[294]Simmons, 53 Hastings L.J. 1303, 1358 n.99 (2002).

[295]See § 2.7(f).

[296]See § 2.7(f).

[297]Nguyen, 7 Va.J.L. & Tech (Summer 2002), par. 9.

Other Supreme Court decisions also lend support to the conclusion that use of facial recognition technology for purposes of identification is not a search. Of particular importance is *United States v. Dionisio*,[298] where the Court in holding that obtaining a voice sample was no search drew an analogy between the sound of one's voice and one's facial features: "Like a man's facial characteristics, * * * his voice is repeatedly produced for others to hear. No person can have a reasonable expectation that others will not know the sound of his voice, any more than he can reasonably expect that his face will be a mystery to the world." So too, facial recognition technology used for identification lacks those features the Court has stressed in other cases finding the investigative technique at issue to be a search. Illustrative is *Skinner v. Railway Labor Executives' Association*,[299] concluding that breath, blood and urine testing all constitute searches because they implicate "similar concerns about bodily integrity and * * * can reveal a host of private medical facts about [a person], including whether he or she is epileptic, pregnant, or diabetic." Perhaps unlike some other forms biometric identification,[300] facial scanning does not "appear to involve the requisite level of physical intrusion or have the ability to reveal private medical facts."[301] Finally, there is the admittedly troubling assertion in *Dow Chemical Co. v. United States*[302] that surveillance might become a search if the government employed "highly sophisticated surveillance equipment not generally available to the public," which would not tip the scales in favor of search as to facial recognition technology because that equipment does not fit within the suggested *Dow* exception.[303]

This is not to suggest that the concerns that have been voiced about facial recognition technology are without substance, but only that those concerns cannot comfortably be fit into extant Fourth Amendment jurisprudence. What those concerns come down to, in the final analysis, is the potential loss of anonymity

---

[298]United States v. Dionisio, 410 U.S. 1, 93 S.Ct. 764, 35 L.Ed.2d 67 (1973).

[299]Skinner v. Railway Labor Executives' Ass'n, 489 U.S. 602, 109 S.Ct. 1402, 103 L.Ed.2d 639 (1989).

[300]Comment, 20 Temp.Envtl.L. & Tech.J. 251, 260–61 (2002), concludes that in light of "recent medical evidence" it should be concluded that "fingerprints, retina and iris scans * * * constitute Fourth Amendment searches because of the ability of these biometric measures to reveal personal medical information,"

[301]Comment, 20 Temp.Envtl.L. & Tech.J. 251, 261 (2002).

[302]Dow Chemical Co. v. United States, 476 U.S. 227, 106 S.Ct. 1819, 90 L.Ed.2d 226 (1986).

[303]"FaceIt technology has been widely advertised to various clientele, including government, private corporations, banks, and office buildings. FaceIt technology is also 'inexpensive' and is compatible with 'any standard off the shelf hardware.' Technology as user-friendly and as easily available to the general public, corporations, and business as FaceIt is likely to tilt this factor in favor of constitutionality under current jurisprudence." Nguyen, 7 Va.J.L. & Tech. (Summer 2002), par. 17.

from the use of such technology.[304] But a right of anonymity is not clearly recognized under the Fourth Amendment[305] (although a powerful argument that it should be has been made[306]); to the extent it has some constitutional status, it resides in the First Amendment.[307] As for the extent to which anonymity is jeopardized by the use of facial recognition technology, this obviously depends upon the manner in which it is utilized. In those early uses receiving considerable publicity, it appears that the cameras were used with software that searched data bases *only* for "the faces of wanted criminals" and that when "no match was found, the scanned image was deleted."[308] If this procedure is adhered to, it would appear that no objectionable infringement of any right to anonymity has occurred, as only those individuals as to whom a probable cause judgment had been previously made have been identified.[309] So viewed, the practice has yet another Fourth Amendment analogy, which is to the case of *United States v. Place*,[310] where in holding the dog sniff at issue there was no search because it involved no physical intrusion and uncovered only the likely presence of contraband, the Court emphasized that the investigative procedure was "so limited both in the manner in which the information is obtained and in the content of the information revealed by the procedure."

The legitimate concerns about facial recognition technology, then, involve potential uses of the equipment in ways other than described above. One risk is that the technology could be used to

---

[304]See, e.g., Nguyen, 7 Va.J.L. & Tech. (Summer 2002), par. 45.

[305]Thus, Comment, 34 U.Tol.L. Rev. 351, 355 (2003), laments "the courts' unwillingness to advance the scope of the Fourth Amendment to privacy interests beyond one's physical person and one's home, i.e., to definitively protect intangible privacy interests (such as anonymity) while in public."

[306]See Slobogin, Public Privacy: Camera Surveillance of Public Places and the Right to Anonymity, 72 Miss.L.J. 213 (2002).

[307]"The First Amendment affects potential privacy-enhancing rules in at least three ways: (1) most prohibitions on private data-gathering in public (i.e. surveillance) risk violating the First Amendment (conversely, most government surveillance in public appears to be unconstrained by the Fourth Amendment); (2) the First Amendment may impose limits on the extent to which legislatures may re-strict the collection and sale of personal data in connection with commercial transactions; and (3) the First Amendment right to freedom of association imposes some limits on the extent to which the government may observe and profile citizens, if only by creating a right to anonymity in some cases." Froomkin, The Death of Privacy?, 52 Stan.L.Rev. 1461, 1506 (2000). See also Solove, The First Amendment as Criminal Procedure, 82 NYU L.Rev. 112 (2007).

[308]Taslitz, The Fourth Amendment in the Twenty-First Century: Technology, Privacy, and Human Emotions, 65 Law & Contemp.Probs. 125 (Spring 2002).

[309]It is at least arguable that also defensible would be the use of such technology at high-risk locations (e.g., airports) to match faces of those only suspected of criminality.

[310]United States v. Place, 462 U.S. 696, 103 S.Ct. 2637, 77 L.Ed.2d 110 (1983).

locate members of the public generally, or could be targeted at certain groups. " 'Once the new surveillance systems become institutionalized and taken for granted in a democratic society,' they can be 'used against those with the "wrong" political beliefs; against racial, ethnic, or religious minorities; and against those with lifestyles that offend the majority.' "[311] And this risk is compounded as the use of facial recognition technology grows, for "a networked system could identify an individual in one location on a specific date, and identify that same person at a different location afterwards."[312] "Once it becomes possible to bank all these images, and to call them up by physical typology, it will be feasible to set up an electronic sentry system giving police access to every citizen's comings and goings."[313] It is this "tracking" capability of the system,[314] then, that is the ultimate concern—a tracking so pervasive in its nature as to far surpass that allowed by the Court in *Knotts* (and thus of the "dragnet" nature that the Court there said would be another matter as far as the reach of the Fourth Amendment goes[315]), as well as a tracking so intense that it appears comparable to the activity that five concurring Justices in *United States v. Jones*[316] declared ought to be deemed a search.[317]

One other camera identification technique deserves mention here, namely, what is commonly referred to as the "red light camera system."[318] It is "a program designed to reduce the number of drivers running red lights by placing electronic cameras at intersections to catch violators. * * * The cameras at the monitored intersections are linked to and operated by a computer that connects to the traffic light's control box and sensors in the road. [R]ed light cameras only photograph the rear of a violator's vehicle. Technicians from the private company that installs and maintains the camera system view each photograph for accuracy and use a '[s]pecial scanner' to zoom in on the violator's license

---

[311]Note, 9 So.Cal.Interdisc.L.J. 295, 328 (1999), quoting MIT Prof. Gary T. Marx.

[312]Comment, 20 J.Marshall J.Computer & Info.L. 321, 343 (2002).

[313]Boal, Spycam City, Village Voice, Oct. 6, 1998, at 38.

[314]While "company officials have argued that individuals are only identified and not tracked, [they] have also admitted that FaceIt technology has such capabilities. If this is the case, then tracking, or following individuals would be a very easy matter. Authorities can simply enter a person's face print and 'reverse engineer' the identity of these individuals, by searching data from previous movements—to see

who they have met with, what they have done, and so on." Nguyen, 7 Va.J.L. & Tech. (Summer 2002), par. 28.

[315]See Fretty, 16 Va.J.L. & Tech. 430, 450–51 (2011).

[316]United States v. Jones, __ U.S. __, 132 S.Ct. 945, 181 L.Ed.2d 911 (2012).

[317]See note 271 supra.

[318]Glancy, Privacy on the Open Road, 30 Ohio N.U.L.Rev. 295, 318–19 (2004); Naumchik, Stop! Photographic Enforcement of Red Lights, 30 McGeorge L.Rev. 833 (1999); Comment, 33 U.Tol.L.Rev. 815 (2003); Recent Development, 80 N.C.L.Rev. 1879 (2002).

plate. After determining that the photograph is accurate, the private company mails the vehicle's owner a citation."[319] In light of what was said above regarding use of facial identification technology to identify offenders, it is apparent that such use of red light cameras does not constitute a Fourth Amendment search. Indeed, the red light camera situation represents an easier case, whether viewed from a Fourth Amendment or loss-of-anonymity standpoint, when it is considered that states may legitimately require "that all cars have license plates placed on the outside of the car,"[320] that there is no justified expectation of privacy in identification numbers of vehicles viewable from outside the vehicle,[321] and that the photographs are only of those vehicles which are apparently at that very moment involved in a violation of the law.[322] However, if a network of vehicle-identification cameras (perhaps also having face-recognition capability as well) were utilized to keep track of people's movements while they are in public,[323] that would constitute such a serious intrusion upon justified privacy expectations that, as noted above, such use should definitely be deemed a search.[324]

Such a judgment would seem appropriate as to the data collection aspect of ALPR (Automated License Plate Recognition) technology, more benignly used to determine that a particular vehicle at a particular location is connected to past criminality.[325] As one commentator has noted,

> many departments across the country are using ALPR not just for observational comparison, but also for *indiscriminate data collection*. When used in this manner, ALPR systems not only flag passing cars that match a criminal database, but also record the

---

[319]Recent Development, 80 N.C.L. Rev. 1879, 1881–82 (2002).

[320]Comment, 33 U.Tol.L.Rev. 815, 828 (2003).

[321]New York v. Class, 475 U.S. 106, 106 S.Ct. 960, 89 L.Ed.2d 81 (1986).

[322]Comment, 33 U.Tol.L.Rev. 815, 839 (2003).

[323]"Police can envision limited domestic uses for an urban surveillance system the Pentagon is developing * * *, which is designed to track and analyze the movements of every vehicle in a city. * * *

"The project's centerpiece would be groundbreaking computer software capable of automatically identifying vehicles by size, color, shape and license tag, or drivers and passengers by face. The proposed software also would provide instant alerts after detecting a vehicle with a license plate

on a watch-list, or search months of records to locate and compare vehicles spotted near terrorist attacks, according to interviews and contracting documents reviewed by The Associated Press. * * *

"Scientists and privacy experts are concerned about the potential impact of the emerging * * * technologies if they are applied to civilians by commercial or government agencies outside the Pentagon." Urban Surveillance System Planned, Champaign-Urbana News-Gazette, July 2, 2003, p. A03, col. 2.

[324]And, if sufficiently long-term, would appear to be the type of activity that the five concurring Justices in United States v. Jones, ___ U.S. ___, 132 S.Ct. 945, 181 L.Ed.2d 911 (2012), indicated should be deemed a search. See note 2082 supra.

[325]See § 2.5, text at note 29.

exact time and location of *all passing cars* into a searchable database, regardless of any evidence of wrongdoing. This data can be kept on file indefinitely. In communities with extensive, integrated networks of ALPR cameras, this could potentially amount of mass surveillance of an entire community. * * * Theoretically, by mounting ALPR at every intersection and on every police car in a city,[326] it is conceivable that the police could begin to compile thousands of discrete data points about an individual's public movements. As the number of these discrete data points increases, law enforcement can ultimately create an incredibly accurate and arguably pervasive record of a person's movements over months, or even years.[327]

---

[326]"There are 238 license plate readers in use in New York City"; "130 are mobile," "mounted on the back of police cars," and "108 cameras are set up at fixed posts at city bridges and tunnels and above thoroughfares." Baker, Camera Scans of Car Plates Are Reshaping Police Inquiries, http:// www.nytimes.com/2011/04/12/nyregion/12plates.html (posted 4/11/11).

[327]Rushin, The Judicial Response to Mass Police Surveillance, http://www.jltp.uiuc.edu/works/Rushin/index.htm (posted 3/16/11), appearing in slightly revised form at 2011 U.Ill.J.L.Tech. & Pol'y 281.